CCENT®

W9-AYV-155

ICND1

Study Guide

Third Edition

CCENT®
Cisco Certified Entry Networking Technician ICND1
Study Guide
Third Edition

Todd Lammle

SYBEX®
A Wiley Brand

Senior Acquisitions Editor: Kenyon Brown
Development Editor: Kim Wimpsett
Technical Editors: Todd Montgomery
Production Editor: Christine O'Connor
Copy Editor: Judy Flynn
Editorial Manager: Mary Beth Wakefield
Production Manager: Kathleen Wisor
Executive Editor : Jim Minatel
Book Designers: Judy Fung and Bill Gibson
Proofreader: Josh Chase, Word One New York
Indexer: John Sleeva
Project Coordinator, Cover: Brent Savage
Cover Designer: Wiley
Cover Image: Getty Images Inc./Jeremy Woodhouse

Copyright © 2016 by John Wiley & Sons, Inc., Indianapolis, Indiana

Published simultaneously in Canada

Manufactured in the United States of America

ISBN: 978-1-119-28878-7
ISBN: 978-1-119-28879-4 (ebk.)
ISBN: 978-1-119-28880-0 (ebk.)

Manufactured in the United States of America

For general information on our other products and services or to obtain technical support, please contact our Customer Care Department within the U.S. at (877) 762-2974, outside the U.S. at (317) 572-3993 or fax (317) 572-4002.

Wiley publishes in a variety of print and electronic formats and by print-on-demand. Some material included with standard print versions of this book may not be included in e-books or in print-on-demand. If this book refers to media such as a CD or DVD that is not included in the version you purchased, you may download this material at http://booksupport.wiley.com. For more information about Wiley products, visit www.wiley.com.

Library of Congress Control Number: 2016942433

10 9 8 7 6 5 4 3

Acknowledgments

There are many people that work to put a book together, and as an author, I dedicated an enormous amount of time to write this book, but it would have never been published without the dedicated, hard work of many other people.

Kenyon Brown, my acquisitions editor, is instrumental to my success in the world of Cisco certification. Ken, I look forward to our continued progress together in both the print and video markets!

Christine O'Connor, my production editor, and Judy Flynn, my copyeditor, were my rock and foundation for formatting and intense editing of every page in this book. This amazing team gives me the confidence to help keep me moving during the difficult and very long days, week after week. How Christine stays so organized with all my changes, as well as making sure every figure is in the right place in the book is still a mystery to me! You're amazing, Christine! Thank you! Judy understands my writing style so well now, after doing at least a dozen books with me, that she even sometimes finds a technical error that may have slipped through as I was going through the material. Thank you, Judy, for doing such a great job! I truly thank you both.

About the Author

Todd Lammle is the authority on Cisco certification and internetworking and is Cisco certified in most Cisco certification categories. He is a world-renowned author, speaker, trainer, and consultant. Todd has three decades of experience working with LANs, WANs, and large enterprise licensed and unlicensed wireless networks, and lately he's been implementing large Cisco Firepower networks. His years of real-world experience are evident in his writing; he is not just an author but an experienced networking engineer with very practical experience working on the largest networks in the world, at such companies as Xerox, Hughes Aircraft, Texaco, AAA, Cisco, and Toshiba, among many others. Todd has published over 60 books, including the very popular *CCNA: Cisco Certified Network Associate Study Guide, CCNA Wireless Study Guide, CCNA Data Center Study Guide,* and *SSFIPS (Firepower)*, all from Sybex. He runs an international consulting and training company based in Colorado, Texas, and San Francisco.

You can reach Todd through his webesite at `www.lammle.com/ccna`.

Contents at a Glance

Contents

Chapter 7   Managing a Cisco Internetwork   271

Introduction

Welcome to the exciting world of Cisco certification! If you've picked up this book because you want to improve yourself and your life with a better, more satisfying, and secure job, you've done the right thing. Whether you're striving to enter the thriving, dynamic IT sector or seeking to enhance your skill set and advance your position within it, being Cisco certified can seriously stack the odds in your favor to help you attain your goals!

Cisco certifications are powerful instruments of success that also markedly improve your grasp of all things internetworking. As you progress through this book, you'll gain a complete understanding of networking that reaches far beyond Cisco devices. By the end of this book, you'll comprehensively know how disparate network topologies and technologies work together to form the fully operational networks that are vital to today's very way of life in the developed world. The knowledge and expertise you'll gain here is essential for and relevant to every networking job and is why Cisco certifications are in such high demand—even at companies with few Cisco devices!

Although it's now common knowledge that Cisco rules routing and switching, the fact that it also rocks the voice, data center, and service provider worlds is also well recognized. And Cisco certifications reach way beyond the popular but less extensive certifications like those offered by CompTIA and Microsoft to equip you with indispensable insight into today's vastly complex networking realm. Essentially, by deciding to become Cisco certified, you're proudly announcing that you want to become an unrivaled networking expert—a goal that this book will get you well on your way to achieving. Congratulations in advance on the beginning of your brilliant future!

For up-to-the-minute updates covering additions or modifications to the Cisco certification exams, as well as additional study tools, videos, review questions, and bonus materials, be sure to visit the Todd Lammle websites and forum at www.lammle.com/ccna.

Cisco's Network Certifications

It used to be that to secure the holy grail of Cisco certifications—the CCIE—you passed only one written test before being faced with a grueling, formidable hands-on lab. This intensely daunting, all-or-nothing approach made it nearly impossible to succeed and predictably didn't work out too well for most people. Cisco responded to this issue by creating a series of new certifications, which not only made it easier to eventually win the highly coveted CCIE prize, it gave employers a way to accurately rate and measure the skill levels of prospective and current employees. This exciting paradigm shift in Cisco's certification path truly opened doors that few were allowed through before!

Beginning in 1998, obtaining the Cisco Certified Network Associate (CCNA) certification was the first milestone in the Cisco certification climb, as well as the official prerequisite to each of the more advanced levels. But that changed in 2007, when Cisco announced the Cisco Certified Entry Network Technician (CCENT) certification. And then in May 2016, Cisco once again proclaimed updates to the CCENT and CCNA Routing and Switching (R/S) tests. Now the Cisco certification process looks like Figure I.1.

FIGURE I.1   The Cisco certification path

	Entry	Associate	Professional	Expert
Architect				Board Exam
Cloud		210–451 CLDFND 210–455 CLDADM	300–460 CLDINF 300–465 CLDDES	
Collaboration		210–060 CICD 210–065 CIVND	300–070 CIPTV1 300–075 CIPTV2 300–080 CTCOLLAB 300–085 CAPPS	Written Exam Lab Exam
Data Center		640–911 DCICN 640–916 DCICT	642–999 DCUCI 642–997 DCUFI 642–998 DCUCD 642–996 DCUFD 642–035 DCUCT 642–980 DCUFT	Written Exam Lab Exam
Design	100–105 ICND1	210–310 DESGN	300–320 ARCH 300–101 ROUTE 300–115 SWITCH	Written Exam Practical Exam
Routing & Switching	100–105 ICND1	100–105 ICND1 200–105 ICND2 200–125 CCNA	300–101 ROUTE 300–115 SWITCH 300–135 TSHOOT	Written Exam Lab Exam
Security	100–105 ICND1	210–260 IINS	300–206 SENSS 300–207 SITCS 300–208 SISAS 300–209 SIMOS	Written Exam Lab Exam
Service Provider		640–875 SPNGN1 640–878 SPNGN2	642–883 SPROUTE 642–885 SPADVROUTE 642–887 SPCORE 642–889 SPEDGE	Written Exam Lab Exam
Wireless	100–105 ICND1	200–355 WIFUND	642–732 CUWSS 642–742 IUWVN 642–747 IUWMS 642–737 IAUWS	Written Exam Lab Exam
Other Certifications	100–105 ICND1 640–692 RSTECH 010–151 DECTECH 640–792 TPTECH			

The Cisco R/S path is by far the most popular and could very well remain so, but soon you'll see the Data Center path become more and more of a focus as companies migrate to data center technologies. The Security track also actually does provide a good job opportunity as well. Still, understanding the foundation of R/S before attempting any other certification track is something I highly recommend.

Even so, and as the figure shows, you only need your CCENT certification to get underway for most of the tracks.

Cisco Certified Entry Network Technician (CCENT)

Don't be fooled by the oh-so-misleading name of this first certification because it absolutely isn't entry level! Okay—maybe entry level for Cisco's certification path, but definitely not for someone without experience trying to break into the highly lucrative yet challenging IT job market! For the uninitiated, the CompTIA A+ and Network+ certifications aren't official prerequisites, but know that Cisco does expect you to have that type and level of experience before embarking on your Cisco certification journey.

All of this gets us to 2016, when the climb to Cisco supremacy just got much harder again. The innocuous-sounding siren's call of the CCENT can lure you to some serious trouble if you're not prepared, because it's actually much harder than the old CCNA ever was. This will rapidly become apparent once you start studying, but be encouraged! The fact that the certification process is getting harder really works better for you in the long run, because that which is harder to obtain only becomes that much more valuable when you finally do, right? Yes, indeed!

Another important factor to keep in mind is that the Interconnection Cisco Network Devices Part 1 (ICND1) exam, which is the required exam for the CCENT certification, costs $150 per attempt, and it's anything but easy to pass! The good news is that this book will guide you step-by-step in building a strong foundation in routing and switching technologies. You really need to build on a strong technical foundation and stay away from exam cram type books, suspicious online material, and the like. They can help somewhat, but understand that you'll pass the Cisco certification exams only if you have a strong foundation and that you'll get that solid foundation only by reading as much as you can, performing the written labs and review questions in this book, and practicing lots and lots of hands-on labs. Additional practice exam questions, videos, and labs are offered on my website, and what seems like a million other sites offer additional material that can help you study.

However, there is one way to skip the CCENT exam and still meet the prerequisite before moving on to any other certification track, and that path is through the CCNA R/S Composite exam. First, I'll discuss the Interconnecting Cisco Network Devices Part 2 (ICND2) exam, and then I'll tell you about the CCNA Composite exam, which will provide you, when successful, with both the CCENT and the CCNA R/S certification.

Cisco Certified Network Associate Routing and Switching (CCNA R/S)

Once you have achieved your CCENT certification, you can take the ICND2 (200-105) exam in order to achieve your CCNA R/S certification, which is the most popular certification Cisco has by far because it's the most sought-after certification by all employers.

As with the CCENT, the ICND2 exam is also $150 per attempt—although thinking you can just skim a book and pass any of these exams would probably be a really expensive mistake! The CCENT/CCNA exams are extremely hard and cover a lot of material, so you have to really know your stuff. Taking a Cisco class or spending months with hands-on experience is definitely a requirement to succeed when faced with this monster!

And once you have your CCNA, you don't have to stop there—you can choose to continue and achieve an even higher certification, called the Cisco Certified Network Professional (CCNP). There are various ones, as shown in Figure I.1. The CCNP R/S is still the most popular, with Security certifications coming in at a close second. And I've got to tell you that the Data Center certification will be catching up fast. Also good to know is that anyone with a CCNP R/S has all the skills and knowledge needed to attempt the notoriously dreaded but coveted CCIE R/S lab. But just becoming a CCNA R/S can land you that job you've dreamed about and that's what this book is all about: helping you to get and keep a great job!

Still, why take two exams to get your CCNA if you don't have to? Cisco still has the CCNA Composite (200-125) exam that, if passed, will land you with your CCENT and your CCNA R/S via only one test, priced accordingly at $300. Some people like the one-test approach, and some people like the two-test approach.

Why Become a CCENT and CCNA R/S?

Cisco, like Microsoft and other vendors that provide certification, has created the certification process to give administrators a set of skills and to equip prospective employers with a way to measure those skills or match certain criteria. And as you probably know, becoming a CCNA R/S is certainly the initial, key step on a successful journey toward a new, highly rewarding, and sustainable networking career.

The CCNA program was created to provide a solid introduction not only to the Cisco Internetwork Operating System (IOS) and Cisco hardware but also to internetworking in general, making it helpful to you in areas that are not exclusively Cisco's. And regarding today's certification process, it's not unrealistic that network managers—even those without Cisco equipment—require Cisco certifications for their job applicants.

Rest assured that if you make it through the CCNA and are still interested in Cisco and internetworking, you're headed down a path to certain success!

What Skills Do You Need to Become a CCNA R/S?

This ICND1 exam (100-105) tests a candidate for the knowledge and skills required to successfully install, operate, and troubleshoot a small branch office network. The exam includes questions on the operation of IP data networks, LAN switching technologies, IPv6, IP routing technologies, IP services, network device security, and basic troubleshooting. The ICND2 exam (exam 200-105) tests a candidate for the knowledge and skills required to successfully install, operate, and troubleshoot a small- to medium-size enterprise branch network. The exam includes questions on LAN switching technologies, IP routing technologies, IP services (FHRP, SNMP v2 and v3), Cloud, ACI as well as troubleshooting, and WAN technologies.

How Do You Become a CCNA R/S

If you want to go straight for our CCNA R/S and take only one exam, all you have to do is pass the CCNA Composite exam (200-125). Oh, but don't you wish it were that easy? True, it's just one test, but it's a whopper, and to pass it you must possess enough knowledge to understand what the test writers are saying, and you need to know everything I mentioned previously, in the sections on the ICND1 and ICND2 exams! Hey, it's hard, but it can be done!

What does the CCNA Composite exam (200-125) cover? Pretty much the same topics covered in the ICND1 and ICND2 exams. Candidates can prepare for this exam by taking the Todd Lammle authorized Cisco boot camps. 200-125 tests a candidate's knowledge and skills required to install, operate, and troubleshoot a small- to medium-size enterprise branch network.

While you can take the Composite exam to get your CCNA, it's good to know that Cisco offers the two-step process I discussed earlier in this introduction. And this book covers both those exams too! It may be easier than taking that one ginormous exam for you, but don't think the two-test method is easy. It takes work! However, it can be done; you just need to stick with your studies.

The two-test method involves passing the following:

- Exam 100-105: Interconnecting Cisco Networking Devices Part 1 (ICND1)
- Exam 200-105: Interconnecting Cisco Networking Devices Part 2 (ICND2)

I can't stress this point enough: It's critical that you have some hands-on experience with Cisco routers. If you can get a hold of some basic routers and switches, you're set, but if you can't, I've worked hard to provide hundreds of configuration examples throughout this book to help network administrators, or people who want to become network administrators, learn the skills they need to pass the CCENT and CCNA R/S exams. In addition, a simulator called LammleSim IOS version is available for free with the purchase of this book. This small simulator will run through all the hands-on labs found in this book—Nice, huh?

 For Cisco certification hands-on training alone which includes CCNA videos and practice test questions all from CCSI Todd Lammle, please see www.lammle.com/ccna.

What Does This Book Cover?

This book covers everything you need to know to pass the ICND1 (100-105). The INCD2 book and composite CCNA book are both available on Amazon as well. But regardless of which path you choose, as I've said, taking plenty of time to study and practice with routers or a router simulator is the real key to success.

   You will learn the following information in this book:

Chapter 1: Internetworking   In Chapter 1, you will learn the basics of the Open Systems Interconnection (OSI) model the way Cisco wants you to learn it. There are written labs and plenty of review questions to help you. Do not even think of skipping the fundamental written labs in this chapter!

Chapter 2: Ethernet Networking and Data Encapsulation   This chapter will provide you with the Ethernet foundation you need in order to pass both the CCENT and CCNA exams. Data encapsulation is discussed in detail in this chapter as well. And as with the other chapters, this chapter includes written labs and review questions to help you.

Chapter 3: Introduction to TCP/IP   This chapter provides you with the background necessary for success on the exam as well as in the real world with a thorough presentation of TCP/IP. This in-depth chapter covers the very beginnings of the Internet Protocol stack and goes all the way to IP addressing and understanding the difference between a network address and a broadcast address before finally ending with network troubleshooting. Don't skip the two written labs and 20 review questions.

Chapter 4: Easy Subnetting   You'll actually be able to subnet a network in your head after reading this chapter if you really want to! And you'll find plenty of help in this chapter as long as you don't skip the written labs and review questions at the end.

Chapter 5: VLSMs, Summarization, and Troubleshooting TCP/IP   Here, you'll find out all about variable length subnet masks (VLSMs) and how to design a network using VLSMs. This chapter will finish with summarization techniques and configurations. As with Chapter 4, plenty of help is there for you if you don't skip the written lab and review questions.

Chapter 6: Cisco's Internetworking Operating System (IOS)   This chapter introduces you to the Cisco Internetworking Operating System (IOS) and command-line interface (CLI). In this chapter you'll learn how to turn on a router and configure the basics of the IOS, including setting passwords, banners, and more. Hands-on labs will help you gain a firm grasp of the concepts taught in the chapter. Before you go through the hands-on labs, be sure to complete the written lab and review questions.

Chapter 7: Managing a Cisco Internetwork   This chapter provides you with the management skills needed to run a Cisco IOS network. Backing up and restoring the IOS, as well as router configuration, are covered, as are the troubleshooting tools necessary to keep a network up and running. As always, before tackling the hands-on labs in this chapter, complete the written labs and review questions.

Chapter 8: Managing Cisco Devices   This chapter describes the boot process of Cisco routers, the configuration register, and how to manage Cisco IOS files. The chapter finishes with a section on Cisco's new licensing strategy for IOS. Hands-on and written labs, along with review questions, will help you build a strong foundation for the objectives covered in this chapter.

Chapter 9: IP Routing   This is a fun chapter because we will begin to build our network, add IP addresses, and route data between routers. You will also learn about static, default, and dynamic routing using RIP and RIPv2. Hands-on labs, a written lab, and the review questions will help you fully nail down IP routing.

Chapter 10: Layer 2 Switching   This chapter sets you up with the solid background you need on layer 2 switching, how switches perform address learning and make forwarding and filtering decisions. In addition, switch port security with MAC addresses is covered in detail. As always, go through the hands-on labs, written lab, and review questions to make sure you've really got layer 2 switching down!

Chapter 11: VLANs and Inter-VLAN Routing   Here I cover virtual VLANs and how to use them in your internetwork. This chapter covers the nitty-gritty of VLANs and the different concepts and protocols used with VLANs. I'll also guide you through troubleshooting techniques in this all-important chapter. The hands-on labs, written lab, and review questions are there to reinforce the VLAN material.

Chapter 12: Security   This chapter covers security and access lists, which are created on routers to filter the network. IP standard, extended, and named access lists are covered in detail. Written and hands-on labs, along with review questions, will help you study for the security and access-list portion of the Cisco exams.

Chapter 13: Network Address Translation (NAT)   New information, commands, troubleshooting, and detailed written labs, review questions, hands-on labs will help you nail the NAT CCENT objectives.

Chapter 14: Internet Protocol Version 6 (IPv6)   This is a fun chapter chock-full of some great information. IPv6 is not the big, bad scary creature that most people think it is, and it's a really important objective on the latest exam, so study this chapter carefully—don't just skim it. And make sure you hit those two written labs, review questions, and hands-on labs hard!

Appendix A: Answers to Written Labs   This appendix contains the answers to the book's written labs.

Appendix B: Answers to Review Questions   This appendix provides the answers to the end-of-chapter review questions.

Appendix C: Disabling and Configuring Network Services   Appendix C takes a look at the basic services you should disable on your routers to make your network less of a target for denial of service (DoS) attacks and break-in attempts.

Be sure to check the announcements section of my forum at www.lammle .com/ccna to find out how to download bonus material I created specifically for this book.

Interactive Online Learning Environment and Test Bank

I've worked hard to provide some really great tools to help you with your certification process. The interactive online learning environment that accompanies the *CCENT ICND1 Study Guide, Exam 100-105, Third Edition*, provides a test bank with study tools to help you prepare for the certification exam—and increase your chances of passing it the first time! The test bank includes the following:

Sample tests   All of the questions in this book are provided, including the assessment test, which you'll find at the end of this introduction, and the chapter tests that include the review questions at the end of each chapter. In addition, there is a practice exam with 50 questions. Use these questions to test your knowledge of the study guide material. The online test bank runs on multiple devices.

Flashcards   The online text bank includes over 50 flashcards specifically written to hit you hard, so don't get discouraged if you don't ace your way through them at first! They're there to ensure that you're really ready for the exam. And no worries—armed with the review questions, practice exams, and flashcards, you'll be more than prepared when exam day comes! Questions are provided in digital flashcard format (a question followed by a single correct answer). You can use the flashcards to reinforce your learning and provide last-minute test prep before the exam.

Glossary   A glossary of key terms from this book and their definitions are available as a fully searchable PDF.

30 Days of Free Video Training from ITPro.TV and Sybex   Take your exam prep to a new level! Through expert live and pre-recorded interactive learning, you will receive an additional 12 hours of expert CCENT ICND1 training from the subject-matter experts at ITPro.TV.

Go to http://www.wiley.com/go/sybextestprep to register and gain access to this interactive online learning environment and test bank with study tools.

In addition to the online test bank, I have provided additional study material that'll help you get the most out of your exam preparation:

Todd Lammle Bonus Material and Labs   Be sure to check the www.lammle.com/ccna for directions on how to download all the latest bonus material created specifically to help you study for your CCENT ICND1 exam.

How to Use This Book

If you want a solid foundation for the serious effort of preparing for the Interconnecting Cisco Network Devices Part 1 exam, then look no further. I've spent hundreds of hours putting together this book with the sole intention of helping you to pass the Cisco exam, as well as really learn how to correctly configure Cisco routers and switches!

This book is loaded with valuable information, and you will get the most out of your study time if you understand why the book is organized the way it is.

So to maximize your benefit from this book, I recommend the following study method:

1. Take the assessment test that's provided at the end of this introduction. (The answers are at the end of the test.) It's okay if you don't know any of the answers; that's why you bought this book! Carefully read over the explanations for any questions you get wrong and note the chapters in which the material relevant to them is covered. This information should help you plan your study strategy.

2. Study each chapter carefully, making sure you fully understand the information and the test objectives listed at the beginning of each one. Pay extra-close attention to any chapter that includes material covered in questions you missed.

3. Complete the written labs at the end of each chapter. (Answers to these appear in Appendix A.) Do *not* skip these written exercises because they directly relate to the Cisco exams and what you must glean from the chapters in which they appear. Do not just skim these labs! Make sure you completely understand the reason for each correct answer.

4. Complete all hands-on labs in each chapter, referring to the text of the chapter so that you understand the reason for each step you take. Try to get your hands on some real equipment, but if you don't have Cisco equipment available, try the LammleSim IOS version, which you can use for the hands-on labs found only in this book. These labs will equip you with everything you need for all your Cisco certification goals.

5. Answer all of the review questions related to each chapter. (The answers appear in Appendix B.) Note the questions that confuse you, and study the topics they cover again until the concepts are crystal clear. And again—do not just skim these questions! Make sure you fully comprehend the reason for each correct answer. Remember that these will not be the exact questions you will find on the exam, but they're written to help you understand the chapter material and ultimately pass the exam!

6. Try your hand at the bonus practice questions that are exclusive to this book. The questions can be found only at http://www.wiley.com/go/sybextestprep. And be sure to check out www.lammle.com/ccna for the most up-to-date Cisco exam prep questions, videos, Todd Lammle boot camps, and more.

7. Test yourself using all the flashcards, which are also found on the download link. These are brand-new and updated flashcards to help you prepare for the CCENT and are a wonderful study tool!

To learn every bit of the material covered in this book, you'll have to apply yourself regularly, and with discipline. Try to set aside the same time period every day to study, and select a comfortable and quiet place to do so. I'm confident that if you work hard, you'll be surprised at how quickly you learn this material!

If you follow these steps and really study—*doing hands-on labs every single day* in addition to using the review questions, the practice exams, the Todd Lammle video sections, and the electronic flashcards, as well as all the written labs—it would actually be hard to fail the Cisco exams. But understand that studying for the Cisco exams is a lot like getting in shape—if you do not go to the gym every day, it's not going to happen!

Where Do You Take the Exams?

You may take the ICND1, ICND2, or CCNA R/S Composite or any Cisco exam at any of the Pearson VUE authorized testing centers. For information, check www.vue.com or call 877-404-EXAM (3926).

To register for a Cisco exam, follow these steps:

1. Determine the number of the exam you want to take. (The ICND1 exam number is 100-105, ICND2 is 100-205, and CCNA R/S Composite is 200-125.)

2. Register with the nearest Pearson VUE testing center. At this point, you will be asked to pay in advance for the exam. At the time of this writing, the ICND1 and ICND2 exams are $150, and the CCNA R/S Composite exam is $300. The exams must be taken within one year of payment. You can schedule exams up to six weeks in advance or as late as the day you want to take it—but if you fail a Cisco exam, you must wait five days before you will be allowed to retake it. If something comes up and you need to cancel or reschedule your exam appointment, contact Pearson VUE at least 24 hours in advance.

3. When you schedule the exam, you'll get instructions regarding all appointment and cancellation procedures, the ID requirements, and information about the testing-center location.

Tips for Taking Your Cisco Exams

The Cisco exams contain about 40 to 50 questions and must be completed in about 90 minutes or less. This information can change per exam. You must get a score of about 85 percent to pass this exam, but again, each exam can be different.

Many questions on the exam have answer choices that at first glance look identical—especially the syntax questions! So remember to read through the choices carefully because close just doesn't cut it. If you get commands in the wrong order or forget one measly character, you'll get the question wrong. So, to practice, do the hands-on exercises at the end of this book's chapters over and over again until they feel natural to you.

Also, never forget that the right answer is the Cisco answer. In many cases, more than one appropriate answer is presented, but the *correct* answer is the one that Cisco recommends. On the exam, you will always be told to pick one, two, or three options, never "choose all that apply." The Cisco exam may include the following test formats:

- Multiple-choice single answer
- Multiple-choice multiple answer
- Drag-and-drop
- Router simulations

Cisco proctored exams will not show the steps to follow in completing a router interface configuration, but they do allow partial command responses. For example, show run, sho running, or sh running-config would be acceptable.

Here are some general tips for exam success:

- Arrive early at the exam center so you can relax and review your study materials.

- Read the questions *carefully*. Don't jump to conclusions. Make sure you're clear about *exactly* what each question asks. "Read twice, answer once," is what I always tell my students.

- When answering multiple-choice questions that you're not sure about, use the process of elimination to get rid of the obviously incorrect answers first. Doing this greatly improves your odds if you need to make an educated guess.

- You can no longer move forward and backward through the Cisco exams, so double-check your answer before clicking Next since you can't change your mind.

After you complete an exam, you'll get immediate, online notification of your pass or fail status, a printed examination score report that indicates your pass or fail status, and your exam results by section. (The test administrator will give you the printed score report.) Test scores are automatically forwarded to Cisco within five working days after you take the test, so you don't need to send your score to them. If you pass the exam, you'll receive confirmation from Cisco, typically within two to four weeks, sometimes a bit longer.

ICND1 (100-105) Exam Objectives

Exam objectives are subject to change at any time without prior notice and at Cisco's sole discretion. Please visit Cisco's certification website (www.cisco.com/web/learning) for the latest information on the ICND1 exam.

Operation of IP Data Networks	Chapter(s)
Recognize the purpose and functions of various network devices, such as Routers, Switches, Bridges, and Hubs.	1, 2
Select the components required to meet a given network specification.	1, 2
Identify common applications and their impact on the network.	1, 3
Describe the purpose and basic operation of the protocols in the OSI and TCP/IP models.	1, 3
Predict the data flow between two hosts across a network.	1, 2, 13
Identify the appropriate media, cables, ports, and connectors, to connect Cisco network devices to other network devices and hosts in a LAN.	2
LAN Switching Technologies	
Determine the technology and media access control method for Ethernet networks.	2
Identify basic switching concepts and the operation of Cisco switches.	2, 10

- Collision domains
- Broadcast domains
- Types of switching
- CAM table

Configure and verify initial switch-configuration including remote access management.	6, 10

- Cisco IOS commands to perform basic switch setup

Verify network status and switch-operation using basic utilities, such as ping, Telnet, and SSH.	7, 10
Describe how VLANs create logically separate networks and the need for routing between them.	11

- Explain network segmentation and basic traffic management concepts.

Configure and verify VLANs.	11
Configure and verify trunking on Cisco switches.	11

- DTP
- Auto negotiation

IP addressing (IPv4/IPv6)

Describe the operation and necessity of using private and public IP addresses for IPv4 addressing.	3, 4
Identify the appropriate IPv6-addressing scheme to satisfy addressing requirements in a LAN/WAN environment.	14
Identify the appropriate IPv4-addressing scheme using VLSM and summarization to satisfy addressing requirements in a LAN/WAN environment.	5

Operation of IP Data Networks	Chapter(s)
Describe the technological requirements for running IPv6 in conjunction with IPv4 such as dual stack.	14
Describe IPv6 addresses.	14

- Global unicast
- Multicast
- Link local
- Unique local
- eui-64
- Autoconfiguration

IP Routing Technologies

Describe basic routing concepts.	8

- CEF
- Packet forwarding
- Router lookup process

Configure and verify utilizing the CLI to set the basic router configuration.	6, 7

- Cisco IOS commands to perform basic router setup

Configure and verify the operation status of an Ethernet interface.	6
Verify router configuration and network connectivity.	6, 7

- Cisco IOS commands to review basic router information and network connectivity

Configure and verify routing configuration for a static or default route given specific routing requirements.	8
Differentiate methods of routing and routing protocols.	8

- Static vs dynamic
- Link state vs distance vector
- Next-hop
- IP routing table
- Passive interfaces

Configure and verify OSPF (single area)	9, 14

- Benefit of single area
- Configure OSPFv2
- Configure OSPFv3
- Router ID
- Passive interface

Operation of IP Data Networks	Chapter(s)
Configure and verify interVLAN routing (router on a stick).	11

- Subinterfaces
- Upstream routing
- Encapsulation

Configure SVI interfaces.	11

IP Services

Configure and verify DHCP (IOS Router).	7

- Configuring router interfaces to use DHCP
- DHCP options
- Excluded addresses
- Lease time

Describe the types, features, and applications of ACLs.	12

- Standard
- Sequence numbers
- Editing
- Extended
- Named
- Numbered
- Log option

Configure and verify ACLs in a network environment.	12

- Named
- Numbered
- Log option

Identify the basic operation of NAT	13

- Purpose
- Pool
- Static
- 1 to 1
- Overloading
- Source addressing
- One-way NAT

Configure and verify NAT for given network requirements.	13
Configure and verify NTP as a client.	7

Operation of IP Data Networks	Chapter(s)
Network Device Security	
Configure and verify network device security features such as:	6

- Device password security
- Enable secret vs enable
- Transport
- Disable Telnet
- SSH
- VTYs
- Physical security
- Service password
- External authentication methods

Configure and verify switch port security features, such as:	10

- Sticky MAC
- MAC address limitation
- Static/dynamic
- Violation modes
- Err disable
- Shutdown
- Protect restrict
- Shutdown unused ports
- Err disable recovery
- Assign unused ports to an unused VLAN
- Setting native VLAN to other than VLAN 1

Configure and verify ACLs to filter network traffic.	12
Configure and verify ACLs to limit Telnet and SSH access to the router.	12
Troubleshooting	
Troubleshoot and correct common problems associated with IP addressing and host configurations.	5
Troubleshoot and resolve VLAN problems.	11

- Identify that VLANs are configured
- Port membership correct
- IP address configured

Operation of IP Data Networks	Chapter(s)
Troubleshoot and resolve trunking problems on Cisco switches.	11

- Correct trunk states
- Correct encapsulation configured
- Correct VLANS allowed

Troubleshoot and resolve ACL issues.	12

- Statistics
- Permitted networks
- Direction
- Interface

Troubleshoot and resolve Layer 1 problems.

- Framing   6
- CRC
- Runts
- Giants
- Dropped packets
- Late collision
- Input/Output errors

Assessment Test

1. You reload a router with a configuration register setting of 0x2101. What will the router do when it reloads?

    A. The router enters setup mode.

    B. The router enters ROM monitor mode.

    C. The router boots the mini-IOS in ROM.

    D. The router expands the first IOS in flash memory into RAM.

2. Which of the following commands provides the product ID and serial number of a router?

    A. `show license`

    B. `show license feature`

    C. `show version`

    D. `show license udi`

3. Which command allows you to view the technology options and licenses that are supported on your router along with several status variables?

    A. show license

    B. show license feature

    C. show license udi

    D. show version

4. You want to send a console message to a syslog server, but you only want to send status messages of 3 and lower. Which of the following commands will you use?

    A. logging trap emergencies

    B. logging trap errors

    C. logging trap debugging

    D. logging trap notifications

    E. logging trap critical

    F. logging trap warnings

    G. logging trap alerts

5. IPv6 unicast routing is running on the Corp router. Which of the following addresses would show up with the show ipv6 int brief command?

    ```
    Corp#sh int f0/0
    FastEthernet0/0 is up, line protocol is up
      Hardware is AmdFE, address is 000d.bd3b.0d80 (bia 000d.bd3b.0d80)
    [output cut]
    ```

    A. FF02::3c3d:0d:bdff:fe3b:0d80

    B. FE80::3c3d:2d:bdff:fe3b:0d80

    C. `FE80::3c3d:0d:bdff:fe3b:0d80`

    D. `FE80::3c3d:2d:ffbd:3bfe:0d80`

6. A host sends a type of NDP message providing the MAC address that was requested. Which type of NDP was sent?

    A. NA

    B. RS

    C. RA

    D. NS

7. Each field in an IPv6 address is how many bits long?

    A. 4

    B. 16

    C. 32

    D. 128

8. What does the command `routerA(config)#line cons 0` allow you to perform next?

    A. Set the Telnet password.

    B. Shut down the router.

    C. Set your console password.

    D. Disable console connections.

9. Which two statements describe the IP address 10.16.3.65/23? (Choose two.)

    A. The subnet address is 10.16.3.0 255.255.254.0.

    B. The lowest host address in the subnet is 10.16.2.1 255.255.254.0.

    C. The last valid host address in the subnet is 10.16.2.254 255.255.254.0.

    D. The broadcast address of the subnet is 10.16.3.255 255.255.254.0.

    E. The network is not subnetted.

10. On which interface do you configure an IP address for a switch?

    A. `int fa0/0`

    B. `int vty 0 15`

    C. `int vlan 1`

    D. `int s/0/0`

11. Which of the following is the valid host range for the subnet on which the IP address 192.168.168.188 255.255.255.192 resides?

    A. 192.168.168.129–190

    B. 192.168.168.129–191

    C. 192.168.168.128–190

    D. 192.168.168.128–192

12. Which of the following is considered to be the inside host's address after translation?

    A. Inside local

    B. Outside local

    C. Inside global

    D. Outside global

13. Your inside locals are not being translated to the inside global addresses. Which of the following commands will show you if your inside globals are allowed to use the NAT pool?

```
ip nat pool Corp 198.18.41.129 198.18.41.134 netmask 255.255.255.248
ip nat inside source list 100 int s0/0 Corp overload
```

    A. `debug ip nat`

    B. `show access-list`

    C. `show ip nat translation`

    D. `show ip nat statistics`

14. How many collision domains are created when you segment a network with a 12-port switch?

    A. 1

    B. 2

    C. 5

    D. 12

15. Which of the following commands will allow you to set your Telnet password on a Cisco router?

    A. `line telnet 0 4`

    B. `line aux 0 4`

    C. `line vty 0 4`

    D. `line con 0`

16. Which router command allows you to view the entire contents of all access lists?

    A. `show all access-lists`

    B. `show access-lists`

    C. `show ip interface`

    D. `show interface`

17. What does a VLAN do?

    A. Acts as the fastest port to all servers

    B. Provides multiple collision domains on one switch port

    C. Breaks up broadcast domains in a layer 2 switch internetwork

    D. Provides multiple broadcast domains within a single collision domain

18. If you wanted to delete the configuration stored in NVRAM, choose the best answer for the Cisco objectives.

   A. `erase startup`

   B. `delete running`

   C. `erase flash`

   D. `erase running`

19. Which protocol is used to send a destination network unknown message back to originating hosts?

   A. TCP

   B. ARP

   C. ICMP

   D. BootP

20. Which class of IP address provides 15 bits for subnetting?

   A. A

   B. B

   C. C

   D. D

21. There are three possible routes for a router to reach a destination network. The first route is from OSPF with a metric of 782. The second route is from RIPv2 with a metric of 4. The third is from EIGRP with a composite metric of 20514560. Which route will be installed by the router in its routing table?

   A. RIPv2

   B. EIGRP

   C. OSPF

   D. All three

22. Which one of the following is true regarding VLANs?

   A. Two VLANs are configured by default on all Cisco switches.

   B. VLANs only work if you have a complete Cisco switched internetwork. No off-brand switches are allowed.

   C. You should not have more than 10 switches in the same VTP domain.

   D. You need to have a trunk link configured between switches in order to send information about more than one VLAN down the link.

23. How many broadcast domains are created when you segment a network with a 12-port switch?

   A. 1

   B. 2

   C. 5

   D. 12

24. What protocols are used to configure trunking on a switch? (Choose two.)

    A. VLAN Trunking Protocol

    B. VLAN

    C. 802.1q

    D. ISL

25. What is a stub network?

    A. A network with more than one exit point

    B. A network with more than one exit and entry point

    C. A network with only one entry and no exit point

    D. A network that has only one entry and exit point

26. Where is a hub specified in the OSI model?

    A. Session layer

    B. Physical layer

    C. Data Link layer

    D. Application layer

27. What are the two main types of access control lists (ACLs)? (Choose two.)

    A. Standard

    B. IEEE

    C. Extended

    D. Specialized

28. Which of the following is the best summarization of the following networks: 192.168.128.0 through 192.168.159.0?

    A. 192.168.0.0/24

    B. 192.168.128.0/16

    C. 192.168.128.0/19

    D. 192.168.128.0/20

29. What command is used to create a backup configuration?

    A. `copy running backup`

    B. `copy running-config startup-config`

    C. `config mem`

    D. `wr net`

30. 1000Base-T is which IEEE standard?

    A. 802.3f

    B. 802.3z

    C. 802.3ab

    D. 802.3ae

Answers to Assessment Test

1. C. 2100 boots the router into ROM monitor mode, 2101 loads the mini-IOS from ROM, and 2102 is the default and loads the IOS from flash. See Chapter 8 for more information.

2. D. The show license udi command displays the unique device identifier (UDI) of the router, which comprises the product ID (PID) and serial number of the router. See Chapter 8 for more information.

3. B. The show license feature command allows you to view the technology package licenses and feature licenses that are supported on your router along with several status variables related to software activation and licensing, both licensed and unlicensed features. See Chapter 8 for more information.

4. B. There are eight different trap levels. If you choose, for example, level 3, level 0 through level 3 messages will be displayed. See Chapter 8 for more information.

5. B. This can be a hard question if you don't remember to invert the 7th bit of the first octet in the MAC address! Always look for the 7th bit when studying for the Cisco R/S, and when using eui-64, invert it. The eui-64 autoconfiguration then inserts an FF:FE in the middle of the 48-bit MAC address to create a unique IPv6 address. See Chapter 14 for more information.

6. A. The NDP neighbor advertisement (NA) contains the MAC address. A neighbor solicitation (NS) was initially sent asking for the MAC address. See Chapter 14 for more information.

7. B. Each field in an IPv6 address is 16 bits long. An IPv6 address has eight fields for a total of 128 bits. See Chapter 14 for more information.

8. C. The command line console 0 places you at a prompt where you can then set your console user-mode password. See Chapter 6 for more information.

9. B, D. The mask 255.255.254.0 (/23) used with a Class A address means that there are 15 subnet bits and 9 host bits. The block size in the third octet is 2 (256 – 254). So this makes the subnets in the interesting octet 0, 2, 4, 6, etc., all the way to 254. The host 10.16.3.65 is in the 2.0 subnet. The next subnet is 4.0, so the broadcast address for the 2.0 subnet is 3.255. The valid host addresses are 2.1 through 3.254. See Chapter 4 for more information.

10. C. The IP address is configured under a logical interface, called a management domain or VLAN 1, by default. See Chapter 10 for more information.

11. A. 256 – 192 = 64, so 64 is our block size. Just count in increments of 64 to find our subnet: 64 + 64 = 128. 128 + 64 = 192. The subnet is 128, the broadcast address is 191, and the valid host range is the numbers in between, or 129–190. See Chapter 4 for more information.

12. C. An inside global address is considered to be the IP address of the host on the private network after translation. See Chapter 13 for more information.

13. B. Once you create your pool, the command ip nat inside source must be used to say which inside locals are allowed to use the pool. In this question, we need to see if access list 100 is configured correctly, if at all, so show access-list is the best answer. See Chapter 13 for more information.

14. D. Layer 2 switching creates individual collision domains per port. See Chapter 1 for more information.

15. C. The command `line vty 0 4` places you in a prompt that will allow you to set or change your Telnet password. See Chapter 6 for more information.

16. B. To see the contents of all access lists, use the `show access-lists` command. See Chapter 12 for more information.

17. C. VLANs break up broadcast domains at layer 2. See Chapter 11 for more information.

18. A. The command `erase startup-config` deletes the configuration stored in NVRAM. See Chapter 6 for more information.

19. C. ICMP is the protocol at the Network layer that is used to send messages back to an originating router. See Chapter 3 for more information.

20. A. Class A addressing provides 22 bits for host subnetting. Class B provides 16 bits, but only 14 are available for subnetting. Class C provides only 6 bits for subnetting. See Chapter 3 for more information.

21. B. Only the EIGRP route will be placed in the routing table because EIGRP has the lowest administrative distance (AD), and that is always used before metrics. See Chapter 9 for more information.

22. D. Switches send information about only one VLAN down a link unless it is configured as a trunk link. See Chapter 11 for more information.

23. A. By default, switches break up collision domains on a per-port basis but are one large broadcast domain. See Chapter 1 for more information.

24. C, D. VLAN Trunking Protocol (VTP) is not right because it has nothing to do with trunking except that it sends VLAN information across a trunk link. 802.1q and ISL encapsulations are used to configure trunking on a port. See Chapter 11 for more information.

25. D. Stub networks have only one connection to an internetwork. Default routes should be set on a stub network or network loops may occur; however, there are exceptions to this rule. See Chapter 9 for more information.

26. B. Hubs regenerate electrical signals, which are specified at the Physical layer. See Chapter 1 for more information.

27. A, C. Standard and extended access control lists (ACLs) are used to configure security on a router. See Chapter 12 for more information.

28. C. If you start at 192.168.128.0 and go through 192.168.159.0, you can see that this is a block of 32 in the third octet. Since the network address is always the first one in the range, the summary address is 192.168.128.0. What mask provides a block of 32 in the third octet? The answer is 255.255.224.0, or /19. See Chapter 5 for more information.

29. B. The command to back up the configuration on a router is `copy running-config startup-config`. See Chapter 7 for more information.

30. C. IEEE 802.3ab is the standard for 1 Gbps on twisted-pair. See Chapter 2 for more information.

Chapter

1

Internetworking

THE FOLLOWING ICND1 EXAM TOPICS ARE COVERED IN THIS CHAPTER:

✓ **Network Fundamentals**

- 1.3 Describe the impact of infrastructure components in an enterprise network

    - 1.3.a Firewalls

    - 1.3.b Access points

    - 1.3.c Wireless controllers

- 1.5 Compare and contrast network topologies

    - 1.5.a Star

    - 1.5.b Mesh

    - 1.5.c Hybrid

Welcome to the exciting world of internetworking. This first chapter will serve as an internetworking review by focusing on how to connect networks together using Cisco routers and switches, and I've written it with the assumption that you have some simple basic networking knowledge. The emphasis of this review will be on the Cisco CCENT and/or CCNA Routing and Switching (CCNA R/S) objectives, on which you'll need a solid grasp in order to succeed in getting your certifications.

Let's start by defining exactly what an internetwork is: You create an internetwork when you connect two or more networks via a router and configure a logical network addressing scheme with a protocol such as IP or IPv6.

We'll also dissect the Open Systems Interconnection (OSI) model, and I'll describe each part of it to you in detail because you really need complete, reliable knowledge of it. Understanding the OSI model is key for the solid foundation you'll need to build upon with the more advanced Cisco networking knowledge gained as you become increasingly more skilled.

The OSI model has seven hierarchical layers that were developed to enable different networks to communicate reliably between disparate systems. Since this book is centering upon all things CCNA, it's crucial for you to understand the OSI model as Cisco sees it, so that's how I'll be presenting the seven layers to you.

After you finish reading this chapter, you'll encounter review questions and written labs. These are given to you to really lock the information from this chapter into your memory. So don't skip them!

To find up-to-the-minute updates for this chapter, please see www.lammle .com/ccna or the book's web page via www.sybex.com/go/ccna.

Internetworking Basics

Before exploring internetworking models and the OSI model's specifications, you need to grasp the big picture and the answer to this burning question: Why is it so important to learn Cisco internetworking anyway?

Networks and networking have grown exponentially over the past 20 years, and understandably so. They've had to evolve at light speed just to keep up with huge increases in basic, mission-critical user needs (e.g., the simple sharing of data and printers) as well as greater burdens like multimedia remote presentations and conferencing. Unless everyone who needs to share network resources is located in the same office space—an increasingly uncommon situation—the challenge is to connect relevant networks so all users can share the wealth of whatever services and resources are required.

Figure 1.1 shows a basic *local area network (LAN)* that's connected using a *hub*, which is basically just an antiquated device that connects wires together. Keep in mind that a simple network like this would be considered one collision domain and one broadcast domain. No worries if you have no idea what I mean by that because coming up soon, I'm going to talk about collision and broadcast domains enough to make you dream about them!

FIGURE 1.1   A very basic network

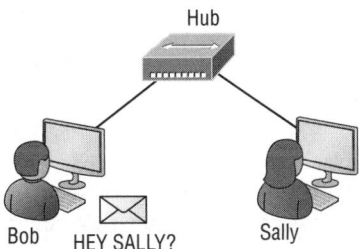

Things really can't get much simpler than this. And yes, though you can still find this configuration in some home networks, even many of those as well as the smallest business networks are more complicated today. As we move through this book, I'll just keep building upon this tiny network a bit at a time until we arrive at some really nice, robust, and current network designs—the types that will help you get your certification and a job!

But as I said, we'll get there one step at a time, so let's get back to the network shown in Figure 1.1 with this scenario: Bob wants to send Sally a file, and to complete that goal in this kind of network, he'll simply broadcast that he's looking for her, which is basically just shouting out over the network. Think of it like this: Bob walks out of his house and yells down a street called Chaos Court in order to contact Sally. This might work if Bob and Sally were the only ones living there, but not so much if it's crammed with homes and all the others living there are always hollering up and down the street to their neighbors just like Bob. Nope, Chaos Court would absolutely live up to its name, with all those residents going off whenever they felt like it—and believe it or not, our networks actually still work this way to a degree! So, given a choice, would you stay in Chaos Court, or would you pull up stakes and move on over to a nice new modern community called Broadway Lanes, which offers plenty of amenities and room for your home plus future additions all on nice, wide streets that can easily handle all present and future traffic? If you chose the latter, good choice... so did Sally, and she now lives a much quieter life, getting letters (packets) from Bob instead of a headache!

The scenario I just described brings me to the basic point of what this book and the Cisco certification objectives are really all about. My goal of showing you how to create efficient networks and segment them correctly in order to minimize all the chaotic yelling and screaming going on in them is a universal theme throughout my CCENT and CCNA series books. It's just inevitable that you'll have to break up a large network into a bunch of smaller ones at some point to match a network's equally inevitable growth, and as that expansion occurs, user response time simultaneously dwindles to a frustrating crawl. But if you master the vital technology and skills I have in store for you in this series, you'll be well equipped to rescue your network and its users by creating an efficient new network neighborhood to give them key amenities like the bandwidth they need to meet their evolving demands.

And this is no joke; most of us think of growth as good—and it can be—but as many of us experience daily when commuting to work, school, etc., it can also mean your LAN's traffic congestion can reach critical mass and grind to a complete halt! Again, the solution to this problem begins with breaking up a massive network into a number of smaller ones—something called *network segmentation*. This concept is a lot like planning a new community or modernizing an existing one. More streets are added, complete with new intersections and traffic signals, plus post offices are built with official maps documenting all those street names and directions on how to get to each. You'll need to effect new laws to keep order to it all and provide a police station to protect this nice new neighborhood as well. In a networking neighborhood environment, all of this is carried out using devices like *routers*, *switches*, and *bridges*.

So let's take a look at our new neighborhood now, because the word has gotten out; many more hosts have moved into it, so it's time to upgrade that new high-capacity infrastructure that we promised to handle the increase in population. Figure 1.2 shows a network that's been segmented with a switch, making each network segment that connects to the switch its own separate collision domain. Doing this results in a lot less yelling!

FIGURE 1.2 A switch can break up collision domains.

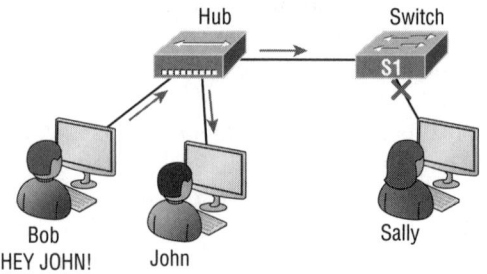

This is a great start, but I really want you to make note of the fact that this network is still one, single broadcast domain, meaning that we've really only decreased our screaming and yelling, not eliminated it. For example, if there's some sort of vital announcement that everyone in our neighborhood needs to hear about, it will definitely still get loud! You can see that the hub used in Figure 1.2 just extended the one collision domain from the switch port. The result is that John received the data from Bob but, happily, Sally did not. This is good because Bob intended to talk with John directly, and if he had needed to send a broadcast instead, everyone, including Sally, would have received it, possibly causing unnecessary congestion.

Here's a list of some of the things that commonly cause LAN traffic congestion:

- Too many hosts in a collision or broadcast domain
- Broadcast storms

- Too much multicast traffic

- Low bandwidth

- Adding hubs for connectivity to the network

- A bunch of ARP broadcasts

Take another look at Figure 1.2 and make sure you see that I extended the main hub from Figure 1.1 to a switch in Figure 1.2. I did that because hubs don't segment a network; they just connect network segments. Basically, it's an inexpensive way to connect a couple of PCs, and again, that's great for home use and troubleshooting, but that's about it!

As our planned community starts to grow, we'll need to add more streets with traffic control, and even some basic security. We'll achieve this by adding routers because these convenient devices are used to connect networks and route packets of data from one network to another. Cisco became the de facto standard for routers because of its unparalleled selection of high-quality router products and fantastic service. So never forget that by default, routers are basically employed to efficiently break up a *broadcast domain*—the set of all devices on a network segment, which are allowed to "hear" all broadcasts sent out on that specific segment.

Figure 1.3 depicts a router in our growing network, creating an internetwork and breaking up broadcast domains.

FIGURE 1.3   Routers create an internetwork.

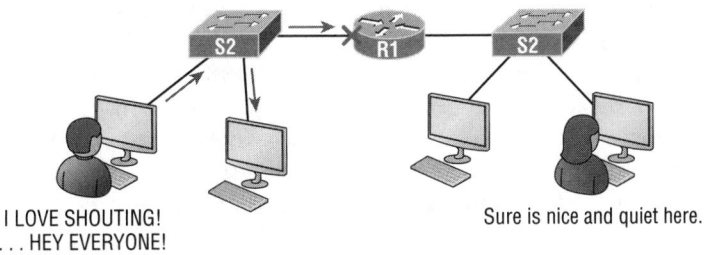

I LOVE SHOUTING!
. . . HEY EVERYONE!

Sure is nice and quiet here.

The network in Figure 1.3 is actually a pretty cool little network. Each host is connected to its own collision domain because of the switch, and the router has created two broadcast domains. So now our Sally is happily living in peace in a completely different neighborhood, no longer subjected to Bob's incessant shouting! If Bob wants to talk with Sally, he has to send a packet with a destination address using her IP address—he cannot broadcast for her!

But there's more… routers provide connections to *wide area network (WAN)* services as well via a serial interface for WAN connections—specifically, a V.35 physical interface on a Cisco router.

Let me make sure you understand why breaking up a broadcast domain is so important. When a host or server sends a network broadcast, every device on the network must read and process that broadcast—unless you have a router. When the router's interface receives this broadcast, it can respond by basically saying, "Thanks, but no thanks," and discard the broadcast without forwarding it on to other networks. Even though routers are known for breaking up broadcast domains by default, it's important to remember that they break up collision domains as well.

There are two advantages to using routers in your network:

- They don't forward broadcasts by default.
- They can filter the network based on layer 3 (Network layer) information such as an IP address.

Here are four ways a router functions in your network:

- Packet switching
- Packet filtering
- Internetwork communication
- Path selection

I'll tell you all about the various layers later in this chapter, but for now, it's helpful to think of routers as layer 3 switches. Unlike plain-vanilla layer 2 switches, which forward or filter frames, routers (layer 3 switches) use logical addressing and provide an important capacity called *packet switching*. Routers can also provide packet filtering via access lists, and when routers connect two or more networks together and use logical addressing (IP or IPv6), you then have an *internetwork*. Finally, routers use a routing table, which is essentially a map of the internetwork, to make best path selections for getting data to its proper destination and properly forward packets to remote networks.

Conversely, we don't use layer 2 switches to create internetworks because they don't break up broadcast domains by default. Instead, they're employed to add functionality to a network LAN. The main purpose of these switches is to make a LAN work better—to optimize its performance—providing more bandwidth for the LAN's users. Also, these switches don't forward packets to other networks like routers do. Instead, they only "switch" frames from one port to another within the switched network. And don't worry, even though you're probably thinking, "Wait—what are frames and packets?" I promise to completely fill you in later in this chapter. For now, think of a packet as a package containing data.

Okay, so by default, switches break up collision domains, but what are these things? *Collision domain* is an Ethernet term used to describe a network scenario in which one device sends a packet out on a network segment and every other device on that same segment is forced to pay attention no matter what. This isn't very efficient because if a different device tries to transmit at the same time, a collision will occur, requiring both devices to retransmit, one at a time—not good! This happens a lot in a hub environment, where each host segment connects to a hub that represents only one collision domain and a single broadcast domain. By contrast, each and every port on a switch represents its own collision domain, allowing network traffic to flow much more smoothly.

 Switches create separate collision domains within a single broadcast domain. Routers provide a separate broadcast domain for each interface. Don't let this ever confuse you!

The term *bridging* was introduced before routers and switches were implemented, so it's pretty common to hear people referring to switches as bridges. That's because bridges and switches basically do the same thing—break up collision domains on a LAN. Note to self that you cannot buy a physical bridge these days, only LAN switches, which use bridging technologies. This does not mean that you won't still hear Cisco and others refer to LAN switches as multiport bridges now and then.

But does it mean that a switch is just a multiple-port bridge with more brainpower? Well, pretty much, only there are still some key differences. Switches do provide a bridging function, but they do that with greatly enhanced management ability and features. Plus, most bridges had only 2 or 4 ports, which is severely limiting. Of course, it was possible to get your hands on a bridge with up to 16 ports, but that's nothing compared to the hundreds of ports available on some switches!

You would use a bridge in a network to reduce collisions within broadcast domains and to increase the number of collision domains in your network. Doing this provides more bandwidth for users. And never forget that using hubs in your Ethernet network can contribute to congestion. As always, plan your network design carefully!

Figure 1.4 shows how a network would look with all these internetwork devices in place. Remember, a router doesn't just break up broadcast domains for every LAN interface, it breaks up collision domains too.

FIGURE 1.4   Internetworking devices

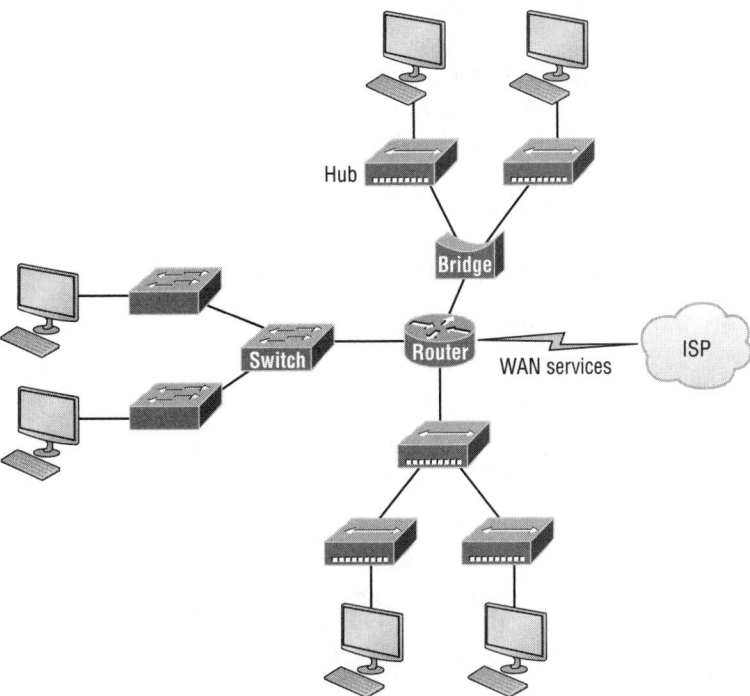

Looking at Figure 1.4, did you notice that the router has the center stage position and connects each physical network together? I'm stuck with using this layout because of the ancient bridges and hubs involved. I really hope you don't run across a network like this, but it's still really important to understand the strategic ideas that this figure represents!

See that bridge up at the top of our internetwork shown in Figure 1.4? It's there to connect the hubs to a router. The bridge breaks up collision domains, but all the hosts connected to both hubs are still crammed into the same broadcast domain. That bridge also created only three collision domains, one for each port, which means that each device connected to a hub is in the same collision domain as every other device connected to that same hub. This is really lame and to be avoided if possible, but it's still better than having one collision domain for all hosts! So don't do this at home; it's a great museum piece and a wonderful example of what not to do, but this inefficient design would be terrible for use in today's networks! It does show us how far we've come though, and again, the foundational concepts it illustrates are really important for you to get.

And I want you to notice something else: The three interconnected hubs at the bottom of the figure also connect to the router. This setup creates one collision domain and one broadcast domain and makes that bridged network, with its two collision domains, look majorly better by contrast!

> Don't misunderstand… bridges/switches are used to segment networks, but they will not isolate broadcast or multicast packets.

The best network connected to the router is the LAN switched network on the left. Why? Because each port on that switch breaks up collision domains. But it's not all good—all devices are still in the same broadcast domain. Do you remember why this can be really bad? Because all devices must listen to all broadcasts transmitted, that's why! And if your broadcast domains are too large, the users have less bandwidth and are required to process more broadcasts. Network response time eventually will slow to a level that could cause riots and strikes, so it's important to keep your broadcast domains small in the vast majority of networks today.

Once there are only switches in our example network, things really change a lot! Figure 1.5 demonstrates a network you'll typically stumble upon today.

FIGURE 1.5   Switched networks creating an internetwork

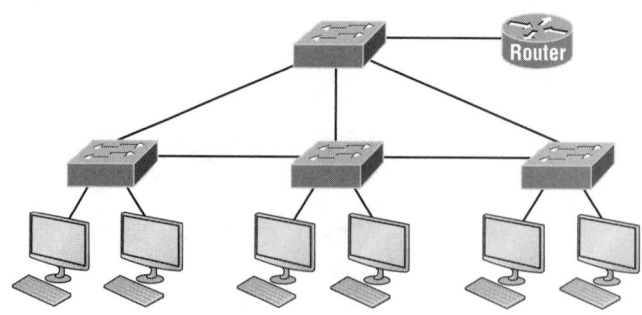

Here I've placed the LAN switches at the center of this network world, with the router connecting the logical networks. If I went ahead and implemented this design, I'll have created something called virtual LANs, or VLANs, which are used when you logically break up broadcast domains in a layer 2, switched network. It's really important to understand that even in a switched network environment, you still need a router to provide communication between VLANs. Don't forget that!

Still, clearly the best network design is the one that's perfectly configured to meet the business requirements of the specific company or client it serves, and it's usually one in which LAN switches exist in harmony with routers strategically placed in the network. It's my hope that this book will help you understand the basics of routers and switches so you can make solid, informed decisions on a case-by-case basis and be able to achieve that goal! But I digress...

So let's go back to Figure 1.4 now for a minute and really scrutinize it because I want to ask you this question: How many collision domains and broadcast domains are really there in this internetwork? I hope you answered nine collision domains and three broadcast domains! The broadcast domains are definitely the easiest to spot because only routers break up broadcast domains by default, and since there are three interface connections, that gives you three broadcast domains. But do you see the nine collision domains? Just in case that's a no, I'll explain. The all-hub network at the bottom is one collision domain; the bridge network on top equals three collision domains. Add in the switch network of five collision domains—one for each switch port—and you get a total of nine!

While we're at this, in Figure 1.5, each port on the switch is a separate collision domain, and each VLAN would be a separate broadcast domain. So how many collision domains do you see here? I'm counting 12—remember that connections between the switches are considered a collision domain! Since the figure doesn't show any VLAN information, we can assume the default of one broadcast domain is in place.

Before we move on to Internetworking Models, let's take a look at a few more network devices that we'll find in pretty much every network today as shown in Figure 1.6.

FIGURE 1.6   Other devices typically found in our internetworks today.

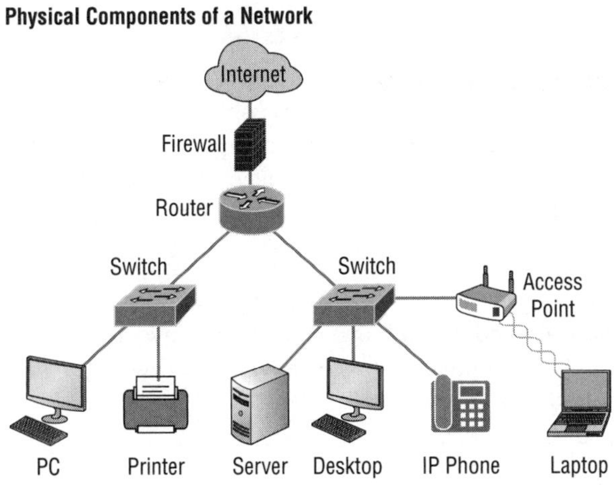

Physical Components of a Network

Taking off from the switched network in Figure 1.5, you'll find WLAN devices, including AP's and wireless controllers, and firewalls. You'd be hard pressed not to find these devices in your networks today.

Let's look closer at these devices:

- WLAN devices: These devices connect wireless devices such as computers, printers, and tablets to the network. Since pretty much every device manufactured today has a wireless NIC, you just need to configure a basic access point (AP) to connect to a traditional wired network.

- Access Points or APs: These devices allow wireless devices to connect to a wired network and extend a collision domain from a switch, and are typically in their own broadcast domain or what we'll refer to as a Virtual LAN (VLAN). An AP can be a simple standalone device, but today they are usually managed by wireless controllers either in house or through the internet.

- WLAN Controllers: These are the devices that network administrators or network operations centers use to manage access points in medium to large to extremely large quantities. The WLAN controller automatically handles the configuration of wireless access points and was typically used only in larger enterprise systems. However, with Cisco's acquisition of Meraki systems, you can easily manage a small to medium sized wireless network via the cloud using their simple to configure web controller system.

- Firewalls: These devices are network security systems that monitor and control the incoming and outgoing network traffic based on predetermined security rules, and is usually an Intrusion Protection System (IPS). Cisco Adaptive Security Appliance (ASA) firewall typically establishes a barrier between a trusted, secure internal network and the Internet, which is not secure or trusted. Cisco's new acquisition of Sourcefire put them in the top of the market with Next Generation Firewalls (NGFW) and Next Generation IPS (NGIPS), which Cisco now just calls Firepower. Cisco new Firepower runs on dedicated appliances, Cisco's ASA's, ISR routers and even on Meraki products.

🌐 Real World Scenario

Should I Replace My Existing 10/100 Mbps Switches?

Let's say you're a network administrator at a large company. The boss comes to you and says that he got your requisition to buy a bunch of new switches but he's really freaking out about the price tag! Should you push it—do you really need to go this far?

Absolutely! Make your case and go for it because the newest switches add really huge capacity to a network that older 10/100 Mbps switches just can't touch. And yes, five-year-old switches are considered pretty Pleistocene these days. But in reality, most of us just don't have an unlimited budget to buy all new gigabit switches; however, 10/100 switches are just not good enough in today's networks.

> Another good question: Do you really need low-latency 1 Gbps or better switch ports for all your users, servers, and other devices? Yes, you *absolutely* need new higher-end switches! This is because servers and hosts are no longer the bottlenecks of our internetworks, our routers and switches are—especially legacy ones. We now need gigabit on the desktop and on every router interface; 10 Gbps is now the minimum between switch uplinks, so go to 40 or even 100 Gbps as uplinks if you can afford it.
>
> Go ahead. Put in that requisition for all new switches. You'll be a hero before long!

Okay, so now that you've gotten a pretty thorough introduction to internetworking and the various devices that populate an internetwork, it's time to head into exploring the internetworking models.

Internetworking Models

First a little history: When networks first came into being, computers could typically communicate only with computers from the same manufacturer. For example, companies ran either a complete DECnet solution or an IBM solution, never both together. In the late 1970s, the *Open Systems Interconnection (OSI) reference model* was created by the International Organization for Standardization (ISO) to break through this barrier.

The OSI model was meant to help vendors create interoperable network devices and software in the form of protocols so that different vendor networks could work in peaceable accord with each other. Like world peace, it'll probably never happen completely, but it's still a great goal!

Anyway the OSI model is the primary architectural model for networks. It describes how data and network information are communicated from an application on one computer through the network media to an application on another computer. The OSI reference model breaks this approach into layers.

Coming up, I'll explain the layered approach to you plus how we can use it to help us troubleshoot our internetworks.

 Goodness! ISO, OSI, and soon you'll hear about IOS! Just remember that the ISO created the OSI and that Cisco created the Internetworking Operating System (IOS), which is what this book is all-so-about.

The Layered Approach

Understand that a *reference model* is a conceptual blueprint of how communications should take place. It addresses all the processes required for effective communication and divides them into logical groupings called *layers*. When a communication system is designed in this manner, it's known as a hierarchical or *layered architecture*.

Think of it like this: You and some friends want to start a company. One of the first things you'll do is sort out every task that must be done and decide who will do what. You would move on to determine the order in which you would like everything to be done with careful consideration of how all your specific operations relate to each other. You would then organize everything into departments (e.g., sales, inventory, and shipping), with each department dealing with its specific responsibilities and keeping its own staff busy enough to focus on their own particular area of the enterprise.

In this scenario, departments are a metaphor for the layers in a communication system. For things to run smoothly, the staff of each department has to trust in and rely heavily upon those in the others to do their jobs well. During planning sessions, you would take notes, recording the entire process to guide later discussions and clarify standards of operation, thereby creating your business blueprint—your own reference model.

And once your business is launched, your department heads, each armed with the part of the blueprint relevant to their own department, will develop practical ways to implement their distinct tasks. These practical methods, or protocols, will then be compiled into a standard operating procedures manual and followed closely because each procedure will have been included for different reasons, delimiting their various degrees of importance and implementation. All of this will become vital if you form a partnership or acquire another company because then it will be really important that the new company's business model is compatible with yours!

Models happen to be really important to software developers too. They often use a reference model to understand computer communication processes so they can determine which functions should be accomplished on a given layer. This means that if someone is creating a protocol for a certain layer, they only need to be concerned with their target layer's function. Software that maps to another layer's protocols and is specifically designed to be deployed there will handle additional functions. The technical term for this idea is *binding*. The communication processes that are related to each other are bound, or grouped together, at a particular layer.

Advantages of Reference Models

The OSI model is hierarchical, and there are many advantages that can be applied to any layered model, but as I said, the OSI model's primary purpose is to allow different vendors' networks to interoperate.

Here's a list of some of the more important benefits of using the OSI layered model:

- It divides the network communication process into smaller and simpler components, facilitating component development, design, and troubleshooting.

- It allows multiple-vendor development through the standardization of network components.

- It encourages industry standardization by clearly defining what functions occur at each layer of the model.

- It allows various types of network hardware and software to communicate.

- It prevents changes in one layer from affecting other layers to expedite development.

The OSI Reference Model

One of best gifts the OSI specifications gives us is paving the way for the data transfer between disparate hosts running different operating systems, like Unix hosts, Windows machines, Macs, smartphones, and so on.

And remember, the OSI is a logical model, not a physical one. It's essentially a set of guidelines that developers can use to create and implement applications to run on a network. It also provides a framework for creating and implementing networking standards, devices, and internetworking schemes.

The OSI has seven different layers, divided into two groups. The top three layers define how the applications within the end stations will communicate with each other as well as with users. The bottom four layers define how data is transmitted end to end.

Figure 1.7 shows the three upper layers and their functions.

FIGURE 1.7   The upper layers

Application	• Provides a user interface
Presentation	• Presents data • Handles processing such as encryption
Session	• Keeps different applications' data separate

When looking at Figure 1.6, understand that users interact with the computer at the Application layer and also that the upper layers are responsible for applications communicating between hosts. None of the upper layers knows anything about networking or network addresses because that's the responsibility of the four bottom layers.

In Figure 1.8, which shows the four lower layers and their functions, you can see that it's these four bottom layers that define how data is transferred through physical media like wire, cable, fiber optics, switches, and routers. These bottom layers also determine how to rebuild a data stream from a transmitting host to a destination host's application.

FIGURE 1.8   The lower layers

Transport	• Provides reliable or unreliable delivery • Performs error correction before retransmit
Network	• Provides logical addressing, which routers use for path determination
Data Link	• Combines packets into bytes and bytes into frames • Provides access to media using MAC address • Performs error detection not correction
Physical	• Moves bits between devices • Specifies voltage, wire speed, and pinout of cables

The following network devices operate at all seven layers of the OSI model:

- *Network management stations (NMSs)*
- Web and application servers
- Gateways (not default gateways)
- Servers
- Network hosts

Basically, the ISO is pretty much the Emily Post of the network protocol world. Just as Ms. Post wrote the book setting the standards—or protocols—for human social interaction, the ISO developed the OSI reference model as the precedent and guide for an open network protocol set. Defining the etiquette of communication models, it remains the most popular means of comparison for protocol suites today.

The OSI reference model has the following seven layers:

- Application layer (layer 7)
- Presentation layer (layer 6)
- Session layer (layer 5)
- Transport layer (layer 4)
- Network layer (layer 3)
- Data Link layer (layer 2)
- Physical layer (layer 1)

Some people like to use a mnemonic to remember the seven layers, such as **All People Seem To Need Data Processing**. Figure 1.9 shows a summary of the functions defined at each layer of the OSI model.

FIGURE 1.9 OSI layer functions

Application	• File, print, message, database, and application services
Presentation	• Data encryption, compression, and translation services
Session	• Dialog control

Transport	• End-to-end connection
Network	• Routing

Data Link	• Framing
Physical	• Physical topology

I've separated the seven-layer model into three different functions: the upper layers, the middle layers, and the bottom layers. The upper layers communicate with the user interface and application, the middle layers do reliable communication and routing to a remote network, and the bottom layers communicate to the local network.

With this in hand, you're now ready to explore each layer's function in detail!

The Application Layer

The *Application layer* of the OSI model marks the spot where users actually communicate to the computer and comes into play only when it's clear that access to the network will be needed soon. Take the case of Internet Explorer (IE). You could actually uninstall every trace of networking components like TCP/IP, the NIC card, and so on and still use IE to view a local HTML document. But things would get ugly if you tried to do things like view a remote HTML document that must be retrieved because IE and other browsers act on these types of requests by attempting to access the Application layer. So basically, the Application layer is working as the interface between the actual application program and the next layer down by providing ways for the application to send information down through the protocol stack. This isn't actually part of the layered structure, because browsers don't live in the Application layer, but they interface with it as well as the relevant protocols when asked to access remote resources.

Identifying and confirming the communication partner's availability and verifying the required resources to permit the specified type of communication to take place also occurs at the Application layer. This is important because, like the lion's share of browser functions, computer applications sometimes need more than desktop resources. It's more typical than you would think for the communicating components of several network applications to come together to carry out a requested function. Here are a few good examples of these kinds of events:

- File transfers
- Email
- Enabling remote access
- Network management activities
- Client/server processes
- Information location

Many network applications provide services for communication over enterprise networks, but for present and future internetworking, the need is fast developing to reach beyond the limits of current physical networking.

The Application layer works as the interface between actual application programs. This means end-user programs like Microsoft Word don't reside at the Application layer, they interface with the Application layer protocols. Later, in Chapter 3, "Introduction to TCP/IP," I'll talk in detail about a few important programs that actually reside at the Application layer, like Telnet, FTP, and TFTP.

The Presentation Layer

The *Presentation layer* gets its name from its purpose: It presents data to the Application layer and is responsible for data translation and code formatting. Think of it as the OSI model's translator, providing coding and conversion services. One very effective way of ensuring a successful data transfer is to convert the data into a standard format before transmission. Computers are configured to receive this generically formatted data and then reformat it back into its native state to read it. An example of this type of translation service occurs when translating old Extended Binary Coded Decimal Interchange Code (EBCDIC) data to ASCII, the American Standard Code for Information Interchange (often pronounced "askee"). So just remember that by providing translation services, the Presentation layer ensures that data transferred from the Application layer of one system can be read by the Application layer of another one.

With this in mind, it follows that the OSI would include protocols that define how standard data should be formatted, so key functions like data compression, decompression, encryption, and decryption are also associated with this layer. Some Presentation layer standards are involved in multimedia operations as well.

The Session Layer

The *Session layer* is responsible for setting up, managing, and dismantling sessions between Presentation layer entities and keeping user data separate. Dialog control between devices also occurs at this layer.

Communication between hosts' various applications at the Session layer, as from a client to a server, is coordinated and organized via three different modes: *simplex*, *half-duplex*, and *full-duplex*. Simplex is simple one-way communication, kind of like saying something and not getting a reply. Half-duplex is actual two-way communication, but it can take place in only one direction at a time, preventing the interruption of the transmitting device. It's like when pilots and ship captains communicate over their radios, or even a walkie-talkie. But full-duplex is exactly like a real conversation where devices can transmit and receive at the same time, much like two people arguing or interrupting each other during a telephone conversation.

The Transport Layer

The *Transport layer* segments and reassembles data into a single data stream. Services located at this layer take all the various data received from upper-layer applications, then combine it into the same, concise data stream. These protocols provide end-to-end data transport services and can establish a logical connection between the sending host and destination host on an internetwork.

A pair of well-known protocols called TCP and UDP are integral to this layer, but no worries if you're not already familiar with them because I'll bring you up to speed later, in Chapter 3. For now, understand that although both work at the Transport layer, TCP is known as a reliable service but UDP is not. This distinction gives application developers more options because they have a choice between the two protocols when they are designing products for this layer.

The Transport layer is responsible for providing mechanisms for multiplexing upper-layer applications, establishing sessions, and tearing down virtual circuits. It can also hide the details of network-dependent information from the higher layers as well as provide transparent data transfer.

> The term *reliable networking* can be used at the Transport layer. Reliable networking requires that acknowledgments, sequencing, and flow control will all be used.

The Transport layer can be either connectionless or connection-oriented, but because Cisco really wants you to understand the connection-oriented function of the Transport layer, I'm going to go into that in more detail here.

Connection-Oriented Communication

For reliable transport to occur, a device that wants to transmit must first establish a connection-oriented communication session with a remote device—its peer system—known as a *call setup* or a *three-way handshake*. Once this process is complete, the data transfer occurs, and when it's finished, a call termination takes place to tear down the virtual circuit.

Figure 1.10 depicts a typical reliable session taking place between sending and receiving systems. In it, you can see that both hosts' application programs begin by notifying their individual operating systems that a connection is about to be initiated. The two operating systems communicate by sending messages over the network confirming that the transfer is approved and that both sides are ready for it to take place. After all of this required synchronization takes place, a connection is fully established and the data transfer begins. And by the way, it's really helpful to understand that this virtual circuit setup is often referred to as overhead!

FIGURE 1.10   Establishing a connection-oriented session

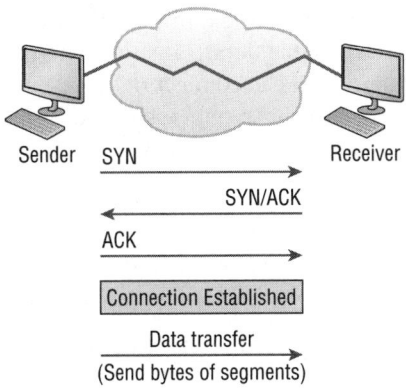

Okay, now while the information is being transferred between hosts, the two machines periodically check in with each other, communicating through their protocol software to ensure that all is going well and that the data is being received properly.

Here's a summary of the steps in the connection-oriented session—that three-way handshake—pictured in Figure 1.9:

- The first "connection agreement" segment is a request for *synchronization (SYN)*.

- The next segments *acknowledge (ACK)* the request and establish connection parameters—the rules—between hosts. These segments request that the receiver's sequencing is synchronized here as well so that a bidirectional connection can be formed.

- The final segment is also an acknowledgment, which notifies the destination host that the connection agreement has been accepted and that the actual connection has been established. Data transfer can now begin.

Sounds pretty simple, but things don't always flow so smoothly. Sometimes during a transfer, congestion can occur because a high-speed computer is generating data traffic a lot faster than the network itself can process it! And a whole bunch of computers simultaneously sending datagrams through a single gateway or destination can also jam things up pretty badly. In the latter case, a gateway or destination can become congested even though no single source caused the problem. Either way, the problem is basically akin to a freeway bottleneck—too much traffic for too small a capacity. It's not usually one car that's the problem; it's just that there are way too many cars on that freeway at once!

But what actually happens when a machine receives a flood of datagrams too quickly for it to process? It stores them in a memory section called a *buffer*. Sounds great; it's just that this buffering action can solve the problem only if the datagrams are part of a small burst. If the datagram deluge continues, eventually exhausting the device's memory, its flood capacity will be exceeded and it will dump any and all additional datagrams it receives just like an inundated overflowing bucket!

Flow Control

Since floods and losing data can both be tragic, we have a fail-safe solution in place known as *flow control*. Its job is to ensure data integrity at the Transport layer by allowing applications to request reliable data transport between systems. Flow control prevents a sending host on one side of the connection from overflowing the buffers in the receiving host. Reliable data transport employs a connection-oriented communications session between systems, and the protocols involved ensure that the following will be achieved:

- The segments delivered are acknowledged back to the sender upon their reception.

- Any segments not acknowledged are retransmitted.

- Segments are sequenced back into their proper order upon arrival at their destination.

- A manageable data flow is maintained in order to avoid congestion, overloading, or worse, data loss.

The purpose of flow control is to provide a way for the receiving device to control the amount of data sent by the sender.

Because of the transport function, network flood control systems really work well. Instead of dumping and losing data, the Transport layer can issue a "not ready" indicator to the sender, or potential source of the flood. This mechanism works kind of like a stop-light, signaling the sending device to stop transmitting segment traffic to its overwhelmed peer. After the peer receiver processes the segments already in its memory reservoir—its buffer—it sends out a "ready" transport indicator. When the machine waiting to transmit the rest of its datagrams receives this "go" indicator, it resumes its transmission. The process is pictured in Figure 1.11.

FIGURE 1.11 Transmitting segments with flow control

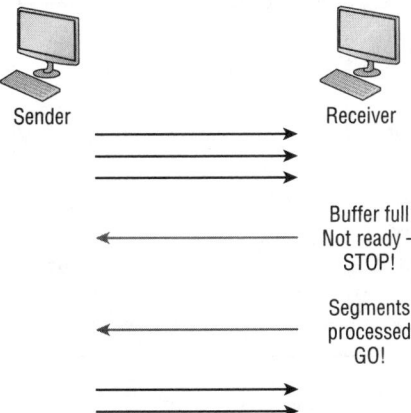

In a reliable, connection-oriented data transfer, datagrams are delivered to the receiving host hopefully in the same sequence they're transmitted. A failure will occur if any data segments are lost, duplicated, or damaged along the way—a problem solved by having the receiving host acknowledge that it has received each and every data segment.

A service is considered connection-oriented if it has the following characteristics:

- A virtual circuit, or "three-way handshake," is set up.
- It uses sequencing.
- It uses acknowledgments.
- It uses flow control.

The types of flow control are buffering, windowing, and congestion avoidance.

Windowing

Ideally, data throughput happens quickly and efficiently. And as you can imagine, it would be painfully slow if the transmitting machine had to actually wait for an acknowledgment after sending each and every segment! The quantity of data segments, measured in bytes, that the transmitting machine is allowed to send without receiving an acknowledgment is called a *window*.

 Windows are used to control the amount of outstanding, unacknowledged data segments.

The size of the window controls how much information is transferred from one end to the other before an acknowledgement is required. While some protocols quantify information depending on the number of packets, TCP/IP measures it by counting the number of bytes.

As you can see in Figure 1.12, there are two window sizes—one set to 1 and one set to 3.

FIGURE 1.12 Windowing

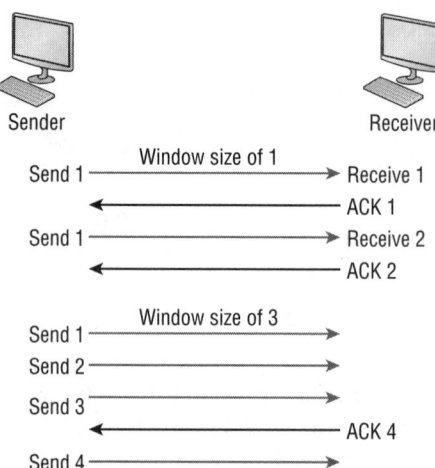

If you've configured a window size of 1, the sending machine will wait for an acknowledgment for each data segment it transmits before transmitting another one but will allow three to be transmitted before receiving an acknowledgement if the window size is set to 3.

In this simplified example, both the sending and receiving machines are workstations. Remember that in reality, the transmission isn't based on simple numbers but in the amount of bytes that can be sent!

 If a receiving host fails to receive all the bytes that it should acknowledge, the host can improve the communication session by decreasing the window size.

Acknowledgments

Reliable data delivery ensures the integrity of a stream of data sent from one machine to the other through a fully functional data link. It guarantees that the data won't be duplicated or lost. This is achieved through something called *positive acknowledgment with retransmission*—a technique that requires a receiving machine to communicate with the transmitting source by sending an acknowledgment message back to the sender when it receives data. The sender documents each segment measured in bytes, then sends and waits for this acknowledgment before sending the next segment. Also important is that when it sends a segment, the transmitting machine starts a timer and will retransmit if it expires before it gets an acknowledgment back from the receiving end. Figure 1.13 shows the process I just described.

FIGURE 1.13   Transport layer reliable delivery

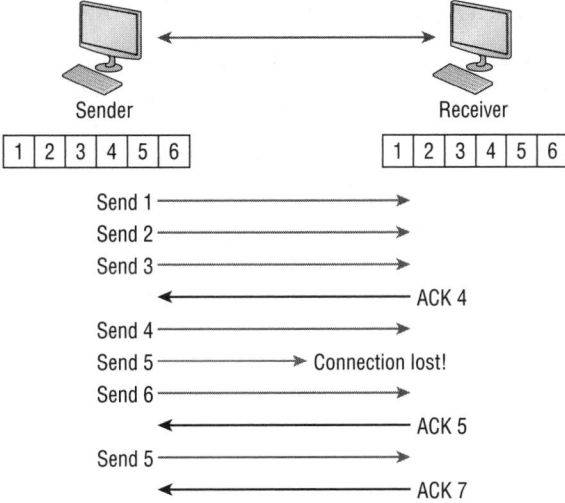

In the figure, the sending machine transmits segments 1, 2, and 3. The receiving node acknowledges that it has received them by requesting segment 4 (what it is expecting next). When it receives the acknowledgment, the sender then transmits segments 4, 5, and 6. If segment 5 doesn't make it to the destination, the receiving node acknowledges that event with a request for the segment to be re-sent. The sending machine will then resend the lost segment and wait for an acknowledgment, which it must receive in order to move on to the transmission of segment 7.

The Transport layer, working in tandem with the Session layer, also separates the data from different applications, an activity known as *session multiplexing*, and it happens when a client connects to a server with multiple browser sessions open. This is exactly what's taking place when you go someplace online like Amazon and click multiple links, opening them simultaneously to get information when comparison shopping. The client data from each browser session must be separate when the server application receives it, which is pretty slick technologically speaking, and it's the Transport layer to the rescue for that juggling act!

The Network Layer

The *Network layer*, or layer 3, manages device addressing, tracks the location of devices on the network, and determines the best way to move data. This means that it's up to the Network layer to transport traffic between devices that aren't locally attached. Routers, which are layer 3 devices, are specified at this layer and provide the routing services within an internetwork.

Here's how that works: first, when a packet is received on a router interface, the destination IP address is checked. If the packet isn't destined for that particular router, it will look up the destination network address in the routing table. Once the router chooses an exit interface, the packet will be sent to that interface to be framed and sent out on the local network. If the router can't find an entry for the packet's destination network in the routing table, the router drops the packet.

Data and route update packets are the two types of packets used at the Network layer:

Data Packets   These are used to transport user data through the internetwork. Protocols used to support data traffic are called routed protocols, and IP and IPv6 are key examples. I'll cover IP addressing in Chapter 3, "Introduction to TCP/IP," and Chapter 4, "Easy Subnetting," and I'll cover IPv6 in Chapter 14, "Internet Protocol Version 6 (IPv6)."

Route Update Packets   These packets are used to update neighboring routers about the networks connected to all routers within the internetwork. Protocols that send route update packets are called routing protocols; the most critical ones for CCNA are RIPv2, EIGRP, and OSPF. Route update packets are used to help build and maintain routing tables.

Figure 1.14 shows an example of a routing table. The routing table each router keeps and refers to includes the following information:

FIGURE 1.14   Routing table used in a router

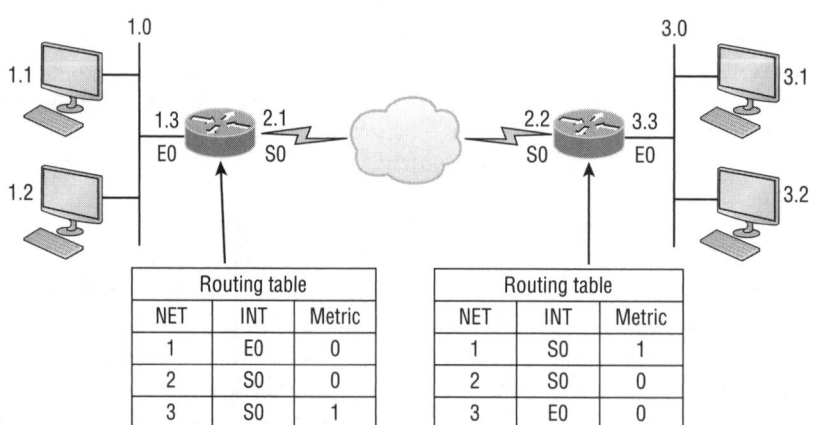

Routing table		
NET	INT	Metric
1	E0	0
2	S0	0
3	S0	1

Routing table		
NET	INT	Metric
1	S0	1
2	S0	0
3	E0	0

Network Addresses   Protocol-specific network addresses. A router must maintain a routing table for individual routing protocols because each routed protocol keeps track of a network with a different addressing scheme. For example, the routing tables for IP and IPv6 are completely different, so the router keeps a table for each one. Think of it as a street sign in each of the different languages spoken by the American, Spanish, and French people living on a street; the street sign would read Cat/Gato/Chat.

Interface   The exit interface a packet will take when destined for a specific network.

Metric   The distance to the remote network. Different routing protocols use different ways of computing this distance. I'm going to cover routing protocols thoroughly in Chapter 9, "IP Routing." For now, know that some routing protocols like the Routing Information Protocol, or RIP, use hop count, which refers to the number of routers a packet passes through en route to a remote network. Others use bandwidth, delay of the line, or even tick count (1/18 of a second) to determine the best path for data to get to a given destination.

And as I mentioned earlier, routers break up broadcast domains, which means that by default, broadcasts aren't forwarded through a router. Do you remember why this is a good thing? Routers also break up collision domains, but you can also do that using layer 2 (Data Link layer) switches. Because each interface in a router represents a separate network, it must be assigned unique network identification numbers, and each host on the network connected to that router must use the same network number. Figure 1.15 shows how a router works in an internetwork.

FIGURE 1.15   A router in an internetwork. Each router LAN interface is a broadcast domain. Routers break up broadcast domains by default and provide WAN services.

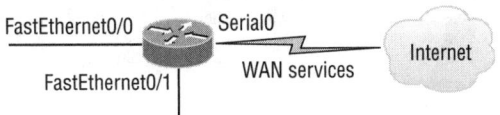

Here are some router characteristics that you should never forget:

- Routers, by default, will not forward any broadcast or multicast packets.
- Routers use the logical address in a Network layer header to determine the next-hop router to forward the packet to.
- Routers can use access lists, created by an administrator, to control security based on the types of packets allowed to enter or exit an interface.
- Routers can provide layer 2 bridging functions if needed and can simultaneously route through the same interface.
- Layer 3 devices—in this case, routers—provide connections between *virtual LANs (VLANs).*
- Routers can provide *quality of service (QoS)* for specific types of network traffic.

The Data Link Layer

The *Data Link layer* provides for the physical transmission of data and handles error notification, network topology, and flow control. This means that the Data Link layer will ensure that messages are delivered to the proper device on a LAN using hardware addresses and will translate messages from the Network layer into bits for the Physical layer to transmit.

The Data Link layer formats the messages, each called a *data frame*, and adds a customized header containing the hardware destination and source address. This added information forms a sort of capsule that surrounds the original message in much the same way that engines, navigational devices, and other tools were attached to the lunar modules of the Apollo project. These various pieces of equipment were useful only during certain stages of space flight and were stripped off the module and discarded when their designated stage was completed. The process of data traveling through networks is similar.

Figure 1.16 shows the Data Link layer with the Ethernet and IEEE specifications. When you check it out, notice that the IEEE 802.2 standard is used in conjunction with and adds functionality to the other IEEE standards. (You'll read more about the important IEEE 802 standards used with the Cisco objectives in Chapter 2, "Ethernet Networking and Data Encapsulation.")

FIGURE 1.16 Data Link layer

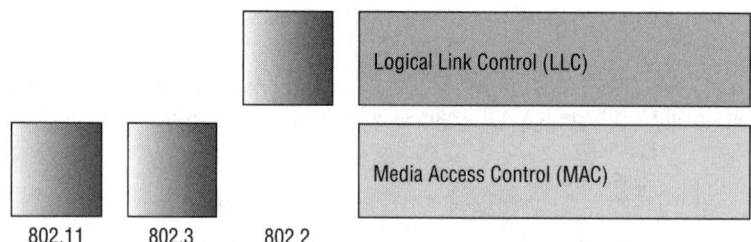

It's important for you to understand that routers, which work at the Network layer, don't care at all about where a particular host is located. They're only concerned about where networks are located and the best way to reach them—including remote ones. Routers are totally obsessive when it comes to networks, which in this case is a good thing! It's the Data Link layer that's responsible for the actual unique identification of each device that resides on a local network.

For a host to send packets to individual hosts on a local network as well as transmit packets between routers, the Data Link layer uses hardware addressing. Each time a packet is sent between routers, it's framed with control information at the Data Link layer, but that information is stripped off at the receiving router and only the original packet is left completely intact. This framing of the packet continues for each hop until the packet is finally delivered to the correct receiving host. It's really important to understand that the packet itself is never altered along the route; it's only encapsulated with the type of control information required for it to be properly passed on to the different media types.

The IEEE Ethernet Data Link layer has two sublayers:

Media Access Control (MAC)   Defines how packets are placed on the media. Contention for media access is "first come/first served" access where everyone shares the same bandwidth—hence the name. Physical addressing is defined here as well as logical topologies. What's a logical topology? It's the signal path through a physical topology. Line discipline, error notification (but not correction), the ordered delivery of frames, and optional flow control can also be used at this sublayer.

Logical Link Control (LLC)   Responsible for identifying Network layer protocols and then encapsulating them. An LLC header tells the Data Link layer what to do with a packet once a frame is received. It works like this: a host receives a frame and looks in the LLC header to find out where the packet is destined—for instance, the IP protocol at the Network layer. The LLC can also provide flow control and sequencing of control bits.

The switches and bridges I talked about near the beginning of the chapter both work at the Data Link layer and filter the network using hardware (MAC) addresses. I'll talk about these next.

As data is encoded with control information at each layer of the OSI model, the data is named with something called a protocol data unit (PDU). At the Transport layer, the PDU is called a segment, at the Network layer it's a packet, at the Data Link a frame, and at the Physical layer it's called bits. This method of naming the data at each layer is covered thoroughly in Chapter 2.

Switches and Bridges at the Data Link Layer

Layer 2 switching is considered hardware-based bridging because it uses specialized hardware called an *application-specific integrated circuit (ASIC)*. ASICs can run up to high gigabit speeds with very low latency rates.

Latency is the time measured from when a frame enters a port to when it exits a port.

Bridges and switches read each frame as it passes through the network. The layer 2 device then puts the source hardware address in a filter table and keeps track of which port the frame was received on. This information (logged in the bridge's or switch's filter table) is what helps the machine determine the location of the specific sending device. Figure 1.17 shows a switch in an internetwork and how John is sending packets to the Internet and Sally doesn't hear his frames because she is in a different collision domain. The destination frame goes directly to the default gateway router, and Sally doesn't see John's traffic, much to her relief.

FIGURE 1.17   A switch in an internetwork

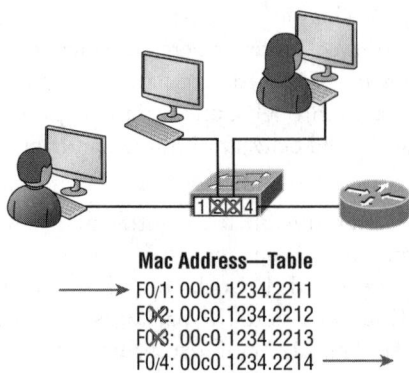

Mac Address—Table
⟶   F0/1: 00c0.1234.2211
FO/2: 00c0.1234.2212
FO/3: 00c0.1234.2213
F0/4: 00c0.1234.2214 ⟶

The real estate business is all about location, location, location, and it's the same way for both layer 2 and layer 3 devices. Though both need to be able to negotiate the network, it's crucial to remember that they're concerned with very different parts of it. Primarily, layer 3 machines (such as routers) need to locate specific networks, whereas layer 2 machines (switches and bridges) need to eventually locate specific devices. So, networks are to routers as individual devices are to switches and bridges. And routing tables that "map" the internetwork are for routers as filter tables that "map" individual devices are for switches and bridges.

After a filter table is built on the layer 2 device, it will forward frames only to the segment where the destination hardware address is located. If the destination device is on the same segment as the frame, the layer 2 device will block the frame from going to any other segments. If the destination is on a different segment, the frame can be transmitted only to that segment. This is called *transparent bridging.*

When a switch interface receives a frame with a destination hardware address that isn't found in the device's filter table, it will forward the frame to all connected segments. If the unknown device that was sent the "mystery frame" replies to this forwarding action, the switch updates its filter table regarding that device's location. But in the event the destination address of the transmitting frame is a broadcast address, the switch will forward all broadcasts to every connected segment by default.

All devices that the broadcast is forwarded to are considered to be in the same broadcast domain. This can be a problem because layer 2 devices propagate layer 2 broadcast storms that can seriously choke performance, and the only way to stop a broadcast storm from propagating through an internetwork is with a layer 3 device—a router!

The biggest benefit of using switches instead of hubs in your internetwork is that each switch port is actually its own collision domain. Remember that a hub creates one large collision domain, which is not a good thing! But even armed with a switch, you still don't get to just break up broadcast domains by default because neither switches nor bridges will do that. They'll simply forward all broadcasts instead.

Another benefit of LAN switching over hub-centered implementations is that each device on every segment plugged into a switch can transmit simultaneously. Well, at least they can as long as there's only one host on each port and there isn't a hub plugged into a switch port! As you might have guessed, this is because hubs allow only one device per network segment to communicate at a time.

The Physical Layer

Finally arriving at the bottom, we find that the *Physical layer* does two things: it sends bits and receives bits. Bits come only in values of 1 or 0—a Morse code with numerical values. The Physical layer communicates directly with the various types of actual communication media. Different kinds of media represent these bit values in different ways. Some use audio tones, while others employ *state transitions*—changes in voltage from high to low and low to high. Specific protocols are needed for each type of media to describe the proper bit patterns to be used, how data is encoded into media signals, and the various qualities of the physical media's attachment interface.

The Physical layer specifies the electrical, mechanical, procedural, and functional requirements for activating, maintaining, and deactivating a physical link between end systems. This layer is also where you identify the interface between the *data terminal equipment (DTE)* and the *data communication equipment (DCE)*. (Some old phone-company employees still call DCE "data circuit-terminating equipment.") The DCE is usually located at the service provider, while the DTE is the attached device. The services available to the DTE are most often accessed via a modem or *channel service unit/data service unit (CSU/DSU)*.

The Physical layer's connectors and different physical topologies are defined by the OSI as standards, allowing disparate systems to communicate. The Cisco exam objectives are interested only in the IEEE Ethernet standards.

Hubs at the Physical Layer

A hub is really a multiple-port repeater. A repeater receives a digital signal, reamplifies or regenerates that signal, then forwards the signal out the other port without looking at any data. A hub does the same thing across all active ports: any digital signal received from a segment on a hub port is regenerated or reamplified and transmitted out all other ports on the hub. This means all devices plugged into a hub are in the same collision domain as well as in the same broadcast domain. Figure 1.18 shows a hub in a network and how when one host transmits, all other hosts must stop and listen.

FIGURE 1.18   A hub in a network

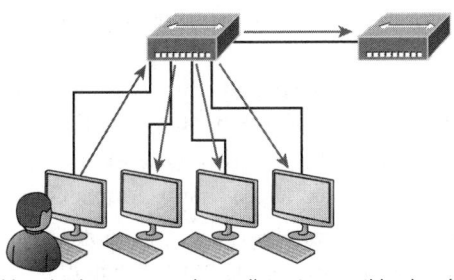

I love it when everyone has to listen to everything I say!

Hubs, like repeaters, don't examine any of the traffic as it enters or before it's transmitted out to the other parts of the physical media. And every device connected to the hub, or hubs, must listen if a device transmits. A physical star network, where the hub is a central device and cables extend in all directions out from it, is the type of topology a hub creates. Visually, the design really does resemble a star, whereas Ethernet networks run a logical bus topology, meaning that the signal has to run through the network from end to end.

Hubs and repeaters can be used to enlarge the area covered by a single LAN segment, but I really do not recommend going with this configuration! LAN switches are affordable for almost every situation and will make you much happier.

Topologies at the Physical layer

One last thing I want to discuss at the Physical layer is topologies, both physical and logical. Understand that every type of network has both a physical and a logical topology.

- The physical topology of a network refers to the physical layout of the devices, but mostly the cabling and cabling layout.

- The logical topology defines the logical path on which the signal will travel on the physical topology.

    Figure 1.19 shows the four types of topologies.

FIGURE 1.19   Physical vs. Logical Topolgies

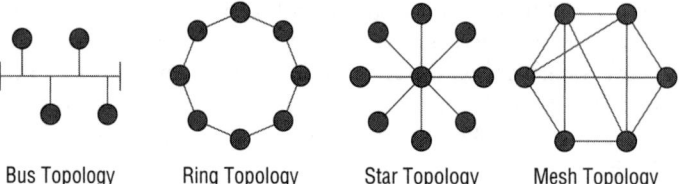

- Physical topology is the physical layout of the devices and cabling.
- The primary physical topology categories are bus, ring, star, and mesh.

Bus Topology   Ring Topology   Star Topology   Mesh Topology

Here are the topology types, although the most common, and pretty much the only network we use today is a physical star, logical bus technology, which is considered a hybrid topology (think Ethernet):

- Bus: In a bus topology, every workstation is connected to a single cable, meaning every host is directly connected to every other workstation in the network.

- Ring: In a ring topology, computers and other network devices are cabled together in a way that the last device is connected to the first to form a circle or ring.

- Star: The most common physical topology is a star topology, which is your Ethernet switching physical layout. A central cabling device (switch) connects the computers and other network devices together. This category includes star and extended star topologies. Physical connection is commonly made using twisted-pair wiring.

- Mesh: In a mesh topology, every network device is cabled together with connection to each other. Redundant links increase reliability and self-healing. The physical connection is commonly made using fiber or twisted-pair wiring.

- Hybrid: Ethernet uses a physical star layout (cables come from all directions), and the signal travels end-to-end, like a bus route.

Summary

Whew! I know this seemed like the chapter that wouldn't end, but it did—and you made it through! You're now armed with a ton of fundamental information; you're ready to build upon it and are well on your way to certification.

I started by discussing simple, basic networking and the differences between collision and broadcast domains.

I then discussed the OSI model—the seven-layer model used to help application developers design applications that can run on any type of system or network. Each layer has its special jobs and select responsibilities within the model to ensure that solid, effective communications do, in fact, occur. I provided you with complete details of each layer and discussed how Cisco views the specifications of the OSI model.

In addition, each layer in the OSI model specifies different types of devices, and I described the different devices used at each layer.

Remember that hubs are Physical layer devices and repeat the digital signal to all segments except the one from which it was received. Switches segment the network using hardware addresses and break up collision domains. Routers break up broadcast domains as well as collision domains and use logical addressing to send packets through an internetwork.

Exam Essentials

Identify the possible causes of LAN traffic congestion.   Too many hosts in a broadcast domain, broadcast storms, multicasting, and low bandwidth are all possible causes of LAN traffic congestion.

Describe the difference between a collision domain and a broadcast domain.   *Collision domain* is an Ethernet term used to describe a network collection of devices in which one particular device sends a packet on a network segment, forcing every other device on that same segment to pay attention to it. With a broadcast domain, a set of all devices on a network hears all broadcasts sent on all segments.

Differentiate a MAC address and an IP address and describe how and when each address type is used in a network.   A MAC address is a hexadecimal number identifying the physical connection of a host. MAC addresses are said to operate on layer 2 of the OSI model. IP addresses, which can be expressed in binary or decimal format, are logical identifiers that are said to be on layer 3 of the OSI model. Hosts on the same physical segment locate one another with MAC addresses, while IP addresses are used when they reside on different LAN segments or subnets.

Understand the difference between a hub, a bridge, a switch, and a router.   A hub creates one collision domain and one broadcast domain. A bridge breaks up collision domains but creates one large broadcast domain. They use hardware addresses to filter the network. Switches are really just multiple-port bridges with more intelligence; they break up collision domains but create one large broadcast domain by default. Bridges and switches use hardware addresses to filter the network. Routers break up broadcast domains (and collision domains) and use logical addressing to filter the network.

Identify the functions and advantages of routers.   Routers perform packet switching, filtering, and path selection, and they facilitate internetwork communication. One advantage of routers is that they reduce broadcast traffic.

Differentiate connection-oriented and connectionless network services and describe how each is handled during network communications.   Connection-oriented services use acknowledgments and flow control to create a reliable session. More overhead is used than in a connectionless network service. Connectionless services are used to send data with no acknowledgments or flow control. This is considered unreliable.

Define the OSI layers, understand the function of each, and describe how devices and networking protocols can be mapped to each layer.   You must remember the seven layers of the OSI model and what function each layer provides. The Application, Presentation, and Session layers are upper layers and are responsible for communicating from a user interface to an application. The Transport layer provides segmentation, sequencing, and virtual circuits. The Network layer provides logical network addressing and routing through an internetwork. The Data Link layer provides framing and placing of data on the network medium. The Physical layer is responsible for taking 1s and 0s and encoding them into a digital signal for transmission on the network segment.

Written Labs

In this section, you'll complete the following labs to make sure you've got the information and concepts contained within them fully dialed in:

> Lab 1.1: OSI Questions
>
> Lab 1.2: Defining the OSI Layers and Devices
>
> Lab 1.3: Identifying Collision and Broadcast Domains

You can find the answers to these labs in Appendix A, "Answers to Written Labs."

Written Lab 1.1: OSI Questions

Answer the following questions about the OSI model:

1. Which layer chooses and determines the availability of communicating partners along with the resources necessary to make the connection, coordinates partnering

applications, and forms a consensus on procedures for controlling data integrity and error recovery?

2. Which layer is responsible for converting data packets from the Data Link layer into electrical signals?

3. At which layer is routing implemented, enabling connections and path selection between two end systems?

4. Which layer defines how data is formatted, presented, encoded, and converted for use on the network?

5. Which layer is responsible for creating, managing, and terminating sessions between applications?

6. Which layer ensures the trustworthy transmission of data across a physical link and is primarily concerned with physical addressing, line discipline, network topology, error notification, ordered delivery of frames, and flow control?

7. Which layer is used for reliable communication between end nodes over the network and provides mechanisms for establishing, maintaining, and terminating virtual circuits; transport-fault detection and recovery; and controlling the flow of information?

8. Which layer provides logical addressing that routers will use for path determination?

9. Which layer specifies voltage, wire speed, and cable pinouts and moves bits between devices?

10. Which layer combines bits into bytes and bytes into frames, uses MAC addressing, and provides error detection?

11. Which layer is responsible for keeping the data from different applications separate on the network?

12. Which layer is represented by frames?

13. Which layer is represented by segments?

14. Which layer is represented by packets?

15. Which layer is represented by bits?

16. Rearrange the following in order of encapsulation:

    Packets

    Frames

    Bits

    Segments

17. Which layer segments and reassembles data into a data stream?

18. Which layer provides the physical transmission of the data and handles error notification, network topology, and flow control?

19. Which layer manages logical device addressing, tracks the location of devices on the internetwork, and determines the best way to move data?

20. What is the bit length and expression form of a MAC address?

Written Lab 1.2: Defining the OSI Layers and Devices

Fill in the blanks with the appropriate layer of the OSI or hub, switch, or router device.

Description	Device or OSI Layer
This device sends and receives information about the Network layer.	
This layer creates a virtual circuit before transmitting between two end stations.	
This device uses hardware addresses to filter a network.	
Ethernet is defined at these layers.	
This layer supports flow control, sequencing, and acknowledgments.	
This device can measure the distance to a remote network.	
Logical addressing is used at this layer.	
Hardware addresses are defined at this layer.	
This device creates one collision domain and one broadcast domain.	
This device creates many smaller collision domains, but the network is still one large broadcast domain.	
This device can never run full-duplex.	
This device breaks up collision domains and broadcast domains.	

Written Lab 1.3: Identifying Collision and Broadcast Domains

1. In the following exhibit, identify the number of collision domains and broadcast domains in each specified device. Each device is represented by a letter:

    A. Hub

    B. Bridge

    C. Switch

    D. Router

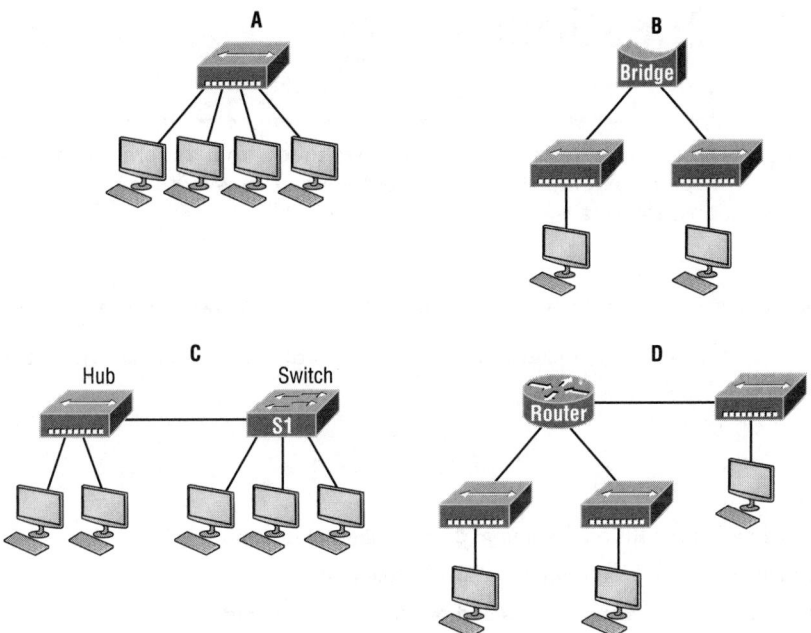

Review Questions

The following questions are designed to test your understanding of this chapter's material. For more information on how to get additional questions, please see www.lammle.com/ccna.

You can find the answers to these questions in Appendix B, "Answers to Review Questions."

1. Which of the following statements is/are true with regard to the device shown here? (Choose all that apply.)

    A.   It includes one collision domain and one broadcast domain.

    B.   It includes 10 collision domains and 10 broadcast domains.

    C.   It includes 10 collision domains and one broadcast domain.

    D.   It includes one collision domain and 10 broadcast domains.

2. With respect to the OSI model, which one of the following is the correct statement about PDUs?

    A.   A segment contains IP addresses.

    B.   A packet contains IP addresses.

    C.   A segment contains MAC addresses.

    D.   A packet contains MAC addresses.

3. You are the Cisco administrator for your company. A new branch office is opening and you are selecting the necessary hardware to support the network. There will be two groups of computers, each organized by department. The Sales group computers will be assigned IP addresses ranging from 192.168.1.2 to 192.168.1.50. The Accounting group will be assigned IP addresses ranging from 10.0.0.2 to 10.0.0.50. What type of device should you select to connect the two groups of computers so that data communication can occur?

    A.   Hub

    B.   Switch

    C.   Router

    D.   Bridge

4. The most effective way to mitigate congestion on a LAN would be to _____.

    A.   Upgrade the network cards

    B.   Change the cabling to CAT 6

   C. Replace the hubs with switches

   D. Upgrade the CPUs in the routers

5. In the following work area, draw a line from the OSI model layer to its PDU.

Layer	Description
Transport	Bits
Data Link	Segment
Physical	Packet
Network	Frame

6. What is a function of the WLAN Controller?

   A. To monitor and control the incoming and outgoing network traffic

   B. To automatically handle the configuration of wireless access points

   C. To allow wireless devices to connect to a wired network

   D. To connect networks and intelligently choose the best paths between networks

7. You need to provide network connectivity to 150 client computers that will reside in the same subnetwork, and each client computer must be allocated dedicated bandwidth. Which device should you use to accomplish the task?

   A. Hub

   B. Switch

   C. Router

   D. Bridge

8. In the following work area, draw a line from the OSI model layer definition on the left to its description on the right.

Layer	Description
Transport	Framing
Physical	End-to-end connection
Data Link	Routing
Network	Conversion to bits

9. What is the function of a firewall?

   A. To automatically handle the configuration of wireless access points

   B. To allow wireless devices to connect to a wired network

   C. To monitor and control the incoming and outgoing network traffic

   D. To connect networks and intelligently choose the best paths between networks

10. Which layer in the OSI reference model is responsible for determining the availability of the receiving program and checking to see whether enough resources exist for that communication?

  A. Transport

  B. Network

  C. Presentation

  D. Application

11. Which of the following correctly describe steps in the OSI data encapsulation process? (Choose two.)

  A. The Transport layer divides a data stream into segments and may add reliability and flow control information.

  B. The Data Link layer adds physical source and destination addresses and an FCS to the segment.

  C. Packets are created when the Network layer encapsulates a frame with source and destination host addresses and protocol-related control information.

  D. Packets are created when the Network layer adds layer 3 addresses and control information to a segment.

  E. The Presentation layer translates bits into voltages for transmission across the physical link.

12. Which of the following layers of the OSI model was later subdivided into two layers?

  A. Presentation

  B. Transport

  C. Data Link

  D. Physical

13. What is a function of an access point (AP)?

  A. To monitor and control the incoming and outgoing network traffic

  B. To automatically handle the configuration of wireless access point

  C. To allow wireless devices to connect to a wired network

  D. To connect networks and intelligently choose the best paths between networks

14. A _____ is an example of a device that operates only at the physical layer.

  A. Hub

  B. Switch

  C. Router

  D. Bridge

15. Which of the following is *not* a benefit of using a reference model?

  A. It divides the network communication process into smaller and simpler components.

  B. It encourages industry standardization.

    C. It enforces consistency across vendors.

    D. It allows various types of network hardware and software to communicate.

16. Which of the following statements is not true with regard to routers?

    A. They forward broadcasts by default.

    B. They can filter the network based on Network layer information.

    C. They perform path selection.

    D. They perform packet switching.

17. Switches break up _____ domains, and routers break up _____ domains.

    A. broadcast, broadcast

    B. collision, collision

    C. collision, broadcast

    D. broadcast, collision

18. How many collision domains are present in the following diagram?

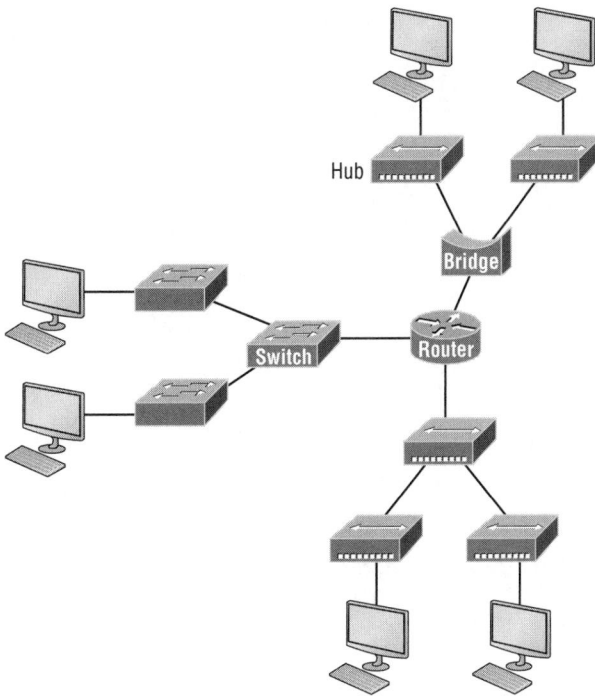

    A. 8

    B. 9

    C. 10

    D. 11

19. Which of the following layers of the OSI model is not involved in defining how the applications within the end stations will communicate with each other as well as with users?

    A. Transport

    B. Application

    C. Presentation

    D. Session

20. Which of the following is the *only* device that operates at all layers of the OSI model?

    A. Network host

    B. Switch

    C. Router

    D. Bridge

Chapter

2

Ethernet Networking and Data Encapsulation

THE FOLLOWING ICND1 EXAM TOPICS ARE COVERED IN THIS CHAPTER:

✓ **Network Fundamentals**

- ▪ 1.6 Select the appropriate cabling type based on implementation requirements

- ▪ 1.4 Compare and contrast collapsed core and three-tier architectures

✓ **LAN Switching Technologies**

- ▪ 2.2 Interpret Ethernet frame format

Before we begin exploring a set of key foundational topics like the TCP/IP DoD model, IP addressing, subnetting, and routing in the upcoming chapters, I really want you to grasp the big picture of LANs conceptually. The role Ethernet plays in today's networks as well as what Media Access Control (MAC) addresses are and how they are used are two more critical networking basics you'll want a solid understanding of as well.

We'll cover these important subjects and more in this chapter, beginning with Ethernet basics and the way MAC addresses are used on an Ethernet LAN, and then we'll focus in on the actual protocols used with Ethernet at the Data Link layer. To round out this discussion, you'll also learn about some very important Ethernet specifications.

You know by now that there are a whole bunch of different devices specified at the various layers of the OSI model and that it's essential to be really familiar with the many types of cables and connectors employed to hook them up to the network correctly. I'll review the types of cabling used with Cisco devices in this chapter, demonstrate how to connect to a router or switch, plus show you how to connect a router or switch via a console connection.

I'll also introduce you to a vital process of encoding data as it makes its way down the OSI stack, known as encapsulation.

I'm not nagging at all here—okay, maybe just a little, but promise that you'll actually work through the four written labs and 20 review questions I added to the end of this chapter just for you. You'll be so happy you did because they're written strategically to make sure all the important material covered in this chapter gets locked in, vault-tight into your memory. So don't skip them!

To find up-to-the-minute updates for this chapter, please see www.lammle .com/ccna or the book's web page via www.sybex.com/go/ccna.

Ethernet Networks in Review

Ethernet is a contention-based media access method that allows all hosts on a network to share the same link's bandwidth. Some reasons it's so popular are that Ethernet is really pretty simple to implement and it makes troubleshooting fairly straightforward as well. Ethernet is also readily scalable, meaning that it eases the process of integrating new technologies into an existing network infrastructure, like upgrading from Fast Ethernet to Gigabit Ethernet.

Ethernet uses both Data Link and Physical layer specifications, so you'll be presented with information relative to both layers, which you'll need to effectively implement, troubleshoot, and maintain an Ethernet network.

Collision Domain

In Chapter 1, "Internetworking," you learned that the Ethernet term *collision domain* refers to a network scenario wherein one device sends a frame out on a physical network segment forcing every other device on the same segment to pay attention to it. This is bad because if two devices on a single physical segment just happen to transmit simultaneously, it will cause a collision and require these devices to retransmit. Think of a collision event as a situation where each device's digital signals totally interfere with one another on the wire. Figure 2.1 shows an old, legacy network that's a single collision domain where only one host can transmit at a time.

FIGURE 2.1   Legacy collision domain design

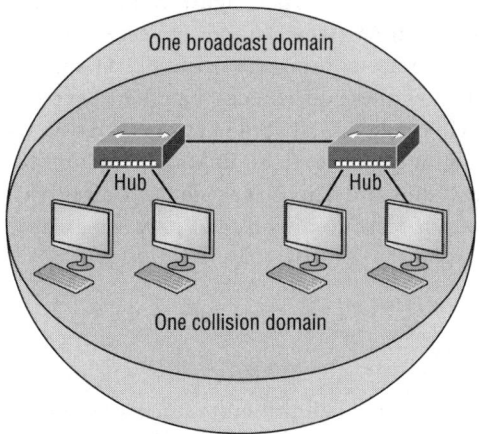

The hosts connected to each hub are in the same collision domain, so if one of them transmits, all the others must take the time to listen for and read the digital signal. It is easy to see how collisions can be a serious drag on network performance, so I'll show you how to strategically avoid them soon!

Okay—take another look at the network pictured in Figure 2.1. True, it has only one collision domain, but worse, it's also a single broadcast domain—what a mess! Let's check out an example, in Figure 2.2, of a typical network design still used today and see if it's any better.

FIGURE 2.2   A typical network you'd see today

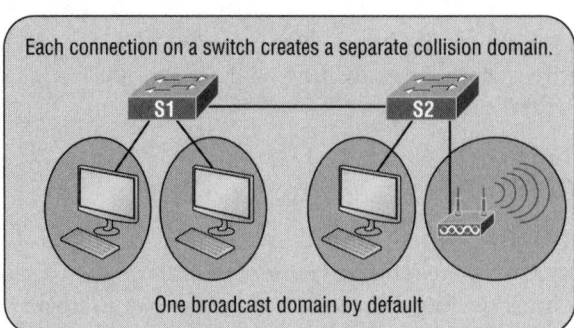

Because each port off a switch is a single collision domain, we gain more bandwidth for users, which is a great start. But switches don't break up broadcast domains by default, so this is still only one broadcast domain, which is not so good. This can work in a really small network, but to expand it at all, we would need to break up the network into smaller broadcast domains or our users won't get enough bandwidth! And you're probably wondering about that device in the lower-right corner, right? Well, that's a *wireless access point*, which is sometimes referred as an AP (which stands for access point). It's a wireless device that allows hosts to connect wirelessly using the IEEE 802.11 specification and I added it to the figure to demonstrate how these devices can be used to extend a collision domain. But still, understand that APs don't actually segment the network, they only extend them, meaning our LAN just got a lot bigger, with an unknown amount of hosts that are all still part of one measly broadcast domain! This clearly demonstrates why it's so important to understand exactly what a broadcast domain is, and now is a great time to talk about them in detail.

Broadcast Domain

Let me start by giving you the formal definition: *broadcast domain* refers to a group of devices on a specific network segment that hear all the broadcasts sent out on that specific network segment.

But even though a broadcast domain is usually a boundary delimited by physical media like switches and routers, the term can also refer to a logical division of a network segment, where all hosts can communicate via a Data Link layer, hardware address broadcast.

Figure 2.3 shows how a router would create a broadcast domain boundary.

Here you can see there are two router interfaces giving us two broadcast domains, and I count 10 switch segments, meaning we've got 10 collision domains.

The design depicted in Figure 2.3 is still in use today, and routers will be around for a long time, but in the latest, modern switched networks, it's important to create small broadcast domains. We achieve this by building virtual LANs (VLANs) within our switched networks, which I'll demonstrate shortly. Without employing VLANs in today's switched environments, there wouldn't be much bandwidth available to individual users. Switches break up collision domains with each port, which is awesome, but they're still only one broadcast domain by default! It's also one more reason why it's extremely important to design our networks very carefully.

FIGURE 2.3   A router creates broadcast domain boundaries.

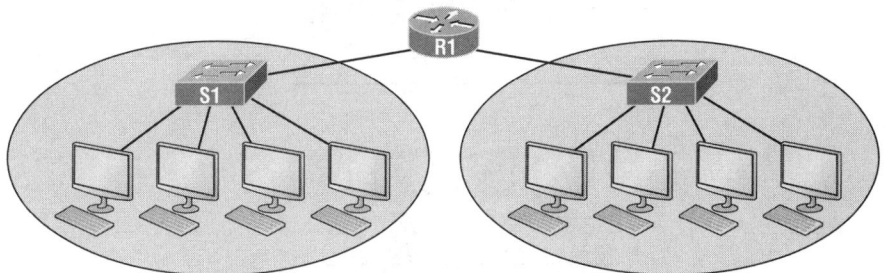

Two broadcast domains. How many collision domains do you see?

And key to carefully planning your network design is never to allow broadcast domains to grow too large and get out of control. Both collision and broadcast domains can easily be controlled with routers and VLANs, so there's just no excuse to allow user bandwidth to slow to a painful crawl when there are plenty of tools in your arsenal to prevent the suffering!

An important reason for this book's existence is to ensure that you really get the foundational basics of Cisco networks nailed down so you can effectively design, implement, configure, troubleshoot, and even dazzle colleagues and superiors with elegant designs that lavish your users with all the bandwidth their hearts could possibly desire.

To make it to the top of that mountain, you need more than just the basic story, so let's move on to explore the collision detection mechanism used in half-duplex Ethernet.

CSMA/CD

Ethernet networking uses a protocol called *Carrier Sense Multiple Access with Collision Detection (CSMA/CD)*, which helps devices share the bandwidth evenly while preventing two devices from transmitting simultaneously on the same network medium. CSMA/CD was actually created to overcome the problem of the collisions that occur when packets are transmitted from different nodes at the same time. And trust me—good collision management is crucial, because when a node transmits in a CSMA/CD network, all the other nodes on the network receive and examine that transmission. Only switches and routers can effectively prevent a transmission from propagating throughout the entire network!

So, how does the CSMA/CD protocol work? Let's start by taking a look at Figure 2.4.

FIGURE 2.4   CSMA/CD

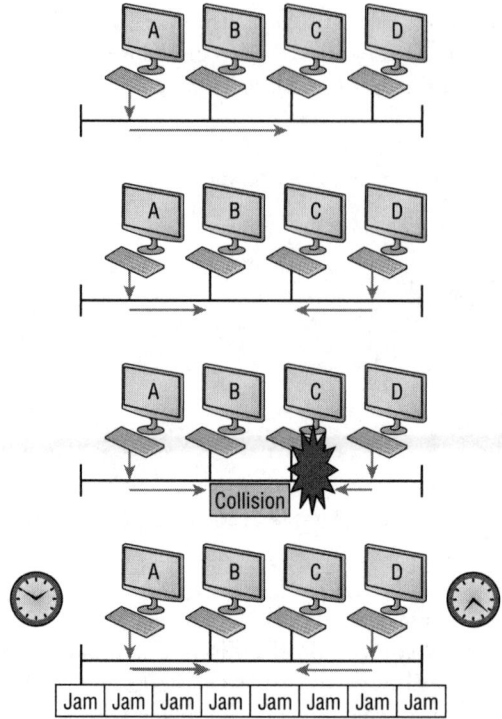

When a host wants to transmit over the network, it first checks for the presence of a digital signal on the wire. If all is clear and no other host is transmitting, the host will then proceed with its transmission.

But it doesn't stop there. The transmitting host constantly monitors the wire to make sure no other hosts begin transmitting. If the host detects another signal on the wire, it sends out an extended jam signal that causes all nodes on the segment to stop sending data—think busy signal.

The nodes respond to that jam signal by waiting a bit before attempting to transmit again. Backoff algorithms determine when the colliding stations can retransmit. If collisions keep occurring after 15 tries, the nodes attempting to transmit will then time out. Half-duplex can be pretty messy!

When a collision occurs on an Ethernet LAN, the following happens:

1. A jam signal informs all devices that a collision occurred.

2. The collision invokes a random backoff algorithm.

3. Each device on the Ethernet segment stops transmitting for a short time until its backoff timer expires.

4. All hosts have equal priority to transmit after the timers have expired.

The ugly effects of having a CSMA/CD network sustain heavy collisions are delay, low throughput, and congestion.

Backoff on an Ethernet network is the retransmission delay that's enforced when a collision occurs. When that happens, a host will resume transmission only after the forced time delay has expired. Keep in mind that after the backoff has elapsed, all stations have equal priority to transmit data.

At this point, let's take a minute to talk about Ethernet in detail at both the Data Link layer (layer 2) and the Physical layer (layer 1).

Half- and Full-Duplex Ethernet

Half-duplex Ethernet is defined in the original IEEE 802.3 Ethernet specification, which differs a bit from how Cisco describes things. Cisco says Ethernet uses only one wire pair with a digital signal running in both directions on the wire. Even though the IEEE specifications discuss the half-duplex process somewhat differently, it's not actually a full-blown technical disagreement. Cisco is really just talking about a general sense of what's happening with Ethernet.

Half-duplex also uses the CSMA/CD protocol I just discussed to help prevent collisions and to permit retransmitting if one occurs. If a hub is attached to a switch, it must operate in half-duplex mode because the end stations must be able to detect collisions. Figure 2.5 shows a network with four hosts connected to a hub.

FIGURE 2.5 Half-duplex example

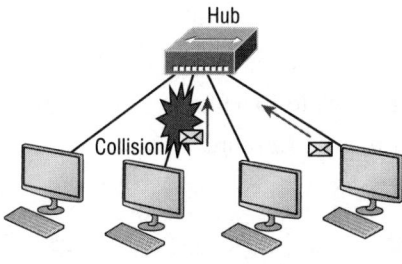

The problem here is that we can only run half-duplex, and if two hosts communicate at the same time there will be a collision. Also, half-duplex Ethernet is only about 30 to 40 percent efficient because a large 100Base-T network will usually only give you 30 to 40 Mbps, at most, due to overhead.

But full-duplex Ethernet uses two pairs of wires at the same time instead of a single wire pair like half-duplex. And full-duplex uses a point-to-point connection between the transmitter of the transmitting device and the receiver of the receiving device. This means that full-duplex data transfers happen a lot faster when compared to half-duplex transfers. Also, because the transmitted data is sent on a different set of wires than the received data, collisions won't happen. Figure 2.6 shows four hosts connected to a switch, plus a hub. Definitely try not to use hubs if you can help it!

FIGURE 2.6   Full-duplex example

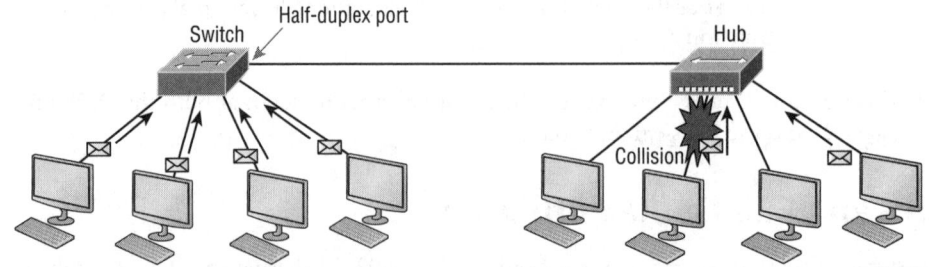

Theoretically all hosts connected to the switch in Figure 2.6 can communicate at the same time because they can run full-duplex. Just keep in mind that the switch port connecting to the hub as well as the hosts connecting to that hub must run at half-duplex.

The reason you don't need to worry about collisions is because now it's like a freeway with multiple lanes instead of the single-lane road provided by half-duplex. Full-duplex Ethernet is supposed to offer 100 percent efficiency in both directions—for example, you can get 20 Mbps with a 10 Mbps Ethernet running full-duplex, or 200 Mbps for Fast Ethernet. But this rate is known as an aggregate rate, which translates as "you're supposed to get" 100 percent efficiency. No guarantees, in networking as in life!

You can use full-duplex Ethernet in at least the following six situations:

- With a connection from a switch to a host
- With a connection from a switch to a switch
- With a connection from a host to a host
- With a connection from a switch to a router
- With a connection from a router to a router
- With a connection from a router to a host

   Full-duplex Ethernet requires a point-to-point connection when only two nodes are present. You can run full-duplex with just about any device except a hub.

Now this may be a little confusing because this begs the question that if it's capable of all that speed, why wouldn't it actually deliver? Well, when a full-duplex Ethernet port is powered on, it first connects to the remote end and then negotiates with the other end of the Fast Ethernet link. This is called an *auto-detect mechanism*. This mechanism first decides on the exchange capability, which means it checks to see if it can run at 10, 100, or even 1000 Mbps. It then checks to see if it can run full-duplex, and if it can't, it will run half-duplex.

> Remember that half-duplex Ethernet shares a collision domain and provides a lower effective throughput than full-duplex Ethernet, which typically has a private per-port collision domain plus a higher effective throughput.

Last, remember these important points:

- There are no collisions in full-duplex mode.
- A dedicated switch port is required for each full-duplex node.
- The host network card and the switch port must be capable of operating in full-duplex mode.
- The default behavior of 10Base-T and 100Base-T hosts is 10 Mbps half-duplex if the autodetect mechanism fails, so it is always good practice to set the speed and duplex of each port on a switch if you can.

Now let's take a look at how Ethernet works at the Data Link layer.

Ethernet at the Data Link Layer

Ethernet at the Data Link layer is responsible for Ethernet addressing, commonly referred to as MAC or hardware addressing. Ethernet is also responsible for framing packets received from the Network layer and preparing them for transmission on the local network through the Ethernet contention-based media access method.

Ethernet Addressing

Here's where we get into how Ethernet addressing works. It uses the *Media Access Control (MAC)* address burned into each and every Ethernet network interface card (NIC). The MAC, or hardware, address is a 48-bit (6-byte) address written in a hexadecimal format.

Figure 2.7 shows the 48-bit MAC addresses and how the bits are divided.

FIGURE 2.7 Ethernet addressing using MAC addresses

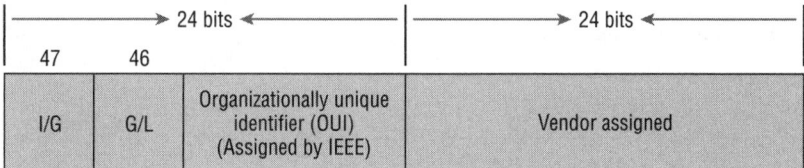

Example: 0000.0c12.3456

The *organizationally unique identifier (OUI)* is assigned by the IEEE to an organization. It's composed of 24 bits, or 3 bytes, and it in turn assigns a globally administered address also made up of 24 bits, or 3 bytes, that's supposedly unique to each and every adapter an organization manufactures. Surprisingly, there's no guarantee when it comes to that unique claim! Okay, now look closely at the figure. The high-order bit is the Individual/Group (I/G) bit. When it has a value of 0, we can assume that the address is the MAC address of a device and that it may well appear in the source portion of the MAC header. When it's a 1, we can assume that the address represents either a broadcast or multicast address in Ethernet.

The next bit is the Global/Local bit, sometimes called the G/L bit or U/L bit, where U means *universal*. When set to 0, this bit represents a globally administered address, as assigned by the IEEE, but when it's a 1, it represents a locally governed and administered address. The low-order 24 bits of an Ethernet address represent a locally administered or manufacturer-assigned code. This portion commonly starts with 24 0s for the first card made and continues in order until there are 24 1s for the last (16,777,216th) card made. You'll find that many manufacturers use these same six hex digits as the last six characters of their serial number on the same card.

Let's stop for a minute and go over some addressing schemes important in the Ethernet world.

Binary to Decimal and Hexadecimal Conversion

Before we get into working with the TCP/IP protocol and IP addressing, which we'll do in Chapter 3, "Introduction to TCP/IP," it's really important for you to truly grasp the differences between binary, decimal, and hexadecimal numbers and how to convert one format into the other.

We'll start with binary numbering, which is really pretty simple. The digits used are limited to either a 1 or a 0, and each digit is called a *bit*, which is short for *binary digit*. Typically, you group either 4 or 8 bits together, with these being referred to as a nibble and a byte, respectively.

The interesting thing about binary numbering is how the value is represented in a decimal format—the typical decimal format being the base-10 number scheme that we've all used since kindergarten. The binary numbers are placed in a value spot, starting at the right and moving left, with each spot having double the value of the previous spot.

Table 2.1 shows the decimal values of each bit location in a nibble and a byte. Remember, a nibble is 4 bits and a byte is 8 bits.

TABLE 2.1   Binary values

Nibble Values	Byte Values
8 4 2 1	128 64 32 16 8 4 2 1

What all this means is that if a one digit (1) is placed in a value spot, then the nibble or byte takes on that decimal value and adds it to any other value spots that have a 1. If a zero (0) is placed in a bit spot, you don't count that value.

Let me clarify this a little. If we have a 1 placed in each spot of our nibble, we would then add up 8 + 4 + 2 + 1 to give us a maximum value of 15. Another example for our nibble values would be 1001, meaning that the 8 bit and the 1 bit are turned on, which equals a decimal value of 9. If we have a nibble binary value of 0110, then our decimal value would be 6, because the 4 and 2 bits are turned on.

But the *byte* decimal values can add up to a number that's significantly higher than 15. This is how: If we counted every bit as a one (1), then the byte binary value would look like the following example because, remember, 8 bits equal a byte:

11111111

We would then count up every bit spot because each is turned on. It would look like this, which demonstrates the maximum value of a byte:

128 + 64 + 32 + 16 + 8 + 4 + 2 + 1 = 255

There are plenty of other decimal values that a binary number can equal. Let's work through a few examples:

10010110

Which bits are on? The 128, 16, 4, and 2 bits are on, so we'll just add them up: 128 + 16 + 4 + 2 = 150.

01101100

Which bits are on? The 64, 32, 8, and 4 bits are on, so we just need to add them up: 64 + 32 + 8 + 4 = 108.

11101000

Which bits are on? The 128, 64, 32, and 8 bits are on, so just add the values up: 128 + 64 + 32 + 8 = 232.

I highly recommend that you memorize Table 2.2 before braving the IP sections in Chapter 3, "Introduction to TCP/IP," and Chapter 4, "Easy Subnetting"!

TABLE 2.2   Binary to decimal memorization chart

Binary Value	Decimal Value
10000000	128
11000000	192
11100000	224
11110000	240

TABLE 2.2   Binary to decimal memorization chart *(continued)*

Binary Value	Decimal Value
11111000	248
11111100	252
11111110	254
11111111	255

Hexadecimal addressing is completely different than binary or decimal—it's converted by reading nibbles, not bytes. By using a nibble, we can convert these bits to hex pretty simply. First, understand that the hexadecimal addressing scheme uses only the characters 0 through 9. Because the numbers 10, 11, 12, and so on can't be used (because they are two-digit numbers), the letters *A*, *B*, *C*, *D*, *E*, and *F* are used instead to represent 10, 11, 12, 13, 14, and 15, respectively.

> *Hex* is short for *hexadecimal*, which is a numbering system that uses the first six letters of the alphabet, *A* through *F*, to extend beyond the available 10 characters in the decimal system. These values are not case sensitive.

Table 2.3 shows both the binary value and the decimal value for each hexadecimal digit.

TABLE 2.3   Hex to binary to decimal chart

Hexadecimal Value	Binary Value	Decimal Value
0	0000	0
1	0001	1
2	0010	2
3	0011	3
4	0100	4
5	0101	5
6	0110	6
7	0111	7

Hexadecimal Value	Binary Value	Decimal Value
8	1000	8
9	1001	9
A	1010	10
B	1011	11
C	1100	12
D	1101	13
E	1110	14
F	1111	15

Did you notice that the first 10 hexadecimal digits (0–9) are the same value as the decimal values? If not, look again because this handy fact makes those values super easy to convert!

Now suppose you have something like this: 0x6A. This is important because sometimes Cisco likes to put *0x* in front of characters so you know that they are a hex value. It doesn't have any other special meaning. So what are the binary and decimal values? All you have to remember is that each hex character is one nibble and that two hex characters joined together make a byte. To figure out the binary value, put the hex characters into two nibbles and then join them together into a byte. Six equals 0110, and A, which is 10 in hex, equals 1010, so the complete byte would be 01101010.

To convert from binary to hex, just take the byte and break it into nibbles. Let me clarify this.

Say you have the binary number 01010101. First, break it into nibbles—0101 and 0101—with the value of each nibble being 5 since the 1 and 4 bits are on. This makes the hex answer 0x55. And in decimal format, the binary number is 01010101, which converts to 64 + 16 + 4 + 1 = 85.

Here's another binary number:

11001100

Your answer would be 1100 = 12 and 1100 = 12, so therefore, it's converted to CC in hex. The decimal conversion answer would be 128 + 64 + 8 + 4 = 204.

One more example, then we need to get working on the Physical layer. Suppose you had the following binary number:

10110101

The hex answer would be 0xB5, since 1011 converts to B and 0101 converts to 5 in hex value. The decimal equivalent is 128 + 32 + 16 + 4 + 1 = 181.

Make sure you check out Written Lab 2.1 for more practice with binary/decimal/hex conversion!

Ethernet Frames

The Data Link layer is responsible for combining bits into bytes and bytes into frames. Frames are used at the Data Link layer to encapsulate packets handed down from the Network layer for transmission on a type of media access.

The function of Ethernet stations is to pass data frames between each other using a group of bits known as a MAC frame format. This provides error detection from a *cyclic redundancy check (CRC)*. But remember—this is error detection, not error correction. An example of a typical Ethernet frame used today is shown in Figure 2.8.

FIGURE 2.8   Typical Ethernet frame format

Ethernet_II

Preamble 7 bytes	SFD 1 byte	Destination 6 bytes	Source 6 bytes	Type 2 bytes	Data and Pad 46 – 1500 bytes	FCS 4 bytes

Packet

Encapsulating a frame within a different type of frame is called *tunneling.*

Following are the details of the various fields in the typical Ethernet frame type:

Preamble   An alternating 1,0 pattern provides a 5 MHz clock at the start of each packet, which allows the receiving devices to lock the incoming bit stream.

Start Frame Delimiter (SFD)/Synch   The preamble is seven octets and the SFD is one octet (synch). The SFD is 10101011, where the last pair of 1s allows the receiver to come into the alternating 1,0 pattern somewhere in the middle and still sync up to detect the beginning of the data.

Destination Address (DA)   This transmits a 48-bit value using the least significant bit (LSB) first. The DA is used by receiving stations to determine whether an incoming packet is addressed to a particular node. The destination address can be an individual address or a broadcast or multicast MAC address. Remember that a broadcast is all 1s—all *F*s in hex—and is sent to all devices. A multicast is sent only to a similar subset of nodes on a network.

Source Address (SA)   The SA is a 48-bit MAC address used to identify the transmitting device, and it uses the least significant bit first. Broadcast and multicast address formats are illegal within the SA field.

Length or Type   802.3 uses a Length field, but the Ethernet_II frame uses a Type field to identify the Network layer protocol. The old, original 802.3 cannot identify the upper-layer protocol and must be used with a proprietary LAN—IPX, for example.

Data   This is a packet sent down to the Data Link layer from the Network layer. The size can vary from 46 to 1,500 bytes.

Frame Check Sequence (FCS)   FCS is a field at the end of the frame that's used to store the cyclic redundancy check (CRC) answer. The CRC is a mathematical algorithm that's run when each frame is built based on the data in the frame. When a receiving host receives the frame and runs the CRC, the answer should be the same. If not, the frame is discarded, assuming errors have occurred.

Let's pause here for a minute and take a look at some frames caught on my trusty network analyzer. You can see that the frame below has only three fields: Destination, Source, and Type, which is shown as Protocol Type on this particular analyzer:

```
Destination:   00:60:f5:00:1f:27
Source:        00:60:f5:00:1f:2c
Protocol Type: 08-00 IP
```

This is an Ethernet_II frame. Notice that the Type field is IP, or 08-00, mostly just referred to as 0x800 in hexadecimal.

The next frame has the same fields, so it must be an Ethernet_II frame as well:

```
Destination:   ff:ff:ff:ff:ff:ff Ethernet Broadcast
Source:        02:07:01:22:de:a4
Protocol Type: 08-00 IP
```

Did you notice that this frame was a broadcast? You can tell because the destination hardware address is all 1s in binary, or all *F*s in hexadecimal.

Let's take a look at one more Ethernet_II frame. I'll talk about this next example again when we use IPv6 in Chapter 14, "Internet Protocol Version 6 (IPv6)," but you can see that the Ethernet frame is the same Ethernet_II frame used with the IPv4 routed protocol. The Type field has 0x86dd when the frame is carrying IPv6 data, and when we have IPv4 data, the frame uses 0x0800 in the protocol field:

```
Destination: IPv6-Neighbor-Discovery_00:01:00:03 (33:33:00:01:00:03)
Source: Aopen_3e:7f:dd (00:01:80:3e:7f:dd)
Type: IPv6 (0x86dd)
```

This is the beauty of the Ethernet_II frame. Because of the Type field, we can run any Network layer routed protocol and the frame will carry the data because it can identify the Network layer protocol!

Ethernet at the Physical Layer

Ethernet was first implemented by a group called DIX, which stands for Digital, Intel, and Xerox. They created and implemented the first Ethernet LAN specification, which the IEEE used to create the IEEE 802.3 committee. This was a 10 Mbps network that ran on coax and then eventually twisted-pair and fiber physical media.

The IEEE extended the 802.3 committee to three new committees known as 802.3u (Fast Ethernet), 802.3ab (Gigabit Ethernet on category 5), and then finally one more, 802.3ae (10 Gbps over fiber and coax). There are more standards evolving almost daily, such as the new 100 Gbps Ethernet (802.3ba)!

When designing your LAN, it's really important to understand the different types of Ethernet media available to you. Sure, it would be great to run Gigabit Ethernet to each desktop and 10 Gbps between switches, but you would need to figure out how to justify the cost of that network today! However, if you mix and match the different types of Ethernet media methods currently available, you can come up with a cost-effective network solution that works really great.

The *EIA/TIA* (Electronic Industries Alliance and the newer Telecommunications Industry Association) is the standards body that creates the Physical layer specifications for Ethernet. The EIA/TIA specifies that Ethernet use a *registered jack (RJ) connector* on *unshielded twisted-pair (UTP)* cabling (RJ45). But the industry is moving toward simply calling this an 8-pin modular connector.

Every Ethernet cable type that's specified by the EIA/TIA has inherent attenuation, which is defined as the loss of signal strength as it travels the length of a cable and is measured in decibels (dB). The cabling used in corporate and home markets is measured in categories. A higher-quality cable will have a higher-rated category and lower attenuation. For example, category 5 is better than category 3 because category 5 cables have more wire twists per foot and therefore less crosstalk. Crosstalk is the unwanted signal interference from adjacent pairs in the cable.

Here is a list of some of the most common IEEE Ethernet standards, starting with 10 Mbps Ethernet:

10Base-T (IEEE 802.3)   10 Mbps using category 3 unshielded twisted pair (UTP) wiring for runs up to 100 meters. Unlike with the 10Base-2 and 10Base-5 networks, each device must connect into a hub or switch, and you can have only one host per segment or wire. It uses an RJ45 connector (8-pin modular connector) with a physical star topology and a logical bus.

100Base-TX (IEEE 802.3u)   100Base-TX, most commonly known as Fast Ethernet, uses EIA/TIA category 5, 5E, or 6 UTP two-pair wiring. One user per segment; up to 100 meters long. It uses an RJ45 connector with a physical star topology and a logical bus.

100Base-FX (IEEE 802.3u)   Uses fiber cabling 62.5/125-micron multimode fiber. Point-to-point topology; up to 412 meters long. It uses ST and SC connectors, which are media-interface connectors.

1000Base-CX (IEEE 802.3z)   Copper twisted-pair, called twinax, is a balanced coaxial pair that can run only up to 25 meters and uses a special 9-pin connector known as the High Speed Serial Data Connector (HSSDC). This is used in Cisco's new Data Center technologies.

1000Base-T (IEEE 802.3ab)   Category 5, four-pair UTP wiring up to 100 meters long and up to 1 Gbps.

1000Base-SX (IEEE 802.3z)   The implementation of 1 Gigabit Ethernet running over multimode fiber-optic cable instead of copper twisted-pair cable, using short wavelength laser. Multimode fiber (MMF) using 62.5- and 50-micron core; uses an 850 nanometer (nm) laser and can go up to 220 meters with 62.5-micron, 550 meters with 50-micron.

1000Base-LX (IEEE 802.3z)   Single-mode fiber that uses a 9-micron core and 1300 nm laser and can go from 3 kilometers up to 10 kilometers.

1000Base-ZX (Cisco standard)   1000BaseZX, or 1000Base-ZX, is a Cisco specified standard for Gigabit Ethernet communication. 1000BaseZX operates on ordinary single-mode fiber-optic links with spans up to 43.5 miles (70 km).

10GBase-T (802.3.an)   10GBase-T is a standard proposed by the IEEE 802.3an committee to provide 10 Gbps connections over conventional UTP cables, (category 5e, 6, or 7 cables). 10GBase-T allows the conventional RJ45 used for Ethernet LANs and can support signal transmission at the full 100-meter distance specified for LAN wiring.

If you want to implement a network medium that is not susceptible to electromagnetic interference (EMI), fiber-optic cable provides a more secure, long-distance cable that is not susceptible to EMI at high speeds.

Armed with the basics covered so far in this chapter, you're equipped to go to the next level and put Ethernet to work using various Ethernet cabling.

 Real World Scenario

Interference or Host Distance Issue?

Quite a few years ago, I was consulting at a very large aerospace company in the Los Angeles area. In the very busy warehouse, they had hundreds of hosts providing many different services to the various departments working in that area.

However, a small group of hosts had been experiencing intermittent outages that no one could explain since most hosts in the same area had no problems whatsoever. So I decided to take a crack at this problem and see what I could find.

First, I traced the backbone connection from the main switch to multiple switches in the warehouse area. Assuming that the hosts with the issues were connected to the same switch, I traced each cable, and much to my surprise they were connected to various switches! Now my interest really peaked because the simplest issue had been eliminated right off the bat. It wasn't a simple switch problem!

I continued to trace each cable one by one, and this is what I found:

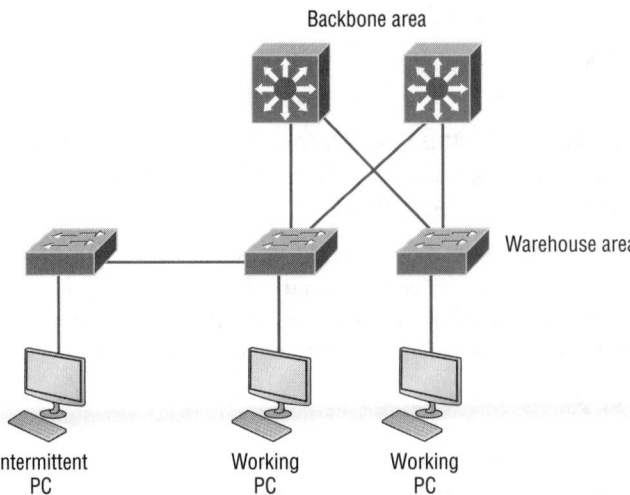

As I drew this network out, I noticed that they had many repeaters in place, which isn't a cause for immediate suspicion since bandwidth was not their biggest requirement here. So I looked deeper still. At this point, I decided to measure the distance of one of the intermittent hosts connecting to their hub/repeater.

This is what I measured. Can you see the problem?

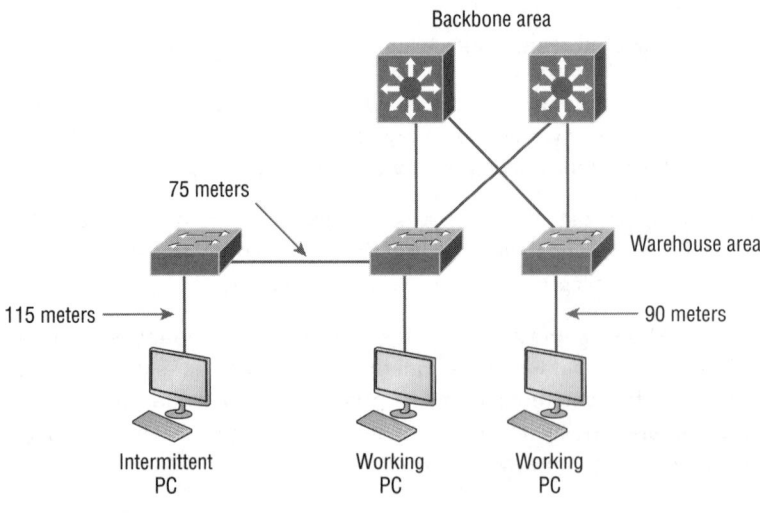

Having a hub or repeater in your network isn't a problem, unless you need better bandwidth (which they didn't in this case), but the distance was! It's not always easy to tell how far away a host is from its connection in an extremely large area, so these hosts ended up having a connection past the 100-meter Ethernet specification, which created a problem for the hosts not cabled correctly. Understand that this didn't stop the hosts from completely working, but the workers felt the hosts stopped working when they were at their most stressful point of the day. Sure, that makes sense, because whenever my host stops working, that becomes my most stressful part of the day!

Ethernet Cabling

A discussion about Ethernet cabling is an important one, especially if you are planning on taking the Cisco exams. You need to really understand the following three types of cables:

- Straight-through cable
- Crossover cable
- Rolled cable

We will look at each in the following sections, but first, let's take a look at the most common Ethernet cable used today, the category 5 Enhanced Unshielded Twisted Pair (UTP), shown in Figure 2.9.

FIGURE 2.9   Category 5 Enhanced UTP cable

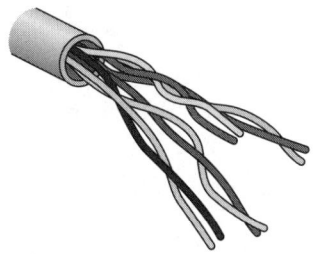

The category 5 Enhanced UTP cable can handle speeds up to a gigabit with a distance of up to 100 meters. Typically we'd use this cable for 100 Mbps and category 6 for a gigabit, but the category 5 Enhanced is rated for gigabit speeds and category 6 is rated for 10 Gbps!

Straight-Through Cable

The *straight-through cable* is used to connect the following devices:

- Host to switch or hub
- Router to switch or hub

Four wires are used in straight-through cable to connect Ethernet devices. It's relatively simple to create this type, and Figure 2.10 shows the four wires used in a straight-through Ethernet cable.

FIGURE 2.10   Straight-through Ethernet cable

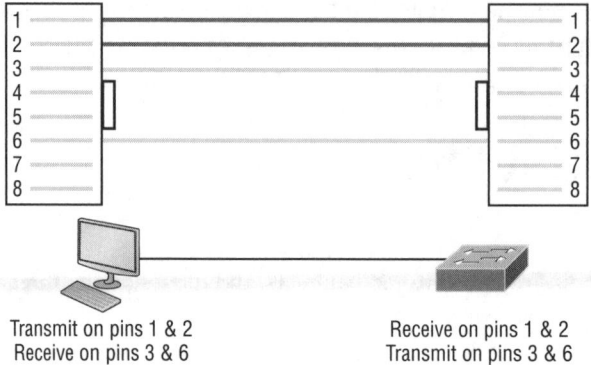

Transmit on pins 1 & 2
Receive on pins 3 & 6

Receive on pins 1 & 2
Transmit on pins 3 & 6

Notice that only pins 1, 2, 3, and 6 are used. Just connect 1 to 1, 2 to 2, 3 to 3, and 6 to 6 and you'll be up and networking in no time. However, remember that this would be a 10/100 Mbps Ethernet-only cable and wouldn't work with gigabit, voice, or other LAN or WAN technology.

Crossover Cable

The *crossover cable* can be used to connect the following devices:

- Switch to switch
- Hub to hub
- Host to host
- Hub to switch
- Router direct to host
- Router to router

The same four wires used in the straight-through cable are used in this cable—we just connect different pins together. Figure 2.11 shows how the four wires are used in a crossover Ethernet cable.

FIGURE 2.11   Crossover Ethernet cable

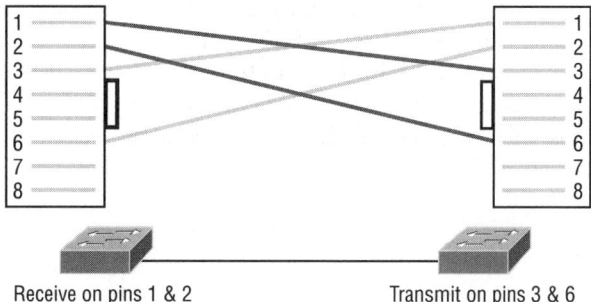

Receive on pins 1 & 2   Transmit on pins 3 & 6

Notice that instead of connecting 1 to 1, 2 to 2, and so on, here we connect pins 1 to 3 and 2 to 6 on each side of the cable. Figure 2.12 shows some typical uses of straight-through and crossover cables.

FIGURE 2.12   Typical uses for straight-through and cross-over Ethernet cables

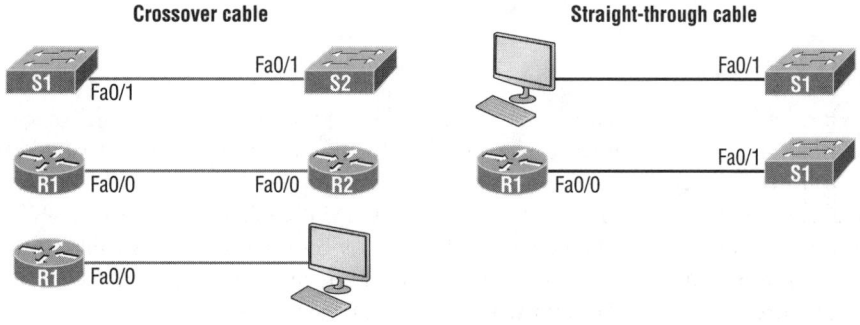

The crossover examples in Figure 2.12 are switch port to switch port, router Ethernet port to router Ethernet port, and router Ethernet port to PC Ethernet port. For the straight-through examples I used PC Ethernet to switch port and router Ethernet port to switch port.

It's very possible to connect a straight-through cable between two switches, and it will start working because of autodetect mechanisms called auto-mdix. But be advised that the CCNA objectives do not typically consider autodetect mechanisms valid between devices!

UTP Gigabit Wiring (1000Base-T)

In the previous examples of 10Base-T and 100Base-T UTP wiring, only two wire pairs were used, but that is not good enough for Gigabit UTP transmission.

1000Base-T UTP wiring (Figure 2.13) requires four wire pairs and uses more advanced electronics so that each and every pair in the cable can transmit simultaneously. Even so, gigabit wiring is almost identical to my earlier 10/100 example, except that we'll use the other two pairs in the cable.

FIGURE 2.13   UTP Gigabit crossover Ethernet cable

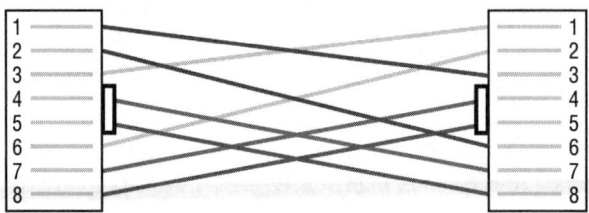

For a straight-through cable it's still 1 to 1, 2 to 2, and so on up to pin 8. And in creating the gigabit crossover cable, you'd still cross 1 to 3 and 2 to 6, but you would add 4 to 7 and 5 to 8—pretty straightforward!

Rolled Cable

Although *rolled cable* isn't used to connect any Ethernet connections together, you can use a rolled Ethernet cable to connect a host EIA-TIA 232 interface to a router console serial communication (COM) port.

If you have a Cisco router or switch, you would use this cable to connect your PC, Mac, or a device like an iPad to the Cisco hardware. Eight wires are used in this cable to connect serial devices, although not all eight are used to send information, just as in Ethernet networking. Figure 2.14 shows the eight wires used in a rolled cable.

FIGURE 2.14   Rolled Ethernet cable

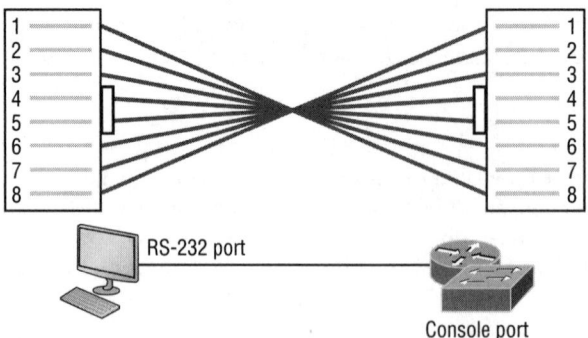

These are probably the easiest cables to make because you just cut the end off on one side of a straight-through cable, turn it over, and put it back on—with a new connector, of course!

Okay, once you have the correct cable connected from your PC to the Cisco router or switch console port, you can start your emulation program such as PuTTY or SecureCRT to create a console connection and configure the device. Set the configuration as shown in Figure 2.15.

FIGURE 2.15   Configuring your console emulation program

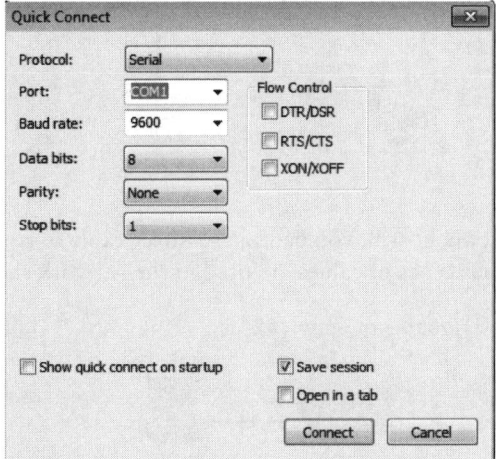

Notice that Baud Rate is set to 9600, Data Bits to 8, Parity to None, and no Flow Control options are set. At this point, you can click Connect and press the Enter key and you should be connected to your Cisco device console port.

Figure 2.16 shows a nice new 2960 switch with two console ports.

FIGURE 2.16   A Cisco 2960 console connections

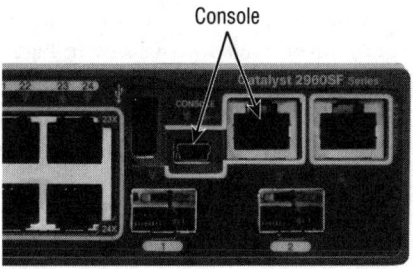

Notice there are two console connections on this new switch—a typical original RJ45 connection and the newer mini type-B USB console. Remember that the new USB port supersedes the RJ45 port if you just happen to plug into both at the same time, and the USB port can have speeds up to 115,200 Kbps, which is awesome if you have to use Xmodem to update an IOS. I've even seen some cables that work on iPhones and iPads and allow them to connect to these mini USB ports!

Now that you've seen the various RJ45 unshielded twisted-pair (UTP) cables, what type of cable is used between the switches in Figure 2.17?

FIGURE 2.17   RJ45 UTP cable question #1

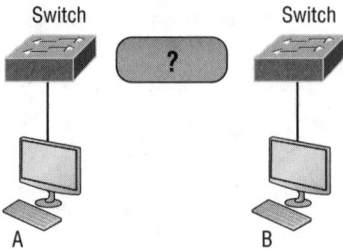

In order for host A to ping host B, you need a crossover cable to connect the two switches together. But what types of cables are used in the network shown in Figure 2.18?

FIGURE 2.18   RJ45 UTP cable question #2

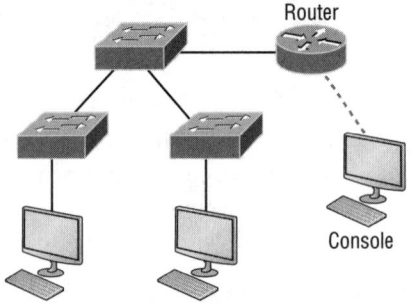

In Figure 2.18, there's a whole menu of cables in use. For the connection between the switches, we'd obviously use a crossover cable like we saw in Figure 2.13. The trouble is that you must understand that we have a console connection that uses a rolled cable. Plus, the connection from the router to the switch is a straight-through cable, as is true for the hosts to the switches. Keep in mind that if we had a serial connection, which we don't, we would use a V.35 to connect us to a WAN.

Fiber Optic

Fiber-optic cabling has been around for a long time and has some solid standards. The cable allows for very fast transmission of data, is made of glass (or even plastic!), is very thin, and works as a waveguide to transmit light between two ends of the fiber. Fiber optics has been used to go very long distances, as in intercontinental connections, but it is becoming more and more popular in Ethernet LAN networks due to the fast speeds available and because, unlike UTP, it's immune to interference like cross-talk.

Some main components of this cable are the core and the cladding. The core will hold the light and the cladding confines the light in the core. The tighter the cladding, the smaller the core, and when the core is small, less light will be sent, but it can go faster and farther!

In Figure 2.19 you can see that there is a 9-micron core, which is very small and can be measured against a human hair, which is 50 microns.

FIGURE 2.19   Typical fiber cable

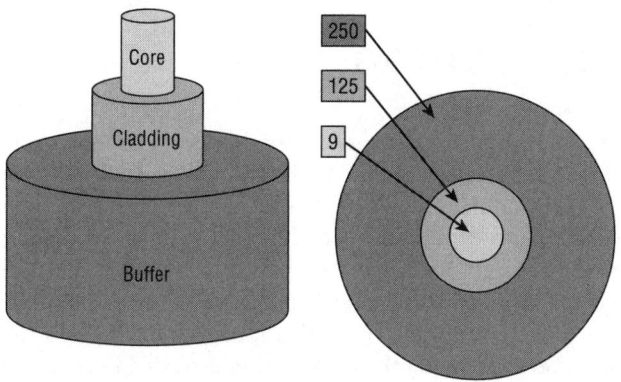

Dimensions are in um (10⁻⁶ meters). Not to scale.

The cladding is 125 microns, which is actually a fiber standard that allows manufacturers to make connectors for all fiber cables. The last piece of this cable is the buffer, which is there to protect the delicate glass.

There are two major types of fiber optics: single-mode and multimode. Figure 2.20 shows the differences between multimode and single-mode fibers.

FIGURE 2.20   Multimode and single-mode fibers

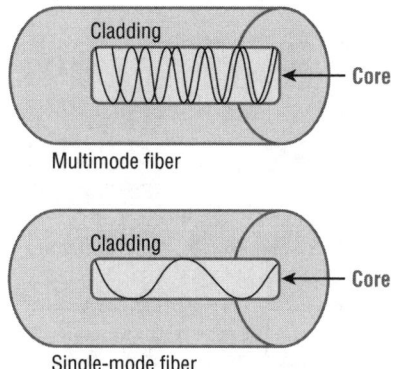

Single-mode is more expensive, has a tighter cladding, and can go much farther distances than multimode. The difference comes in the tightness of the cladding, which makes a smaller core, meaning that only one mode of light will propagate down the fiber. Multimode is looser and has a larger core so it allows multiple light particles to travel down the glass. These particles have to be put back together at the receiving end, so distance is less than that with single-mode fiber, which allows only very few light particles to travel down the fiber.

There are about 70 different connectors for fiber, and Cisco uses a few different types. Looking back at Figure 2.16, the two bottom ports are referred to as Small Form-Factor Pluggables, or SFPs.

Data Encapsulation

When a host transmits data across a network to another device, the data goes through a process called *encapsulation* and is wrapped with protocol information at each layer of the OSI model. Each layer communicates only with its peer layer on the receiving device.

To communicate and exchange information, each layer uses *protocol data units (PDUs)*. These hold the control information attached to the data at each layer of the model. They are usually attached to the header in front of the data field but can also be at the trailer, or end, of it.

Each PDU attaches to the data by encapsulating it at each layer of the OSI model, and each has a specific name depending on the information provided in each header. This PDU information is read only by the peer layer on the receiving device. After its read, it's stripped off and the data is then handed to the next layer up.

Figure 2.21 shows the PDUs and how they attach control information to each layer. This figure demonstrates how the upper-layer user data is converted for transmission on the network. The data stream is then handed down to the Transport layer, which sets up a virtual circuit to the receiving device by sending over a synch packet. Next, the data stream is broken up into smaller pieces, and a Transport layer header is created and attached to the header of the data field; now the piece of data is called a *segment* (a PDU). Each segment can be sequenced so the data stream can be put back together on the receiving side exactly as it was transmitted.

FIGURE 2.21 Data encapsulation

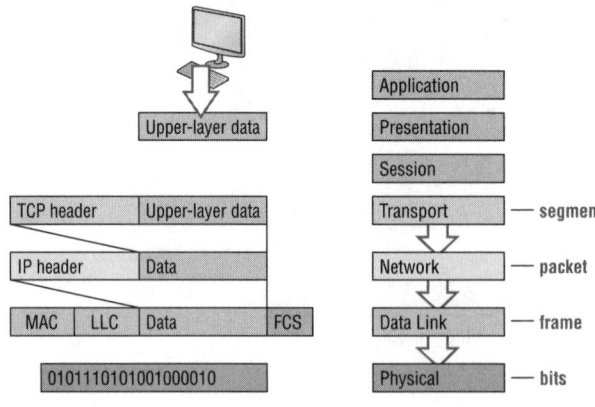

Each segment is then handed to the Network layer for network addressing and routing through the internetwork. Logical addressing (for example, IP and IPv6) is used to get each segment to the correct network. The Network layer protocol adds a control header to the segment handed down from the Transport layer, and what we have now is called a *packet* or *datagram*. Remember that the Transport and Network layers work together to rebuild a data stream on a receiving host, but it's not part of their work to place their PDUs on a local network segment—which is the only way to get the information to a router or host.

It's the Data Link layer that's responsible for taking packets from the Network layer and placing them on the network medium (cable or wireless). The Data Link layer encapsulates each packet in a *frame*, and the frame's header carries the hardware addresses of the source and destination hosts. If the destination device is on a remote network, then the frame is sent to a router to be routed through an internetwork. Once it gets to the destination network, a new frame is used to get the packet to the destination host.

To put this frame on the network, it must first be put into a digital signal. Since a frame is really a logical group of 1s and 0s, the physical layer is responsible for encoding these digits into a digital signal, which is read by devices on the same local network. The receiving devices will synchronize on the digital signal and extract (decode) the 1s and 0s from the digital signal. At this point, the devices reconstruct the frames, run a CRC, and then check their answer against the answer in the frame's FCS field. If it matches, the packet is pulled from the frame and what's left of the frame is discarded. This process is called *de-encapsulation*. The packet is handed to the Network layer, where the address is checked. If the address matches, the segment is pulled from the packet and what's left of the packet is discarded. The segment is processed at the Transport layer, which rebuilds the data stream and acknowledges to the transmitting station that it received each piece. It then happily hands the data stream to the upper-layer application.

At a transmitting device, the data encapsulation method works like this:

1. User information is converted to data for transmission on the network.

2. Data is converted to segments, and a reliable connection is set up between the transmitting and receiving hosts.

3. Segments are converted to packets or datagrams, and a logical address is placed in the header so each packet can be routed through an internetwork.

4. Packets or datagrams are converted to frames for transmission on the local network. Hardware (Ethernet) addresses are used to uniquely identify hosts on a local network segment.

5. Frames are converted to bits, and a digital encoding and clocking scheme is used.

To explain this in more detail using the layer addressing, I'll use Figure 2.22.

Remember that a data stream is handed down from the upper layer to the Transport layer. As technicians, we really don't care who the data stream comes from because that's really a programmer's problem. Our job is to rebuild the data stream reliably and hand it to the upper layers on the receiving device.

FIGURE 2.22 PDU and layer addressing

Segment		Source port	Destination port	...	Data	

Packet	Source IP	Destination IP	Protocol	...	Segment	

Frame	Destination MAC	Source MAC	Ether-Field	Packet	FCS	

Bits	1011011100011110000

Before we go further in our discussion of Figure 2.22, let's discuss port numbers and make sure you understand them. The Transport layer uses port numbers to define both the virtual circuit and the upper-layer processes, as you can see from Figure 2.23.

FIGURE 2.23 Port numbers at the Transport layer

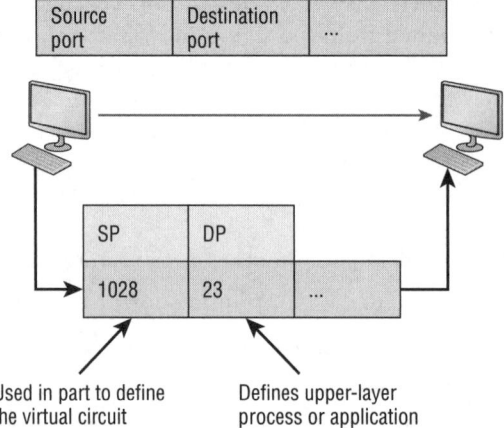

Source port	Destination port	...

SP	DP	
1028	23	...

Used in part to define the virtual circuit

Defines upper-layer process or application

When using a connection-oriented protocol like TCP, the Transport layer takes the data stream, makes segments out of it, and establishes a reliable session by creating a virtual circuit. It then sequences (numbers) each segment and uses acknowledgments and flow control. If you're using TCP, the virtual circuit is defined by the source and destination port number plus the source and destination IP address and called a socket. Understand that the host just makes this up, starting at port number 1024 because 0 through 1023 are reserved for well-known port numbers. The destination port number defines the upper-layer process or application that the data stream is handed to when the data stream is reliably rebuilt on the receiving host.

Now that you understand port numbers and how they are used at the Transport layer, let's go back to Figure 2.22. Once the Transport layer header information is added to the piece of data, it becomes a segment that's handed down to the Network layer along with the destination IP address. As you know, the destination IP address was handed down from the upper layers to the Transport layer with the data stream and was identified via name resolution at the upper layers—probably with DNS.

The Network layer adds a header and adds the logical addressing such as IP addresses to the front of each segment. Once the header is added to the segment, the PDU is called a packet. The packet has a protocol field that describes where the segment came from (either UDP or TCP) so it can hand the segment to the correct protocol at the Transport layer when it reaches the receiving host.

The Network layer is responsible for finding the destination hardware address that dictates where the packet should be sent on the local network. It does this by using the Address Resolution Protocol (ARP)—something I'll talk about more in Chapter 3. IP at the Network layer looks at the destination IP address and compares that address to its own source IP address and subnet mask. If it turns out to be a local network request, the hardware address of the local host is requested via an ARP request. If the packet is destined for a host on a remote network, IP will look for the IP address of the default gateway (router) instead.

The packet, along with the destination hardware address of either the local host or default gateway, is then handed down to the Data Link layer. The Data Link layer will add a header to the front of the packet and the piece of data then becomes a frame. It's called a frame because both a header and a trailer are added to the packet, which makes it look like it's within bookends—a frame—as shown in Figure 2.22. The frame uses an Ether-Type field to describe which protocol the packet came from at the Network layer. Now a cyclic redundancy check is run on the frame, and the answer to the CRC is placed in the Frame Check Sequence field found in the trailer of the frame.

The frame is now ready to be handed down, one bit at a time, to the Physical layer, which will use bit-timing rules to encode the data in a digital signal. Every device on the network segment will receive the digital signal and synchronize with the clock and extract the 1s and 0s from the digital signal to build a frame. After the frame is rebuilt, a CRC is run to make sure the frame is in proper order. If everything turns out to be all good, the hosts will check the destination MAC and IP addresses to see if the frame is for them.

If all this is making your eyes cross and your brain freeze, don't freak. I'll be going over exactly how data is encapsulated and routed through an internetwork later, in Chapter 9, "IP Routing."

The Cisco Three-Layer Hierarchical Model

Most of us were exposed to hierarchy early in life. Anyone with older siblings learned what it was like to be at the bottom of the hierarchy. Regardless of where you first discovered the concept of hierarchy, most of us experience it in many aspects of our lives. It's *hierarchy* that helps us understand where things belong, how things fit together, and what functions go where. It brings order to otherwise complex models. If you want a pay raise, for instance, hierarchy dictates that you ask your boss, not your subordinate, because that's the person whose role it is to grant or deny your request. So basically, understanding hierarchy helps us discern where we should go to get what we need.

Hierarchy has many of the same benefits in network design that it does in other areas of life. When used properly, it makes networks more predictable and helps us define which areas should perform certain functions. Likewise, you can use tools such as access lists at certain levels in hierarchical networks and avoid them at others.

Let's face it: Large networks can be extremely complicated, with multiple protocols, detailed configurations, and diverse technologies. Hierarchy helps us summarize a complex collection of details into an understandable model, bringing order from the chaos. Then, as specific configurations are needed, the model dictates the appropriate manner in which to apply them.

The Cisco hierarchical model can help you design, implement, and maintain a scalable, reliable, cost-effective hierarchical internetwork. Cisco defines three layers of hierarchy, as shown in Figure 2.24, each with specific functions.

FIGURE 2.24   The Cisco hierarchical model

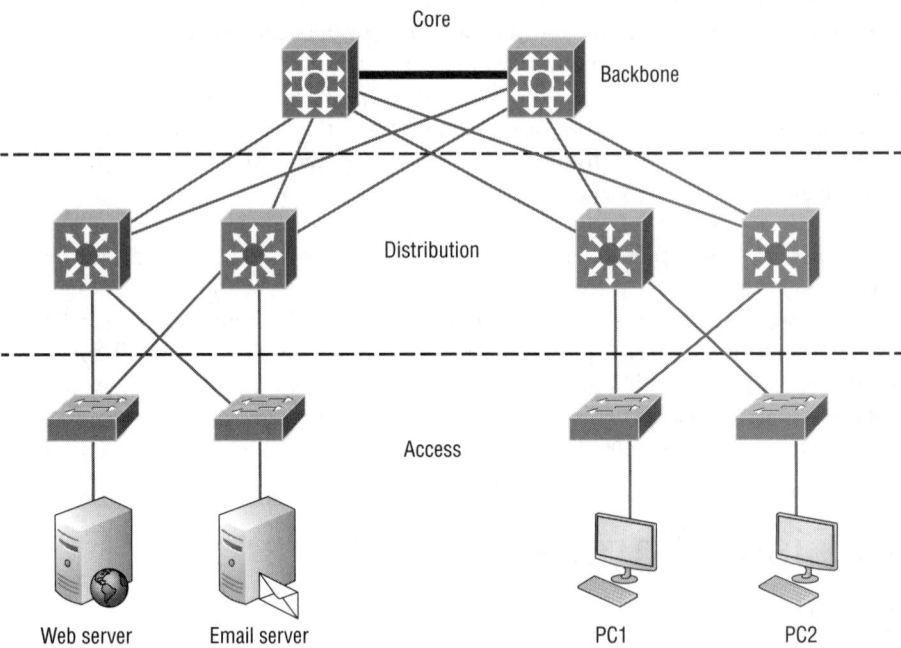

Each layer has specific responsibilities. Keep in mind that the three layers are logical and are not necessarily physical devices. Consider the OSI model, another logical hierarchy. Its seven layers describe functions but not necessarily protocols, right? Sometimes a protocol maps to more than one layer of the OSI model, and sometimes multiple protocols communicate within a single layer. In the same way, when we build physical implementations of hierarchical networks, we may have many devices in a single layer, or there may be a single device performing functions at two layers. Just remember that the definition of the layers is logical, not physical!

So let's take a closer look at each of the layers now.

The Core Layer

The *core layer* is literally the core of the network. At the top of the hierarchy, the core layer is responsible for transporting large amounts of traffic both reliably and quickly. The only purpose of the network's core layer is to switch traffic as fast as possible. The traffic transported across the core is common to a majority of users. But remember that user data is processed at the distribution layer, which forwards the requests to the core if needed.

If there's a failure in the core, *every single user* can be affected! This is why fault tolerance at this layer is so important. The core is likely to see large volumes of traffic, so speed and latency are driving concerns here. Given the function of the core, we can now consider some design specifics. Let's start with some things we don't want to do:

- Never do anything to slow down traffic. This includes making sure you don't use access lists, perform routing between virtual local area networks, or implement packet filtering.

- Don't support workgroup access here.

- Avoid expanding the core (e.g., adding routers when the internetwork grows). If performance becomes an issue in the core, give preference to upgrades over expansion.

    Here's a list of things that we want to achieve as we design the core:

- Design the core for high reliability. Consider data-link technologies that facilitate both speed and redundancy, like Gigabit Ethernet with redundant links or even 10 Gigabit Ethernet.

- Design with speed in mind. The core should have very little latency.

- Select routing protocols with lower convergence times. Fast and redundant data-link connectivity is no help if your routing tables are shot!

The Distribution Layer

The *distribution layer* is sometimes referred to as the *workgroup layer* and is the communication point between the access layer and the core. The primary functions of the distribution layer are to provide routing, filtering, and WAN access and to determine how packets can access the core, if needed. The distribution layer must determine the fastest way that network service requests are handled—for example, how a file request is forwarded to a server. After the distribution layer determines the best path, it forwards the request to the core layer if necessary. The core layer then quickly transports the request to the correct service.

The distribution layer is where we want to implement policies for the network because we are allowed a lot of flexibility in defining network operation here. There are several things that should generally be handled at the distribution layer:

- Routing
- Implementing tools (such as access lists), packet filtering, and queuing
- Implementing security and network policies, including address translation and firewalls
- Redistributing between routing protocols, including static routing
- Routing between VLANs and other workgroup support functions
- Defining broadcast and multicast domains

Key things to avoid at the distribution layer are those that are limited to functions that exclusively belong to one of the other layers!

The Access Layer

The *access layer* controls user and workgroup access to internetwork resources. The access layer is sometimes referred to as the *desktop layer*. The network resources most users need will be available locally because the distribution layer handles any traffic for remote services.

The following are some of the functions to be included at the access layer:

- Continued (from distribution layer) use of access control and policies
- Creation of separate collision domains (microsegmentation/switches)
- Workgroup connectivity into the distribution layer
- Device connectivity
- Resiliency and security services
- Advanced technology capabilities (voice/video, etc.)

Technologies like Gigabit or Fast Ethernet switching are frequently seen in the access layer.

I can't stress this enough—just because there are three separate levels does not imply three separate devices! There could be fewer or there could be more. After all, this is a *layered* approach.

Summary

In this chapter, you learned the fundamentals of Ethernet networking, how hosts communicate on a network. You discovered how CSMA/CD works in an Ethernet half-duplex network.

I also talked about the differences between half- and full-duplex modes, and we discussed the collision detection mechanism called CSMA/CD.

I described the common Ethernet cable types used in today's networks in this chapter as well, and by the way, you'd be wise to study that section really well!

Important enough to not gloss over, this chapter provided an introduction to encapsulation. Encapsulation is the process of encoding data as it goes down the OSI stack.

Last, I covered the Cisco three-layer hierarchical model. I described in detail the three layers and how each is used to help design and implement a Cisco internetwork.

Exam Essentials

Describe the operation of Carrier Sense Multiple Access with Collision Detection (CSMA/CD).   CSMA/CD is a protocol that helps devices share the bandwidth evenly without having two devices transmit at the same time on the network medium. Although it does not eliminate collisions, it helps to greatly reduce them, which reduces retransmissions, resulting in a more efficient transmission of data for all devices.

Differentiate half-duplex and full-duplex communication and define the requirements to utilize each method.   Full-duplex Ethernet uses two pairs of wires at the same time instead of one wire pair like half-duplex. Full-duplex allows for sending and receiving at the same time, using different wires to eliminate collisions, while half-duplex can send or receive but not at the same time and still can suffer collisions. To use full-duplex, the devices at both ends of the cable must be capable of and configured to perform full-duplex.

Describe the sections of a MAC address and the information contained in each section.   The MAC, or hardware, address is a 48-bit (6-byte) address written in a hexadecimal format. The first 24 bits, or 3 bytes, are called the organizationally unique identifier (OUI), which is assigned by the IEEE to the manufacturer of the NIC. The balance of the number uniquely identifies the NIC.

Identify the binary and hexadecimal equivalent of a decimal number.   Any number expressed in one format can also be expressed in the other two. The ability to perform this conversion is critical to understanding IP addressing and subnetting. Be sure to go through the written labs covering binary to decimal to hexadecimal conversion.

Identify the fields in the Data Link portion of an Ethernet frame.   The fields in the Data Link portion of a frame include the preamble, Start Frame Delimiter, destination MAC address, source MAC address, Length or Type, Data, and Frame Check Sequence.

Identify the IEEE physical standards for Ethernet cabling.   These standards describe the capabilities and physical characteristics of various cable types and include but are not limited to 10Base-2, 10Base-5, and 10Base-T.

Differentiate types of Ethernet cabling and identify their proper application.   The three types of cables that can be created from an Ethernet cable are straight-through (to connect a PC's or router's Ethernet interface to a hub or switch), crossover (to connect hub to hub, hub to switch, switch to switch, or PC to PC), and rolled (for a console connection from a PC to a router or switch).

Describe the data encapsulation process and the role it plays in packet creation.   Data encapsulation is a process whereby information is added to the frame from each layer of the OSI model. This is also called packet creation. Each layer communicates only with its peer layer on the receiving device.

Understand how to connect a console cable from a PC to a router and switch.   Take a rolled cable and connect it from the COM port of the host to the console port of a router. Start your emulations program such as putty or SecureCRT and set the bits per second to 9600 and flow control to None.

Identify the layers in the Cisco three-layer model and describe the ideal function of each layer.   The three layers in the Cisco hierarchical model are the core (responsible for transporting large amounts of traffic both reliably and quickly), distribution (provides routing, filtering, and WAN access), and access (workgroup connectivity into the distribution layer).

Written Labs

In this section, you'll complete the following labs to make sure you've got the information and concepts contained within them fully dialed in:

Lab 2.1: Binary/Decimal/Hexadecimal Conversion

Lab 2.2: CSMA/CD Operations

Lab 2.3: Cabling

Lab 2.4: Encapsulation

You can find the answers to these labs in Appendix A, "Answers to Written Labs."

Written Lab 2.1: Binary/Decimal/Hexadecimal Conversion

1. Convert from decimal IP address to binary format.

    Complete the following table to express 192.168.10.15 in binary format.

128	64	32	16	8	4	2	1	Binary

Complete the following table to express 172.16.20.55 in binary format.

128	64	32	16	8	4	2	1	Binary

Complete the following table to express 10.11.12.99 in binary format.

128	64	32	16	8	4	2	1	Binary

2. Convert the following from binary format to decimal IP address.

Complete the following table to express 11001100.00110011.10101010.01010101 in decimal IP address format.

128	64	32	16	8	4	2	1	Decimal

Complete the following table to express 11000110.11010011.00111001.11010001 in decimal IP address format.

128	64	32	16	8	4	2	1	Decimal

Complete the following table to express 10000100.11010010.10111000.10100110 in decimal IP address format.

128	64	32	16	8	4	2	1	Decimal

3. Convert the following from binary format to hexadecimal.

Complete the following table to express 11011000.00011011.00111101.01110110 in hexadecimal.

128	64	32	16	8	4	2	1	Hexadecimal

Complete the following table to express 11001010.11110101.10000011.11101011 in hexadecimal.

128	64	32	16	8	4	2	1	Hexadecimal

Complete the following table to express 10000100.11010010.01000011.10110011 in hexadecimal.

128	64	32	16	8	4	2	1	Hexadecimal

Written Lab 2.2: CSMA/CD Operations

Carrier Sense Multiple Access with Collision Detection (CSMA/CD) helps to minimize collisions in the network, thereby increasing data transmission efficiency. Place the following steps of its operation in the order in which they occur after a collision.

- All hosts have equal priority to transmit after the timers have expired.
- Each device on the Ethernet segment stops transmitting for a short time until the timers expire.
- The collision invokes a random backoff algorithm.
- A jam signal informs all devices that a collision occurred.

Written Lab 2.3: Cabling

For each of the following situations, determine whether a straight-through, crossover, or rolled cable would be used.

1. Host to host
2. Host to switch or hub
3. Router direct to host
4. Switch to switch
5. Router to switch or hub
6. Hub to hub
7. Hub to switch
8. Host to a router console serial communication (COM) port

Written Lab 2.4: Encapsulation

Place the following steps of the encapsulation process in the proper order.

- Packets or datagrams are converted to frames for transmission on the local network. Hardware (Ethernet) addresses are used to uniquely identify hosts on a local network segment.
- Segments are converted to packets or datagrams, and a logical address is placed in the header so each packet can be routed through an internetwork.
- User information is converted to data for transmission on the network.
- Frames are converted to bits, and a digital encoding and clocking scheme is used.
- Data is converted to segments, and a reliable connection is set up between the transmitting and receiving hosts.

Review Questions

The following questions are designed to test your understanding of this chapter's material. For more information on how to get additional questions, please see www.lammle.com/ccna.

You can find the answers to these questions in Appendix B, "Answers to Review Questions."

1. In the accompanying graphic, what is the name for the section of the MAC address marked as unknown?

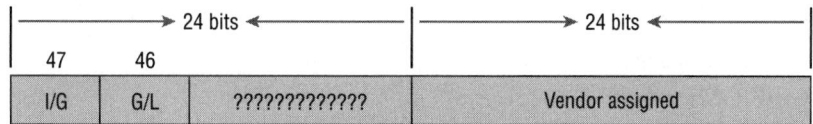

Example: 0000.0c12.3456

   A. IOS
   B. OSI
   C. ISO
   D. OUI

2. _____ on an Ethernet network is the retransmission delay that's enforced when a collision occurs.
   A. Backoff
   B. Carrier sense
   C. Forward delay
   D. Jamming

3. On which type of device could the situation shown in the diagram occur?

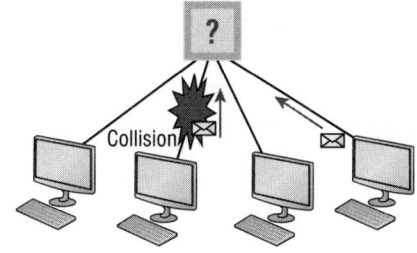

  A. Hub

  B. Switch

  C. Router

  D. Bridge

4. In the Ethernet II frame shown here, what is the function of the section labeled "FCS"?

Ethernet_II

Preamble 7 bytes	SFD 1 byte	Destination 6 bytes	Source 6 bytes	Type 2 bytes	Data and Pad 46 – 1500 bytes	FCS 4 bytes

  A. Allows the receiving devices to lock the incoming bit stream.

  B. Error detection

  C. Identifies the upper-layer protocol

  D. Identifies the transmitting device

5. A network interface port has collision detection and carrier sensing enabled on a shared twisted-pair network. From this statement, what is known about the network interface port?

  A. This is a 10 Mbps switch port.

  B. This is a 100 Mb/s switch port.

  C. This is an Ethernet port operating at half-duplex.

  D. This is an Ethernet port operating at full-duplex.

  E. This is a port on a network interface card in a PC.

6. For what two purposes does the Ethernet protocol use physical addresses? (Choose two.)

  A. To uniquely identify devices at layer 2

  B. To allow communication with devices on a different network

  C. To differentiate a layer 2 frame from a layer 3 packet

  D. To establish a priority system to determine which device gets to transmit first

  E. To allow communication between different devices on the same network

  F. To allow detection of a remote device when its physical address is unknown

7. Between which systems could you use a cable that uses the pinout pattern shown here?

    A. With a connection from a switch to a switch

    B. With a connection from a router to a router

    C. With a connection from a host to a host

    D. With a connection from a host to a switch

8. In an Ethernet network, under what two scenarios can devices transmit? (Choose two.)

    A. When they receive a special token

    B. When there is a carrier

    C. When they detect that no other devices are sending

    D. When the medium is idle

    E. When the server grants access

9. What type of cable uses the pinout shown here?

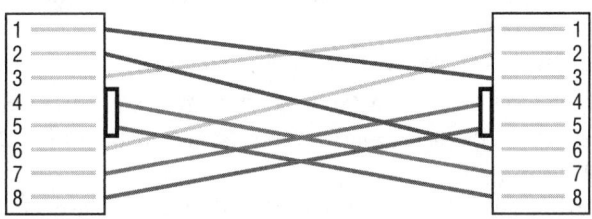

    A. Fiber optic

    B. Crossover Gigabit Ethernet cable

    C. Straight-through Fast Ethernet

    D. Coaxial

10. When configuring a terminal emulation program, which of the following is an incorrect setting?

    A. Bit rate: 9600

    B. Parity: None

    C. Flow control: None

    D. Data bits: 1

11. Which part of a MAC address indicates whether the address is a locally or globally administered address?

    A. FCS

    B. I/G bit

    C. OUI

    D. U/L bit

12. What cable type uses the pinout arrangement shown below?

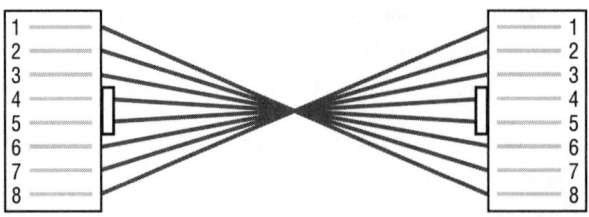

- **A.** Fiber optic
- **B.** Rolled
- **C.** Straight-through
- **D.** Crossover

13. Which of the following is *not* one of the actions taken in the operation of CSMA/CD when a collision occurs?

- **A.** A jam signal informs all devices that a collision occurred.
- **B.** The collision invokes a random backoff algorithm on the systems involved in the collision.
- **C.** Each device on the Ethernet segment stops transmitting for a short time until its back-off timer expires.
- **D.** All hosts have equal priority to transmit after the timers have expired.

14. Which of the following statements is *false* with regard to Ethernet?

- **A.** There are very few collisions in full-duplex mode.
- **B.** A dedicated switch port is required for each full-duplex node.
- **C.** The host network card and the switch port must be capable of operating in full-duplex mode to use full-duplex.
- **D.** The default behavior of 10Base-T and 100Base-T hosts is 10 Mbps half-duplex if the autodetect mechanism fails.

15. In the following diagram, identify the cable types required for connections A and B.

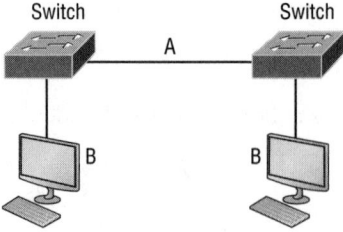

- **A.** A= crossover, B= crossover
- **B.** A= crossover, B= straight-through
- **C.** A= straight-through, B= straight-through
- **D.** A= straight-through, B= crossover

16. In the following image, match the cable type to the standard with which it goes.

1000Base-T	IEEE 802.3u
1000Base-SX	IEEE 802.3
10Base-T	IEEE 802.3ab
100Base-TX	IEEE 802.3z

17. The cable used to connect to the console port on a router or switch is called a _____ cable.
   A. Crossover
   B. Rollover
   C. Straight-through
   D. Full-duplex

18. Which of the following items does a socket comprise?
   A. IP address and MAC address
   B. IP address and port number
   C. Port number and MAC address
   D. MAC address and DLCI

19. Which of the following hexadecimal numbers converts to 28 in decimal?
   A. 1c
   B. 12
   C. 15
   D. ab

20. What cable type is shown in the following graphic?

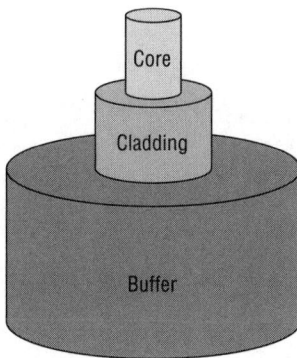

   A. Fiber optic
   B. Rollover
   C. Coaxial
   D. Full-duplex

Chapter

3

Introduction to TCP/IP

THE FOLLOWING ICND1 EXAM TOPICS ARE COVERED IN THIS CHAPTER:

✓ **Network Fundamentals**

- ▪ 1.1 Compare and contrast OSI and TCP/IP models

- ▪ 1.2 Compare and contrast TCP and UDP protocols

- ▪ 1.7 Apply troubleshooting methodologies to resolve problems

- ▪ 1.7.a Perform fault isolation and document

- ▪ 1.7.b Resolve or escalate

- ▪ 1.7.c Verify and monitor resolution

- ▪ 1.9 Compare and contrast IPv4 address types

  - ▪ 1.9.a Unicast

  - ▪ 1.9.b Broadcast

  - ▪ 1.9.c Multicast

- ▪ 1.10 Describe the need for private IPv4 addressing

The *Transmission Control Protocol/Internet Protocol (TCP/IP)* suite was designed and implemented by the Department of Defense (DoD) to ensure and preserve data integrity as well as maintain communications in the event of catastrophic war. So it follows that if designed and implemented correctly, a TCP/IP network can be a secure, dependable and resilient one. In this chapter, I'll cover the protocols of TCP/IP, and throughout this book, you'll learn how to create a solid TCP/IP network with Cisco routers and switches.

We'll begin by exploring the DoD's version of TCP/IP, then compare that version and its protocols with the OSI reference model that we discussed earlier.

Once you understand the protocols and processes used at the various levels of the DoD model, we'll take the next logical step by delving into the world of IP addressing and the different classes of IP addresses used in networks today.

 Subnetting is so vital, it will be covered in its own chapter, Chapter 4, "Easy Subnetting."

Because having a good grasp of the various IPv4 address types is critical to understanding IP addressing, subnetting, and variable length subnet masks (VLSMs), we'll explore these key topics in detail, ending this chapter by discussing the various types of IPv4 addresses that you'll need to have down for the exam.

I'm not going to cover Internet Protocol version 6 in this chapter because we'll get into that later, in Chapter 14, "Internet Protocol Version 6 (IPv6)." And just so you know, you'll simply see Internet Protocol version 4 written as just IP, rarely as IPv4.

 To find up-to-the-minute updates for this chapter, please see www.lammle .com/ccna or the book's web page via www.sybex.com/go/ccna.

Introducing TCP/IP

TCP/IP is at the very core of all things networking, so I really want to ensure that you have a comprehensive and functional command of it. I'll start by giving you the whole TCP/IP backstory, including its inception, and then move on to describe the important technical goals as defined by its original architects. And of course I'll include how TCP/IP compares to the theoretical OSI model.

A Brief History of TCP/IP

TCP first came on the scene way back in 1973, and in 1978, it was divided into two distinct protocols: TCP and IP. Later, in 1983, TCP/IP replaced the Network Control Protocol (NCP) and was authorized as the official means of data transport for anything connecting to ARPAnet, the Internet's ancestor. The DoD's Advanced Research Projects Agency (ARPA) created this ancient network way back in 1957 in a cold war reaction to the Soviet's launching of *Sputnik*. Also in 1983, ARPA was redubbed DARPA and divided into ARPAnet and MILNET until both were finally dissolved in 1990.

It may be counterintuitive, but most of the development work on TCP/IP happened at UC Berkeley in Northern California, where a group of scientists were simultaneously working on the Berkeley version of UNIX, which soon became known as the Berkeley Software Distribution (BSD) series of UNIX versions. Of course, because TCP/IP worked so well, it was packaged into subsequent releases of BSD Unix and offered to other universities and institutions if they bought the distribution tape. So basically, BSD Unix bundled with TCP/IP began as shareware in the world of academia. As a result, it became the foundation for the tremendous success and unprecedented growth of today's Internet as well as smaller, private and corporate intranets.

As usual, what started as a small group of TCP/IP aficionados evolved, and as it did, the US government created a program to test any new published standards and make sure they passed certain criteria. This was to protect TCP/IP's integrity and to ensure that no developer changed anything too dramatically or added any proprietary features. It's this very quality—this open-systems approach to the TCP/IP family of protocols—that sealed its popularity because this quality guarantees a solid connection between myriad hardware and software platforms with no strings attached.

TCP/IP and the DoD Model

The DoD model is basically a condensed version of the OSI model that comprises four instead of seven layers:

- Process/Application layer
- Host-to-Host layer or Transport layer
- Internet layer
- Network Access layer or Link layer

Figure 3.1 offers a comparison of the DoD model and the OSI reference model. As you can see, the two are similar in concept, but each has a different number of layers with different names. Cisco may at times use different names for the same layer, such as both "Host-to-Host" and Transport" at the layer above the Internet layer, as well as "Network Access" and "Link" used to describe the bottom layer.

FIGURE 3.1 The DoD and OSI models

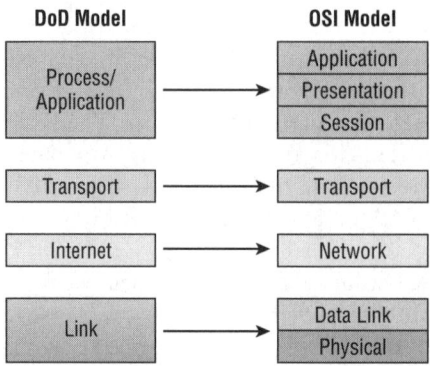

 When the different protocols in the IP stack are discussed, the layers of the OSI and DoD models are interchangeable. In other words, be prepared for the exam objectives to call the Host-to-Host layer the Transport layer!

A vast array of protocols join forces at the DoD model's *Process/Application layer.* These processes integrate the various activities and duties spanning the focus of the OSI's corresponding top three layers (Application, Presentation, and Session). We'll focus on a few of the most important applications found in the CCNA objectives. In short, the Process/Application layer defines protocols for node-to-node application communication and controls user-interface specifications.

The *Host-to-Host layer or Transport layer* parallels the functions of the OSI's Transport layer, defining protocols for setting up the level of transmission service for applications. It tackles issues like creating reliable end-to-end communication and ensuring the error-free delivery of data. It handles packet sequencing and maintains data integrity.

The *Internet layer* corresponds to the OSI's Network layer, designating the protocols relating to the logical transmission of packets over the entire network. It takes care of the addressing of hosts by giving them an IP (Internet Protocol) address and handles the routing of packets among multiple networks.

At the bottom of the DoD model, the *Network Access layer or Link layer* implements the data exchange between the host and the network. The equivalent of the Data Link and Physical layers of the OSI model, the Network Access layer oversees hardware addressing and defines protocols for the physical transmission of data. The reason TCP/IP became so popular is because there were no set physical layer specifications, so it could run on any existing or future physical network!

The DoD and OSI models are alike in design and concept and have similar functions in similar layers. Figure 3.2 shows the TCP/IP protocol suite and how its protocols relate to the DoD model layers.

FIGURE 3.2   The TCP/IP protocol suite

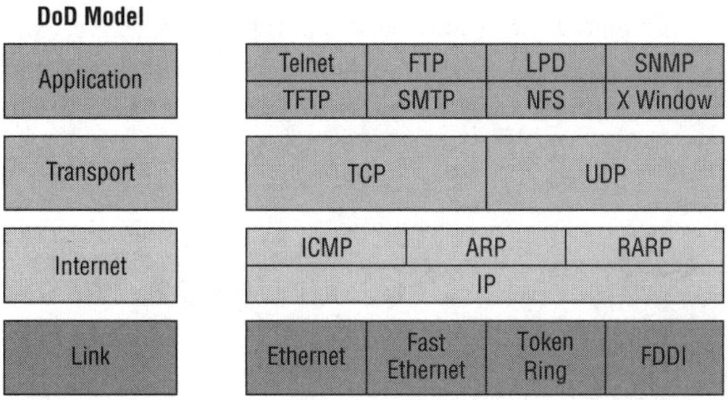

DoD Model

DoD Model					
Application	Telnet	FTP	LPD	SNMP	
	TFTP	SMTP	NFS	X Window	
Transport	TCP		UDP		
Internet	ICMP	ARP		RARP	
	IP				
Link	Ethernet	Fast Ethernet	Token Ring	FDDI	

In the following sections, we will look at the different protocols in more detail, beginning with those found at the Process/Application layer.

The Process/Application Layer Protocols

Coming up, I'll describe the different applications and services typically used in IP networks, and although there are many more protocols defined here, we'll focus in on the protocols most relevant to the CCNA objectives. Here's a list of the protocols and applications we'll cover in this section:

- Telnet
- SSH
- FTP
- TFTP
- SNMP
- HTTP
- HTTPS
- NTP
- DNS
- DHCP/BootP
- APIPA

Telnet

Telnet was one of the first Internet standards, developed in 1969, and is the chameleon of protocols—its specialty is terminal emulation. It allows a user on a remote client machine, called the Telnet client, to access the resources of another machine, the Telnet server, in order to access a command-line interface. Telnet achieves this by pulling a fast one on the Telnet server and making the client machine appear as though it were a terminal directly attached to the local network. This projection is actually a software image—a virtual terminal that can interact with the chosen remote host. A drawback is that there are no encryption techniques available within the Telnet protocol, so everything must be sent in clear text, including passwords! Figure 3.3 shows an example of a Telnet client trying to connect to a Telnet server.

FIGURE 3.3 Telnet

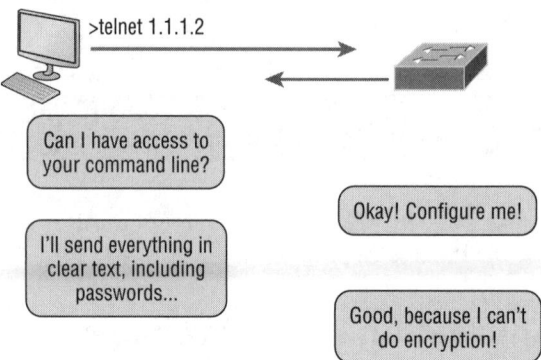

These emulated terminals are of the text-mode type and can execute defined procedures such as displaying menus that give users the opportunity to choose options and access the applications on the duped server. Users begin a Telnet session by running the Telnet client software and then logging into the Telnet server. Telnet uses an 8-bit, byte-oriented data connection over TCP, which makes it very thorough. It's still in use today because it is so simple and easy to use, with very low overhead, but again, with everything sent in clear text, it's not recommended in production.

Secure Shell (SSH)

Secure Shell (SSH) protocol sets up a secure session that's similar to Telnet over a standard TCP/IP connection and is employed for doing things like logging into systems, running programs on remote systems, and moving files from one system to another. And it does all of this while maintaining an encrypted connection. Figure 3.4 shows a SSH client trying to connect to a SSH server. The client must send the data encrypted!

You can think of it as the new-generation protocol that's now used in place of the antiquated and very unused rsh and rlogin—even Telnet.

File Transfer Protocol (FTP)

File Transfer Protocol (FTP) actually lets us transfer files, and it can accomplish this between any two machines using it. But FTP isn't just a protocol; it's also a program. Operating as a protocol, FTP is used by applications. As a program, it's employed by users to perform file tasks by hand. FTP also allows for access to both directories and files and can accomplish certain types of directory operations, such as relocating into different ones (Figure 3.5).

FIGURE 3.4   Secure Shell

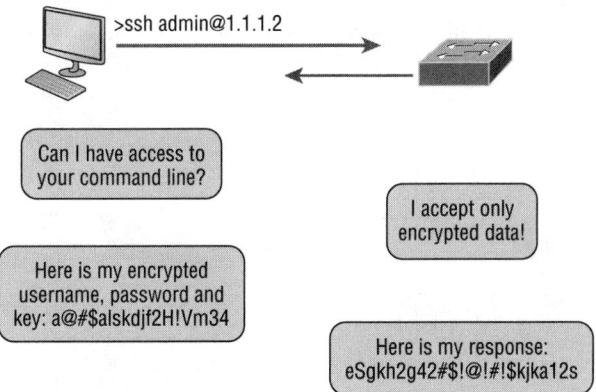

FIGURE 3.5   FTP

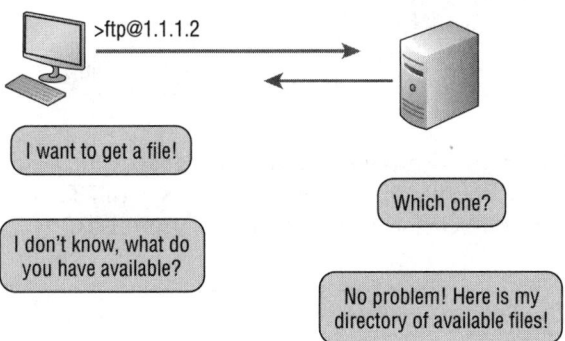

But accessing a host through FTP is only the first step. Users must then be subjected to an authentication login that's usually secured with passwords and usernames implemented by system administrators to restrict access. You can get around this somewhat by adopting the username *anonymous*, but you'll be limited in what you'll be able to access.

Even when employed by users manually as a program, FTP's functions are limited to listing and manipulating directories, typing file contents, and copying files between hosts. It can't execute remote files as programs.

Trivial File Transfer Protocol (TFTP)

Trivial File Transfer Protocol (TFTP) is the stripped-down, stock version of FTP, but it's the protocol of choice if you know exactly what you want and where to find it because it's fast and so easy to use!

But TFTP doesn't offer the abundance of functions that FTP does because it has no directory-browsing abilities, meaning that it can only send and receive files (Figure 3.6). Still, it's heavily used for managing file systems on Cisco devices, as I'll show you in Chapter 7, "Managing a Cisco Internetwork."

FIGURE 3.6   TFTP

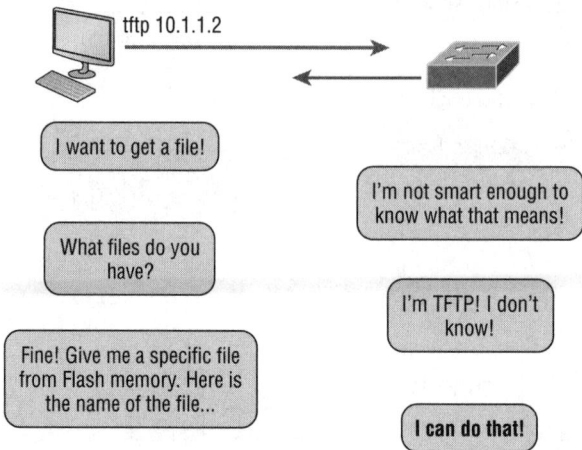

This compact little protocol also skimps in the data department, sending much smaller blocks of data than FTP. Also, there's no authentication as with FTP, so it's even more insecure, and few sites support it because of the inherent security risks.

 **Real World Scenario**

When Should You Use FTP?

Let's say everyone at your San Francisco office needs a 50 GB file emailed to them right away. What do you do? Many email servers would reject that email due to size limits (a lot of ISPs don't allow files larger than 5 MB or 10 MB to be emailed), and even if there are no size limits on the server, it would still take a while to send this huge file. FTP to the rescue!

If you need to give someone a large file or you need to get a large file from someone, FTP is a nice choice. To use FTP, you would need to set up an FTP server on the Internet so that the files can be shared.

Besides resolving size issues, FTP is faster than email. In addition, because it uses TCP and is connection-oriented, if the session dies, FTP can sometimes start up where it left off. Try that with your email client!

Simple Network Management Protocol (SNMP)

Simple Network Management Protocol (SNMP) collects and manipulates valuable network information, as you can see in Figure 3.7. It gathers data by polling the devices on the network from a network management station (NMS) at fixed or random intervals, requiring them to disclose certain information, or even asking for certain information from the device. In addition, network devices can inform the NMS station about problems as they occur so the network administrator is alerted.

FIGURE 3.7   SNMP

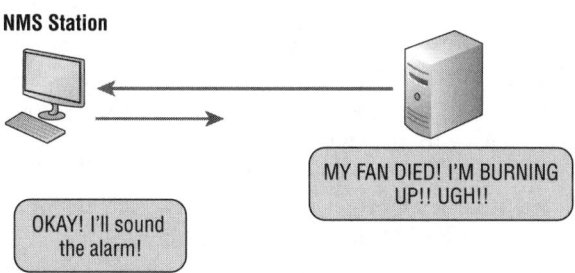

When all is well, SNMP receives something called a *baseline*—a report delimiting the operational traits of a healthy network. This protocol can also stand as a watchdog over the network, quickly notifying managers of any sudden turn of events. These network watchdogs are called *agents*, and when aberrations occur, agents send an alert called a *trap* to the management station.

SNMP Versions 1, 2, and 3

SNMP versions 1 and 2 are pretty much obsolete. This doesn't mean you won't see them in a network now and then, but you'll only come across v1 rarely, if ever. SNMPv2 provided improvements, especially in performance. But one of the best additions was called GETBULK, which allowed a host to retrieve a large amount of data at once. Even so, v2 never really caught on in the networking world and SNMPv3 is now the standard. Unlike v1, which used only UDP, v3 uses both TCP and UDP and added even more security, message integrity, authentication, and encryption.

Hypertext Transfer Protocol (HTTP)

All those snappy websites comprising a mélange of graphics, text, links, ads, and so on rely on the *Hypertext Transfer Protocol (HTTP)* to make it all possible (Figure 3.8). It's used to manage communications between web browsers and web servers and opens the right resource when you click a link, wherever that resource may actually reside.

FIGURE 3.8   HTTP

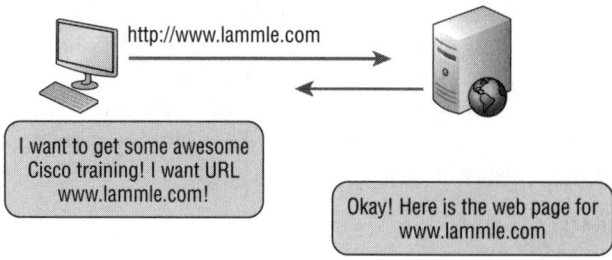

In order for a browser to display a web page, it must find the exact server that has the right web page, plus the exact details that identify the information requested. This information must be then be sent back to the browser. Nowadays, it's highly doubtful that a web server would have only one page to display!

Your browser can understand what you need when you enter a Uniform Resource Locator (URL), which we usually refer to as a web address, such as, for example, `http://www.lammle.com/forum` and `http://www.lammle.com/blog`.

So basically, each URL defines the protocol used to transfer data, the name of the server, and the particular web page on that server.

Hypertext Transfer Protocol Secure (HTTPS)

Hypertext Transfer Protocol Secure (HTTPS) is also known as Secure Hypertext Transfer Protocol. It uses Secure Sockets Layer (SSL). Sometimes you'll see it referred to as SHTTP or S-HTTP, which were slightly different protocols, but since Microsoft supported HTTPS, it became the de facto standard for securing web communication. But no matter—as indicated, it's a secure version of HTTP that arms you with a whole bunch of security tools for keeping transactions between a web browser and a server secure.

It's what your browser needs to fill out forms, sign in, authenticate, and encrypt an HTTP message when you do things online like make a reservation, access your bank, or buy something.

Network Time Protocol (NTP)

Kudos to Professor David Mills of the University of Delaware for coming up with this handy protocol that's used to synchronize the clocks on our computers to one standard time source (typically, an atomic clock). *Network Time Protocol (NTP)* works by synchronizing devices to ensure that all computers on a given network agree on the time (Figure 3.9).

This may sound pretty simple, but it's very important because so many of the transactions done today are time and date stamped. Think about databases—a server can get messed up pretty badly and even crash if it's out of sync with the machines connected to it by even mere seconds! You can't have a transaction entered by a machine at, say, 1:50 a.m. when the server records that transaction as having occurred at 1:45 a.m. So basically, NTP works to prevent a "back to the future *sans* DeLorean" scenario from bringing down the network—very important indeed!

FIGURE 3.9   NTP

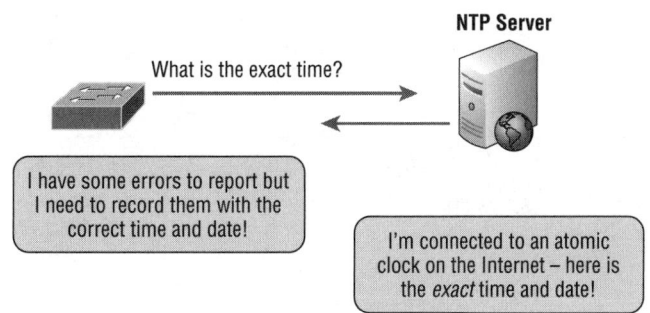

I'll tell you a lot more about NTP in Chapter 7, including how to configure this protocol in a Cisco environment.

Domain Name Service (DNS)

Domain Name Service (DNS) resolves hostnames—specifically, Internet names, such as www.lammle.com. But you don't have to actually use DNS. You just type in the IP address of any device you want to communicate with and find the IP address of a URL by using the Ping program. For example, >ping www.cisco.com will return the IP address resolved by DNS.

An IP address identifies hosts on a network and the Internet as well, but DNS was designed to make our lives easier. Think about this: What would happen if you wanted to move your web page to a different service provider? The IP address would change and no one would know what the new one is. DNS allows you to use a domain name to specify an IP address. You can change the IP address as often as you want and no one will know the difference.

To resolve a DNS address from a host, you'd typically type in the URL from your favorite browser, which would hand the data to the Application layer interface to be transmitted on the network. The application would look up the DNS address and send a UDP request to your DNS server to resolve the name (Figure 3.10).

If your first DNS server doesn't know the answer to the query, then the DNS server forwards a TCP request to its root DNS server. Once the query is resolved, the answer is transmitted back to the originating host, which means the host can now request the information from the correct web server.

DNS is used to resolve a *fully qualified domain name (FQDN)*—for example, www .lammle.com or todd.lammle.com. An FQDN is a hierarchy that can logically locate a system based on its domain identifier.

If you want to resolve the name *todd*, you either must type in the FQDN of todd .lammle.com or have a device such as a PC or router add the suffix for you. For example, on a Cisco router, you can use the command ip domain-name lammle.com to append each request with the lammle.com domain. If you don't do that, you'll have to type in the FQDN to get DNS to resolve the name.

FIGURE 3.10   DNS

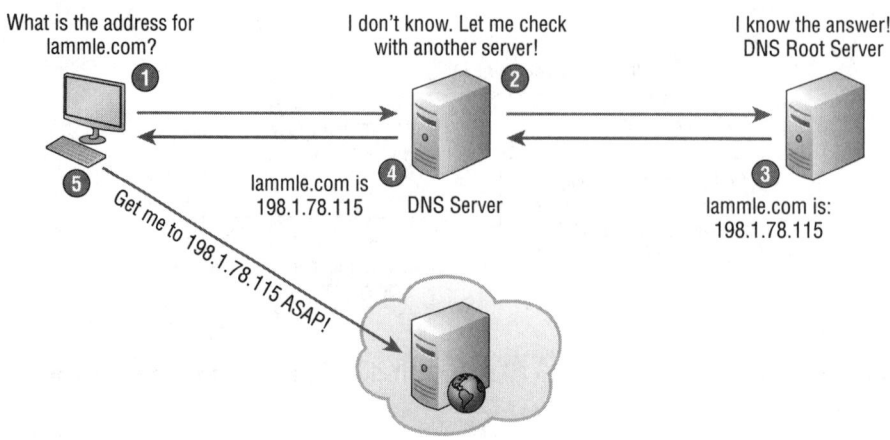

An important thing to remember about DNS is that if you can ping a device with an IP address but cannot use its FQDN, then you might have some type of DNS configuration failure.

Dynamic Host Configuration Protocol (DHCP)/Bootstrap Protocol (BootP)

Dynamic Host Configuration Protocol (DHCP) assigns IP addresses to hosts. It allows for easier administration and works well in small to very large network environments. Many types of hardware can be used as a DHCP server, including a Cisco router.

DHCP differs from BootP in that BootP assigns an IP address to a host but the host's hardware address must be entered manually in a BootP table. You can think of DHCP as a dynamic BootP. But remember that BootP is also used to send an operating system that a host can boot from. DHCP can't do that.

But there's still a lot of information a DHCP server can provide to a host when the host is requesting an IP address from the DHCP server. Here's a list of the most common types of information a DHCP server can provide:

- IP address
- Subnet mask
- Domain name
- Default gateway (routers)
- DNS server address
- WINS server address

A client that sends out a DHCP Discover message in order to receive an IP address sends out a broadcast at both layer 2 and layer 3.

- The layer 2 broadcast is all *F*s in hex, which looks like this: ff:ff:ff:ff:ff:ff.
- The layer 3 broadcast is 255.255.255.255, which means all networks and all hosts.

DHCP is connectionless, which means it uses User Datagram Protocol (UDP) at the Transport layer, also known as the Host-to-Host layer, which we'll talk about later.

Seeing is believing, so here's an example of output from my analyzer showing the layer 2 and layer 3 broadcasts:

```
Ethernet II, Src: 0.0.0.0 (00:0b:db:99:d3:5e),Dst: Broadcast(ff:ff:ff:ff:ff:ff)
Internet Protocol, Src: 0.0.0.0 (0.0.0.0),Dst: 255.255.255.255(255.255.255.255)
```

The Data Link and Network layers are both sending out "all hands" broadcasts saying, "Help—I don't know my IP address!"

 DHCP will be discussed in more detail, including configuration on a Cisco router and switch, in Chapter 7, "Managing a Cisco Internetwork," and Chapter 9, "IP Routing."

Figure 3.11 shows the process of a client/server relationship using a DHCP connection.

FIGURE 3.11   DHCP client four-step process

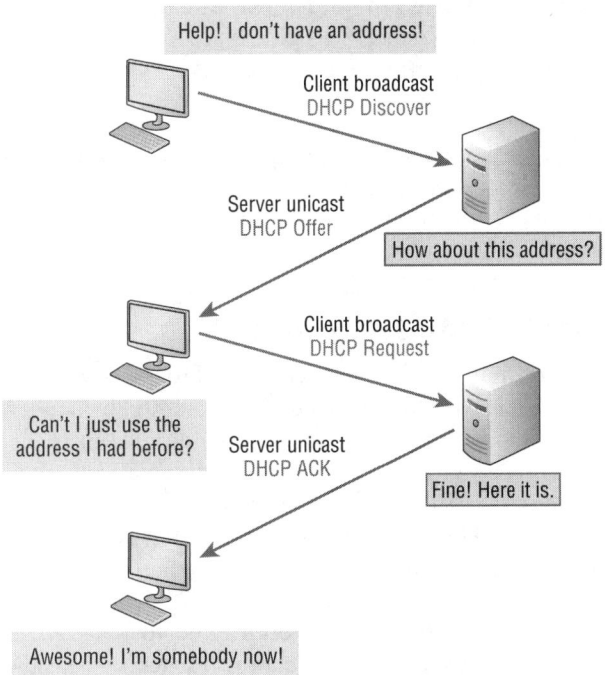

This is the four-step process a client takes to receive an IP address from a DHCP server:

1. The DHCP client broadcasts a DHCP Discover message looking for a DHCP server (Port 67).

2. The DHCP server that received the DHCP Discover message sends a layer 2 unicast DHCP Offer message back to the host.

3. The client then broadcasts to the server a DHCP Request message asking for the offered IP address and possibly other information.

4. The server finalizes the exchange with a unicast DHCP Acknowledgment message.

DHCP Conflicts

A DHCP address conflict occurs when two hosts use the same IP address. This sounds bad, and it is! We'll never even have to discuss this problem once we get to the chapter on IPv6!

During IP address assignment, a DHCP server checks for conflicts using the Ping program to test the availability of the address before it's assigned from the pool. If no host replies, then the DHCP server assumes that the IP address is not already allocated. This helps the server know that it's providing a good address, but what about the host? To provide extra protection against that terrible IP conflict issue, the host can broadcast for its own address!

A host uses something called a gratuitous ARP to help avoid a possible duplicate address. The DHCP client sends an ARP broadcast out on the local LAN or VLAN using its newly assigned address to solve conflicts before they occur.

So, if an IP address conflict is detected, the address is removed from the DHCP pool (scope), and it's really important to remember that the address will not be assigned to a host until the administrator resolves the conflict by hand!

Please see Chapter 9, "IP Routing," to check out a DHCP configuration on a Cisco router and also to find out what happens when a DHCP client is on one side of a router but the DHCP server is on the other side on a different network!

Automatic Private IP Addressing (APIPA)

Okay, so what happens if you have a few hosts connected together with a switch or hub and you don't have a DHCP server? You can add IP information by hand, known as *static IP addressing*, but later Windows operating systems provide a feature called Automatic Private IP Addressing (APIPA). With APIPA, clients can automatically self-configure an IP address and subnet mask—basic IP information that hosts use to communicate—when a DHCP server isn't available. The IP address range for APIPA is 169.254.0.1 through 169.254.255.254. The client also configures itself with a default Class B subnet mask of 255.255.0.0.

But when you're in your corporate network working and you have a DHCP server running, and your host shows that it's using this IP address range, it means that either your

DHCP client on the host is not working or the server is down or can't be reached due to some network issue. Believe me—I don't know anyone who's seen a host in this address range and has been happy about it!

Now, let's take a look at the Transport layer, or what the DoD calls the Host-to-Host layer.

The Host-to-Host or Transport Layer Protocols

The main purpose of the Host-to-Host layer is to shield the upper-layer applications from the complexities of the network. This layer says to the upper layer, "Just give me your data stream, with any instructions, and I'll begin the process of getting your information ready to send."

Coming up, I'll introduce you to the two protocols at this layer:

- Transmission Control Protocol (TCP)
- User Datagram Protocol (UDP)

In addition, we'll look at some of the key host-to-host protocol concepts, as well as the port numbers.

Remember, this is still considered layer 4, and Cisco really likes the way layer 4 can use acknowledgments, sequencing, and flow control.

Transmission Control Protocol (TCP)

Transmission Control Protocol (TCP) takes large blocks of information from an application and breaks them into segments. It numbers and sequences each segment so that the destination's TCP stack can put the segments back into the order the application intended. After these segments are sent on the transmitting host, TCP waits for an acknowledgment of the receiving end's TCP virtual circuit session, retransmitting any segments that aren't acknowledged.

Before a transmitting host starts to send segments down the model, the sender's TCP stack contacts the destination's TCP stack to establish a connection. This creates a *virtual circuit*, and this type of communication is known as *connection-oriented*. During this initial handshake, the two TCP layers also agree on the amount of information that's going to be sent before the recipient's TCP sends back an acknowledgment. With everything agreed upon in advance, the path is paved for reliable communication to take place.

TCP is a full-duplex, connection-oriented, reliable, and accurate protocol, but establishing all these terms and conditions, in addition to error checking, is no small task. TCP is very complicated, and so not surprisingly, it's costly in terms of network overhead. And since today's networks are much more reliable than those of yore, this added reliability is often unnecessary. Most programmers use TCP because it removes a lot of programming work, but for real-time video and VoIP, *User Datagram Protocol (UDP)* is often better because using it results in less overhead.

TCP Segment Format

Since the upper layers just send a data stream to the protocols in the Transport layers, I'll use Figure 3.12 to demonstrate how TCP segments a data stream and prepares it for the Internet layer. When the Internet layer receives the data stream, it routes the segments as packets through an internetwork. The segments are handed to the receiving host's Host-to-Host layer protocol, which rebuilds the data stream for the upper-layer applications or protocols.

FIGURE 3.12   TCP segment format

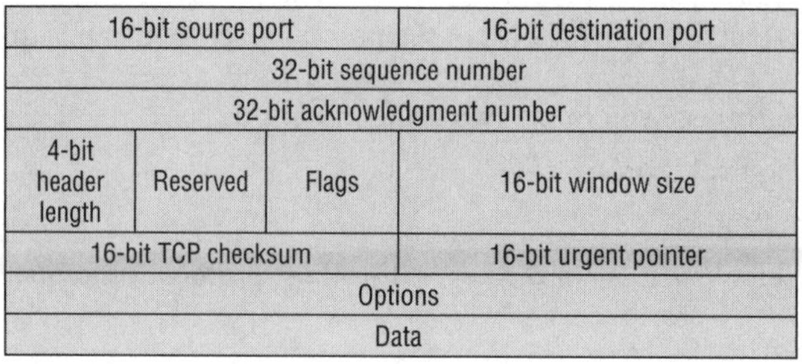

16-bit source port			16-bit destination port	
32-bit sequence number				
32-bit acknowledgment number				
4-bit header length	Reserved	Flags	16-bit window size	
16-bit TCP checksum			16-bit urgent pointer	
Options				
Data				

Figure 3.12 shows the TCP segment format and shows the different fields within the TCP header. This isn't important to memorize for the Cisco exam objectives, but you need to understand it well because it's really good foundational information.

The TCP header is 20 bytes long, or up to 24 bytes with options. You need to understand what each field in the TCP segment is in order to build a strong educational foundation:

Source port   This is the port number of the application on the host sending the data, which I'll talk about more thoroughly a little later in this chapter.

Destination port   This is the port number of the application requested on the destination host.

Sequence number   A number used by TCP that puts the data back in the correct order or retransmits missing or damaged data during a process called sequencing.

Acknowledgment number   The value is the TCP octet that is expected next.

Header length   The number of 32-bit words in the TCP header, which indicates where the data begins. The TCP header (even one including options) is an integral number of 32 bits in length.

Reserved   Always set to zero.

Code bits/flags   Controls functions used to set up and terminate a session.

Window   The window size the sender is willing to accept, in octets.

Checksum   The cyclic redundancy check (CRC), used because TCP doesn't trust the lower layers and checks everything. The CRC checks the header and data fields.

Urgent   A valid field only if the Urgent pointer in the code bits is set. If so, this value indicates the offset from the current sequence number, in octets, where the segment of non-urgent data begins.

Options   May be 0, meaning that no options have to be present, or a multiple of 32 bits. However, if any options are used that do not cause the option field to total a multiple of 32 bits, padding of 0s must be used to make sure the data begins on a 32-bit boundary. These boundaries are known as words.

Data   Handed down to the TCP protocol at the Transport layer, which includes the upper-layer headers.

Let's take a look at a TCP segment copied from a network analyzer:

```
TCP - Transport Control Protocol
   Source Port:       5973
   Destination Port: 23
   Sequence Number:  1456389907
   Ack Number:       1242056456
   Offset:           5
   Reserved:         %000000
   Code:             %011000
         Ack is valid
         Push Request
   Window:           61320
   Checksum:         0x61a6
   Urgent Pointer:   0
   No TCP Options
   TCP Data Area:
   vL.5.+.5.+.5.+.5  76 4c 19 35 11 2b 19 35 11 2b 19 35 11
     2b 19 35 +. 11 2b 19
   Frame Check Sequence: 0x0d00000f
```

Did you notice that everything I talked about earlier is in the segment? As you can see from the number of fields in the header, TCP creates a lot of overhead. Again, this is why application developers may opt for efficiency over reliability to save overhead and go with UDP instead. It's also defined at the Transport layer as an alternative to TCP.

User Datagram Protocol (UDP)

User Datagram Protocol (UDP) is basically the scaled-down economy model of TCP, which is why UDP is sometimes referred to as a thin protocol. Like a thin person on a park bench, a thin protocol doesn't take up a lot of room—or in this case, require much bandwidth on a network.

UDP doesn't offer all the bells and whistles of TCP either, but it does do a fabulous job of transporting information that doesn't require reliable delivery, using far less network resources. (UDP is covered thoroughly in Request for Comments 768.)

So clearly, there are times that it's wise for developers to opt for UDP rather than TCP, one of them being when reliability is already taken care of at the Process/Application layer. Network File System (NFS) handles its own reliability issues, making the use of TCP both impractical and redundant. But ultimately, it's up to the application developer to opt for using UDP or TCP, not the user who wants to transfer data faster!

UDP does *not* sequence the segments and does not care about the order in which the segments arrive at the destination. UDP just sends the segments off and forgets about them. It doesn't follow through, check up on them, or even allow for an acknowledgment of safe arrival—complete abandonment. Because of this, it's referred to as an unreliable protocol. This does not mean that UDP is ineffective, only that it doesn't deal with reliability issues at all.

Furthermore, UDP doesn't create a virtual circuit, nor does it contact the destination before delivering information to it. Because of this, it's also considered a *connectionless* protocol. Since UDP assumes that the application will use its own reliability method, it doesn't use any itself. This presents an application developer with a choice when running the Internet Protocol stack: TCP for reliability or UDP for faster transfers.

It's important to know how this process works because if the segments arrive out of order, which is commonplace in IP networks, they'll simply be passed up to the next layer in whatever order they were received. This can result in some seriously garbled data! On the other hand, TCP sequences the segments so they get put back together in exactly the right order, which is something UDP just can't do.

UDP Segment Format

Figure 3.13 clearly illustrates UDP's markedly lean overhead as compared to TCP's hungry requirements. Look at the figure carefully—can you see that UDP doesn't use windowing or provide for acknowledgments in the UDP header?

FIGURE 3.13 UDP segment

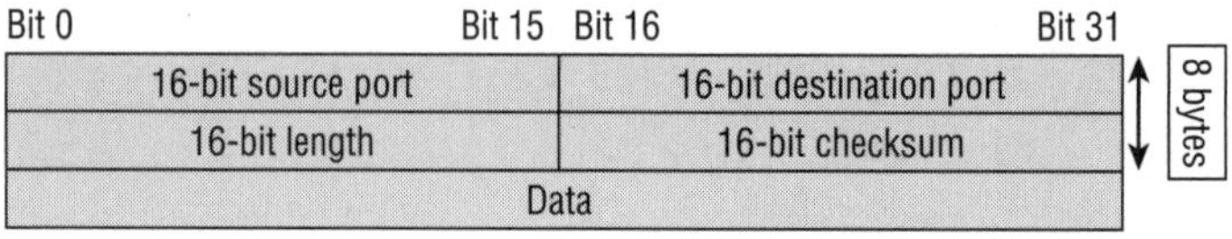

It's important for you to understand what each field in the UDP segment is:

Source port Port number of the application on the host sending the data

Destination port Port number of the application requested on the destination host

Length Length of UDP header and UDP data

Checksum Checksum of both the UDP header and UDP data fields

Data Upper-layer data

UDP, like TCP, doesn't trust the lower layers and runs its own CRC. Remember that the Frame Check Sequence (FCS) is the field that houses the CRC, which is why you can see the FCS information.

The following shows a UDP segment caught on a network analyzer:

```
UDP - User Datagram Protocol
 Source Port:       1085
 Destination Port: 5136
 Length:           41
 Checksum:         0x7a3c
 UDP Data Area:
 ..Z......00 01 5a 96 00 01 00 00 00 00 00 11 0000 00
 ...C..2._C._C  2e 03 00 43 02 1e 32 0a 00 0a 00 80 43 00 80
Frame Check Sequence: 0x00000000
```

Notice that low overhead! Try to find the sequence number, ack number, and window size in the UDP segment. You can't because they just aren't there!

Key Concepts of Host-to-Host Protocols

Since you've now seen both a connection-oriented (TCP) and connectionless (UDP) protocol in action, it's a good time to summarize the two here. Table 3.1 highlights some of the key concepts about these two protocols for you to memorize.

TABLE 3.1   Key features of TCP and UDP

TCP	UDP
Sequenced	Unsequenced
Reliable	Unreliable
Connection-oriented	Connectionless
Virtual circuit	Low overhead
Acknowledgments	No acknowledgment
Windowing flow control	No windowing or flow control of any type

And if all this isn't quite clear yet, a telephone analogy will really help you understand how TCP works. Most of us know that before you speak to someone on a phone, you must first establish a connection with that other person no matter where they are. This is akin to establishing a virtual circuit with the TCP protocol. If you were giving someone important information during your conversation, you might say things like, "You know? or "Did you get that?" Saying things like this is a lot like a TCP acknowledgment—it's designed to get you verification. From time to time, especially on mobile phones, people ask, "Are you still there?" People end their conversations with a "Goodbye" of some kind, putting closure on the phone call, which you can think of as tearing down the virtual circuit that was created for your communication session. TCP performs these types of functions.

Conversely, using UDP is more like sending a postcard. To do that, you don't need to contact the other party first, you simply write your message, address the postcard, and send it off. This is analogous to UDP's connectionless orientation. Since the message on the postcard is probably not a matter of life or death, you don't need an acknowledgment of its receipt. Similarly, UDP does not involve acknowledgments.

Let's take a look at another figure, one that includes TCP, UDP, and the applications associated to each protocol: Figure 3.14 (discussed in the next section).

FIGURE 3.14   Port numbers for TCP and UDP

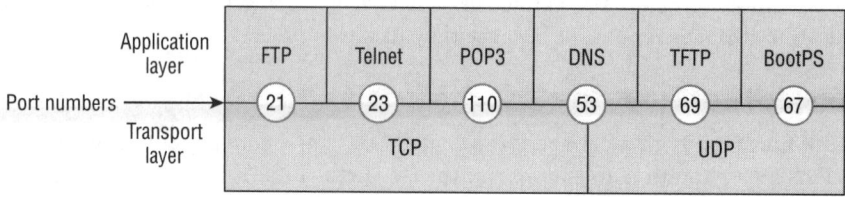

Port Numbers

TCP and UDP must use *port numbers* to communicate with the upper layers because these are what keep track of different conversations crossing the network simultaneously. Originating-source port numbers are dynamically assigned by the source host and will equal some number starting at 1024. Port number 1023 and below are defined in RFC 3232 (or just see www.iana.org), which discusses what we call well-known port numbers.

Virtual circuits that don't use an application with a well-known port number are assigned port numbers randomly from a specific range instead. These port numbers identify the source and destination application or process in the TCP segment.

 The Requests for Comments (RFCs) form a series of notes about the Internet (originally the ARPAnet) started in 1969. These notes discuss many aspects of computer communication, focusing on networking protocols, procedures, programs, and concepts, but they also include meeting notes, opinions, and sometimes even humor. You can find the RFCs by visiting www.iana.org.

Figure 3.14 illustrates how both TCP and UDP use port numbers. I'll cover the different port numbers that can be used next:

- Numbers below 1024 are considered well-known port numbers and are defined in RFC 3232.

- Numbers 1024 and above are used by the upper layers to set up sessions with other hosts and by TCP and UDP to use as source and destination addresses in the segment.

TCP Session: Source Port

Let's take a minute to check out analyzer output showing a TCP session I captured with my analyzer software session now:

```
TCP - Transport Control Protocol
  Source Port:       5973
  Destination Port: 23
  Sequence Number:  1456389907
  Ack Number:       1242056456
  Offset:           5
  Reserved:         %000000
  Code:             %011000
       Ack is valid
       Push Request
  Window:           61320
  Checksum:         0x61a6
  Urgent Pointer:   0
  No TCP Options
  TCP Data Area:
  vL.5.+.5.+.5.+.5  76 4c 19 35 11 2b 19 35 11 2b 19 35 11
   2b 19 35 +. 11 2b 19
Frame Check Sequence: 0x0d00000f
```

Notice that the source host makes up the source port, which in this case is 5973. The destination port is 23, which is used to tell the receiving host the purpose of the intended connection (Telnet).

By looking at this session, you can see that the source host makes up the source port by using numbers from 1024 to 65535. But why does the source make up a port number? To differentiate between sessions with different hosts because how would a server know where information is coming from if it didn't have a different number from a sending host? TCP and the upper layers don't use hardware and logical addresses to understand the sending host's address as the Data Link and Network layer protocols do. Instead, they use port numbers.

TCP Session: Destination Port

You'll sometimes look at an analyzer and see that only the source port is above 1024 and the destination port is a well-known port, as shown in the following trace:

```
TCP - Transport Control Protocol
  Source Port:       1144
  Destination Port: 80 World Wide Web HTTP
  Sequence Number:  9356570
  Ack Number:       0
```

```
Offset:             7
Reserved:           %000000
Code:               %000010
     Synch Sequence
Window:             8192
Checksum:           0x57E7
Urgent Pointer:     0
TCP Options:
 Option Type: 2 Maximum Segment Size
   Length:    4
   MSS:       536
 Option Type: 1 No Operation
 Option Type: 1 No Operation
 Option Type: 4
   Length:    2
   Opt Value:
 No More HTTP Data
Frame Check Sequence: 0x43697363
```

And sure enough, the source port is over 1024, but the destination port is 80, indicating an HTTP service. The server, or receiving host, will change the destination port if it needs to.

In the preceding trace, a "SYN" packet is sent to the destination device. This Synch (as shown in the output) sequence is what's used to inform the remote destination device that it wants to create a session.

TCP Session: Syn Packet Acknowledgment

The next trace shows an acknowledgment to the SYN packet:

```
TCP - Transport Control Protocol
 Source Port:       80 World Wide Web HTTP
 Destination Port: 1144
 Sequence Number:  2873580788
 Ack Number:       9356571
 Offset:           6
 Reserved:         %000000
 Code:             %010010
     Ack is valid
     Synch Sequence
 Window:           8576
 Checksum:         0x5F85
 Urgent Pointer:   0
```

```
TCP Options:
  Option Type: 2 Maximum Segment Size
    Length:    4
    MSS:       1460
  No More HTTP Data
Frame Check Sequence: 0x6E203132
```

Notice the `Ack is valid`, which means that the source port was accepted and the device agreed to create a virtual circuit with the originating host.

And here again, you can see that the response from the server shows that the source is 80 and the destination is the 1144 sent from the originating host—all's well!

Table 3.2 gives you a list of the typical applications used in the TCP/IP suite by showing their well-known port numbers and the Transport layer protocols used by each application or process. It's really key to memorize this table.

TABLE 3.2   Key protocols that use TCP and UDP

TCP	UDP
Telnet 23	SNMP 161
SMTP 25	TFTP 69
HTTP 80	DNS 53
FTP 20, 21	BooTPS/DHCP 67
DNS 53	
HTTPS 443	NTP 123
SSH 22	
POP3 110	
IMAP4 143	

Notice that DNS uses both TCP and UDP. Whether it opts for one or the other depends on what it's trying to do. Even though it's not the only application that can use both protocols, it's certainly one that you should make sure to remember in your studies.

What makes TCP reliable is sequencing, acknowledgments, and flow control (windowing). UDP does not have reliability.

Okay—I want to discuss one more item before we move down to the Internet layer—session multiplexing. Session multiplexing is used by both TCP and UDP and basically allows a single computer, with a single IP address, to have multiple sessions occurring simultaneously. Say you go to www.lammle.com and are browsing and then you click a link to another page. Doing this opens another session to your host. Now you go to www.lammle.com/forum from another window and that site opens a window as well. Now you have three sessions open using one IP address because the Session layer is sorting the separate requests based on the Transport layer port number. This is the job of the Session layer: to keep application layer data separate!

The Internet Layer Protocols

In the DoD model, there are two main reasons for the Internet layer's existence: routing and providing a single network interface to the upper layers.

None of the other upper- or lower-layer protocols have any functions relating to routing—that complex and important task belongs entirely to the Internet layer. The Internet layer's second duty is to provide a single network interface to the upper-layer protocols. Without this layer, application programmers would need to write "hooks" into every one of their applications for each different Network Access protocol. This would not only be a pain in the neck, but it would lead to different versions of each application—one for Ethernet, another one for wireless, and so on. To prevent this, IP provides one single network interface for the upper-layer protocols. With that mission accomplished, it's then the job of IP and the various Network Access protocols to get along and work together.

All network roads don't lead to Rome—they lead to IP. And all the other protocols at this layer, as well as all those at the upper layers, use it. Never forget that. All paths through the DoD model go through IP. Here's a list of the important protocols at the Internet layer that I'll cover individually in detail coming up:

- Internet Protocol (IP)
- Internet Control Message Protocol (ICMP)
- Address Resolution Protocol (ARP)

Internet Protocol (IP)

Internet Protocol (IP) essentially is the Internet layer. The other protocols found here merely exist to support it. IP holds the big picture and could be said to "see all," because it's aware of all the interconnected networks. It can do this because all the machines on the network have a software, or logical, address called an IP address, which we'll explore more thoroughly later in this chapter.

For now, understand that IP looks at each packet's address. Then, using a routing table, it decides where a packet is to be sent next, choosing the best path to send it upon. The protocols of the Network Access layer at the bottom of the DoD model don't possess IP's enlightened scope of the entire network; they deal only with physical links (local networks).

Identifying devices on networks requires answering these two questions: Which network is it on? And what is its ID on that network? The first answer is the *software address*, or *logical address*. You can think of this as the part of the address that specifies the correct street. The second answer is the hardware address, which goes a step further to specify the correct mailbox. All hosts on a network have a logical ID called an IP address. This is the software, or logical, address and contains valuable encoded information, greatly simplifying the complex task of routing. (IP is discussed in RFC 791.)

IP receives segments from the Host-to-Host layer and fragments them into datagrams (packets) if necessary. IP then reassembles datagrams back into segments on the receiving side. Each datagram is assigned the IP address of the sender and that of the recipient. Each router or switch (layer 3 device) that receives a datagram makes routing decisions based on the packet's destination IP address.

Figure 3.15 shows an IP header. This will give you a picture of what the IP protocol has to go through every time user data that is destined for a remote network is sent from the upper layers.

FIGURE 3.15   IP header

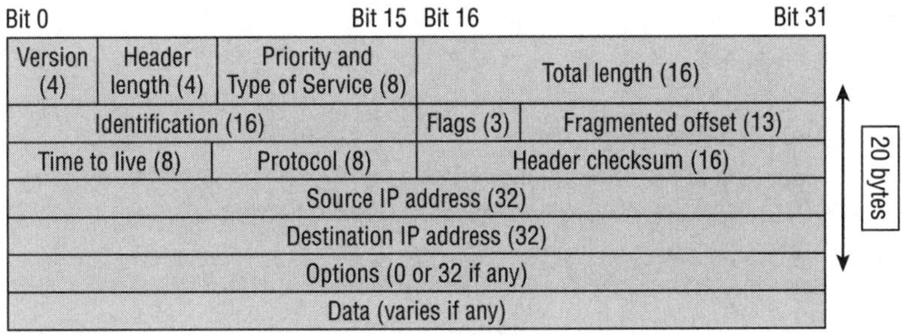

The following fields make up the IP header:

Version   IP version number.

Header length   Header length (HLEN) in 32-bit words.

Priority and Type of Service   Type of Service tells how the datagram should be handled. The first 3 bits are the priority bits, now called the differentiated services bits.

Total length   Length of the packet, including header and data.

Identification   Unique IP-packet value used to differentiate fragmented packets from different datagrams.

Flags   Specifies whether fragmentation should occur.

Fragment offset   Provides fragmentation and reassembly if the packet is too large to put in a frame. It also allows different maximum transmission units (MTUs) on the Internet.

Time To Live   The time to live (TTL) is set into a packet when it is originally generated. If it doesn't get to where it's supposed to go before the TTL expires, boom—it's gone. This stops IP packets from continuously circling the network looking for a home.

Protocol   Port of upper-layer protocol; for example, TCP is port 6 or UDP is port 17. Also supports Network layer protocols, like ARP and ICMP, and can be referred to as the Type field in some analyzers. We'll talk about this field more in a minute.

Header checksum   Cyclic redundancy check (CRC) on header only.

Source IP address   32-bit IP address of sending station.

Destination IP address   32-bit IP address of the station this packet is destined for.

Options   Used for network testing, debugging, security, and more.

Data   After the IP option field, will be the upper-layer data.

Here's a snapshot of an IP packet caught on a network analyzer. Notice that all the header information discussed previously appears here:

```
IP Header - Internet Protocol Datagram
 Version:              4
 Header Length:        5
 Precedence:           0
 Type of Service:      %000
 Unused:               %00
 Total Length:         187
 Identifier:           22486
 Fragmentation Flags:  %010 Do Not Fragment
 Fragment Offset:      0
 Time To Live:         60
 IP Type:              0x06 TCP
 Header Checksum:      0xd031
 Source IP Address:    10.7.1.30
 Dest. IP Address:     10.7.1.10
 No Internet Datagram Options
```

The Type field is typically a Protocol field, but this analyzer sees it as an IP Type field. This is important. If the header didn't carry the protocol information for the next layer, IP wouldn't know what to do with the data carried in the packet. The preceding example clearly tells IP to hand the segment to TCP.

Figure 3.16 demonstrates how the Network layer sees the protocols at the Transport layer when it needs to hand a packet up to the upper-layer protocols.

FIGURE 3.16   The Protocol field in an IP header

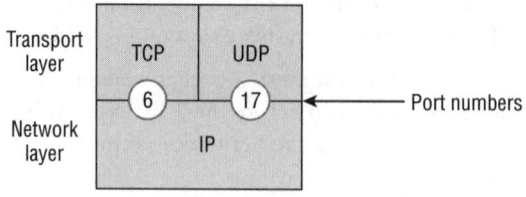

In this example, the Protocol field tells IP to send the data to either TCP port 6 or UDP port 17. But it will be UDP or TCP only if the data is part of a data stream headed for an upper-layer service or application. It could just as easily be destined for Internet Control Message Protocol (ICMP), Address Resolution Protocol (ARP), or some other type of Network layer protocol.

Table 3.3 is a list of some other popular protocols that can be specified in the Protocol field.

TABLE 3.3   Possible protocols found in the Protocol field of an IP header

Protocol	Protocol Number
ICMP	1
IP in IP (tunneling)	4
TCP	6
UDP	17
EIGRP	88
OSPF	89
IPv6	41
GRE	47
Layer 2 tunnel (L2TP)	115

You can find a complete list of Protocol field numbers at www.iana.org/assignments/protocol-numbers.

Internet Control Message Protocol (ICMP)

Internet Control Message Protocol (ICMP) works at the Network layer and is used by IP for many different services. ICMP is basically a management protocol and messaging service provider for IP. Its messages are carried as IP datagrams. RFC 1256 is an annex to ICMP, which gives hosts extended capability in discovering routes to gateways.

ICMP packets have the following characteristics:

- They can provide hosts with information about network problems.
- They are encapsulated within IP datagrams.

The following are some common events and messages that ICMP relates to:

Destination unreachable   If a router can't send an IP datagram any further, it uses ICMP to send a message back to the sender, advising it of the situation. For example, take a look at Figure 3.17, which shows that interface e0 of the Lab_B router is down.

FIGURE 3.17   ICMP error message is sent to the sending host from the remote router.

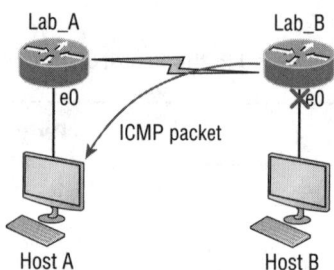

When Host A sends a packet destined for Host B, the Lab_B router will send an ICMP destination unreachable message back to the sending device, which is Host A in this example.

Buffer full/source quench   If a router's memory buffer for receiving incoming datagrams is full, it will use ICMP to send out this message alert until the congestion abates.

Hops/time exceeded   Each IP datagram is allotted a certain number of routers, called hops, to pass through. If it reaches its limit of hops before arriving at its destination, the last router to receive that datagram deletes it. The executioner router then uses ICMP to send an obituary message, informing the sending machine of the demise of its datagram.

Ping   Packet Internet Groper (Ping) uses ICMP echo request and reply messages to check the physical and logical connectivity of machines on an internetwork.

Traceroute   Using ICMP time-outs, Traceroute is used to discover the path a packet takes as it traverses an internetwork.

Traceroute is usually just called trace. Microsoft Windows uses tracert to allow you to verify address configurations in your internetwork.

The following data is from a network analyzer catching an ICMP echo request:

```
Flags:          0x00
 Status:         0x00
 Packet Length: 78
 Timestamp:     14:04:25.967000 12/20/03
Ethernet Header
 Destination: 00:a0:24:6e:0f:a8
```

```
Source:        00:80:c7:a8:f0:3d
Ether-Type:    08-00 IP
IP Header - Internet Protocol Datagram
Version:               4
Header Length:         5
Precedence:            0
Type of Service:       %000
Unused:                %00
Total Length:          60
Identifier:            56325
Fragmentation Flags:   %000
Fragment Offset:       0
Time To Live:          32
IP Type:               0x01 ICMP
Header Checksum:       0x2df0
Source IP Address:     100.100.100.2
Dest. IP Address:      100.100.100.1
No Internet Datagram Options
ICMP - Internet Control Messages Protocol
ICMP Type:         8 Echo Request
Code:              0
Checksum:          0x395c
Identifier:        0x0300
Sequence Number:   4352
ICMP Data Area:
abcdefghijklmnop  61 62 63 64 65 66 67 68 69 6a 6b 6c 6d 6e 6f 70
qrstuvwabcdefghi  71 72 73 74 75 76 77 61 62 63 64 65 66 67 68 69
Frame Check Sequence: 0x00000000
```

Notice anything unusual? Did you catch the fact that even though ICMP works at the Internet (Network) layer, it still uses IP to do the Ping request? The Type field in the IP header is 0x01, which specifies that the data we're carrying is owned by the ICMP protocol. Remember, just as all roads lead to Rome, all segments or data *must* go through IP!

 The Ping program uses the alphabet in the data portion of the packet as a payload, typically around 100 bytes by default, unless, of course, you are pinging from a Windows device, which thinks the alphabet stops at the letter *W* (and doesn't include *X, Y,* or *Z*) and then starts at *A* again. Go figure!

If you remember reading about the Data Link layer and the different frame types in Chapter 2, "Ethernet Networking and Data Encapsulation," you should be able to look at the preceding trace and tell what type of Ethernet frame this is. The only fields are destination hardware address, source hardware address, and Ether-Type. The only frame that uses an Ether-Type field exclusively is an Ethernet_II frame.

We'll move on soon, but before we get into the ARP protocol, let's take another look at ICMP in action. Figure 3.18 shows an internetwork—it has a router, so it's an internetwork, right?

FIGURE 3.18   ICMP in action

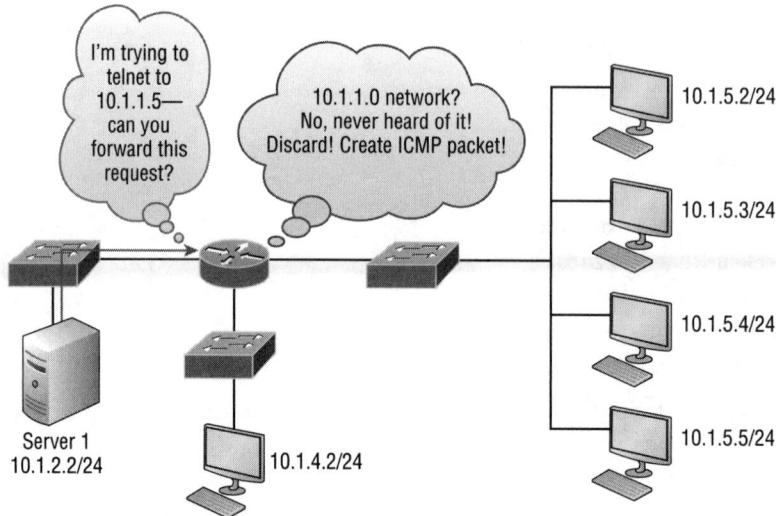

Server 1 (10.1.2.2) telnets to 10.1.1.5 from a DOS prompt. What do you think Server 1 will receive as a response? Server 1 will send the Telnet data to the default gateway, which is the router, and the router will drop the packet because there isn't a network 10.1.1.0 in the routing table. Because of this, Server 1 will receive an ICMP destination unreachable back from the router.

Address Resolution Protocol (ARP)

Address Resolution Protocol (ARP) finds the hardware address of a host from a known IP address. Here's how it works: When IP has a datagram to send, it must inform a Network Access protocol, such as Ethernet or wireless, of the destination's hardware address on the local network. Remember that it has already been informed by upper-layer protocols of the destination's IP address. If IP doesn't find the destination host's hardware address in the ARP cache, it uses ARP to find this information.

As IP's detective, ARP interrogates the local network by sending out a broadcast asking the machine with the specified IP address to reply with its hardware address. So basically, ARP translates the software (IP) address into a hardware address—for example, the destination machine's Ethernet adapter address—and from it, deduces its whereabouts on the LAN by broadcasting for this address. Figure 3.19 shows how an ARP broadcast looks to a local network.

FIGURE 3.19   Local ARP broadcast

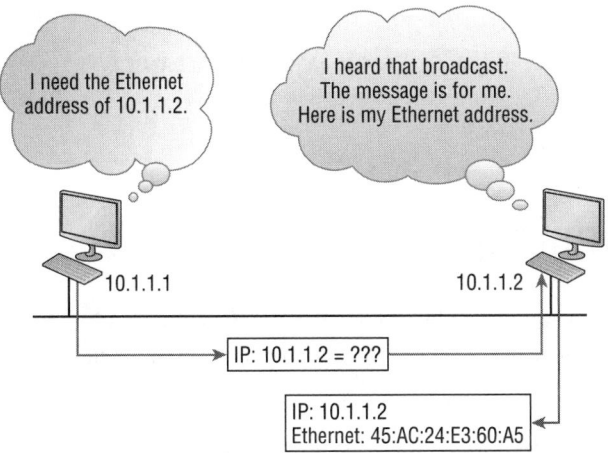

 ARP resolves IP addresses to Ethernet (MAC) addresses.

The following trace shows an ARP broadcast—notice that the destination hardware address is unknown and is all *F*s in hex (all 1s in binary)—and is a hardware address broadcast:

```
Flags:          0x00
Status:         0x00
Packet Length:  64
Timestamp:      09:17:29.574000 12/06/03
Ethernet Header
Destination:    FF:FF:FF:FF:FF:FF Ethernet Broadcast
Source:         00:A0:24:48:60:A5
Protocol Type:  0x0806 IP ARP
ARP - Address Resolution Protocol
Hardware:                1 Ethernet (10Mb)
Protocol:                0x0800 IP
Hardware Address Length: 6
Protocol Address Length: 4
Operation:               1 ARP Request
Sender Hardware Address: 00:A0:24:48:60:A5
Sender Internet Address: 172.16.10.3
```

```
Target Hardware Address: 00:00:00:00:00:00 (ignored)
Target Internet Address: 172.16.10.10
Extra bytes (Padding):
............... 0A 0A 0A 0A 0A 0A 0A 0A 0A 0A 0A 0A 0A
  0A 0A 0A 0A 0A
Frame Check Sequence: 0x00000000
```

IP Addressing

One of the most important topics in any discussion of TCP/IP is IP addressing. An *IP address* is a numeric identifier assigned to each machine on an IP network. It designates the specific location of a device on the network.

An IP address is a software address, not a hardware address—the latter is hard-coded on a network interface card (NIC) and used for finding hosts on a local network. IP addressing was designed to allow hosts on one network to communicate with a host on a different network regardless of the type of LANs the hosts are participating in.

Before we get into the more complicated aspects of IP addressing, you need to understand some of the basics. First I'm going to explain some of the fundamentals of IP addressing and its terminology. Then you'll learn about the hierarchical IP addressing scheme and private IP addresses.

IP Terminology

Throughout this chapter you're being introduced to several important terms that are vital to understanding the Internet Protocol. Here are a few to get you started:

Bit   A bit is one digit, either a 1 or a 0.

Byte   A byte is 7 or 8 bits, depending on whether parity is used. For the rest of this chapter, always assume a byte is 8 bits.

Octet   An octet, made up of 8 bits, is just an ordinary 8-bit binary number. In this chapter, the terms *byte* and *octet* are completely interchangeable.

Network address   This is the designation used in routing to send packets to a remote network—for example, 10.0.0.0, 172.16.0.0, and 192.168.10.0.

Broadcast address   The address used by applications and hosts to send information to all nodes on a network is called the broadcast address. Examples of layer 3 broadcasts include 255.255.255.255, which is any network, all nodes; 172.16.255.255, which is all subnets and hosts on network 172.16.0.0; and 10.255.255.255, which broadcasts to all subnets and hosts on network 10.0.0.0.

The Hierarchical IP Addressing Scheme

An IP address consists of 32 bits of information. These bits are divided into four sections, referred to as octets or bytes, with each containing 1 byte (8 bits). You can depict an IP address using one of three methods:

- Dotted-decimal, as in 172.16.30.56

- Binary, as in 10101100.00010000.00011110.00111000

- Hexadecimal, as in AC.10.1E.38

All these examples represent the same IP address. Pertaining to IP addressing, hexadecimal isn't used as often as dotted-decimal or binary, but you still might find an IP address stored in hexadecimal in some programs.

The 32-bit IP address is a structured or hierarchical address, as opposed to a flat or nonhierarchical address. Although either type of addressing scheme could have been used, *hierarchical addressing* was chosen for a good reason. The advantage of this scheme is that it can handle a large number of addresses, namely 4.3 billion (a 32-bit address space with two possible values for each position—either 0 or 1—gives you 2^{32}, or 4,294,967,296). The disadvantage of the flat addressing scheme, and the reason it's not used for IP addressing, relates to routing. If every address were unique, all routers on the Internet would need to store the address of each and every machine on the Internet. This would make efficient routing impossible, even if only a fraction of the possible addresses were used!

The solution to this problem is to use a two- or three-level hierarchical addressing scheme that is structured by network and host or by network, subnet, and host.

This two- or three-level scheme can also be compared to a telephone number. The first section, the area code, designates a very large area. The second section, the prefix, narrows the scope to a local calling area. The final segment, the customer number, zooms in on the specific connection. IP addresses use the same type of layered structure. Rather than all 32 bits being treated as a unique identifier, as in flat addressing, a part of the address is designated as the network address and the other part is designated as either the subnet and host or just the node address.

Next, we'll cover IP network addressing and the different classes of address we can use to address our networks.

Network Addressing

The *network address* (which can also be called the network number) uniquely identifies each network. Every machine on the same network shares that network address as part of its IP address. For example, in the IP address 172.16.30.56, 172.16 is the network address.

The *node address* is assigned to, and uniquely identifies, each machine on a network. This part of the address must be unique because it identifies a particular machine—an individual—as opposed to a network, which is a group. This number can also be referred to as a *host address*. In the sample IP address 172.16.30.56, the 30.56 specifies the node address.

The designers of the Internet decided to create classes of networks based on network size. For the small number of networks possessing a very large number of nodes, they created the rank *Class A network*. At the other extreme is the *Class C network*, which is reserved for the numerous networks with a small number of nodes. The class distinction for networks between very large and very small is predictably called the *Class B network*.

Subdividing an IP address into a network and node address is determined by the class designation of one's network. Figure 3.20 summarizes the three classes of networks used to address hosts—a subject I'll explain in much greater detail throughout this chapter.

FIGURE 3.20   Summary of the three classes of networks

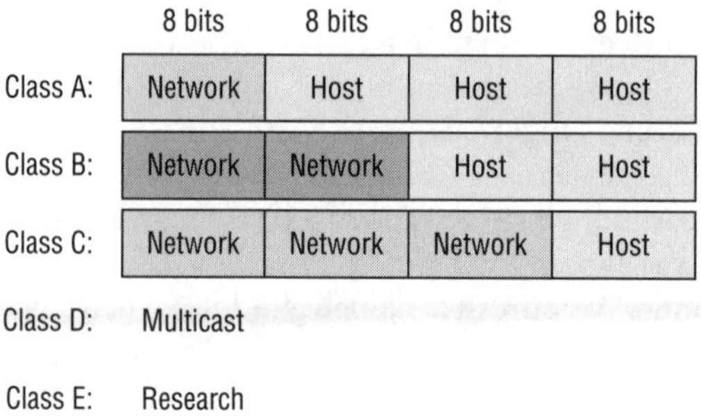

To ensure efficient routing, Internet designers defined a mandate for the leading-bits section of the address for each different network class. For example, since a router knows that a Class A network address always starts with a 0, the router might be able to speed a packet on its way after reading only the first bit of its address. This is where the address schemes define the difference between a Class A, a Class B, and a Class C address. Coming up, I'll discuss the differences between these three classes, followed by a discussion of the Class D and Class E addresses. Classes A, B, and C are the only ranges that are used to address hosts in our networks.

Network Address Range: Class A

The designers of the IP address scheme decided that the first bit of the first byte in a Class A network address must always be off, or 0. This means a Class A address must be between 0 and 127 in the first byte, inclusive.

Consider the following network address:

0xxxxxxx

If we turn the other 7 bits all off and then turn them all on, we'll find the Class A range of network addresses:

00000000 = 0
01111111 = 127

So, a Class A network is defined in the first octet between 0 and 127, and it can't be less or more. Understand that 0 and 127 are not valid in a Class A network because they're reserved addresses, which I'll explain soon.

Network Address Range: Class B

In a Class B network, the RFCs state that the first bit of the first byte must always be turned on but the second bit must always be turned off. If you turn the other 6 bits all off and then all on, you will find the range for a Class B network:

```
10000000 = 128
10111111 = 191
```

As you can see, a Class B network is defined when the first byte is configured from 128 to 191.

Network Address Range: Class C

For Class C networks, the RFCs define the first 2 bits of the first octet as always turned on, but the third bit can never be on. Following the same process as the previous classes, convert from binary to decimal to find the range. Here's the range for a Class C network:

```
11000000 = 192
11011111 = 223
```

So, if you see an IP address that starts at 192 and goes to 223, you'll know it is a Class C IP address.

Network Address Ranges: Classes D and E

The addresses between 224 to 255 are reserved for Class D and E networks. Class D (224–239) is used for multicast addresses and Class E (240–255) for scientific purposes, but I'm not going into these types of addresses because they are beyond the scope of knowledge you need to gain from this book.

Network Addresses: Special Purpose

Some IP addresses are reserved for special purposes, so network administrators can't ever assign these addresses to nodes. Table 3.4 lists the members of this exclusive little club and the reasons why they're included in it.

TABLE 3.4 Reserved IP addresses

Address	Function
Network address of all 0s	Interpreted to mean "this network or segment."
Network address of all 1s	Interpreted to mean "all networks."
Network 127.0.0.1	Reserved for loopback tests. Designates the local node and allows that node to send a test packet to itself without generating network traffic.

TABLE 3.4   Reserved IP addresses *(continued)*

Address	Function
Node address of all 0s	Interpreted to mean "network address" or any host on a specified network.
Node address of all 1s	Interpreted to mean "all nodes" on the specified network; for example, 128.2.255.255 means "all nodes" on network 128.2 (Class B address).
Entire IP address set to all 0s	Used by Cisco routers to designate the default route. Could also mean "any network."
Entire IP address set to all 1s (same as 255.255.255.255)	Broadcast to all nodes on the current network; sometimes called an "all 1s broadcast" or local broadcast.

Class A Addresses

In a Class A network address, the first byte is assigned to the network address and the three remaining bytes are used for the node addresses. The Class A format is as follows:

network.node.node.node

For example, in the IP address 49.22.102.70, the 49 is the network address and 22.102.70 is the node address. Every machine on this particular network would have the distinctive network address of 49.

Class A network addresses are 1 byte long, with the first bit of that byte reserved and the 7 remaining bits available for manipulation (addressing). As a result, the maximum number of Class A networks that can be created is 128. Why? Because each of the 7 bit positions can be either a 0 or a 1, thus 2^7, or 128.

To complicate matters further, the network address of all 0s (0000 0000) is reserved to designate the default route (see Table 3.4 in the previous section). Additionally, the address 127, which is reserved for diagnostics, can't be used either, which means that you can really only use the numbers 1 to 126 to designate Class A network addresses. This means the actual number of usable Class A network addresses is 128 minus 2, or 126.

The IP address 127.0.0.1 is used to test the IP stack on an individual node and cannot be used as a valid host address. However, the loopback address creates a shortcut method for TCP/IP applications and services that run on the same device to communicate with each other.

Each Class A address has 3 bytes (24-bit positions) for the node address of a machine. This means there are 2^{24}—or 16,777,216—unique combinations and, therefore, precisely that many possible unique node addresses for each Class A network. Because node addresses with the two patterns of all 0s and all 1s are reserved, the actual maximum usable number of nodes for a Class A network is 2^{24} minus 2, which equals 16,777,214. Either way, that's a huge number of hosts on a single network segment!

Class A Valid Host IDs

Here's an example of how to figure out the valid host IDs in a Class A network address:

- All host bits off is the network address: 10.0.0.0.
- All host bits on is the broadcast address: 10.255.255.255.

The valid hosts are the numbers in between the network address and the broadcast address: 10.0.0.1 through 10.255.255.254. Notice that 0s and 255s can be valid host IDs. All you need to remember when trying to find valid host addresses is that the host bits can't all be turned off or on at the same time.

Class B Addresses

In a Class B network address, the first 2 bytes are assigned to the network address and the remaining 2 bytes are used for node addresses. The format is as follows:

network.network.node.node

For example, in the IP address 172.16.30.56, the network address is 172.16 and the node address is 30.56.

With a network address being 2 bytes (8 bits each), you get 2^{16} unique combinations. But the Internet designers decided that all Class B network addresses should start with the binary digit 1, then 0. This leaves 14 bit positions to manipulate, therefore 16,384, or 2^{14} unique Class B network addresses.

A Class B address uses 2 bytes for node addresses. This is 2^{16} minus the two reserved patterns of all 0s and all 1s for a total of 65,534 possible node addresses for each Class B network.

Class B Valid Host IDs

Here's an example of how to find the valid hosts in a Class B network:

- All host bits turned off is the network address: 172.16.0.0.
- All host bits turned on is the broadcast address: 172.16.255.255.

The valid hosts would be the numbers in between the network address and the broadcast address: 172.16.0.1 through 172.16.255.254.

Class C Addresses

The first 3 bytes of a Class C network address are dedicated to the network portion of the address, with only 1 measly byte remaining for the node address. Here's the format:

network.network.network.node

Using the example IP address 192.168.100.102, the network address is 192.168.100 and the node address is 102.

In a Class C network address, the first three bit positions are always the binary 110. The calculation is as follows: 3 bytes, or 24 bits, minus 3 reserved positions leaves 21 positions. Hence, there are 2^{21}, or 2,097,152, possible Class C networks.

Each unique Class C network has 1 byte to use for node addresses. This leads to 2^8, or 256, minus the two reserved patterns of all 0s and all 1s, for a total of 254 node addresses for each Class C network.

Class C Valid Host IDs

Here's an example of how to find a valid host ID in a Class C network:

- All host bits turned off is the network ID: 192.168.100.0.

- All host bits turned on is the broadcast address: 192.168.100.255.

The valid hosts would be the numbers in between the network address and the broadcast address: 192.168.100.1 through 192.168.100.254.

Private IP Addresses (RFC 1918)

The people who created the IP addressing scheme also created private IP addresses. These addresses can be used on a private network, but they're not routable through the Internet. This is designed for the purpose of creating a measure of well-needed security, but it also conveniently saves valuable IP address space.

If every host on every network was required to have real routable IP addresses, we would have run out of IP addresses to hand out years ago. But by using private IP addresses, ISPs, corporations, and home users only need a relatively tiny group of bona fide IP addresses to connect their networks to the Internet. This is economical because they can use private IP addresses on their inside networks and get along just fine.

To accomplish this task, the ISP and the corporation—the end user, no matter who they are—need to use something called *Network Address Translation (NAT)*, which basically takes a private IP address and converts it for use on the Internet. NAT is covered in Chapter 13, "Network Address Translation (NAT)." Many people can use the same real IP address to transmit out onto the Internet. Doing things this way saves megatons of address space—good for us all!

The reserved private addresses are listed in Table 3.5.

TABLE 3.5   Reserved IP address space

Address Class	Reserved Address Space
Class A	10.0.0.0 through 10.255.255.255
Class B	172.16.0.0 through 172.31.255.255
Class C	192.168.0.0 through 192.168.255.255

 You must know your private address space to become Cisco certified!

So, What Private IP Address Should I Use?

That's a really great question: Should you use Class A, Class B, or even Class C private addressing when setting up your network? Let's take Acme Corporation in SF as an example. This company is moving into a new building and needs a whole new network. It has 14 departments, with about 70 users in each. You could probably squeeze one or two Class C addresses to use, or maybe you could use a Class B, or even a Class A just for fun.

The rule of thumb in the consulting world is, when you're setting up a corporate network—regardless of how small it is—you should use a Class A network address because it gives you the most flexibility and growth options. For example, if you used the 10.0.0.0 network address with a /24 mask, then you'd have 65,536 networks, each with 254 hosts. Lots of room for growth with that network!

But if you're setting up a home network, you'd opt for a Class C address because it is the easiest for people to understand and configure. Using the default Class C mask gives you one network with 254 hosts—plenty for a home network.

With the Acme Corporation, a nice 10.1.x.0 with a /24 mask (the x is the subnet for each department) makes this easy to design, install, and troubleshoot.

IPv4 Address Types

Most people use the term *broadcast* as a generic term, and most of the time, we understand what they mean—but not always! For example, you might say, "The host broadcasted through a router to a DHCP server," but, well, it's pretty unlikely that this would ever really happen. What you probably mean—using the correct technical jargon—is, "The DHCP client broadcasted for an IP address and a router then forwarded this as a unicast packet to the DHCP server." Oh, and remember that with IPv4, broadcasts are pretty important, but with IPv6, there aren't any broadcasts sent at all—now there's something to look forward to reading about in Chapter 14!

Okay, I've referred to IP addresses throughout the preceding chapters and now all throughout this chapter, and even showed you some examples. But I really haven't gone into the different terms and uses associated with them yet, and it's about time I did. So here are the address types that I'd like to define for you:

Loopback (localhost)   Used to test the IP stack on the local computer. Can be any address from 127.0.0.1 through 127.255.255.254.

Layer 2 broadcasts   These are sent to all nodes on a LAN.

Broadcasts (layer 3)   These are sent to all nodes on the network.

Unicast   This is an address for a single interface, and these are used to send packets to a single destination host.

Multicast   These are packets sent from a single source and transmitted to many devices on different networks. Referred to as "one-to-many."

Layer 2 Broadcasts

First, understand that layer 2 broadcasts are also known as hardware broadcasts—they only go out on a LAN, but they don't go past the LAN boundary (router).

The typical hardware address is 6 bytes (48 bits) and looks something like 45:AC:24:E3:60:A5. The broadcast would be all 1s in binary, which would be all *F*s in hexadecimal, as in ff:ff:ff:ff:ff:ff and shown in Figure 3.21.

FIGURE 3.21   Local layer 2 broadcasts

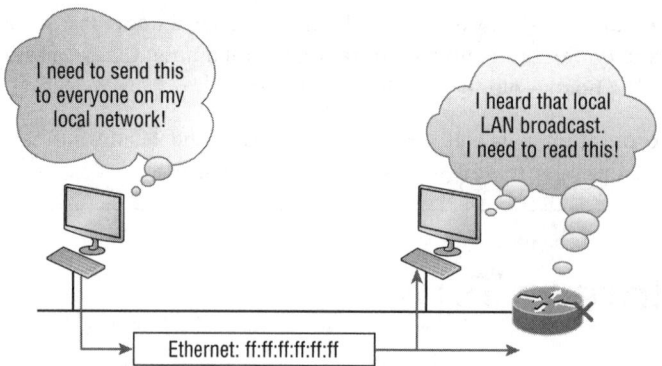

Every network interface card (NIC) will receive and read the frame, including the router, since this was a layer 2 broadcast, but the router would never, ever forward this!

Layer 3 Broadcasts

Then there are the plain old broadcast addresses at layer 3. Broadcast messages are meant to reach all hosts on a broadcast domain. These are the network broadcasts that have all host bits on.

Here's an example that you're already familiar with: The network address of 172.16.0.0 255.255.0.0 would have a broadcast address of 172.16.255.255—all host bits on. Broadcasts can also be "any network and all hosts," as indicated by 255.255.255.255, and shown in Figure 3.22.

FIGURE 3.22   Layer 3 broadcasts

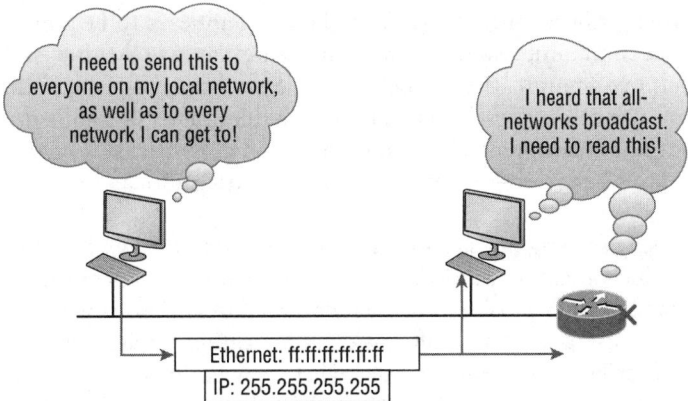

In Figure 3.22, all hosts on the LAN will get this broadcast on their NIC, including the router, but by default the router would never forward this packet.

Unicast Address

A unicast is defined as a single IP address that's assigned to a network interface card and is the destination IP address in a packet—in other words, it's used for directing packets to a specific host.

In Figure 3.23, both the MAC address and the destination IP address are for a single NIC on the network. All hosts on the broadcast domain would receive this frame and accept it. Only the destination NIC of 10.1.1.2 would accept the packet; the other NICs would discard the packet.

FIGURE 3.23   Unicast address

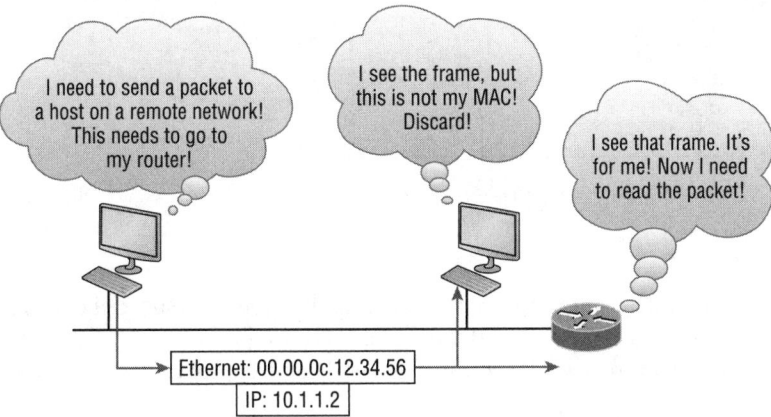

Multicast Address

Multicast is a different beast entirely. At first glance, it appears to be a hybrid of unicast and broadcast communication, but that isn't quite the case. Multicast does allow point-to-multipoint communication, which is similar to broadcasts, but it happens in a different manner. The crux of *multicast* is that it enables multiple recipients to receive messages without flooding the messages to all hosts on a broadcast domain. However, this is not the default behavior—it's what we *can* do with multicasting if it's configured correctly!

Multicast works by sending messages or data to IP *multicast group* addresses. Unlike with broadcasts, which aren't forwarded, routers then forward copies of the packet out to every interface that has hosts *subscribed* to that group address. This is where multicast differs from broadcast messages—with multicast communication, copies of packets, in theory, are sent only to subscribed hosts. For example, when I say in theory, I mean that the hosts will receive a multicast packet destined for 224.0.0.10. This is an EIGRP packet, and only a router running the EIGRP protocol will read these. All hosts on the broadcast LAN, and Ethernet is a broadcast multi-access LAN technology, will pick up the frame, read the destination address, then immediately discard the frame unless they're in the multicast group. This saves PC processing, not LAN bandwidth. Be warned though—multicasting can cause some serious LAN congestion if it's not implemented carefully! Figure 3.24 shows a Cisco router sending an EIGRP multicast packet on the local LAN and only the other Cisco router will accept and read this packet.

FIGURE 3.24   EIGRP multicast example

There are several different groups that users or applications can subscribe to. The range of multicast addresses starts with 224.0.0.0 and goes through 239.255.255.255. As you can see, this range of addresses falls within IP Class D address space based on classful IP assignment.

Summary

If you made it this far and understood everything the first time through, you should be extremely proud of yourself! We really covered a lot of ground in this chapter, but understand that the information in it is critical to being able to navigate well through the rest of this book.

If you didn't get a complete understanding the first time around, don't stress. It really wouldn't hurt you to read this chapter more than once. There is still a lot of ground to cover, so make sure you've got this material all nailed down. That way, you'll be ready for more, and just so you know, there's a lot more! What we're doing up to this point is building a solid foundation to build upon as you advance.

With that in mind, after you learned about the DoD model, the layers, and associated protocols, you learned about the oh-so-important topic of IP addressing. I discussed in detail the difference between each address class, how to find a network address and broadcast address, and what denotes a valid host address range. I can't stress enough how important it is for you to have this critical information unshakably understood before moving on to Chapter 4!

Since you've already come this far, there's no reason to stop now and waste all those brainwaves and new neural connections. So don't stop—go through the written labs and review questions at the end of this chapter and make sure you understand each answer's explanation. The best is yet to come!

Exam Essentials

Differentiate between the DoD and the OSI network models.   The DoD model is a condensed version of the OSI model, composed of four layers instead of seven, but is nonetheless like the OSI model in that it can be used to describe packet creation and devices and protocols can be mapped to its layers.

Identify Process/Application layer protocols.   Telnet is a terminal emulation program that allows you to log into a remote host and run programs. File Transfer Protocol (FTP) is a connection-oriented service that allows you to transfer files. Trivial FTP (TFTP) is a connectionless file transfer program. Simple Mail Transfer Protocol (SMTP) is a sendmail program.

Identify Host-to-Host layer protocols.   Transmission Control Protocol (TCP) is a connection-oriented protocol that provides reliable network service by using acknowledgments and flow control. User Datagram Protocol (UDP) is a connectionless protocol that provides low overhead and is considered unreliable.

Identify Internet layer protocols.   Internet Protocol (IP) is a connectionless protocol that provides network address and routing through an internetwork. Address Resolution Protocol (ARP) finds a hardware address from a known IP address. Reverse ARP (RARP) finds an IP address from a known hardware address. Internet Control Message Protocol (ICMP) provides diagnostics and destination unreachable messages.

Describe the functions of DNS and DHCP in the network.   Dynamic Host Configuration Protocol (DHCP) provides network configuration information (including IP addresses) to hosts, eliminating the need to perform the configurations manually. Domain Name Service (DNS) resolves hostnames—both Internet names such as www.lammle.com and device names such as Workstation 2—to IP addresses, eliminating the need to know the IP address of a device for connection purposes.

Identify what is contained in the TCP header of a connection-oriented transmission.   The fields in the TCP header include the source port, destination port, sequence number, acknowledgment number, header length, a field reserved for future use, code bits, window size, checksum, urgent pointer, options field, and finally, the data field.

Identify what is contained in the UDP header of a connectionless transmission.   The fields in the UDP header include only the source port, destination port, length, checksum, and data. The smaller number of fields as compared to the TCP header comes at the expense of providing none of the more advanced functions of the TCP frame.

Identify what is contained in the IP header.   The fields of an IP header include version, header length, priority or type of service, total length, identification, flags, fragment offset, time to live, protocol, header checksum, source IP address, destination IP address, options, and finally, data.

Compare and contrast UDP and TCP characteristics and features.   TCP is connection-oriented, acknowledged, and sequenced and has flow and error control, while UDP is connectionless, unacknowledged, and not sequenced and provides no error or flow control.

Understand the role of port numbers.   Port numbers are used to identify the protocol or service that is to be used in the transmission.

Identify the role of ICMP.   Internet Control Message Protocol (ICMP) works at the Network layer and is used by IP for many different services. ICMP is a management protocol and messaging service provider for IP.

Define the Class A IP address range.   The IP range for a Class A network is 1–126. This provides 8 bits of network addressing and 24 bits of host addressing by default.

Define the Class B IP address range.   The IP range for a Class B network is 128–191. Class B addressing provides 16 bits of network addressing and 16 bits of host addressing by default.

Define the Class C IP address range.   The IP range for a Class C network is 192 through 223. Class C addressing provides 24 bits of network addressing and 8 bits of host addressing by default.

Identify the private IP ranges.   The Class A private address range is 10.0.0.0 through 10.255.255.255. The Class B private address range is 172.16.0.0 through 172.31.255.255. The Class C private address range is 192.168.0.0 through 192.168.255.255.

Understand the difference between a broadcast, unicast, and multicast address.   A broadcast is to all devices in a subnet, a unicast is to one device, and a multicast is to some but not all devices.

Written Labs

In this section, you'll complete the following labs to make sure you've got the information and concepts contained within them fully dialed in:

Lab 3.1: TCP/IP

Lab 3.2: Mapping Applications to the DoD Model

You can find the answers to these labs in Appendix A, "Answers to Written Labs."

Written Lab 3.1: TCP/IP

Answer the following questions about TCP/IP:

1. What is the Class C address range in decimal and in binary?
2. What layer of the DoD model is equivalent to the Transport layer of the OSI model?
3. What is the valid range of a Class A network address?
4. What is the 127.0.0.1 address used for?
5. How do you find the network address from a listed IP address?
6. How do you find the broadcast address from a listed IP address?
7. What is the Class A private IP address space?
8. What is the Class B private IP address space?
9. What is the Class C private IP address space?
10. What are all the available characters that you can use in hexadecimal addressing?

Written Lab 3.2: Mapping Applications to the DoD Model

The four layers of the DoD model are Process/Application, Host-to-Host, Internet, and Network Access. Identify the layer of the DoD model on which each of these protocols operates.

1. Internet Protocol (IP)
2. Telnet
3. FTP
4. SNMP
5. DNS
6. Address Resolution Protocol (ARP)
7. DHCP/BootP
8. Transmission Control Protocol (TCP)
9. X Window

10. User Datagram Protocol (UDP)
11. NFS
12. Internet Control Message Protocol (ICMP)
13. Reverse Address Resolution Protocol (RARP)
14. Proxy ARP
15. TFTP
16. SMTP
17. LPD

Review Questions

The following questions are designed to test your understanding of this chapter's material. For more information on how to get additional questions, please see www.lammle.com/ccna.

You can find the answers to these questions in Appendix B, "Answers to Review Questions."

1. What must happen if a DHCP IP conflict occurs?

   A. Proxy ARP will fix the issue.

   B. The client uses a gratuitous ARP to fix the issue.

   C. The administrator must fix the conflict by hand at the DHCP server.

   D. The DHCP server will reassign new IP addresses to both computers.

2. Which of the following Application layer protocols sets up a secure session that's similar to Telnet?

   A. FTP

   B. SSH

   C. DNS

   D. DHCP

3. Which of the following mechanisms is used by the client to avoid a duplicate IP address during the DHCP process?

   A. Ping

   B. Traceroute

   C. Gratuitous ARP

   D. Pathping

4. What protocol is used to find the hardware address of a local device?

   A. RARP

   B. ARP

   C. IP

   D. ICMP

   E. BootP

5. Which of the following are layers in the TCP/IP model? (Choose three.)
   A. Application
   B. Session
   C. Transport
   D. Internet
   E. Data Link
   F. Physical

6. Which class of IP address provides a maximum of only 254 host addresses per network ID?
   A. Class A
   B. Class B
   C. Class C
   D. Class D
   E. Class E

7. Which of the following describe the DHCP Discover message? (Choose two.)
   A. It uses ff:ff:ff:ff:ff:ff as a layer 2 broadcast.
   B. It uses UDP as the Transport layer protocol.
   C. It uses TCP as the Transport layer protocol.
   D. It does not use a layer 2 destination address.

8. Which layer 4 protocol is used for a Telnet connection?
   A. IP
   B. TCP
   C. TCP/IP
   D. UDP
   E. ICMP

9. Private IP addressing was specified in RFC _____ .

10. Which of the following services use TCP? (Choose three.)
    A. DHCP
    B. SMTP
    C. SNMP
    D. FTP
    E. HTTP
    F. TFTP

11. Which Class of IP addresses uses the pattern shown here?

Network	Network	Network	Host

   A. Class A

   B. Class B

   C. Class C

   D. Class D

12. Which of the following is an example of a multicast address?

   A. 10.6.9.1

   B. 192.168.10.6

   C. 224.0.0.10

   D. 172.16.9.5

13. The following illustration shows a data structure header. What protocol is this header from?

16-Bit Source Port			16-Bit Destination Port	
32-Bit Sequence Number				
32-Bit Acknowledgement Number				
4-Bit Header Length	Reserved	Flags	16-Bit Window Size	
16-bit TCP Checksum			16-bit Urgent Pointer	
Options				
Data				

   A. IP

   B. ICMP

   C. TCP

   D. UDP

   E. ARP

   F. RARP

14. If you use either Telnet or FTP, what layer are you using to generate the data?

   A. Application

   B. Presentation

   C. Session

   D. Transport

15. The DoD model (also called the TCP/IP stack) has four layers. Which layer of the DoD model is equivalent to the Network layer of the OSI model?

   A. Application

   B. Host-to-Host

   C. Internet

   D. Network Access

16. Which two of the following are private IP addresses?

   A. 12.0.0.1

   B. 168.172.19.39

   C. 172.20.14.36

   D. 172.33.194.30

   E. 192.168.24.43

17. What layer in the TCP/IP stack is equivalent to the Transport layer of the OSI model?

   A. Application

   B. Host-to-Host

   C. Internet

   D. Network Access

18. Which statements are true regarding ICMP packets? (Choose two.)

   A. ICMP guarantees datagram delivery.

   B. ICMP can provide hosts with information about network problems.

   C. ICMP is encapsulated within IP datagrams.

   D. ICMP is encapsulated within UDP datagrams.

19. What is the address range of a Class B network address in binary?

   A. 01xxxxxx

   B. 0xxxxxxx

   C. 10xxxxxx

   D. 110xxxxx

20. Drag the steps in the DHCP process and place them in the correct order on the right.

DHCPOffer	Drop Target A
DHCPDiscover	Drop Target B
DHCPAck	Drop Target C
DHCPRequest	Drop Target D

Chapter
4

Easy Subnetting

THE FOLLOWING ICND1 EXAM TOPICS ARE COVERED IN THIS CHAPTER:

✓ **Network Fundamentals**

- 1.8 Configure, verify, and troubleshoot IPv4 addressing and subnetting

We'll pick up right where we left off in the last chapter and continue to explore the world of IP addressing. I'll open this chapter by telling you how to subnet an IP network—an indispensably crucial skill that's central to mastering networking in general! Forewarned is forearmed, so prepare yourself because being able to subnet quickly and accurately is pretty challenging and you'll need time to practice what you've learned to really nail it. So be patient and don't give up on this key aspect of networking until your skills are seriously sharp. I'm not kidding—this chapter is so important you should really just graft it into your brain!

So be ready because we're going to hit the ground running and thoroughly cover IP subnetting from the very start. And though I know this will sound weird to you, you'll be much better off if you just try to forget everything you've learned about subnetting before reading this chapter—especially if you've been to an official Cisco or Microsoft class! I think these forms of special torture often do more harm than good and sometimes even scare people away from networking completely. Those that survive and persevere usually at least question the sanity of continuing to study in this field. If this is you, relax, breathe, and know that you'll find that the way I tackle the issue of subnetting is relatively painless because I'm going to show you a whole new, much easier method to conquer this monster!

After working through this chapter, and I can't say this enough, after working through the extra study material at the end as well, you'll be able to tame the IP addressing/subnetting beast—just don't give up! I promise that you'll be really glad you didn't. It's one of those things that once you get it down, you'll wonder why you used to think it was so hard!

To find up-to-the minute updates for this chapter, please see www.lammle.com/ccna or the book's web page at www.sybex.com/go/ccna.

Subnetting Basics

In Chapter 3, "Introduction to TCP/IP," you learned how to define and find the valid host ranges used in a Class A, Class B, and Class C network address by turning the host bits all off and then all on. This is very good, but here's the catch: you were defining only one network, as shown in Figure 4.1.

FIGURE 4.1   One network

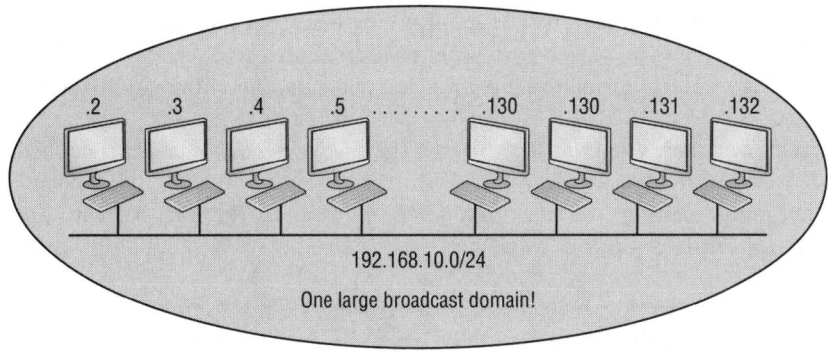

By now you know that having one large network is not a good thing because the first three chapters you just read were veritably peppered with me incessantly telling you that! But how would you fix the out-of-control problem that Figure 4.1 illustrates? Wouldn't it be nice to be able to break up that one, huge network address and create four manageable networks from it? You betcha it would, but to make that happen, you would need to apply the infamous trick of *subnetting* because it's the best way to break up a giant network into a bunch of smaller ones. Take a look at Figure 4.2 and see how this might look.

FIGURE 4.2   Multiple networks connected together

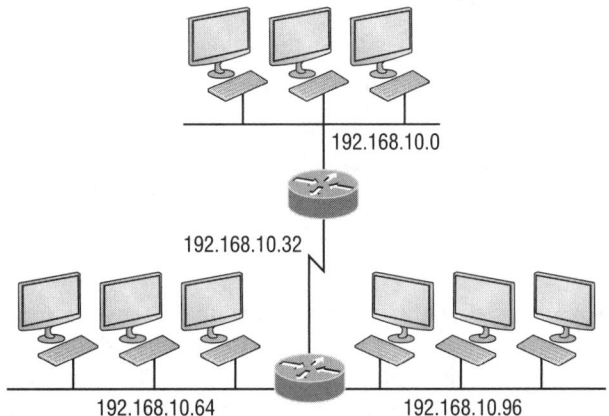

What are those 192.168.10.*x* addresses shown in the figure? Well that is what this chapter will explain—how to make one network into many networks!

Let's take off from where we left in Chapter 3 and start working in the host section (host bits) of a network address, where we can borrow bits to create subnets.

How to Create Subnets

Creating subnetworks is essentially the act of taking bits from the host portion of the address and reserving them to define the subnet address instead. Clearly this will result in fewer bits being available for defining your hosts, which is something you'll always want to keep in mind.

Later in this chapter, I'll guide you through the entire process of creating subnets starting with Class C addresses. As always in networking, before you actually implement anything, including subnetting, you must first determine your current requirements and make sure to plan for future conditions as well.

> In this first section, we'll be discussing classful routing, which refers to the fact that all hosts (nodes) in the network are using the exact same subnet mask. Later, when we move on to cover variable length subnet masks (VLSMs), I'll tell you all about classless routing, which is an environment wherein each network segment *can* use a different subnet mask.

To create a subnet, we'll start by fulfilling these three steps:

1. Determine the number of required network IDs:
   - One for each LAN subnet
   - One for each wide area network connection
2. Determine the number of required host IDs per subnet:
   - One for each TCP/IP host
   - One for each router interface
3. Based on the previous requirements, create the following:
   - A unique subnet mask for your entire network
   - A unique subnet ID for each physical segment
   - A range of host IDs for each subnet

Subnet Masks

For the subnet address scheme to work, every machine on the network must know which part of the host address will be used as the subnet address. This condition is met by assigning a *subnet mask* to each machine. A subnet mask is a 32-bit value that allows the device that's receiving IP packets to distinguish the network ID portion of the IP address from the host ID portion of the IP address. This 32-bit subnet mask is composed of 1s and 0s, where the 1s represent the positions that refer to the network subnet addresses.

Not all networks need subnets, and if not, it really means that they're using the default subnet mask, which is basically the same as saying that a network doesn't have a subnet address. Table 4.1 shows the default subnet masks for Classes A, B, and C.

TABLE 4.1 Default subnet mask

Class	Format	Default Subnet Mask
A	*network.node.node.node*	255.0.0.0
B	*network.network.node.node*	255.255.0.0
C	*network.network.network.node*	255.255.255.0

Although you can use any mask in any way on an interface, typically it's not usually good to mess with the default masks. In other words, you don't want to make a Class B subnet mask read 255.0.0.0, and some hosts won't even let you type it in. But these days, most devices will. For a Class A network, you wouldn't change the first byte in a subnet mask because it should read 255.0.0.0 at a minimum. Similarly, you wouldn't assign 255.255.255.255 because this is all 1s, which is a broadcast address. A Class B address starts with 255.255.0.0, and a Class C starts with 255.255.255.0, and for the CCNA especially, there is no reason to change the defaults!

Understanding the Powers of 2

Powers of 2 are important to understand and memorize for use with IP subnetting. Reviewing powers of 2, remember that when you see a number noted with an exponent, it means you should multiply the number by itself as many times as the upper number specifies. For example, 2^3 is 2 x 2 x 2, which equals 8. Here's a list of powers of 2 to commit to memory:

$2^1 = 2$

$2^2 = 4$

$2^3 = 8$

$2^4 = 16$

$2^5 = 32$

$2^6 = 64$

$2^7 = 128$

$2^8 = 256$

$2^9 = 512$

$2^{10} = 1{,}024$

$2^{11} = 2{,}048$

$2^{12} = 4,096$

$2^{13} = 8,192$

$2^{14} = 16,384$

Memorizing these powers of 2 is a good idea, but it's not absolutely necessary. Just remember that since you're working with powers of 2, each successive power of 2 is double the previous one.

It works like this—all you have to do to remember the value of 2^9 is to first know that $2^8 = 256$. Why? Because when you double 2 to the eighth power (256), you get 2^9 (or 512). To determine the value of 2^{10}, simply start at $2^8 = 256$, and then double it twice.

You can go the other way as well. If you needed to know what 2^6 is, for example, you just cut 256 in half two times: once to reach 2^7 and then one more time to reach 2^6.

Classless Inter-Domain Routing (CIDR)

Another term you need to familiarize yourself with is *Classless Inter-Domain Routing (CIDR)*. It's basically the method that Internet service providers (ISPs) use to allocate a number of addresses to a company, a home—their customers. They provide addresses in a certain block size, something I'll talk about in greater detail soon.

When you receive a block of addresses from an ISP, what you get will look something like this: 192.168.10.32/28. This is telling you what your subnet mask is. The slash notation (/) means how many bits are turned on (1s). Obviously, the maximum could only be /32 because a byte is 8 bits and there are 4 bytes in an IP address: (4 × 8 = 32). But keep in mind that regardless of the class of address, the largest subnet mask available relevant to the Cisco exam objectives can only be a /30 because you've got to keep at least 2 bits for host bits.

Take, for example, a Class A default subnet mask, which is 255.0.0.0. This tells us that the first byte of the subnet mask is all ones (1s), or 11111111. When referring to a slash notation, you need to count all the 1 bits to figure out your mask. The 255.0.0.0 is considered a /8 because it has 8 bits that are 1s—that is, 8 bits that are turned on.

A Class B default mask would be 255.255.0.0, which is a /16 because 16 bits are ones (1s): 11111111.11111111.00000000.00000000.

Table 4.2 has a listing of every available subnet mask and its equivalent CIDR slash notation.

TABLE 4.2   CIDR values

Subnet Mask	CIDR Value
255.0.0.0	/8
255.128.0.0	/9

Subnet Mask	CIDR Value
255.192.0.0	/10
255.224.0.0	/11
255.240.0.0	/12
255.248.0.0	/13
255.252.0.0	/14
255.254.0.0	/15
255.255.0.0	/16
255.255.128.0	/17
255.255.192.0	/18
255.255.224.0	/19
255.255.240.0	/20
255.255.248.0	/21
255.255.252.0	/22
255.255.254.0	/23
255.255.255.0	/24
255.255.255.128	/25
255.255.255.192	/26
255.255.255.224	/27
255.255.255.240	/28
255.255.255.248	/29
255.255.255.252	/30

The /8 through /15 can only be used with Class A network addresses. /16 through /23 can be used by Class A and B network addresses. /24 through /30 can be used by Class A, B, and C network addresses. This is a big reason why most companies use Class A network addresses. Since they can use all subnet masks, they get the maximum flexibility in network design.

> No, you cannot configure a Cisco router using this slash format. But wouldn't that be nice? Nevertheless, it's *really* important for you to know subnet masks in the slash notation (CIDR).

IP Subnet-Zero

Even though ip subnet-zero is not a new command, Cisco courseware and Cisco exam objectives didn't used to cover it. Know that Cisco certainly covers it now! This command allows you to use the first and last subnet in your network design. For instance, the Class C mask of 255.255.255.192 provides subnets 64 and 128, another facet of subnetting that we'll discuss more thoroughly later in this chapter. But with the ip subnet-zero command, you now get to use subnets 0, 64, 128, and 192. It may not seem like a lot, but this provides two more subnets for every subnet mask we use.

Even though we don't discuss the command-line interface (CLI) until Chapter 6, "Cisco's Internetworking Operating System (IOS)," it's important for you to be at least a little familiar with this command at this point:

```
Router#sh running-config
Building configuration...
Current configuration : 827 bytes
!
hostname Pod1R1
!
ip subnet-zero
!
```

This router output shows that the command ip subnet-zero is enabled on the router. Cisco has turned this command on by default starting with Cisco IOS version 12.*x* and now we're running 15.*x* code.

When taking your Cisco exams, make sure you read very carefully to see if Cisco is asking you *not* to use ip subnet-zero. There are actually instances where this may happen.

Subnetting Class C Addresses

There are many different ways to subnet a network. The right way is the way that works best for you. In a Class C address, only 8 bits are available for defining the hosts. Remember that subnet bits start at the left and move to the right, without skipping bits. This means that the only Class C subnet masks can be the following:

```
Binary      Decimal  CIDR
------------------------------------------------------------
00000000 = 255.255.255.0      /24
10000000 = 255.255.255.128    /25
11000000 = 255.255.255.192    /26
11100000 = 255.255.255.224    /27
11110000 = 255.255.255.240    /28
11111000 = 255.255.255.248    /29
11111100 = 255.255.255.252    /30
```

We can't use a /31 or /32 because, as I've said, we must have at least 2 host bits for assigning IP addresses to hosts. But this is only mostly true. Certainly we can never use a /32 because that would mean zero host bits available, yet Cisco has various forms of the IOS, as well as the new Cisco Nexus switches operating system, that support the /31 mask. The /31 is above the scope of the CCENT and CCNA objectives, so we won't be covering it in this book.

Coming up, I'm going to teach you that significantly less painful method of subnetting I promised you at the beginning of this chapter, which makes it ever so much easier to subnet larger numbers in a flash. Excited? Good! Because I'm not kidding when I tell you that you absolutely need to be able to subnet quickly and accurately to succeed in the networking real world and on the exam too!

Subnetting a Class C Address—The Fast Way!

When you've chosen a possible subnet mask for your network and need to determine the number of subnets, valid hosts, and the broadcast addresses of a subnet that mask will provide, all you need to do is answer five simple questions:

- How many subnets does the chosen subnet mask produce?
- How many valid hosts per subnet are available?
- What are the valid subnets?
- What's the broadcast address of each subnet?
- What are the valid hosts in each subnet?

This is where you'll be really glad you followed my advice and took the time to memorize your powers of 2. If you didn't, now would be a good time... Just refer back to the sidebar "Understanding the Powers of 2" earlier if you need to brush up. Here's how you arrive at the answers to those five big questions:

- *How many subnets?* 2^x = number of subnets. x is the number of masked bits, or the 1s. For example, in 11000000, the number of 1s gives us 2^2 subnets. So in this example, there are 4 subnets.

- *How many hosts per subnet?* $2^y - 2$ = number of hosts per subnet. y is the number of unmasked bits, or the 0s. For example, in 11000000, the number of 0s gives us $2^6 - 2$ hosts, or 62 hosts per subnet. You need to subtract 2 for the subnet address and the broadcast address, which are not valid hosts.

- *What are the valid subnets?* 256 – subnet mask = block size, or increment number. An example would be the 255.255.255.192 mask, where the interesting octet is the fourth octet (interesting because that is where our subnet numbers are). Just use this math: 256 – 192 = 64. The block size of a 192 mask is always 64. Start counting at zero in blocks of 64 until you reach the subnet mask value and these are your subnets in the fourth octet: 0, 64, 128, 192. Easy, huh?

- *What's the broadcast address for each subnet?* Now here's the really easy part. Since we counted our subnets in the last section as 0, 64, 128, and 192, the broadcast address is always the number right before the next subnet. For example, the 0 subnet has a broadcast address of 63 because the next subnet is 64. The 64 subnet has a broadcast address of 127 because the next subnet is 128, and so on. Remember, the broadcast address of the last subnet is always 255.

- *What are the valid hosts?* Valid hosts are the numbers between the subnets, omitting the all-0s and all-1s. For example, if 64 is the subnet number and 127 is the broadcast address, then 65–126 is the valid host range. Your valid range is *always* the group of numbers between the subnet address and the broadcast address.

If you're still confused, don't worry because it really isn't as hard as it seems to be at first—just hang in there! To help lift any mental fog, try a few of the practice examples next.

Subnetting Practice Examples: Class C Addresses

Here's your opportunity to practice subnetting Class C addresses using the method I just described. This is so cool. We're going to start with the first Class C subnet mask and work through every subnet that we can, using a Class C address. When we're done, I'll show you how easy this is with Class A and B networks too!

Practice Example #1C: 255.255.255.128 (/25)

Since 128 is 10000000 in binary, there is only 1 bit for subnetting and 7 bits for hosts. We're going to subnet the Class C network address 192.168.10.0.

    192.168.10.0 = Network address

    255.255.255.128 = Subnet mask

Now, let's answer our big five:

- *How many subnets?* Since 128 is 1 bit on (10000000), the answer would be $2^1 = 2$.

- *How many hosts per subnet?* We have 7 host bits off (10000000), so the equation would be $2^7 - 2 = 126$ hosts. Once you figure out the block size of a mask, the amount of hosts is always the block size minus 2. No need to do extra math if you don't need to!

- *What are the valid subnets?* 256 – 128 = 128. Remember, we'll start at zero and count in our block size, so our subnets are 0, 128. By just counting your subnets when counting in your block size, you really don't need to do steps 1 and 2. We can see we have two subnets, and in the step before this one, just remember that the amount of hosts is always the block size minus 2, and in this example, that gives us 2 subnets, each with 126 hosts.

- *What's the broadcast address for each subnet?* The number right before the value of the next subnet is all host bits turned on and equals the broadcast address. For the zero subnet, the next subnet is 128, so the broadcast of the 0 subnet is 127.

- *What are the valid hosts?* These are the numbers between the subnet and broadcast address. The easiest way to find the hosts is to write out the subnet address and the broadcast address, which makes valid hosts completely obvious. The following table shows the 0 and 128 subnets, the valid host ranges of each, and the broadcast address of both subnets:

Subnet	0	128
First host	1	129
Last host	126	254
Broadcast	127	255

Looking at a Class C /25, it's pretty clear that there are two subnets. But so what—why is this significant? Well actually, it's not because that's not the right question. What you really want to know is what you would do with this information!

I know this isn't exactly everyone's favorite pastime, but what we're about to do is really important, so bear with me; we're going to talk about subnetting—period. The key to understanding subnetting is to understand the very reason you need to do it, and I'm going to demonstrate this by going through the process of building a physical network.

Okay—because we added that router shown in Figure 4.3, in order for the hosts on our internetwork to communicate, they must now have a logical network addressing scheme. We could use IPv6, but IPv4 is still the most popular for now. It's also what we're studying at the moment, so that's what we're going with.

FIGURE 4.3 Implementing a Class C /25 logical network

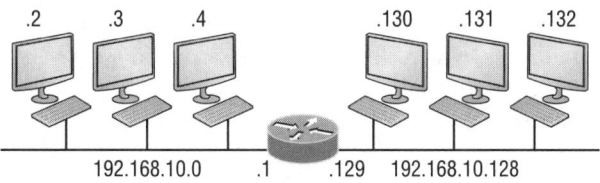

```
Router#show ip route
 [output cut]
C 192.168.10.0 is directly connected to Ethernet 0
C 192.168.10.128 is directly connected to Ethernet 1
```

Looking at Figure 4.3, you can see that there are two physical networks, so we're going to implement a logical addressing scheme that allows for two logical networks. As always, it's a really good idea to look ahead and consider likely short- and long-term growth scenarios, but for this example in this book, a /25 gets it done.

Figure 4.3 shows us that both subnets have been assigned to a router interface, which creates our broadcast domains and assigns our subnets. Use the command show ip route to see the routing table on a router. Notice that instead of one large broadcast domain, there are now two smaller broadcast domains, providing for up to 126 hosts in each. The C in the router output translates to "directly connected network," and we can see we have two of those with two broadcast domains and that we created and implemented them. So congratulations—you did it! You have successfully subnetted a network and applied it to a network design. Nice! Let's do it again.

Practice Example #2C: 255.255.255.192 (/26)

This time, we're going to subnet the network address 192.168.10.0 using the subnet mask 255.255.255.192.

192.168.10.0 = Network address

255.255.255.192 = Subnet mask

Now, let's answer the big five:

- *How many subnets?* Since 192 is 2 bits on (**11000000**), the answer would be $2^2 = 4$ subnets.

- *How many hosts per subnet?* We have 6 host bits off (**11000000**), giving us $2^6 - 2 = 62$ hosts. The amount of hosts is always the block size minus 2.

- *What are the valid subnets?* 256 – 192 = 64. Remember to start at zero and count in our block size. This means our subnets are 0, 64, 128, and 192. We can see we have a block size of 64, so we have 4 subnets, each with 62 hosts.

- *What's the broadcast address for each subnet?* The number right before the value of the next subnet is all host bits turned on and equals the broadcast address. For the zero subnet, the next subnet is 64, so the broadcast address for the zero subnet is 63.

- *What are the valid hosts?* These are the numbers between the subnet and broadcast address. As I said, the easiest way to find the hosts is to write out the subnet address and the broadcast address, which clearly delimits our valid hosts. The following table shows the 0, 64, 128, and 192 subnets, the valid host ranges of each, and the broadcast address of each subnet:

The subnets (do this first)	0	64	128	192
Our first host (perform host addressing last)	1	65	129	193
Our last host	62	126	190	254
The broadcast address (do this second)	63	127	191	255

Again, before getting into the next example, you can see that we can now subnet a /26 as long as we can count in increments of 64. And what are you going to do with this fascinating information? Implement it! We'll use Figure 4.4 to practice a /26 network implementation.

FIGURE 4.4   Implementing a class C /26 (with three networks)

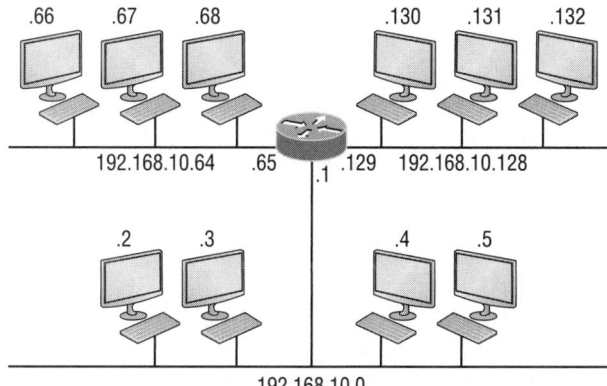

```
Router#show ip route
[output cut]
C 192.168.10.0 is directly connected to Ethernet 0
C 192.168.10.64 is directly connected to Ethernet 1
C 192.168.10.128 is directly connected to Ethernet 2
```

The /26 mask provides four subnetworks, and we need a subnet for each router interface. With this mask, in this example, we actually have room with a spare subnet to add to another router interface in the future. Always plan for growth if possible!

Practice Example #3C: 255.255.255.224 (/27)

This time, we'll subnet the network address 192.168.10.0 and subnet mask 255.255.255.224.

> 192.168.10.0 = Network address
>
> 255.255.255.224 = Subnet mask

- *How many subnets?* 224 is 11100000, so our equation would be $2^3 = 8$.

- *How many hosts?* $2^5 - 2 = 30$.

- *What are the valid subnets?* 256 − 224 = 32. We just start at zero and count to the subnet mask value in blocks (increments) of 32: 0, 32, 64, 96, 128, 160, 192, and 224.

- *What's the broadcast address for each subnet (always the number right before the next subnet)?*

- *What are the valid hosts (the numbers between the subnet number and the broadcast address)?*

To answer the last two questions, first just write out the subnets, then write out the broadcast addresses—the number right before the next subnet. Last, fill in the host addresses. The following table gives you all the subnets for the 255.255.255.224 Class C subnet mask:

The subnet address	0	32	64	96	128	160	192	224
The first valid host	1	33	65	97	129	161	193	225
The last valid host	30	62	94	126	158	190	222	254
The broadcast address	31	63	95	127	159	191	223	255

In practice example #3C, we're using a 255.255.255.224 (/27) network, which provides eight subnets as shown previously. We can take these subnets and implement them as shown in Figure 4.5 using any of the subnets available.

FIGURE 4.5   Implementing a Class C /27 logical network

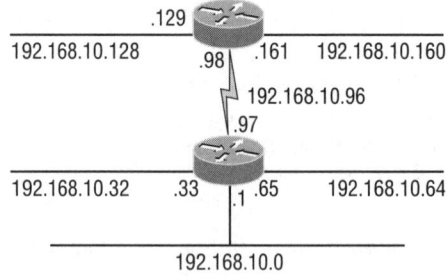

```
Router#show ip route
[output cut]
C 192.168.10.0 is directly connected to Ethernet 0
C 192.168.10.32 is directly connected to Ethernet 1
C 192.168.10.64 is directly connected to Ethernet 2
C 192.168.10.96 is directly connected to Serial 0
```

Notice that used six of the eight subnets available for my network design. The lightning bolt symbol in the figure represents a wide area network (WAN) such as a T1 or other serial connection through an ISP or telco. In other words, something you don't own, but it's still a subnet just like any LAN connection on a router. As usual, I used the first valid host in each subnet as the router's interface address. This is just a rule of thumb; you can use any address in the valid host range as long as you remember what address you configured so you can set the default gateways on your hosts to the router address.

Practice Example #4C: 255.255.255.240 (/28)

Let's practice another one:

    192.168.10.0 = Network address

    255.255.255.240 = Subnet mask

- *Subnets?* 240 is 11110000 in binary. $2^4 = 16$.

- *Hosts?* 4 host bits, or $2^4 - 2 = 14$.

- *Valid subnets?* $256 - 240 = 16$. Start at 0: $0 + 16 = 16$. $16 + 16 = 32$. $32 + 16 = 48$. $48 + 16 = 64$. $64 + 16 = 80$. $80 + 16 = 96$. $96 + 16 = 112$. $112 + 16 = 128$. $128 + 16 = 144$. $144 + 16 = 160$. $160 + 16 = 176$. $176 + 16 = 192$. $192 + 16 = 208$. $208 + 16 = 224$. $224 + 16 = 240$.

- *Broadcast address for each subnet?*

- *Valid hosts?*

To answer the last two questions, check out the following table. It gives you the subnets, valid hosts, and broadcast addresses for each subnet. First, find the address of each subnet using the block size (increment). Second, find the broadcast address of each subnet increment, which is always the number right before the next valid subnet, and then just fill in the host addresses. The following table shows the available subnets, hosts, and broadcast addresses provided from a Class C 255.255.255.240 mask.

Subnet	0	16	32	48	64	80	96	112	128	144	160	176	192	208	224	240
First host	1	17	33	49	65	81	97	113	129	145	161	177	193	209	225	241
Last host	14	30	46	62	78	94	110	126	142	158	174	190	206	222	238	254
Broadcast	15	31	47	63	79	95	111	127	143	159	175	191	207	223	239	255

Cisco has figured out that most people cannot count in 16s and therefore have a hard time finding valid subnets, hosts, and broadcast addresses with the Class C 255.255.255.240 mask. You'd be wise to study this mask.

Practice Example #5C: 255.255.255.248 (/29)

Let's keep practicing:

192.168.10.0 = Network address

255.255.255.248 = Subnet mask

- *Subnets?* 248 in binary = 11111000. $2^5 = 32$.

- *Hosts?* $2^3 - 2 = 6$.

- *Valid subnets?* $256 - 248 = 0, 8, 16, 24, 32, 40, 48, 56, 64, 72, 80, 88, 96, 104, 112, 120, 128, 136, 144, 152, 160, 168, 176, 184, 192, 200, 208, 216, 224, 232, 240,$ and 248.

- *Broadcast address for each subnet?*

- *Valid hosts?*

Take a look at the following table. It shows some of the subnets (first four and last four only), valid hosts, and broadcast addresses for the Class C 255.255.255.248 mask:

Subnet	0	8	16	24	...	224	232	240	248
First host	1	9	17	25	...	225	233	241	249
Last host	6	14	22	30	...	230	238	246	254
Broadcast	7	15	23	31	...	231	239	247	255

If you try to configure a router interface with the address 192.168.10.6 255.255.255.248 and receive the following error, It means that ip subnet-zero is not enabled:

```
Bad mask /29 for address 192.168.10.6
```

You must be able to subnet to see that the address used in this example is in the zero subnet!

Practice Example #6C: 255.255.255.252 (/30)

Okay—just one more:

192.168.10.0 = Network address

255.255.255.252 = Subnet mask

- *Subnets?* 64.
- *Hosts?* 2.
- *Valid subnets?* 0, 4, 8, 12, etc., all the way to 252.
- *Broadcast address for each subnet? (Always the number right before the next subnet.)*
- *Valid hosts?* (The numbers between the subnet number and the broadcast address.)

The following table shows you the subnet, valid host, and broadcast address of the first four and last four subnets in the 255.255.255.252 Class C subnet:

Subnet	0	4	8	12	...	240	244	248	252
First host	1	5	9	13	...	241	245	249	253
Last host	2	6	10	14	...	242	246	250	254
Broadcast	3	7	11	15	...	243	247	251	255

You are the network administrator for Acme Corporation in San Francisco, with dozens of WAN links connecting to your corporate office. Right now your network is a classful network, which means that the same subnet mask is on each host and router interface. You've read about classless routing, where you can have different sized masks, but don't know what to use on your point-to-point WAN links. Is the 255.255.255.252 (/30) a helpful mask in this situation?

Yes, this is a very helpful mask in wide area networks and of course with any type of point-to-point link!

If you were to use the 255.255.255.0 mask in this situation, then each network would have 254 hosts. But you use only 2 addresses with a WAN or point-to-point link, which is a waste of 252 hosts per subnet! If you use the 255.255.255.252 mask, then each subnet has only 2 hosts, and you don't want to waste precious addresses. This is a really important subject, one that we'll address in a lot more detail in the section on VLSM network design in the next chapter!

Subnetting in Your Head: Class C Addresses

It really is possible to subnet in your head? Yes, and it's not all that hard either—take the following example:

192.168.10.50 = Node address

255.255.255.224 = Subnet mask

First, determine the subnet and broadcast address of the network in which the previous IP address resides. You can do this by answering question 3 of the big 5 questions: 256 – 224 = 32. 0, 32, 64, and so on. The address of 50 falls between the two subnets of 32 and 64 and must be part of the 192.168.10.32 subnet. The next subnet is 64, so the broadcast address of the 32 subnet is 63. Don't forget that the broadcast address of a subnet is always the number right before the next subnet. The valid host range equals the numbers between the subnet and broadcast address, or 33–62. This is too easy!

Let's try another one. We'll subnet another Class C address:

192.168.10.50 = Node address

255.255.255.240 = Subnet mask

What is the subnet and broadcast address of the network of which the previous IP address is a member? 256 – 240 = 16. Now just count by our increments of 16 until we pass the host address: 0, 16, 32, 48, 64. Bingo—the host address is between the 48 and 64 subnets. The subnet is 192.168.10.48, and the broadcast address is 63 because the next subnet is 64. The valid host range equals the numbers between the subnet number and the broadcast address, or 49–62.

Let's do a couple more to make sure you have this down.

You have a node address of 192.168.10.174 with a mask of 255.255.255.240. What is the valid host range?

The mask is 240, so we'd do a 256 – 240 = 16. This is our block size. Just keep adding 16 until we pass the host address of 174, starting at zero, of course: 0, 16, 32, 48, 64, 80, 96, 112, 128, 144, 160, 176. The host address of 174 is between 160 and 176, so the subnet is 160. The broadcast address is 175; the valid host range is 161–174. That was a tough one!

One more—just for fun. This one is the easiest of all Class C subnetting:

192.168.10.17 = Node address

255.255.255.252 = Subnet mask

What is the subnet and broadcast address of the subnet in which the previous IP address resides? 256 – 252 = 0 (always start at zero unless told otherwise). 0, 4, 8, 12, 16, 20, etc. You've got it! The host address is between the 16 and 20 subnets. The subnet is 192.168.10.16, and the broadcast address is 19. The valid host range is 17–18.

Now that you're all over Class C subnetting, let's move on to Class B subnetting. But before we do, let's go through a quick review.

What Do We Know?

Okay—here's where you can really apply what you've learned so far and begin committing it all to memory. This is a very cool section that I've been using in my classes for years. It will really help you nail down subnetting for good!

When you see a subnet mask or slash notation (CIDR), you should know the following:

/25 What do we know about a /25?

- 128 mask
- 1 bit on and 7 bits off (10000000)
- Block size of 128
- Subnets 0 and 128
- 2 subnets, each with 126 hosts

/26 What do we know about a /26?

- 192 mask
- 2 bits on and 6 bits off (11000000)

- Block size of 64
- Subnets 0, 64, 128, 192
- 4 subnets, each with 62 hosts

/27 What do we know about a /27?

- 224 mask
- 3 bits on and 5 bits off (11100000)
- Block size of 32
- Subnets 0, 32, 64, 96, 128, 160, 192, 224
- 8 subnets, each with 30 hosts

/28 What do we know about a /28?

- 240 mask
- 4 bits on and 4 bits off
- Block size of 16
- Subnets 0, 16, 32, 48, 64, 80, 96, 112, 128, 144, 160, 176, 192, 208, 224, 240
- 16 subnets, each with 14 hosts

/29 What do we know about a /29?

- 248 mask
- 5 bits on and 3 bits off
- Block size of 8
- Subnets 0, 8, 16, 24, 32, 40, 48, etc.
- 32 subnets, each with 6 hosts

/30 What do we know about a /30?

- 252 mask
- 6 bits on and 2 bits off
- Block size of 4
- Subnets 0, 4, 8, 12, 16, 20, 24, etc.
- 64 subnets, each with 2 hosts

Table 4.3 puts all of the previous information into one compact little table. You should practice writing this table out on scratch paper, and if you can do it, write it down before you start your exam!

TABLE 4.3   What do you know?

CIDR Notation	Mask	Bits	Block Size	Subnets	Hosts
/25	128	1 bit on and 7 bits off	128	0 and 128	2 subnets, each with 126 hosts
/26	192	2 bits on and 6 bits off	64	0, 64, 128, 192	4 subnets, each with 62 hosts
/27	224	3 bits on and 5 bits off	32	0, 32, 64, 96, 128, 160, 192, 224	8 subnets, each with 30 hosts
/28	240	4 bits on and 4 bits off	16	0, 16, 32, 48, 64, 80, 96, 112, 128, 144, 160, 176, 192, 208, 224, 240	16 subnets, each with 14 hosts
/29	248	5 bits on and 3 bits off	8	0, 8, 16, 24, 32, 40, 48, etc.	32 subnets, each with 6 hosts
/30	252	6 bits on and 2 bits off	4	0, 4, 8, 12, 16, 20, 24, etc.	64 subnets, each with 2 hosts

Regardless of whether you have a Class A, Class B, or Class C address, the /30 mask will provide you with only two hosts, ever. As suggested by Cisco, this mask is suited almost exclusively for use on point-to-point links.

If you can memorize this "What Do We Know?" section, you'll be much better off in your day-to-day job and in your studies. Try saying it out loud, which helps you memorize things—yes, your significant other and/or coworkers will think you've lost it, but they probably already do if you're in the networking field anyway. And if you're not yet in the networking field but are studying all this to break into it, get used to it!

It's also helpful to write these on some type of flashcards and have people test your skill. You'd be amazed at how fast you can get subnetting down if you memorize block sizes as well as this "What Do We Know?" section.

Subnetting Class B Addresses

Before we dive into this, let's look at all the possible Class B subnet masks first. Notice that we have a lot more possible subnet masks than we do with a Class C network address:

```
255.255.0.0      (/16)
255.255.128.0    (/17)        255.255.255.0      (/24)
255.255.192.0    (/18)        255.255.255.128    (/25)
```

```
255.255.224.0  (/19)      255.255.255.192  (/26)
255.255.240.0  (/20)      255.255.255.224  (/27)
255.255.248.0  (/21)      255.255.255.240  (/28)
255.255.252.0  (/22)      255.255.255.248  (/29)
255.255.254.0  (/23)      255.255.255.252  (/30)
```

We know the Class B network address has 16 bits available for host addressing. This means we can use up to 14 bits for subnetting because we need to leave at least 2 bits for host addressing. Using a /16 means you are not subnetting with Class B, but it *is* a mask you can use!

> By the way, do you notice anything interesting about that list of subnet values—a pattern, maybe? Ah ha! That's exactly why I had you memorize the binary-to-decimal numbers earlier in Chapter 2, "Ethernet Networking and Data Encapsulation." Since subnet mask bits start on the left and move to the right and bits can't be skipped, the numbers are always the same regardless of the class of address. If you haven't already, memorize this pattern!

The process of subnetting a Class B network is pretty much the same as it is for a Class C, except that you have more host bits and you start in the third octet.

Use the same subnet numbers for the third octet with Class B that you used for the fourth octet with Class C, but add a zero to the network portion and a 255 to the broadcast section in the fourth octet. The following table shows you an example host range of two subnets used in a Class B 240 (/20) subnet mask:

Subnet address	16.0	32.0
Broadcast address	31.255	47.255

Just add the valid hosts between the numbers and you're set!

> The preceding example is true only until you get up to /24. After that, it's numerically exactly like Class C.

Subnetting Practice Examples: Class B Addresses

The following sections will give you an opportunity to practice subnetting Class B addresses. Again, I have to mention that this is the same as subnetting with Class C, except we start in the third octet—with the exact same numbers!

Practice Example #1B: 255.255.128.0 (/17)

172.16.0.0 = Network address

255.255.128.0 = Subnet mask

- *Subnets?* 2^1 = 2 (same amount as Class C).
- *Hosts?* 2^{15} − 2 = 32,766 (7 bits in the third octet, and 8 in the fourth).
- *Valid subnets?* 256 − 128 = 128. 0, 128. Remember that subnetting is performed in the third octet, so the subnet numbers are really 0.0 and 128.0, as shown in the next table. These are the exact numbers we used with Class C; we use them in the third octet and add a 0 in the fourth octet for the network address.
- *Broadcast address for each subnet?*
- *Valid hosts?*

The following table shows the two subnets available, the valid host range, and the broadcast address of each:

Subnet	0.0	128.0
First host	0.1	128.1
Last host	127.254	255.254
Broadcast	127.255	255.255

Okay, notice that we just added the fourth octet's lowest and highest values and came up with the answers. And again, it's done exactly the same way as for a Class C subnet. We just used the same numbers in the third octet and added 0 and 255 in the fourth octet—pretty simple, huh? I really can't say this enough: it's just not that hard. The numbers never change; we just use them in different octets!

Question: Using the previous subnet mask, do you think 172.16.10.0 is a valid host address? What about 172.16.10.255? Can 0 and 255 in the fourth octet ever be a valid host address? The answer is absolutely, yes, those are valid hosts! Any number between the subnet number and the broadcast address is always a valid host.

Practice Example #2B: 255.255.192.0 (/18)

172.16.0.0 = Network address

255.255.192.0 = Subnet mask

- *Subnets?* 2^2 = 4.
- *Hosts?* 2^{14} − 2 = 16,382 (6 bits in the third octet, and 8 in the fourth).

- *Valid subnets?* 256 – 192 = 64. 0, 64, 128, 192. Remember that the subnetting is performed in the third octet, so the subnet numbers are really 0.0, 64.0, 128.0, and 192.0, as shown in the next table.
- *Broadcast address for each subnet?*
- *Valid hosts?*

The following table shows the four subnets available, the valid host range, and the broadcast address of each:

Subnet	0.0	64.0	128.0	192.0
First host	0.1	64.1	128.1	192.1
Last host	63.254	127.254	191.254	255.254
Broadcast	63.255	127.255	191.255	255.255

Again, it's pretty much the same as it is for a Class C subnet—we just added 0 and 255 in the fourth octet for each subnet in the third octet.

Practice Example #3B: 255.255.240.0 (/20)

172.16.0.0 = Network address

255.255.240.0 = Subnet mask

- *Subnets?* 2^4 = 16.
- *Hosts?* $2^{12} - 2$ = 4094.
- *Valid subnets?* 256 – 240 = 0, 16, 32, 48, etc., up to 240. Notice that these are the same numbers as a Class C 240 mask—we just put them in the third octet and add a 0 and 255 in the fourth octet.
- *Broadcast address for each subnet?*
- *Valid hosts?*

The following table shows the first four subnets, valid hosts, and broadcast addresses in a Class B 255.255.240.0 mask:

Subnet	0.0	16.0	32.0	48.0
First host	0.1	16.1	32.1	48.1
Last host	15.254	31.254	47.254	63.254
Broadcast	15.255	31.255	47.255	63.255

Practice Example #4B: 255.255.248.0 (/21)

172.16.0.0 = Network address

255.255.248.0 = Subnet mask

- *Subnets?* $2^5 = 32$.
- *Hosts?* $2^{11} - 2 = 2046$.
- *Valid subnets?* 256 − 248 = 0, 8, 16, 24, 32, etc., up to 248.
- *Broadcast address for each subnet?*
- *Valid hosts?*

The following table shows the first five subnets, valid hosts, and broadcast addresses in a Class B 255.255.248.0 mask:

Subnet	0.0	8.0	16.0	24.0	32.0
First host	0.1	8.1	16.1	24.1	32.1
Last host	7.254	15.254	23.254	31.254	39.254
Broadcast	7.255	15.255	23.255	31.255	39.255

Practice Example #5B: 255.255.252.0 (/22)

172.16.0.0 = Network address

255.255.252.0 = Subnet mask

- *Subnets?* $2^6 = 64$.
- *Hosts?* $2^{10} - 2 = 1022$.
- *Valid subnets?* 256 − 252 = 0, 4, 8, 12, 16, etc., up to 252.
- *Broadcast address for each subnet?*
- *Valid hosts?*

The following table shows the first five subnets, valid hosts, and broadcast addresses in a Class B 255.255.252.0 mask:

Subnet	0.0	4.0	8.0	12.0	16.0
First host	0.1	4.1	8.1	12.1	16.1
Last host	3.254	7.254	11.254	15.254	19.254
Broadcast	3.255	7.255	11.255	15.255	19.255

Practice Example #6B: 255.255.254.0 (/23)

172.16.0.0 = Network address

255.255.254.0 = Subnet mask

- *Subnets?* $2^7 = 128$.
- *Hosts?* $2^9 - 2 = 510$.
- *Valid subnets?* $256 - 254 = 0, 2, 4, 6, 8$, etc., up to 254.
- *Broadcast address for each subnet?*
- *Valid hosts?*

The following table shows the first five subnets, valid hosts, and broadcast addresses in a Class B 255.255.254.0 mask:

Subnet	0.0	2.0	4.0	6.0	8.0
First host	0.1	2.1	4.1	6.1	8.1
Last host	1.254	3.254	5.254	7.254	9.254
Broadcast	1.255	3.255	5.255	7.255	9.255

Practice Example #7B: 255.255.255.0 (/24)

Contrary to popular belief, 255.255.255.0 used with a Class B network address is not called a Class B network with a Class C subnet mask. It's amazing how many people see this mask used in a Class B network and think it's a Class C subnet mask. This is a Class B subnet mask with 8 bits of subnetting—it's logically different from a Class C mask. Subnetting this address is fairly simple:

172.16.0.0 = Network address

255.255.255.0 = Subnet mask

- *Subnets?* $2^8 = 256$.
- *Hosts?* $2^8 - 2 = 254$.
- *Valid subnets?* $256 - 255 = 1. 0, 1, 2, 3$, etc., all the way to 255.
- *Broadcast address for each subnet?*
- *Valid hosts?*

The following table shows the first four and last two subnets, the valid hosts, and the broadcast addresses in a Class B 255.255.255.0 mask:

Subnet	0.0	1.0	2.0	3.0	...	254.0	255.0
First host	0.1	1.1	2.1	3.1	...	254.1	255.1
Last host	0.254	1.254	2.254	3.254	...	254.254	255.254
Broadcast	0.255	1.255	2.255	3.255	...	254.255	255.255

Practice Example #8B: 255.255.255.128 (/25)

This is actually one of the hardest subnet masks you can play with. And worse, it actually is a really good subnet to use in production because it creates over 500 subnets with 126 hosts for each subnet—a nice mixture. So, don't skip over it!

> 172.16.0.0 = Network address
>
> 255.255.255.128 = Subnet mask

- *Subnets?* $2^9 = 512$.
- *Hosts?* $2^7 - 2 = 126$.
- *Valid subnets?* Now for the tricky part. $256 - 255 = 1$. 0, 1, 2, 3, etc., for the third octet. But you can't forget the one subnet bit used in the fourth octet. Remember when I showed you how to figure one subnet bit with a Class C mask? You figure this the same way. You actually get two subnets for each third octet value, hence the 512 subnets. For example, if the third octet is showing subnet 3, the two subnets would actually be 3.0 and 3.128.
- *Broadcast address for each subnet?* The numbers right before the next subnet.
- *Valid hosts?* The numbers between the subnet numbers and the broadcast address.

The following graphic shows how you can create subnets, valid hosts, and broadcast addresses using the Class B 255.255.255.128 subnet mask. The first eight subnets are shown, followed by the last two subnets:

Subnet	0.0	0.128	1.0	1.128	2.0	2.128	3.0	3.128	...	255.0	255.128
First host	0.1	0.129	1.1	1.129	2.1	2.129	3.1	3.129	...	255.1	255.129
Last host	0.126	0.254	1.126	1.254	2.126	2.254	3.126	3.254	...	255.126	255.254
Broadcast	0.127	0.255	1.127	1.255	2.127	2.255	3.127	3.255	...	255.127	255.255

Practice Example #9B: 255.255.255.192 (/26)

Now, this is where Class B subnetting gets easy. Since the third octet has a 255 in the mask section, whatever number is listed in the third octet is a subnet number. And now that we have a subnet number in the fourth octet, we can subnet this octet just as we did with Class C subnetting. Let's try it out:

> 172.16.0.0 = Network address
>
> 255.255.255.192 = Subnet mask

- *Subnets?* $2^{10} = 1024$.
- *Hosts?* $2^6 - 2 = 62$.
- *Valid subnets?* $256 - 192 = 64$. The subnets are shown in the following table. Do these numbers look familiar?
- *Broadcast address for each subnet?*
- *Valid hosts?*

The following table shows the first eight subnet ranges, valid hosts, and broadcast addresses:

Subnet	0.0	0.64	0.128	0.192	1.0	1.64	1.128	1.192
First host	0.1	0.65	0.129	0.193	1.1	1.65	1.129	1.193
Last host	0.62	0.126	0.190	0.254	1.62	1.126	1.190	1.254
Broadcast	0.63	0.127	0.191	0.255	1.63	1.127	1.191	1.255

Notice that for each subnet value in the third octet, you get subnets 0, 64, 128, and 192 in the fourth octet.

Practice Example #10B: 255.255.255.224 (/27)

This one is done the same way as the preceding subnet mask, except that we just have more subnets and fewer hosts per subnet available.

172.16.0.0 = Network address

255.255.255.224 = Subnet mask

- *Subnets?* $2^{11} = 2048$.
- *Hosts?* $2^5 - 2 = 30$.
- *Valid subnets?* $256 - 224 = 32$. 0, 32, 64, 96, 128, 160, 192, 224.
- *Broadcast address for each subnet?*
- *Valid hosts?*

The following table shows the first eight subnets:

Subnet	0.0	0.32	0.64	0.96	0.128	0.160	0.192	0.224
First host	0.1	0.33	0.65	0.97	0.129	0.161	0.193	0.225
Last host	0.30	0.62	0.94	0.126	0.158	0.190	0.222	0.254
Broadcast	0.31	0.63	0.95	0.127	0.159	0.191	0.223	0.255

This next table shows the last eight subnets:

Subnet	255.0	255.32	255.64	255.96	255.128	255.160	255.192	255.224
First host	255.1	255.33	255.65	255.97	255.129	255.161	255.193	255.225
Last host	255.30	255.62	255.94	255.126	255.158	255.190	255.222	255.254
Broadcast	255.31	255.63	255.95	255.127	255.159	255.191	255.223	255.255

Subnetting in Your Head: Class B Addresses

Are you nuts? Subnet Class B addresses in our heads? It's actually easier than writing it out—I'm not kidding! Let me show you how:

Question: What is the subnet and broadcast address of the subnet in which 172.16.10.33 /27 resides?

Answer: The interesting octet is the fourth one. 256 − 224 = 32. 32 + 32 = 64. You've got it: 33 is between 32 and 64. But remember that the third octet is considered part of the subnet, so the answer would be the 10.32 subnet. The broadcast is 10.63, since 10.64 is the next subnet. That was a pretty easy one.

Question: What subnet and broadcast address is the IP address 172.16.66.10 255.255.192.0 (/18) a member of?

Answer: The interesting octet here is the third octet instead of the fourth one. 256 − 192 = 64. 0, 64, 128. The subnet is 172.16.64.0. The broadcast must be 172.16.127.255 since 128.0 is the next subnet.

Question: What subnet and broadcast address is the IP address 172.16.50.10 255.255.224.0 (/19) a member of?

Answer: 256 − 224 = 0, 32, 64 (remember, we always start counting at 0). The subnet is 172.16.32.0, and the broadcast must be 172.16.63.255 since 64.0 is the next subnet.

Question: What subnet and broadcast address is the IP address 172.16.46.255 255.255.240.0 (/20) a member of?

Answer: 256 − 240 = 16. The third octet is important here: 0, 16, 32, 48. This subnet address must be in the 172.16.32.0 subnet, and the broadcast must be 172.16.47.255 since 48.0 is the next subnet. So, yes, 172.16.46.255 is a valid host.

Question: What subnet and broadcast address is the IP address 172.16.45.14 255.255.255.252 (/30) a member of?

Answer: Where is our interesting octet? 256 − 252 = 0, 4, 8, 12, 16—the fourth. The subnet is 172.16.45.12, with a broadcast of 172.16.45.15 because the next subnet is 172.16.45.16.

Question: What is the subnet and broadcast address of the host 172.16.88.255/20?

Answer: What is a /20 written out in dotted decimal? If you can't answer this, you can't answer this question, can you? A /20 is 255.255.240.0, gives us a block size of 16 in the third octet, and since no subnet bits are on in the fourth octet, the answer is always 0 and 255 in the fourth octet: 0, 16, 32, 48, 64, 80, 96. Because 88 is between 80 and 96, the subnet is 80.0 and the broadcast address is 95.255.

Question: A router receives a packet on an interface with a destination address of 172.16.46.191/26. What will the router do with this packet?

Answer: Discard it. Do you know why? 172.16.46.191/26 is a 255.255.255.192 mask, which gives us a block size of 64. Our subnets are then 0, 64, 128 and 192. 191 is the broadcast address of the 128 subnet, and by default, a router will discard any broadcast packets.

Subnetting Class A Addresses

You don't go about Class A subnetting any differently than Classes B and C, but there are 24 bits to play with instead of the 16 in a Class B address and the 8 in a Class C address.

Let's start by listing all the Class A masks:

```
255.0.0.0       (/8)
255.128.0.0     (/9)        255.255.240.0    (/20)
255.192.0.0     (/10)       255.255.248.0    (/21)
255.224.0.0     (/11)       255.255.252.0    (/22)
255.240.0.0     (/12)       255.255.254.0    (/23)
255.248.0.0     (/13)       255.255.255.0    (/24)
255.252.0.0     (/14)       255.255.255.128  (/25)
255.254.0.0     (/15)       255.255.255.192  (/26)
255.255.0.0     (/16)       255.255.255.224  (/27)
255.255.128.0   (/17)       255.255.255.240  (/28)
255.255.192.0   (/18)       255.255.255.248  (/29)
255.255.224.0   (/19)       255.255.255.252  (/30)
```

That's it. You must leave at least 2 bits for defining hosts. I hope you can see the pattern by now. Remember, we're going to do this the same way as a Class B or C subnet. It's just that, again, we simply have more host bits and we just use the same subnet numbers we used with Class B and C, but we start using these numbers in the second octet. However, the reason Class A addresses are so popular to implement is because they give the most flexibility. You can subnet in the second, third or fourth octet. I'll show you this in the next examples.

Subnetting Practice Examples: Class A Addresses

When you look at an IP address and a subnet mask, you must be able to distinguish the bits used for subnets from the bits used for determining hosts. This is imperative. If you're still struggling with this concept, please reread the section "IP Addressing" in Chapter 3. It shows you how to determine the difference between the subnet and host bits and should help clear things up.

Practice Example #1A: 255.255.0.0 (/16)

Class A addresses use a default mask of 255.0.0.0, which leaves 22 bits for subnetting because you must leave 2 bits for host addressing. The 255.255.0.0 mask with a Class A address is using 8 subnet bits:

- *Subnets?* 2^8 = 256.
- *Hosts?* 2^{16} − 2 = 65,534.
- *Valid subnets?* What is the interesting octet? 256 − 255 = 1. 0, 1, 2, 3, etc. (all in the second octet). The subnets would be 10.0.0.0, 10.1.0.0, 10.2.0.0, 10.3.0.0, etc., up to 10.255.0.0.
- *Broadcast address for each subnet?*
- *Valid hosts?*

The following table shows the first two and the last two subnets, the valid host range and the broadcast addresses for the private Class A 10.0.0.0 network:

Subnet	10.0.0.0	10.1.0.0	...	10.254.0.0	10.255.0.0
First host	10.0.0.1	10.1.0.1	...	10.254.0.1	10.255.0.1
Last host	10.0.255.254	10.1.255.254	...	10.254.255.254	10.255.255.254
Broadcast	10.0.255.255	10.1.255.255	...	10.254.255.255	10.255.255.255

Practice Example #2A: 255.255.240.0 (/20)

255.255.240.0 gives us 12 bits of subnetting and leaves us 12 bits for host addressing.

- *Subnets?* 2^{12} = 4096.
- *Hosts?* 2^{12} − 2 = 4094.
- *Valid subnets?* What is your interesting octet? 256 − 240 = 16. The subnets in the second octet are a block size of 1 and the subnets in the third octet are 0, 16, 32, etc.
- *Broadcast address for each subnet?*
- *Valid hosts?*

The following table shows some examples of the host ranges—the first three subnets and the last subnet:

Subnet	10.0.0.0	10.0.16.0	10.0.32.0	...	10.255.240.0
First host	10.0.0.1	10.0.16.1	10.0.32.1	...	10.255.240.1
Last host	10.0.15.254	10.0.31.254	10.0.47.254	...	10.255.255.254
Broadcast	10.0.15.255	10.0.31.255	10.0.47.255	...	10.255.255.255

Practice Example #3A: 255.255.255.192 (/26)

Let's do one more example using the second, third, and fourth octets for subnetting:

- *Subnets?* 2^{18} = 262,144.

- *Hosts?* $2^6 - 2$ = 62.

- *Valid subnets?* In the second and third octet, the block size is 1, and in the fourth octet, the block size is 64.

- *Broadcast address for each subnet?*

- *Valid hosts?*

The following table shows the first four subnets and their valid hosts and broadcast addresses in the Class A 255.255.255.192 mask:

Subnet	10.0.0.0	10.0.0.64	10.0.0.128	10.0.0.192
First host	10.0.0.1	10.0.0.65	10.0.0.129	10.0.0.193
Last host	10.0.0.62	10.0.0.126	10.0.0.190	10.0.0.254
Broadcast	10.0.0.63	10.0.0.127	10.0.0.191	10.0.0.255

This table shows the last four subnets and their valid hosts and broadcast addresses:

Subnet	10.255.255.0	10.255.255.64	10.255.255.128	10.255.255.192
First host	10.255.255.1	10.255.255.65	10.255.255.129	10.255.255.193
Last host	10.255.255.62	10.255.255.126	10.255.255.190	10.255.255.254
Broadcast	10.255.255.63	10.255.255.127	10.255.255.191	10.255.255.255

Subnetting in Your Head: Class A Addresses

Again, I know this sounds hard, but as with Class C and Class B, the numbers are the same; we just start in the second octet. What makes this easy? You only need to worry about the octet that has the largest block size, which is typically called the interesting octet, and one that is something other than 0 or 255, such as, for example, 255.255.240.0 (/20) with a Class A network. The second octet has a block size of 1, so any number listed in that octet is a subnet. The third octet is a 240 mask, which means we have a block size of 16 in the third octet. If your host ID is 10.20.80.30, what is your subnet, broadcast address, and valid host range?

The subnet in the second octet is 20 with a block size of 1, but the third octet is in block sizes of 16, so we'll just count them out: 0, 16, 32, 48, 64, 80, 96… voilà! By the way, you can count by 16s by now, right? Good! This makes our subnet 10.20.80.0, with a broadcast address of 10.20.95.255 because the next subnet is 10.20.96.0. The valid host range is 10.20.80.1 through 10.20.95.254. And yes, no lie! You really can do this in your head if you just get your block sizes nailed!

Let's practice on one more, just for fun!

Host IP: 10.1.3.65/23

First, you can't answer this question if you don't know what a /23 is. It's 255.255.254.0. The interesting octet here is the third one: 256 − 254 = 2. Our subnets in the third octet are 0, 2, 4, 6, etc. The host in this question is in subnet 2.0, and the next subnet is 4.0, so that makes the broadcast address 3.255. And any address between 10.1.2.1 and 10.1.3.254 is considered a valid host.

Summary

Did you read Chapters 3 and 4 and understand everything on the first pass? If so, that is fantastic—congratulations! However, you probably really did get lost a couple of times. No worries because as I told you, that's what usually happens. Don't waste time feeling bad if you have to read each chapter more than once, or even 10 times, before you're truly good to go. If you do have to read the chapters more than once, you'll be seriously better off in the long run even if you were pretty comfortable the first time through!

This chapter provided you with an important understanding of IP subnetting—the painless way! And when you've got the key material presented in this chapter really nailed down, you should be able to subnet IP addresses in your head.

This chapter is extremely essential to your Cisco certification process, so if you just skimmed it, please go back, read it thoroughly, and don't forget to do all the written labs too!

Exam Essentials

Identify the advantages of subnetting.   Benefits of subnetting a physical network include reduced network traffic, optimized network performance, simplified management, and facilitated spanning of large geographical distances.

Describe the effect of the `ip subnet-zero` command.   This command allows you to use the first and last subnet in your network design.

Identify the steps to subnet a classful network.   Understand how IP addressing and subnetting work. First, determine your block size by using the 256-subnet mask math. Then count your subnets and determine the broadcast address of each subnet—it is always the number right before the next subnet. Your valid hosts are the numbers between the subnet address and the broadcast address.

Determine possible block sizes.   This is an important part of understanding IP addressing and subnetting. The valid block sizes are always 2, 4, 8, 16, 32, 64, 128, etc. You can determine your block size by using the 256-subnet mask math.

Describe the role of a subnet mask in IP addressing.   A subnet mask is a 32-bit value that allows the recipient of IP packets to distinguish the network ID portion of the IP address from the host ID portion of the IP address.

Understand and apply the $2^x - 2$ formula.   Use this formula to determine the proper subnet mask for a particular size network given the application of that subnet mask to a particular classful network.

Explain the impact of Classless Inter-Domain Routing (CIDR).   CIDR allows the creation of networks of a size other than those allowed with the classful subnetting by allowing more than the three classful subnet masks.

Written Labs

In this section, you'll complete the following labs to make sure you've got the information and concepts contained within them fully dialed in:

Lab 4.1: Written Subnet Practice #1

Lab 4.2: Written Subnet Practice #2

Lab 4.3: Written Subnet Practice #3

You can find the answers to these labs in Appendix A, "Answers to Written Labs."

Written Lab 4.1: Written Subnet Practice #1

Write the subnet, broadcast address, and a valid host range for question 1 through question 6. Then answer the remaining questions.

1. 192.168.100.25/30
2. 192.168.100.37/28
3. 192.168.100.66/27
4. 192.168.100.17/29
5. 192.168.100.99/26
6. 192.168.100.99/25
7. You have a Class B network and need 29 subnets. What is your mask?
8. What is the broadcast address of 192.168.192.10/29?
9. How many hosts are available with a Class C /29 mask?
10. What is the subnet for host ID 10.16.3.65/23?

Written Lab 4.2: Written Subnet Practice #2

Given a Class B network and the net bits identified (CIDR), complete the following table to identify the subnet mask and the number of host addresses possible for each mask.

Classful Address	Subnet Mask	Number of Hosts per Subnet ($2^x - 2$)
/16		
/17		
/18		
/19		
/20		
/21		
/22		
/23		
/24		
/25		
/26		
/27		
/28		
/29		
/30		

Written Lab 4.3: Written Subnet Practice #3

Complete the following based on the decimal IP address.

Decimal IP Address	Address Class	Number of Subnet and Host Bits	Number of Subnets (2^x)	Number of Hosts ($2^x - 2$)
10.25.66.154/23				
172.31.254.12/24				
192.168.20.123/28				
63.24.89.21/18				
128.1.1.254/20				
208.100.54.209/30				

Review Questions

The following questions are designed to test your understanding of this chapter's material. For more information on how to get additional questions, please see www.lammle.com/ccna.

You can find the answers to these questions in Appendix B, "Answers to Review Questions."

1. What is the maximum number of IP addresses that can be assigned to hosts on a local subnet that uses the 255.255.255.224 subnet mask?

   A. 14

   B. 15

   C. 16

   D. 30

   E. 31

   F. 62

2. You have a network that needs 29 subnets while maximizing the number of host addresses available on each subnet. How many bits must you borrow from the host field to provide the correct subnet mask?

   A. 2

   B. 3

   C. 4

   D. 5

   E. 6

   F. 7

3. What is the subnetwork address for a host with the IP address 200.10.5.68/28?

   A. 200.10.5.56

   B. 200.10.5.32

   C. 200.10.5.64

   D. 200.10.5.0

4. The network address of 172.16.0.0/19 provides how many subnets and hosts?

   A. 7 subnets, 30 hosts each

   B. 7 subnets, 2,046 hosts each

   C. 7 subnets, 8,190 hosts each

   D. 8 subnets, 30 hosts each

E.   8 subnets, 2,046 hosts each

F.   8 subnets, 8,190 hosts each

5.   Which two statements describe the IP address 10.16.3.65/23? (Choose two.)

A.   The subnet address is 10.16.3.0 255.255.254.0.

B.   The lowest host address in the subnet is 10.16.2.1 255.255.254.0.

C.   The last valid host address in the subnet is 10.16.2.254 255.255.254.0.

D.   The broadcast address of the subnet is 10.16.3.255 255.255.254.0.

E.   The network is not subnetted.

6.   If a host on a network has the address 172.16.45.14/30, what is the subnetwork this host belongs to?

A.   172.16.45.0

B.   172.16.45.4

C.   172.16.45.8

D.   172.16.45.12

E.   172.16.45.16

7.   Which mask should you use on point-to-point links in order to reduce the waste of IP addresses?

A.   /27

B.   /28

C.   /29

D.   /30

E.   /31

8.   What is the subnetwork number of a host with an IP address of 172.16.66.0/21?

A.   172.16.36.0

B.   172.16.48.0

C.   172.16.64.0

D.   172.16.0.0

9.   You have an interface on a router with the IP address of 192.168.192.10/29. Including the router interface, how many hosts can have IP addresses on the LAN attached to the router interface?

A.   6

B.   8

C.   30

D.   62

E.   126

10. You need to configure a server that is on the subnet 192.168.19.24/29. The router has the first available host address. Which of the following should you assign to the server?

    A. 192.168.19.0 255.255.255.0

    B. 192.168.19.33 255.255.255.240

    C. 192.168.19.26 255.255.255.248

    D. 192.168.19.31 255.255.255.248

    E. 192.168.19.34 255.255.255.240

11. You have an interface on a router with the IP address of 192.168.192.10/29. What is the broadcast address the hosts will use on this LAN?

    A. 192.168.192.15

    B. 192.168.192.31

    C. 192.168.192.63

    D. 192.168.192.127

    E. 192.168.192.255

12. You need to subnet a network that has 5 subnets, each with at least 16 hosts. Which classful subnet mask would you use?

    A. 255.255.255.192

    B. 255.255.255.224

    C. 255.255.255.240

    D. 255.255.255.248

13. You configure a router interface with the IP address 192.168.10.62 255.255.255.192 and receive the following error:

    ```
    Bad mask /26 for address 192.168.10.62
    ```

    Why did you receive this error?

    A. You typed this mask on a WAN link and that is not allowed.

    B. This is not a valid host and subnet mask combination.

    C. `ip subnet-zero` is not enabled on the router.

    D. The router does not support IP.

14. If an Ethernet port on a router were assigned an IP address of 172.16.112.1/25, what would be the valid subnet address of this interface?

    A. 172.16.112.0

    B. 172.16.0.0

    C. 172.16.96.0

    D. 172.16.255.0

    E. 172.16.128.0

15. Using the following illustration, what would be the IP address of E0 if you were using the eighth subnet? The network ID is 192.168.10.0/28 and you need to use the last available IP address in the range. The zero subnet should not be considered valid for this question.

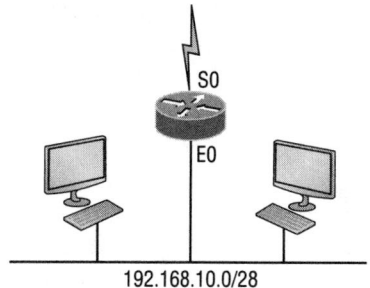

192.168.10.0/28

  A. 192.168.10.142
  B. 192.168.10.66
  C. 192.168.100.254
  D. 192.168.10.143
  E. 192.168.10.126

16. Using the illustration from the previous question, what would be the IP address of S0 if you were using the first subnet? The network ID is 192.168.10.0/28 and you need to use the last available IP address in the range. Again, the zero subnet should not be considered valid for this question.

  A. 192.168.10.24
  B. 192.168.10.62
  C. 192.168.10.30
  D. 192.168.10.127

17. You have a network in your data center that needs 310 hosts. Which mask should you use so you waste the least amount of addresses?

  A. 255.255.255.0
  B. 255.255.254.0
  C. 255.255.252.0
  D. 255.255.248.0

18. You have a network with a host address of 172.16.17.0/22. From the following options, which is another valid host address in the same subnet?

  A. 172.16.17.1 255.255.255.252
  B. 172.16.0.1 255.255.240.0
  C. 172.16.20.1 255.255.254.0
  D. 172.16.16.1 255.255.255.240

    E.   172.16.18.255 255.255.252.0

    F.   172.16.0.1 255.255.255.0

19. Your router has the following IP address on Ethernet0: 172.16.2.1/23. Which of the following can be valid host IDs on the LAN interface attached to the router? (Choose two.)

    A.   172.16.0.5

    B.   172.16.1.100

    C.   172.16.1.198

    D.   172.16.2.255

    E.   172.16.3.0

    F.   172.16.3.255

20. Given an IP address 172.16.28.252 with a subnet mask of 255.255.240.0, what is the correct network address?

    A.   172.16.16.0

    B.   172.16.0.0

    C.   172.16.24.0

    D.   172.16.28.0

Chapter

5

VLSMs, Summarization, and Troubleshooting TCP/IP

THE FOLLOWING ICND1 EXAM TOPICS ARE COVERED IN THIS CHAPTER:

✓ **Network Fundamentals**

- 1.7 Apply troubleshooting methodologies to resolve problems

- 1.7.a Perform fault isolation and document

- 1.7.b Resolve or escalate

- 1.7.c Verify and monitor resolution

- 1.8 Configure, verify, and troubleshoot IPv4 addressing and subnetting

Now that IP addressing and subnetting have been thoroughly covered in the last two chapters, you're fully prepared and ready to learn all about variable length subnet masks (VLSMs). I'll also show you how to design and implement a network using VLSM in this chapter. After ensuring you've mastered VLSM design and implementation, I'll demonstrate how to summarize classful boundaries.

We'll wrap up the chapter by going over IP address troubleshooting, focusing on the steps Cisco recommends to follow when troubleshooting an IP network.

So get psyched because this chapter will give you powerful tools to hone your knowledge of IP addressing and networking and seriously refine the important skills you've gained so far. So stay with me—I guarantee that your hard work will pay off! Ready? Let's go!

To find up-to-the minute updates for this chapter, please see www.lammle.com/ccna or the book's web page at www.sybex.com/go/ccna.

Variable Length Subnet Masks (VLSMs)

Teaching you a simple way to create many networks from a large single network using subnet masks of different lengths in various kinds of network designs is what my primary focus will be in this chapter. Doing this is called VLSM networking, and it brings up another important subject I mentioned in Chapter 4, "Easy Subnetting," classful and classless networking.

Older routing protocols like Routing Information Protocol version 1 (RIPv1) do not have a field for subnet information, so the subnet information gets dropped. This means that if a router running RIP has a subnet mask of a certain value, it assumes that *all* interfaces within the classful address space have the same subnet mask. This is called classful routing, and RIP is considered a classful routing protocol. We'll cover RIP and the difference between classful and classless networks later on in Chapter 9, "IP Routing," but for now, just remember that if you try to mix and match subnet mask lengths in a network that's running an old routing protocol, such as RIP, it just won't work!

However, classless routing protocols do support the advertisement of subnet information, which means you can use VLSM with routing protocols such as RIPv2, Enhanced

Interior Gateway Protocol (EIGRP), and Open Shortest Path First (OSPF). The benefit of this type of network is that it saves a bunch of IP address space.

As the name suggests, VLSMs can use subnet masks with different lengths for different router interfaces. Check out Figure 5.1 to see an example of why classful network designs are inefficient.

FIGURE 5.1   Typical classful network

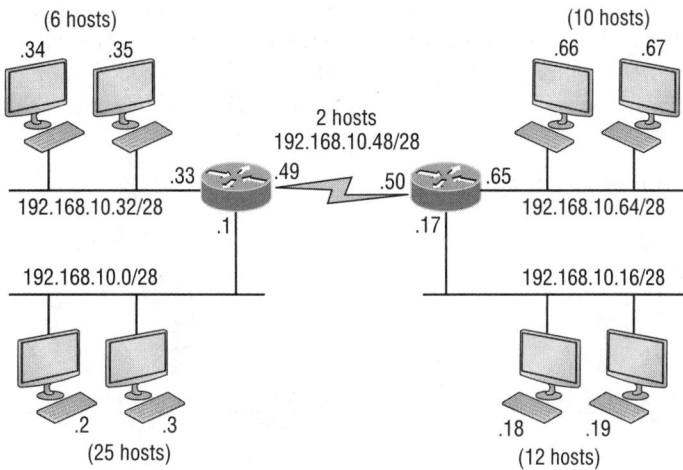

Looking at Figure 5.1, you can see that there are two routers, each with two LANs and connected together with a WAN serial link. In a typical classful network design that's running RIP, you could subnet a network like this:

192.168.10.0 = Network

255.255.255.240 (/28) = Mask

Our subnets would be—you know this part, right?— 0, 16, 32, 48, 64, 80, etc., which allows us to assign 16 subnets to our internetwork. But how many hosts would be available on each network? Well, as you know by now, each subnet provides only 14 hosts, so each LAN has only 14 valid hosts available (don't forget that the router interface needs an address too and is included in the amount of needed valid hosts). This means that one LAN doesn't even have enough addresses needed for all the hosts, and this network as it is shown would not work as addressed in the figure! Since the point-to-point WAN link also has 14 valid hosts, it would be great to be able to nick a few valid hosts from that WAN link to give to our LANs!

All hosts and router interfaces have the same subnet mask—again, known as classful routing—and if we want this network to be efficient, we would definitely need to add different masks to each router interface.

But that's not our only problem—the link between the two routers will never use more than two valid hosts! This wastes valuable IP address space, and it's the big reason you need to learn about VLSM network design.

VLSM Design

Let's take Figure 5.1 and use a classless design instead, which will become the new network shown in Figure 5.2. In the previous example, we wasted address space—one LAN didn't have enough addresses because every router interface and host used the same subnet mask. Not so good. A better solution would be to provide for only the needed number of hosts on each router interface, and we're going to use VLSMs to achieve that goal.

FIGURE 5.2   Classless network design

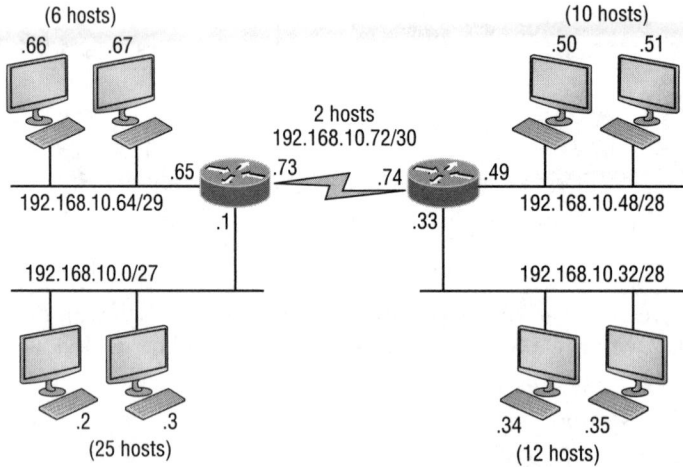

Now remember that we can use different size masks on each router interface. If we use a /30 on our WAN links and a /27, /28, and /29 on our LANs, we'll get 2 hosts per WAN interface and 30, 14, and 6 hosts per LAN interface—nice (remember to count your router interface as a host)! This makes a huge difference—not only can we get just the right amount of hosts on each LAN, we still have room to add more WANs and LANs using this same network!

To implement a VLSM design on your network, you need to have a routing protocol that sends subnet mask information with the route updates. The protocols that do that are RIPv2, EIGRP, and OSPF. Remember, RIPv1 will not work in classless networks, so it's considered a classful routing protocol.

Implementing VLSM Networks

To create VLSMs quickly and efficiently, you need to understand how block sizes and charts work together to create the VLSM masks. Table 5.1 shows you the block sizes used when creating VLSMs with Class C networks. For example, if you need 25 hosts, then you'll need a block size of 32. If you need 11 hosts, you'll use a block size of 16. Need 40 hosts? Then you'll need a block of 64. You cannot just make up block sizes—they've got to be the block sizes shown in Table 5.1. So memorize the block sizes in this table—it's easy. They're the same numbers we used with subnetting!

TABLE 5.1   Block sizes

Prefix	Mask	Hosts	Block Size
/25	128	126	128
/26	192	62	64
/27	224	30	32
/28	240	14	16
/29	248	6	8
/30	252	2	4

The next step is to create a VLSM table. Figure 5.3 shows you the table used in creating a VLSM network. The reason we use this table is so we don't accidentally overlap networks.

You'll find the sheet shown in Figure 5.3 very valuable because it lists every block size you can use for a network address. Notice that the block sizes start at 4 and advance all the way up to a block size of 128. If you have two networks with block sizes of 128, you can have only 2 networks. With a block size of 64, you can have only 4, and so on, all the way to 64 networks using a block size of 4. Of course, this is assuming you're using the ip subnet-zero command in your network design.

So now all you need to do is fill in the chart in the lower-left corner, then add the subnets to the worksheet and you're good to go!

Based on what you've learned so far about block sizes and the VLSM table, let's create a VLSM network using a Class C network address 192.168.10.0 for the network in Figure 5.4, then fill out the VLSM table, as shown in Figure 5.5.

In Figure 5.4, we have four WAN links and four LANs connected together, so we need to create a VLSM network that will save address space. Looks like we have two block sizes of 32, a block size of 16, and a block size of 8, and our WANs each have a block size of 4. Take a look and see how I filled out our VLSM chart in Figure 5.5.

FIGURE 5.3 The VLSM table

Subnet	Mask	Subnets	Hosts	Block
/25	128	2	126	128
/26	192	4	62	64
/27	224	8	30	32
/28	240	16	14	16
/29	248	32	6	8
/30	252	64	2	4

Network	Hosts	Block	Subnet	Mask
A				
B				
C				
D				
E				
F				
G				
H				
I				
J				
K				
L				

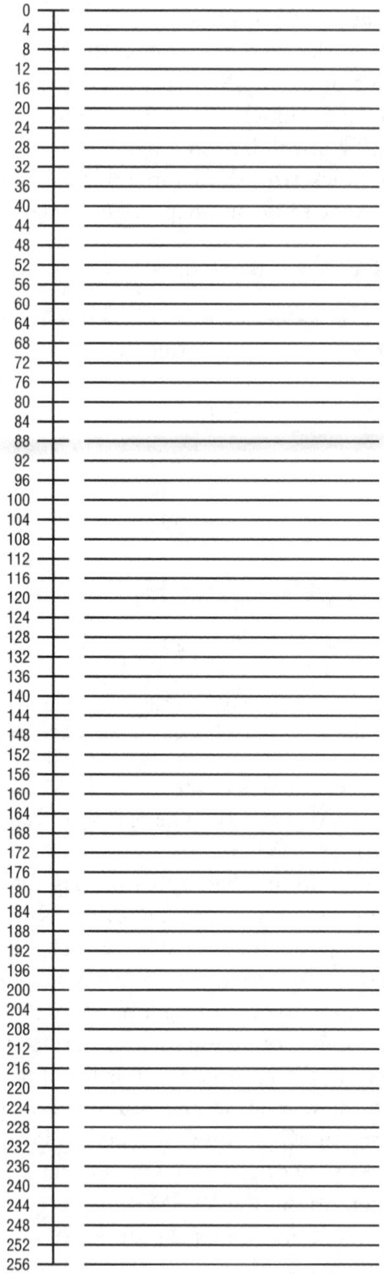

0
4
8
12
16
20
24
28
32
36
40
44
48
52
56
60
64
68
72
76
80
84
88
92
96
100
104
108
112
116
120
124
128
132
136
140
144
148
152
156
160
164
168
172
176
180
184
188
192
196
200
204
208
212
216
220
224
228
232
236
240
244
248
252
256

FIGURE 5.4   VLSM network example 1

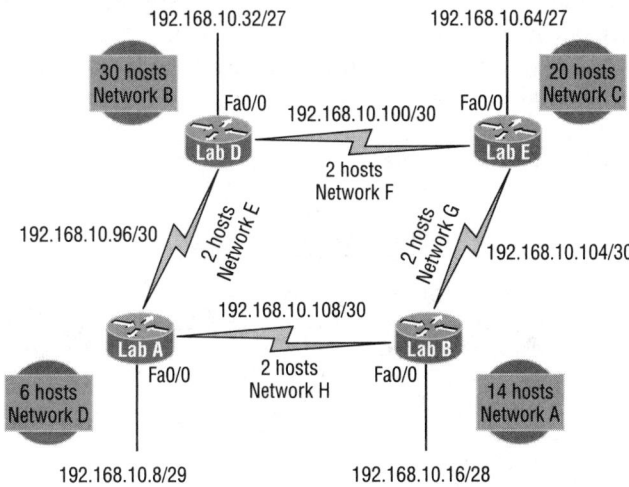

FIGURE 5.5   VLSM table example 1

Subnet	Mask	Subnets	Hosts	Block
/25	128	2	126	128
/26	192	4	62	64
/27	224	8	30	32
/28	240	16	14	16
/29	248	32	6	8
/30	252	64	2	4

Network	Hosts	Block	Subnet	Mask
A	14	16	/28	240
B	30	32	/27	224
C	20	32	/27	224
D	6	8	/29	248
E	2	4	/30	252
F	2	4	/30	252
G	2	4	/30	252
H	2	4	/30	252

```
  0 ──┬──────────────────────────────────
  4 ──┤
  8 ──┤
 12 ──┤        D — 192.168.10.8/29
 16 ──┤
 20 ──┤
 24 ──┤        A — 192.168.10.16/28
 28 ──┤
 32 ──┤
 36 ──┤
 40 ──┤
 44 ──┤
 48 ──┤        B — 192.168.10.32/27
 52 ──┤
 56 ──┤
 60 ──┤
 64 ──┤
 68 ──┤
 72 ──┤
 76 ──┤
 80 ──┤        C — 192.168.10.64/27
 84 ──┤
 88 ──┤
 92 ──┤
 96 ──┤        E — 192.168.10.96/30
100 ──┤        F — 192.168.10.100/30
104 ──┤        G — 192.168.10.104/30
108 ──┤        H — 192.168.10.108/30
112 ──┤
116 ──┤
120 ──┤
124 ──┤
128 ──┤
132 ──┤
136 ──┤
140 ──┤
144 ──┤
148 ──┴──────────────────────────────────
          ---output cut---
```

There are two important things to note here. The first is that we still have plenty of room for growth with this VLSM network design. The second point is that we could never achieve this goal with one subnet mask using classful routing.

Let's do another one. Figure 5.6 shows a network with 11 networks, two block sizes of 64, one of 32, five of 16, and three of 4.

FIGURE 5.6 VLSM network example 2

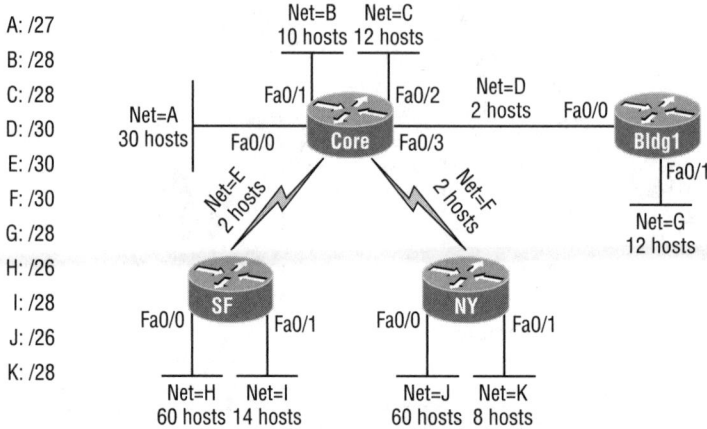

First, create your VLSM table and use your block size chart to fill in the table with the subnets you need. Figure 5.7 shows a possible solution.

Notice that I filled in this entire chart and only have room for one more block size of 4. You can only gain that amount of address space savings with a VLSM network!

Keep in mind that it doesn't matter where you start your block sizes as long as you always begin counting from zero. For example, if you had a block size of 16, you must start at 0 and incrementally progress from there—0, 16, 32, 48, and so on. You can't start with a block size of 16 or some value like 40, and you can't progress using anything but increments of 16.

Here's another example. If you had block sizes of 32, start at zero like this: 0, 32, 64, 96, etc. Again, you don't get to start wherever you want; you must always start counting from zero. In the example in Figure 5.7, I started at 64 and 128, with my two block sizes of 64. I didn't have much choice because my options are 0, 64, 128, and 192. However, I added the block size of 32, 16, 8, and 4 elsewhere, but they were always in the correct increments required of the specific block size. Remember that if you always start with the largest blocks first, then make your way to the smaller blocks sizes, you will automatically fall on an increment boundary. It also guarantees that you are using your address space in the most effective way.

Okay—you have three locations you need to address, and the IP network you have received is 192.168.55.0 to use as the addressing for the entire network. You'll use ip sub-net-zero and RIPv2 as the routing protocol because RIPv2 supports VLSM networks but

FIGURE 5.7 VLSM table example 2

Subnet	Mask	Subnets	Hosts	Block
/25	128	2	126	128
/26	192	4	62	64
/27	224	8	30	32
/28	240	16	14	16
/29	248	32	6	8
/30	252	64	2	4

Network	Hosts	Block	Subnet	Mask
A				
B				
C				
D				
E				
F				
G				
H				
I				
J				
K				

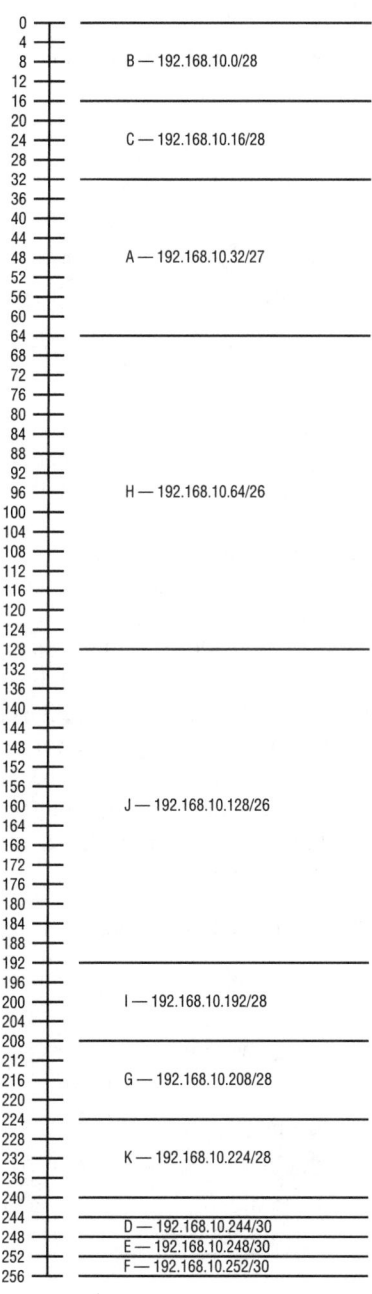

RIPv1 does not. Figure 5.8 shows the network diagram and the IP address of the RouterA S0/0 interface.

FIGURE 5.8 VLSM design example 1

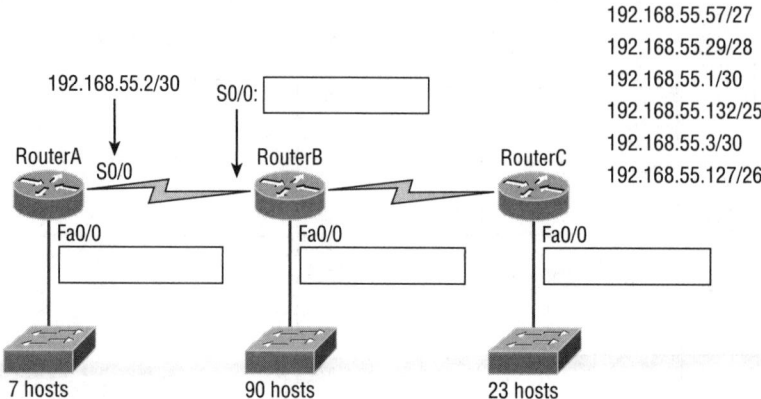

From the list of IP addresses on the right of the figure, which IP address do you think will be placed in each router's FastEthernet 0/0 interface and serial 0/0 of RouterB?

To answer this, look for clues in Figure 5.8. The first is that interface S0/0 on RouterA has IP address 192.168.55.2/30 assigned, which makes for an easy answer because A /30 is 255.255.255.252, which gives you a block size of 4. Your subnets are 0, 4, 8, etc. Since the known host has an IP address of 2, the only other valid host in the zero subnet is 1, so the third answer down is the right one for the S0/0 interface of RouterB.

The next clues are the listed number of hosts for each of the LANs. RouterA needs 7 hosts—a block size of 16 (/28). RouterB needs 90 hosts—a block size of 128 (/25). And RouterC needs 23 hosts—a block size of 32 (/27).

Figure 5.9 illustrates this solution.

FIGURE 5.9 Solution to VLSM design example 1

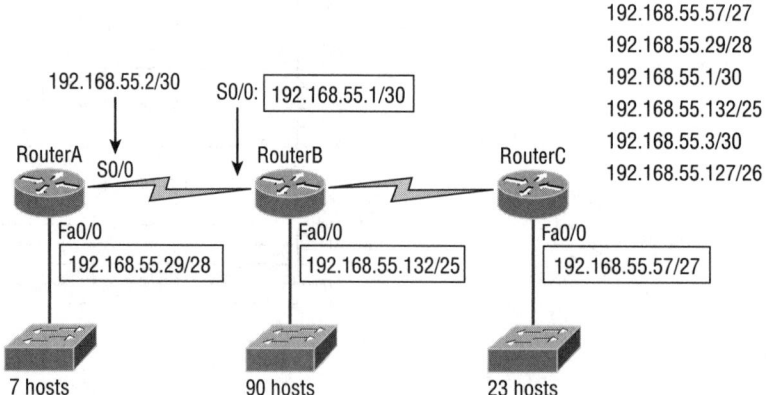

This is actually pretty simple because once you've figured out the block size needed for each LAN, all you need to get to the right solution is to identify proper clues and, of course, know your block sizes well!

One last example of VLSM design before we move on to summarization. Figure 5.10 shows three routers, all running RIPv2. Which Class C addressing scheme would you use to maintain the needs of this network while saving as much address space as possible?

FIGURE 5.10 VLSM design example 2

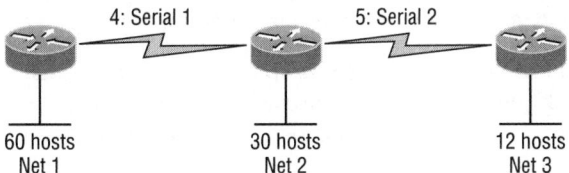

This is actually a pretty clean network design that's just waiting for you to fill out the chart. There are block sizes of 64, 32, and 16 and two block sizes of 4. Coming up with the right solution should be a slam dunk! Take a look at my answer in Figure 5.11.

FIGURE 5.11 Solution to VLSM design example 2

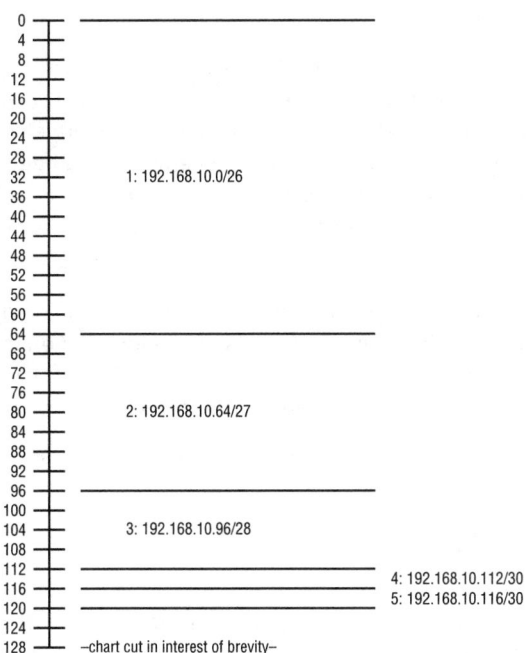

My solution began at subnet 0, and I used the block size of 64. Clearly, I didn't have to go with a block size of 64 because I could've chosen a block size of 4 instead. But I didn't because I usually like to start with the largest block size and move to the smallest. With that done, I added the block sizes of 32 and 16 as well as the two block sizes of 4. This solution is optimal because it still leaves lots of room to add subnets to this network!

Why Bother with VLSM Design?

You have just been hired by a new company and need to add on to their existing network. There are no restrictions to prevent you from starting over with a completely new IP address scheme. Should you use a VLSM classless network or opt for a classful network?

Let's say you happen to have plenty of address space because you're using the Class A 10.0.0.0 private network address, so you really can't imagine that you'd ever run out of IP addresses. So why would you want to bother with the VLSM design process in this environment?

Good question! Here's your answer...

By creating contiguous blocks of addresses to specific areas of your network, you can then easily summarize the network and keep route updates with a routing protocol to a minimum. Why would anyone want to advertise hundreds of networks between buildings when you can just send one summary route between buildings and achieve the same result? This approach will optimize the network's performance dramatically!

To make sure this is clear, let me take a second to explain summary routes. Summarization, also called supernetting, provides route updates in the most efficient way possible by advertising many routes in one advertisement instead of individually. This saves a ton of bandwidth and minimizes router processing. As always, you need to use blocks of addresses to configure your summary routes and watch your network's performance hum along efficiently! And remember, block sizes are used in all sorts of networks anyway.

Still, it's important to understand that summarization works only if you design your network properly. If you carelessly hand out IP subnets to any location on the network, you'll quickly notice that you no longer have any summary boundaries. And you won't get very far creating summary routes without those, so watch your step!

Summarization

Summarization, also called route aggregation, allows routing protocols to advertise many networks as one address. The purpose of this is to reduce the size of routing tables on routers to save memory, which also shortens the amount of time IP requires to parse the routing table when determining the best path to a remote network.

Figure 5.12 shows how a summary address would be used in an internetwork.

FIGURE 5.12   Summary address used in an internetwork

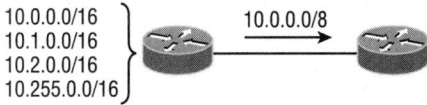

Summarization is pretty straightforward because all you really need to have down is a solid understanding of the block sizes we've been using for subnetting and VLSM design. For example, if you wanted to summarize the following networks into one network advertisement, you just have to find the block size first, which will make it easy to find your answer:

192.168.16.0 through network 192.168.31.0

Okay—so what's the block size? Well, there are exactly 16 Class C networks, which fit neatly into a block size of 16.

Now that we've determined the block size, we just need to find the network address and mask used to summarize these networks into one advertisement. The network address used to advertise the summary address is always the first network address in the block—in this example, 192.168.16.0. To figure out a summary mask, we just need to figure out which mask will get us a block size of 16. If you came up with 240, you got it right! 240 would be placed in the third octet, which is exactly the octet where we're summarizing, so the mask would be 255.255.240.0.

Here's another example:

Networks 172.16.32.0 through 172.16.50.0

This isn't as clean as the previous example because there are two possible answers. Here's why: Since you're starting at network 32, your options for block sizes are 4, 8, 16, 32, 64, etc., and block sizes of 16 and 32 could work as this summary address. Let's explore your two options:

- If you went with a block size of 16, then the network address would be 172.16.32.0 with a mask of 255.255.240.0 (240 provides a block of 16). The problem is that this only summarizes from 32 to 47, which means that networks 48 through 50 would be advertised as single networks. Even so, this could still be a good solution depending on your network design.

- If you decided to go with a block size of 32 instead, then your summary address would still be 172.16.32.0, but the mask would be 255.255.224.0 (224 provides a block of 32). The possible problem with this answer is that it will summarize networks 32 through 63 and we only have networks 32 to 50. No worries if you're planning on adding networks 51 to 63 later into the same network, but you could have serious problems in your internetwork if somehow networks 51 to 63 were to show up and be advertised from somewhere else in your network! So even though this option does allow for growth, it's a lot safer to go with option #1.

Let's take a look at another example: Your summary address is 192.168.144.0/20, so what's the range of host addresses that would be forwarded according to this summary? The /20 provides a summary address of 192.168.144.0 and mask of 255.255.240.0.

The third octet has a block size of 16, and starting at summary address 144, the next block of 16 is 160, so your network summary range is 144 to 159 in the third octet. This is why it comes in handy to be able to count in 16s!

A router with this summary address in the routing table will forward any packet having destination IP addresses of 192.168.144.1 through 192.168.159.254.

Only two more summarization examples, then we'll move on to troubleshooting.

In summarization example 4, Figure 5.13, the Ethernet networks connected to router R1 are being summarized to R2 as 192.168.144.0/20. Which range of IP addresses will R2 forward to R1 according to this summary?

FIGURE 5.13   Summarization example 4

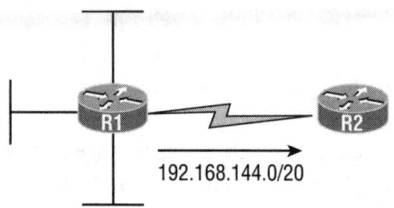

192.168.144.0/20

No worries—solving this is easier than it looks initially. The question actually has the summary address listed in it: 192.168.144.0/20. You already know that /20 is 255.255.240.0, which means you've got a block size of 16 in the third octet. Starting at 144, which is also right there in the question, makes the next block size of 16 equal 160. You can't go above 159 in the third octet, so the IP addresses that will be forwarded are 192.168.144.1 through 192.168.159.254.

Okay, last one. In Figure 5.14, there are five networks connected to router R1. What's the best summary address to R2?

FIGURE 5.14   Summarization example 5

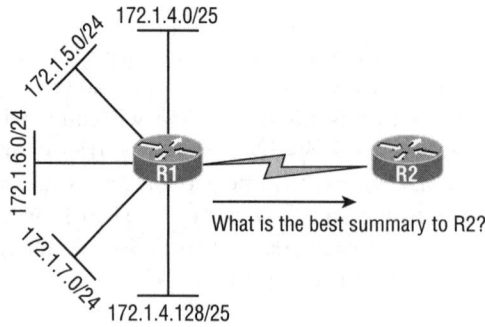

172.1.5.0/24   172.1.4.0/25
172.1.6.0/24
172.1.7.0/24   172.1.4.128/25

What is the best summary to R2?

I'll be honest with you—this is a much harder question than the one in Figure 5.13, so you're going to have to look carefully to see the answer. A good approach here would be to write down all the networks and see if you can find anything in common with all of them:

- 172.1.4.128/25
- 172.1.7.0/24
- 172.1.6.0/24
- 172.1.5.0/24
- 172.1.4.0/25

Do you see an octet that looks interesting to you? I do. It's the third octet. 4, 5, 6, 7, and yes, it's a block size of 4. So you can summarize 172.1.4.0 using a mask of 255.255.252.0, meaning you would use a block size of 4 in the third octet. The IP addresses forwarded with this summary would be 172.1.4.1 through 172.1.7.254.

To summarize the summarization section, if you've nailed down your block sizes, then finding and applying summary addresses and masks is a relatively straightforward task. But you're going to get bogged down pretty quickly if you don't know what a /20 is or if you can't count by 16s!

Troubleshooting IP Addressing

Because running into trouble now and then in networking is a given, being able to trouble-shoot IP addressing is clearly a vital skill. I'm not being negative here—just realistic. The positive side to this is that if you're the one equipped with the tools to diagnose and clear up the inevitable trouble, you get to be the hero when you save the day! Even better? You can usually fix an IP network regardless of whether you're on site or at home!

So this is where I'm going to show you the "Cisco way" of troubleshooting IP addressing. Let's use Figure 5.15 as an example of your basic IP trouble—poor Sally can't log in to the Windows server. Do you deal with this by calling the Microsoft team to tell them their server is a pile of junk and causing all your problems? Though tempting, a better approach is to first double-check and verify your network instead.

FIGURE 5.15   Basic IP troubleshooting

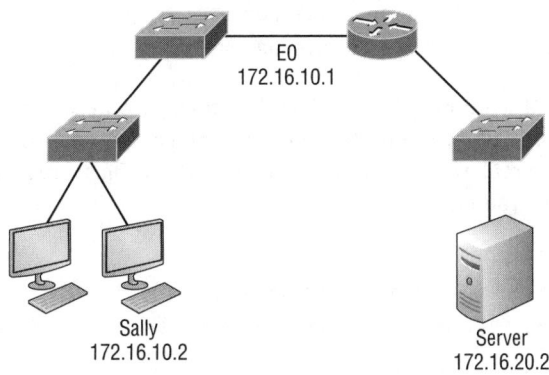

Okay, let's get started by going through the troubleshooting steps that Cisco recommends. They're pretty simple, but important nonetheless. Pretend you're at a customer host and they're complaining that they can't communicate to a server that just happens to be on a remote network. Here are the four troubleshooting steps Cisco recommends:

1. Open a Command window and ping 127.0.0.1. This is the diagnostic, or loopback, address, and if you get a successful ping, your IP stack is considered initialized. If it fails, then you have an IP stack failure and need to reinstall TCP/IP on the host.

    ```
    C:\>ping 127.0.0.1
    Pinging 127.0.0.1 with 32 bytes of data:
    Reply from 127.0.0.1: bytes=32 time<1ms TTL=128
    Reply from 127.0.0.1: bytes=32 time<1ms TTL=128
    Reply from 127.0.0.1: bytes=32 time<1ms TTL=128
    Reply from 127.0.0.1: bytes=32 time<1ms TTL=128
    Ping statistics for 127.0.0.1:
        Packets: Sent &#x0003D; 4, Received = 4, Lost = 0 (0% loss),
    Approximate round trip times in milli-seconds:
        Minimum = 0ms, Maximum = 0ms, Average = 0ms
    ```

2. From the Command window, ping the IP address of the local host (we'll assume correct configuration here, but always check the IP configuration too!). If that's successful, your network interface card (NIC) is functioning. If it fails, there is a problem with the NIC. Success here doesn't just mean that a cable is plugged into the NIC, only that the IP protocol stack on the host can communicate to the NIC via the LAN driver.

    ```
    C:\>ping 172.16.10.2
    Pinging 172.16.10.2 with 32 bytes of data:
    Reply from 172.16.10.2: bytes=32 time<1ms TTL=128
    Reply from 172.16.10.2: bytes=32 time<1ms TTL=128
    Reply from 172.16.10.2: bytes=32 time<1ms TTL=128
    Reply from 172.16.10.2: bytes=32 time<1ms TTL=128
    Ping statistics for 172.16.10.2:
        Packets: Sent = 4, Received = 4, Lost = 0 (0% loss),
    Approximate round trip times in milli-seconds:
        Minimum = 0ms, Maximum = 0ms, Average = 0ms
    ```

3. From the Command window, ping the default gateway (router). If the ping works, it means that the NIC is plugged into the network and can communicate on the local network. If it fails, you have a local physical network problem that could be anywhere from the NIC to the router.

    ```
    C:\>ping 172.16.10.1
    Pinging 172.16.10.1 with 32 bytes of data:
    Reply from 172.16.10.1: bytes=32 time<1ms TTL=128
    ```

```
Reply from 172.16.10.1: bytes=32 time<1ms TTL=128
Reply from 172.16.10.1: bytes=32 time<1ms TTL=128
Reply from 172.16.10.1: bytes=32 time<1ms TTL=128
Ping statistics for 172.16.10.1:
    Packets: Sent = 4, Received = 4, Lost = 0 (0% loss),
Approximate round trip times in milli-seconds:
    Minimum = 0ms, Maximum = 0ms, Average = 0ms
```

4. If steps 1 through 3 were successful, try to ping the remote server. If that works, then you know that you have IP communication between the local host and the remote server. You also know that the remote physical network is working.

```
C:\>ping 172.16.20.2
Pinging 172.16.20.2 with 32 bytes of data:
Reply from 172.16.20.2: bytes=32 time<1ms TTL=128
Reply from 172.16.20.2: bytes=32 time<1ms TTL=128
Reply from 172.16.20.2: bytes=32 time<1ms TTL=128
Reply from 172.16.20.2: bytes=32 time<1ms TTL=128
Ping statistics for 172.16.20.2:
    Packets: Sent = 4, Received = 4, Lost = 0 (0% loss),
Approximate round trip times in milli-seconds:
    Minimum = 0ms, Maximum = 0ms, Average = 0ms
```

If the user still can't communicate with the server after steps 1 through 4 have been completed successfully, you probably have some type of name resolution problem and need to check your Domain Name System (DNS) settings. But if the ping to the remote server fails, then you know you have some type of remote physical network problem and need to go to the server and work through steps 1 through 3 until you find the snag.

Before we move on to determining IP address problems and how to fix them, I just want to mention some basic commands that you can use to help troubleshoot your network from both a PC and a Cisco router. Keep in mind that though these commands may do the same thing, they're implemented differently.

ping   Uses ICMP echo request and replies to test if a node IP stack is initialized and alive on the network.

traceroute   Displays the list of routers on a path to a network destination by using TTL time-outs and ICMP error messages. This command will not work from a command prompt.

tracert   Same function as traceroute, but it's a Microsoft Windows command and will not work on a Cisco router.

arp -a   Displays IP-to-MAC-address mappings on a Windows PC.

show ip arp   Same function as arp -a, but displays the ARP table on a Cisco router. Like the commands traceroute and tracert, arp -a and show ip arp are not interchangeable through DOS and Cisco.

`ipconfig /all` Used only from a Windows command prompt; shows you the PC network configuration.

Once you've gone through all these steps and, if necessary, used the appropriate commands, what do you do when you find a problem? How do you go about fixing an IP address configuration error? Time to cover the next step—determining and fixing the issue at hand!

Determining IP Address Problems

It's common for a host, router, or other network device to be configured with the wrong IP address, subnet mask, or default gateway. Because this happens way too often, you must know how to find and fix IP address configuration errors.

A good way to start is to draw out the network and IP addressing scheme. If that's already been done, consider yourself lucky because though sensible, it's rarely done. Even if it is, it's usually outdated or inaccurate anyway. So either way, it's a good idea to bite the bullet and start from scratch.

I'll show you how a great way to draw out your network using the Cisco Discovery Protocol (CDP) soon, in Chapter 7, "Managing a Cisco Internetwork."

Once you have your network accurately drawn out, including the IP addressing scheme, you need to verify each host's IP address, mask, and default gateway address to establish the problem. Of course, this is assuming that you don't have a physical layer problem, or if you did, that you've already fixed it.

Let's check out the example illustrated in Figure 5.16.

FIGURE 5.16 IP address problem 1

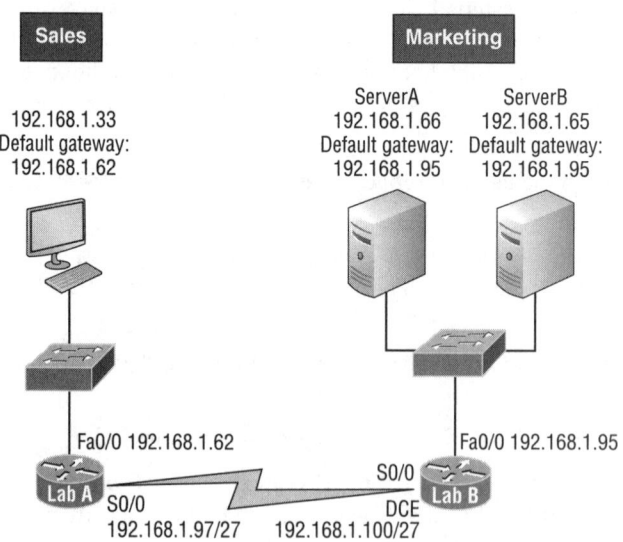

A user in the sales department calls and tells you that she can't get to ServerA in the marketing department. You ask her if she can get to ServerB in the marketing department, but she doesn't know because she doesn't have rights to log on to that server. What do you do?

First, guide your user through the four troubleshooting steps you learned in the preceding section. Okay—let's say steps 1 through 3 work but step 4 fails. By looking at the figure, can you determine the problem? Look for clues in the network drawing. First, the WAN link between the Lab A router and the Lab B router shows the mask as a /27. You should already know that this mask is 255.255.255.224 and determine that all networks are using this mask. The network address is 192.168.1.0. What are our valid subnets and hosts? 256 – 224 = 32, so this makes our subnets 0, 32, 64, 96, 128, etc. So, by looking at the figure, you can see that subnet 32 is being used by the sales department. The WAN link is using subnet 96, and the marketing department is using subnet 64.

Now you've got to establish what the valid host ranges are for each subnet. From what you learned at the beginning of this chapter, you should now be able to easily determine the subnet address, broadcast addresses, and valid host ranges. The valid hosts for the Sales LAN are 33 through 62, and the broadcast address is 63 because the next subnet is 64, right? For the Marketing LAN, the valid hosts are 65 through 94 (broadcast 95), and for the WAN link, 97 through 126 (broadcast 127). By closely examining the figure, you can determine that the default gateway on the Lab B router is incorrect. That address is the broadcast address for subnet 64, so there's no way it could be a valid host!

If you tried to configure that address on the Lab B router interface, you'd receive a bad mask error. Cisco routers don't let you type in subnet and broadcast addresses as valid hosts!

Did you get all that? Let's try another one to make sure. Figure 5.17 shows a network problem.

FIGURE 5.17 IP address problem 2

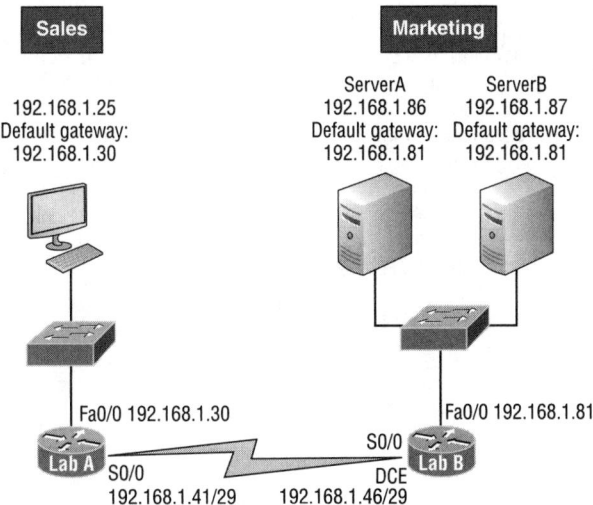

A user in the Sales LAN can't get to ServerB. You have the user run through the four basic troubleshooting steps and find that the host can communicate to the local network but not to the remote network. Find and define the IP addressing problem.

If you went through the same steps used to solve the last problem, you can see that first, the WAN link again provides the subnet mask to use— /29, or 255.255.255.248. Assuming classful addressing, you need to determine what the valid subnets, broadcast addresses, and valid host ranges are to solve this problem.

The 248 mask is a block size of 8 (256 − 248 = 8, as discussed in Chapter 4), so the subnets both start and increment in multiples of 8. By looking at the figure, you see that the Sales LAN is in the 24 subnet, the WAN is in the 40 subnet, and the Marketing LAN is in the 80 subnet. Can you see the problem yet? The valid host range for the Sales LAN is 25–30, and the configuration appears correct. The valid host range for the WAN link is 41–46, and this also appears correct. The valid host range for the 80 subnet is 81–86, with a broadcast address of 87 because the next subnet is 88. ServerB has been configured with the broadcast address of the subnet.

Okay, now that you can figure out misconfigured IP addresses on hosts, what do you do if a host doesn't have an IP address and you need to assign one? What you need to do is scrutinize the other hosts on the LAN and figure out the network, mask, and default gateway. Let's take a look at a couple of examples of how to find and apply valid IP addresses to hosts.

You need to assign a server and router IP addresses on a LAN. The subnet assigned on that segment is 192.168.20.24/29. The router needs to be assigned the first usable address and the server needs the last valid host ID. What is the IP address, mask, and default gateway assigned to the server?

To answer this, you must know that a /29 is a 255.255.255.248 mask, which provides a block size of 8. The subnet is known as 24, the next subnet in a block of 8 is 32, so the broadcast address of the 24 subnet is 31 and the valid host range is 25–30.

Server IP address: 192.168.20.30

Server mask: 255.255.255.248

Default gateway: 192.168.20.25 (router's IP address)

Take a look at Figure 5.18 and solve this problem.

FIGURE 5.18   Find the valid host #1

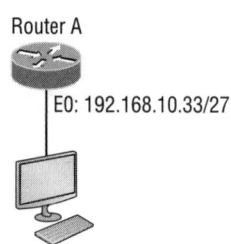

Router A

E0: 192.168.10.33/27

Look at the router's IP address on Ethernet0. What IP address, subnet mask, and valid host range could be assigned to the host?

The IP address of the router's Ethernet0 is 192.168.10.33/27. As you already know, a /27 is a 224 mask with a block size of 32. The router's interface is in the 32 subnet. The next subnet is 64, so that makes the broadcast address of the 32 subnet 63 and the valid host range 33–62.

Host IP address: 192.168.10.34–62 (any address in the range except for 33, which is assigned to the router)

Mask: 255.255.255.224

Default gateway: 192.168.10.33

Figure 5.19 shows two routers with Ethernet configurations already assigned. What are the host addresses and subnet masks of HostA and HostB?

FIGURE 5.19   Find the valid host #2

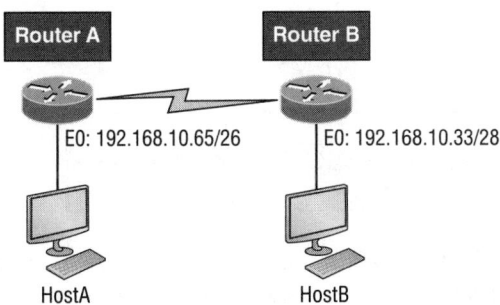

Router A has an IP address of 192.168.10.65/26 and Router B has an IP address of 192.168.10.33/28. What are the host configurations? Router A Ethernet0 is in the 192.168.10.64 subnet and Router B Ethernet0 is in the 192.168.10.32 network.

Host A IP address: 192.168.10.66–126

Host A mask: 255.255.255.192

Host A default gateway: 192.168.10.65

Host B IP address: 192.168.10.34–46

Host B mask: 255.255.255.240

Host B default gateway: 192.168.10.33

Just a couple more examples before you can put this chapter behind you—hang in there!

Figure 5.20 shows two routers. You need to configure the S0/0 interface on RouterA. The IP address assigned to the serial link is 172.16.17.0/22. What IP address can be assigned?

FIGURE 5.20   Find the valid host address #3

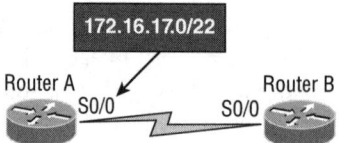

First, know that a /22 CIDR is 255.255.252.0, which makes a block size of 4 in the third octet. Since 17 is listed, the available range is 16.1 through 19.254, so in this example, the IP address S0/0 could be 172.16.18.255 since that's within the range.

Okay, last one! You need to find a classful network address that has one Class C network ID and you need to provide one usable subnet per city while allowing enough usable host addresses for each city specified in Figure 5.21. What is your mask?

FIGURE 5.21   Find the valid subnet mask

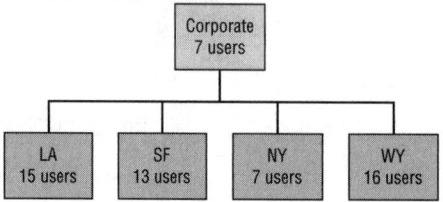

Actually, this is probably the easiest thing you've done all day! I count 5 subnets needed, and the Wyoming office needs 16 users—always look for the network that needs the most hosts! What block size is needed for the Wyoming office? Your answer is 32. You can't use a block size of 16 because you always have to subtract 2. What mask provides you with a block size of 32? 224 is your answer because this provides 8 subnets, each with 30 hosts.

You're done—the diva has sung and the chicken has safely crossed the road...whew! Time to take a break, but skip the shot and the beer if that's what you had in mind because you need to have your head straight to go through the written lab and review questions next!

Summary

Again, if you got to this point without getting lost along the way a few times, you're awesome, but if you did get lost, don't stress because most people do! Just be patient with yourself and go back over the material that tripped you up until it's all crystal clear. You'll get there!

This chapter provided you with keys to understanding the oh-so-very-important topic of variable length subnet masks. You should also know how to design and implement simple VLSM networks and be clear on summarization as well.

And make sure you understand and memorize Cisco's troubleshooting methods. You must remember the four steps that Cisco recommends to take when trying to narrow down exactly where a network and/or IP addressing problem is and then know how to proceed systematically to fix it. In addition, you should be able to find valid IP addresses and subnet masks by looking at a network diagram.

Exam Essentials

Describe the benefits of variable length subnet masks (VLSMs).   VLSMs enable the creation of subnets of specific sizes and allow the division of a classless network into smaller networks that do not need to be equal in size. This makes use of the address space more efficient because many times IP addresses are wasted with classful subnetting.

Understand the relationship between the subnet mask value and the resulting block size and the allowable IP addresses in each resulting subnet.   The relationship between the classful network being subdivided and the subnet mask used determines the number of possible hosts or the block size. It also determines where each subnet begins and ends and which IP addresses cannot be assigned to a host within each subnet.

Describe the process of summarization or route aggregation and its relationship to subnetting.   Summarization is the combining of subnets derived from a classful network for the purpose of advertising a single route to neighboring routers instead of multiple routes, reducing the size of routing tables and speeding the route process.

Calculate the summary mask that will advertise a single network representing all subnets.   The network address used to advertise the summary address is always the first network address in the block of subnets. The mask is the subnet mask value that yields the same block size.

Remember the four diagnostic steps.   The four simple steps that Cisco recommends for troubleshooting are ping the loopback address, ping the NIC, ping the default gateway, and ping the remote device.

Identify and mitigate an IP addressing problem.   Once you go through the four troubleshooting steps that Cisco recommends, you must be able to determine the IP addressing problem by drawing out the network and finding the valid and invalid hosts addressed in your network.

Understand the troubleshooting tools that you can use from your host and a Cisco router.   The ping 127.0.0.1 command tests your local IP stack, and tracert is a Windows command to track the path a packet takes through an internetwork to a destination. Cisco routers use the command traceroute, or just trace for short. Don't confuse the Windows and Cisco commands. Although they produce the same output, they don't work from the same prompts. The command ipconfig /all will display your PC network configuration from a DOS prompt, and arp -a (again from a DOS prompt) will display IP-to-MAC-address mapping on a Windows PC.

Written Lab 5

In this section, you'll complete the following lab to make sure you've got the information and concepts contained within them fully dialed in:

Lab 5.1: Summarization Practice

You can find the answers to this lab in Appendix A, "Answers to Written Labs."

Lab 5.1: Summarization Practice

For each of the following sets of networks, determine the summary address and the mask to be used that will summarize the subnets.

1. 192.168.1.0/24 through 192.168.12.0/24
2. 172.144.0.0 through 172.159.0.0
3. 192.168.32.0 through 192.168.63.0
4. 192.168.96.0 through 192.168.111.0
5. 66.66.0.0 through 66.66.15.0
6. 192.168.1.0 through 192.168.120.0
7. 172.16.1.0 through 172.16.7.0
8. 192.168.128.0 through 192.168.190.0
9. 53.60.96.0 through 53.60.127.0
10. 172.16.10.0 through 172.16.63.0

Review Questions

 The following questions are designed to test your understanding of this chapter's material. For more information on how to get additional questions, please see www.lammle.com/ccna.

You can find the answers to these questions in Appendix B, "Answers to Review Questions."

1. On a VLSM network, which mask should you use on point-to-point WAN links in order to reduce the waste of IP addresses?

   A. /27

   B. /28

   C. /29

   D. /30

   E. /31

2. In the network shown in the diagram, how many computers could be in Network B?

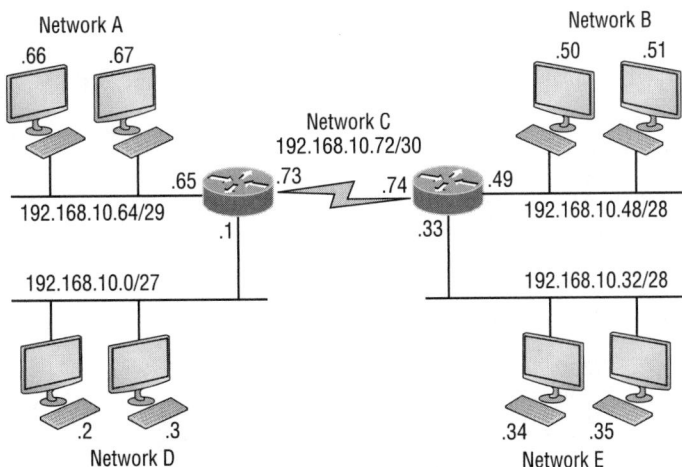

   A. 6

   B. 12

   C. 14

   D. 30

3. In the following diagram, in order to have IP addressing that's as efficient as possible, which network should use a /29 mask?

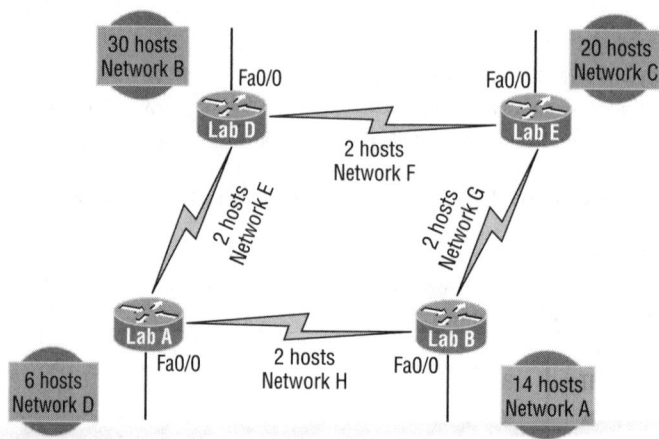

   A. A

   B. B

   C. C

   D. D

4. To use VLSM, what capability must the routing protocols in use possess?

   A. Support for multicast

   B. Multiprotocol support

   C. Transmission of subnet mask information

   D. Support for unequal load balancing

5. What summary address would cover all the networks shown and advertise a single, efficient route to Router B that won't advertise more networks than needed?

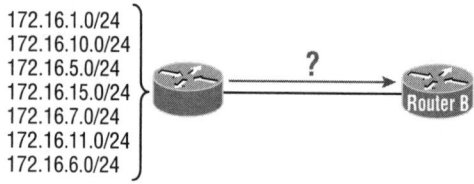

   A. 172.16.0.0/24

   B. 172.16.1.0/24

   C. 172.16.0.0/24

   D. 172.16.0.0/20

   E. 172.16.16.0/28

   F. 172.16.0.0/27

6. In the following diagram, what is the most likely reason the station cannot ping outside of its network?

Router A

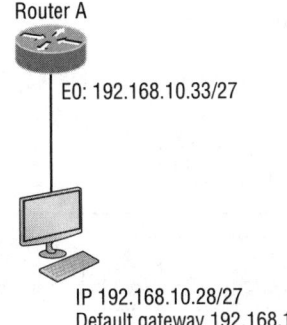

E0: 192.168.10.33/27

IP 192.168.10.28/27
Default gateway 192.168.10.33/27

   A. The IP address is incorrect on interface E0 of the router.

   B. The default gateway address is incorrect on the station.

   C. The IP address on the station is incorrect.

   D. The router is malfunctioning.

7. If a host is configured with an incorrect default gateway and all the other computers and router are known to be configured correctly, which of the following statements is TRUE?

   A. Host A cannot communicate with the router.

   B. Host A can communicate with other hosts in the same subnet.

   C. Host A can communicate with hosts in other subnets.

   D. Host A can communicate with no other systems.

8. Which of the following troubleshooting steps, if completed successfully, also confirms that the other steps will succeed as well?

   A. Ping a remote computer.

   B. Ping the loopback address.

   C. Ping the NIC.

   D. Ping the default gateway.

9. When a ping to the local host IP address fails, what can you assume?

   A. The IP address of the local host is incorrect.

   B. The IP address of the remote host is incorrect.

   C. The NIC is not functional.

   D. The IP stack has failed to initialize.

10. When a ping to the local host IP address succeeds but a ping to the default gateway IP address fails, what can you rule out? (Choose all that apply.)

   A. The IP address of the local host is incorrect.

   B. The IP address of the gateway is incorrect.

   C. The NIC is not functional.

   D. The IP stack has failed to initialize.

11. Which of the networks in the diagram could use a /29 mask?

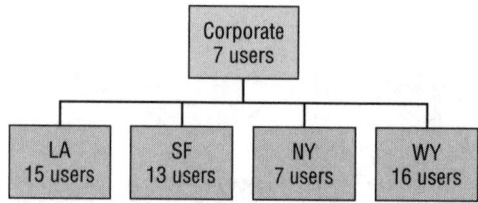

   A. Corporate

   B. LA

   C. SF

   D. NY

   E. None

12. What network service is the most likely problem if you can ping a computer by IP address but not by name?

   A. DNS

   B. DHCP

   C. ARP

   D. ICMP

13. When you issue the ping command, what protocol are you using?

   A. DNS

   B. DHCP

   C. ARP

   D. ICMP

14. Which of the following commands displays the networks traversed on a path to a network destination?

   A. ping

   B. traceroute

   C. pingroute

   D. pathroute

15. What command generated the output shown below?

```
Reply from 172.16.10.2: bytes=32 time<1ms TTL=128
Reply from 172.16.10.2: bytes=32 time<1ms TTL=128
Reply from 172.16.10.2: bytes=32 time<1ms TTL=128
Reply from 172.16.10.2: bytes=32 time<1ms TTL=128
```

   A. traceroute

   B. show ip route

   C. ping

   D. pathping

16. In the work area, match the command to its function on the right.

traceroute	=	Displays the list of routers on a path to a network destination
arp -	=	Displays IP-to_MAC
show ip arp	=	Cisco router ARP table
ipconfig /asll	=	PC Net config

17. Which of the following network addresses correctly summarizes the three networks shown below efficiently?

10.0.0.0/16

10.1.0.0/16

10.2.0.0/16

   A. 10.0.0.0/15

   B. 10.1.0.0/8

   C. 10.0.0.0/14

   D. 10.0.0.8/16

18. What command displays the ARP table on a Cisco router?

   A. show ip arp

   B. traceroute

   C. arp -a

   D. tracert

19. What switch must be added to the `ipconfig` command on a PC to verify DNS configuration?

   A. /dns

   B. -dns

   C. /all

   D. showall

20. Which of the following is the best summarization of the following networks: 192.168.128.0 through 192.168.159.0?

   A. 192.168.0.0/24

   B. 192.168.128.0/16

   C. 192.168.128.0/19

   D. 192.168.128.0/20

Chapter

6

Cisco's Internetworking Operating System (IOS)

THE FOLLOWING ICND1 EXAM TOPICS ARE COVERED IN THIS CHAPTER:

- ✓ 2.0 LAN Switching Technologies

- ✓ 2.3 Troubleshoot interface and cable issues (collisions, errors, duplex, speed)

- ✓ 5.0 Infrastructure Management

- ✓ 5.3 Configure and verify initial device configuration

- ✓ 5.4 Configure, verify, and troubleshoot basic device hardening

- ✓ 5.4.a Local authentication

- ✓ 5.4.b Secure password

- ✓ 5.4.c Access to device

  - 5.4.c. (i) Voice

  - 5.4.c. (ii) Video

- ✓ 5.4.c. (iii) Data

- ✓ 5.4.d Source address Telnet/SSH

- ✓ 5.4.e Login banner

- ✓ 5.6 Use Cisco IOS tools to troubleshoot and resolve problems

  - 5.6.a Ping and traceroute with extended option

  - 5.6.b Terminal monitor

  - 5.6.c Log events

It's time to introduce you to the Cisco Internetwork Operating System (IOS). The IOS is what runs Cisco routers as well as Cisco's switches, and it's also what we use to configure these devices.

So that's what you're going to learn about in this chapter. I'm going to show you how to configure a Cisco IOS device using the Cisco IOS command-line interface (CLI). Once proficient with this interface, you'll be able to configure hostnames, banners, passwords, and more as well as troubleshoot skillfully using the Cisco IOS.

We'll also begin the journey to mastering the basics of router and switch configurations plus command verifications in this chapter.

I'll start with a basic IOS switch to begin building the network we'll use throughout this book for configuration examples. Don't forget—I'll be using both switches and routers throughout this chapter, and we configure these devices pretty much the same way. Things diverge when we get to the interfaces where the differences between the two become key, so pay attention closely when we get to that point!

Just as it was with preceding chapters, the fundamentals presented in this chapter are important building blocks to have solidly in place before moving on to the more advanced material coming up in the next ones.

To find up-to-the minute updates for this chapter, please see www.lammle .com/ccna or the book's web page at www.sybex.com/go/ccna.

The IOS User Interface

The *Cisco Internetwork Operating System (IOS)* is the kernel of Cisco routers as well as all current Catalyst switches. In case you didn't know, a kernel is the elemental, indispensable part of an operating system that allocates resources and manages tasks like low-level hardware interfaces and security.

Coming up, I'll show you the Cisco IOS and how to configure a Cisco switch using the *command-line interface (CLI)*. By using the CLI, we can provide access to a Cisco device and provide voice, video, and data service. … The configurations you'll see in this chapter are exactly the same as they are on a Cisco router.

Cisco IOS

The Cisco IOS is a proprietary kernel that provides routing, switching, internetworking, and telecommunications features. The first IOS was written by William Yeager in 1986 and enabled networked applications. It runs on most Cisco routers as well as a growing number of Cisco Catalyst switches, like the Catalyst 2960 and 3560 series switches used in this book. And it's an essential for the Cisco exam objectives!

Here's a short list of some important things that the Cisco router IOS software is responsible for:

- Carrying network protocols and functions
- Connecting high-speed traffic between devices
- Adding security to control access and stopping unauthorized network use
- Providing scalability for ease of network growth and redundancy
- Supplying network reliability for connecting to network resources

You can access the Cisco IOS through the console port of a router or switch, from a modem into the auxiliary (or aux) port on a router, or even through Telnet and Secure Shell (SSH). Access to the IOS command line is called an *EXEC session*.

Connecting to a Cisco IOS Device

We connect to a Cisco device to configure it, verify its configuration, and check statistics, and although there are different approaches to this, the first place you would usually connect to is the console port. The *console port* is usually an RJ45, 8-pin modular connection located at the back of the device, and there may or may not be a password set on it by default.

Look back into Chapter 2, "Ethernet Networking and Data Encapsulation," to review how to configure a PC and enable it to connect to a router console port.

You can also connect to a Cisco router through an *auxiliary port*, which is really the same thing as a console port, so it follows that you can use it as one. The main difference with an auxiliary port is that it also allows you to configure modem commands so that a modem can be connected to the router. This is a cool feature because it lets you dial up a remote router and attach to the auxiliary port if the router is down and you need to configure it remotely, *out-of-band*. One of the differences between Cisco routers and switches is that switches do not have an auxiliary port.

The third way to connect to a Cisco device is *in-band*, through the program *Telnet* or *Secure Shell (SSH)*. In-band means configuring the device via the network, the opposite of *out-of-band*. We covered Telnet and SSH in Chapter 3, "Introduction to TCP/IP," and in this chapter, I'll show you how to configure access to both of these protocols on a Cisco device.

Figure 6.1 shows an illustration of a Cisco 2960 switch. Really focus in on all the different kinds of interfaces and connections! On the right side is the 10/100/1000 uplink. You can use either the UTP port or the fiber port, but not both at the same time.

FIGURE 6.1 A Cisco 2960 switch

The 3560 switch I'll be using in this book looks a lot like the 2960, but it can perform layer 3 switching, unlike the 2960, which is limited to only layer 2 functions.

I also want to take a moment and tell you about the 2800 series router because that's the router series I'll be using in this book. This router is known as an Integrated Services Router (ISR) and Cisco has updated it to the 2900 series, but I still have plenty of 2800 series routers in my production networks. Figure 6.2 shows a new 1900 series router. The new ISR series of routers are nice; they are so named because many services, like security, are built into them. The ISR series router is a modular device, much faster and a lot sleeker than the older 2600 series routers, and it's elegantly designed to support a broad new range of interface options. The new ISR series router can offer multiple serial interfaces, which can be used for connecting a T1 using a serial V.35 WAN connection. And multiple Fast Ethernet or Gigabit Ethernet ports can be used on the router, depending on the model. This router also has one console via an RJ45 connector and another through the USB port. There is also an auxiliary connection to allow a console connection via a remote modem.

FIGURE 6.2 A new Cisco 1900 router

You need to keep in mind that for the most part, you get some serious bang for your buck with the 2800/2900—unless you start adding a bunch of interfaces to it. You've got to pony up for each one of those little beauties, so this can really start to add up and fast!

A couple of other series of routers that will set you back a lot less than the 2800 series are the 1800/1900s, so look into these routers if you want a less-expensive alternative to the 2800/2900 but still want to run the same IOS.

So even though I'm going to be using mostly 2800 series routers and 2960/3560 switches throughout this book to demonstrate examples of IOS configurations, I want to point out that the particular *router* model you use to practice for the Cisco exam isn't really important. The *switch* types are, though—you definitely need a couple 2960 switches as well as a 3560 switch if you want to measure up to the exam objectives!

You can find more information about all Cisco routers at www.cisco.com/en/US/products/hw/routers/index.html.

Bringing Up a Switch

When you first bring up a Cisco IOS device, it will run a power-on self-test—a POST. Upon passing that, the machine will look for and then load the Cisco IOS from flash memory if an IOS file is present, then expand it into RAM. As you probably know, flash memory is electronically erasable programmable read-only memory—an EEPROM. The next step is for the IOS to locate and load a valid configuration known as the startup-config that will be stored in *nonvolatile RAM (NVRAM)*.

Once the IOS is loaded and up and running, the startup-config will be copied from NVRAM into RAM and from then on referred to as the running-config.

But if a valid startup-config isn't found in NVRAM, your switch will enter setup mode, giving you a step-by-step dialog to help configure some basic parameters on it.

You can also enter setup mode at any time from the command line by typing the command **setup** from privileged mode, which I'll get to in a minute. Setup mode only covers some basic commands and generally isn't really all that helpful. Here's an example:

```
Would you like to enter the initial configuration dialog? [yes/no]: y

At any point you may enter a question mark '?' for help.
Use ctrl-c to abort configuration dialog at any prompt.
Default settings are in square brackets '[]'.


Basic management setup configures only enough connectivity
for management of the system, extended setup will ask you
to configure each interface on the system

Would you like to enter basic management setup? [yes/no]: y
Configuring global parameters:

  Enter host name [Switch]: Ctrl+C
Configuration aborted, no changes made.
```

> You can exit setup mode at any time by pressing Ctrl+C.

I highly recommend going through setup mode once, then never again because you should always use the CLI instead!

Command-Line Interface (CLI)

I sometimes refer to the CLI as "cash line interface" because the ability to create advanced configurations on Cisco routers and switches using the CLI will earn you some decent cash!

Entering the CLI

After the interface status messages appear and you press Enter, the Switch> prompt will pop up. This is called *user exec mode*, or user mode for short, and although it's mostly used to view statistics, it is also a stepping stone along the way to logging in to *privileged exec mode*, called privileged mode for short.

You can view and change the configuration of a Cisco router only while in privileged mode, and you enter it via the enable command like this:

```
Switch>enable
Switch#
```

The Switch# prompt signals you're in privileged mode where you can both view and change the switch configuration. You can go back from privileged mode into user mode by using the disable command:

```
Switch#disable
Switch>
```

You can type **logout** from either mode to exit the console:

```
Switch>logout
Switch con0 is now available
Press RETURN to get started.
```

Next, I'll show how to perform some basic administrative configurations.

Overview of Router Modes

To configure from a CLI, you can make global changes to the router by typing **configure terminal** or just **config t**. This will get you into global configuration mode where you can make changes to the running-config. Commands run from global configuration mode are predictably referred to as global commands, and they are typically set only once and affect the entire router.

Type **config** from the privileged-mode prompt and then press Enter to opt for the default of terminal like this:

```
Switch#config
Configuring from terminal, memory, or network [terminal]? [press enter]
Enter configuration commands, one per line.  End with CNTL/Z.
Switch(config)#
```

At this point, you make changes that affect the router as a whole (globally), hence the term *global configuration mode*. For instance, to change the running-config—the current configuration running in dynamic RAM (DRAM)—use the configure terminal command, as I just demonstrated.

CLI Prompts

Let's explore the different prompts you'll encounter when configuring a switch or router now, because knowing them well will really help you orient yourself and recognize exactly where you are at any given time while in configuration mode. I'm going to demonstrate some of the prompts used on a Cisco switch and cover the various terms used along the way. Make sure you're very familiar with them, and always check your prompts before making any changes to a router's configuration!

We're not going to venture into every last obscure command prompt you could potentially come across in the configuration mode world because that would get us deep into territory that's beyond the scope of this book. Instead, I'm going to focus on the prompts you absolutely must know to pass the exam plus the very handy and seriously vital ones you'll need and use the most in real-life networking—the cream of the crop.

Don't freak! It's not important that you understand exactly what each of these command prompts accomplishes just yet because I'm going to completely fill you in on all of them really soon. For now, relax and focus on just becoming familiar with the different prompts available and all will be well!

Interfaces

To make changes to an interface, you use the `interface` command from global configuration mode:

```
Switch(config)#interface ?
  Async           Async interface
  BVI             Bridge-Group Virtual Interface
  CTunnel         CTunnel interface
  Dialer          Dialer interface
  FastEthernet    FastEthernet IEEE 802.3
  Filter          Filter interface
  Filtergroup     Filter Group interface
  GigabitEthernet GigabitEthernet IEEE 802.3z
  Group-Async     Async Group interface
  Lex             Lex interface
  Loopback        Loopback interface
  Null            Null interface
  Port-channel    Ethernet Channel of interfaces
  Portgroup       Portgroup interface
  Pos-channel     POS Channel of interfaces
  Tunnel          Tunnel interface
```

```
  Vif              PGM Multicast Host interface
  Virtual-Template  Virtual Template interface
  Virtual-TokenRing  Virtual TokenRing
  Vlan             Catalyst Vlans
  fcpa             Fiber Channel
  range            interface range command
Switch(config)#interface fastEthernet 0/1
Switch(config-if)#)
```

Did you notice that the prompt changed to Switch(config-if)#? This tells you that you're in *interface configuration mode*. And wouldn't it be nice if the prompt also gave you an indication of what interface you were configuring? Well, at least for now we'll have to live without the prompt information, because it doesn't. But it should already be clear to you that you really need to pay attention when configuring an IOS device!

Line Commands

To configure user-mode passwords, use the line command. The prompt then becomes Switch(config-line)#:

```
Switch(config)#line ?
  <0-16>   First Line number
  console  Primary terminal line
  vty      Virtual terminal
Switch(config)#line console 0
Switch(config-line)#
```

The line console 0 command is a global command, and sometimes you'll also hear people refer to global commands as major commands. In this example, any command typed from the (config-line) prompt is known as a subcommand.

Access List Configurations

To configure a standard named access list, you'll need to get to the prompt Switch(config-std-nacl)#:

```
Switch#config t
Switch(config)#ip access-list standard Todd
Switch(config-std-nacl)#
```

What you see here is a typical basic standard ACL prompt. There are various ways to configure access lists, and the prompts are only slightly different from this particular example.

Routing Protocol Configurations

I need to point out that we don't use routing or router protocols on 2960 switches, but we can and will use them on my 3560 switches. Here is an example of configuring routing on a layer 3 switch:

```
Switch(config)#router rip
IP routing not enabled
Switch(config)#ip routing
Switch(config)#router rip
Switch(config-router)#
```

Did you notice that the prompt changed to Switch(config-router)#? To make sure you achieve the objectives specific to the Cisco exam and this book, I'll configure static routing, RIPv2, and RIPng. And don't worry—I'll explain all of these in detail soon, in Chapter 9, "IP Routing," and Chapter 14, "Internet Protocol Version 6 (IPv6)"!

Defining Router Terms

Table 6.1 defines some of the terms I've used so far.

TABLE 6.1   Router terms

Mode	Definition
User exec mode	Limited to basic monitoring commands
Privileged exec mode	Provides access to all other router commands
Global configuration mode	Commands that affect the entire system
Specific configuration modes	Commands that affect interfaces/processes only
Setup mode	Interactive configuration dialog

Editing and Help Features

The Cisco advanced editing features can also help you configure your router. If you type in a question mark (?) at any prompt, you'll be given a list of all the commands available from that prompt:

```
Switch#?
Exec commands:
  access-enable    Create a temporary Access-List entry
  access-template  Create a temporary Access-List entry
  archive          manage archive files
  cd               Change current directory
  clear            Reset functions
  clock            Manage the system clock
  cns              CNS agents
```

```
configure        Enter configuration mode
connect          Open a terminal connection
copy             Copy from one file to another
debug            Debugging functions (see also 'undebug')
delete           Delete a file
diagnostic       Diagnostic commands
dir              List files on a filesystem
disable          Turn off privileged commands
disconnect       Disconnect an existing network connection
dot1x            IEEE 802.1X Exec Commands
enable           Turn on privileged commands
eou              EAPoUDP
erase            Erase a filesystem
exit             Exit from the EXEC
--More-- ?
Press RETURN for another line, SPACE for another page, anything else to quit
```

And if this is not enough information for you, you can press the spacebar to get another whole page of information, or you can press Enter to go one command at a time. You can also press Q, or any other key for that matter, to quit and return to the prompt. Notice that I typed a question mark (?) at the more prompt and it told me what my options were from that prompt.

Here's a shortcut: To find commands that start with a certain letter, use the letter and the question mark with no space between them, like this:

```
Switch#c?
cd        clear  clock  cns  configure
connect   copy
Switch#c
```

Okay, see that? By typing **c?**, I got a response listing all the commands that start with *c*. Also notice that the Switch#**c** prompt reappears after the list of commands is displayed. This can be really helpful when you happen to be working with long commands but you're short on patience and still need the next possible one. It would get old fast if you actually had to retype the entire command every time you used a question mark!

So with that, let's find the next command in a string by typing the first command and then a question mark:

```
Switch#clock ?
  set  Set the time and date

Switch#clock set ?
  hh:mm:ss  Current Time

Switch#clock set 2:34 ?
% Unrecognized command
```

```
Switch#clock set 2:34:01 ?
  <1-31>  Day of the month
  MONTH   Month of the year

Switch#clock set 2:34:01 21 july ?
  <1993-2035>  Year

Switch#clock set 2:34:01 21 august 2013
Switch#
00:19:45: %SYS-6-CLOCKUPDATE: System clock has been updated from 00:19:45
UTC Mon Mar 1 1993 to 02:34:01 UTC Wed Aug 21 2013, configured from console
by console.
```

I entered the **clock ?** command and got a list of the next possible parameters plus what they do. Make note of the fact that you can just keep typing a command, a space, and then a question mark until <cr> (carriage return) is your only option left.

And if you're typing commands and receive

```
Switch#clock set 11:15:11
% Incomplete command.
```

no worries—that's only telling you that the command string simply isn't complete quite yet. All you need to do is to press the up arrow key to redisplay the last command entered and then continue with the command by using your question mark.

But if you get the error

```
Switch(config)#access-list 100 permit host 1.1.1.1 host 2.2.2.2
                                          ^
% Invalid input detected at '^' marker.
```

all is not well because it means you actually have entered a command incorrectly. See that little caret—the ^? It's a very helpful tool that marks the exact point where you blew it and made a mess.

Here's another example of when you'll see that caret:

```
Switch#sh fastethernet 0/0
         ^
% Invalid input detected at '^' marker.
```

This command looks right, but be careful! The problem is that the full command is show interface fastethernet 0/0.

Now if you receive the error

```
Switch#sh cl
% Ambiguous command:  "sh cl"
```

you're being told that there are multiple commands that begin with the string you entered and it's not unique. Use the question mark to find the exact command you need:

```
Switch#sh cl?
class-map  clock  cluster
```

Case in point: There are three commands that start with show cl.

Table 6.2 lists the enhanced editing commands available on a Cisco router.

TABLE 6.2   Enhanced editing commands

Command	Meaning
Ctrl+A	Moves your cursor to the beginning of the line
Ctrl+E	Moves your cursor to the end of the line
Esc+B	Moves back one word
Ctrl+B	Moves back one character
Ctrl+F	Moves forward one character
Esc+F	Moves forward one word
Ctrl+D	Deletes a single character
Backspace	Deletes a single character
Ctrl+R	Redisplays a line
Ctrl+U	Erases a line
Ctrl+W	Erases a word
Ctrl+Z	Ends configuration mode and returns to EXEC
Tab	Finishes typing a command for you

Another really cool editing feature you need to know about is the automatic scrolling of long lines. In the following example, the command I typed reached the right margin and automatically moved 11 spaces to the left. How do I know this? Because the dollar sign [$] is telling me that the line has been scrolled to the left:

```
Switch#config t
Switch(config)#$ 100 permit ip host 192.168.10.1 192.168.10.0 0.0.0.255
```

You can review the router-command history with the commands shown in Table 6.3.

TABLE 6.3   IOS-command history

Command	Meaning
Ctrl+P or up arrow	Shows last command entered
Ctrl+N or down arrow	Shows previous commands entered
show history	Shows last 20 commands entered by default
show terminal	Shows terminal configurations and history buffer size
terminal history size	Changes buffer size (max 256)

The following example demonstrates the show history command as well as how to change the history's size. It also shows how to verify the history with the show terminal command. First, use the show history command, which will allow you to see the last 20 commands that were entered on the router (even though my particular router reveals only 10 commands because that's all I've entered since rebooting it). Check it out:

```
Switch#sh history
  sh fastethernet 0/0
  sh ru
  sh cl
  config t
  sh history
  sh flash
  sh running-config
  sh startup-config
  sh ver
  sh history
```

Okay—now, we'll use the show terminal command to verify the terminal history size:

```
Switch#sh terminal
Line 0, Location: "", Type: ""
Length: 24 lines, Width: 80 columns
Baud rate (TX/RX) is 9600/9600, no parity, 2 stopbits, 8 databits
Status: PSI Enabled, Ready, Active, Ctrl-c Enabled, Automore On
  0x40000
Capabilities: none
Modem state: Ready
```

```
[output cut]
Modem type is unknown.
Session limit is not set.
Time since activation: 00:17:22
Editing is enabled.
History is enabled, history size is 10.
DNS resolution in show commands is enabled
Full user help is disabled
Allowed input transports are none.
Allowed output transports are telnet.
Preferred transport is telnet.
No output characters are padded
No special data dispatching characters
```

When Should I Use the Cisco Editing Features?

You'll find yourself using a couple of editing features quite often and some not so much, if at all. Understand that Cisco didn't make these up; these are just old Unix commands! Even so, Ctrl+A is still a really helpful way to negate a command.

For example, if you were to put in a long command and then decide you didn't want to use that command in your configuration after all, or if it didn't work, then you could just press your up arrow key to show the last command entered, press Ctrl+A, type **no** and then a space, press Enter—and poof! The command is negated. This doesn't work on every command, but it works on a lot of them and saves some serious time!

Administrative Configurations

Even though the following sections aren't critical to making a router or switch *work* on a network, they're still really important. I'm going to guide you through configuring specific commands that are particularly helpful when administering your network.

You can configure the following administrative functions on a router and switch:

- Hostnames
- Banners
- Passwords
- Interface descriptions

Remember, none of these will make your routers or switches work better or faster, but trust me, your life will be a whole lot better if you just take the time to set these configurations on each of your network devices. This is because doing so makes trouble-shooting and maintaining your network a great deal easier—seriously! In this next section, I'll be demonstrating commands on a Cisco switch, but understand that these commands are used in the exact same way on a Cisco router.

Hostnames

We use the hostname command to set the identity of the router and switch. This is only locally significant, meaning it doesn't affect how the router or switch performs name lookups or how the device actually works on the internetwork. But the hostname is still important in routes because it's often used for authentication in many wide area networks (WANs). Here's an example:

```
Switch#config t
Switch(config)#hostname Todd
Todd(config)#hostname Chicago
Chicago(config)#hostname Todd
Todd(config)#
```

I know it's pretty tempting to configure the hostname after your own name, but it's usually a much better idea to name the device something that relates to its physical location. A name that maps to where the device lives will make finding it a whole lot easier, which among other things, confirms that you're actually configuring the correct device. Even though it seems like I'm completely ditching my own advice by naming mine *Todd*, I'm not, because this particular device really does live in "Todd's" office. Its name perfectly maps to where it is, so it won't be confused with those in the other networks I work with!

Banners

A very good reason for having a *banner* is to give any and all who dare attempt to telnet or sneak into your internetwork a little security notice. And they're very cool because you can create and customize them so that they'll greet anyone who shows up on the router with exactly the information you want them to have!

Here are the three types of banners you need to be sure you're familiar with:

- Exec process creation banner
- Login banner
- Message of the day banner

And you can see them all illustrated in the following code:

```
Todd(config)#banner ?
  LINE         c banner-text c, where 'c' is a delimiting character
  exec         Set EXEC process creation banner
```

```
incoming          Set incoming terminal line banner
login             Set login banner
motd              Set Message of the Day banner
prompt-timeout    Set Message for login authentication timeout
slip-ppp          Set Message for SLIP/PPP
```

Message of the day (MOTD) banners are the most widely used banners because they give a message to anyone connecting to the router via Telnet or an auxiliary port or even through a console port as seen here:

```
Todd(config)#banner motd ?
LINE c banner-text c, where 'c' is a delimiting character
Todd(config)#banner motd #
Enter TEXT message. End with the character '#'.
$ Acme.com network, then you must disconnect immediately.
#
```

Todd(config)#**^Z** (Press the control key + z keys to return to privileged mode)

```
Todd#exit
con0 is now available
Press RETURN to get started.
If you are not authorized to be in Acme.com network, then you
must disconnect immediately.
Todd#
```

This MOTD banner essentially tells anyone connecting to the device to get lost if they're not on the guest list. The part to focus upon here is the delimiting character, which is what informs the router the message is done. Clearly, you can use any character you want for it except for the delimiting character in the message itself. Once the message is complete, press Enter, then the delimiting character, and then press Enter again. Everything will still work if you don't follow this routine unless you have more than one banner. If that's the case, make sure you do follow it or your banners will all be combined into one message and put on a single line!

You can set a banner on one line like this:

```
Todd(config)#banner motd x Unauthorized access prohibited! x
```

Let's take a minute to go into more detail about the other two types of banners I mentioned:

Exec banner   You can configure a line-activation (exec) banner to be displayed when EXEC processes such as a line activation or an incoming connection to a VTY line have been created. Simply initiating a user exec session through a console port will activate the exec banner.

Login banner   You can configure a login banner for display on all connected terminals. It will show up after the MOTD banner but before the login prompts. This login banner can't be disabled on a per-line basis, so to globally disable it you've got to delete it with the no banner login command.

Here's what a login banner output looks like:

```
!
banner login ^C
------------------------------------------------------------------------
Cisco Router and Security Device Manager (SDM) is installed on this device.
This feature requires the one-time use of the username "cisco"
with the password "cisco". The default username and password
have a privilege level of 15.
Please change these publicly known initial credentials using
SDM or the IOS CLI.
Here are the Cisco IOS commands.
username <myuser>  privilege 15 secret 0 <mypassword>
no username cisco
Replace <myuser> and <mypassword> with the username and
password you want to use.
For more information about SDM please follow the instructions
in the QUICK START GUIDE for your router or go to http://www.cisco.com/go/sdm
------------------------------------------------------------------------
^C
!
```

The previous login banner should look pretty familiar to anyone who's ever logged into an ISR router because it's the banner Cisco has in the default configuration for its ISR routers.

Remember that the login banner is displayed before the login prompts and after the MOTD banner.

Setting Passwords

There are five passwords you'll need to secure your Cisco routers: console, auxiliary, telnet/SSH (VTY), enable password, and enable secret. The enable secret and enable password are the ones used to set the password for securing privileged mode. Once the `enable` commands are set, users will be prompted for a password. The other three are used to configure a password when user mode is accessed through the console port, through the auxiliary port, or via Telnet.

Let's take a look at each of these now.

Enable Passwords

You set the enable passwords from global configuration mode like this:

```
Todd(config)#enable ?
 last-resort Define enable action if no TACACS servers
            respond
```

```
password    Assign the privileged level password
secret      Assign the privileged level secret
use-tacacs  Use TACACS to check enable passwords
```

The following list describes the enable password parameters:

last-resort   This allows you to still enter the device if you set up authentication through a TACACS server and it's not available. It won't be used if the TACACS server is working.

password   This sets the enable password on older, pre-10.3 systems and isn't ever used if an enable secret is set.

secret   The newer, encrypted password that overrides the enable password if it has been set.

use-tacacs   This tells the router or switch to authenticate through a TACACS server. It comes in really handy when you have lots of routers because changing the password on a multitude of them can be insanely tedious. It's much easier to simply go through the TACACS server and change the password only once!

Here's an example that shows how to set the enable passwords:

```
Todd(config)#enable secret todd
Todd(config)#enable password todd
The enable password you have chosen is the same as your
    enable secret. This is not recommended. Re-enter the
    enable password.
```

If you try to set the enable secret and enable passwords the same, the device will give you a polite warning to change the second password. Make a note to yourself that if there aren't any old legacy routers involved, you don't even bother to use the enable password!

User-mode passwords are assigned via the line command like this:

```
Todd(config)#line ?
  <0-16>   First Line number
  console  Primary terminal line
  vty      Virtual terminal
```

And these two lines are especially important for the exam objectives:

console   Sets a console user-mode password.

vty   Sets a Telnet password on the device. If this password isn't set, then by default, Telnet can't be used.

To configure user-mode passwords, choose the line you want and configure it using the login command to make the switch prompt for authentication. Let's focus in on the configuration of individual lines now.

Console Password

We set the console password with the `line console 0` command, but look at what happened when I tried to type **line console ?** from the (config-line)# prompt—I received an error! Here's the example:

```
Todd(config-line)#line console ?
% Unrecognized command
Todd(config-line)#exit
Todd(config)#line console ?
  <0-0>  First Line number
Todd(config)#line console 0
Todd(config-line)#password console
Todd(config-line)#login
```

You can still type **line console 0** and that will be accepted, but the help screens just don't work from that prompt. Type **exit** to go back one level, and you'll find that your help screens now work. This is a "feature." Really.

Because there's only one console port, I can only choose line console 0. You can set all your line passwords to the same password, but doing this isn't exactly a brilliant security move!

And it's also important to remember to apply the `login` command or the console port won't prompt for authentication. The way Cisco has this process set up means you can't set the `login` command before a password is set on a line because if you set it but don't then set a password, that line won't be usable. You'll actually get prompted for a password that doesn't exist, so Cisco's method isn't just a hassle; it makes sense and is a feature after all!

Definitely remember that although Cisco has this "password feature" on its routers starting with IOS 12.2 and above, it's not included in older IOSs.

Okay, there are a few other important commands you need to know regarding the console port.

For one, the `exec-timeout 0 0` command sets the time-out for the console EXEC session to zero, ensuring that it never times out. The default time-out is 10 minutes.

If you're feeling mischievous, try this on people at work: Set the `exec-timeout` command to 0 1. This will make the console time out in 1 second, and to fix it, you have to continually press the down arrow key while changing the time-out time with your free hand!

`Logging synchronous` is such a cool command that it should be a default, but it's not. It's great because it's the antidote for those annoying console messages that disrupt the input you're trying to type. The messages will still pop up, but at least you get returned to your device prompt without your input being interrupted! This makes your input messages oh-so-much easier to read!

Here's an example of how to configure both commands:

```
Todd(config-line)#line con 0
Todd(config-line)#exec-timeout ?
  <0-35791>  Timeout in minutes
Todd(config-line)#exec-timeout 0 ?
  <0-2147483>  Timeout in seconds
  <cr>
Todd(config-line)#exec-timeout 0 0
Todd(config-line)#logging synchronous
```

> You can set the console to go from never timing out (0 0) to timing out in 35,791 minutes and 2,147,483 seconds. Remember that the default is 10 minutes.

Telnet Password

To set the user-mode password for Telnet access into the router or switch, use the line vty command. IOS switches typically have 16 lines, but routers running the Enterprise edition have considerably more. The best way to find out how many lines you have is to use that handy question mark like this:

```
Todd(config-line)#line vty 0 ?
% Unrecognized command
Todd(config-line)#exit
Todd(config)#line vty 0 ?
  <1-15>  Last Line number
  <cr>
Todd(config)#line vty 0 15
Todd(config-line)#password telnet
Todd(config-line)#login
```

This output clearly shows that you cannot get help from your (config-line)# prompt. You must go back to global config mode in order to use the question mark (?).

So what will happen if you try to telnet into a device that doesn't have a VTY password set? You'll receive an error saying the connection has been refused because the password isn't set. So, if you telnet into a switch and receive a message like this one that I got from Switch B

```
Todd#telnet SwitchB
Trying SwitchB (10.0.0.1)…Open

Password required, but none set
[Connection to SwitchB closed by foreign host]
Todd#
```

it means the switch doesn't have the VTY password set. But you can still get around this and tell the switch to allow Telnet connections without a password by using the no login command:

```
SwitchB(config-line)#line vty 0 15
SwitchB(config-line)#no login
```

> **WARNING**   I definitely do not recommend using the no login command to allow Telnet connections without a password, unless you're in a testing or classroom environment. In a production network, always set your VTY password!

After your IOS devices are configured with an IP address, you can use the Telnet program to configure and check your routers instead of having to use a console cable. You can use the Telnet program by typing **telnet** from any command prompt (DOS or Cisco). I'll cover all things Telnet more thoroughly in Chapter 7, "Managing a Cisco Internetwork."

Auxiliary Password

To configure the auxiliary password on a router, go into global configuration mode and type **line aux ?**. And by the way, you won't find these ports on a switch. This output shows that you only get a choice of 0–0, which is because there's only one port:

```
Todd#config t
Todd(config)#line aux ?
  <0-0>  First Line number
Todd(config)#line aux 0
Todd(config-line)#login
% Login disabled on line 1, until 'password' is set
Todd(config-line)#password aux
Todd(config-line)#login
```

Setting Up Secure Shell (SSH)

I strongly recommend using Secure Shell (SSH) instead of Telnet because it creates a more secure session. The Telnet application uses an unencrypted data stream, but SSH uses encryption keys to send data so your username and password aren't sent in the clear, vulnerable to anyone lurking around!

Here are the steps for setting up SSH:

1. Set your hostname:

   ```
   Router(config)#hostname Todd
   ```

2. Set the domain name—both the hostname and domain name are required for the encryption keys to be generated:

    `Todd(config)#ip domain-name Lammle.com`

3. Set the username to allow SSH client access:

    `Todd(config)#username Todd password Lammle`

4. Generate the encryption keys for securing the session:

    ```
    Todd(config)#crypto key generate rsa
    The name for the keys will be: Todd.Lammle.com
    Choose the size of the key modulus in the range of 360 to
    4096 for your General Purpose Keys. Choosing a key modulus
    Greater than 512 may take a few minutes.

    How many bits in the modulus [512]: 1024
    % Generating 1024 bit RSA keys, keys will be non-exportable...
    [OK] (elapsed time was 6 seconds)

    Todd(config)#
    1d14h: %SSH-5-ENABLED: SSH 1.99 has been enabled*June 24
    19:25:30.035: %SSH-5-ENABLED: SSH 1.99 has been enabled
    ```

5. Enable SSH version 2 on the device—not mandatory, but strongly suggested:

    `Todd(config)#ip ssh version 2`

6. Connect to the VTY lines of the switch or router:

    `Todd(config)#line vty 0 15`

7. Tell the lines to use the local database for password:

    `Todd(config-line)#login local`

8. Configure your access protocols:

    ```
    Todd(config-line)#transport input ?
      all     All protocols
      none    No protocols
      ssh     TCP/IP SSH protocol
      telnet  TCP/IP Telnet protocol
    ```

    Beware of this next line, and make sure you never use it in production because it's a horrendous security risk:

    `Todd(config-line)#transport input all`

I recommend using the next line to secure your VTY lines with SSH:

```
Todd(config-line)#transport input ssh ?
  telnet  TCP/IP Telnet protocol
  <cr>
```

I actually do use Telnet once in a while when a situation arises that specifically calls for it. It just doesn't happen very often. But if you want to go with Telnet, here's how you do that:

```
Todd(config-line)#transport input ssh telnet
```

Know that if you don't use the keyword telnet at the end of the command string, then only SSH will work on the device. You can go with either, just so long as you understand that SSH is way more secure than Telnet.

Encrypting Your Passwords

Because only the enable secret password is encrypted by default, you'll need to manually configure the user-mode and enable passwords for encryption.

Notice that you can see all the passwords except the enable secret when performing a show running-config on a switch:

```
Todd#sh running-config
Building configuration...

Current configuration : 1020 bytes
!
! Last configuration change at 00:03:11 UTC Mon Mar 1 1993
!
version 15.0
no service pad
service timestamps debug datetime msec
service timestamps log datetime msec
no service password-encryption
!
hostname Todd
!
enable secret 4 ykw.3/tgsOuy9.6qmgG/EeYOYgBvfX4v.S8UNA9Rddg
enable password todd
!
[output cut]
!
line con 0
```

```
 password console
 login
line vty 0 4
 password telnet
 login
line vty 5 15
 password telnet
 login
!
end
```

To manually encrypt your passwords, use the service password-encryption command. Here's how:

```
Todd#config t
Todd(config)#service password-encryption
Todd(config)#exit
Todd#show run
Building configuration...
!
!
enable secret 4 ykw.3/tgsOuy9.6qmgG/EeYOYgBvfX4v.S8UNA9Rddg
enable password 7 1506040800
!
[output cut]
!
!
line con 0
 password 7 050809013243420C
 login
line vty 0 4
 password 7 06120A2D424B1D
 login
line vty 5 15
 password 7 06120A2D424B1D
 login
!
end
Todd#config t
Todd(config)#no service password-encryption
Todd(config)#^Z
Todd#
```

Nicely done—the passwords will now be encrypted. All you need to do is encrypt the passwords, perform a show run, then turn off the command if you want. This output clearly shows us that the enable password and the line passwords are all encrypted.

Before we move on to find out how to set descriptions on your interfaces, I want to stress some points about password encryption. As I said, if you set your passwords and then turn on the service password-encryption command, you have to perform a show running-config before you turn off the encryption service or your passwords won't be encrypted. You don't have to turn off the encryption service at all—you'd only do that if your switch is running low on processes. And if you turn on the service before you set your passwords, then you don't even have to view them to have them encrypted.

Descriptions

Setting descriptions on an interface is another administratively helpful thing, and like the hostname, it's also only locally significant. One case where the description command comes in really handy is when you want to keep track of circuit numbers on a switch or a router's serial WAN port.

Here's an example on my switch:

```
Todd#config t
Todd(config)#int fa0/1
Todd(config-if)#description Sales VLAN Trunk Link
Todd(config-if)#^Z
Todd#
```

And on a router serial WAN:

```
Router#config t
Router(config)#int s0/0/0
Router(config-if)#description WAN to Miami
Router(config-if)#^Z
```

You can view an interface's description with either the show running-config command or the show interface—even with the show interface description command:

```
Todd#sh run
Building configuration...

Current configuration : 855 bytes
!
interface FastEthernet0/1
 description Sales VLAN Trunk Link
!
 [output cut]
```

```
Todd#sh int f0/1
FastEthernet0/1 is up, line protocol is up (connected)
  Hardware is Fast Ethernet, address is ecc8.8202.8282 (bia ecc8.8202.8282)
  Description: Sales VLAN Trunk Link
  MTU 1500 bytes, BW 100000 Kbit/sec, DLY 100 usec,
 [output cut]
```

```
Todd#sh int description
Interface                    Status        Protocol Description
Vl1                          up            up
Fa0/1                        up            up       Sales VLAN Trunk Link
Fa0/2                        up            up
```

 Real World Scenario

description: A Helpful Command

Bob, a senior network admin at Acme Corporation in San Francisco, has over 50 WAN links to branches throughout the United States and Canada. Whenever an interface goes down, Bob wastes lots of time trying to figure out the circuit number and the phone number of the provider of his ailing WAN link.

This kind of scenario shows just how helpful the interface description command can be. It would save Bob a lot of work because he could use it on his most important switch LAN links to find out exactly where every interface is connected. Bob's life would also be made a lot easier by adding circuit numbers to each and every WAN interface on his routers, along with the phone number of the responsible provider.

So if Bob had just taken time in advance to preventively add this information to his interfaces, he would have saved himself an ocean of stress and a ton of precious time when his WAN links inevitably go down!

Doing the *do* Command

In every previous example so far, we've had to run all show commands from privileged mode. But I've got great news—beginning with IOS version 12.3, Cisco has finally added a command to the IOS that allows you to view the configuration and statistics from within configuration mode!

In fact, with any IOS, you'd get the following error if you tried to view the configuration from global config:

```
Todd(config)#sh run
              ^
% Invalid input detected at '^' marker.
```

Compare that to the output I get from entering that same command on my router that's running the 15.0 IOS using the "do" syntax:

```
Todd(config)#do show run
Building configuration...

Current configuration : 759 bytes
!
version 15.0
no service pad
service timestamps debug datetime msec
service timestamps log datetime msec
no service password-encryption
!
hostname Todd
!
boot-start-marker
boot-end-marker
!
[output cut]
```

So now you can pretty much run any command from any configuration prompt—nice, huh? Looking back through all those examples for encrypting our passwords, you can see that the do command would definitely have gotten the party started sooner, making this innovation one to celebrate for sure!

Router and Switch Interfaces

Interface configuration is arguably the most important router configuration because without interfaces, a router is a pretty useless object. Furthermore, interface configurations must be totally precise to enable communication with other devices. Network layer addresses, media type, bandwidth, and other administrator commands are all used to configure an interface.

On a layer 2 switch, interface configurations typically involve a lot less work than router interface configuration. Check out the output from the powerful verification command show ip interface brief, which reveals all the interfaces on my 3560 switch:

```
Todd#sh ip interface brief
Interface          IP-Address       OK? Method Status        Protocol
Vlan1              192.168.255.8    YES DHCP   up                    up
FastEthernet0/1    unassigned       YES unset  up                    up
FastEthernet0/2    unassigned       YES unset  up                    up
```

FastEthernet0/3	unassigned	YES unset	down	down
FastEthernet0/4	unassigned	YES unset	down	down
FastEthernet0/5	unassigned	YES unset	up	up
FastEthernet0/6	unassigned	YES unset	up	up
FastEthernet0/7	unassigned	YES unset	down	down
FastEthernet0/8	unassigned	YES unset	down	down
GigabitEthernet0/1	unassigned	YES unset	down	down

The previous output shows the default routed port found on all Cisco switches (VLAN 1), plus nine switch FastEthernet interface ports, with one port being a Gigabit Ethernet port used for uplinks to other switches.

Different routers use different methods to choose the interfaces used on them. For instance, the following command shows one of my 2800 ISR Cisco routers with two FastEthernet interfaces along with two serial WAN interfaces:

```
Router>sh ip int brief
Interface       IP-Address      OK? Method Status                Protocol
FastEthernet0/0 192.168.255.11  YES DHCP   up                    up
FastEthernet0/1 unassigned      YES unset  administratively down down
Serial0/0/0     unassigned      YES unset  administratively down down
Serial0/1/0     unassigned      YES unset  administratively down down
Router>
```

Previously, we always used the interface type *number* sequence to configure an interface, but the newer routers come with an actual physical slot and include a port number on the module plugged into it. So on a modular router, the configuration would be interface *type slot/port*, as demonstrated here:

```
Todd#config t
Todd(config)#interface GigabitEthernet 0/1
Todd(config-if)#
```

You can see that we are now at the Gigabit Ethernet slot 0, port 1 prompt, and from here we can make configuration changes to the interface. Make note of the fact that you can't just type **int gigabitethernet 0**. No shortcuts on the slot/port—you've got to type the slot/port variables in the command: ***type slot/port*** or, for example, **int gigabitethernet 0/1** (or just **int g0/1**).

Once in interface configuration mode, we can configure various options. Keep in mind that speed and duplex are the two factors to be concerned with for the LAN:

```
Todd#config t
Todd(config)#interface GigabitEthernet 0/1
Todd(config-if)#speed 1000
Todd(config-if)#duplex full
```

So what's happened here? Well basically, this has shut off the auto-detect mechanism on the port, forcing it to only run gigabit speeds at full duplex. For the ISR series router, it's basically the same, but you get even more options! The LAN interfaces are the same, but the rest of the modules are different—they use three numbers instead of two. The three numbers used here can represent slot/subslot/port, but this depends on the card used in the ISR router. For the objectives, you just need to remember this: The first 0 is the router itself. You then choose the slot and then the port. Here's an example of a serial interface on my 2811:

```
Todd(config)#interface serial ?
  <0-2>  Serial interface number
Todd(config)#interface serial 0/0/?
  <0-1>  Serial interface number
Todd(config)#interface serial 0/0/0
Todd(config-if)#
```

This might look a little dicey to you, but I promise it's really not that hard! It helps to remember that you should always view the output of the show ip interface brief command or a show running-config output first so you know the exact interfaces you have to deal with. Here's one of my 2811's output that has even more serial interfaces installed:

```
Todd(config-if)#do show run
Building configuration...
[output cut]
!
interface FastEthernet0/0
 no ip address
 shutdown
 duplex auto
 speed auto
!
interface FastEthernet0/1
 no ip address
 shutdown
 duplex auto
 speed auto
!
interface Serial0/0/0
 no ip address
 shutdown
 no fair-queue
!
```

```
interface Serial0/0/1
 no ip address
 shutdown
!
interface Serial0/1/0
 no ip address
 shutdown
!
interface Serial0/2/0
 no ip address
 shutdown
 clock rate 2000000
!
 [output cut]
```

For the sake of brevity, I didn't include my complete running-config, but I've displayed all you really need. You can see the two built-in FastEthernet interfaces, the two serial interfaces in slot 0 (0/0/0 and 0/0/1), the serial interface in slot 1 (0/1/0), and the serial interface in slot 2 (0/2/0). And once you see the interfaces like this, it makes it a lot easier to understand how the modules are inserted into the router.

Just understand that if you type **interface e0** on an old 2500 series router, **interface fastethernet 0/0** on a modular router (such as the 2800 series router), or **interface serial 0/1/0** on an ISR router, all you're actually doing is choosing an interface to configure. Essentially, they're all configured the same way after that.

Let's delve deeper into our router interface discussion by exploring how to bring up the interface and set an IP address on it next.

Bringing Up an Interface

You can disable an interface with the interface command shutdown and enable it with the no shutdown command. Just to remind you, all switch ports are enabled by default and all router ports are disabled by default, so we're going to talk more about router ports than switch ports in the next few sections.

If an interface is shut down, it'll display as administratively down when you use the show interfaces command (sh int for short):

```
Router#sh int f0/0
FastEthernet0/1 is administratively down, line protocol is down
[output cut]
```

Another way to check an interface's status is via the show running-config command. You can bring up the router interface with the no shutdown command (no shut for short):

```
Router(config)#int f0/0
Router(config-if)#no shutdown
```

```
*August 21 13:45:08.455: %LINK-3-UPDOWN: Interface FastEthernet0/0,
    changed state to up
Router(config-if)#do show int f0/0
FastEthernet0/0 is up, line protocol is up
[output cut]
```

Configuring an IP Address on an Interface

Even though you don't have to use IP on your routers, it's usually what everyone uses. To configure IP addresses on an interface, use the ip address command from interface configuration mode and remember that you do not set an IP address on a layer 2 switch port!

```
Todd(config)#int f0/1
Todd(config-if)#ip address 172.16.10.2 255.255.255.0
```

Also, don't forget to enable the interface with the no shutdown command. Remember to look at the command show interface *int* output to see if the interface is administratively shut down or not. Show ip int brief and show running-config will also give you this information.

 The ip address *address mask* command starts the IP processing on the router interface. Again, you do not configure an IP address on a layer 2 switch interface!

Okay—now if you want to add a second subnet address to an interface, you have to use the secondary parameter. If you type another IP address and press Enter, it will replace the existing primary IP address and mask. This is definitely one of the Cisco IOS's coolest features!

So let's try it. To add a secondary IP address, just use the secondary parameter:

```
Todd(config-if)#ip address 172.16.20.2 255.255.255.0 ?
  secondary  Make this IP address a secondary address
  <cr>
Todd(config-if)#ip address 172.16.20.2 255.255.255.0 secondary
Todd(config-if)#do sh run
Building configuration...
[output cut]

interface FastEthernet0/1
 ip address 172.16.20.2 255.255.255.0 secondary
 ip address 172.16.10.2 255.255.255.0
 duplex auto
 speed auto
!
```

But I've got to stop here to tell you that I really wouldn't recommend having multiple IP addresses on an interface because it's really inefficient. I showed you how anyway just in case you someday find yourself dealing with an MIS manager who's in love with really bad network design and makes you administer it! And who knows? Maybe someone will ask you about it someday and you'll get to seem really smart because you know this.

Using the Pipe

No, not that pipe. I mean the output modifier. Although, I've got to say that some of the router configurations I've seen in my career make me wonder! Anyway, this pipe (|) allows us to wade through all the configurations or other long outputs and get straight to our goods fast. Here's an example:

```
Router#sh run | ?
  append    Append redirected output to URL (URLs supporting append
            operation only)
  begin     Begin with the line that matches
  exclude   Exclude lines that match
  include   Include lines that match
  redirect  Redirect output to URL
  section   Filter a section of output
  tee       Copy output to URL

Router#sh run | begin interface
interface FastEthernet0/0
 description Sales VLAN
 ip address 10.10.10.1 255.255.255.248
 duplex auto
 speed auto
!
interface FastEthernet0/1
 ip address 172.16.20.2 255.255.255.0 secondary
 ip address 172.16.10.2 255.255.255.0
 duplex auto
 speed auto
!
interface Serial0/0/0
 description Wan to SF circuit number 6fdda 12345678
 no ip address
!
```

So basically, the pipe symbol—the output modifier—is what you need to help you get where you want to go light years faster than mucking around in a router's entire configuration. I use it a lot when scrutinizing a large routing table to find out whether a certain route is in the routing table. Here's an example:

```
Todd#sh ip route | include 192.168.3.32
R       192.168.3.32 [120/2] via 10.10.10.8, 00:00:25, FastEthernet0/0
Todd#
```

First, you need to know that this routing table had over 100 entries, so without my trusty pipe, I'd probably still be looking through that output! It's a powerfully efficient tool that saves you major time and effort by quickly finding a line in a configuration—or as the preceding example shows, a single route within a huge routing table.

Give yourself a little time to play around with the pipe command to get the hang of it and you'll be naturally high on your newfound ability to quickly parse through router output!

Serial Interface Commands

But wait! Before you just jump in and configure a serial interface, you need some key information, like knowing the interface will usually be attached to a CSU/DSU type of device that provides clocking for the line to the router. Check out Figure 6.3 for an example.

FIGURE 6.3 A typical WAN connection. Clocking is typically provided by a DCE network to routers. In nonproduction environments, a DCE network is not always present.

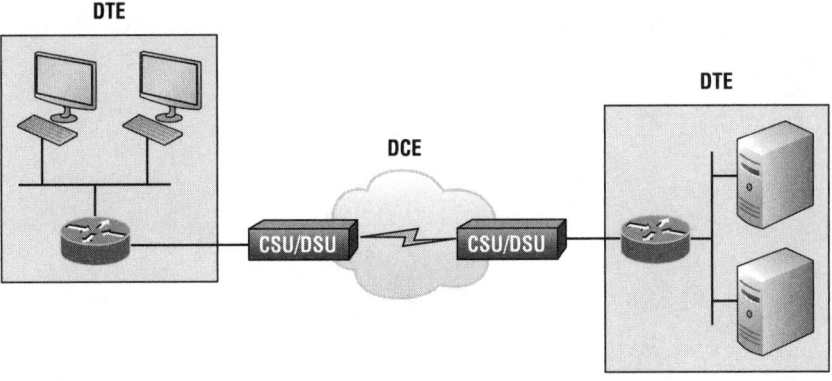

Here you can see that the serial interface is used to connect to a DCE network via a CSU/DSU that provides the clocking to the router interface. But if you have a back-to-back configuration, such as one that's used in a lab environment like the one in Figure 6.4, one end—the data communication equipment (DCE) end of the cable—must provide clocking!

FIGURE 6.4   Providing clocking on a nonproduction network

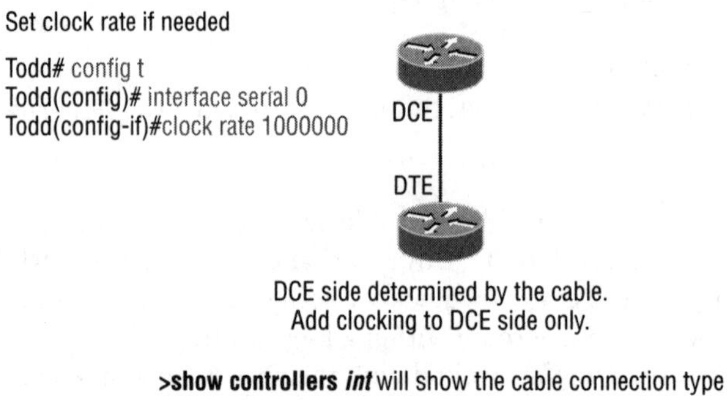

Set clock rate if needed

Todd# config t
Todd(config)# interface serial 0
Todd(config-if)#clock rate 1000000

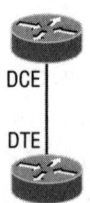

DCE

DTE

DCE side determined by the cable.
Add clocking to DCE side only.

>show controllers *int* will show the cable connection type

By default, Cisco router serial interfaces are all data terminal equipment (DTE) interfaces, which means that you must configure an interface to provide clocking if you need
it to act like a DCE device. Again, you would not provide clocking on a production WAN
serial connection because you would have a CSU/DSU connected to your serial interface, as
shown in Figure 6.3.

You configure a DCE serial interface with the clock rate command:

```
Router#config t
Enter configuration commands, one per line.  End with CNTL/Z.
Router(config)#int s0/0/0
Router(config-if)#clock rate ?
      Speed (bits per second)
  1200
  2400
  4800
  9600
  14400
  19200
  28800
  32000
  38400
  48000
  56000
  57600
  64000
  72000
  115200
  125000
  128000
```

```
148000
192000
250000
256000
384000
500000
512000
768000
800000
1000000
2000000
4000000
5300000
8000000
```

```
<300-8000000>    Choose clockrate from list above
Router(config-if)#clock rate 1000000
```

The clock rate command is set in bits per second. Besides looking at the cable end to check for a label of DCE or DTE, you can see if a router's serial interface has a DCE cable connected with the show controllers *int* command:

```
Router#sh controllers s0/0/0
Interface Serial0/0/0
Hardware is GT96K
DTE V.35idb at 0x4342FCB0, driver data structure at 0x434373D4
```

Here is an example of an output depicting a DCE connection:

```
Router#sh controllers s0/2/0
Interface Serial0/2/0
Hardware is GT96K
DCE V.35, clock rate 1000000
```

The next command you need to get acquainted with is the bandwidth command. Every Cisco router ships with a default serial link bandwidth of T1 (1.544 Mbps). But this has nothing to do with how data is transferred over a link. The bandwidth of a serial link is used by routing protocols such as EIGRP and OSPF to calculate the best cost path to a remote network. So if you're using RIP routing, the bandwidth setting of a serial link is irrelevant since RIP uses only hop count to determine this.

You may be rereading this part and thinking, "Huh? What? Routing protocols? Metrics?" But don't freak! I'm going over all of that soon in Chapter 9.

Here's an example of using the bandwidth command:

```
Router#config t
Router(config)#int s0/0/0
Router(config-if)#bandwidth ?
  <1-10000000>  Bandwidth in kilobits
  inherit       Specify that bandwidth is inherited
  receive       Specify receive-side bandwidth
Router(config-if)#bandwidth 1000
```

Did you notice that, unlike the clock rate command, the bandwidth command is configured in kilobits per second?

 After going through all these configuration examples regarding the clock rate command, understand that the new ISR routers automatically detect DCE connections and set clock rate to 2000000. But know that you still need to understand the clock rate command for the Cisco objectives, even though the new routers set it for you automatically!

Viewing, Saving, and Erasing Configurations

If you run through setup mode, you'll be asked if you want to use the configuration you just created. If you say yes, the configuration running in DRAM that's known as the running-config will be copied into NVRAM, and the file will be named startup-config. Hopefully, you'll be smart and always use the CLI, not setup mode!

You can manually save the file from DRAM, which is usually just called RAM, to NVRAM by using the copy running-config startup-config command. You can use the shortcut copy run start as well:

```
Todd#copy running-config startup-config
Destination filename [startup-config]? [press enter]
Building configuration...
[OK]
Todd#
Building configuration...
```

When you see a question with an answer in [], it means that if you just press Enter, you're choosing the default answer.

Also, when the command asks for the destination filename, the default answer is startup-config. The reason it asks is because you can copy the configuration to pretty much anywhere you want. Take a look at the output from my switch:

Todd#**copy running-config ?**

```
flash:          Copy to flash: file system
ftp:            Copy to ftp: file system
http:           Copy to http: file system
https:          Copy to https: file system
null:           Copy to null: file system
nvram:          Copy to nvram: file system
rcp:            Copy to rcp: file system
running-config  Update (merge with) current system configuration
scp:            Copy to scp: file system
startup-config  Copy to startup configuration
syslog:         Copy to syslog: file system
system:         Copy to system: file system
tftp:           Copy to tftp: file system
tmpsys:         Copy to tmpsys: file system
vb:             Copy to vb: file system
```

To reassure you, we'll get deeper into how and where to copy files in Chapter 7.

For now, you can view the files by typing **show running-config** or **show startup-config** from privileged mode. The sh run command, which is a shortcut for show running-config, tells us that we're viewing the current configuration:

Todd#**sh run**
```
Building configuration...

Current configuration : 855 bytes
!
! Last configuration change at 23:20:06 UTC Mon Mar 1 1993
!
version 15.0
[output cut]
```

The sh start command—one of the shortcuts for the show startup-config command—shows us the configuration that will be used the next time the router is reloaded. It also tells us how much NVRAM is being used to store the startup-config file. Here's an example:

Todd#**sh start**
```
Using 855 out of 524288 bytes
!
```

```
! Last configuration change at 23:20:06 UTC Mon Mar 1 1993
!
version 15.0
[output cut]
```

But beware—if you try and view the configuration and see

Todd#**sh start**
```
startup-config is not present
```

you have not saved your running-config to NVRAM, or you've deleted the backup configuration! Let me talk about just how you would do that now.

Deleting the Configuration and Reloading the Device

You can delete the startup-config file by using the erase startup-config command:

Todd#**erase start**
```
% Incomplete command.
```

First, notice that you can no longer use the shortcut commands for erasing the backup configuration. This started in IOS 12.4 with the ISR routers.

Todd#**erase startup-config**
```
Erasing the nvram filesystem will remove all configuration files! Continue?
[confirm]
[OK]
Erase of nvram: complete
Todd#
*Mar  5 01:59:45.206: %SYS-7-NV_BLOCK_INIT: Initialized the geometry of nvram
```
Todd#**reload**
```
Proceed with reload? [confirm]
```

Now if you reload or power the router down after using the erase startup-config command, you'll be offered setup mode because there's no configuration saved in NVRAM. You can press Ctrl+C to exit setup mode at any time, but the reload command can only be used from privileged mode.

At this point, you shouldn't use setup mode to configure your router. So just say **no** to setup mode, because it's there to help people who don't know how to use the command line interface (CLI), and this no longer applies to you. Be strong—you can do it!

Verifying Your Configuration

Obviously, show running-config would be the best way to verify your configuration and show startup-config would be the best way to verify the configuration that'll be used the next time the router is reloaded—right?

Well, once you take a look at the running-config, if all appears well, you can verify your configuration with utilities like Ping and Telnet. Ping is a program that uses ICMP echo requests and replies, which we covered in Chapter 3. For review, Ping sends a packet to a remote host, and if that host responds, you know that it's alive. But you don't know if it's alive and also *well*; just because you can ping a Microsoft server does not mean you can log in! Even so, Ping is an awesome starting point for troubleshooting an internetwork.

Did you know that you can ping with different protocols? You can, and you can test this by typing **ping ?** at either the router user-mode or privileged-mode prompt:

```
Todd#ping ?
  WORD  Ping destination address or hostname
  clns  CLNS echo
  ip    IP echo
  ipv6  IPv6 echo
  tag   Tag encapsulated IP echo
  <cr>
```

If you want to find a neighbor's Network layer address, either you go straight to the router or switch itself or you can type **show cdp entry * protocol** to get the Network layer addresses you need for pinging.

You can also use an extended ping to change the default variables, as shown here:

```
Todd#ping
Protocol [ip]:
Target IP address: 10.1.1.1
Repeat count [5]:
% A decimal number between 1 and 2147483647.
Repeat count [5]: 5000
Datagram size [100]:
% A decimal number between 36 and 18024.
Datagram size [100]: 1500
Timeout in seconds [2]:
Extended commands [n]: y
Source address or interface: FastEthernet 0/1
Source address or interface: Vlan 1
Type of service [0]:
Set DF bit in IP header? [no]:
Validate reply data? [no]:
Data pattern [0xABCD]:
Loose, Strict, Record, Timestamp, Verbose[none]:
Sweep range of sizes [n]:
Type escape sequence to abort.
Sending 5000, 1500-byte ICMP Echos to 10.1.1.1, timeout is 2 seconds:
Packet sent with a source address of 10.10.10.1
```

Notice that by using the question mark, I was able to determine that extended ping allows you to set the repeat count higher than the default of 5 and the datagram size larger.

This raises the MTU and allows for a more accurate testing of throughput. The source interface is one last important piece of information I'll pull out of the output. You can choose which interface the ping is sourced from, which is really helpful in certain diagnostic situations. Using my switch to display the extended ping capabilities, I had to use my only routed port, which is named VLAN 1, by default.

However, if you want to use a different diagnostic port, you can create a logical interface called a loopback interface as so:

```
Todd(config)#interface loopback ?
  <0-2147483647>  Loopback interface number

Todd(config)#interface loopback 0
*May 19 03:06:42.697: %LINEPROTO-5-UPDOWN: Line prot
 changed state to ups
Todd(config-if)#ip address 20.20.20.1 255.255.255.0
```

Now I can use this port for diagnostics, and even as my source port of my ping or traceroute, as so:

```
Todd#ping
Protocol [ip]:
Target IP address: 10.1.1.1
Repeat count [5]:
Datagram size [100]:
Timeout in seconds [2]:
Extended commands [n]: y
Source address or interface: 20.20.20.1
Type of service [0]:
Set DF bit in IP header? [no]:
Validate reply data? [no]:
Data pattern [0xABCD]:
Loose, Strict, Record, Timestamp, Verbose[none]:
Sweep range of sizes [n]:
Type escape sequence to abort.
Sending 5, 100-byte ICMP Echos to 10.1.1.1, timeout is 2 seconds:
Packet sent with a source address of 20.20.20.1
```

The logical interface are great for diagnostics and for using them in our home labs where we don't have any real interfaces to play with, but we'll also use them in our OSPF configurations in ICND2.

Cisco Discovery Protocol (CDP) is covered in Chapter 7.

Traceroute uses ICMP with IP time to live (TTL) time-outs to track the path a given packet takes through an internetwork. This is in contrast to Ping, which just finds the host and responds. Traceroute can also be used with multiple protocols. Check out this output:

```
Todd#traceroute ?
  WORD       Trace route to destination address or hostname
  aaa        Define trace options for AAA events/actions/errors
  appletalk  AppleTalk Trace
  clns       ISO CLNS Trace
  ip         IP Trace
  ipv6       IPv6 Trace
  ipx        IPX Trace
  mac        Trace Layer2 path between 2 endpoints
  oldvines   Vines Trace (Cisco)
  vines      Vines Trace (Banyan)
  <cr>
```

And as with ping, we can perform an extended traceroute using additional parameters, typically used to change the source interface:

```
Todd#traceroute
Protocol [ip]:
Target IP address: 10.1.1.1
Source address: 172.16.10.1
Numeric display [n]:
Timeout in seconds [3]:
Probe count [3]:
Minimum Time to Live [1]: 255
Maximum Time to Live [30]:
Type escape sequence to abort.
Tracing the route to 10.1.1.1
```

Telnet, FTP, and HTTP are really the best tools because they use IP at the Network layer and TCP at the Transport layer to create a session with a remote host. If you can telnet, ftp, or http into a device, you know that your IP connectivity just has to be solid!

```
Todd#telnet ?
  WORD IP address or hostname of a remote system
  <cr>
Todd#telnet 10.1.1.1
```

When you telnet into a remote device, you won't see console messages by default. For example, you will not see debugging output. To allow console messages to be sent to your Telnet session, use the terminal monitor command, as shown on the SF router.

```
SF#terminal monitor
```

From the switch or router prompt, you just type a hostname or IP address and it will assume you want to telnet—you don't need to type the actual command, telnet.

Coming up, I'll show you how to verify the interface statistics.

Verifying with the *show interface* Command

Another way to verify your configuration is by typing show interface commands, the first of which is the show interface ? command. Doing this will reveal all the available interfaces to verify and configure.

 The show interfaces command, plural, displays the configurable parameters and statistics of all interfaces on a router.

This command comes in really handy when you're verifying and troubleshooting router and network issues.

The following output is from my freshly erased and rebooted 2811 router:

```
Router#sh int ?
  Async              Async interface
  BVI                Bridge-Group Virtual Interface
  CDMA-Ix            CDMA Ix interface
  CTunnel            CTunnel interface
  Dialer             Dialer interface
  FastEthernet       FastEthernet IEEE 802.3
  Loopback           Loopback interface
  MFR                Multilink Frame Relay bundle interface
  Multilink          Multilink-group interface
  Null               Null interface
  Port-channel       Ethernet Channel of interfaces
  Serial             Serial
  Tunnel             Tunnel interface
  Vif                PGM Multicast Host interface
  Virtual-PPP        Virtual PPP interface
  Virtual-Template   Virtual Template interface
  Virtual-TokenRing  Virtual TokenRing
  accounting         Show interface accounting
  counters           Show interface counters
  crb                Show interface routing/bridging info
  dampening          Show interface dampening info
  description        Show interface description
  etherchannel       Show interface etherchannel information
  irb                Show interface routing/bridging info
  mac-accounting     Show interface MAC accounting info
```

mpls-exp	Show interface MPLS experimental accounting info
precedence	Show interface precedence accounting info
pruning	Show interface trunk VTP pruning information
rate-limit	Show interface rate-limit info
status	Show interface line status
summary	Show interface summary
switching	Show interface switching
switchport	Show interface switchport information
trunk	Show interface trunk information
|	Output modifiers
<cr>	

The only "real" physical interfaces are FastEthernet, Serial, and Async—the rest are all logical interfaces or commands you can use to verify with.

The next command is show interface fastethernet 0/0. It reveals the hardware address, logical address, and encapsulation method as well as statistics on collisions, as seen here:

```
Router#sh int f0/0
FastEthernet0/0 is up, line protocol is up
  Hardware is MV96340 Ethernet, address is 001a.2f55.c9e8 (bia 001a.2f55.c9e8)
  Internet address is 192.168.1.33/27
  MTU 1500 bytes, BW 100000 Kbit, DLY 100 usec,
     reliability 255/255, txload 1/255, rxload 1/255
  Encapsulation ARPA, loopback not set
  Keepalive set (10 sec)
  Auto-duplex, Auto Speed, 100BaseTX/FX
  ARP type: ARPA, ARP Timeout 04:00:00
  Last input never, output 00:02:07, output hang never
  Last clearing of "show interface" counters never
  Input queue: 0/75/0/0 (size/max/drops/flushes); Total output drops: 0
  Queueing strategy: fifo
  Output queue: 0/40 (size/max)
  5 minute input rate 0 bits/sec, 0 packets/sec
  5 minute output rate 0 bits/sec, 0 packets/sec
     0 packets input, 0 bytes
     Received 0 broadcasts, 0 runts, 0 giants, 0 throttles
     0 input errors, 0 CRC, 0 frame, 0 overrun, 0 ignored
     0 watchdog
     0 input packets with dribble condition detected
     16 packets output, 960 bytes, 0 underruns
     0 output errors, 0 collisions, 0 interface resets
     0 babbles, 0 late collision, 0 deferred
```

```
      0 lost carrier, 0 no carrier
      0 output buffer failures, 0 output buffers swapped out
Router#
```

You probably guessed that we're going to go over the important statistics from this output, but first, just for fun, I've got to ask you, which subnet is FastEthernet 0/0 a member of and what's the broadcast address and valid host range?

I'm serious—you really have to be able to nail these things NASCAR-fast! Just in case you didn't, the address is 192.168.1.33/27. And I've gotta be honest—if you don't know what a /27 is at this point, you'll need a miracle to pass the exam! That or you need to actually read this book. (As a quick reminder, a /27 is 255.255.255.224.) The fourth octet is a block size of 32. The subnets are 0, 32, 64, etc.; the FastEthernet interface is in the 32 subnet; the broadcast address is 63; and the valid hosts are 33–62. All good now?

> **NOTE**   If you struggled with any of this, please save yourself from certain doom and get yourself back into Chapter 4, "Easy Subnetting," now! Read and reread it until you've got it dialed in!

Okay—back to the output. The preceding interface is working and looks to be in good shape. The show interfaces command will show you if you're receiving errors on the interface, and it will also show you the maximum transmission unit (MTU). MTU is the maximum packet size allowed to transmit on that interface, bandwidth (BW) is for use with routing protocols, and 255/255 means that reliability is perfect! The load is 1/255, meaning no load.

Continuing through the output, can you figure out the bandwidth of the interface? Well, other than the easy giveaway of the interface being called a "FastEthernet" interface, we can see that the bandwidth is 100000 Kbit, which is 100,000,000. Kbit means to add three zeros, which is 100 Mbits per second, or FastEthernet. Gigabit would be 1000000 Kbits per second.

Be sure you don't miss the output errors and collisions, which show 0 in my output. If these numbers are increasing, then you have some sort of Physical or Data Link layer issue. Check your duplex! If you have one side as half-duplex and one at full-duplex, your interface will work, albeit really slow and those numbers will be increasing fast!

The most important statistic of the show interface command is the output of the line and Data Link protocol status. If the output reveals that FastEthernet 0/0 is up and the line protocol is up, then the interface is up and running:

```
Router#sh int fa0/0
FastEthernet0/0 is up, line protocol is up
```

The first parameter refers to the Physical layer, and it's up when it receives carrier detect. The second parameter refers to the Data Link layer, and it looks for keepalives from the connecting end. Keepalives are important because they're used between devices to make sure connectivity hasn't been dropped.

Here's an example of where your problem will often be found—on serial interfaces:

```
Router#sh int s0/0/0
Serial0/0 is up, line protocol is down
```

If you see that the line is up but the protocol is down, as displayed here, you're experiencing a clocking (keepalive) or framing problem—possibly an encapsulation mismatch. Check the keepalives on both ends to make sure they match. Make sure that the clock rate is set, if needed, and that the encapsulation type is equal on both ends. The preceding output tells us that there's a Data Link layer problem.

If you discover that both the line interface and the protocol are down, it's a cable or interface problem. The following output would indicate a Physical layer problem:

```
Router#sh int s0/0/0
Serial0/0 is down, line protocol is down
```

As you'll see next, if one end is administratively shut down, the remote end would present as down and down:

```
Router#sh int s0/0/0
Serial0/0 is administratively down, line protocol is down
```

To enable the interface, use the command no shutdown from interface configuration mode.

The next show interface serial 0/0/0 command demonstrates the serial line and the maximum transmission unit (MTU)—1,500 bytes by default. It also shows the default bandwidth (BW) on all Cisco serial links, which is 1.544 Kbps. This is used to determine the bandwidth of the line for routing protocols like EIGRP and OSPF. Another important configuration to notice is the keepalive, which is 10 seconds by default. Each router sends a keepalive message to its neighbor every 10 seconds, and if both routers aren't configured for the same keepalive time, it won't work! Check out this output:

```
Router#sh int s0/0/0
Serial0/0 is up, line protocol is up
 Hardware is HD64570
 MTU 1500 bytes, BW 1544 Kbit, DLY 20000 usec,
   reliability 255/255, txload 1/255, rxload 1/255
 Encapsulation HDLC, loopback not set, keepalive set
  (10 sec)
 Last input never, output never, output hang never
 Last clearing of "show interface" counters never
 Queueing strategy: fifo
 Output queue 0/40, 0 drops; input queue 0/75, 0 drops
 5 minute input rate 0 bits/sec, 0 packets/sec
 5 minute output rate 0 bits/sec, 0 packets/sec
  0 packets input, 0 bytes, 0 no buffer
```

```
Received 0 broadcasts, 0 runts, 0 giants, 0 throttles
0 input errors, 0 CRC, 0 frame, 0 overrun, 0 ignored,
0 abort
0 packets output, 0 bytes, 0 underruns
0 output errors, 0 collisions, 16 interface resets
0 output buffer failures, 0 output buffers swapped out
0 carrier transitions
DCD=down DSR=down DTR=down RTS=down CTS=down
```

You can clear the counters on the interface by typing the command **clear counters**:

```
Router#clear counters ?
  Async             Async interface
  BVI               Bridge-Group Virtual Interface
  CTunnel           CTunnel interface
  Dialer            Dialer interface
  FastEthernet      FastEthernet IEEE 802.3
  Group-Async       Async Group interface
  Line              Terminal line
  Loopback          Loopback interface
  MFR               Multilink Frame Relay bundle interface
  Multilink         Multilink-group interface
  Null              Null interface
  Serial            Serial
  Tunnel            Tunnel interface
  Vif               PGM Multicast Host interface
  Virtual-Template  Virtual Template interface
  Virtual-TokenRing Virtual TokenRing
  <cr>
```

```
Router#clear counters s0/0/0
Clear "show interface" counters on this interface
  [confirm][enter]
Router#
00:17:35: %CLEAR-5-COUNTERS: Clear counter on interface
  Serial0/0/0 by console
Router#
```

Troubleshooting with the *show interfaces* Command

Let's take a look at the output of the show interfaces command one more time before I move on. There are some statistics in this output that are important for the Cisco objectives.

```
275496 packets input, 35226811 bytes, 0 no buffer
   Received 69748 broadcasts (58822 multicasts)
```

```
0 runts, 0 giants, 0 throttles
0 input errors, 0 CRC, 0 frame, 0 overrun, 0 ignored
0 watchdog, 58822 multicast, 0 pause input
0 input packets with dribble condition detected
2392529 packets output, 337933522 bytes, 0 underruns
0 output errors, 0 collisions, 1 interface resets
0 babbles, 0 late collision, 0 deferred
0 lost carrier, 0 no carrier, 0 PAUSE output
0 output buffer failures, 0 output buffers swapped out
```

Finding where to start when troubleshooting an interface can be the difficult part, but certainly we'll look for the number of input errors and CRCs right away. Typically we'd see those statistics increase with a duplex error, but it could be another Physical layer issue such as the cable might be receiving excessive interference or the network interface cards might have a failure. Typically you can tell if it is interference when the CRC and input errors output grow but the collision counters do not.

Let's take a look at some of the output:

No buffer   This isn't a number you want to see incrementing. This means you don't have any buffer room left for incoming packets. Any packets received once the buffers are full are discarded. You can see how many packets are dropped with the ignored output.

Ignored   If the packet buffers are full, packets will be dropped. You see this increment along with the no buffer output. Typically if the no buffer and ignored outputs are incrementing, you have some sort of broadcast storm on your LAN. This can be caused by a bad NIC or even a bad network design.

I'll repeat this because it is so important for the exam objectives: Typically if the no buffer and ignored outputs are incrementing, you have some sort of broadcast storm on your LAN. This can be caused by a bad NIC or even a bad network design.

Runts   Frames that did not meet the minimum frame size requirement of 64 bytes. Typically caused by collisions.

Giants   Frames received that are larger than 1518 bytes

Input Errors   This is the total of many counters: runts, giants, no buffer, CRC, frame, overrun, and ignored counts.

CRC   At the end of each frame is a Frame Check Sequence (FCS) field that holds the answer to a cyclic redundancy check (CRC). If the receiving host's answer to the CRC does not match the sending host's answer, then a CRC error will occur.

Frame   This output increments when frames received are of an illegal format, or not complete, which is typically incremented when a collision occurs.

Packets Output   Total number of packets (frames) forwarded out to the interface.

Output Errors   Total number of packets (frames) that the switch port tried to transmit but for which some problem occurred.

Collisions   When transmitting a frame in half-duplex, the NIC listens on the receiving pair of the cable for another signal. If a signal is transmitted from another host, a collision has occurred. This output should not increment if you are running full-duplex.

Late Collisions   If all Ethernet specifications are followed during the cable install, all collisions should occur by the 64th byte of the frame. If a collision occurs after 64 bytes, the late collisions counter increments. This counter will increment on a duplex mismatched interface, or if cable length exceeds specifications.

 A duplex mismatch causes late collision errors at the end of the connection. To avoid this situation, manually set the duplex parameters of the switch to match the attached device.

A duplex mismatch is a situation in which the switch operates at full-duplex and the connected device operates at half-duplex, or vice versa. The result of a duplex mismatch is extremely slow performance, intermittent connectivity, and loss of connection. Other possible causes of data-link errors at full-duplex are bad cables, a faulty switch port, or NIC software or hardware issues. Use the show interface command to verify the duplex settings.

If the mismatch occurs between two Cisco devices with Cisco Discovery Protocol enabled, you will see Cisco Discovery Protocol error messages on the console or in the logging buffer of both devices.

```
%CDP-4-DUPLEX_MISMATCH: duplex mismatch discovered on FastEthernet0/2 (not
half duplex)
```

Cisco Discovery Protocol is useful for detecting errors and for gathering port and system statistics on nearby Cisco devices. CDP is covered in Chapter 7.

Verifying with the *show ip interface* Command

The show ip interface command will provide you with information regarding the layer 3 configurations of a router's interface, such as the IP address and subnet mask, MTU, and if an access list is set on the interface:

```
Router#sh ip interface
FastEthernet0/0 is up, line protocol is up
  Internet address is 1.1.1.1/24
  Broadcast address is 255.255.255.255
  Address determined by setup command
  MTU is 1500 bytes
```

```
    Helper address is not set
    Directed broadcast forwarding is disabled
    Outgoing access list is not set
    Inbound  access list is not set
    Proxy ARP is enabled
    Security level is default
    Split horizon is enabled
[output cut]
```

The status of the interface, the IP address and mask, information on whether an access list is set on the interface, and basic IP information are all included in this output.

Using the *show ip interface brief* Command

The show ip interface brief command is probably one of the best commands that you can ever use on a Cisco router or switch. This command provides a quick overview of the devices interfaces, including the logical address and status:

```
Router#sh ip int brief
Interface        IP-Address    OK? Method Status     Protocol
FastEthernet0/0  unassigned    YES unset  up             up
FastEthernet0/1  unassigned    YES unset  up             up
Serial0/0/0      unassigned    YES unset  up             down
Serial0/0/1      unassigned    YES unset  administratively down down
Serial0/1/0      unassigned    YES unset  administratively down down
Serial0/2/0      unassigned    YES unset  administratively down down
```

Remember, administratively down means that you need to type no shutdown in order to enable the interface. Notice that Serial0/0/0 is up/down, which means that the Physical layer is good and carrier detect is sensed but no keepalives are being received from the remote end. In a nonproduction network, like the one I am working with, this tells us the clock rate hasn't been set.

Verifying with the *show protocols* Command

The show protocols command is also a really helpful command that you'd use in order to quickly see the status of layers 1 and 2 of each interface as well as the IP addresses used.

Here's a look at one of my production routers:

```
Router#sh protocols
Global values:
  Internet Protocol routing is enabled
Ethernet0/0 is administratively down, line protocol is down
Serial0/0 is up, line protocol is up
  Internet address is 100.30.31.5/24
```

```
Serial0/1 is administratively down, line protocol is down
Serial0/2 is up, line protocol is up
  Internet address is 100.50.31.2/24
Loopback0 is up, line protocol is up
  Internet address is 100.20.31.1/24
```

The show ip interface brief and show protocols commands provide the layer 1 and layer 2 statistics of an interface as well as the IP addresses. The next command, show controllers, only provides layer 1 information. Let's take a look.

Using the *show controllers* Command

The show controllers command displays information about the physical interface itself. It'll also give you the type of serial cable plugged into a serial port. Usually, this will only be a DTE cable that plugs into a type of data service unit (DSU).

```
Router#sh controllers serial 0/0
HD unit 0, idb = 0x1229E4, driver structure at 0x127E70
buffer size 1524 HD unit 0, V.35 DTE cable
```

```
Router#sh controllers serial 0/1
HD unit 1, idb = 0x12C174, driver structure at 0x131600
buffer size 1524 HD unit 1, V.35 DCE cable
```

Notice that serial 0/0 has a DTE cable, whereas the serial 0/1 connection has a DCE cable. Serial 0/1 would have to provide clocking with the clock rate command. Serial 0/0 would get its clocking from the DSU.

Let's look at this command again. In Figure 6.5, see the DTE/DCE cable between the two routers? Know that you will not see this in production networks!

FIGURE 6.5 Where do you configure clocking? Use the show controllers command on each router's serial interface to find out.

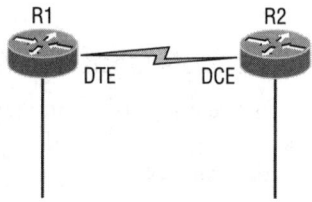

Router R1 has a DTE connection, which is typically the default for all Cisco routers. Routers R1 and R2 can't communicate. Check out the output of the show controllers s0/0 command here:

```
R1#sh controllers serial 0/0
HD unit 0, idb = 0x1229E4, driver structure at 0x127E70
buffer size 1524 HD unit 0, V.35 DCE cable
```

The show controllers s0/0 command reveals that the interface is a V.35 DCE cable. This means that R1 needs to provide clocking of the line to router R2. Basically, the interface has the wrong label on the cable on the R1 router's serial interface. But if you add clocking on the R1 router's serial interface, the network should come right up.

Let's check out another issue in Figure 6.6 that you can solve by using the show controllers command. Again, routers R1 and R2 can't communicate.

FIGURE 6.6 By looking at R1, the show controllers command reveals that R1 and R2 can't communicate.

R1   R2

S0/0   S0/0

Here's the output of R1's show controllers s0/0 command and show ip interface s0/0:

R1#**sh controllers s0/0**
HD unit 0, idb = 0x1229E4, driver structure at 0x127E70
buffer size 1524 HD unit 0,
DTE V.35 clocks stopped
cpb = 0xE2, eda = 0x4140, cda = 0x4000

R1#**sh ip interface s0/0**
Serial0/0 is up, line protocol is down
  Internet address is 192.168.10.2/24
  Broadcast address is 255.255.255.255

If you use the show controllers command and the show ip interface command, you'll see that router R1 isn't receiving the clocking of the line. This network is a nonproduction network, so no CSU/DSU is connected to provide clocking for it. This means the DCE end of the cable will be providing the clock rate—in this case, the R2 router. The show ip interface indicates that the interface is up but the protocol is down, which means that no keepalives are being received from the far end. In this example, the likely culprit is the result of bad cable, or simply the lack of clocking.

Summary

This was a fun chapter! I showed you a lot about the Cisco IOS, and I really hope you gained a lot of insight into the Cisco router world. I started off by explaining the Cisco Internetwork Operating System (IOS) and how you can use the IOS to run and configure Cisco routers. You learned how to bring a router up and what setup mode does. Oh, and by the way, since you can now basically configure Cisco routers, you should never use setup mode, right?

After I discussed how to connect to a router with a console and LAN connection, I covered the Cisco help features and how to use the CLI to find commands and command parameters. In addition, I discussed some basic show commands to help you verify your configurations.

Administrative functions on a router help you administer your network and verify that you are configuring the correct device. Setting router passwords is one of the most important configurations you can perform on your routers. I showed you the five passwords you must set, plus I introduced you to the hostname, interface description, and banners as tools to help you administer your router.

Well, that concludes your introduction to the Cisco IOS. And, as usual, it's super-important for you to have the basics that we went over in this chapter down rock-solid before you move on to the following chapters!

Exam Essentials

Describe the responsibilities of the IOS.   The Cisco router IOS software is responsible for network protocols and providing supporting functions, connecting high-speed traffic between devices, adding security to control access and prevent unauthorized network use, providing scalability for ease of network growth and redundancy, and supplying network reliability for connecting to network resources.

List the options available to connect to a Cisco device for management purposes.   The three options available are the console port, auxiliary port, and in-band communication, such as Telnet, SSH, and HTTP. Don't forget, a Telnet connection is not possible until an IP address has been configured and a Telnet password has been configured.

Understand the boot sequence of a router.   When you first bring up a Cisco router, it will run a power-on self-test (POST), and if that passes, it will look for and load the Cisco IOS from flash memory, if a file is present. The IOS then proceeds to load and looks for a valid configuration in NVRAM called the startup-config. If no file is present in NVRAM, the router will go into setup mode.

Describe the use of setup mode.   Setup mode is automatically started if a router boots and no startup-config is in NVRAM. You can also bring up setup mode by typing **setup** from privileged mode. Setup provides a minimum amount of configuration in an easy format for someone who does not understand how to configure a Cisco router from the command line.

Differentiate user, privileged, and global configuration modes, both visually and from a command capabilities perspective.   User mode, indicated by the **routername>** prompt, provides a command-line interface with very few available commands by default. User mode does not allow the configuration to be viewed or changed. Privileged mode, indicated by the **routername#** prompt, allows a user to both view and change the configuration of a router. You can enter privileged mode by typing the command **enable** and entering the enable password or enable secret password, if set. Global configuration mode, indicated by the **routername(config)#** prompt, allows configuration changes to be made that apply to the entire router (as opposed to a configuration change that might affect only one interface, for example).

Recognize additional prompts available in other modes and describe their use.   Additional modes are reached via the global configuration prompt, **routername(config)#**, and their prompts include interface, **router(config-if)#**, for making interface settings; line configuration mode, **router(config-line)#**, used to set passwords and make other settings to various connection methods; and routing protocol modes for various routing protocols; **router(config-router)#**, used to enable and configure routing protocols.

Access and utilize editing and help features.   Make use of typing a question mark at the end of commands for help in using the commands. Additionally, understand how to filter command help with the same question mark and letters. Use the command history to retrieve commands previously utilized without retyping. Understand the meaning of the caret when an incorrect command is rejected. Finally, identify useful hot key combinations.

Identify the information provided by the show version **command.**   The show version command will provide basic configuration for the system hardware as well as the software version, the names and sources of configuration files, the configuration register setting, and the boot images.

Set the hostname of a router.   The command sequence to set the hostname of a router is as follows:

```
enable
config t
hostname Todd
```

Differentiate the enable password and enable secret password.   Both of these passwords are used to gain access into privileged mode. However, the enable secret password is newer and is always encrypted by default. Also, if you set the enable password and then set the enable secret, only the enable secret will be used.

Describe the configuration and use of banners.   Banners provide information to users accessing the device and can be displayed at various login prompts. They are configured with the banner command and a keyword describing the specific type of banner.

Set the enable secret on a router.   To set the enable secret, you use the global config command enable secret. Do not use enable secret password *password* or you will set your password to *password password*. Here is an example:

```
enable
config t
enable secret todd
```

Set the console password on a router.   To set the console password, use the following sequence:

```
enable
config t
line console 0
password todd
login
```

Set the Telnet password on a router.   To set the Telnet password, the sequence is as follows:

```
enable
config t
line vty 0 4
password todd
login
```

Describe the advantages of using Secure Shell and list its requirements.   Secure Shell (SSH) uses encrypted keys to send data so that usernames and passwords are not sent in the clear. It requires that a hostname and domain name be configured and that encryption keys be generated.

Describe the process of preparing an interface for use.   To use an interface, you must configure it with an IP address and subnet mask in the same subnet of the hosts that will be connecting to the switch that is connected to that interface. It also must be enabled with the no shutdown command. A serial interface that is connected back to back with another router serial interface must also be configured with a clock rate on the DCE end of the serial cable.

Understand how to troubleshoot a serial link problem.   If you type **show interface serial 0/0** and see down, line protocol is down, this will be considered a Physical layer problem. If you see it as up, line protocol is down, then you have a Data Link layer problem.

Understand how to verify your router with the show interfaces **command.**   If you type **show interfaces**, you can view the statistics for the interfaces on the router, verify whether the interfaces are shut down, and see the IP address of each interface.

Describe how to view, edit, delete, and save a configuration.   The show running-config command is used to view the current configuration being used by the router. The show startup-config command displays the last configuration that was saved and is the one that will be used at next startup. The copy running-config startup-config command is used to save changes made to the running configuration in NVRAM. The erase startup-config command deletes the saved configuration and will result in the invocation of the setup menu when the router is rebooted because there will be no configuration present.

Written Lab 6: IOS Understanding

In this section, you'll complete the following lab to make sure you've got the information and concepts contained within them fully dialed in:

Lab 6.1: IOS Understanding

You can find the answers to this lab in Appendix A, "Answers to Written Labs."

Write out the command or commands for the following questions:

1. What command is used to set a serial interface to provide clocking to another router at 1000 Kb?

2. If you telnet into a switch and get the response connection refused, password not set, what commands would you execute on the destination device to stop receiving this message and not be prompted for a password?

3. If you type **show int fastethernet 0/1** and notice the port is administratively down, what commands would you execute to enable the interface?

4. If you wanted to delete the configuration stored in NVRAM, what command(s) would you type?

5. If you wanted to set the user-mode password to *todd* for the console port, what command(s) would you type?

6. If you wanted to set the enable secret password to *cisco*, what command(s) would you type?

7. If you wanted to determine if serial interface 0/2 on your router should provide clocking, what command would you use?

8. What command would you use to see the terminal history size?

9. You want to reinitialize the switch and totally replace the running-config with the current startup-config. What command will you use?

10. How would you set the name of a switch to *Sales*?

Hands-on Labs

In this section, you will perform commands on a Cisco switch (or you can use a router) that will help you understand what you learned in this chapter.

You'll need at least one Cisco device—two would be better, three would be outstanding. The hands-on labs in this section are included for use with real Cisco routers, but all of these labs work with the LammleSim IOS version (see www.lammle.com/ccna) or use the Cisco Packet Tracer router simulator. Last, for the Cisco exam it doesn't matter what model of switch or router you use with these labs, as long as you're running IOS 12.2 or newer. Yes, I know the objectives are 15 code, but that is not important for any of these labs.

It is assumed that the device you're going to use has no current configuration present. If necessary, erase any existing configuration with Hands-on Lab 6.1; otherwise, proceed to Hands-on Lab 6.2:

Lab 6.1: Erasing an Existing Configuration

Lab 6.2: Exploring User, Privileged, and Configuration Modes

Lab 6.3: Using the Help and Editing Features

Lab 6.4: Saving a Configuration

Lab 6.5: Setting Passwords

Lab 6.6: Setting the Hostname, Descriptions, IP Address, and Clock Rate

Hands-on Lab 6.1: Erasing an Existing Configuration

The following lab may require the knowledge of a username and password to enter privileged mode. If the router has a configuration with an unknown username and password for privileged mode, this procedure will not be possible. It is possible to erase a configuration without a privileged mode password, but the exact steps depend on the model and will not be covered until Chapter 7.

1. Start the switch up and when prompted, press Enter.

2. At the Switch> prompt, type **enable**.

3. If prompted, enter the username and press Enter. Then enter the correct password and press Enter.

4. At the privileged mode prompt, type **erase startup-config**.

5. At the privileged mode prompt, type **reload**, and when prompted to save the configuration, type **n** for no.

Hands-on Lab 6.2: Exploring User, Privileged, and Configuration Modes

In the following lab, you'll explore user, privileged, and configuration modes:

1. Plug the switch in, or turn the router on. If you just erased the configuration as in Hands-on Lab 6.1, when prompted to continue with the configuration dialog, enter **n** for no and press Enter. When prompted, press Enter to connect to your router. This will put you into user mode.

2. At the Switch> prompt, type a question mark (**?**).

3. Notice the -more- at the bottom of the screen.

4. Press the Enter key to view the commands line by line. Press the spacebar to view the commands a full screen at a time. You can type **q** at any time to quit.

5. Type **enable** or **en** and press Enter. This will put you into privileged mode where you can change and view the router configuration.

6. At the Switch# prompt, type a question mark (**?**). Notice how many options are available to you in privileged mode.

7. Type **q** to quit.

8. Type **config** and press Enter.

9. When prompted for a method, press Enter to configure your router using your terminal (which is the default).

10. At the Switch(config)# prompt, type a question mark (**?**), then **q** to quit, or press the spacebar to view the commands.

11. Type **interface f0/1** or **int f0/1** (or even **int gig0/1**) and press Enter. This will allow you to configure interface FastEthernet 0/1 or Gigabit 0/1.

12. At the Switch(config-if)# prompt, type a question mark (**?**).

13. If using a router, type **int s0/0**, **interface s0/0** or even **interface s0/0/0** and press Enter. This will allow you to configure interface serial 0/0. Notice that you can go from interface to interface easily.

14. Type **encapsulation ?**.

15. Type **exit**. Notice how this brings you back one level.

16. Press Ctrl+Z. Notice how this brings you out of configuration mode and places you back into privileged mode.

17. Type **disable**. This will put you into user mode.

18. Type **exit**, which will log you out of the router or switch.

Hands-on Lab 6.3: Using the Help and Editing Features

This lab will provide hands-on experience with Cisco's help and editing features.

1. Log into your device and go to privileged mode by typing **en** or **enable**.

2. Type a question mark (**?**).

3. Type **cl?** and then press Enter. Notice that you can see all the commands that start with *cl*.

4. Type **clock ?** and press Enter.

> Notice the difference between steps 3 and 4. Step 3 has you type letters with no space and a question mark, which will give you all the commands that start with *cl*. Step 4 has you type a command, space, and question mark. By doing this, you will see the next available parameter.

5. Set the clock by typing **clock ?** and, following the help screens, setting the time and date. The following steps walk you through setting the date and time.

6. Type **clock ?**.

7. Type **clock set ?**.

8. Type **clock set 10:30:30 ?**.

9. Type **clock set 10:30:30 14 May ?**.

10. Type **clock set 10:30:30 14 May 2011**.

11. Press Enter.

12. Type **show clock** to see the time and date.

13. From privileged mode, type **show access-list 10**. Don't press Enter.

14. Press Ctrl+A. This takes you to the beginning of the line.

15. Press Ctrl+E. This should take you back to the end of the line.

16. Ctrl+A takes your cursor back to the beginning of the line, and then Ctrl+F moves your cursor forward one character.

17. Press Ctrl+B, which will move you back one character.

18. Press Enter, then press Ctrl+P. This will repeat the last command.

19. Press the up arrow key on your keyboard. This will also repeat the last command.

20. Type **sh history**. This shows you the last 10 commands entered.

21. Type **terminal history size ?**. This changes the history entry size. The ? is the number of allowed lines.

22. Type **show terminal** to gather terminal statistics and history size.

23. Type **terminal no editing**. This turns off advanced editing. Repeat steps 14 through 18 to see that the shortcut editing keys have no effect until you type **terminal editing**.

24. Type **terminal editing** and press Enter to re-enable advanced editing.

25. Type **sh run**, then press your Tab key. This will finish typing the command for you.

26. Type **sh start**, then press your Tab key. This will finish typing the command for you.

Hands-on Lab 6.4: Saving a Configuration

In this lab, you will get hands-on experience saving a configuration:

1. Log into your device and go into privileged mode by typing **en** or **enable**, then press Enter.

2. To see the configuration stored in NVRAM, type **sh start** and press Tab and Enter, or type **show startup-config** and press Enter. However, if no configuration has been saved, you will get an error message.

3. To save a configuration to NVRAM, which is known as startup-config, you can do one of the following:

   ▪ Type **copy run start** and press Enter.

   ▪ Type **copy running**, press Tab, type **start**, press Tab, and press Enter.

   ▪ Type **copy running-config startup-config** and press Enter.

4. Type **sh start**, press Tab, then press Enter.

5. Type **sh run**, press Tab, then press Enter.

6. Type **erase startup-config**, press Tab, then press Enter.

7. Type **sh start**, press Tab, then press Enter. The router will either tell you that NVRAM is not present or display some other type of message, depending on the IOS and hardware.

8. Type **reload**, then press Enter. Acknowledge the reload by pressing Enter. Wait for the device to reload.

9. Say no to entering setup mode, or just press Ctrl+C.

Hands-on Lab 6.5: Setting Passwords

This hands-on lab will have you set your passwords.

1. Log into the router and go into privileged mode by typing **en** or **enable**.

2. Type **config t** and press Enter.

3. Type **enable ?**.

4. Set your enable secret password by typing **enable secret *password*** (the third word should be your own personalized password) and pressing Enter. Do not add the parameter password after the parameter secret (this would make your password the word *password*). An example would be enable secret todd.

5. Now let's see what happens when you log all the way out of the router and then log in. Log out by pressing Ctrl+Z, and then type **exit** and press Enter. Go to privileged mode. Before you are allowed to enter privileged mode, you will be asked for a password. If you successfully enter the secret password, you can proceed.

6. Remove the secret password. Go to privileged mode, type **config t**, and press Enter. Type **no enable secret** and press Enter. Log out and then log back in again; now you should not be asked for a password.

7. One more password used to enter privileged mode is called the enable password. It is an older, less secure password and is not used if an enable secret password is set. Here is an example of how to set it:

```
config t
enable password todd1
```

8. Notice that the enable secret and enable passwords are different. They should never be set the same. Actually, you should never use the enable password, only enable secret.

9. Type **config t** to be at the right level to set your console and auxiliary passwords, then type **line ?**.

10. Notice that the parameters for the line commands are auxiliary, vty, and console. You will set all three if you're on a router; if you're on a switch, only the console and VTY lines are available.

11. To set the Telnet or VTY password, type **line vty 0 4** and then press Enter. The 0 4 is the range of the five available virtual lines used to connect with Telnet. If you have an enterprise IOS, the number of lines may vary. Use the question mark to determine the last line number available on your router.

12. The next command is used to set the authentication on or off. Type **login** and press Enter to prompt for a user-mode password when telnetting into the device. You will not be able to telnet into a Cisco device if the password is not set.

> You can use the no `login` command to disable the user-mode password prompt when using Telnet. Do not do this in production!

13. One more command you need to set for your VTY password is password. Type **password** *password* to set the password. (*password* is your password.)

14. Here is an example of how to set the VTY password:

```
config t
line vty 0 4
password todd
login
```

15. Set your auxiliary password by first typing **line auxiliary 0** or **line aux 0** (if you are using a router).

16. Type **login**.

17. Type **password** *password*.

18. Set your console password by first typing **line console 0** or **line con 0**.

19. Type **login**.

20. Type **password** *password*. Here is an example of the last two command sequences:

```
config t
line con 0
password todd1
login
line aux 0
password todd
login
```

21. You can add the Exec-timeout 0 0 command to the console 0 line. This will stop the console from timing out and logging you out. The command sequence will now look like this:

```
config t
line con 0
password todd2
```

```
login
exec-timeout 0 0
```

22. Set the console prompt to not overwrite the command you're typing with console messages by using the command `logging synchronous`.

```
config t
line con 0
logging synchronous
```

Hands-on Lab 6.6: Setting the Hostname, Descriptions, IP Address, and Clock Rate

This lab will have you set your administrative functions on each device.

1. Log into the switch or router and go into privileged mode by typing **en** or **enable**. If required, enter a username and password.

2. Set your hostname by using the `hostname` command. Notice that it is one word. Here is an example of setting your hostname on your router, but the switch uses the exact same command:

```
Router#config t
Router(config)#hostname RouterA
RouterA(config)#
```

Notice that the hostname of the router changed in the prompt as soon as you pressed Enter.

3. Set a banner that the network administrators will see by using the `banner` command, as shown in the following steps.

4. Type **config t**, then **banner ?**.

5. Notice that you can set at least four different banners. For this lab we are only interested in the login and message of the day (MOTD) banners.

6. Set your MOTD banner, which will be displayed when a console, auxiliary, or Telnet connection is made to the router, by typing this:

```
config t
banner motd #
This is an motd banner
#
```

7. The preceding example used a # sign as a delimiting character. This tells the router when the message is done. You cannot use the delimiting character in the message itself.

8. You can remove the MOTD banner by typing the following command:

```
config t
no banner motd
```

9. Set the login banner by typing this:

```
config t
banner login #
This is a login banner
#
```

10. The login banner will display immediately after the MOTD but before the user-mode password prompt. Remember that you set your user-mode passwords by setting the console, auxiliary, and VTY line passwords.

11. You can remove the login banner by typing this:

```
config t
no banner login
```

12. You can add an IP address to an interface with the ip address command if you are using a router. You need to get into interface configuration mode first; here is an example of how you do that:

```
config t
int f0/1
ip address 1.1.1.1 255.255.0.0
no shutdown
```

Notice that the IP address (1.1.1.1) and subnet mask (255.255.0.0) are configured on one line. The no shutdown (or no shut for short) command is used to enable the interface. All interfaces are shut down by default on a router. If you are on a layer 2 switch, you can set an IP address only on the VLAN 1 interface.

13. You can add identification to an interface by using the description command. This is useful for adding information about the connection. Here is an example:

```
config t
int f0/1
ip address 2.2.2.1 255.255.0.0
no shut
description LAN link to Finance
```

14. You can add the bandwidth of a serial link as well as the clock rate when simulating a DCE WAN link on a router. Here is an example:

```
config t
int s0/0
bandwidth 1000
clock rate 1000000
```

Review Questions

 The following questions are designed to test your understanding of this chapter's material. For more information on how to get additional questions, please see www.lammle.com/ccna.

You can find the answers to these questions in Appendix B, "Answers to Review Questions."

1. You type **show interfaces fa0/1** and get this output:

```
275496 packets input, 35226811 bytes, 0 no buffer
    Received 69748 broadcasts (58822 multicasts)
    0 runts, 0 giants, 0 throttles
    111395 input errors, 511987 CRC, 0 frame, 0 overrun, 0 ignored
    0 watchdog, 58822 multicast, 0 pause input
    0 input packets with dribble condition detected
    2392529 packets output, 337933522 bytes, 0 underruns
    0 output errors, 0 collisions, 1 interface resets
    0 babbles, 0 late collision, 0 deferred
    0 lost carrier, 0 no carrier, 0 PAUSE output
    0 output buffer failures, 0 output buffers swapped out
```

What could the problem possibly be with this interface?

A. Speed mismatch on directly connected interfaces

B. Collisions causing CRC errors

C. Frames received are too large

D. Interference on the Ethernet cable

2. The output of the show running-config command comes from _____.

A. NVRAM

B. Flash

C. RAM

D. Firmware

3. Which two of the following commands are required when configuring SSH on your router? (Choose two.)

A. enable secret *password*

B. exec-timeout 0 0

    C. `ip domain-name` *name*

    D. `username` *name* `password` *password*

    E. `ip ssh version 2`

4. Which command will show you whether a DTE or a DCE cable is plugged into serial 0/0 on your router's WAN port?

    A. `sh int s0/0`

    B. `sh int serial0/0`

    C. `show controllers s0/0`

    D. `show serial0/0 controllers`

5. In the work area, drag the router term to its definition on the right.

Mode	Definition
user exec mode	Commands that affect the entire system
privileged exec mode	Commands that affect interfaces/processes only
Global configuration mode	Interactive configuration dialog
Specific configuration modes	Provides access to all other router commands
Setup mode	Limited to basic monitoring commands

6. Using the given output, what type of interface is shown?

```
[output cut]
Hardware is MV96340 Ethernet, address is 001a.2f55.c9e8 (bia 001a.2f55.c9e8)
Internet address is 192.168.1.33/27
MTU 1500 bytes, BW 100000 Kbit, DLY 100 usec,
    reliability 255/255, txload 1/255, rxload 1/255
```

    A. 10 Mb

    B. 100 Mb

    C. 1000 Mb

    D. 1000 MB

7. Which of the following commands will configure all the default VTY ports on a switch?

    A. `Switch#`**`line vty 0 4`**

    B. `Switch(config)#`**`line vty 0 4`**

    C. `Switch(config-if)#`**`line console 0`**

    D. `Switch(config)#`**`line vty all`**

8. Which of the following commands sets the privileged mode password to Cisco and encrypts the password?

    A. `enable secret password Cisco`

    B. `enable secret cisco`

    C. `enable secret Cisco`

    D. `enable password Cisco`

9. If you wanted administrators to see a message when logging into the switch, which command would you use?

    A. `message banner motd`

    B. `banner message motd`

    C. `banner motd`

    D. `message motd`

10. Which of the following prompts indicates that the switch is currently in privileged mode?

    A. `Switch(config)#`

    B. `Switch>`

    C. `Switch#`

    D. `Switch(config-if)`

11. What command do you type to save the configuration stored in RAM to NVRAM?

    A. `Switch(config)#`**`copy current to starting`**

    B. `Switch#`**`copy starting to running`**

    C. `Switch(config)#`**`copy running-config startup-config`**

    D. `Switch#`**`copy run start`**

12. You try to telnet into SF from router Corp and receive this message:

    ```
    Corp#telnet SF
    Trying SF (10.0.0.1)...Open

    Password required, but none set
    [Connection to SF closed by foreign host]
    Corp#
    ```

    Which of the following sequences will address this problem correctly?

    A. `Corp(config)#line console 0`
        `Corp(config-line)#password` *password*
        `Corp(config-line)#login`

    B. `SF config)#line console 0`
        `SF(config-line)#enable secret` *password*
        `SF(config-line)#login`

C. `Corp(config)#line vty 0 4`

   `Corp(config-line)#password` *password*

   `Corp(config-line)#login`

D. `SF(config)#line vty 0 4`

   `SF(config-line)#password` *password*

   `SF(config-line)#login`

13. Which command will delete the contents of NVRAM on a switch?

   A. `delete NVRAM`

   B. `delete startup-config`

   C. `erase flash`

   D. `erase startup-config`

   E. `erase start`

14. What is the problem with an interface if you type **show interface g0/1** and receive the following message?

   `Gigabit 0/1 is administratively down, line protocol is down`

   A. The keepalives are different times.

   B. The administrator has the interface shut down.

   C. The administrator is pinging from the interface.

   D. No cable is attached.

15. Which of the following commands displays the configurable parameters and statistics of all interfaces on a switch?

   A. `show running-config`

   B. `show startup-config`

   C. `show interfaces`

   D. `show versions`

16. If you delete the contents of NVRAM and reboot the switch, what mode will you be in?

   A. Privileged mode

   B. Global mode

   C. Setup mode

   D. NVRAM loaded mode

17. You type the following command into the switch and receive the following output:

   `Switch#show fastethernet 0/1`

   `                ^`

   `% Invalid input detected at '^' marker.`

Why was this error message displayed?

A. You need to be in privileged mode.

B. You cannot have a space between `fastethernet` and `0/1`.

C. The switch does not have a FastEthernet 0/1 interface.

D. Part of the command is missing.

18. You type **Switch#sh r** and receive a `% ambiguous command` error. Why did you receive this message?

A. The command requires additional options or parameters.

B. There is more than one show command that starts with the letter *r*.

C. There is no show command that starts with *r*.

D. The command is being executed from the wrong mode.

19. Which of the following commands will display the current IP addressing and the layer 1 and 2 status of an interface? (Choose two.)

A. `show version`

B. `show interfaces`

C. `show controllers`

D. `show ip interface`

E. `show running-config`

20. At which layer of the OSI model would you assume the problem is if you type **show interface serial 1** and receive the following message?

`Serial1 is down, line protocol is down`

A. Physical layer

B. Data Link layer

C. Network layer

D. None; it is a router problem.

Chapter 7

Managing a Cisco Internetwork

THE FOLLOWING ICND1 EXAM TOPICS ARE COVERED IN THIS CHAPTER:

✓ **2.0 LAN Switching Technologies**

- 2.6 Configure and verify Layer 2 protocols
  - 2.6.a Cisco Discovery Protocol
  - 2.6.b LLDP

✓ **4.0 Infrastructure Services**

- 4.1 Describe DNS lookup operation
- 4.2 Troubleshoot client connectivity issues involving DNS
- 4.3 Configure and verify DHCP on a router (excluding static reservations)
  - 4.3.a Server
  - 4.3.b Relay
  - 4.3.c Client
  - 4.3.d TFTP, DNS, and gateway options
- 4.4 Troubleshoot client- and router-based DHCP connectivity issues
- 4.5 Configure and verify NTP operating in client/server mode

✓ **5.0 Infrastructure Management**

- 5.1 Configure and verify device-monitoring using syslog
- 5.2 Configure and verify device management
  - 5.2.a Backup and restore device configuration
  - 5.2.b Using Cisco Discovery Protocol and LLDP for device discovery
  - 5.2.d Logging
  - 5.2.e Timezone
  - 5.2.f Loopback

Here in Chapter 7, I'm going to show you how to manage Cisco routers and switches on an internetwork. You'll be learning about the main components of a router, as well as the router boot sequence. You'll also find out how to manage Cisco devices by using the copy command with a TFTP host and how to configure DHCP and NTP, plus you'll get a survey of the Cisco Discovery Protocol (CDP). I'll also show you how to resolve hostnames.

I'll wrap up the chapter by guiding you through some important Cisco IOS troubleshooting techniques to ensure that you're well equipped with these key skills.

To find up-to-the minute updates for this chapter, please see www.lammle .com/ccna or the book's web page at www.sybex.com/go/ccna.

The Internal Components of a Cisco Router and Switch

Unless you happen to be really savvy about the inner and outer workings of all your car's systems and its machinery and how all of that technology works together, you'll take it to someone who *does* know how to keep it maintained, figure out what's wrong when it stops running, and get it up and running again. It's the same deal with Cisco networking devices—you need to know all about their major components, pieces, and parts as well as what they all do and why and how they all work together to make a network work. The more solid your knowledge, the more expert you are about these things and the better equipped you'll be to configure and troubleshoot a Cisco internetwork. Toward that goal, study Table 7.1 for an introductory description of a Cisco router's major components.

TABLE 7.1 Cisco router components

Component	Description
Bootstrap	Stored in the microcode of the ROM, the bootstrap is used to bring a router up during initialization. It boots the router up and then loads the IOS.
POST (power-on self-test)	Also stored in the microcode of the ROM, the POST is used to check the basic functionality of the router hardware and determines which interfaces are present.

Component	Description
ROM monitor	Again, stored in the microcode of the ROM, the ROM monitor is used for manufacturing, testing, and troubleshooting, as well as running a mini-IOS when the IOS in flash fails to load.
Mini-IOS	Called the RXBOOT or bootloader by Cisco, the mini-IOS is a small IOS in ROM that can be used to bring up an interface and load a Cisco IOS into flash memory. The mini-IOS can also perform a few other maintenance operations.
RAM (random access memory)	Used to hold packet buffers, ARP cache, routing tables, and also the software and data structures that allow the router to function. Running-config is stored in RAM, and most routers expand the IOS from flash into RAM upon boot.
ROM (read-only memory)	Used to start and maintain the router. Holds the POST and the bootstrap program as well as the mini-IOS.
Flash memory	Stores the Cisco IOS by default. Flash memory is not erased when the router is reloaded. It is EEPROM (electronically erasable programmable read-only memory) created by Intel.
NVRAM (nonvolatile RAM)	Used to hold the router and switch configuration. NVRAM is not erased when the router or switch is reloaded. Does not store an IOS. The configuration register is stored in NVRAM.
Configuration register	Used to control how the router boots up. This value can be found as the last line of the show version command output and by default is set to 0x2102, which tells the router to load the IOS from flash memory as well as to load the configuration from NVRAM.

The Router and Switch Boot Sequence

When a Cisco device boots up, it performs a series of steps, called the *boot sequence*, to test the hardware and load the necessary software. The boot sequence comprises the following steps, as shown in Figure 7.1:

1. The IOS device performs a POST, which tests the hardware to verify that all components of the device are present and operational. The post takes stock of the different interfaces on the switch or router, and it's stored in and runs from read-only memory (ROM).

2. The bootstrap in ROM then locates and loads the Cisco IOS software by executing programs responsible for finding where each IOS program is located. Once they are found, it then loads the proper files. By default, the IOS software is loaded from flash memory in all Cisco devices.

FIGURE 7.1   Router bootup process

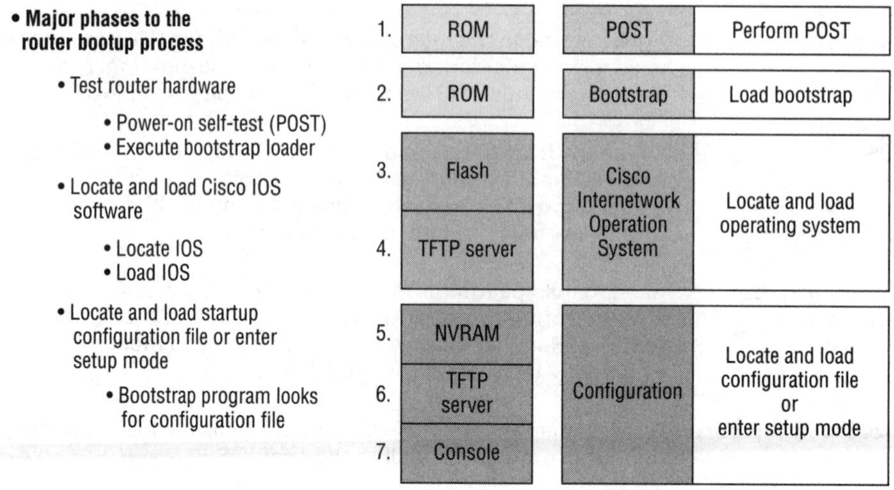

Major phases to the router bootup process		

- **Major phases to the router bootup process**
  - Test router hardware
    - Power-on self-test (POST)
    - Execute bootstrap loader
  - Locate and load Cisco IOS software
    - Locate IOS
    - Load IOS
  - Locate and load startup configuration file or enter setup mode
    - Bootstrap program looks for configuration file

#			
1.	ROM	POST	Perform POST
2.	ROM	Bootstrap	Load bootstrap
3.	Flash	Cisco Internetwork Operation System	Locate and load operating system
4.	TFTP server		
5.	NVRAM	Configuration	Locate and load configuration file or enter setup mode
6.	TFTP server		
7.	Console		

3. The IOS software then looks for a valid configuration file stored in NVRAM. This file is called startup-config and will be present only if an administrator has copied the running-config file into NVRAM.

4. If a startup-config file is found in NVRAM, the router or switch will copy it, place it in RAM, and name the file the running-config. The device will use this file to run, and the router/switch should now be operational. If a startup-config file is not in NVRAM, the router will broadcast out any interface that detects carrier detect (CD) for a TFTP host looking for a configuration, and when that fails (typically it will fail—most people won't even realize the router has attempted this process), it will start the setup mode configuration process.

The default order of an IOS loading from a Cisco device begins with flash, then TFTP server, and finally, ROM.

Backing Up and Restoring the Cisco Configuration

Any changes that you make to the configuration are stored in the running-config file. And if you don't enter a copy run start command after you make a change to running-config, that change will totally disappear if the device reboots or gets powered down. As always, backups are good, so you'll want to make another backup of the configuration information just in case the router or switch completely dies on you. Even if your machine is healthy and happy, it's good to have a backup for reference and documentation reasons!

Next, I'll cover how to copy the configuration of a router to a TFTP server as well as how to restore that configuration.

Backing Up the Cisco Configuration

To copy the configuration from an IOS device to a TFTP server, you can use either the copy running-config tftp or the copy startup-config tftp command. Either one will back up the router configuration that's currently running in DRAM or one that's stored in NVRAM.

Verifying the Current Configuration

To verify the configuration in DRAM, use the show running-config command (sh run for short) like this:

```
Router#show running-config
Building configuration...

Current configuration : 855 bytes
!
version 15.0
```

The current configuration information indicates that the router is running version 15.0 of the IOS.

Verifying the Stored Configuration

Next, you should check the configuration stored in NVRAM. To see this, use the show startup-config command (sh start for short) like this:

```
Router#sh start
Using 855 out of 524288 bytes
!
! Last configuration change at 04:49:14 UTC Fri Mar 5 1993
!
version 15.0
```

The first line shows you how much room your backup configuration is taking up. Here, we can see that NVRAM is about 524 KB and that only 855 bytes of it are being used. But memory is easier to reveal via the show version command when you're using an ISR router.

If you're not sure that the files are the same and the running-config file is what you want to go with, then use the copy running-config startup-config command. This will help you ensure that both files are in fact the same. I'll guide you through this in the next section.

Copying the Current Configuration to NVRAM

By copying running-config to NVRAM as a backup, as shown in the following output, you ensure that your running-config will always be reloaded if the router gets rebooted. Starting in the 12.0 IOS, you'll be prompted for the filename you want to use:

```
Router#copy running-config startup-config
Destination filename [startup-config]?[enter]
Building configuration...
[OK]
```

The reason the filename prompt appears is that there are now so many options you can use when using the copy command—check it out:

```
Router#copy running-config ?
  flash:          Copy to flash: file system
  ftp:            Copy to ftp: file system
  http:           Copy to http: file system
  https:          Copy to https: file system
  null:           Copy to null: file system
  nvram:          Copy to nvram: file system
  rcp:            Copy to rcp: file system
  running-config  Update (merge with) current system configuration
  scp:            Copy to scp: file system
  startup-config  Copy to startup configuration
  syslog:         Copy to syslog: file system
  system:         Copy to system: file system
  tftp:           Copy to tftp: file system
  tmpsys:         Copy to tmpsys: file system
```

Copying the Configuration to a TFTP Server

Once the file is copied to NVRAM, you can make a second backup to a TFTP server by using the copy running-config tftp command, or copy run tftp for short. I'm going to set the hostname to Todd before I run this command:

```
Todd#copy running-config tftp
Address or name of remote host []? 10.10.10.254
Destination filename [todd-confg]?
!!
776 bytes copied in 0.800 secs (970 bytes/sec)
```

If you have a hostname already configured, the command will automatically use the hostname plus the extension -confg as the name of the file.

Restoring the Cisco Configuration

What do you do if you've changed your running-config file and want to restore the configuration to the version in the startup-config file? The easiest way to get this done is to use the copy startup-config running-config command, or copy start run for short, but this will work only if you copied running-config into NVRAM before you made any changes! Of course, a reload of the device will work too!

If you did copy the configuration to a TFTP server as a second backup, you can restore the configuration using the copy tftp running-config command (copy tftp run for short), or the copy tftp startup-config command (copy tftp start for short), as shown in the following output. Just so you know, the old command we used to use for this is config net:

```
Todd#copy tftp running-config
Address or name of remote host []?10.10.10.254
Source filename []?todd-confg
Destination filename[running-config]?[enter]
Accessing tftp://10.10.10.254/todd-confg...
Loading todd-confg from 10.10.10.254 (via FastEthernet0/0):
!!
[OK - 776 bytes]
776 bytes copied in 9.212 secs (84 bytes/sec)
Todd#
*Mar  7 17:53:34.071: %SYS-5-CONFIG_I: Configured from
    tftp://10.10.10.254/todd-confg by console
```

Okay that the configuration file is an ASCII text file ... meaning that before you copy the configuration stored on a TFTP server back to a router, you can make changes to the file with any text editor.

> Remember that when you copy or merge a configuration from a TFTP server to a freshly erased and rebooted router's RAM, the interfaces are shut down by default and you must manually enable each interface with the no shutdown command.

Erasing the Configuration

To delete the startup-config file on a Cisco router or switch, use the command erase startup-config, like this:

```
Todd#erase startup-config
Erasing the nvram filesystem will remove all configuration files!
    Continue? [confirm][enter]
```

```
[OK]
Erase of nvram: complete
*Mar  7 17:56:20.407: %SYS-7-NV_BLOCK_INIT: Initialized the geometry of nvram
Todd#reload
System configuration has been modified. Save? [yes/no]:n
Proceed with reload? [confirm][enter]
 *Mar  7 17:56:31.059: %SYS-5-RELOAD: Reload requested by console.
   Reload Reason: Reload Command.
```

This command deletes the contents of NVRAM on the switch and router. If you type **reload** while in privileged mode and say no to saving changes, the switch or router will reload and come up into setup mode.

Configuring DHCP

We went over DHCP in Chapter 3, "Introduction to TCP/IP," where I described how it works and what happens when there's a conflict. At this point, you're ready to learn how to configure DHCP on Cisco's IOS as well as how to configure a DHCP forwarder for when your hosts don't live on the same LAN as the DHCP server. Do you remember the four-step process hosts used to get an address from a server? If not, now would be a really great time to head back to Chapter 3 and thoroughly review that before moving on with this!

To configure a DHCP server for your hosts, you need the following information at minimum:

Network and mask for each LAN Network ID, also called a scope. All addresses in a subnet can be leased to hosts by default.

Reserved/excluded addresses Reserved addresses for printers, servers, routers, etc. These addresses will not be handed out to hosts. I usually reserve the first address of each subnet for the router, but you don't have to do this.

Default router This is the router's address for each LAN.

DNS address A list of DNS server addresses provided to hosts so they can resolve names.

Here are your configuration steps:

1. Exclude the addresses you want to reserve. The reason you do this step first is because as soon as you set a network ID, the DHCP service will start responding to client requests.

2. Create your pool for each LAN using a unique name.

3. Choose the network ID and subnet mask for the DHCP pool that the server will use to provide addresses to hosts.

4. Add the address used for the default gateway of the subnet.

5. Provide the DNS server address(es).

6. If you don't want to use the default lease time of 24 hours, you need to set the lease time in days, hours, and minutes.

I'll configure the switch in Figure 7.2 to be the DHCP server for the Sales wireless LAN.

FIGURE 7.2 DHCP configuration example on a switch

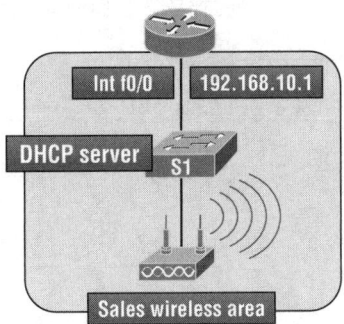

Understand that this configuration could just have easily been placed on the router in Figure 7.2. Here's how we'll configure DHCP using the 192.168.10.0/24 network ID:

```
Switch(config)#ip dhcp excluded-address 192.168.10.1 192.168.10.10
Switch(config)#ip dhcp pool Sales_Wireless
Switch(dhcp-config)#network 192.168.10.0 255.255.255.0
Switch(dhcp-config)#default-router 192.168.10.1
Switch(dhcp-config)#dns-server 4.4.4.4
Switch(dhcp-config)#lease 3 12 15
Switch(dhcp-config)#option 66 ascii tftp.lammle.com
```

First, you can see that I reserved 10 addresses in the range for the router, servers, and printers, etc. I then created the pool named Sales_Wireless, added the default gateway and DNS server, and set the lease to 3 days, 12 hours, and 15 minutes (which isn't really significant because I just set it that way for demonstration purposes). Lastly, I provided an example on you how you would set option 66, which is sending a TFTP server address to a DHCP client. Typically used for VoIP phones, or auto installs, and needs to be listed as a FQDN. Pretty straightforward, right? The switch will now respond to DHCP client requests. But what happens if we need to provide an IP address from a DHCP server to a host that's not in our broadcast domain, or if we want to receive a DHCP address for a client from a remote server?

DHCP Relay

If you need to provide addresses from a DHCP server to hosts that aren't on the same LAN as the DHCP server, you can configure your router interface to relay or forward the DHCP client requests, as shown in Figure 7.3. If we don't provide this service, our router would receive the DHCP client broadcast, promptly discard it, and the remote host would never receive an address—unless we added a DHCP server on every broadcast domain! Let's take a look at how we would typically configure DHCP service in today's networks.

FIGURE 7.3   Configuring a DHCP relay

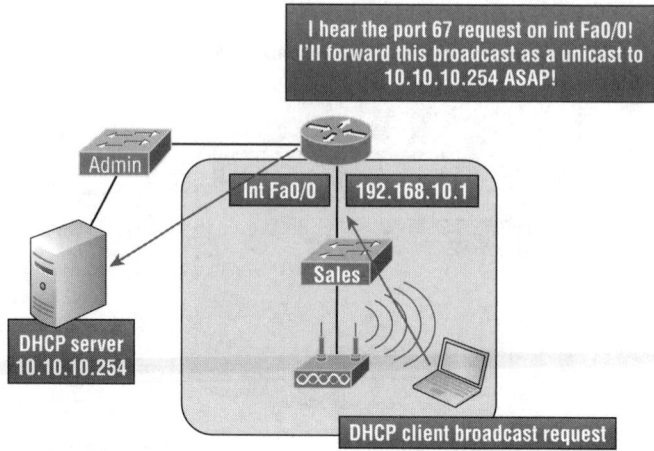

So we know that because the hosts off the router don't have access to a DHCP server, the router will simply drop their client request broadcast messages by default. To solve this problem, we can configure the Fa0/0 interface of the router to accept the DHCP client requests and forward them to the DHCP server like this:

```
Router#config t
Router(config)#interface fa0/0
Router(config-if)#ip helper-address 10.10.10.254
```

Now I know that was a pretty simple example, and there are definitely other ways to configure the relay, but rest assured that I've covered the objectives for you. Also, I want you to know that ip helper-address forwards more than just DHCP client requests, so be sure to research this command before you implement it! Now that I've demonstrated how to create the DHCP service, let's take a minute to verify DHCP before moving on to NTP.

Verifying DHCP on Cisco IOS

There are some really useful verification commands to use on a Cisco IOS device for monitoring and verifying a DHCP service. You'll get to see the output for these commands when I build the network in Chapter 9, "IP Routing," and add DHCP to the two remote LANs. I just want you to begin getting familiar with them, so here's a list of four very important ones and what they do:

show ip dhcp binding   Lists state information about each IP address currently leased to a client.

show ip dhcp pool [poolname]   Lists the configured range of IP addresses, plus statistics for the number of currently leased addresses and the high watermark for leases from each pool.

show ip dhcp server statistics   Lists DHCP server statistics—a lot of them!

show ip dhcp conflict   If someone statically configures an IP address on a LAN and the DHCP server hands out that same address, you'll end up with a duplicate address. This isn't good, which is why this command is so helpful!

Again, no worries because we'll cover these vital commands thoroughly in Chapter 9.

Syslog

Reading system messages from a switch's or router's internal buffer is the most popular and efficient method of seeing what's going on with your network at a particular time. But the best way is to log messages to a *syslog* server, which stores messages from you and can even time-stamp and sequence them for you, and it's easy to set up and configure!

Syslog allows you to display, sort, and even search messages, all of which makes it a really great troubleshooting tool. The search feature is especially powerful because you can use keywords and even severity levels. Plus, the server can email admins based on the severity level of the message.

Network devices can be configured to generate a syslog message and forward it to various destinations. These four examples are popular ways to gather messages from Cisco devices:

- Logging buffer (on by default)
- Console line (on by default)
- Terminal lines (using the `terminal monitor` command)
- Syslog server

As you already know, all system messages and debug output generated by the IOS go out only the console port by default and are also logged in buffers in RAM. And you also know that Cisco routers aren't exactly shy about sending messages! To send a message to the VTY lines, use the `terminal monitor` command. We'll also add a small configuration needed for syslog, which I'll show you soon in the configuration section.

So by default, we'd see something like this on our console line:

```
*Oct 21 17:33:50.565:%LINK-5-CHANGED:Interface FastEthernet0/0, changed
state to administratively down
*Oct 21 17:33:51.565:%LINEPROTO-5-UPDOWN:Line protocol on Interface
FastEthernet0/0, changed state to down
```

And the Cisco router would send a general version of the message to the syslog server that would be formatted into something like this:

```
Seq no:timestamp: %facility-severity-MNEMONIC:description
```

The system message format can be broken down in this way:

seq no   This stamp logs messages with a sequence number, but not by default. If you want this output, you've got to configure it.

Timestamp   Data and time of the message or event, which again will show up only if configured.

Facility   The facility to which the message refers.

Severity   A single-digit code from 0 to 7 that indicates the severity of the message.

MNEMONIC   Text string that uniquely describes the message.

Description   Text string containing detailed information about the event being reported.

The severity levels, from the most severe level to the least severe, are explained in Table 7.2. Informational is the default and will result in all messages being sent to the buffers and console.

TABLE 7.2   Severity levels

Severity Level	Explanation
Emergency (severity 0)	System is unusable.
Alert (severity 1)	Immediate action is needed.
Critical (severity 2)	Critical condition.
Error (severity 3)	Error condition.
Warning (severity 4)	Warning condition.
Notification (severity 5)	Normal but significant condition.
Informational (severity 6)	Normal information message.
Debugging (severity 7)	Debugging message.

If you are studying for your Cisco exam, you need to memorize Table 7.2 using this acronym: Every Awesome Cisco Engineer Will Need Icecream Daily.

Understand that only emergency-level messages will be displayed if you've configured severity level 0. But if, for example, you opt for level 4 instead, level 0 through 4 will be displayed, giving you emergency, alert, critical, error, and warning messages too. Level 7 is the highest-level security option and displays everything, but be warned that going with it could have a serious impact on the performance of your device. So always use debugging commands carefully, with an eye on the messages you really need to meet your specific business requirements!

Configuring and Verifying Syslog

As I said, Cisco devices send all log messages of the severity level you've chosen to the console. They'll also go to the buffer, and both happen by default. Because of this, it's good to know that you can disable and enable these features with the following commands:

```
Router(config)#logging ?
  Hostname or A.B.C.D  IP address of the logging host
  buffered             Set buffered logging parameters
  buginf               Enable buginf logging for debugging
  cns-events           Set CNS Event logging level
  console              Set console logging parameters
  count                Count every log message and timestamp last occurrence
  esm                  Set ESM filter restrictions
  exception            Limit size of exception flush output
  facility             Facility parameter for syslog messages
  filter               Specify logging filter
  history              Configure syslog history table
  host                 Set syslog server IP address and parameters
  monitor              Set terminal line (monitor) logging parameters
  on                   Enable logging to all enabled destinations
  origin-id            Add origin ID to syslog messages
  queue-limit          Set logger message queue size
  rate-limit           Set messages per second limit
  reload               Set reload logging level
  server-arp           Enable sending ARP requests for syslog servers when
                       first configured
  source-interface     Specify interface for source address in logging
                       transactions
  trap                 Set syslog server logging level
  userinfo             Enable logging of user info on privileged mode enabling

Router(config)#logging console
Router(config)#logging buffered
```

Wow—as you can see in this output, there are plenty of options you can use with the logging command! The preceding configuration enabled the console and buffer to receive all log messages of all severities, and don't forget that this is the default setting for all Cisco IOS devices. If you want to disable the defaults, use the following commands:

```
Router(config)#no logging console
Router(config)#no logging buffered
```

I like leaving the console and buffer commands on in order to receive the logging info, but that's up to you. You can see the buffers with the show logging command here:

```
Router#sh logging
Syslog logging: enabled (11 messages dropped, 1 messages rate-limited,
                0 flushes, 0 overruns, xml disabled, filtering disabled)
   Console logging: level debugging, 29 messages logged, xml disabled,
                    filtering disabled
   Monitor logging: level debugging, 0 messages logged, xml disabled,
                    filtering disabled
   Buffer logging: level debugging, 1 messages logged, xml disabled,
                   filtering disabled
   Logging Exception size (4096 bytes)
   Count and timestamp logging messages: disabled
No active filter modules.

   Trap logging: level informational, 33 message lines logged

Log Buffer (4096 bytes):
*Jun 21 23:09:37.822: %SYS-5-CONFIG_I: Configured from console by console
Router#
```

The default trap (message from device to NMS) level is debugging, but you can change this too. And now that you've seen the system message format on a Cisco device, I want to show you how you can also control the format of your messages via sequence numbers and time stamps, which aren't enabled by default. We'll begin with a basic, simple example of how to configure a device to send messages to a syslog server, demonstrated in Figure 7.4.

FIGURE 7.4   Messages sent to a syslog server

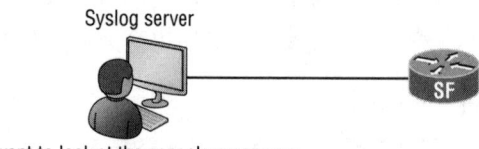

Syslog server

I want to look at the console messages
of the SF router from last night.

A syslog server saves copies of console messages and can time-stamp them for viewing at a later time. This is actually pretty easy to configure, and here's how doing that would look on the SF router:

```
SF(config)#logging 172.16.10.1
SF(config)#logging informational
```

This is awesome—now all the console messages will be stored in one location to be viewed at your convenience! I typically use the logging host ip_address command, but logging IP_address without the host keyword gets the same result.

We can limit the amount of messages sent to the syslog server, based on severity, with the following command:

```
SF(config)#logging trap ?
  <0-7>          Logging severity level
  alerts         Immediate action needed          (severity=1)
  critical       Critical conditions              (severity=2)
  debugging      Debugging messages               (severity=7)
  emergencies    System is unusable               (severity=0)
  errors         Error conditions                 (severity=3)
  informational  Informational messages           (severity=6)
  notifications  Normal but significant conditions (severity=5)
  warnings       Warning conditions               (severity=4)
  <cr>
SF(config)#logging trap informational
```

Notice that we can use either the number or the actual severity level name—and they are in alphabetical order, not severity order, which makes it even harder to memorize the order! (Thanks, Cisco!) Since I went with severity level 6 (Informational), I'll receive messages for levels 0 through 6. These are referred to as local levels as well, such as, for example, local6—no difference.

Now let's configure the router to use sequence numbers:

```
SF(config)#no service timestamps
SF(config)#service sequence-numbers
SF(config)#^Z
000038: %SYS-5-CONFIG_I: Configured from console by console
```

When you exit configuration mode, the router will send a message like the one shown in the preceding code lines. Without the time stamps enabled, we'll no longer see a time and date, but we will see a sequence number.

So we now have the following:

- Sequence number: 000038
- Facility: %SYS

- Severity level: 5
- MNEMONIC: CONFIG_I
- Description: Configured from console by console

I want to stress that of all of these, the severity level is what you need to pay attention to the most for the Cisco exams as well as for a means to control the amount of messages sent to the syslog server.

Network Time Protocol (NTP)

Network Time Protocol provides pretty much what it describes: time to all your network devices. To be more precise, NTP synchronizes clocks of computer systems over packet-switched, variable-latency data networks.

Typically you'll have an NTP server that connects through the Internet to an atomic clock. This time can then be synchronized through the network to keep all routers, switches, servers, etc. receiving the same time information.

Correct network time within the network is important:

- Correct time allows the tracking of events in the network in the correct order.
- Clock synchronization is critical for the correct interpretation of events within the syslog data.
- Clock synchronization is critical for digital certificates.

Making sure all your devices have the correct time is especially helpful for your routers and switches for looking at logs regarding security issues or other maintenance issues. Routers and switches issue log messages when different events take place—for example, when an interface goes down and then back up. As you already know, all messages generated by the IOS go only to the console port by default. However, as shown in Figure 7.4, those console messages can be directed to a syslog server.

A syslog server saves copies of console messages and can time-stamp them so you can view them at a later time. This is actually rather easy to do. Here would be your configuration on the SF router:

```
SF(config)#service timestamps log datetime msec
```

Even though I had the messages time-stamped with the command service timestamps log datetime msec, this doesn't mean that we'll know the exact time if using default clock sources.

To make sure all devices are synchronized with the same time information, we'll configure our devices to receive the accurate time information from a centralized server, as shown here in the following command and in Figure 7.5:

```
SF(config)#ntp server 172.16.10.1 version 4
```

FIGURE 7.5   Synchronizing time information

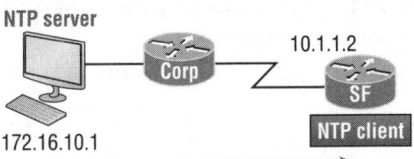

Here is the exact time and date!

Just use that one simple command on all your devices and each network device on your network will then have the same exact time and date information. You can then rest assured that your time stamps are accurate. You can also make your router or switch be an NTP server with the ntp master command.

To verify that our NTP client is receiving clocking information, we use the following commands:

```
SF#sh ntp ?
  associations  NTP associations
  status        NTP status  status     VTP domain status


SF#sh ntp status
Clock is unsynchronized, stratum 16, no reference clock
nominal freq is 119.2092 Hz, actual freq is 119.2092 Hz, precision is 2**18
reference time is 00000000.00000000 (00:00:00.000 UTC Mon Jan 1 1900)
clock offset is 0.0000 msec, root delay is 0.00 msec
S1#sh ntp associations

address     ref clock     st  when  poll reach  delay  offset    disp
~172.16.10.1  0.0.0.0            16    -    64    0     0.0    0.00  16000.
 * master (synced), # master (unsynced), + selected, - candidate, ~ configured
```

You can see in the example that the NTP client in SF is not synchronized with the server by using the show ntp status command. The stratum value is a number from 1 to 15, and a lower stratum value indicates a higher NTP priority; 16 means there is no clocking received.

There are many other configurations of an NTP client that are available, such as authentication of NTP so a router or switch isn't fooled into changing the time of an attack, for example.

Exploring Connected Devices Using CDP and LLDP

Cisco Discovery Protocol (CDP) is a proprietary Layer 2 protocol designed by Cisco to help administrators collect information about locally attached Cisco devices. Armed with CDP, you can gather hardware and protocol information about neighbor devices, which is crucial information to have when troubleshooting and documenting the network. Another dynamic discovery protocol is Link Layer Discovery Protocol (LLDP), but instead of being proprietary like CDP, it is vendor independent.

Let's start by exploring the CDP timer and CDP commands we'll need to verify our network.

Getting CDP Timers and Holdtime Information

The show cdp command (sh cdp for short) gives you information about two CDP global parameters that can be configured on Cisco devices:

- *CDP timer* delimits how often CDP packets are transmitted out all active interfaces.

- *CDP holdtime* delimits the amount of time that the device will hold packets received from neighbor devices.

Both Cisco routers and switches use the same parameters. Check out Figure 7.6 to see how CDP works within a switched network that I set up for my switching labs in this book.

FIGURE 7.6   Cisco Discovery Protocol

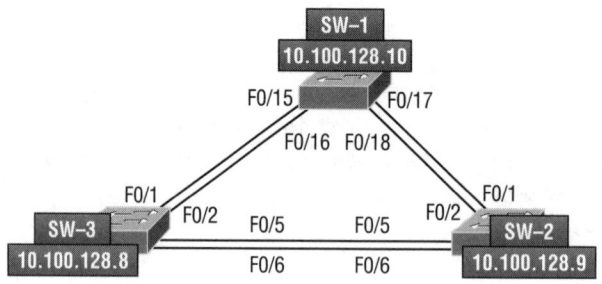

The output on my 3560 SW-3 looks like this:

```
SW-3#sh cdp
Global CDP information:
        Sending CDP packets every 60 seconds
        Sending a holdtime value of 180 seconds
        Sending CDPv2 advertisements is enabled
```

This output tells us that the default transmits every 60 seconds and will hold packets from a neighbor in the CDP table for 180 seconds. I can use the global commands cdp holdtime and cdp timer to configure the CDP holdtime and timer on a router if necessary like this:

```
SW-3(config)#cdp ?
  advertise-v2   CDP sends version-2 advertisements
  holdtime       Specify the holdtime (in sec) to be sent in packets
```

```
run            Enable CDP
timer          Specify the rate at which CDP packets are sent (in sec)
tlv            Enable exchange of specific tlv information
```

```
SW-3(config)#cdp holdtime ?
  <10-255> Length of time (in sec) that receiver must keep this packet
```

```
SW-3(config)#cdp timer ?
  <5-254>  Rate at which CDP packets are sent (in  sec)
```

You can turn off CDP completely with the no cdp run command from global configuration mode of a router and enable it with the cdp run command:

```
SW-3(config)#no cdp run
SW-3(config)#cdp run
```

To turn CDP off or on for an interface, use the no cdp enable and cdp enable commands.

Gathering Neighbor Information

The show cdp neighbor command (sh cdp nei for short) delivers information about directly connected devices. It's important to remember that CDP packets aren't passed through a Cisco switch and that you only see what's directly attached. So this means that if your router is connected to a switch, you won't see any of the Cisco devices connected beyond that switch!

The following output shows the show cdp neighbor command I used on my SW-3:

```
SW-3#sh cdp neighbors
Capability Codes: R - Router, T - Trans Bridge, B - Source Route Bridge
                  S - Switch, H - Host, I - IGMP, r - Repeater, P - Phone,
                  D - Remote, C - CVTA, M - Two-port Mac Relay Device ID
Local Intrfce    Holdtme    Capability  Platform  Port ID
SW-1  Fas 0/1    170          S I       WS-C3560- Fas 0/15
SW-1  Fas 0/2    170          S I       WS-C3560- Fas 0/16
SW-2  Fas 0/5    162          S I       WS-C3560- Fas 0/5
SW-2  Fas 0/6    162          S I       WS-C3560- Fas 0/6
```

Okay—we can see that I'm directly connected with a console cable to the SW-3 switch and also that SW-3 is directly connected to two other switches. However, do we really need the figure to draw out our network? We don't! CDP allows me to see who my directly connected neighbors are and gather information about them. From the SW-3 switch, we can see that there are two connections to SW-1 and two connections to SW-2. SW-3 connects to SW-1 with ports Fas 0/1 and Fas 0/2, and we have connections to SW-2 with local interfaces Fas 0/5 and Fas 0/6. Both the SW-1 and SW-2 switches are 3650 switches, and SW-1 is using ports Fas 0/15 and Fas 0/16 to connect to SW-3. SW-2 is using ports Fas 0/5 and Fas 0/6.

To sum this up, the device ID shows the configured hostname of the connected device, that the local interface is our interface, and the port ID is the remote devices' directly connected interface. Remember that all you get to view are directly connected devices!

Table 7.3 summarizes the information displayed by the show cdp neighbor command for each device.

TABLE 7.3   Output of the **show cdp neighbors** command

Field	Description
Device ID	The hostname of the device directly connected.
Local Interface	The port or interface on which you are receiving the CDP packet.
Holdtime	The remaining amount of time the router will hold the information before discarding it if no more CDP packets are received.
Capability	The capability of the neighbor—the router, switch, or repeater. The capability codes are listed at the top of the command output.
Platform	The type of Cisco device directly connected. In the previous output, the SW-3 shows it's directly connected to two 3560 switches.
Port ID	The neighbor device's port or interface on which the CDP packets are multicast.

It's imperative that you can look at the output of a show cdp neighbors command and decipher the information gained about the neighbor device's capability, whether it's a router or switch, the model number (platform), your port connecting to that device (local interface), and the port of the neighbor connecting to you (port ID).

Another command that will deliver the goods on neighbor information is the show cdp neighbors detail command (show cdp nei de for short). This command can be run on both routers and switches, and it displays detailed information about each device connected to the device you're running the command on. Check out the router output in Listing 7.1.

Listing 7.1: Showing CDP neighbors

```
SW-3#sh cdp neighbors detail
-------------------------
Device ID: SW-1
```

```
Entry address(es):
  IP address: 10.100.128.10
Platform: cisco WS-C3560-24TS,  Capabilities: Switch IGMP
Interface: FastEthernet0/1,  Port ID (outgoing port): FastEthernet0/15
Holdtime : 137 sec

Version :
Cisco IOS Software, C3560 Software (C3560-IPSERVICESK9-M), Version 12.2(55)SE7,
RELEASE SOFTWARE (fc1)
Technical Support: http://www.cisco.com/techsupport
Copyright (c) 1986-2013 by Cisco Systems, Inc.
Compiled Mon 28-Jan-13 10:10 by prod_rel_team

advertisement version: 2
Protocol Hello:  OUI=0x00000C, Protocol ID=0x0112; payload len=27, value=0000000
0FFFFFFFF010221FF000000000000001C575EC880Fc00f000
VTP Management Domain: 'NULL'
Native VLAN: 1
Duplex: full
Power Available TLV:

    Power request id: 0, Power management id: 1, Power available: 0, Power
management level: -1
Management address(es):
  IP address: 10.100.128.10
-------------------------

[ouput cut]

-------------------------
Device ID: SW-2
Entry address(es):
  IP address: 10.100.128.9
Platform: cisco WS-C3560-8PC,  Capabilities: Switch IGMP
Interface: FastEthernet0/5,  Port ID (outgoing port): FastEthernet0/5
Holdtime : 129 sec

Version :
Cisco IOS Software, C3560 Software (C3560-IPBASE-M), Version 12.2(35)SE5,
RELEASE SOFTWARE (fc1)
Copyright (c) 1986-2007 by Cisco Systems, Inc.
Compiled Thu 19-Jul-07 18:15 by nachen

advertisement version: 2
Protocol Hello:  OUI=0x00000C, Protocol ID=0x0112; payload len=27, value=0000000
0FFFFFFFF010221FF000000000000B41489D91880Fc00f000
VTP Management Domain: 'NULL'
```

```
Native VLAN: 1
Duplex: full
Power Available TLV:

    Power request id: 0, Power management id: 1, Power available: 0, Power
management level: -1
Management address(es):
  IP address: 10.100.128.9
[output cut]
```

So what's revealed here? First, we've been given the hostname and IP address of all directly connected devices. And in addition to the same information displayed by the show cdp neighbors command (see Table 7.3), the show cdp neighbors detail command tells us about the IOS version and IP address of the neighbor device—that's quite a bit!

The show cdp entry * command displays the same information as the show cdp neighbors detail command. There isn't any difference between these commands.

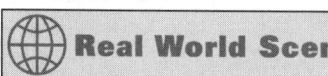

Real World Scenario

CDP Can Save Lives!

Karen has just been hired as a senior network consultant at a large hospital in Dallas, Texas, so she's expected to be able to take care of any problem that rears its ugly head. As if that weren't enough pressure, she also has to worry about the horrid possibility that people won't receive correct health care solutions—even the correct medications—if the network goes down. Talk about a potential life-or-death situation!

But Karen is confident and begins her job optimistically. Of course, it's not long before the network reveals that it has a few problems. Unfazed, she asks one of the junior administrators for a network map so she can troubleshoot the network. This person tells her that the old senior administrator, who she replaced, had them with him and now no one can find them. The sky begins to darken!

Doctors are calling every couple of minutes because they can't get the necessary information they need to take care of their patients. What should she do?

It's CDP to the rescue! And it's a gift that this hospital happens to be running Cisco routers and switches exclusively, because CDP is enabled by default on all Cisco devices. Karen is also in luck because the disgruntled former administrator didn't turn off CDP on any devices before he left!

So all Karen has to do now is to use the show cdp neighbor detail command to find all the information she needs about each device to help draw out the hospital network, bringing it back up to speed so the personnel who rely upon it can get on to the important business of saving lives!

The only snag for you nailing this in your own network is if you don't know the passwords of all those devices. Your only hope then is to somehow find out the access passwords or to perform password recovery on them.

So, use CDP—you never know when you may end up saving someone's life.

By the way, this is a true story!

Documenting a Network Topology Using CDP

With that moving real-life scenario in mind, I'm now going to show you how to document a sample network by using CDP. You'll learn to determine the appropriate router types, interface types, and IP addresses of various interfaces using only CDP commands and the show running-config command. And you can only console into the Lab_A router to document the network. You'll have to assign any remote routers the next IP address in each range. We'll use a different figure for this example—Figure 7.7— to help us to complete the necessary documentation.

FIGURE 7.7   Documenting a network topology using CDP

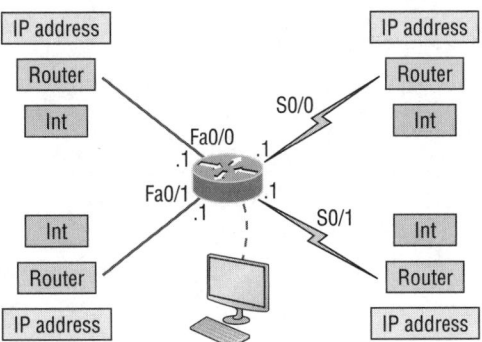

In this output, you can see that you have a router with four interfaces: two Fast Ethernet and two serial. First, determine the IP addresses of each interface by using the show running-config command like this:

```
Lab_A#sh running-config
Building configuration...

Current configuration : 960 bytes
!
version 12.2
service timestamps debug uptime
service timestamps log uptime
```

```
no service password-encryption
!
hostname Lab_A
!
ip subnet-zero
!
!
interface FastEthernet0/0
 ip address 192.168.21.1 255.255.255.0
 duplex auto
!
interface FastEthernet0/1
 ip address 192.168.18.1 255.255.255.0
 duplex auto
!
interface Serial0/0
ip address 192.168.23.1 255.255.255.0
!
interface Serial0/1
ip address 192.168.28.1 255.255.255.0
!
ip classless
!
line con 0
line aux 0
line vty 0 4
!
end
```

With this step completed, you can now write down the IP addresses of the Lab_A router's four interfaces. Next, you must determine the type of device on the other end of each of these interfaces. It's easy—just use the show cdp neighbors command:

```
Lab_A#sh cdp neighbors
Capability Codes: R - Router, T - Trans Bridge, B - Source Route Bridge
S - Switch, H - Host, I - IGMP, r - Repeater
Device ID    Local Intrfce    Holdtme    Capability Platform   Port ID
Lab_B        Fas 0/0          178        R          2501       E0
Lab_C        Fas 0/1          137        R          2621       Fa0/0
Lab_D        Ser 0/0          178        R          2514       S1
Lab_E        Ser 0/1          137        R          2620       S0/1
```

Wow—looks like we're connected to some old routers! But it's not our job to judge. Our mission is to draw out our network, so it's good that we've got some nice information to meet the challenge with now. By using both the show running-config and show cdp neighbors commands, we know about all the IP addresses of the Lab_A router, the types of routers connected to each of the Lab_A router's links, and all the interfaces of the remote routers.

Now that we're equipped with all the information gathered via show running-config and show cdp neighbors, we can accurately create the topology in Figure 7.8.

FIGURE 7.8   Network topology documented

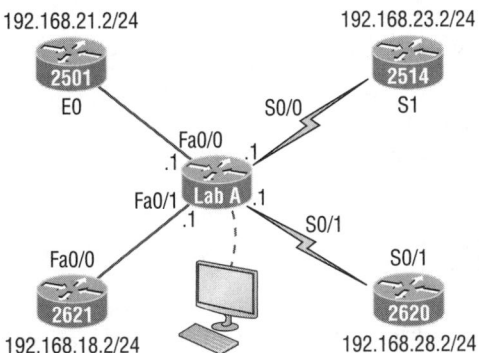

If we needed to, we could've also used the show cdp neighbors detail command to view the neighbor's IP addresses. But since we know the IP addresses of each link on the Lab_A router, we already know what the next available IP address is going to be.

Link Layer Discovery Protocol (LLDP)

Before moving on from CDP, I want to tell you about a nonproprietary discovery protocol that provides pretty much the same information as CDP but works in multi-vendor networks.

The IEEE created a new standardized discovery protocol called 802.1AB for Station and Media Access Control Connectivity Discovery. We'll just call it *Link Layer Discovery Protocol (LLDP)*.

LLDP defines basic discovery capabilities, but it was also enhanced to specifically address the voice application, and this version is called LLDP-MED (Media Endpoint Discovery). It's good to remember that LLDP and LLDP-MED are not compatible.

LLDP has the following configuration guidelines and limitations:

- LLDP must be enabled on the device before you can enable or disable it on any interface.
- LLDP is supported only on physical interfaces.
- LLDP can discover up to one device per port.
- LLDP can discover Linux servers.

You can turn off LLDP completely with the no lldp run command from global configuration mode of a device and enable it with the lldp run command, which enables it on all interfaces as well:

```
SW-3(config)#no lldp run
SW-3(config)#lldp run
```

To turn LLDP off or on for an interface, use the lldp transmit and lldp receive commands.

```
SW-3(config-if)#no lldp transmit
SW-3(config-if)#no lldp receive

SW-3(config-if)#lldp transmit
SW-3(config-if)#lldp receive
```

Using Telnet

As part of the TCP/IP protocol suite, *Telnet* is a virtual terminal protocol that allows you to make connections to remote devices, gather information, and run programs.

After your routers and switches are configured, you can use the Telnet program to reconfigure and/or check up on them without using a console cable. You run the Telnet program by typing **telnet** from any command prompt (Windows or Cisco), but you need to have VTY passwords set on the IOS devices for this to work.

Remember, you can't use CDP to gather information about routers and switches that aren't directly connected to your device. But you can use the Telnet application to connect to your neighbor devices and then run CDP on those remote devices to get information on them.

You can issue the telnet command from any router or switch prompt. In the following code, I'm trying to telnet from switch 1 to switch 3:

```
SW-1#telnet 10.100.128.8
Trying 10.100.128.8 ... Open

Password required, but none set

[Connection to 10.100.128.8 closed by foreign host]
```

Oops—clearly, I didn't set my passwords—how embarrassing! Remember that the VTY ports are default configured as login, meaning that we have to either set the VTY passwords or use the no login command. If you need to review the process of setting passwords, take a quick look back in Chapter 6, "Cisco's Internetworking Operating System (IOS)."

 If you can't telnet into a device, it could be that the password on the remote device hasn't been set. It's also quite possible that an access control list is filtering the Telnet session.

On a Cisco device, you don't need to use the telnet command; you can just type in an IP address from a command prompt and the router will assume that you want to telnet to the device. Here's how that looks using just the IP address:

```
SW-1#10.100.128.8
Trying 10.100.128.8... Open

Password required, but none set

[Connection to 10.100.128.8 closed by foreign host]
SW-1#
```

Now would be a great time to set those VTY passwords on the SW-3 that I want to telnet into. Here's what I did on the switch named SW-3:

```
SW-3(config)#line vty 0 15
SW-3(config-line)#login
SW-3(config-line)#password telnet
SW-3(config-line)#login
SW-3(config-line)#^Z
```

Now let's try this again. This time, I'm connecting to SW-3 from the SW-1 console:

```
SW-1#10.100.128.8
Trying 10.100.128.8 ... Open

User Access Verification

Password:
SW-3>
```

Remember that the VTY password is the user-mode password, not the enable-mode password. Watch what happens when I try to go into privileged mode after telnetting into the switch:

```
SW-3>en
% No password set
SW-3>
```

It's totally slamming the door in my face, which happens to be a really nice security feature! After all, you don't want just anyone telnetting into your device and typing the enable command to get into privileged mode now, do you? You've got to set your enable-mode password or enable secret password to use Telnet to configure remote devices.

 When you telnet into a remote device, you won't see console messages by default. For example, you will not see debugging output. To allow console messages to be sent to your Telnet session, use the `terminal monitor` command.

Using the next group of examples, I'll show you how to telnet into multiple devices simultaneously as well as how to use hostnames instead of IP addresses.

Telnetting into Multiple Devices Simultaneously

If you telnet to a router or switch, you can end the connection by typing **exit** at any time. But what if you want to keep your connection to a remote device going while still coming back to your original router console? To do that, you can press the Ctrl+Shift+6 key combination, release it, and then press X.

Here's an example of connecting to multiple devices from my SW-1 console:

```
SW-1#10.100.128.8
Trying 10.100.128.8... Open

User Access Verification

Password:
SW-3>Ctrl+Shift+6
SW-1#
```

Here you can see that I telnetted to SW-1 and then typed the password to enter user mode. Next, I pressed Ctrl+Shift+6, then X, but you won't see any of that because it doesn't show on the screen output. Notice that my command prompt now has me back at the SW-1 switch.

Now let's run through some verification commands.

Checking Telnet Connections

If you want to view the connections from your router or switch to a remote device, just use the show sessions command. In this case, I've telnetted into both the SW-3 and SW-2 switches from SW1:

```
SW-1#sh sessions
Conn Host            Address          Byte  Idle Conn Name
   1 10.100.128.9    10.100.128.9     0          10.100.128.9
*  2 10.100.128.8    10.100.128.8     0          10.100.128.8
SW-1#
```

See that asterisk (*) next to connection 2? It means that session 2 was the last session I connected to. You can return to your last session by pressing Enter twice. You can also return to any session by typing the number of the connection and then Enter.

Checking Telnet Users

You can reveal all active consoles and VTY ports in use on your router with the show users command:

```
SW-1#sh users
    Line        User        Host(s)              Idle        Location
*   0 con 0                 10.100.128.9         00:00:01
                           10.100.128.8         00:01:06
```

In the command's output, con represents the local console, and we can see that the console session is connected to two remote IP addresses—in other words, two devices.

Closing Telnet Sessions

You can end Telnet sessions a few different ways. Typing exit or disconnect are probably the two quickest and easiest.

To end a session from a remote device, use the exit command:

```
SW-3>exit
[Connection to 10.100.128.8 closed by foreign host]
SW-1#
```

To end a session from a local device, use the disconnect command:

```
SW-1#sh session
Conn Host            Address           Byte  Idle Conn Name
   *2 10.100.128.9    10.100.128.9      0          10.100.128.9
SW-1#disconnect ?
  <2-2>  The number of an active network connection
  qdm    Disconnect QDM web-based clients
  ssh    Disconnect an active SSH connection
SW-1#disconnect 2
Closing connection to 10.100.128.9 [confirm][enter]
```

In this example, I used session number 2 because that was the connection I wanted to conclude. As demonstrated, you can use the show sessions command to see the connection number.

Resolving Hostnames

If you want to use a hostname instead of an IP address to connect to a remote device, the device that you're using to make the connection must be able to translate the hostname to an IP address.

There are two ways to resolve hostnames to IP addresses. The first is by building a host table on each router, and the second is to build a Domain Name System (DNS) server. The latter method is similar to creating a dynamic host table, assuming that you're dealing with dynamic DNS.

Building a Host Table

An important factor to remember is that although a host table provides name resolution, it does that only on the specific router that it was built upon. The command you use to build a host table on a router looks this:

```
ip host host_name [tcp_port_number] ip_address
```

The default is TCP port number 23, but you can create a session using Telnet with a different TCP port number if you want. You can also assign up to eight IP addresses to a hostname.

Here's how I configured a host table on the SW-1 switch with two entries to resolve the names for the SW-2 and SW-3:

```
SW-1#config t
SW-1(config)#ip host SW-2 ?
  <0-65535>   Default telnet port number
  A.B.C.D     Host IP address
  additional  Append addresses

SW-1(config)#ip host SW-2 10.100.128.9
SW-1(config)#ip host SW-3 10.100.128.8
```

Notice that I can just keep adding IP addresses to reference a unique host, one after another. To view our newly built host table, I'll just use the show hosts command:

```
SW-1(config)#do sho hosts
Default domain is not set
Name/address lookup uses domain service
Name servers are 255.255.255.255

Codes: u - unknown, e - expired, * - OK, ? - revalidate
       t - temporary, p - permanent
```

```
Host                    Port  Flags      Age Type  Address(es)
SW-3                    None  (perm, OK)  0   IP    10.100.128.8
SW-2                    None  (perm, OK)  0   IP    10.100.128.9
```

In this output, you can see the two hostnames plus their associated IP addresses. The perm in the Flags column means that the entry has been manually configured. If it read temp, it would be an entry that was resolved by DNS.

> The show hosts command provides information on temporary DNS entries and permanent name-to-address mappings created using the ip host command.

To verify that the host table resolves names, try typing the hostnames at a router prompt. Remember that if you don't specify the command, the router will assume you want to telnet.

In the following example, I'll use the hostnames to telnet into the remote devices and press Ctrl+Shift+6 and then X to return to the main console of the SW-1 router:

```
SW-1#sw-3
Trying SW-3 (10.100.128.8)... Open


User Access Verification


Password:
SW-3> Ctrl+Shift+6
SW-1#
```

It worked—I successfully used entries in the host table to create a session to the SW-3 device by using the name to telnet into it. And just so you know, names in the host table are not case sensitive.

Notice that the entries in the following show sessions output now display the hostnames and IP addresses instead of just the IP addresses:

```
SW-1#sh sessions
Conn Host               Address          Byte  Idle Conn Name
   1 SW-3               10.100.128.8     0     1    SW-3
*  2 SW-2               10.100.128.9     0     1    SW-2
SW-1#
```

If you want to remove a hostname from the table, all you need to do is use the no ip host command like this:

```
SW-1(config)#no ip host SW-3
```

The drawback to going with this host table method is that you must create a host table on each router in order to be able to resolve names. So clearly, if you have a whole bunch of routers and want to resolve names, using DNS is a much better option!

Using DNS to Resolve Names

If you have a lot of devices, you don't want to create a host table in each one of them unless you've also got a lot of time to waste. Since most of us don't, I highly recommend using a DNS server to resolve hostnames instead!

Anytime a Cisco device receives a command it doesn't understand, it will try to resolve it through DNS by default. Watch what happens when I type the special command todd at a Cisco router prompt:

```
SW-1#todd
Translating "todd"...domain server (255.255.255.255)
% Unknown command or computer name, or unable to find
  computer address
SW-1#
```

Because it doesn't know my name or the command I'm trying to type, it tries to resolve this through DNS. This is really annoying for two reasons: first, because it doesn't know my name <grin>, and second, because I need to hang out and wait for the name lookup to time out. You can get around this and prevent a time-consuming DNS lookup by using the no ip domain-lookup command on your router from global configuration mode.

So if you have a DNS server on your network, you'll need to add a few commands to make DNS name resolution work well for you:

- The first command is ip domain-lookup, which is turned on by default. It needs to be entered only if you previously turned it off with the no ip domain-lookup command. The command can be used without the hyphen as well with the syntax ip domain lookup.

- The second command is ip name-server. This sets the IP address of the DNS server. You can enter the IP addresses of up to six servers.

- The last command is ip domain-name. Although this command is optional, you really need to set it because it appends the domain name to the hostname you type in. Since DNS uses a fully qualified domain name (FQDN) system, you must have a second-level DNS name, in the form *domain.com*.

Here's an example of using these three commands:

```
SW-1#config t
SW-1(config)#ip domain-lookup
SW-1(config)#ip name-server ?
  A.B.C.D  Domain server IP address (maximum of 6)
SW-1(config)#ip name-server 4.4.4.4
```

```
SW-1(config)#ip domain-name lammle.com
SW-1(config)#^Z
```

After the DNS configurations have been set, you can test the DNS server by using a host-name to ping or telnet into a device like this:

```
SW-1#ping SW-3
Translating "SW-3"...domain server (4.4.4.4) [OK]
Type escape sequence to abort.
Sending 5, 100-byte ICMP Echos to 10.100.128.8, timeout is
  2 seconds:
!!!!!
Success rate is 100 percent (5/5), round-trip min/avg/max
  = 28/31/32 ms
```

Notice that the router uses the DNS server to resolve the name.

After a name is resolved using DNS, use the show hosts command to verify that the device cached this information in the host table. If I hadn't used the ip domain-name lammle.com command, I would have needed to type in ping sw-3.lammle.com, which is kind of a hassle.

 Real World Scenario

Should You Use a Host Table or a DNS Server?

Karen has finally finished mapping her network via CDP and the hospital's staff is now much happier. But Karen is still having a difficult time administering the network because she has to look at the network drawing to find an IP address every time she needs to tel-net to a remote router.

Karen was thinking about putting host tables on each router, but with literally hundreds of routers, this is a daunting task and not the best solution. What should she do?

Most networks have a DNS server now anyway, so adding a hundred or so hostnames into it would be much easier—certainly better than adding these hostnames to each and every router! She can just add the three commands on each router and voilà—she's resolving names!

Using a DNS server makes it easy to update any old entries too. Remember, for even one little change, her alternative would be to go to each and every router to manually update its table if she's using static host tables.

Keep in mind that this has nothing to do with name resolution on the network and noth-ing to do with what a host on the network is trying to accomplish. You only use this method when you're trying to resolve names from the router console.

Checking Network Connectivity and Troubleshooting

You can use the ping and traceroute commands to test connectivity to remote devices, and both of them can be used with many protocols, not just IP. But don't forget that the show ip route command is a great troubleshooting command for verifying your routing table and the show interfaces command will reveal the status of each interface to you.

I'm not going to get into the show interfaces commands here because we've already been over that in Chapter 6. But I am going to go over both the debug command and the show processes command, both of which come in very handy when you need to troubleshoot a router.

Using the *ping* Command

So far, you've seen lots of examples of pinging devices to test IP connectivity and name resolution using the DNS server. To see all the different protocols that you can use with the *Ping* program, type **ping ?**:

```
SW-1#ping ?
  WORD  Ping destination address or hostname
  clns  CLNS echo
  ip    IP echo
  ipv6  IPv6 echo
  tag   Tag encapsulated IP echo
  <cr>
```

The ping output displays the minimum, average, and maximum times it takes for a ping packet to find a specified system and return. Here's an example:

```
SW-1#ping SW-3
Translating "SW-3"...domain server (4.4.4.4) [OK]
Type escape sequence to abort.
Sending 5, 100-byte ICMP Echos to 10.100.128.8, timeout is
  2 seconds:
!!!!!
Success rate is 100 percent (5/5), round-trip min/avg/max
  = 28/31/32 ms
```

This output tells us that the DNS server was used to resolve the name, and the device was pinged in a minimum of 28 ms (milliseconds), an average of 31 ms, and up to 32 ms. This network has some latency!

The ping command can be used in user and privileged mode but not configuration mode!

Using the *traceroute* Command

Traceroute—the traceroute command, or trace for short—shows the path a packet takes to get to a remote device. It uses time to live (TTL), time-outs, and ICMP error messages to outline the path a packet takes through an internetwork to arrive at a remote host.

The trace command, which you can deploy from either user mode or privileged mode, allows you to figure out which router in the path to an unreachable network host should be examined more closely as the probable cause of your network's failure.

To see the protocols that you can use with the traceroute command, type **traceroute ?**:

```
SW-1#traceroute ?
  WORD       Trace route to destination address or hostname
  appletalk  AppleTalk Trace
  clns       ISO CLNS Trace
  ip         IP Trace
  ipv6       IPv6 Trace
  ipx        IPX Trace
  mac        Trace Layer2 path between 2 endpoints
  oldvines   Vines Trace (Cisco)
  vines      Vines Trace (Banyan)
  <cr>
```

The traceroute command shows the hop or hops that a packet traverses on its way to a remote device.

Do not get confused! You can't use the tracert command; that's a Windows command. For a router, use the traceroute command!

Here's an example of using tracert on a Windows prompt—notice that the command is tracert, not traceroute:

```
C:\>tracert www.whitehouse.gov

Tracing route to a1289.g.akamai.net [69.8.201.107]
over a maximum of 30 hops:

  1     *        *        *      Request timed out.
  2    53 ms    61 ms    53 ms  hlrn-dsl-gw15-207.hlrn.qwest.net [207.225.112.207]
```

```
3    53 ms    55 ms    54 ms  hlrn-agw1.inet.qwest.net [71.217.188.113]
4    54 ms    53 ms    54 ms  hlr-core-01.inet.qwest.net [205.171.253.97]
5    54 ms    53 ms    54 ms  apa-cntr-01.inet.qwest.net [205.171.253.26]
6    54 ms    53 ms    53 ms  63.150.160.34
7    54 ms    54 ms    53 ms  www.whitehouse.gov [69.8.201.107]

Trace complete.
```

Okay, let's move on now and talk about how to troubleshoot your network using the debug command.

Debugging

Debug is a useful troubleshooting command that's available from the privileged exec mode of Cisco IOS. It's used to display information about various router operations and the related traffic generated or received by the router, plus any error messages.

Even though it's a helpful, informative tool, there are a few important facts that you need to know about it. Debug is regarded as a very high-overhead task because it can consume a huge amount of resources and the router is forced to process-switch the packets being debugged. So you don't just use debug as a monitoring tool—it's meant to be used for a short period of time and only as a troubleshooting tool. It's highly useful for discovering some truly significant facts about both working and faulty software and/or hardware components, but remember to limit its use as the beneficial troubleshooting tool it's designed to be.

Because debugging output takes priority over other network traffic, and because the debug all command generates more output than any other debug command, it can severely diminish the router's performance—even render it unusable! Because of this, it's nearly always best to use more specific debug commands.

As you can see from the following output, you can't enable debugging from user mode, only privileged mode:

```
SW-1>debug ?
% Unrecognized command
SW-1>en
SW-1#debug ?
  aaa                 AAA Authentication, Authorization and Accounting
  access-expression   Boolean access expression
  adjacency           adjacency
  aim                 Attachment Information Manager
  all                 Enable all debugging
  archive             debug archive commands
  arp                 IP ARP and HP Probe transactions
  authentication      Auth Manager debugging
  auto                Debug Automation
```

```
beep                BEEP debugging
bgp                 BGP information
bing                Bing(d) debugging
call-admission      Call admission control
cca                 CCA activity
cdp                 CDP information
cef                 CEF address family independent operations
cfgdiff             debug cfgdiff commands
cisp                CISP debugging
clns                CLNS information
cluster             Cluster information
cmdhd               Command Handler
cns                 CNS agents
condition           Condition
configuration       Debug Configuration behavior
[output cut]
```

If you've got the freedom to pretty much take out a router or switch and you really want to have some fun with debugging, use the debug all command:

```
Sw-1#debug all
```

```
This may severely impact network performance. Continue? (yes/[no]):yes
All possible debugging has been turned on
```

At this point my switch overloaded and crashed and I had to reboot it. Try this on your switch at work and see if you get the same results. Just kidding!

To disable debugging on a router, just use the command no in front of the debug command:

```
SW-1#no debug all
```

I typically just use the undebug all command since it is so easy when using the shortcut:

```
SW-1#un all
```

Remember that instead of using the debug all command, it's usually a much better idea to use specific commands—and only for short periods of time. Here's an example:

```
S1#debug ip icmp
ICMP packet debugging is on
S1#ping 192.168.10.17
```

```
Type escape sequence to abort.
Sending 5, 100-byte ICMP Echos to 192.168.10.17, timeout is 2 seconds:
!!!!!
```

```
Success rate is 100 percent (5/5), round-trip min/avg/max = 1/1/1 ms
S1#
1w4d: ICMP: echo reply sent, src 192.168.10.17, dst 192.168.10.17
1w4d: ICMP: echo reply rcvd, src 192.168.10.17, dst 192.168.10.17
1w4d: ICMP: echo reply sent, src 192.168.10.17, dst 192.168.10.17
1w4d: ICMP: echo reply rcvd, src 192.168.10.17, dst 192.168.10.17
1w4d: ICMP: echo reply sent, src 192.168.10.17, dst 192.168.10.17
1w4d: ICMP: echo reply rcvd, src 192.168.10.17, dst 192.168.10.17
1w4d: ICMP: echo reply sent, src 192.168.10.17, dst 192.168.10.17
1w4d: ICMP: echo reply rcvd, src 192.168.10.17, dst 192.168.10.17
1w4d: ICMP: echo reply sent, src 192.168.10.17, dst 192.168.10.17
1w4d: ICMP: echo reply rcvd, src 192.168.10.17, dst 192.168.10.17
SW-1#un all
```

I'm sure you can see that the debug command is one powerful command. And because of this, I'm also sure you realize that before you use any of the debugging commands, you should make sure you check the CPU utilization capacity of your router. This is important because in most cases, you don't want to negatively impact the device's ability to process the packets on your internetwork. You can determine a specific router's CPU utilization information by using the show processes command.

> Remember, when you telnet into a remote device, you will not see console messages by default! For example, you will not see debugging output. To allow console messages to be sent to your Telnet session, use the terminal monitor command.

Using the *show processes* Command

As I've said, you've really got to be careful when using the debug command on your devices. If your router's CPU utilization is consistently at 50 percent or more, it's probably not a good idea to type in the debug all command unless you want to see what a router looks like when it crashes!

So what other approaches can you use? Well, the show processes (or show processes cpu) is a good tool for determining a given router's CPU utilization. Plus, it'll give you a list of active processes along with their corresponding process ID, priority, scheduler test (status), CPU time used, number of times invoked, and so on. Lots of great stuff! Plus, this command is super handy when you want to evaluate your router's performance and CPU utilization and are otherwise tempted to reach for the debug command!

Okay—what do you see in the following output? The first line shows the CPU utilization output for the last 5 seconds, 1 minute, and 5 minutes. The output provides 5%/0% in front of the CPU utilization for the last 5 seconds: The first number equals the total utilization, and the second one indicates the utilization due to interrupt routines. Take a look:

```
SW-1#sh processes
CPU utilization for five seconds: 5%/0%; one minute: 7%; five minutes: 8%
 PID QTy       PC Runtime(ms)  Invoked   uSecs   Stacks   TTY Process
   1 Cwe 29EBC58       0       22        0  5236/6000    0 Chunk Manager
   2 Csp 1B9CF10     241   206881        1  2516/3000    0 Load Meter
   3 Hwe 1F108D0       0        1        0  8768/9000    0 Connection Mgr
   4 Lst 29FA5C4 9437909   454026    20787  5540/6000    0 Check heaps
   5 Cwe 2A02468       0        2        0  5476/6000    0 Pool Manager
   6 Mst 1E98F04       0        2        0  5488/6000    0 Timers
   7 Hwe 13EB1B4    3686   101399       36  5740/6000    0 Net Input
   8 Mwe 13BCD84       0        1        0 23668/24000   0 Crash writer
   9 Mwe 1C591B4    4346    53691       80  4896/6000    0 ARP Input
  10 Lwe 1DA1504       0        1        0  5760/6000    0 CEF MIB API
  11 Lwe 1E76ACC       0        1        0  5764/6000    0 AAA_SERVER_DEADT
  12 Mwe 1E6F980       0        2        0  5476/6000    0 AAA high-capacit
  13 Mwe 1F56F24       0        1        0 11732/12000   0 Policy Manager [output cut]
```

So basically, the output from the show processes command reveals that our router is happily able to process debugging commands without being overloaded—nice!

Summary

In this chapter, you learned how Cisco routers are configured and how to manage those configurations.

We covered the internal components of a router, including ROM, RAM, NVRAM, and flash.

Next, you found out how to back up and restore the configuration of a Cisco router and switch.

You also learned how to use CDP and Telnet to gather information about remote devices. Finally, you discovered how to resolve hostnames and use the ping and trace commands to test network connectivity as well as how to use the debug and show processes commands—well done!

Exam Essentials

Define the Cisco router components.   Describe the functions of the bootstrap, POST, ROM monitor, mini-IOS, RAM, ROM, flash memory, NVRAM, and the configuration register.

Identify the steps in the router boot sequence.   The steps in the boot sequence are POST, loading the IOS, and copying the startup configuration from NVRAM to RAM.

Save the configuration of a router or switch.   There are a couple of ways to do this, but the most common method, as well as the most tested, is copy running-config startup-config.

Erase the configuration of a router or switch.   Type the privileged-mode command erase startup-config and reload the router.

Understand the various levels of syslog.   It's rather simple to configure syslog; however, there are a bunch of options you have to remember for the exam. To configure basic syslog with debugging as the default level, it's just this one command:

```
SF(config)#logging 172.16.10.1
```

However, you must remember all eight options:

```
SF(config)#logging trap ?
  <0-7>          Logging severity level
  alerts         Immediate action needed           (severity=1)
  critical       Critical conditions               (severity=2)
  debugging      Debugging messages                (severity=7)
  emergencies    System is unusable                (severity=0)
  errors         Error conditions                  (severity=3)
  informational  Informational messages            (severity=6)
  notifications  Normal but significant conditions (severity=5)
  warnings       Warning conditions                (severity=4)
  <cr>
```

Understand how to configure NTP.   It's pretty simple to configure NTP, just like it was syslog, but we don't have to remember a bunch of options! It's just telling the syslog to mark the time and date and enabling NTP:

```
SF(config)#service timestamps log datetime msec
SF(config)#ntp server 172.16.10.1 version 4
```

Describe the value of CDP and LLDP.   Cisco Discovery Protocol can be used to help you document as well as troubleshoot your network; also, LLDP is a nonproprietary protocol that can provide the same information as CDP.

List the information provided by the output of the show cdp neighbors command.   The show cdp neighbors command provides the following information: device ID, local interface, holdtime, capability, platform, and port ID (remote interface).

Understand how to establish a Telnet session with multiple routers simultaneously.   If you telnet to a router or switch, you can end the connection by typing **exit** at any time.

However, if you want to keep your connection to a remote device but still come back to your original router console, you can press the Ctrl+Shift+6 key combination, release it, and then press X.

Identify current Telnet sessions. The command show sessions will provide you with information about all the currently active sessions your router has with other routers.

Build a static host table on a router. By using the global configuration command ip host *host_name ip_address*, you can build a static host table on your router. You can apply multiple IP addresses against the same host entry.

Verify the host table on a router. You can verify the host table with the show hosts command.

Describe the function of the ping command. Packet Internet Groper (ping) uses ICMP echo requests and ICMP echo replies to verify an active IP address on a network.

Ping a valid host ID from the correct prompt. You can ping an IP address from a router's user mode or privileged mode but not from configuration mode, unless you use the do command. You must ping a valid address, such as 1.1.1.1.

Written Labs 7

In this section, you'll complete the following labs to make sure you've got the information and concepts contained within them fully dialed in:

Lab 7.1: IOS Management

Lab 7.2: Router Memory

You can find the answers to these labs in Appendix A, "Answers to Written Labs."

Written Lab 7.1: IOS Management

Write the answers to the following questions:

1. What is the command to copy the startup-config file to DRAM?

2. What command can you use to see the neighbor router's IP address from your router prompt?

3. What command can you use to see the hostname, local interface, platform, and remote port of a neighbor router?

4. What keystrokes can you use to telnet into multiple devices simultaneously?

5. What command will show you your active Telnet connections to neighbor and remote devices?

6. What command can you use to merge a backup configuration with the configuration in RAM?

7. What protocol can be used on a network to synchronize clock and date information?

8. What command is used by a router to forward a DHCP client request to a remote DHCP server?

9. What command enables your switch or router to receive clock and date information and synchronize with the NTP server?

10. Which NTP verification command will show the reference master for the client?

Written Lab 7.2: Router Memory

Identify the location in a router where each of the following files is stored by default.

1. Cisco IOS

2. Bootstrap

3. Startup configuration

4. POST routine

5. Running configuration

6. ARP cache

7. Mini-IOS

8. ROM Monitor

9. Routing tables

10. Packet buffers

Hands-on Labs

To complete the labs in this section, you need at least one router or switch (three would be best) and at least one PC running as a TFTP server. TFTP server software must be installed and running on the PC. For this lab, it is also assumed that your PC and the Cisco devices are connected together with a switch and that all interfaces (PC NIC and router interfaces) are in the same subnet. You can alternately connect the PC directly to the router or connect the routers directly to one another (use a crossover cable in that case). Remember that the labs listed here were created for use with real routers but can easily be used with the LammleSim IOS Version (see www.lammle.com/ccna) or you can use the Cisco Packet Tracer router simulator. Last, although it doesn't matter if you are using a switch or router in these labs, I'm just going to use my routers, but feel free to use your switch to go through these labs!

Here is a list of the labs in this chapter:

Lab 7.1: Backing Up the Router Configuration

Lab 7.2: Using the Cisco Discovery Protocol (CDP)

Lab 7.3: Using Telnet

Lab 7.4: Resolving Hostnames

Hands-on Lab 7.1: Backing Up the Router Configuration

In this lab, you'll back up the router configuration:

1. Log into your router and go into privileged mode by typing **en** or **enable**.

2. Ping the TFTP server to make sure you have IP connectivity.

3. From RouterB, type **copy run tftp**.

4. When prompted, type the IP address of the TFTP server (for example, 172.16.30.2) and press Enter.

5. By default, the router will prompt you for a filename. The hostname of the router is followed by the suffix -confg (yes, I spelled that correctly). You can use any name you want.

   ```
   Name of configuration file to write [RouterB-confg]?
   ```

   Press Enter to accept the default name.

   ```
   Write file RouterB-confg on host 172.16.30.2? [confirm]
   ```

   Press Enter to confirm.

Hands-on Lab 7.2: Using the Cisco Discovery Protocol (CDP)

CDP is an important objective for the Cisco exams. Please go through this lab and use CDP as much as possible during your studies.

1. Log into your router and go into privileged mode by typing **en** or **enable**.

2. From the router, type **sh cdp** and press Enter. You should see that CDP packets are being sent out to all active interfaces every 60 seconds and the holdtime is 180 seconds (these are the defaults).

3. To change the CDP update frequency to 90 seconds, type **cdp timer 90** in global configuration mode.

   ```
   Router#config t
   Enter configuration commands, one per line.  End with
     CNTL/Z.
   Router(config)#cdp timer ?
     <5-900>  Rate at which CDP packets are sent (in sec)
   Router(config)#cdp timer 90
   ```

4. Verify that your CDP timer frequency has changed by using the command **show cdp** in privileged mode.

```
Router#sh cdp
Global CDP information:
Sending CDP packets every 90 seconds
Sending a holdtime value of 180 seconds
```

5. Now use CDP to gather information about neighbor routers. You can get the list of available commands by typing **sh cdp ?**.

```
Router#sh cdp ?
  entry      Information for specific neighbor entry
  interface CDP interface status and configuration
  neighbors CDP neighbor entries
  traffic    CDP statistics
  <cr>
```

6. Type **sh cdp int** to see the interface information plus the default encapsulation used by the interface. It also shows the CDP timer information.

7. Type **sh cdp entry *** to see complete CDP information received from all devices.

8. Type **show cdp neighbors** to gather information about all connected neighbors. (You should know the specific information output by this command.)

9. Type **show cdp neighbors detail**. Notice that it produces the same output as show cdp entry *.

Hands-on Lab 7.3: Using Telnet

Secure Shell was covered in Chapter 6, and it is what you should use for remote access into a Cisco device. However, the Cisco objectives cover Telnet configuration, so let's do a lab on Telnet!

1. Log into your router and go into privileged mode by typing **en** or **enable**.

2. From RouterA, telnet into your remote router (RouterB) by typing **telnet** *ip_address* from the command prompt. Type **exit** to disconnect.

3. Now type in RouterB's IP address from RouterA's command prompt. Notice that the router automatically tries to telnet to the IP address you specified. You can use the telnet command or just type in the IP address.

4. From RouterB, press Ctrl+Shift+6 and then X to return to RouterA's command prompt. Now telnet into your third router, RouterC. Press Ctrl+Shift+6 and then X to return to RouterA.

5. From RouterA, type **show sessions**. Notice your two sessions. You can press the number displayed to the left of the session and press Enter twice to return to that session. The asterisk shows the default session. You can press Enter twice to return to that session.

6. Go to the session for your RouterB. Type **show users**. This shows the console connection and the remote connection. You can use the disconnect command to clear the session or just type **exit** from the prompt to close your session with RouterB.

7. Go to RouterC's console port by typing **show sessions** on the first router and using the connection number to return to RouterC. Type **show user** and notice the connection to your first router, RouterA.

8. Type **clear line line_number** to disconnect the Telnet session.

Hands-on Lab 7.4: Resolving Hostnames

It's best to use a DNS server for name resolution, but you can also create a local hosts table to resolve names. Let's take a look.

1. Log into your router and go into privileged mode by typing **en** or **enable**.

2. From RouterA, type **todd** and press Enter at the command prompt. Notice the error you receive and the delay. The router is trying to resolve the hostname to an IP address by looking for a DNS server. You can turn this feature off by using the no ip domain-lookup command from global configuration mode.

3. To build a host table, you use the ip host command. From RouterA, add a host table entry for RouterB and RouterC by entering the following commands:

```
ip host routerb ip_address
ip host routerc ip_address
```

Here is an example:

```
ip host routerb 172.16.20.2
ip host routerc 172.16.40.2
```

4. Test your host table by typing **ping routerb** from the privileged mode prompt (not the config prompt).

```
RouterA#ping routerb
Type escape sequence to abort.
Sending 5, 100-byte ICMP Echos to 172.16.20.2, timeout
  is 2 seconds:
!!!!!
Success rate is 100 percent (5/5), round-trip
  min/avg/max = 4/4/4 ms
```

5. Test your host table by typing **ping routerc**.

```
RouterA#ping routerc
Type escape sequence to abort.
Sending 5, 100-byte ICMP Echos to 172.16.40.2, timeout
```

```
 is 2 seconds:
!!!!!
Success rate is 100 percent (5/5), round-trip
  min/avg/max = 4/6/8 ms
```

6. Telnet to RouterB and keep your session to RouterB open to RouterA by pressing Ctrl+Shift+6, then X.

7. Telnet to RouterC by typing **routerc** at the command prompt.

8. Return to RouterA and keep the session to RouterC open by pressing Ctrl+Shift+6, then X.

9. View the host table by typing **show hosts** and pressing Enter.

```
Default domain is not set
Name/address lookup uses domain service
Name servers are 255.255.255.255
Host                Flags       Age Type   Address(es)
routerb             (perm, OK)  0   IP     172.16.20.2
routerc             (perm, OK)  0   IP     172.16.40.2
```

Review Questions

The following questions are designed to test your understanding of this chapter's material. For more information on how to get additional questions, please see www.lammle.com/ccna.

You can find the answers to these questions in Appendix B, "Answers to Review Questions."

1. Which of the following is a standards-based protocol that provides dynamic network discovery?

   A. DHCP

   B. LLDP

   C. DDNS

   D. SSTP

   E. CDP

2. Which command can be used to determine a router's CPU utilization?

   A. `show version`

   B. `show controllers`

   C. `show processes cpu`

   D. `show memory`

3. You are troubleshooting a connectivity problem in your corporate network and want to isolate the problem. You suspect that a router on the route to an unreachable network is at fault. What IOS user exec command should you issue?

   A. `Router>ping`

   B. `Router>trace`

   C. `Router>show ip route`

   D. `Router>show interface`

   E. `Router>show cdp neighbors`

4. You copy a configuration from a network host to a router's RAM. The configuration looks correct, yet it is not working at all. What could the problem be?

   A. You copied the wrong configuration into RAM.

   B. You copied the configuration into flash memory instead.

   C. The copy did not override the `shutdown` command in running-config.

   D. The IOS became corrupted after the `copy` command was initiated.

5. In the following command, what does the IP address 10.10.10.254 refer to?

```
Router#config t
Router(config)#interface fa0/0
Router(config-if)#ip helper-address 10.10.10.254
```

A. IP address of the ingress interface on the router

B. IP address of the egress interface on the router

C. IP address of the next hop on the path to the DHCP server

D. IP address of the DHCP server

6. The corporate office sends you a new router to connect, but upon connecting the console cable, you see that there is already a configuration on the router. What should be done before a new configuration is entered in the router?

A. RAM should be erased and the router restarted.

B. Flash should be erased and the router restarted.

C. NVRAM should be erased and the router restarted.

D. The new configuration should be entered and saved.

7. What command can you use to determine the IP address of a directly connected neighbor?

A. show cdp

B. show cdp neighbors

C. show cdp neighbors detail

D. show neighbor detail

8. According to the output, what interface does SW-2 use to connect to SW-3?

```
SW-3#sh cdp neighbors
Capability Codes: R - Router, T - Trans Bridge, B - Source Route BridgeS -
Switch, H - Host, I - IGMP, r - Repeater, P - Phone, D - Remote, C - CVTA,
M - Two-port Mac Relay Device ID
Local Intrfce    Holdtme    Capability  Platform   Port ID
SW-1   Fas 0/1      170          S I      WS-C3560- Fas 0/15
SW-1   Fas 0/2      170          S I      WS-C3560- Fas 0/16
SW-2   Fas 0/5      162          S I      WS-C3560- Fas 0/2
```

A. Fas 0/1

B. Fas 0/16

C. Fas 0/2

D. Fas 0/5

9. Which of the following commands enables syslog on a Cisco device with debugging as the level?

A. syslog 172.16.10.1

B. logging 172.16.10.1

C. remote console 172.16.10.1 syslog debugging

D. transmit console messages level 7 172.16.10.1

10. You save the configuration on a router with the `copy running-config startup-config` command and reboot the router. The router, however, comes up with a blank configuration. What can the problem be?

   A. You didn't boot the router with the correct command.

   B. NVRAM is corrupted.

   C. The configuration register setting is incorrect.

   D. The newly upgraded IOS is not compatible with the hardware of the router.

   E. The configuration you saved is not compatible with the hardware.

11. If you want to have more than one Telnet session open at the same time, what keystroke combination would you use?

   A. Tab+spacebar

   B. Ctrl+X, then 6

   C. Ctrl+Shift+X, then 6

   D. Ctrl+Shift+6, then X

12. You are unsuccessful in telnetting into a remote device from your switch, but you could telnet to the router earlier. However, you can still ping the remote device. What could the problem be? (Choose two.)

   A. IP addresses are incorrect.

   B. Access control list is filtering Telnet.

   C. There is a defective serial cable.

   D. The VTY password is missing.

13. What information is displayed by the `show hosts` command? (Choose two.)

   A. Temporary DNS entries

   B. The names of the routers created using the `hostname` command

   C. The IP addresses of workstations allowed to access the router

   D. Permanent name-to-address mappings created using the `ip host` command

   E. The length of time a host has been connected to the router via Telnet

14. Which three commands can be used to check LAN connectivity problems on an enterprise switch? (Choose three.)

   A. `show interfaces`

   B. `show ip route`

   C. `tracert`

   D. `ping`

   E. `dns lookups`

15. What is the default syslog facility level?

   A. local4

   B. local5

    C. local6

    D. local7

16. You telnet into a remote device and type debug ip icmp, but no output from the debug command is seen. What could the problem be?

    A. You must type the show ip icmp command first.

    B. IP addressing on the network is incorrect.

    C. You must use the terminal monitor command.

    D. Debug output is sent only to the console.

17. Which three statements about syslog utilization are true? (Choose three.)

    A. Utilizing syslog improves network performance.

    B. The syslog server automatically notifies the network administrator of network problems.

    C. A syslog server provides the storage space necessary to store log files without using router disk space.

    D. There are more syslog messages available within Cisco IOS than there are comparable SNMP trap messages.

    E. Enabling syslog on a router automatically enables NTP for accurate time stamping.

    F. A syslog server helps in aggregation of logs and alerts.

18. You need to gather the IP address of a remote switch that is located in Hawaii. What can you do to find the address?

    A. Fly to Hawaii, console into the switch, then relax and have a drink with an umbrella in it.

    B. Issue the show ip route command on the router connected to the switch.

    C. Issue the show cdp neighbor command on the router connected to the switch.

    D. Issue the show ip arp command on the router connected to the switch.

    E. Issue the show cdp neighbors detail command on the router connected to the switch.

19. You need to configure all your routers and switches so they synchronize their clocks from one time source. What command will you type for each device?

    A. clock synchronization ip_address

    B. ntp master ip_address

    C. sync ntp ip_address

    D. ntp server ip_address version number

20. A network administrator enters the following command on a router: logging trap 3. What are three message types that will be sent to the syslog server? (Choose three.)

    A. Informational

    B. Emergency

    C. Warning

    D. Critical

    E. Debug

    F. Error

Chapter

8

Managing Cisco Devices

THE FOLLOWING ICND1 EXAM TOPICS ARE COVERED IN THIS CHAPTER:

✓ **5.0 Infrastructure Management**

- 5.2 Configure and verify device management

    - 5.2.c Licensing

- 5.5 Perform device maintenance

    - 5.5.a Cisco IOS upgrades and recovery (SCP, FTP, TFTP, and MD5 verify)

    - 5.5.b Password recovery and configuration register

    - 5.5.c File system management

Here in Chapter 8, I'm going to show you how to manage Cisco routers on an internetwork. The Internetwork Operating System (IOS) and configuration files reside in different locations in a Cisco device, so it's really important to understand both where these files are located and how they work.

You'll be learning about the configuration register, including how to use the configuration register for password recovery.

Finally, I'll cover how to verify licenses on the ISRG2 routers as well as how to install a permanent license and configure evaluation features in the latest universal images.

To find up-to-the-minute updates for this chapter, please see www.lammle .com/ccna or the book's web page at www.sybex.com/go/ccna.

Managing the Configuration Register

All Cisco routers have a 16-bit software register that's written into NVRAM. By default, the *configuration register* is set to load the Cisco IOS from *flash memory* and to look for and load the startup-config file from NVRAM. In the following sections, I am going to discuss the configuration register settings and how to use these settings to provide password recovery on your routers.

Understanding the Configuration Register Bits

The 16 bits (2 bytes) of the configuration register are read from 15 to 0, from left to right. The default configuration setting on Cisco routers is 0x2102. This means that bits 13, 8, and 1 are on, as shown in Table 8.1. Notice that each set of 4 bits (called a nibble) is read in binary with a value of 8, 4, 2, 1.

TABLE 8.1   The configuration register bit numbers

Configuration Register	2				1				0				2			
Bit number	15	14	13	12	11	10	9	8	7	6	5	4	3	2	1	0
Binary	0	0	1	0	0	0	0	1	0	0	0	0	0	0	1	0

Add the prefix *0x* to the configuration register address. The *0x* means that the digits that follow are in hexadecimal.

Table 8.2 lists the software configuration bit meanings. Notice that bit 6 can be used to ignore the NVRAM contents. This bit is used for password recovery—something I'll go over with you soon in the section "Recovering Passwords," later in this chapter.

Remember that in hex, the scheme is 0–9 and A–F (A = 10, B = 11, C = 12, D = 13, E = 14, and F = 15). This means that a 210F setting for the configuration register is actually 210(15), or 1111 in binary.

TABLE 8.2   Software configuration meanings

Bit	Hex	Description
0–3	0x0000–0x000F	Boot field (see Table 8.3).
6	0x0040	Ignore NVRAM contents.
7	0x0080	OEM bit enabled.
8	0x101	Break disabled.
10	0x0400	IP broadcast with all zeros.
5, 11–12	0x0800–0x1000	Console line speed.
13	0x2000	Boot default ROM software if network boot fails.
14	0x4000	IP broadcasts do not have net numbers.
15	0x8000	Enable diagnostic messages and ignore NVRAM contents.

The boot field, which consists of bits 0–3 in the configuration register (the last 4 bits), controls the router boot sequence and locates the Cisco IOS. Table 8.3 describes the boot field bits.

TABLE 8.3 The boot field (configuration register bits 00–03)

Boot Field	Meaning	Use
00	ROM monitor mode	To boot to ROM monitor mode, set the configuration register to 2100. You must manually boot the router with the b command. The router will show the `rommon>` prompt.
01	Boot image from ROM	To boot the mini-IOS image stored in ROM, set the configuration register to 2101. The router will show the `Router(boot)>` prompt. The mini-IOS is not available in all routers and is also referred to as RXBOOT.
02–F	Specifies a default boot filename	Any value from 2102 through 210F tells the router to use the boot commands specified in NVRAM.

Checking the Current Configuration Register Value

You can see the current value of the configuration register by using the show version command (sh version or show ver for short), as demonstrated here:

```
Router>sh version
Cisco IOS Software, 2800 Software (C2800NM-ADVSECURITYK9-M),
Version 15.1(4)M6, RELEASE SOFTWARE (fc2)
[output cut]
Configuration register is 0x2102
```

The last information given from this command is the value of the configuration register. In this example, the value is 0x2102—the default setting. The configuration register setting of 0x2102 tells the router to look in NVRAM for the boot sequence.

Notice that the show version command also provides the IOS version, and in the preceding example, it shows the IOS version as 15.1(4)M6.

The show version command will display system hardware configuration information, system serial number, the software version, and the names of the boot images on a router.

To change the configuration register, use the config-register command from global configuration mode:

```
Router(config)#config-register 0x2142
Router(config)#do sh ver
```

[output cut]
Configuration register is 0x2102 (will be 0x2142 at next reload)

It's important that you are careful when you set the configuration register!

 If you save your configuration and reload the router and it comes up in setup mode, the configuration register setting is probably incorrect.

Boot System Commands

Did you know that you can configure your router to boot another IOS if the flash is corrupted? Well, you can. You can boot all of your routers from a TFTP server, but it's old school, and people just don't do it anymore; it's just for backup in case of failure.

There are some boot commands you can play with that will help you manage the way your router boots the Cisco IOS—but please remember, we're talking about the router's IOS here, *not* the router's configuration!

```
Router>en
Router#config t
Enter configuration commands, one per line.  End with CNTL/Z.
Router(config)#boot ?
  bootstrap  Bootstrap image file
  config     Configuration file
  host       Router-specific config file
  network    Network-wide config file
  system     System image file
```

The boot command truly gives you a wealth of options, but first, I'll show you the typical settings that Cisco recommends. So let's get started—the boot system command will allow you to tell the router which system IOS file to boot from flash memory. Remember that the router, by default, boots the first system IOS file found in flash. You can change that with the following commands, as shown in the output:

```
Router(config)#boot system ?
  WORD   TFTP filename or URL
  flash  Boot from flash memory
  ftp    Boot from a server via ftp
  mop    Boot from a Decnet MOP server
  rcp    Boot from a server via rcp
  rom    Boot from rom
  tftp   Boot from a tftp server
Router(config)#boot system flash c2800nm-advsecurityk9-mz.151-4.M6.bin
```

Notice I could boot from FLASH, FTP, ROM, TFTP, or another useless options. The command I used configures the router to boot the IOS listed in it. This is a helpful command for when you load a new IOS into flash and want to test it, or even when you want to totally change which IOS is loading by default.

The next command is considered a fallback routine, but as I said, you can make it a permanent way to have your routers boot from a TFTP host. Personally, I wouldn't necessarily recommend doing this (single point of failure); I'm just showing you that it's possible:

```
Router(config)#boot system tftp ?
  WORD  System image filename
Router(config)#boot system tftp c2800nm-advsecurityk9-mz.151-4.M6.bin?
  Hostname or A.B.C.D  Address from which to download the file
  <cr>
Router(config)#boot system tftp c2800nm-advsecurityk9-mz.151-4.M6.bin 1.1.1.2
Router(config)#
```

As your last recommended fallback option—the one to go to if the IOS in flash doesn't load and the TFTP host does not produce the IOS—load the mini-IOS from ROM like this:

```
Router(config)#boot system rom
Router(config)#do show run | include boot system
boot system flash c2800nm-advsecurityk9-mz.151-4.M6.bin
boot system tftp c2800nm-advsecurityk9-mz.151-4.M6.bin 1.1.1.2
boot system rom
Router(config)#
```

If the preceding configuration is set, the router will try to boot from the TFTP server if flash fails, and if the TFTP boot fails, the mini-IOS will load after six unsuccessful attempts of trying to locate the TFTP server.

In the next section, I'll show you how to load the router into ROM monitor mode so you can perform password recovery.

Recovering Passwords

If you're locked out of a router because you forgot the password, you can change the configuration register to help you get back on your feet. As I said earlier, bit 6 in the configuration register is used to tell the router whether to use the contents of NVRAM to load a router configuration.

The default configuration register value is 0x2102, meaning that bit 6 is off. With the default setting, the router will look for and load a router configuration stored in NVRAM (startup-config). To recover a password, you need to turn on bit 6. Doing this will tell the router to ignore the NVRAM contents. The configuration register value to turn on bit 6 is 0x2142.

Here are the main steps to password recovery:

1. Boot the router and interrupt the boot sequence by performing a break, which will take the router into ROM monitor mode.

2. Change the configuration register to turn on bit 6 (with the value 0x2142).

3. Reload the router.

4. Say "no" to entering setup mode, then enter privileged mode.

5. Copy the startup-config file to running-config, and don't forget to verify that your interfaces are re-enabled.

6. Change the password.

7. Reset the configuration register to the default value.

8. Save the router configuration.

9. Reload the router (optional).

I'm going to cover these steps in more detail in the following sections. I'll also show you the commands to restore access to ISR series routers.

You can enter ROM monitor mode by pressing Ctrl+Break or Ctrl+Shift+6, then b, during router bootup. But if the IOS is corrupt or missing, if there's no network connectivity available to find a TFTP host, or if the mini-IOS from ROM doesn't load (meaning the default router fallback failed), the router will enter ROM monitor mode by default.

Interrupting the Router Boot Sequence

Your first step is to boot the router and perform a break. This is usually done by pressing the Ctrl+Break key combination when using HyperTerminal (personally, I use SecureCRT or PuTTY) while the router first reboots.

```
System Bootstrap, Version 15.1(4)M6, RELEASE SOFTWARE (fc2)
Copyright (c) 1999 by cisco Systems, Inc.
TAC:Home:SW:IOS:Specials for info
PC = 0xfff0a530, Vector = 0x500, SP = 0x680127b0
C2800 platform with 32768 Kbytes of main memory
PC = 0xfff0a530, Vector = 0x500, SP = 0x80004374
monitor: command "boot" aborted due to user interrupt
rommon 1 >
```

Notice the line monitor: command "boot" aborted due to user interrupt. At this point, you will be at the rommon 1> prompt, which is called the ROM monitor mode.

Changing the Configuration Register

As I explained earlier, you can change the configuration register from within the IOS by using the config-register command. To turn on bit 6, use the configuration register value 0x2142.

> Remember that if you change the configuration register to 0x2142, the startup-config will be bypassed and the router will load into setup mode.

To change the bit value on a Cisco ISR series router, you just enter the following command at the rommon 1> prompt:

```
rommon 1 >confreg 0x2142
You must reset or power cycle for new config to take effect
rommon 2 >reset
```

Reloading the Router and Entering Privileged Mode

At this point, you need to reset the router like this:

- From the ISR series router, type **I** (for initialize) or **reset**.

- From an older series router, type **I**.

The router will reload and ask if you want to use setup mode (because no startup-config is used). Answer no to entering setup mode, press Enter to go into user mode, and then type **enable** to go into privileged mode.

Viewing and Changing the Configuration

Now you're past the point where you would need to enter the user-mode and privileged-mode passwords in a router. Copy the startup-config file to the running-config file:

```
copy startup-config running-config
```

Or use the shortcut:

```
copy start run
```

The configuration is now running in *random access memory (RAM)*, and you're in privileged mode, meaning that you can now view and change the configuration. But you can't view the enable secret setting for the password since it is encrypted. To change the password, do this:

```
config t
enable secret todd
```

Resetting the Configuration Register and Reloading the Router

After you're finished changing passwords, set the configuration register back to the default value with the config-register command:

```
config t
config-register 0x2102
```

It's important to remember to enable your interfaces after copying the configuration from NVRAM to RAM.

Finally, save the new configuration with a copy `running-config startup-config` and use `reload` to reload the router.

 If you save your configuration and reload the router and it comes up in setup mode, the configuration register setting is probably incorrect.

To sum this up, we now have Cisco's suggested IOS backup routine configured on our router: flash, TFTP host, ROM.

Backing Up and Restoring the Cisco IOS

Before you upgrade or restore a Cisco IOS, you really should copy the existing file to a *TFTP host* as a backup just in case the new image crashes and burns.

And you can use any TFTP host to accomplish this. By default, the flash memory in a router is used to store the Cisco IOS. In the following sections, I'll describe how to check the amount of flash memory, how to copy the Cisco IOS from flash memory to a TFTP host, and how to copy the IOS from a TFTP host to flash memory.

But before you back up an IOS image to a network server on your intranet, you've got to do these three things:

- Make sure you can access the network server.
- Ensure that the network server has adequate space for the code image.
- Verify the file naming and path requirements.

You can connect your laptop or workstation's Ethernet port directly to a router's Ethernet interface, as shown in Figure 8.1.

FIGURE 8.1   Copying an IOS from a router to a TFTP host

Copy the IOS to a TFTP host.
Router# copy flash tftp
- IP address of the TFTP server
- IOS filename

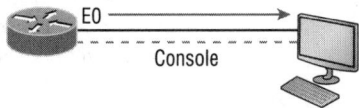

```
RouterX#copy flash tftp:
Source filename [] ?c2800nm-ipbase-mz.124-5a.bin
Address or name of remote host [] ? 10.1.1.1
Destination filename [c2800nm-ipbase-mz.124-5a.bin] [enter]
!!!!!!!!!!!!!!!!!!!!!!!!!!!!!!!!!!!!!!!!!!!!!!!!!!!!!!!!!!!!!!!!!<output omitted>
12094416 bytes copied in 98.858 secs (122341 bytes/sec)
RouterX#
```

- TFTP server software must be running on the PC.
- The PC must be on the same subnet as the router's E0 interface.
- The `copy flash tftp` command must be supplied the IP address of the PC.

You need to verify the following before attempting to copy the image to or from the router:

- TFTP server software must be running on the laptop or workstation.

- The Ethernet connection between the router and the workstation must be made with a crossover cable.

- The workstation must be on the same subnet as the router's Ethernet interface.

- The copy `flash tftp` command must be supplied the IP address of the workstation if you are copying from the router flash.

- And if you're copying "into" flash, you need to verify that there's enough room in flash memory to accommodate the file to be copied.

Verifying Flash Memory

Before you attempt to upgrade the Cisco IOS on your router with a new IOS file, it's a good idea to verify that your flash memory has enough room to hold the new image. You verify the amount of flash memory and the file or files being stored in flash memory by using the show flash command (sh flash for short):

```
Router#sh flash
-#- --length-- -----date/time------ path
1    45392400 Apr 14 2013 05:31:44 +00:00 c2800nm-advsecurityk9-mz.151-4.M6.bin

18620416 bytes available (45395968 bytes used)
```

There are about 45 MB of flash used, but there are still about 18 MB available. If you want to copy a file into flash that is more than 18 MB in size, the router will ask you if you want to erase flash. Be careful here!

> The show flash command will display the amount of memory consumed by the current IOS image as well as tell you if there's enough room available to hold both current and new images. You should know that if there's not enough room for both the old and new image you want to load, the old image will be erased!

The amount of RAM and flash is actually easy to tally using the show version command on routers:

```
Router#show version
[output cut]
System returned to ROM by power-on
System image file is "flash:c2800nm-advsecurityk9-mz.151-4.M6.bin"
[output cut]
```

Cisco 2811 (revision 1.0) with 249856K/12288K bytes of memory.
Processor board ID FTX1049A1AB
2 FastEthernet interfaces
2 Serial(sync/async) interfaces
1 Virtual Private Network (VPN) Module
DRAM configuration is 64 bits wide with parity enabled.
239K bytes of non-volatile configuration memory.
62720K bytes of ATA CompactFlash (Read/Write)

The second highlighted line shows us that this router has about 256 MB of RAM, and you can see that the amount of flash shows up on the last line. By estimating up, we get the amount of flash to 64 MB.

Notice in the first highlighted line that the filename in this example is c2800nm-advsecurity k9-mz.151-4.M6.bin. The main difference in the output of the show flash and show version commands is that the show flash command displays all files in flash memory and the show version command shows the actual name of the file used to run the router and the location from which it was loaded, which is flash memory.

Backing Up the Cisco IOS

To back up the Cisco IOS to a TFTP server, you use the copy flash tftp command. It's a straightforward command that requires only the source filename and the IP address of the TFTP server.

The key to success in this backup routine is to make sure you've got good, solid connectivity to the TFTP server. Check this by pinging the TFTP device from the router console prompt like this:

```
Router#ping 1.1.1.2
Type escape sequence to abort.
Sending 5, 100-byte ICMP Echos to 1.1.1.2, timeout
  is 2 seconds:
!!!!!
Success rate is 100 percent (5/5), round-trip min/avg/max
  = 4/4/8 ms
```

After you ping the TFTP server to make sure that IP is working, you can use the copy flash tftp command to copy the IOS to the TFTP server as shown next:

```
Router#copy flash tftp
Source filename []?c2800nm-advsecurityk9-mz.151-4.M6.bin
Address or name of remote host []?1.1.1.2
Destination filename [c2800nm-advsecurityk9-mz.151-4.M6.bin]?[enter]
!!!!!!!!!!!!!!!!!!!!!!!!!!!!!!!!!!!!!!!!!!!!!!!!!!!!!!!!!!!!!!!!!!!!!!!!!!!!!!!!!!!!!
45395968 bytes copied in 123.724 secs (357532 bytes/sec)
Router#
```

Just copy the IOS filename from either the show flash or show version command and then paste it when prompted for the source filename.

In the preceding example, the contents of flash memory were copied successfully to the TFTP server. The address of the remote host is the IP address of the TFTP host, and the source filename is the file in flash memory.

WARNING   Many newer Cisco routers have removable memory. You may see names for this memory such as flash0:, in which case the command in the preceding example would be copy flash0: tftp:. Alternately, you may see it as usbflash0:.

Restoring or Upgrading the Cisco Router IOS

What happens if you need to restore the Cisco IOS to flash memory to replace an original file that has been damaged or if you want to upgrade the IOS? You can download the file from a TFTP server to flash memory by using the copy tftp flash command. This command requires the IP address of the TFTP host and the name of the file you want to download.

However, since IOS's can be very large today, we may want to use something other than tftp, which is unreliable and can only transfer smaller files. Check this out:

```
Corp#copy ?
  /erase          Erase destination file system.
  /error          Allow to copy error file.
  /noverify       Don't verify image signature before reload.
  /verify         Verify image signature before reload.
  archive:        Copy from archive: file system
  cns:            Copy from cns: file system
  flash:          Copy from flash: file system
  ftp:            Copy from ftp: file system
  http:           Copy from http: file system
  https:          Copy from https: file system
  null:           Copy from null: file system
  nvram:          Copy from nvram: file system
  rcp:            Copy from rcp: file system
  running-config  Copy from current system configuration
  scp:            Copy from scp: file system
  startup-config  Copy from startup configuration
  system:         Copy from system: file system
  tar:            Copy from tar: file system
  tftp:           Copy from tftp: file system
  tmpsys:         Copy from tmpsys: file system
  xmodem:         Copy from xmodem: file system
  ymodem:         Copy from ymodem: file system
```

You can see from the output above that we have many options, and for the larger files we'll use ftp: or scp: to copy our IOS into or from routers and switches, and you can even perform an MD5 verification with the /verify at the end of a command.

Let's just use tftp for our examples in the chapter because it's easiest. But before you begin, make sure the file you want to place in flash memory is in the default TFTP directory on your host. When you issue the command, TFTP won't ask you where the file is, so if the file you want to use isn't in the default directory of the TFTP host, this just won't work.

```
Router#copy tftp flash
Address or name of remote host []?1.1.1.2
Source filename []?c2800nm-advsecurityk9-mz.151-4.M6.bin
Destination filename [c2800nm-advsecurityk9-mz.151-4.M6.bin]?[enter]
%Warning: There is a file already existing with this name
Do you want to over write? [confirm][enter]
Accessing tftp://1.1.1.2/ c2800nm-advsecurityk9-mz.151-4.M6.bin...
Loading c2800nm-advsecurityk9-mz.151-4.M6.bin from 1.1.1.2 (via
    FastEthernet0/0): !!!!!!!!!!!!!!!!!!!!!!!!!!!!!!!!!!!!!!!!!!!!!!!!!!!!!!!!!!!!!!!
[OK - 21710744 bytes]

45395968 bytes copied in 82.880 secs (261954 bytes/sec)
Router#
```

In the preceding example, I copied the same file into flash memory, so it asked me if I wanted to overwrite it. Remember that we are "playing" with files in flash memory. If I had just corrupted my file by overwriting it, I won't know for sure until I reboot the router. Be careful with this command! If the file is corrupted, you'll need to do an IOS-restore from ROM monitor mode.

If you are loading a new file and you don't have enough room in flash memory to store both the new and existing copies, the router will ask to erase the contents of flash memory before writing the new file into flash memory, and if you are able to copy the IOS without erasing the old version, then make sure you remember to use the boot system flash: *ios-file* command.

A Cisco router can become a TFTP server host for a router system image that's run in flash memory. The global configuration command is tftp-server flash: *ios-file*.

 **Real World Scenario**

It's Monday Morning and You Just Upgraded Your IOS

You came in early to work to upgrade the IOS on your router. After the upgrade, you reload the router and the router now shows the rommon> prompt.

It seems that you're about to have a bad day! This is what I call an RGE: a resume-generating event! So, now what do you do? Just keep calm and chive on! Follow these steps to save your job:

rommon 1 > **tftpdnld**

Missing or illegal ip address for variable IP_ADDRESS
Illegal IP address.

usage: tftpdnld [-hr]
  Use this command for disaster recovery only to recover an image via TFTP.
  Monitor variables are used to set up parameters for the transfer.
  (Syntax: "VARIABLE_NAME=value" and use "set" to show current variables.)
  "ctrl-c" or "break" stops the transfer before flash erase begins.

  The following variables are REQUIRED to be set for tftpdnld:
            IP_ADDRESS: The IP address for this unit
        IP_SUBNET_MASK: The subnet mask for this unit
       DEFAULT_GATEWAY: The default gateway for this unit
           TFTP_SERVER: The IP address of the server to fetch from
             TFTP_FILE: The filename to fetch

  The following variables are OPTIONAL:
[unneeded output cut]
rommon 2 >**set IP_Address:1.1.1.1**
rommon 3 >**set IP_SUBNET_MASK:255.0.0.0**
rommon 4 >**set DEFAULT_GATEWAY:1.1.1.2**
rommon 5 >**set TFTP_SERVER:1.1.1.2**
rommon 6 >**set TFTP_FILE: flash:c2800nm-advipservicesk9-mz.124-12.bin**
rommon 7 >**tftpdnld**

From here you can see the variables you need to configure using the set command; be sure you use ALL_CAPS with these commands as well as underscore (_). From here, you need to set the IP address, mask, and default gateway of your router, then the IP address of the TFTP host, which in this example is a directly connected router that I made a TFTP server with this command:

Router(config)#**tftp-server flash:c2800nm-advipservicesk9-mz.124-12.bin**

And finally, you set the IOS filename of the file on your TFTP server. Whew! Job saved.

There is one other way you can restore the IOS on a router, but it takes a while. You can use what is called the Xmodem protocol to actually upload an IOS file into flash memory through the console port. You'd use the Xmodem through the console port procedure if you had no network connectivity to the router or switch.

Using the Cisco IOS File System (Cisco IFS)

Cisco has created a file system called Cisco IFS that allows you to work with files and directories just as you would from a Windows DOS prompt. The commands you use are dir, copy, more, delete, erase or format, cd and pwd, and mkdir and rmdir.

Working with IFS gives you the ability to view all files, even those on remote servers. And you definitely want to find out if an image on one of your remote servers is valid before you copy it, right? You also need to know how big it is—size matters here! It's also a really good idea to take a look at the remote server's configuration and make sure it's all good before loading that file on your router.

It's very cool that IFS makes the file system user interface universal—it's not platform specific anymore. You now get to use the same syntax for all your commands on all of your routers, no matter the platform!

Sound too good to be true? Well, it kind of is because you'll find out that support for all commands on each file system and platform just isn't there. But it's really no big deal since various file systems differ in the actions they perform; the commands that aren't relevant to a particular file system are the very ones that aren't supported on that file system. Be assured that any file system or platform will fully support all the commands you need to manage it.

Another cool IFS feature is that it cuts down on all those obligatory prompts for a lot of the commands. If you want to enter a command, all you have to do is type all the necessary info straight into the command line—no more jumping through hoops of prompts! So, if you want to copy a file to an FTP server, all you'd do is first indicate where the desired source file is on your router, pinpoint where the destination file is to be on the FTP server, determine the username and password you're going to use when you want to connect to that server, and type it all in on one line—sleek! And for those of you resistant to change, you can still have the router prompt you for all the information it needs and enjoy entering a more elegantly minimized version of the command than you did before.

But even in spite of all this, your router might still prompt you—even if you did everything right in your command line. It comes down to how you've got the file prompt command configured and which command you're trying to use. But no worries—if that happens, the default value will be entered right there in the command, and all you have to do is hit Enter to verify the correct values.

IFS also lets you explore various directories and inventory files in any directory you want. Plus, you can make subdirectories in flash memory or on a card, but you only get to do that if you're working on one of the more recent platforms.

And get this—the new file system interface uses URLs to determine the whereabouts of a file. So just as they pinpoint places on the Web, URLs now indicate where files are on your Cisco router, or even on a remote file server! You just type URLs right into your commands to identify where the file or directory is. It's really that easy—to copy a file from one place to another, you simply enter the copy *source-url destination-url* command—sweet! IFS URLs are a tad different than what you're used to though, and there's an array of formats to use that vary depending on where, exactly, the file is that you're after.

We're going to use Cisco IFS commands pretty much the same way that we used the copy command in the IOS section earlier:

- For backing up the IOS
- For upgrading the IOS
- For viewing text files

Okay—with all that down, let's take a look at the common IFS commands available to us for managing the IOS. I'll get into configuration files soon, but for now I'm going to get you started with going over the basics used to manage the new Cisco IOS.

dir   Same as with Windows, this command lets you view files in a directory. Type **dir**, hit Enter, and by default you get the contents of the flash:/ directory output.

copy   This is one popular command, often used to upgrade, restore, or back up an IOS. But as I said, when you use it, it's really important to focus on the details—what you're copying, where it's coming from, and where it's going to land.

more   Same as with Unix, this will take a text file and let you look at it on a card. You can use it to check out your configuration file or your backup configuration file. I'll go over it more when we get into actual configuration.

show file   This command will give you the skinny on a specified file or file system, but it's kind of obscure because people don't use it a lot.

delete   Three guesses—yep, it deletes stuff. But with some types of routers, not as well as you'd think. That's because even though it whacks the file, it doesn't always free up the space it was using. To actually get the space back, you have to use something called the squeeze command too.

erase/format   Use these with care—make sure that when you're copying files, you say no to the dialog that asks you if you want to erase the file system! The type of memory you're using determines if you can nix the flash drive or not.

cd/pwd   Same as with Unix and DOS, cd is the command you use to change directories. Use the pwd command to print (show) the working directory.

mkdir/rmdir   Use these commands on certain routers and switches to create and delete directories—the mkdir command for creation and the rmdir command for deletion. Use the cd and pwd commands to change into these directories.

The Cisco IFS uses the alternate term system:running-config as well as nvram:startup-config when copying the configurations on a router, although it is not mandatory that you use this naming convention.

Using the Cisco IFS to Upgrade an IOS

Let's take a look at some of these Cisco IFS commands on my ISR router (1841 series) with a hostname of R1.

We'll start with the pwd command to verify our default directory and then use the dir command to verify its contents (flash:/):

```
R1#pwd
flash:
R1#dir
Directory of flash:/
    1  -rw-    13937472  Dec 20 2006 19:58:18 +00:00  c1841-ipbase-
    mz.124-1c.bin
    2  -rw-        1821  Dec 20 2006 20:11:24 +00:00  sdmconfig-18xx.cfg
    3  -rw-     4734464  Dec 20 2006 20:12:00 +00:00  sdm.tar
    4  -rw-      833024  Dec 20 2006 20:12:24 +00:00  es.tar
    5  -rw-     1052160  Dec 20 2006 20:12:50 +00:00  common.tar
    6  -rw-        1038  Dec 20 2006 20:13:10 +00:00  home.shtml
    7  -rw-      102400  Dec 20 2006 20:13:30 +00:00  home.tar
    8  -rw-      491213  Dec 20 2006 20:13:56 +00:00  128MB.sdf
    9  -rw-     1684577  Dec 20 2006 20:14:34 +00:00  securedesktop-
    ios-3.1.1.27-k9.pkg
   10  -rw-      398305  Dec 20 2006 20:15:04 +00:00  sslclient-win-1.1.0.154.pkg

32071680 bytes total (8818688 bytes free)
```

What we can see here is that we have the basic IP IOS (c1841-ipbase-mz.124-1c.bin). Looks like we need to upgrade our 1841. You've just got to love how Cisco puts the IOS type in the filename now! First, let's check the size of the file that's in flash with the show file command (show flash would also work):

```
R1#show file info flash:c1841-ipbase-mz.124-1c.bin
flash:c1841-ipbase-mz.124-1c.bin:
  type is image (elf) []
  file size is 13937472 bytes, run size is 14103140 bytes
  Runnable image, entry point 0x8000F000, run from ram
```

With a file that size, the existing IOS will have to be erased before we can add our new IOS file (c1841-advipservicesk9-mz.124-12.bin), which is over 21 MB. We'll use the delete command, but remember, we can play with any file in flash memory and nothing serious will happen until we reboot—that is, if we made a mistake. So obviously, and as I pointed out earlier, we need to be very careful here!

```
R1#delete flash:c1841-ipbase-mz.124-1c.bin
Delete filename [c1841-ipbase-mz.124-1c.bin]?[enter]
Delete flash:c1841-ipbase-mz.124-1c.bin? [confirm][enter]
R1#sh flash
```

```
-#- --length-- -----date/time------ path
1         1821 Dec 20 2006 20:11:24 +00:00 sdmconfig-18xx.cfg
2      4734464 Dec 20 2006 20:12:00 +00:00 sdm.tar
3       833024 Dec 20 2006 20:12:24 +00:00 es.tar
4      1052160 Dec 20 2006 20:12:50 +00:00 common.tar
5         1038 Dec 20 2006 20:13:10 +00:00 home.shtml
6       102400 Dec 20 2006 20:13:30 +00:00 home.tar
7       491213 Dec 20 2006 20:13:56 +00:00 128MB.sdf
8      1684577 Dec 20 2006 20:14:34 +00:00 securedesktop-ios-3.1.1.27-k9.pkg
9       398305 Dec 20 2006 20:15:04 +00:00 sslclient-win-1.1.0.154.pkg
22757376 bytes available (9314304 bytes used)
R1#sh file info flash:c1841-ipbase-mz.124-1c.bin
%Error opening flash:c1841-ipbase-mz.124-1c.bin (File not found)
R1#
```

So with the preceding commands, we deleted the existing file and then verified the deletion by using both the show flash and show file commands. We'll add the new file with the copy command, but again, we need to make sure to be careful because this way isn't any safer than the first method I showed you earlier:

```
R1#copy tftp://1.1.1.2/c1841-advipservicesk9-mz.124-12.bin/ flash:/
    c1841-advipservicesk9-mz.124-12.bin
Source filename [/c1841-advipservicesk9-mz.124-12.bin/]?[enter]
Destination filename [c1841-advipservicesk9-mz.124-12.bin]?[enter]
Loading /c1841-advipservicesk9-mz.124-12.bin/ from 1.1.1.2 (via
    FastEthernet0/0): !!!!!!!!!!!!!!!!!!!!!!!!!!!!!!!!!!!!!!!!
[output cut]
!!!!!!!!!!!!!!!!!!!!!!!!!!!!!!!!!!!!!!!!!!!!!!!!!!!!!!
[OK - 22103052 bytes]
22103052 bytes copied in 72.008 secs (306953 bytes/sec)
R1#sh flash
-#- --length-- -----date/time------ path
1         1821 Dec 20 2006 20:11:24 +00:00 sdmconfig-18xx.cfg
2      4734464 Dec 20 2006 20:12:00 +00:00 sdm.tar
3       833024 Dec 20 2006 20:12:24 +00:00 es.tar
4      1052160 Dec 20 2006 20:12:50 +00:00 common.tar
5         1038 Dec 20 2006 20:13:10 +00:00 home.shtml
6       102400 Dec 20 2006 20:13:30 +00:00 home.tar
7       491213 Dec 20 2006 20:13:56 +00:00 128MB.sdf
8      1684577 Dec 20 2006 20:14:34 +00:00 securedesktop-ios-3.1.1.27-k9.pkg
9       398305 Dec 20 2006 20:15:04 +00:00 sslclient-win-1.1.0.154.pkg
```

```
10    22103052 Mar 10 2007 19:40:50 +00:00 c1841-advipservicesk9-mz.124-12.bin
651264 bytes available (31420416 bytes used)
R1#
```

We can also check the file information with the show file command:

```
R1#sh file information flash:c1841-advipservicesk9-mz.124-12.bin
flash:c1841-advipservicesk9-mz.124-12.bin:
  type is image (elf) []
  file size is 22103052 bytes, run size is 22268736 bytes
  Runnable image, entry point 0x8000F000, run from ram
```

Remember that the IOS is expanded into RAM when the router boots, so the new IOS will not run until you reload the router.

I really recommend experimenting with the Cisco IFS commands on a router just to get a good feel for them because, as I've said, they can definitely give you some grief if not executed properly!

> I mention "safer methods" a lot in this chapter. Clearly, I've caused myself some serious pain by not being careful enough when working in flash memory! I cannot stress this enough—pay attention when messing around with flash memory!

One of the brilliant features of the ISR routers is that they use the physical flash cards that are accessible from the front or back of any router. These typically have a name like usbflash0:, so to view the contents, you'd type **dir usbflash0:**, for example. You can pull these flash cards out, put them in an appropriate slot in your PC, and the card will show up as a drive. You can then add, change, and delete files. Just put the flash card back in your router and power up—instant upgrade. Nice!

Licensing

IOS licensing is now done quite differently than it was with previous versions of the IOS. Actually, there was no licensing before the new 15.0 IOS code, just your word and honor, and we can only guess based on how all products are downloaded on the Internet daily how well that has worked out for Cisco!

Starting with the IOS 15.0 code, things are much different—almost too different. I can imagine that Cisco will come back toward the middle on its licensing issues, so that the administration and management won't be as detailed as it is with the new 15.0 code license is now; but you can be the judge of that after reading this section.

A new ISR router is pre-installed with the software images and licenses that you ordered, so as long as you ordered and paid for everything you need, you're set! If not, you can just install another license, which can be a tad tedious at first—enough so that installing a license was made an objective on the Cisco exam! Of course, it can be done, but it definitely requires some effort. As is typical with Cisco, if you spend enough money on their products, they tend to make it easier on you and your administration, and the licensing for the newest IOS is no exception, as you'll soon see.

On a positive note, Cisco provides evaluation licenses for most software packages and features that are supported on the hardware you purchased, and it's always nice to be able to try it out before you buy. Once the temporary license expires after 60 days, you need to acquire a permanent license in order to continue to use the extended features that aren't available in your current version. This method of licensing allows you to enable a router to use different parts of the IOS. So, what happens after 60 days? Well, nothing—back to the honor system for now. This is now called *Right-To-Use (RTU) licensing*, and it probably won't always be available via your honor, but for now it is.

But that's not the best part of the new licensing features. Prior to the 15.0 code release, there were eight different software feature sets for each hardware router type. With the IOS 15.0 code, the packaging is now called a *universal image*, meaning all feature sets are available in one file with all features packed neatly inside. So instead of the pre-15.0 IOS file packages of one image per feature set, Cisco now just builds one universal image that includes all of them in the file. Even so, we still need a different universal image per router model or series, just not a different image for each feature set as we did with previous IOS versions.

To use the features in the IOS software, you must unlock them using the software activation process. Since all features available are inside the universal image already, you can just unlock the features you need as you need them, and of course pay for these features when you determine that they meet your business requirements. All routers come with something called the IP Base licensing, which is the prerequisite for installing all other features.

There are three different technology packages available for purchase that can be installed as additional feature packs on top of the prerequisite IP Base (default), which provides entry-level IOS functionality. These are as follows:

Data: MPLS, ATM, and multiprotocol support

Unified Communications: VoIP and IP telephony

Security: Cisco IOS Firewall, IPS, IPsec, 3DES, and VPN

For example, if you need MPLS and IPsec, you'll need the default IP Base, Data, and Security premium packages unlocked on your router.

To obtain the license, you'll need the unique device identifier (UDI), which has two components: the product ID (PID) and the serial number of the router. The show license UDI command provides this information in an output as shown:

```
Router#sh license udi
Device#   PID                 SN              UDI
--------------------------------------------------------------------
*0        CISCO2901/K9        FTX1641Y07J     CISCO2901/K9:FTX1641Y07J
```

After the time has expired for your 60-day evaluation period, you can either obtain the license file from the Cisco License Manager (CLM), which is an automated process, or use the manual process through the Cisco Product License Registration portal. Typically only larger companies will use the CLM because you'd need to install software on a server, which then keeps track of all your licenses for you. If you have just a few licenses that you use, you can opt for the manual web browser process found on the Cisco Product License Registration portal and then just add in a few CLI commands. After that, you just basically keep track of putting all the different license features together for each device you manage. Although this sounds like a lot of work, you don't need to perform these steps often. But clearly, going with the CLM makes a lot of sense if you have bunches of licenses to manage because it will put together all the little pieces of licensing for each router in one easy process.

When you purchase the software package with the features that you want to install, you need to permanently activate the software package using your UDI and the *product authorization key (PAK)* that you received with your purchase. This is essentially your receipt acknowledging that you purchased the license. You then need to connect the license with a particular router by combining the PAK and the UDI, which you do online at the Cisco Product License Registration portal (www.cisco.com/go/license). If you haven't already registered the license on a different router, and it is valid, Cisco will then email you your permanent license, or you can download it from your account.

But wait! You're still not done. You now need to activate the license on the router. Whew... maybe it's worthwhile to install the CLM on a server after all! Staying with the manual method, you need to make the new license file available to the router either via a USB port on the router or through a TFTP server. Once it's available to the router, you'll use the license install command from privileged mode.

Assuming that you copied the file into flash memory, the command would look like something like this:

```
Router#license install ?
    archive:  Install from archive: file system
    flash:    Install from flash: file system
    ftp:      Install from ftp: file system
    http:     Install from http: file system
    https:    Install from https: file system
    null:     Install from null: file system
    nvram:    Install from nvram: file system
    rcp:      Install from rcp: file system
    scp:      Install from scp: file system
    syslog:   Install from syslog: file system
    system:   Install from system: file system
    tftp:     Install from tftp: file system
    tmpsys:   Install from tmpsys: file system
    xmodem:   Install from xmodem: file system
    ymodem:   Install from ymodem: file system
Router#license install flash:FTX1628838P_201302111432454180.lic
```

```
Installing licenses from "flash::FTX1628838P_201302111432454180.lic"
Installing...Feature:datak9...Successful:Supported
1/1 licenses were successfully installed
0/1 licenses were existing licenses
0/1 licenses were failed to install
April 12 2:31:19.786: %LICENSE-6-INSTALL: Feature datak9 1.0 was
installed in this device. UDI=CISCO2901/K9:FTX1628838P; StoreIndex=1:Primary
License Storage

April 12 2:31:20.078: %IOS_LICENSE_IMAGE_APPLICATION-6-LICENSE_LEVEL: Module name
=c2800 Next reboot level = datak9 and License = datak9
```

You need to reboot to have the new license take effect. Now that you have your license installed and running, how do you use Right-To-Use licensing to check out new features on your router? Let's look into that now.

Right-To-Use Licenses (Evaluation Licenses)

Originally called evaluation licenses, Right-To-Use (RTU) licenses are what you need when you want to update your IOS to load a new feature but either don't want to wait to get the license or just want to test if this feature will truly meet your business requirements. This makes sense because if Cisco made it complicated to load and check out a feature, they could potentially miss out on a sale! Of course if the feature does work for you, they'll want you to buy a permanent license, but again, this is on the honor system at the time of this writing.

Cisco's license model allows you to install the feature you want without a PAK. The Right-To-Use license works for 60 days before you would need to install your permanent license. To enable the Right-To-Use license you would use the license boot module command. The following demonstrates starting the Right-To-Use license on my 2900 series router, enabling the security module named securityk9:

```
Router(config)#license boot module c2900 technology-package securityk9
PLEASE READ THE FOLLOWING TERMS CAREFULLY. INSTALLING THE LICENSE OR LICENSE KEY
PROVIDED FOR ANY CISCO PRODUCT FEATURE OR USING
SUCHPRODUCT FEATURE CONSTITUTES YOUR FULL ACCEPTANCE OF THE
FOLLOWING TERMS. YOU MUST NOT PROCEED FURTHER IF YOU ARE NOT WILLING
TO BE BOUND BY ALL THE TERMS SET FORTH HEREIN.
[output cut]
Activation of the software command line interface will be evidence of
your acceptance of this agreement.

ACCEPT? [yes/no]: yes
```

```
% use 'write' command to make license boot config take effect on next boot
Feb 12 01:35:45.060: %IOS_LICENSE_IMAGE_APPLICATION-6-LICENSE_LEVEL:
Module name =c2900 Next reboot level = securityk9 and License = securityk9

Feb 12 01:35:45.524: %LICENSE-6-EULA_ACCEPTED: EULA for feature
securityk9 1.0 has been accepted. UDI=CISCO2901/K9:FTX1628838P;
StoreIndex=0:Built-In License Storage
```

Once the router is reloaded, you can use the security feature set. And it is really nice that you don't need to reload the router again if you choose to install a permanent license for this feature. The show license command shows the licenses installed on the router:

```
Router#show license
Index 1 Feature: ipbasek9
      Period left: Life time
      License Type: Permanent
      License State: Active, In Use
      License Count: Non-Counted
      License Priority: Medium
Index 2 Feature: securityk9
      Period left: 8 weeks  2 days
      Period Used: 0  minute  0  second
      License Type: EvalRightToUse
      License State: Active, In Use
      License Count: Non-Counted
      License Priority: None
Index 3 Feature: uck9
      Period left: Life time
      License Type: Permanent
      License State: Active, In Use
      License Count: Non-Counted
      License Priority: Medium
Index 4 Feature: datak9
      Period left: Not Activated
      Period Used: 0  minute  0  second
      License Type: EvalRightToUse
      License State: Not in Use, EULA not accepted
      License Count: Non-Counted
      License Priority: None
Index 5 Feature: gatekeeper
  [output cut]
```

You can see in the preceding output that the ipbasek9 is permanent and the securityk9 has a license type of EvalRightToUse. The show license feature command provides the same information as show license, but it's summarized into one line as shown in the next output:

```
Router#sh license feature
```

Feature name	Enforcement	Evaluation	Subscription	Enabled	RightToUse
ipbasek9	no	no	no	yes	no
securityk9	yes	yes	no	no	yes
uck9	yes	yes	no	yes	yes
datak9	yes	yes	no	no	yes
gatekeeper	yes	yes	no	no	yes
SSL_VPN	yes	yes	no	no	yes
ios-ips-update	yes	yes	yes	no	yes
SNASw	yes	yes	no	no	yes
hseck9	yes	no	no	no	no
cme-srst	yes	yes	no	yes	yes
WAAS_Express	yes	yes	no	no	yes
UCVideo	yes	yes	no	no	yes

The show version command also shows the license information at the end of the command output:

```
Router#show version
[output cut]
License Info:

License UDI:

-----------------------------------------------
Device#    PID                 SN
-----------------------------------------------
*0         CISCO2901/K9        FTX1641Y07J


Technology Package License Information for Module:'c2900'
```

Technology	Technology-package Current	Type	Technology-package Next reboot
ipbase	ipbasek9	Permanent	ipbasek9
security	None	None	None

uc	uck9	Permanent	uck9
data	None	None	None

Configuration register is 0x2102

The show version command shows if the license was activated. Don't forget, you'll need to reload the router to have the license features take effect if the license evaluation is not already active.

Backing Up and Uninstalling the License

It would be a shame to lose your license if it has been stored in flash and your flash files become corrupted. So always back up your IOS license!

If your license has been saved in a location other than flash, you can easily back it up to flash memory via the license save command:

Router#**license save flash:Todd_License.lic**

The previous command will save your current license to flash. You can restore your license with the license install command I demonstrated earlier.

There are two steps to uninstalling the license on a router. First, to uninstall the license you need to disable the technology package, using the no license boot module command with the keyword disable at the end of the command line:

Router#**license boot module c2900 technology-package securityk9 disable**

The second step is to clear the license. To achieve this from the router, use the license clear command and then remove the license with the no license boot module command:

Router#**license clear securityk9**
Router#**config t**
Router(config)#**no license boot module c2900 technology-package securityk9 disable**
Router(config)#**exit**
Router#**reload**

After you run through the preceding commands, the license will be removed from your router.

Here's a summary of the license commands I used in this chapter. These are important commands to have down and you really need to understand these to meet the Cisco objectives:

- show license determines the licenses that are active on your system. It also displays a group of lines for each feature in the currently running IOS image along with several status variables related to software activation and licensing, both licensed and unlicensed features.

- `show license feature` allows you to view the technology package licenses and feature licenses that are supported on your router along with several status variables related to software activation and licensing. This includes both licensed and unlicensed features.

- `show license udi` displays the unique device identifier (UDI) of the router, which comprises the product ID (PID) and serial number of the router.

- `show version` displays various pieces of information about the current IOS version, including the licensing details at the end of the command's output.

- `license install` *url* installs a license key file into a router.

- `license boot module` installs a Right-To-Use license feature on a router.

To help you organize a large amount of licenses, search on `Cisco.com` for the Cisco Smart Software Manager. This web page enables you to manage all your licenses from one centralized website. With Cisco Smart Software Manager, you organize and view your licenses in groups that are called *virtual accounts*, which are collections of licenses and product instances.

Summary

You now know how Cisco routers are configured and how to manage those configurations.

This chapter covered the internal components of a router, which included ROM, RAM, NVRAM, and flash.

In addition, I covered what happens when a router boots and which files are loaded at that time. The configuration register tells the router how to boot and where to find files. You learned how to change and verify the configuration register settings for password recovery purposes. I also showed you how to manage these files using the CLI and IFS.

Finally, the chapter covered licensing with the new 15.0 code, including how to install a permanent license and a Right-To-Use license to install features for 60 days. I also showed you the verification commands used to see what licenses are installed and to verify their status.

Exam Essentials

Define the Cisco router components.   Describe the functions of the bootstrap, POST, ROM monitor, mini-IOS, RAM, ROM, flash memory, NVRAM, and the configuration register.

Identify the steps in the router boot sequence.   The steps in the boot sequence are POST, loading the IOS, and copying the startup configuration from NVRAM to RAM.

Understand configuration register commands and settings.   The 0x2102 setting is the default on all Cisco routers and tells the router to look in NVRAM for the boot sequence. 0x2101 tells the router to boot from ROM, and 0x2142 tells the router not to load the startup-config in NVRAM to provide password recovery.

Perform password recovery.   The steps in the password recovery process are interrupt the router boot sequence, change the configuration register, reload the router and enter privileged mode, copy the startup-config file to running-config and verify that your interfaces are re-enabled, change/set the password, save the new configuration, reset the configuration register, and reload the router.

Back up an IOS image.   By using the privileged-mode command copy flash tftp, you can back up a file from flash memory to a TFTP (network) server.

Restore or upgrade an IOS image.   By using the privileged-mode command copy tftp flash, you can restore or upgrade a file from a TFTP (network) server to flash memory.

Describe best practices to prepare to back up an IOS image to a network server.   Make sure that you can access the network server, ensure that the network server has adequate space for the code image, and verify the file naming and path requirement.

Understand and use Cisco IFS file system management commands.   The commands to use are dir, copy, more, delete, erase or format, cd and pwd, and mkdir and rmdir, as well as system:running-config and nvram:startup-config.

Remember how to install a permanent and Right-To-Use license.   To install a permanent license on a router, use the install license url command. To install an evaluation feature, use the license boot module command.

Remember the verification commands used for licensing in the new ISR G2 routers.   The show license command determines the licenses that are active on your system. The show license feature command allows you to view the technology package licenses and feature licenses that are supported on your router. The show license udi command displays the unique device identifier (UDI) of the router, which comprises the product ID (PID) and serial number of the router, and the show version command displays information about the current IOS version, including the licensing details at the end of the command's output.

Written Lab 8

You can find the answers to this labs in Appendix A, "Answers to Written Labs."

In this section, you'll complete the following lab to make sure you've got the information and concepts contained within them fully dialed in:

Lab 8.1: IOS Management

Written Lab 8.1: IOS Management

Write the answers to the following questions:

1. What is the command to copy a Cisco IOS to a TFTP server?
2. What do you set the configuration register setting to in order to boot the mini-IOS in ROM?
3. What is the configuration register setting to tell the router to look in NVRAM for the boot sequence?
4. What do you set the configuration register setting to in order to boot to ROM monitor mode?
5. What is used with a PAK to generate a license file?
6. What is the configuration register setting for password recovery?
7. Which command can change the location from which the system loads the IOS?
8. What is the first step of the router boot sequence?
9. What command can you use to upgrade a Cisco IOS?
10. Which command determines the licenses that are active on your system?

Hands-on Labs

To complete the labs in this section, you need at least one router (three would be best) and at least one PC running as a TFTP server. TFTP server software must be installed and running on the PC. For these labs, it is also assumed that your PC and the router(s) are connected together with a switch or hub and that all interfaces (PC NIC and router interfaces) are in the same subnet. You can alternately connect the PC directly to the router or connect the routers directly to one another (use a crossover cable in that case). Remember that the labs listed here were created for use with real routers but can easily be used with the LammleSim IOS version (found at www.lammle.com/ccna) or Cisco's Packet Tracer program.

Here is a list of the labs in this chapter:

Lab 8.1: Backing Up Your Router IOS

Lab 8.2: Upgrading or Restoring Your Router IOS

Hands-on Lab 8.1: Backing Up Your Router IOS

In this lab, we'll be backing up the IOS from flash to a TFTP host.

1. Log into your router and go into privileged mode by typing **en** or **enable**.
2. Make sure you can connect to the TFTP server that is on your network by pinging the IP address from the router console.

3. Type **show flash** to see the contents of flash memory.

4. Type **show version** at the router privileged-mode prompt to get the name of the IOS currently running on the router. If there is only one file in flash memory, the show flash and show version commands show the same file. Remember that the show version command shows you the file that is currently running and the show flash command shows you all of the files in flash memory.

5. Once you know you have good Ethernet connectivity to the TFTP server and you also know the IOS filename, back up your IOS by typing **copy flash tftp**. This command tells the router to copy a specified file from flash memory (this is where the IOS is stored by default) to a TFTP server.

6. Enter the IP address of the TFTP server and the source IOS filename. The file is now copied and stored in the TFTP server's default directory.

Hands-on Lab 8.2: Upgrading or Restoring Your Router IOS

In this lab, we'll be copying an IOS from a TFTP host to flash memory.

1. Log into your router and go into privileged mode by typing **en** or **enable**.

2. Make sure you can connect to the TFTP server by pinging the IP address of the server from the router console.

3. Once you know you have good Ethernet connectivity to the TFTP server, type the **copy tftp flash** command.

4. Confirm that the router will not function during the restore or upgrade by following the prompts provided on the router console. It is possible this prompt may not occur.

5. Enter the IP address of the TFTP server.

6. Enter the name of the IOS file you want to restore or upgrade.

7. Confirm that you understand that the contents of flash memory will be erased if there is not enough room in flash to store the new image.

8. Watch in amazement as your IOS is deleted out of flash memory and your new IOS is copied to flash memory.

If the file that was in flash memory is deleted but the new version wasn't copied to flash memory, the router will boot from ROM monitor mode. You'll need to figure out why the copy operation did not take place.

Review Questions

The following questions are designed to test your understanding of this chapter's material. For more information on how to get additional questions, please see www.lammle.com/ccna.

You can find the answers to these questions in Appendix B, "Answers to Review Questions."

1. What does the command `confreg 0x2142` provide?

   A. It is used to restart the router.

   B. It is used to bypass the configuration in NVRAM.

   C. It is used to enter ROM monitor mode.

   D. It is used to view the lost password.

2. Which command will copy the IOS to a backup host on your network?

   A. `transfer IOS to 172.16.10.1`

   B. `copy run start`

   C. `copy tftp flash`

   D. `copy start tftp`

   E. `copy flash tftp`

3. What command is used to permanently install a license on an ISR2 router?

   A. `install license`

   B. `license install`

   C. `boot system license`

   D. `boot license module`

4. You type the following into the router and reload. What will the router do?

   ```
   Router(config)#boot system flash c2800nm-advsecurityk9-mz.151-4.M6.bin
   Router(config)#config-register 0x2101
   Router(config)#do sh ver
   [output cut]
   Configuration register is 0x2102 (will be 0x2101 at next reload)
   ```

   A. The router will expand and run the `c2800nm-advsecurityk9-mz.151-4.M6.bin` IOS from flash memory.

   B. The router will go into setup mode.

   C. The router will load the mini-IOS from ROM.

   D. The router will enter ROM monitor mode.

5. A network administrator wants to upgrade the IOS of a router without removing the image currently installed. What command will display the amount of memory consumed by the current IOS image and indicate whether there is enough room available to hold both the current and new images?

   A. `show version`

   B. `show flash`

   C. `show memory`

   D. `show buffers`

   E. `show running-config`

6. The corporate office sends you a new router to connect, but upon connecting the console cable, you see that there is already a configuration on the router. What should be done before a new configuration is entered in the router?

   A. RAM should be erased and the router restarted.

   B. Flash should be erased and the router restarted.

   C. NVRAM should be erased and the router restarted.

   D. The new configuration should be entered and saved.

7. Which command loads a new version of the Cisco IOS into a router?

   A. `copy flash ftp`

   B. `copy nvram flash`

   C. `copy flash tftp`

   D. `copy tftp flash`

8. Which command will show you the IOS version running on your router?

   A. `sh IOS`

   B. `sh flash`

   C. `sh version`

   D. `sh protocols`

9. What should the configuration register value be after you successfully complete the password recovery procedure and return the router to normal operation?

   A. 0x2100

   B. 0x2101

   C. 0x2102

   D. 0x2142

10. You save the configuration on a router with the `copy running-config startup-config` command and reboot the router. The router, however, comes up with a blank configuration. What can the problem be?

   A. You didn't boot the router with the correct command.

   B. NVRAM is corrupted.

   C. The configuration register setting is incorrect.

   D. The newly upgraded IOS is not compatible with the hardware of the router.

   E. The configuration you saved is not compatible with the hardware.

11. Which command will install a Right-To-Use license so you can use an evaluation version of a feature?

   A. `install Right-To-Use license feature` *feature*

   B. `install temporary feature` *feature*

   C. `license install feature`

   D. `license boot module`

12. Which command determines the licenses that are active on your system along with several status variables?

   A. `show license`

   B. `show license feature`

   C. `show license udi`

   D. `show version`

13. Which command allows you to view the technology package licenses and feature licenses that are supported on your router along with several status variables?

   A. `show license`

   B. `show license feature`

   C. `show license udi`

   D. `show version`

14. Which command displays the unique device identifier that comprises the product ID and serial number of the router?

   A. `show license`

   B. `show license feature`

   C. `show license udi`

   D. `show version`

15. Which command displays various pieces of information about the current IOS version, including the licensing details at the end of the command's output?

   A. `show license`

   B. `show license feature`

   C. `show license udi`

   D. `show version`

16. Which command backs up your license to flash memory?

   A. `copy tftp flash`

   B. `save license flash`

C. `license save flash`

D. `copy license flash`

17. Which command displays the configuration register setting?

    A. `show ip route`

    B. `show boot version`

    C. `show version`

    D. `show flash`

18. What two steps are needed to remove a license from a router? (Choose two.)

    A. Use the `erase flash:license` command.

    B. Reload the system.

    C. Use the `license boot` command with the `disable` variable at the end of the command line.

    D. Clear the license with the `license clear` command.

19. You have your laptop directly connected into a router's Ethernet port. Which of the following are among the requirements for the `copy flash tftp` command to be successful? (Choose three.)

    A. TFTP server software must be running on the router.

    B. TFTP server software must be running on your laptop.

    C. The Ethernet cable connecting the laptop directly into the router's Ethernet port must be a straight-through cable.

    D. The laptop must be on the same subnet as the router's Ethernet interface.

    E. The `copy flash tftp` command must be supplied the IP address of the laptop.

    F. There must be enough room in the flash memory of the router to accommodate the file to be copied.

20. The configuration register setting of 0x2102 provides what function to a router?

    A. Tells the router to boot into ROM monitor mode

    B. Provides password recovery

    C. Tells the router to look in NVRAM for the boot sequence

    D. Boots the IOS from a TFTP server

    E. Boots an IOS image stored in ROM

Chapter

9

IP Routing

THE FOLLOWING ICND1 EXAM TOPICS ARE COVERED IN THIS CHAPTER:

✓ **3.0 Routing Technologies**

- 3.1 Describe the routing concepts
    - 3.1.a Packet handling along the path through a network
    - 3.1.b Forwarding decision based on route lookup
    - 3.1.c Frame rewrite
- 3.2 Interpret the components of routing table
    - 3.2.a Prefix
    - 3.2.b Network mask
    - 3.2.c Next hop
    - 3.2.d Routing protocol code
    - 3.2.e Administrative distance
    - 3.2.f Metric
    - 3.2.g Gateway of last resort
- 3.3 Describe how a routing table is populated by different routing information sources
    - 3.3.a Admin distance
- 3.5 Compare and contrast static routing and dynamic routing
- 3.6 Configure, verify, and troubleshoot IPv4 and IPv6 static routing
    - 3.6.a Default route
    - 3.6.b Network route
    - 3.6.c Host route
    - 3.6.d Floating static
- 3.7 Configure, verify, and troubleshoot RIPv2 for IPv4 (excluding authentication, filtering, manual summarization, redistribution)

It's time now to turn our focus toward the core topic of the ubiquitous IP routing process. It's integral to networking because it pertains to all routers and configurations that use it, which is easily the lion's share. IP routing is basically the process of moving packets from one network to another network using routers. And by routers, I mean Cisco routers, of course! However, the terms *router* and *layer 3 device* are interchangeable, and throughout this chapter when I use the term *router*, I am referring to any layer 3 device.

Before jumping into this chapter, I want to make sure you understand the difference between a *routing protocol* and a *routed protocol*. Routers use routing protocols to dynamically find all networks within the greater internetwork and to ensure that all routers have the same routing table. Routing protocols are also employed to determine the best path a packet should take through an internetwork to get to its destination most efficiently. RIP, RIPv2, EIGRP, and OSPF are great examples of the most common routing protocols.

Once all routers know about all networks, a routed protocol can be used to send user data (packets) through the established enterprise. Routed protocols are assigned to an interface and determine the method of packet delivery. Examples of routed protocols are IP and IPv6.

I'm pretty confident I don't have to underscore how crucial it is for you to have this chapter's material down to a near instinctive level. IP routing is innately what Cisco routers do, and they do it very well, so having a firm grasp of the fundamentals and basics of this topic is vital if you want to excel during the exam and in a real-world networking environment as well!

In this chapter, I'm going to show you how to configure and verify IP routing with Cisco routers and guide you through these five key subjects:

- Routing basics
- The IP routing process
- Static routing
- Default routing
- Dynamic routing

I want to start by nailing down the basics of how packets actually move through an internetwork, so let's get started!

To find up-to-the-minute updates for this chapter, please see www.lammle .com/ccna or the book's web page at www.sybex.com/go/ccna.

Routing Basics

Once you create an internetwork by connecting your WANs and LANs to a router, you'll need to configure logical network addresses, like IP addresses, to all hosts on that internetwork for them to communicate successfully throughout it.

The term *routing* refers to taking a packet from one device and sending it through the network to another device on a different network. Routers don't really care about hosts—they only care about networks and the best path to each one of them. The logical network address of the destination host is key to getting packets through a routed network. It's the hardware address of the host that's used to deliver the packet from a router and ensure it arrives at the correct destination host.

Routing is irrelevant if your network has no routers because their job is to route traffic to all the networks in your internetwork, but this is rarely the case! So here's an important list of the minimum factors a router must know to be able to effectively route packets:

- Destination address
- Neighbor routers from which it can learn about remote networks
- Possible routes to all remote networks
- The best route to each remote network
- How to maintain and verify routing information

The router learns about remote networks from neighboring routers or from an administrator. The router then builds a routing table, which is basically a map of the internetwork, and it describes how to find remote networks. If a network is directly connected, then the router already knows how to get to it.

But if a network isn't directly connected to the router, the router must use one of two ways to learn how to get to the remote network. The *static routing* method requires someone to hand-type all network locations into the routing table, which can be a pretty daunting task when used on all but the smallest of networks!

Conversely, when *dynamic routing* is used, a protocol on one router communicates with the same protocol running on neighboring routers. The routers then update each other about all the networks they know about and place this information into the routing table. If a change occurs in the network, the dynamic routing protocols automatically inform all routers about the event. If static routing is used, the administrator is responsible for updating all changes by hand onto all routers. Most people usually use a combination of dynamic and static routing to administer a large network.

Before we jump into the IP routing process, let's take a look at a very simple example that demonstrates how a router uses the routing table to route packets out of an interface. We'll be going into a more detailed study of the process soon, but I want to show you something called the "longest match rule" first. With it, IP will scan a routing table to find the longest match as compared to the destination address of a packet. Let's take a look at Figure 9.1 to get a picture of this process.

FIGURE 9.1   A simple routing example

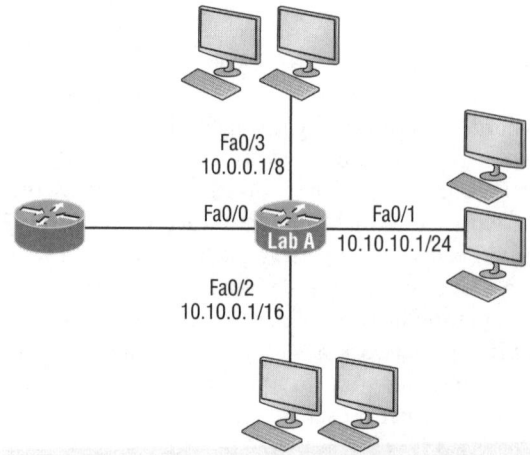

Figure 9.1 shows a simple network. Lab_A has four interfaces. Can you see which interface will be used to forward an IP datagram to a host with a destination IP address of 10.10.10.30?

By using the command show ip route on a router, we can see the routing table (map of the internetwork) that Lab_A has used to make its forwarding decisions:

```
Lab_A#sh ip route
Codes: L - local, C - connected, S - static,
[output cut]
        10.0.0.0/8 is variably subnetted, 6 subnets, 4 masks
C       10.0.0.0/8 is directly connected, FastEthernet0/3
L       10.0.0.1/32 is directly connected, FastEthernet0/3
C       10.10.0.0/16 is directly connected, FastEthernet0/2
L       10.10.0.1/32 is directly connected, FastEthernet0/2
C       10.10.10.0/24 is directly connected, FastEthernet0/1
L       10.10.10.1/32 is directly connected, FastEthernet0/1
S*      0.0.0.0/0 is directly connected, FastEthernet0/0
```

The C in the routing table output means that the networks listed are "directly connected," and until we add a routing protocol like RIPv2, OSPF, etc. to the routers in our internetwork, or enter static routes, only directly connected networks will show up in our routing table. But wait—what about that L in the routing table—that's new, isn't it? Yes it is, because in the new Cisco IOS 15 code, Cisco defines a different route, called a local host route. Each local route has a /32 prefix, defining a route just for the one address. So in this example, the router has relied upon these routes that list their own local IP addresses to more efficiently forward packets to the router itself.

So let's get back to the original question: By looking at the figure and the output of the routing table, can you determine what IP will do with a received packet that has a destination IP address of 10.10.10.30? The answer is that the router will packet-switch the packet to interface FastEthernet 0/1, which will frame the packet and then send it out on the network segment. This is referred to as frame rewrite. Based upon the longest match rule, IP would look for 10.10.10.30, and if that isn't found in the table, then IP would search for 10.10.10.0, then 10.10.0.0, and so on until a route is discovered.

Here's another example: Based on the output of the next routing table, which interface will a packet with a destination address of 10.10.10.14 be forwarded from?

```
Lab_A#sh ip route
[output cut]
Gateway of last resort is not set
C       10.10.10.16/28 is directly connected, FastEthernet0/0
L       10.10.10.17/32 is directly connected, FastEthernet0/0
C       10.10.10.8/29 is directly connected, FastEthernet0/1
L       10.10.10.9/32 is directly connected, FastEthernet0/1
C       10.10.10.4/30 is directly connected, FastEthernet0/2
L       10.10.10.5/32 is directly connected, FastEthernet0/2
C       10.10.10.0/30 is directly connected, Serial 0/0
L       10.10.10.1/32 is directly connected, Serial0/0
```

To figure this out, look closely at the output until you see that the network is subnetted and each interface has a different mask. And I have to tell you—you just can't answer this question if you can't subnet! 10.10.10.14 would be a host in the 10.10.10.8/29 subnet that's connected to the FastEthernet0/1 interface. Don't freak if you're struggling and don't get this! Instead, just go back and reread Chapter 4, "Easy Subnetting," until it becomes clear to you.

The IP Routing Process

The IP routing process is fairly simple and doesn't change, regardless of the size of your network. For a good example of this fact, I'll use Figure 9.2 to describe step-by-step what happens when Host A wants to communicate with Host B on a different network.

FIGURE 9.2   IP routing example using two hosts and one router

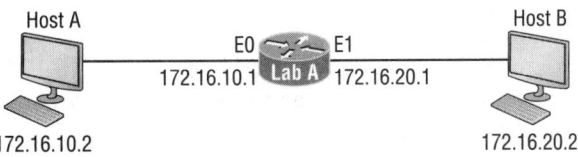

In Figure 9.2 a user on Host_A pinged Host_B's IP address. Routing doesn't get any simpler than this, but it still involves a lot of steps, so let's work through them now:

1. Internet Control Message Protocol (ICMP) creates an echo request payload, which is simply the alphabet in the data field.

2. ICMP hands that payload to Internet Protocol (IP), which then creates a packet. At a minimum, this packet contains an IP source address, an IP destination address, and a Protocol field with 01h. Don't forget that Cisco likes to use *0x* in front of hex characters, so this could also look like 0x01. This tells the receiving host to whom it should hand the payload when the destination is reached—in this example, ICMP.

3. Once the packet is created, IP determines whether the destination IP address is on the local network or a remote one.

4. Since IP has determined that this is a remote request, the packet must be sent to the default gateway so it can be routed to the remote network. The Registry in Windows is parsed to find the configured default gateway.

5. The default gateway of Host_A is configured to 172.16.10.1. For this packet to be sent to the default gateway, the hardware address of the router's interface Ethernet 0, which is configured with the IP address of 172.16.10.1, must be known. Why? So the packet can be handed down to the Data Link layer, framed, and sent to the router's interface that's connected to the 172.16.10.0 network. Because hosts communicate only via hardware addresses on the local LAN, it's important to recognize that for Host_A to communicate to Host_B, it has to send packets to the Media Access Control (MAC) address of the default gateway on the local network.

> MAC addresses are always local on the LAN and never go through and
> past a router.

6. Next, the Address Resolution Protocol (ARP) cache of the host is checked to see if the IP address of the default gateway has already been resolved to a hardware address.

    If it has, the packet is then free to be handed to the Data Link layer for framing. Remember that the hardware destination address is also handed down with that packet. To view the ARP cache on your host, use the following command:

```
C:\>arp -a
Interface: 172.16.10.2 --- 0x3
  Internet Address      Physical Address      Type
  172.16.10.1           00-15-05-06-31-b0     dynamic
```

    If the hardware address isn't already in the ARP cache of the host, an ARP broadcast will be sent out onto the local network to search for the 172.16.10.1 hardware address. The router then responds to the request and provides the hardware address of Ethernet 0, and the host caches this address.

7. Once the packet and destination hardware address are handed to the Data Link layer, the LAN driver is used to provide media access via the type of LAN being used, which

is Ethernet in this case. A frame is then generated, encapsulating the packet with control information. Within that frame are the hardware destination and source addresses plus, in this case, an Ether-Type field, which identifies the specific Network layer protocol that handed the packet to the Data Link layer. In this instance, it's IP. At the end of the frame is something called a Frame Check Sequence (FCS) field that houses the result of the cyclic redundancy check (CRC). The frame would look something like what I've detailed in Figure 9.3. It contains Host A's hardware (MAC) address and the destination hardware address of the default gateway. It does not include the remote host's MAC address—remember that!

FIGURE 9.3   Frame used from Host A to the Lab_A router when Host B is pinged

Destination MAC (router's E0 MAC address)	Source MAC (Host A MAC address)	Ether-Type field	Packet	FCS CRC

8. Once the frame is completed, it's handed down to the Physical layer to be put on the physical medium (in this example, twisted-pair wire) one bit at a time.

9. Every device in the collision domain receives these bits and builds the frame. They each run a CRC and check the answer in the FCS field. If the answers don't match, the frame is discarded.

   ▪ If the CRC matches, then the hardware destination address is checked to see if it matches (which, in this example, is the router's interface Ethernet 0).

   ▪ If it's a match, then the Ether-Type field is checked to find the protocol used at the Network layer.

10. The packet is pulled from the frame, and what is left of the frame is discarded. The packet is handed to the protocol listed in the Ether-Type field—it's given to IP.

11. IP receives the packet and checks the IP destination address. Since the packet's destination address doesn't match any of the addresses configured on the receiving router itself, the router will look up the destination IP network address in its routing table.

12. The routing table must have an entry for the network 172.16.20.0 or the packet will be discarded immediately and an ICMP message will be sent back to the originating device with a destination network unreachable message.

13. If the router does find an entry for the destination network in its table, the packet is switched to the exit interface—in this example, interface Ethernet 1. The following output displays the Lab_A router's routing table. The C means "directly connected." No routing protocols are needed in this network since all networks (all two of them) are directly connected.

```
Lab_A>sh ip route
C      172.16.10.0 is directly connected,   Ethernet0
L      172.16.10.1/32 is directly connected, Ethernet0
C      172.16.20.0 is directly connected,   Ethernet1
L      172.16.20.1/32 is directly connected, Ethernet1
```

14. The router packet-switches the packet to the Ethernet 1 buffer.

15. The Ethernet 1 buffer needs to know the hardware address of the destination host and first checks the ARP cache.

- If the hardware address of Host_B has already been resolved and is in the router's ARP cache, then the packet and the hardware address will be handed down to the Data Link layer to be framed. Let's take a look at the ARP cache on the Lab_A router by using the show ip arp command:

```
Lab_A#sh ip arp
Protocol  Address      Age(min)  Hardware Addr   Type   Interface
Internet  172.16.20.1  -         00d0.58ad.05f4  ARPA   Ethernet1
Internet  172.16.20.2  3         0030.9492.a5dd  ARPA   Ethernet1
Internet  172.16.10.1  -         00d0.58ad.06aa  ARPA   Ethernet0
Internet  172.16.10.2  12        0030.9492.a4ac  ARPA   Ethernet0
```

The dash (-) signifies that this is the physical interface on the router. This output shows us that the router knows the 172.16.10.2 (Host_A) and 172.16.20.2 (Host_B) hardware addresses. Cisco routers will keep an entry in the ARP table for 4 hours.

- Now if the hardware address hasn't already been resolved, the router will send an ARP request out E1 looking for the 172.16.20.2 hardware address. Host_B responds with its hardware address, and the packet and destination hardware addresses are then both sent to the Data Link layer for framing.

16. The Data Link layer creates a frame with the destination and source hardware addresses, Ether-Type field, and FCS field at the end. The frame is then handed to the Physical layer to be sent out on the physical medium one bit at a time.

17. Host_B receives the frame and immediately runs a CRC. If the result matches the information in the FCS field, the hardware destination address will then be checked next. If the host finds a match, the Ether-Type field is then checked to determine the protocol that the packet should be handed to at the Network layer—IP in this example.

18. At the Network layer, IP receives the packet and runs a CRC on the IP header. If that passes, IP then checks the destination address. Since a match has finally been made, the Protocol field is checked to find out to whom the payload should be given.

19. The payload is handed to ICMP, which understands that this is an echo request. ICMP responds to this by immediately discarding the packet and generating a new payload as an echo reply.

20. A packet is then created including the source and destination addresses, Protocol field, and payload. The destination device is now Host_A.

21. IP then checks to see whether the destination IP address is a device on the local LAN or on a remote network. Since the destination device is on a remote network, the packet needs to be sent to the default gateway.

22. The default gateway IP address is found in the Registry of the Windows device, and the ARP cache is checked to see if the hardware address has already been resolved from an IP address.

23. Once the hardware address of the default gateway is found, the packet and destination hardware addresses are handed down to the Data Link layer for framing.

24. The Data Link layer frames the packet of information and includes the following in the header:

   ▪ The destination and source hardware addresses

   ▪ The Ether-Type field with 0x0800 (IP) in it

   ▪ The FCS field with the CRC result in tow

25. The frame is now handed down to the Physical layer to be sent out over the network medium one bit at a time.

26. The router's Ethernet 1 interface receives the bits and builds a frame. The CRC is run, and the FCS field is checked to make sure the answers match.

27. Once the CRC is found to be okay, the hardware destination address is checked. Since the router's interface is a match, the packet is pulled from the frame and the Ether-Type field is checked to determine which protocol the packet should be delivered to at the Network layer.

28. The protocol is determined to be IP, so it gets the packet. IP runs a CRC check on the IP header first and then checks the destination IP address.

IP does not run a complete CRC as the Data Link layer does—it only checks the header for errors.

Since the IP destination address doesn't match any of the router's interfaces, the routing table is checked to see whether it has a route to 172.16.10.0. If it doesn't have a route over to the destination network, the packet will be discarded immediately. I want to take a minute to point out that this is exactly where the source of confusion begins for a lot of administrators because when a ping fails, most people think the packet never reached the destination host. But as we see here, that's not *always* the case. All it takes for this to happen is for even just one of the remote routers to lack a route back to the originating host's network and—*poof!*—the packet is dropped on the *return trip*, not on its way to the host!

Just a quick note to mention that when (and if) the packet is lost on the way back to the originating host, you will typically see a request timed-out message because it is an unknown error. If the error occurs because of a known issue, such as if a route is not in the routing table on the way to the destination device, you will see a destination unreachable message. This should help you determine if the problem occurred on the way to the destination or on the way back.

29. In this case, the router happens to know how to get to network 172.16.10.0—the exit interface is Ethernet 0—so the packet is switched to interface Ethernet 0.

30. The router then checks the ARP cache to determine whether the hardware address for 172.16.10.2 has already been resolved.

31. Since the hardware address to 172.16.10.2 is already cached from the originating trip to Host_B, the hardware address and packet are then handed to the Data Link layer.

32. The Data Link layer builds a frame with the destination hardware address and source hardware address and then puts IP in the Ether-Type field. A CRC is run on the frame and the result is placed in the FCS field.

33. The frame is then handed to the Physical layer to be sent out onto the local network one bit at a time.

34. The destination host receives the frame, runs a CRC, checks the destination hardware address, then looks into the Ether-Type field to find out to whom to hand the packet.

35. IP is the designated receiver, and after the packet is handed to IP at the Network layer, it checks the Protocol field for further direction. IP finds instructions to give the payload to ICMP, and ICMP determines the packet to be an ICMP echo reply.

36. ICMP acknowledges that it has received the reply by sending an exclamation point (!) to the user interface. ICMP then attempts to send four more echo requests to the destination host.

You've just experienced Todd's 36 easy steps to understanding IP routing. The key point here is that if you had a much larger network, the process would be the *same*. It's just that the larger the internetwork, the more hops the packet goes through before it finds the destination host.

It's super-important to remember that when Host_A sends a packet to Host_B, the destination hardware address used is the default gateway's Ethernet interface. Why? Because frames can't be placed on remote networks—only local networks. So packets destined for remote networks must go through the default gateway.

Let's take a look at Host_A's ARP cache now:

```
C:\ >arp -a
Interface: 172.16.10.2 --- 0x3
  Internet Address      Physical Address       Type
  172.16.10.1           00-15-05-06-31-b0      dynamic
  172.16.20.1           00-15-05-06-31-b0      dynamic
```

Did you notice that the hardware (MAC) address that Host_A uses to get to Host_B is the Lab_A E0 interface? Hardware addresses are *always* local, and they never pass through a router's interface. Understanding this process is as important as air to you, so carve this into your memory!

The Cisco Router Internal Process

One more thing before we get to testing your understanding of my 36 steps of IP routing. I think it's important to explain how a router forwards packets internally. For IP to look up a destination address in a routing table on a router, processing in the router must take place, and if there are tens of thousands of routes in that table, the amount of CPU time would be enormous. It results in a potentially overwhelming amount of overhead—think about a router at your ISP that has to calculate millions of packets per second and even subnet to find the correct exit interface! Even with the little network I'm using in this book, lots of processing would need to be done if there were actual hosts connected and sending data.

Cisco uses three types of packet-forwarding techniques.

Process switching   This is actually how many people see routers to this day, because it's true that routers actually did perform this type of bare-bones packet switching back in 1990 when Cisco released their very first router. But those days when traffic demands were unimaginably light are long gone—not in today's networks! This process is now extremely complex and involves looking up every destination in the routing table and finding the exit interface for every packet. This is pretty much how I just explained the process in my 36 steps. But even though what I wrote was absolutely true in concept, the internal process requires much more than packet-switching technology today because of the millions of packets per second that must now be processed. So Cisco came up with some other technologies to help with the "big process problem."

Fast switching   This solution was created to make the slow performance of process switching faster and more efficient. Fast switching uses a cache to store the most recently used destinations so that lookups are not required for every packet. By caching the exit interface of the destination device, as well as the layer 2 header, performance was dramatically improved, but as our networks evolved with the need for even more speed, Cisco created yet another technology!

Cisco Express Forwarding (CEF)   This is Cisco's newer creation, and it's the default packet-forwarding method used on all the latest Cisco routers. CEF makes many different cache tables to help improve performance and is change triggered, not packet triggered. Translated, this means that when the network topology changes, the cache changes along with it.

To see which packet switching method your router interface is using, use the command show ip interface.

Testing Your IP Routing Understanding

Since understanding IP routing is super-important, it's time for that little test I talked about earlier on how well you've got the IP routing process down so far. I'm going to do that by having you look at a couple of figures and answer some very basic IP routing questions based upon them.

Figure 9.4 shows a LAN connected to RouterA that's connected via a WAN link to RouterB. RouterB has a LAN connected with an HTTP server attached.

FIGURE 9.4 IP routing example 1

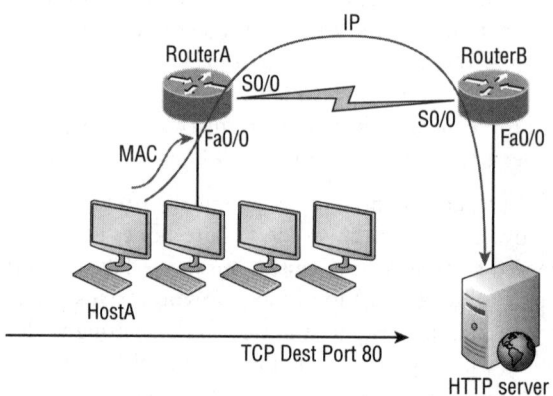

The critical information you want to obtain by looking at this figure is exactly how IP routing will occur in this example. Let's determine the characteristics of a frame as it leaves HostA. Okay—we'll cheat a bit. I'll give you the answer, but then you should go back over the figure and see if you can answer example 2 without looking at my three-step answer!

1. The destination address of a frame from HostA would be the MAC address of Router A's Fa0/0 interface.

2. The destination address of a packet would be the IP address of the HTTP server's network interface card (NIC).

3. The destination port number in the segment header would be 80.

That was a pretty simple, straightforward scenario. One thing to remember is that when multiple hosts are communicating to a server using HTTP, they must all use a different source port number. The source and destination IP addresses and port numbers are how the server keeps the data separated at the Transport layer.

Let's complicate matters by adding another device into the network and then see if you can find the answers. Figure 9.5 shows a network with only one router but two switches.

FIGURE 9.5 IP routing example 2

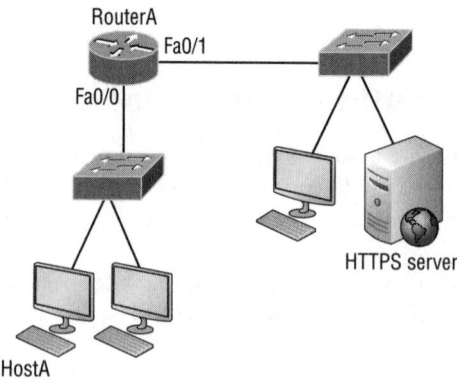

The key thing to understand about the IP routing process in this scenario is what happens when HostA sends data to the HTTPS server? Here's your answer:

1. The destination address of a frame from HostA would be the MAC address of RouterA's Fa0/0 interface.

2. The destination address of a packet is the IP address of the HTTPS server's network interface card (NIC).

3. The destination port number in the segment header will have a value of 443.

Did you notice that the switches weren't used as either a default gateway or any other destination? That's because switches have nothing to do with routing. I wonder how many of you chose the switch as the default gateway (destination) MAC address for HostA? If you did, don't feel bad—just take another look to see where you went wrong and why. It's very important to remember that the destination MAC address will always be the router's interface—if your packets are destined for outside the LAN, as they were in these last two examples!

Before moving on into some of the more advanced aspects of IP routing, let's look at another issue. Take a look at the output of this router's routing table:

```
Corp#sh ip route
[output cut]
R     192.168.215.0 [120/2] via 192.168.20.2, 00:00:23, Serial0/0
R     192.168.115.0 [120/1] via 192.168.20.2, 00:00:23, Serial0/0
R     192.168.30.0 [120/1] via 192.168.20.2, 00:00:23, Serial0/0
C     192.168.20.0 is directly connected, Serial0/0
L     192.168.20.1/32 is directly connected, Serial0/0
C     192.168.214.0 is directly connected, FastEthernet0/0
L     192.168.214.1/32 is directly connected, FastEthernet0/0
```

What do we see here? If I were to tell you that the corporate router received an IP packet with a source IP address of 192.168.214.20 and a destination address of 192.168.22.3, what do you think the Corp router will do with this packet?

If you said, "The packet came in on the FastEthernet 0/0 interface, but because the routing table doesn't show a route to network 192.168.22.0 (or a default route), the router will discard the packet and send an ICMP destination unreachable message back out to interface FastEthernet 0/0," you're a genius! The reason that's the correct answer is because that's the source LAN where the packet originated from.

Now, let's check out the next figure and talk about the frames and packets in detail. We're not really going over anything new here; I'm just making sure you totally, completely, thoroughly, fully understand basic IP routing! It is the crux of this book, and the topic the exam objectives are geared toward. It's all about IP routing, which means you need to be all over this stuff! We'll use Figure 9.6 for the next few scenarios.

FIGURE 9.6 Basic IP routing using MAC and IP addresses

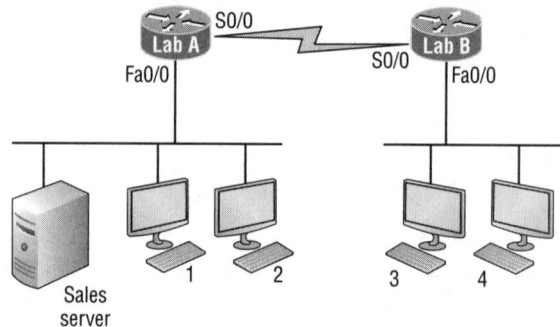

Referring to Figure 9.6, here's a list of all the answers to questions you need inscribed in your brain:

1. In order to begin communicating with the Sales server, Host 4 sends out an ARP request. How will the devices exhibited in the topology respond to this request?

2. Host 4 has received an ARP reply. Host 4 will now build a packet, then place this packet in the frame. What information will be placed in the header of the packet that leaves Host 4 if Host 4 is going to communicate to the Sales server?

3. The Lab_A router has received the packet and will send it out Fa0/0 onto the LAN toward the server. What will the frame have in the header as the source and destination addresses?

4. Host 4 is displaying two web documents from the Sales server in two browser windows at the same time. How did the data find its way to the correct browser windows?

The following should probably be written in a teensy font and put upside down in another part of the book so it would be really hard for you to cheat and peek, but since I'm not that mean and you really need to have this down, here are your answers in the same order that the scenarios were just presented:

1. In order to begin communicating with the server, Host 4 sends out an ARP request. How will the devices exhibited in the topology respond to this request? Since MAC addresses must stay on the local network, the Lab_B router will respond with the MAC address of the Fa0/0 interface and Host 4 will send all frames to the MAC address of the Lab_B Fa0/0 interface when sending packets to the Sales server.

2. Host 4 has received an ARP reply. Host 4 will now build a packet, then place this packet in the frame. What information will be placed in the header of the packet that leaves Host 4 if Host 4 is going to communicate to the Sales server? Since we're now talking about packets, not frames, the source address will be the IP address of Host 4 and the destination address will be the IP address of the Sales server.

3. Finally, the Lab_A router has received the packet and will send it out Fa0/0 onto the LAN toward the server. What will the frame have in the header as the source and

destination addresses? The source MAC address will be the Lab_A router's Fa0/0 interface, and the destination MAC address will be the Sales server's MAC address because all MAC addresses must be local on the LAN.

4.   Host 4 is displaying two web documents from the Sales server in two different browser windows at the same time. How did the data find its way to the correct browser windows? TCP port numbers are used to direct the data to the correct application window.

Great! But we're not quite done yet. I've got a few more questions for you before you actually get to configure routing in a real network. Ready? Figure 9.7 shows a basic network, and Host 4 needs to get email. Which address will be placed in the destination address field of the frame when it leaves Host 4?

FIGURE 9.7   Testing basic routing knowledge

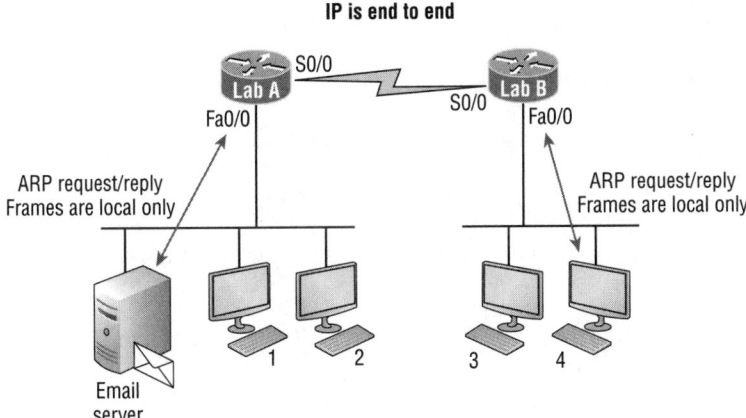

The answer is that Host 4 will use the destination MAC address of the Fa0/0 interface on the Lab_B router—you knew that, right? Look at Figure 9.7 again: What if Host 4 needs to communicate with Host 1—not the server, but with Host 1. Which OSI layer 3 source address will be found in the packet header when it reaches Host 1?

Hopefully you've got this: At layer 3, the source IP address will be Host 4 and the destination address in the packet will be the IP address of Host 1. Of course, the destination MAC address from Host 4 will always be the Fa0/0 address of the Lab_B router, right? And since we have more than one router, we'll need a routing protocol that communicates between both of them so that traffic can be forwarded in the right direction to reach the network that Host 1 is connected to.

Okay—one more scenario and you're on your way to being an IP routing machine! Again, using Figure 9.7, Host 4 is transferring a file to the email server connected to the Lab_A router. What would be the layer 2 destination address leaving Host 4? Yes, I've asked this question more than once. But not this one: What will be the source MAC address when the frame is received at the email server?

Hopefully, you answered that the layer 2 destination address leaving Host 4 is the MAC address of the Fa0/0 interface on the Lab_B router and that the source layer 2 address that the email server will receive is the Fa0/0 interface of the Lab_A router.

If you did, you're ready to discover how IP routing is handled in a larger network environment!

Configuring IP Routing

It's time to get serious and configure a real network. Figure 9.8 shows three routers: Corp, SF, and LA. Remember that, by default, these routers only know about networks that are directly connected to them. I'll continue to use this figure and network throughout the rest of the chapters in this book. As I progress through this book, I'll add more routers and switches as needed.

FIGURE 9.8   Configuring IP routing

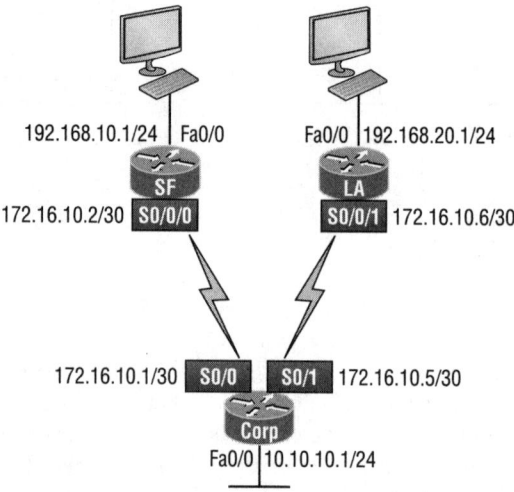

As you might guess, I've got quite a nice collection of routers for us to play with. But you don't need a closet full of devices to perform most, if not all, of the commands we'll use in this book. You can get by nicely with pretty much any router or even with a good router simulator.

Getting back to business, the Corp router has two serial interfaces, which will provide a WAN connection to the SF and LA router and two Fast Ethernet interfaces as well. The two remote routers have two serial interfaces and two Fast Ethernet interfaces.

The first step for this project is to correctly configure each router with an IP address on each interface. The following list shows the IP address scheme I'm going to use to configure the network. After we go over how the network is configured, I'll cover how to configure

IP routing. Pay attention to the subnet masks—they're important! The LANs all use a /24 mask, but the WANs are using a /30.

Corp

- Serial 0/0: 172.16.10.1/30
- Serial 0/1: 172.16.10.5/30
- Fa0/0: 10.10.10.1/24

SF

- S0/0/0: 172.16.10.2/30
- Fa0/0: 192.168.10.1/24

LA

- S0/0/0: 172.16.10.6/30
- Fa0/0: 192.168.20.1/24

The router configuration is really a pretty straightforward process since you just need to add IP addresses to your interfaces and then perform a no shutdown on those same interfaces. It gets a tad more complex later on, but for right now, let's configure the IP addresses in the network.

Corp Configuration

We need to configure three interfaces to configure the Corp router. And configuring the hostnames of each router will make identification much easier. While we're at it, let's set the interface descriptions, banner, and router passwords too because it's a really good idea to make a habit of configuring these commands on every router!

To get started, I performed an erase startup-config on the router and reloaded, so we'll start in setup mode. I chose no when prompted to enter setup mode, which will get us straight to the username prompt of the console. I'm going to configure all my routers this same way.

Here's how what I just did looks:

```
        --- System Configuration Dialog ---
Would you like to enter the initial configuration dialog? [yes/no]: n

Press RETURN to get started!
Router>en
Router#config t
Router(config)#hostname Corp
Corp(config)#enable secret GlobalNet
Corp(config)#no ip domain-lookup
Corp(config)#int f0/0
Corp(config-if)#desc Connection to LAN BackBone
```

```
Corp(config-if)#ip address 10.10.10.1 255.255.255.0
Corp(config-if)#no shut
Corp(config-if)#int s0/0
Corp(config-if)#desc WAN connection to SF
Corp(config-if)#ip address 172.16.10.1 255.255.255.252
Corp(config-if)#no shut
Corp(config-if)#int s0/1
Corp(config-if)#desc WAN connection to LA
Corp(config-if)#ip address 172.16.10.5 255.255.255.252
Corp(config-if)#no shut
Corp(config-if)#line con 0
Corp(config-line)#password console
Corp(config-line)#logging
Corp(config-line)#logging sync
Corp(config-line)#exit
Corp(config)#line vty 0 ?
  <1-181>  Last Line number
  <cr>
Corp(config)#line vty 0 181
Corp(config-line)#password telnet
Corp(config-line)#login
Corp(config-line)#exit
Corp(config)#banner motd # This is my Corp Router #
Corp(config)#^Z
Corp#copy run start
Destination filename [startup-config]?
Building configuration...
[OK]
Corp# [OK]
```

Let's talk about the configuration of the Corp router. First, I set the hostname and enable secret, but what is that no ip domain-lookup command? That command stops the router from trying to resolve hostnames, which is an annoying feature unless you've configured a host table or DNS. Next, I configured the three interfaces with descriptions and IP addresses and enabled them with the no shutdown command. The console and VTY passwords came next, but what is that logging sync command under the console line? The logging synchronous command stops console messages from writing over what you are typing in, meaning it's a sanity-saving command that you'll come to love! Last, I set my banner and then saved my configs.

> **NOTE**   If you're having a hard time understanding this configuration process, refer back to Chapter 6, "Cisco's Internetworking Operating System (IOS)."

To view the IP routing tables created on a Cisco router, use the command show ip route. Here's the command's output:

```
Corp#sh ip route
Codes: L - local, C - connected, S - static, R - RIP, M - mobile, B - BGP
   D - EIGRP, EX - EIGRP external, O - OSPF, IA - OSPF inter area
   N1 - OSPF NSSA external type 1, N2 - OSPF NSSA external type 2
   E1 - OSPF external type 1, E2 - OSPF external type 2
   i - IS-IS, su - IS-IS summary, L1 - IS-IS level-1, L2 - IS-IS level-2
   ia - IS-IS inter area, * - candidate default, U - per-user static route
   o - ODR, P - periodic downloaded static route, H - NHRP, l - LISP
   + - replicated route, % - next hop override
Gateway of last resort is not set


      10.0.0.0/24 is subnetted, 1 subnets
C        10.10.10.0 is directly connected, FastEthernet0/0
L        10.10.10.1/32 is directly connected, FastEthernet0/0
Corp#
```

It's important to remember that only configured, directly connected networks are going to show up in the routing table. So why is it that only the FastEthernet 0/0 interface shows up in the table? No worries—that's just because you won't see the serial interfaces come up until the other side of the links are operational. As soon as we configure our SF and LA routers, those interfaces should pop right up!

But did you notice the C on the left side of the output of the routing table? When you see that there, it means that the network is directly connected. The codes for each type of connection are listed at the top of the show ip route command, along with their descriptions.

> For brevity, the codes at the top of the output will be cut in the rest of this chapter.

SF Configuration

Now we're ready to configure the next router—SF. To make that happen correctly, keep in mind that we have two interfaces to deal with: Serial 0/0/0 and FastEthernet 0/0. So let's make sure we don't forget to add the hostname, passwords, interface descriptions, and banners to the router configuration. As I did with the Corp router, I erased the configuration and reloaded since this router had already been configured before.

Here's the configuration I used:

```
R1#erase start
% Incomplete command.
```

```
R1#erase startup-config
Erasing the nvram filesystem will remove all configuration files!
   Continue? [confirm][enter]
[OK]
Erase of nvram: complete
R1#reload
Proceed with reload? [confirm][enter]
[output cut]
%Error opening tftp://255.255.255.255/network-confg (Timed out)
%Error opening tftp://255.255.255.255/cisconet.cfg (Timed out)


       --- System Configuration Dialog ---


Would you like to enter the initial configuration dialog? [yes/no]: n
```

Before we move on, let's talk about this output for a second. First, notice that beginning with IOS 12.4, ISR routers will no longer take the command erase start. The router has only one command after erase that starts with *s*, as shown here:

```
Router#erase s?
startup-config
```

I know, you'd think that the IOS would continue to accept the command, but nope—sorry! The second thing I want to point out is that the output tells us the router is looking for a TFTP host to see if it can download a configuration. When that fails, it goes straight into setup mode. This gives you a great picture of the Cisco router default boot sequence we talked about in Chapter 7, "Managing a Cisco Internetwork."

Let's get back to configuring our router:

```
Press RETURN to get started!
Router#config t
Router(config)#hostname SF
SF(config)#enable secret GlobalNet
SF(config)#no ip domain-lookup
SF(config)#int s0/0/0
SF(config-if)#desc WAN Connection to Corp
SF(config-if)#ip address 172.16.10.2 255.255.255.252
SF(config-if)#no shut
SF(config-if)#clock rate 1000000
SF(config-if)#int f0/0
SF(config-if)#desc SF LAN
SF(config-if)#ip address 192.168.10.1 255.255.255.0
SF(config-if)#no shut
```

```
SF(config-if)#line con 0
SF(config-line)#password console
SF(config-line)#login
SF(config-line)#logging sync
SF(config-line)#exit
SF(config)#line vty 0 ?
  <1-1180>  Last Line number
  <cr>
SF(config)#line vty 0 1180
SF(config-line)#password telnet
SF(config-line)#login
SF(config-line)#banner motd #This is the SF Branch router#
SF(config)#exit
SF#copy run start
Destination filename [startup-config]?
Building configuration...
 [OK]
```

Let's take a look at our configuration of the interfaces with the following two commands:

```
SF#sh run | begin int
interface FastEthernet0/0
 description SF LAN
 ip address 192.168.10.1 255.255.255.0
 duplex auto
 speed auto
!
interface FastEthernet0/1
 no ip address
 shutdown
 duplex auto
 speed auto
!
interface Serial0/0/0
 description WAN Connection to Corp
 ip address 172.16.10.2 255.255.255.252
 clock rate 1000000
!
SF#sh ip int brief
Interface           IP-Address      OK? Method Status          Protocol
FastEthernet0/0     192.168.10.1    YES manual up              up
```

```
FastEthernet0/1        unassigned     YES unset  administratively down down
Serial0/0/0            172.16.10.2    YES manual up                      up
Serial0/0/1            unassigned     YES unset  administratively down down
SF#
```

Now that both ends of the serial link are configured, the link comes up. Remember, the up/up status for the interfaces are Physical/Data Link layer status indicators that don't reflect the layer 3 status! I ask students in my classes, "If the link shows up/up, can you ping the directly connected network?" And they say, "Yes!" The correct answer is, "I don't know," because we can't see the layer 3 status with this command. We only see layers 1 and 2 and verify that the IP addresses don't have a typo. This is really important to understand!

The show ip route command for the SF router reveals the following:

```
SF#sh ip route
C    192.168.10.0/24 is directly connected, FastEthernet0/0
L    192.168.10.1/32 is directly connected, FastEthernet0/0
     172.16.0.0/30 is subnetted, 1 subnets
C        172.16.10.0 is directly connected, Serial0/0/0
L        172.16.10.2/32 is directly connected, Serial0/0/0
```

Notice that router SF knows how to get to networks 172.16.10.0/30 and 192.168.10.0/24; we can now ping to the Corp router from SF:

```
SF#ping 172.16.10.1

Type escape sequence to abort.
Sending 5, 100-byte ICMP Echos to 172.16.10.1, timeout is 2 seconds:
!!!!!
Success rate is 100 percent (5/5), round-trip min/avg/max = 1/3/4 ms
```

Now let's head back to the Corp router and check out the routing table:

```
Corp>sh ip route
     172.16.0.0/30 is subnetted, 1 subnets
C        172.16.10.0 is directly connected, Serial0/0
L        172.16.10.1/32 is directly connected, Serial0/0
     10.0.0.0/24 is subnetted, 1 subnets
C        10.10.10.0 is directly connected, FastEthernet0/0
L        10.10.10.1/32 is directly connected, FastEthernet0/0
```

On the SF router's serial interface 0/0/0 is a DCE connection, which means a clock rate needs to be set on the interface. Remember that you don't need to use the clock rate command in production. While true, it's still imperative that you know how/when you can use it and that you understand it really well when studying for your CCNA exam!

We can see our clocking with the show controllers command:

```
SF#sh controllers s0/0/0
Interface Serial0/0/0
Hardware is GT96K
DCE V.35, clock rate 1000000

Corp>sh controllers s0/0
Interface Serial0/0
Hardware is PowerQUICC MPC860
DTE V.35 TX and RX clocks detected.
```

Since the SF router has a DCE cable connection, I needed to add clock rate to this interface because DTE receives clock. Keep in mind that the new ISR routers will autodetect this and set the clock rate to 2000000. And you still need to make sure you're able to find an interface that is DCE and set clocking to meet the objectives.

Since the serial links are showing up, we can now see both networks in the Corp routing table. And once we configure LA, we'll see one more network in the routing table of the Corp router. The Corp router can't see the 192.168.10.0 network because we don't have any routing configured yet—routers see only directly connected networks by default.

LA Configuration

To configure LA, we're going to do pretty much the same thing we did with the other two routers. There are two interfaces to deal with, Serial 0/0/1 and FastEthernet 0/0, and again, we'll be sure to add the hostname, passwords, interface descriptions, and a banner to the router configuration:

```
Router(config)#hostname LA
LA(config)#enable secret GlobalNet
LA(config)#no ip domain-lookup
LA(config)#int s0/0/1
LA(config-if)#ip address 172.16.10.6 255.255.255.252
LA(config-if)#no shut
LA(config-if)#clock rate 1000000
LA(config-if)#description WAN To Corporate
LA(config-if)#int f0/0
LA(config-if)#ip address 192.168.20.1 255.255.255.0
LA(config-if)#no shut
LA(config-if)#description LA LAN
LA(config-if)#line con 0
LA(config-line)#password console
LA(config-line)#login
```

```
LA(config-line)#logging sync
LA(config-line)#exit
LA(config)#line vty 0 ?
  <1-1180>  Last Line number
  <cr>
LA(config)#line vty 0 1180
LA(config-line)#password telnet
LA(config-line)#login
LA(config-line)#exit
LA(config)#banner motd #This is my LA Router#
LA(config)#exit
LA#copy run start
Destination filename [startup-config]?
Building configuration...
[OK]
```

Nice—everything was pretty straightforward. The following output, which I gained via the show ip route command, displays the directly connected networks of 192.168.20.0 and 172.16.10.0:

```
LA#sh ip route
     172.16.0.0/30 is subnetted, 1 subnets
C       172.16.10.4 is directly connected, Serial0/0/1
L       172.16.10.6/32 is directly connected, Serial0/0/1
C    192.168.20.0/24 is directly connected, FastEthernet0/0
L    192.168.20.1/32 is directly connected, FastEthernet0/0
```

So now that we've configured all three routers with IP addresses and administrative functions, we can move on to deal with routing. But I want to do one more thing on the SF and LA routers—since this is a very small network, let's build a DHCP server on the Corp router for each LAN.

Configuring DHCP on Our Corp Router

While it's true that I could approach this task by going to each remote router and creating a pool, why bother with all that when I can easily create two pools on the Corp router and have the remote routers forward requests to the Corp router? Of course, you remember how to do this from Chapter 7!

Let's give it a shot:

```
Corp#config t
Corp(config)#ip dhcp excluded-address 192.168.10.1
Corp(config)#ip dhcp excluded-address 192.168.20.1
Corp(config)#ip dhcp pool SF_LAN
Corp(dhcp-config)#network 192.168.10.0 255.255.255.0
Corp(dhcp-config)#default-router 192.168.10.1
```

```
Corp(dhcp-config)#dns-server 4.4.4.4
Corp(dhcp-config)#exit
Corp(config)#ip dhcp pool LA_LAN
Corp(dhcp-config)#network 192.168.20.0 255.255.255.0
Corp(dhcp-config)#default-router 192.168.20.1
Corp(dhcp-config)#dns-server 4.4.4.4
Corp(dhcp-config)#exit
Corp(config)#exit
Corp#copy run start
Destination filename [startup-config]?
Building configuration...
```

Creating DHCP pools on a router is actually a simple process, and you would go about the configuration the same way on any router you wish to add a DHCP pool to. To designate a router as a DHCP server, you just create the pool name, add the network/subnet and the default gateway, and then exclude any addresses that you don't want handed out. You definitely want to make sure you've excluded the default gateway address, and you'd usually add a DNS server as well. I always add any exclusions first, and remember that you can conveniently exclude a range of addresses on a single line. Soon, I'll demonstrate those verification commands I promised I'd show you back in Chapter 7, but first, we need to figure out why the Corp router still can't get to the remote networks by default!

Now I'm pretty sure I configured DHCP correctly, but I just have this nagging feeling I forgot something important. What could that be? Well, the hosts are remote across a router, so what would I need to do that would allow them to get an address from a DHCP server? If you concluded that I've got to configure the SF and LA F0/0 interfaces to forward the DHCP client requests to the server, you got it!

Here's how we'd go about doing that:

```
LA#config t
LA(config)#int f0/0
LA(config-if)#ip helper-address 172.16.10.5

SF#config t
SF(config)#int f0/0
SF(config-if)#ip helper-address 172.16.10.1
```

I'm pretty sure I did this correctly, but we won't know until I have some type of routing configured and working. So let's get to that next!

Configuring IP Routing in Our Network

So is our network really good to go? After all, I've configured it with IP addressing, administrative functions, and even clocking that will automatically occur with the ISR routers. But how will our routers send packets to remote networks when they get their destination information by looking into their tables that only include directions about directly connected networks? And you know routers promptly discard packets they receive with addresses for networks that aren't listed in their routing table!

So we're not exactly ready to rock after all. But we will be soon because there are several ways to configure the routing tables to include all the networks in our little internetwork so that packets will be properly forwarded. As usual, one size fits all rarely fits at all, and what's best for one network isn't necessarily what's best for another. That's why understanding the different types of routing will be really helpful when choosing the best solution for your specific environment and business requirements.

These are the three routing methods I'm going to cover with you:

- Static routing
- Default routing
- Dynamic routing

We're going to start with the first way and implement static routing on our network, because if you can implement static routing *and* make it work, you've demonstrated that you definitely have a solid understanding of the internetwork. So let's get started.

Static Routing

Static routing is the process that ensues when you manually add routes in each router's routing table. Predictably, there are pros and cons to static routing, but that's true for all routing approaches.

Here are the pros:

- There is no overhead on the router CPU, which means you could probably make do with a cheaper router than you would need for dynamic routing.

- There is no bandwidth usage between routers, saving you money on WAN links as well as minimizing overhead on the router since you're not using a routing protocol.

- It adds security because you, the administrator, can be very exclusive and choose to allow routing access to certain networks only.

And here are the cons:

- Whoever the administrator is must have a vault-tight knowledge of the internetwork and how each router is connected in order to configure routes correctly. If you don't have a good, accurate map of your internetwork, things will get very messy quickly!

- If you add a network to the internetwork, you have to tediously add a route to it on all routers by hand, which only gets increasingly insane as the network grows.

- Due to the last point, it's just not feasible to use it in most large networks because maintaining it would be a full-time job in itself.

But that list of cons doesn't mean you get to skip learning all about it mainly because of that first disadvantage I listed—the fact that you must have such a solid understanding of a network to configure it properly and that your administrative knowledge has to practically verge on the supernatural! So let's dive in and develop those skills. Starting at the beginning, here's the command syntax you use to add a static route to a routing table from global config:

```
ip route [destination_network] [mask] [next-hop_address or
    exitinterface] [administrative_distance] [permanent]
```

This list describes each command in the string:

ip route   The command used to create the static route.

destination_network   The network you're placing in the routing table.

mask   The subnet mask being used on the network.

next-hop_address   This is the IP address of the next-hop router that will receive packets and forward them to the remote network, which must signify a router interface that's on a directly connected network. You must be able to successfully ping the router interface before you can add the route. Important note to self is that if you type in the wrong next-hop address or the interface to the correct router is down, the static route will show up in the router's configuration but not in the routing table.

exitinterface   Used in place of the next-hop address if you want, and shows up as a directly connected route.

administrative_distance   By default, static routes have an administrative distance of 1 or 0 if you use an exit interface instead of a next-hop address. You can change the default value by adding an administrative weight at the end of the command. I'll talk a lot more about this later in the chapter when we get to the section on dynamic routing.

permanent   If the interface is shut down or the router can't communicate to the next-hop router, the route will automatically be discarded from the routing table by default. Choosing the permanent option keeps the entry in the routing table no matter what happens.

Before I guide you through configuring static routes, let's take a look at a sample static route to see what we can find out about it:

```
Router(config)#ip route 172.16.3.0 255.255.255.0 192.168.2.4
```

- The ip route command tells us simply that it's a static route.
- 172.16.3.0 is the remote network we want to send packets to.
- 255.255.255.0 is the mask of the remote network.
- 192.168.2.4 is the next hop, or router, that packets will be sent to.

But what if the static route looked like this instead?

```
Router(config)#ip route 172.16.3.0 255.255.255.0 192.168.2.4 150
```

That 150 at the end changes the default administrative distance (AD) of 1 to 150. As I said, I'll talk much more about AD when we get into dynamic routing, but for now, just remember that the AD is the trustworthiness of a route, where 0 is best and 255 is worst.

One more example, then we'll start configuring:

```
Router(config)#ip route 172.16.3.0 255.255.255.0 s0/0/0
```

Instead of using a next-hop address, we can use an exit interface that will make the route show up as a directly connected network. Functionally, the next hop and exit interface work exactly the same.

To help you understand how static routes work, I'll demonstrate the configuration on the internetwork shown previously in Figure 9.8. Here it is again in Figure 9.9 to save you the trouble of having to go back and forth to view the same figure.

FIGURE 9.9   Our internetwork

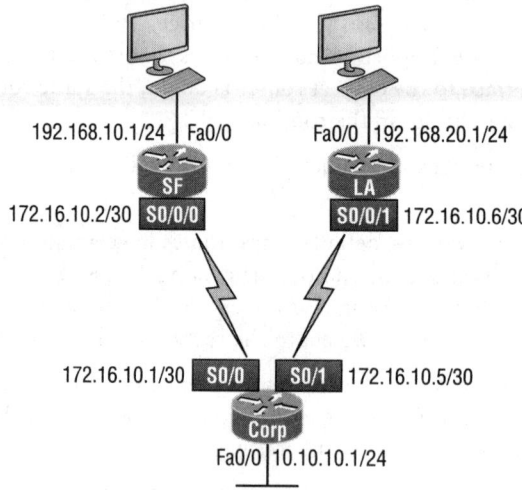

Corp

Each routing table automatically includes directly connected networks. To be able to route to all indirectly connected networks within the internetwork, the routing table must include information that describes where these other networks are located and how to get to them.

The Corp router is connected to three networks. For the Corp router to be able to route to all networks, the following networks have to be configured into its routing table:

- 192.168.10.0
- 192.168.20.0

The following router output shows the static routes on the Corp router and the routing table after the configuration. For the Corp router to find the remote networks, I had to place an entry into the routing table describing the remote network, the remote mask, and where to send the packets. I am going to add a 150 at the end of each line to raise the administrative distance. You'll see why soon when we get to dynamic routing. Many times this is also referred to as a floating static route because the static route has a higher administrative distance than any routing protocol and will only be used if the routes found with the routing protocols go down. Here's the output:

```
Corp#config t
Corp(config)#ip route 192.168.10.0 255.255.255.0 172.16.10.2 150
Corp(config)#ip route 192.168.20.0 255.255.255.0 s0/1 150
Corp(config)#do show run | begin ip route
ip route 192.168.10.0 255.255.255.0 172.16.10.2 150
ip route 192.168.20.0 255.255.255.0 Serial0/1 150
```

I needed to use different paths for networks 192.168.10.0 and 192.168.20.0, so I used a next-hop address for the SF router and an exit interface for the LA router. After the router has been configured, you can just type **show ip route** to see the static routes:

```
Corp(config)#do show ip route
S    192.168.10.0/24 [150/0] via 172.16.10.2
     172.16.0.0/30 is subnetted, 2 subnets
C       172.16.10.4 is directly connected, Serial0/1
L       172.16.10.5/32 is directly connected, Serial0/1
C       172.16.10.0 is directly connected, Serial0/0
L       172.16.10.1/32 is directly connected, Serial0/0
S    192.168.20.0/24 is directly connected, Serial0/1
     10.0.0.0/24 is subnetted, 1 subnets
C       10.10.10.0 is directly connected, FastEthernet0/0
L       10.10.10.1/32 is directly connected, FastEthernet0/0
```

The Corp router is configured to route and know all routes to all networks. But can you see a difference in the routing table for the routes to SF and LA? That's right! The next-hop configuration showed up as via, and the route configured with an exit interface configuration shows up as static but also as directly connected! This demonstrates how they are functionally the same but will display differently in the routing table.

Understand that if the routes don't appear in the routing table, it's because the router can't communicate with the next-hop address you've configured. But you can still use the permanent parameter to keep the route in the routing table even if the next-hop device can't be contacted.

The S in the first routing table entry means that the route is a static entry. The [150/0] stands for the administrative distance and metric to the remote network, respectively.

Okay—we're good. The Corp router now has all the information it needs to communicate with the other remote networks. Still, keep in mind that if the SF and LA routers aren't configured with all the same information, the packets will be discarded. We can fix this by configuring static routes.

Don't stress about the 150 at the end of the static route configuration at all, because I promise to get to it really soon in *this* chapter, not a later one! You really don't need to worry about it at this point.

SF

The SF router is directly connected to networks 172.16.10.0/30 and 192.168.10.0/24, which means I've got to configure the following static routes on the SF router:

- 10.10.10.0/24
- 192.168.20.0/24
- 172.16.10.4/30

The configuration for the SF router is revealed in the following output. Remember that we'll never create a static route to any network we're directly connected to as well as the fact that we must use the next hop of 172.16.10.1 since that's our only router connection. Let's check out the commands:

```
SF(config)#ip route 10.10.10.0 255.255.255.0 172.16.10.1 150
SF(config)#ip route 172.16.10.4 255.255.255.252 172.16.10.1 150
SF(config)#ip route 192.168.20.0 255.255.255.0 172.16.10.1 150
SF(config)#do show run | begin ip route
ip route 10.10.10.0 255.255.255.0 172.16.10.1 150
ip route 172.16.10.4 255.255.255.252 172.16.10.1 150
ip route 192.168.20.0 255.255.255.0 172.16.10.1 150
```

By looking at the routing table, you can see that the SF router now understands how to find each network:

```
SF(config)#do show ip route
C    192.168.10.0/24 is directly connected, FastEthernet0/0
L    192.168.10.1/32 is directly connected, FastEthernet0/0
     172.16.0.0/30 is subnetted, 3 subnets
S       172.16.10.4 [150/0] via 172.16.10.1
C       172.16.10.0 is directly connected, Serial0/0/0
L       172.16.10.2/32 is directly connected, Serial0/0
S    192.168.20.0/24 [150/0] via 172.16.10.1
     10.0.0.0/24 is subnetted, 1 subnets
S       10.10.10.0 [150/0] via 172.16.10.1
```

And we now can rest assured that the SF router has a complete routing table as well. As soon as the LA router has all the networks in its routing table, SF will be able to communicate with all remote networks!

LA

The LA router is directly connected to 192.168.20.0/24 and 172.16.10.4/30, so these are the routes that must be added:

- 10.10.10.0/24
- 172.16.10.0/30
- 192.168.10.0/24

And here's the LA router's configuration:

```
LA#config t
LA(config)#ip route 10.10.10.0 255.255.255.0 172.16.10.5 150
LA(config)#ip route 172.16.10.0 255.255.255.252 172.16.10.5 150
LA(config)#ip route 192.168.10.0 255.255.255.0 172.16.10.5 150
LA(config)#do show run | begin ip route
ip route 10.10.10.0 255.255.255.0 172.16.10.5 150
ip route 172.16.10.0 255.255.255.252 172.16.10.5 150
ip route 192.168.10.0 255.255.255.0 172.16.10.5 150
```

This output displays the routing table on the LA router:

```
LA(config)#do sho ip route
S    192.168.10.0/24 [150/0] via 172.16.10.5
     172.16.0.0/30 is subnetted, 3 subnets
C       172.16.10.4 is directly connected, Serial0/0/1
L       172.16.10.6/32 is directly connected, Serial0/0/1
S       172.16.10.0 [150/0] via 172.16.10.5
C    192.168.20.0/24 is directly connected, FastEthernet0/0
L    192.168.20.1/32 is directly connected, FastEthernet0/0
     10.0.0.0/24 is subnetted, 1 subnets
S       10.10.10.0 [150/0] via 172.16.10.5
```

LA now shows all five networks in the internetwork, so it too can now communicate with all routers and networks. But before we test our little network, as well as our DHCP server, let's cover one more topic.

Default Routing

The SF and LA routers that I've connected to the Corp router are considered stub routers. A *stub* indicates that the networks in this design have only one way out to reach all other networks, which means that instead of creating multiple static routes, we can just use a single default route. This default route is used by IP to forward any packet with a destination not found in the routing table, which is why it is also called a gateway of last resort. Here's the configuration I could have done on the LA router instead of typing in the static routes due to its stub status:

```
LA#config t
LA(config)#no ip route 10.10.10.0 255.255.255.0 172.16.10.5 150
LA(config)#no ip route 172.16.10.0 255.255.255.252 172.16.10.5 150
LA(config)#no ip route 192.168.10.0 255.255.255.0 172.16.10.5 150
LA(config)#ip route 0.0.0.0 0.0.0.0 172.16.10.5
LA(config)#do sho ip route
[output cut]
```

```
Gateway of last resort is 172.16.10.5 to network 0.0.0.0
172.16.0.0/30 is subnetted, 1 subnets
C       172.16.10.4 is directly connected, Serial0/0/1
L       172.16.10.6/32 is directly connected, Serial0/0/1
C    192.168.20.0/24 is directly connected, FastEthernet0/0
L    192.168.20.0/32 is directly connected, FastEthernet0/0
S*   0.0.0.0/0 [1/0] via 172.16.10.5
```

Okay—I've removed all the initial static routes I had configured, and adding a default route is a lot easier than typing a bunch of static routes! Can you see the default route listed last in the routing table? The S* shows that as a candidate for the default route. And I really want you to notice that the gateway of last resort is now set too. Everything the router receives with a destination not found in the routing table will be forwarded to 172.16.10.5. You need to be careful where you place default routes because you can easily create a network loop!

So we're there—we've configured all our routing tables! All the routers have the correct routing table, so all routers and hosts should be able to communicate without a hitch—for now. But if you add even one more network or another router to the internetwork, you'll have to update each and every router's routing tables by hand—ugh! Not really a problem at all if you've got a small network like we do, but it would be a time-consuming monster if you're dealing with a large internetwork!

Verifying Your Configuration

But we're not done yet—once all the routers' routing tables are configured, they must be verified. The best way to do this, besides using the show ip route command, is via Ping. I'll start by pinging from the Corp router to the SF router.

Here's the output I got:

```
Corp#ping 192.168.10.1
Type escape sequence to abort.
Sending 5, 100-byte ICMP Echos to 192.168.10.1, timeout is 2 seconds:
!!!!!
Success rate is 100 percent (5/5), round-trip min/avg/max = 4/4/4 ms
Corp#
```

Here you can see that I pinged from the Corp router to the remote interface of the SF router. Now let's ping the remote network on the LA router, and after that, we'll test our DHCP server and see if that is working too!

```
Corp#ping 192.168.20.1
Type escape sequence to abort.
Sending 5, 100-byte ICMP Echos to 192.168.20.1, timeout is 2 seconds:
!!!!!
Success rate is 100 percent (5/5), round-trip min/avg/max = 1/2/4 ms
Corp#
```

And why not test my configuration of the DHCP server on the Corp router while we're at it? I'm going to go to each host on the SF and LA routers and make them DHCP clients. By the way, I'm using an old router to represent "hosts," which just happens to work great for studying purposes. Here's how I did that:

```
SF_PC(config)#int e0
SF_PC(config-if)#ip address dhcp
SF_PC(config-if)#no shut
Interface Ethernet0 assigned DHCP address 192.168.10.8, mask 255.255.255.0
LA_PC(config)#int e0
LA_PC(config-if)#ip addr dhcp
LA_PC(config-if)#no shut
Interface Ethernet0 assigned DHCP address 192.168.20.4, mask 255.255.255.0
```

Nice! Don't you love it when things just work the first time? Sadly, this just isn't exactly a realistic expectation in the networking world, so we must be able to troubleshoot and verify our networks. Let's verify our DHCP server with a few of the commands you learned back in Chapter 7:

```
Corp#sh ip dhcp binding
Bindings from all pools not associated with VRF:
IP address          Client-ID/              Lease expiration       Type
                    Hardware address/
                    User name
192.168.10.8        0063.6973.636f.2d30.    Sept 16 2013 10:34 AM  Automatic
                    3035.302e.3062.6330.
                    2e30.3063.632d.4574.
                    30
192.168.20.4        0063.6973.636f.2d30.    Sept 16 2013 10:46 AM  Automatic
                    3030.322e.3137.3632.
                    2e64.3032.372d.4574.
                    30
```

We can see from earlier that our little DHCP server is working! Let's try another couple of commands:

```
Corp#sh ip dhcp pool SF_LAN
Pool SF_LAN :
 Utilization mark (high/low)    : 100 / 0
 Subnet size (first/next)       : 0 / 0
 Total addresses                : 254
 Leased addresses               : 3
 Pending event                  : none
 1 subnet is currently in the pool :
```

```
Current index          IP address range                      Leased addresses
192.168.10.9           192.168.10.1    - 192.168.10.254      3
```

```
Corp#sh ip dhcp conflict
IP address          Detection method   Detection time        VRF
```

The last command would tell us if we had two hosts with the same IP address, so it's good news because there are no conflicts reported! Two detection methods are used to confirm this:

- A ping from the DHCP server to make sure no other host responds before handing out an address
- A gratuitous ARP from a host that receives a DHCP address from the server

The DHCP client will send an ARP request with its new IP address looking to see if anyone responds, and if so, it will report the conflict to the server.

Okay, since we can communicate from end to end and to each host without a problem while receiving DHCP addresses from our server, I'd say our static and default route configurations have been a success—cheers!

Dynamic Routing

Dynamic routing is when protocols are used to find networks and update routing tables on routers. This is whole lot easier than using static or default routing, but it will cost you in terms of router CPU processing and bandwidth on network links. A routing protocol defines the set of rules used by a router when it communicates routing information between neighboring routers.

The routing protocol I'm going to talk about in this chapter is Routing Information Protocol (RIP) versions 1 and 2.

Two types of routing protocols are used in internetworks: *interior gateway protocols (IGPs)* and *exterior gateway protocols (EGPs)*. IGPs are used to exchange routing information with routers in the same *autonomous system (AS)*. An AS is either a single network or a collection of networks under a common administrative domain, which basically means that all routers sharing the same routing-table information are in the same AS. EGPs are used to communicate between ASs. An example of an EGP is Border Gateway Protocol (BGP), which we're not going to bother with because it's beyond the scope of this book.

Since routing protocols are so essential to dynamic routing, I'm going to give you the basic information you need to know about them next. Later on in this chapter, we'll focus on configuration.

Routing Protocol Basics

There are some important things you should know about routing protocols before we get deeper into RIP routing. Being familiar with administrative distances and the three different kinds of routing protocols, for example. Let's take a look.

Administrative Distances

The *administrative distance (AD)* is used to rate the trustworthiness of routing information received on a router from a neighbor router. An administrative distance is an integer from 0 to 255, where 0 is the most trusted and 255 means no traffic will be passed via this route.

If a router receives two updates listing the same remote network, the first thing the router checks is the AD. If one of the advertised routes has a lower AD than the other, then the route with the lowest AD will be chosen and placed in the routing table.

If both advertised routes to the same network have the same AD, then routing protocol metrics like *hop count* and/or the bandwidth of the lines will be used to find the best path to the remote network. The advertised route with the lowest metric will be placed in the routing table, but if both advertised routes have the same AD as well as the same metrics, then the routing protocol will load-balance to the remote network, meaning the protocol will send data down each link.

Table 9.1 shows the default administrative distances that a Cisco router uses to decide which route to take to a remote network.

TABLE 9.1   Default administrative distances

Route Source	Default AD
Connected interface	0
Static route	1
External BGP	20
EIGRP	90
OSPF	110
RIP	120
External EIGRP	170
Internal BGP	200
Unknown	255 (This route will never be used.)

If a network is directly connected, the router will always use the interface connected to the network. If you configure a static route, the router will then believe that route over any other ones it learns about. You can change the administrative distance of static routes, but by default, they have an AD of 1. In our previous static route configuration, the AD of each route is set at 150. This AD allows us to configure routing protocols without having to remove the static routes because it's nice to have them there for backup in case the routing protocol experiences some kind of failure.

If you have a static route, an RIP-advertised route, and an EIGRP-advertised route listing the same network, which route will the router go with? That's right—by default, the router will always use the static route unless you change its AD—which we did!

Routing Protocols

There are three classes of routing protocols:

Distance vector   The distance-vector protocols in use today find the best path to a remote network by judging distance. In RIP routing, each instance where a packet goes through a router is called a hop, and the route with the least number of hops to the network will be chosen as the best one. The vector indicates the direction to the remote network. RIP is a distance-vector routing protocol and periodically sends out the entire routing table to directly connected neighbors.

Link state   In link-state protocols, also called shortest-path-first (SPF) protocols, the routers each create three separate tables. One of these tables keeps track of directly attached neighbors, one determines the topology of the entire internetwork, and one is used as the routing table. Link-state routers know more about the internetwork than any distance-vector routing protocol ever could. OSPF is an IP routing protocol that's completely link-state. Link-state routing tables are not exchanged periodically. Instead, triggered updates containing only specific link-state information are sent. Periodic keepalives that are small and efficient, in the form of hello messages, are exchanged between directly connected neighbors to establish and maintain neighbor relationships.

Advanced distance vector   Advanced distance-vector protocols use aspects of both distance-vector and link-state protocols, and EIGRP is a great example. EIGRP may act like a link-state routing protocol because it uses a Hello protocol to discover neighbors and form neighbor relationships and because only partial updates are sent when a change occurs. However, EIGRP is still based on the key distance-vector routing protocol principle that information about the rest of the network is learned from directly connected neighbors.

There's no set of rules to follow that dictate exactly how to broadly configure routing protocols for every situation. It's a task that really must be undertaken on a case-by-case basis, with an eye on specific requirements of each one. If you understand how the different routing protocols work, you can make good, solid decisions that will solidly meet the individual needs of any business!

Routing Information Protocol (RIP)

Routing Information Protocol (RIP) is a true distance-vector routing protocol. RIP sends the complete routing table out of all active interfaces every 30 seconds. It relies on hop count to determine the best way to a remote network, but it has a maximum allowable hop count of 15 by default, so a destination of 16 would be considered unreachable. RIP works okay in very small networks, but it's super inefficient on large networks with slow WAN links or on networks with a large number of routers installed and completely useless on networks that have links with variable bandwidths!

RIP version 1 uses only *classful routing*, which means that all devices in the network must use the same subnet mask. This is because RIP version 1 doesn't send updates with subnet mask information in tow. RIP version 2 provides something called *prefix routing* and does send subnet mask information with its route updates. This is called *classless routing*.

So, with that let's configure our current network with RIPv2, before we move onto the next chapter.

Configuring RIP Routing

To configure RIP routing, just turn on the protocol with the `router rip` command and tell the RIP routing protocol the networks to advertise. Remember that with static routing, we always configured remote networks and never typed a route to our directly connected networks? Well, dynamic routing is carried out the complete opposite way. You would never type a *remote* network under your routing protocol—only enter your directly connected networks! Let's configure our three-router internetwork, revisited in Figure 9.9, with RIP routing.

Corp

RIP has an administrative distance of 120. Static routes have an administrative distance of 1 by default, and since we currently have static routes configured, the routing tables won't be populated with RIP information by default. We're still good though because I added the 150 to the end of each static route!

You can add the RIP routing protocol by using the `router rip` command and the `network` command. The `network` command tells the routing protocol which classful network to advertise. By doing this, you're activating the RIP routing process on the interfaces whose addressing falls within the specified classful networks configured with the `network` command under the RIP routing process.

Look at the Corp router configuration to see how easy this is. Oh wait—first, I want to verify my directly connected networks so I know what to configure RIP with:

```
Corp#sh ip int brief
Interface       IP-Address    OK? Method Status                Protocol
FastEthernet0/0 10.10.10.1    YES manual up                    up
Serial0/0       172.16.10.1   YES manual up                    up
FastEthernet0/1 unassigned    YES unset  administratively down down
Serial0/1       172.16.10.5   YES manual up                    up
Corp#config t
Corp(config)#router rip
Corp(config-router)#network 10.0.0.0
Corp(config-router)#network 172.16.0.0
Corp(config-router)#version 2
Corp(config-router)#no auto-summary
```

That's it—really! Typically just two or three commands and you're done, which sure makes your job a lot easier than dealing with static routes, doesn't it? Be sure to keep in mind the extra router CPU process and bandwidth that you're consuming.

Anyway, so what exactly did I do here? I enabled the RIP routing protocol, added my directly connected networks, made sure I was only running RIPv2, which is a classless routing protocol, and then I disabled auto-summary. We typically don't want our routing protocols summarizing for us because it's better to do that manually and both RIP and EIGRP (before 15.x code) auto-summarize by default. So a general rule of thumb is to disable auto-summary, which allows them to advertise subnets.

Notice I didn't type in subnets, only the classful network address, which is betrayed by the fact that all subnet bits and host bits are off! That's because with dynamic routing, it's not my job and it's up to the routing protocol to find the subnets and populate the routing tables. And since we have no router buddies running RIP, we won't see any RIP routes in the routing table yet.

> Remember that RIP uses the classful address when configuring the net-
> work address. To clarify this, refer to the example in our network with an
> address of 172.16.0.0/24 using subnets 172.16.10.0 and 172.16.20.0. You
> would only type in the classful network address of 172.16.0.0 and let RIP
> find the subnets and place them in the routing table. This doesn't mean
> you are running a classful routing protocol; this is just the way that both
> RIP and EIGRP are configured.

SF

Let's configure our SF router now, which is connected to two networks. We need to config-ure both directly connected classful networks, not subnets:

```
SF#sh ip int brief
Interface       IP-Address     OK? Method Status                Protocol
FastEthernet0/0 192.168.10.1   YES manual up                    up
FastEthernet0/1 unassigned     YES unset  administratively down down
Serial0/0/0     172.16.10.2    YES manual up                    up
Serial0/0/1     unassigned     YES unset  administratively down down
SF#config
SF(config)#router rip
SF(config-router)#network 192.168.10.0
SF(config-router)#network 172.16.0.0
SF(config-router)#version 2
SF(config-router)#no auto-summary
SF(config-router)#do show ip route
C    192.168.10.0/24 is directly connected, FastEthernet0/0
L    192.168.10.1/32 is directly connected, FastEthernet0/0
```

```
     172.16.0.0/30 is subnetted, 3 subnets
R       172.16.10.4 [120/1] via 172.16.10.1, 00:00:08, Serial0/0/0
C       172.16.10.0 is directly connected, Serial0/0/0
L       172.16.10.2/32 is directly connected, Serial0/0
S     192.168.20.0/24 [150/0] via 172.16.10.1
     10.0.0.0/24 is subnetted, 1 subnets
R       10.10.10.0 [120/1] via 172.16.10.1, 00:00:08, Serial0/0/0
```

That was pretty straightforward. Let's talk about this routing table. Since we have one RIP buddy out there with whom we are exchanging routing tables, we can see the RIP networks coming from the Corp router. All the other routes still show up as static and local. RIP also found both connections through the Corp router to networks 10.10.10.0 and 172.16.10.4. But we're not done yet!

LA

Let's configure our LA router with RIP, only I'm going to remove the default route first, even though I don't have to. You'll see why soon:

```
LA#config t
LA(config)#no ip route 0.0.0.0 0.0.0.0
LA(config)#router rip
LA(config-router)#network 192.168.20.0
LA(config-router)#network 172.16.0.0
LA(config-router)#no auto
LA(config-router)#vers 2
LA(config-router)#do show ip route
R     192.168.10.0/24 [120/2] via 172.16.10.5, 00:00:10, Serial0/0/1
     172.16.0.0/30 is subnetted, 3 subnets
C       172.16.10.4 is directly connected, Serial0/0/1
L       172.16.10.6/32 is directly connected, Serial0/0/1
R       172.16.10.0 [120/1] via 172.16.10.5, 00:00:10, Serial0/0/1
C     192.168.20.0/24 is directly connected, FastEthernet0/0
L     192.168.20.1/32 is directly connected, FastEthernet0/0
     10.0.0.0/24 is subnetted, 1 subnets
R       10.10.10.0 [120/1] via 172.16.10.5, 00:00:10, Serial0/0/1
```

The routing table is sprouting new R's as we add RIP buddies! We can still see that all routes are in the routing table.

This output shows us basically the same routing table and the same entries that it had when we were using static routes—except for those R's. An R indicates that the networks were added dynamically using the RIP routing protocol. The [120/1] is the administrative distance of the route (120) along with the metric, which for RIP is the number of hops to that remote network (1). From the Corp router, all networks are one hop away.

So, while yes, it's true that RIP has worked in our little internetwork, it's just not a great solution for most enterprises. Its maximum hop count of only 15 is a highly limiting factor. And it performs full routing-table updates every 30 seconds, which would bring a larger internetwork to a painful crawl in no time!

There's still one more thing I want to show you about RIP routing tables and the parameters used to advertise remote networks. Using a different router on a different network as an example for a second, look into the following output. Can you spot where the following routing table shows [120/15] in the 10.1.3.0 network metric? This means that the administrative distance is 120, the default for RIP, but the hop count is 15. Remember that each time a router sends out an update to a neighbor router, the hop count goes up by one incrementally for each route! Here's that output now:

```
Router#sh ip route
     10.0.0.0/24 is subnetted, 12 subnets
C       10.1.11.0 is directly connected, FastEthernet0/1
L       10.1.11.1/32 is directly connected, FastEthernet0/1
C       10.1.10.0 is directly connected, FastEthernet0/0
L       10.1.10.1/32 is directly connected, FastEthernet/0/0
R       10.1.9.0 [120/2] via 10.1.5.1, 00:00:15, Serial0/0/1
R       10.1.8.0 [120/2] via 10.1.5.1, 00:00:15, Serial0/0/1
R       10.1.12.0 [120/1] via 10.1.11.2, 00:00:00, FastEthernet0/1
R       10.1.3.0 [120/15] via 10.1.5.1, 00:00:15, Serial0/0/1
R       10.1.2.0 [120/1] via 10.1.5.1, 00:00:15, Serial0/0/1
R       10.1.1.0 [120/1] via 10.1.5.1, 00:00:15, Serial0/0/1
R       10.1.7.0 [120/2] via 10.1.5.1, 00:00:15, Serial0/0/1
R       10.1.6.0 [120/2] via 10.1.5.1, 00:00:15, Serial0/0/1
C       10.1.5.0 is directly connected, Serial0/0/1
L       10.1.5.1/32 is directly connected, Serial0/0/1
R       10.1.4.0 [120/1] via 10.1.5.1, 00:00:15, Serial0/0/1
```

So this [120/15] is really bad. We're basically doomed because the next router that receives the table from this router will just discard the route to network 10.1.3.0 since the hop count would rise to 16, which is invalid!

> If a router receives a routing update that contains a higher-cost path to a network that's already in its routing table, the update will be ignored.

Holding Down RIP Propagations

You probably don't want your RIP network advertised everywhere on your LAN and WAN. There's enough stress in networking already and not a whole lot to be gained by advertising your RIP network to the Internet!

There are a few different ways to stop unwanted RIP updates from propagating across your LANs and WANs, and the easiest one is through the passive-interface command. This command prevents RIP update broadcasts from being sent out of a specified interface but still allows that same interface to receive RIP updates.

Here's an example of how to configure a passive-interface on the Corp router's Fa0/1 interface, which we will pretend is connected to a LAN that we don't want RIP on (and the interface isn't shown in the figure):

```
Corp#config t
Corp(config)#router rip
Corp(config-router)#passive-interface FastEthernet 0/1
```

This command will stop RIP updates from being propagated out of FastEthernet interface 0/1, but it can still receive RIP updates.

 Real World Scenario

Should We Really Use RIP in an Internetwork?

You have been hired as a consultant to install a couple of Cisco routers into a growing network. They have a couple of old Unix routers that they want to keep in the network. These routers do not support any routing protocol except RIP. I guess this means you just have to run RIP on the entire network. If you were balding before, your head now shines like chrome.

No need for hairs abandoning ship though—you can run RIP on a router connecting that old network, but you certainly don't need to run RIP throughout the whole internetwork!

You can do what is called *redistribution*, which is basically translating from one type of routing protocol to another. This means that you can support those old routers using RIP but use something much better like Enhanced IGRP on the rest of your network.

This will prevent RIP routes from being sent all over the internetwork gobbling up all that precious bandwidth!

Advertising a Default Route Using RIP

Now I'm going to guide you through how to advertise a way out of your autonomous system to other routers, and you'll see this is completed the same way with OSPF. Imagine that our Corp router's Fa0/0 interface is connected to some type of Metro-Ethernet as a connection to the Internet. This is a pretty common configuration today that uses a LAN interface to connect to the ISP instead of a serial interface.

If we do add an Internet connection to Corp, all routers in our AS (SF and LA) must know where to send packets destined for networks on the Internet or they'll just drop the packets when they get a remote request. One solution to this little hitch would be to place a default route on every router and funnel the information to Corp, which in turn would have a default route to the ISP. Most people do this type of configuration in small- to medium-size networks because it actually works pretty well!

But since I'm running RIPv2 on all routers, I'll just add a default route on the Corp router to our ISP, as I would normally. I'll then add another command to advertise my network to the other routers in the AS as the default route to show them where to send packets destined for the Internet.

Here's my new Corp configuration:

```
Corp(config)#ip route 0.0.0.0 0.0.0.0 fa0/0
Corp(config)#router rip
Corp(config-router)#default-information originate
```

Now, let's take a look at the last entry found in the Corp routing table:

```
S*   0.0.0.0/0 is directly connected, FastEthernet0/0
```

Let's see if the LA router can see this same entry:

```
LA#sh ip route
Gateway of last resort is 172.16.10.5 to network 0.0.0.0

R    192.168.10.0/24 [120/2] via 172.16.10.5, 00:00:04, Serial0/0/1
     172.16.0.0/30 is subnetted, 2 subnets
C       172.16.10.4 is directly connected, Serial0/0/1
L       172.16.10.5/32 is directly connected, Serial0/0/1
R       172.16.10.0 [120/1] via 172.16.10.5, 00:00:04, Serial0/0/1
C    192.168.20.0/24 is directly connected, FastEthernet0/0
L    192.168.20.1/32 is directly connected, FastEthernet0/0
     10.0.0.0/24 is subnetted, 1 subnets
R       10.10.10.0 [120/1] via 172.16.10.5, 00:00:04, Serial0/0/1
R    192.168.218.0/24 [120/3] via 172.16.10.5, 00:00:04, Serial0/0/1
R    192.168.118.0/24 [120/2] via 172.16.10.5, 00:00:05, Serial0/0/1
R*   0.0.0.0/0 [120/1] via 172.16.10.5, 00:00:05, Serial0/0/1
```

Can you see that last entry? It screams that it's an RIP injected route, but it's also a default route, so our default-information originate command is working! Last, notice that the gateway of last resort is now set as well.

If all of what you've learned is clear and understood, congratulations—you're ready to move on to the next chapter right after you go through the written and hands-on labs, and while you're at it, don't forget the review questions!

Summary

This chapter covered IP routing in detail. Again, it's extremely important to fully understand the basics we covered in this chapter because everything that's done on a Cisco router will typically have some kind of IP routing configured and running.

You learned how IP routing uses frames to transport packets between routers and to the destination host. From there, we configured static routing on our routers and discussed the administrative distance used by IP to determine the best route to a destination network. You found out that if you have a stub network, you can configure default routing, which sets the gateway of last resort on a router.

We then discussed dynamic routing, specifically RIPv2 and how it works on an internetwork, which is not very well!

Exam Essentials

Describe the basic IP routing process.   You need to remember that the frame changes at each hop but that the packet is never changed or manipulated in any way until it reaches the destination device (the TTL field in the IP header is decremented for each hop, but that's it!).

List the information required by a router to successfully route packets.   To be able to route packets, a router must know, at a minimum, the destination address, the location of neighboring routers through which it can reach remote networks, possible routes to all remote networks, the best route to each remote network, and how to maintain and verify routing information.

Describe how MAC addresses are used during the routing process.   A MAC (hardware) address will only be used on a local LAN. It will never pass a router's interface. A frame uses MAC (hardware) addresses to send a packet on a LAN. The frame will take the packet to either a host on the LAN or a router's interface (if the packet is destined for a remote network). As packets move from one router to another, the MAC addresses used will change, but normally the original source and destination IP addresses within the packet will not.

View and interpret the routing table of a router.   Use the show ip route command to view the routing table. Each route will be listed along with the source of the routing information. A C to the left of the route will indicate directly connected routes, and other letters next to the route can also indicate a particular routing protocol that provided the information, such as, for example, R for RIP.

Differentiate the three types of routing.   The three types of routing are static (in which routes are manually configured at the CLI), dynamic (in which the routers share routing information via a routing protocol), and default routing (in which a special route is configured for all traffic without a more specific destination network found in the table).

Compare and contrast static and dynamic routing. Static routing creates no routing update traffic and creates less overhead on the router and network links, but it must be configured manually and does not have the ability to react to link outages. Dynamic routing creates routing update traffic and uses more overhead on the router and network links.

Configure static routes at the CLI. The command syntax to add a route is
`ip route [destination_network] [mask] [next-hop_address or exitinterface]`
`[administrative_distance] [permanent]`.

Create a default route. To add a default route, use the command syntax `ip route`
`0.0.0.0 0.0.0.0 ip-address` or `exit interface type and number`.

Understand administrative distance and its role in the selection of the best route.
Administrative distance (AD) is used to rate the trustworthiness of routing information received on a router from a neighbor router. Administrative distance is an integer from 0 to 255, where 0 is the most trusted and 255 means no traffic will be passed via this route. All routing protocols are assigned a default AD, but it can be changed at the CLI.

Differentiate distance-vector, link-state, and hybrid routing protocols. Distance-vector routing protocols make routing decisions based on hop count (think RIP), while link-state routing protocols are able to consider multiple factors such as bandwidth available and building a topology table. Hybrid routing protocols exhibit characteristics of both types.

Configure RIPv2 routing. To configure RIP routing, first you must be in global configuration mode and then you type the command `router rip`. Then you add all directly connected networks, making sure to use the classful address and the `version 2` command and to disable auto-summarization with the `no auto-summary` command.

Written Lab 9

In this section, you'll complete the following lab to make sure you've got the information and concepts contained within them fully dialed in:

Lab 9.1: IP Routing

You can find the answers to this lab in Appendix A, "Answers to Written Labs."
Write the answers to the following questions:

1. At the appropriate command prompt, create a static route to network 172.16.10.0/24 with a next-hop gateway of 172.16.20.1 and an administrative distance of 150.

2. When a PC sends a packet to another PC in a remote network, what destination addresses will be in the frame that it sends to its default gateway?

3. At the appropriate command prompt, create a default route to 172.16.40.1.

4. On which type of network is a default route most beneficial?

5. At the appropriate command prompt, display the routing table on your router.

6. When creating a static or default route, you don't have to use the next-hop IP address; you can use the _____.

7. True/False: To reach a remote host, you must know the MAC address of the remote host.

8. True/False: To reach a remote host, you must know the IP address of the remote host.

9. At the appropriate command prompt(s), prevent a router from propagating RIP information out serial 1.

10. True/False: RIPv2 is considered classless.

Hands-on Labs

In the following hands-on labs, you will configure a network with three routers. These exercises assume all the same setup requirements as the labs found in earlier chapters. You can use real routers, the LammleSim IOS version found at www.lammle.com/ccna, or the Cisco Packet Tracer program to run these labs.

This chapter includes the following labs:

Lab 9.1: Creating Static Routes

Lab 9.2: Configuring RIP Routing

The internetwork shown in the following graphic will be used to configure all routers.

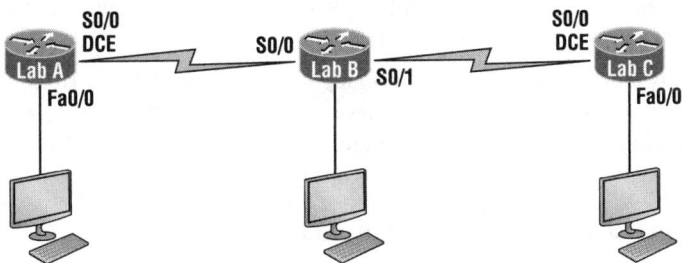

Table 9.2 shows our IP addresses for each router (each interface uses a /24 mask).

TABLE 9.2   Our IP addresses

Router	Interface	IP Address
Lab_A	Fa0/0	172.16.10.1
Lab_A	S0/0	172.16.20.1
Lab_B	S0/0	172.16.20.2
Lab_B	S0/1	172.16.30.1
Lab_C	S0/0	172.16.30.2
Lab_C	Fa0/0	172.16.40.1

These labs were written without using the LAN interface on the Lab_B router. You can choose to add that LAN into the labs if necessary. Also, if you have enough LAN interfaces, then you don't need to add the serial interfaces into this lab. Using all LAN interfaces is fine.

Hands-on Lab 9.1: Creating Static Routes

In this lab, you will create a static route in all three routers so that the routers see all networks. Verify with the Ping program when complete.

1. The Lab_A router is connected to two networks, 172.16.10.0 and 172.16.20.0. You need to add routes to networks 172.16.30.0 and 172.16.40.0. Use the following commands to add the static routes:

```
Lab_A#config t
Lab_A(config)#ip route 172.16.30.0 255.255.255.0
   172.16.20.2
Lab_A(config)#ip route 172.16.40.0 255.255.255.0
   172.16.20.2
```

2. Save the current configuration for the Lab_A router by going to privileged mode, typing **copy run start**, and pressing Enter.

3. On the Lab_B router, you have direct connections to networks 172.16.20.0 and 172.16.30.0. You need to add routes to networks 172.16.10.0 and 172.16.40.0. Use the following commands to add the static routes:

```
Lab_B#config t
Lab_B(config)#ip route 172.16.10.0 255.255.255.0
   172.16.20.1
Lab_B(config)#ip route 172.16.40.0 255.255.255.0
   172.16.30.2
```

4. Save the current configuration for router Lab_B by going to the enabled mode, typing **copy run start**, and pressing Enter.

5. On router Lab_C, create a static route to networks 172.16.10.0 and 172.16.20.0, which are not directly connected. Create static routes so that router Lab_C can see all networks, using the commands shown here:

```
Lab_C#config t
Lab_C(config)#ip route 172.16.10.0 255.255.255.0
   172.16.30.1
Lab_C(config)#ip route 172.16.20.0 255.255.255.0
   172.16.30.1
```

6. Save the current configuration for router Lab_C by going to the enable mode, typing **copy run start**, and pressing Enter.

7. Check your routing tables to make sure all four networks show up by executing the **show ip route** command.

8. Now ping from each router to your hosts and from each router to each router. If it is set up correctly, it will work.

Hands-on Lab 9.2: Configuring RIP Routing

In this lab, we will use the dynamic routing protocol RIP instead of static routing.

1. Remove any static routes or default routes configured on your routers by using the no ip route command. For example, here is how you would remove the static routes on the Lab_A router:

```
Lab_A#config t
Lab_A(config)#no ip route 172.16.30.0 255.255.255.0
  172.16.20.2
Lab_A(config)#no ip route 172.16.40.0 255.255.255.0
  172.16.20.2
```

Do the same thing for routers Lab_B and Lab_C. Verify that only your directly connected networks are in the routing tables.

2. After your static and default routes are clear, go into configuration mode on router Lab_A by typing **config t**.

3. Tell your router to use RIP routing by typing **router rip** and pressing Enter, as shown here:

```
config t
router rip
```

4. Add the network number for the networks you want to advertise. Since router Lab_A has two interfaces that are in two different networks, you must enter a network statement using the network ID of the network in which each interface resides. Alternately, you could use a summarization of these networks and use a single statement, minimizing the size of the routing table. Since the two networks are 172.16.10.0/24 and 172.16.20.0/24, the network summarization 172.16.0.0 would include both subnets. Do this by typing **network 172.16.0.0** and pressing Enter.

5. Press Ctrl+Z to get out of configuration mode.

6. The interfaces on Lab_B and Lab_C are in the 172.16.20.0/24 and 172.16.30.0/24 networks; therefore, the same summarized network statement will work there as well. Type the same commands, as shown here:

```
Config t
Router rip
network 172.16.0.0
```

7. Verify that RIP is running at each router by typing the following commands at each router:

   show ip protocols

   (Should indicate to you that RIP is present on the router.)

   show ip route

   (Should have routes present with an R to the left of them.)

   show running-config or show run

   (Should indicate that RIP is present and the networks are being advertised.)

8. Save your configurations by typing **copy run start** or **copy running-config startup-config** and pressing Enter at each router.

9. Verify the network by pinging all remote networks and hosts.

Review Questions

 The following questions are designed to test your understanding of this chapter's material. For more information on how to get additional questions, please see www.lammle.com/ccna.

You can find the answers to these questions in Appendix B, "Answers to Review Questions."

1. What command was used to generate the following output?

```
Codes: L - local, C - connected, S - static,
[output cut]
        10.0.0.0/8 is variably subnetted, 6 subnets, 4 masks
C       10.0.0.0/8 is directly connected, FastEthernet0/3
L       10.0.0.1/32 is directly connected, FastEthernet0/3
C       10.10.0.0/16 is directly connected, FastEthernet0/2
L       10.10.0.1/32 is directly connected, FastEthernet0/2
C       10.10.10.0/24 is directly connected, FastEthernet0/1
L       10.10.10.1/32 is directly connected, FastEthernet0/1
S*      0.0.0.0/0 is directly connected, FastEthernet0/0
```

2. You are viewing the routing table and you see an entry 10.1.1.1/32. What legend code would you expect to see next to this route?

    A. C

    B. L

    C. S

    D. D

3. Which of the following statements are true regarding the command ip route 172.16.4.0 255.255.255.0 192.168.4.2? (Choose two.)

    A. The command is used to establish a static route.

    B. The default administrative distance is used.

    C. The command is used to configure the default route.

    D. The subnet mask for the source address is 255.255.255.0.

    E. The command is used to establish a stub network.

4. What destination addresses will be used by HostA to send data to the HTTPS server as shown in the following network? (Choose two.)

    A. The IP address of the switch

    B. The MAC address of the remote switch

    C. The IP address of the HTTPS server

    D. The MAC address of the HTTPS server

    E. The IP address of RouterA's Fa0/0 interface

    F. The MAC address of RouterA's Fa0/0 interface

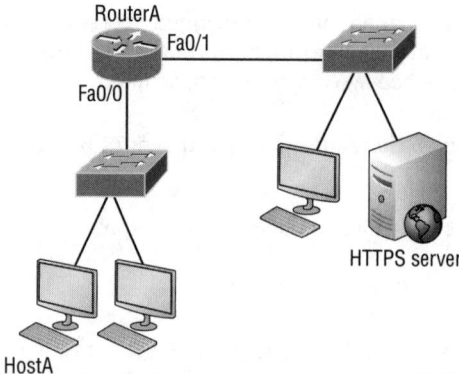

5. Using the output shown, what protocol was used to learn the MAC address for 172.16.10.1?

```
Interface: 172.16.10.2 --- 0x3
  Internet Address      Physical Address      Type
  172.16.10.1           00-15-05-06-31-b0     dynamic
```

    A. ICMP

    B. ARP

    C. TCP

    D. UDP

6. Which of the following is called an advanced distance-vector routing protocol?

    A. OSPF

    B. EIGRP

    C. BGP

    D. RIP

7. When a packet is routed across a network, the _____ in the packet changes at every hop while the _____ does not.

    A. MAC address, IP address

    B. IP address, MAC address

    C. Port number, IP address

    D. IP address, port number

8. Which statements are true regarding classless routing protocols? (Choose two.)

   A. The use of discontiguous networks is not allowed.

   B. The use of variable length subnet masks is permitted.

   C. RIPv1 is a classless routing protocol.

   D. IGRP supports classless routing within the same autonomous system.

   E. RIPv2 supports classless routing.

9. Which two of the following are true regarding the distance-vector and link-state routing protocols? (Choose two.)

   A. Link state sends its complete routing table out of all active interfaces at periodic time intervals.

   B. Distance vector sends its complete routing table out of all active interfaces at periodic time intervals.

   C. Link state sends updates containing the state of its own links to all routers in the internetwork.

   D. Distance vector sends updates containing the state of its own links to all routers in the internetwork.

10. When a router looks up the destination in the routing table for every single packet, it is called _____ .

    A. dynamic switching

    B. fast switching

    C. process switching

    D. Cisco Express Forwarding

11. What type(s) of route is the following? (Choose all that apply.)

    ```
    S*   0.0.0.0/0 [1/0] via 172.16.10.5
    ```

    A. Default

    B. Subnetted

    C. Static

    D. Local

12. A network administrator views the output from the show ip route command. A network that is advertised by both RIP and EIGRP appears in the routing table flagged as an EIGRP route. Why is the RIP route to this network not used in the routing table?

    A. EIGRP has a faster update timer.

    B. EIGRP has a lower administrative distance.

    C. RIP has a higher metric value for that route.

    D. The EIGRP route has fewer hops.

    E. The RIP path has a routing loop.

13. Which of the following is *not* an advantage of static routing?

    A. Less overhead on the router CPU

    B. No bandwidth usage between routers

    C. Adds security

    D. Recovers automatically from lost routes

14. What metric does RIPv2 use to find the best path to a remote network?

    A. Hop count

    B. MTU

    C. Cumulative interface delay

    D. Load

    E. Path bandwidth value

15. The Corporate router receives an IP packet with a source IP address of 192.168.214.20 and a destination address of 192.168.22.3. Looking at the output from the Corp router, what will the router do with this packet?

```
Corp#sh ip route
[output cut]
R    192.168.215.0 [120/2] via 192.168.20.2, 00:00:23, Serial0/0
R    192.168.115.0 [120/1] via 192.168.20.2, 00:00:23, Serial0/0
R    192.168.30.0 [120/1] via 192.168.20.2, 00:00:23, Serial0/0
C    192.168.20.0 is directly connected, Serial0/0
C    192.168.214.0 is directly connected, FastEthernet0/0
```

    A. The packet will be discarded.

    B. The packet will be routed out of the S0/0 interface.

    C. The router will broadcast looking for the destination.

    D. The packet will be routed out of the Fa0/0 interface.

16. If your routing table has a static, an RIP, and an EIGRP route to the same network, which route will be used to route packets by default?

    A. Any available route

    B. RIP route

    C. Static route

    D. EIGRP route

    E. They will all load-balance.

17. Which of the following is an EGP?

    A. RIPv2

    B. EIGRP

    C. BGP

    D. RIP

18. Which of the following is an advantage of static routing?

  A. Less overhead on the router CPU

  B. No bandwidth usage between routers

  C. Adds security

  D. Recovers automatically from lost routes

19. What command produced the following output?

```
Interface          IP-Address      OK? Method Status                 Protocol
FastEthernet0/0    192.168.10.1    YES manual up                     up
FastEthernet0/1    unassigned      YES unset  administratively down  down
Serial0/0/0        172.16.10.2     YES manual up                     up
Serial0/0/1        unassigned      YES unset  administratively down  down
```

  A. show ip route

  B. show interfaces

  C. show ip interface brief

  D. show ip arp

20. What does the 150 at the end of the following command mean?

```
Router(config)#ip route 172.16.3.0 255.255.255.0 192.168.2.4 150
```

  A. Metric

  B. Administrative distance

  C. Hop count

  D. Cost

Chapter

10

Layer 2 Switching

THE FOLLOWING ICND1 EXAM TOPICS ARE COVERED IN THIS CHAPTER:

✓ **2.0 LAN Switching Technologies**

- 2.1 Describe and verify switching concepts
    - 2.1.a MAC learning and aging
    - 2.1.b Frame switching
    - 2.1.c Frame flooding
    - 2.1.d MAC address table
- 2.7 Configure, verify, and troubleshoot port security
    - 2.7.a Static
    - 2.7.b Dynamic
    - 2.7.c Sticky
    - 2.7.d Max MAC addresses
    - 2.7.e Violation actions
    - 2.7.f Err-disable recovery

When people at Cisco discuss switching in regards to the Cisco exam objectives, they're talking about layer 2 switching unless they say otherwise. Layer 2 switching is the process of using the hardware address of devices on a LAN to segment a network. Since you've got the basic idea of how that works nailed down by now, we're going to dive deeper into the particulars of layer 2 switching to ensure that your concept of how it works is solid and complete.

You already know that we rely on switching to break up large collision domains into smaller ones and that a collision domain is a network segment with two or more devices sharing the same bandwidth. A hub network is a typical example of this type of technology. But since each port on a switch is actually its own collision domain, we were able to create a much better Ethernet LAN network by simply replacing our hubs with switches!

Switches truly have changed the way networks are designed and implemented. If a pure switched design is properly implemented, it absolutely will result in a clean, cost-effective, and resilient internetwork. In this chapter, we'll survey and compare how networks were designed before and after switching technologies were introduced.

I'll be using three switches to begin our configuration of a switched network, and we'll actually continue with their configurations in Chapter 11, "VLANs and Inter-VLAN Routing."

To find up-to-the-minute updates for this chapter, please see www.lammle.com/ccna or the book's web page at www.sybex.com/go/ccna.

Switching Services

Unlike old bridges, which used software to create and manage a Content Addressable Memory (CAM) filter table, our new, fast switches use application-specific integrated circuits (ASICs) to build and maintain their MAC filter tables. But it's still okay to think of a layer 2 switch as a multiport bridge because their basic reason for being is the same: to break up collision domains.

Layer 2 switches and bridges are faster than routers because they don't take up time looking at the Network layer header information. Instead, they look at the frame's hardware addresses before deciding to either forward, flood, or drop the frame.

Unlike hubs, switches create private, dedicated collision domains and provide independent bandwidth exclusive on each port.

Here's a list of four important advantages we gain when using layer 2 switching:

- Hardware-based bridging (ASICs)

- Wire speed

- Low latency

- Low cost

A big reason layer 2 switching is so efficient is that no modification to the data packet takes place. The device only reads the frame encapsulating the packet, which makes the switching process considerably faster and less error-prone than routing processes are.

And if you use layer 2 switching for both workgroup connectivity and network segmentation (breaking up collision domains), you can create more network segments than you can with traditional routed networks. Plus, layer 2 switching increases bandwidth for each user because, again, each connection, or interface into the switch, is its own, self-contained collision domain.

Three Switch Functions at Layer 2

There are three distinct functions of layer 2 switching that are vital for you to remember: *address learning*, *forward/filter decisions*, and *loop avoidance*.

Address learning   Layer 2 switches remember the source hardware address of each frame received on an interface and enter this information into a MAC database called a forward/filter table.

Forward/filter decisions   When a frame is received on an interface, the switch looks at the destination hardware address, then chooses the appropriate exit interface for it in the MAC database. This way, the frame is only forwarded out of the correct destination port.

Loop avoidance   If multiple connections between switches are created for redundancy purposes, network loops can occur. Spanning Tree Protocol (STP) is used to prevent network loops while still permitting redundancy.

Next, I'm going to talk about address learning and forward/filtering decisions. Loop avoidance is beyond the scope of the objectives being covered in this chapter.

Address Learning

When a switch is first powered on, the MAC forward/filter table (CAM) is empty, as shown in Figure 10.1.

FIGURE 10.1 Empty forward/filter table on a switch

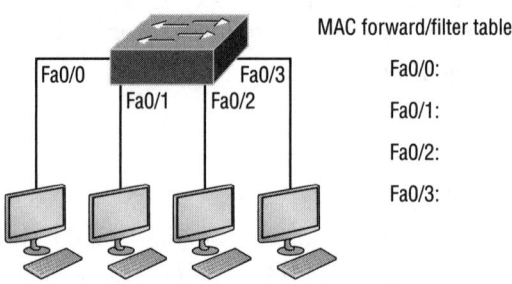

When a device transmits and an interface receives a frame, the switch places the frame's source address in the MAC forward/filter table, allowing it to refer to the precise interface the sending device is located on. The switch then has no choice but to flood the network with this frame out of every port except the source port because it has no idea where the destination device is actually located.

If a device answers this flooded frame and sends a frame back, then the switch will take the source address from that frame and place that MAC address in its database as well, associating this address with the interface that received the frame. Because the switch now has both of the relevant MAC addresses in its filtering table, the two devices can now make a point-to-point connection. The switch doesn't need to flood the frame as it did the first time because now the frames can and will only be forwarded between these two devices. This is exactly why layer 2 switches are so superior to hubs. In a hub network, all frames are forwarded out all ports every time—no matter what. Figure 10.2 shows the processes involved in building a MAC database.

FIGURE 10.2 How switches learn hosts' locations

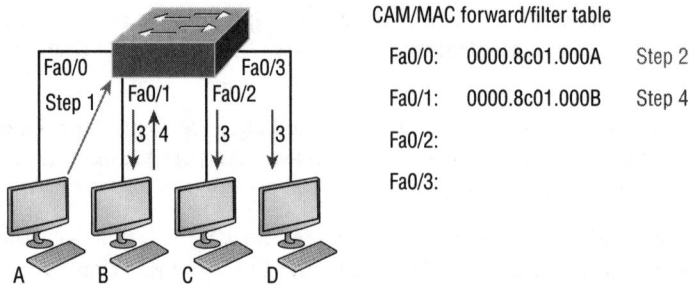

In this figure, you can see four hosts attached to a switch. When the switch is powered on, it has nothing in its MAC address forward/filter table, just as in Figure 10.1. But when the hosts start communicating, the switch places the source hardware address of each frame into the table along with the port that the frame's source address corresponds to.

Let me give you an example of how a forward/filter table is populated using Figure 10.2:

1. Host A sends a frame to Host B. Host A's MAC address is 0000.8c01.000A; Host B's MAC address is 0000.8c01.000B.

2. The switch receives the frame on the Fa0/0 interface and places the source address in the MAC address table.

3. Since the destination address isn't in the MAC database, the frame is forwarded out all interfaces except the source port.

4. Host B receives the frame and responds to Host A. The switch receives this frame on interface Fa0/1 and places the source hardware address in the MAC database.

5. Host A and Host B can now make a point-to-point connection and only these specific devices will receive the frames. Hosts C and D won't see the frames, nor will their MAC addresses be found in the database because they haven't sent a frame to the switch yet.

If Host A and Host B don't communicate to the switch again within a certain time period, the switch will flush their entries from the database to keep it as current as possible.

Forward/Filter Decisions

When a frame arrives at a switch interface, the destination hardware address is compared to the forward/filter MAC database. If the destination hardware address is known and listed in the database, the frame is only sent out of the appropriate exit interface. The switch won't transmit the frame out any interface except for the destination interface, which preserves bandwidth on the other network segments. This process is called *frame filtering*.

But if the destination hardware address isn't listed in the MAC database, then the frame will be flooded out all active interfaces except the interface it was received on. If a device answers the flooded frame, the MAC database is then updated with the device's location— its correct interface.

If a host or server sends a broadcast on the LAN, by default, the switch will flood the frame out all active ports except the source port. Remember, the switch creates smaller collision domains, but it's always still one large broadcast domain by default.

In Figure 10.3, Host A sends a data frame to Host D. What do you think the switch will do when it receives the frame from Host A?

FIGURE 10.3   Forward/filter table

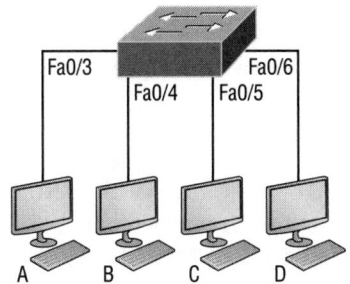

Switch# show mac address-table

VLAN	Mac Address	Ports
1	0005.dccb.d74b	Fa0/4
1	000a.f467.9e80	Fa0/5
1	000a.f467.9e8b	Fa0/6

Let's examine Figure 10.4 to find the answer.

FIGURE 10.4   Forward/filter table answer

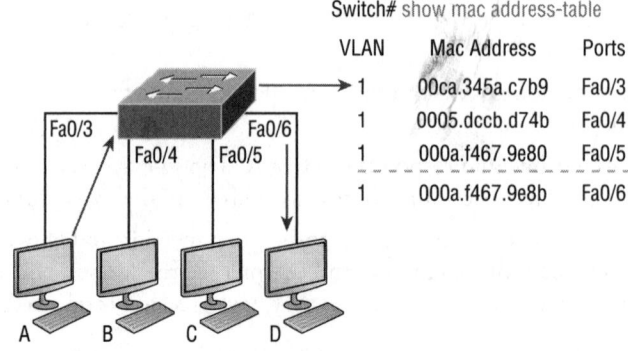

Since Host A's MAC address is not in the forward/filter table, the switch will add the source address and port to the MAC address table, then forward the frame to Host D. It's really important to remember that the source MAC is always checked first to make sure it's in the CAM table. After that, if Host D's MAC address wasn't found in the forward/filter table, the switch would've flooded the frame out all ports except for port Fa0/3 because that's the specific port the frame was received on.

Now let's take a look at the output that results from using a show mac address-table command:

```
Switch#sh mac address-table
Vlan    Mac Address      Type      Ports
----    -----------      --------  -----
   1    0005.dccb.d74b   DYNAMIC   Fa0/1
   1    000a.f467.9e80   DYNAMIC   Fa0/3
   1    000a.f467.9e8b   DYNAMIC   Fa0/4
   1    000a.f467.9e8c   DYNAMIC   Fa0/3
   1    0010.7b7f.c2b0   DYNAMIC   Fa0/3
   1    0030.80dc.460b   DYNAMIC   Fa0/3
   1    0030.9492.a5dd   DYNAMIC   Fa0/1
   1    00d0.58ad.05f4   DYNAMIC   Fa0/1
```

But let's say the preceding switch received a frame with the following MAC addresses:

Source MAC: **0005.dccb.d74b**

Destination MAC: **000a.f467.9e8c**

How will the switch handle this frame? The right answer is that the destination MAC address will be found in the MAC address table and the frame will only be forwarded out Fa0/3. Never forget that if the destination MAC address isn't found in the forward/filter table, the frame will be forwarded out all of the switch's ports except for the one on which it was originally received in an attempt to locate the destination device. Now that you can see the MAC address table and how switches add host addresses to the forward filter table, how do think we can secure it from unauthorized users?

Port Security

It's usually not a good thing to have your switches available for anyone to just plug into and play around with. I mean, we worry about wireless security, so why wouldn't we demand switch security just as much, if not more?

But just how do we actually prevent someone from simply plugging a host into one of our switch ports—or worse, adding a hub, switch, or access point into the Ethernet jack in their office? By default, MAC addresses will just dynamically appear in your MAC forward/filter database and you can stop them in their tracks by using port security!

Figure 10.5 shows two hosts connected to the single switch port Fa0/3 via either a hub or access point (AP).

FIGURE 10.5   "Port security" on a switch port restricts port access by MAC address.

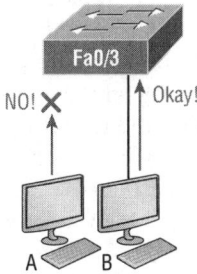

Port Fa0/3 is configured to observe and allow only certain MAC addresses to associate with the specific port, so in this example, Host A is denied access, but Host B is allowed to associate with the port.

By using port security, you can limit the number of MAC addresses that can be assigned dynamically to a port, set static MAC addresses, and—here's my favorite part—set penalties for users who abuse your policy! Personally, I like to have the port shut down when the security policy is violated. Making abusers bring me a memo from their boss explaining why they violated the security policy brings with it a certain poetic justice, which is nice. And I'll also require something like that before I'll enable their port again. Things like this really seem to help people remember to behave!

This is all good, but you still need to balance your particular security needs with the time that implementing and managing them will realistically require. If you have tons of time on your hands, then go ahead and seriously lock your network down vault-tight! If you're busy like the rest of us, I'm here to reassure you that there are ways to secure things nicely without being totally overwhelmed with a massive amount of administrative overhead. First, and painlessly, always remember to shut down unused ports or assign them to an unused VLAN. All ports are enabled by default, so you need to make sure there's no access to unused switch ports!

Here are your options for configuring port security:

```
Switch#config t
Switch(config)#int f0/1
Switch(config-if)#switchport mode access
Switch(config-if)#switchport port-security
Switch(config-if)#switchport port-security ?
  aging           Port-security aging commands
  mac-address     Secure mac address
  maximum         Max secure addresses
  violation       Security violation mode
  <cr>
```

Most Cisco switches ship with their ports in desirable mode, which means that those ports will desire to trunk when sensing that another switch has just been connected. So first, we need to change the port out from desirable mode and make it an access port instead. If we don't do that, we won't be able to configure port security on it at all! Once that's out of the way, we can move on using our port-security commands, never forgetting that we must enable port security on the interface with the basic command switchport port-security. Notice that I did this after I made the port an access port!

The preceding output clearly illustrates that the switchport port-security command can be used with four options. You can use the switchport port-security mac-address *mac-address* command to assign individual MAC addresses to each switch port, but be warned because if you go with that option, you had better have boatloads of time on your hands!

You can configure the device to take one of the following actions when a security violation occurs by using the switchport port-security command:

- Protect: The protect violation mode drops packets with unknown source addresses until you remove enough secure MAC addresses to drop below the maximum value.

- Restrict: The restrict violation mode also drops packets with unknown source addresses until you remove enough secure MAC addresses to drop below the maximum value. However, it also generates a log message, causes the security violation counter to increment, and sends an SNMP trap.

- Shutdown: Shutdown is the default violation mode. The shutdown violation mode puts the interface into an error-disabled state immediately. The entire port is shut down. Also, in this mode, the system generates a log message, sends an SNMP trap, and increments the violation counter. To make the interface usable, you must perform a shut/no shut on the interface.

If you want to set up a switch port to allow only one host per port and make sure the port will shut down if this rule is violated, use the following commands like this:

```
Switch(config-if)#switchport port-security maximum 1
Switch(config-if)#switchport port-security violation shutdown
```

These commands really are probably the most popular because they prevent random users from connecting to a specific switch or access point that's in their office. The port security default that's immediately set on a port when it's enabled is maximum 1 and violation shutdown. This sounds okay, but the drawback to this is that it only allows a single MAC address to be used on the port, so if anyone, including you, tries to add another host on that segment, the switch port will immediately enter error-disabled state and the port will turn amber. And when that happens, you have to manually go into the switch and re-enable the port by cycling it with a shutdown and then a no shutdown command.

Probably one of my favorite commands is the sticky command, and not just because it's got a cool name. It also makes very cool things happen! You can find this command under the mac-address command:

```
Switch(config-if)#switchport port-security mac-address sticky
Switch(config-if)#switchport port-security maximum 2
Switch(config-if)#switchport port-security violation shutdown
```

Basically, with the sticky command you can provide static MAC address security without having to type in absolutely everyone's MAC address on the network. I like things that save me time like that!

In the preceding example, the first two MAC addresses coming into the port "stick" to it as static addresses and will be placed in the running-config, but when a third address tried to connect, the port would shut down immediately.

I'll be going over port security CCENT objectives again in the configuration examples later in this chapter. They're important!

Let me show you one more example. Figure 10.6 displays a host in a company lobby that needs to be secured against the Ethernet cable used by anyone other than a single authorized individual.

FIGURE 10.6   Protecting a PC in a lobby

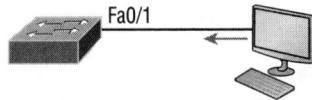

Fa0/1

What can you do to ensure that only the MAC address of the lobby PC is allowed by switch port Fa0/1?

The solution is pretty straightforward because in this case, the defaults for port security will work well. All I have left to do is add a static MAC entry:

```
Switch(config-if)#switchport port-security
Switch(config-if)#switchport port-security violation restrict
Switch(config-if)#switchport port-security mac-address aa.bb.cc.dd.ee.ff
```

To protect the lobby PC, we would set the maximum allowed MAC addresses to 1 and the violation to restrict so the port didn't get shut down every time someone tried to use the Ethernet cable (which would be constantly). By using violation restrict, the unauthorized frames would just be dropped. But did you notice that I enabled port-security and then set a static MAC address? Remember that as soon as you enable port-security on a port, it defaults to violation shutdown and a maximum of 1. So all I needed to do was change the violation mode and add the static MAC address and our business requirement is solidly met!

 Real World Scenario

Lobby PC Always Being Disconnected Becomes a Security Risk

At a large Fortune 50 company in San Jose, California, there was a PC in the lobby that held the company directory. With no security guard present in the lobby, the Ethernet cable connecting the PC was free game to all vendors, contractors, and visitors waiting in the lobby.

Port security to the rescue! When port security was enabled on the port with the switchport port-security command, the switch port connecting to the PC was automatically secured with the defaults of allowing only one MAC address to associate to the port and violation shutdown. However, the port was always going into err-shutdown mode whenever anyone tried to use the Ethernet port. When the violation mode was changed to restrict and a static MAC address was set for the port with the switchport port-security mac-address command, only the Lobby PC was able to connect and communicate on the network! Problem solved!

Loop Avoidance

Redundant links between switches are important to have in place because they help prevent nasty network failures in the event that one link stops working.

But while it's true that redundant links can be extremely helpful, they can also cause more problems than they solve! This is because frames can be flooded down all redundant links simultaneously, creating network loops as well as other evils. Here's a list of some of the ugliest problems that can occur:

- If no loop avoidance schemes are put in place, the switches will flood broadcasts endlessly throughout the internetwork. This is sometimes referred to as a *broadcast storm*. Most of the time, they're referred to in very unprintable ways! Figure 10.7 illustrates how a broadcast can be propagated throughout the network. Observe how a frame is continually being flooded through the internetwork's physical network media.

FIGURE 10.7   Broadcast storm

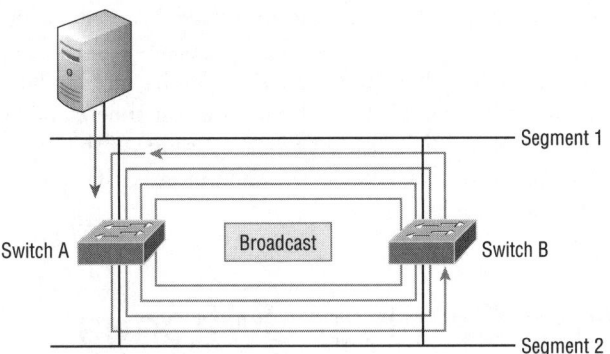

- A device can receive multiple copies of the same frame because that frame can arrive from different segments at the same time. Figure 10.8 demonstrates how a whole bunch of frames can arrive from multiple segments simultaneously. The server in the figure sends a unicast frame to Router C. Because it's a unicast frame, Switch A forwards the frame and Switch B provides the same service—it forwards the unicast. This is bad because it means that Router C receives that unicast frame twice, causing additional overhead on the network.

FIGURE 10.8   Multiple frame copies

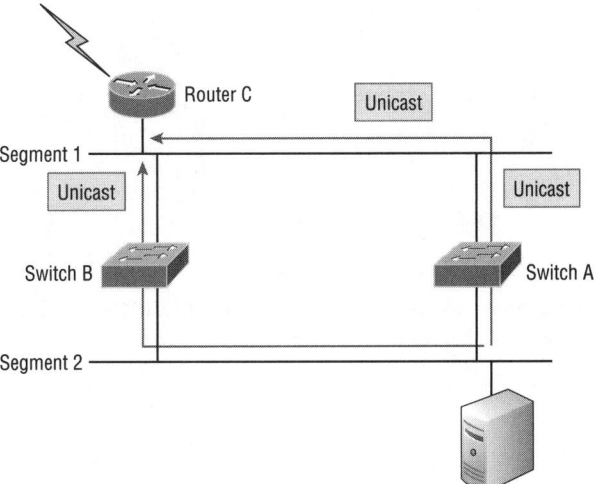

- You may have thought of this one: The MAC address filter table could be totally confused about the source device's location because the switch can receive the frame from more than one link. Worse, the bewildered switch could get so caught up in constantly updating the MAC filter table with source hardware address locations that it will fail to forward a frame! This is called thrashing the MAC table.

- One of the most vile events is when multiple loops propagate throughout a network. Loops can occur within other loops, and if a broadcast storm were to occur simultaneously, the network wouldn't be able to perform frame switching—period!

All of these problems spell disaster or close, and they're all evil situations that must be avoided or fixed somehow. That's where the Spanning Tree Protocol comes into play. It was actually developed to solve each and every one of the problems I just told you about!

Now that I explained the issues that can occur when you have redundant links, or when you have links that are improperly implemented, I'm sure you understand how vital it is to prevent them. However, the best solutions are beyond the scope of this chapter and among the territory covered in the more advanced Cisco exam objectives. For now, let's focus on configuring some switching!

Configuring Catalyst Switches

Cisco Catalyst switches come in many flavors; some run 10 Mbps, while others can speed all the way up to 10 Gbps or higher switched ports with a combination of twisted-pair and fiber. These newer switches, like the 3850, also have more intelligence, so they can give you data fast—mixed media services, too!

With that in mind, it's time to show you how to start up and configure a Cisco Catalyst switch using the command-line interface (CLI). After you get the basic commands down in this chapter, I'll show you how to configure virtual LANs (VLANs) plus Inter-Switch Link (ISL) and 802.1q trunking in the next one.

Here's a list of the basic tasks we'll be covering next:

- Administrative functions
- Configuring the IP address and subnet mask
- Setting the IP default gateway
- Setting port security
- Testing and verifying the network

 You can learn all about the Cisco family of Catalyst switches at www.cisco .com/en/US/products/hw/switches/index.html.

Catalyst Switch Configuration

But before we actually get into configuring one of the Catalyst switches, I've got to fill you in regarding the boot process of these switches, just as I did with the routers in Chapter 7, "Managing a Cisco Internetwork." Figure 10.9 shows a typical Cisco Catalyst switch, and I need to tell you about the different interfaces and features of this device.

FIGURE 10.9   A Cisco Catalyst switch

The first thing I want to point out is that the console port for the Catalyst switches are typically located on the back of the switch. Yet, on a smaller switch like the 3560 shown in the figure, the console is right in the front to make it easier to use. (The eight-port 2960 looks exactly the same.) If the POST completes successfully, the system LED turns green, but if the POST fails, it will turn amber. And seeing that amber glow is an ominous thing—typically fatal. So you may just want to keep a spare switch around—especially in case it's a production switch that's croaked! The bottom button is used to show you which lights are providing Power over Ethernet (PoE). You can see this by pressing the Mode button. The PoE is a very nice feature of these switches. It allows me to power my access point and phone by just connecting them into the switch with an Ethernet cable—sweet.

Just as we did with the routers we configured in Chapter 9, "IP Routing," we'll use a diagram and switch setup in this chapter as well as in Chapter 11. Figure 10.10 shows the switched network we'll be working on.

FIGURE 10.10   Our switched network

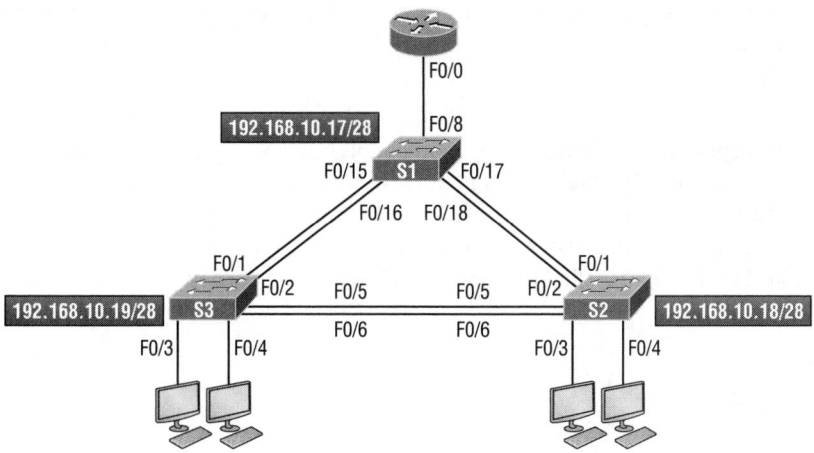

I'm going to use three 3560 switches, which I also used for demonstration in Chapter 6, "Cisco's Internetworking Operating System (IOS)," and Chapter 7. You can use any layer 2 switches for this chapter to follow the configuration, but when we get to Chapter 11, you'll need at least one router as well as a layer 3 switch, like my 3560.

Now if we connect our switches to each other, as shown in Figure 10.10, remember that first we'll need a crossover cable between the switches. My 3560 switches autodetect the connection type, so I was able to use straight-through cables. But not all switches autodetect the cable type. Different switches have different needs and abilities, so just keep this in mind when connecting your various switches together. Make a note that in the Cisco exam objectives, switches never autodetect!

When you first connect the switch ports to each other, the link lights are amber and then turn green, indicating normal operation. What you're actually watching is spanning-tree converging, and this process takes around 50 seconds with no extensions enabled. But if you connect into a switch port and the switch port LED is alternating green and amber, it means the port is experiencing errors. If this happens, check the host NIC or the cabling, possibly even the duplex settings on the port to make sure they match the host setting.

Do We Need to Put an IP Address on a Switch?

Absolutely not! Switches have all ports enabled and ready to rock. Take the switch out of the box, plug it in, and the switch starts learning MAC addresses in the CAM. So why would I need an IP address since switches are providing layer 2 services? Because you still need it for in-band management purposes! Telnet, SSH, SNMP, etc. all need an IP address in order to communicate with the switch through the network (in-band). Remember, since all ports are enabled by default, you need to shut down unused ports or assign them to an unused VLAN for security reasons.

So where do we put this management IP address the switch needs for management purposes? On what is predictably called the management VLAN interface—a routed interface on every Cisco switch and called interface VLAN 1. This management interface can be changed, and Cisco recommends that you do change this to a different management interface for security purposes. No worries—I'll demonstrate how to do this in Chapter 11.

Let's configure our switches now so you can watch how I configure the management interfaces on each switch.

S1

We're going to begin our configuration by connecting into each switch and setting the administrative functions. We'll also assign an IP address to each switch, but as I said, doing that isn't really necessary to make our network function. The only reason we're going to do that is so we can manage/administer it remotely, via Telnet for example. Let's use a simple IP scheme like 192.168.10.16/28. This mask should be familiar to you! Check out the following output:

```
Switch>en
Switch#config t
```

```
Switch(config)#hostname S1
S1(config)#enable secret todd
S1(config)#int f0/15
S1(config-if)#description 1st connection to S3
S1(config-if)#int f0/16
S1(config-if)#description 2nd connection to S3
S1(config-if)#int f0/17
S1(config-if)#description 1st connection to S2
S1(config-if)#int f0/18
S1(config-if)#description 2nd connection to S2
S1(config-if)#int f0/8
S1(config-if)#desc Connection to IVR
S1(config-if)#line con 0
S1(config-line)#password console
S1(config-line)#login
S1(config-line)#line vty 0 15
S1(config-line)#password telnet
S1(config-line)#login
S1(config-line)#int vlan 1
S1(config-if)#ip address 192.168.10.17 255.255.255.240
S1(config-if)#no shut
S1(config-if)#exit
S1(config)#banner motd #this is my S1 switch#
S1(config)#exit
S1#copy run start
Destination filename [startup-config]? [enter]
Building configuration...
[OK]
S1#
```

The first thing to notice about this is that there's no IP address configured on the switch's physical interfaces. Since all ports on a switch are enabled by default, there's not really a whole lot to configure! The IP address is configured under a logical interface, called a management domain or VLAN. You can use the default VLAN 1 to manage a switched network just as we're doing here, or you can opt to use a different VLAN for management.

The rest of the configuration is basically the same as the process you go through for router configuration. So remember... no IP addresses on physical switch interfaces, no routing protocols, and so on. We're performing layer 2 switching at this point, not routing! Also, make a note to self that there is no AUX port on Cisco switches.

S2

Here is the S2 configuration:

```
Switch#config t
Switch(config)#hostname S2
S2(config)#enable secret todd
S2(config)#int f0/1
S2(config-if)#desc 1st connection to S1
S2(config-if)#int f0/2
S2(config-if)#desc 2nd connection to s2
S2(config-if)#int f0/5
S2(config-if)#desc 1st connection to S3
S2(config-if)#int f0/6
S2(config-if)#desc 2nd connection to s3
S2(config-if)#line con 0
S2(config-line)#password console
S2(config-line)#login
S2(config-line)#line vty 0 15
S2(config-line)#password telnet
S2(config-line)#login
S2(config-line)#int vlan 1
S2(config-if)#ip address 192.168.10.18 255.255.255.240
S2(config)#exit
S2#copy run start
Destination filename [startup-config]?[enter]
Building configuration...
[OK]
S2#
```

We should now be able to ping from S2 to S1. Let's try it:

```
S2#ping 192.168.10.17

Type escape sequence to abort.
Sending 5, 100-byte ICMP Echos to 192.168.10.17, timeout is 2 seconds:
.!!!!
Success rate is 80 percent (4/5), round-trip min/avg/max = 1/1/1 ms
S2#
```

Okay—now why did I get only four pings to work instead of five? The first period [.] is a time-out, but the exclamation point [!] is a success.

It's a good question, and here's your answer: the first ping didn't work because of the time that ARP takes to resolve the IP address to its corresponding hardware MAC address.

S3

Check out the S3 switch configuration:

```
Switch>en
Switch#config t
SW-3(config)#hostname S3
S3(config)#enable secret todd
S3(config)#int f0/1
S3(config-if)#desc 1st connection to S1
S3(config-if)#int f0/2
S3(config-if)#desc 2nd connection to S1
S3(config-if)#int f0/5
S3(config-if)#desc 1st connection to S2
S3(config-if)#int f0/6
S3(config-if)#desc 2nd connection to S2
S3(config-if)#line con 0
S3(config-line)#password console
S3(config-line)#login
S3(config-line)#line vty 0 15
S3(config-line)#password telnet
S3(config-line)#login
S3(config-line)#int vlan 1
S3(config-if)#ip address 192.168.10.19 255.255.255.240
S3(config-if)#no shut
S3(config-if)#banner motd #This is the S3 switch#
S3(config)#exit
S3#copy run start
Destination filename [startup-config]?[enter]
Building configuration...
[OK]
S3#
```

Now let's ping to S1 and S2 from the S3 switch and see what happens:

```
S3#ping 192.168.10.17
Type escape sequence to abort.
Sending 5, 100-byte ICMP Echos to 192.168.10.17, timeout is 2 seconds:
.!!!!
Success rate is 80 percent (4/5), round-trip min/avg/max = 1/3/9 ms
```

```
S3#ping 192.168.10.18
Type escape sequence to abort.
Sending 5, 100-byte ICMP Echos to 192.168.10.18, timeout is 2 seconds:
.!!!!
Success rate is 80 percent (4/5), round-trip min/avg/max = 1/3/9 ms
S3#sh ip arp
Protocol  Address          Age (min)  Hardware Addr   Type   Interface
Internet  192.168.10.17           0   001c.575e.c8c0  ARPA   Vlan1
Internet  192.168.10.18           0   b414.89d9.18c0  ARPA   Vlan1
Internet  192.168.10.19           -   ecc8.8202.82c0  ARPA   Vlan1
S3#
```

In the output of the show ip arp command, the dash (-) in the minutes column means that it is the physical interface of the device.

Now, before we move on to verifying the switch configurations, there's one more command you need to know about, even though we don't really need it in our current network because we don't have a router involved. It's the ip default-gateway command. If you want to manage your switches from outside your LAN, you must set a default gateway on the switches just as you would with a host, and you do this from global config. Here's an example where we introduce our router with an IP address using the last IP address in our subnet range:

```
S3#config t
S3(config)#ip default-gateway 192.168.10.30
```

Now that we have all three switches basically configured, let's have some fun with them!

Port Security

A secured switch port can associate anywhere from 1 to 8,192 MAC addresses, but the 3560s I am using can support only 6,144, which seems like way more than enough to me. You can choose to allow the switch to learn these values dynamically, or you can set static addresses for each port using the switchport port-security mac-address *mac-address* command.

So let's set port security on our S3 switch now. Ports Fa0/3 and Fa0/4 will have only one device connected in our lab. By using port security, we're assured that no other device can connect once our hosts in ports Fa0/3 and in Fa0/4 are connected. Here's how to easily do that with just a couple commands:

```
S3#config t
S3(config)#int range f0/3-4
S3(config-if-range)#switchport mode access
S3(config-if-range)#switchport port-security
S3(config-if-range)#do show port-security int f0/3
```

```
Port Security             : Enabled
Port Status               : Secure-down
Violation Mode            : Shutdown
Aging Time                : 0 mins
Aging Type                : Absolute
SecureStatic Address Aging : Disabled
Maximum MAC Addresses     : 1
Total MAC Addresses       : 0
Configured MAC Addresses  : 0
Sticky MAC Addresses      : 0
Last Source Address:Vlan  : 0000.0000.0000:0
Security Violation Count  : 0
```

The first command sets the mode of the ports to "access" ports. These ports must be access or trunk ports to enable port security. By using the command `switchport port-security` on the interface, I've enabled port security with a maximum MAC address of 1 and violation of shutdown. These are the defaults, and you can see them in the high-lighted output of the `show port-security int f0/3` command in the preceding code.

Port security is enabled, as displayed on the first line, but the second line shows Secure-down because I haven't connected my hosts into the ports yet. Once I do, the status will show Secure-up and would become Secure-shutdown if a violation occurs.

I've just got to point out this all-so-important fact one more time: It's very important to remember that you can set parameters for port security but it won't work until you enable port security at the interface level. Notice the output for port F0/6:

```
S3#config t
S3(config)#int range f0/6
S3(config-if-range)#switchport mode access
S3(config-if-range)#switchport port-security violation restrict
S3(config-if-range)#do show port-security int f0/6
Port Security             : Disabled
Port Status               : Secure-up
Violation Mode            : restrict
[output cut]
```

Port Fa0/6 has been configured with a violation of restrict, but the first line shows that port security has not been enabled on the port yet. Remember, you must use this command at interface level to enable port security on a port:

```
S3(config-if-range)#switchport port-security
```

There are two other modes you can use instead of just shutting down the port. The restrict and protect modes mean that another host can connect up to the maximum MAC addresses allowed, but after the maximum has been met, all frames will just be dropped and the port won't be shut down. Additionally, both the restrict and shutdown violation modes alert you via SNMP that a violation has occurred on a port. You can then call the abuser and tell them they're so busted—you can see them, you know what they did, and they're in serious trouble!

If you've configured ports with the violation shutdown command, then the ports will look like this when a violation occurs:

```
S3#sh port-security int f0/3
Port Security              : Enabled
Port Status                : Secure-shutdown
Violation Mode             : Shutdown
Aging Time                 : 0 mins
Aging Type                 : Absolute
SecureStatic Address Aging : Disabled
Maximum MAC Addresses      : 1
Total MAC Addresses        : 2
Configured MAC Addresses   : 0
Sticky MAC Addresses       : 0
Last Source Address:Vlan   : 0013:0ca69:00bb3:00ba8:1
Security Violation Count   : 1
```

Here you can see that the port is in Secure-shutdown mode and the light for the port would be amber. To enable the port again, you'd need to do the following:

```
S3(config-if)#shutdown
S3(config-if)#no shutdown
```

Let's verify our switch configurations before we move onto VLANs in the next chapter. Beware that even though some switches will show err-disabled instead of Secure-shutdown as my switch shows, there is no difference between the two.

Verifying Cisco Catalyst Switches

The first thing I like to do with any router or switch is to run through the configurations with a show running-config command. Why? Because doing this gives me a really great overview of each device. But it is time consuming, and showing you all the configs would take up way too many pages in this book. Besides, we can instead run other commands that will still stock us up with really good information.

For example, to verify the IP address set on a switch, we can use the show interface command. Here's the output:

```
S3#sh int vlan 1
Vlan1 is up, line protocol is up
  Hardware is EtherSVI, address is ecc8.8202.82c0 (bia ecc8.8202.82c0)
```

```
Internet address is 192.168.10.19/28
MTU 1500 bytes, BW 1000000 Kbit/sec, DLY 10 usec,
    reliability 255/255, txload 1/255, rxload 1/255
Encapsulation ARPA, loopback not set
[output cut]
```

The previous output shows the interface is in up/up status. Remember to always check this interface, either with this command or the show ip interface brief command. Lots of people tend to forget that this interface is shutdown by default.

 Never forget that IP addresses aren't needed on a switch for it to operate. The only reason we would set an IP address, mask, and default gateway is for management purposes.

show mac address-table

I'm sure you remember being shown this command earlier in the chapter. Using it displays the forward filter table, also called a content addressable memory (CAM) table. Here's the output from the S1 switch:

```
S3#sh mac address-table
        Mac Address Table
-------------------------------------------

Vlan    Mac Address     Type       Ports
----    -----------     --------   -----
 All    0100.0ccc.cccc  STATIC     CPU
[output cut]
   1    000e.83b2.e34b  DYNAMIC    Fa0/1
   1    0011.1191.556f  DYNAMIC    Fa0/1
   1    0011.3206.25cb  DYNAMIC    Fa0/1
   1    001a.2f55.c9e8  DYNAMIC    Fa0/1
   1    001a.4d55.2f7e  DYNAMIC    Fa0/1
   1    001c.575e.c891  DYNAMIC    Fa0/1
   1    b414.89d9.1886  DYNAMIC    Fa0/5
   1    b414.89d9.1887  DYNAMIC    Fa0/6
```

The switches use things called base MAC addresses, which are assigned to the CPU. The first one listed is the base mac address of the switch. From the preceding output, you can see that we have six MAC addresses dynamically assigned to Fa0/1, meaning that port Fa0/1 is connected to another switch. Ports Fa0/5 and Fa0/6 only have one MAC address assigned, and all ports are assigned to VLAN 1.

Let's take a look at the S2 switch CAM and see what we can find out.

```
S2#sh mac address-table
         Mac Address Table
-------------------------------------------
Vlan    Mac Address     Type        Ports
----    -----------     --------    -----
 All    0100.0ccc.cccc  STATIC      CPU
[output cut
   1    000e.83b2.e34b  DYNAMIC     Fa0/5
   1    0011.1191.556f  DYNAMIC     Fa0/5
   1    0011.3206.25cb  DYNAMIC     Fa0/5
   1    001a.4d55.2f7e  DYNAMIC     Fa0/5
   1    581f.aaff.86b8  DYNAMIC     Fa0/5
   1    ecc8.8202.8286  DYNAMIC     Fa0/5
   1    ecc8.8202.82c0  DYNAMIC     Fa0/5
Total Mac Addresses for this criterion: 27
S2#
```

This output tells us that we have seven MAC addresses assigned to Fa0/5, which is our connection to S3. But where's port 6? Since port 6 is a redundant link to S3, STP placed Fa0/6 into blocking mode.

Assigning Static MAC Addresses

You can set a static MAC address in the MAC address table, but like setting static MAC port security without the sticky command, it's a ton of work. Just in case you want to do it, here's how it's done:

```
S3(config)#mac address-table ?
  aging-time    Set MAC address table entry maximum age
  learning      Enable MAC table learning feature
  move          Move keyword
  notification  Enable/Disable MAC Notification on the switch
  static        static keyword
```

```
S3(config)#mac address-table static aaaa.bbbb.cccc vlan 1 int fa0/7
S3(config)#do show mac address-table
         Mac Address Table
-------------------------------------------
Vlan    Mac Address     Type        Ports
----    -----------     --------    -----
 All    0100.0ccc.cccc  STATIC      CPU
[output cut]
   1    000e.83b2.e34b  DYNAMIC     Fa0/1
   1    0011.1191.556f  DYNAMIC     Fa0/1
```

```
  1    0011.3206.25cb    DYNAMIC    Fa0/1
  1    001a.4d55.2f7e    DYNAMIC    Fa0/1
  1    001b.d40a.0538    DYNAMIC    Fa0/1
  1    001c.575e.c891    DYNAMIC    Fa0/1
  1    aaaa.bbbb.0ccc    STATIC     Fa0/7
[output cut]
Total Mac Addresses for this criterion: 59
```

As shown on the left side of the output, you can see that a static MAC address has now been assigned permanently to interface Fa0/7 and that it's also been assigned to VLAN 1 only.

Now admit it—this chapter had a lot of great information, and you really did learn a lot and, well, maybe even had a little fun along the way too! You've now configured and verified all switches and set port security. That means you're now ready to learn all about virtual LANs! I'm going to save all our switch configurations so we'll be able to start right from here in Chapter 11.

Summary

In this chapter, I talked about the differences between switches and bridges and how they both work at layer 2. They create MAC address forward/filter tables in order to make decisions on whether to forward or flood a frame.

Although everything in this chapter is important, I wrote two port-security sections— one to provide a foundation and one with a configuration example. You must know both these sections in detail.

I also covered some problems that can occur if you have multiple links between bridges (switches).

Finally, I covered detailed configuration of Cisco's Catalyst switches, including verifying the configuration.

Exam Essentials

Remember the three switch functions.   Address learning, forward/filter decisions, and loop avoidance are the functions of a switch.

Remember the command `show mac address-table`.   The command show mac address-table will show you the forward/filter table used on the LAN switch.

Understand the reason for port security.   Port security restricts access to a switch based on MAC addresses.

Know the command to enable port security. To enable port security on a port, you must first make sure the port is an access port with `switchport mode access` and then use the `switchport port-security` command at the interface level. You can set the port security parameters before or after enabling port security.

Know the commands to verify port security. To verify port security, use the `show port-security`, `show port-security interface` *interface*, and `show running-config` commands.

Written Lab 10

In this section, you'll complete the following lab to make sure you've got the information and concepts contained within them fully dialed in:

Lab 10.1: Layer 2 Switching

You can find the answers to this lab in Appendix A, "Answers to Written Labs."

Write the answers to the following questions:

1. What command will show you the forward/filter table?
2. If a destination MAC address is not in the forward/filter table, what will the switch do with the frame?
3. What are the three switch functions at layer 2?
4. If a frame is received on a switch port and the source MAC address is not in the forward/filter table, what will the switch do?
5. What are the default modes for a switch port configured with port security?
6. Which two violation modes send out an SNMP trap?
7. Which violation mode drops packets with unknown source addresses until you remove enough secure MAC addresses to drop below the maximum but also generates a log message, causes the security violation counter to increment, and sends an SNMP trap but does not disable the port?
8. What does the `sticky` keyword in the `port-security` command provide?
9. What two commands can you use to verify that port security has been configured on a port FastEthernet 0/12 on a switch?
10. True/False: The layer 2 switch must have an IP address set and the PCs connecting to the switch must use that address as their default gateway.

Hands-on Labs

In this section, you will use the following switched network to configure your switching labs. You can use any Cisco switches to do this lab, as well as LammleSim IOS version simulator found at www.lammle.com/ccna. They do not need to be multilayer switches, just layer 2 switches.

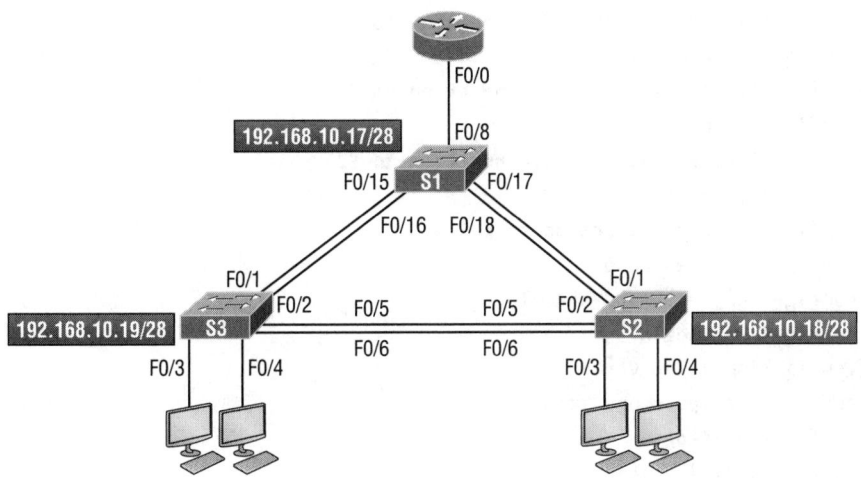

The first lab (Lab 10.1) requires you to configure three switches, and then you will verify them in Lab 10.2.

The labs in this chapter are as follows:

Hands-on Lab 10.1: Configuring Layer 2 Switches

Hands-on Lab 10.2: Verifying Layer 2 Switches

Hands-on Lab 10.3: Configuring Port Security

Lab 10.1: Configuring Layer 2 Switches

In this lab, you will configure the three switches in the graphic:

1. Connect to the S1 switch and configure the following, not in any particular order:

    - Hostname
    - Banner
    - Interface description
    - Passwords
    - IP address, subnet mask, default gateway

```
Switch>en
Switch#config t
Switch(config)#hostname S1
S1(config)#enable secret todd
S1(config)#int f0/15
S1(config-if)#description 1st connection to S3
S1(config-if)#int f0/16
```

```
S1(config-if)#description 2nd connection to S3
S1(config-if)#int f0/17
S1(config-if)#description 1st connection to S2
S1(config-if)#int f0/18
S1(config-if)#description 2nd connection to S2
S1(config-if)#int f0/8
S1(config-if)#desc Connection to IVR
S1(config-if)#line con 0
S1(config-line)#password console
S1(config-line)#login
S1(config-line)#line vty 0 15
S1(config-line)#password telnet
S1(config-line)#login
S1(config-line)#int vlan 1
S1(config-if)#ip address 192.168.10.17 255.255.255.240
S1(config-if)#no shut
S1(config-if)#exit
S1(config)#banner motd #this is my S1 switch#
S1(config)#exit
S1#copy run start
Destination filename [startup-config]? [enter]
Building configuration...
```

2. Connect to the S2 switch and configure all the settings you used in step 1. Do not forget to use a different IP address on the switch.

3. Connect to the S3 switch and configure all the settings you used in steps 1 and 2. Do not forget to use a different IP address on the switch.

Lab 10.2: Verifying Layer 2 Switches

Once you configure a device, you must be able to verify it.

1. Connect to each switch and verify the management interface.

   ```
   S1#sh interface vlan 1
   ```

2. Connect to each switch and verify the CAM.

   ```
   S1#sh mac address-table
   ```

3. Verify your configurations with the following commands:

   ```
   S1#sh running-config
   S1#sh ip int brief
   ```

Lab 10.3: Configuring Port Security

Port security is a big Cisco objective. Do not skip this lab!

1. Connect to your S3 switch.

2. Configure port Fa0/3 with port security.

    ```
    S3#config t
    S(config)#int fa0/3
    S3(config-if#Switchport mode access
    S3(config-if#switchport port-security
    ```

3. Check your default setting for port security.

    ```
    S3#show port-security int f0/3
    ```

4. Change the settings to have a maximum of two MAC addresses that can associate to interface Fa0/3.

    ```
    S3#config t
    S(config)#int fa0/3
    S3(config-if#switchport port-security maximum 2
    ```

5. Change the violation mode to restrict.

    ```
    S3#config t
    S(config)#int fa0/3
    S3(config-if#switchport port-security violation restrict
    ```

6. Verify your configuration with the following commands:

    ```
    S3#show port-security
    S3#show port-security int fa0/3
    S3#show running-config
    ```

Review Questions

 The following questions are designed to test your understanding of this chapter's material. For more information on how to get additional questions, please see www.lammle.com/ccna.

You can find the answers to these questions in Appendix B, "Answers to Review Questions."

1. Which of the following statements is *not* true with regard to layer 2 switching?

   A. Layer 2 switches and bridges are faster than routers because they don't take up time looking at the Data Link layer header information.

   B. Layer 2 switches and bridges look at the frame's hardware addresses before deciding to either forward, flood, or drop the frame.

   C. Switches create private, dedicated collision domains and provide independent bandwidth on each port.

   D. Switches use application-specific integrated circuits (ASICs) to build and maintain their MAC filter tables.

2. List the two commands that generated the last entry in the MAC address table shown.

```
Mac Address Table
-------------------------------------------

Vlan    Mac Address      Type       Ports
----    -----------      --------   -----
 All    0100.0ccc.cccc   STATIC     CPU
[output cut]
   1    000e.83b2.e34b   DYNAMIC    Fa0/1
   1    0011.1191.556f   DYNAMIC    Fa0/1
   1    0011.3206.25cb   DYNAMIC    Fa0/1
   1    001a.4d55.2f7e   DYNAMIC    Fa0/1
   1    001b.d40a.0538   DYNAMIC    Fa0/1
   1    001c.575e.c891   DYNAMIC    Fa0/1
   1    aaaa.bbbb.0ccc   STATIC     Fa0/7
```

3. In the diagram shown, what will the switch do if a frame with a destination MAC address of 000a.f467.63b1 is received on Fa0/4? (Choose all that apply.)

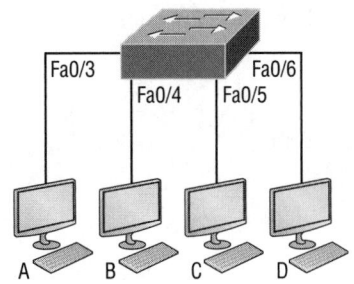

Switch# show mac address-table

VLAN	Mac Address	Ports
1	0005.dccb.d74b	Fa0/4
1	000a.f467.9e80	Fa0/5
1	000a.f467.9e8b	Fa0/6

A. Drop the frame.

B. Send the frame out of Fa0/3.

C. Send the frame out of Fa0/4.

D. Send the frame out of Fa0/5.

E. Send the frame out of Fa0/6.

4. Write the command that generated the following output.

```
        Mac Address Table
-------------------------------------------

Vlan    Mac Address     Type        Ports
----    -----------     --------    -----
All     0100.0ccc.cccc  STATIC      CPU
[output cut]
  1     000e.83b2.e34b  DYNAMIC     Fa0/1
  1     0011.1191.556f  DYNAMIC     Fa0/1
  1     0011.3206.25cb  DYNAMIC     Fa0/1
  1     001a.2f55.c9e8  DYNAMIC     Fa0/1
  1     001a.4d55.2f7e  DYNAMIC     Fa0/1
  1     001c.575e.c891  DYNAMIC     Fa0/1
  1     b414.89d9.1886  DYNAMIC     Fa0/5
  1     b414.89d9.1887  DYNAMIC     Fa0/6
```

5. In the work area in the following graphic, draw the functions of a switch from the list on the left to the right.

Address learning	Target 1
Packet forwarding	Target 2
Layer 3 security	Target 3
Forward/filter decisions	
Loop avoidance	

6. What statement(s) is/are true about the output shown here? (Choose all that apply.)

```
S3#sh port-security int f0/3
Port Security              : Enabled
Port Status               : Secure-shutdown
Violation Mode            : Shutdown
Aging Time                : 0 mins
Aging Type                : Absolute
SecureStatic Address Aging : Disabled
Maximum MAC Addresses     : 1
Total MAC Addresses       : 2
Configured MAC Addresses  : 0
Sticky MAC Addresses      : 0
Last Source Address:Vlan  : 0013:0ca69:00bb3:00ba8:1
Security Violation Count  : 1
```

    A. The port light for F0/3 will be amber in color.

    B. The F0/3 port is forwarding frames.

    C. This problem will resolve itself in a few minutes.

    D. This port requires the shutdown command to function.

7. Write the command that would limit the number of MAC addresses allowed on a port to 2. Write only the command and not the prompt.

8. Which of the following commands in this configuration is a prerequisite for the other commands to function?

```
S3#config t
S(config)#int fa0/3
S3(config-if#switchport port-security
S3(config-if#switchport port-security maximum 3
S3(config-if#switchport port-security violation restrict
S3(config-if#Switchport mode-security aging time 10
```

    A. switchport mode-security aging time 10

    B. switchport port-security

    C. switchport port-security maximum 3

    D. switchport port-security violation restrict

9. Which if the following is *not* an issue addressed by STP?

    A. Broadcast storms

    B. Gateway redundancy

   C. A device receiving multiple copies of the same frame

   D. Constant updating of the MAC filter table

10. What issue that arises when redundancy exists between switches is shown in the figure?

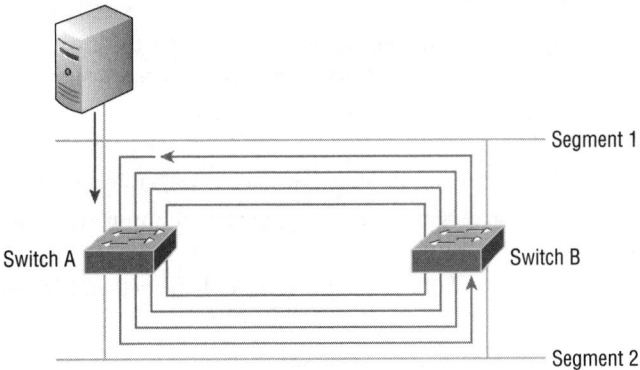

   A. Broadcast storm

   B. Routing loop

   C. Port violation

   D. Loss of gateway

11. Which two of the following switch port violation modes will alert you via SNMP that a violation has occurred on a port?

   A. `restrict`

   B. `protect`

   C. `shutdown`

   D. `err-disable`

12. _____ is the loop avoidance mechanism used by switches.

13. Write the command that must be present on any switch that you need to manage from a different subnet.

14. On which default interface have you configured an IP address for a switch?

   A. `int fa0/0`

   B. `int vty 0 15`

   C. `int vlan 1`

   D. `int s/0/0`

15. Which Cisco IOS command is used to verify the port security configuration of a switch port?

   A. `show interfaces port-security`

   B. `show port-security interface`

    C. `show ip interface`

    D. `show interfaces switchport`

16. Write the command that will save a dynamically learned MAC address in the running-configuration of a Cisco switch?

17. Which of the following methods will ensure that only one specific host can connect to port F0/3 on a switch? (Choose two. Each correct answer is a separate solution.)

    A. Configure port security on F0/3 to accept traffic other than that of the MAC address of the host.

    B. Configure the MAC address of the host as a static entry associated with port F0/3.

    C. Configure an inbound access control list on port F0/3 limiting traffic to the IP address of the host.

    D. Configure port security on F0/3 to accept traffic only from the MAC address of the host.

18. What will be the effect of executing the following command on port F0/1?

```
switch(config-if)# switchport port-security mac-address 00C0.35F0.8301
```

    A. The command configures an inbound access control list on port F0/1, limiting traffic to the IP address of the host.

    B. The command expressly prohibits the MAC address of 00c0.35F0.8301 as an allowed host on the switch port.

    C. The command encrypts all traffic on the port from the MAC address of 00c0.35F0.8301.

    D. The command statically defines the MAC address of 00c0.35F0.8301 as an allowed host on the switch port.

19. The conference room has a switch port available for use by the presenter during classes, and each presenter uses the same PC attached to the port. You would like to prevent other PCs from using that port. You have completely removed the former configuration in order to start anew. Which of the following steps is *not* required to prevent any other PCs from using that port?

    A. Enable port security.

    B. Assign the MAC address of the PC to the port.

    C. Make the port an access port.

    D. Make the port a trunk port.

20. Write the command required to disable the port if a security violation occurs. Write only the command and not the prompt.

Chapter

11

VLANs and Inter-VLAN Routing

THE FOLLOWING ICND1 EXAM TOPICS ARE COVERED IN THIS CHAPTER:

✓ **2.0 LAN Switching Technologies**

- 2.4 Configure, verify, and troubleshoot VLANs (normal range) spanning multiple switches
  - 2.4.a Access ports (data and voice)
  - 2.4.b Default VLAN
- 2.5 Configure, verify, and troubleshoot interswitch connectivity
  - 2.5.a Trunk ports
  - 2.5.b 802.1Q
  - 2.5.c Native VLAN

✓ **3.0 Routing Technologies**

- 3.4 Configure, verify, and troubleshoot inter-VLAN routing
  - 3.4.a Router on a stick

I know I keep telling you this, but so you never forget it, here I go, one last time: By default, switches break up collision domains and routers break up broadcast domains. Okay, I feel better! Now we can move on.

In contrast to the networks of yesterday that were based on collapsed backbones, today's network design is characterized by a flatter architecture—thanks to switches. So now what? How do we break up broadcast domains in a pure switched internetwork? By creating virtual local area networks (VLANs). A VLAN is a logical grouping of network users and resources connected to administratively defined ports on a switch. When you create VLANs, you're given the ability to create smaller broadcast domains within a layer 2 switched internetwork by assigning different ports on the switch to service different subnetworks. A VLAN is treated like its own subnet or broadcast domain, meaning that frames broadcast onto the network are only switched between the ports logically grouped within the same VLAN.

So, does this mean we no longer need routers? Maybe yes; maybe no. It really depends on what your particular networking needs and goals are. By default, hosts in a specific VLAN can't communicate with hosts that are members of another VLAN, so if you want inter-VLAN communication, the answer is that you still need a router or Inter-VLAN Routing (IVR).

In this chapter, you're going to comprehensively learn exactly what a VLAN is and how VLAN memberships are used in a switched network. You'll also become well-versed in what a trunk link is and how to configure and verify them.

I'll finish this chapter by demonstrating how you can make inter-VLAN communication happen by introducing a router into a switched network. Of course, we'll configure our familiar switched network layout we used in the last chapter for creating VLANs and for implementing trunking and Inter-VLAN routing on a layer 3 switch by creating switched virtual interfaces (SVIs).

To find up-to-the-minute updates for this chapter, please see www.lammle .com/ccna or the book's web page at www.sybex.com/go/ccna.

VLAN Basics

Figure 11.1 illustrates the flat network architecture that used to be so typical for layer 2 switched networks. With this configuration, every broadcast packet transmitted is seen by every device on the network regardless of whether the device needs to receive that data or not.

FIGURE 11.1   Flat network structure

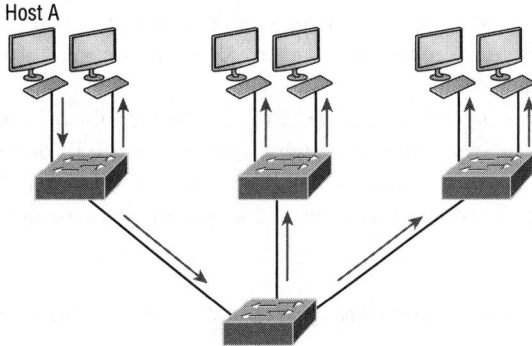

By default, routers allow broadcasts to occur only within the originating network, while switches forward broadcasts to all segments. Oh, and by the way, the reason it's called a *flat network* is because it's one *broadcast domain*, not because the actual design is physically flat. In Figure 11.1 we see Host A sending out a broadcast and all ports on all switches forwarding it—all except the port that originally received it.

Now check out Figure 11.2. It pictures a switched network and shows Host A sending a frame with Host D as its destination. Clearly, the important factor here is that the frame is only forwarded out the port where Host D is located.

FIGURE 11.2   The benefit of a switched network

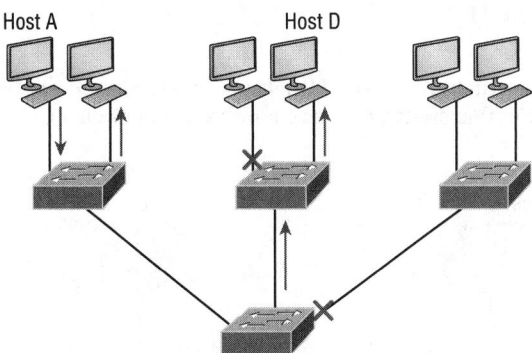

This is a huge improvement over the old hub networks, unless having one *collision domain* by default is what you really want for some reason!

Okay—you already know that the biggest benefit gained by having a layer 2 switched network is that it creates individual collision domain segments for each device plugged into each port on the switch. This scenario frees us from the old Ethernet density constraints and makes us able to build larger networks. But too often, each new advance comes with new issues. For instance, the more users and devices that populate and use a network, the more broadcasts and packets each switch must handle.

And there's another big issue—security! This one is real trouble because within the typical layer 2 switched internetwork, all users can see all devices by default. And you can't stop devices from broadcasting, plus you can't stop users from trying to respond to broadcasts. This means your security options are dismally limited to placing passwords on your servers and other devices.

But wait—there's hope if you create a *virtual LAN (VLAN)*! You can solve many of the problems associated with layer 2 switching with VLANs, as you'll soon see.

VLANs work like this: Figure 11.3 shows all hosts in this very small company connected to one switch, meaning all hosts will receive all frames, which is the default behavior of all switches.

FIGURE 11.3   One switch, one LAN: Before VLANs, there were no separations between hosts.

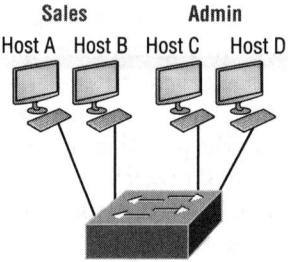

If we want to separate the host's data, we could either buy another switch or create virtual LANs, as shown in Figure 11.4.

FIGURE 11.4   One switch, two virtual LANs (*logical* separation between hosts): Still physically one switch, but this switch acts as many separate devices.

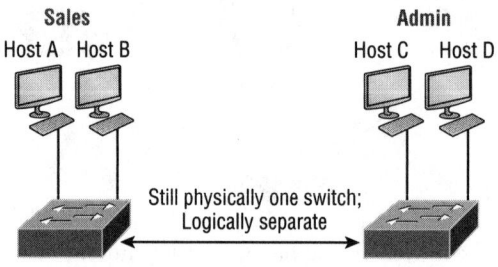

In Figure 11.4, I configured the switch to be two separate LANs, two subnets, two broadcast domains, two VLANs—they all mean the same thing—without buying another switch. We can do this 1,000 times on most Cisco switches, which saves thousands of dollars and more!

Notice that even though the separation is virtual and the hosts are all still connected to the same switch, the LANs can't send data to each other by default. This is because they are still separate networks, but no worries—we'll get into inter-VLAN communication later in this chapter.

Here's a short list of ways VLANs simplify network management:

- Network adds, moves, and changes are achieved with ease by just configuring a port into the appropriate VLAN.

- A group of users that need an unusually high level of security can be put into its own VLAN so that users outside of that VLAN can't communicate with the group's users.

- As a logical grouping of users by function, VLANs can be considered independent from their physical or geographic locations.

- VLANs greatly enhance network security if implemented correctly.

- VLANs increase the number of broadcast domains while decreasing their size.

Coming up, we'll thoroughly explore the world of switching, and you learn exactly how and why switches provide us with much better network services than hubs can in our networks today.

Broadcast Control

Broadcasts occur in every protocol, but how often they occur depends upon three things:

- The type of protocol

- The application(s) running on the internetwork

- How these services are used

Some older applications have been rewritten to reduce their bandwidth consumption, but there's a new generation of applications that are so bandwidth greedy they'll consume any and all they can find. These gluttons are the legion of multimedia applications that use both broadcasts and multicasts extensively. As if they weren't enough trouble, factors like faulty equipment, inadequate segmentation, and poorly designed firewalls can seriously compound the problems already caused by these broadcast-intensive applications. All of this has added a major new dimension to network design and presents a bunch of new challenges for an administrator. Positively making sure your network is properly segmented so you can quickly isolate a single segment's problems to prevent them from propagating throughout your entire internetwork is now imperative. And the most effective way to do that is through strategic switching and routing!

Since switches have become more affordable, most everyone has replaced their flat hub networks with pure switched network and VLAN environments. All devices within a VLAN are members of the same broadcast domain and receive all broadcasts relevant to it. By default, these broadcasts are filtered from all ports on a switch that aren't members of the same VLAN. This is great because you get all the benefits you would with a switched design without getting hit with all the problems you'd have if all your users were in the same broadcast domain—sweet!

Security

But there's always a catch, right? Time to get back to those security issues. A flat internetwork's security used to be tackled by connecting hubs and switches together with routers. So it was basically the router's job to maintain security. This arrangement was pretty ineffective for several reasons. First, anyone connecting to the physical network could access the network resources located on that particular physical LAN. Second, all anyone had to do to observe any and all traffic traversing that network was to simply plug a network analyzer into the hub. And similar to that last, scary, fact, users could easily join a workgroup by just plugging their workstations into the existing hub. That's about as secure as a barrel of honey in a bear enclosure!

But that's exactly what makes VLANs so cool. If you build them and create multiple broadcast groups, you can still have total control over each port and user! So the days when anyone could just plug their workstations into any switch port and gain access to network resources are history because now you get to control each port and any resources it can access.

And that's not even all—VLANs can be created in harmony with a specific user's need for the network resources. Plus, switches can be configured to inform a network management station about unauthorized access to those vital network resources. And if you need inter-VLAN communication, you can implement restrictions on a router to make sure this all happens securely. You can also place restrictions on hardware addresses, protocols, and applications. *Now* we're talking security—our honey barrel is now sealed tightly, made of solid titanium and wrapped in razor wire!

Flexibility and Scalability

If you've been paying attention so far, you know that layer 2 switches only read frames for filtering because they don't look at the Network layer protocol. You also know that by default, switches forward broadcasts to all ports. But if you create and implement VLANs, you're essentially creating smaller broadcast domains at layer 2.

As a result, broadcasts sent out from a node in one VLAN won't be forwarded to ports configured to belong to a different VLAN. But if we assign switch ports or users to VLAN groups on a switch or on a group of connected switches, we gain the flexibility to exclusively add only the users we want to let into that broadcast domain regardless of their physical location. This setup can also work to block broadcast storms caused by a faulty network interface card (NIC) as well as prevent an intermediate device from propagating broadcast storms throughout the entire internetwork. Those evils can still happen on the VLAN where the problem originated, but the disease will be fully contained in that one ailing VLAN!

Another advantage is that when a VLAN gets too big, you can simply create more VLANs to keep the broadcasts from consuming too much bandwidth. The fewer users in a VLAN, the fewer users affected by broadcasts. This is all good, but you seriously need to keep network services in mind and understand how the users connect to these services when creating a VLAN. A good strategy is to try to keep all services, except for the email and Internet access that everyone needs, local to all users whenever possible.

Identifying VLANs

Switch ports are layer 2–only interfaces that are associated with a physical port that can belong to only one VLAN if it's an access port or all VLANs if it's a trunk port.

Switches are definitely pretty busy devices. As myriad frames are switched throughout the network, switches have to be able to keep track of all of them, plus understand what to do with them depending on their associated hardware addresses. And remember—frames are handled differently according to the type of link they're traversing.

There are two different types of ports in a switched environment. Let's take a look at the first type in Figure 11.5.

FIGURE 11.5   Access ports

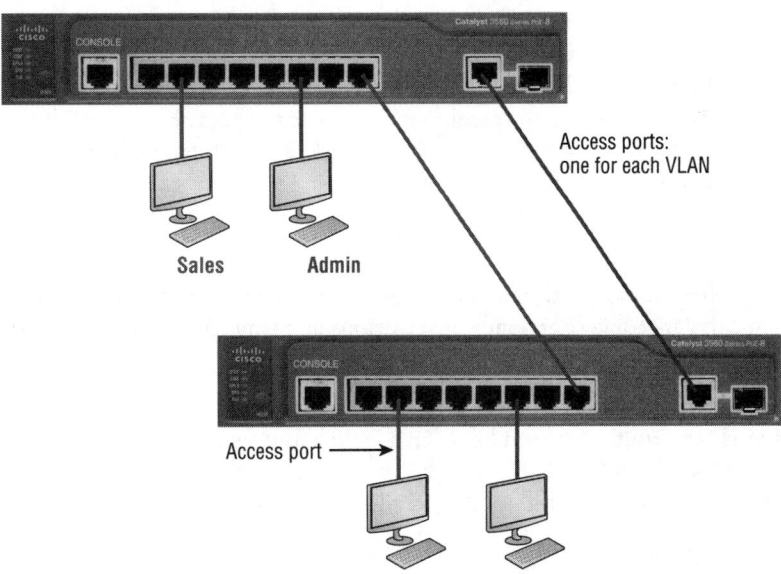

Notice there are access ports for each host and an access port between switches—one for each VLAN.

Access ports   An *access port* belongs to and carries the traffic of only one VLAN. Traffic is both received and sent in native formats with no VLAN information (tagging) whatsoever. Anything arriving on an access port is simply assumed to belong to the VLAN assigned to the port. Because an access port doesn't look at the source address, tagged traffic—a frame with added VLAN information—can be correctly forwarded and received only on trunk ports.

With an access link, this can be referred to as the *configured VLAN* of the port. Any device attached to an *access link* is unaware of a VLAN membership—the device just assumes it's part of some broadcast domain. But it doesn't have the big picture, so it doesn't understand the physical network topology at all.

Another good bit of information to know is that switches remove any VLAN information from the frame before it's forwarded out to an access-link device. Remember that access-link devices can't communicate with devices outside their VLAN unless the packet is routed. Also, you can only create a switch port to be either an access port or a trunk port— not both. So you've got to choose one or the other and know that if you make it an access port, that port can be assigned to one VLAN only. In Figure 11.5, only the hosts in the Sales VLAN can talk to other hosts in the same VLAN. This is the same with the Admin VLAN, and they can both communicate to hosts on the other switch because of an access link for each VLAN configured between switches.

> **Voice access ports**   Not to confuse you, but all that I just said about the fact that an access port can be assigned to only one VLAN is really only sort of true. Nowadays, most switches will allow you to add a second VLAN to an access port on a switch port for your voice traffic, called the voice VLAN. The voice VLAN used to be called the auxiliary VLAN, which allowed it to be overlaid on top of the data VLAN, enabling both types of traffic to travel through the same port. Even though this is technically considered to be a different type of link, it's still just an access port that can be configured for both data and voice VLANs. This allows you to connect both a phone and a PC device to one switch port but still have each device in a separate VLAN.

Trunk ports   Believe it or not, the term *trunk port* was inspired by the telephone system trunks, which carry multiple telephone conversations at a time. So it follows that trunk ports can similarly carry multiple VLANs at a time as well.

A *trunk link* is a 100, 1,000, or 10,000 Mbps point-to-point link between two switches, between a switch and router, or even between a switch and server, and it carries the traffic of multiple VLANs—from 1 to 4,094 VLANs at a time. But the amount is really only up to 1,001 unless you're going with something called extended VLANs.

Instead of an access link for each VLAN between switches, we'll create a trunk link, demonstrated in Figure 11.6.

FIGURE 11.6 VLANs can span across multiple switches by using trunk links, which carry traffic for multiple VLANs.

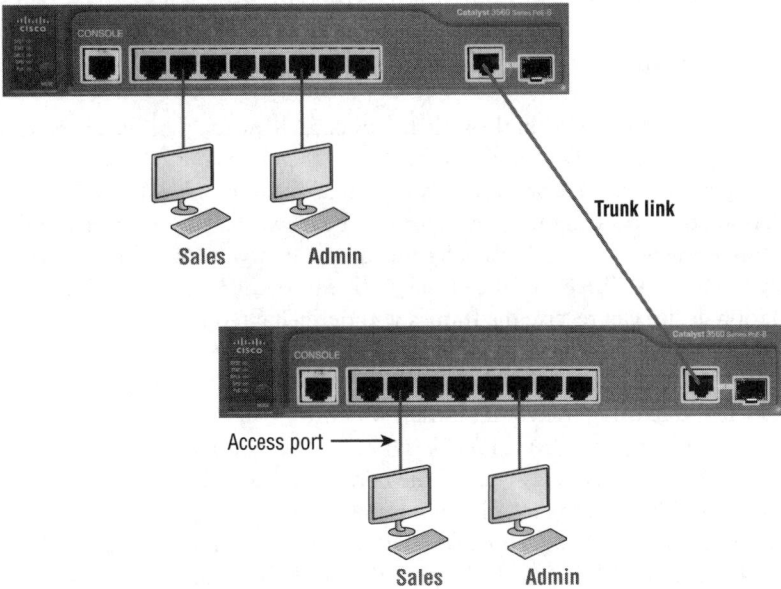

Trunking can be a real advantage because with it, you get to make a single port part of a whole bunch of different VLANs at the same time. This is a great feature because you can actually set ports up to have a server in two separate broadcast domains simultaneously so your users won't have to cross a layer 3 device (router) to log in and access it. Another benefit to trunking comes into play when you're connecting switches. Trunk links can carry the frames of various VLANs across them, but by default, if the links between your switches aren't trunked, only information from the configured access VLAN will be switched across that link.

It's also good to know that all VLANs send information on a trunked link unless you clear each VLAN by hand, and no worries, I'll show you how to clear individual VLANs from a trunk in a bit.

Okay—it's finally time to tell you about frame tagging and the VLAN identification methods used in it across our trunk links.

Frame Tagging

As you now know, you can set up your VLANs to span more than one connected switch. You can see that going on in Figure 11.6, which depicts hosts from two VLANs spread across two switches. This flexible, power-packed capability is probably the main advantage to implementing VLANs, and we can do this with up to a thousand VLANs and thousands upon thousands of hosts!

All this can get kind of complicated—even for a switch—so there needs to be a way for each one to keep track of all the users and frames as they travel the switch fabric and VLANs. When I say, "switch fabric," I'm just referring to a group of switches that share the same VLAN information. And this just happens to be where *frame tagging* enters the scene. This frame identification method uniquely assigns a user-defined VLAN ID to each frame.

Here's how it works: Once within the switch fabric, each switch that the frame reaches must first identify the VLAN ID from the frame tag. It then finds out what to do with the frame by looking at the information in what's known as the filter table. If the frame reaches a switch that has another trunked link, the frame will be forwarded out of the trunk-link port.

Once the frame reaches an exit that's determined by the forward/filter table to be an access link matching the frame's VLAN ID, the switch will remove the VLAN identifier. This is so the destination device can receive the frames without being required to understand their VLAN identification information.

Another great thing about trunk ports is that they'll support tagged and untagged traffic simultaneously if you're using 802.1q trunking, which we will talk about next. The trunk port is assigned a default port VLAN ID (PVID) for a VLAN upon which all untagged traffic will travel. This VLAN is also called the native VLAN and is always VLAN 1 by default, but it can be changed to any VLAN number.

Similarly, any untagged or tagged traffic with a NULL (unassigned) VLAN ID is assumed to belong to the VLAN with the port default PVID. Again, this would be VLAN 1 by default. A packet with a VLAN ID equal to the outgoing port native VLAN is sent untagged and can communicate to only hosts or devices in that same VLAN. All other VLAN traffic has to be sent with a VLAN tag to communicate within a particular VLAN that corresponds with that tag.

VLAN Identification Methods

VLAN identification is what switches use to keep track of all those frames as they're traversing a switch fabric. It's how switches identify which frames belong to which VLANs, and there's more than one trunking method.

Inter-Switch Link (ISL)

Inter-Switch Link (ISL) is a way of explicitly tagging VLAN information onto an Ethernet frame. This tagging information allows VLANs to be multiplexed over a trunk link through an external encapsulation method. This allows the switch to identify the VLAN membership of a frame received over the trunked link.

By running ISL, you can interconnect multiple switches and still maintain VLAN information as traffic travels between switches on trunk links. ISL functions at layer 2 by encapsulating a data frame with a new header and by performing a new cyclic redundancy check (CRC).

Of note is that ISL is proprietary to Cisco switches and is pretty versatile as well. ISL can be used on a switch port, router interfaces, and server interface cards to trunk a server.

Although some Cisco switches still support ISL frame tagging, Cisco is moving toward using only 802.1q.

IEEE 802.1q

Created by the IEEE as a standard method of frame tagging, IEEE 802.1q actually inserts a field into the frame to identify the VLAN. If you're trunking between a Cisco switched link and a different brand of switch, you've got to use 802.1q for the trunk to work.

Unlike ISL, which encapsulates the frame with control information, 802.1q inserts an 802.1q field along with tag control information, as shown in Figure 11.7.

FIGURE 11.7   IEEE 802.1q encapsulation with and without the 802.1q tag

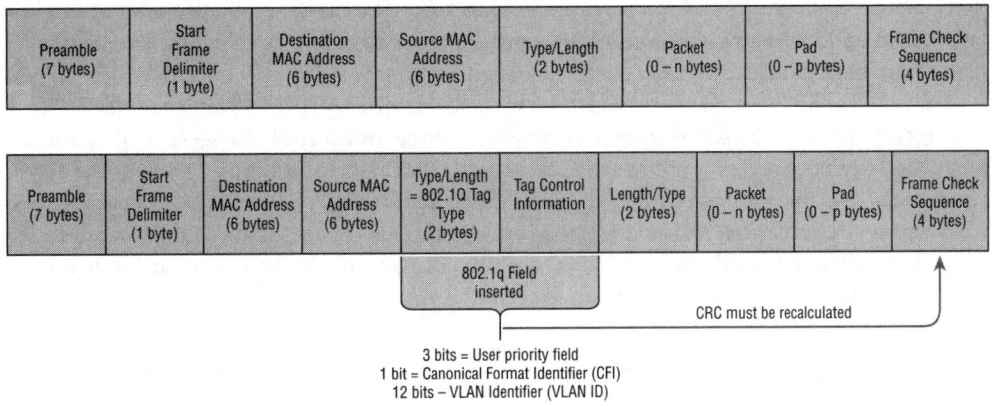

For the Cisco exam objectives, it's only the 12-bit VLAN ID that matters. This field identifies the VLAN and can be 2 to the 12th, minus 2 for the 0 and 4,095 reserved VLANs, which means an 802.1q tagged frame can carry information for 4,094 VLANs.

It works like this: You first designate each port that's going to be a trunk with 802.1q encapsulation. The other ports must be assigned a specific VLAN ID in order for them to communicate. VLAN 1 is the default native VLAN, and when using 802.1q, all traffic for a native VLAN is untagged. The ports that populate the same trunk create a group with this native VLAN and each port gets tagged with an identification number reflecting that. Again the default is VLAN 1. The native VLAN allows the trunks to accept information that was received without any VLAN identification or frame tag.

Most 2960 model switches only support the IEEE 802.1q trunking protocol, but the 3560 will support both the ISL and IEEE methods, which you'll see later in this chapter.

The basic purpose of ISL and 802.1q frame-tagging methods is to provide inter-switch VLAN communication. Remember that any ISL or 802.1q frame tagging is removed if a frame is forwarded out an access link—tagging is used internally and across trunk links only!

Routing between VLANs

Hosts in a VLAN live in their own broadcast domain and can communicate freely. VLANs create network partitioning and traffic separation at layer 2 of the OSI, and as I said when I told you why we still need routers, if you want hosts or any other IP-addressable device to communicate between VLANs, you must have a layer 3 device to provide routing.

For this, you can use a router that has an interface for each VLAN or a router that supports ISL or 802.1q routing. The least expensive router that supports ISL or 802.1q routing is the 2600 series router. You'd have to buy that from a used-equipment reseller because they are end-of-life, or EOL. I'd recommend at least a 2800 as a bare minimum, but even that only supports 802.1q; Cisco is really moving away from ISL, so you probably should only be using 802.1q anyway. Some 2800s may support both ISL and 802.1q; I've just never seen it supported.

Anyway, as shown in Figure 11.8, if you had two or three VLANs, you could get by with a router equipped with two or three FastEthernet connections. And 10Base-T is okay for home study purposes, and I mean only for your studies, but for anything else I'd highly recommend Gigabit interfaces for real power under the hood!

What we see in Figure 11.8 is that each router interface is plugged into an access link. This means that each of the routers' interface IP addresses would then become the default gateway address for each host in each respective VLAN.

FIGURE 11.8   Router connecting three VLANs together for inter-VLAN communication, one router interface for each VLAN

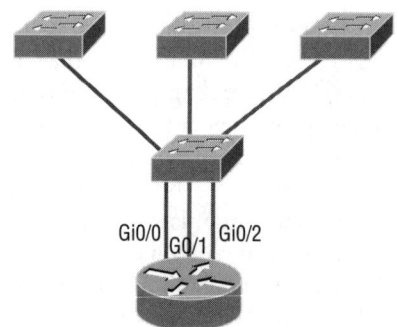

If you have more VLANs available than router interfaces, you can configure trunking on one FastEthernet interface or buy a layer 3 switch, like the old and now cheap 3560 or a higher-end switch like a 3850. You could even opt for a 6800 if you've got money to burn!

Instead of using a router interface for each VLAN, you can use one FastEthernet interface and run ISL or 802.1q trunking. Figure 11.9 shows how a FastEthernet interface on a router will look when configured with ISL or 802.1q trunking. This allows all VLANs to communicate through one interface. Cisco calls this a router on a stick (ROAS).

FIGURE 11.9   Router on a stick: single router interface connecting all three VLANs together for inter-VLAN communication

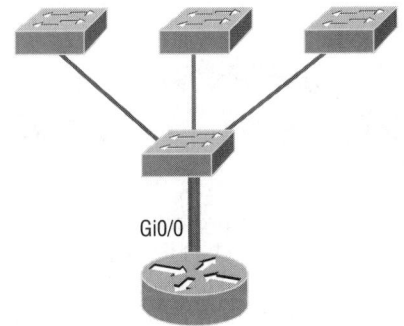

Gi0/0

I really want to point out that this creates a potential bottleneck, as well as a single point of failure, so your host/VLAN count is limited. To how many? Well, that depends on your traffic level. To really make things right, you'd be better off using a higher-end switch and routing on the backplane. But if you just happen to have a router sitting around, configuring this method is free, right?

Figure 11.10 shows how we would create a router on a stick using a router's physical interface by creating logical interfaces—one for each VLAN.

FIGURE 11.10   A router creates logical interfaces.

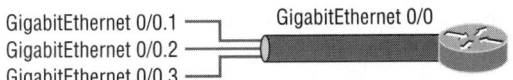

GigabitEthernet 0/0.1 ⏋
GigabitEthernet 0/0.2 —   GigabitEthernet 0/0
GigabitEthernet 0/0.3 ⏌

Here we see one physical interface divided into multiple subinterfaces, with one subnet assigned per VLAN, each subinterface being the default gateway address for each VLAN/subnet. An encapsulation identifier must be assigned to each subinterface to define the VLAN ID of that subinterface. In the next section where I'll configure VLANs and inter-VLAN routing, I'll configure our switched network with a router on a stick and demonstrate this configuration for you.

But wait, there's still one more way to go about routing! Instead of using an external router interface for each VLAN, or an external router on a stick, we can configure logical interfaces on the backplane of the layer 3 switch; this is called inter-VLAN routing (IVR), and it's configured with a switched virtual interface (SVI). Figure 11.11 shows how hosts see these virtual interfaces.

FIGURE 11.11 With IVR, routing runs on the backplane of the switch, and it appears to the hosts that a router is present.

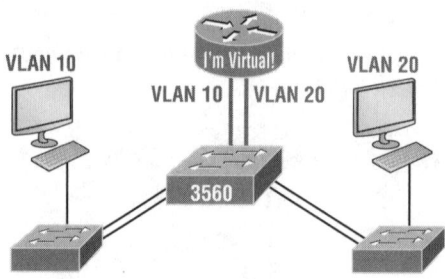

In Figure 11.11, it appears there's a router present, but there is no physical router present as there was when we used router on a stick. The IVR process takes little effort and is easy to implement, which makes it very cool! Plus, it's a lot more efficient for inter-VLAN routing than an external router is. To implement IVR on a multilayer switch, we just need to create logical interfaces in the switch configuration for each VLAN. We'll configure this method in a minute, but first let's take our existing switched network from Chapter 10, "Layer 2 Switching," and add some VLANs, then configure VLAN memberships and trunk links between our switches.

Configuring VLANs

Now this may come as a surprise to you, but configuring VLANs is actually pretty easy. It's just that figuring out which users you want in each VLAN is not, and doing that can eat up a lot of your time! But once you've decided on the number of VLANs you want to create and established which users you want belonging to each one, it's time to bring your first VLAN into the world.

To configure VLANs on a Cisco Catalyst switch, use the global config vlan command. In the following example, I'm going to demonstrate how to configure VLANs on the S1 switch by creating three VLANs for three different departments—again, remember that VLAN 1 is the native and management VLAN by default:

```
S1(config)#vlan ?
    WORD        ISL VLAN IDs 1-4094
    access-map  Create vlan access-map or enter vlan access-map command mode
    dot1q       dot1q parameters
    filter      Apply a VLAN Map
    group       Create a vlan group
    internal    internal VLAN
```

```
S1(config)#vlan 2
S1(config-vlan)#name Sales
S1(config-vlan)#vlan 3
S1(config-vlan)#name Marketing
S1(config-vlan)#vlan 4
S1(config-vlan)#name Accounting
S1(config-vlan)#vlan 5
S1(config-vlan)#name Voice
S1(config-vlan)#^Z
S1#
```

In this output, you can see that you can create VLANs from 1 to 4094. But this is only mostly true. As I said, VLANs can really only be created up to 1001, and you can't use, change, rename, or delete VLANs 1 or 1002 through 1005 because they're reserved. The VLAN numbers above 1005 are called extended VLANs and won't be saved in the database unless your switch is set to what is called VLAN Trunking Protocol (VTP) transparent mode. You won't see these VLAN numbers used too often in production. Here's an example of me attempting to set my S1 switch to VLAN 4000 when my switch is set to VTP server mode (the default VTP mode):

```
S1#config t
S1(config)#vlan 4000
S1(config-vlan)#^Z
% Failed to create VLANs 4000
Extended VLAN(s) not allowed in current VTP mode.
%Failed to commit extended VLAN(s) changes.
```

After you create the VLANs that you want, you can use the show vlan command to check them out. But notice that, by default, all ports on the switch are in VLAN 1. To change the VLAN associated with a port, you need to go to each interface and specifically tell it which VLAN to be a part of.

 Remember that a created VLAN is unused until it is assigned to a switch port or ports and that all ports are always assigned in VLAN 1 unless set otherwise.

Once the VLANs are created, verify your configuration with the show vlan command (sh vlan for short):

```
S1#sh vlan
VLAN Name                             Status    Ports
---- -------------------------------- --------- -------------------------------
1    default                          active    Fa0/1, Fa0/2, Fa0/3, Fa0/4
                                                Fa0/5, Fa0/6, Fa0/7, Fa0/8
                                                Fa0/9, Fa0/10, Fa0/11, Fa0/12
```

```
                                      Fa0/13, Fa0/14, Fa0/19, Fa0/20
                                      Fa0/21, Fa0/22, Fa0/23, Gi0/1
                                      Gi0/2
2      Sales                          active
3      Marketing                      active
4      Accounting                     active
5      Voice                          active
[output cut]
```

This may seem repetitive, but it's important, and I want you to remember it: You can't change, delete, or rename VLAN 1 because it's the default VLAN and you just can't change that—period. It's also the native VLAN of all switches by default, and Cisco recommends that you use it as your management VLAN. If you're worried about security issues, then change it! Basically, any ports that aren't specifically assigned to a different VLAN will be sent down to the native VLAN—VLAN 1.

In the preceding S1 output, you can see that ports Fa0/1 through Fa0/14, Fa0/19 through 23, and Gi0/1 and Gi0/2 uplinks are all in VLAN 1. But where are ports 15 through 18? First, understand that the command show vlan only displays access ports, so now that you know what you're looking at with the show vlan command, where do you think ports Fa15–18 are? That's right! They are trunked ports. Cisco switches run a proprietary protocol called *Dynamic Trunk Protocol (DTP)*, and if there is a compatible switch connected, they will start trunking automatically, which is precisely where my four ports are. You have to use the show interfaces trunk command to see your trunked ports like this:

```
S1# show interfaces trunk
Port       Mode          Encapsulation  Status     Native vlan
Fa0/15     desirable     n-isl          trunking   1
Fa0/16     desirable     n-isl          trunking   1
Fa0/17     desirable     n-isl          trunking   1
Fa0/18     desirable     n-isl          trunking   1

Port       Vlans allowed on trunk
Fa0/15     1-4094
Fa0/16     1-4094
Fa0/17     1-4094
Fa0/18     1-4094

[output cut]
```

This output reveals that the VLANs from 1 to 4094 are allowed across the trunk by default. Another helpful command, which is also part of the Cisco exam objectives, is the show interfaces *interface* switchport command:

```
S1#sh interfaces fastEthernet 0/15 switchport
Name: Fa0/15
Switchport: Enabled
```

```
Administrative Mode: dynamic desirable
Operational Mode: trunk
Administrative Trunking Encapsulation: negotiate
Operational Trunking Encapsulation: isl
Negotiation of Trunking: On
Access Mode VLAN: 1 (default)
Trunking Native Mode VLAN: 1 (default)
Administrative Native VLAN tagging: enabled
Voice VLAN: none
[output cut]
```

The highlighted output shows us the administrative mode of dynamic desirable, that the port is a trunk port, and that DTP was used to negotiate the frame-tagging method of ISL. It also predictably shows that the native VLAN is the default of 1.

Now that we can see the VLANs created, we can assign switch ports to specific ones. Each port can be part of only one VLAN, with the exception of voice access ports. Using trunking, you can make a port available to traffic from all VLANs. I'll cover that next.

Assigning Switch Ports to VLANs

You configure a port to belong to a VLAN by assigning a membership mode that specifies the kind of traffic the port carries plus the number of VLANs it can belong to. You can also configure each port on a switch to be in a specific VLAN (access port) by using the interface switchport command. You can even configure multiple ports at the same time with the interface range command.

In the next example, I'll configure interface Fa0/3 to VLAN 3. This is the connection from the S3 switch to the host device:

```
S3#config t
S3(config)#int fa0/3
S3(config-if)#switchport ?
  access        Set access mode characteristics of the interface
  autostate     Include or exclude this port from vlan link up calculation
  backup        Set backup for the interface
  block         Disable forwarding of unknown uni/multi cast addresses
  host          Set port host
  mode          Set trunking mode of the interface
  nonegotiate   Device will not engage in negotiation protocol on this
                interface
  port-security Security related command
  priority      Set appliance 802.1p priority
  private-vlan  Set the private VLAN configuration
```

```
protected      Configure an interface to be a protected port
trunk          Set trunking characteristics of the interface
voice          Voice appliance attributes voice
```

Well now, what do we have here? There's some new stuff showing up in our output now. We can see various commands—some that I've already covered, but no worries because I'm going to cover the access, mode, nonegotiate, and trunk commands very soon. Let's start with setting an access port on S1, which is probably the most widely used type of port you'll find on production switches that have VLANs configured:

```
S3(config-if)#switchport mode ?
    access          Set trunking mode to ACCESS unconditionally
  dot1q-tunnel  set trunking mode to TUNNEL unconditionally
  dynamic         Set trunking mode to dynamically negotiate access or trunk mode
  private-vlan  Set private-vlan mode
  trunk           Set trunking mode to TRUNK unconditionally

S3(config-if)#switchport mode access
S3(config-if)#switchport access vlan 3
S3(config-if)#switchport voice vlan 5
```

By starting with the switchport mode access command, you're telling the switch that this is a nontrunking layer 2 port. You can then assign a VLAN to the port with the switchport access command, as well as configure the same port to be a member of a different type of VLAN, called the voice VLAN. This allows you to connect a laptop into a phone, and the phone into a single switch port. Remember, you can choose many ports to configure simultaneously with the interface range command.

Let's take a look at our VLANs now:

```
S3#show vlan
VLAN Name                     Status     Ports
---- ----------------------   --------   ------------------------------
1    default                  active     Fa0/4, Fa0/5, Fa0/6, Fa0/7
                                         Fa0/8, Fa0/9, Fa0/10, Fa0/11,
                                         Fa0/12, Fa0/13, Fa0/14, Fa0/19,
                                         Fa0/20, Fa0/21, Fa0/22, Fa0/23,
                                         Gi0/1 ,Gi0/2
2    Sales                    active
3    Marketing                active     Fa0/3
5    Voice                    active     Fa0/3
```

Notice that port Fa0/3 is now a member of VLAN 3 and VLAN 5—two different types of VLANs. But, can you tell me where ports 1 and 2 are? And why aren't they showing up in the output of show vlan? That's right, because they are trunk ports!

We can also see this with the show interfaces *interface* switchport command:

```
S3#sh int fa0/3 switchport
Name: Fa0/3
```

```
Switchport: Enabled
```
Administrative Mode: static access
Operational Mode: static access
```
Administrative Trunking Encapsulation: negotiate
Negotiation of Trunking: Off
```
Access Mode VLAN: 3 (Marketing)
```
Trunking Native Mode VLAN: 1 (default)
Administrative Native VLAN tagging: enabled
```
Voice VLAN: 5 (Voice)

The highlighted output shows that Fa0/3 is an access port and a member of VLAN 3 (Marketing), as well as a member of the Voice VLAN 5.

That's it. Well, sort of. If you plugged devices into each VLAN port, they can only talk to other devices in the same VLAN. But as soon as you learn a bit more about trunking, we're going to enable inter-VLAN communication!

Configuring Trunk Ports

The 2960 switch only runs the IEEE 802.1q encapsulation method. To configure trunking on a FastEthernet port, use the interface command switchport mode trunk. It's a tad different on the 3560 switch.

The following switch output shows the trunk configuration on interfaces Fa0/15–18 as set to trunk:

```
S1(config)#int range f0/15-18
S1(config-if-range)#switchport trunk encapsulation dot1q
S1(config-if-range)#switchport mode trunk
```

If you have a switch that only runs the 802.1q encapsulation method, then you wouldn't use the encapsulation command as I did in the preceding output. Let's check out our trunk ports now:

```
S1(config-if-range)#do sh int f0/15 swi
Name: Fa0/15
Switchport: Enabled
```
Administrative Mode: trunk
Operational Mode: trunk
Administrative Trunking Encapsulation: dot1q
```
Operational Trunking Encapsulation: dot1q
Negotiation of Trunking: On
Access Mode VLAN: 1 (default)
Trunking Native Mode VLAN: 1 (default)
Administrative Native VLAN tagging: enabled
Voice VLAN: none
```

Notice that port Fa0/15 is a trunk and running 802.1q. Let's take another look:

```
S1(config-if-range)#do sh int trunk
Port          Mode              Encapsulation  Status        Native vlan
Fa0/15        on                802.1q         trunking      1
Fa0/16        on                802.1q         trunking      1
Fa0/17        on                802.1q         trunking      1
Fa0/18        on                802.1q         trunking      1
Port          Vlans allowed on trunk
Fa0/15        1-4094
Fa0/16        1-4094
Fa0/17        1-4094
Fa0/18        1-4094
```

Take note of the fact that ports 15–18 are now in the trunk mode of on and the encapsulation is now 802.1q instead of the negotiated ISL. Here's a description of the different options available when configuring a switch interface:

switchport mode access   I discussed this in the previous section, but this puts the interface (access port) into permanent nontrunking mode and negotiates to convert the link into a nontrunk link. The interface becomes a nontrunk interface regardless of whether the neighboring interface is a trunk interface. The port would be a dedicated layer 2 access port.

switchport mode dynamic auto   This mode makes the interface able to convert the link to a trunk link. The interface becomes a trunk interface if the neighboring interface is set to trunk or desirable mode. The default is dynamic auto on a lot of Cisco switches, but that default trunk method is changing to dynamic desirable on most new models.

switchport mode dynamic desirable   This one makes the interface actively attempt to convert the link to a trunk link. The interface becomes a trunk interface if the neighboring interface is set to trunk, desirable, or auto mode. I used to see this mode as the default on some switches, but not any longer. This is now the default switch port mode for all Ethernet interfaces on all new Cisco switches.

switchport mode trunk   Puts the interface into permanent trunking mode and negotiates to convert the neighboring link into a trunk link. The interface becomes a trunk interface even if the neighboring interface isn't a trunk interface.

switchport nonegotiate   Prevents the interface from generating DTP frames. You can use this command only when the interface switchport mode is access or trunk. You must manually configure the neighboring interface as a trunk interface to establish a trunk link.

Dynamic Trunking Protocol (DTP) is used for negotiating trunking on a link between two devices as well as negotiating the encapsulation type of either 802.1q or ISL. I use the nonegotiate command when I want dedicated trunk ports; no questions asked.

To disable trunking on an interface, use the switchport mode access command, which sets the port back to a dedicated layer 2 access switch port.

Defining the Allowed VLANs on a Trunk

As I've mentioned, trunk ports send and receive information from all VLANs by default, and if a frame is untagged, it's sent to the management VLAN. Understand that this applies to the extended range VLANs too.

But we can remove VLANs from the allowed list to prevent traffic from certain VLANs from traversing a trunked link. I'll show you how you'd do that, but first let me again demonstrate that all VLANs are allowed across the trunk link by default:

```
S1#sh int trunk
[output cut]
Port        Vlans allowed on trunk
Fa0/15      1-4094
Fa0/16      1-4094
Fa0/17      1-4094
Fa0/18      1-4094
S1(config)#int f0/15
S1(config-if)#switchport trunk allowed vlan 4,6,12,15
S1(config-if)#do show int trunk
[output cut]
Port        Vlans allowed on trunk
Fa0/15      4,6,12,15
Fa0/16      1-4094
Fa0/17      1-4094
Fa0/18      1-4094
```

The preceding command affected the trunk link configured on S1 port F0/15, causing it to permit all traffic sent and received for VLANs 4, 6, 12, and 15. You can try to remove VLAN 1 on a trunk link, but it will still send and receive management like CDP, DTP, and VTP, so what's the point?

To remove a range of VLANs, just use the hyphen:

```
S1(config-if)#switchport trunk allowed vlan remove 4-8
```

If by chance someone has removed some VLANs from a trunk link and you want to set the trunk back to default, just use this command:

```
S1(config-if)#switchport trunk allowed vlan all
```

Next, I want to show you how to configure a native VLAN for a trunk before we start routing between VLANs.

Changing or Modifying the Trunk Native VLAN

You can change the trunk port native VLAN from VLAN 1, which many people do for security reasons. To change the native VLAN, use the following command:

```
S1(config)#int f0/15
S1(config-if)#switchport trunk native vlan ?
  <1-4094>  VLAN ID of the native VLAN when this port is in trunking mode

S1(config-if)#switchport trunk native vlan 4
1w6d: %CDP-4-NATIVE_VLAN_MISMATCH: Native VLAN mismatch discovered on
FastEthernet0/15 (4), with S3 FastEthernet0/1 (1).
```

So we've changed our native VLAN on our trunk link to 4, and by using the show running-config command, I can see the configuration under the trunk link:

```
S1#sh run int f0/15
Building configuration...

Current configuration : 202 bytes
!
interface FastEthernet0/15
 description 1st connection to S3
 switchport trunk encapsulation dot1q
 switchport trunk native vlan 4
 switchport trunk allowed vlan 4,6,12,15
 switchport mode trunk
end

S1#!
```

Oops—wait a minute! You didn't think it would be this easy and would just start working, did you? Of course not! Here's the rub: If all switches don't have the same native VLAN configured on the given trunk links, then we'll start to receive this error, which happened immediately after I entered the command:

```
1w6d: %CDP-4-NATIVE_VLAN_MISMATCH: Native VLAN mismatch discovered
on FastEthernet0/15 (4), with S3 FastEthernet0/1 (1).
```

Actually, this is a good, noncryptic error, so either we can go to the other end of our trunk link(s) and change the native VLAN or we set the native VLAN back to the default to fix it. Here's how we'd do that:

```
S1(config-if)#no switchport trunk native vlan
1w6d: %SPANTREE-2-UNBLOCK_CONSIST_PORT: Unblocking FastEthernet0/15
on VLAN0004. Port consistency restored.
```

Now our trunk link is using the default VLAN 1 as the native VLAN. Just remember that all switches on a given trunk must use the same native VLAN or you'll have some serious management problems. These issues won't affect user data, just management traffic between switches. Now, let's mix it up by connecting a router into our switched network and configure inter-VLAN communication.

Configuring Inter-VLAN Routing

By default, only hosts that are members of the same VLAN can communicate. To change this and allow inter-VLAN communication, you need a router or a layer 3 switch. I'm going to start with the router approach.

To support ISL or 802.1q routing on a FastEthernet interface, the router's interface is divided into logical interfaces—one for each VLAN—as was shown in Figure 11.10. These are called *subinterfaces*. From a FastEthernet or Gigabit interface, you can set the interface to trunk with the encapsulation command:

```
ISR#config t
ISR(config)#int f0/0.1
ISR(config-subif)#encapsulation ?
  dot1Q  IEEE 802.1Q Virtual LAN
ISR(config-subif)#encapsulation dot1Q ?
  <1-4094>  IEEE 802.1Q VLAN ID
```

Notice that my 2811 router (named ISR) only supports 802.1q. We'd need an older-model router to run the ISL encapsulation, but why bother?

The subinterface number is only locally significant, so it doesn't matter which subinterface numbers are configured on the router. Most of the time, I'll configure a subinterface with the same number as the VLAN I want to route. It's easy to remember that way since the subinterface number is used only for administrative purposes.

It's really important that you understand that each VLAN is actually a separate subnet. True, I know—they don't *have* to be. But it really is a good idea to configure your VLANs as separate subnets, so just do that. Before we move on, I want to define *upstream routing*. This is a term used to define the router on a stick. This router will provide inter-VLAN routing, but it can also be used to forward traffic upstream from the switched network to other parts of the corporate network or Internet.

Now, I need to make sure you're fully prepared to configure inter-VLAN routing as well as determine the IP addresses of hosts connected in a switched VLAN environment. And as always, it's also a good idea to be able to fix any problems that may arise. To set you up for success, let me give you few examples.

First, start by looking at Figure 11.12 and read the router and switch configuration within it. By this point in the book, you should be able to determine the IP address, masks, and default gateways of each of the hosts in the VLANs.

FIGURE 11.12   Configuring inter-VLAN example 1

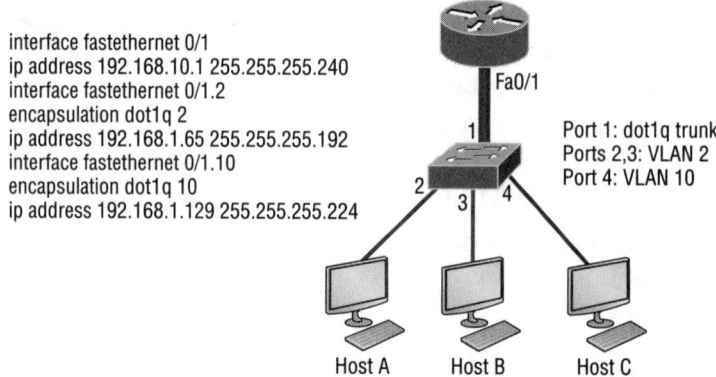

```
interface fastethernet 0/1
ip address 192.168.10.1 255.255.255.240
interface fastethernet 0/1.2
encapsulation dot1q 2
ip address 192.168.1.65 255.255.255.192
interface fastethernet 0/1.10
encapsulation dot1q 10
ip address 192.168.1.129 255.255.255.224
```

Fa0/1

Port 1: dot1q trunk
Ports 2,3: VLAN 2
Port 4: VLAN 10

Host A   Host B   Host C

The next step is to figure out which subnets are being used. By looking at the router configuration in the figure, you can see that we're using 192.168.10.0/28 for VLAN1, 192.168.1.64/26 with VLAN 2, and 192.168.1.128/27 for VLAN 10.

By looking at the switch configuration, you can see that ports 2 and 3 are in VLAN 2 and port 4 is in VLAN 10. This means that Host A and Host B are in VLAN 2 and Host C is in VLAN 10.

But wait—what's that IP address doing there under the physical interface? Can we even do that? Sure we can! If we place an IP address under the physical interface, the result is that frames sent from the IP address would be untagged. So what VLAN would those frames be a member of? By default, they would belong to VLAN 1, our management VLAN. This means the address 192.168.10.1/28 is my native VLAN IP address for this switch.

Here's what the hosts' IP addresses should be:

Host A: 192.168.1.66, 255.255.255.192, default gateway 192.168.1.65

Host B: 192.168.1.67, 255.255.255.192, default gateway 192.168.1.65

Host C: 192.168.1.130, 255.255.255.224, default gateway 192.168.1.129

The hosts could be any address in the range—I just chose the first available IP address after the default gateway address. That wasn't so hard, was it?

Now, again using Figure 11.12, let's go through the commands necessary to configure switch port 1 so it will establish a link with the router and provide inter-VLAN communication using the IEEE version for encapsulation. Keep in mind that the commands can vary slightly depending on what type of switch you're dealing with.

For a 2960 switch, use the following:

```
2960#config t
2960(config)#interface fa0/1
2960(config-if)#switchport mode trunk
```

That's it! As you already know, the 2960 switch can only run the 802.1q encapsulation, so there's no need to specify it. You can't anyway. For a 3560, it's basically the same, but because it can run ISL and 802.1q, you have to specify the trunking encapsulation protocol you're going to use.

> Remember that when you create a trunked link, all VLANs are allowed to pass data by default.

Let's take a look at Figure 11.13 and see what we can determine. This figure shows three VLANs, with two hosts in each of them. The router in Figure 11.13 is connected to the Fa0/1 switch port, and VLAN 4 is configured on port F0/6.

When looking at this diagram, keep in mind that these three factors are what Cisco expects you to know:

- The router is connected to the switch using subinterfaces.

- The switch port connecting to the router is a trunk port.

- The switch ports connecting to the clients and the hub are access ports, not trunk ports.

FIGURE 11.13   Inter-VLAN example 2

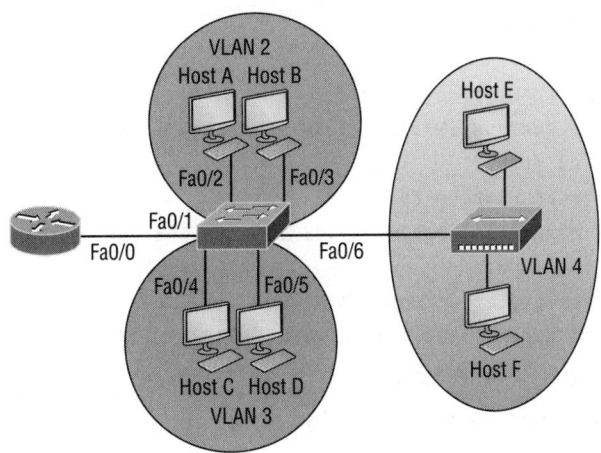

The configuration of the switch would look something like this:

```
2960#config t
2960(config)#int f0/1
2960(config-if)#switchport mode trunk
```

```
2960(config-if)#int f0/2
2960(config-if)#switchport access vlan 2
2960(config-if)#int f0/3
2960(config-if)#switchport access vlan 2
2960(config-if)#int f0/4
2960(config-if)#switchport access vlan 3
2960(config-if)#int f0/5
2960(config-if)#switchport access vlan 3
2960(config-if)#int f0/6
2960(config-if)#switchport access vlan 4
```

Before we configure the router, we need to design our logical network:

VLAN 1: 192.168.10.0/28

VLAN 2: 192.168.10.16/28

VLAN 3: 192.168.10.32/28

VLAN 4: 192.168.10.48/28

The configuration of the router would then look like this:

```
ISR#config t
ISR(config)#int fa0/0
ISR(config-if)#ip address 192.168.10.1 255.255.255.240
ISR(config-if)#no shutdown
ISR(config-if)#int f0/0.2
ISR(config-subif)#encapsulation dot1q 2
ISR(config-subif)#ip address 192.168.10.17 255.255.255.240
ISR(config-subif)#int f0/0.3
ISR(config-subif)#encapsulation dot1q 3
ISR(config-subif)#ip address 192.168.10.33 255.255.255.240
ISR(config-subif)#int f0/0.4
ISR(config-subif)#encapsulation dot1q 4
ISR(config-subif)#ip address 192.168.10.49 255.255.255.240
```

Notice I didn't tag VLAN 1. Even though I could have created a subinterface and tagged VLAN 1, it's not necessary with 802.1q because untagged frames are members of the native VLAN.

The hosts in each VLAN would be assigned an address from their subnet range, and the default gateway would be the IP address assigned to the router's subinterface in that VLAN.

Now, let's take a look at another figure and see if you can determine the switch and router configurations without looking at the answer—no cheating! Figure 11.14 shows a router connected to a 2960 switch with two VLANs. One host in each VLAN is assigned an IP address. What would your router and switch configurations be based on these IP addresses?

FIGURE 11.14   Inter-VLAN example 3

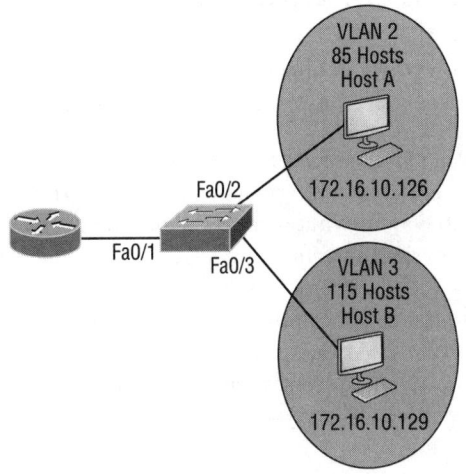

Since the hosts don't list a subnet mask, you have to look for the number of hosts used in each VLAN to figure out the block size. VLAN 2 has 85 hosts and VLAN 3 has 115 hosts. Each of these will fit in a block size of 128, which is a /25 mask, or 255.255.255.128.

You should know by now that the subnets are 0 and 128; the 0 subnet (VLAN 2) has a host range of 1–126, and the 128 subnet (VLAN 3) has a range of 129–254. You can almost be fooled since Host A has an IP address of 126, which makes it *almost* seem that Host A and B are in the same subnet. But they're not, and you're way too smart by now to be fooled by this one!

Here is the switch configuration:

```
2960#config t
2960(config)#int f0/1
2960(config-if)#switchport mode trunk
2960(config-if)#int f0/2
2960(config-if)#switchport access vlan 2
2960(config-if)#int f0/3
2960(config-if)#switchport access vlan 3
```

Here is the router configuration:

```
ISR#config t
ISR(config)#int f0/0
```

```
ISR(config-if)#ip address 192.168.10.1 255.255.255.0
ISR(config-if)#no shutdown
ISR(config-if)#int f0/0.2
ISR(config-subif)#encapsulation dot1q 2
ISR(config-subif)#ip address 172.16.10.1 255.255.255.128
ISR(config-subif)#int f0/0.3
ISR(config-subif)#encapsulation dot1q 3
ISR(config-subif)#ip address 172.16.10.254 255.255.255.128
```

I used the first address in the host range for VLAN 2 and the last address in the range for VLAN 3, but any address in the range would work. You would just have to configure the host's default gateway to whatever you make the router's address. Also, I used a different subnet for my physical interface, which is my management VLAN router's address.

Now, before we go on to the next example, I need to make sure you know how to set the IP address on the switch. Since VLAN 1 is typically the administrative VLAN, we'll use an IP address from out of that pool of addresses. Here's how to set the IP address of the switch (not nagging, but you really should already know this!):

```
2960#config t
2960(config)#int vlan 1
2960(config-if)#ip address 192.168.10.2 255.255.255.0
2960(config-if)#no shutdown
2960(config-if)#exit
2960(config)#ip default-gateway 192.168.10.1
```

Yes, you have to execute a no shutdown on the VLAN interface and set the ip default-gateway address to the router.

One more example, and then we'll move on to IVR using a multilayer switch—another important subject that you definitely don't want to miss! In Figure 11.15 there are two VLANs, plus the management VLAN 1. By looking at the router configuration, what's the IP address, subnet mask, and default gateway of Host A? Use the last IP address in the range for Host A's address.

If you really look carefully at the router configuration (the hostname in this configuration is just Router), there's a simple and quick answer. All subnets are using a /28, which is a 255.255.255.240 mask. This is a block size of 16. The router's address for VLAN 2 is in subnet 128. The next subnet is 144, so the broadcast address of VLAN 2 is 143 and the valid host range is 129–142. So the host address would be this:

IP address: 192.168.10.142

Mask: 255.255.255.240

Default gateway: 192.168.10.129

FIGURE 11.15   Inter-VLAN example 4

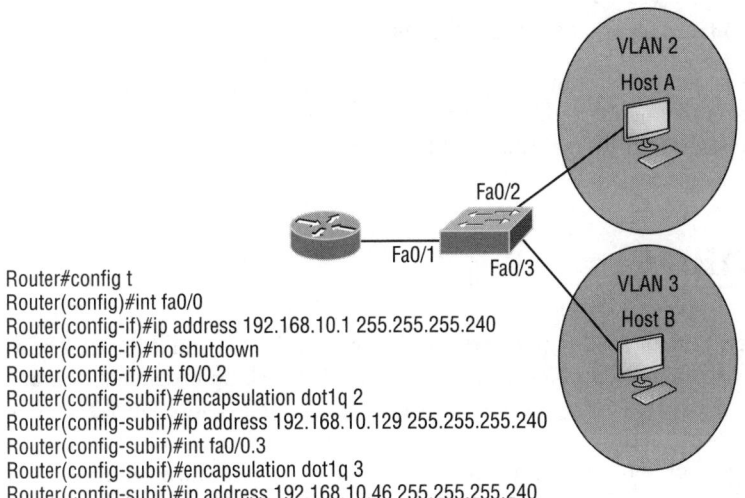

```
Router#config t
Router(config)#int fa0/0
Router(config-if)#ip address 192.168.10.1 255.255.255.240
Router(config-if)#no shutdown
Router(config-if)#int f0/0.2
Router(config-subif)#encapsulation dot1q 2
Router(config-subif)#ip address 192.168.10.129 255.255.255.240
Router(config-subif)#int fa0/0.3
Router(config-subif)#encapsulation dot1q 3
Router(config-subif)#ip address 192.168.10.46 255.255.255.240
```

This section was probably the hardest part of this entire book, and I honestly created the simplest configuration you can possibly get away with using to help you through it!

I'll use Figure 11.16 to demonstrate configuring inter-VLAN routing (IVR) with a multi-layer switch, which is often referred to as a switched virtual interface (SVI). I'm going to use the same network that I used to discuss a multilayer switch back in Figure 11.11, and I'll use this IP address scheme: 192.168.*x*.0/24, where *x* represents the VLAN subnet. In my example this will be the same as the VLAN number.

FIGURE 11.16   Inter-VLAN routing with a multilayer switch

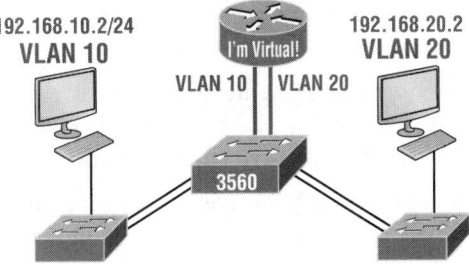

The hosts are already configured with the IP address, subnet mask, and default gateway address using the first address in the range. Now I just need to configure the routing on the switch, which is pretty simple actually:

```
S1(config)#ip routing
S1(config)#int vlan 10
```

```
S1(config-if)#ip address 192.168.10.1 255.255.255.0
S1(config-if)#int vlan 20
S1(config-if)#ip address 192.168.20.1 255.255.255.0
```

And that's it! Enable IP routing and create one logical interface for each VLAN using the interface vlan number command and voilà! You've now accomplished making inter-VLAN routing work on the backplane of the switch!

Summary

In this chapter, I introduced you to the world of virtual LANs and described how Cisco switches can use them. We talked about how VLANs break up broadcast domains in a switched internetwork—a very important, necessary thing because layer 2 switches only break up collision domains, and by default, all switches make up one large broadcast domain. I also described access links to you, and we went over how trunked VLANs work across a FastEthernet or faster link.

Trunking is a crucial technology to understand really well when you're dealing with a network populated by multiple switches that are running several VLANs.

You were also presented with some key troubleshooting and configuration examples for access and trunk ports, configuring trunking options, and a huge section on IVR.

Exam Essentials

Understand the term *frame tagging.* *Frame tagging* refers to VLAN identification; this is what switches use to keep track of all those frames as they're traversing a switch fabric. It's how switches identify which frames belong to which VLANs.

Understand the 802.1q VLAN identification method. This is a nonproprietary IEEE method of frame tagging. If you're trunking between a Cisco switched link and a different brand of switch, you have to use 802.1q for the trunk to work.

Remember how to set a trunk port on a 2960 switch. To set a port to trunking on a 2960, use the switchport mode trunk command.

Remember to check a switch port's VLAN assignment when plugging in a new host. If you plug a new host into a switch, then you must verify the VLAN membership of that port. If the membership is different than what is needed for that host, the host will not be able to reach the needed network services, such as a workgroup server or printer.

Remember how to create a Cisco router on a stick to provide inter-VLAN communication. You can use a Cisco FastEthernet or Gigabit Ethernet interface to provide inter-VLAN routing. The switch port connected to the router must be a trunk port; then you must create virtual interfaces (subinterfaces) on the router port for each VLAN connecting to it. The hosts in each VLAN will use this subinterface address as their default gateway address.

Remember how to provide inter-VLAN routing with a layer 3 switch.   You can use a layer 3 (multilayer) switch to provide IVR just as with a router on a stick, but using a layer 3 switch is more efficient and faster. First you start the routing process with the command ip routing, then create a virtual interface for each VLAN using the command interface vlan *vlan*, and then apply the IP address for that VLAN under that logical interface.

Written Lab 11

In this section, you'll complete the following lab to make sure you've got the information and concepts contained within them fully dialed in:

Lab 11.1: VLANs
You can find the answers to this lab in Appendix A, "Answers to Written Labs."
Write the answers to the following questions:

1. True/False: To provide IVR with a layer 3 switch, you place an IP address on each interface of the switch.

2. What protocol will stop loops in a layer 2 switched network?

3. VLANs break up _____ domains in a layer 2 switched network.

4. Which VLAN numbers are reserved by default?

5. If you have a switch that provides both ISL and 802.1q frame tagging, what command under the trunk interface will make the trunk use 802.1q?

6. What does trunking provide?

7. How many VLANs can you create on an IOS switch by default?

8. True/False: The 802.1q encapsulation is removed from the frame if the frame is forwarded out an access link.

9. What type of link on a switch is a member of only one VLAN?

10. You want to change from the default of VLAN 1 to VLAN 4 for untagged traffic. What command will you use?

Hands-on Labs

In these labs, you will use three switches and a router. To perform the last lab, you'll need a layer 3 switch.

Lab 11.1: Configuring and Verifying VLANs
Lab 11.2: Configuring and Verifying Trunk Links

Lab 11.3: Configuring Router on a Stick Routing

Lab 11.4: Configuring IVR with a Layer 3 Switch

In these labs, I'll use the following layout:

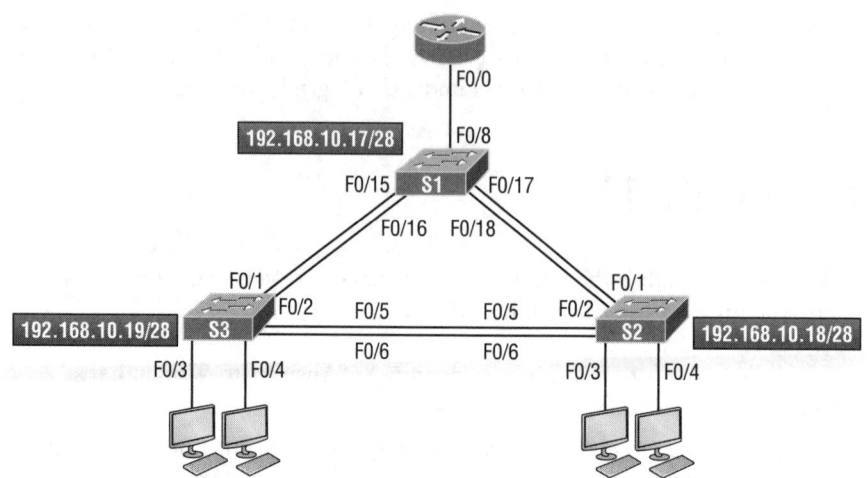

Hands-on Lab 11.1: Configuring and Verifying VLANs

This lab will have you configure VLANs from global configuration mode and then verify the VLANs.

1. Configure two VLANs on each switch, VLAN 10 and VLAN 20.

   ```
   S1(config)#vlan 10
   S1(config-vlan)#vlan 20

   S2(config)#vlan 10
   S2(config-vlan)#vlan 20

   S3(config)#vlan 10
   S3(config-vlan)#vlan 20
   ```

2. Use the show vlan and show vlan brief commands to verify your VLANs. Notice that all interfaces are in VLAN 1 by default.

   ```
   S1#sh vlan
   S1#sh vlan brief
   ```

Hands-on Lab 11.2: Configuring and Verifying Trunk Links

This lab will have you configure trunk links and then verify them.

1. Connect to each switch and configure trunking on all switch links. If you are using a switch that supports both 802.1q and ISL frame tagging, then use the encapsulation command; if not, then skip that command.

   ```
   S1#config t
   S1(config)#interface fa0/15
   S1(config-if)#switchport trunk encapsulation ?
     dot1q  Interface uses only 802.1q trunking encapsulation when trunking
     isl    Interface uses only ISL trunking encapsulation when trunking
     negotiate  Device will negotiate trunking encapsulation with peer on
   interface
   ```

   Again, if you typed the previous and received an error, then your switch does not support both encapsulation methods:

   ```
   S1 (config-if)#switchport trunk encapsulation dot1q
   S1 (config-if)#switchport mode trunk
   S1 (config-if)#interface fa0/16
   S1 (config-if)#switchport trunk encapsulation dot1q
   S1 (config-if)#switchport mode trunk
   S1 (config-if)#interface fa0/17
   S1 (config-if)#switchport trunk encapsulation dot1q
   S1 (config-if)#switchport mode trunk
   S1 (config-f)#interface fa0/18
   S1 (config-if)#switchport trunk encapsulation dot1q
   S1 (config-if)#switchport mode trunk
   ```

2. Configure the trunk links on your other switches.

3. On each switch, verify your trunk ports with the show interface trunk command:

   ```
   S1#show interface trunk
   ```

4. Verify the switchport configuration with the following:

   ```
   S1#show interface interface switchport
   ```

   The second *interface* in the command is a variable, such as Fa0/15.

Hands-on Lab 11.3: Configuring Router on a Stick Routing

In this lab, you'll use the router connected to port F0/8 of switch S1 to configure ROAS.

1. Configure the F0/0 of the router with two subinterfaces to provide inter-VLAN routing using 802.1q encapsulation. Use 172.16.10.0/24 for your management VLAN, 10.10.10.0/24 for VLAN 10, and 20.20.20.0/24 for VLAN 20.

```
Router#config t
Router (config)#int f0/0
Router (config-if)#ip address 172.16.10.1 255.255.255.0
Router (config-if)#interface f0/0.10
Router (config-subif)#encapsulation dot1q 10
Router (config-subif)#ip address 10.10.10.1 255.255.255.0
Router (config-subif)#interface f0/0.20
Router (config-subif)#encapsulation dot1q 20
Router (config-subif)#ip address 20.20.20.1 255.255.255.0
```

2. Verify the configuration with the show running-config command.

3. Configure trunking on interface F0/8 of the S1 switch connecting to your router.

4. Verify that your VLANs are still configured on your switches with the sh vlan command.

5. Configure your hosts to be in VLAN 10 and VLAN 20 with the switchport access vlan x command.

6. Ping from your PC to the router's subinterface configured for your VLAN.

7. Ping from your PC to your PC in the other VLAN. You are now routing through the router!

Hands-on Lab 11.4: Configuring IVR with a Layer 3 Switch

In this lab, you will disable the router and use the S1 switch to provide inter-VLAN routing by creating SVI's.

1. Connect to the S1 switch and make interface F0/8 an access port, which will make the router stop providing inter-VLAN routing.

2. Enable IP routing on the S1 switch.

```
S1(config)#ip routing
```

3. Create two new interfaces on the S1 switch to provide IVR.

```
S1(config)#interface vlan 10
S1(config-if)#ip address 10.10.10.1 255.255.255.0
S1(config-if)#interface vlan 20
S1(config-if)#ip address 20.20.20.1 255.255.255.0
```

4. Clear the ARP cache on the switch and hosts.

```
S1#clear arp
```

5. Ping from your PC to the router's subinterface configured for your VLAN.

6. Ping from your PC to your PC in the other VLAN. You are now routing through the S1 switch!

Review Questions

The following questions are designed to test your understanding of this chapter's material. For more information on how to get additional questions, please see www.lammle.com/ccna.

You can find the answers to these questions in Appendix B, "Answers to Review Questions."

1. Which of the following statements is true with regard to VLANs?

   A. VLANs greatly reduce network security.

   B. VLANs increase the number of collision domains while decreasing their size.

   C. VLANs decrease the number of broadcast domains while decreasing their size.

   D. Network adds, moves, and changes are achieved with ease by just configuring a port into the appropriate VLAN.

2. Write the command that must be present for this layer 3 switch to provide inter-VLAN routing between the two VLANs created with these commands:

   ```
   S1(config)#int vlan 10
   S1(config-if)#ip address 192.168.10.1 255.255.255.0
   S1(config-if)#int vlan 20
   S1(config-if)#ip address 192.168.20.1 255.255.255.0
   ```

3. In the following diagram, how must the port on each end of the line be configured to carry traffic between the four hosts?

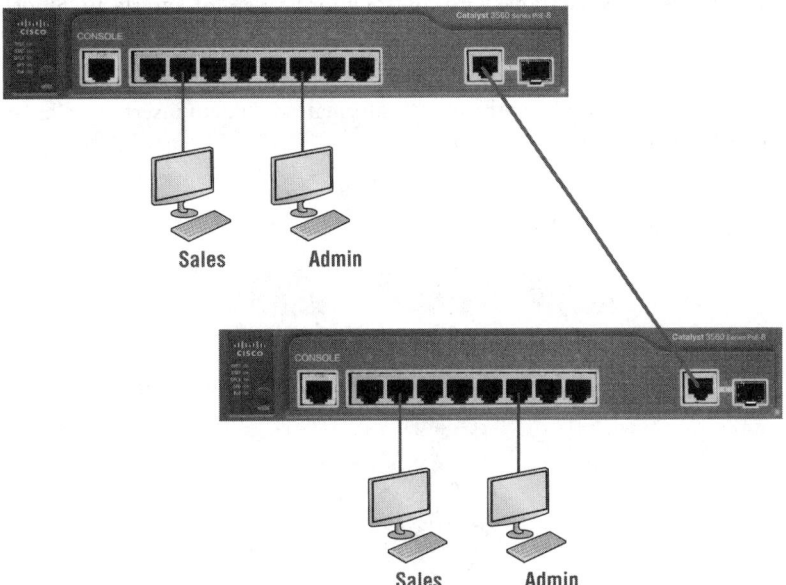

     A. Access port

     B. 10 GB

     C. Trunk

     D. Spanning

4. What is the only type of *second* VLAN of which an access port can be a member?

     A. Secondary

     B. Voice

     C. Primary

     D. Trunk

5. In the following configuration, what command is missing in the creation of the VLAN interface?

```
2960#config t
2960(config)#int vlan 1
2960(config-if)#ip address 192.168.10.2 255.255.255.0
2960(config-if)#exit
2960(config)#ip default-gateway 192.168.10.1
```

     A. `no shutdown` under int vlan 1

     B. `encapsulation dot1q 1` under int vlan 1

     C. `switchport access vlan 1`

     D. `passive-interface`

6. Which of the following statements is true with regard to ISL and 802.1q?

     A. 802.1q encapsulates the frame with control information; ISL inserts an ISL field along with tag control information.

     B. 802.1q is Cisco proprietary.

     C. ISL encapsulates the frame with control information; 802.1q inserts an 802.1q field along with tag control information.

     D. ISL is a standard.

7. What concept is depicted in the diagram?

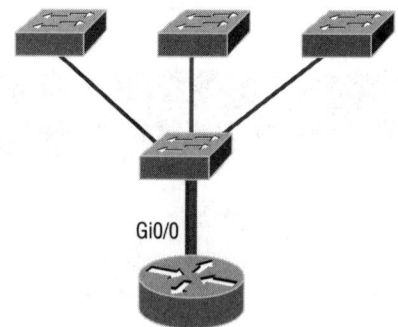

    A. Multiprotocol routing

    B. Passive interface

    C. Gateway redundancy

    D. Router on a stick

8. Write the command that places an interface into VLAN 2. Write only the command and not the prompt.

9. Write the command that generated the following output:

```
VLAN Name                            Status    Ports
---- -------------------------------- --------- ------------------------
1    default                          active    Fa0/1, Fa0/2, Fa0/3, Fa0/4
                                                Fa0/5, Fa0/6, Fa0/7, Fa0/8
                                                Fa0/9, Fa0/10, Fa0/11, Fa0/12
                                                Fa0/13, Fa0/14, Fa0/19, Fa0/20
                                                Fa0/21, Fa0/22, Fa0/23, Gi0/1
                                                Gi0/2
2    Sales                            active
3    Marketing                        active
4    Accounting                       active
[output cut]
```

10. In the configuration and diagram shown, what command is missing to enable inter-VLAN routing between VLAN 2 and VLAN 3?

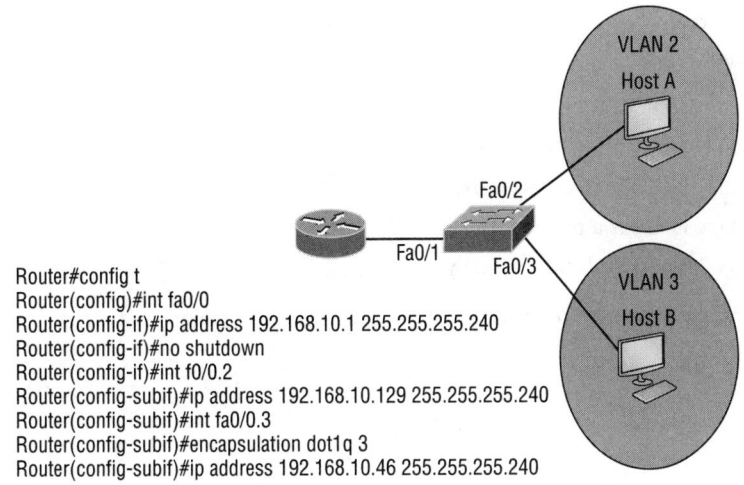

```
Router#config t
Router(config)#int fa0/0
Router(config-if)#ip address 192.168.10.1 255.255.255.240
Router(config-if)#no shutdown
Router(config-if)#int f0/0.2
Router(config-subif)#ip address 192.168.10.129 255.255.255.240
Router(config-subif)#int fa0/0.3
Router(config-subif)#encapsulation dot1q 3
Router(config-subif)#ip address 192.168.10.46 255.255.255.240
```

    A. `encapsulation dot1q 3` under int f0/0.2

    B. `encapsulation dot1q 2` under int f0/0.2

    C. `no shutdown` under int f0/0.2

    D. `no shutdown` under int f0/0.3

11. Based on the configuration shown here, what statement is true?

```
S1(config)#ip routing
S1(config)#int vlan 10
S1(config-if)#ip address 192.168.10.1 255.255.255.0
S1(config-if)#int vlan 20
S1(config-if)#ip address 192.168.20.1 255.255.255.0
```

   A. This is a multilayer switch.

   B. The two VLANs are in the same subnet.

   C. Encapsulation must be configured.

   D. VLAN 10 is the management VLAN.

12. What is true of the output shown here?

```
S1#sh vlan
```

```
VLAN Name                   Status    Ports
---- --------------------   --------- ------------------------------
1    default                active    Fa0/1, Fa0/2, Fa0/3, Fa0/4
                                      Fa0/5, Fa0/6, Fa0/7, Fa0/8
                                      Fa0/9, Fa0/10, Fa0/11, Fa0/12
                                      Fa0/13, Fa0/14, Fa0/19, Fa0/20,
                                      Fa0/22, Fa0/23, Gi0/1, Gi0/2

2    Sales                  active
3    Marketing              active    Fa0/21
4    Accounting             active
[output cut]
```

   A. Interface F0/15 is a trunk port.

   B. Interface F0/17 is an access port.

   C. Interface F0/21 is a trunk port.

   D. VLAN 1 was populated manually.

13. 802.1q untagged frames are members of the _____ VLAN.

   A. Auxiliary

   B. Voice

   C. Native

   D. Private

14. Write the command that generated the following output. Write only the command and not the prompt:

```
Name: Fa0/15
Switchport: Enabled
Administrative Mode: dynamic desirable
Operational Mode: trunk
Administrative Trunking Encapsulation: negotiate
Operational Trunking Encapsulation: isl
Negotiation of Trunking: On
Access Mode VLAN: 1 (default)
Trunking Native Mode VLAN: 1 (default)
Administrative Native VLAN tagging: enabled
Voice VLAN: none
[output cut]
```

15. In the switch output of question 12, how many broadcast domains are shown?

   A. 1

   B. 2

   C. 4

   D. 1001

16. In the diagram, what should be the default gateway address of Host B?

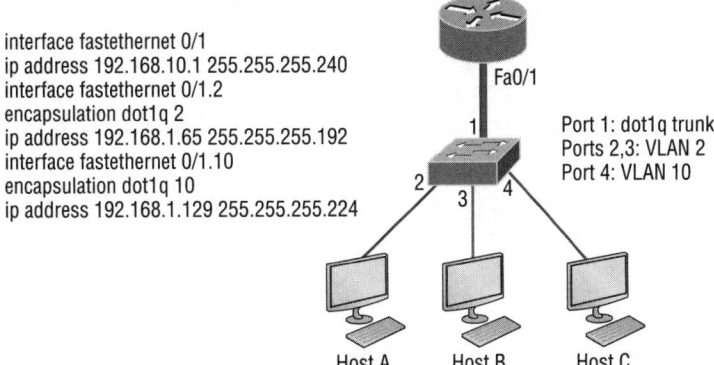

   A. 192.168.10.1

   B. 192.168.1.65

   C. 192.168.1.129

   D. 192.168.1.2

17. What is the purpose of frame tagging in virtual LAN (VLAN) configurations?

    A. Inter-VLAN routing

    B. Encryption of network packets

    C. Frame identification over trunk links

    D. Frame identification over access links

18. Write the command to create VLAN 2 on a layer 2 switch. Write only the command and not the prompt.

19. Which statement is true regarding 802.1q frame tagging?

    A. 802.1q adds a 26-byte trailer and 4-byte header.

    B. 802.1q uses a native VLAN.

    C. The original Ethernet frame is not modified.

    D. 802.1q only works with Cisco switches.

20. Write the command that prevents an interface from generating DTP frames. Write only the command and not the prompt.

Chapter

12

Security

THE FOLLOWING ICND1 EXAM TOPICS ARE COVERED IN THIS CHAPTER:

✓ **4.0 Infrastructure Services**

- 4.6 Configure, verify, and troubleshoot IPv4 standard numbered and named access list for routed interfaces

If you're a sys admin, it's my guess that shielding sensitive, critical data, as well as your network's resources, from every possible evil exploit is a top priority of yours, right? Good to know you're on the right page because Cisco has some really effective security solutions to equip you with the tools you'll need to make this happen in a very real way!

The first power tool I'm going to hand you is known as the access control list (ACL). Being able to execute an ACL proficiently is an integral part of Cisco's security solution, so I'm going to begin by showing you how to create and implement simple ACLs. From there, I'll move to demonstrating more advanced ACLs and describe how to implement them strategically to provide serious armor for an internetwork in today's challenging, high-risk environment.

In Appendix C, "Disabling and Configuring Network Services," I'll show you how to mitigate most security-oriented network threats. Make sure you don't skip this appendix because it is chock full of great security information, and the information it contains is part of the Cisco exam objectives as well!

The proper use and configuration of access lists is a vital part of router configuration because access lists are such versatile networking accessories. Contributing mightily to the efficiency and operation of your network, access lists give network managers a huge amount of control over traffic flow throughout the enterprise. With access lists, we can gather basic statistics on packet flow and security policies can be implemented. These dynamic tools also enable us to protect sensitive devices from the dangers of unauthorized access.

In this chapter, we'll cover ACLs for TCP/IP as well as explore effective ways available to us for testing and monitoring how well applied access lists are functioning. We'll begin now by discussing key security measures deployed using hardware devices and VLANs and then I'll introduce you to ACLs.

To find up-to-the-minute updates for this chapter, please see www.lammle .com/ccna or the book's web page at www.sybex.com/go/ccna.

Perimeter, Firewall, and Internal Routers

You see this a lot—typically, in medium to large enterprise networks—the various strategies for security are based on some mix of internal and perimeter routers plus firewall devices. Internal routers provide additional security by screening traffic to various parts of the protected corporate network, and they achieve this using access lists. You can see where each of these types of devices would be found in Figure 12.1.

FIGURE 12.1   A typical secured network

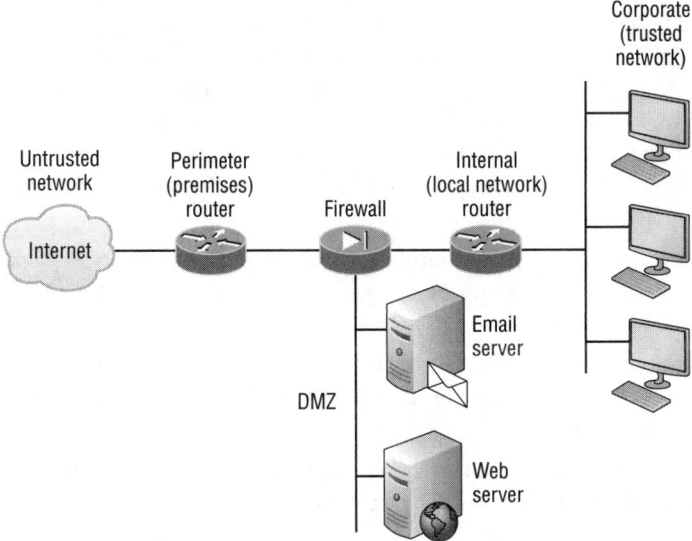

I'll use the terms *trusted network* and *untrusted network* throughout this chapter, so it's important that you can see where they're found in a typical secured network. The demilitarized zone (DMZ) can be global (real) Internet addresses or private addresses, depending on how you configure your firewall, but this is typically where you'll find the HTTP, DNS, email, and other Internet-type corporate servers.

As you now know, instead of using routers, we can create VLANs with switches on the inside trusted network. Multilayer switches containing their own security features can sometimes replace internal (LAN) routers to provide higher performance in VLAN architectures.

Let's look at some ways of protecting the internetwork using access lists.

Introduction to Access Lists

An *access list* is essentially a list of conditions that categorize packets, and they really come in handy when you need to exercise control over network traffic. An ACL would be your tool of choice for decision making in these situations.

One of the most common and easiest-to-understand uses of access lists is to filter unwanted packets when implementing security policies. For example, you can set them up to make very specific decisions about regulating traffic patterns so that they'll allow only certain hosts to access web resources on the Internet while restricting others. With the right combination of access lists, network managers arm themselves with the power to enforce nearly any security policy they can invent.

Creating access lists is really a lot like programming a series of if-then statements—if a given condition is met, then a given action is taken. If the specific condition isn't met, nothing happens and the next statement is evaluated. Access-list statements are basically packet filters that packets are compared against, categorized by, and acted upon accordingly. Once the lists are built, they can be applied to either inbound or outbound traffic on any interface. Applying an access list causes the router to analyze every packet crossing that interface in the specified direction and take the appropriate action.

There are three important rules that a packet follows when it's being compared with an access list:

- The packet is always compared with each line of the access list in sequential order—it will always start with the first line of the access list, move on to line 2, then line 3, and so on.

- The packet is compared with lines of the access list only until a match is made. Once it matches the condition on a line of the access list, the packet is acted upon and no further comparisons take place.

- There is an implicit "deny" at the end of each access list—this means that if a packet doesn't match the condition on any of the lines in the access list, the packet will be discarded.

Each of these rules has some powerful implications when filtering IP packets with access lists, so keep in mind that creating effective access lists definitely takes some practice.

There are two main types of access lists:

Standard access lists   These ACLs use only the source IP address in an IP packet as the condition test. All decisions are made based on the source IP address. This means that standard access lists basically permit or deny an entire suite of protocols. They don't distinguish between any of the many types of IP traffic such as Web, Telnet, UDP, and so on.

Extended access lists   Extended access lists can evaluate many of the other fields in the layer 3 and layer 4 headers of an IP packet. They can evaluate source and destination IP addresses, the Protocol field in the Network layer header, and the port number at the Transport layer header. This gives extended access lists the ability to make much more granular decisions when controlling traffic.

Named access lists   Hey, wait a minute—I said there were only two types of access lists but listed three! Well, technically there really are only two since *named access lists* are either standard or extended and not actually a distinct type. I'm just distinguishing them because they're created and referred to differently than standard and extended access lists are, but they're still functionally the same.

   We'll cover these types of access lists in more depth later in the chapter.

Once you create an access list, it's not really going to do anything until you apply it. Yes, they're there on the router, but they're inactive until you tell that router what to do with them. To use an access list as a packet filter, you need to apply it to an interface on the router where you want the traffic filtered. And you've got to specify which direction of traffic you want the access list applied to. There's a good reason for this—you may want different controls in place for traffic leaving your enterprise destined for the Internet than you'd want for traffic coming into your enterprise from the Internet. So, by specifying the direction of traffic, you can and must use different access lists for inbound and outbound traffic on a single interface:

Inbound access lists   When an access list is applied to inbound packets on an interface, those packets are processed through the access list before being routed to the outbound interface. Any packets that are denied won't be routed because they're discarded before the routing process is invoked.

Outbound access lists   When an access list is applied to outbound packets on an interface, packets are routed to the outbound interface and then processed through the access list before being queued.

There are some general access-list guidelines that you should keep in mind when creating and implementing access lists on a router:

- You can assign only one access list per interface per protocol per direction. This means that when applying IP access lists, you can have only one inbound access list and one outbound access list per interface.

When you consider the implications of the implicit deny at the end of any access list, it makes sense that you can't have multiple access lists applied on the same interface in the same direction for the same protocol. That's because any packets that don't match some condition in the first access list would be denied and there wouldn't be any packets left over to compare against a second access list!

- Organize your access lists so that the more specific tests are at the top.
- Anytime a new entry is added to the access list, it will be placed at the bottom of the list, which is why I highly recommend using a text editor for access lists.
- You can't remove one line from an access list. If you try to do this, you will remove the entire list. This is why it's best to copy the access list to a text editor before trying to edit the list. The only exception is when you're using named access lists.

You can edit, add, or delete a single line from a named access list. I'll show you how shortly.

- Unless your access list ends with a `permit any` command, all packets will be discarded if they do not meet any of the list's tests. This means every list should have at least one `permit` statement or it will deny all traffic.

- Create access lists and then apply them to an interface. Any access list applied to an interface without access-list test statements present will not filter traffic.

- Access lists are designed to filter traffic going through the router. They will not filter traffic that has originated from the router.

- Place IP standard access lists as close to the destination as possible. This is the reason we don't really want to use standard access lists in our networks. You can't put a standard access list close to the source host or network because you can only filter based on source address and all destinations would be affected as a result.

- Place IP extended access lists as close to the source as possible. Since extended access lists can filter on very specific addresses and protocols, you don't want your traffic to traverse the entire network just to be denied. By placing this list as close to the source address as possible, you can filter traffic before it uses up precious bandwidth.

Before I move on to demonstrate how to configure basic and extended ACLs, let's talk about how they can be used to mitigate the security threats I mentioned earlier.

Mitigating Security Issues with ACLs

The most common attack is a denial of service (DoS) attack. Although ACLs can help with a DoS, you really need an intrusion detection system (IDS) and intrusion prevention system (IPS) to help prevent these common attacks. Cisco sells the Adaptive Security Appliance (ASA), which has IDS/IPS modules, but lots of other companies sell IDS/IPS products too.

Here's a list of the many security threats you can mitigate with ACLs:

- IP address spoofing, inbound

- IP address spoofing, outbound

- Denial of service (DoS) TCP SYN attacks, blocking external attacks

- DoS TCP SYN attacks, using TCP Intercept

- DoS smurf attacks

- Denying/filtering ICMP messages, inbound

- Denying/filtering ICMP messages, outbound

- Denying/filtering Traceroute

> This is not an "introduction to security" book, so you may have to research some of the preceding terms if you don't understand them.

It's generally a bad idea to allow into a private network any external IP packets that contain the source address of any internal hosts or networks—just don't do it!

Here's a list of rules to live by when configuring ACLs from the Internet to your production network to mitigate security problems:

- Deny any source addresses from your internal networks.

- Deny any local host addresses (127.0.0.0/8).

- Deny any reserved private addresses (RFC 1918).
- Deny any addresses in the IP multicast address range (224.0.0.0/4).

None of these source addresses should be ever be allowed to enter your internetwork. Now finally, let's get our hands dirty and configure some basic and advanced access lists!

Standard Access Lists

Standard IP access lists filter network traffic by examining the source IP address in a packet. You create a *standard IP access list* by using the access-list numbers 1–99 or numbers in the expanded range of 1300–1999 because the type of ACL is generally differentiated using a number. Based on the number used when the access list is created, the router knows which type of syntax to expect as the list is entered. By using numbers 1–99 or 1300–1999, you're telling the router that you want to create a standard IP access list, so the router will expect syntax specifying only the source IP address in the test lines.

The following output displays a good example of the many access-list number ranges that you can use to filter traffic on your network. The IOS version delimits the protocols you can specify access for:

```
Corp(config)#access-list ?

  <1-99>           IP standard access list
  <100-199>        IP extended access list
  <1000-1099>      IPX SAP access list
  <1100-1199>      Extended 48-bit MAC address access list
  <1200-1299>      IPX summary address access list
  <1300-1999>      IP standard access list (expanded range)
  <200-299>        Protocol type-code access list
  <2000-2699>      IP extended access list (expanded range)
  <2700-2799>      MPLS access list
  <300-399>        DECnet access list
  <700-799>        48-bit MAC address access list
  <800-899>        IPX standard access list
  <900-999>        IPX extended access list
  dynamic-extended Extend the dynamic ACL absolute timer
  rate-limit       Simple rate-limit specific access list
```

Wow—there certainly are lot of old protocols listed in that output! IPX and DECnet would no longer be used in any of today's networks. Let's take a look at the syntax used when creating a standard IP access list:

```
Corp(config)#access-list 10 ?
  deny    Specify packets to reject
```

```
permit  Specify packets to forward
remark  Access list entry comment
```

As I said, by using the access-list numbers 1–99 or 1300–1999, you're telling the router that you want to create a standard IP access list, which means you can only filter on source IP address.

Once you've chosen the access-list number, you need to decide whether you're creating a permit or deny statement. I'm going to create a deny statement now:

```
Corp(config)#access-list 10 deny ?
  Hostname or A.B.C.D  Address to match
  any                  Any source host
  host                 A single host address
```

The next step is more detailed because there are three options available in it:

1. The first option is the any parameter, which is used to permit or deny any source host or network.

2. The second choice is to use an IP address to specify either a single host or a range of them.

3. The last option is to use the host command to specify a specific host only.

The any command is pretty obvious—any source address matches the statement, so every packet compared against this line will match. The host command is relatively simple too, as you can see here:

```
Corp(config)#access-list 10 deny host ?
  Hostname or A.B.C.D  Host address
Corp(config)#access-list 10 deny host 172.16.30.2
```

This tells the list to deny any packets from host 172.16.30.2. The default parameter is host. In other words, if you type **access-list 10 deny 172.16.30.2**, the router assumes you mean host 172.16.30.2 and that's exactly how it will show in your running-config.

But there's another way to specify either a particular host or a range of hosts, and it's known as wildcard masking. In fact, to specify any range of hosts, you must use wildcard masking in the access list.

So exactly what is wildcard masking? Coming up, I'm going to show you using a standard access list example. I'll also guide you through how to control access to a virtual terminal.

Wildcard Masking

Wildcards are used with access lists to specify an individual host, a network, or a specific range of a network or networks. The block sizes you learned about earlier used to specify a range of addresses are key to understanding wildcards.

Let me pause here for a quick review of block sizes before we go any further. I'm sure you remember that the different block sizes available are 64, 32, 16, 8, and 4. When you need to specify a range of addresses, you choose the next-largest block size for your needs. So if you need to specify 34 networks, you need a block size of 64. If you want to specify 18 hosts, you need a block size of 32. If you specify only 2 networks, then go with a block size of 4.

Wildcards are used with the host or network address to tell the router a range of available addresses to filter. To specify a host, the address would look like this:

```
172.16.30.5 0.0.0.0
```

The four zeros represent each octet of the address. Whenever a zero is present, it indicates that the octet in the address must match the corresponding reference octet exactly. To specify that an octet can be any value, use the value 255. Here's an example of how a /24 subnet is specified with a wildcard mask:

```
172.16.30.0 0.0.0.255
```

This tells the router to match up the first three octets exactly, but the fourth octet can be any value.

Okay—that was the easy part. But what if you want to specify only a small range of subnets? This is where block sizes come in. You have to specify the range of values in a block size, so you can't choose to specify 20 networks. You can only specify the exact amount that the block size value allows. This means that the range would have to be either 16 or 32, but not 20.

Let's say that you want to block access to the part of the network that ranges from 172.16.8.0 through 172.16.15.0. To do that, you would go with a block size of 8, your network number would be 172.16.8.0, and the wildcard would be 0.0.7.255. The 7.255 equals the value the router will use to determine the block size. So together, the network number and the wildcard tell the router to begin at 172.16.8.0 and go up a block size of eight addresses to network 172.16.15.0.

This really is easier than it looks! I could certainly go through the binary math for you, but no one needs that kind of pain because all you have to do is remember that the wildcard is always one number less than the block size. So, in our example, the wildcard would be 7 since our block size is 8. If you used a block size of 16, the wildcard would be 15. Easy, right?

Just to make you've got this, we'll go through some examples that will definitely help you nail it down. The following example tells the router to match the first three octets exactly but that the fourth octet can be anything:

```
Corp(config)#access-list 10 deny 172.16.10.0 0.0.0.255
```

The next example tells the router to match the first two octets and that the last two octets can be any value:

```
Corp(config)#access-list 10 deny 172.16.0.0 0.0.255.255
```

Now, try to figure out this next line:

```
Corp(config)#access-list 10 deny 172.16.16.0 0.0.3.255
```

This configuration tells the router to start at network 172.16.16.0 and use a block size of 4. The range would then be 172.16.16.0 through 172.16.19.255, and by the way, the Cisco objectives seem to really like this one!

Let's keep practicing. What about this next one?

```
Corp(config)#access-list 10 deny 172.16.16.0 0.0.7.255
```

This example reveals an access list starting at 172.16.16.0 going up a block size of 8 to 172.16.23.255.

Let's keep at it... What do you think the range of this one is?

```
Corp(config)#access-list 10 deny 172.16.32.0 0.0.15.255
```

This one begins at network 172.16.32.0 and goes up a block size of 16 to 172.16.47.255. You're almost done practicing! After a couple more, we'll configure some real ACLs.

```
Corp(config)#access-list 10 deny 172.16.64.0 0.0.63.255
```

This example starts at network 172.16.64.0 and goes up a block size of 64 to 172.16.127.255.

What about this last example?

```
Corp(config)#access-list 10 deny 192.168.160.0 0.0.31.255
```

This one shows us that it begins at network 192.168.160.0 and goes up a block size of 32 to 192.168.191.255.

Here are two more things to keep in mind when working with block sizes and wildcards:

- Each block size must start at 0 or a multiple of the block size. For example, you can't say that you want a block size of 8 and then start at 12. You must use 0–7, 8–15, 16–23, etc. For a block size of 32, the ranges are 0–31, 32–63, 64–95, etc.

- The command any is the same thing as writing out the wildcard 0.0.0.0 255.255.255.255.

Wildcard masking is a crucial skill to master when creating IP access lists, and it's used identically when creating standard and extended IP access lists.

Standard Access List Example

In this section, you'll learn how to use a standard access list to stop specific users from gaining access to the Finance department LAN.

In Figure 12.2, a router has three LAN connections and one WAN connection to the Internet. Users on the Sales LAN should not have access to the Finance LAN, but they should be able to access the Internet and the marketing department files. The Marketing LAN needs to access the Finance LAN for application services.

FIGURE 12.2   IP access list example with three LANs and a WAN connection

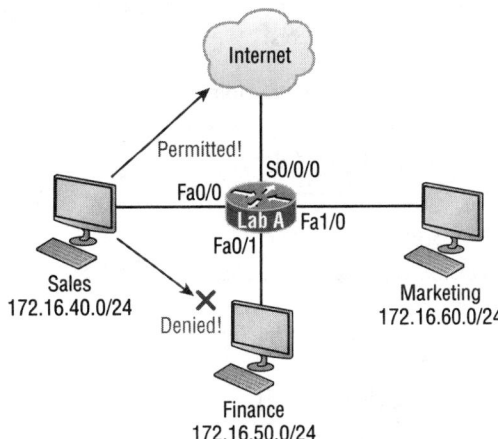

We can see that the following standard IP access list is configured on the router:

```
Lab_A#config t
Lab_A(config)#access-list 10 deny 172.16.40.0 0.0.0.255
Lab_A(config)#access-list 10 permit any
```

It's very important to remember that the any command is the same thing as saying the following using wildcard masking:

```
Lab_A(config)#access-list 10 permit 0.0.0.0 255.255.255.255
```

Since the wildcard mask says that none of the octets are to be evaluated, every address matches the test condition, so this is functionally doing the same as using the any keyword.

At this point, the access list is configured to deny source addresses from the Sales LAN to the Finance LAN and to allow everyone else. But remember, no action will be taken until the access list is applied on an interface in a specific direction!

But where should this access list be placed? If you place it as an incoming access list on Fa0/0, you might as well shut down the FastEthernet interface because all of the Sales LAN devices will be denied access to all networks attached to the router. The best place to apply this access list is on the Fa0/1 interface as an outbound list:

```
Lab_A(config)#int fa0/1
Lab_A(config-if)#ip access-group 10 out
```

Doing this completely stops traffic from 172.16.40.0 from getting out FastEthernet0/1. It has no effect on the hosts from the Sales LAN accessing the Marketing LAN and the Internet because traffic to those destinations doesn't go through interface Fa0/1. Any packet trying to exit out Fa0/1 will have to go through the access list first. If there were an inbound list placed on F0/0, then any packet trying to enter interface F0/0 would have to go through the access list before being routed to an exit interface.

Now, let's take a look at another standard access list example. Figure 12.3 shows an internetwork of two routers with four LANs.

FIGURE 12.3   IP standard access list example 2

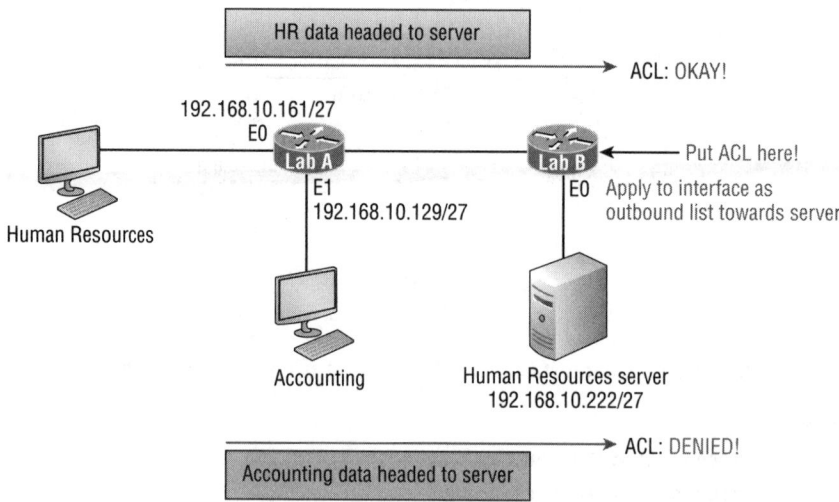

Now we're going to stop the Accounting users from accessing the Human Resources server attached to the Lab_B router but allow all other users access to that LAN using a standard ACL. What kind of standard access list would we need to create and where would we place it to achieve our goals?

The real answer is that we should use an extended access list and place it closest to the source! But this question specifies using a standard access list, and as a rule, standard ACLs are placed closest to the destination. In this example, Ethernet 0 is the outbound interface on the Lab_B router and here's the access list that should be placed on it:

```
Lab_B#config t
Lab_B(config)#access-list 10 deny 192.168.10.128 0.0.0.31
Lab_B(config)#access-list 10 permit any
Lab_B(config)#interface Ethernet 0
Lab_B(config-if)#ip access-group 10 out
```

Keep in mind that to be able to answer this question correctly, you really need to understand subnetting, wildcard masks, and how to configure and implement ACLs. The accounting subnet is the 192.168.10.128/27, which is a 255.255.255.224, with a block size of 32 in the fourth octet.

With all this in mind and before we move on to restricting Telnet access on a router, let's take a look at one more standard access list example. This one is going to require some thought. In Figure 12.4, you have a router with four LAN connections and one WAN connection to the Internet.

FIGURE 12.4   IP standard access list example 3

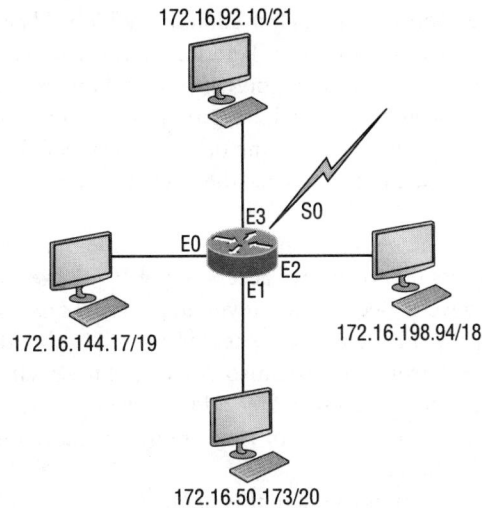

172.16.92.10/21

E3   S0
E0
E2
E1

172.16.144.17/19

172.16.198.94/18

172.16.50.173/20

Okay—you need to write an access list that will stop access from each of the four LANs shown in the diagram to the Internet. Each of the LANs reveals a single host's IP address, which you need to use to determine the subnet and wildcards of each LAN to configure the access list.

Here is an example of what your answer should look like, beginning with the network on E0 and working through to E3:

```
Router(config)#access-list 1 deny 172.16.128.0 0.0.31.255
Router(config)#access-list 1 deny 172.16.48.0 0.0.15.255
Router(config)#access-list 1 deny 172.16.192.0 0.0.63.255
Router(config)#access-list 1 deny 172.16.88.0 0.0.7.255
Router(config)#access-list 1 permit any
Router(config)#interface serial 0
Router(config-if)#ip access-group 1 out
```

Sure, you could have done this with one line:

```
Router(config)#access-list 1 deny 172.16.0.0 0.0.255.255
```

But what fun is that?

And remember the reasons for creating this list. If you actually applied this ACL on the router, you'd effectively shut down access to the Internet, so why even have an Internet connection? I included this exercise so you can practice how to use block sizes with access lists, which is vital for succeeding when you take the Cisco exam!

Controlling VTY (Telnet/SSH) Access

Trying to stop users from telnetting or trying to SSH to a router is really challenging because any active interface on a router is fair game for VTY/SSH access. Creating an extended IP ACL that limits access to every IP address on the router may sound like a solution, but if you did that, you'd have to apply it inbound on every interface, which really wouldn't scale well if you happen to have dozens, even hundreds, of interfaces, now would it? And think of all the latency dragging down your network as a result of each and every router checking every packet just in case the packet was trying to access your VTY lines—horrible!

Don't give up—there's always a solution! And in this case, a much better one, which employs a standard IP access list to control access to the VTY lines themselves.

Why does this work so well? Because when you apply an access list to the VTY lines, you don't need to specify the protocol since access to the VTY already implies terminal access via the Telnet or SSH protocols. You also don't need to specify a destination address because it really doesn't matter which interface address the user used as a target for the Telnet session. All you really need control of is where the user is coming from, which is betrayed by their source IP address.

You need to do these two things to make this happen:

1. Create a standard IP access list that permits only the host or hosts you want to be able to telnet into the routers.

2. Apply the access list to the VTY line with the `access-class in` command.

Here, I'm allowing only host 172.16.10.3 to telnet into a router:

```
Lab_A(config)#access-list 50 permit host 172.16.10.3
Lab_A(config)#line vty 0 4
Lab_A(config-line)#access-class 50 in
```

Because of the implied deny any at the end of the list, the ACL stops any host from telnetting into the router except the host 172.16.10.3, regardless of the individual IP address on the router being used as a target. It's a good idea to include an admin subnet address as the source instead of a single host, but the reason I demonstrated this was to show you how to create security on your VTY lines without adding latency to your router.

Real World Scenario

Should You Secure Your VTY Lines on a Router?

You're monitoring your network and notice that someone has telnetted into your core router by using the show users command. You use the disconnect command and they're disconnected from the router, but you notice that they're right back in there a few minutes later. You consider putting an ACL on the router interfaces, but you don't want to add latency on each interface since your router is already pushing a lot of packets. At this point, you think about putting an access list on the VTY lines themselves, but not having done this before, you're not sure if this is a safe alternative to putting an ACL on each interface. Would placing an ACL on the VTY lines be a good idea for this network?

Yes—absolutely! And the access-class command covered in this chapter is the way to do it. Why? Because it doesn't use an access list that just sits on an interface looking at every packet, resulting in unnecessary overhead and latency.

When you put the access-class in command on the VTY lines, only packets trying to telnet into the router will be checked and compared, providing easy-to-configure yet solid security for your router!

 Just a reminder—Cisco recommends using Secure Shell (SSH) instead of Telnet on the VTY lines of a router, as we covered in Chapter 6, "Cisco's Internetworking Operating System (IOS)," so review that chapter if you need a refresher on SSH and how to configure it on your routers and switches.

Extended Access Lists

Let's go back to the standard IP access list example where you had to block all access from the Sales LAN to the finance department and add a new requirement. You now must allow Sales to gain access to a certain server on the Finance LAN but not to other network services for security reasons. What's the solution? Applying a standard IP access list won't allow users to get to one network service but not another because a standard ACL won't allow you to make decisions based on both source and destination addresses. It makes decisions based only on source address, so we need another way to achieve our new goal—but what is it?

Using an *extended access list* will save the day because extended ACLs allow us to specify source and destination addresses as well as the protocol and port number that identify the upper-layer protocol or application. An extended ACL is just what we need to affectively allow users access to a physical LAN while denying them access to specific hosts— even specific services on those hosts!

Yes, I am well aware there are no ICND1 objectives for extended access lists, but you need to understand Extended ACL's for when you get to ICND2 troubleshooting, so I added foundation here.

We're going to take a look at the commands we have in our arsenal, but first, you need to know that you must use the extended access-list range from 100 to 199. The 2000–2699 range is also available for extended IP access lists.

After choosing a number in the extended range, you need to decide what type of list entry to make. For this example, I'm going with a deny list entry:

```
Corp(config)#access-list 110 ?
  deny      Specify packets to reject
  dynamic   Specify a DYNAMIC list of PERMITs or DENYs
  permit    Specify packets to forward
  remark    Access list entry comment
```

And once you've settled on the type of ACL, you then need to select a protocol field entry:

```
Corp(config)#access-list 110 deny ?
  <0-255>   An IP protocol number
  ahp       Authentication Header Protocol
  eigrp     Cisco's EIGRP routing protocol
  esp       Encapsulation Security Payload
  gre       Cisco's GRE tunneling
  icmp      Internet Control Message Protocol
  igmp      Internet Gateway Message Protocol
  ip        Any Internet Protocol
  ipinip    IP in IP tunneling
  nos       KA9Q NOS compatible IP over IP tunneling
  ospf      OSPF routing protocol
  pcp       Payload Compression Protocol
  pim       Protocol Independent Multicast
  tcp       Transmission Control Protocol
  udp       User Datagram Protocol
```

If you want to filter by Application layer protocol, you have to choose the appropriate layer 4 transport protocol after the `permit` or `deny` statement. For example, to filter Telnet or FTP, choose TCP since both Telnet and FTP use TCP at the Transport layer. Selecting IP wouldn't allow you to specify a particular application protocol later and only filter based on source and destination addresses.

So now, let's filter an Application layer protocol that uses TCP by selecting TCP as the protocol and indicating the specific destination TCP port at the end of the line. Next, we'll be prompted for the source IP address of the host or network and we'll choose the any command to allow any source address:

```
Corp(config)#access-list 110 deny tcp ?
  A.B.C.D  Source address
  any      Any source host
  host     A single source host
```

After we've selected the source address, we can then choose the specific destination address:

```
Corp(config)#access-list 110 deny tcp any ?
  A.B.C.D  Destination address
  any      Any destination host
  eq       Match only packets on a given port number
  gt       Match only packets with a greater port number
  host     A single destination host
  lt       Match only packets with a lower port number
  neq      Match only packets not on a given port number
  range    Match only packets in the range of port numbers
```

In this output, you can see that any source IP address that has a destination IP address of 172.16.30.2 has been denied:

```
Corp(config)#access-list 110 deny tcp any host 172.16.30.2 ?
  ack          Match on the ACK bit
  dscp         Match packets with given dscp value
  eq           Match only packets on a given port number
  established  Match established connections
  fin          Match on the FIN bit
  fragments    Check non-initial fragments
  gt           Match only packets with a greater port number
  log          Log matches against this entry
  log-input    Log matches against this entry, including input interface
  lt           Match only packets with a lower port number
  neq          Match only packets not on a given port number
  precedence   Match packets with given precedence value
  psh          Match on the PSH bit
  range        Match only packets in the range of port numbers
  rst          Match on the RST bit
  syn          Match on the SYN bit
```

```
time-range    Specify a time-range
tos           Match packets with given TOS value
urg           Match on the URG bit
<cr>
```

And once we have the destination host addresses in place, we just need to specify the type of service to deny using the equal to command, entered as eq. The following help screen reveals the options available now. You can choose a port number or use the application name:

```
Corp(config)#access-list 110 deny tcp any host 172.16.30.2 eq ?
  <0-65535>     Port number
  bgp           Border Gateway Protocol (179)
  chargen       Character generator (19)
  cmd           Remote commands (rcmd, 514)
  daytime       Daytime (13)
  discard       Discard (9)
  domain        Domain Name Service (53)
  drip          Dynamic Routing Information Protocol (3949)
  echo          Echo (7)
  exec          Exec (rsh, 512)
  finger        Finger (79)
  ftp           File Transfer Protocol (21)
  ftp-data      FTP data connections (20)
  gopher        Gopher (70)
  hostname      NIC hostname server (101)
  ident         Ident Protocol (113)
  irc           Internet Relay Chat (194)
  klogin        Kerberos login (543)
  kshell        Kerberos shell (544)
  login         Login (rlogin, 513)
  lpd           Printer service (515)
  nntp          Network News Transport Protocol (119)
  pim-auto-rp   PIM Auto-RP (496)
  pop2          Post Office Protocol v2 (109)
  pop3          Post Office Protocol v3 (110)
  smtp          Simple Mail Transport Protocol (25)
  sunrpc        Sun Remote Procedure Call (111)
  syslog        Syslog (514)
  tacacs        TAC Access Control System (49)
  talk          Talk (517)
  telnet        Telnet (23)
```

time	Time (37)
uucp	Unix-to-Unix Copy Program (540)
whois	Nicname (43)
www	World Wide Web (HTTP, 80)

Now let's block Telnet (port 23) to host 172.16.30.2 only. If the users want to use FTP, fine—that's allowed. The `log` command is used to log messages every time the access list entry is hit. This can be an extremely cool way to monitor inappropriate access attempts, but be careful because in a large network, this command can overload your console's screen with messages!

Here's our result:

```
Corp(config)#access-list 110 deny tcp any host 172.16.30.2 eq 23 log
```

This line says to deny any source host trying to telnet to destination host 172.16.30.2. Keep in mind that the next line is an implicit deny by default. If you apply this access list to an interface, you might as well just shut the interface down because by default, there's an implicit deny `all` at the end of every access list. So we've got to follow up the access list with the following command:

```
Corp(config)#access-list 110 permit ip any any
```

The IP in this line is important because it will permit the IP stack. If TCP was used instead of IP in this line, then UDP, etc. would all be denied. Remember, the `0.0.0.0 255.255.255.255` is the same command as any, so the command could also look like this:

```
Corp(config)#access-list 110 permit ip 0.0.0.0 255.255.255.255
0.0.0.0 255.255.255.255
```

But if you did this, when you looked at the running-config, the commands would be replaced with the any any. I like efficiency so I'll just use the any command because it requires less typing.

As always, once our access list is created, we must apply it to an interface with the same command used for the IP standard list:

```
Corp(config-if)#ip access-group 110 in
```

Or this:

```
Corp(config-if)#ip access-group 110 out
```

Next, we'll check out some examples of how to use an extended access list.

Extended Access List Example 1

For our first scenario, we'll use Figure 12.5. What do we need to do to deny access to a host at 172.16.50.5 on the finance department LAN for both Telnet and FTP services? All other services on this and all other hosts are acceptable for the sales and marketing departments to access.

FIGURE 12.5   Extended ACL example 1

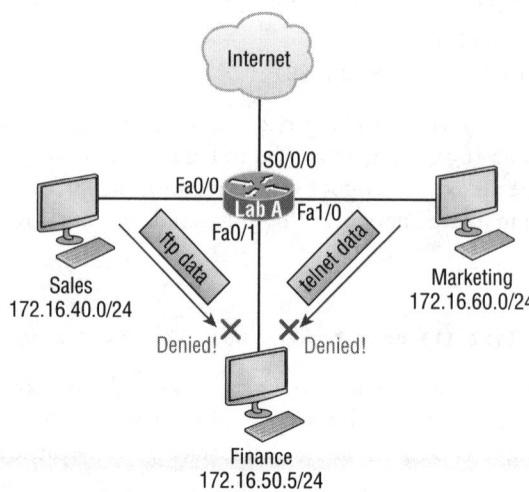

Here's the ACL we must create:

```
Lab_A#config t
Lab_A(config)#access-list 110 deny tcp any host 172.16.50.5 eq 21
Lab_A(config)#access-list 110 deny tcp any host 172.16.50.5 eq 23
Lab_A(config)#access-list 110 permit ip any any
```

The access-list 110 tells the router we're creating an extended IP ACL. The tcp is the protocol field in the Network layer header. If the list doesn't say tcp here, you cannot filter by TCP port numbers 21 and 23 as shown in the example. Remember that these values indicate FTP and Telnet, which both use TCP for connection-oriented services. The any command is the source, which means any source IP address, and the host is the destination IP address. This ACL says that all IP traffic will be permitted from any host except FTP and Telnet to host 172.16.50.5 from any source.

 Remember that instead of the host 172.16.50.5 command when we created the extended access list, we could have entered 172.16.50.5 0.0.0.0. There would be no difference in the result other than the router would change the command to host 172.16.50.5 in the running-config.

After the list is created, it must be applied to the FastEthernet 0/1 interface outbound because we want to block all traffic from getting to host 172.16.50.5 and performing FTP and Telnet. If this list was created to block access only from the Sales LAN to host 172.16.50.5, then we'd have put this list closer to the source, or on FastEthernet 0/0. In that situation, we'd apply the list to inbound traffic. This highlights the fact that you really need to analyze each situation carefully before creating and applying ACLs!

Now let's go ahead and apply the list to interface Fa0/1 to block all outside FTP and Telnet access to the host 172.16.50.5:

```
Lab_A(config)#int fa0/1
Lab_A(config-if)#ip access-group 110 out
```

Extended Access List Example 2

We're going to use Figure 12.4 again, which has four LANs and a serial connection. We need to prevent Telnet access to the networks attached to the E1 and E2 interfaces.

The configuration on the router would look something like this, although the answer can vary:

```
Router(config)#access-list 110 deny tcp any 172.16.48.0 0.0.15.255
eq 23
Router(config)#access-list 110 deny tcp any 172.16.192.0 0.0.63.255
eq 23
Router(config)#access-list 110 permit ip any any
Router(config)#interface Ethernet 1
Router(config-if)#ip access-group 110 out
Router(config-if)#interface Ethernet 2
Router(config-if)#ip access-group 110 out
```

Here are the key factors to understand from this list:

- First, you need to verify that the number range is correct for the type of access list you are creating. In this example, it's extended, so the range must be 100–199.

- Second, you must verify that the protocol field matches the upper-layer process or application, which in this case, is TCP port 23 (Telnet).

 The protocol parameter must be TCP since Telnet uses TCP. If it were TFTP instead, then the protocol parameter would have to be UDP because TFTP uses UDP at the Transport layer.

- Third, verify that the destination port number matches the application you're filtering for. In this case, port 23 matches Telnet, which is correct, but know that you can also type **telnet** at the end of the line instead of 23.

- Finally, the test statement permit ip any any is important to have there at the end of the list because it means to enable all packets other than Telnet packets destined for the LANs connected to Ethernet 1 and Ethernet 2.

Extended Access List Example 3

I want to guide you through one more extended ACL example before we move on to named ACLs. Figure 12.6 displays the network we're going to use for this last scenario.

FIGURE 12.6   Extended ACL example 3

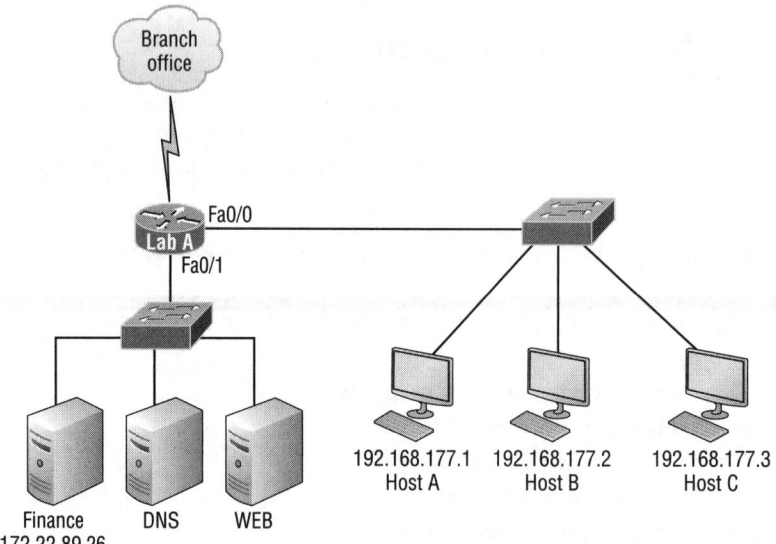

In this example, we're going to allow HTTP access to the Finance server from source Host B only. All other traffic will be permitted. We need to be able to configure this in only three test statements, and then we'll need to add the interface configuration.

Let's take what we've learned and knock this one out:

```
Lab_A#config t
Lab_A(config)#access-list 110 permit tcp host 192.168.177.2 host 172.22.89.26 eq 80
Lab_A(config)#access-list 110 deny tcp any host 172.22.89.26 eq 80
Lab_A(config)#access-list 110 permit ip any any
```

This is really pretty simple! First we need to permit Host B HTTP access to the Finance server. But since all other traffic must be allowed, we must detail who cannot HTTP to the Finance server, so the second test statement is there to deny anyone else from using HTTP on the Finance server. Finally, now that Host B can HTTP to the Finance server and everyone else can't, we'll permit all other traffic with our third test statement.

Not so bad—this just takes a little thought! But wait—we're not done yet because we still need to apply this to an interface. Since extended access lists are typically applied closest to the source, we should simply place this inbound on F0/0, right? Well, this is one time we're not going to follow the rules. Our challenge required us to allow only HTTP traffic to the Finance server from Host B. If we apply the ACL inbound on Fa0/0, then the branch office would be able to access the Finance server and perform HTTP. So in this example, we need to place the ACL closest to the destination:

```
Lab_A(config)#interface fastethernet 0/1
Lab_A(config-if)#ip access-group 110 out
```

Perfect! Now let's get into how to create ACLs using names.

Named ACLs

As I said earlier, *named* access lists are just another way to create standard and extended access lists. In medium to large enterprises, managing ACLs can become a real hassle over time! A handy way to make things easier is to copy the access list to a text editor, edit the list, then paste the new list back into the router, which works pretty well if it weren't for the "pack rat" mentality. It's really common to think things like, "What if I find a problem with the new list and need to back out of the change?" This and other factors cause people to hoard unapplied ACLs, and over time, they can seriously build up on a router, leading to more questions, like, "What were these ACLs for? Are they important? Do I need them?" All good questions, and named access lists are the answer to this problem!

And of course, this kind of thing can also apply to access lists that are up and running. Let's say you come into an existing network and are looking at access lists on a router. Suppose you find an access list 177, which happens to be an extended access list that's a whopping 93 lines long. This leads to more of the same bunch of questions and can even lead to needless existential despair! Instead, wouldn't it be a whole lot easier to identify an access with a name like "FinanceLAN" rather than one mysteriously dubbed "177"?

To our collective relief, named access lists allow us to use names for creating and applying either standard or extended access lists. There's really nothing new or different about these ACLs aside from being readily identifiable in a way that makes sense to humans, but there are some subtle changes to the syntax. So let's re-create the standard access list we created earlier for our test network in Figure 12.2 using a named access list:

```
Lab_A#config t
Lab_A(config)# ip access-list ?
  extended     Extended Access List
  log-update   Control access list log updates
  logging      Control access list logging
  resequence   Resequence Access List
  standard     Standard Access List
```

Notice that I started by typing **ip access-list**, not **access-list**. Doing this allows me to enter a named access list. Next, I'll need to specify it as a standard access list:

```
Lab_A(config)#ip access-list standard ?
  <1-99>       Standard IP access-list number
```

```
<1300-1999>  Standard IP access-list number (expanded range)
WORD         Access-list name
```

```
Lab_A(config)#ip access-list standard BlockSales
Lab_A(config-std-nacl)#
```

I've specified a standard access list, then added the name, BlockSales. I definitely could've used a number for a standard access list, but instead, I chose to use a nice, clear, descriptive name. And notice that after entering the name, I hit Enter and the router prompt changed. This confirms that I'm now in named access list configuration mode and that I'm entering the named access list:

```
Lab_A(config-std-nacl)#?
Standard Access List configuration commands:
  default  Set a command to its defaults
  deny     Specify packets to reject
  exit     Exit from access-list configuration mode
  no       Negate a command or set its defaults
  permit   Specify packets to forward
```

```
Lab_A(config-std-nacl)#deny 172.16.40.0 0.0.0.255
Lab_A(config-std-nacl)#permit any
Lab_A(config-std-nacl)#exit
Lab_A(config)#^Z
Lab_A#
```

So I've entered the access list and then exited configuration mode. Next, I'll take a look at the running configuration to verify that the access list is indeed in the router:

```
Lab_A#sh running-config | begin ip access
ip access-list standard BlockSales
 deny    172.16.40.0 0.0.0.255
 permit any
!
```

And there it is: the BlockSales access list has truly been created and is in the running-config of the router. Next, I'll need to apply the access list to the correct interface:

```
Lab_A#config t
Lab_A(config)#int fa0/1
Lab_A(config-if)#ip access-group BlockSales out
```

Clear skies! At this point, we've re-created the work done earlier using a named access list. But let's take our IP extended example, shown in Figure 12.6, and redo that list using a named ACL instead as well.

Same business requirements: Allow HTTP access to the Finance server from source Host B only. All other traffic is permitted.

```
Lab_A#config t
Lab_A(config)#ip access-list extended 110
Lab_A(config-ext-nacl)#permit tcp host 192.168.177.2 host 172.22.89.26 eq 80
Lab_A(config-ext-nacl)#deny tcp any host 172.22.89.26 eq 80
Lab_A(config-ext-nacl)#permit ip any any
Lab_A(config-ext-nacl)#int fa0/1
Lab_A(config-if)#ip access-group 110 out
```

Okay—true—I named the extended list with a number, but sometimes it's okay to do that! I'm guessing that named ACLs don't seem all that exciting or different to you, do they? Maybe not in this configuration, except that I don't need to start every line with access-list 110, which is nice. But where named ACLs really shine is that they allow us to insert, delete, or edit a single line. That isn't just nice, it's wonderful! Numbered ACLs just can't compare with that, and I'll demonstrate this in a minute.

Remarks

The remark keyword is really important because it arms you with the ability to include comments—remarks—regarding the entries you've made in both your IP standard and extended ACLs. Remarks are very cool because they efficiently increase your ability to examine and understand your ACLs to superhero level! Without them, you'd be caught in a quagmire of potentially meaningless numbers without anything to help you recall what all those numbers mean.

Even though you have the option of placing your remarks either before or after a permit or deny statement, I totally recommend that you choose to position them consistently so you don't get confused about which remark is relevant to a specific permit or deny statement.

To get this going for both standard and extended ACLs, just use the access-list access-list number remark remark global configuration command like this:

```
R2#config t
R2(config)#access-list 110 remark Permit Bob from Sales Only To Finance
R2(config)#access-list 110 permit ip host 172.16.40.1 172.16.50.0 0.0.0.255
R2(config)#access-list 110 deny ip 172.16.40.0 0.0.0.255 172.16.50.0 0.0.0.255
R2(config)#ip access-list extended No_Telnet
R2(config-ext-nacl)#remark Deny all of Sales from Telnetting to Marketing
R2(config-ext-nacl)#deny tcp 172.16.40.0 0.0.0.255 172.16.60.0 0.0.0.255 eq 23
R2(config-ext-nacl)#permit ip any any
R2(config-ext-nacl)#do show run
[output cut]
!
```

```
ip access-list extended No_Telnet
 remark Stop all of Sales from Telnetting to Marketing
 deny   tcp 172.16.40.0 0.0.0.255 172.16.60.0 0.0.0.255 eq telnet
 permit ip any any
!
access-list 110 remark Permit Bob from Sales Only To Finance
access-list 110 permit ip host 172.16.40.1 172.16.50.0 0.0.0.255
access-list 110 deny   ip 172.16.40.0 0.0.0.255 172.16.50.0 0.0.0.255
access-list 110 permit ip any any
!
```

Sweet—I was able to add a remark to both an extended list and a named access list. Keep in mind that you cannot see these remarks in the output of the show access-list command, which we'll cover next, because they only show up in the running-config.

Speaking of ACLs, I still need to show you how to monitor and verify them. This is an important topic, so pay attention!

Monitoring Access Lists

It's always good to be able to verify a router's configuration. Table 12.1 lists the commands that we can use to achieve that.

TABLE 12.1   Commands used to verify access-list configuration

Command	Effect
show access-list	Displays all access lists and their parameters configured on the router. Also shows statistics about how many times the line either permitted or denied a packet. This command does not show you which interface the list is applied on.
show access-list 110	Reveals only the parameters for access list 110. Again, this command will not reveal the specific interface the list is set on.
show ip access-list	Shows only the IP access lists configured on the router.
show ip interface	Displays which interfaces have access lists set on them.
show running-config	Shows the access lists and the specific interfaces that have ACLs applied on them.

We've already used the show running-config command to verify that a named access list was in the router, so now let's take a look at the output from some of the other commands.

The show access-list command will list all ACLs on the router, whether they're applied to an interface or not:

```
Lab_A#show access-list
Standard IP access list 10
    10 deny    172.16.40.0, wildcard bits 0.0.0.255
    20 permit any
Standard IP access list BlockSales
    10 deny    172.16.40.0, wildcard bits 0.0.0.255
    20 permit any
Extended IP access list 110
    10 deny tcp any host 172.16.30.5 eq ftp
    20 deny tcp any host 172.16.30.5 eq telnet
    30 permit ip any any
    40 permit tcp host 192.168.177.2 host 172.22.89.26 eq www
    50 deny tcp any host 172.22.89.26 eq www
Lab_A#
```

First, notice that access list 10 as well as both of our named access lists appear on this list—remember, my extended named ACL was named 110! Second, notice that even though I entered actual numbers for TCP ports in access list 110, the show command gives us the protocol names rather than TCP ports for serious clarity.

But wait! The best part is those numbers on the left side: 10, 20, 30, etc. Those are called sequence numbers, and they allow us to edit our named ACL. Here's an example where I added a line into the named extended ACL 110:

```
Lab_A (config)#ip access-list extended 110
Lab_A (config-ext-nacl)#21 deny udp any host 172.16.30.5 eq 69
Lab_A#show access-list
[output cut]
Extended IP access list 110
    10 deny tcp any host 172.16.30.5 eq ftp
    20 deny tcp any host 172.16.30.5 eq telnet
    21 deny udp any host 172.16.30.5 eq tftp
    30 permit ip any any
    40 permit tcp host 192.168.177.2 host 172.22.89.26 eq www
    50 deny tcp any host 172.22.89.26 eq www
```

You can see that I added line 21. I could have deleted a line or edited an existing line as well—very nice!

Here's the output of the show ip interface command:

```
Lab_A#show ip interface fa0/1
FastEthernet0/1 is up, line protocol is up
  Internet address is 172.16.30.1/24
  Broadcast address is 255.255.255.255
  Address determined by non-volatile memory
  MTU is 1500 bytes
  Helper address is not set
  Directed broadcast forwarding is disabled
  Outgoing access list is 110
  Inbound access list is not set
  Proxy ARP is enabled
  Security level is default
  Split horizon is enabled
[output cut]
```

Be sure to notice the bold line indicating that the outgoing list on this interface is 110, yet the inbound access list isn't set. What happened to BlockSales? I had configured that outbound on Fa0/1! That's true, I did, but I configured my extended named ACL 110 and applied it to Fa0/1 as well. You can't have two lists on the same interface, in the same direction, so what happened here is that my last configuration overwrote the BlockSales configuration.

And as I've already mentioned, you can use the show running-config command to see any and all access lists.

Summary

In this chapter you learned how to configure standard access lists to properly filter IP traffic. You discovered what a standard access list is and how to apply it to a Cisco router to add security to your network. You also learned how to configure extended access lists to further filter IP traffic. We also covered the key differences between standard and extended access lists as well as how to apply them to Cisco routers.

Moving on, you found out how to configure named access lists and apply them to interfaces on the router and learned that named access lists offer the huge advantage of being easily identifiable and, therefore, a whole lot easier to manage than mysterious access lists that are simply referred to by obscure numbers.

Appendix C, "Disabling and Configuring Network Services," which takes off from this chapter, has a fun section in it: turning off default services. I've always found performing this administration task fun, and the auto secure command can help us configure basic, much-needed security on our routers.

The chapter wrapped up by showing you how to monitor and verify selected access-list configurations on a router.

Exam Essentials

Remember the standard and extended IP access-list number ranges.   The number ranges you can use to configure a standard IP access list are 1–99 and 1300–1999. The number ranges for an extended IP access list are 100–199 and 2000–2699.

Understand the term implicit deny.   At the end of every access list is an *implicit deny*. What this means is that if a packet does not match any of the lines in the access list, it will be discarded. Also, if you have nothing but deny statements in your list, the list will not permit any packets.

Understand the standard IP access-list configuration command.   To configure a standard IP access list, use the access-list numbers 1–99 or 1300–1999 in global configuration mode. Choose permit or deny, then choose the source IP address you want to filter on using one of the three techniques covered in this chapter.

Understand the extended IP access-list configuration command.   To configure an extended IP access list, use the access-list numbers 100–199 or 2000–2699 in global configuration mode. Choose permit or deny, the Network layer protocol field, the source IP address you want to filter on, the destination address you want to filter on, and finally, the Transport layer port number if TCP or UDP has been specified as the protocol.

Remember the command to verify an access list on a router interface.   To see whether an access list is set on an interface and in which direction it is filtering, use the show ip interface command. This command will not show you the contents of the access list, merely which access lists are applied on the interface.

Remember the command to verify the access-list configuration.   To see the configured access lists on your router, use the show access-list command. This command will not show you which interfaces have an access list set.

Written Lab 12

In this section, you'll complete the following lab to make sure you've got the information and concepts contained within them fully dialed in:

Lab 12.1: Security

The answers to this lab can be found in Appendix A, "Answers to Written Labs."

In this section, write the answers to the following questions:

1. What command would you use to configure a standard IP access list to prevent all machines on network 172.16.0.0/16 from accessing your Ethernet network?

2. What command would you use to apply the access list you created in question 1 to an Ethernet interface outbound?

3. What command(s) would you use to create an access list that denies host 192.168.15.5 access to an Ethernet network?

4. Which command verifies that you've entered the access list correctly?

5. What two tools can help notify and prevent DoS attacks?

6. What command(s) would you use to create an extended access list that stops host 172.16.10.1 from telnetting to host 172.16.30.5?

7. What command would you use to set an access list on a VTY line?

8. Write the same standard IP access list you wrote in question 1 but this time as a named access list.

9. Write the command to apply the named access list you created in question 8 to an Ethernet interface outbound.

10. Which command verifies the placement and direction of an access list?

Hands-on Labs

In this section, you will complete two labs. To complete these labs, you will need at least three routers. You can easily perform these labs with the Cisco Packet Tracer program. If you are studying to take your Cisco exam, you really need to do these labs!

Lab 12.1: Standard IP Access Lists

Lab 12.2: Extended IP Access Lists

All of the labs will use the following diagram for configuring the routers.

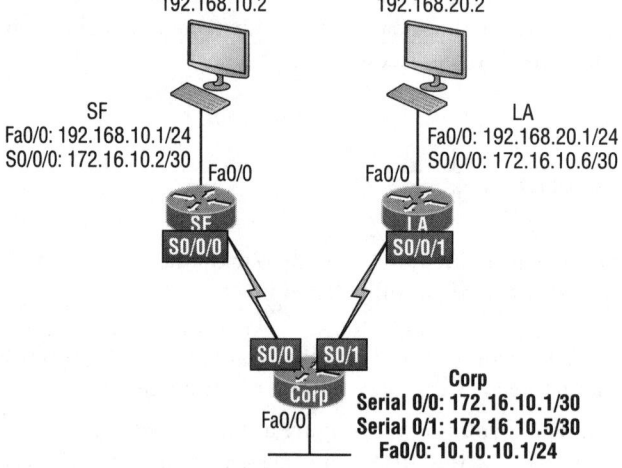

Hands-on Lab 12.1: Standard IP Access Lists

In this lab, you will allow only packets from a single host on the SF LAN to enter the LA LAN.

1. Go to LA router and enter global configuration mode by typing **config t**.

2. From global configuration mode, type **access-list ?** to get a list of all the different access lists available.

3. Choose an access-list number that will allow you to create an IP standard access list. This is a number between 1 and 99 or 1300 and 1399.

4. Choose to permit host 192.168.10.2, which is the host address:

   ```
   LA(config)#access-list 10 permit 192.168.20.2 ?
     A.B.C.D  Wildcard bits
     <cr>
   ```

   To specify only host 192.168.20.2, use the wildcards 0.0.0.0:

   ```
   LA(config)#access-list 10 permit 192.168.20.2
     0.0.0.0
   ```

5. Now that the access list is created, you must apply it to an interface to make it work:

   ```
   LA(config)#int f0/0
   Lab_A(config-if)#ip access-group 10 out
   ```

6. Verify your access list with the following commands:

   ```
   LA#sh access-list
   Standard IP access list 10
       permit 192.168.20.2
   LA#sh run
   [output cut]
   interface FastEthernet0/0
    ip address 192.168.20.1 255.255.255.0
    ip access-group 10 out
   ```

7. Test your access list by pinging from 192.168.10.2 to 192.168.20.2.

8. If you have another host on the LA LAN, ping that address, which should fail if your ACL is working.

Hands-on Lab 12.2: Extended IP Access Lists

In this lab, you will use an extended IP access list to stop host 192.168.10.2 from creating a Telnet session to router LA (172.16.10.6). However, the host still should be able to ping the LA router. IP extended lists should be placed close to the source, so add the extended list on router SF. Pay attention to the log command used in step 6. It is a Cisco objective!

1. Remove any access lists on SF and add an extended list to SF.

2. Choose a number to create an extended IP list. The IP extended lists use 100–199 or 2000–2699.

3. Use a deny statement. (You'll add a permit statement in step 7 to allow other traffic to still work.)

```
SF(config)#access-list 110 deny ?
  <0-255>  An IP protocol number
  ahp      Authentication Header Protocol
  eigrp    Cisco's EIGRP routing protocol
  esp      Encapsulation Security Payload
  gre      Cisco's GRE tunneling
  icmp     Internet Control Message Protocol
  igmp     Internet Gateway Message Protocol
  igrp     Cisco's IGRP routing protocol
  ip       Any Internet Protocol
  ipinip   IP in IP tunneling
  nos      KA9Q NOS compatible IP over IP tunneling
  ospf     OSPF routing protocol
  pcp      Payload Compression Protocol
  tcp      Transmission Control Protocol
  udp      User Datagram Protocol
```

4. Since you are going to deny Telnet, you must choose TCP as a Transport layer protocol:

```
SF(config)#access-list 110 deny tcp ?
  A.B.C.D  Source address
  any      Any source host
  host     A single source host
```

5. Add the source IP address you want to filter on, then add the destination host IP address. Use the host command instead of wildcard bits.

```
SF(config)#access-list 110 deny tcp host
  192.168.10.2 host 172.16.10.6 ?
  ack            Match on the ACK bit
```

```
eq              Match only packets on a given port
                number
established     Match established connections
fin             Match on the FIN bit
fragments       Check fragments
gt              Match only packets with a greater
                port number
log             Log matches against this entry
log-input       Log matches against this entry,
                including input interface
lt              Match only packets with a lower port
                number
neq             Match only packets not on a given
                port number
precedence      Match packets with given precedence
                value
psh             Match on the PSH bit
range           Match only packets in the range of
                port numbers
rst             Match on the RST bit
syn             Match on the SYN bit
tos             Match packets with given TOS value
urg             Match on the URG bit
<cr>
```

6. At this point, you can add the eq telnet command to filter host 192.168.10.2 from telnetting to 172.16.10.6. The log command can also be used at the end of the command so that whenever the access-list line is hit, a log will be generated on the console.

```
SF(config)#access-list 110 deny tcp host
   192.168.10.2 host 172.16.10.6 eq telnet log
```

7. It is important to add this line next to create a permit statement. (Remember that 0.0.0.0 255.255.255.255 is the same as the any command.)

```
SF(config)#access-list 110 permit ip any 0.0.0.0
   255.255.255.255
```

You must create a permit statement; if you just add a deny statement, nothing will be permitted at all. Please see the sections earlier in this chapter for more detailed information on the deny any command implied at the end of every ACL.

8. Apply the access list to the FastEthernet0/0 on SF to stop the Telnet traffic as soon as it hits the first router interface.

```
SF(config)#int f0/0
SF(config-if)#ip access-group 110 in
SF(config-if)#^Z
```

9. Try telnetting from host 192.168.10.2 to LA using the destination IP address of 172.16.10.6. This should fail, but the ping command should work.

10. On the console of SF, because of the log command, the output should appear as follows:

```
01:11:48: %SEC-6-IPACCESSLOGP: list 110 denied tcp
   192.168.10.2(1030) -> 172.16.10.6(23), 1 packet
01:13:04: %SEC-6-IPACCESSLOGP: list 110 denied tcp
   192.168.10.2(1030) -> 172.16.10.6(23), 3 packets
```

Review Questions

 The following questions are designed to test your understanding of this chapter's material. For more information on how to get additional questions, please see www.lammle.com/ccna.

You can find the answers to these questions in Appendix B, "Answers to Review Questions."

1. Which of the following statements is false when a packet is being compared to an access list?

   A. It's always compared with each line of the access list in sequential order.

   B. Once the packet matches the condition on a line of the access list, the packet is acted upon and no further comparisons take place.

   C. There is an implicit "deny" at the end of each access list.

   D. Until all lines have been analyzed, the comparison is not over.

2. You need to create an access list that will prevent hosts in the network range of 192.168.160.0 to 192.168.191.0. Which of the following lists will you use?

   A. `access-list 10 deny 192.168.160.0 255.255.224.0`

   B. `access-list 10 deny 192.168.160.0 0.0.191.255`

   C. `access-list 10 deny 192.168.160.0 0.0.31.255`

   D. `access-list 10 deny 192.168.0.0 0.0.31.255`

3. You have created a named access list called BlockSales. Which of the following is a valid command for applying this to packets trying to enter interface Fa0/0 of your router?

   A. `(config)#ip access-group 110 in`

   B. `(config-if)#ip access-group 110 in`

   C. `(config-if)#ip access-group Blocksales in`

   D. `(config-if)#BlockSales ip access-list in`

4. Which access list statement will permit all HTTP sessions to network 192.168.144.0/24 containing web servers?

   A. `access-list 110 permit tcp 192.168.144.0 0.0.0.255 any eq 80`

   B. `access-list 110 permit tcp any 192.168.144.0 0.0.0.255 eq 80`

   C. `access-list 110 permit tcp 192.168.144.0 0.0.0.255 192.168.144.0 0.0.0.255 any eq 80`

   D. `access-list 110 permit udp any 192.168.144.0 eq 80`

5. Which of the following access lists will allow only HTTP traffic into network 196.15.7.0?

   A. `access-list 100 permit tcp any 196.15.7.0 0.0.0.255 eq www`

   B. `access-list 10 deny tcp any 196.15.7.0 eq www`

   C. `access-list 100 permit 196.15.7.0 0.0.0.255 eq www`

    D. `access-list 110 permit ip any 196.15.7.0 0.0.0.255`

    E. `access-list 110 permit www 196.15.7.0 0.0.0.255`

6. What router command allows you to determine whether an IP access list is enabled on a particular interface?

    A. `show ip port`

    B. `show access-lists`

    C. `show ip interface`

    D. `show access-lists interface`

7. In the work area, connect the `show` command to its function on the right.

show access-list	Shows only the parameters for the access list 110. This command does not show you the interface the list is set on.
show access-list 110	Shows only the IP access lists configured on the router.
show ip access-list	Shows which interfaces have access lists set.
show ip interface	Displays all access lists and their parameters configured on the router. This command does not show you which interface the list is set on.

8. If you wanted to deny all Telnet connections to only network 192.168.10.0, which command could you use?

    A. `access-list 100 deny tcp 192.168.10.0 255.255.255.0 eq telnet`

    B. `access-list 100 deny tcp 192.168.10.0 0.255.255.255 eq telnet`

    C. `access-list 100 deny tcp any 192.168.10.0 0.0.0.255 eq 23`

    D. `access-list 100 deny 192.168.10.0 0.0.0.255 any eq 23`

9. If you wanted to deny FTP access from network 200.200.10.0 to network 200.199.11.0 but allow everything else, which of the following command strings is valid?

    A. `access-list 110 deny 200.200.10.0 to network 200.199.11.0 eq ftp`

        `access-list 111 permit ip any 0.0.0.0 255.255.255.255`

    B. `access-list 1 deny ftp 200.200.10.0 200.199.11.0 any any`

    C. `access-list 100 deny tcp 200.200.10.0 0.0.0.255 200.199.11.0 0.0.0.255 eq ftp`

    D. `access-list 198 deny tcp 200.200.10.0 0.0.0.255 200.199.11.0 0.0.0.255 eq ftp`

        `access-list 198 permit ip any 0.0.0.0 255.255.255.255`

10. You want to create an extended access list that denies the subnet of the following host: 172.16.50.172/20. Which of the following would you start your list with?

    A. `access-list 110 deny ip 172.16.48.0 255.255.240.0 any`

    B. `access-list 110 udp deny 172.16.0.0 0.0.255.255 ip any`

   C. `access-list 110 deny tcp 172.16.64.0 0.0.31.255 any eq 80`

   D. `access-list 110 deny ip 172.16.48.0 0.0.15.255 any`

11. Which of the following is the wildcard (inverse) version of a /27 mask?

   A. 0.0.0.7

   B. 0.0.0.31

   C. 0.0.0.27

   D. 0.0.31.255

12. You want to create an extended access list that denies the subnet of the following host: 172.16.198.94/19. Which of the following would you start your list with?

   A. `access-list 110 deny ip 172.16.192.0 0.0.31.255 any`

   B. `access-list 110 deny ip 172.16.0.0 0.0.255.255 any`

   C. `access-list 10 deny ip 172.16.172.0 0.0.31.255 any`

   D. `access-list 110 deny ip 172.16.188.0 0.0.15.255 any`

13. The following access list has been applied to an interface on a router:

    ```
    access-list 101 deny tcp 199.111.16.32 0.0.0.31 host 199.168.5.60
    ```

    Which of the following IP addresses will be blocked because of this single rule in the list? (Choose all that apply.)

   A. 199.111.16.67

   B. 199.111.16.38

   C. 199.111.16.65

   D. 199.11.16.54

14. Which of the following commands connects access list 110 inbound to interface Ethernet0?

   A. `Router(config)#ip access-group 110 in`

   B. `Router(config)#ip access-list 110 in`

   C. `Router(config-if)#ip access-group 110 in`

   D. `Router(config-if)#ip access-list 110 in`

15. What is the effect of this single-line access list?

    ```
    access-list 110 deny ip 172.16.10.0 0.0.0.255 host 1.1.1.1
    ```

   A. Denies only the computer at 172.16.10

   B. Denies all traffic

   C. Denies the subnet 172.16.10.0/26

   D. Denies the subnet 172.16.10.0/25

16. You configure the following access list. What will the result of this access list be?

    ```
    access-list 110 deny tcp 10.1.1.128 0.0.0.63 any eq smtp
    access-list 110 deny tcp any any eq 23
    ```

```
int ethernet 0
ip access-group 110 out
```

   A. Email and Telnet will be allowed out E0.

   B. Email and Telnet will be allowed in E0.

   C. Everything but email and Telnet will be allowed out E0.

   D. No IP traffic will be allowed out E0.

17. Which of the following series of commands will restrict Telnet access to the router?

   A. `Lab_A(config)#access-list 10 permit 172.16.1.1`
   `Lab_A(config)#line con 0`
   `Lab_A(config-line)#ip access-group 10 in`

   B. `Lab_A(config)#access-list 10 permit 172.16.1.1`
   `Lab_A(config)#line vty 0 4`
   `Lab_A(config-line)#access-class 10 out`

   C. `Lab_A(config)#access-list 10 permit 172.16.1.1`
   `Lab_A(config)#line vty 0 4`
   `Lab_A(config-line)#access-class 10 in`

   D. `Lab_A(config)#access-list 10 permit 172.16.1.1`
   `Lab_A(config)#line vty 0 4`
   `Lab_A(config-line)#ip access-group 10 in`

18. Which of the following is true regarding access lists applied to an interface?

   A. You can place as many access lists as you want on any interface until you run out of memory.

   B. You can apply only one access list on any interface.

   C. One access list may be configured, per direction, for each layer 3 protocol configured on an interface.

   D. You can apply two access lists to any interface.

19. What is the most common attack on a network today?

   A. Lock picking

   B. Naggle

   C. DoS

   D. `auto secure`

20. You need to stop DoS attacks in real time and have a log of anyone who has tried to attack your network. What should you do your network?

   A. Add more routers.

   B. Use the `auto secure` command.

   C. Implement IDS/IPS.

   D. Configure Naggle.

Chapter

13

Network Address Translation (NAT)

THE FOLLOWING ICND1 EXAM TOPICS ARE COVERED IN THIS CHAPTER:

✓ **4.0 Infrastructure Services**

- 4.7 Configure, verify, and troubleshoot inside source NAT

  - 4.7.a Static

  - 4.7.b Pool

  - 4.7.c PAT

In this chapter, we're going to dig into Network Address Translation (NAT), Dynamic NAT, and Port Address Translation (PAT), also known as NAT Overload. Of course, I'll demonstrate all the NAT commands. I also provided some fantastic hands-on labs for you to configure at the end of this chapter, so be sure not to miss those!

It's important to understand the Cisco objectives for this chapter. They are very straightforward: you have hosts on your inside Corporate network using RFC 1918 addresses and you need to allow those hosts access to the Internet by configuring NAT translations. With that objective in mind, that will be my direction with this chapter.

Because we'll be using ACLs in our NAT configurations, it's important that you're really comfortable with the skills you learned in the previous chapter before proceeding with this one.

To find up-to-the-minute updates for this chapter, please see www.lammle .com/ccna or the book's web page at www.sybex.com/go/ccna.

When Do We Use NAT?

Network Address Translation (NAT) is similar to Classless Inter-Domain Routing (CIDR) in that the original intention for NAT was to slow the depletion of available IP address space by allowing multiple private IP addresses to be represented by a much smaller number of public IP addresses.

Since then, it's been discovered that NAT is also a useful tool for network migrations and mergers, server load sharing, and creating "virtual servers." So in this chapter, I'm going to describe the basics of NAT functionality and the terminology common to NAT.

Because NAT really decreases the overwhelming amount of public IP addresses required in a networking environment, it comes in really handy when two companies that have duplicate internal addressing schemes merge. NAT is also a great tool to use when an organization changes its Internet service provider (ISP) but the networking manager needs to avoid the hassle of changing the internal address scheme.

Here's a list of situations when NAT can be especially helpful:

- When you need to connect to the Internet and your hosts don't have globally unique IP addresses

- When you've changed to a new ISP that requires you to renumber your network
- When you need to merge two intranets with duplicate addresses

You typically use NAT on a border router. For example, in Figure 13.1, NAT is used on the Corporate router connected to the Internet.

FIGURE 13.1   Where to configure NAT

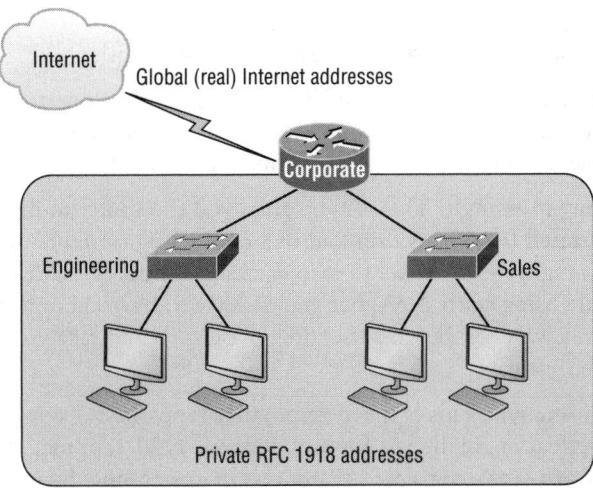

Now you may be thinking, "NAT's totally cool and I just gotta have it!" But don't get too excited yet because there are some serious snags related to using NAT that you need to understand first. Don't get me wrong—it can truly be a lifesaver sometimes, but NAT has a bit of a dark side you need to know about too. For the pros and cons linked to using NAT, check out Table 13.1.

TABLE 13.1   Advantages and disadvantages of implementing NAT

Advantages	Disadvantages
Conserves legally registered addresses.	Translation results in switching path delays.
Remedies address overlap events.	Causes loss of end-to-end IP traceability
Increases flexibility when connecting to the Internet.	Certain applications will not function with NAT enabled
Eliminates address renumbering as a network evolves.	Complicates tunneling protocols such as IPsec because NAT modifies the values in the header

The most obvious advantage associated with NAT is that it allows you to conserve your legally registered address scheme. But a version of it known as PAT is also why we've only just recently run out of IPv4 addresses. Without NAT/PAT, we'd have run out of IPv4 addresses more than a decade ago!

Types of Network Address Translation

In this section, I'm going to go over the three types of NATs with you:

Static NAT (one-to-one)   This type of NAT is designed to allow one-to-one mapping between local and global addresses. Keep in mind that the static version requires you to have one real Internet IP address for every host on your network.

Dynamic NAT (many-to-many)   This version gives you the ability to map an unregistered IP address to a registered IP address from out of a pool of registered IP addresses. You don't have to statically configure your router to map each inside address to an individual outside address as you would using static NAT, but you do have to have enough real, bona fide IP addresses for everyone who's going to be sending packets to and receiving them from the Internet at the same time.

Overloading (one-to-many)   This is the most popular type of NAT configuration. Understand that overloading really is a form of dynamic NAT that maps multiple unregistered IP addresses to a single registered IP address (many-to-one) by using different source ports. Now, why is this so special? Well, because it's also known as *Port Address Translation (PAT)*, which is also commonly referred to as NAT Overload. Using PAT allows you to permit thousands of users to connect to the Internet using only one real global IP address—pretty slick, right? Seriously, NAT Overload is the real reason we haven't run out of valid IP addresses on the Internet. Really—I'm not joking!

I'll show you how to configure all three types of NAT throughout this chapter and at the end of this chapter with the hands-on labs.

NAT Names

The names we use to describe the addresses used with NAT are fairly straightforward. Addresses used after NAT translations are called *global addresses*. These are usually the public addresses used on the Internet, which you don't need if you aren't going on the Internet.

Local addresses are the ones we use before NAT translation. This means that the inside local address is actually the private address of the sending host that's attempting to get to the Internet. The outside local address would typically be the router interface connected to your ISP and is also usually a public address used as the packet begins its journey.

After translation, the inside local address is then called the *inside global address* and the outside global address then becomes the address of the destination host. Check out Table 13.2, which lists all this terminology and offers a clear picture of the various names used with NAT. Keep in mind that these terms and their definitions can vary somewhat based on implementation. The table shows how they're used according to the Cisco exam objectives.

TABLE 13.2   NAT terms

Names	Meaning
Inside local	Source host inside address before translation—typically an RFC 1918 address.
Outside local	Address of an outside host as it appears to the inside network. This is usually the address of the router interface connected to ISP—the actual Internet address.
Inside global	Source host address used after translation to get onto the Internet. This is also the actual Internet address.
Outside global	Address of outside destination host and, again, the real Internet address.

How NAT Works

Okay, it's time to look at how this whole NAT thing works. I'm going to start by using Figure 13.2 to describe basic NAT translation.

FIGURE 13.2   Basic NAT translation

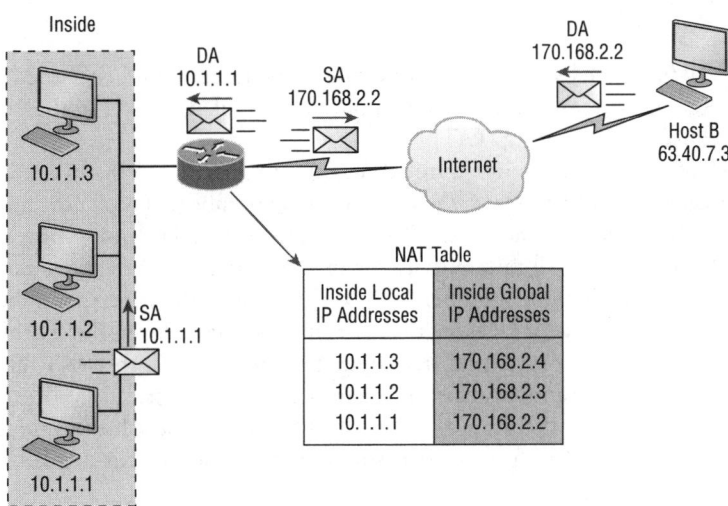

In this figure, we can see host 10.1.1.1 sending an Internet-bound packet to the border router configured with NAT. The router identifies the source IP address as an inside local IP address destined for an outside network, translates the source IP address in the packet, and documents the translation in the NAT table.

The packet is sent to the outside interface with the new translated source address. The external host returns the packet to the destination host and the NAT router translates the inside global IP address back to the inside local IP address using the NAT table. This is as simple as it gets!

Let's take a look at a more complex configuration using overloading, also referred to as PAT. I'll use Figure 13.3 to demonstrate how PAT works by having an inside host HTTP to a server on the Internet.

FIGURE 13.3   NAT overloading example (PAT)

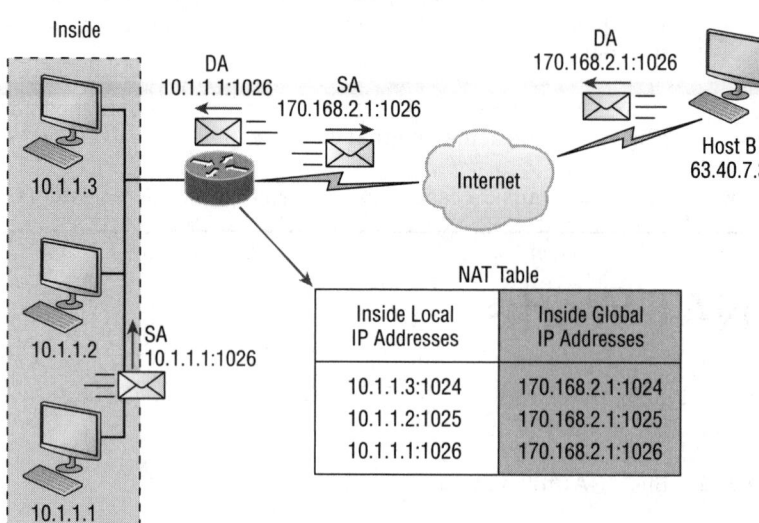

With PAT, all inside hosts get translated to one single IP address, hence the term *overloading*. Again, the reason we've just run out of available global IP addresses on the Internet is because of overloading (PAT).

Take a look at the NAT table in Figure 13.3 again. In addition to the inside local IP address and inside global IP address, we now have port numbers. These port numbers help the router identify which host should receive the return traffic. The router uses the source port number from each host to differentiate the traffic from each of them. Understand that the packet has a destination port number of 80 when it leaves the router, and the HTTP server sends back the data with a destination port number of 1026, in this example. This allows the NAT translation router to differentiate between hosts in the NAT table and then translate the destination IP address back to the inside local address.

Port numbers are used at the Transport layer to identify the local host in this example. If we had to use real global IP addresses to identify the source hosts, that's called *static NAT* and we would run out of addresses. PAT allows us to use the Transport layer to identify the hosts, which in turn allows us to theoretically use up to about 65,000 hosts with only one real IP address!

Static NAT Configuration

Let's take a look at a simple example of a basic static NAT configuration:

```
ip nat inside source static 10.1.1.1 170.46.2.2
!
interface Ethernet0
 ip address 10.1.1.10 255.255.255.0
 ip nat inside
!
interface Serial0
 ip address 170.46.2.1 255.255.255.0
 ip nat outside
!
```

In the preceding router output, the ip nat inside source command identifies which IP addresses will be translated. In this configuration example, the ip nat inside source command configures a static translation between the inside local IP address 10.1.1.1 and the outside global IP address 170.46.2.2.

Scrolling farther down in the configuration, we find an ip nat command under each interface. The ip nat inside command identifies that interface as the inside interface. The ip nat outside command identifies that interface as the outside interface. When you look back at the ip nat inside source command, you can see that the command is referencing the inside interface as the source or starting point of the translation. You could also use the command like this: ip nat outside source. This option indicates the interface that you designated as the outside interface should become the source or starting point for the translation.

Dynamic NAT Configuration

Basically, dynamic NAT really means we have a pool of addresses that we'll use to provide real IP addresses to a group of users on the inside. Because we don't use port numbers, we must have real IP addresses for every user who's trying to get outside the local network simultaneously.

Here is a sample output of a dynamic NAT configuration:

```
ip nat pool todd 170.168.2.3 170.168.2.254
    netmask 255.255.255.0
ip nat inside source list 1 pool todd
```

```
!
interface Ethernet0
 ip address 10.1.1.10 255.255.255.0
 ip nat inside
!
interface Serial0
 ip address 170.168.2.1 255.255.255.0
 ip nat outside
!
access-list 1 permit 10.1.1.0 0.0.0.255
!
```

The `ip nat inside source list 1 pool todd` command tells the router to translate IP addresses that match `access-list 1` to an address found in the IP NAT pool named todd. Here the ACL isn't there to filter traffic for security reasons by permitting or denying traffic. In this case, it's there to select or designate what we often call interesting traffic. When interesting traffic has been matched with the access list, it's pulled into the NAT process to be translated. This is actually a common use for access lists, which aren't always just stuck with the dull job of just blocking traffic at an interface!

The command `ip nat pool todd 170.168.2.3 170.168.2.254 netmask 255.255.255.0` creates a pool of addresses that will be distributed to the specific hosts that require global addresses. When troubleshooting NAT for the Cisco objectives, always check this pool to confirm that there are enough addresses in it to provide translation for all the inside hosts. Last, check to make sure the pool names match exactly on both lines, remembering that they are case sensitive; if they don't, the pool won't work!

PAT (Overloading) Configuration

This last example shows how to configure inside global address overloading. This is the typical form of NAT that we would use today. It's actually now rare to use static or dynamic NAT unless it is for something like statically mapping a server, for example.

Here is a sample output of a PAT configuration:

```
ip nat pool globalnet 170.168.2.1 170.168.2.1 netmask 255.255.255.0
ip nat inside source list 1 pool globalnet overload
!
interface Ethernet0/0
 ip address 10.1.1.10 255.255.255.0
 ip nat inside
!
interface Serial0/0
 ip address 170.168.2.1 255.255.255.0
 ip nat outside
!
access-list 1 permit 10.1.1.0 0.0.0.255
```

The nice thing about PAT is that these are only a few differences between this configuration and the previous dynamic NAT configuration:

- Our pool of addresses has shrunk to only one IP address.

- We included the `overload` keyword at the end of our `ip nat inside source` command.

A really key factor to see in the example is that the one IP address that's in the pool for us to use is the IP address of the outside interface. This is perfect if you are configuring NAT Overload for yourself at home or for a small office that only has one IP address from your ISP. You could, however, use an additional address such as 170.168.2.2 if you had that address available to you as well, and doing that could prove very helpful in a very large implementation where you've got such an abundance of simultaneously active internal users that you need to have more than one overloaded IP address on the outside!

Simple Verification of NAT

As always, once you've chosen and configured the type of NAT you're going to run, which is typically PAT, you must be able to verify your configuration.

To see basic IP address translation information, use the following command:

```
Router#show ip nat translations
```

When looking at the IP NAT translations, you may see many translations from the same host to the corresponding host at the destination. Understand that this is typical when there are many connections to the same server.

You can also verify your NAT configuration via the `debug ip nat` command. This output will show the sending address, the translation, and the destination address on each debug line:

```
Router#debug ip nat
```

But wait—how do you clear your NAT entries from the translation table? Just use the `clear ip nat translation` command, and if you want to clear all entries from the NAT table, just use an asterisk (*) at the end of the command.

Testing and Troubleshooting NAT

Cisco's NAT gives you some serious power—and it does so without much effort, because the configurations are really pretty simple. But we all know nothing's perfect, so in case something goes wrong, you can figure out some of the more common culprits by running through this list of potential causes:

- Check the dynamic pools. Are they composed of the right scope of addresses?

- Check to see if any dynamic pools overlap.

- Check to see if the addresses used for static mapping and those in the dynamic pools overlap.

- Ensure that your access lists specify the correct addresses for translation.

- Make sure there aren't any addresses left out that need to be there, and ensure that none are included that shouldn't be.

- Check to make sure you've got both the inside and outside interfaces delimited properly.

A key thing to keep in mind is that one of the most common problems with a new NAT configuration often isn't specific to NAT at all—it usually involves a routing blooper. So, because you're changing a source or destination address in a packet, make sure your router still knows what to do with the new address after the translation!

The first command you should typically use is the show ip nat translations command:

```
Router#show ip nat trans
Pro    Inside global    Inside local    Outside local    Outside global
---    192.2.2.1        10.1.1.1        ---              ---
---    192.2.2.2        10.1.1.2        ---              ---
```

After checking out this output, can you tell me if the configuration on the router is static or dynamic NAT? The answer is yes, either static or dynamic NAT is configured because there's a one-to-one translation from the inside local to the inside global. Basically, by looking at the output, you can't tell if it's static or dynamic per se, but you absolutely can tell that you're not using PAT because there are no port numbers.

Let's take a look at another output:

```
Router#sh ip nat trans
Pro Inside global        Inside local        Outside local       Outside global
tcp 170.168.2.1:11003   10.1.1.1:11003      172.40.2.2:23       172.40.2.2:23
tcp 170.168.2.1:1067    10.1.1.1:1067       172.40.2.3:23       172.40.2.3:23
```

Okay, you can easily see that the previous output is using NAT Overload (PAT). The protocol in this output is TCP, and the inside global address is the same for both entries.

Supposedly the sky's the limit regarding the number of mappings the NAT table can hold. But this is reality, so things like memory and CPU, or even the boundaries set in place by the scope of available addresses or ports, can cause limitations on the actual number of entries. Consider that each NAT mapping devours about 160 bytes of memory. And sometimes the amount of entries must be limited for the sake of performance or because of policy restrictions, but this doesn't happen very often. In situations like these, just go to the ip nat translation max-entries command for help.

Another handy command for troubleshooting is show ip nat statistics. Deploying this gives you a summary of the NAT configuration, and it will count the number of active translation types too. Also counted are hits to an existing mapping as well any misses, with the latter causing an attempt to create a mapping. This command will also reveal expired translations. If you want to check into dynamic pools, their types, the total available addresses, how many addresses have been allocated and how many have failed, plus the number of translations that have occurred, just use the pool keyword after statistics.

Here is an example of the basic NAT debugging command:

```
Router#debug ip nat
NAT: s=10.1.1.1->192.168.2.1, d=172.16.2.2 [0]
NAT: s=172.16.2.2, d=192.168.2.1->10.1.1.1 [0]
NAT: s=10.1.1.1->192.168.2.1, d=172.16.2.2 [1]
NAT: s=10.1.1.1->192.168.2.1, d=172.16.2.2 [2]
NAT: s=10.1.1.1->192.168.2.1, d=172.16.2.2 [3]
NAT*: s=172.16.2.2, d=192.168.2.1->10.1.1.1 [1]
```

Notice the last line in the output and how the NAT at the beginning of the line has an asterisk (*). This means the packet was translated and fast-switched to the destination. What's fast-switched? Well in brief, fast-switching has gone by several aliases such as cache-based switching and this nicely descriptive name, "route once switch many." The fast-switching process is used on Cisco routers to create a cache of layer 3 routing information to be accessed at layer 2 so packets can be forwarded quickly through a router without the routing table having to be parsed for every packet. As packets are packet switched (looked up in the routing table), this information is stored in the cache for later use if needed for faster routing processing.

Let's get back to verifying NAT. Did you know you can manually clear dynamic NAT entries from the NAT table? You can, and doing this can come in seriously handy if you need to get rid of a specific rotten entry without sitting around waiting for the timeout to expire! A manual clear is also really useful when you want to clear the whole NAT table to reconfigure a pool of addresses.

You also need to know that the Cisco IOS software just won't allow you to change or delete an address pool if any of that pool's addresses are mapped in the NAT table. The clear ip nat translations command clears entries—you can indicate a single entry via the global and local address and through TCP and UDP translations, including ports, or you can just type in an asterisk (*) to wipe out the entire table. But know that if you do that, only dynamic entries will be cleared because this command won't remove static entries.

Oh, and there's more—any outside device's packet destination address that happens to be responding to any inside device is known as the inside global (IG) address. This means that the initial mapping has to be held in the NAT table so that all packets arriving from a specific connection get translated consistently. Holding entries in the NAT table also cuts down on repeated translation operations happening each time the same inside machine sends packets to the same outside destinations on a regular basis.

Let me clarify: When an entry is placed into the NAT table the first time, a timer begins ticking and its duration is known as the translation timeout. Each time a packet for a given entry translates through the router, the timer gets reset. If the timer expires, the entry will be unceremoniously removed from the NAT table and the dynamically assigned address will then be returned to the pool. Cisco's default translation timeout is 86,400 seconds (24 hours), but you can change that with the ip nat translation timeout command.

Before we move on to the configuration section and actually use the commands I just talked about, let's go through a couple of NAT examples and see if you can figure out the best configuration to go with. To start, look at Figure 13.4 and ask yourself two things: Where would you implement NAT in this design? What type of NAT would you configure?

FIGURE 13.4 NAT example

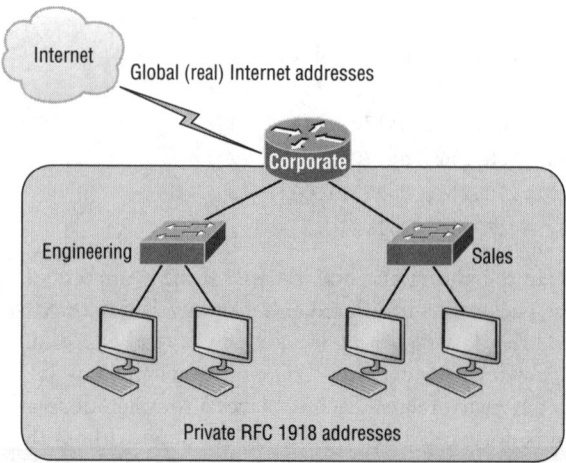

Global (real) Internet addresses

Private RFC 1918 addresses

In Figure 13.4, the NAT configuration would be placed on the corporate router, just as I demonstrated with Figure 13.1, and the configuration would be dynamic NAT with over-load (PAT). In this next NAT example, what type of NAT is being used?

```
ip nat pool todd-nat 170.168.10.10 170.168.10.20 netmask 255.255.255.0
ip nat inside source list 1 pool todd-nat
```

The preceding command uses dynamic NAT without PAT. The pool in the command gives the answer away as dynamic, plus there's more than one address in the pool and there is no overload command at the end of our ip nat inside source command. This means we are not using PAT!

In the next NAT example, refer to Figure 13.5 and see if you can come up with the configuration needed.

FIGURE 13.5 Another NAT example

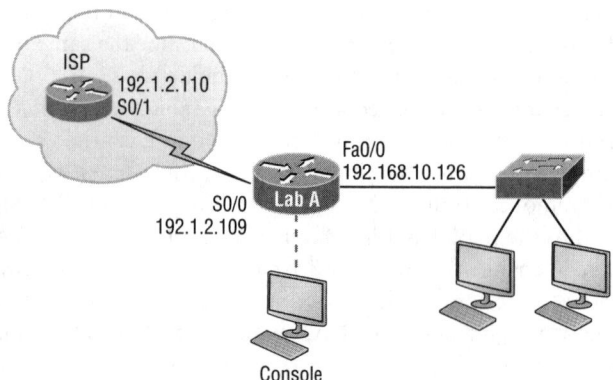

ISP
192.1.2.110
S0/1

Fa0/0
192.168.10.126

S0/0
192.1.2.109

Lab A

Console

Figure 13.5 shows a border router that needs to be configured with NAT and allow the use of six public IP addresses to the inside locals, 192.1.2.109 through 192.1.2.114. However, on the inside network, you have 62 hosts that use the private addresses of 192.168.10.65 through 192.168.10.126. What would your NAT configuration be on the border router?

Actually, two different answers would both work here, but the following would be my first choice based on the exam objectives:

```
ip nat pool Todd 192.1.2.109 192.1.2.109 netmask 255.255.255.248
access-list 1 permit 192.168.10.64 0.0.0.63
ip nat inside source list 1 pool Todd overload
```

The command ip nat pool Todd 192.1.2.109 192.1.2.109 netmask 255.255.255.248 sets the pool name as Todd and creates a dynamic pool of only one address using NAT address 192.1.2.109. Instead of the netmask command, you can use the prefix-length 29 statement. Just in case you're wondering, you cannot do this on router interfaces as well!

The second answer would get you the exact same result of having only 192.1.2.109 as your inside global, but you can type this in and it will also work: ip nat pool Todd 192.1.2.109 192.1.2.114 netmask 255.255.255.248. But this option really is a waste because the second through sixth addresses would only be used if there was a conflict with a TCP port number. You would use something like what I've shown in this example if you literally had about ten thousand hosts with one Internet connection! You would need it to help with the TCP-Reset issue when two hosts are trying to use the same source port number and get a negative acknowledgment (NAK). But in our example, we've only got up to 62 hosts connecting to the Internet at the same time, so having more than one inside global gets us nothing!

If you're fuzzy on the second line where the access list is set in the NAT configuration, do a quick review of Chapter 12, "Security." But this isn't difficult to grasp because it's easy to see in this access-list line that it's just the *network number* and *wildcard* used with that command. I always say, "Every question is a subnet question," and this one is no exception. The inside locals in this example were 192.168.10.65–126, which is a block of 64, or a 255.255.255.192 mask. As I've said in pretty much every chapter, you really need to be able to subnet quickly!

The command ip nat inside source list 1 pool Todd overload sets the dynamic pool to use PAT by using the overload command.

And be sure to add the ip nat inside and ip nat outside statements on the appropriate interfaces.

If you're planning on testing for any Cisco exam, configure the hands-on labs at the end of this chapter until you're really comfortable with doing that!

One more example, and then you are off to the written lab, hands-on labs, and review questions.

The network in Figure 13.6 is already configured with IP addresses as shown in the figure, and there is only one configured host. However, you need to add 25 more hosts to the LAN. Now, all 26 hosts must be able to get to the Internet at the same time.

FIGURE 13.6 Last NAT example

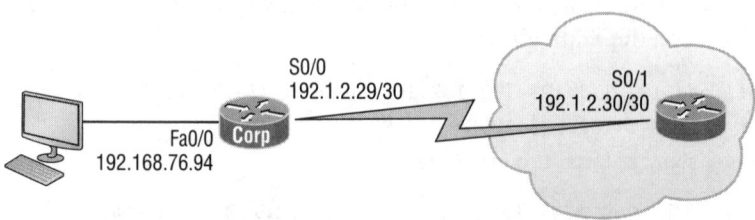

By looking at the configured network, use only the following inside addresses to configure NAT on the Corp router to allow all hosts to reach the Internet:

- Inside globals: 198.18.41.129 through 198.18.41.134
- Inside locals: 192.168.76.65 through 192.168.76.94

This one is a bit more challenging because all we have to help us figure out the configuration is the inside globals and the inside locals. But even meagerly armed with these crumbs of information, plus the IP addresses of the router interfaces shown in the figure, we can still configure this correctly.

To do that, we must first determine what our block sizes are so we can get our subnet mask for our NAT pool. This will also equip us to configure the wildcard for the access list.

You should easily be able to see that the block size of the inside globals is 8 and the block size of the inside locals is 32. Know that it's critical not to stumble on this foundational information!

So we can configure NAT now that we have our block sizes:

```
ip nat pool Corp 198.18.41.129 198.18.41.134 netmask 255.255.255.248
ip nat inside source list 1 pool Corp overload
access-list 1 permit 192.168.76.64 0.0.0.31
```

Since we had a block of only 8 for our pool, we had to use the overload command to make sure all 26 hosts can get to the Internet at the same time.

There is one other simple way to configure NAT, and I use this command at my home office to connect to my ISP. One command line and it's done! Here it is:

```
ip nat inside source list 1 int s0/0/0 overload
```

I can't say enough how much I love efficiency, and being able to achieve something cool using one measly line always makes me happy! My one little powerfully elegant line essentially says, "Use my outside local as my inside global and overload it." Nice! Of course, I still had to create ACL 1 and add the inside and outside interface commands to the configuration, but this is a really nice, fast way to configure NAT if you don't have a pool of addresses to use.

Summary

Now this really was a fun chapter. Come on—admit it! You learned a lot about Network Address Translation (NAT) and how it's configured as static and dynamic as well as with Port Address Translation (PAT), also called NAT Overload.

I also described how each flavor of NAT is used in a network as well as how each type is configured.

We finished up by going through some verification and troubleshooting commands. Now don't forget to practice all the wonderfully helpful labs until you've got them nailed down tight!

Exam Essentials

Understand the term *NAT*.   This may come as news to you, because I didn't—okay, failed to—mention it earlier, but NAT has a few nicknames. In the industry, it's referred to as network masquerading, IP-masquerading, and (for those who are besieged with OCD and compelled to spell everything out) Network Address Translation. Whatever you want to dub it, basically, they all refer to the process of rewriting the source/destination addresses of IP packets when they go through a router or firewall. Just focus on the process that's occurring and your understanding of it (i.e., the important part) and you're on it for sure!

Remember the three methods of NAT.   The three methods are static, dynamic, and overloading; the latter is also called PAT.

Understand static NAT.   This type of NAT is designed to allow one-to-one mapping between local and global addresses.

Understand dynamic NAT.   This version gives you the ability to map a range of unregistered IP addresses to a registered IP address from out of a pool of registered IP addresses.

Understand overloading.   Overloading really is a form of dynamic NAT that maps multiple unregistered IP addresses to a single registered IP address (many-to-one) by using different ports. It's also known as *PAT*.

Written Lab 13

In this section, you'll complete the following lab to make sure you've got the information and concepts contained within it fully dialed in:

Lab 13.1: NAT

You can find the answers to this lab in Appendix A, "Answers to Written Labs."

In this section, write the answers to the following questions:

1. What type of address translation can use only one address to allow thousands of hosts to be translated globally?

2. What command can you use to show the NAT translations as they occur on your router?

3. What command will show you the translation table?

4. What command will clear all your NAT entries from the translation table?

5. An inside local is before or after translation?

6. An inside global is before or after translation?

7. Which command can be used for troubleshooting and displays a summary of the NAT configuration as well as counts of active translation types and hits to an existing mapping?

8. What commands must be used on your router interfaces before NAT will translate addresses?

9. In the following output, what type of NAT is being used?

   ```
   ip nat pool todd-nat 170.168.10.10 170.168.10.20 netmask 255.255.255.0
   ```

10. Instead of the netmask command, you can use the _____ statement.

Hands-on Labs

I am going to use some basic routers for these labs, but really, almost any Cisco router will work. Also, you can use the LammleSim IOS version to run through all the labs in this (and every) chapter in this book.

Here is a list of the labs in this chapter:

Lab 13.1: Preparing for NAT

Lab 13.2: Configuring Dynamic NAT

Lab 13.3: Configuring PAT

I am going to use the network shown in the following diagram for our hands-on labs. I highly recommend you connect up some routers and run through these labs. You will configure NAT on router Lab_A to translate the private IP address of 192.168.10.0 to a public address of 171.16.10.0.

Table 13.3 shows the commands we will use and the purpose of each command.

TABLE 13.3   Command summary for NAT/PAT hands-on labs

Command	Purpose
ip nat inside source list *acl* pool *name*	Translates IPs that match the ACL to the pool
ip nat inside source static *inside_addr outside_addr*	Statically maps an inside local address to an out-side global address
ip nat pool *name*	Creates an address pool
ip nat inside	Sets an interface to be an inside interface
ip nat outside	Sets an interface to be an outside interface
show ip nat translations	Shows current NAT translations

Lab 13.1: Preparing for NAT

In this lab, you'll set up your routers with IP addresses and RIP routing.

1. Configure the routers with the IP addresses listed in the following table:

Router	Interface	IP Address
ISP	S0	171.16.10.1/24
Lab_A	S0/2	171.16.10.2/24
Lab_A	S0/0	192.168.20.1/24
Lab_B	S0	192.168.20.2/24
Lab_B	E0	192.168.30.1/24
Lab_C	E0	192.168.30.2/24

After you configure IP addresses on the routers, you should be able to ping from router to router, but since we do not have a routing protocol running until the next step, you can verify only from one router to another but not through the network until RIP is set up. You can use any routing protocol you wish; I am just using RIP for simplicity's sake to get this up and running.

2. On Lab_A, configure RIP routing, set a passive interface, and configure the default network.

```
Lab_A#config t
Lab_A(config)#router rip
```

```
Lab_A(config-router)#network 192.168.20.0
Lab_A(config-router)#network 171.16.0.0
Lab_A(config-router)#passive-interface s0/2
Lab_A(config-router)#exit
Lab_A(config)#ip default-network 171.16.10.1
```

The passive-interface command stops RIP updates from being sent to the ISP and
the ip default-network command advertises a default network to the other routers so
they know how to get to the Internet.

3.   On Lab_B, configure RIP routing:

```
Lab_B#config t
Lab_B(config)#router rip
Lab_B(config-router)#network 192.168.30.0
Lab_B(config-router)#network 192.168.20.0
```

4.   On Lab_C, configure RIP routing:

```
Lab_C#config t
Lab_C(config)#router rip
Lab_C(config-router)#network 192.168.30.0
```

5.   On the ISP router, configure a default route to the corporate network:

```
ISP#config t
ISP(config)#ip route 0.0.0.0 0.0.0.0 s0
```

6.   Configure the ISP router so you can telnet into the router without being prompted for a
     password:

```
ISP#config t
ISP(config)#line vty 0 4
ISP(config-line)#no login
```

7.   Verify that you can ping from the ISP router to the Lab_C router and from the Lab_C
     router to the ISP router. If you cannot, troubleshoot your network.

Lab 13.2: Configuring Dynamic NAT

In this lab, you'll configure dynamic NAT on the Lab_A router.

1.   Create a pool of addresses called GlobalNet on the Lab_A router. The pool should
     contain a range of addresses of 171.16.10.50 through 171.16.10.55.

```
Lab_A(config)#ip nat pool GlobalNet 171.16.10.50 171.16.10.55
net 255.255.255.0
```

2. Create access list 1. This list permits traffic from the 192.168.20.0 and 192.168.30.0 network to be translated.

```
Lab_A(config)#access-list 1 permit 192.168.20.0 0.0.0.255
Lab_A(config)#access-list 1 permit 192.168.30.0 0.0.0.255
```

3. Map the access list to the pool that was created.

```
Lab_A(config)#ip nat inside source list 1 pool GlobalNet
```

4. Configure serial 0/0 as an inside NAT interface.

```
Lab_A(config)#int s0/0
Lab_A(config-if)#ip nat inside
```

5. Configure serial 0/2 as an outside NAT interface.

```
Lab_A(config-if)#int s0/2
Lab_A(config-if)#ip nat outside
```

6. Move the console connection to the Lab_C router. Log in to the Lab_C router. Telnet from the Lab_C router to the ISP router.

```
Lab_C#telnet 171.16.10.1
```

7. Move the console connection to the Lab_B router. Log in to the Lab_B router. Telnet from the Lab_B router to the ISP router.

```
Lab_B#telnet 171.16.10.1
```

8. Execute the command **show users** from the ISP router. (This shows who is accessing the VTY lines.)

```
ISP#show users
```

    a. What does it show as your source IP address?_____

    b. What is your real source IP address?_____

The show users output should look something like this:

```
ISP>sh users
    Line        User      Host(s)            Idle       Location
   0 con 0                idle               00:03:32
   2 vty 0                idle               00:01:33 171.16.10.50
*  3 vty 1                idle               00:00:09 171.16.10.51
   Interface User     Mode                  Idle Peer Address
ISP>
```

NOTE   Notice that there is a one-to-one translation. This means you must have a real IP address for every host that wants to get to the Internet, which is not typically possible.

9. Leave the session open on the ISP router and connect to Lab_A. (Use **Ctrl+Shift+6**, let go, and then press **X**.)

10. Log in to your Lab_A router and view your current translations by entering the show ip nat translations command. You should see something like this:

```
Lab_A#sh ip nat translations
Pro Inside global    Inside local     Outside local    Outside global
--- 171.16.10.50     192.168.30.2     ---              ---
--- 171.16.10.51     192.168.20.2     ---              ---
Lab_A#
```

11. If you turn on debug ip nat on the Lab_A router and then ping through the router, you will see the actual NAT process take place, which will look something like this:

```
00:32:47: NAT*: s=192.168.30.2->171.16.10.50, d=171.16.10.1 [5]
00:32:47: NAT*: s=171.16.10.1, d=171.16.10.50->192.168.30.2
```

Lab 13.3: Configuring PAT

In this lab, you'll configure PAT on the Lab_A router. We will use PAT because we don't want a one-to-one translation, which uses just one IP address for every user on the network.

1. On the Lab_A router, delete the translation table and remove the dynamic NAT pool.

```
Lab_A#clear ip nat translations *
Lab_A#config t
Lab_A(config)#no ip nat pool GlobalNet 171.16.10.50
171.16.10.55 netmask 255.255.255.0
Lab_A(config)#no ip nat inside source list 1 pool GlobalNet
```

2. On the Lab_A router, create a NAT pool with one address called Lammle. The pool should contain a single address, 171.16.10.100. Enter the following command:

```
Lab_A#config t
Lab_A(config)#ip nat pool Lammle 171.16.10.100 171.16.10.100
net 255.255.255.0
```

3. Create access list 2. It should permit networks 192.168.20.0 and 192.168.30.0 to be translated.

```
Lab_A(config)#access-list 2 permit 192.168.20.0 0.0.0.255
Lab_A(config)#access-list 2 permit 192.168.30.0 0.0.0.255
```

4. Map access list 2 to the new pool, allowing PAT to occur by using the overload command.

    ```
    Lab_A(config)#ip nat inside source list 2 pool Lammle overload
    ```

5. Log in to the Lab_C router and telnet to the ISP router; also, log in to the Lab_B router and telnet to the ISP router.

6. From the ISP router, use the show users command. The output should look like this:

```
ISP>sh users
    Line        User        Host(s)             Idle        Location
*   0 con 0                 idle                00:00:00
    2 vty 0                 idle                00:00:39 171.16.10.100
    4 vty 2                 idle                00:00:37 171.16.10.100

    Interface  User    Mode            Idle Peer Address

ISP>
```

7. From the Lab_A router, use the show ip nat translations command.

```
Lab_A#sh ip nat translations
Pro Inside global   Inside local   Outside local Outside global
tcp 171.16.10.100:11001 192.168.20.2:11001 171.16.10.1:23
171.16.10.1:23
tcp 171.16.10.100:11002 192.168.30.2:11002 171.16.10.1:23
171.16.10.1:23
```

8. Also make sure the debug ip nat command is on for the Lab_A router. If you ping from the Lab_C router to the ISP router, the output will look like this:

```
01:12:36: NAT: s=192.168.30.2->171.16.10.100, d=171.16.10.1 [35]
01:12:36: NAT*: s=171.16.10.1, d=171.16.10.100->192.168.30.2 [35]
01:12:36: NAT*: s=192.168.30.2->171.16.10.100, d=171.16.10.1 [36]
01:12:36: NAT*: s=171.16.10.1, d=171.16.10.100->192.168.30.2 [36]
01:12:36: NAT*: s=192.168.30.2->171.16.10.100, d=171.16.10.1 [37]
01:12:36: NAT*: s=171.16.10.1, d=171.16.10.100->192.168.30.2 [37]
01:12:36: NAT*: s=192.168.30.2->171.16.10.100, d=171.16.10.1 [38]
01:12:36: NAT*: s=171.16.10.1, d=171.16.10.100->192.168.30.2 [38]
01:12:37: NAT*: s=192.168.30.2->171.16.10.100, d=171.16.10.1 [39]
01:12:37: NAT*: s=171.16.10.1, d=171.16.10.100->192.168.30.2 [39]
```

Review Questions

The following questions are designed to test your understanding of this chapter's material. For more information on how to get additional questions, please see www.lammle.com/ccna.

You can find the answers to these questions in Appendix B, "Answers to Review Questions."

1. Which of the following are disadvantages of using NAT? (Choose three.)
   A. Translation introduces switching path delays.
   B. NAT conserves legally registered addresses.
   C. NAT causes loss of end-to-end IP traceability.
   D. NAT increases flexibility when connecting to the Internet.
   E. Certain applications will not function with NAT enabled.
   F. NAT reduces address overlap occurrence.

2. Which of the following are advantages of using NAT? (Choose three.)
   A. Translation introduces switching path delays.
   B. NAT conserves legally registered addresses.
   C. NAT causes loss of end-to-end IP traceability.
   D. NAT increases flexibility when connecting to the Internet.
   E. Certain applications will not function with NAT enabled.
   F. NAT remedies address overlap occurrence.

3. Which command will allow you to see real-time translations on your router?
   A. `show ip nat translations`
   B. `show ip nat statistics`
   C. `debug ip nat`
   D. `clear ip nat translations *`

4. Which command will show you all the translations active on your router?
   A. `show ip nat translations`
   B. `show ip nat statistics`
   C. `debug ip nat`
   D. `clear ip nat translations *`

5. Which command will clear all the translations active on your router?
   A. `show ip nat translations`
   B. `show ip nat statistics`

C. debug ip nat

D. clear ip nat translations *

6. Which command will show you the summary of the NAT configuration?

   A. show ip nat translations

   B. show ip nat statistics

   C. debug ip nat

   D. clear ip nat translations *

7. Which command will create a dynamic pool named Todd that will provide you with 30 global addresses?

   A. ip nat pool Todd 171.16.10.65 171.16.10.94 net 255.255.255.240

   B. ip nat pool Todd 171.16.10.65 171.16.10.94 net 255.255.255.224

   C. ip nat pool todd 171.16.10.65 171.16.10.94 net 255.255.255.224

   D. ip nat pool Todd 171.16.10.1 171.16.10.254 net 255.255.255.0

8. Which of the following are methods of NAT? (Choose three.)

   A. Static

   B. IP NAT pool

   C. Dynamic

   D. NAT double-translation

   E. Overload

9. When creating a pool of global addresses, which of the following can be used instead of the netmask command?

   A. / (slash notation)

   B. prefix-length

   C. no mask

   D. block-size

10. Which of the following would be a good starting point for troubleshooting if your router is not translating?

   A. Reboot.

   B. Call Cisco.

   C. Check your interfaces for the correct configuration.

   D. Run the debug all command.

11. Which of the following would be good reasons to run NAT? (Choose three.)

   A. You need to connect to the Internet and your hosts don't have globally unique IP addresses.

   B. You change to a new ISP that requires you to renumber your network.

   C. You don't want any hosts connecting to the Internet.

   D. You require two intranets with duplicate addresses to merge.

12. Which of the following is considered to be the inside host's address after translation?

    A. Inside local

    B. Outside local

    C. Inside global

    D. Outside global

13. Which of the following is considered to be the inside host's address before translation?

    A. Inside local

    B. Outside local

    C. Inside global

    D. Outside global

14. By looking at the following output, determine which of the following commands would allow dynamic translations?

```
Router#show ip nat trans
Pro    Inside global    Inside local    Outside local Outside global
---    1.1.128.1        10.1.1.1        ---           ---
---    1.1.130.178      10.1.1.2        ---           ---
---    1.1.129.174      10.1.1.10       ---           ---
---    1.1.130.101      10.1.1.89       ---           ---
---    1.1.134.169      10.1.1.100      ---           ---
---    1.1.135.174      10.1.1.200      ---           ---
```

    A. `ip nat inside source pool todd 1.1.128.1 1.1.135.254 prefix-length 19`

    B. `ip nat pool todd 1.1.128.1 1.1.135.254 prefix-length 19`

    C. `ip nat pool todd 1.1.128.1 1.1.135.254 prefix-length 18`

    D. `ip nat pool todd 1.1.128.1 1.1.135.254 prefix-length 21`

15. Your inside locals are not being translated to the inside global addresses. Which of the following commands will show you if your inside globals are allowed to use the NAT pool?

```
ip nat pool Corp 198.18.41.129 198.18.41.134 netmask 255.255.255.248
ip nat inside source list 100 int s0/0 Corp overload
```

    A. `debug ip nat`

    B. `show access-list`

    C. `show ip nat translation`

    D. `show ip nat statistics`

16. Which command would you place on the interface of a private network?

    A. `ip nat inside`

    B. `ip nat outside`

    C. `ip outside global`

    D. `ip inside local`

17. Which command would you place on an interface connected to the Internet?

    A. `ip nat inside`

    B. `ip nat outside`

    C. `ip outside global`

    D. `ip inside local`

18. Port Address Translation is also called what?

    A. NAT Fast

    B. NAT Static

    C. NAT Overload

    D. Overloading Static

19. What does the asterisk (*) represent in the following output?

```
NAT*: s=172.16.2.2, d=192.168.2.1->10.1.1.1 [1]
```

    A. The packet was destined for a local interface on the router.

    B. The packet was translated and fast-switched to the destination.

    C. The packet attempted to be translated but failed.

    D. The packet was translated but there was no response from the remote host.

20. Which of the following needs to be added to the configuration to enable PAT?

```
ip nat pool Corp 198.18.41.129 198.18.41.134 netmask 255.255.255.248
access-list 1 permit 192.168.76.64 0.0.0.31
```

    A. `ip nat pool inside overload`

    B. `ip nat inside source list 1 pool Corp overload`

    C. `ip nat pool outside overload`

    D. `ip nat pool Corp 198.41.129 net 255.255.255.0 overload`

Chapter 14

Internet Protocol Version 6 (IPv6)

THE FOLLOWING ICND1 EXAM TOPICS ARE COVERED IN THIS CHAPTER:

✓ **1.11 Identify the appropriate IPv6 addressing scheme to satisfy addressing requirements in a LAN/WAN environment**

✓ **1.12 Configure, verify, and troubleshoot IPv6 addressing**

✓ **1.13 Configure and verify IPv6 Stateless Address Auto Configuration**

✓ **1.14 Compare and contrast IPv6 address types**

- 1.14.a Global unicast
- 1.14.b Unique local
- 1.14.c Link local
- 1.14.d Multicast
- 1.14.e Modified EUI 64
- 1.14.f Autoconfiguration
- 1.14.g Anycast

✓ **3.6 Configure, verify, and troubleshoot IPv4 and IPv6 static routing**

- 3.6.a Default route

We've covered a lot of ground in this book, and though the journey has been tough at times, it's been well worth it! But our networking expedition isn't quite over yet because we still have the vastly important frontier of IPv6 to explore. There's still some expansive territory to cover with this sweeping new subject, so gear up and get ready to discover all you need to know about IPv6. Understanding IPv6 is vital now, so you'll be much better equipped and prepared to meet today's real-world networking challenges as well as to ace the exam. This final chapter is packed and brimming with all the IPv6 information you'll need to complete your Cisco exam trek successfully, so get psyched—we're in the home stretch!

I probably don't need to say this, but I will anyway because I really want to go the distance and do everything I can to ensure that you arrive and achieve . . . You absolutely must have a solid hold on IPv4 by now, but if you're still not confident with it, or feel you could use a refresher, just page back to the chapters on TCP/IP and subnetting. And if you're not crystal clear on the address problems inherent to IPv4, you really need to review Chapter 13, "Network Address Translation (NAT)", before we decamp for this chapter's IPv6 summit push!

People refer to IPv6 as "the next-generation Internet protocol," and it was originally created as the solution to IPv4's inevitable and impending address-exhaustion crisis. Though you've probably heard a thing or two about IPv6 already, it has been improved even further in the quest to bring us the flexibility, efficiency, capability, and optimized functionality that can effectively meet our world's seemingly insatiable thirst for ever-evolving technologies and increasing access. The capacity of its predecessor, IPv4, pales wan and ghostly in comparison, which is why IPv4 is destined to fade into history completely, making way for IPv6 and the future.

The IPv6 header and address structure has been completely overhauled, and many of the features that were basically just afterthoughts and addenda in IPv4 are now included as full-blown standards in IPv6. It's power-packed, well equipped with robust and elegant features, poised and prepared to manage the mind-blowing demands of the Internet to come!

After an introduction like that, I understand if you're a little apprehensive, but I promise—really—to make this chapter and its VIP topic pretty painless for you. In fact, you might even find yourself actually enjoying it—I definitely did! Because IPv6 is so complex, while still being so elegant, innovative, and powerful, it fascinates me like some weird combination of a sleek, new Aston Martin and a riveting futuristic novel. Hopefully you'll experience this chapter as an awesome ride and enjoy reading it as much as I did writing it!

To find up-to-the-minute updates for this chapter, please see www.lammle .com/ccna or the book's web page at www.sybex.com/go/ccna.

Why Do We Need IPv6?

Well, the short answer is because we need to communicate and our current system isn't really cutting it anymore. It's kind of like the Pony Express trying to compete with airmail! Consider how much time and effort we've been investing for years while we scratch our heads to resourcefully come up with slick new ways to conserve bandwidth and IP addresses. Sure, variable length subnet masks (VLSMs) are wonderful and cool, but they're really just another invention to help us cope while we desperately struggle to overcome the worsening address drought.

I'm not exaggerating, at all, about how dire things are getting, because it's simply reality. The number of people and devices that connect to networks increases dramatically each and every day, which is not a bad thing. We're just finding new and exciting ways to communicate to more people, more often, which is good thing. And it's not likely to go away or even decrease in the littlest bit, because communicating and making connections are, in fact, basic human needs—they're in our very nature. But with our numbers increasing along with the rising tide of people joining the communications party increasing as well, the forecast for our current system isn't exactly clear skies and smooth sailing. IPv4, upon which our ability to do all this connecting and communicating is presently dependent, is quickly running out of addresses for us to use.

IPv4 has only about 4.3 billion addresses available—in theory—and we know that we don't even get to use most of those! Sure, the use of Classless Inter-Domain Routing (CIDR) and Network Address Translation (NAT) has helped to extend the inevitable dearth of addresses, but we will still run out of them, and it's going to happen within a few years. China is barely online, and we know there's a huge population of people and corporations there that surely want to be. There are myriad reports that give us all kinds of numbers, but all you really need to think about to realize that I'm not just being an alarmist is this: there are about 7 billion people in the world today, and it's estimated that only just over 10 percent of that population is currently connected to the Internet—wow!

That statistic is basically screaming at us the ugly truth that based on IPv4's capacity, every person can't even have a computer, let alone all the other IP devices we use with them! I have more than one computer, and it's pretty likely that you do too, and I'm not even including phones, laptops, game consoles, fax machines, routers, switches, and a mother lode of other devices we use every day into the mix! So I think I've made it pretty clear that we've got to do something before we run out of addresses and lose the ability to connect with each other as we know it. And that "something" just happens to be implementing IPv6.

The Benefits and Uses of IPv6

So what's so fabulous about IPv6? Is it really the answer to our coming dilemma? Is it really worth it to upgrade from IPv4? All good questions—you may even think of a few more. Of course, there's going to be that group of people with the time-tested "resistance to change syndrome," but don't listen to them. If we had done that years ago, we'd still be waiting weeks, even months for our mail to arrive via horseback. Instead, just know that the answer is a resounding *yes*, it is really the answer, and it is worth the upgrade! Not only does IPv6 give us lots of addresses (3.4×10^{38} = definitely enough), there are tons of other features built into this version that make it well worth the cost, time, and effort required to migrate to it.

Today's networks, as well as the Internet, have a ton of unforeseen requirements that simply weren't even considerations when IPv4 was created. We've tried to compensate with a collection of add-ons that can actually make implementing them more difficult than they would be if they were required by a standard. By default, IPv6 has improved upon and included many of those features as standard and mandatory. One of these sweet new standards is IPsec—a feature that provides end-to-end security.

But it's the efficiency features that are really going to rock the house! For starters, the headers in an IPv6 packet have half the fields, and they are aligned to 64 bits, which gives us some seriously souped-up processing speed. Compared to IPv4, lookups happen at light speed! Most of the information that used to be bound into the IPv4 header was taken out, and now you can choose to put it, or parts of it, back into the header in the form of optional extension headers that follow the basic header fields.

And of course there's that whole new universe of addresses—the 3.4×10^{38} I just mentioned—but where did we get them? Did some genie just suddenly arrive and make them magically appear? That huge proliferation of addresses had to come from somewhere! Well it just so happens that IPv6 gives us a substantially larger address space, meaning the address itself is a whole lot bigger—four times bigger as a matter of fact! An IPv6 address is actually 128 bits in length, and no worries—I'm going to break down the address piece by piece and show you exactly what it looks like coming up in the section "IPv6 Addressing and Expressions." For now, let me just say that all that additional room permits more levels of hierarchy inside the address space and a more flexible addressing architecture. It also makes routing much more efficient and scalable because the addresses can be aggregated a lot more effectively. And IPv6 also allows multiple addresses for hosts and networks. This is especially important for enterprises veritably drooling for enhanced access and availability. Plus, the new version of IP now includes an expanded use of multicast communication—one device sending to many hosts or to a select group—that joins in to seriously boost efficiency on networks because communications will be more specific.

IPv4 uses broadcasts quite prolifically, causing a bunch of problems, the worst of which is of course the dreaded broadcast storm. This is that uncontrolled deluge of forwarded broadcast traffic that can bring an entire network to its knees and devour every last bit of bandwidth! Another nasty thing about broadcast traffic is that it interrupts each and every device on the network. When a broadcast is sent out, every machine has to stop what it's doing and respond to the traffic whether the broadcast is relevant to it or not.

But smile assuredly, everyone. There's no such thing as a broadcast in IPv6 because it uses multicast traffic instead. And there are two other types of communications as well: unicast, which is the same as it is in IPv4, and a new type called *anycast*. Anycast communication allows the same address to be placed on more than one device so that when traffic is sent to the device service addressed in this way, it's routed to the nearest host that shares the same address. And this is just the beginning—we'll get into the various types of communication later in the section called "Address Types."

IPv6 Addressing and Expressions

Just as understanding how IP addresses are structured and used is critical with IPv4 addressing, it's also vital when it comes to IPv6. You've already read about the fact that at 128 bits, an IPv6 address is much larger than an IPv4 address. Because of this, as well as the new ways the addresses can be used, you've probably guessed that IPv6 will be more complicated to manage. But no worries! As I said, I'll break down the basics and show you what the address looks like and how you can write it as well as many of its common uses. It's going to be a little weird at first, but before you know it, you'll have it nailed!

So let's take a look at Figure 14.1, which has a sample IPv6 address broken down into sections.

FIGURE 14.1   IPv6 address example

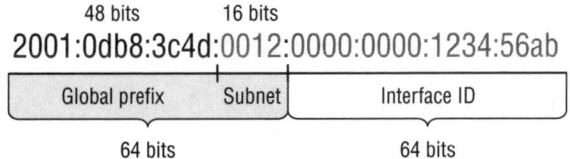

As you can clearly see, the address is definitely much larger. But what else is different? Well, first, notice that it has eight groups of numbers instead of four and also that those groups are separated by colons instead of periods. And hey, wait a second . . . there are letters in that address! Yep, the address is expressed in hexadecimal just like a MAC address is, so you could say this address has eight 16-bit hexadecimal colon-delimited blocks. That's already quite a mouthful, and you probably haven't even tried to say the address out loud yet!

There are four hexadecimal characters (16 bits) in each IPv6 field (with eight fields total), separated by colons.

Shortened Expression

The good news is there are a few tricks to help rescue us when writing these monster addresses. For one thing, you can actually leave out parts of the address to abbreviate it, but to get away with doing that you have to follow a couple of rules. First, you can drop any leading zeros in each of the individual blocks. After you do that, the sample address from earlier would then look like this:

`2001:db8:3c4d:12:0:0:1234:56ab`

That's a definite improvement—at least we don't have to write all of those extra zeros! But what about whole blocks that don't have anything in them except zeros? Well, we can kind of lose those too—at least some of them. Again referring to our sample address, we can remove the two consecutive blocks of zeros by replacing them with a doubled colon, like this:

`2001:db8:3c4d:12::1234:56ab`

Cool—we replaced the blocks of all zeros with a doubled colon. The rule you have to follow to get away with this is that you can replace only one contiguous block of such zeros in an address. So if my address has four blocks of zeros and each of them were separated, I just don't get to replace them all because I can replace only one contiguous block with a doubled colon. Check out this example:

`2001:0000:0000:0012:0000:0000:1234:56ab`

And just know that you *can't* do this:

`2001::12::1234:56ab`

Instead, the best you can do is this:

`2001::12:0:0:1234:56ab`

The reason the preceding example is our best shot is that if we remove two sets of zeros, the device looking at the address will have no way of knowing where the zeros go back in. Basically, the router would look at the incorrect address and say, "Well, do I place two blocks into the first set of doubled colons and two into the second set, or do I place three blocks into the first set and one block into the second set?" And on and on it would go because the information the router needs just isn't there.

Address Types

We're all familiar with IPv4's unicast, broadcast, and multicast addresses that basically define who or at least how many other devices we're talking to. But as I mentioned, IPv6 modifies that trio and introduces the anycast. Broadcasts, as we know them, have been eliminated in IPv6 because of their cumbersome inefficiency and basic tendency to drive us insane!

So let's find out what each of these types of IPv6 addressing and communication methods do for us:

Unicast   Packets addressed to a unicast address are delivered to a single interface. For load balancing, multiple interfaces across several devices can use the same address, but we'll call that an anycast address. There are a few different types of unicast addresses, but we don't need to get further into that here.

Global unicast addresses (2000::/3)   These are your typical publicly routable addresses and they're the same as in IPv4. Global addresses start at 2000::/3. Figure 14.2 shows how a unicast address breaks down. The ISP can provide you with a minimum /48 network ID, which in turn provides you 16-bits to create a unique 64-bit router interface address. The last 64-bits are the unique host ID.

FIGURE 14.2   IPv6 global unicast addresses

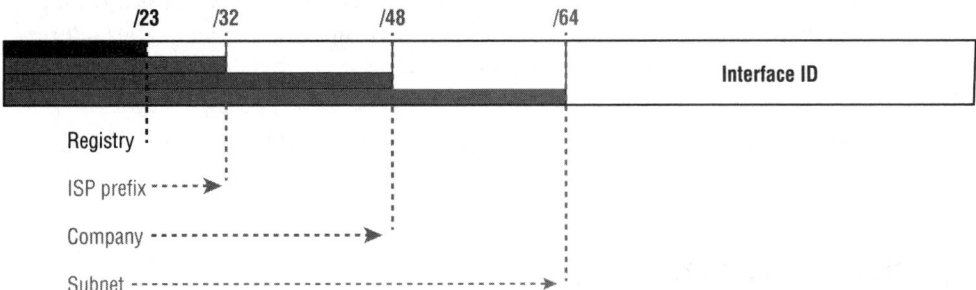

Link-local addresses (FE80::/10)   These are like the Automatic Private IP Address (APIPA) addresses that Microsoft uses to automatically provide addresses in IPv4 in that they're not meant to be routed. In IPv6 they start with FE80::/10, as shown in Figure 14.3. Think of these addresses as handy tools that give you the ability to throw a temporary LAN together for meetings or create a small LAN that's not going to be routed but still needs to share and access files and services locally.

FIGURE 14.3   IPv6 link local FE80::/10: The first 10 bits define the address type.

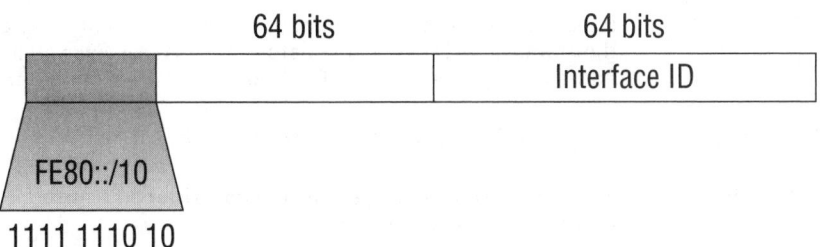

Unique local addresses (FC00::/7)   These addresses are also intended for nonrouting purposes over the Internet, but they are nearly globally unique, so it's unlikely you'll ever have one of them overlap. Unique local addresses were designed to replace site-local addresses, so they basically do almost exactly what IPv4 private addresses do: allow communication throughout a site while being routable to multiple local networks. Site-local addresses were deprecated as of September 2004.

Multicast (FF00::/8)   Again, as in IPv4, packets addressed to a multicast address are delivered to all interfaces tuned into the multicast address. Sometimes people call them "one-to-many" addresses. It's really easy to spot a multicast address in IPv6 because they always start with *FF*. We'll get deeper into multicast operation coming up, in "How IPv6 Works in an Internetwork."

Anycast   Like multicast addresses, an anycast address identifies multiple interfaces on multiple devices. But there's a big difference: the anycast packet is delivered to only one device—actually, to the closest one it finds defined in terms of routing distance. And again, this address is special because you can apply a single address to more than one host. These are referred to as "one-to-nearest" addresses. Anycast addresses are typically only configured on routers, never hosts, and a source address could never be an anycast address. Of note is that the IETF did reserve the top 128 addresses for each /64 for use with anycast addresses.

You're probably wondering if there are any special, reserved addresses in IPv6 because you know they're there in IPv4. Well there are—plenty of them! Let's go over those now.

Special Addresses

I'm going to list some of the addresses and address ranges (in Table 14.1) that you should definitely make sure to remember because you'll eventually use them. They're all special or reserved for a specific use, but unlike IPv4, IPv6 gives us a galaxy of addresses, so reserving a few here and there doesn't hurt at all!

TABLE 14.1   Special IPv6 addresses

Address	Meaning
0:0:0:0:0:0:0:0	Equals ::. This is the equivalent of IPv4's 0.0.0.0 and is typically the source address of a host before the host receives an IP address when you're using DHCP-driven stateful configuration.
0:0:0:0:0:0:0:1	Equals ::1. The equivalent of 127.0.0.1 in IPv4.
0:0:0:0:0:0:192.168.100.1	This is how an IPv4 address would be written in a mixed IPv6/IPv4 network environment.
2000::/3	The global unicast address range.
FC00::/7	The unique local unicast range.
FE80::/10	The link-local unicast range.
FF00::/8	The multicast range.

Address	Meaning
3FFF:FFFF::/32	Reserved for examples and documentation.
2001:0DB8::/32	Also reserved for examples and documentation.
2002::/16	Used with 6-to-4 tunneling, which is an IPv4-to-IPv6 transition system. The structure allows IPv6 packets to be transmitted over an IPv4 network without the need to configure explicit tunnels.

When you run IPv4 and IPv6 on a router, you have what is called "dual-stack."

Let me show you how IPv6 actually works in an internetwork. We all know how IPv4 works, so let's see what's new!

How IPv6 Works in an Internetwork

It's time to explore the finer points of IPv6. A great place to start is by showing you how to address a host and what gives it the ability to find other hosts and resources on a network.

I'll also demonstrate a device's ability to automatically address itself—something called stateless autoconfiguration—plus another type of autoconfiguration known as stateful. Keep in mind that stateful autoconfiguration uses a DHCP server in a very similar way to how it's used in an IPv4 configuration. I'll also show you how Internet Control Message Protocol (ICMP) and multicasting works for us in an IPv6 network environment.

Manual Address Assignment

In order to enable IPv6 on a router, you have to use the `ipv6 unicast-routing` global configuration command:

```
Corp(config)#ipv6 unicast-routing
```

By default, IPv6 traffic forwarding is disabled, so using this command enables it. Also, as you've probably guessed, IPv6 isn't enabled by default on any interfaces either, so we have to go to each interface individually and enable it.

There are a few different ways to do this, but a really easy way is to just add an address to the interface. You use the interface configuration command `ipv6 address <ipv6prefix>/<prefix-length>` [eui-64] to get this done.

Here's an example:

```
Corp(config-if)#ipv6 address 2001:db8:3c4d:1:0260:d6FF.FE73:1987/64
```

You can specify the entire 128-bit global IPv6 address as I just demonstrated with the preceding command, or you can use the EUI-64 option. Remember, the EUI-64 (extended unique identifier) format allows the device to use its MAC address and pad it to make the interface ID. Check it out:

```
Corp(config-if)#ipv6 address 2001:db8:3c4d:1::/64 eui-64
```

As an alternative to typing in an IPv6 address on a router, you can enable the interface instead to permit the application of an automatic link-local address.

To configure a router so that it uses only link-local addresses, use the `ipv6 enable` interface configuration command:

```
Corp(config-if)#ipv6 enable
```

 Remember, if you have only a link-local address, you will be able to communicate only on that local subnet.

Stateless Autoconfiguration (eui-64)

Autoconfiguration is an especially useful solution because it allows devices on a network to address themselves with a link-local unicast address as well as with a global unicast address. This process happens through first learning the prefix information from the router and then appending the device's own interface address as the interface ID. But where does it get that interface ID? Well, you know every device on an Ethernet network has a physical MAC address, which is exactly what's used for the interface ID. But since the interface ID in an IPv6 address is 64 bits in length and a MAC address is only 48 bits, where do the extra 16 bits come from? The MAC address is padded in the middle with the extra bits—it's padded with FFFE.

For example, let's say I have a device with a MAC address that looks like this: 0060:d673:1987. After it's been padded, it would look like this: 0260:d6FF:FE73:1987. Figure 14.4 illustrates what an EUI-64 address looks like.

FIGURE 14.4   EUI-64 interface ID assignment

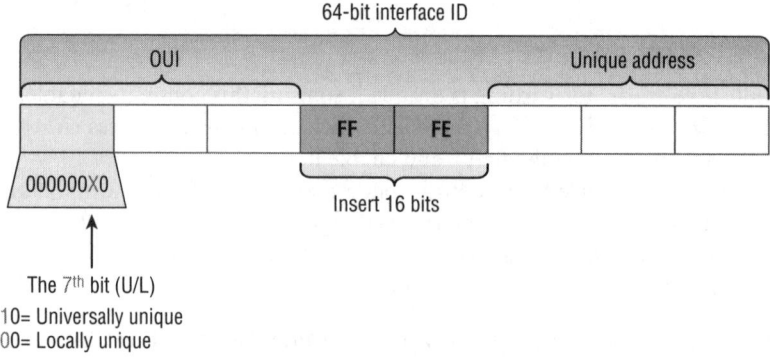

So where did that 2 in the beginning of the address come from? Another good question. You see that part of the process of padding, called modified EUI-64 format, changes a bit to specify if the address is locally unique or globally unique. And the bit that gets changed is the 7th bit in the address.

The reason for modifying the U/L bit is that, when using manually assigned addresses on an interface, it means you can simply assign the address 2001:db8:1:9::1/64 instead of the much longer 2001:db8:1:9:0200::1/64. Also, if you are going to manually assign a link-local address, you can assign the short address fe80::1 instead of the long fe80::0200:0:0:1 or fe80:0:0:0:0200::1. So, even though at first glance it seems the IETF made this harder for you to simply understand IPv6 addressing by flipping the 7th bit, in reality this made addressing much simpler. Also, since most people don't typically override the burned-in address, the U/L bit is a 0, which means that you'll see this inverted to a 1 most of the time. But because you're studying the Cisco exam objectives, you'll need to look at inverting it both ways.

Here are a few examples:

- MAC address 0090:2716:fd0f

- IPv6 EUI-64 address: 2001:0db8:0:1:0290:27ff:fe16:fd0f

That one was easy! Too easy for the Cisco exam, so let's do another:

- MAC address aa12:bcbc:1234

- IPv6 EUI-64 address: 2001:0db8:0:1:a812:bcff:febc:1234

10101010 represents the first 8 bits of the MAC address (aa), which when inverting the 7th bit becomes 10101000. The answer becomes A8. I can't tell you how important this is for you to understand, so bear with me and work through a couple more!

- MAC address 0c0c:dede:1234

- IPv6 EUI-64 address: 2001:0db8:0:1:0e0c:deff:fede:1234

0c is 00001100 in the first 8 bits of the MAC address, which then becomes 00001110 when flipping the 7th bit. The answer is then 0e. Let's practice one more:

- MAC address 0b34:ba12:1234

- IPv6 EUI-64 address: 2001:0db8:0:1:0934:baff:fe12:1234

0b in binary is 00001011, the first 8 bits of the MAC address, which then becomes 00001001. The answer is 09.

> Pay extra-special attention to this EUI-64 address assignment and be able to convert the 7th bit based on the EUI-64 rules! Written Lab 14.2 will help you practice this.

To perform autoconfiguration, a host goes through a basic two-step process:

1. First, the host needs the prefix information, similar to the network portion of an IPv4 address, to configure its interface, so it sends a router solicitation (RS) request for it. This RS is then sent out as a multicast to all routers (FF02::2). The actual information

being sent is a type of ICMP message, and like everything in networking, this ICMP message has a number that identifies it. The RS message is ICMP type 133.

2. The router answers back with the required prefix information via a router advertisement (RA). An RA message also happens to be a multicast packet that's sent to the all-nodes multicast address (FF02::1) and is ICMP type 134. RA messages are sent on a periodic basis, but the host sends the RS for an immediate response so it doesn't have to wait until the next scheduled RA to get what it needs.

These two steps are shown in Figure 14.5.

FIGURE 14.5 Two steps to IPv6 autoconfiguration

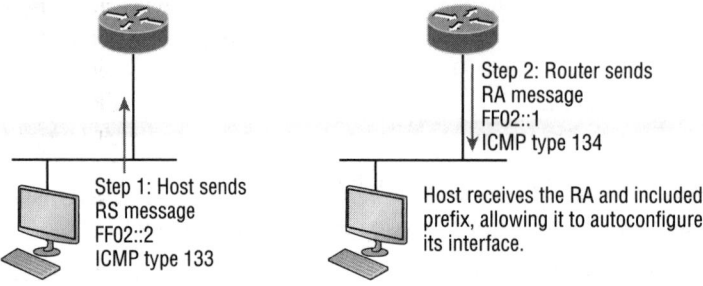

By the way, this type of autoconfiguration is also known as stateless autoconfiguration because it doesn't contact or connect to and receive any further information from the other device. We'll get to stateful configuration when we talk about DHCPv6 next.

But before we do that, first take a look at Figure 14.6. In this figure, the Branch router needs to be configured, but I just don't feel like typing in an IPv6 address on the interface connecting to the Corp router. I also don't feel like typing in any routing commands, but I need more than a link-local address on that interface, so I'm going to have to do something! So basically, I want to have the Branch router work with IPv6 on the internetwork with the least amount of effort from me. Let's see if I can get away with that.

FIGURE 14.6 IPv6 autoconfiguration example

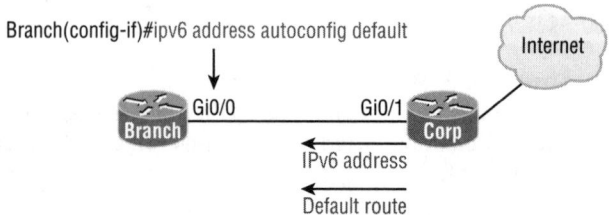

Ah ha—there is an easy way! I love IPv6 because it allows me to be relatively lazy when dealing with some parts of my network, yet it still works really well. By using the command ipv6 address autoconfig, the interface will listen for RAs and then, via the EUI-64 format, it will assign itself a global address—sweet!

This is all really great, but you're hopefully wondering what that default is doing there at the end of the command. If so, good catch! It happens to be a wonderful, optional part of the command that smoothly delivers a default route received from the Corp router, which will be automatically injected into my routing table and set as the default route—so easy!

DHCPv6 (Stateful)

DHCPv6 works pretty much the same way DHCP does in v4, with the obvious difference that it supports IPv6's new addressing scheme. And it might come as a surprise, but there are a couple of other options that DHCP still provides for us that autoconfiguration doesn't. And no, I'm not kidding— in autoconfiguration, there's absolutely no mention of DNS servers, domain names, or many of the other options that DHCP has always generously provided for us via IPv4. This is a big reason that the odds favor DHCP's continued use into the future in IPv6 at least partially—maybe even most of the time!

Upon booting up in IPv4, a client sends out a DHCP Discover message looking for a server to give it the information it needs. But remember, in IPv6, the RS and RA process happens first, so if there's a DHCPv6 server on the network, the RA that comes back to the client will tell it if DHCP is available for use. If a router isn't found, the client will respond by sending out a DHCP Solicit message, which is actually a multicast message addressed with a destination of ff02::1:2 that calls out, "All DHCP agents, both servers and relays."

It's good to know that there's some support for DHCPv6 in the Cisco IOS even though it's limited. This rather miserly support is reserved for stateless DHCP servers and tells us it doesn't offer any address management of the pool or the options available for configuring that address pool other than the DNS, domain name, default gateway, and SIP servers.

This means that you're definitely going to need another server around to supply and dispense all the additional, required information—maybe to even manage the address assignment, if needed!

 Remember for the objectives that both stateless and stateful autoconfiguration can dynamically assign IPv6 addresses.

IPv6 Header

An IPv4 header is 20 bytes long, so since an IPv6 address is four times the size of IPv4 at 128 bits, its header must then be 80 bytes long, right? That makes sense and is totally intuitive, but it's also completely wrong! When IPv6 designers devised the header, they created fewer, streamlined fields that would also result in a faster routed protocol at the same time. Let's take a look at the streamlined IPv6 header using Figure 14.7.

FIGURE 14.7   IPv6 header

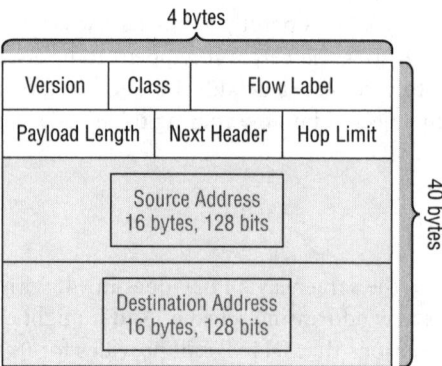

The basic IPv6 header contains eight fields, making it only twice as large as an IP header at 40 bytes. Let's zoom in on these fields:

Version   This 4-bit field contains the number 6, instead of the number 4 as in IPv4.

Traffic Class   This 8-bit field is like the Type of Service (ToS) field in IPv4.

Flow Label   This new field, which is 24 bits long, is used to mark packets and traffic flows. A flow is a sequence of packets from a single source to a single destination host, an anycast or multicast address. The field enables efficient IPv6 flow classification.

Payload Length   IPv4 had a total length field delimiting the length of the packet. IPv6's payload length describes the length of the payload only.

Next Header   Since there are optional extension headers with IPv6, this field defines the next header to be read. This is in contrast to IPv4, which demands static headers with each packet.

Hop Limit   This field specifies the maximum number of hops that an IPv6 packet can traverse.

For objectives remember that the Hop Limit field is equivalent to the TTL field in IPv4's header, and the Extension header (after the destination address and not shown in the figure) is used instead of the IPv4 Fragmentation field.

Source Address   This field of 16 bytes, or 128 bits, identifies the source of the packet.

Destination Address   This field of 16 bytes, or 128 bits, identifies the destination of the packet.

There are also some optional extension headers following these eight fields, which carry other Network layer information. These header lengths are not a fixed number—they're of variable size.

So what's different in the IPv6 header from the IPv4 header? Let's look at that:

- The Internet Header Length field was removed because it is no longer required. Unlike the variable-length IPv4 header, the IPv6 header is fixed at 40 bytes.

- Fragmentation is processed differently in IPv6 and does not need the Flags field in the basic IPv4 header. In IPv6, routers no longer process fragmentation; the host is responsible for fragmentation.

- The Header Checksum field at the IP layer was removed because most Data Link layer technologies already perform checksum and error control, which forces formerly optional upper-layer checksums (UDP, for example) to become mandatory.

 For the objectives, remember that unlike IPv4 headers, IPv6 headers have a fixed length, use an extension header instead of the IPv4 Fragmentation field, and eliminate the IPv4 checksum field.

It's time to move on to talk about another IPv4 familiar face and find out how a certain very important, built-in protocol has evolved in IPv6.

ICMPv6

IPv4 used the ICMP workhorse for lots of tasks, including error messages like destination unreachable and troubleshooting functions like Ping and Traceroute. ICMPv6 still does those things for us, but unlike its predecessor, the v6 flavor isn't implemented as a separate layer 3 protocol. Instead, it's an integrated part of IPv6 and is carried after the basic IPv6 header information as an extension header. And ICMPv6 gives us another really cool feature—by default, it prevents IPv6 from doing any fragmentation through an ICMPv6 process called path MTU discovery. Figure 14.8 shows how ICMPv6 has evolved to become part of the IPv6 packet itself.

FIGURE 14.8   ICMPv6

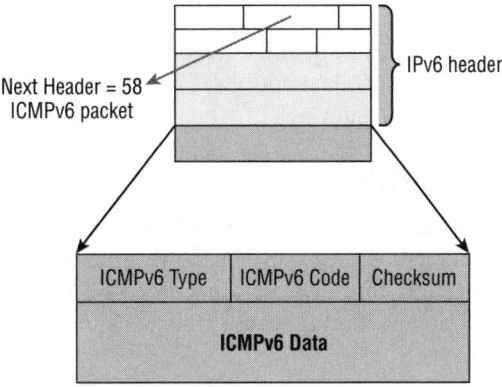

The ICMPv6 packet is identified by the value 58 in the Next Header field, located inside the ICMPv6 packet. The Type field identifies the particular kind of ICMP message that's being carried, and the Code field further details the specifics of the message. The Data field contains the ICMPv6 payload.

Table 14.2 shows the ICMP Type codes.

TABLE 14.2   ICMPv6 types

ICMPv6 Type	Description
1	Destination Unreachable
128	Echo Request
129	Echo Reply
133	Router Solicitation
134	Router Advertisement
135	Neighbor Solicitation
136	Neighbor Advertisement

And this is how it works: The source node of a connection sends a packet that's equal to the MTU size of its local link's MTU. As this packet traverses the path toward its destination, any link that has an MTU smaller than the size of the current packet will force the intermediate router to send a "packet too big" message back to the source machine. This message tells the source node the maximum size the restrictive link will allow and asks the source to send a new, scaled-down packet that can pass through. This process will continue until the destination is finally reached, with the source node now sporting the new path's MTU. So now, when the rest of the data packets are transmitted, they'll be protected from fragmentation.

ICMPv6 is used for router solicitation and advertisement, for neighbor solicitation and advertisement (i.e., finding the MAC data addresses for IPv6 neighbors), and for redirecting the host to the best router (default gateway).

Neighbor Discovery (NDP)

ICMPv6 also takes over the task of finding the address of other devices on the local link. The Address Resolution Protocol is used to perform this function for IPv4, but that's been renamed neighbor discovery (ND) in ICMPv6. This process is now achieved via a multicast address called the solicited-node address because all hosts join this multicast group upon connecting to the network.

Neighbor discovery enables these functions:

- Determining the MAC address of neighbors
- Router solicitation (RS) FF02::2 type code 133
- Router advertisements (RA) FF02::1 type code 134
- Neighbor solicitation (NS) Type code 135
- Neighbor advertisement (NA) Type code 136
- Duplicate address detection (DAD)

The part of the IPv6 address designated by the 24 bits farthest to the right is added to the end of the multicast address FF02:0:0:0:0:1:FF/104 prefix and is referred to as the *solicited-node address*. When this address is queried, the corresponding host will send back its layer 2 address.

Devices can find and keep track of other neighbor devices on the network in pretty much the same way. When I talked about RA and RS messages earlier and told you that they use multicast traffic to request and send address information, that too is actually a function of ICMPv6—specifically, neighbor discovery.

In IPv4, the protocol IGMP was used to allow a host device to tell its local router that it was joining a multicast group and would like to receive the traffic for that group. This IGMP function has been replaced by ICMPv6, and the process has been renamed multicast listener discovery.

With IPv4, our hosts could have only one default gateway configured, and if that router went down we had to either fix the router, change the default gateway, or run some type of virtual default gateway with other protocols created as a solution for this inadequacy in IPv4. Figure 14.9 shows how IPv6 devices find their default gateways using neighbor discovery.

FIGURE 14.9   Router solicitation (RS) and router advertisement (RA)

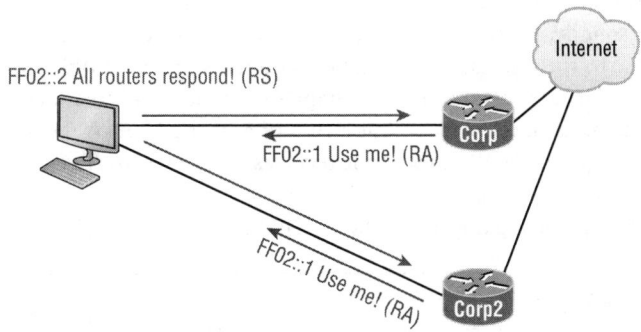

IPv6 hosts send a router solicitation (RS) onto their data link asking for all routers to respond, and they use the multicast address FF02::2 to achieve this. Routers on the same link respond with a unicast to the requesting host, or with a router advertisement (RA) using FF02::1.

But that's not all! Hosts also can send solicitations and advertisements between themselves using a neighbor solicitation (NS) and neighbor advertisement (NA), as shown in Figure 14.10. Remember that RA and RS gather or provide information about routers, and NS and NA gather information about hosts. Remember that a "neighbor" is a host on the same data link or VLAN.

FIGURE 14.10 Neighbor solicitation (NS) and neighbor advertisement (NA)

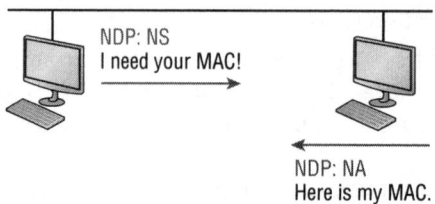

Solicited-Node and Multicast Mapping over Ethernet

If an IPv6 address is known, then the associated IPv6 solicited-node multicast address is known, and if an IPv6 multicast address is known, then the associated Ethernet MAC address is known.

For example, the IPv6 address 2001:DB8:2002:F:2C0:10FF:FE18:FC0F will have a known solicited-node address of FF02::1:FF18:FC0F.

Now we'll form the multicast Ethernet addresses by adding the last 32 bits of the IPv6 multicast address to 33:33.

For example, if the IPv6 solicited-node multicast address is FF02::1:FF18:FC0F, the associated Ethernet MAC address is 33:33:FF:18:FC:0F and is a virtual address.

Duplicate Address Detection (DAD)

So what do you think are the odds that two hosts will assign themselves the same random IPv6 address? Personally, I think you could probably win the lotto every day for a year and still not come close to the odds against two hosts on the same data link duplicating an IPv6 address! Still, to make sure this doesn't ever happen, duplicate address detection (DAD) was created, which isn't an actual protocol, but a function of the NS/NA messages. Figure 14.11 shows how a host sends an NDP NS when it receives or creates an IPv6 address.

FIGURE 14.11 Duplicate address detection (DAD)

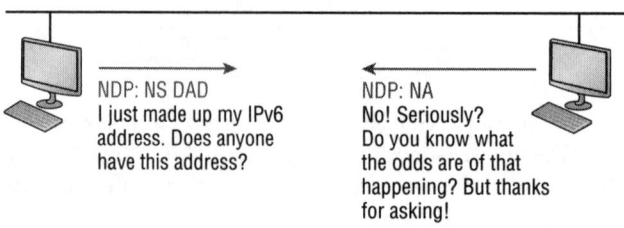

When hosts make up or receive an IPv6 address, they send three DADs out via NDP NS asking if anyone has this same address. The odds are unlikely that this will ever happen, but they ask anyway.

Remember for the objectives that ICMPv6 uses type 134 for router advertisement messages, and the advertised prefix must be 64 bits in length.

IPv6 Routing Protocols

All of the routing protocols we've already discussed have been tweaked and upgraded for use in IPv6 networks, so it figures that many of the functions and configurations that you've already learned will be used in almost the same way as they are now. Knowing that broadcasts have been eliminated in IPv6, it's safe to conclude that any protocols relying entirely on broadcast traffic will go the way of the dodo. But unlike with the dodo, it'll be really nice to say goodbye to these bandwidth-hogging, performance-annihilating little gremlins!

The routing protocols we'll still use in IPv6 have been renovated and given new names. Even though this chapter's focus is on the Cisco exam objectives, which cover only static and default routing, I want to discuss a few of the more important ones too.

First on the list is the IPv6 RIPng (next generation). Those of you who've been in IT for a while know that RIP has worked pretty well for us on smaller networks. This happens to be the very reason it didn't get whacked and will still be around in IPv6. And we still have EIGRPv6 because EIGRP already had protocol-dependent modules and all we had to do was add a new one to it to fit in nicely with the IPv6 protocol. Rounding out our group of protocol survivors is OSPFv3—that's not a typo, it really is v3! OSPF for IPv4 was actually v2, so when it got its upgrade to IPv6, it became OSPFv3. Lastly, for the new objectives, we'll list MP-BGP4 as a multiprotocol BGP-4 protocol for IPv6. Please understand for the objectives at this point in the book, we only need to understand static and default routing.

Static Routing with IPv6

Okay, now don't let the heading of this section scare you into looking on Monster.com for some job that has nothing to do with networking! I know that static routing has always run a chill up our collective spines because it's cumbersome, difficult, and really easy to screw up. And I won't lie to you—it's certainly not any easier with IPv6's longer addresses, but you can do it!

We know that to make static routing work, whether in IP or IPv6, you need these three tools:

- An accurate, up-to-date network map of your entire internetwork
- Next-hop address and exit interface for each neighbor connection
- All the remote subnet IDs

Of course, we don't need to have any of these for dynamic routing, which is why we mostly use dynamic routing. It's just so awesome to have the routing protocol do all that work for us by finding all the remote subnets and automatically placing them into the routing table!

Figure 14.12 shows a really good example of how to use static routing with IPv6. It really doesn't have to be that hard, but just as with IPv4, you absolutely need an accurate network map to make static routing work!

FIGURE 14.12   IPv6 static and default routing

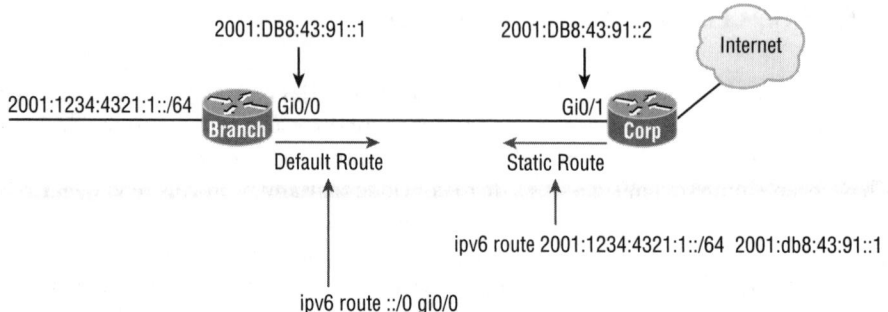

So here's what I did: First, I created a static route on the Corp router to the remote network 2001:1234:4321:1::/64 using the next hop address. I could've just as easily used the Corp router's exit interface. Next, I just set up a default route for the Branch router with ::/0 and the Branch exit interface of Gi0/0—not so bad!

Configuring IPv6 on Our Internetwork

We're going to continue working on the same internetwork we've been configuring throughout this book, as shown in Figure 14.13. Let's add IPv6 to the Corp, SF, and LA routers by using a simple subnet scheme of 11, 12, 13, 14, and 15. After that, we'll add the OSPFv3 routing protocol. Notice in Figure 14.13 how the subnet numbers are the same on each end of the WAN links. Keep in mind that we'll finish this chapter by running through some verification commands.

As usual, I'll start with the Corp router:

```
Corp#config t
Corp(config)#ipv6 unicast-routing
Corp(config)#int f0/0
Corp(config-if)#ipv6 address 2001:db8:3c4d:11::/64 eui-64
Corp(config-if)#int s0/0
Corp(config-if)#ipv6 address 2001:db8:3c4d:12::/64 eui-64
```

```
Corp(config-if)#int s0/1
Corp(config-if)#ipv6 address 2001:db8:3c4d:13::/64 eui-64
Corp(config-if)#^Z
Corp#copy run start
Destination filename [startup-config]?[enter]
Building configuration...
[OK]
```

FIGURE 14.13   Our internetwork

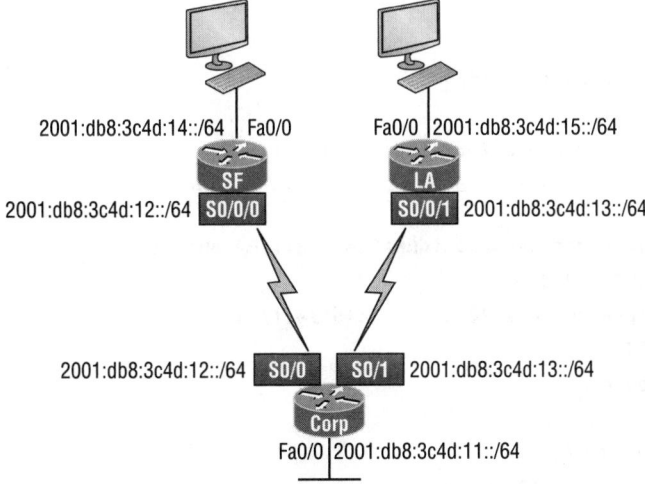

Pretty simple! In the previous configuration, I only changed the subnet address for each interface slightly. Let's take a look at the routing table now:

```
Corp(config-if)#do sho ipv6 route
C    2001:DB8:3C4D:11::/64 [0/0]
     via ::, FastEthernet0/0
L    2001:DB8:3C4D:11:20D:BDFF:FE3B:D80/128 [0/0]
     via ::, FastEthernet0/0
C    2001:DB8:3C4D:12::/64 [0/0]
     via ::, Serial0/0
L    2001:DB8:3C4D:12:20D:BDFF:FE3B:D80/128 [0/0]
     via ::, Serial0/0
C    2001:DB8:3C4D:13::/64 [0/0]
     via ::, Serial0/1
L    2001:DB8:3C4D:13:20D:BDFF:FE3B:D80/128 [0/0]
     via ::, Serial0/1
```

```
L    FE80::/10 [0/0]
       via ::, Null0
L    FF00::/8 [0/0]
       via ::, Null0
Corp(config-if)#
```

Alright, but what's up with those two addresses for each interface? One shows C for connected, one shows L. The connected address indicates the IPv6 address I configured on each interface and the L is the link-local that's been automatically assigned. Notice in the link-local address that the FF:FE is inserted into the address to create the EUI-64 address.

Let's configure the SF router now:

```
SF#config t
SF(config)#ipv6 unicast-routing
SF(config)#int s0/0/0
SF(config-if)#ipv6 address 2001:db8:3c4d:12::/64
% 2001:DB8:3C4D:12::/64 should not be configured on Serial0/0/0, a subnet router
anycast
SF(config-if)#ipv6 address 2001:db8:3c4d:12::/64 eui-64
SF(config-if)#int fa0/0
SF(config-if)#ipv6 address 2001:db8:3c4d:14::/64 eui-64
SF(config-if)#^Z
SF#show ipv6 route
C    2001:DB8:3C4D:12::/64 [0/0]
       via ::, Serial0/0/0
L    2001:DB8:3C4D:12::/128 [0/0]
       via ::, Serial0/0/0
L    2001:DB8:3C4D:12:21A:2FFF:FEE7:4398/128 [0/0]
       via ::, Serial0/0/0
C    2001:DB8:3C4D:14::/64 [0/0]
       via ::, FastEthernet0/0
L    2001:DB8:3C4D:14:21A:2FFF:FEE7:4398/128 [0/0]
       via ::, FastEthernet0/0
L    FE80::/10 [0/0]
       via ::, Null0
L    FF00::/8 [0/0]
       via ::, Null0
```

Did you notice that I used the exact IPv6 subnet addresses on each side of the serial link? Good . . . but wait—what's with that anycast error I received when trying to configure the interfaces on the SF router? I didn't meant to create that error; it happened because I forgot to add the eui-64 at the end of the address. Still, what's behind that error? An anycast address is a host address of all 0s, meaning the last 64 bits are all off, but by typing in /64 without the eui-64, I was telling the interface that the unique identifier would be nothing but zeros, and that's not allowed!

Let's configure the LA router now, and then add OSPFv3:

```
SF#config t
SF(config)#ipv6 unicast-routing
SF(config)#int s0/0/1
SF(config-if)#ipv6 address 2001:db8:3c4d:13::/64 eui-64
SF(config-if)#int f0/0
SF(config-if)#ipv6 address 2001:db8:3c4d:15::/64 eui-64
SF(config-if)#do show ipv6 route
C    2001:DB8:3C4D:13::/64 [0/0]
     via ::, Serial0/0/1
L    2001:DB8:3C4D:13:21A:6CFF:FEA1:1F48/128 [0/0]
     via ::, Serial0/0/1
C    2001:DB8:3C4D:15::/64 [0/0]
     via ::, FastEthernet0/0
L    2001:DB8:3C4D:15:21A:6CFF:FEA1:1F48/128 [0/0]
     via ::, FastEthernet0/0
L    FE80::/10 [0/0]
     via ::, Null0
L    FF00::/8 [0/0]
     via ::, Null0
```

This looks good, but I want you to notice that I used the exact same IPv6 subnet addresses on each side of the links from the Corp router to the SF router as well as from the Corp to the LA router.

Configuring Routing on Our Internetwork

I'll start at the Corp router and add simple static routes. Check it out:

```
Corp(config)#ipv6 route 2001:db8:3c4d:14::/64  2001:DB8:3C4D:12:21A:2FFF:
FEE7:4398 150
Corp(config)#ipv6 route 2001:DB8:3C4D:15::/64 s0/1 150
Corp(config)#do sho ipv6 route static
[output cut]
S    2001:DB8:3C4D:14::/64 [150/0]
     via 2001:DB8:3C4D:12:21A:2FFF:FEE7:4398
```

Okay—I agree that first static route line was pretty long because I used the next-hop address, but notice that I used the exit interface on the second entry. But it still wasn't really all that hard to create the longer static route entry. I just went to the SF router, used the command show ipv6 int brief, and then copied and pasted the interface address used for the next hop. You'll get used to IPv6 addresses (You'll get used to doing a lot of copy/paste moves!).

Now since I put an AD of 150 on the static routes, once I configure a routing protocol such as OSPF, they'll be replaced with an OSPF injected route. Let's go to the SF and LA routers and put a single entry in each router to get to remote subnet 11.

```
SF(config)#ipv6 route 2001:db8:3c4d:11::/64 s0/0/0 150
```

That's it! I'm going to head over to LA and put a default route on that router now:

```
LA(config)#ipv6 route ::/0 s0/0/1
```

Let's take a peek at the Corp router's routing table and see if our static routes are in there.

```
Corp#sh ipv6 route static
[output cut]
S   2001:DB8:3C4D:14::/64 [150/0]
     via 2001:DB8:3C4D:12:21A:2FFF:FEE7:4398
S   2001:DB8:3C4D:15::/64 [150/0]
     via ::, Serial0/1
```

Voilà! I can see both of my static routes in the routing table, so IPv6 can now route to those networks. But we're not done because we still need to test our network! First I'm going to go to the SF router and get the IPv6 address of the Fa0/0 interface:

```
SF#sh ipv6 int brief
FastEthernet0/0            [up/up]
    FE80::21A:2FFF:FEE7:4398
    2001:DB8:3C4D:14:21A:2FFF:FEE7:4398
FastEthernet0/1            [administratively down/down]
Serial0/0/0               [up/up]
    FE80::21A:2FFF:FEE7:4398
    2001:DB8:3C4D:12:21A:2FFF:FEE7:4398
```

Next, I'm going to go back to the Corporate router and ping that remote interface by copying and pasting in the address. No sense doing all that typing when copy/paste works great!

```
Corp#ping ipv6 2001:DB8:3C4D:14:21A:2FFF:FEE7:4398
Type escape sequence to abort.
Sending 5, 100-byte ICMP Echos to 2001:DB8:3C4D:14:21A:2FFF:FEE7:4398, timeout
is 2 seconds:
!!!!!
```

Success rate is 100 percent (5/5), round-trip min/avg/max = 0/0/0 ms
Corp#

We can see that static route worked, so next, I'll go get the IPv6 address of the LA router
and ping that remote interface as well:

LA#**sh ipv6 int brief**
FastEthernet0/0   [up/up]
    FE80::21A:6CFF:FEA1:1F48
    2001:DB8:3C4D:15:21A:6CFF:FEA1:1F48
Serial0/0/1   [up/up]
    FE80::21A:6CFF:FEA1:1F48
    2001:DB8:3C4D:13:21A:6CFF:FEA1:1F48

It's time to head over to Corp and ping LA:

Corp#**ping ipv6 2001:DB8:3C4D:15:21A:6CFF:FEA1:1F48**
Type escape sequence to abort.
Sending 5, 100-byte ICMP Echos to 2001:DB8:3C4D:15:21A:6CFF:FEA1:1F48, timeout
is 2 seconds:
!!!!!
Success rate is 100 percent (5/5), round-trip min/avg/max = 4/4/4 ms
Corp#

Now let's use one of my favorite commands:

Corp#**sh ipv6 int brief**
FastEthernet0/0   [up/up]
    FE80::20D:BDFF:FE3B:D80
    2001:DB8:3C4D:11:20D:BDFF:FE3B:D80
Serial0/0   [up/up]
    FE80::20D:BDFF:FE3B:D80
    2001:DB8:3C4D:12:20D:BDFF:FE3B:D80
FastEthernet0/1   [administratively down/down]
    unassigned
Serial0/1   [up/up]
    FE80::20D:BDFF:FE3B:D80
    2001:DB8:3C4D:13:20D:BDFF:FE3B:D80
Loopback0   [up/up]
    unassigned
Corp#

What a nice output! All our interfaces are up/up, and we can see the link-local and
assigned global address.

Static routing really isn't so bad with IPv6! I'm not saying I'd like to do this in a ginor-mous network—no way—I wouldn't want to opt for doing that with IPv4 either! But you can see that it can be done. Also, notice how easy it was to ping an IPv6 address. Copy/paste really is your friend!

Before we finish the chapter, let's add another router to our network and connect it to the Corp Fa0/0 LAN. For our new router I really don't feel like doing any work, so I'll just type this:

```
Boulder#config t
Boulder(config)#int f0/0
Boulder(config-if)#ipv6 address autoconfig default
```

Nice and easy! This configures stateless autoconfiguration on the interface, and the default keyword will advertise itself as the default route for the local link!

I hope you found this chapter as rewarding as I did. The best thing you can do to learn IPv6 is to get some routers and just go at it. Don't give up because it's seriously worth your time!

Summary

This last chapter introduced you to some very key IPv6 structural elements as well as how to make IPv6 work within a Cisco internetwork. You now know that even when covering and configuring IPv6 basics, there's still a great deal to understand—and we just scratched the surface! But you're still well equipped with all you need to meet the Cisco exam objectives.

You learned the vital reasons why we need IPv6 and the benefits associated with it. I covered IPv6 addressing and the importance of using the shortened expressions. As I covered addressing with IPv6, I also showed you the different address types, plus the special addresses reserved in IPv6.

IPv6 will mostly be deployed automatically, meaning hosts will employ autoconfigura-tion. I demonstrated how IPv6 utilizes autoconfiguration and how it comes into play when configuring a Cisco router. You also learned that in IPv6, we can and still should use a DHCP server to the router to provide options to hosts just as we've been doing for years with IPv4—not necessarily IPv6 addresses, but other mission-critical options like providing a DNS server address.

From there, I discussed the evolution of some more integral and familiar protocols like ICMP and OSPF. They've been upgraded to work in the IPv6 environment, but these net-working workhorses are still vital and relevant to operations, and I detailed how ICMP works with IPv6, followed by how to configure OSPFv3. I wrapped up this pivotal chapter by demonstrating key methods to use when verifying that all is running correctly in your IPv6 network. So take some time and work through all the essential study material, especially the written labs, to ensure that you meet your networking goals!

Exam Essentials

Understand why we need IPv6.   Without IPv6, the world would be depleted of IP addresses.

Understand link-local.   Link-local is like an IPv4 private IP address, but it can't be routed at all, not even in your organization.

Understand unique local.   This, like link-local, is like a private IP address in IPv4 and cannot be routed to the Internet. However, the difference between link-local and unique local is that unique local can be routed within your organization or company.

Remember IPv6 addressing.   IPv6 addressing is not like IPv4 addressing. IPv6 addressing has much more address space, is 128 bits long, and represented in hexadecimal, unlike IPv4, which is only 32 bits long and represented in decimal.

Understand and be able to read a EUI-64 address with the 7th bit inverted.   Hosts can use autoconfiguration to obtain an IPv6 address, and one of the ways it can do that is through what is called EUI-64. This takes the unique MAC address of a host and inserts FF:FE in the middle of the address to change a 48-bit MAC address to a 64-bit interface ID. In addition to inserting the 16 bits into the interface ID, the 7th bit of the 1st byte is inverted, typically from a 0 to a 1. Practice this with Written Lab 14.2.

Written Labs 14

In this section, you'll complete the following labs to make sure you've got the information and concepts contained within them fully dialed in:

    Lab 14.1: IPv6

    Lab 14.2: Converting EUI addresses

    You can find the answers to these labs in Appendix A, "Answers to Written Labs."

Written Lab 14.1

In this section, write the answers to the following IPv6 questions:

1.   Which two ICMPv6 types are used for testing IPv6 reachability?
2.   What is the corresponding Ethernet address for FF02:0000:0000:0000:0000:0001:FF 17:FC0F?
3.   Which type of address is not meant to be routed?
4.   What type of address is this: FE80::/10?
5.   Which type of address is meant to be delivered to multiple interfaces?

6. Which type of address identifies multiple interfaces, but packets are delivered only to the first address it finds?

7. Which routing protocol uses multicast address FF02::5?

8. IPv4 had a loopback address of 127.0.0.1. What is the IPv6 loopback address?

9. What does a link-local address always start with?

10. Which IPv6 address is the all-router multicast group?

Written Lab 14.2

In this section, you will practice inverting the 7th bit of a EUI-64 address. Use the prefix 2001:db8:1:1/64 for each address.

1. Convert the following MAC address into a EUI-64 address: 0b0c:abcd:1234.

2. Convert the following MAC address into a EUI-64 address: 060c:32f1:a4d2.

3. Convert the following MAC address into a EUI-64 address: 10bc:abcd:1234.

4. Convert the following MAC address into a EUI-64 address: 0d01:3a2f:1234.

5. Convert the following MAC address into a EUI-64 address: 0a0c.abac.caba.

Hands-on Labs

You'll need at least three routers to complete these labs; five would be better, but if you are using the LammleSim IOS version, then these lab layouts are preconfigured for you. This section will have you configure the following labs:

Lab 14.1: Manual and Stateful Autoconfiguration

Lab 14.2: Static and Default Routing

Here is our network:

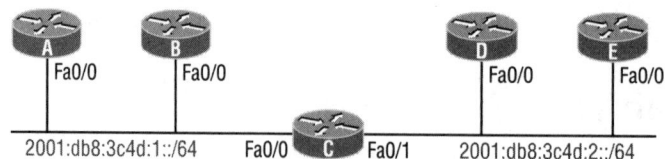

Hands-on Lab 14.1: Manual and Stateful Autoconfiguration

In this lab, you will configure the C router with manual IPv6 addresses on the Fa0/0 and Fa0/1 interfaces and then configure the other routers to automatically assign themselves an IPv6 address.

1. Log in to the C router and configure IPv6 addresses on each interface based on the subnets (1 and 2) shown in the graphic.

   ```
   C(config)#ipv6 unicast-routing
   C(config)#int fa0/0
   C(config-if)#ipv6 address 2001:db8:3c4d:1::1/64
   C(config-if)#int fa0/1
   C(config-if)#ipv6 address 2001:db8:3c4d:2::1/64
   ```

2. Verify the interfaces with the show ipv6 route connected and sho ipv6 int brief commands.

   ```
   C(config-if)#do show ipv6 route connected
   [output cut]
   C   2001:DB8:3C4D:1::/64 [0/0]
        via ::, FastEthernet0/0
   C   2001:DB8:3C4D:2::/64 [0/0]
        via ::, FastEthernet0/0
   C(config-if)#sh ipv6 int brief
   FastEthernet0/0              [up/up]
       FE80::20D:BDFF:FE3B:D80
       2001:DB8:3C4D:1::1
   FastEthernet0/1              [up/up]
       FE80::20D:BDFF:FE3B:D81
       2001:DB8:3C4D:2::1
   Loopback0                    [up/up]
       Unassigned
   ```

3. Go to your other routers and configure the Fa0/0 on each router to autoconfigure an IPv6 address.

   ```
   A(config)#ipv6 unicast-routing
   A(config)#int f0/0
   A(config-if)#ipv6 address autoconfig
   A(config-if)#no shut

   B(config)#ipv6 unicast-routing
   B(config)#int fa0/0
   B(config-if)#ipv6 address autoconfig
   B(config-if)#no shut

   D(config)#ipv6 unicast-routing
   D(config)#int fa0/0
   D(config-if)#ipv6 address autoconfig
   D(config-if)#no shut
   ```

```
E(config)#ipv6 unicast-routing
E(config)#int fa0/0
E(config-if)#ipv6 address autoconfig
E(config-if)#no shut
```

4. Verify that your routers received an IPv6 address.

   ```
   A#sh ipv6 int brief
   FastEthernet0/0                [up/up]
       FE80::20D:BDFF:FE3B:C20
       2001:DB8:3C4D:1:20D:BDFF:FE3B:C20
   ```

   Continue to verify your addresses on all your other routers.

Hands-on Lab 14.2: Static and Default Routing

Router C is directly connected to both subnets, so no routing of any type needs to be configured. However, all the other routers are connected to only one subnet, so at least one route needs to be configured on each router.

1. On the A router, configure a static route to the 2001:db8:3c4d:2::/64 subnet.

   ```
   A(config)#ipv6 route 2001:db8:3c4d:2::/64 fa0/0
   ```

2. On the B router, configure a default route.

   ```
   B(config)#ipv6 route ::/0 fa0/0
   ```

3. On the D router, create a static route to the remote subnet.

   ```
   D(config)#ipv6 route 2001:db8:3c4d:1::/64 fa0/0
   ```

4. On the E router, create a static route to the remote subnet.

   ```
   E(config)#ipv6 route 2001:db8:3c4d:1::/64 fa0/0
   ```

5. Verify your configurations with a show running-config and show ipv6 route.

6. Ping from router D to router A. First, you need to get router A's IPv6 address with a show ipv6 int brief command. Here is an example:

   ```
   A#sh ipv6 int brief
   FastEthernet0/0                [up/up]
       FE80::20D:BDFF:FE3B:C20
       2001:DB8:3C4D:1:20D:BDFF:FE3B:C20
   ```

7. Now go to router D and ping the IPv6 address from router A:

   ```
   D#ping ipv6 2001:DB8:3C4D:1:20D:BDFF:FE3B:C20
   Type escape sequence to abort.
   Sending 5, 100-byte ICMP Echos to 2001:DB8:3C4D:1:20D:BDFF:FE3B:C20, timeout
   is 2 seconds:
   !!!!!
   Success rate is 100 percent (5/5), round-trip min/avg/max = 0/2/4 ms
   ```

Review Questions

The following questions are designed to test your understanding of this chapter's material. For more information on how to get additional questions, please see www.lammle.com/ccna.

The answers to these questions can be found in Appendix B, "Answers to Chapter Review Questions."

1. How is an EUI-64 format interface ID created from a 48-bit MAC address?

    A. By appending 0xFF to the MAC address

    B. By prefixing the MAC address with 0xFFEE

    C. By prefixing the MAC address with 0xFF and appending 0xFF to it

    D. By inserting 0xFFFE between the upper 3 bytes and the lower 3 bytes of the MAC address

    E. By prefixing the MAC address with 0xF and inserting 0xF after each of its first three bytes

2. Which option is a valid IPv6 address?

    A. 2001:0000:130F::099a::12a

    B. 2002:7654:A1AD:61:81AF:CCC1

    C. FEC0:ABCD:WXYZ:0067::2A4

    D. 2004:1:25A4:886F::1

3. Which three statements about IPv6 prefixes are true? (Choose three.)

    A. FF00:/8 is used for IPv6 multicast.

    B. FE80::/10 is used for link-local unicast.

    C. FC00::/7 is used in private networks.

    D. 2001::1/127 is used for loopback addresses.

    E. FE80::/8 is used for link-local unicast.

    F. FEC0::/10 is used for IPv6 broadcast.

4. What are three approaches that are used when migrating from an IPv4 addressing scheme to an IPv6 scheme? (Choose three.)

    A. Enable dual-stack routing.

    B. Configure IPv6 directly.

    C. Configure IPv4 tunnels between IPv6 islands.

    D. Use proxying and translation to translate IPv6 packets into IPv4 packets.

    E. Statically map IPv4 addresses to IPv6 addresses.

    F. Use DHCPv6 to map IPv4 addresses to IPv6 addresses.

5. Which two statements about IPv6 router advertisement messages are true? (Choose two.)

    A. They use ICMPv6 type 134.

    B. The advertised prefix length must be 64 bits.

    C. The advertised prefix length must be 48 bits.

    D. They are sourced from the configured IPv6 interface address.

    E. Their destination is always the link-local address of the neighboring node.

6. Which of the following is true when describing an IPv6 anycast address?

    A. One-to-many communication model

    B. One-to-nearest communication model

    C. Any-to-many communication model

    D. A unique IPv6 address for each device in the group

    E. The same address for multiple devices in the group

    F. Delivery of packets to the group interface that is closest to the sending device

7. You want to ping the loopback address of your IPv6 local host. What will you type?

    A. `ping 127.0.0.1`

    B. `ping 0.0.0.0`

    C. `ping ::1`

    D. `trace 0.0.::1`

8. What are three features of the IPv6 protocol? (Choose three.)

    A. Optional IPsec

    B. Autoconfiguration

    C. No broadcasts

    D. Complicated header

    E. Plug-and-play

    F. Checksums

9. Which two statements describe characteristics of IPv6 unicast addressing? (Choose two.)

    A. Global addresses start with 2000::/3.

    B. Link-local addresses start with FE00:/12.

    C. Link-local addresses start with FF00::/10.

    D. There is only one loopback address and it is ::1.

    E. If a global address is assigned to an interface, then that is the only allowable address for the interface.

10. A host sends a router solicitation (RS) on the data link. What destination address is sent with this request?

    A. FF02::A

    B. FF02::9

   C. FF02::2

   D. FF02::1

   E. FF02::5

11. What are two valid reasons for adopting IPv6 over IPv4? (Choose two.)

   A. No broadcast

   B. Change of source address in the IPv6 header

   C. Change of destination address in the IPv6 header

   D. No password required for Telnet access

   E. Autoconfiguration

   F. NAT

12. A host sends a type of NDP message providing the MAC address that was requested. Which type of NDP was sent?

   A. NA

   B. RS

   C. RA

   D. NS

13. Which is known as "one-to-nearest" addressing in IPv6?

   A. Global unicast

   B. Anycast

   C. Multicast

   D. Unspecified address

14. Which of the following statements about IPv6 addresses are true? (Choose two.)

   A. Leading zeros are required.

   B. Two colons (::) are used to represent successive hexadecimal fields of zeros.

   C. Two colons (::) are used to separate fields.

   D. A single interface will have multiple IPv6 addresses of different types.

15. Which three ways are an IPv6 header simpler than an IPv4 header? (Choose three.)

   A. Unlike IPv4 headers, IPv6 headers have a fixed length.

   B. IPv6 uses an extension header instead of the IPv4 Fragmentation field.

   C. IPv6 headers eliminate the IPv4 Checksum field.

   D. IPv6 headers use the Fragment Offset field in place of the IPv4 Fragmentation field.

   E. IPv6 headers use a smaller Option field size than IPv4 headers.

   F. IPv6 headers use a 4-bit TTL field, and IPv4 headers use an 8-bit TTL field.

16. Which of the following descriptions about IPv6 is correct?

   A. Addresses are not hierarchical and are assigned at random.

   B. Broadcasts have been eliminated and replaced with multicasts.

    C. There are 2.7 billion addresses.

    D. An interface can only be configured with one IPv6 address.

17. How many bits are in an IPv6 address field?

    A. 24

    B. 4

    C. 3

    D. 16

    E. 32

    F. 128

18. Which of the following correctly describe characteristics of IPv6 unicast addressing? (Choose two.)

    A. Global addresses start with 2000::/3.

    B. Link-local addresses start with FF00::/10.

    C. Link-local addresses start with FE00:/12.

    D. There is only one loopback address and it is ::1.

19. Which of the following statements are true of IPv6 address representation? (Choose two.)

    A. The first 64 bits represent the dynamically created interface ID.

    B. A single interface may be assigned multiple IPv6 addresses of any type.

    C. Every IPv6 interface contains at least one loopback address.

    D. Leading zeroes in an IPv6 16-bit hexadecimal field are mandatory.

20. Which command enables IPv6 forwarding on a Cisco router?

    A. `ipv6 local`

    B. `ipv6 host`

    C. `ipv6 unicast-routing`

    D. `ipv6 neighbor`

Appendix A

Answers to Written Labs

Chapter 1: Internetworking

Written Lab 1.1: OSI Questions

1. The Application layer is responsible for finding the network resources broadcast from a server and adding flow control and error control (if the application developer chooses).

2. The Physical layer takes frames from the Data Link layer and encodes the 1s and 0s into a digital or analog (Ethernet or wireless) signal for transmission on the network medium.

3. The Network layer provides routing through an internetwork and logical addressing.

4. The Presentation layer makes sure that data is in a readable format for the Application layer.

5. The Session layer sets up, maintains, and terminates sessions between applications.

6. PDUs at the Data Link layer are called frames and provide physical addressing plus other options to place packets on the network medium.

7. The Transport layer uses virtual circuits to create a reliable connection between two hosts.

8. The Network layer provides logical addressing, typically IP addressing and routing.

9. The Physical layer is responsible for the electrical and mechanical connections between devices.

10. The Data Link layer is responsible for the framing of data packets.

11. The Session layer creates sessions between different hosts' applications.

12. The Data Link layer frames packets received from the Network layer.

13. The Transport layer segments user data.

14. The Network layer creates packets out of segments handed down from the Transport layer.

15. The Physical layer is responsible for transporting 1s and 0s (bits) in a digital signal.

16. Segments, packets, frames, bits

17. Transport

18. Data Link

19. Network

20. 48 bits (6 bytes) expressed as a hexadecimal number

Written Lab 1.2: Defining the OSI Layers and Devices

Description	Device or OSI Layer
This device sends and receives information about the Network layer.	Router
This layer creates a virtual circuit before transmitting between two end stations.	Transport
This device uses hardware addresses to filter a network.	Bridge or switch
Ethernet is defined at these layers.	Data Link and Physical
This layer supports flow control, sequencing, and acknowledgments.	Transport
This device can measure the distance to a remote network.	Router
Logical addressing is used at this layer.	Network
Hardware addresses are defined at this layer.	Data Link (MAC sub-layer)
This device creates one collision domain and one broadcast domain.	Hub
This device creates many smaller collision domains, but the network is still one large broadcast domain.	Switch or bridge
This device can never run full-duplex.	Hub
This device breaks up collision domains and broadcast domains.	Router

Written Lab 1.3: Identifying Collision and Broadcast Domains

A. Hub: One collision domain, one broadcast domain

B. Bridge: Two collision domains, one broadcast domain

C. Switch: Four collision domains, one broadcast domain

D. Router: Three collision domains, three broadcast domains

Chapter 2: Ethernet Networking and Data Encapsulation

Written Lab 2.1: Binary/Decimal/Hexadecimal Conversion

1.

Decimal	128	64	32	16	8	4	2	1	Binary
192	1	1	0	0	0	0	0	0	11000000
168	1	0	1	0	1	0	0	0	10101000
10	0	0	0	0	1	0	1	0	00001010
15	0	0	0	0	1	1	1	1	00001111
Decimal	128	64	32	16	8	4	2	1	Binary
172	1	0	1	0	1	1	0	0	10101100
16	0	0	0	1	0	0	0	0	00010000
20	0	0	0	1	0	1	0	0	00010100
55	0	0	1	1	0	1	1	1	00110111
Decimal	128	64	32	16	8	4	2	1	Binary
10	0	0	0	0	1	0	1	0	00001010
11	0	0	0	0	1	0	1	1	00001011
12	0	0	0	0	1	1	0	0	00001100
99	0	1	1	0	0	0	1	1	01100011

2.

Binary	128	64	32	16	8	4	2	1	Decimal
11001100	1	1	0	0	1	1	0	0	204
00110011	0	0	1	1	0	0	1	1	51
10101010	1	0	1	0	1	0	1	0	170
01010101	0	1	0	1	0	1	0	1	85

Binary	128	64	32	16	8	4	2	1	Decimal
11000110	1	1	0	0	0	1	1	0	198
11010011	1	1	0	1	0	0	1	1	211
00111001	0	0	1	1	1	0	0	1	57
11010001	1	1	0	1	0	0	0	1	209
Binary	128	64	32	16	8	4	2	1	Decimal
10000100	1	0	0	0	0	1	0	0	132
11010010	1	1	0	1	0	0	1	0	210
10111000	1	0	1	1	1	0	0	0	184
10100110	1	0	1	0	0	1	1	0	166

3.

Binary	128	64	32	16	8	4	2	1	Hexadecimal
11011000	1	1	0	1	1	0	0	0	D8
00011011	0	0	0	1	1	0	1	1	1B
00111101	0	0	1	1	1	1	0	1	3D
01110110	0	1	1	1	0	1	1	0	76
Binary	128	6	32	16	8	4	2	1	Hexadecimal
11001010	1	1	0	0	1	0	1	0	CA
11110101	1	1	1	1	0	1	0	1	F5
10000011	1	0	0	0	0	0	1	1	83
11101011	1	1	1	0	1	0	1	1	EB
Binary	128	64	32	16	8	4	2	1	Hexadecimal
10000100	1	0	0	0	0	1	0	0	84
11010010	1	1	0	1	0	0	1	0	D2
01000011	0	1	0	0	0	0	1	1	43
10110011	1	0	1	1	0	0	1	1	B3

Written Lab 2.2: CSMA/CD Operations

When a collision occurs on an Ethernet LAN, the following happens:

1. A jam signal informs all devices that a collision occurred.

2. The collision invokes a random backoff algorithm.

3. Each device on the Ethernet segment stops transmitting for a short time until the timers expire.

4. All hosts have equal priority to transmit after the timers have expired.

Written Lab 2.3: Cabling

1. Crossover

2. Straight-through

3. Crossover

4. Crossover

5. Straight-through

6. Crossover

7. Crossover

8. Rolled

Written Lab 2.4: Encapsulation

At a transmitting device, the data encapsulation method works like this:

1. User information is converted to data for transmission on the network.

2. Data is converted to segments, and a reliable connection is set up between the transmitting and receiving hosts.

3. Segments are converted to packets or datagrams, and a logical address is placed in the header so each packet can be routed through an internetwork.

4. Packets or datagrams are converted to frames for transmission on the local network. Hardware (Ethernet) addresses are used to uniquely identify hosts on a local network segment.

5. Frames are converted to bits, and a digital encoding and clocking scheme is used.

Chapter 3: Introduction to TCP/IP

Written Lab 3.1: TCP/IP

1. 192 through 223, 110*xxxxx*

2. Host-to-Host or Transport

3. 1 through 126

4. Loopback or diagnostics

5. Turn all host bits off.

6. Turn all host bits on.

7. 10.0.0.0 through 10.255.255.255

8. 172.16.0.0 through 172.31.255.255

9. 192.168.0.0 through 192.168.255.255

10. 0 through 9 and *A, B, C, D, E,* and *F*

Written Lab 3.2: Mapping Applications to the DoD Model

1. Internet

2. Process/Application

3. Process/Application

4. Process/Application

5. Process/Application

6. Internet

7. Process/Application

8. Host-to-host/Transport

9. Process/Application

10. Host-to-host/Transport

11. Process/Application

12. Internet

13. Internet

14. Internet

15. Process/Application

16. Process/Application

17. Process/Application

Chapter 4: Easy Subnetting

Written Lab 4.1: Written Subnet Practice #1

1. 192.168.100.25/30. A /30 is 255.255.255.252. The valid subnet is 192.168.100.24, broadcast is 192.168.100.27, and valid hosts are 192.168.100.25 and 26.

2. 192.168.100.37/28. A /28 is 255.255.255.240. The fourth octet is a block size of 16. Just count by 16s until you pass 37. 0, 16, 32, 48. The host is in the 32 subnet, with a broadcast address of 47. Valid hosts 33–46.

3. A /27 is 255.255.255.224. The fourth octet is a block size of 32. Count by 32s until you pass the host address of 66. 0, 32, 64, 96. The host is in the 64 subnet, and the broadcast address is 95. Valid host range is 65–94.

4. 192.168.100.17/29. A /29 is 255.255.255.248. The fourth octet is a block size of 8. 0, 8, 16, 24. The host is in the 16 subnet, broadcast of 23. Valid hosts 17–22.

5. 192.168.100.99/26. A /26 is 255.255.255.192. The fourth octet has a block size of 64. 0, 64, 128. The host is in the 64 subnet, broadcast of 127. Valid hosts 65–126.

6. 192.168.100.99/25. A /25 is 255.255.255.128. The fourth octet is a block size of 128. 0, 128. The host is in the 0 subnet, broadcast of 127. Valid hosts 1–126.

7. A default Class B is 255.255.0.0. A Class B 255.255.255.0 mask is 256 subnets, each with 254 hosts. We need fewer subnets. If we used 255.255.240.0, this provides 16 subnets. Let's add one more subnet bit. 255.255.248.0. This is 5 bits of subnetting, which provides 32 subnets. This is our best answer, a /21.

8. A /29 is 255.255.255.248. This is a block size of 8 in the fourth octet. 0, 8, 16. The host is in the 8 subnet, broadcast is 15.

9. A /29 is 255.255.255.248, which is 5 subnet bits and 3 host bits. This is only 6 hosts per subnet.

10. A /23 is 255.255.254.0. The third octet is a block size of 2. 0, 2, 4. The subnet is in the 16.2.0 subnet; the broadcast address is 16.3.255.

Written Lab 4.2: Written Subnet Practice #2

Classful Address	Subnet Mask	Number of Hosts per Subnet ($2^x - 2$)
/16	255.255.0.0	65,534
/17	255.255.128.0	32,766
/18	255.255.192.0	16,382
/19	255.255.224.0	8,190
/20	255.255.240.0	4,094
/21	255.255.248.0	2,046
/22	255.255.252.0	1,022
/23	255.255.254.0	510
/24	255.255.255.0	254
/25	255.255.255.128	126
/26	255.255.255.192	62
/27	255.255.255.224	30
/28	255.255.255.240	14
/29	255.255.255.248	6
/30	255.255.255.252	2

Written Lab 4.3: Written Subnet Practice #3

Decimal IP Address	Address Class	Number of Subnet and Host Bits	Number of Subnets ($2x$)	Number of Hosts ($2x - 2$)
10.25.66.154/23	A	15/9	32,768	510
172.31.254.12/24	B	8/8	256	254
192.168.20.123/28	C	4/4	16	14
63.24.89.21/18	A	10/14	1,024	16,382
128.1.1.254/20	B	4/12	16	4,094
208.100.54.209/30	C	6/2	64	2

Chapter 5: VLSMs, Summarization and Troubleshooting TCP/IP

1. 192.168.0.0/20

2. 172.144.0.0 255.240.0.0

3. 192.168.32.0 255.255.224.0

4. 192.168.96.0 255.255.240.0

5. 66.66.0.0 255.255.240.0

6. 192.168.0.0/17

7. 172.16.0.0 255.255.248.0

8. 192.168.128.0 255.255.192.0

9. 53.60.96.0 255.255.224.0

10. 172.16.0.0 255.255.192.0

Chapter 6: Cisco's Internetworking Operating System (IOS)

Written Lab 6: Cisco IOS

1. Router(config)#**clock rate 1000000**

2. Switch#**config t**
    switch config)# **line vty 0 15**
    switch(config-line)# **no login**

3. Switch#**config t**
    Switch(config)# **int f0/1**
    Switch(config-if)# **no shutdown**

4. Switch#**erase startup-config**

5. Switch#**config t**
    Switch(config)#**line console 0**

```
     Switch(config-line)#password todd
     Switch(config-line)#login
```

6. `Switch#config t`
    `Switch(config)# enable secret cisco`

7. `Router#show controllers serial 0/2`

8. `Switch#show terminal`

9. `Switch#reload`

10. `Switch#config t`
    `Switch(config)#hostname Sales`

Chapter 7: Managing a Cisco Internetwork

Written Lab 7.1: IOS Management

1. `copy start run`

2. `show cdp neighbor detail` or `show cdp entry *`

3. `show cdp neighbor`

4. Ctrl+Shift+6, then X

5. `show sessions`

6. Either `copy tftp run` or `copy start run`

7. NTP

8. `ip helper-address`

9. `ntp server` *ip_address* `version 4`

10. `show ntp status`

Written Lab 7.2: Router Memory

1. Flash memory

2. ROM

3. NVRAM

4. ROM

5. RAM

6. RAM

7. ROM

8. ROM

9. RAM

10. RAM

Chapter 8: Managing Cisco Devices

Written Lab 8.1: IOS Management

1. `copy flash tftp`

2. 0x2101

3. 0x2102

4. 0x2100

5. UDI

6. 0x2142

7. `boot system`

8. POST test

9. `copy tftp flash`

10. `show license`

Chapter 9: IP Routing

1. router(config)#**ip route 172.16.10.0 255.255.255.0 172.16.20.1 150**

2. It will use the gateway interface MAC at L2 and the actual destination IP at L3.

3. router(config)#**ip route 0.0.0.0 0.0.0.0 172.16.40.1**

4. Stub network

5. Router#**show ip route**

6. Exit interface

7. False. The MAC address would be the local router interface, not the remote host.

8. True

9. router(config)#**router rip**
    router(config-router)#**passive-interface S1**

10. True

Chapter 10: Layer 2 Switching

1. show mac address-table

2. Flood the frame out all ports except the port on which it was received

3. Address learning, forward/filter decisions, and loop avoidance

4. It will add the source MAC address in the forward/filter table and associate it with the port on which the frame was received.

5. Maximum 1, violation shutdown

6. Restrict and shutdown

7. Restrict

8. The addition of dynamically learned addresses to the running-configuration

9. Show port-security interface fastethernet 0/12 and show running-config

10. False

Chapter 11: VLANs and InterVLAN Routing

1. False! You do not provide an IP address under any physical port.

2. STP

3. Broadcast

4. VLAN 1 is the default VLAN and cannot be changed, renamed, or deleted. VLANs 1002–1005 are reserved, and VLANs 1006–4094 are extended VLANs and can only be configured if you are in VTP transparent mode. You can only configure VLANs 2–1001 by default.

5. `switchport trunk encapsulation dot1q`

6. Trunking sends information about all or many VLANs across a single link.

7. 1000 (2 to 1001). VLAN 1 is the default VLAN and cannot be changed, renamed, or deleted. VLANs 1002–1005 are reserved, and VLANs 1006–4094 are extended VLANs and can only be configured if you are in VTP transparent mode.

8. True

9. Access link

10. `switchport trunk native vlan 4`

Chapter 12: Security

1. `access-list 10 deny 172.16.0.0 0.0.255.255`
   `access-list 10 permit any`

2. `ip access-group 10 out`

3. `access-list 10 deny host 192.168.15.5`
   `access-list 10 permit any`

4. `show access-lists`

5. IDS, IPS

6. `access-list 110 deny tcp host`
   `172.16.10.1 host  172.16.30.5 eq 23`
   `access-list 110 permit ip any any`

7. `line vty 0 4`
   `access-class 110 in`

8. `ip access-list standard No172Net`
   `deny 172.16.0.0 0.0.255.255`
   `permit any`

9. `ip access-group No172Net out`

10. `show ip interfaces`

Chapter 13: Network Address Translation (NAT)

1. Port Address Translation (PAT), also called NAT Overload

2. `debug ip nat`

3. `show ip nat translations`

4. `clear ip nat translations *`

5. Before

6. After

7. `show ip nat statistics`

8. The `ip nat inside` and `ip nat outside` commands

9. Dynamic NAT

10. `prefix-length`

Chapter 14: Internet Protocol Version 6 (IPv6)

Written Lab 14.1: IPv6 Foundation

1. 128 and 129

2. 33-33-FF-17-FC-0F

3. Link-local

4. Link-local

5. Multicast

6. Anycast

7. OSPFv3

8. ::1

9. FE80::/10

10. FF02::2

Written Lab 14.2: EUI-64 Format

1. 2001:db8:1:1:090c:abff:fecd:1234

2. 2001:db8:1:1:040c:32ff:fef1:a4d2

3. 2001:db8:1:1:12:abff:fecd:1234

4. 2001:db8:1:1:0f01:3aff:fe2f:1234

5. 2001:db8:1:1:080c:abff:feac:caba

Appendix

B

Answers to Review Questions

Chapter 1: Internetworking

1.   A. The device shown is a hub and hubs place all ports in the same broadcast domain and the same collision domain.

2.   B. The contents of a protocol data unit (PDU) depend on the PDU because they are created in a specific order and their contents are based on that order. A packet will contain IP addresses but not MAC addresses because MAC addresses are not present until the PDU becomes a frame.

3.   C. You should select a router to connect the two groups. When computers are in different subnets, as these two groups are, you will require a device that can make decisions based on IP addresses. Routers operate at layer 3 of the Open Systems Interconnect (OSI) model and make data-forwarding decisions based on layer 3 networking information, which are IP addresses. They create routing tables that guide them in forwarding traffic out of the proper interface to the proper subnet.

4.   C. Replacing the hub with a switch would reduce collisions and retransmissions, which would have the most impact on reducing congestion.

5.   Answer:

Layer	Description
Transport	Bits
Data Link	Segment
Physical	Packet
Network	Frame

The given layers of the OSI model use the PDUs shown in the above diagram.

6.   B. Wireless LAN Controllers are used to manage anywhere from a few access points to thousands. The AP's are completely managed from the controller and are considered lightweight or dumb AP's as they have no configuration on the AP itself.

7.   B. You should use a switch to accomplish the task in this scenario. A switch is used to provide dedicated bandwidth to each node by eliminating the possibility of collisions on the switch port where the node resides. Switches work at layer 2 in the Open Systems Interconnection (OSI) model and perform the function of separating collision domains.

8.

Answer:

Transport	End-to-end connection
Physical	Conversion to bits
Data Link	Framing
Network	Routing

The listed layers of the OSI model have the functions shown in the diagram above.

9. C. Firewalls are used to connect our trusted internal network such as the DMZ, to the untrusted outside network—typically the internet.

10. D. The Application layer is responsible for identifying and establishing the availability of the intended communication partner and determining whether sufficient resources for the intended communication exist.

11. A, D. The Transport layer segments data into smaller pieces for transport. Each segment is assigned a sequence number so that the receiving device can reassemble the data on arrival. The Network layer (layer 3) has two key responsibilities. First, this layer controls the logical addressing of devices. Second, the Network layer determines the best path to a particular destination network and routes the data appropriately.

12. C. The IEEE Ethernet Data Link layer has two sublayers, the Media Access Control (MAC) layer and the Logical Link Control (LLC) layer.

13. C. Wireless AP's are very popular today and will be going away about the same time that rock n' roll does. The idea behind these devices (which are layer 2 bridge devices) is to connect wireless products to the wired Ethernet network. The wireless AP will create a single collision domain and is typically its own dedicated broadcast domain as well.

14. A. Hubs operate on the Physical Layer as they have no intelligence and send all traffic in all directions.

15. C. While it is true that the OSI model's primary purpose is to allow different vendors' networks to interoperate, there is no requirement that vendors follow the model.

16. A. Routers by default do NOT forward broadcasts.

17. C. Switches create separate collision domains within a single broadcast domain. Routers provide a separate broadcast domain for each interface.

18. B. The all-hub network at the bottom is one collision domain; the bridge network on top equals three collision domains. Add in the switch network of five collision domains—one for each switch port—and you get a total of nine.

19. A. The top three layers define how the applications within the end stations will communicate with each other as well as with users.

20. A. The following network devices operate at all seven layers of the OSI model: network management stations (NMSs), gateways (not default gateways), servers, and network hosts.

Chapter 2: Ethernet Networking and Data Encapsulation

1. D. The organizationally unique identifier (OUI) is assigned by the IEEE to an organization composed of 24 bits, or 3 bytes, which in turn assigns a globally administered address also comprising 24 bits, or 3 bytes, that's supposedly unique to each and every adapter it manufactures.

2. A. Backoff on an Ethernet network is the retransmission delay that's enforced when a collision occurs. When that happens, a host will only resume transmission after the forced time delay has expired. Keep in mind that after the backoff has elapsed, all stations have equal priority to transmit data.

3. A. When using a hub, all ports are in the same collision domain, which will introduce collisions as shown between devices connected to the same hub.

4. B. FCS is a field at the end of the frame that's used to store the cyclic redundancy check (CRC) answer. The CRC is a mathematical algorithm that's based on the data in the frame and run when each frame is built. When a receiving host receives the frame and runs the CRC, the answer should be the same. If not, the frame is discarded, assuming errors have occurred.

5. C. Half-duplex Ethernet networking uses a protocol called Carrier Sense Multiple Access with Collision Detection (CSMA/CD), which helps devices share the bandwidth evenly while preventing two devices from transmitting simultaneously on the same network medium.

6. A, E. Physical addresses or MAC addresses are used to identify devices at layer 2. MAC addresses are only used to communicate on the same network. To communicate on different network, we have to use layer 3 addresses (IP addresses).

7. D. The cable shown is a straight-through cable, which is used between dissimilar devices.

8. C, D. An Ethernet network is a shared environment, so all devices have the right to access the medium. If more than one device transmits simultaneously, the signals collide and cannot reach the destination.If a device detects another device is sending, it will wait for a specified amount of time before attempting to transmit.

   When there is no traffic detected, a device will transmit its message. While this transmission is occurring, the device continues to listen for traffic or collisions on the LAN. After the message is sent, the device returns to its default listening mode.

9. B. In creating the gigabit crossover cable, you'd still cross 1 to 3 and 2 to 6, but you would add 4 to 7 and 5 to 8.

10. D. When you set up the connection, use these settings:

- Bits per sec: 9600
- Data bits: 8
- Parity: None
- Stop bits: 1
- Flow control: None

11. D. When set to 0, this bit represents a globally administered address, as specified by the IEEE, but when it's a 1, it represents a locally governed and administered address.

12. B. You can use a rolled Ethernet cable to connect a host EIA-TIA 232 interface to a router console serial communication (COM) port.

13. B. The collision will invoke a backoff algorithm on all systems, not ju
in the collision.

14. A. There are no collisions in full-duplex mode.

15. B. The connection between the two switches requires a crossover an
the hosts to the switches requires a straight-through.

16. The given cable types are matched with their standards in the follow

IEEE 802.3u	100Base-Tx
IEEE 802.3	10Base-T
IEEE 802.3ab	1000Base-T
IEEE 802.3z	1000Base-SX

17. B. Although rolled cable isn't used to connect any Ethernet connections together, you can use a rolled Ethernet cable to connect a host EIA-TIA 232 interface to a router console serial communication (COM) port.

18. B. If you're using TCP, the virtual circuit is defined by the source and destination port number plus the source and destination IP address and called a *socket*.

19. A. The hex value 1c is converted as 28 in decimal.

20. A. Fiber-optic cables are the only ones that have a core surrounded by a material called cladding.

Chapter 3: Introduction to TCP/IP

1. C. If a DHCP conflict is detected, either by the server sending a ping and getting a response or by a host using a gratuitous ARP (arp'ing for its own IP address and seeing if a host responds), then the server will hold that address and not use it again until it is fixed by an administrator.

2. B. Secure Shell (SSH) protocol sets up a secure session that's similar to Telnet over a standard TCP/IP connection and is employed for doing things like logging into systems, running programs on remote systems, and moving files from one system to another.

3. C. A host uses something called a gratuitous ARP to help avoid a possible duplicate address. The DHCP client sends an ARP broadcast out on the local LAN or VLAN using its newly assigned address to help solve conflicts before they occur.

4. B. Address Resolution Protocol (ARP) is used to find the hardware address from a known IP address.

5. A, C, D. The listed answers are from the OSI model and the question asked about the TCP/IP protocol stack (DoD model). Yes, it is normal for the objectives to have this type of question. However, let's just look for what is wrong. First, the Session layer is not in the TCP/IP model; neither are the Data Link and Physical layers. This leaves us with the Transport layer (Host-to-Host in the DoD model), Internet layer (Network layer in the OSI), and Application layer (Application/Process in the DoD). Remember, the CCENT objectives can list the layers as OSI layers or DoD layers at any time, regardless of what the question is asking.

6. C. A Class C network address has only 8 bits for defining hosts: $2^8 - 2 = 256$.

7. A, B. A client that sends out a DHCP Discover message in order to receive an IP address sends out a broadcast at both layer 2 and layer 3. The layer 2 broadcast is all Fs in hex, or FF:FF:FF:FF:FF:FF. The layer 3 broadcast is 255.255.255.255, which means any networks and all hosts. DHCP is connectionless, which means it uses User Datagram Protocol (UDP) at the Transport layer, also called the Host-to-Host layer.

8. B. Although Telnet does use TCP and IP (TCP/IP), the question specifically asks about layer 4, and IP works at layer 3. Telnet uses TCP at layer 4.

9. RFC 1918. These addresses can be used on a private network, but they're not routable through the Internet.

10. B, D, E. SMTP, FTP, and HTTP use TCP.

11. C. Class C addresses devote 24 bits to the network portion and 8 bits to the host portion.

12. C. The range of multicast addresses starts with 224.0.0.0 and goes through 239.255.255.255.

13. C. First, you should know easily that only TCP and UDP work at the Transport layer, so now you have a 50/50 shot. However, since the header has sequencing, acknowledgment, and window numbers, the answer can only be TCP.

14. A. Both FTP and Telnet use TCP at the Transport layer; however, they both are Application layer protocols, so the Application layer is the best answer for this question.

15. C. The four layers of the DoD model are Application/Process, Host-to-Host, Internet, and Network Access. The Internet layer is equivalent to the Network layer of the OSI model.

16. C, E. The Class A private address range is 10.0.0.0 through 10.255.255.255. The Class B private address range is 172.16.0.0 through 172.31.255.255, and the Class C private address range is 192.168.0.0 through 192.168.255.255.

17. B. The four layers of the TCP/IP stack (also called the DoD model) are Application/Process, Host-to-Host (also called Transport on the objectives), Internet, and Network Access/Link. The Host-to-Host layer is equivalent to the Transport layer of the OSI model.

18. B, C. ICMP is used for diagnostics and destination unreachable messages. ICMP is encapsulated within IP datagrams, and because it is used for diagnostics, it will provide hosts with information about network problems.

19. C. The range of a Class B network address is 128–191. This makes our binary range 10*xxxxxx*.

20.

Answer
DHCPDiscover
DHCPOffer
DHCPRequest
DHCPAck

The steps are as shown in the answer diagram.

Chapter 4: Easy Subnetting

1. D. A /27 (255.255.255.224) is 3 bits on and 5 bits off. This provides 8 subnets, each with 30 hosts. Does it matter if this mask is used with a Class A, B, or C network address? Not at all. The number of subnet bits would never change.

2. D. A 240 mask is 4 subnet bits and provides 16 subnets, each with 14 hosts. We need more subnets, so let's add subnet bits. One more subnet bit would be a 248 mask. This provides 5 subnet bits (32 subnets) with 3 host bits (6 hosts per subnet). This is the best answer.

3. C. This is a pretty simple question. A /28 is 255.255.255.240, which means that our block size is 16 in the fourth octet. 0, 16, 32, 48, 64, 80, etc. The host is in the 64 subnet.

4. C. A CIDR address of /19 is 255.255.224.0. This is a Class B address, so that is only 3 subnet bits, but it provides 13 host bits, or 8 subnets, each with 8,190 hosts.

5. B, D. The mask 255.255.254.0 (/23) used with a Class A address means that there are 15 subnet bits and 9 host bits. The block size in the third octet is 2 (256 − 254). So this makes the subnets in the interesting octet 0, 2, 4, 6, etc., all the way to 254. The host 10.16.3.65 is in the 2.0 subnet. The next subnet is 4.0, so the broadcast address for the 2.0 subnet is 3.255. The valid host addresses are 2.1 through 3.254.

6. D. A /30, regardless of the class of address, has a 252 in the fourth octet. This means we have a block size of 4 and our subnets are 0, 4, 8, 12, 16, etc. Address 14 is obviously in the 12 subnet.

7. D. A point-to-point link uses only two hosts. A /30, or 255.255.255.252, mask provides two hosts per subnet.

8. C. A /21 is 255.255.248.0, which means we have a block size of 8 in the third octet, so we just count by 8 until we reach 66. The subnet in this question is 64.0. The next subnet is 72.0, so the broadcast address of the 64 subnet is 71.255.

9. A. A /29 (255.255.255.248), regardless of the class of address, has only 3 host bits. Six is the maximum number of hosts on this LAN, including the router interface.

10. C. A /29 is 255.255.255.248, which is a block size of 8 in the fourth octet. The subnets are 0, 8, 16, 24, 32, 40, etc. 192.168.19.24 is the 24 subnet, and since 32 is the next subnet, the broadcast address for the 24 subnet is 31. 192.168.19.26 is the only correct answer.

11. A. A /29 (255.255.255.248) has a block size of 8 in the fourth octet. This means the subnets are 0, 8, 16, 24, etc. 10 is in the 8 subnet. The next subnet is 16, so 15 is the broadcast address.

12. B. You need 5 subnets, each with at least 16 hosts. The mask 255.255.255.240 provides 16 subnets with 14 hosts—this will not work. The mask 255.255.255.224 provides 8 subnets, each with 30 hosts. This is the best answer.

13. C. First, you cannot answer this question if you can't subnet. The 192.168.10.62 with a mask of 255.255.255.192 is a block size of 64 in the fourth octet. The host 192.168.10.62 is in the zero subnet, and the error occurred because ip subnet-zero is not enabled on the router.

14. A. A /25 mask is 255.255.255.128. Used with a Class B network, the third and fourth octets are used for subnetting with a total of 9 subnet bits, 8 bits in the third octet and 1 bit in the fourth octet. Since there is only 1 bit in the fourth octet, the bit is either off or on—which is a value of 0 or 128. The host in the question is in the 0 subnet, which has a broadcast address of 127 since 112.128 is the next subnet.

15. A. A /28 is a 255.255.255.240 mask. Let's count to the ninth subnet (we need to find the broadcast address of the eighth subnet, so we need to count to the ninth subnet). Starting at 16 (remember, the question stated that we will not use subnet zero, so we start at 16, not 0), we have 16, 32, 48, 64, 80, 96, 112, 128, 144, etc. The eighth subnet is 128 and the next subnet is 144, so our broadcast address of the 128 subnet is 143. This makes the host range 129–142. 142 is the last valid host.

16. C. A /28 is a 255.255.255.240 mask. The first subnet is 16 (remember that the question stated not to use subnet zero) and the next subnet is 32, so our broadcast address is 31. This makes our host range 17–30. 30 is the last valid host.

17. B. We need 9 host bits to answer this question, which is a /23.

18. E. A Class B network ID with a /22 mask is 255.255.252.0, with a block size of 4 in the third octet. The network address in the question is in subnet 172.16.16.0 with a broadcast address of 172.16.19.255. Only option E has the correct subnet mask listed, and 172.16.18.255 is a valid host.

19. D, E. The router's IP address on the E0 interface is 172.16.2.1/23, which is 255.255.254.0. This makes the third octet a block size of 2. The router's interface is in the 2.0 subnet, and the broadcast address is 3.255 because the next subnet is 4.0. The valid host range is 2.1 through 3.254. The router is using the first valid host address in the range.

20. A. For this example, the network range is 172.16.16.1 to 172.16.31.254, the network address is 172.16.16.0, and the broadcast IP address is 172.16.31.255.

Chapter 5: VLSMs, Summarization, and Troubleshooting TCP/IP

1. D. A point-to-point link uses only two hosts. A /30, or 255.255.255.252, mask provides two hosts per subnet.

2. C. Using a /28 mask, there are 4 bits available for hosts. Two-to-the-fourth power minus 2 = 14, or block size −2.

3. D. For 6 hosts we need to leave 3 bits in the host portion since 2 to the third power = 8 and 8 minus 2 is 6. With 3 bits for the host portion, that leaves 29 bits for the mask, or /29.

4. C. To use VLSM, the routing protocols in use possess the capability to transmit subnet mask information.

5. D. In a question like this, you need to look for an interesting octet where you can combine networks. In this example, the third octet has all our subnets, so we just need to find our block size now. If we used a block of 8 starting at 172.16.0.0/19, then we cover 172.16.0.0 through 172.16.7.255. However, if we used 172.16.0.0/20, then we'd cover a block of 16, which would be from 172.16.0.0 through 172.16.15.255, which is the best answer.

6. C. The IP address of the station and the gateway are not in the same network. Since the address of the gateway is correct on the station, it is *most likely* the IP address of the station is incorrect.

7. B. With an incorrect gateway, Host A will not be able to communicate with the router or beyond the router but will be able to communicate within the subnet.

8. A. Pinging the remote computer would fail if any of the other steps fail.

9. C. When a ping to the local host IP address fails, you can assume the NIC is not functional.

10. C, D. If a ping to the local host succeeds, you can rule out IP stack or NIC failure.

11. E. A /29 mask yields only 6 addresses, so none of the networks could use it.

12. A. The most likely problem if you can ping a computer by IP address but not by name is a failure of DNS.

13. D. When you issue the ping command, you are using the ICMP protocol.

14. B. The traceroute command displays the networks traversed on a path to a network destination.

15. C. The ping command tests connectivity to another station. The full command is shown below.

```
C:\>ping 172.16.10.2
Pinging 172.16.10.2 with 32 bytes of data:
Reply from 172.16.10.2: bytes=32 time<1ms TTL=128
Reply from 172.16.10.2: bytes=32 time<1ms TTL=128
Reply from 172.16.10.2: bytes=32 time<1ms TTL=128
Reply from 172.16.10.2: bytes=32 time<1ms TTL=128
Ping statistics for 172.16.10.2:
    Packets: Sent = 4, Received = 4, Lost = 0 (0% loss),
Approximate round trip times in milli-seconds:
    Minimum = 0ms, Maximum = 0ms, Average = 0ms
```

16.

traceroute	Displays the list of routers on a path to a network destination
arp -a	Displays IP-to-MAC-address mappings on a Windows PC
show ip arp	Displays the ARP table on a Cisco router
ipconfig /all	Shows you the PC network configuration

The commands use the functions described in the answer table.

17. C. The interesting octet in this example is the second octet, and it is a block size of four starting at 10.0.0.0. By using a 255.252.0.0 mask, we are telling the summary to use a block size of four in the second octet. This will cover 10.0.0.0 through 10.3.255.255. This is the best answer.

18. A. The command that displays the ARP table on a Cisco router is show ip arp.

19. C. The /all switch must be added to the ipconfig command on a PC to verify DNS configuration.

20. C. If you start at 192.168.128.0 and go through 192.168.159.0, you can see this is a block of 32 in the third octet. Since the network address is always the first one in the range, the summary address is 192.168.128.0. What mask provides a block of 32 in the third octet? The answer is 255.255.224.0, or /19.

Chapter 6: Cisco's Internetworking Operating System (IOS)

1. D. Typically, we'd see the input errors and CRC statistics increase with a duplex error, but it could be another Physical layer issue such as the cable might be receiving excessive interference or the network interface cards might have a failure. Typically, you can tell if it is interference when the CRC and input errors output grow but the collision counters do not, which is the case with this question.

2. C. Once the IOS is loaded and up and running, the startup-config will be copied from NVRAM into RAM and from then on, referred to as the running-config.

3. C, D. To configure SSH on your router, you need to set the username command, the ip domain-name, login local, and the transport input ssh under the VTY lines and the crypto key command. However, SSH version 2 is suggested but not required.

4. C. The show controllers serial 0/0 command will show you whether either a DTE or DCE cable is connected to the interface. If it is a DCE connection, you need to add clocking with the clock rate command.

5.

Mode	Definition
User EXEC mode	Commands that affect the entire system
Privileged EXEC mode	Commands that affect interfaces/processes only
Global configuration mode	Interactive configuration dialog
Specific configuration modes	Provides access to all other router commands
Setup mode	Limited to basic monitoring commands

User exec mode is limited to basic monitoring commands; privileged exec mode provides access to all other router commands. Specific configuration modes include the commands that affect a specific interface or process, while global configuration mode allows commands that affect the entire system. Setup mode is where you access the interactive configuration dialog.

6. B. The bandwidth shown is 100000 kbits a second, which is a FastEthernet port, or 100 Mbs.

7.   B. From global configuration mode, use the `line vty 0 4` command to set all five default VTY lines. However, you would typically always set all lines, not just the defaults.

8.   C. The enable secret password is case sensitive, so the second option is wrong. To set the enable secret password, use the `enable secret` *password* command from global configuration mode. This password is automatically encrypted.

9.   C. The banner motd sets a message of the day for administrators when they login to a switch or router.

10. C. The prompts offered as options indicate the following modes:

```
Switch(config)# is global configuration mode.
Switch> is user mode.
Switch# is privileged mode.
Switch(config-if)# is interface configuration mode.
```

11. D. To copy the running-config to NVRAM so that it will be used if the router is restarted, use the `copy running-config startup-config` command in privileged mode (copy run start for short).

12. D. To allow a VTY (Telnet) session into your router, you must set the VTY password. Option C is wrong because it is setting the password on the wrong router. Notice that you have to set the password before you set the login command.

13. C. Wireless AP's are very popular today and will be going away about the same time that rock n' roll does. The idea behind these devices (which are layer 2 bridge devices) is to connect wireless products to the wired Ethernet network. The wireless AP will create a single collision domain and is typically its own dedicated broadcast domain as well.

14. B. If an interface is shut down, the `show interface` command will show the interface as administratively down. (It is possible that no cable is attached, but you can't tell that from this message.)

15. C. With the `show interfaces` command, you can view the configurable parameters, get statistics for the interfaces on the switch, check for input and CRC errors, and verify if the interfaces are shut down.

16. C. If you delete the startup-config and reload the switch, the device will automatically enter setup mode. You can also type **setup** from privileged mode at any time.

17. D. You can view the interface statistics from user mode, but the command is show interface fastethernet 0/0.

18. B. The `% ambiguous command` error means that there is more than one possible show command that starts with *r*. Use a question mark to find the correct command.

19. B, D. The commands show interfaces and show ip interface will show you the layer 1 and 2 status and the IP addresses of your router's interfaces.

20. A. If you see that a serial interface and the protocol are both down, then you have a Physical layer problem. If you see serial1 is up, line protocol is down, then you are not receiving (Data Link) keepalives from the remote end.

Chapter 7: Managing a Cisco Internetwork

1. B. The IEEE created a new standardized discovery protocol called 802.1AB for Station and Media Access Control Connectivity Discovery. We'll just call it Link Layer Discovery Protocol (LLDP).

2. C. The show processes (or show processes cpu) is a good tool for determining a given router's CPU utilization. When it is high, it is not a good time to execute a debug command.

3. B. The command traceroute (trace for short), which can be issued from user mode or privileged mode, is used to find the path a packet takes through an internetwork and will also show you where the packet stops because of an error on a router.

4. C. Since the configuration looks correct, you probably didn't screw up the copy job. However, when you perform a copy from a network host to a router, the interfaces are automatically shut down and need to be manually enabled with the no shutdown command.

5. D. Specifying the address of the DHCP server allows the router to relay broadcast traffic destined for a DHCP server to that server.

6. C. Before you start to configure the router, you should erase the NVRAM with the erase startup-config command and then reload the router using the reload command.

7. C. This command can be run on both routers and switches and it displays detailed information about each device connected to the device you're running the command on, including the IP address.

8. C. The Port ID column describes the interfaces on the remote device end of the connection.

9. B. Syslog levels range from 0–7, and level 7 (known as Debugging or local7) is the default if you were to use the logging ip_address command from global config.

10. C. If you save a configuration and reload the router and it comes up either in setup mode or as a blank configuration, chances are the configuration register setting is incorrect.

11. D. To keep open one or more Telnet sessions, use the Ctrl+Shift+6 and then X keystroke combination.

12. B, D. The best answers, the ones you need to remember, are that either an access control list is filtering the Telnet session or the VTY password is not set on the remote device.

13. A, D. The show hosts command provides information on temporary DNS entries and permanent name-to-address mappings created using the ip host command.

14. A, B, D. The tracert command is a Windows command and will not work on a router or switch! IOS uses the traceroute command.

15. D. By default, Cisco IOS devices use facility local7. Moreover, most Cisco devices provide options to change the facility level from their default value.

16. C. To see console messages through your Telnet session, you must enter the terminal monitor command.

17. C, D, F. There are significantly more syslog messages available within IOS as compared to SNMP Trap messages. System logging is a method of collecting messages from devices to a server running a syslog daemon. Logging to a central syslog server helps in aggregation of logs and alerts.

18. E. Although option A is certainly the "best" answer, unfortunately option E will work just fine and your boss would probably prefer you to use the show cdp neighbors detail command.

19. D. To enable a device to be an NTP client, use the ntp server *IP_address* version *number* command at global configuration mode. That's all there is to it! Assuming your NTP server is working of course.

20. B, D, F. If you specify a level with the "logging trap *level*" command, that level and all the higher levels will be logged. For example, by using the logging trap 3 command, emergencies, alerts, critical, and error messages will be logged. Only three of these were listed as possible options.

Chapter 8: Managing Cisco Devices

1. B. The default configuration setting is 0x2102, which tells the router to load the IOS from flash and the configuration from NVRAM. 0x2142 tells the router to bypass the configuration in NVRAM so that you can perform password recovery.

2. E. To copy the IOS to a backup host, which is stored in flash memory by default, use the copy flash tftp command.

3. B. To install a new license on an ISR G2 router, use the license install url command.

4. C. The configuration register provides the boot commands, and 0x2101 tells the router to boot the mini-IOS, if found, and not to load a file from flash memory. Many newer routers do not have a mini-IOS, so as an alternative, the router would end up in ROM monitor mode if the mini-IOS is not found. However, option C is the best answer for this question.

5. B. The show flash command will provide you with the current IOS name and size and the size of flash memory.

6. C. Before you start to configure the router, you should erase the NVRAM with the `erase startup-config` command and then reload the router using the `reload` command.

7. D. The command `copy tftp flash` will allow you to copy a new IOS into flash memory on your router.

8. C. The best answer is `show version`, which shows you the IOS file running currently on your router. The `show flash` command shows you the contents of flash memory, not which file is running.

9. C. All Cisco routers have a default configuration register setting of 0x2102, which tells the router to load the IOS from flash memory and the configuration from NVRAM.

10. C. If you save a configuration and reload the router and it comes up either in setup mode or as a blank configuration, chances are the configuration register setting is incorrect.

11. D. The `license boot module` command installs a Right-To-Use license feature on a router.

12. A. The `show license` command determines the licenses that are active on your system. It also displays a group of lines for each feature in the currently running IOS image along with several status variables related to software activation and licensing, both licensed and unlicensed features.

13. B. The `show license feature` command allows you to view the technology package licenses and feature licenses that are supported on your router along with several status variables related to software activation and licensing, both licensed and unlicensed features.

14. C. The `show license udi` command displays the unique device identifier (UDI) of the router, which comprises the product ID (PID) and serial number of the router.

15. D. The `show version` command displays various pieces of information about the current IOS version, including the licensing details at the end of the command's output.

16. C. The `license save flash` command allows you to back up your license to flash memory.

17. C. The `show version` command provides you with the current configuration register setting.

18. C, D. The two steps to remove a license are to first disable the technology package and then clear the license.

19. B, D, E. Before you back up an IOS image to a laptop directly connected to a router's Ethernet port, make sure that the TFTP server software is running on your laptop, that the Ethernet cable is a "crossover," and that the laptop is in the same subnet as the router's Ethernet port, and then you can use the `copy flash tftp` command from your laptop.

20. C. The default configuration setting of 0x2102 tells the router to look in NVRAM for the boot sequence.

Chapter 9: IP Routing

1. `show ip route`

   The `ip route` command is used to display the routing table of a router.

2. B. In the new 15 IOS code, Cisco defines a different route called a local route. Each has a /32 prefix defining a route just for the one address, which is the router's interface.

3. A, B. Although option D almost seems right, it is not; the mask option is the mask used on the remote network, not the source network. Since there is no number at the end of the static route, it is using the default administrative distance of 1.

4. C, F. The switches are not used as either a default gateway or other destination. Switches have nothing to do with routing. It is very important to remember that the destination MAC address will always be the router's interface. The destination address of a frame, from HostA, will be the MAC address of the Fa0/0 interface of RouterA. The destination address of a packet will be the IP address of the network interface card (NIC) of the HTTPS server. The destination port number in the segment header will have a value of 443 (HTTPS).

5. B. This mapping was learned dynamically, which means it was learned through ARP.

6. B. Hybrid protocols use aspects of both distance vector and link state—for example, EIGRP. Be advised, however, that Cisco typically just calls EIGRP an advanced distance-vector routing protocol. Do not be misled by the way the question is worded. Yes, I know that MAC addresses are not in a packet. You must read the question to understand of what it is really asking.

7. A. Since the destination MAC address is different at each hop, it must keep changing. The IP address, which is used for the routing process, does not.

8. B, E. Classful routing means that all hosts in the internetwork use the same mask and that only default masks are in use. Classless routing means that you can use variable length subnet masks (VLSMs).

9. B, C. The distance-vector routing protocol sends its complete routing table out of all active interfaces at periodic time intervals. Link-state routing protocols send updates containing the state of their own links to all routers in the internetwork.

10. C. This is how most people see routers, and certainly they could do this type of plain ol' packet switching in 1990 when Cisco released their very first router and traffic was seriously slow, but not in today's networks! This process involves looking up every destination in the routing table and finding the exit interface for every packet.

11. A, C. The S* shows that this is a candidate for default route and that it was configured manually.

12. B. RIP has an administrative distance (AD) of 120, while EIGRP has an administrative distance of 90, so the router will discard any route with a higher AD than 90 to that same network.

13. D. Recovery from a lost route requires manual intervention by a human to replace the lost route.

14. A. RIPv1 and RIPv2 only use the lowest hop count to determine the best path to a remote network.

15. A. Since the routing table shows no route to the 192.168.22.0 network, the router will discard the packet and send an ICMP destination unreachable message out of interface FastEthernet 0/0, which is the source LAN from which the packet originated.

16. C. Static routes have an administrative distance of 1 by default. Unless you change this, a static route will always be used over any other dynamically learned route. EIGRP has an administrative distance of 90, and RIP has an administrative distance of 120, by default.

17. C. BGP is the only EGP listed.

18. A, B, C. Recovery from a lost route requires manual intervention by a human to replace the lost route. The advantages are less overhead on the router and network as well as more security.

19. C. The `show ip interface brief` command displays a concise summary of the interfaces.

20. B. The 150 at the end changes the default administrative distance (AD) of 1 to 150.

Chapter 10: Layer 2 Switching

1. A. Layer 2 switches and bridges are faster than routers because they don't take up time looking at the Network Layer header information. They do make use of the Data Link layer information.

2. `mac address-table static aaaa.bbbb.cccc vlan 1 int fa0/7`

You can set a static MAC address in the MAC address table, and when done, it will appear as a static entry in the table.

3. B, D, E. Since the MAC address is not present in the table, it will send the frame out of all ports in the same VLAN with the exception of the port on which it was received.

4. `show mac address-table`

This command displays the forward filter table, also called a Content Addressable Memory (CAM) table.

5.

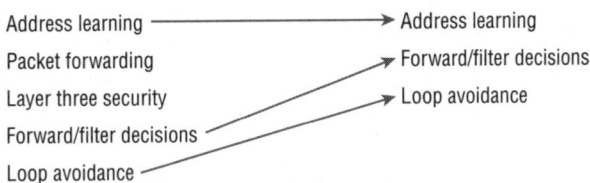

The three functions are address learning, forward/filter decisions, and loop avoidance.

6. A, D. In the output shown, you can see that the port is in Secure-shutdown mode and the light for the port would be amber. To enable the port again, you'd need to do the following:

```
S3(config-if)#shutdown
S3(config-if)#no shutdown
```

7. `switchport port-security maximum 2`

The maximum setting of 2 means only two MAC addresses can be used on that port; if the user tries to add another host on that segment, the switch port will take the action specified. In the `port-security violation` command.

8. B. The `switchport port-security` command enables port security, which is a prerequisite for the other commands to function.

9. B. Gateway redundancy is not an issue addressed by STP.

10. A. If no loop avoidance schemes are put in place, the switches will flood broadcasts endlessly throughout the internetwork. This is sometimes referred to as a broadcast storm.

11. B, C. Shutdown and protect mode will alert you via SNMP that a violation has occurred on a port.

12. Spanning Tree Protocol (STP) STP is a switching loop avoidance scheme use by switches.

13. `ip default-gateway`

If you want to manage your switches from outside your LAN, you need to set a default gateway on the switches, just as you would with a host.

14. C. The IP address is configured under a logical interface, called a management domain or VLAN 1.

15. B. The `show port-security interface` command displays the current port security and status of a switch port, as in this sample output:

```
Switch# show port-security interface fastethernet0/1
Port Security: Enabled
Port status: SecureUp
Violation mode: Shutdown
Maximum MAC Addresses: 2
Total MAC Addresses: 2
Configured MAC Addresses: 2
Aging Time: 30 mins
Aging Type: Inactivity
SecureStatic address aging: Enabled
Security Violation count: 0
```

16. `switchport port-security mac-address sticky`

Issuing the `switchport port-security mac-address sticky` command will allow a switch to save a dynamically learned MAC address in the running-configuration of the switch, which prevents the administrator from having to document or configure specific MAC addresses.

17. B, D. To limit connections to a specific host, you should configure the MAC address of the host as a static entry associated with the port, although be aware that this host can still connect to any other port, but no other port can connect to F0/3, in this example. Another solution would be to configure port security to accept traffic only from the MAC address of the host. By default, an unlimited number of MAC addresses can be learned on a single switch port, whether it is configured as an access port or a trunk port. Switch ports can be secured by defining one or more specific MAC addresses that should be allowed to connect and by defining violation policies (such as disabling the port) to be enacted if additional hosts try to gain a connection.

18. D. The command statically defines the MAC address of 00c0.35F0.8301 as an allowed host on the switch port. By default, an unlimited number of MAC addresses can be learned on a single switch port, whether it is configured as an access port or a trunk port. Switch ports can be secured by defining one or more specific MAC addresses that should be allowed to connect, and violation policies (such as disabling the port) if additional hosts try to gain a connection.

19. D. You would not make the port a trunk. In this example, this switchport is a member of one VLAN. However, you can configure port security on a trunk port, but again, that's not valid for this question.

20. `switchport port-security violation shutdown`

This command is used to set the reaction of the switch to a port violation of shutdown.

Chapter 11: VLANs and InterVLAN Routing

1. D. Here's a list of ways VLANs simplify network management:

- Network adds, moves, and changes are achieved with ease by just configuring a port into the appropriate VLAN.

- A group of users that need an unusually high level of security can be put into its own VLAN so that users outside of the VLAN can't communicate with them.

- As a logical grouping of users by function, VLANs can be considered independent from their physical or geographic locations.

- VLANs greatly enhance network security if implemented correctly.

- VLANs increase the number of broadcast domains while decreasing their size.

2. `ip routing`

Routing must be enabled on the layer 3 switch.

3. C. VLANs can span across multiple switches by using trunk links, which carry traffic for multiple VLANs.

4. B. While in all other cases access ports can be a member of only one VLAN, most switches will allow you to add a second VLAN to an access port on a switch port for your voice traffic; it's called the voice VLAN. The voice VLAN used to be called the auxiliary VLAN, which allowed it to be overlaid on top of the data VLAN, enabling both types of traffic through the same port.

5. A. Yes, you have to do a no shutdown on the VLAN interface.

6. C. Unlike ISL which encapsulates the frame with control information, 802.1q inserts an 802.1q field along with tag control information.

7. D. Instead of using a router interface for each VLAN, you can use one FastEthernet interface and run ISL or 802.1q trunking. This allows all VLANs to communicate through one interface. Cisco calls this a "router on a stick."

8. switchport access vlan 2

This command is executed under the interface (switch port) that is being placed in the VLAN.

9. show vlan

After you create the VLANs that you want, you can use the show vlan command to check them out.

10. B. The encapsulation command specifying the VLAN for the subinterface must be present under both subinterfaces.

11. A. With a multilayer switch, enable IP routing and create one logical interface for each VLAN using the interface vlan number command and you're now doing inter-VLAN routing on the backplane of the switch!

12. A. Ports Fa0/15–18 are not present in any VLANs. They are trunk ports.

13. C. Untagged frames are members of the native VLAN, which by default is VLAN 1.

14. sh interfaces fastEthernet 0/15 switchport

This show interfaces interface switchport command shows us the administrative mode of dynamic desirable and that the port is a trunk port, DTP was used to negotiate the frame tagging method of ISL, and the native VLAN is the default of 1.

15. C. A VLAN is a broadcast domain on a layer 2 switch. You need a separate address space (subnet) for each VLAN. There are four VLANs, so that means four broadcast domains/subnets.

16. B. The host's default gateway should be set to the IP address of the subinterface that is associated with the VLAN of which the host is a member, in this case VLAN 2.

17. C. Frame tagging is used when VLAN traffic travels over a trunk link. Trunk links carry frames for multiple VLANs. Therefore, frame tags are used for identification of frames from different VLANs.

18. vlan 2

To configure VLANs on a Cisco Catalyst switch, use the global config vlan command.

19. B. 802.1q uses the native VLAN.

20. switchport nonegotiate

You can use this command only when the interface switchport mode is access or trunk. You must manually configure the neighboring interface as a trunk interface to establish a trunk link.

Chapter 12: Security

1. D. It's compared with lines of the access list only until a match is made. Once the packet matches the condition on a line of the access list, the packet is acted upon and no further comparisons take place.

2. C. The range of 192.168.160.0 to 192.168.191.0 is a block size of 32. The network address is 192.168.160.0 and the mask would be 255.255.224.0, which for an access list must be a wildcard format of 0.0.31.255. The 31 is used for a block size of 32. The wildcard is always one less than the block size.

3. C. Using a named access list just replaces the number used when applying the list to the router's interface. `ip access-group Blocksales in` is correct.

4. B. The list must specify TCP as the Transport layer protocol and use a correct wildcard mask (in this case 0.0.0.255), and it must specify the destination port (80). It also should specify any as the set of computers allowed to have this access.

5. A. The first thing to check in a question like this is the access-list number. Right away, you can see that the second option is wrong because it is using a standard IP access-list number. The second thing to check is the protocol. If you are filtering by upper-layer protocol, then you must be using either UDP or TCP; this eliminates the fourth option. The third and last answers have the wrong syntax.

6. C. Of the available choices, only the `show ip interface` command will tell you which interfaces have access lists applied. `show access-lists` will not show you which interfaces have an access list applied.

7.

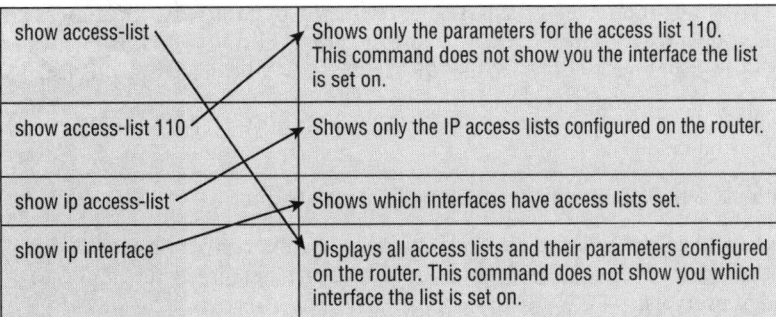

The command `show access-list` displays all access lists and their parameters configured on the router; it does not show you which interface the list is set on. `show access-list 110` shows only the parameters for the access list 110 and, again, does not tell you which interface the list is set on. `show ip access-list` reveals only the IP access lists configured on the router. Finally, `show ip interface` shows which interfaces have access lists set.

The functions of each command are as shown in the solution graphic.

8. C. The extended access list ranges are 100–199 and 2000–2699, so the access-list number of 100 is valid. Telnet uses TCP, so the protocol TCP is valid. Now you just need to look for the source and destination address. Only the third option has the correct sequence of parameters. Option B may work, but the question specifically states "only" to network 192.168.10.0, and the wildcard in option B is too broad.

9. D. Extended IP access lists use numbers 100–199 and 2000–2699 and filter based on source and destination IP address, protocol number, and port number. The last option is correct because of the second line that specifies permit ip any any. (I used 0.0.0.0 255.255.255.255, which is the same as the any option.) The third option does not have this, so it would deny access but not allow everything else.

10. D. First, you must know that a /20 is 255.255.240.0, which is a block size of 16 in the third octet. Counting by 16s, this makes our subnet 48 in the third octet, and the wildcard for the third octet would be 15 since the wildcard is always one less than the block size.

11. B. To find the wildcard (inverse) version of this mask, the zero and one bits are simply reversed as follows:

11111111.11111111.11111111.11100000 (27 one bits, or /27)

00000000.00000000.00000000.00011111 (wildcard/inverse mask)

12. A. First, you must know that a /19 is 255.255.224.0, which is a block size of 32 in the third octet. Counting by 32s, this makes our subnet 192 in the third octet, and the wildcard for the third octet would be 31 since the wildcard is always one less than the block size.

13. B, D. The scope of an access list is determined by the wildcard mask and the network address to which it is applied. For example, in this case the starting point of the list of addresses affected by the mask is the network ID 192.111.16.32. The wildcard mask is 0.0.0.31. Adding the value of the last octet in the mask to the network address (32 + 31 = 63) tells you where the effects of the access list ends, which is 199.111.16.63. Therefore, all addresses in the range 199.111.16.32–199.111.16.63 will be denied by this list.

14. C. To place an access list on an interface, use the ip access-group command in interface configuration mode.

15. B. With no permit statement, the ACL will deny all traffic.

16. D. If you add an access list to an interface and you do not have at least one permit statement, then you will effectively shut down the interface because of the implicit deny any at the end of every list.

17. C. Telnet access to the router is restricted by using either a standard or extended IP access list inbound on the VTY lines of the router. The command access-class is used to apply the access list to the VTY lines.

18. C. A Cisco router has rules regarding the placement of access lists on a router interface. You can place one access list per direction for each layer 3 protocol configured on an interface.

19. C. The most common attack on a network today is a denial of service (DoS) because it is the easiest attack to achieve.

20. C. Implementing intrusion detection services and intrusion prevention services will help notify you and stop attacks in real time.

Chapter 13: Network Address Translation (NAT)

1. A, C, E. NAT is not perfect and can cause some issues in some networks, but most networks work just fine. NAT can cause delays and troubleshooting problems, and some applications just won't work.

2. B, D, F. NAT is not perfect, but there are some advantages. It conserves global addresses, which allow us to add millions of hosts to the Internet without "real" IP addresses. This provides flexibility in our corporate networks. NAT can also allow you to use the same subnet more than once in the same network without overlapping networks.

3. C. The command debug ip nat will show you in real time the translations occurring on your router.

4. A. The command show ip nat translations will show you the translation table containing all the active NAT entries.

5. D. The command clear ip nat translations * will clear all the active NAT entries in your translation table.

6. B. The show ip nat statistics command displays a summary of the NAT configuration as well as counts of active translation types, hits to an existing mapping, misses (an attempt to create a mapping), and expired translations.

7. B. The command ip nat pool *name* creates the pool that hosts can use to get onto the global Internet. What makes option B correct is that the range 171.16.10.65 through 171.16.10.94 includes 30 hosts, but the mask has to match 30 hosts as well, and that mask is 255.255.255.224. Option C is wrong because there is a lowercase t in the pool name. Pool names are case sensitive.

8. A, C, E. You can configure NAT three ways on a Cisco router: static, dynamic, and NAT Overload (PAT).

9. B. Instead of the netmask command, you can use the prefix-length *length* statement.

10. C. In order for NAT to provide translation services, you must have ip nat inside and ip nat outside configured on your router's interfaces.

11. A, B, D. The most popular use of NAT is if you want to connect to the Internet and you don't want hosts to have global (real) IP addresses, but options B and D are correct as well.

12. C. An inside global address is considered to be the IP address of the host on the private network after translation.

13. A. An inside local address is considered to be the IP address of the host on the private network before translation.

14. D. What we need to figure out for this question is only the inside global pool. Basically we start at 1.1.128.1 and end at 1.1.135.174; our block size is 8 in the third octet, or /21. Always look for your block size and the interesting octet and you can find your answer every time.

15. B. Once you create your pool, the command `ip nat inside source` must be used to say which inside locals are allowed to use the pool. In this question we need to see if access-list 100 is configured correctly, if at all, so `show access-list` is the best answer.

16. A. You must configure your interfaces before NAT will provide any translations. On the inside network interfaces, you would use the command `ip nat inside`. On the outside network interfaces, you will use the command `ip nat outside`.

17. B. You must configure your interfaces before NAT will provide any translations. On the inside networks you would use the command `ip nat inside`. On the outside network interfaces, you will use the command `ip nat outside`.

18. C. Another term for Port Address Translation is *NAT Overload* because that is the keyword used to enable port address translation.

19. B. Fast-switching is used on Cisco routers to create a type of route cache in order to quickly forward packets through a router without having to parse the routing table for every packet. As packets are processed-switched (looked up in the routing table), this information is stored in the cache for later use if needed for faster routing processing.

20. B. Once you create a pool for the inside locals to use to get out to the global Internet, you must configure the command to allow them access to the pool. The `ip nat inside source list` *number pool-name* `overload` command has the correct sequence for this question.

Chapter 14: Internet Protocol Version 6 (IPv6)

1. D. The modified EUI-64 format interface identifier is derived from the 48-bit link-layer (MAC) address by inserting the hexadecimal number FFFE between the upper 3 bytes (OUI field) and the lower 3 bytes (serial number) of the link layer address.

2. D. An IPv6 address is represented as eight groups of four hexadecimal digits, each group representing 16 bits (two octets). The groups are separated by colons (:). Option A has two double colons, B doesn't have 8 fields, and option C has invalid hex characters.

3. A, B, C. This question is easier to answer if you just take out the wrong options. First, the loopback is only ::1, so that makes option D wrong. Link local is FE80::/10, not /8 and there are no broadcasts..

4. A, C, D. Several methods are used in terms of migration, including tunneling, translators, and dual-stack. Tunnels are used to carry one protocol inside another, while translators simply translate IPv6 packets into IPv4 packets. Dual-stack uses a combination of both native IPv4 and IPv6. With dual-stack, devices are able to run IPv4 and IPv6 together, and if IPv6 communication is possible, that is the preferred protocol. Hosts can simultaneously reach IPv4 and IPv6 content.

5. A, B. ICMPv6 router advertisements use type 134 and must be at least 64 bits in length.

6. B, E, F. Anycast addresses identify multiple interfaces, which is somewhat similar to multi-cast addresses; however, the big difference is that the anycast packet is only delivered to one address, the first one it finds defined in terms of routing distance. This address can also be called one-to-one-of-many, or one-to-nearest.

7. C. The loopback address with IPv4 is 127.0.0.1. With IPv6, that address is ::1.

8. B, C, E. An important feature of IPv6 is that it allows the plug-and-play option to the network devices by allowing them to configure themselves independently. It is possible to plug a node into an IPv6 network without requiring any human intervention. IPv6 does not implement traditional IP broadcasts.

9. A, D. The loopback address is ::1, link-local starts with FE80::/10, site-local addresses start with FEC0::/10, global addresses start with 200::/3, and multicast addresses start with FF00::/8.

10. C. A router solicitation is sent out using the all-routers multicast address of FF02::2. The router can send a router advertisement to all hosts using the FF02::1 multicast address.

11. A, E. IPv6 does not use broadcasts, and autoconfiguration is a feature of IPV6 that allows for hosts to automatically obtain an IPv6 address.

12. A. The NDP neighbor advertisement (NA) contains the MAC address. A neighbor solicitation (NS) was initially sent asking for the MAC address.

13. B. IPv6 anycast addresses are used for one-to-nearest communication, meaning an anycast address is used by a device to send data to one specific recipient (interface) that is the closest out of a group of recipients (interfaces).

14. B, D. To shorten the written length of an IPv6 address, successive fields of zeros may be replaced by double colons. In trying to shorten the address further, leading zeros may also be removed. Just as with IPv4, a single device's interface can have more than one address; with IPv6 there are more types of addresses and the same rule applies. There can be link-local, global unicast, multicast, and anycast addresses all assigned to the same interface.

15. A, B, C. The Internet Header Length field was removed because it is no longer required. Unlike the variable-length IPv4 header, the IPv6 header is fixed at 40 bytes. Fragmentation is processed differently in IPv6 and does not need the Flags field in the basic IPv4 header. In IPv6, routers no longer process fragmentation; the host is responsible for fragmentation. The Header Checksum field at the IP layer was removed because most Data Link layer technologies already perform checksum and error control, which forces formerly optional upper-layer checksums (UDP, for example) to become mandatory.

16. B. There are no broadcasts with IPv6. Unicast, multicast, anycast, global, and link-local unicast are used.

17. D. This question asked how many bits in a field, not how many bits in an IPv6 address. There are 16 bits (four hex characters) in an IPv6 field and there are eight fields.

18. A, D. Global addresses start with 2000::/3, link-locals start with FE80::/10, loopback is ::1, and unspecified is just two colons (::). Each interface will have a loopback address automatically configured.

19. B, C. If you verify your IP configuration on your host, you'll see that you have multiple IPv6 addresses, including a loopback address. The last 64 bits represent the dynamically created interface ID, and leading zeros are not mandatory in a 16-bit IPv6 field.

20. C. To enable IPv6 routing on the Cisco router, use the following command from global config:

```
ipv6 unicast-routing
```

If this command is not recognized, your version of IOS does not support IPv6.

Appendix

C

Disabling and Configuring Network Services

By default, the Cisco IOS runs some services that are unnecessary to its normal operation, and if you don't disable them, they can be easy targets for denial-of-service (DoS) attacks and break-in attempts.

DoS attacks are the most common attacks because they are the easiest to perform. Using software and/or hardware tools such as an intrusion detection system (IDS) and intrusion prevention system (IPS) tools can both warn and stop these simple, but harmful, attacks. However, if we can't implement IDS/IPS, there are some basic commands we can use on our router to make them more safe. Keep in mind, though, that nothing will make you completely safe in today's networks.

Let's take a look at the basic services we should disable on our routers.

Blocking SNMP Packets

The Cisco IOS default configurations permit remote access from any source, so unless you're either way too trusting or insane, it should be totally obvious to you that those configurations need a bit of attention. You've got to restrict them. If you don't, the router will be a pretty easy target for an attacker who wants to log in to it. This is where access lists come into the game—they can really protect you.

If you place the following command on the serial0/0 interface of the perimeter router, it'll stop any SNMP packets from entering the router or the DMZ. (You'd also need to have a permit command along with this list to really make it work, but this is just an example.)

```
Lab_B(config)#access-list 110 deny udp any any eq snmp
Lab_B(config)#interface s0/0
Lab_B(config-if)#access-group 110 in
```

Disabling Echo

In case you don't know this already, small services are servers (daemons) running in the router that are quite useful for diagnostics. And here we go again—by default, the Cisco router has a series of diagnostic ports enabled for certain UDP and TCP services, including echo, chargen, and discard.

When a host attaches to those ports, a small amount of CPU is consumed to service these requests. All a single attacking device needs to do is send a whole slew of requests with different, random, phony source IP addresses to overwhelm the router, making it slow down or even fail. You can use the no version of these commands to stop a chargen attack:

```
Lab_B(config)#no service tcp-small-servers
Lab_B(config)#no service udp-small-servers
```

Finger is a utility program designed to allow users of Unix hosts on the Internet to get information about each other:

```
Lab_B(config)#no service finger
```

This matters because the finger command can be used to find information about all users on the network and/or the router. It's also why you should disable it. The finger command is the remote equivalent to issuing the show users command on the router.

Here are the TCP small services:

Echo Echoes back whatever you type. Type the command **telnet x.x.x.x echo ?** to see the options.

Chargen Generates a stream of ASCII data. Type the command **telnet x.x.x.x chargen ?** to see the options.

Discard Throws away whatever you type. Type the command **telnet x.x.x.x discard ?** to see the options.

Daytime Returns the system date and time, if correct. It is correct if you are running NTP or have set the date and time manually from the EXEC level. Type the command **telnet x.x.x.x daytime ?** to see the options.

The UDP small services are as follows:

Echo Echoes the payload of the datagram you send.

Discard Silently pitches the datagram you send.

Chargen Pitches the datagram you send and responds with a 72-character string of ASCII characters terminated with a CR+LF.

Turning off BootP and Auto-Config

Again, by default, the Cisco router also offers the BootP service as well as remote auto-configuration. To disable these functions on your Cisco router, use the following commands:

```
Lab_B(config)#no ip boot server
Lab_B(config)#no service config
```

Disabling the HTTP Interface

The `ip http server` command may be useful for configuring and monitoring the router, but the cleartext nature of HTTP can obviously be a security risk. To disable the HTTP process on your router, use the following command:

```
Lab_B(config)#no ip http server
```

To enable an HTTP server on a router for AAA, use the global configuration command `ip http server`.

Disabling IP Source Routing

The IP header source-route option allows the source IP host to set a packet's route through the IP network. With IP source routing enabled, packets containing the source-route option are forwarded to the router addresses specified in the header. Use the following command to disable any processing of packets with source-routing header options:

```
Lab_B(config)#no ip source-route
```

Disabling Proxy ARP

Proxy ARP is the technique in which one host—usually a router—answers ARP requests intended for another machine. By "faking" its identity, the router accepts responsibility for getting those packets to the "real" destination. Proxy ARP can help machines on a subnet reach remote subnets without configuring routing or a default gateway. The following command disables proxy ARP:

```
Lab_B(config)#interface fa0/0
Lab_B(config-if)#no ip proxy-arp
```

Apply this command to all your router's LAN interfaces.

Disabling Redirect Messages

ICMP redirect messages are used by routers to notify hosts on the data link that a better route is available for a particular destination. To disable the redirect messages so bad people can't draw out your network topology with this information, use the following command:

```
Lab_B(config)#interface s0/0
Lab_B(config-if)#no ip redirects
```

Apply this command to all your router's interfaces. However, just understand that if this is configured, legitimate user traffic may end up taking a suboptimal route. Use caution when disabling this command.

Disabling the Generation of ICMP Unreachable Messages

The no ip unreachables command prevents the perimeter router from divulging topology information by telling external hosts which subnets are not configured. This command is used on a router's interface that is connected to an outside network:

```
Lab_B(config)#interface s0/0
Lab_B(config-if)#no ip unreachables
```

Again, apply this to all the interfaces of your router that connect to the outside world.

Disabling Multicast Route Caching

The multicast route cache lists multicast routing cache entries. These packets can be read, and so they create a security problem. To disable the multicast route caching, use the following command:

```
Lab_B(config)#interface s0/0
Lab_B(config-if)#no ip mroute-cache
```

Apply this command to all the interfaces of the router. However, use caution when disabling this command because it may slow legitimate multicast traffic.

Disabling the Maintenance Operation Protocol (MOP)

The Maintenance Operation Protocol (MOP) works at the Data Link and Network layers in the DECnet protocol suite and is used for utility services like uploading and downloading system software, remote testing, and problem diagnosis. So, who uses DECnet? Anyone with their hands up? I didn't think so. To disable this service, use the following command:

```
Lab_B(config)#interface s0/0
Lab_B(config-if)#no mop enabled
```

Apply this command to all the interfaces of the router.

Turning Off the X.25 PAD Service

Packet assembler/disassembler (PAD) connects asynchronous devices like terminals and computers to public/private X.25 networks. Since every computer in the world is pretty much IP savvy, and X.25 has gone the way of the dodo bird, there is no reason to leave this service running. Use the following command to disable the PAD service:

```
Lab_B(config)#no service pad
```

Enabling the Nagle TCP Congestion Algorithm

The Nagle TCP congestion algorithm is useful for small packet congestion, but if you're using a higher setting than the default MTU of 1,500 bytes, it can create an above-average traffic load. To enable this service, use the following command:

```
Lab_B(config)#service nagle
```

It is important to understand that the Nagle congestion service can break X Window connections to an X server, so don't use it if you're using X Window.

Logging Every Event

Used as a syslog server, the Cisco ACS server can log events for you to verify. Use the logging trap debugging or logging trap *level* command and the logging *ip_address* command to turn this feature on:

```
Lab_B(config)#logging trap debugging
Lab_B(config)#logging 192.168.254.251
Lab_B(config)#exit
Lab_B#sh logging
Syslog logging: enabled (0 messages dropped, 0 flushes, 0 overruns)
    Console logging: level debugging, 15 messages logged
    Monitor logging: level debugging, 0 messages logged
    Buffer logging: disabled
    Trap logging: level debugging, 19 message lines logged
        Logging to 192.168.254.251, 1 message lines logged
```

The show logging command provides you with statistics of the logging configuration on the router.

Disabling Cisco Discovery Protocol

Cisco Discovery Protocol (CDP) does just that—it's a Cisco proprietary protocol that discovers directly connected Cisco devices on the network. But because it's a Data Link layer protocol, it can't find Cisco devices on the other side of a router. Plus, by default, Cisco switches don't forward CDP packets, so you can't see Cisco devices attached to any other port on a switch.

When you are bringing up your network for the first time, CDP can be a really helpful protocol for verifying it. But since you're going to be thorough and document your network, you don't need the CDP after that. And because CDP does discover Cisco routers and switches on your network, you should disable it. You do that in global configuration mode, which turns off CDP completely for your router or switch:

```
Lab_B(config)#no cdp run
```

Or, you can turn off CDP on each individual interface using the following command:

```
Lab_B(config-if)#no cdp enable
```

Disabling the Default Forwarded UDP Protocols

When you use the ip helper-address command as follows on an interface, your router will forward UDP broadcasts to the listed server or servers:

```
Lab_B(config)#interface f0/0
Lab_B(config-if)#ip helper-address 192.168.254.251
```

You would generally use the ip helper-address command when you want to forward DHCP client requests to a DHCP server. The problem is that not only does this forward port 67 (BootP server request), it forwards seven other ports by default as well. To disable the unused ports, use the following commands:

```
Lab_B(config)#no ip forward-protocol udp 69
Lab_B(config)#no ip forward-protocol udp 53
Lab_B(config)#no ip forward-protocol udp 37
Lab_B(config)#no ip forward-protocol udp 137
```

```
Lab_B(config)#no ip forward-protocol udp 138
Lab_B(config)#no ip forward-protocol udp 68
Lab_B(config)#no ip forward-protocol udp 49
```

Now, only the BootP server request (67) will be forwarded to the DHCP server. If you want to forward a certain port—say, TACACS+, for example—use the following command:

```
Lab_B(config)#ip forward-protocol udp 49
```

Cisco's *auto secure*

Okay, so ACLs seem like a lot of work and so does turning off all those services I just discussed. But you do want to secure your router with ACLs, especially on your interface connected to the Internet. However, you are just not sure what the best approach should be, or maybe you just don't want to miss happy hour with your buddies because you're creating ACLs and turning off default services all night long.

Either way, Cisco has a solution that is a good start, and it's darn easy to implement. The command is called auto secure, and you just run it from privileged mode as shown:

```
R1#auto secure
                --- AutoSecure Configuration ---

*** AutoSecure configuration enhances the security of
the router, but it will not make it absolutely resistant
to all security attacks ***

AutoSecure will modify the configuration of your device.
All configuration changes will be shown. For a detailed
explanation of how the configuration changes enhance
security and any possible side effects, please refer to Cisco.com
for Autosecure documentation.
At any prompt you may enter '?' for help.
Use ctrl-c to abort this session at any prompt.

Gathering information about the router for AutoSecure
Is this router connected to internet? [no]: yes
Enter the number of interfaces facing the internet [1]: [enter]
Interface              IP-Address      OK? Method Status                Protocol
FastEthernet0/0        10.10.10.1      YES NVRAM  up                    up
Serial0/0              1.1.1.1         YES NVRAM  down                  down
FastEthernet0/1        unassigned      YES NVRAM  administratively down down
Serial0/1              unassigned      YES NVRAM  administratively down down
Enter the interface name that is facing the internet: serial0/0
```

```
Securing Management plane services…

Disabling service finger
Disabling service pad
Disabling udp & tcp small servers
Enabling service password encryption
Enabling service tcp-keepalives-in
Enabling service tcp-keepalives-out
Disabling the cdp protocol

Disabling the bootp server
Disabling the http server
Disabling the finger service
Disabling source routing
Disabling gratuitous arp

Here is a sample Security Banner to be shown
at every access to device. Modify it to suit your
enterprise requirements.

Authorized Access only
   This system is the property of So-&-So-Enterprise.
   UNAUTHORIZED ACCESS TO THIS DEVICE IS PROHIBITED.
   You must have explicit permission to access this
   device. All activities performed on this device
   are logged. Any violations of access policy will result
   in disciplinary action.

Enter the security banner {Put the banner between
k and k, where k is any character}:
#
```
If you are not part of the www.globalnettc.com domain, disconnect now!
```
#
Enable secret is either not configured or
 is the same as enable password
Enter the new enable secret: [password not shown]
% Password too short - must be at least 6 characters. Password configuration
failed
Enter the new enable secret: [password not shown]
Confirm the enable secret : [password not shown]
Enter the new enable password: [password not shown]
Confirm the enable password: [password not shown]
Configuration of local user database
Enter the username: Todd
```

```
Enter the password: [password not shown]
Confirm the password: [password not shown]
Configuring AAA local authentication
Configuring Console, Aux and VTY lines for
local authentication, exec-timeout, and transport
Securing device against Login Attacks
Configure the following parameters
Blocking Period when Login Attack detected: ?
% A decimal number between 1 and 32767.
Blocking Period when Login Attack detected: 100
Maximum Login failures with the device: 5
Maximum time period for crossing the failed login attempts: 10
Configure SSH server? [yes]: [enter to take default of yes]
Enter the domain-name: lammle.com
Configuring interface specific AutoSecure services
Disabling the following ip services on all interfaces:

 no ip redirects
 no ip proxy-arp
 no ip unreachables
 no ip directed-broadcast
 no ip mask-reply
Disabling mop on Ethernet interfaces

Securing Forwarding plane services...

Enabling CEF (This might impact the memory requirements for your platform)
Enabling unicast rpf on all interfaces connected
to internet

Configure CBAC Firewall feature? [yes/no]:
Configure CBAC Firewall feature? [yes/no]: no
Tcp intercept feature is used prevent tcp syn attack
on the servers in the network. Create autosec_tcp_intercept_list
to form the list of servers to which the tcp traffic is to
be observed

Enable tcp intercept feature? [yes/no]: yes
```

And that's it—all the services I mentioned earlier are disabled, plus some! By saving the configuration that the auto secure command created, you can then take a look at your running-config to see your new configuration. It's a long one!

Although it is tempting to run out to happy hour right now, you still need to verify your security and add your internal access-list configurations to your intranet.

Index

Note to the Reader: Throughout this index boldfaced page numbers indicate primary discussions of a topic. Italicized page numbers indicate illustrations.

Comprehensive Online Learning Environment

Register on Sybex.com to gain access to the comprehensive online interactive learning environment and test bank to help you study for your CCENT ICND1 exam.

The online test bank includes the following:

- **Chapter Tests** to reinforce what you learned
- **Practice Exam** to test your knowledge of the material
- **Electronic Flashcards** to reinforce your learning and provide last-minute test prep before the exam
- **Searchable Glossary** gives you instant access to the key terms you'll need to know for the exam

Go to `http://www.wiley.com/go/sybextestprep` **to register and gain access to this comprehensive study tool package.**

30 Days Free On-Demand Video Training and Hands-on Labs

ITProTV and Sybex have partnered to provide 30 days access to 12 hours of CCENT ICND1 video training and all of ITProTV's other premium on-demand video, vLabs, and practice tests covering IT certifications and technical skills. ITProTV provides a unique, custom learning environment for IT professionals and students alike, looking to validate their skills through vendor certifications. On-demand courses provide over 1,000 hours of video training with new courses being added every month, while labs and practice exams provide additional hands-on experience. Register at the Sybex interactive learning environment for more information on this offer and to start your 30 day free trial membership today.

W9-BAC-844

solutions@syngress.com

With more than 1,500,000 copies of our MCSE, MCSD, CompTIA, and Cisco study guides in print, we continue to look for ways we can better serve the information needs of our readers. One way we do that is by listening.

Readers like yourself have been telling us they want an Internet-based service that would extend and enhance the value of our books. Based on reader feedback and our own strategic plan, we have created a Web site that we hope will exceed your expectations.

Solutions@syngress.com is an interactive treasure trove of useful information focusing on our book topics and related technologies. The site offers the following features:

- One-year warranty against content obsolescence due to vendor product upgrades. You can access online updates for any affected chapters.

- "Ask the Author" customer query forms that enable you to post questions to our authors and editors.

- Exclusive monthly mailings in which our experts provide answers to reader queries and clear explanations of complex material.

- Regularly updated links to sites specially selected by our editors for readers desiring additional reliable information on key topics.

Best of all, the book you're now holding is your key to this amazing site. Just go to **www.syngress.com/solutions**, and keep this book handy when you register to verify your purchase.

Thank you for giving us the opportunity to serve your needs. And be sure to let us know if there's anything else we can do to help you get the maximum value from your investment. We're listening.

www.syngress.com/solutions

SYNGRESS®

MANAGING
Cisco Network Security Second Edition

Eric Knipp

Brian Browne

Woody Weaver

C. Tate Baumrucker

Larry Chaffin

Jamie Caesar

Vitaly Osipov

Edgar Danielyan Technical Editor

KEY	SERIAL NUMBER
001	42397FGT54
002	56468932HF
003	FT6Y78934N
004	2648K9244T
005	379KS4F772
006	V6762SD445
007	99468ZZ652
008	748B783B66
009	834BS4782Q
010	X7RF563WS9

PUBLISHED BY
Syngress Publishing, Inc.
800 Hingham Street
Rockland, MA 02370

Managing Cisco® Network Security, Second Edition

Printed in the United States of America

1 2 3 4 5 6 7 8 9 0

ISBN: 1-931836-56-6

Technical Editor: Edgar Danielyan   Cover Designer: Michael Kavish
Technical Reviewer: Sean Thurston   Page Layout and Art by: Shannon Tozier
Acquisitions Editor: Catherine B. Nolan   Copy Editor: Michael McGee
Developmental Editor: Jonathan Babcock   Indexer: Nara Wood

Distributed by Publishers Group West in the United States and Jaguar Book Group in Canada.

Acknowledgments

We would like to acknowledge the following people for their kindness and support in making this book possible.

Ralph Troupe, Rhonda St. John, Emlyn Rhodes, and the team at Callisma for their invaluable insight into the challenges of designing, deploying and supporting world-class enterprise networks.

Karen Cross, Lance Tilford, Meaghan Cunningham, Kim Wylie, Harry Kirchner, Kevin Votel, Kent Anderson, Frida Yara, Bill Getz, Jon Mayes, John Mesjak, Peg O'Donnell, Sandra Patterson, Betty Redmond, Roy Remer, Ron Shapiro, Patricia Kelly, Andrea Tetrick, Jennifer Pascal, Doug Reil, and David Dahl of Publishers Group West for sharing their incredible marketing experience and expertise.

Jacquie Shanahan, AnnHelen Lindeholm, David Burton, Febea Marinetti, and Rosie Moss of Elsevier Science for making certain that our vision remains worldwide in scope.

Annabel Dent and Paul Barry of Elsevier Science/Harcourt Australia for all their help.

David Buckland, Wendi Wong, Marie Chieng, Lucy Chong, Leslie Lim, Audrey Gan, and Joseph Chan of Transquest Publishers for the enthusiasm with which they receive our books.

Kwon Sung June at Acorn Publishing for his support.

Ethan Atkin at Cranbury International for his help in expanding the Syngress program.

Jackie Gross, Gayle Voycey, Alexia Penny, Anik Robitaille, Craig Siddall, Darlene Morrow, Iolanda Miller, Jane Mackay, and Marie Skelly at Jackie Gross & Associates for all their help and enthusiasm representing our product in Canada.

Lois Fraser, Connie McMenemy, Shannon Russell and the rest of the great folks at Jaguar Book Group for their help with distribution of Syngress books in Canada.

Thank you to our hard-working colleagues at New England Fulfillment & Distribution who manage to get all our books sent pretty much everywhere in the world. Thank you to Debbie "DJ" Ricardo, Sally Greene, Janet Honaker, and Peter Finch.

Contributors

F. William Lynch (SCSA, CCNA, LPI-I, MCSE, MCP, Linux+, A+)
is co-author of *Hack Proofing Sun Solaris 8* (Syngress Publishing, ISBN:
1-928994-44-X), and *Hack Proofing Your Network, Second Edition* (Syngress
Publishing, ISBN: 1-928994-70-9). He is an independent security and
systems administration consultant and specializes in firewalls, virtual private networks, security auditing, documentation, and systems performance
analysis. William has served as a consultant to multinational corporations
and the federal government including the Centers for Disease Control
and Prevention headquarters in Atlanta, GA as well as various airbases of
the United States Air Force. He is also the Founder and Director of the
MRTG-PME project, which uses the MRTG engine to track systems
performance of various UNIX-like operating systems. William holds a
bachelor's degree in Chemical Engineering from the University of
Dayton in Dayton, OH and a master's of Business Administration from
Regis University in Denver, CO.

Robert "Woody" Weaver (CISSP) is a Principal Architect and the Field
Practice Leader for Security at Callisma. As an information systems security professional, Woody's responsibilities include field delivery and professional services product development. His background includes a decade as
a tenured professor teaching mathematics and computer science, as the
most senior network engineer for Williams Communications in the San
Jose/San Francisco Bay area, providing client services for their network
integration arm, and as Vice President of Technology for Fullspeed
Network Services, a regional systems integrator. Woody received a bachelor's of Science from Caltech, and a Ph.D. from Ohio State. He currently
works out of the Washington, DC metro area.

Larry Chaffin (CCNA, CCDA, CCNA-WAN, CCDP-WAN, CSS1,
NNCDS, JNCIS) is a Consultant with Callisma. He currently provides
strategic design and technical consulting to all Callisma clients. His specialties include Cisco WAN routers, Cisco PIX Firewall, Cisco VPN, ISP

design and implementation, strategic network planning, network architecture and design, and network troubleshooting and optimization. He also provides Technical Training for Callisma in all technology areas that include Cisco, Juniper, Microsoft, and others. Larry's background includes positions as a Senior LAN/WAN Engineer at WCOM-UUNET, and he also is a freelance sports writer for *USA Today* and ESPN.

Eric Knipp (CCNP, CCDP, CCNA, CCDA, MCSE, MCP+I) is a Consultant with Callisma. He is currently engaged in a broadband optimization project for a major US backbone service provider. He specializes in IP telephony and convergence, Cisco routers, LAN switches, as well as Microsoft NT, and network design and implementation. He has also passed both the CCIE Routing and Switching written exam as well as the CCIE Communications and Services Optical qualification exam. Eric is currently preparing to take the CCIE lab later this year. Eric's background includes positions as a project manager for a major international law firm and as a project manager for NORTEL. He is co-author on the previously published *Cisco AVVID and IP Telephony Design and Implementation* (Syngress Publishing, ISBN: 1-928994-83-0), and the forthcoming book *Configuring IPv6 for Cisco IOS* (Syngress Publishing, ISBN: 1-928994-84-9).

Jamie Caesar (CCNP) is the Senior Network Engineer for INFO1 Inc., located in Norcross, GA. INFO1 is a national provider of electronic services to the credit industry and a market leader in electronic credit solutions. INFO1 provides secure WAN connectivity to customers for e-business services. Jamie contributes his time with enterprise connectivity architecture, security, deployment, and project management for all WAN services. His contributions enable INFO1 to provide mission-critical, 24/7 services to customers across all of North America. Jamie holds a bachelor's degree in Electrical Engineering from Georgia Tech. He resides outside Atlanta, GA with his wife, Julie.

Vitaly Osipov (CISSP, CCSA, CCSE) is a Security Specialist with a technical profile. He has spent the last five years consulting various companies in Eastern, Central, and Western Europe on information security issues. Last year Vitaly was busy with the development of managed security service for a data center in Dublin, Ireland. He is a regular contributor to various infosec-related mailing lists and recently co-authored *Check Point NG Certified Security Administrator Study Guide*. Vitaly has a degree in mathematics. Currently he lives in the British Isles.

C. Tate Baumrucker (CISSP, CCNP, Sun Enterprise Engineer, MCSE) is a Senior Consultant with Callisma. He is responsible for leading engineering teams in the design and implementation of complex and highly available systems infrastructures and networks. Tate is industry recognized as a subject matter expert in security and LAN/WAN support systems such as HTTP, SMTP, DNS, and DHCP. He has spent eight years providing technical consulting services in enterprise and service provider industries for companies including American Home Products, Blue Cross and Blue Shield of Alabama, Amtrak, Iridium, National Geographic, Geico, GTSI, Adelphia Communications, Digex, Cambrian Communications, and BroadBand Office.

Brian Browne (CISSP) is a Senior Consultant with Callisma. He provides senior-level strategic and technical security consulting to Callisma clients, has 12 years of experience in the field of information systems security, and is skilled in all phases of the security lifecycle. A former independent consultant, Brian has provided security consulting for multiple Fortune 500 clients, and has been published in *Business Communications Review*. His security experience includes network security, firewall architectures, virtual private networks (VPNs), intrusion detection systems, UNIX security, Windows NT security, and public key infrastructure (PKI). Brian resides in Willow Grove, PA with his wife, Lisa and daughter, Marisa.

Technical Reviewer

Sean Thurston (CCDP, CCNP, MCSE, MCP+I) is an employee of Western Wireless, a leading provider of communications services in the Western United States. His specialties include implementation of multi-vendor routing and switching equipment and XoIP (Everything over IP installations). Sean's background includes positions as a Technical Analyst for Sprint-Paranet and the Director of a brick-and-mortar advertising dot com. Sean is also a contributing author to *Building a Cisco Network for Windows 2000* (Syngress Publishing, ISBN: 1-928994-00-8) and *Cisco AVVID & IP Telephony Design and Implementation* (Syngress Publishing, ISBN: 1-928994-83-0). Sean lives in Renton, WA with his fiancée, Kerry. He is currently pursuing his CCIE.

Technical Editor

Edgar Danielyan (CCNP Security, CCDP, CSE, SCNA) is a self-employed consultant, author, and editor specializing in security, UNIX, and internetworking. He is the author of *Solaris 8 Security* available from New Riders, and has contributed his expertise as a Technical Editor of several books on security and networking including *Hack Proofing Linux* (Syngress Publishing, ISBN: 1-928994-34-2) and *Hack Proofing Your Web Applications* (Syngress Publishing, ISBN: 1-928994-31-8). Edgar is also a member of the ACM, IEEE, IEEE Computer Society, ISACA, SAGE, and the USENIX Association.

Contents

**Remote Dial-in User
System**

Remote Dial-in User
System (RADIUS) is an
open standard and
available from many
vendors:

- RADIUS uses UDP, so it
  only offers best effort
  delivery at a lower
  overhead.

- RADIUS encrypts only
  the password sent
  between the Cisco
  access client and
  RADIUS server. RADIUS
  does not provide
  encryption between
  the workstation and
  the Cisco access client.

- RADIUS does not
  support multiple
  protocols, and only
  works on IP networks.

- RADIUS does not
  provide the ability to
  control the commands
  that can be executed
  on a router: It provides
  authentication, but not
  authorization to Cisco
  devices.

Answers to Your Frequently Asked Questions

Q: Is a vulnerability assessment program expensive?

A: Not necessarily. The Cisco product is not terribly expensive, and there exist open source solutions which are free to use. The actual assessment program is probably less expensive than the remediation efforts: Maintaining all your hosts on an ongoing basis is a steep maintenance requirement, and one that not all enterprises have accepted. But ever since the summer of 2001, there has been clear evidence that you have to manage your hosts and keep their patch levels up-to-date just to stay in business.

NOTE

Make sure the COM port properties in the terminal emulation program match the following values:

- 9600 baud
- 8 data bits
- No parity
- 1 stop bit
- Hardware flow control

Chapter 4 Traffic Filtering in the Cisco Internetwork Operating System   163

Logging Commands

There are also eight different levels of messages, which will be listed from most severe (Emergency - Level 0) to least severe (Debugging - Level 7):

- Emergency – Level 0

- Alerts – Level 1

- Critical – Level 2

- Errors – Level 3

- Warning – Level 4

- Notification – Level 5

- Informational – Level 6

- Debugging – Level 7

Chapter 5 Network Address Translation/Port Address Translation

Configuration Commands

Before NAT can be implemented, the "inside" and "outside" networks must be defined. To define the "inside" and "outside" networks, use the *ip nat* command.

```
ip nat inside |
    outside
```

- **Inside** Indicates the interface is connected to the inside network (the network is subject to NAT translation).

- **Outside** Indicates the interface is connected to the outside network.

Chapter 6 Cryptography   273

Encryption Key Types

Cryptography uses two types of keys: *symmetric* and *asymmetric*. Symmetric keys have been around the longest; they utilize a single key for both the encryption and decryption of the ciphertext. This type of key is called a *secret key*, because you must keep it secret. Otherwise, anyone in possession of the key can decrypt messages that have been encrypted with it. The algorithms used in symmetric key encryption have, for the most part, been around for many years and are well known, so the only thing that is secret is the key being used. Indeed, all of the really useful algorithms in use today are completely open to the public.

LocalDirector Product Overview

The LocalDirector product is available in three different ranges:

- **LocalDirector 416**
  This is both the entry-level product as well as the medium-size product. It supports up to 90 Mbps throughput and 7,000 connections per second.

- **LocalDirector 430**
  This is the high-end product. It supports up to 400 Mbps throughput and 30,000 connections per second.

- **LocalDirector 417**
  Newer platform with different mounting features. It is even more productive than 430 series and has more memory—two Fast Ethernet and one Gigabit Ethernet interfaces.

Chapter 8 Virtual Private Networks and Remote Access

Overview of the Different VPN Technologies

- A *peer* VPN model is one in which the path determination at the network layer is done on a hop-by-hop basis.

- An *overlay* VPN model is one in which path determination at the network layer is done on a "cut-through" basis to another edge node (customer site).

- Link Layer VPNs are implemented at link layer (Layer 2) of the OSI Reference model.

WARNING

The SRVTAB is the core of Kerberos security. Using TFTP to transfer this key is an IMPORTANT security risk! Be very careful about the networks in which this file crosses when transferred from the server to the router. To minimize the security risk, use a cross-over cable that is directly connected from a PC to the router's Ethernet interface. Configure both interfaces with IP addresses in the same subnet. By doing this, it is physically impossible for anyone to capture the packets as they are transferred from the Kerberos server to the router.

FlowWall Security

FlowWall provides intelligent flow inspection technology that screens for all common DoS attacks, such as SYN floods, ping floods, smurfs, and abnormal or malicious connection attempts. It does this by discarding packets that have the following characteristics:

- Frame length is too short.

- Frame is fragmented.

- Source IP address = IP destination (LAND attack).

- Source address = Cisco address, or the source is a subnet broadcast.

- Source address is not a unicast address.

- Source IP address is a loop-back address.

- Destination IP address is a loop-back address.

- Destination address is not a valid unicast or multicast address.

Searching the Network for Vulnerabilities

There are three primary steps in creating a session to search your network for vulnerabilities:

1. Identifying the network addresses to scan

2. Identifying vulnerabilities to scan by specifying the TCP and UDP ports (and any active probe settings)

3. Scheduling the session

Frequently Asked Questions

Q: Which IDS platforms are supported in CSPM?

A: Only Cisco Secure IDS sensors (former NetRanger sensors) are supported, either in standalone configuration or as Catalyst 6000 blades. Embedded IDS features of Cisco PIX firewalls and Cisco IOS routers are not supported.

**Distributed Denial of
Service Attacks**

Recently, distributed denial of service (DDoS) attacks have become more common. Typical tools used by attackers are Trinoo, TFN, TFN2K and Stacheldraht ("barbed wire" in German). How does a DDoS attack work? The attacker gains access to a Client PC. From there, the cracker can use tools to send commands to the nodes. These nodes then flood or send malformed packets to the victim. Coordinated traceroutes from several sources are used to probe the same target to construct a table of routes for the network. This information is then used as the basis for further attacks.

Network Security Management

To overcome security management issues, Cisco has developed several security management applications including these:

- PIX Device Manager

- CiscoWorks2000 Access Control Lists Manager

- Cisco Secure Policy Manager

- Cisco Secure Access Control Server

Understanding Security Fundamentals and Principles of Protection

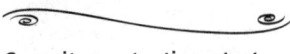

Security protection starts with the preservation of the *confidentiality*, *integrity*, and *availability* (CIA) of data and computing resources. These three tenets of information security, often referred to as "The Big Three," are sometimes represented by the CIA triad.

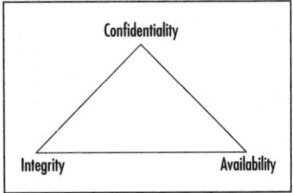

Foreword

Today's Security Environment

Information security has become an extremely important topic for everyone over the past few years. In today's environment the number of touch points between an organization's information assets and the outside world has drastically increased: millions of customers can interact via a Web site, thousands of employees and partners may connect using Virtual Private Network s (VPNs), and dozens of critical applications may be completely outsourced to application service providers (ASPs). The deployment of wireless LANs also means that users no longer even need a physical connection to the network to gain access.

In addition to an explosion of touch points, we are faced with an infinitively complex and rapidly changing web of networks, applications, systems, client software, and service providers. Under these circumstances, absolute security cannot be guaranteed since it's impossible to test the security implications of every configuration combination of hardware and software under every set of conditions.

A critical strategy for reducing security risk is to practice defense-in-depth. The essence of defense-in-depth is to create an architecture that incorporates multiple layers of security protection. Recognizing this requirement, Cisco Systems has placed a high priority on security and offers a wide range of stand-alone and integrated security products. *Managing Cisco Network Security, Second Edition* is important to anyone involved with Cisco networks, as it provides practical information on using a broad spectrum of Cisco's security products. Security is not just for "security geeks" anymore. It is an absolute requirement of all network engineers, system administrators, and other technical staff to understand how best to implement security.

About This Book

In addition to providing a general understanding of IP network security and the threat environment, this book offers detailed and practical information on how to use Cisco's suite of security products. Callisma's contributing authors are industry experts with real world implementation experience. Each chapter will guide you through a particular aspect of security, from the family of PIX firewalls, to the Cisco Secure Intrusion Detection System (IDS), to traffic filtering in IOS, to the Cisco Secure Policy Manager (CSPM). In reading this book, you will obtain a firm understanding of how to secure your Cisco network.

About Callisma

Callisma is setting a new standard for network consulting, helping today's enterprises and service providers design and deploy networks that deliver strategic business value. By providing its clients with a broad base of technical practices, a flexible, results-oriented engagement style, and the highest quality documentation and communication, Callisma delivers superior solutions—on time and on budget. Callisma practices include IP Telephony, Internetworking, Optical Networking, Operations Management, Project Management, and Security and Storage Networking. Callisma is headquartered in Silicon Valley, with offices located throughout the United States. For more information, visit the Callisma Web site at www.callisma.com or call 888-805-7075

—Ralph Troupe
President and CEO, Callisma

## Chapter 1

Introduction to IP Network Security

Solutions in this chapter:

- **What Role Does Security Play in a Network?**

- **The Fundamentals of Networking**

- **Where Does Security Fit in?**

- **Cisco IP Security Hardware and Software**

☑ **Summary**

☑ **Solutions Fast Track**

☑ **Frequently Asked Questions**

Introduction

This book is intended to help people implement IP network security in a Cisco environment. It will provide the language, architectural framework, technical insight, technical configuration, and practical advice to ensure best practice security implementation. Successfully digesting the material presented in this book will allow you to protect your environment and client services using a wide array of Cisco security technologies and equipment.

What Role Does Security Play in a Network?

This book is about IP network security. Though you probably already know something about networking, we'll go over some of the language to be sure we are all working from the same concepts. Let's begin by discussing what we are trying to accomplish with IP network security.

Goals

The goals of security usually boil down to three things, represented by the acronym CIA:

- **Confidentiality** Confidentiality protects sensitive information from unauthorized disclosure or intelligible interception. Information should only be seen by the intended parties in a conversation, not by eavesdroppers.

- **Integrity** Integrity ensures that information or software is complete, accurate, and authentic (in other words, it isn't altered without authorization). We want to ensure mechanisms are in place to protect against accidental or malicious changes, and may wish to produce documented trails of which communications have occurred.

- **Availability** Availability ensures that information and services are accessible and functional when needed and authorized. There is a related concept of trust. The formal definition of trust concerns the extent to which someone who relies on a system can have confidence that the system meets its specifications (that is, the system does what it claims to do and does not perform unwanted functions).

Different systems and businesses will place differing levels of importance on each of these three characteristics. For example, while Internet service providers (ISPs) may be concerned with confidentiality and integrity, they will be more concerned with protecting availability for their customers. The military, by contrast, places more emphasis on confidentiality, with its system of classifications of information, and the clearances for people who need to access it. Most businesses must be concerned with all three elements, but will be concerned primarily with the integrity of their data.

Confidentiality

Confidentiality protects sensitive information from unauthorized disclosure or intelligible interception. Cryptography and access control are used to protect confidentiality. The effort applied to protecting confidentiality depends on the sensitivity of the information and the likelihood of it being observed or intercepted.

Damage & Defense...

Cleartext Passwords

Passing passwords in cleartext that permits administrative access to systems is a severe security risk. Use access control mechanisms, and where possible, encryption controls (such as SSH) to communicate with infrastructure devices. Many Cisco devices will support SSH with a modern image.

Network encryption can be applied at any level in the protocol stack. Applications can provide end-to-end encryption, but each application must be adapted to provide this service. Encryption at the transport layer is used frequently today. Virtual private networks (VPNs) can be used to establish secure channels of communication between two sites or between an end user and a site. (VPNs are covered in more detail in Chapter 5.) Encryption can be used at the OSI data-link layer, but doesn't scale easily; every networking device in the communication pathway would have to participate in the encryption scheme. Data-link layer encryption is making a comeback in the area of wireless security, such as in IEEE 802.11. Physical security, meanwhile, is used to prevent unauthorized access to network ports or equipment rooms. One of the risks at the physical level is violation of access control through the attachment of promiscuous packet capture devices to the network, particularly with the widespread use of open source tools such as Ethereal (www.ethereal.com) and tcpdump (www.tcpdump.org) that permits nearly any host to become a packet decoder.

Integrity

Integrity ensures that information or software is complete, accurate, and authentic. We want to keep unauthorized people or processes from making any changes to the system, and keep authorized users from making changes that exceed their authority. These changes may be intentional or unintentional, and similar mechanisms can protect a system from both.

For network integrity, we need to ensure that the message received is the same message that was sent. The content of the message must be complete and unmodified, and that the link is between a valid source and destination nodes. Connection integrity can be provided by cryptography and routing control. Simple integrity assurance methods to detect incidental changes, like adding up all the bytes in a message and recording that as an element in the packet, are used in everyday IP flows. More robust approaches, such as taking the output from a hash function like message digest (version) 5 (MD5) or secure hash algorithim (SHA) and adding that to the message, as is used in IPSec, can detect attempted malicious changes to a communication.

For host integrity, cryptography can also come to the rescue. Using a secure hash can identify whether an unauthorized change has occurred. However, of fundamental importance are careful use of audit trails to determine what changed, when the change occurred, and who made the change. Sound security design includes a centralized log server, and policy and procedure around safe handling of audit data.

Integrity also extends to the software images for network devices that are transporting data. The images must be verified as authentic, and that they have not been modified or corrupted. Just as a transported IP packet has a checksum to verify it wasn't accidentally damaged in transit, Cisco provides a checksum for IOS images. When copying an image into flash memory, verify that the checksum of the bundled image matches the checksum listed in the README file that comes with the upgrade.

Availability

Availability ensures that information and services are accessible and functional when needed. Redundancy, fault tolerance, reliability, failover, backups, recovery, resilience, and load balancing are the network design concepts used to assure availability. If systems aren't available, then integrity and confidentiality won't matter. Build networks that provide high availability.

Your customers or end users will perceive availability as being the entire system—application, servers, network, and workstation. If they can't run their applications, then it is not available. To provide high availability, ensure that security processes are reliable and responsive. Modular systems and software, including security systems, need to be interoperable.

Denial of service (DoS) attacks are aimed at crippling the availability of networks and servers, and can create severe losses for organizations. In February, 2000, large Web sites such as Yahoo!, eBay, Amazon, CNN, ZDNet, E★Trade, Excite, and Buy.com were knocked offline or had their availability reduced to about 10 percent for many hours by distributed denial of service attacks (DDoS). The attacks were not particularly sophisticated—they were launched by a teenager—but were disastrously effective.

NOTE

Having a good inventory and documentation of your network is important for day-to-day operations, but in a disaster, you can't depend on having it available. Business Continuity/Disaster Recovery is an important aspect of security design. Store the configurations and software images of network devices *offsite* with your backups from servers, and keep them up to date. Include documentation about the architecture of your network. All of this documentation should be available in printed form because electronic versions may be unavailable or difficult to locate in an emergency. Such information will save valuable time in a crisis.

Cisco makes many products designed for high hardware availability. These devices are characterized by a long mean time between failure (MTBF) with redundant power supplies, and hot-swappable cards or modules. For example, devices that provide 99.999 percent availability would have about five minutes downtime per year.

Availability of individual devices can be enhanced by their configuration. Using features such as redundant uplinks with Hot Standby Router Protocol (HSRP), fast convergent Spanning Tree, or Fast EtherChannel provide a failover if one link should fail. Uninterruptible power supplies (UPSs) and backup generators are used to protect mission-critical equipment in the event of a power outage. These are not security features per se—and in some instances may work against security, such as using HSRP to force a router offline to allow the bypassing of access controls—but are a valid part of a security design.

Although not covered in this book, Cisco IOS includes reliability features such as:

- Hot Standby Router Protocol (HSRP)
- Simple Server Redundancy Protocol (SSRP)
- Deterministic Load Distribution (DLD)

Philosophy

The underlying philosophy behind security is different from what most network managers face. There are three common perspectives behind the design of networks:

- **User perspective** Get it out fast, and as inexpensively as possible. Make it work. If it breaks, fix it.

- **Operations management perspective** Get it out to meet all needs, and do it as reliably as possible. Document how it's working. Don't let it break, or at least recover from breaks transparently.

- **Security perspective** Get it out in a controlled fashion, meeting authorized needs. Allow only authorized services to work. If it breaks, make sure it fails in a fashion that doesn't allow unauthorized services.

The way to think of the user perspective is to imagine you are programming a computer: Write code to make it work, and move on. If the code is a little buggy, that's okay—it's less expensive, and you get most of what you need. The way to think of the operations management perspective is to see yourself programming Murphy's computer: Write code with the understanding that things will break at the worst possible time, and deal with it gracefully. You spend time developing useful error messages, and help the user understand what is happening inside the program. It costs more, but it's a better "quality" program. The way to think of the security perspective is to imagine yourself programming Satan's computer: Write code with the understanding that there is an actively malicious agent at the heart of the environment trying to break things; protect yourself and your clients. You spend time checking for buffer overflows or impossible inputs. It's more difficult of course, but hey, it's a dangerous world out there...

None of these perspectives is best; they all have advantages. Working from an operations management perspective is expensive; it means you usually have to buy two of everything, provide redundant routes, and spend time thinking about command and management issues. Working from a security perspective is inconvenient; in addition to the increased complexities, we often have to reduce features and try to streamline systems to provide the necessary controls. Maintaining all three perspectives simultaneously is the challenge that network managers face.

Cisco has documented its fundamental blueprints in the SAFE program (see www.cisco.com/warp/public/779/largeent/issues/security/safebprint.html for further information). A quick summary might state that security does not come from a single product but is based upon a triad of people, processes, and technology; and that security should not be in a single location but be handled by a distributed, defense-in-depth approach that's spread across the enterprise. Though security policy and its procedural issues are outside the scope of this book, be warned that some sidebars may creep into these pages from time to time. What we will do is show how the various pieces of security technology can be deployed across your environment to enhance your security posture.

What if I Don't Deploy Security?

Security costs significant money, and is rather inconvenient. These are rather good reasons not to deploy security, and for many enterprises that was the standard operating procedure. Unfortunately, that turned out to be a shortsighted decision. According to an Information Week / Price Waterhouse Cooper survey (the Security Benchmarking Service), losses due to security breaches cost over 1.39 *trillion* dollars last year. The Computer Security Institue (CSI)/FBI survey showed that the average annual loss per company exceeded *two million* dollars. One interesting study is Egghead Software: On the day a security breach was announced, their stock dropped 25 percent, and they never recovered. What is a fourth of your company's capitalization? If you can reduce or eliminate this number, that can fund a pretty significant security program.

An effective security program *can* make a difference. Computer Economics estimated the three most costly mobile code events were CodeRed and its variants at 2.62 billion dollars; SirCam at 1.15 billion dollars; and Nimda at 635 million dollars. The first and last could have been stopped by an effective vulnerability assessment program, such as a solid Cisco Secure Scanner deployment, while the SirCam could have been stopped by an effective antivirus filtering program at the perimeter of the network.

Some enterprises argue that they aren't a target, so they don't have to protect themselves. How wrong they are. Automated tools probe the Internet looking for vulnerable hosts. If you put an unpatched Microsoft Internet Information Server (IIS) on the Internet, (even via dialup or DSL) you have between 30 minutes and two hours, on average, before a Nimda probe will compromise your machine. Script kiddies and commercial crooks alike look for innocuous hosts, called *zombies*, that they can compromise and control to use in attacks on other systems. Even if you don't handle credit card information, if you care about your system being available for your own use, you have to take steps, and if you care about the "public health" of the Internet, you have to be diligent.

The Fundamentals of Networking

Information security deals primarily with the CIA of information. IP network security addresses these issues as information passes over IP networks. Consequently, to talk about security we first have to talk about IP networking.

A good place to start is the underlying information architecture on which networking is based. A good reference point is the Department of Defense (DoD) networking model; this was the original seed for the ideas on which the Internet was founded, and IP protocols tend to be based upon this model.

The four layers of the DoD model, moving up from low-level transport to high-level application are:

- **Network Access Layer** Describes how computers talk to other locally attached devices. Focuses on issues of frames, which is the fundamental data unit passed along a physical network interface. In network security, we look at media, hub, and switch issues for security.

- **Internetwork Layer** Describes how frames are encapsulated into packets, and packets into datagrams; and how the datagram is transported between local networks. In network security, we look at switches, routers, and firewalls, such as the Cisco PIX for security.

- **Host-to-Host Transport Layer** Describes how hosts can achieve a reliable information stream. In network security, we look at routers, firewalls, and application devices such as load balancers or content managers, in conjunction with detective controls such as an Intrusion Detection System (IDS—for example, the Cisco Secure IDS) for security.

- **Process Application Layer** Describes how end users and end applications interact with the transported data. In network security, we look at end applications, together with IDS and Vulnerability Assessment tools such as the Cisco Secure Scanner, as well as auxiliary applications such as authentication servers like Cisco Secure Access Control Server (ACS).

Security can be applied in each layer and at the interface between layers; for example:

- **Network Access Layer** Examples of network access security issues are physical media access address resolution protocols and broadcast issues (for example, Address Resolution Protocol (ARP) cache poisoning and Virtual LANs (VLANs)/Multiprotocol Label Swtiching (MPLS) design).

- **Internetwork Layer** Examples of internetwork layer issues are packet routing security and transport control issues (for instance, IP address spoofing, IP address-based Access Control Lists (ACLs), source routing, fragment handling, and ICMP message handling).

- **Host-to-Lost Layer** Examples of host-to-host transport layer issues are communication stream initialization, transport confidentiality and integrity, and communication stream closure (for example, three-way handshake spoofing, packet snooping, and session hijacking).

- **Process Application Layer** Examples would be the SMTP or HTTP protocols (such as unsolicited commercial e-mail eradication or mobile code stripping).

Where Does Security Fit in?

To protect your infrastructure, you must apply security in layers. This layered approach is also called defense in depth. The idea is that you create multiple systems, so that a failure in one of them does not leave you vulnerable, but is caught in the next layer. You should create appropriate barriers inside your system so intruders that gain access to one part of it, do not automatically acquire access to the rest of the system. Use firewalls to minimize the exposure of private servers from public networks. Firewalls are the first line of defense. Packet filtering on routers can supplement the protection of firewalls and provide internal access boundaries.

Access to hosts that contain confidential information needs to be carefully controlled. Inventory the hosts on your network, and use this list to categorize the protection they will need. Some hosts will be used to providing public access, such as the corporate Web site or online storefront. Others will contain confidential information that may be used only by a single department or workgroup.

Plan the type of access needed and determine the boundaries of access control for these resources.

A good way to develop a defense in depth is to look at each layer of the DoD model, and apply security accordingly.

Network Access Layer Security

Network access layer security is done locally. One form of security addresses point-to-point communication, such as over a leased line or Frame Relay permanent virtual circuit. Dedicated hardware devices attached to each end of the link do encryption and decryption. Military, governments, and banking are the most common users of this approach. Though it is not scalable to large internetworks, because the packets are not routable in their encrypted state, this method does have the advantage that an eavesdropper cannot determine the source or destination addresses in the packets. It can also be used for upper-layer protocols.

A second form of security addresses controlling access to the shared media of the local LAN. At its simplest, if you have two machines that shouldn't communicate without controls (for example, a machine that handles Top Secret data and a machine that handles Unclassified data), don't put them on the same LAN. The military is known for building completely separate and partitioned networks, and having people with two machines on their desk to prevent information from spilling from one network into the other. Even in networks with less stringent requirements, the modern style is to develop separate, out-of-band management networks for controlling infrastructure equipment.

Configuring & Implementing...

NSA Router Security Guides

The National Security Agency of the United States has developed guidance on deploying Cisco routers in a secure fashion. They provide strategic design elements and tactical configurations for Cisco equipment. As of this writing, the guides are available online at http://nsa2 .www.conxion.com/cisco/index.html.

In a modern enterprise, it's not always possible to completely isolate machines on separate networks. They may need to communicate directly, or we may not have the resources to deploy separate routers, switches, and communication channels for all the equipment. In that environment, the most reasonable solution is judicious use of VLANs and virtual wide area networks through MPLS. For example, suppose you want to manage your firewalls, routers, switches, IDS, and other security devices from a management station on your desktop. You could buy a separate T1 to connect to your remote sites, and run separate wires to management interfaces on all these devices. Since that isn't practical, you can use MPLS and VLAN tags, combined with physically isolating management interfaces on separate switched ports, to provide that virtually partitioned network.

NOTE

Don't carry this process to the extreme. In security, there is a concept known as the Trusted Computing Base (TCB), its formal definition being "The totality of protection mechanisms within a computer system, including hardware, firmware, and software, the combination of which is responsible for enforcing a security policy." (Orange book). The goal is to make the TCB as small as possible—and ensure the components of the TCB are security devices, carefully reviewed, and so on.

For critical placements, you want the TCB to be the firewall and its software, and nothing else. It's important to remember that a switch is not a security device. As the SAFE architecture notes, "Avoid using VLANs as the sole method of securing access between two subnets. The capability for human error, combined with understanding that VLANs and VLAN tagging protocols were not designed with security in mind, makes their use in sensitive environments inadvisable. When VLANs are needed in security deployments, be sure to pay close attention to the configurations and guidelines mentioned above."

So, don't interconnect the router outside your firewall with a device inside the firewall via VLANs—there is a risk that if the switch is compromised, the firewall will be bypassed and the security of the whole enterprise will be placed in jeopardy. Make reasonable tradeoffs in the way of convenience, elegant design, and security.

Internetwork Layer Security

The easiest place to enforce a technical control is at the Internetwork layer—since you can inspect and forbid information from passing between separate networks and machines. Controlling access to the network with firewalls, routers, switches, remote access servers, and authentication servers can reduce the traffic getting to critical hosts to just authorized users and services. Security considerations can have an effect on the physical design of the network. Networks can be segmented to provide separation of responsibility. Departments, such as finance, research, or engineering, can be restricted so only the people that need access to particular resources can enter a network. You need to know the specifications that will be used to purchase network equipment, software features or revision levels that need to be used, and any specialized devices used to provide encryption, quality of service, or access control. You need to determine the resources to protect, the origin of threats against them, and where your network security perimeters should be located. Install devices and configurations at the perimeter—the internetwork layer between networks—that meets your security requirements.

Jon Postel, one of the godfathers of the Internet, wrote: "be conservative in what you do, be liberal in what you accept from others." Unfortunately, this principle of robustness has lead to security problems, particularly at the application and internetwork layers. At the Internetwork layer, it is important to validate the information you receive before routing. Of special importance is preventing simple fraud: a particularly pernicious problem today is based upon the *smurf* attack. This is a variant of the real-world "pizza order" attack, where you call a dozen pizza delivery companies and have them all deliver a pizza to someone's home at the same time. In a smurf attack, one computer makes requests for service from a large number of sites on the behalf of another host. There are details in terms of minimization of the bandwidth consumed by the attacker and maximization of the tidal wave of responses that hits the victim host, but it's all based upon sending outgoing requests as if for another person. If the pizza company could use caller ID to not accept requests from places other than where the call originates, the "pizza order" attack would fail. Similarly, if end routers did not route packets that could not have originated locally, the smurf attack would never get off the ground. In a modern internetworking environment, be cautious in what you accept from others; if it doesn't make sense, log it and drop it.

Access Control Lists

Access Control Lists (ACLs) are an effective way to address the filtering problem mentioned earlier. ACLs are packet filters that can be implemented on routers and similar devices to control the source and destination IP addresses allowed to pass through the gateway. Standard access lists can filter on source address. Extended access lists can filter ICMP, IGMP, or IP protocols at the Network layer. ICMP can be filtered based on the specific message. IP filtering can include port numbers at the transport (TCP/UDP) layer to allow or disallow specific services between particular addresses. Access lists can also control other routed protocols such as AppleTalk or IPX, and they are your first and best way to eliminate inappropriate traffic.

Configuring & Implementing…

Martian Filtering

The router requirements of RFC 1812 talk about "martian filtering," and notes "A router SHOULD NOT forward any packet that has an invalid IP source address or a source address on network 0." Large chunks of IP space—not just the RFC 1918's of the 10, 172.16, and 192.168 networks, are invalid addresses and should be dropped. An effective way of achieving this is to null route the logon, like this:

```
ip route 1.0.0.0 255.0.0.0 null0
ip route 2.0.0.0 255.0.0.0 null0
ip route 5.0.0.0 255.0.0.0 null0
ip route 7.0.0.0 255.0.0.0 null0
ip route 10.0.0.0 255.0.0.0 null0
ip route 23.0.0.0 255.0.0.0 null0
ip route 27.0.0.0 255.0.0.0 null0
ip route 31.0.0.0 255.0.0.0 null0
ip route 36.0.0.0 255.0.0.0 null0
ip route 37.0.0.0 255.0.0.0 null0
ip route 39.0.0.0 255.0.0.0 null0
ip route 41.0.0.0 255.0.0.0 null0
ip route 42.0.0.0 255.0.0.0 null0
```

An extremely useful consensus document on secure router templates for the Internet is Rob Thomas' *Secure IOS Template*, available at www.cymru.com/~robt/Docs/Articles/secure-ios-template.html.

Host-to-host Layer Security

Host-to-host layer security can be applied to secure traffic for all applications or transport protocols in the above layers. Applications do not need to be modified since they communicate with the Transport layer above. Confidentiality and integrity are easily obtained through encryption and authentication protocols, and availability and other reliability issues are addressed through reliable transport protocols.

IPSec

The security architecture for IP (IPSec) is a suite of security services for traffic at the IP layer. It is an open standard, defined in RFC 2401 and several following RFCs. It has received widespread adoption, and clients are generally available for many hosts and network infrastructure devices. It is integrated into Cisco IOS, and available on most routers and firewalls. It is the single most common, least expensive, and most widely deployed technical security control at the host-to-host layer.

IPSec protocols can supply access control, authentication, data integrity, and confidentiality for each IP packet between two participating network nodes. IPSec can be used between two hosts (including clients), a gateway and a host, or two gateways. No modification of network hardware or software is required to route IPSec. Applications and upper-level protocols can thus be used unchanged.

IPSec adds two security protocols to IP, Authentication Header (AH) and Encapsulating Security Payload (ESP). AH provides connectionless integrity, data origin authentication, and anti-replay service for the IP packet. AH does not encrypt the data, but any modification of the data would be detected. ESP provides confidentiality through the encryption of the payload. Access control is provided through the use and management of keys to control participation in traffic flows.

IPSec was designed to be flexible so different security needs could be accommodated. The security services can be tailored to the particular needs of each connection by using AH or ESP separately for their individual functions, or combining the protocols to provide the full range of protection offered by IPSec. Multiple cryptographic algorithms are supported. The algorithms that must be present in any implementation of IPSec are listed next. The null algorithms provide no protection, but are used for consistent negotiation by the protocols. AH and ESP cannot both be null at the same time.

- Data Encryption Standard (DES) in Cipher Block Chaining (CBC) mode

- HMAC (Hash Message Authentication Codes) with MD5
- HMAC with SHA
- Null Authentication Algorithm
- Null Encryption Algorithm

A security association (SA) forms an agreement between two systems participating in an IPSec connection. A security association represents a simplex connection to provide a security service using a selected policy and keys, between two nodes. A Security Parameter Index (SPI), an IP destination address, and a protocol identifier are used to identify a particular SA. The SPI is an arbitrary, 32-bit value selected by the destination system that uniquely identifies a particular security association among several associations that may exist on a specific node. The protocol identifier can indicate either AH or ESP, but not both. Separate security associations are created for each protocol, and for each direction between systems. If two systems were using AH and ESP in both directions, then they would form four security associations.

Each protocol supports a transport mode and a tunnel mode of operation. The transport mode is between two hosts. These hosts are the endpoints for the cryptographic functions being used. Tunnel mode is an IP tunnel, and is used whenever either end of the security association is a security gateway. A security gateway is an intermediate system, such as a router or firewall, which implements IPSec protocols. A security association between a host and a security gateway must use tunnel mode. If the connection traffic is destined for the gateway itself, such as management traffic, then the gateway is treated as a host, because it is the endpoint of the communication.

In transport mode, the AH or ESP header is inserted after the IP header, but before any upper-layer protocol headers. As shown in Figure 1.1, AH authenticates the original IP header, but does not protect the fields that are modified in the course of routing IP packets. ESP only protects what comes after the ESP header. If the security policy between two nodes requires a combination of security services, the AH header appears first after the IP header, followed by the ESP header. This combination of security associations is called an *SA bundle*.

In tunnel mode, the original IP header and payload are encapsulated by the IPSec protocols. A new IP header that specifies the IPSec tunnel destination is prepended to the packet. The original IP header and its payload are protected by the AH or ESP headers. From Figure 1.2, you can see that, as in transport mode, AH offers some protection for the entire packet, but does not protect the fields that are modified in the course of routing IP packets between the IPSec tunnel endpoints. It does, however, completely protect the original IP header.

Figure 1.1 The IPSec Transport Mode in IPv4

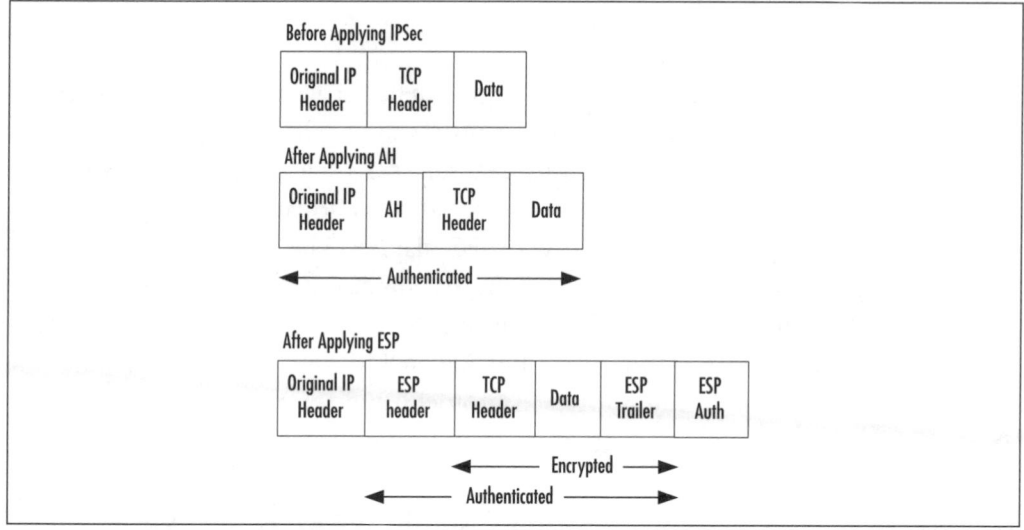

Figure 1.2 The IPSec Tunnel Mode in IPv4

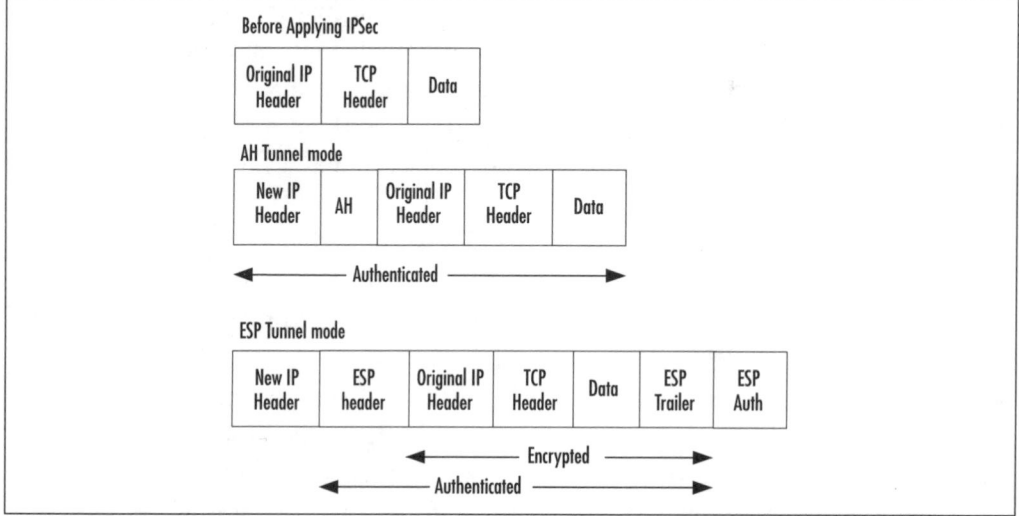

Key management is another major component of IPSec. Manual techniques are allowed in the IPSec standard, and might be acceptable for configuring one or two gateways, but typing in keys and data is not practical in most environments. The Internet Key Exchange (IKE) provides automated, bidirectional SA management, key generation, and key management. IKE negotiates in two phases. Phase 1 negotiates a secure, authenticated channel over which the two systems can communicate for further negotiations. They agree on the encryption algorithm, hash algorithm, authentication method, and Diffie-Hellman group to exchange keys and information. A single phase 1 association can be used for multiple phase 2 negotiations. Phase 2 negotiates the services that define the security associations used by IPSec. They agree on IPSec protocol, hash algorithm, and encryption algorithm. Multiple security associations will result from phase 2 negotiations. An SA is created for the inbound and outbound of each protocol used.

Process Application Layer Security

Any vendor's software is susceptible to harboring security vulnerabilities. Security can be seen as an arms race, with the bad guys exploiting vulnerabilities and the good guys patching them. Every day, Web sites that track security vulnerabilities, such as CERT, are reporting new vulnerability discoveries in operating systems, application software, server software, and even in security software or devices. Last year, CERT advertised an average of over six vulnerabilities a day. Figure 1.3 shows the increase in reported incidents over the years.

Figure 1.3 CERT Reporting Statistics

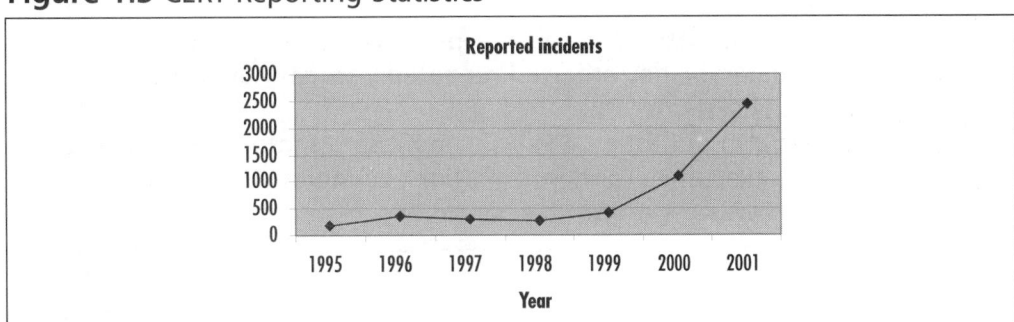

Patches are implemented for these known bugs, but new vulnerability discoveries continue. Sometimes patches fix one bug, only to introduce another. Even open source software that has been widely used for ten years is not immune to harboring serious vulnerabilities. In June 2000, CERT reported that MIT Kerberos had multiple buffer overflow vulnerabilities that could be used to gain root access, and in Feb of 2002, widespread vulnerabilities were announced in the fundamental ASN.1 encoding schema common to all SNMP agents, allowing the compromise of nearly all infrastructure devices across the Internet.

Many sites do not keep up when it comes to applying patches and so leave their systems with known vulnerabilities. It is important to keep all of your software up to date. Many of the most damaging attacks have occurred in end-user software such as electronic mail clients. Attacks can be directed at any software and can seriously affect your network.

The default configuration of hosts makes them easy to get up and running, but many default services are unnecessary. These unnecessary services increase the vulnerabilities of the system. On each host, all unnecessary services should be shut down. Misconfigured hosts also increase the risk of an unauthorized access. All default passwords and community names must be changed.

NOTE

The SANS (System Administration, Networking, and Security) Institute in conjunction with the National Infrastructure Protection Center (NIPC) has created a list of the top 20 Internet security threats as determined by a group of security experts. The list is maintained at www.sans.org/top20.htm. This guide is an excellent list of the most urgent and critical vulnerabilities to repair on your systems. Two of the problems listed earlier—unnecessary default services and default passwords—are on this list.

This effort was started because experience has shown that a small number of vulnerabilities are used repeatedly to gain unauthorized access to many systems.

SANS has also published a list of the most common mistakes made by end users, executives, and information technology personnel. It is available at www.sans.org/mistakes.htm.

The increased complexity of systems, the shortage of well-trained administrators, and a lack of resources all contribute to reducing the security of hosts and applications. We cannot depend on hosts to protect themselves from all threats. A useful approach is to use automated scanning devices, such as Cisco Secure Scanner (formerly NetSonar) to help identify the vulnerabilities from a network perspective, and work with the information owner to apply the necessary remediation.

All is not lost, however. Application layer security can provide end-to-end security from an application running on one host through the network to the application on another host. It does not care about the underlying transport mechanism. Complete coverage of security requirements, integrity, confidentiality and non-repudiation, can be provided at this layer. Applications have a fine granularity of control over the nature and content of the transactions. However, application layer security is not a general solution, because each application and client must be adapted to provide the security services. Several examples of application security extensions are described next.

PGP

Phil Zimmerman created Pretty Good Privacy (PGP) in 1991. It is widely used by individuals worldwide for privacy and the digital signing of e-mail messages. PGP provides end-to-end security from the sender to the receiver. It can also be used to encrypt files. PGP has traditionally used RSA public key cryptography to exchange keys, and IDEA to encrypt messages.

PGP uses a Web of trust or network trust model, where any users can vouch for the identity of other users. Getting the public keys of the intended person can be difficult to achieve in a secure manner. You can get a person's public key directly from that person, and then communicate the hash of the key in an out-of-band pathway. Keys are stored in files called key rings. Some Internet servers, in fact, have public key rings. They do not authenticate the keys—merely store them. You should not trust keys that have an unknown heritage.

S-HTTP

S-HTTP is not widely used, but it was designed to provide security for Web-based applications. Secure HTTP is a secure message-oriented communications protocol, and can transmit individual messages securely. It provides transaction confidentiality, authentication, and message integrity, and extends HTTP to include tags for encrypted and secure transactions. S-HTTP is implemented in some commercial Web servers and most browsers. As an S-HTTP server, it negotiates with the client for the type of encryption that will be used, several types of which exist.

S-HTTP does not require clients to have public key certificates because it can use symmetric keys to provide private transactions. The symmetric keys would be provided in advance using out of band communication.

Secure Sockets Layer and Transport Layer Security

Secure Sockets Layer (SSL) was designed by Netscape and is widely used on the Internet for Web transactions such as sending credit card data. It can be utilized for other protocols as well, such as Telnet, FTP, LDAP, IMAP, and SMTP, but these are not commonly used. Transport Layer Security (TLS), on the other hand, is an open, IETF-proposed standard based on SSL 3.0. RFCs 2246, 2712, 2817, and 2818 define TLS. The name is misleading, since TLS happens well above the transport layer. The two protocols are not interoperable, but TLS has the capability to drop down into SSL 3.0 mode for backwards compatibility, and both can provide security for a single TCP session.

SSL and TLS provide a connection between a client and a server, over which any amount of data can be sent securely. Server and browser generally must be SSL- or TLS-enabled to facilitate secure Web connections, while applications generally must be SSL- or TLS-enabled to allow their use of the secure connection. However, a recent trend is to use dedicated SSL accelerators as VPN terminators, passing the content on to an end server; the Cisco Content Services Switch Secure Content Accelerator 1100 is an example of this technique.

For the browser and server to communicate securely, each needs to have the shared session key. SSL/TLS use public key encryption to exchange session keys during communication initialization. When a browser is installed on a workstation, it generates a unique private/public key pair.

The Secure Shell Protocol

The Secure Shell protocol (SSH) is specified in a set of Internet draft documents. SSH provides secure remote login and other secure network services over an insecure network. It's being promoted free as a means for reducing cleartext passwords on networks. One excellent Windows client is PuTTY, available at www.chiark.greenend.org.uk/~sgtatham/putty. The IOS on a modern Cisco router supports SSH, but only SSH version 1. SSH version 2 is completely rewritten to use different security protocols and has added public key cryptography. Both versions provide confidentiality of passwords and other commands during sessions.

The SSH protocol provides channels for establishing secure, interactive shell sessions and tunneling other TCP applications. There are three major components to SSH:

- **Transport layer protocol** Provides authentication, confidentiality, and integrity for the server. It can also compress the data stream. The SSH transport runs on top of TCP. The transport protocol negotiates the key exchange method, public key, symmetric encryption, authentication, and hash algorithms.

- **User authentication protocol** Authenticates the user-level client to the server and runs on top of the SSH transport layer. It assumes that the transport layer provides integrity and confidentiality. The method of authentication is negotiated between the server and the client.

- **Connection protocol** Multiplexes an encrypted tunnel into several channels. It is run on top of SSH transport and authentication protocols. The two ends negotiate the channel, window size, and type of data. The connection protocol can tunnel X11 or any arbitrary TCP port traffic.

Figure 1.4 shows how various security controls can interact with network traffic, and shows several of the areas where controls can be placed—from directly encrypting signals as they are applied to the Network Access Layer (link encryption) all the way up to encrypting the contents of a mail message (PGP):

Figure 1.4 The Layers of Security Controls

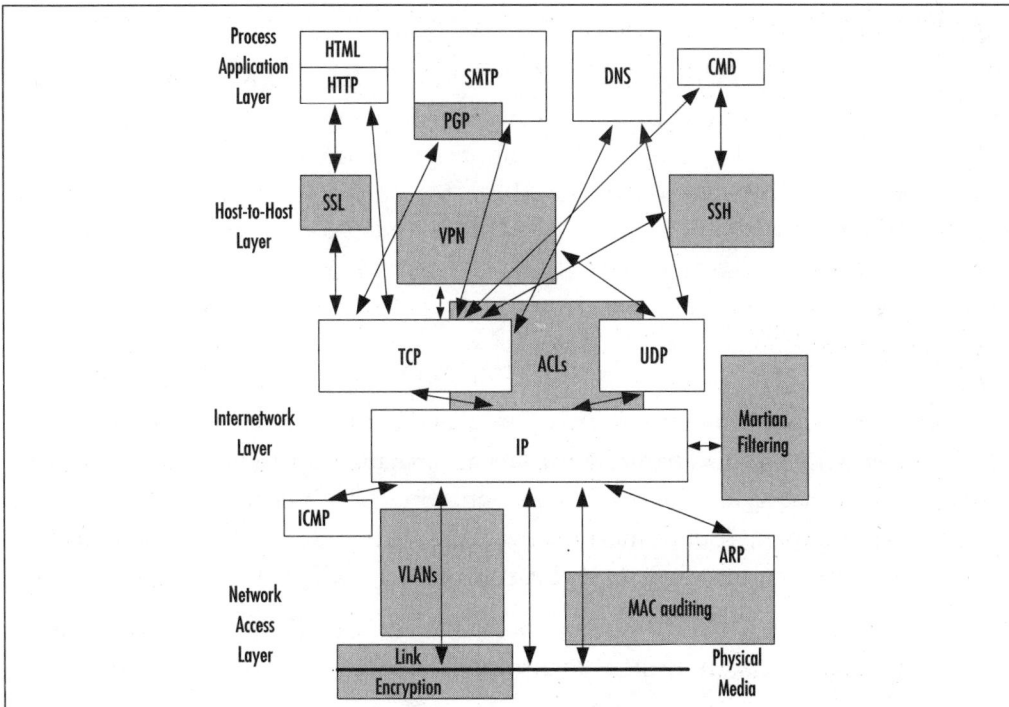

Authentication

Authentication can be used as a security control at any layer in the protocol stack, but is typically deployed at the application process layer. (Often, the application process layer then makes changes to controls at the internetworking layer, establishing sessions or opening ACLs to permit traffic.)

Authentication can be provided locally on each device on your network, but using an authentication server offers improved scalability, flexibility, and control. Firewalls, routers, and remote access servers enforce network access security. Configuring these devices to use one, centralized database of accounts is easier on the administrator and the users who may access the network through multiple pathways.

A Cisco Network Access Server (NAS), firewall, or router acts as the client and requests authentication from an authentication server. The access server or router will prompt the user for a username and password, and then verifies the password with the authentication server. TACACS+, RADIUS, and Kerberos are widely used authentication servers supported by Cisco. TACACS+ and RADIUS can also provide services for authorization, and accounting.

Terminal Access Controller Access System Plus

Terminal Access Controller Access System Plus (TACACS+) is an enhanced version of TACACS developed by Cisco. The enhancements include the separation of authentication, authorization, and accounting into three distinct functions. These services can be used independently or together. For example, Kerberos could be used for authentication, and TACACS+ used for authorization and accounting. Some of the characteristics of TACACS+ are:

- While older versions of TACACS and RADIUS use UDP for transport, TACACS+ uses TCP (port 49) for reliable and acknowledged transport.

- TACACS+ can encrypt the entire payload of the packet, so it protects the password, username, and other information sent between the Cisco access client and the server. The encryption can be turned off for troubleshooting. Communication from the workstation to the Cisco client providing access services is not encrypted.

- TACACS+ supports multiple protocols such as IP, AppleTalk Remote Access (ARA), Novell, Asynchronous Services Interface (NASI), X.25 PAD connection, and NetBIOS.

- You can use TACACS+ to provide greater control over router management in either nonprivileged or privileged mode, because you can authenticate individual users or groups rather than a shared password. Router commands can be specified explicitly on the TACACS+ server to allow specific commands.

Remote Dial-in User System

Remote Dial-in User System (RADIUS) is an open standard and available from many vendors. It was originally designed for ISPs to support dial-in clients, and provides the authorization and billing information for those needs. RADIUS can be a good choice in a heterogeneous network environment because of its widespread support, but some vendors have implemented proprietary attributes in RADIUS that hinder interoperability.

- RADIUS uses UDP, so it only offers best effort delivery at a lower overhead.

- For authentication, RADIUS encrypts only the password sent between the Cisco access client and RADIUS server. RADIUS does not provide encryption between the workstation and the Cisco access client.

- RADIUS does not support multiple protocols, and only works on IP networks.

- RADIUS does not provide the ability to control the commands that can be executed on a router: It provides authentication, but not authorization to Cisco devices.

Kerberos

Kerberos protocol can be used for network authentication and host authentication. It uses a *trusted third-party* approach, where users identify themselves to a central server, and the server then provides "tickets," that the user can present to gain access to servers; the end server trusts that the Kerberos server is granting authority correctly.

    A Kerberos realm includes all users, hosts and network services that are registered with a Kerberos server. Kerberos uses symmetric key cryptography and stores a shared key for each user and each network resource that is participating in its realm. Host-based applications must be "kerberized," with modules adapted to use the Kerberos protocol. Kerberized versions of Telnet, ftp, mail, and several others exist, and APIs exist for updating code. Every user and network resource needs a Kerberos account. Kerberos stores all passwords encrypted with a single system key. If that system key is compromised, all passwords need to be recreated.

    The process of authenticating using Kerberos involves three systems: a client, a network resource, and the Kerberos server. The Kerberos server is called the Key Distribution Center (KDC). The KDC has two functions: an Authentication

Service (AS) and a Ticket Granting Service (TGS). The basic process is a six-step sequence:

1. **Alice to KDC** Hi, I'm Alice. Could I have access to the AS?

2. **AS to Alice** Here is your "ticket-granting ticket." If you aren't Alice, it's useless. If you are Alice, decrypt this, and come back with the answer.

3. **Alice to TGS** Okay, I figured out your secret. Give me a "service-granting ticket" so I can talk to server Bob.

4. **TGS to Alice** You have it! It's encrypted using the same mechanism as before, and then encrypted with Bob's password. This ticket will be accepted by Bob for eight hours.

5. **Client to Bob** The KDC gave me this ticket, and it is encrypted using your password. Validate me.

6. **Bob to Alice** Hello, Alice! I've decrypted what you got from the KDC, I trust the KDC, and he trusts you, so your access is granted. It is worth noting that under Kerberos, passwords are never sent in the clear; there is a preshared secret between the client and the KDC, and the client uses that to unlock the "ticket-granting ticket." This allows the client to request tickets that can be provided to individual servers to obtain that service.

As an example, let's look at remote network access. The remote user establishes a PPP connection to the boundary device, and the device prompts the user for username and password. The device, acting as the client, requests a ticket-granting ticket from the Kerberos authentication server. If the user has an account, the authentication server generates a session key, and sends a ticket-granting ticket (TGT) to the client encrypted with the password stored on the AS for that account. The Cisco access server will attempt to decrypt the TGT with the password that the user entered. The TGT is a credential that specifies the user's verified identity, the Kerberos server identity, and the expiration time of the ticket. By default, tickets expire after eight hours. The TGT is encrypted with a key known only to the ticket-granting server and the authentication server. The TGT is presented back to the TGS with a request for access to the Cisco access server. Now the roles reverse, and the Cisco access server becomes the server. The Cisco access server accepts the service ticket, decrypts it to verify it is valid, and provides service. If successful, the user is authenticated to the access server, and the user's workstation becomes part of the protected network.

Note that at this point, the only authenticated "user" is the Cisco access server. Users, who want to access services that are part of the Kerberos realm on the network, must now re-authenticate against the Kerberos server and get authorization to access the services. The user first gets a ticket-granting ticket as previously described, which is used to request access to other services. The difference is that the client is now the user's workstation.

More details on AAA can be found in Chapter 9.

OSI Model

The DoD model is very helpful for thinking about security. Unfortunately, it's the Betamax of security models—internetworking professionals tend to prefer the OSI model; it adds more specific layers at the low and high ends, and more naturally maps to certain kinds of equipment. It is worth reviewing the OSI model to set up the language that will be used in the later chapters of the book, and to correspond to materials you will read elsewhere.

The OSI Reference Model consists of seven layers:

- The physical layer (Layer 1)

- The data-link layer (Layer 2)

- The network layer (Layer 3)

- The transport layer (Layer 4)

- The session layer (Layer 5)

- The presentation layer (Layer 6)

- The application layer (Layer 7).

This convention has been developed to provide an initial framework to simplify network design and to provide a systematic approach to troubleshooting. As our discussion progresses, the functionality of each layer and how these layers communicate will become increasingly clear. The OSI model was an extension of the more Internet focused DoD model, and provides additional structure, particularly at the higher layers.

A nice mnemonic for the OSI layers is the expression "All People Seem To Need Data Processing." The first initials correspond to "Application, Presentation, Session, Transport, Network, Data, Physical."

In our discussion of how each layer functions, we look at the parallels between human communication and that of computer systems, breaking down the communication process into its components to allow more granular comparisons. Imagine yourself as a student in a classroom listening to an instructor's lecture. This constitutes our example of human communication; we then address how computer communications correspond to that example. Keep in mind that when we talk about computer systems communicating, we are really referring to one device talking to another.

Layer 1: The Physical Layer

The *physical layer* is identified as the physical medium that facilitates communication. In our classroom example, air is considered the physical medium. It carries the sound waves produced by the instructor to the students. Both the air and the sound waves being transmitted are considered part of the physical layer. In the computer world, where traditional wired technology is implemented, copper is the primary mode of transmission. It carries a designated electrical pattern to the other computers in the local network. Again, the electrical waves are a component of the physical layer. This layer is also responsible for specifying the shape and intensity of the electrical wave.

Layer 2: The Data-link Layer

The *data-link layer,* in our human analogy, formats thoughts passed from the instructor's brain into a simplified, and hopefully more organized structure. The structures at this phase are blocks of verbal syllables. These syllables are the simplest elements of the message from the higher layers. In order to ensure that the instructor emits sound waves comprehensible to the audience, there is a "think before you speak" process, the human equivalent of error checking. This layer then hands these blocks of syllables, or *frames*, to the physical layer, which translates these messages into sounds that the students can understand. Lastly, sound waves are produced from the instructor and transmitted via air compression waves to the intended audience—the students in the class.

Another characteristic of communication at this layer, called *flow control*, is evidenced when a student has a question during a lecture. The instructor can either stop the lecture and address the question immediately or request that the student hold the question until the instructor is finished—that is, the instructor is managing the flow of the lecture. This function is important because it optimizes communication within the classroom. The instructor might think that the material needs to be presented in its entirety to maximize the level of understanding. On the other hand, the instructor could find that questions from the audience enhance the lecture. The flow of the class all depends on the instructor.

These same attributes are found in the computer world as well. Information from higher-level layers is formatted into frames, just as the instructor's concept from the instructor's mental processes is formatted into syllables the instructor speaks. In addition to formatting, the intended destination (the students) and source identifier (their instructor) are attached. The destination and source information are represented as addresses, formally referred to as *media access control* (MAC) addresses. The Ethernet MAC address is a 48-bit number known as the hardware address, which is mostly unique and that is "burned into" the device. Also included in the frame created by the data-link layer is the *cyclical redundancy checksum* (CRC). The CRC provides a metric allowing the receiving device a way of determining whether the data has been damaged in the transmission process or in transit. This parallels the "think before you speak" process, making sure that the instructor didn't mumble (valid transmission) and loud noises didn't drown out the lecture (not damaged during transit). Note that in our example, the destination address is a *broadcast address*, intended for multiple recipients. In the Ethernet world, this is achieved by using a special MAC—either the all 1s MAC as a general broadcast, or through the use of a specialized MAC and techniques such as group messaging controls to indicate the intended audience.

Damage & Defense...

Hardware Address Spoofing

Hardware MAC addresses are supposed to be unique, and some systems use them as unique security identifiers. The problem is that the transmitted address can be manipulated by software. Sometimes this is a good thing: if a network is designed with a particular fixed MAC address in mind, and a piece of hardware fails, then another device can "take over" that role—this is used for highly available systems or to comply with licensing constraints. It can also be used to indicate particular functions—for example, one popular "sticky honeypot" uses a forged MAC address for its virtual hosts. On the other hand, if a system trusts a MAC address to identify a host, and someone else interferes with that process—either by interrupting the hardware address resolution request or killing the victim host and spoofing its address—unintentional and inappropriate communications may occur.

The physical layer is actually divided into two sublayers: the logical link control (LLC) and the MAC. The LLC is the liaison between the protocols within the network layer and the media access control sublayer. The media access controls access the physical medium. An example of a protocol that works with MAC is the carrier sense multiple access/collision detect (CSMA/CD). This protocol performs a measure of flow control.

NOTE

Watch for unusual changes in the physical port locations of your hardware addresses. If devices "move around" mysteriously or large numbers of devices suddenly appear, you probably have a network problem or a security event.

Layer 3: The Network Layer

The primary function of the *network layer* is to determine the best-known path for information to reach its intended destination. In our classroom example, the information is intended for the local audience. The instructor knows that all the students in the class are there to hear the information in the lecture. The information is formatted, error-checked, and translated into a message via the data-link layer. Subsequently, the frame is transmitted into the physical medium. Because the students are local, no particular treatment is required; they are directly available to hear the message.

What if there is an emergency phone message for the instructor? The person taking the call knows the instructor and the location of the classroom and will deliver the information. The messenger knows the information in the message is important and needs to find the best—in this case, the fastest—way to the classroom. Perhaps the elevator is the fastest, but there are many students in the building, which could cause delay. The stairs seem to be the most reliable and the fastest route. These decisions are similar to the decisions the network layer makes in order to deliver traffic as effectively as possible.

The network layer deals with *packets*, which are eventually encapsulated into frames by the data-link layer. The packets contain information from the layer above the network layer. This is also where the logical IP addresses reside. They are considered logical because, unlike the MAC address that is permanently "burned" into the network interface card (NIC), IP addressing provides a method of grouping devices regardless of their physical location. This is an important aspect of network design.

Layer 4: The Transport Layer

The *transport layer* provides methods of flow control, ordering of received data, and acknowledgement of correctly received data. It relates to our classroom scenario in that it establishes the way that the instructor presents the lecture. For instance, the instructor might look to the audience for an indication of whether or not they understand the lecture. The instructor could invite questions, look for body language indicating agreement, or perhaps even count sleeping students. The instructor attempts to give each student a chance to be involved in the lecture emulating one-on-one attention. On the other hand, it is also possible that the instructor does not desire feedback and will lecture regardless of audience reactions. This type of presentation could be necessary when there is an excessive amount of information and inadequate time to present the material. These two approaches are both appropriate for certain situations and audiences. You will see this type of communication in the computer world as well.

The transport layer can be categorized into *connection-oriented* and *connectionless* protocols. An example of a connection-oriented protocol is TCP. The term *connection-oriented* refers to communications that establish an interaction between the two ends of the connection; they shake hands and agree upon some basic conventions, and then pass along service information about the ongoing communication. It implies a level of reliability and a guarantee of delivery of services, much like the first method of presentation in the classroom. The processes involved in the protocol function to provide a virtual one-on-one appearance. Connectionless protocols, like UDP, do not provide these measures of reliability. In a connectionless communication, information is simply dropped on the wire and a "best effort" delivery is assumed to get the information to its recipient. This method is analogous to the second method in our classroom example, in which the instructor continues to lecture whether the students hear and understand everything or not. Generally speaking, what is lost in reliability is gained in efficiency; connectionless protocols are generally chosen when high throughput is necessary and some information loss is acceptable.

Designing & Planning...

ISN Spoofing

As part of the connection establishment process, a TCP session identifies an initial sequence number (ISN) that is used to provide a marker into how much data has been transmitted and received. Because this is information negotiated as part of the session, some people assume that possession of the ISN means that you are rightfully one of the parties of the communication.

The problem is that ISNs are often predictable. Originally, ISNs were designed to be clock-driven—which provides uniqueness, but also a high degree of predictability. Later implementations simply used the next available number, so systems that were relatively quiet were easily predicted. A malicious user would use this predictability to forge a communication from a trusted host, bypassing local security measures. The most famous of these was Kevin Mitnick, who used this technique to steal research data, documented in Tsutomu Shimomura and John Markoff's book, *Takedown*.

NOTE

Don't assume that because a TCP session has been successfully established, the end IP addresses are valid. Enforce IP address antispoofing techniques whenever possible to prevent rogue packets from coming onto your network.

Layer 5: The Session Layer

The *session layer* establishes the parameters of any upcoming communication. The parameters include the language that will be used and the style of the lecture (whether or not questions are acceptable intermittently or need to be held until the end of the lecture)—those being parameters that need to be predetermined. Another issue to resolve is setting time limits: When the lecture will conclude, for example, which could be at an established time or simply whenever all the topics and questions have been addressed. These parameters are established to set the expectations for everyone involved, a critical aspect of effective communication.

These types of parameters are also established prior to the exchange of data among computer systems. First, protocols need to be agreed on. Some examples of session-layer protocols are Network File System (NFS), Structured Query Language (SQL), and X Windows. Protocols are important because if the devices are not using the same protocols, they are essentially speaking different languages. Next, they decide on the communication flow. There are three types: *single mode*, *half-duplex mode*, and *full-duplex mode*. Single-mode communication occurs when only one device at a time transmits information, and it transmits until all the information has been completely sent. Half-duplex mode occurs when the devices take turns transmitting. This is comparable to a conversation between two people using walkie-talkies in which only one person can talk at any given time. (If both people push the Talk button at the same time, neither person will hear anything.) Full-duplex mode occurs when the devices transmit and receive simultaneously. An example of full-duplex communication is when two people talk on a phone—both parties can talk at the same time.

Once all the preliminary details have been established, data exchange can proceed. After the exchange is complete, the devices systematically disengage the session.

The session layer can be either *connection-oriented* or *connectionless*. A connection-oriented session contains checkpoints or activity management. This system provides a way to efficiently retransmit any data that is lost or is erroneous on receipt. It is efficient because only the data that needs to be transmitted is sent, rather than the entire session. Connectionless sessions, as with IP and UDP, are a best-effort delivery. As with the two other examples, in a connectionless session, the layer above (the presentation layer) is responsible for providing reliability.

Layer 6: The Presentation Layer

The *presentation layer* establishes the way in which information is presented, typically for display or printing. Data encryption and character set conversion (such as ASCII to EBCDIC) are usually associated with this layer. The primary reason for someone to attend a class is that the presentation of information is designed to help that person learn. Students could, theoretically, pick up the literature and learn the material on their own; however, the value comes with the instructor's interpretation of the material. The instructor translates the information in such a way that students understand it. The presentation layer provides this functionality in computer systems.

The presentation layer translates information in a way that the application layer understands. Likewise, this layer translates information from the application layer to the session layer. Some examples of presentation layer protocols are SSL, HTTP/ HTML (agent), FTP (server), AppleTalk Filing Protocol, Telnet, and so on.

Layer 7: The Application Layer

The *application layer* is where user space programs make requests of network services. In our metaphor, this represents the overall point or concept of the instructor's lecture—this is what use the student makes of the lecture. All the layers of communication we have talked about to this point are transparent to the student, for the most part. However, the overall effectiveness of the course could depend on the way the material is communicated and how the class is structured. For instance, if the instructor is difficult to understand, for whatever reason, the content of the material is meaningless to the students. The same is true if the situation were reversed: the instructor could be a sensational communicator, but if the material being covered is inappropriate for the desired goal of the class, the content is worthless.

A good example of an application layer protocol is the HTTP/HTML browser. The end look and feel of a Web page is highly dependent upon the application. Using Microsoft Internet Explorer may cause certain things to break that look normal under Netscape; using lynx provides a text-based view; other browsers are designed for the visually impaired, and read the text out loud or provide displays to Braille screens. The end-user experience is very different in each case—but if we looked at what is happening on the network, it's still the same HTTP GET requests.

Another good example is FTP. At the application layer, an FTP server provides a user interface. You can see the output from an FTP command line client next:

```
ftp> help
Commands may be abbreviated. Commands are:
!              delete         literal        prompt         send
?              debug          ls             put            status
append         dir            mdelete        pwd            trace
ascii          disconnect     mdir           quit           type
bell           get            mget           quote          user
binary         glob           mkdir          recv           verbose
bye            hash           mls            remotehelp
cd             help           mput           rename
close          lcd            open           rmdir
```

Some of these commands are completely local—for example, the command *help* produced the output shown in the code and no network traffic. However, several correspond to a network interface, as specified in various RFCs. These are listed in Table 1.1 that follows.

Table 1.1 FTP Session Layer Commands

Type of Command	Applicable Commands
Access Control Commands	USER, PASS, ACCT, CWD, CDUP, SMNT, REIN, QUIT
Transfer Parameter Commands	PORT, PASV, TYPE, STRU, MODE
FTP Service Commands	RETR, STOR, STOU, APPE, ALLO, REST, RNFR, RNTO, ABOR, DELE, RMD, MKD, PWD, LIST, NLST, SITE, SYST, STAT, HELP, NOOP

Take a look at this output:

```
ftp> ascii
200 Type set to A.
ftp> get icmpmask.c
200 PORT command successful.
150 Opening ASCII mode data connection for icmpmask.c (7565 bytes).
226 Transfer complete.
ftp: 7852 bytes received in 1.09Seconds 7.20Kbytes/sec.
```

It was produced by the following TCP stream:

```
C: TYPE A
S: 200 Type set to A.
C: PORT 165,247,113,42,9,142
S: 200 PORT command successful.
C: RETR icmpmask.c
S: 150 Opening ASCII mode data connection for icmpmask.c (7565 bytes).
S: 226 Transfer complete.
```

Thus FTP is both a Layer 6 (session) and Layer 7 (application) layer protocol.

Some protocols exist only at Layer 7. For example, online gaming, such as Doom, typically only has one standard client, so all requests are handled directly by the application.

How the OSI Model Works

Now that we've looked at the overview of the OSI model with metaphors to make things more natural, let's address some of the specifics of IP communication over Ethernet networks.

Transport Layer Protocols

The transport layer provides duplex, end-to-end data transport services between applications. Data sent from the application layer is divided into segments appropriate in size for the network technology being used. TCP and UDP are the protocols used at this layer.

TCP

TCP provides reliable service by being connection-oriented and including error detection and correction. The connected nature of TCP is used only for two end points to communicate with each other. The connection must be established before a data transfer can occur, and transfers are acknowledged throughout the process. Acknowledgements assure that data is being received properly. The acknowledgement process provides robustness in the face of network congestion or communication unreliability. TCP also determines when the transfer ends and closes the connection, thus freeing up resources on the systems. Checksums assure that the data has not been accidentally modified during transit. Figure 1.5, taken from RFC 793, shows the format of the TCP header.

Figure 1.5 The TCP Header

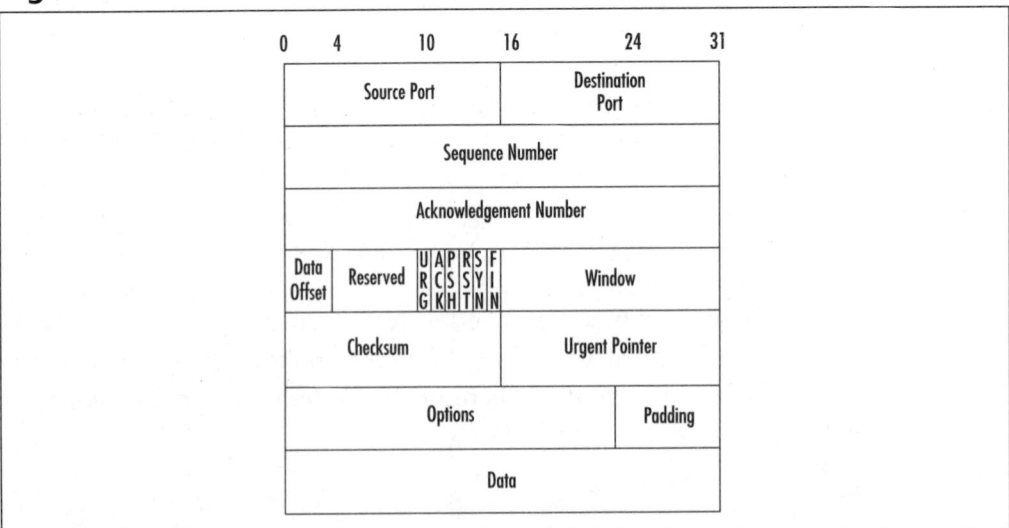

TCP ports are used to multiplex this protocol layer to the layer above with multiple applications on the same host. A source port and a destination port are associated with the sending and receiving applications, respectively. The ports from 0 to 1023 are Well Known Ports, and are assigned by Internet Assigned Numbers Authority (IANA). Ports from 1024 to 49151 are Registered Ports, while ports from 49152 through 65535 are Dynamic/Private Ports. The Well Known and Registered Port numbers are available at www.isi.edu/in-notes/iana/assignments/port-numbers.

Bits 10 through 15 at word offset 3 correspond to the TCP control bits, or flags. They provide information about the importance of the Sequence Number, Acknowledgement Number, and Urgent Pointer fields. They also provide information about how the packet should be treated by the receiving host. These are reflected in Table 1.2.

Table 1.2 TCP Control Bits

Control Bit	Description
URG	Urgent control bit indicates that Urgent Pointer is a valid offset to add to the Sequence Number. The sender of data can indicate to the receiver that there is urgent data pending.
ACK	Acknowledgement control bit indicates that the Acknowledgement Number contains the value of the next sequence number the sender of the segment is expecting to receive. ACK is always set for an established connection.
PSH	Push all data received to this point up to the receiving application. This function expedites the delivery of urgent data to the destination.
RST	Reset the connection. This function flushes all queued segments waiting for transmission or retransmission, and puts the receiver in listen mode.
SYN	Synchronize sequence numbers. The SYN control bit indicates that the Sequence Number contains the initial sequence number.
FIN	Sender has finished sending data. The FIN control bit is set by the application closing its connection.

The sequence numbers allow recovery by TCP from data that was lost, damaged, duplicated, or delivered out of order. Each host in the TCP connection selects an Initial Sequence Number (ISN), and these are synchronized during the establishment of the connection. The sequence number is incremented for each byte of data transmitted across the TCP connection, including the SYN and FIN flags. Sequence numbers are 32 bits and will wrap around to zero when they overflow. The ISN should be unpredictable for a given TCP connection. Some TCP implementations have exhibited vulnerabilities of predictable sequence numbers. Predicting the sequence number can allow an attacker to impersonate a host.

The acknowledgement number has a valid entry when the ACK flag is on. It contains the next sequence number that the receiver is expecting. Since every data segment sent over a TCP connection has a sequence number, it also has an acknowledgement number.

The ACK and RST play a role in determining whether a connection is established or being established. Cisco uses the established keyword in Access Control Lists (ACLs) to check whether the ACK or RST flags are set. If either flag is set, the packet meets the test as established. If neither the ACK nor the RST flags are set, then this packet is not part of an existing connection, but an attempt to establish a new connection to the device at the destination TCP address.

Damage & Defense...

Penetrating "Established" ACLs

One problem with using simple ACLs for a network firewall is that inbound at your perimeter router you have to allow "established" packets, as noted above. Unfortunately, this means a crafted packet that has an ACK bit set will pass through to an end host. This allows various sorts of network mapping to occur, and is a demonstration of why keeping state, either through stateful packet filters or application gateways, is needed to fully conceal protected networks.

HTTP, SMTP, FTP, Telnet, and rlogin are examples of applications that use TCP for transport. Applications that need reliability support from the transport layer use Remote Procedure Calls (RPC) over TCP. Applications that do not depend on the transport layer for reliability use RPC over UDP.

TCP Connections

Figure 1.6 shows the establishment of a TCP/IP connection. Establishing a TCP connection requires three segments, known as the "three-way handshake."

1. To initiate the connection, the source host sends a SYN segment (SYN flag is set), and an ISN in the sequence number field to the destination port and host address.

2. The destination host responds with a segment containing its initial sequence number, and both the SYN and ACK flags set. The acknowledgement number will be the source's sequence number, incremented by one.

3. The source host acknowledges the SYN from the destination host by replying with an ACK segment and an acknowledgement number that is the destination's sequence number incremented by one.

Figure 1.6 Establishing a TCP Connection

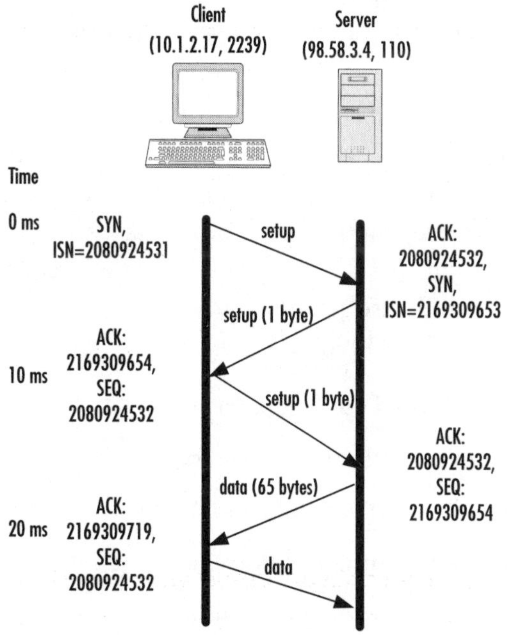

This sequence—SYN, SYN-ACK, ACK—characterizes the handshake.

This diagram represents the first few packets in a TCP session. The packets marked "setup" represent the establishment of the TCP session. The packets marked "data" represent the first few packets in the data stream. In this case, the session represents a typical Windows POP3 session between a host on a private network and a server on the Internet. The host establishes a local socket using its IP address (here, 10.1.2.17) and an ephemeral port, chosen for this session (here, 2239). The server, at IP address 98.58.3.4, is listening on port 110.

The client generates a packet with source IP 10.1.2.17, source port 2239, and destination address 98.58.3.4, destination port 110. The sequence number field is filled with an Initial Sequence Number chosen randomly—for this example, the ISN is 2080924531. Note that the ISNs are 32-bit unsigned integers, between zero and about four billion, and so, in general, are quite large. The acknowledgement number field is not used in the initial packet; by convention it is set to zero. The data offset field is set to a value that describes where in the TCP packet the data begins; in the sample diagram describing packets above, the offset would be 6 (since there is one 32-bit word consisting of options plus padding); other implementations will vary. The reserved field must be set to zero. With regards to the control fields, the SYN bit (offset 4, bit 14) is set to one; all other bits are set to zero. The window size is set to a value suitable for the client; 16K is typical. The checksum is computed based upon the TCP packet plus the source and destination address, the protocol, and the TCP length. Since the Urgent control bit is not set, the urgent pointer field is conventionally set to zero. The options field is set to implementation-specific values; communicating the maximum segment size is common. In this case, there will be no data (other than the fact of the SYN request) so the data field will be empty, and our packet is ready for transmission!

When the client receives the packet, it will make note of the request for communication. It will store in its TCP acceptance queue a request with sequence number 2080924531. It will also generate an ISN for its data; in this case, the randomly chosen number is 2169309653. Filling in the fields one at a time:

- Source port: 110 (its POP3 server)
- Destination port: 2239 (client request)
- Sequence number: 2169309653 (its ISN)
- Acknowledgement number: 2080924532 (client's ISN + 1)
- Data offset: 5 (depends on TCP implementation)
- Reserved: 0 (always)
- Control Bits: SYN, ACK (acknowledging the client data, requesting client synchronize)
- Window size: 17520 (depends upon server implementation)
- Checksum (computed based upon packet values)
- Urgent pointer: 0 (urgent control bit not set)
- Options, padding: Depends upon TCP implementation
- Data: Empty (no data yet)

When the client receives the SYN-ACK, the client needs to acknowledge the server request. Back comes a packet with only the ACK bit set, with sequence number set to its ISN + 1, and acknowledging client's ISN + 1.

Once a TCP connection between the two systems exists, data can be transferred. As data is sent, the sequence number is incremented to track the number of bytes. In the previous example, the first packet after establishment sends 65 bytes of data. Acknowledgement segments from the destination host increment the acknowledgement number as bytes of data are received; in this case, the client ACKs reception through 2169309719 = 2169309654 + 65 bytes.

The states that TCP goes through in establishing its connection allows firewalls to easily recognize new connections versus existing connections. Access lists on routers also use these flags in the TCP header to determine whether the connection is established.

A socket is the combination of IP address and TCP port. A local and remote socket pair (quadruplet) determines a connection between two hosts uniquely:

- The source IP address
- The source TCP port
- The destination IP address
- The destination TCP port

Firewalls can use this quadruplet to track the many connections on which they are making forwarding decisions at a very granular level. During the establishment of the connection, the firewall will learn the dynamic port assigned to the client for a particular connection. For the period of time that the connection exists, the dynamic port is allowed through the firewall. Once the connection is finished, the client port will be closed. By tracking the state of a particular connection in this way, security policy rules don't need to compensate for dynamic port assignments.

UDP

UDP is a simple, unreliable transport service. It is connectionless, so delivery is not assured. Look at the simple design of the UDP header in Figure 1.7, and you will understand the efficiency of this protocol. Since connections aren't set up and torn down, there is very little overhead. Lost, damaged, or out of order segments will not be retransmitted unless the application layer requests it. UDP is used for fast, simple messages sent from one host to another. Due to its simplicity, UDP packets are more easily spoofed than TCP packets. If reliable or ordered delivery of data is needed, applications should use TCP.

Figure 1.7 The UDP Header

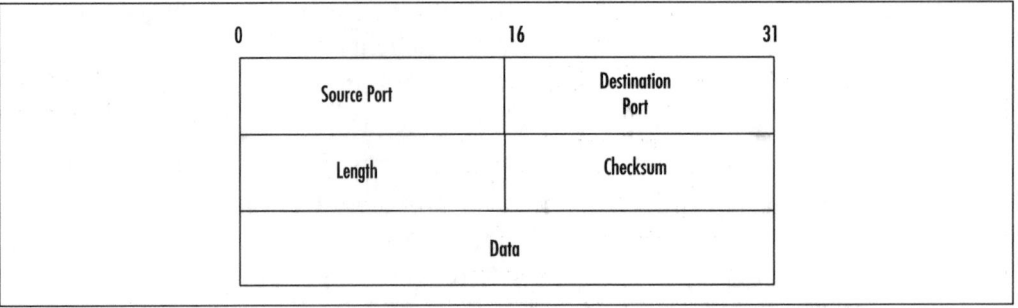

Simple Network Management Protocol (SNMP), Trivial File Transfer Protocol (TFTP), BOOTstrap Protocol (BOOTP), Network File System (NFS), and Dynamic Host Control Protocol (DHCP) are examples of applications that use UDP for transport. UDP is also used for multimedia applications. Unlike the connection-oriented TCP which can only connect between two hosts, UDP can broadcast or multicast to many systems at once. The small overhead of UDP eases the network load when running time-sensitive data such as audio or video.

The Internet Layer

The Internet layer is responsible for addressing, routing, error notification, and hop-by-hop fragmentation and reassembly. It manages the delivery of information from host to host. Fragmentation could occur at this layer because different network technologies have a different Maximum Transmission Unit (MTU). IP, ICMP, and ARP are protocols used at this layer.

IP

IP is an unreliable, routable packet delivery protocol. All upper layer protocols use IP to send and receive packets, which receives segments from the transport layer, fragments them into packets, and passes them to the network layer.

The IP address is a logical address assigned to each node on a TCP/IP network. IP addressing is designed to allow routing of packets across internetworks. Since IP addresses are easy to change or spoof, they should not be relied upon to provide identification in untrusted environments. As shown in Figure 1.8, the source and destination addresses are included in the IP header.

Figure 1.8 The IP Header

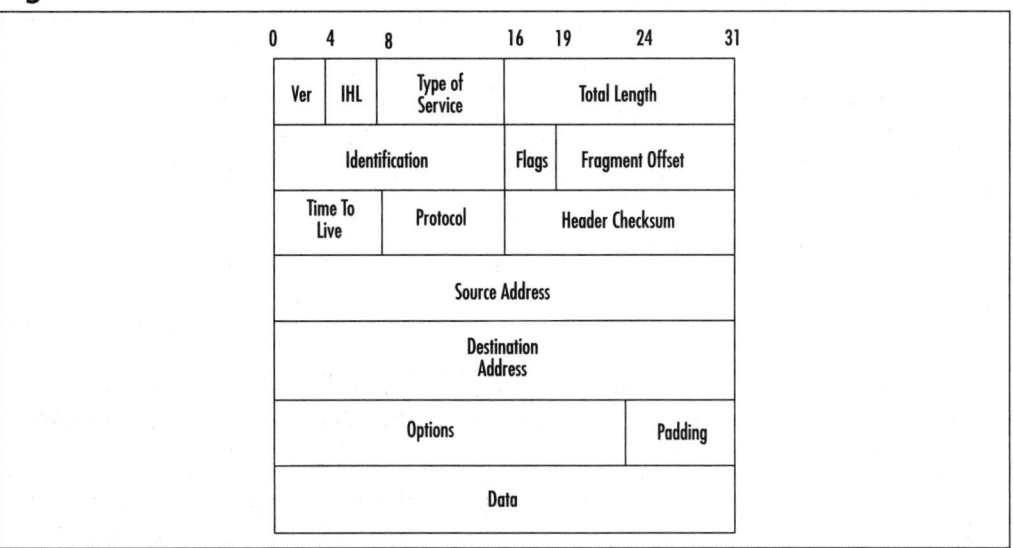

Let's take a look at each of these fields in Figure 1.8:

- *Ver* documents the IP version number. This template is for IP version 4, commonly deployed across the Internet.

- *IHL* is the Internet Header Length, in 32-bit words, and points to the beginning of the data segment. Note that the minimum valid IHL is 5, when there are no options.

- The *Type of Service* provides a suggestion for the desired quality of service. Across the Internet, no particular type of service can be guaranteed; generally, this field is set to zero.

- The *Total Length* specifies the length of the datagram. Based upon size, the largest datagram is 65535 bytes; this does (rarely) occur across some cores. Typically, the largest size one sees is 1500.

- The *Identification* field provides a unique identifier prepared by the sender to help in the reassembly of packets.

- There are three *Flags*. The first bit is reserved, and always set to zero. The second bit is the "Don't Fragment" bit, set if routers are not permitted to fragment the packet as it is passed along. The third bit is the "More Fragments" bit, set if additional fragments of this packet exist, or unset if this is the last fragment in the packet.

- The *Fragment Offset* field suggests where this packet exists in the datastream, measured in units of eight octets. The first fragment has offset zero.

- The *Time To Live* field indicates the maximum number of router hops the packet will survive before being discarded. The host generating the packet will set the value to some number—Windows often uses 128, some Unixes use 64—and as the packet is routed, the number is decremented.

- The *protocol* parameter indicates the upper level protocol that is using IP. The decimal value for TCP is 6 and UDP is 17. The list of assigned numbers for this field is available at www.isi.edu/in-notes/iana/assignments/protocol-numbers.

- The *checksum* is computed only on the header, so it does not check the integrity of the data payload.

- The *source address* and *destination address* fields are filled with the IP address of the respective devices; note an IP address is four octets, so this can be viewed as a 32-bit number.

- The *options* field resembles the TCP options field, and similarly allows for zero byte padding to bring options plus *padding* to a multiple of 32 bits.

Damage & Defense...

Penetrating with Sharp Fragments

Because not all links allow transmission of the same size of fragments, occasionally routers have to fragment datagrams (segment the data portion and place them into multiple packets) and end hosts have to reassemble the fragments into the original datagram. Packet reassembly can be a time-consuming task for detective systems, and so malicious users often artificially fragment their packets before delivery to evade firewalls and intrusion detection systems. One trick involved negative packet fragments, to create a packet with rewritten source and destination addresses!

Ensure that your defenses include packet reassembly before passing uncontrolled traffic onto your unsuspecting hosts.

ICMP

ICMP provides diagnostic functions and error reporting for IP. ICMP is protocol type 1. For example, ICMP can provide feedback to a sending host when a destination is unreachable or time is exceeded (TTL=0). A ping is an ICMP echo request message, and the response is an ICMP echo reply.

ARP

ARP is responsible for resolving the logical IP address into the hardware address for the network layer. (Note that an ARP packet is not an IP packet, and works below that layer.) If the destination IP address is on the same subnet as the source host, then IP will use ARP to determine the hardware address of the destination host. If the destination IP address is on a remote subnet, then ARP will be used to determine the hardware address of the default gateway. The ARP cache, a table of translations between IP address and hardware, stores its entries dynamically and flushes them after a short period of time.

SECURITY ALERT!

Some attacks have been based upon gratuitous or forged ARP replies and redirecting IP traffic to a system that sniffs for cleartext passwords or other information. One such attack tool is available at www.monkey.org/~dugsong/dsniff/. This attack disables the benefit of a switched Ethernet environment because ARP requests are broadcast to all local network ports. The spoofing machine can respond with its hardware address and become a man-in-the-middle. Research is being conducted on a new ARP protocol that would be resistant to these types of attacks. However, it is best to assume that switches do not provide access control, and avoid the use of cleartext passwords or other sensitive information.

The Network Layer

The network layer includes the network interface card and device driver. These provide the physical interface to the media of the network. The network layer controls the network hardware, encapsulates and transmits outgoing packets, and accepts and demultiplexes incoming packets. It accepts IP packets from the Internet layer above.

Composition of a Data Packet

In the IP world, the term *data packet* is generic. To be more formal, we often talk about a *protocol data unit* (PDU) that is wrapped into a frame—a representation of the data defined by physical characteristics. Collections of frames are integrated (or sometimes split) with the extraneous framing information removed into datagrams. Using the lecture metaphor again, the underlying thoughts are the PDUs, the physical manifestation of syllables the frames, and the words (an assembled collection of syllables) are the datagram.

Before considering the security of the packet, first we will look at the physical issues of the frame.

Ethernet

Ethernet refers broadly to a wide variety of data link implementations. Originally, this referred to the Dec, Intel, and Xerox implementation of Version 1 or Version 2 Ethernet. When IEEE developed the 802.3 standard, the term was applied to it as well, and characterizes Carrier Sense Multiple Access, Collision Detect (CSMA/CS) technology. Today, this protocol is used as a general reference to several different types of data link protocols, including the 802.3u or *Fast Ethernet* and the 802.3x or *Full Duplex*. It has evolved from transmission rates of 1/10/100 Mbps to 1 Gbps. Ethernet is even used as a model for 802.11, Carrier Sense Multiple Access, Collision Avoidance (CSMA/CA) within wireless networks.

Looking at the structure of an Ethernet frame is important to better understand the functions this layer provides. There are four common types of Ethernet frames found in networks today: Version II, 802.3 SNAP, 802.3 raw, and 802.3 LLC. Figure 1.9 examines the "Original Style," described on Cisco equipment as Ethernet frame type ARPA, which is probably the most common—it is the default in "pure-play IP" Windows NT and 2000 installations.

The Preamble consists of 62 bits of alternating 1s and 0s that allow the NIC to synchronize with the beginning of the frame. The Start Frame Delimiter is the bit pattern 10101011, and indicates the start of the frame. The Ethertype distinguishes between various types of frames, and its values can be found in RFC 1340. For example, IP packets have Ethertype 08 00 while ARP packets have Ethertype 08 03. The Frame Check Sequence (FCS) is a checksum computed by a Cyclic Redundancy Check polynomial (CRC) based upon the address fields, Ethertype, and data, and is designed to detect errors in transmission.

One interesting observation about the structure of Ethernet packets is that the destination MAC comes first in the frame, unlike in IP packet headers. The reason for this engineering is to allow bridges and switches earliest access to the destination so they can copy the packet to the correct port as quickly as possible.

Figure 1.9 An Ethernet Frame: Original Style (Digital, Intel, Xerox)

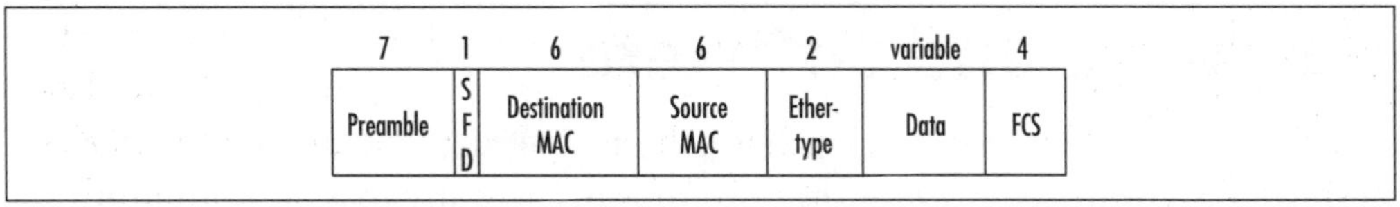

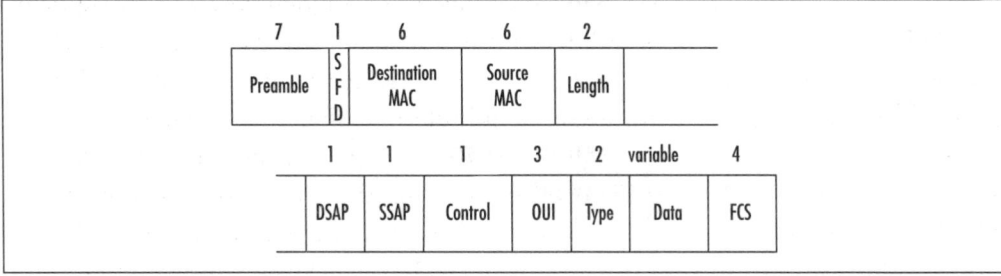

Figure 1.10 examines an 802.3 SNAP Ethernet frame, described on Cisco equipment as Ethernet frame type SNAP. This is an extension of the earlier LLC format, which had only a limited number of Ethertypes.

Figure 1.10 An Ethernet Frame: IEEE-Style SNAP

The new fields here are the Destination and Source Service Access Points, which describe the upper protocol type for the frame; the Control field, generally unused but designed for administrative purposes; the Organizationally Unique Identifier (OUI), to distinguish protocols from different vendors—the OUI is the same value used in the MAC addresses—and finally a two-byte Type identifier to specify the actual protocol, and maintain compatibility with the earlier Ethernet II frame type.

Security in TCP/IP

The Internet provides no guarantee of privacy or integrity for data. Because of this, cryptography should be considered for private, valuable, or vulnerable data. This way, data is encrypted as it is transmitted, and decrypted as it is received. In fact, most layers in the ISO model can be used to provide data integrity and confidentiality. The application of security to each layer has its own particular advantages and disadvantages. The characteristics of security applied at a particular layer provide features that can be used as a decision point in determining the applicability of each technique to solve a particular problem.

Cisco IP Security Hardware and Software

Firewalls are typically placed at borders of security groups to create a security perimeter. Most frequently, they are used to protect an internal network from external access. Firewalls may also be used internally to control network access to specific departments or resources. The Cisco Secure PIX Firewall series of products are dedicated firewall appliances. All models offer VPN, IPSec, and firewall capabilities. The three models, 506, 515, and 520, provide performance levels ranging from small offices up to large enterprises and Internet service providers (ISP). Choose the appropriate model based on the throughput and number of interfaces needed for your application.

Information flow control policies can be enforced consistently across large enterprises and ISPs with the Cisco Secure Policy Manager (CSPM). It can centrally manage up to 500 Cisco Secure PIX firewalls. Organizations providing managed network security to many customers will also appreciate this centralized management feature.

The Cisco Secure PIX Firewall

The Cisco Secure PIX Firewall 506 has two integrated 10BaseT ports. The 515-R is limited to two 10/100 Ethernet interfaces. The 515-UR and the 520 provide up to six 10/100 Ethernet interfaces, while the 520 also gives the option of up to four 4/16 Mbps token ring or two dual-attached, multimode FDDI interfaces.

Common features shared by all models are as follows:

- **Embedded, Real-Time Operating System** The proprietary operating system was developed specifically for the PIX firewall. It provides high performance, and is generally immune to Unix security breaches. The code is a trade secret held by Cisco.

- **Stateful Inspection** Cisco calls it Adaptive Security Algorithm (ASA). ASA tracks the state of connections based upon source address, destination address, sequence numbers, ports numbers, and TCP flags. Forwarding decisions are based on applying the configured security policy to these parameters.

- **VPN Tunnels Using DES or 3DES** This feature provides confidentiality across untrusted networks. The addition of the PIX Private Link encryption card allows the PIX to create and/or terminate VPN tunnels between two PIX firewalls, between a PIX and any Cisco VPN enabled router, and between a PIX and the Cisco Secure VPN Client. The 506 supports up to four VPN peers. The 515 and 520, meanwhile, support up to 256 peers.

- **Java Applet Filter** Java applets can be blocked when delivered in HTTP content. More sophisticated filtering requires a third-party product.

NOTE

There are three basic types of firewalls available today, Packet Filters, Application Gateways, and Hybrids.

- **Packet Filters (PF)** look at various pieces of information and decide whether or not to forward the packet. A PF can be stateless or stateful. In a stateless environment, the PF looks at the protocol, address, or port information and other pieces of information in each packet and makes a forwarding decision for that packet based on static rules. Access Control Lists (ACLs) on routers are an example of stateless packet filters. Access control lists are useful for blocking source or destination addresses, solving the problems of spoofed source addresses, and can restrict the services accessible.

- **Stateful Inspection (SPF)** analyzes all the communication layers, extracts the relevant communication and application state information, and dynamically maintains the state of communications in tables. Forwarding decisions are based upon the configured security policy. Stateful inspection offers flexibility and increased applicability to enforcement of information flow control rules.

- **Application Gateways (AG)** use a specific application for each service that will be forwarded through the firewall. The AG takes requests on one interface, and terminates the service request; it then forwards a request, as appropriate, on to the device on another network. In particular, with a Web server protected by an AG, the Web server sees the IP stack of the AG, not the end client; this means that low-level packet attacks that might pass through a packet filtering firewall will be stopped by the AG. All other things being equal, an AG offers the best security, but you must have an application for each service that will be processed by the firewall.

Most modern firewalls are a hybrid of the three types. For example, the PIX uses primarily packet filtering for reasons of performance. However, some applications (the "fixup commands") invoke application gateways to sanitize particular services. This provides heightened capabilities, such as the Java content blocking ability mentioned earlier.

The 515 and 520 models offer additional features of interest to larger organizations:

- **Network Address Translation (NAT)** NAT conserves the IP address space by translating up to 64,000 internal hosts to a single external IP address. The PIX firewall uses port address translation (PAT) to multiplex each internal host with a different port number. PAT does not work with H.323 applications, multimedia applications, or caching nameservers.

- **Failover/Hot Standby Option** This feature improves availability of the network. It is not available on the 515-R. Cisco has created a Fail-Over Bundle (515-UR only) to add software and a second chassis to create a redundant firewall configuration.

- **Cut-through User Authentication** A cut-through proxy is used to authenticate users with a TACACS+ or RADIUS server. This feature improves performance for authentication, authorization, and accounting. When the username and password are correct, the PIX firewall lets further traffic between the specified authentication server and the connection interact directly.

- **URL Filtering** A NetPartners WebSENSE server is needed to utilize this feature. The PIX firewall permits or denies connections based on the outbound URL requests and the policy on the WebSENSE server.

Table 1.3 compares the performance of the PIX firewalls offered by Cisco.

Table 1.3 Cisco Secure PIX Firewall Performance Comparison

Model	Throughput	Simultaneous Sessions
506	10 Mbps	N/A
515-R	120 Mbps	50,000
515-UR	120 Mbps	125,000
520	370 Mbps	250,000

You will find configuration details on Cisco Secure PIX firewalls in Chapter 3. Additional information on related topics is found in Chapter 8, 9, and 5.

Cisco Secure Integrated Software

Cisco Secure Integrated Software (formerly called Cisco IOS Firewall Feature Set) is a bundle of security features that integrate with Cisco IOS software. It can add firewall, intrusion detection, Data Encryption Standard (DES) (56-bit) encryption, and secure administration capabilities to most of the following routers:

- 800
- UBR900 series
- 1600
- 1720
- 2500
- 2600
- 3600
- 7100
- 7200
- 7500
- RSM (Route Switch Module)

The 800, UBR904, 1600, and 2500 do not support authentication proxy or intrusion detection.

The authentication proxy can use TACACS+ or RADIUS protocols, which can be applied per-user on LAN or dial-up communication links.

The Cisco Secure Intrusion Detection System described next is a separate appliance and merely watches the network traffic. The Cisco Secure Integrated

Software is an integral part of Cisco IOS. This difference can affect performance because the Cisco Secure Integrated Software lies in the critical packet path.

Cisco Secure Integrated VPN Software

Cisco Secure Integrated VPN Software adds 3 DES (168-bit) encryption, and authentication through digital certificates, one-time password tokens, and pre-shared keys to the Cisco Secure Integrated Software features described earlier. The package is available for the following routers:

- 1720
- 2600
- 3600
- 7100

VPNs can be established over remote access, intranet, or extranets.

The Cisco Secure VPN Client

The Cisco Secure VPN Client enables secure connectivity for remote access VPNs. It can be used for applications such as e-commerce, mobile user, and telecommuting. It provides Microsoft Windows 95/98/2000 and NT users with a complete implementation of IPSec, including support for DES (56-bit) and 3DES (168-bit) encryption, and authentication through digital certificates, one-time password tokens, and preshared keys.

The security policy for end-users can be centrally managed, and protected as read-only for the client. This feature prevents users from bypassing the policy that has been put in place and ensures that policy is applied consistently among users.

More details about VPNs can be found in Chapter 8.

Cisco Secure Access Control Server

The Cisco Secure Access Control Server (ACS) provides authentication, authorization, and accounting (AAA) for users accessing network services. Cisco Secure ACS supports TACACS+ and RADIUS protocols, and the Windows NT version can also do pass-through authentication to the NT user accounts. The ACS can be used as a centralized server or a distributed system comprised of multiple ACS systems. It can also interface to other third-party RADIUS or TACACS+ systems in a distributed configuration. In a distributed environment, the ACS can act as a proxy and automatically forward an authentication request to another AAA server.

The accounting function can record each user session that was authenticated by the server. The accounting information can be used by ISPs to provide billing or usage reports for customers. It can also serve as data for security or forensic analysis.

More details about AAA can be found in Chapter 9.

Cisco Secure Scanner

Cisco Secure Scanner (formerly called NetSonar) is a vulnerability assessment tool for network hosts. This scanner software package is available to run on Windows NT, Solaris, and Solaris x86. It will map all devices connected to the scanned network. Vulnerability assessment can be performed on:

- Unix hosts
- Windows NT hosts
- Network TCP/IP hosts
- Mail servers
- Web servers
- FTP servers
- Routers
- Firewalls
- Switches

The scanner comes with a database of known security vulnerabilities. The database contains information about repairing any of the vulnerabilities it finds, and is updated periodically as new vulnerabilities are discovered. You can also create customized scanning rules tailored to your environment or security policies.

More details about Cisco Secure Scanner can be found in Chapter 11.

Cisco Secure Intrusion Detection System

An intrusion detection system (IDS) can help make you aware of the nature and frequency of attacks against your network and systems. From the information provided by the IDS, you can design an appropriate response to reduce the risks to your systems from these attacks.

Cisco Secure Intrusion Detection System (formerly called NetRanger) is a real-time, network intrusion detection system (NIDS) consisting of sensors and one or more managers. A system can be implemented with a single sensor at a strategic location, or multiple sensors placed at many well-chosen locations in the network. Sensors operate in promiscuous mode and passively analyze the network traffic that appears on its interface for unauthorized activity. The IDS sensor will report traffic matching attack signatures to the director. The sensor can also be configured to actively change ACLs on Cisco routers in response to attack signatures, a process called "shunning." The sensor is a hardware and software appliance that is available for five network technologies:

- Ethernet
- Fast Ethernet
- Token Ring
- Single attached FDDI
- Dual attached FDDI

The Cisco Secure Policy Manager (CSPM) is the management station. It receives the alerts from sensors locally or remotely located. You can have one central director—which can be configured to send alarms to a pager or e-mail address—or you can have multiple directors receiving alerts from any of your network sensors.

A recent addition to the IDS product line is the host-based IDS (HIDS), an OEM of Entercept technologies. The host-based approach allows for detection of malicious activity at the target itself—and the HIDS can be configured to prevent malicious activity. These sensors are also controlled by a centralized console mechanism.

More details about intrusion detection can be found in Chapter 13.

Cisco Secure Policy Manager

The Cisco Secure Policy Manager (formerly called Cisco Security Manager) is a comprehensive security management system for Cisco Secure products. You can define, distribute, enforce, and audit security policies for multiple security devices from a central location. Cisco Secure Policy Manager supports IPSec VPN, user authentication, and in a future version will support intrusion detection and vulnerability scanning technologies. Its use on routers requires that Cisco Secure Integrated Software be installed.

Policy Manager centralizes the management of security policies, the monitoring of status, and reporting of policy events. It can help to ensure a consistent application of policies across hundreds of devices, and will save you time by automating portions of the policy creation and distribution.

More details about Cisco Secure Policy Manager can be found in Chapter 12.

Cisco Secure Consulting Services

Cisco Secure Consulting Services are targeted to large corporate and government customers, and though consulting services are beyond the scope of this book, they do round out the Cisco Secure product line for those of you who need expert assistance. It offers two types of professional services:

- **Security Posture Assessments** This service provides comprehensive security analysis of large, complex networks. Cisco will test your network security from the perspective of external attackers, disgruntled employees, or contractors. They will then make recommendations on needed security measures to improve your network security.

- **Incident Control and Recovery** This service is an emergency response to a hostile network incident. Cisco can provide short-notice assistance to restore control and availability of your network.

Summary

Security plays a key role in a network. The fundamental goals of network security usually boil down to three issues, coded by CIA: Confidentiality, Integrity, and Availability of data and services. Confidentiality is usually achieved through access control and encryption. Integrity, meanwhile, is attained by cryptographic means and careful use of audit trails. Lastly, availability is accomplished by using high-quality Cisco equipment configured to carefully provide redundancy, as well as designing services that can survive or rapidly recover from attack.

Security is one of three common perspectives in designing networks. These perspectives are: the user perspective, where the goal is to get a fast, cheap solution; the ops management perspective, where the goal is to get a complete and reliable solution; and the security perspective, where the goal is to get a controlled, authorized solution. All perspectives are valid, and a good network architect will balance all three.

An excellent source of security design is the Cisco SAFE program, available at www.cisco.com/warp/public/779/largeent/issues/security/safebprint.html.

You don't *have* to deploy security. However, this means your site is assuming some significant risks—corporate losses per company per year averaged over two million dollars, according to CSI/FBI statistics. Simple programs can eliminate the most expensive risks, but remember, every enterprise is a target.

One of the most effective ways of thinking about network security is the DoD model. This breaks the net into four layers: Network Access, Internetwork, Host-to-host Transport, and Process Application. Security techniques can be applied at each of these layers to improve the security posture of your network.

At the Network Access Layer, you can control accesses to shared media, and provide link encryptors where appropriate. It's best to partition where possible, virtually using VLAN or MPLS technologies.

At the Internetwork Layer, controls can be enforced over the packets routed between layers. The old adage "be conservative in what you do, be liberal in what you accept from others" needs to be updated: Be cautious in what you accept from others, and if it doesn't make sense, log it and drop it.

At the Host-to-host Layer, transport protocols such as IPSec are widely used and quite effective. IPSec is a flexible protocol that is part of a best practices mechanism for transport across uncontrolled networks. It has two modes: transport mode, useful when both endpoints of the IPSec tunnel are capable of using the data, and tunnel mode, useful as a passive encapsulated, encrypted path across the uncontrolled network.

At the process application layer, the key message is that it is an arms race, and constant vigilance is required. Last year, an average of six vulnerabilities a day were reported. To keep on top of the situation, information owners must consistently update their software with vendor patches, and information security officers should apply vulnerability scanners on a regular basis to identify problems before they are exploited.

Some approaches to providing application security include Pretty Good Privacy (PGP), a standalone encryption package that can be integrated into mail transport and file storage. Secure Sockets Layer (SSL) can provide on-the-fly transport encryption to an application. Secure Shell (SSH), meanwhile, can provide confidentiality and session integrity for a command channel.

Some controls can be applied through all layers. Authentication protocols, for instance, can help with identity management using common authentication protocols such as TACACS+, RADIUS, and Kerberos. TACACS+ is a proprietary protocol that is especially useful in controlling access to Cisco infrastructure equipment. RADIUS is effective in a heterogeneous environment, as it is widely supported. Kerberos, on the other hand, is a sophisticated and trusted third-party solution that does not require passwords be sent in the clear, and has vendor neutral support.

While the DoD model is perhaps best for thinking about security issues, the OSI model is more commonly adopted by internetworkers, and is useful for discussing what occurs with security equipment. The seven layers are: Physical Layer, Data-link Layer, Network Layer, Transport Layer, Session Layer, Presentation Layer, Application Layer. The following is a brief description of each: Physical Layer—handles physical characteristics of signal transport; Data-link Layer—handles encoding and decoding of data from bits into transmitted frames, and address access to the physical layer; Network Layer—handles transport of datagrams across local networks to remote networks; Transport Layer—addresses flow control, ordering of received data, and acknowledgement of data; Session Layer—establishes the parameters of any upcoming communication; Presentation Layer—establishes the way information is presented, typically for display or printing; Application Layer—where user space programs make requests of network services.

Some specific aspects of the OSI model that are important: key layer 4 protocols are TCP and UDP.

TCP provides a reliable, connection-oriented service with data sequencing, congestion control, error detection, and retransmission. TCP communicates on "ports," distinguished by a number between 0 and 65535. It achieves sequencing, congestion control, error detection, and retransmission by sequence numbers and corresponding acknowledgements. Individual flags provide additional information to the receiving host about the nature of the packet. TCP sessions are initialized through three packets, SYN, SYN-ACK, and ACK—known as the "three-way handshake." A TCP session is uniquely identified by the local and remote socket pair.

UDP provides a connectionless but low overhead transport protocol. Some typical applications are SNMP, TFTP, DHCP, and many multimedia applications.

A key Layer 3 protocol is the IP protocol. TCP and UDP packets are encapsulated in IP packets. Other examples of IP packet types are ICMP and ARP.

Firewalls are typically placed at borders of security groups to create a security perimeter, and to offer firewall services such as VPN termination. Information flow control policies can be enforced consistently across large enterprises with a centralized security management platform such as the Cisco Secure Policy Manager. The Cisco Secure Integrated Software (formerly Cisco IOS Firewall Feature Set) allows integration of security controls across the enterprise by building it into the infrastructure. Several models also incorporate native VPNs, which interoperate with the Cisco Secure VPN client. The Cisco Secure ACS allows for centralized authentication of these structures.

Other tools, such as the Cisco Secure Scanner and Cisco Secure IDS, allow for detective analysis of an enterprise environment. Both the Cisco Secure IDS and HIDS allow for detective and preventative controls, unlike most IDSs on the market.

Solutions Fast Track

What Role Does Security Play in a Network?

- ☑ The fundamental goals for a security information processing network generally boil down to the acronym CIA: Confidentiality, Integrity, and Availability.

- ☑ Networks are typically designed from a user perspective—get it out fast and cheap—or from an operations management perspective—get it out reliably, and recover from faults gracefully. Add to this a third perspective: the security perspective—get it out in a controlled fashion, and fail safely.

- ☑ You don't have to deploy security. You can assume the risks yourself, just remember that they are high—average annual costs are around two million dollars per company for security breaches, and in some instances, said security events have destroyed the company.

The Fundamentals of Networking

☑ The DoD network model was the source for the design of the Internet.

☑ It is based upon four layers: the Network Access Layer, Internetwork Layer, Host-to-host Layer, and Process Application Layer.

☑ Security controls typically are applied within a layer.

Where Does Security Fit in?

☑ Applying security at multiple layers—defense in depth—means that a failure in one control doesn't invalidate your security policy. Look back to Figure 1.4 to see the various places security controls can be deployed.

☑ Unlike most security controls that are specific to a single layer, authentication applies at all layers.

☑ While most security types are like the DoD model, most networking types resemble the OSI model. It is based upon seven layers: Physical and Data-Link, corresponding to the Network Access Layer; Network corresponding to the Internetwork Layer; Transport, Session, and Presentation corresponding to the Host-to-Host Layer; and Application corresponding to the Process Application Layer.

☑ Application designers don't want to reinvent the wheel, so instead they generally depend upon two well-defined Transport Layer protocols: TCP and UDP. TCP is used for reliable, connection-oriented traffic; while UDP is employed for efficient, connectionless traffic.

☑ Two additional protocols to be aware of are the ICMP protocol, which provides control messages for IP, and ARP, which provides name services between physical media addresses and IP addresses.

Cisco IP Security Hardware and Software

☑ Cisco's primary appliance for providing information flow control policy enforcement is the PIX firewall. This is an IOS-like, high-performance firewall based upon stateful packet filtering combined with application gateways for specified protocols.

☑ Because Cisco has a wide variety of infrastructure products, Cisco has integrated security features into those devices to provide comprehensive protection for the whole enterprise. Cisco Secure Integrated Software and Integrated VPN Software are IOS features that permit protective and detective controls in the existing router and switch hardware; the VPN client allows termination of IPSec tunnels on end-user equipment.

☑ Authentication is provided by the Cisco Secure ACS, a combination RADIUS and TACACS+ server that runs on Unix or Windows platforms.

☑ The Cisco Secure Scanner (formerly NetSonar) provides vulnerability assessment services to identify problems on hosts before they can be exploited.

☑ The Cisco Secure IDS, both host- and network-based, provides ongoing reporting of intrusions and inappropriate traffic as it occurs.

☑ The Cisco Secure Policy Manager is the management console that provides control features for the security equipment at the site.

Frequently Asked Questions

The following Frequently Asked Questions, answered by the authors of this book, are designed to both measure your understanding of the concepts presented in this chapter and to assist you with real-life implementation of these concepts. To have your questions about this chapter answered by the author, browse to **www.syngress.com/solutions** and click on the **"Ask the Author"** form.

Q: I've deployed a firewall/IDS/VPN. Am I safe now?

A: No. Security is a process, not a product. It takes careful design, integrated personnel support, and multiple technologies. For example, the recent Nimda event would blow through most firewalls protecting corporate Web servers—the exploit was a conventional Web request, and firewalls are designed to allow Web requests into Web servers. Firewalls help with many things, but in this case, you would have needed a vulnerability assessment tool, like the Cisco Secure Scanner, combined with a remediation program, to dodge this particular bullet.

Q: I've deployed a firewall/IDS/VPN. Why should I put ACLs on my routers? Isn't that overkill?

A: Deploying multiple technologies is known as "defense in depth." The idea is that if one defense slips—due to human errors and omissions, or weaknesses in technology—another defense can cover the gap. It's also important to realize that sometimes the router is outside the firewall, and needs protection too, so it doesn't hurt to provide some protections for the firewall as well. Many systems, all working together, make the likelihood of a security incident less likely.

Q: My Web servers are on a service network, protected by a third interface off the PIX. I need to get them to talk to an SQL back-end, which lives within my corporate network. The Web guy wants to put another NIC in the Web server and use that to communicate into my corporate network because he says the PIX is too slow. He says he'll turn off packet routing on the Web server. Should I do that?

A: Some network engineers do use that architecture. It's probably not the best approach, however. The problem is that now the Web server is part of your trusted computing base – if the "Web guy" forgets to turn off packet routing, or for some reason the Web server is compromised, a direct path from the outside will open into the heart of your network. The PIX is a high-performance device. It can generally be quite effective at routing traffic back to the back-end server. An even better approach, however, is to put the SQL servers on their own service network, and enforce traffic to the SQL servers that way. Now, even if the Web server is compromised, the attack is contained. If for some reason something evil breaks out in your user community, the SQL servers are still protected.

Q: I'm designing a high-speed Web farm. Should I put in a PIX?

A: Some network architects use that design. However, consider this: in that environment, the PIX would limit access to Web services, and provide you with an audit trail of the transactions. You can achieve the same facilities with access lists on your routers and host logs on the servers. A careful Web farm design will incorporate load balancers, redundant routers and switches, VPN terminators for management, and IDS for detective controls. Assuming there are ACLs on the perimeter, firewalls are optional.

Q: Which firewall/IDS/VPN should I buy?

A: Your choice of product depends upon many factors, including cost, performance, support, the long-term viability of the company, the feature set, and so on. Cisco has an advantage in several of these arenas, and, of course, if you have a Cisco network already, a reduced number of vendors and the ability to integrate security features into your infrastructure can be very helpful. The best approach, however, is to identify what issues are important to you, and then review how equipment and support compares between vendors on these issues, ranking them accordingly. Be a smart consumer of security, and remember to design security natively and ubiquitously across your network!

## Chapter 2

What Are We Trying to Prevent?

Solutions in this chapter:

- **What Threats Face Your Network?**
- **Malicious Mobile Code**
- **Denial of Service**
- **Detecting Breaches**
- **Preventing Attacks**

☑ **Summary**

☑ **Solutions Fast Track**

☑ **Frequently Asked Questions**

Introduction

An attentive network administrator is always looking for the right strategy for information services security. You need to understand the risks you are facing, and assign resources to reduce and manage those risks. To do this correctly, one needs a *quantitative* security risk assessment. You write down all the potential adverse events, estimate the loss from such events, and calculate the probability of such events occurring. Multiplying the latter and then adding up the results gives a value known as the "Annual Loss Expectation" or "Expected Annual Costs."

For information security, this is a difficult problem on several levels. Writing down every potential adverse event is a complex and time-consuming task. Estimating the loss from such events is no trivial feat either. For risks like fire or earthquake, we at least have data culled over a long period of time. Risks due to information security events, on the other hand, are highly variable, and change over time as new tools emerge and new malicious code is distributed. Insurance companies are busy developing data for new information security insurance, but that data remains regrettably limited.

On the upside, undertakings of this sort produce hard numbers—the kind a CEO can appreciate. It's a type of exercise that can be helpful when considering strategies or identifying where security resources should be deployed. Even a simple first-pass approach—identify the crucial assets, think about what can go wrong for those assets, figure out some likely scenarios and assign likelihood—can help with the decision-making process. Quantitative risk analysis is a path that many enterprises do follow, particularly in high-risk environments such as financial institutions, or highly-regulated environments such as health care.

Given the drawbacks, an alternative *qualitative* security business risk assessment is often more cost effective. The idea here is that probability data and cost impacts are not required, but instead, a rough estimate is employed—for instance, evaluating threats, vulnerabilities, and controls. This allows you to take a look at what risks you are facing (threats), the potential impacts of those threats (vulnerabilities), and potential ways to minimize both the threats and the vulnerabilities (controls). Controls that correspond to events of high probability and high impact are generally worth exploring first, while controls that correspond to events of low probability and low impact are worth examining later. A vulnerability approach is generally followed (rather than an asset protection approach) because the vulnerabilities usually are a smaller set of things to consider, and more directly relate to the controls that will be proposed.

When conducting security environmental vulnerability assessments in a qualitative environment, one associates a Risk Mitigation Factor with each device.

This factor is based upon two elements: The potential impact of the security violation on functional operations (severity of the hazard) and the probability that the violation will occur. The severity of the risk is classified in one of four categories: Critical, Severe, Moderate, and Low. The probability ranking is also categorized in one of four different classifications: Frequent, Probable, Occasional, and Possible. Table 2.1 lists the different levels of risk severity, while Table 2.2 shows the different levels of risk probability.

Table 2.1 Risk Severity

Level of Severity	Description
Critical	Business impact is considered Critical when exploitation of the vulnerability would result in a total system compromise, which may include complete loss of management control and/or use of the compromised system to launch attacks or intrusions against other companies. In addition to direct costs, there may be significant indirect financial loss, due in part to litigation or damaged reputation. An example of vulnerabilities of this nature would be installation of remote control software that would permit a remote intruder full access to the machine.
Severe	The business impact is considered Severe when exploitation of the vulnerability would result in a partial system compromise, potentially losing control over a delivered service or prompting unauthorized distribution of sensitive information. The primary impact of this sort of vulnerability is the direct cost associated with loss of service or information. An example of vulnerabilities of this nature would be a weakness in Web server configuration that allowed for Web page defacement.
Moderate	Impact is considered Moderate when exploitation of the vulnerability would result in degraded performance and loss of system integrity. Primary impact of this sort of vulnerability is the indirect cost associated with event normalization. An example of vulnerabilities of this nature would be a server subject to a Denial of Service attack.
Low	Business impact is considered Low when exploitation of the vulnerability results in degraded performance without loss of integrity, or which prompts an inability to control integrity in a functioning host. The primary impact of this sort of vulnerability is the indirect cost associated with higher maintenance. An example of vulnerabilities of this nature would be user-controlled desktops.

Table 2.2 Risk Probability

Level of Probability	Description
Frequent	The probability is considered Frequent when the event is likely to happen often. This might occur if the vulnerability has been widely publicized, automated tools are available, and/or if a worm using the exploit is available.
Probable	The probability is considered Probable when the event is likely to happen several times during the life cycle of the host system. This might occur because the vulnerability is well known, but "user friendly" exploit tools are not available, and thus require a higher level of skill to compromise the system.
Occasional	The probability is considered Occasional when the event is likely to occur sometime during the host system's life cycle. This would occur when the vulnerability is not well known, or when specific circumstances would be required for a breach (such as a maintenance window when certain protections are not in place).
Possible	The probability is considered Possible when it is unlikely but possible to occur in the system's lifecycle. A classification may be such when the vulnerability is of a theoretical nature and no exploit code is known, or specific circumstances of low probability are required, or when the vulnerability is of a theoretical nature and no way to exploit the vulnerability is currently known.

More information about identifying vulnerabilities is given in Chapter 11, where the Cisco Secure Scanner is discussed.

What Threats Face Your Network?

A threat to your network might come from actual intent to do harm to it, or from a malicious source a user may inadvertently activate. Both arise as a result of violations to a security policy.

Policy is driven by goals. Back in the summer of 1986, Hal Tipton, Richard W. Owen, Jr., and Ross Leo coined the term CIA—Confidentiality, Integrity, and Assurance—as a compact and succinct description of the things that matter in a secure information delivery/processing system. (The fact that it provides a nice chuckle at the expense of the U.S. Central Intelligence Agency only helps to make it more memorable.) Looking at harm from the perspective of a breakdown in CIA is a good way to approach potential problems.

Loss of Confidentiality

Loss of confidentiality is often the most serious form of harm. For example, when a merchant has customer credit card numbers compromised, he can expect a serious loss of customer confidence. The owner of the credit card loses, due to potential charges on their account, and the hassle of getting them cleared. The credit card company loses, due to absorbing the risk of fraud. In December of 2000, Egghead lost control of its 3.7 million customer database. Some clients lost access to their cards during the Christmas season, while the card's issuing companies were forced to cancel and reissue cards. Other credit card companies absorbed the risk of the fraud – and the estimate was that millions of dollars were lost. The biggest loser was Egghead itself: It saw its stock drop twenty-five percent overnight, and shortly thereafter ceased to be a viable company. Loss of confidentiality is usually due to human actions, but at least one worm (SirCam) will actively e-mail out potentially sensitive documents from an infected host.

Loss of Integrity

Loss of integrity is one of the most insidious forms of harm. Perhaps the earliest widespread example was the XM_COMPAT virus, which spread through macro code in Excel during the fall of 1998, making subtle changes to the spreadsheet data it infected. Since the computations of spreadsheets can affect device controls, including medical equipment, this was a potentially life-threatening virus and not easily detected by simple inspection (modern antivirus software easily controls this sort of problem, as long as the signatures are current.)

Another form of loss of integrity arises when authentication systems are poorly designed or are ineffective. If a VPN's server logs are not readily available, you won't be able to tell who is crawling through your system. If passwords are poorly chosen, mail may be compromised, and if something bad does happen, you may lose the ability to associate actions with individuals. Both of these events add to the cost of dealing with network problems.

Loss of Availability

Loss of availability is the most high-profile of the visible forms of harm. This category has its own classification—a denial of service (DoS) attack. More on this type of attack will be described later. Unfortunately, this sort of harm is generally the easiest to execute.

Sources of Threats

Donn Parker, in his book *Fighting Computer Crime, a New Framework for the Protection of Information*, recommends breaking down potential attackers by SKRAM, which stands for skills, knowledge, resources, authority, and motives. For example, one type of person that presents a serious threat to any network is the "script kiddie"—someone who downloads tools written by others, perhaps does some trivial modifications, and then launches those scripts without a deep understanding of their mechanisms or impact. These people are low in skill and authority and usually have limited knowledge of the target. However, they are high in resources, and often operate with a motive more related to chaos than financial gain. Another common threat is the disgruntled system administrator. These people most likely have a high level of skill and possess a deep knowledge of the target with enough authority to do some serious harm. Yet another threat to consider is mobile code, such as viruses, worms, Trojan horses, and the like. These have varying degrees of skill (worms are typically badly coded, and bugs are common) and generally have no particular knowledge of the target. They do have amazing resources, however, based upon the sheer number of machines they can infect and mobilize to help in their malicious work.

In these examples, the primary motive is to sow chaos. Other harm is possible, of course. We are starting to see a rise in computer-based crime: individuals or syndicates that utilize sophisticated programming techniques to commit extortion against information owners. For example, in the fall of 1999 the FBI arrested two members of the "Phonemasters," an international group that penetrated many of the computers at well-known corporations such as MCI, Sprint, AT&T, and Equifax. They stole Sprint calling card numbers that ended up in the hands of organized crime groups in Italy. Even if your network does not have such juicy targets, it can still be used as an attack platform against other systems, as the companies listed here were.

Perhaps an even more curious motive was documented in Clifford Stoll's book, *The Cuckoo's Egg*. There, Soviet foreign intelligence agents tapped into the resources of West German crackers to penetrate United States military and paramilitary organizations. It should not be a surprise that foreign agents might use such methods to acquire private sector intellectual property as well.

A final threat worth describing is automated crime. Over the past half-century, we've used computing technology to automate our business processes. These days, the direct deposit of payroll checks, the ordering of supplies, and other routine business transactions often occur without human intervention. With the proper

SKRAM, payroll checks can be sent to inappropriate accounts, supplies might arrive at inappropriate locations, and other breakdowns in business transactions will occur with the speed and scale of electronic activity. This means new kinds of responses to these threats are required.

Malicious Mobile Code

Malicious code, or malware, is software that does you harm. Malicious mobile code deals with viruses, worms, Trojan horses, and similar problems of rogue code that might compromise your security policy. Because the code is mobile, using your network to cause harm, it's your responsibility to bring it to heel. Due to its ability to infect many computers simultaneously and automatically, the vast resources available to this threat mean you must deal with it seriously in your defense strategies.

Trojan Horses

The term Trojan horse is a reference to a stratagem used in the siege of Troy, as told in the Iliad. The attacking Greeks found the city's walls impenetrable. They built a wooden horse and presented it to the citizens of Troy as a peace offering, concealing a force of one hundred Greek warriors inside. Even though one of the Trojan High Priests, Laocoön, warned against "Greeks bearing gifts," and the King's own daughter, Cassandra, warned of disaster, the horse was brought into the city. Later that night, the warriors concealed within crept out and opened the gates of the city, letting the Greeks in to sack and loot Troy.

In information technology, a Trojan horse is a computer program that appears to have a useful function, but in truth has a hidden and potentially malicious function that evades security mechanisms, sometimes by exploiting legitimate authorizations of the system entity that invoked the program in the first place. IT departments frequently warn their users against accepting files and e-mails from the Internet—yet warnings even from senior executives fail to be heeded. Trojan horses continue to be the most expensive vector for malicious code.

Viruses

A biological virus is a piece of DNA or RNA code that attaches itself to the surface of a healthy cell. The code then injects itself into the cell's functions, causing the cell to produce the viral fragments. In a similar vein, a computer virus is a piece of code that searches out other programs and inserts itself into them; these other programs then become Trojan horses that proceed to infect their neighbors. The chief difference between a computer virus and a Trojan horse is that the virus is not a complete program in and of itself, but requires resources of the victim program to replicate itself. In theory, computer viruses should be more widespread than Trojan horses, since they can reproduce via a wide variety of programs, while Trojans do so via a single program. In practice, computer environments are so highly homogeneous, with similar operating systems and applications, and the human part of the equation is so ready to execute unknown programs, that Trojan horses constitute more serious risks to the enterprise.

Worms

The term worm appears to have originated by John Brunner in his book "Shockwave Rider," a novel written in 1975 which anticipated many of the information tracking and privacy issues of the modern Internet. In the modern parlance, a worm is a computer program that can run independently, can propagate a complete working version of itself onto other hosts on a network, and may consume computer resources destructively. Common vectors today are open (or accessible) network shares and vulnerabilities in network services. As an example, the high profile (and still quite common) Nimda worm used both techniques to spread itself from machine to machine.

Worms can be classified into several subtypes.

- **Intelligent, Data-driven** These use databases provided by the infected host (for example, Outlook mail addresses) to pass code to the victim host. These have the advantage of drawing upon information that the author of the worm code didn't possess, and so can act in unanticipated ways. The may avoid some controls—for example, if you get a piece of mail from someone you know, you are more likely to execute Trojan code. They can be detected through unusual behavior, however. For example, it would be considered unusual for a user to suddenly send e-mails out to the first 50 names in his address book, leading a system administrator to suspect a compromised host.

- **Intelligent, Activity-driven** These sense activity from the infected host (for example, Web page clients, network file shares) to pass code to the victim host. These can be even more subtle; the hidden Trojan transaction is masked by an existing client transaction, so they would bypass controls to detect anomalous activity.

- **Unintelligent** These use search techniques to identify additional targets. They can be identified by a process in which they contact machines that aren't running vulnerable services, or in which they attempt to contact nonexistent IP addresses. This is the most general infective technique, and currently the most destructive.

Designing & Planning…

Tracking and Taming Unintelligent Worms

It is helpful to track attempts to contact a host on unused ports or unused IP addresses, which can indicate either a misconfiguration or a potentially malicious activity. Most worms don't use IP spoofing techniques, so it can be a good way to identify an infected host.

In addition, one can apply inverse TCP quality of service techniques to reduce the infection rate of hosts. Programs such as Tom Liston's LaBrea (at www.hackbusters.com) or the use of Cisco's Network-Based Application Recognition (NBAR) will allow system administrators time to get to the source of infection before it spreads farther.

A worm can be countered at several locations. The most traditional approach is to arrest the worm at the perimeter, through antivirus software on firewalls, mail servers, Web caches, and the like. Layered security through desktop antivirus software is also a common practice; the problem is ensuring that the antivirus software remains current. Perhaps the most cost-effective approach is to engage the end user, and ensure they communicate effectively with the security personnel.

The biggest threat of a worm lies in its automated capability to replicate. With a human attacker, replication works in terms of human reaction times. People have to receive and execute the malicious program. With a worm, the replication works in terms of computer reaction times. In November of 1988, Robert Tappan Morris released the "Great Worm," a coding experiment that was designed to seek out and contact Unix hosts, and then use those hosts to repeat that process. Unfortunately, some coding errors caused multiple copies of the worm to spawn, clogging process tables; like today's Nimda, the worm was everywhere, and sites took the unprecedented step of disconnecting themselves to address event normalization needs. For the first (and hopefully only) time in the history of the Internet, it was down, though not for a long time.

One traditional defense is the use of antivirus signatures at the perimeter. It is important to keep your antivirus software frequently updated, so that when a problem tries to penetrate your perimeter, it is recognized and blocked. When a "day zero" virus is announced, antivirus researchers update their signatures (which typically takes about a day) and the signatures are pushed out to the enforcement points. This keeps your window of exposure small, and hopefully provides a managed risk. However, an interesting paper by Nicholas Weaver at www.cs.berkeley .edu/~nweaver/warhol.html describes Warhol worms, sometimes called Flash worms, which by initially targeting highly connected hosts have the potential to infect every vulnerable machine across the Internet in about 15 minutes. Traditional antivirus approaches can not be successful in this sort of environment.

Current Malicious Code Threats

Commercial antivirus companies provide data on the most frequent malicious code they see from their clients. This information is relevant to the risk probability computation mentioned previously. As of this writing, the most common threats include the following:

1. A JavaScript Trojan horse that alters a browser's home page.
2. A Visual Basic Trojan horse that alters a browser's home page.
3. An e-mail Trojan horse and network shares worm.
4. An e-mail Trojan horse that executes upon viewing in certain mail viewers.
5. The Nimda Trojan horse/worm.
6. An e-mail Visual Basic script Trojan horse.

What should you draw from this list? None of these threats are new; all are based upon virus engines from the previous year. All of these have Trojan components. It should be clear that user education (not just warnings provided by Laocoön) is an important part of your malicious code defense strategy. None of these are viruses—instead, it should be taken as a statement about the efficiency of modern antivirus software rather than the potential vulnerability of the threat model.

Current Malicious Code Impacts

The threat associated with malicious mobile code is very high. Code executed via a Trojan runs with the privileges of the person who launched the code; this means, at the very least, user files are at risk. The second point of the CIA triad is integrity, and it's a crucial breakdown in information integrity. In a modern operating system, protections are in place so that an ordinary user does not have the ability to seriously harm the underlying system—but it turns out that operating system permissions are often frangible. Fred Cohen, one of the early virus researchers, noted in his PhD thesis how Unix viruses can break through the protective mechanisms of Unix operating system permissions. This is a reflection of rule number one of Microsoft's *Ten Immutable Laws of Security*, available at: www.microsoft.com/technet/columns/security/essays/10imlaws.asp

"If a bad guy can persuade you to run his program on your computer, it's not your computer anymore." Theory aside, we do see that the impact is critical. If you place a machine on the Internet, you will be probed on port 80 by a Nimda-infected machine. Nimda installs a "back door," a service that provides remote access to the machine. Take the IP address of the machine that probed you, and you can turn around and exploit that back door, and then use that machine to launch attacks across the Internet.

In 1988, the Great Worm required sites to disconnect themselves from the Internet. In the fall of 1999, Melissa spread like wildfire through e-mail systems globally. In the 11 years since the earlier event, networks had become much more robust, but e-mail was still a weak spot. Again, many enterprises had to shut mail systems down to clear queues and apply protective techniques. In the summer of 2001, Nimda proved an even more dangerous opponent: once infected, Nimda aggressively attempted to contact and infect additional vulnerable servers. The aggression produced ARP storms that brought down cable systems; the traffic overloaded enterprise LANs which prevented any other traffic. Try to imagine the traffic utilization associated with network backups running on every machine across the core of the network during the middle of the day. One representative case is a developer of Web-based customer relationship software, who had about a sixth of their six thousand machines running vulnerable Web servers. They were unable to talk to their clients for four days, during which "all hands on deck" emergency action with staff and outside consultants was carried out. The business impact of four days of downtime, along with the PR impact of a customer relationship management (CRM) developer being unable to talk to customers, is incalculable.

Denial of Service

A network-based denial of service (DoS) attack is a direct attack on system availability. There are two types of denial of service attacks: triggers and floods. The trigger class uses a vulnerability inherent in the operating system or application to make a system or component unavailable. A flood generally uses normal system functions but generates so much traffic that the target is overwhelmed. The target can be a client, service, or system. A target client would be a specific application, such as a Web browser or instant messaging client, which is made unavailable as a result of the attack. A target service would be when the attack prevents normal functioning of a particular service, such as Web browsing or file shares, without harming the underlying operating system. A target system would be when the underlying operating system itself is damaged and the entire host is made unavailable.

A nice example of a trigger attack on a client is a JavaScript bomb: very simply, the requested Web page invokes a new browser window inside a JavaScript loop, as in the following example:

```
<script language="JavaScript">
while(true) window.open("http://www.someone.com");
</script>
```

The effect of this code is to open an endless series of browser windows, exhausting the resources available to the browser. An interesting variant uses a lengthy list of pornographic sites as the URL to be opened, thus not only making the browser unusable but also getting the user in trouble with the local administration when URL filtering software is enabled.

A good example of a trigger attack on a service was seen by many AVVID clients as an incidental consequence of the IIS server attacks, such as CodeRed and Nimda. The Call Manager server is based upon IIS, and as Cisco observed in its security notice www.cisco.com/warp/public/707/cisco-code-red-worm-pub.shtml:

> the management of a Cisco CallManager product is disabled or severely limited until the defaced Web page is removed and the original management Web page is restored. Cisco CSS 11000 Content Services Switch, Cisco IP/VC 3510 H.323 Videoconference Multipoint Control Units, Cisco Aironet Wireless Bridge/Access Point, Cisco IP phone models 7960, 7940, and 7910, and Cisco 600 series DSL routers are vulnerable to a repeatable denial of service until the software is upgraded, or workarounds are applied.

An example of a trigger attack on a target system from a couple of years ago is the "Land" attack. If you craft a SYN packet with a source IP and port equal to the destination IP and port, the operating system may try to synchronize with itself—a Windows 95 PC will freeze and require a reboot, and an NT Workstation will be unusable for about a minute before it recovers.

Flood attacks are less subtle. They attempt to overwhelm by sheer volume of traffic. An example of a flood attack on a client would be to send an overly large mail attachment when an end user is on a dial-up system; if they can't control the browser to delete the rogue file without downloading it, it would deny mail services until the download is completed.

An example of a flood attack on a service would be the "Host Announcement Frame" vulnerability for Microsoft Common Internet File System (CIFS) documented in Microsoft Security Bulletin MS00-036. In essence, what happens is that if someone sends a large number of announcements for hosts, then those announcements need to be processed by a machine that is doing essential tasks, thereby degrading its performance. That host then replicates that information among its peers, again consuming large amounts of network bandwidth. Any other hosts that try to use that service need to process the large tables, degrading their performance. This is a common theme: The best floods have a natural multiplier effect that allows the user to exert a force on the network, while the effect is tenfold more severe.

The most common flood attacks are based upon simple volume-of-traffic tricks. The attacker generates packets, sometimes bouncing them off other hosts to conceal his tracks, and perhaps uses a multiplier trick to make his traffic more effective. The receiver must then deal with this heavy wave of traffic. Two attacks deserve special recognition: the Smurf attack and the SYN flood attack.

The Smurf Attack

The smurf attack uses an unfortunate default behavior of routers to swamp a victim host. Recall that ICMP is used to provide control messages over IP. One control message is an *echo request*, that asks a host to provide an *echo reply*, responding with the body of the message. Here lies the start of the problem: Suppose our evil host wants to take out a target host. He finds a well-connected intermediary, and forges an echo request to the intermediary host apparently from the target host. The intermediary responds, and the target receives a flood of traffic from the intermediary, potentially overwhelming the target. One additional trick makes this more deadly: the original echo request can be targeted not just at a single host, but at a broadcast request—and under a default configuration, *all* hosts on that network will reply. This allows a host to multiply itself by the number of hosts on that network: with a 200-fold multiplication, a single host on a 256K DSL line can saturate a 10Mb Ethernet feed.

The recommended guidance is to prevent broadcast addresses from being expanded, at least from packets on the Internet. On your Cisco routers, for each interface, apply the following configuration:

```
no ip directed-broadcast
```

This will prevent broadcast packets from being converted. Blocking ICMP doesn't help: A variant, *fraggle*, uses UDP packets in a similar fashion to flood hosts. An even more vicious approach, described in CERT advisory CA-1996-01, uses forged packets to activate the *chargen* port, ideally connecting to the *echo* port on the target. The two hosts are then locked in a fatal embrace of a packet stream until one or both of the machines are reset.

The SYN Flood Attack

The SYN flood attack consumes a limited resource on the victim server—the ability to establish TCP sessions—to prevent service. The idea is again fairly simple: Recall that a TCP session begins with a three-packet handshake. The idea is to spoof a new, incoming connection. The SYN packet prompts a response SYN-ACK from the server. The old approach, still followed by the Microsoft IP stack, is to maintain a small list of pending responses so that the server can remember which packets have already been received.

The vulnerability is to thus send a large number of SYN requests without receiving any response. The usual technique is to forge the return address on the request; since the end host doesn't exist, the server is never going to receive a response from its SYN-ACK, thus limiting the resource. In a surprisingly short time, this can prevent a host from accepting connections.

A PIX firewall can provide protection against this sort of attack. In a typical environment, one would specify the target IP with a *static* statement and use ACLs to pass traffic inside. For example, suppose the IP address 63.122.40.140 is a Web server off a DMZ interface of a PIX. The configuration would look something like:

```
static (dmz,outside) 63.122.40.140 63.122.40.140 netmask 255.255.255.255
    10000 500
access-list acl_out permit tcp any host 63.122.40.140 eq www
access-group acl_out in interface outside
```

The key line here is the first one; this allows the IP address 63.122.40.140 to allow traffic through the PIX. (The traffic is limited to Web traffic in the following line.) The last two values provide the protection. The first is the *max_cons* parameter; this is the maximum number of simultaneous connections through the PIX to the Web server. This allows a maximum of 10,000 simultaneous sessions. The second is the *em_limit*, and is the maximum number of uncompleted handshakes that will be passed to the inner host. If the number exceeds this limit, the PIX's TCP Intercept feature takes over. For each SYN received, the PIX captures the request, and responds for the server. It then waits for the handshake, and if the connection was false, doesn't bother the protected server. If the handshake is completed, it opens a connection with the inner host, establishes the handshake in a proxy fashion, and then forwards the packet appropriately.

If you don't have a PIX, another approach is to use an operating system that is not subject to this kind of attack. An approach known as *syn-cookies* uses a specialized ISN to record the state of the handshake. This means that the server does not need to remember any of the SYN packets it has received, therefore there is no resource for the attacker to consume. This is similar to the approach the PIX uses internally in its TCP Intercept feature.

Damage & Defense...

Don't Be a Participant in a Spoofed DoS Attack!

If a flood of traffic hits the victim, there is little they can do—the packets have already overwhelmed their link. To help lessen the damage, everyone should be a good corporate citizen, and prevent inappropriate packets from leaving their network.

The best current practice is to prevent packet spoofing. This is documented in RFC 2267. The idea is to ensure that packets that leave your network are stamped with a return address appropriate for your network. Don't let forged traffic onto the Internet!

Distributed Denial of Service (DDoS) Attacks

As described earlier, a fair amount of technical complexity is required to make these denial of service attacks work. A fair amount of labor is necessary to multiply an individual attacker's bandwidth enough that it swamps the end user. From this, network managers are becoming more and more careful, and denial of service attacks are becoming less and less successful.

Unfortunately, a simpler approach for the bad guys exists. A large number of hosts on the Internet are owned by individuals who do not exert proper care over their systems. They allow their hosts to become compromised, and permit remote-controlled software to be installed. After which, malicious agents can use these systems against others, providing remote computing power to help them facilitate brute force cracking attacks, or enough raw network bandwidth to be used against a host.

In underground parlance, a compromised host is known as a *zombie*, while the surreptitious controller is known as the *zombie master*.

The most famous example of a zombie attack was the spring 2000 attack on Yahoo!, eBay, Amazon, and others. Apparently, a ping flood tool known as *imp* was employed in the attack; the strategy was to launch a combined attack from hundreds of zombies, many located at the University of California in Santa Barbara. The attack hit like sledgehammer, flooding the target sites with hundreds of megabytes per second of traffic, and effectively bringing them to a standstill.

The only way to remedy such attacks is to find each of the zombies and release them from the control of the zombie master—a slow and tedious task. The only way to protect against this kind of traffic is to detect the compromise, and address remediation before the zombie can be put to use. This can be difficult, but, conveniently, it does provide an introduction to the next section.

Detecting Breaches

In any network exposed to an uncontrolled environment like the Internet, there will always be risk of a systems compromise—and over time, that risk approaches a level of certainty. Every system administrator should be prepared to detect breaches, and take appropriate action.

What is the appropriate action? That depends. In some environments, you clean it up and forget about it. It's usually helpful to document the attack, if possible, and report it to the originating ISP: This helps put pressure on the originator, and may reduce further attacks. In some cases, a detailed analysis of the event is prepared, to ensure the proposed remediation will be effective. In still others, detailed forensics with an eye to civil or criminal prosecution is required. This section delves into the detection and documentation of network attacks, as well as the strategies for addressing results.

Initial Detection

The bad way to find out a breach has occurred is to discover that your Web site isn't accessible, your Human Resources database has been zeroed out, or your President's private correspondence is duplicated in everyone's e-mail in-basket. Unfortunately, finding out that site service confidentiality, integrity, or availability has been compromised is not an uncommon way to detect the problem.

A better approach is through the use of file system integrity or network traffic anomaly tools. The former detects changes in the static configuration of a system, while the latter detects changes in network behavior. This sort of preparation allows for a more rapid and effective response to a breach.

File System Integrity Software

The idea behind file system integrity software is to take a snapshot of the configuration and file contents of a device, and then see what changes over time. A fundamental principle of security is that of secure change management: If a system starts in a known secure state, and the only changes to the system occur securely, then the system will always be in a secure state. So, take those snapshots, and periodically compare them against what actually exists on the device. If a change has occurred, and it doesn't match the expected changes as documented under the secure change control process, then you have a problem—either the change control didn't provide accurate documentation, or your systems have been breached.

The first software to perform this task was developed as an academic project by Gene Kim (a student) and Gene Spafford (professor) at Purdue University. The idea is fairly straightforward: develop a size, timestamp, and checksum for every file on the system. If a change occurs, you would like one of these three values to change. Crafting the change so that size and timestamp aren't altered isn't that difficult. However, the third element is what makes the bad guy's job hard: Using a cryptographically strong function to compute the checksum will ensure a change in the file will cause a change in the checksum. The original description of the idea is available at www.cerias.purdue.edu/homes/spaf/tech-reps/gkim. Tripwire still exists in an open source form as well as a commercial product; in addition, there are many other products such as AIDE, or fcheck. There are important details, such as ensuring the signature information is properly protected, that the signatures are computed correctly, that the tool is executed frequently enough to detect changes in near real time, that the results are available to security management in a useful format (and so on)—all of which should be specific to the product.

An alternative approach has recently become popular, based upon something called *host-based intrusion detection*. It boils down to that secure change concept: If we have a piece of software running that detects all inappropriate changes, we are safe. There is a Cisco product, manufactured by Entercept, which not only provides that detective capability, but also has the potential to prevent unauthorized changes from occurring. This change detection approach can provide real-time alerting of a security breach.

Network Traffic Anomaly Tools

A network traffic anomaly tool views traffic or reacts to traffic on the wire, and attempts to determine if something peculiar, abnormal, or otherwise inappropriate is occurring. Several approaches are valid: conventional network intrusion detection, log analysis, and honeypot approaches.

The most commonly deployed tool is a network intrusion detection system (IDS). Again, there is a Cisco product for intrusion detection, the Cisco Secure IDS, which is discussed in more detail in Chapter 13.

Log analysis depends on configuring systems to record traffic that doesn't match normal parameters, and then using scripted tools to analyze the resulting logs. For example, placing a "log" clause on an extended access list will send information about matching traffic via syslog to a central log server. A text-based search of those records can identify unusual traffic.

A honeypot, meanwhile, is a system (or systems) designed to decoy, detect, and trap an attacker on your network. Because these systems are not in use as production servers, simple use is an indication of inappropriate traffic. The systems are thus designed with more alarms than a conventional server, and often contain attractive elements that encourage an attacker to spend time on the system, increasing the likelihood of detection and tracking. An easily deployed tool is Tom Liston's "LaBrea" project, which is a "sticky honeypot" that reacts to TCP connection attempts on unused IP addresses.

Are Forensics Important?

The previous steps for initial detection involved a planning phase. You deployed integrity tools or a detective control, and hoped you found out about the breach before the users did. But perhaps the first inkling of the problem was when you found your Web site defaced. What do you do next?

Before you can answer that, you have to decide if preservation of forensic evidence is a goal. That means collecting data regarding the nature of the attack so you can prove to an independent third party your conclusions about how the attack occurred. Common reasons for preservation of forensic evidence are:

- To determine just how the breach occurred to improve your defenses.

- To document the event for an internal "lessons learned" document.

- To document the event for management to provide a root cause analysis.

- To prepare for a civil or criminal action (including a personnel action).

These require a careful handling of evidence, and correspondingly, a more expensive and time-consuming response to the security event. You should get guidance from management about the most appropriate response; if they want to follow up with legal action and you've already formatted the hard drive containing the breach, you're pretty much out of luck.

Some techniques apply to all levels of forensics. Probably the most important one involves careful documentation. Write everything down! Having good notes available will not only allow for the preparation of any reports required, but also help you review the steps you've followed, and assist in the analysis of the system.

It is worth observing that if you are preparing for legal action, it is important to not merely document what occurred but to preserve evidence. When preparing notes, start with a bound book in which you write your notes, subsequently signing and dating each page as you complete it. When working with hard drives, do not work on the original equipment! Prepare two copies of the disk. Remove the original, tag it, and place it into secure storage. Give one copy back to the information owner so they can get on with business, and retain one scratch copy for your own analysis.

What Are the Key Steps after a Breach Is Detected?

After detecting a breach, several steps should be followed. Precise details will vary depending upon site security policy, the nature of the event, and other constraints, but most should adhere to the following steps:

1. **Identification and Classification** This step requires determining whether or not a breach has actually occurred, and analyzing the circumstances of the breach. If a Web site is defaced, this is clearly a smoking gun. If one of the host integrity or networking intrusion detection tools dispatches an alarm, it may not be as obvious that the event

has occurred. The security analyst needs to review the tool's alarm, and determine if this is inappropriate traffic, or just an artifact of the tool.

2. **Containment** As soon as an event is detected, the next step is usually containment, in order to limit potential damage from the event. You generally want to limit the scope and magnitude of the breach, to keep the cost of event normalization as small as possible.

3. **Eradication** Eradication involves eliminating the cause of the breach. The most complete approach involves finding the human or humans responsible and hauling them into court to prevent them from further action. It is difficult to do this in a timely fashion, unfortunately. For the threats of malware, removing the software or using antivirus software is usually the best approach. For network-based threats, reconfiguring the perimeter as well as applying controls internally is usually effective. Other eradication techniques may depend upon the exact nature of the incident.

4. **Recovery** Recovery is the process of returning status to normal after the event. If it was a simple Web defacement, it may be as easy as restoring the data from a recent backup. In a more complex incident, it may require complete rebuilds of the affected servers. Recovery also means restoring faith in your system, something which may require new procedures or updated software be put in place to ensure the original problem doesn't reoccur.

5. **Follow-up** This final step involves analysis and the production of whatever ongoing reports are required for the future. This is a critical step! There is no better time to improve the security posture of your site than just after an incident. You generally have the attention of the principals involved, and your own attention is closely focused on the security of your environment. It is helpful to estimate the cost involved in the incident, both for future planning issues and to update law enforcement personnel for their own statistics.

Preventing Attacks

You've now seen several of the threats your network faces, and what to do when a breach occurs. While you can never eliminate the need to plan for security breaches, there are several things you can do to prevent certain types of attacks and reduce the likelihood of others.

The easiest step is to reduce vulnerabilities, places where the threat can take hold. There is an old joke in security: Protecting against network threats is often like being with a group of hikers in the woods who suddenly come across a bear. To be safe, you don't have to run faster than the bear—you just have to run faster than your fellow hikers. In a network environment, this means you don't have to be "completely" bulletproof—you just have to offer less vulnerability than the next guy. As a result, worms and other threats that flourish on the Internet will often pass you by for other targets.

The next easiest step is to "keep it simple," and provide a security architecture that is easy to diagnose, and offers enough visibility into your network that you can detect inappropriate activity early in the process. Good use of access controls to partition your network will help with simple, controlled designs.

Another step (generally the most cost-effective but not the easiest to implement) is to develop a culture of security within your company. Get your fellow employees working for you, and you'll have both fewer opportunities for security events and more eyes watching the store.

Perhaps the most important step, and one often overlooked, is clear documentation and explicit policy. Documentation on your intended security policy allows you to plan your security architecture, and helps you recover after an incident. It helps you better understand how you are achieving your goals, and thus allows you to catch errors before the bad guys find them for you!

Reducing Vulnerabilities

The security of a system is never greater than the security of its weakest element. Thus before getting clever about additional security controls, the first step should be to conduct an assessment and clean up any identified vulnerabilities.

This generally is an ongoing process. If you are running a particular service and have applied all known vendor patches, you can consider yourself free of known vulnerabilities to that service, which should provide some peace of mind. Six months later, a bug in the code may have been identified, and a new patch may have been released, which should prompt new activity on your part. Your security should be reviewed periodically over time to determine any new issues.

The easiest way to do this is through an automated tool such as the Cisco Secure Scanner, also known as NetSonar. This is a subscription-based software, where, just as antivirus signatures are maintained over time, Cisco manages the vendor alerts and patch information for you, so all you have to do is keep the scanner current and run it periodically. Automated vulnerability assessment is an easy way to identify problems inherent in the system.

Of course, the scanner doesn't fix problems, it merely identifies them. You must also institute a tracking program, so that when problems are identified, they are remedied. This is not always easy—often security personnel are separate from the people who actually own the assets. You may need cooperation from senior management to encourage other employees throughout the company to patch or otherwise address their system's vulnerabilities. Running the scanner on a regular basis and providing management level reports documenting when a vulnerability was first identified, and when notification to the asset owner occurred is important. It should be combined with an assessment of the risk this poses to the company, and generally prompt executive management to ensure the vulnerability is addressed.

Besides patching necessary systems to the current vendor recommended levels, another important strategy is that of "least privilege." The common concept is that a security architecture should be designed so that each system entity is granted the minimum system resources and authorizations that the entity needs to do its work. For system design, this means you should encourage removal of all unnecessary services on servers. The idea behind this is twofold. First, with fewer services is place, you can spend more time focusing on the security of the services you do provide. Second, fewer services means fewer things to go wrong, thus limiting the number and impact of systemic vulnerabilities.

Providing a Simple
Security Network Architecture

We saw at the beginning of this chapter that an important part of risk management is "what if" planning, trying to understand what can go wrong in a system. If you have a complex environment, there may be too many variables, meaning too many things that can go wrong, preventing you from providing effective analysis. By reducing complexity, you can bring the number of "what ifs" down to a manageable level.

An example of this that nearly everyone follows is the use of firewalls on the perimeter to protect user and host servers. Since we removed all vulnerabilities in the previous step, this really isn't required, right? Wrong. Things still might go wrong. We might miss a vulnerability. Because of this, most people deploy perimeter controls to limit the exposure of their internal machines to the Internet. We would certainly still like to remove vulnerabilities wherever possible, but now we can provide some realistic planning about what might go wrong. The environment has been simplified to the "inside," the "outside," and the traffic that flows between those networks.

This idea can be extended. In the 80s and early 90s, most network designs had the approach we just described: a hostile network (the Internet), a friendly network (the inside), and a DMZ marked by a pair of routers that severely limited traffic between the two zones. Traffic that passed first had to be inspected by an armed guard—a bastion host—before it was allowed transit.

In the late 90s, the style was to introduce a centralized firewall and a services network. The idea would be that if a site wanted to provide public services, they would be isolated to their own network. The public services might access private databases through a three-tier architecture—external client on the Internet, talking to front-end Web server, talking to back-end database. Communication from the Web server back to the database would still be controlled by a firewall, so that in the event the Web server was compromised, this wouldn't provide unfettered access to the database. It also meant you could plan what protections were required, since you had a pretty good idea of the information flow patterns between the hosts because your information flow control policy could be enforced at that central firewall.

The cost of another interface off a firewall has decreased rapidly, and performance through firewalls has increased significantly. The modern style is to provide as many security zones as are required by functional properties or level of trust, and to separate each from the other with an access control device such as a firewall. Firewalls no longer are limited to external perimeters, but multiple, internal firewalls can protect the corporate "crown jewels" from the rest of the network. Also, part of the modern style is to support a partitioned administrative network to manage the infrastructure. Ideally, you would like this to be completely out of band, but in practice, a combination of VLAN and MPLS technologies are used to provide some traffic isolation.

A sample network is shown in Figure 2.1. The scenario is that of an enterprise that has an "operations network," a backbone that directly relates to the operation of the business. For example, a bioinformatics company might need a dedicated network that has a distributed storage network designed to support their internal databases; a circuit design company might need a compute server network; or a manufacturing company might need a fabrication control network. Developers are provided with a test network so they can develop new applications or experiment with existing ones without being required to change control procedures for the production network. In the diagram that follows, the operations network is drawn as distributed, so it can hook up with operations networks at other sites via internal point-to-point links. The scenario also assumes a business-to-business relationship, where the company hosts key servers on their site (the "crown jewel" DMZ) for client services and data. Typical user services are provided, so that individuals can do their local work as well as provide developers access to the test network, and managers access to the admin network.

Figure 2.1 A Sample "Simple" Network Design

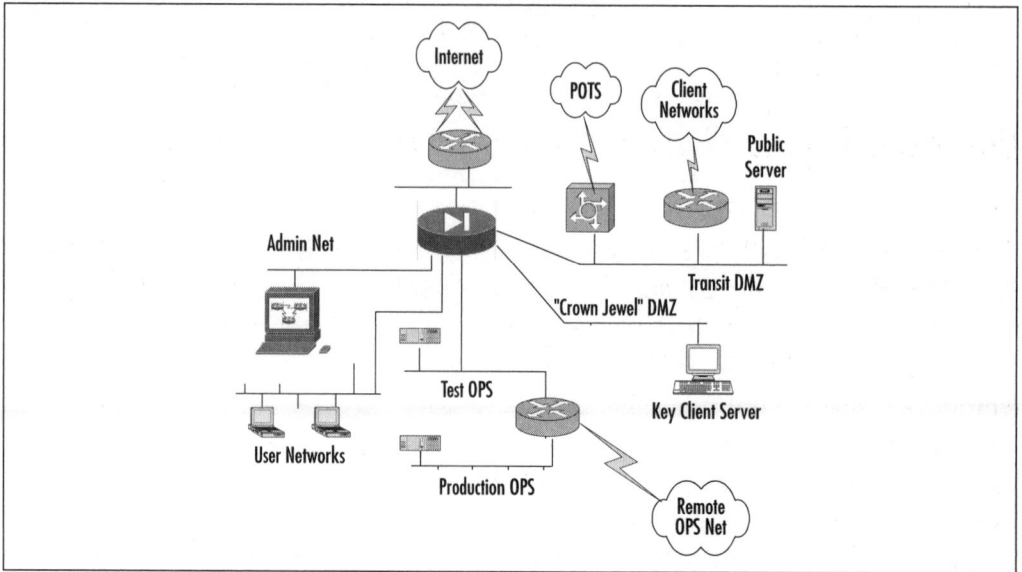

This probably doesn't look that simple. But the simplicity is not in the configuration of the hardware—after all, no firewalls provide a *really* simple network diagram. What it does provide is simplicity in information flow. The outside world (including dial-in or VPN users, clients, and the public) only talks to devices on the transit DMZ. No one talks to the production OPS network except the administration network, and no one talks to the "crown jewel DMZ" except system administrators from the admin network, who are possibly pulling content from the test network. The allowed communication is very controlled, with a limited number of patterns, and it is this simplicity that makes for a secure network.

What if something goes wrong? You have compartmentalization. Suppose a user accidentally executes a Trojan and contaminates his desktop. He would have full access to the other user machines, which could be a problem. Unfortunately, you can't put firewalls everywhere, and if he is an administrator, he might have limited access to the administrator network. Nevertheless, it definitely slows the spread, and if, for example, strong authentication is required to access the administration network, you are protected against all worms and viruses that don't have specific knowledge of your environment. Suppose a developer makes an error of omission on a test machine and it explodes, spewing packets everywhere? No problem, the test network is isolated from the production network (and the rest of the environment). But what if everything goes *really* sour? You can simply power down that central firewall, and provide complete isolation, while still preserving the physical integrity of the production operations net.

Yes, this provides more gear to manage. But in the long run, it offers a simpler security architectural model, and that translates to reduced risk.

Developing a Culture of Security

There is a wonderful apocryphal story of a new security officer who was unhappy that the written security policy of requiring badges for access through the building was not being universally enforced. The rules stated everyone should be badged, and technical controls would control access to certain rooms. However, once inside the perimeter, people would generally flow freely, making it next to impossible to determine if a visitor got away from his escort and was viewing unauthorized materials.

He had an interesting solution. Being new to the company, and not well known, the fellow stopped wearing his badge. Occasionally, someone would stop him and ask for identification. When that did occur, he would produce his identification—and a $20 bill. He would explain who he was, and present the money as a prize for complying with the company guideline on verifying identification. The story got around. He stopped the practice, but compliance remained high: It was a simple object lesson underlining the fact that the company cared about security, that it cared about people wandering the corridors unbadged; and reminded the community that it was their job to help with the enforcement of security.

You may not have $20 bills to hand out, but the concept of engaging the community, and providing a reminder that security matters and that it's a part of everyone's job is an essential element of any security program. It can be relatively inexpensive. Security is a very hot topic at the moment, and makes the front pages of the newspaper all the time. Start a brown bag lunch program, where a talk is provided on current security events, either nationally or within the company, and discuss how the company's policies and procedures might impact those events.

Getting the community on your side has many significant effects. There is the first order effect described previously: People will keep their eyes open, and if you gain their trust and let it be known you are receptive to alerts, you will have a highly effective security event alarming system. It is not at all uncommon for a breach to be detected because a user noticed someone he'd never seen before accessing a service; if that information gets back to you, and you can classify the event, it's a more effective approach than any network or host-based IDS.

A second order effect is even more profound: People start working with the system to get their job done, instead of working around it. Your employees are probably very clever when it comes to getting what they want. Security is generally inconvenient, so employees often try to bypass security to get their jobs done, and that can lead to headaches and vulnerabilities. Get them to work with you, having patience if it takes a little longer to bring a service up or a little more work to gain access to a system, and the vulnerabilities won't occur. A similar effect occurs when you publish policy on acceptable use, and then start providing feedback through technical controls like firewall filtering or an IDS deployment. Provide guidance, and demonstrate that the company takes this seriously, and people start complying with acceptable use guidelines, which will reduce overall maintenance costs dramatically.

Developing a Security Policy

Developing a security policy is the single most important step in security risk management. Security policy is the glue that binds the various efforts together. It provides the statement of goals and intent that the security infrastructure is designed to enforce. In many respects, it is better to have a policy and no firewall rather than firewall and no policy. With policy, you can know what it is you need to do, and take the necessary steps to ensure your goals are achieved. Without policy, any control you deploy will be hit or miss, and there is no guarantee you will achieve your purpose. Because the fundamental issues of security come from control of the details, your overall security is probably weakened.

All sites have some policy, of course. If nothing is written down, then the policy exists in the consensual cultural expectation. People probably have some expectations: That their PC will turn on in the morning, that they can access their e-mail without it being distributed to competitors, that the file they were working on yesterday will still be there and contain the same information when they closed the application. Sometimes policy can be inferred: For example, many sites adopt an "arbitrary network traffic can go out; only a specified set of traffic—mail to the mail server, Web clients to the public Web server can go in as a default information flow-control policy. Most people understand and accept the principle of least permission, and these are probably in the informal policy.

Documentation is important, however. People need guidance on how to handle the information, services, and equipment around them. Is it acceptable to load games on the office PC? Allowing uncontrolled applications runs the risk of a potential loss of system integrity. Many sites discourage such behavior, but then allow it on field worker laptops as an acceptable compromise when it comes to security, utility, and morale. Is it acceptable to receive personal e-mail on your corporate account? Allowing such things runs the risk of increased network utilization, and the transport of Trojans into the corporate network, but at the same time encourages increased literacy and raises morale. Policy needs to be written down so consensual policy can be made clear to all members of the community. Likewise, managers ideally need to make trade-offs to ensure due protection of corporate assets while optimizing worker efficiency.

Policy does not need to be overly complex. Indeed, it's best to make policy short. A policy framework can establish the overall guidelines—to borrow a Judeo-Christian metaphor: The Ten Commandments of security might be better than the security Bible. Most people only need those Ten Commandments. Where necessary, there can be a security Bible, which provides more detailed guidance, and provides documentation on security control configuration or security architecture strategies, but policy, at its best, should be holistically integrated into the people, processes, and technology that provides secure business information flow.

Summary

A professional network administrator or security officer makes plans for their security architecture. Effective planning requires an assessment of the risks. Two types of risk assessment are: quantitative, where hard numbers are developed to identify annual loss expectations and return on security investment; and qualitative, where relative values rank the importance of various threats, vulnerabilities, and controls for planning purposes. Because of the difficulty of the former, the latter is usually followed.

Threats are the actors or programs that may do harm to your network. Harm usually flows from a breakdown in CIA—confidentiality, integrity, and assurance. Loss of confidentiality is often the most serious type of harm: losing control over proprietary or third-party data hurts everyone involved, and can lead to the demise of the company. Loss of integrity is perhaps the most insidious harm: often the most difficult to detect, it means you can't trust your own data. Loss of availability is the most visible kind of harm: not everyone understands how bad things are if a credit card number is lost or a spreadsheet is altered, but if you can't get to your e-mail, it has a personal impact.

Sources of threats come from many categories. A good way to classify threats is via Skills, Knowledge, Resources, Authority, and Motive, which is also known as SKRAM. Examples of threat models are "script kiddies," disgruntled system administrators, dedicated cyber-criminals, foreign intelligences, and even automated programs that attack without human intervention.

A particular example of the latter is malicious mobile code. This is a special case of malicious code, or malware, that can spread across network boundaries to harm your assets. Malicious mobile code is usually broken into one of three types: Trojan horses, viruses, and worms. A Trojan horse is a piece of code that appears to do one thing, but actually has an unsuspected and inappropriate secondary function. A computer virus is a piece of code that is less than a program, but can attach itself to a program to turn it into a Trojan horse. A worm is a complete working program that can propel itself across a network, producing copies and potentially using computer resources destructively. Trojan horses and worms have been responsible for some dramatic losses over the past years, from the Great Worm that caused the Internet to crash in 1988, to Melissa that shut down many e-mail systems in 1999, to modern plagues like Nimda which appear to have permanently polluted port 80 across the Internet.

The threat associated with malicious mobile code is very high. Rule number one of Microsoft's *Ten Immutable Laws of Security* states: If a bad guy can persuade you to run his program on your computer, it's not your computer anymore." This is the integrity that malicious code violates.

Currently, while Trojan horses can be tamed by effective user training, worms must be defended through network means. They can be classified by intelligent worms that are either data-driven (using intelligence inherited from the host configuration) or state-driven (using activity provided by the host). Unintelligent worms simply reproduce through search strategies. Currently, the most widespread technique is the unintelligent worm.

Denial of service attacks, or DoS, are harm caused through loss of availability. Network denial of service attacks are based either on triggers, where a specific circumstance causes the end server to fail, or on floods, where the bulk nature of the communication causes the end server to fail. The target of the DoS can be a client application, a host service, or the entire system. Trigger attacks can have unexpected effects—for example, the Nimda worm caused trigger attacks on some Cisco infrastructure products, prompting instability and failure. Floods can affect a client (for example, an excessively large mail attachment causing a DoS on client mail downloads), a service (for instance, the CIFS Host Announcement Frame vulnerability that can cause Windows Domain Controllers to function poorly), or on a system and infrastructure (such as a smurf attack, which consumes all bandwidth heading toward a site). Floods are particularly difficult to address, as they often have no effective defense.

Of growing concern is the Distributed Denial of Service, or DDoS, attack. The chief problem is that a large number of unsophisticated users have placed their computers on the Internet, allowing unscrupulous attackers to take over their machine. These large numbers of machines can be used to harm networks or systems of networks in very simple ways—by launching DoS floods—and in such a fashion that the end site can not protect itself from the attack.

Any network exposed to an uncontrolled environment will eventually experience a systems compromise. System administrators should prepare to detect and address the breach of security. The first phase should be preparation, so that you find out about the compromise before the end user. Two common techniques are the use of file system integrity software and network traffic anomaly tools. File system integrity software takes a snapshot of the file system, in an efficient manner, and then periodically compares that snapshot against the current status to see what has changed. Network traffic anomaly tools scan traffic and attempt to identify evidence of a breach. System integrity software includes a new approach to host-based intrusion detection, detecting changes as they occur and potentially preventing those changes. Traffic anomaly tools include network intrusion detection systems, log analysis, and honeypots. The Cisco product, Cisco Secure Intrusion Detection System, is an example of a network IDS tool.

If you believe a breach has occurred, then you probably want to do more than just reformat the hard drives and start over. It is usually a good idea to produce a document analyzing the event, and you may also be asked to provide forensic evidence in support of legal action. The first thing to remember if forensics is required (or in most any event handling) is to take detailed and copious notes. The second is that if legal action is anticipated, preserve the evidence. This means carefully handling your notes to ensure they have not been tampered with. Physical evidence, meanwhile, should have the chain of custody preserved: original materials (not copies) should be kept in your possession and not tampered with until they can be placed into a secure storage facility.

After a breach has been detected, there are five steps you should take:

1. **Identification and Classification** Determine the extent and type of the breach.

2. **Containment** Prevent the breach from getting farther into your network.

3. **Eradication** Stop the source of the breach.

4. **Recovery** Return to a known good state.

5. **Follow-up** Use this as an opportunity to understand what went wrong and improve your security.

There are several things you can do to prevent some classes of attacks and reduce the likelihood of others. The easiest step is to reduce the number of vulnerabilities present on your network. This is an ongoing process, due to the continually changing status of software. Ongoing automated vulnerability assessment is an effective tool. The Cisco Secure Scanner (NetSonar) is an effective tool, in conjunction with a vulnerability remediation tracking program, so you can ensure that problems are fixed over time.

The next easiest step is to provide a simple security network architecture, meaning an environment with as few interactions as possible. This is an extension of the security principle of least privilege. Reduce complexity in the number of possible interactions between devices, and you improve control over the network. Provide compartmentalization, so that if something goes wrong, the problem is limited in scope, and controls are put in place to protect critical portions of your network.

A third step is to develop a culture of security. Get users on your side and you will have fewer incidents and more support. The final recommended step is to ensure that policy is developed, kept current, and disseminated to the users to ensure that security people, policy, and technologies at a site are kept consistent and work together.

Solutions Fast Track

What Threats Face Your Network?

☑ The sources of harm are related to the goals of information security: loss of confidentiality, loss of integrity, and loss of availability. Loss of confidentiality is serious and has destroyed companies. Loss of integrity is insidious, and makes your data untrustworthy. Loss of availability has a high visibility among the user community.

☑ There are a wide variety of sources that threats can come from. A good way to classify them is Skills, Knowledge, Resources, Authority, and Motives.

☑ Several kinds of threats include:

- **Script kiddies** Low skills but high resources, with a motive for chaos.

- **Disgruntled system administrators** Large knowledge base due to a position of high authority; motive is revenge.

- **Worms** Similar to script kiddies, but on a potentially wider scale.

- **Organized crime rings** High skills, motive is financial gain.

- **Automated crime** High skills, knowledge; motive is financial gain.

Malicious Mobile Code

☑ Malicious mobile code is usually classified as one of three types: Trojan horse, virus, or worm.

☑ A Trojan horse is a program that seems to do one thing, while performing another unexpected action. Users are notorious for not listening to the advice of system administrators to be on the lookout for Trojan horses.

☑ A virus is a fragment of a computer code that inserts itself into a normal program, turning it into a Trojan horse. At one time, viruses were the most frequent vector for malicious code; today worms and Trojan horses are much more common.

☑ A worm is a complete program that self-replicates over network resources. There is a risk that worms may reproduce so fast that conventional defenses may prove inadequate.

☑ Malicious code is a real and present danger. The fundamental problem is that uncontrolled code is running on your computer. As Microsoft puts it, "If a bad guy can persuade you to run his program on your computer, it's not your computer anymore."

☑ Worms can be classified into intelligent and unintelligent types. Slightly different defensive techniques are used to tame these different classes of worms.

Denial of Service

☑ Denial of service (DoS) attacks are direct attacks on system availability. They fall into two basic types: triggers, which require only a limited amount of traffic to cause a target to fail, and floods, in which the sheer amount of communication prompts failure.

☑ Targets of DoS include client, service, and host(s). An example of a client DoS would be a Web browser open loop, causing the browser to open windows indefinitely until resources were exhausted. An example of a service DoS would be Nimda's attack on Cisco's CallManager product, in which management was unavailable until the system was patched. An example of a host flood would be the massive ICMP floods perpetrated on commercial servers during February of 2001.

☑ Two DoS attacks of particular importance are the smurf attack and the TCP SYN flood attack. You can help protect yourself and others against smurf by removing directed broadcasts from all interfaces. You can protect others and be a good Internet citizen by enforcing antispoofing criteria, as recommended in RFC 2267.

☑ An extension of DoS is the distributed DoS. This occurs when an unscrupulous attacker compromises many individual hosts, called zombies, and then uses those zombies to attack a central target. This is a particularly destructive attack, since all of the zombies have to be addressed before the situation is returned to normal.

Detecting Breaches

☑ Every system will experience breaches. It is a good idea to be prepared and deploy detection software before the breach occurs so you can find it before your users do.

☑ Two types of controls exist: host-based, such as file system integrity; and network-based, such as IDS, log analysis, and honeypots. Cisco has an effective host-based product, manufactured by Entercept, as well as an effective network-based product, the Cisco Secure Intrusion Detection System (IDS).

☑ After detection, an important consideration is forensics. In all cases, take careful notes. If you are going to collect evidence for legal action, be sure to preserve the chain of evidence.

☑ The next steps vary slightly from site to site, but are generally: identification and classification, to determine the nature of the event; containment, to limit the damage; eradication, to eliminate the cause; recovery, to provide event normalization; and follow-up, to find lessons in the event.

Preventing Attacks

☑ The four recommended steps to prevent attacks are: reduce vulnerabilities, provide a simple security network architecture, develop a culture of security, and develop security policy.

☑ Reducing vulnerabilities can be achieved by automated vulnerability programs. The Cisco Secure Scanner (NetSonar) is an effective tool in identifying vulnerabilities. This should be combined with a security event management program to ensure that vulnerabilities are tracked and resolved over time.

☑ A simple network architecture provides heightened control over the network. This reduces the number of vulnerabilities by reducing the complexity of system interactions, and allows for compartmentalization of the site.

☑ A culture of security can enhance your environment in many ways. Getting people on your side will allow them to help support the security environment through shared effort. In addition, people working with the system instead of working around it will mean fewer security exceptions. People will start complying with acceptable use guidelines, which reduces overall maintenance costs dramatically.

☑ All sites have a policy—even if not written down, sites have a way of doing business. Documenting the policy allows for improved planning, clear communications of intent, and thoughtful management guidance to preserve corporate assets and make efficient decisions about corporate culture and worker efficiency.

Frequently Asked Questions

The following Frequently Asked Questions, answered by the authors of this book, are designed to both measure your understanding of the concepts presented in this chapter and to assist you with real-life implementation of these concepts. To have your questions about this chapter answered by the author, browse to **www.syngress.com/solutions** and click on the **"Ask the Author"** form.

Q: I've got antivirus software. Am I safe from malicious code?

A: Not completely. It certainly helps, since many pieces of code circulate over time, and the antivirus software will detect it. You do have to ensure your antivirus software is current, with current signatures, and that it is integrated with your mail client so it prevents the launch of a Trojan horse before clicking it. However, antivirus software won't protect you from flaws in your software—you need to patch your code to current vendor recommended standards. Even then, there is a window of vulnerability in which you might be affected.

Q: Does "virus" mean all of these things, worms and Trojan horses included?

A: The language is flexible, and antivirus software makers provide protection against the three types of malware, so it is natural that their name is associated with all three. However, the mechanisms for infection are different, and the best ways to protect against the codes are different. Because of this, security professionals tend to use the more specific names where possible.

Q: How can I protect against denial of service floods?

A: You can't, completely. If the packet is already crossing your WAN link and saturating it, then blocking it at your perimeter router won't help. Your best protection is a good relationship with your upstream, so they can block it at their routers, and leave your link free for traffic. They can apply specific blocks, or rate limiting techniques to ensure your traffic will continue to flow. Multihoming is also often a good idea, since sometimes you can control the inbound flow of traffic through BGP announcements or the like, and it gives you another tool in combating the flood.

Q: Is a vulnerability assessment program expensive?

A: Not necessarily. The Cisco product is not terribly expensive, and there exist open source solutions which are free to use. The actual assessment program is probably less expensive than the remediation efforts: maintaining all your hosts on an ongoing basis is a steep maintenance requirement, and one that not all enterprises have accepted. But ever since the summer of 2001, there has been clear evidence that you have to manage your hosts and keep their patch levels up-to-date just to stay in business.

Q: Should I use an IDS?

A: Only by sitting down with your security policy can you identify the necessary controls. However, it is worth noting that according to CSI/FBI statistics, about two thirds of all sites have IDSs in place, with another 10 percent due to be installed this year. Market statistics show that IDS products are among the top sellers, and external mandates such as HIPAA and Presidential Decision Directive 63 should provide even more drivers. Another observation is that IDSs are not yet well integrated into the enterprise: only limited traffic is exposed to IDSs, and IDS event management is generally not well operationalized. However, market forces and the effectiveness of an IDS as a tool will lead to improved devices in the near future.

Chapter 3

Cisco PIX Firewall

Solutions in this chapter:

- Overview of the Security Features
- Initial Configuration
- The Command-Line Interface
- Configuring NAT and PAT
- Security Policy Configuration
- PIX Configuration Examples
- Securing and Maintaining the PIX

- ☑ Summary
- ☑ Solutions Fast Track
- ☑ Frequently Asked Questions

Introduction

A firewall can be described as a security mechanism located on a network that protects resources from other networks and individuals. It controls access to a network and enforces a security policy that can be tailored to suit the needs of a company.

There is some confusion on what the difference is between a Cisco PIX firewall and a router. Both devices are capable of filtering traffic with access control lists, and both devices are capable of providing Network Address Translation. PIX go above and beyond simply filtering packets, based on source/destination IP addresses, as well as source/destination TCP/UDP port numbers. PIX are a dedicated hardware device built to provide security. Although a router can also provide some of the functions of a PIX by implementing access control lists, it also has to deal with routing packets from one network to another. Depending on what model of router is being used, access lists tend to burden the CPU, especially if there are numerous access lists that must be referenced for every packet that travels through the router. This can impact the performance of the router, causing other problems such as network convergence time. A router is also unable to provide security features such as URL, ActiveX, and Java filtering, Flood Defender, Flood Guard, and IP Frag Guard, DNS Guard, Mail Guard, Failover, and FTP and URL logging.

Cisco Systems offer a number of security solutions for networks. Included in those solutions are the Cisco Secure PIX Firewall series. The PIX firewall is a dedicated hardware-based firewall that utilizes a version of the Cisco IOS for configuration and operation. This chapter will introduce and discuss security features, Network Address Translation (NAT), Network Address Port Translation (NAPT, referred to as PAT on the PIX firewall IOS), developing a security policy for your network, applying the security policy on the PIX and finally, maintaining your PIX and securing it from unauthorized individuals.

The PIX Firewall series offers several models to meet the needs of networks today. These range from the Enterprise class Secure PIX 535 Firewall to the newly introduced Small Office/Home Office (SOHO) class Secure PIX 501 Firewall model. A specification and description chart is shown in Table 3.1 that follows.

- **Cisco PIX 535 Firewall** Intended for large enterprise and service provider environments. It will provide over 1 Gbps of firewall throughput with the ability to handle up to 500,000 simultaneous connections. Some PIX 535 models include stateful high-availability capabilities, as well as integrated hardware acceleration for VPNs. This provides up to 95 Mbps of 3DES VPN and support for 2,000 IPSec tunnels. The Cisco PIX 535 provides a modular chassis with support for up to ten 10/100 Fast Ethernet interfaces or nine Gigabit Ethernet interfaces.

- **Cisco PIX 525 Firewall** Intended for large enterprise and service provider environments. It will provide over 360 Mbps of firewall throughput with the ability to handle as many as 280,000 simultaneous sessions. Some PIX 525 models include stateful high-availability capabilities, as well as integrated hardware acceleration for VPN. This will provide up to 70 Mbps of 3DES VPN and support for 2,000 IPSec tunnels. The PIX 525 provides a modular chassis with support for up to eight 10/100 Fast Ethernet interfaces or three Gigabit Ethernet interfaces.

- **Cisco PIX 515E Firewall** Intended for small-to-medium business and enterprise environments. It will provide up to 188 Mbps of firewall throughput with the ability to handle as many as 125,000 simultaneous sessions. Many PIX 515E models include stateful high-availability capabilities, as well as integrated support for 2,000 IPSec tunnels. The PIX 515E provides a modular chassis with support for up to six 10/100 Fast Ethernet interfaces.

- **Cisco PIX 506E Firewall** Intended for remote office/branch office environments. These PIX will provide up to 20 Mbps of firewall throughput and 16 Mbps of 3DES VPN throughput. The PIX 506E uses a compact, desktop chassis and provides two auto-sensing 10Base-T interfaces.

- **Cisco PIX 501 Firewall** Intended for small office and enterprise teleworker environments. These PIX will provide up to 10 Mbps of firewall throughput and 3 Mbps of 3DES VPN throughput. The PIX 501 delivers great security in a compact security appliance. It includes an integrated four-port Fast Ethernet (10/100) switch and one 10Base-T interface.

Table 3.1 Specifications for Cisco PIX Firewalls

Description	PIX 501	PIX 506	PIX 515	PIX 525	PIX 535
Processor	133MHz	200MHz	200MHz	350MHz	1GHz
RAM	16MB	32MB	32MB or 64MB	128MB or 256MB	512MB or 1GB

Continued

Table 3.1 Continued

Description	PIX 501	PIX 506	PIX 515	PIX 525	PIX 535
Flash Memory	8MB	8MB	16MB	16MB	16MB
PCI Slots	None	None	2	3	9
Fixed Interfaces	One 10BaseT Ethernet, four-port 10/100 switch	Two 10BaseT Ethernet	Two 10/100 Fast Ethernet	Two 10/100 Fast Ethernet	None
Max Interfaces	One 10BaseT Ethernet, four-port 10/100 switch	Two 10BaseT Ethernet	Six 10/100 Fast Ethernet or Gigabit Ethernet	Eight 10/100 Fast Ethernet or Gigabit Ethernet	Ten 10/100 Fast Ethernet
VPN Accelerator Card	No	No	Yes	Yes	Yes
Failover Support	No	No	Yes; UNRE-STRICTED only	Yes; UNRE-STRICTED only	Yes; UNRE-STRICTED only
Rack Mountable	No	No	Yes	Yes	Yes
Size	Desktop	Desktop	One RU	Two RU	Three RU

Overview of the Security Features

With the enormous growth of the Internet, companies are beginning to depend on having an online presence on the Internet. With that presence, there will be security risks that allow outside individuals to gain access to critical information and resources.

Companies are now faced with the task of implementing security measures to protect their data and resources. The resources to protect can be much diversified, such as Web servers, mail Servers, FTP servers, databases, or any type of networked devices. Figure 3.1 displays a typical company network with access to the Internet via a leased line without a firewall in place.

Figure 3.1 A Typical LAN with no Firewall

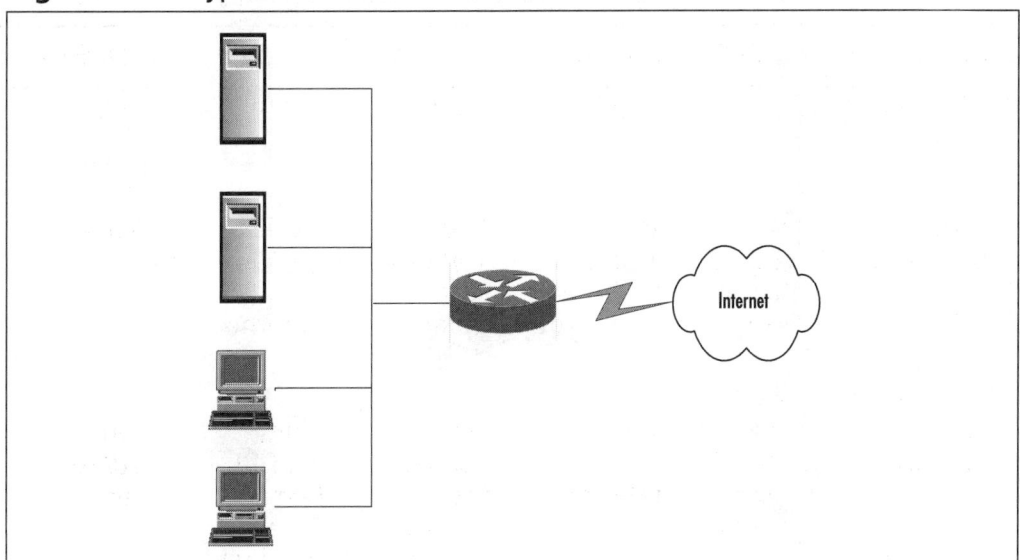

As you can see in Figure 3.1, company XYZ has a direct connection to the Internet. They are also using a class C public IP address space for their network, therefore making it publicly available to anyone who wishes to access it. Without any security measures, individuals are able to access each of the devices on the network with a public IP. Private information can be compromised, while malicious strikes such as denial of service (DoS) attacks may be launched against the company. If a firewall was placed between company XYZ's network and the Internet, security measures could be taken to filter and block unwanted traffic. Without access control at the network perimeter, a company's security relies on the proper configuration and security of each individual host and server. This can be an administrative nightmare if hundreds of devices need to be configured for this purpose.

Routers have the ability to filter traffic based on source address, destination address, and TCP/UDP ports. Using this ability as well as a firewall can provide a more complete security solution for a network.

Another example of how a PIX firewall can secure a network is in a company's intranet. Figure 3.2 illustrates a network in which departments are separated by two different subnets. What is stopping an individual in the Human Resources network from accessing resources on the Finance network? A firewall can be put in place between the two subnets to secure the Finance network from any unauthorized access, or restrict access to certain hosts.

Figure 3.2 A LAN Segmented by a Department with no Firewall

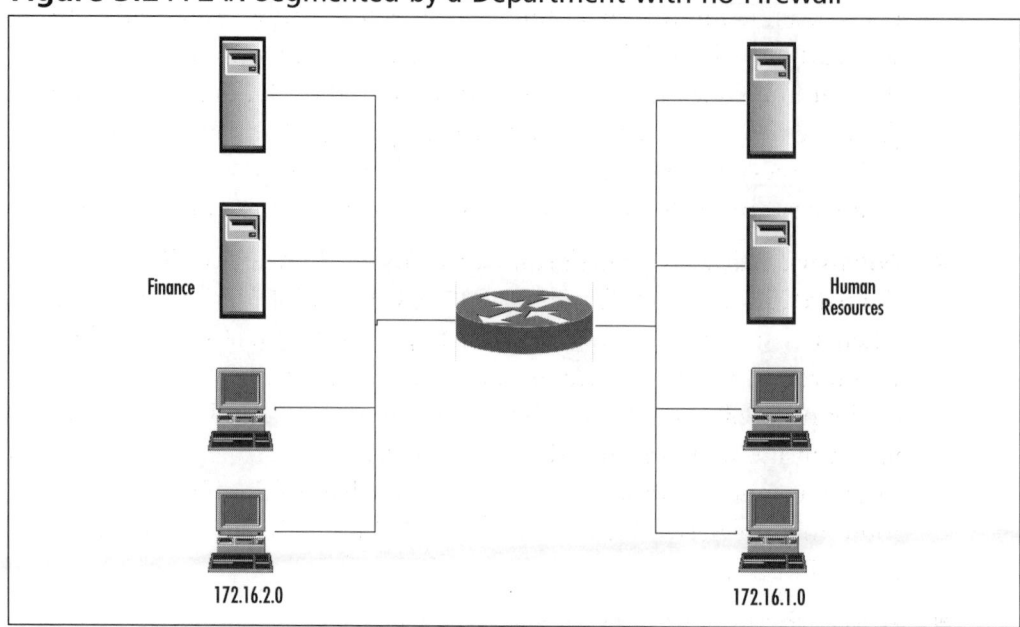

Since the PIX are designed as a security appliance, it provides a wealth of features to secure a network. These features include:

- **Packet filtering** A method for limiting inbound information from the Internet. Packet filters employ access control lists (ACL) similar to those used in routers to accept or deny access based on packet source address, destination address, and TCP/UDP sources and destination ports.

- **Proxy Server** A device that examines higher layers of the Open System Interconnection (OSI) model. This will act as an intermediary between the source and destination by creating a separate connection to each. Optionally, authentication can be achieved by requiring users to authenticate with a secure system by means of a proxy such as a Cisco IOS Firewall Authentication Proxy Server. Some of the drawbacks for this method of security are that it provides authentication at the cost of performance, and a proxy only supports a limited number of protocols.

- **Stateful Filtering** A secure method of analyzing packets and placing extensive information about that packet in a table. Each time a TCP connection is established from an inside host accessing an outside host through the PIX firewall, the information about the connection is automatically logged in a stateful session flow table. The table contains the source and destination addresses, port numbers, TCP sequencing information, and additional flags for each TCP connection associated with that particular host. Inbound packets are compared against the session flows in the table and are permitted through the PIX only if an appropriate connection exists to validate their passage. Without stateful filtering, access lists would have to be configured to allow traffic originating from the inside network to return from the outside network.

- **Network Address Translation and Network Address Port Translation** Another feature of the PIX. Usage of NAT is often mistaken as a security measure. Translating private IP addresses into global IP addresses was implemented to assist in the problem of rapidly depleting public IP addresses. Even though private IP addresses are used for an inside network, an ISP is still directly connected. It is not unheard of that a sloppy routing configuration on behalf of the ISP will leak a route to your network to other clients. NAT will hide your network, but it should not be relied upon as a security measure.

- **IPSec** Provides VPN (Virtual Private Network) access via digital certificates or preshared keys.

- **Flood Defender, Flood Guard, and IP Frag Guard** Features used to protect a network from TCP SYN flood attacks, controlling the AAA service's tolerance for unanswered login attempts, and IP fragmentation attacks.

- **DNS Guard** Identifies an outbound DNS resolve request, and only allows a single DNS response.

- **FTP and URL Logging** Allows you to view inbound and outbound FTP commands entered by users, as well as the URLs they use to access other sites.

- **Mail Guard** Provides safe access for SMTP (Simple Mail Transfer Protocol) connections from the outside to an inside e-mail server.

- **ActiveX Blocking** Blocks HTML *object* commands and comments them out of the HTML Web page.

- **Java Filtering** Allows an administrator to prevent Java applets from being downloaded by a host on the inside network.

- **URL Filtering** When used with NetPartners WebSENSE product, PIX checks outgoing URL requests with policy defined on the WebSENSE server, which runs on either Windows NT/2000 or Unix.

- **AAA** Provides authentication, authorization, and accounting with the aid of an AAA server such as a RADIUS or TACACS+ server.

Differences between PIX OS Version 4.x and Version 5.x

The following describes new features available in the recent release of the PIX OS:

- Cisco IOS Access Lists

- IPSec

- Stateful Failover

- Voice over IP (VoIP) Support

Cisco IOS access lists can now be specified in support of the IPSec feature. In addition, access lists can now be used to specify the type of traffic permitted through the PIX in conjunction with the *access-group* command. PIX OS 4.x used *conduit* and *outbound* statements to limit the type of traffic permitted through the interface. For example, the following command set can be rewritten using *access-list* and *access-group* statements.

```
pixfirewall(config)#write terminal
static (inside,outside) 207.139.221.10 192.168.0.10 netmask
    >255.255.255.255
```

Creates a static translation for private 192.168.0.10 to globally unique IP 207.139.221.10.

```
conduit permit tcp any host 207.139.221.10 eq www
```

Specifies that only HTTP traffic will be permitted to reach host 207.139.221.10.

```
outbound 10 permit any any 80 tcp
outbound 10 permit any any 23 tcp
outbound 10 deny any any any tcp
outbound 10 deny any any any udp
```

Specifies that HTTP and Telnet traffic will be permitted from a higher-level security interface to a lower-level security interface (inside, outside), followed by an explicit *deny all* statement.

```
apply (inside) 10 outgoing_src
```

Applies outbound list 10 to an inside interface. This configuration can be rewritten using *access-list* and *access-group* commands available in 5.x PIX OS.

```
pixfirewall(config)#write terminal
static (inside,outside) 207.139.221.10 192.168.0.10 netmask
   >255.255.255.255
```

This creates a static translation for private 192.168.0.10 to a globally unique IP 207.139.221.10.

```
access-list acl_out permit tcp any any eq www
access-list acl_out permit tcp any any eq telnet
access-list acl_out deny tcp any any
access-list acl_out deny udp any any
```

This specifies that HTTP and Telnet traffic will be permitted, followed by an explicit *deny all* statement:

```
access-list acl_in permit tcp any host 207.139.221.10 eq www
access-list acl_in permit tcp any host 207.139.221.10 eq ftp
```

This specifies that HTTP and FTP traffic will be permitted from any source to host 207.139.221.10.

```
access-group acl_out in interface inside
```

This applies access list *acl_out* to the inside interface.

```
access-group acl_in in interface outside
```

This applies access list acl_in to the outside interface.

The purpose of using the *access-list* and *access-group* commands instead of the *outbound* and *conduit* statements is to provide a common operating environment across various platforms. If an individual is able to implement access lists on a router, then implementing access lists on PIX should be no different.

The IPSec feature is based on the Cisco IOS IPSec implementation and provides functionality with those IPSec-compliant devices. IPSec offers a mechanism for secure data transmission by providing confidentiality, integrity, and authenticity of data across a public IP network. Refer to Chapter 8 for more information on IPSec.

The Stateful Failover feature provides a mechanism for hardware and software redundancy by allowing two identical PIX units to serve the same functionality in case one fails in an unattended environment. One PIX is considered an active unit while the other is in standby mode. In the event the active unit fails, the standby unit will become active, therefore providing redundancy.

PIX provides support for VoIP in its H.323 RAS feature—however, Cisco CallManager is not supported. For more information on VoIP, please refer to Cisco's Web site (www.cisco.com).

Other new commands introduced in the PIX 5.x OS are as follows:

- **ca** Provides access to the IPSec certification authority feature.

- **Clear flashfs** Clears Flash memory. Use before downgrading to any version 4.x release.

- **Crypto-map** Provides IPSec cryptography mapping.

- **Debug crypto ca** Debugs Certification Authority (CA) processing.

- **Debug crypto ipsec** Debugs IPSec processing.

- **Debug crypto isakmp** Debugs ISAKMP processing.

- **Domain-name** Changes the domain name.

- **Failover link** Enables Stateful Failover support.

- **ipsec** Shortened form of the *crypto ipsec* command.

- **Isakmp** Lets you create an IKE security association.

- **Sysopt connection permit-ipsec** Specifies that the PIX implicitly permit IPSec traffic and bypass the checking of the *conduit* or *access-group* commands associated with IPSec connections.

Differences between PIX OS Version 6.0 and Version 5.x

The newest version of Cisco PIX OS is Version 6.0. This version delivers the latest PIX capabilities and security improvements as well as some new features. The following is a list of new features for 6.0:

- PIX Device Manager

- VPN Client v3.x

- CPU Utilization Statistics

- Dynamic Shunning with the Cisco Intrusion Detection System

- Port Address Translations

- Skinny Protocol Support

- Session Initiation Protocol

- Stateful Sharing of HTTP (port 80) Sessions

- Ethernet Interfaces

Each of these new features are discussed in greater detail in the following sections.

Cisco PIX Device Manager

The Cisco PIX Device Manager is a Web browser-based configuration tool that enables you to set up, configure, and monitor your PIX firewall graphically over the Web browser—all without requiring any real knowledge of the command-line interface of the PIX firewall.

VPN Client v3.x

The Cisco VPN Client enables customers to establish secure end-to-end encrypted tunnels. The client can be preconfigured for deployment, and initial logins require very little user help. VPN access policies and configurations are downloaded from the PIX and pushed to the client when a connection is established, allowing simple setup and manageability.

CPU Utilization Statistics

The ability to monitor the CPU load on the PIX firewall has been added to version 6.0. The *show* command and PIX Device Manager can monitor and obtain five-second to five-minute CPU utilization statistics.

Dynamic Shunning with Cisco Intrusion Detection System

This feature allows PIX, when combined with a Cisco Intrusion Detection System Sensor, to dynamically respond to an attacking host by preventing new connections and disallowing packets from any existing connection. A Cisco

Intrusion Detection System device instructs the PIX firewall to shun sources of traffic when those sources of traffic are determined to be malicious by rule. The *shun* command applies a "blocking function" to the interface receiving the attack for a defined period of time by the user. Packets containing the IP source address of the attacking host are dropped and logged until the blocking function is removed by the Cisco Intrusion Detection System. No traffic from that IP source address will be allowed to traverse to the PIX firewall; also, any remaining connections time out. The *shun* command is applied whether or not a connection with the specified host IP address is currently active.

Port Address Translations

The PIX firewall now provides static Port Address Translation capability, enabling you to send multiple inbound TCP or UDP services to different internal hosts through a single global IP address. The global IP address can be a unique address or a shared outbound Port Address Translation.

Skinny Protocol Support

Cisco Secure PIX Firewall application handling has been enhanced to support the Skinny Client Control Protocol used by Cisco IP phones for VoIP call signaling. This capability dynamically opens pinholes for media sessions and Network Address Translation embedded IP addresses. Skinny Client Control Protocol supports IP telephony and can reside in an H.323 environment. An application layer ensures that all Skinny Client Control Protocol signaling and media packets can traverse the PIX firewall and interoperate with H.323 terminals.

Session Initiation Protocol

Session Initiation Protocol as defined by the Internet Engineering Task Force enables call handling sessions, particularly two-party audio conferences. Session Initiation Protocol works with Session Description Protocol, which defines the calls prior to call handling. Using Session Initiation Protocol, the PIX firewall can support VoIP and any proxy server using VoIP.

Stateful Sharing of HTTP (port 80) Sessions

The PIX firewall supports high-availability with the deployment of a redundant hot standby unit. This failover option maintains concurrent connections through automatic stateful synchronization. This ensures that even in the event of a system failure, sessions are maintained, and the transition is completely transparent to network users. PIX Firewall version 6.0 adds the ability to maintain HTTP (port 80) sessions.

Ethernet Interfaces

The PIX Firewall series supports single or four-port 10/100 Fast Ethernet, as well as Gigabit Ethernet network interface cards. The PIX 6.0 on PIX Firewall 535 with an unrestricted license may support up to ten Ethernet interfaces. Restricted licenses can support up to eight interfaces.

Initial Configuration

The initial configuration of the Secure PIX Firewall greatly resembles that of a router. A console cable kit consisting of a rollover cable and DB9/DB25 serial adapter is needed to configure the device out of the box. It is recommended that the initial configuration not take place on a live network until the initial setup has been completed and tested. Initial configuration should take place in a test bed environment, which is isolated from any production network. If initial configuration takes place on a production network and an incorrect IP address that is already in use on the network is assigned to an interface on the PIX, IP address conflicts will occur. It is generally a bad idea to set up a firewall or other security device on a non-isolated network. The default configuration is often not secure and can be compromised between the setup stage and security policy stage. Installing the PIX consists of removing the unit from the packaging, installing any optional hardware, such as an additional NIC, mounting the PIX in a rack (optional), and connecting all the necessary cables such as power and network cables. Once the hardware portion of the PIX setup has been completed, the software portion of the setup can begin.

Before configuring the software, be sure to have a design plan already in place. Items such as IP addresses, security policies, and placement of the PIX should already be mapped out. With a proper design strategy, the basic configuration will only have to be done once to make the PIX functional.

Installing the PIX Software

In this section, we will discuss the initial software configuration of the PIX to allow traffic to pass through it. Other features such as configuring NAT, PAT, and security policies will be covered later in this chapter.

When the PIX is first powered on, the software configuration stored in Flash memory permits the PIX to start up, but will not allow any traffic to pass through it until configured to do so. Newer versions of the PIX OS may be available from Cisco depending on what version shipped with the PIX, so it may be a good idea to complete the basic configuration to establish connectivity and then upgrade the version of the PIX OS.

Connecting to the PIX—Basic Configuration

In order to upgrade the IOS or begin allowing traffic to pass through the PIX, some basic configuration is needed to make the PIX operational.

1. Connect the serial port of your PC to the console port on the PIX firewall with the serial cable supplied with the PIX.

2. Using a Terminal Emulation program such as HyperTerminal, connect to the COM port on the PC.

NOTE

Make sure the COM port properties in the terminal emulation program match the following values:

- 9600 baud
- 8 data bits
- No parity
- 1 stop bit
- Hardware flow control

---

3. Turn on the PIX.

4. Once the PIX has finished booting up, the following prompt will appear:

   ```
   pixfirewall>
   ```

5. Type **enable** and press the **Enter** key. The following prompt appears:

   ```
   Password:
   ```

6. Press the **Enter** key again and you will now be in privileged mode, which is represented by the following prompt:

   ```
   pixfirewall#
   ```

7. Set an enable password by going into configuration mode. A strong, non-guessable password should be chosen. The example uses *<password>* to designate where your password should be typed:

```
pixfirewall#configure terminal
pixfirewall(config)#enable password <password>
```

8. Permit Telnet access to the console from the inside network:

```
pixfirewall(config)#telnet 0.0.0.0 0.0.0.0 inside
```

9. Set the Telnet console password. This password should be different from the enable password chosen in step 7.

```
pixfirewall(config)#passwd   <password>
```

10. Save your changes to your non-volatile RAM (NVRAM) with the *write* command:

```
pixfirewall(config)#write memory
```

NOTE

The configuration used in the following examples is based on IOS version 5.1(1).

Identify Each Interface

On new installations with only two interfaces, PIX will provide names for each interface, by default. These can be viewed with the *show nameif* command. The *show nameif* command output will resemble the following:

```
pixfirewall# show nameif
nameif ethernet0 outside security0
nameif ethernet1 inside security100
```

If additional NICs are going to be used, you must assign a unique name and security value to each additional interface.

The default behavior of the PIX includes blocking traffic originating from the *outside* interface destined for the *inside* interface. Traffic originating from the *inside* interface destined to the *outside* interface will be permitted until access lists are implemented to restrict traffic. The inside interface will be assigned a security value of 100 and the outside interface will be assigned a value of 0. These values are important when creating security policies in which traffic will flow from a lower security interface to a higher security level interface. If additional interfaces are added to the PIX, it is important to properly plan which interfaces will be used for what purposes. For example, in a situation where three interfaces are used to separate an inside network, outside network, and DMZ (Demilitarized Zone; discussed later in this chapter), assign the DMZ interface a security value between the inside and outside interfaces such as 50. This configuration will reflect the purpose of the DMZ, which is a network separated from the inside and outside networks, yet security can still be controlled with the PIX.

In order to assign a name to an interface, use:

Nameif hardware_id name security_level

- **Hardware_id** Either ethernet*n* for Ethernet, or token*x* for Token Ring interfaces where *n* and *x* are the interface numbers.
- **Name** The name to be assigned to the interface.
- **Security_level** A value such as security40 or security60. You can use any security value between 1 and 99.

  ```
  pixfirewall#configure terminal
  pixfirewall(config)#nameif ethernet2 dmz1 security40
  pixfirewall(config)#show nameif
  pixfirewall(config)#nameif ethernet0 outside security0
  pixfirewall(config)#nameif ethernet1 inside security100
  pixfirewall(config)#nameif ethernet2 dmz1 security40
  ```

NOTE

Be sure to use a naming convention that will easily describe the function of each interface. The dmz1 interface represents a "demilitarized zone" which is intended to be an area between the inside and outside networks. This is a common implementation for companies that host Web servers, mail servers, and other resources.

By default, each interface is in a shutdown state and must be made active. Use the *interface* command to activate the interfaces.

Interface hardware_id hardware_speed [**shutdown**]

- **Hardware_id** Either ethernet*n* for Ethernet, or token*x* for Token Ring interfaces where *n* and *x* are the interface numbers.

- **Hardware_speed** Either 4 Mpbs or 16 Mpbs for Token Ring, depending on the line speed of the Token Ring card. If the interface is Ethernet, use auto.

- **Auto** Activates auto-negotiation for the Ethernet 10/100 interface.

- **Shutdown** Disables the interface. When the PIX are configured for the first time, all interfaces will be shut down, by default.

The following examples will enable the *ethernet0* interface into auto-negotiation mode, and the Token Ring interface *token0* into 16 Mbps mode.

```
pixfirewall(config)#interface ethernet0 auto
pixfirewall(config)#interface token0 16mpbs
```

Installing the IOS over TFTP

The following steps will guide you through upgrading the PIX IOS.

1. Download the latest version of the IOS from Cisco's Web site (www.cisco.com).

2. Download and install the TFTP Server application which can also be found on Cisco's Web site. The TFTP server is an application installed on a host computer to provide a TFTP service. This service is used by the PIX firewall to download or upload software images and configuration parameters.

NOTE

You need to download the TFTP server software if you are using a Windows NT/2000 machine as a server. A Unix server has a TFTP server, by default.

3. Make sure the TFTP software is running on a server. Also confirm that the server is on the same subnet as one of the interfaces.

4. Once the connection to the PIX console port has been established, power on the PIX.

5. Immediately send a BREAK character by pressing the **Esc** key. The monitor prompt will appear.

6. Use the *address* command to specify an IP address on the interface in the same network where the TFTP resides.

7. Use the *server* command to specify the IP address of the TFTP server.

8. Use the *file* command to specify the name of the file to download from the TFTP server.

9. If the TFTP server resides on a different subnet then that of the PIX interface, use the *gateway* command to specify the IP address of the default gateway in order to reach the TFTP server.

10. In order to test connectivity, use the *ping* command to ping the TFTP server.

11. Finally, use the *TFTP* command to start the TFTP download of the IOS.

For example, assuming that the TFTP server has been configured with the IP address 172.16.0.39, and that a new software image file *pix512.bin* is stored on that server. We can download this new image on the PIX as follows:

```
monitor>
monitor>address 172.16.0.1
monitor>server 172.16.0.39
monitor>file pix512.bin
monitor>ping 172.16.0.39
Sending 5, 100-byte 0x5b8d ICMP Echoes to 172.16.0.39, timeout is 4
    seconds:
!!!!!
Success rate is 100 percent (5/5)
monitor>tftp
tftp pix512.bin@172.16.0.39
Received 626688 bytes

PIX admin loader (3.0) #0: Mon July 10 10:43:02 PDT 2000
Flash=AT29C040A @ 0x300
Flash version 4.9.9.1, Install version 5.1.2

Installing to flash
```

The following is a list of commands available while in monitor mode:

- **Address** Sets the IP address.

- **File** Specifies the boot file name.

- **Gateway** Sets the IP gateway IP address.

- **Help** Lists help messages.

- **Interface** Specifies the type of interface (Ethernet, Token Ring).

- **Ping** Tests connectivity by issuing echo-requests to specified IP addresses.

- **Help** Lists available commands and syntax.

- **Reload** Halts and reloads system.

- **Server** Specifies the server by IP address in which the TFTP application is running.

- **Tftp** Initiates the TFTP download.

- **Trace** Toggles packet tracing.

The Command-Line Interface

The command-line interface (CLI) used on the PIX is very similar to that used on routers. Three modes exist to perform configuration and troubleshooting steps. These three modes are:

- Unprivileged mode

- Privileged mode

- Configuration mode

When you first initiate a console or Telnet session to the PIX, you will be in user mode. Virtually no commands will be available in user mode. Only the *enable*, *pager*, and *quit* commands are permitted. Once in privileged mode, commands such as *show*, *debug*, and *reload* are available. From privileged mode, configuration tasks may take place by entering the *configure* command, followed by where the PIX will accept configuration commands from. For example, when you first connect to the PIX, either through a Telnet or console session, you will be in user mode (the user mode password must be entered when accessing the PIX by Telnet). User mode is represented by the following prompt:

```
Pixfirewall>
```

In order to access privileged mode, you must type **enable** at the prompt. After providing the required authentication, you will enter privileged mode. Privileged mode is represented by the following prompt:

```
Pixfurewall>enable
Password:  ********
Pixfirewall#
```

If the system did not request a password after typing **enable**, it means no enable password has been configured as described in the *Basic Configuration* section. It is very important that an enable password be configured.

Finally, in order to perform configuration tasks, you must be in configuration mode. This mode is represented by the following prompt:

```
Pixfurewall#configure terminal
Pixfirewall(config)#
```

Table 3.2 lists some of the shortcut key combinations available on the PIX CLI.

Table 3.2 Key Combination Shortcuts

Command	Result
TAB	Completes a command entry
Ctrl+A	Takes cursor to beginning of the line
Ctrl+E	Takes cursor to end of the line
Ctrl+R	Redisplays a line (useful if command gets interrupted by console output)
Arrow up or Ctrl+P	Displays previous line
Arrow up or Ctrl+n	Displays next line
Help or ?	Displays help

IP Configuration

Once the interfaces on the PIX have been named and assigned a security value (additional interfaces only), the IP must be configured on the interfaces in order to allow traffic to pass through the PIX.

IP Addresses

Once the interfaces have been named and are activated, an IP address needs to be assigned to them. To assign an IP address to an interface, use the command:

ip address interface-name netmask

To further explain:

- **Interface-name** The name assigned to the interface using the *nameif* command.

- **Netmask** The network mask assigned to the interface.

```
pixfirewall(config)#interface ethernet0 auto
pixfirewall(config)#interface ethernet1 auto
pixfirewall(config)#ip address inside 172.16.0.1 255.255.255.0
pixfirewall(config)#ip address outside 207.139.221.1 255.255.255.0
pixfirewall(config)#show interface ethernet1
interface ethernet1 "inside" is up, line protocol is up
  Hardware is i82559 ethernet, address is 0050.54ff.2aa9
  IP address 172.16.0.1, subnet mask 255.255.255.0
  MTU 1500 bytes, BW 100000 Kbit full duplex
        147022319 packets input, 3391299957 bytes, 0 no buffer
        Received 12580140 broadcasts, 0 runts, 0 giants
        0 input errors, 0 CRC, 0 frame, 0 overrun, 0 ignored, 0
abort
        166995559 packets output, 1686643683 bytes, 0 underruns
        0 output errors, 0 collisions, 0 interface resets
        0 babbles, 0 late collisions, 0 deferred
        0 lost carrier, 0 no carrier
```

Once the interfaces have been configured, test them to make sure they have been configured properly. A simple connectivity test is to ping another interface on your network or test lab environment. To do this:

Ping interface ip_address

In this case, the following is true:

- **Interface** The interface in which you want the ping to originate from (similar to an extended ping on a router).

- **Ip_address** The target IP address to ping.

```
pixfirewall#ping inside 172.16.0.2
        172.16.0.2 response received — 0ms
        172.16.0.2 response received — 0ms
        172.16.0.2 response received — 0ms
```

If no response is received, confirm that the network cables are connected to the interfaces and the interfaces have been configured correctly.

```
pixfirewall#ping inside 172.16.0.4
        172.16.0.4 NO response received — 940ms
        172.16.0.4 NO response received — 900ms
        172.16.0.4 NO response received — 920ms
```

Default Route

Now that all the interfaces have been configured, a default gateway must be assigned. A typical implementation will have a PIX firewall positioned between the ISP and company's networks (Figure 3.3).

Figure 3.3 Default Route

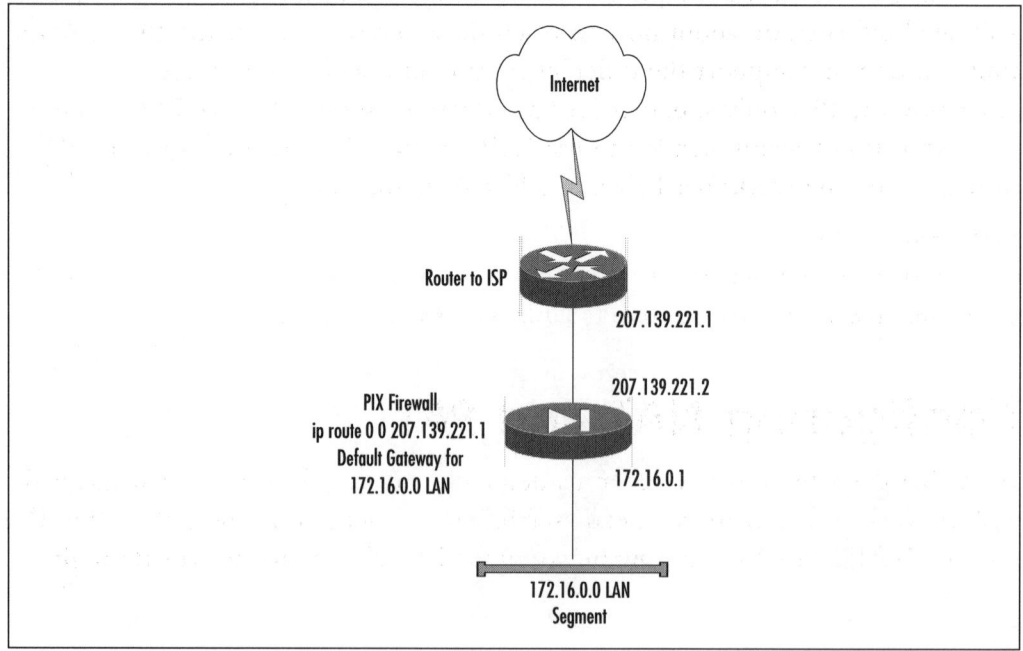

A default gateway must be assigned to the outside interface to allow traffic to reach the ISP. To do this, use the command:

route interface_name ip_address netmask gateway_ip [metric]

To further explain:

- **Interface_name** The internal or external network interface name.

- **Ip_address** ID of the internal or external IP address. Use **0.0.0.0** to specify a default route. The **0.0.0.0** can be abbreviated as **0**.

- **Netmask** Specifies a network mask to apply to *ip_address*. Use **0.0.0.0** to specify a default route. The **0.0.0.0** can be abbreviated as **0**.

- **Gateway_ip** The IP address of the gateway router (the next hop address for this route).

- **Metric** Specifies the number of hops to *gateway_ip*.

    ```
    pixfirewall>enable
    pixfirewall#configure terminal
    pixfirewall(config)#route outside 0 0 207.139.221.1
    ```

If different networks are present on the inside or outside interface, the PIX will need information about how to reach those networks. Since the PIX is not a router, it does not support the different routing protocols a router does. Currently, the PIX only supports RIP as its routing protocol. Since PIX it is not a router, it is not recommended to use RIP. Instead, add static routes to the PIX to make other networks reachable. To add a static route:

```
pixfirewall>enable
pixfirewall#configure terminal
pixfirewall(config)#route inside 192.168.1.0 255.255.255.0 172.16.0.2 1
```

Configuring NAT and PAT

Now that the interfaces have been named and security values have been assigned, and network connectivity has been established by configuring and testing the IP settings, NAT and PAT can now be configured to allow traffic to pass through.

Permit Traffic Through

When an outbound packet arrives at a higher security level interface (inside), the PIX checks the validity of the packet based on the Adaptive Security Algorithm (ASA), and then whether or not a previous packet has come from that host. If no packet has originated from that host, then the packet is for a new connection, and PIX will create a translation in its table for the connection.

The information that PIX stores in the translation table includes the inside IP address and a globally unique IP address assigned by the Network Address Translation, or Network Address Port Translation. The PIX then changes the packet's source IP address to the global address, modifies the checksum and other fields as required, and forwards the packet to the lower security interface (outside, or DMZ).

When an inbound packet arrives at a lower security level interface (outside, or DMZ), it must first pass the PIX Adaptive Security criteria. If the packet passes the security tests (static and Access Control Lists), the PIX removes the destination IP address, and the internal IP address is inserted in its place. The packet is then forwarded to the higher security level interface (inside). Figure 3.4 illustrates the NAT process on the PIX.

Figure 3.4 NAT Example

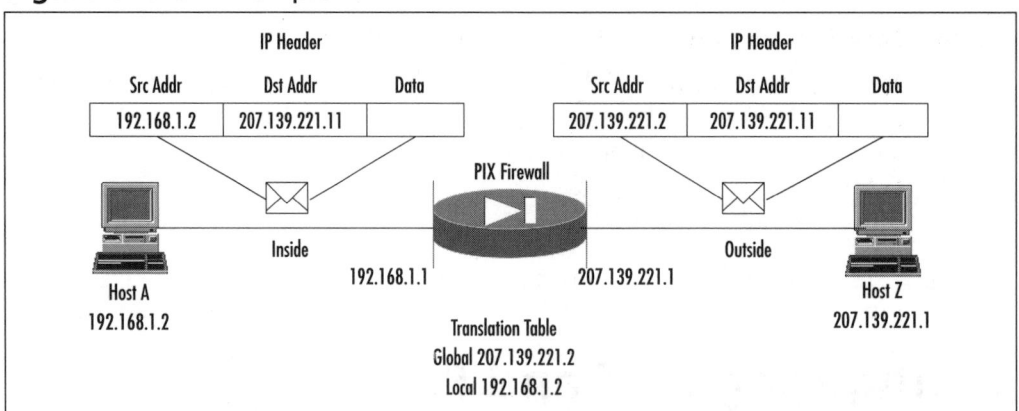

In the example, Host A initiates a session with Host Z. Since Host A is not on the same subnet as host Z, the packet must be routed. When the packet arrives at the inside interface of the PIX, it examines the Source address. NAT has been enabled on the PIX and a global pool of IP addresses has been allocated for translations. The PIX then modifies the IP header and alters the source address of the IP header to an IP address from the global pool of IP addresses. Once the translation occurs, the packet is then routed to Host Z. When Host Z replies to Host A, the PIX examines the packet that arrives on the outside interface. Since there is an active translation for Host A, the PIX knows that packets destined for IP address 207.139.221.2 must be translated back to 192.168.1.2. Once the PIX alters the IP header, it then routes the packet back to Host A. This process occurs until no more traffic needs to be translated between the two devices and the translation times out.

In order to allow traffic to flow from a higher-level security interface to a lower-level security interface (inside, outside), you must use the *nat* and *global* commands. In order to permit traffic from a lower-level security interface to flow through a higher-level security interface, you must use the *access-list* and *access-group* command.

NAT or Network Address Translation is a feature that dynamically maps IP addresses originating from the higher-level security interface into IP addresses on the same subnet as the lower-level security interface. For more information on NAT and PAT, refer to Chapter 5.

To enable NAT on an interface, use the command:

nat [(*interface_name*)] nat_id local_ip [*netmask* [*max_conns* [*em_limit*]]] [**norandomseq**]

To further explain:

- **Interface_name** The internal network interface name.

- **Nat_id** Used in the *global* command statement. All *nat* commands with the same *nat_id* are in the same *nat* group.

- **Local_ip** The internal network IP address to be translated. You can use **0.0.0.0** to allow all hosts to start an outbound connection originating from the inside interface. The **0.0.0.0** IP can be abbreviated as **0**.

- **Netmask** The network mask for *local_ip*. You can also use the **0.0.0.0** to allow all outbound connections originating from the inside interface.

- **Max_cons** The maximum TCP connections limit. The default is 0, which will allow unlimited connections.

- **Em_limit** The embryonic connection limit. The default is also 0, which will allow unlimited connections.

- **Norandomseq** Specifies not to randomize TCP packet sequence numbers. Because this is one of the security features of PIX, it is not recommended this option be used.

```
pixfirewall(config)#nat (inside) 1 0.0.0.0 0.0.0.0
pixfirewall(config)#nat (inside) 2 172.16.0.0 255.255.0.0
```

The first *nat_ id* will translate all traffic from the inside interface, whereas the second *nat_id* will translate only traffic originating from the 172.16.0.0 subnet.

NOTE

When PAT is used, the PIX will keep track of each translation by adding a unique source port number to the source IP address for each translation. This feature is valuable when only limited IP address space is available from the service provider. To display the active translations, use the command *show xlate* from the enable prompt.

Once the traffic to be translated has been specified on the inside interface, it is now time to specify the IP address pool that the inside traffic will be translated to. To do this, the *global* command will be used.

global [(interface_name)] nat_id global_ip[-global_ip] [**netmask** global_mask]

In this case:

- **Interface_name** The external network interface where these global addresses will be used.

- **Nat_id** The number shared with the *nat* command that will group the *nat* and *global* statements together.

- **Global_ip** One or more global IP addresses that the PIX will translate the inside interface traffic to. If the external network interface is connected to the Internet, each global IP must be registered with the Network Information Center (NIC). You can specify either a single IP address or a range of addresses by separating the addresses with a dash (-). You can create a Network Address Port Translation (PAT) by specifying a single IP address in the *global* statement.

- **Global_mask** The network mask for the *global_ip* statement.

```
pixfirewall(config)#global (outside) 1 207.139.221.1-207.139.221.254 netmask
    >255.255.255.0
Global 207.139.221.1-207.139.221.254 will be Network Address Translated
pixfirewall(config)#global (outside) 1 207.139.221.1 255.255.255.255
Global 207.139.221.128 will be Port Address Translated
```

WARNING

If PAT is used, the IP address must be different from the IP address assigned to any of the interfaces on the PIX.

In the first statement, inside IP addresses will be translated to an IP address in the range of 207.139.221.1 to 207.139.221.254. In the second statement, the inside IP address will be port address translated in a single IP address, 207.139.221.128.

NOTE

When NAT is used, the PIX have a specified range of global IP addresses to perform translations with. Once the last available global IP is used, no other traffic from the inside interface will be permitted through until one of the translations times out. It is a good idea to use both a NAT statement followed by a PAT statement. This way, when all IP addresses are used in NAT, the PAT will then be used until a NAT address has timed out. However, keep in mind that not all protocols work with PAT.

Security Policy Configuration

Security policy configuration is probably one of the most important factors in establishing a secure network. The following sections present security strategies and best practice policies that you can implement to ensure the best possible security.

Designing & Planning…

The Importance of Security Policies

A security policy is the most important aspect in network security. As a manager, you must take many things into careful consideration when planning your policy. Tasks such as identifying the resources to protect, balancing security risks with cost/productivity, and the ability to log items are very important. Creating regular reports on usage will assist in identifying possible weaknesses in your security policy. If weaknesses have been overlooked, they can then be quickly remedied. PIX allows you to utilize a feature called a syslog. With the addition of third-party software such as Open Systems Private I, detailed analysis on the contents of a syslog can be achieved. The ability to generate reports on the types of traffic being permitted or denied by the PIX is crucial to a security policy. If you suspect your network is being attacked, the ability to look at logs over certain time periods is invaluable in proving your suspicions.

As a manager, proactive measures are always better then reactive measures. Instead of generating reports and looking for weaknesses after the fact, it may be beneficial to create a strict policy and then remove elements of that policy as necessary. For example, if a company has set up a Web server on the inside network and has used PIX to translate that inside address to a globally unique address on the outside, the server has now become fully exposed. To reduce the risk of the server being compromised, access lists can be used to limit the type of TCP/UDP traffic that will be permitted to reach the server through the PIX. By only allowing HTTP traffic to reach the Web server from the outside network and explicitly denying all other traffic, the risk of it being comprised has been greatly reduced. If the server becomes an FTP server as well as a Web server, the security policy can be modified to permit FTP as well as HTTP traffic to the server from the outside interface by adding another access list which permits FTP traffic. A security policy can take many forms depending on the needs of an organization, and careful planning is a necessity prior to implementing the PIX firewall.

Security Strategies

In order for the PIX to protect a network, managers and administrators must figure out what type of security strategy to employ. Do we deny everything that is not explicitly permitted, or do we allow everything and deny only certain things? The security policy is the most important element when designing a secure network. Without a policy, the necessary devices and configurations cannot be implemented properly. The security policy should aim for a balance between security and cost/productivity. It is impossible for a network to be totally secure, but the security policy should reflect the biggest potential security risks the company is willing to take. For example, by allowing users the ability to browse Web sites to perform research on the Internet, a company opens itself up to numerous security risks that can be exploited. Weigh this against restricting access to browsing Web sites in a company which relies heavily on that information to function. If the security policy is designed and implemented properly, these risks will be minimal. Once a security policy has been established, a firewall can then be used as a tool to implement that security policy. It will not function properly at protecting your network if the security policy is not carefully defined beforehand.

Designing & Planning…

The Cost of Security

One thing to remember when working on your security policy is how much will it cost? This can be the biggest factor in deciding which policy you choose for your company. Here are some questions to ask yourself when pondering the numbers of your future policy:

- Does the cost of protection outweigh the value of what you are trying to protect?
- Could the cost of a one-time security breach and restore of data be more than the cost of a new policy?
- What is the average amount of data you will lose on an annual basis due to security breaches?
- Does a new policy outweigh the cost of all breaches put together?

Deny Everything that Is Not Explicitly Permitted

One of the most common strategies used for security policies, is to permit only certain IP traffic, and deny the rest. For example, Company XYZ wishes to permit HTTP, FTP, and Telnet traffic for users. Managers and administrators agreed that as a company policy only these three types of traffic are to be permitted. All other traffic, such as Real Audio, ICQ, and MSN Messenger, will be blocked. Using Access Control Lists (ACLs) similar to those employed on routers, the PIX will allow an administrator to specify which type of IP traffic to permit or deny based on the destination address/network, source address/network, TCP port number, and UDP port number. This implementation makes configuring the security policy for the administrator very simple. The administrator only has to worry about entering statements to permit HTTP, FTP, and Telnet traffic, and then at the end of the ACL he/she will add an explicit *deny all* statement.

Allow Everything that Is Not Explicitly Denied

On a network where many different types of IP traffic will be permitted, it may be easier for an administrator to use a different approach for a security policy. This strategy is to allow all types of traffic and deny specific IP traffic. For example, if Company XYZ is not concerned as to what types of traffic the users are going to access, but managers and administrators have agreed that since they only have a T1 connection to their Internet service provider that services one thousand users, they do not wish their users to use RealPlayer because it is bandwidth intensive. In order to implement this strategy, only one ACL needs to be implemented on the PIX. This ACL will deny the TCP/UDP port that RealAudio uses while allowing everything else.

> ## WARNING
>
> This is not a recommended strategy. Be sure to carefully plan in advance what types of traffic will be permitted through the firewall. This example was shown as an alternative to the "Deny Everything that Is Not Explicitly Permitted" strategy, and in some network scenarios may be useful. By using this type of implementation in a situation where the ISP charges by the byte may cause quite a shock when the first bill from the ISP arrives. This is also less secure than the deny all, permit some approach.

Identify the Resources to Protect

In the context of a security policy, a resource can be defined as any network device susceptible to attack which can cost a company financially or otherwise. Examples of resources are Web servers, mail servers, database servers, and servers which contain sensitive information such as employee records. If any of these servers are attacked, functionality can be affected which then costs a company money.

It is important to carefully evaluate the assets a company wishes to protect. Are some resources more important that others, therefore requiring higher security? Is a mail server more important to the operation of the company than a print server?

Areas of weakness must also be identified prior to implementing the security policy. If a company uses an ISP for Internet access, a pool of modems for dial-in access, and remote users tunneling into the LAN via the Internet through VPN, each of these points of entry must be looked at as a potential source of security issues. Once weaknesses have been identified, a security policy can be shaped to protect a company's LAN from those various weaknesses. For example, using the previous scenario of an ISP, dial-in access, and remote VPN access, placement of the PIX will be critical to the overall security of the LAN. If the PIX are placed between the LAN and the ISP, how does this protect the LAN from unauthorized dial-in users? By adding an additional NIC to the PIX, a DMZ (covered later) can be used to isolate the dial-in and VPN users from the rest of the LAN. An example of protecting a resource is in a situation where a public Web site is hosted internally by the company. The Web server is definitely considered an asset and must be protected. Because of this, some decisions will need to be made as to how the PIX will secure the Web server. Since only one Web site is hosted by the company, and it uses a private IP address space, a static translation in which the Web server is assigned an internal IP address is then translated by the PIX firewall with a global IP address allowing outside users to gain access to it.

Depending on the security policy, having servers on an internal network which are then translated to global IP addresses may be too risky. An alternative is to implement a demilitarized zone in which the public resources will reside.

Demilitarized Zone

A DMZ (demilitarized zone) is a zone that is logically and physically separated from both the inside network and outside networks. A DMZ can be created by installing additional NICs to the PIX. By creating a DMZ, it allows administrators to remove devices that need to be accessed publicly from the inside and outside zones, and place them into their own zone. By implementing this type of configuration, it helps an administrator establish boundaries on the various zones of their network.

NOTE

Remember that only the PIX 515 and 520 models allow additional interfaces to be added. The PIX 501 is a SOHO class firewall and currently does not support additional interfaces.

Figure 3.5 illustrates how a DMZ is used to secure public resources.

Figure 3.5 Securing Public Resources with a DMZ

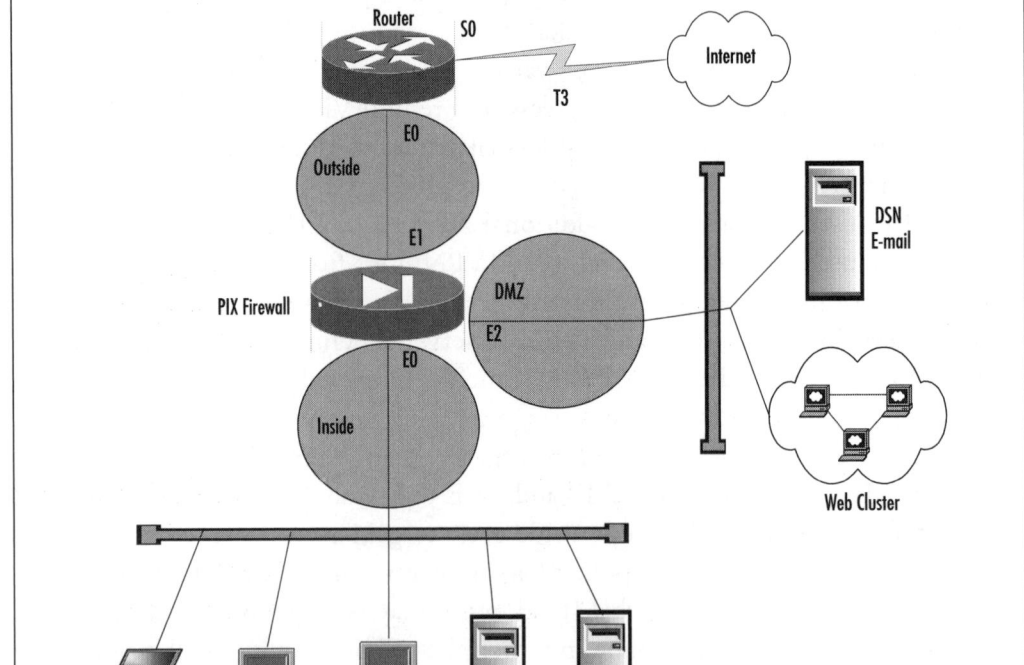

In this scenario, a DMZ has been used to separate the public servers from the inside and outside zones. This will allow administrators to control the flow of traffic destined for the DMZ zone. Since all traffic must pass through the outside interface in order to reach the DMZ, ACLs can be applied to the outside interface specifying the type of traffic permitted to reach the DMZ. For example, since the public servers are Web, e-mail, and DNS servers, HTTP, DNS, and SMTP traffic will be permitted to reach the DMZ. Everything else will be denied.

It is very difficult to secure a server. The Operating System (OS) and software applications can contain bugs and security flaws and need to be continuously updated. As soon as you install a server that offers a public service, there is always a risk the server can be compromised. Creating a new perimeter (DMZ) where the public servers are located, allows more control over the traffic permitted into the internal network. For example, once a DMZ has been set up and the public servers have been removed from the inside network, a rule can be created that denies all traffic destined for the inside network, therefore increasing security.

No matter what type of network a company has, careful planning is needed well in advance to implement a successful security policy. Planning in advance helps avoid making unnecessary changes in the way the PIX operates while in production. If a company continuously alters how resources are to be protected, availability of those resources will fluctuate. In a situation where a company relies heavily on that availability, careless planning may cost the company money.

Identify the Security Services to Implement

Depending on how your security policy is designed will reflect on how you design and implement your network. Various factors such as resources to protect, user authentication, traffic filtering, and confidentiality all come into play when designing the security policy.

Authentication and Authorization

Authentication is a mechanism which verifies a user is who they say they are, authorization is a mechanism which will determine what services a user can employ to access a host. An administrator must design a security policy which specifies the resources that need to be protected, what type of user will be able to access those resources, and which services a user will be able to employ to access those resources. Once a security policy has been outlined, an authentication server such as a RADIUS or TACACS+ server must be put in place in order to implement the security policy.

Once authentication and authorization have been enabled on the PIX, it will provide credential prompts on inbound and outbound connections for FTP, Telnet, and HTTP access. The actual decision about what users are permitted or denied use of, and the services used will be done by the authentication and authorization server. For more information on AAA, please refer to Chapter 6.

Access Control

In a network of any size, various administrators have control over different areas of the network. How does one administrator know where their responsibility stops and another administrator's responsibility begins? It is important to lay out the perimeters either inside a network, or surrounding a network. For example, if a network is connected to the Internet via a T1 leased line, does the administrator maintain the network on the other side of the T1? Probably not. This is where the ISP takes over. Perimeters must be established in order to help design a security policy. By defining perimeters, an administrator can secure resources under their control, which will also aid in the decision of where traffic should be filtered. ACLs are used to permit or deny traffic based on various criteria. These ACLs are used to assist in securing various resources by filtering the traffic that will get to them.

Confidentiality

Confidentiality is achieved by encrypting the information that travels along the network. If an individual used a network monitoring tool, there is a good chance they would be able to look at the data in the packets. An example of this is PAP. When using PPP (Point-to-Point Protocol) with PAP (Password Authentication Protocol), information is sent in clear text during the authentication phase. If a network monitor is used to capture these packets, the password used to authenticate the two parties would be readily available. To remedy this problem CHAP (Challenge Handshake Authentication Protocol) encrypts the negotiation phase. IPSec was developed to provide confidentiality, access control, authentication and integrity for data traversing a network. IPSec is a suite of protocols to assist in the encryption of data across a network. Commonly found in VPN tunnels, IPSec uses various encryption algorithms, keys, and certificates to validate information passed throughout a network. For more information on IPSec, refer to Chapter 5.

URL, ActiveX, and Java Filtering

ACLs are limited to certain criteria; destination address, source address, and ports are all taken into consideration for ACLs. ActiveX blocking occurs by the PIX commenting out HTML *<object>* commands on Web pages. As a technology, ActiveX creates many potential problems for clients—prompting workstations to fail, introducing network security problems, or causing servers to fail.

Java filtering is accomplished by denying applets downloaded to a client once they access a URL.

URLs themselves can also be filtered. Typically a company will introduce an AUP (Acceptable Usage Policy) that dictates usage of the Internet for their employees. This can be somewhat enforced by the PIX as well as third-party applications. The PIX can redirect URL requests to a server running a third-party application. This application will decide whether to permit or deny access to that URL and then pass responses back to the PIX.

> **NOTE**
>
> URL filtering can be accomplished with addition of a server running WebSENSE (www.websense.com). The configuration on the PIX will allow URLs to be forwarded to the WebSENSE server, which will then permit or deny the destination URL.

Implementing the Network Security Policy

Once a security policy has been created, it is now time to implement that security policy on the PIX. In order to completely implement a policy, other devices (such as AAA server and IPSec) will need to be used. This section will cover the commands to enable these features on the PIX, but the actual configuration on other devices will be discussed in later chapters.

Authentication Configuration in PIX

In order to configure Authentication on the PIX, it must first be enabled. To enable AAA authentication, use the *aaa-server* and *aaa* commands.

```
aaa-server group_tag if_name host server_ip key timeout seconds
```

In this case:

- **Group_tag** An alphanumeric string which is the name of the server group. Use the *group_tag* in the *aaa* command to associate *aaa authentication* and *aaa accounting* command statements to an AAA server.

- **If_name** The interface name on which the server resides.

- **Host *server_ip*** The IP address of the TACACS_ or RADIUS server.

- **Key** A case-sensitive, alphanumeric keyword of up to 127 characters. The key must be the same one used on the TACACS+ server.

- **Timeout *seconds*** A retransmit timer that specifies the duration in which the PIX can retry access four times to the AAA server before choosing the next AAA server.

- **Protocol *auth_protocol*** The type of AAA server, either tacacs+ or radius.

```
aaa authentication include | exclude authen_service inbound | outbound |
    if_name local_ip local_mask foreign_ip foreign_mask group_tag
```

In this case:

- **Accounting** Enables or disables accounting services with an authentication server.

- **Include** Creates a new rule with the specified service to include.

- **Exclude** Creates an exception to a previously stated rule by excluding the specified service from authentication, authorization, or accounting to the specified host.

- **Acctg_service** The account service. Accounting is provided for all services, or you can limit it to one or more services. Possible values are *any*, *ftp*, *http*, *telnet,* or *protocol port*.

- **Authentication** Enables or disables user authentication, prompts user for username and password, and verifies information with the authentication server.

- **Authen_service** The application with which a user accesses a network. Use *an*, *ftp*, *http*, or *telnet*.

- **Authorization** Enables or disables TACACS+ user authorization for services (PIX does not support RADIUS authorization).

- **Author_service** The services which require authorization. Use *any*, *ftp*, *http*, *telnet*, or *protocol port*.

- **Inbound** Authenticates or authorizes inbound connections.

- **Outbound** Authenticates or authorizes outbound connections.

- **If_name** The interface name from which users require authentication. Use *if_name* in combination with the *local_ip* address and the *foreign_ip* address to determine where access is sought and from whom.

- **Local_ip** The IP address of the host or network of hosts that you want to be authenticated or authorized. Set this to **0** for all hosts.

- **Local_mask** The network mask of *local_ip*. If IP is 0, use **0**. Use **255.255.255.255** for a host.

- **Foreign_ip** The IP address of the hosts you want to access the *local_ip* address. Use **0** for all hosts and **255.255.255.255** for a single host.

- **Foreign_mask** The network mask of *foreign_ip*. Always specify a specific mask value. Use **0** if the IP address is 0, use **255.255.255.255** for a single host

- **Group_tag** The group tag set with the *aaa-server* command.

```
pixfirewall>enable

pixfirewall#configure terminal

pixfirewall(config)#aaa-server AuthOutbound protocol tacacs+

pixfirewall(config)#aaa-server tacacs+ (inside) host 172.16.0.10
cisco  >timeout 20

pixfirewall(config)#aaa authentication include any outbound 0 0 0 0
>AuthOutbound

pixfirewall(config)#aaa authorization include any outbound 0 0 0 0
```

The first *aaa-server* statement specifies TACACS+ as the authentication protocol to use, and the second *aaa-server* statement specifies the server that is performing the authentication. The last two statements indicate that all traffic outbound will need to be authenticated and authorized.

Access Control Configuration in PIX

Access control can be achieved through the use of ACLs. Similar to those used on routers, ACLs can limit the traffic able to traverse the PIX based on several criteria, including source address, destination address, source TCP/UDP ports, and destination TCP/UDP ports.

In order to implement ACLs on PIX, the *access-list* and *access-group* commands are used:

```
access-list acl_name deny | permit protocol src_addr src_mask operator
    port dest_addr dest_mask operator port
```

- **Acl_name** The name of an access list.

- **Deny** Does not allow a packet to traverse the PIX. By default, PIX denies all inbound packets unless explicitly permitted.

- **Permit** Allows a packet to traverse the PIX.

- **Protocol** The name or number of an IP protocol. It can be one of the keywords, *icmp, ip, tcp,* or *udp.*

- **Src_addr** The address of the network or host from which the packet originated. To specify all networks or hosts, use the keyword *any,* which is equivalent to a source network and mask of 0.0.0.0 0.0.0.0. Use the *host* keyword to specify a single host.

- **Src_mask** The netmask bits to be applied to the *src_addr* if the source address is for a network mask. Do not apply if the source address is a host.

- **Dst_addr** The IP address of the network or host to which the packet is being sent. Like the *src_addr,* the keyword *any* can be applied for a destination and a netmask of 0.0.0.0 0.0.0.0, as well as the *host* abbreviation for a single host.

- **Dst_mask** The netmask bits to be applied to the *dst_addr* if the destination address is for a network mask. Do not apply if the destination address is a host.

- **Operator** A comparison that lets you specify a port or port range. Use without the operator and port to indicate all ports. Use *eq* and *port* to permit or deny access to just that single port. Use *it* to permit or deny access to all ports less than the port specified. Use *gt* and a *port permit,* to deny access to all ports greater than the port you specify. Use *neq* and a *port permit,* or deny access to every port except the ports you specify. Finally, use *range* and *port range* to permit or deny access to only those ports named in the range.

- **Port** Service or services you permit to be used while accessing *src_addr* or *dest_addr.* Specify services by port number or use the literal name.

- **Icmp_type** Permits or denies access to ICMP message types.

    ```
    access-group acl_name in interface interface-name
    ```

- **Acl_name** Name associated with an access list.

- **In interface** Filters inbound packets at the given interface.

- **Interface_name** Name of the network interface.

```
pixfirewall>enable
pixfirewall#configure terminal
pixfirewall(config)#access-list acl_out permit tcp any any eq http
pixfirewall(config)#access-list acl_out permit tcp any any eq ftp
pixfirewall(config)#access-list acl_out permit tcp any any eq ftp-data
pixfirewall(config)#access-list acl_out permit tcp any any eq telnet
pixfirewall(config)#access-list acl_out permit tcp any any eq smtp
pixfirewall(config)#access-list acl_out deny tcp any any
pixfirewall(config)#access-list acl_out deny udp any any
pixfirewall(config)#access-group acl_out in interface inside
```

The *access-list* statements for ACL *acl_out* will permit http, ftp, ftp-data, telnet, and smtp traffic. The last two statements of the *access-list* will explicitly deny all traffic.

The *access-group* statement will apply ACL *acl_out* to the inside interface.

Securing Resources

An example of securing resources would arise if Company XYZ has numerous consultants that need access to a resource on the internal LAN. Previously, the consultants have been using a RAS connection to dial in but have complained several times that the link is too slow for their work. To remedy this, administrators have decided to permit terminal access to the server via the Internet. The internal server is a Windows NT 4.0 Terminal Server and the consultants have been provided with the Terminal Server client. For security reasons, administrators have also requested the IP and subnet from which the consultants are going to be connecting.

This configuration example will explain the commands necessary to protect a server with a private IP address that is translated to a global IP address.

In order to create a translation for an internal IP address to a public IP address, use the *static* command.

static (internal_if_name, external_if_name) global_ip local_ip **netmask**
    network_mask max_conns em_limit **norandomseq**

To further explain:

- **Internal_if_name** The internal network interface name. The higher security level interface you are accessing.

- **External_if_name** The external network interface name. The lower security level interface you are accessing.

- **Global_ip** A global IP address. This address cannot be a Port Address Translation IP address.

- **Local_ip** The local IP address from the inside network.

- **Netmask** Specifies the network mask.

- **Network_mask** Pertains to both *global_ip* and *local_ip*. For host addresses, always use 255.255.255.255. For networks, use the appropriate class mask or subnet mask.

- **Max_cons** The maximum number of connections permitted through the static at the same time.

- **Em_limit** The embryonic connection limit. An embryonic connection is one that has started but not yet completed. Set this limit to prevent attack by a flood of embryonic connections.

- **Norandomseq** Specifies not to randomize the TCP/IP packet's sequence number. Only use this option if another inline firewall is also randomizing sequence numbers. Employing this feature opens a security hole in the PIX.

Once a translation for an internal IP to an external IP has been made, you must specify the type of traffic that will be permitted to access it. To do this, use the *access-list* command.

```
access-list acl_name deny | permit protocol src_addr src_mask operator
    port dest_addr dest_mask operator port
```

- **Acl_name** The name of an access list.

- **Deny** Does not allow a packet to traverse the PIX. By default, PIX denies all inbound packets unless explicitly permitted.

- **Permit** Allows a packet to traverse the PIX.

- **Protocol** The name or number of an IP protocol. It can be one of the keywords, *icmp*, *ip*, *tcp*, or *udp*.

- **Src_addr** The address of the network or host from which the packet originated. To specify all networks or hosts, use the keyword *any*, which is equivalent to a source network and mask of 0.0.0.0 0.0.0.0. Use the *host* keyword to specify a single host.

- **Src_mask** The netmask bits to be applied to the *src_addr* if the source address is for a network mask. Do not apply if the source address is a host.

- **Dst_addr** The IP address of the network or host to which the packet is being sent. Like the *src_addr*, the keyword *any* can be applied for a destination and netmask of 0.0.0.0 0.0.0.0, as well as the *host* abbreviation for a single host.

- **Dst_mask** The netmask bits to be applied to the *dst_addr* if the destination address is for a network mask. Do not apply if the destination address is a host.

- **Operator** A comparison that lets you specify a port or port range. Use without the operator and port to indicate all ports. Use *eq* and port to permit or deny access to just that single port. Use *it* to permit or deny access to all ports less than the port specified. Use *gt* and a port permit or deny access to all ports greater than the port you specify. Use *neq* and a port to permit or deny access to every port except the ports you specify. Finally, use *range* and port range to permit or deny access to only those ports named in the range.

- **Port** A service or services you permit to be used while accessing *src_addr* or *dest_addr*. Specify services by port number or use the literal name.

- **Icmp_type** Permits or denies access to ICMP message types.

```
pixfirewall>enable
pixfirewall#configure terminal
pixfirewall(config)#static (inside,outside) 207.139.221.10 172.16.0.32  >
    netmask 255.255.255.255
pixfirewall(config)#access-list acl_consult permit tcp 198.142.65.0 >
    255.255.255.0 host 207.139.221.10 eq 3389
pixfirewall(config)#access-list acl_consult permit tcp 64.182.95.0 >
    255.255.255.0 host 307.139.221.10 eq 3389
pixfirewall(config)#access-group acl_consult in interface outside
```

The first *static* statement will provide a translation for the inside server with an IP address of 172.16.0.32 to a global IP address of 207.139.221.10.

The *access-list* statements specify that the ACL *acl_consult* will only permit Microsoft Terminal Server client traffic originating from 198.142.65.0 and 64.182.95.0.

NOTE

TCP port 3389 is the corresponding port for Microsoft Terminal Server client. For a listing of valid TCP and UDP port numbers, refer to: www.isi.edu/in-notes/iana/assignments/port-numbers.

Finally, the *access-group* statement will apply the *acl_consult* Access Control List to the outside interface.

It is also important to note that implementing a security policy does not revolve around configuration of the PIX. In the previous example, PIX will not assist as a security measure if the information passed from terminal server to terminal server client is not encrypted. If information is passed as cleartext, a network monitoring tool could be used to capture packets which could then be analyzed by other individuals. Once a consultant has connected to the terminal server, how is the authentication handled? What permissions does that account have? Have various Windows NT security flaws been addressed with the latest service packs?

Confidentiality Configuration in PIX

This configuration example will explain the commands necessary to enable IPSec on the PIX. For more detailed information on IPSec refer to Chapter 5.

URL, ActiveX, and Java Filtering

To implement URL, ActiveX, and Java filtering, use the *filter* command:

```
filter activex port local_ip mask foreign_ip mask
```

In this case:

- **Activex** Blocks outbound ActiveX tags from outbound packets.

- **Port** Filters Activex only at the point which Web traffic is received on the PIX firewall.

- **Local_ip** The IP address of the highest security level interface from which access is sought. You can set this address to **0** to specify all hosts.

- **Mask** The network mask of *local_ip*. You can use **0** to specify all hosts.

- **Foreign_ip** The IP address of the lowest security level interface to which access is sought. You can use **0** to specify all hosts.

- **Foreign_mask** The network mask of *foreign_ip*. Always specify a mask value. You can use **0** to specify all hosts.

filter java port[-port] *local_ip mask foreign_ip mask*

To further explain:

- **Java** Blocks Java applets returning to the PIX firewall as a result of an outbound connection.

- **Port[-port]** Filters Java only on one or more ports on which Java applets may be received.

- **Local_ip** The IP address of the highest security level interface from which access is sought. You can set this address to **0** to specify all hosts.

- **Mask** The network mask of *local_ip*. You can use **0** to specify all hosts.

- **Foreign_ip** The IP address of the lowest security level interface to which access is sought. You can use **0** to specify all hosts.

- **Foreign_mask** The network mask of *foreign_ip*. Always specify a mask value. You can use **0** to specify all hosts.

filter url http|except *local_ip local_mask foreign_ip foreign_mask* [**allow**]

Here we see:

- **url** Filters URLs from data moving through the PIX firewall.

- **http** Filters URL only Filter HTTP URLs.

- **except** Filters URL only and creates an exception to a previous *filter* condition.

- **Local_ip** The IP address of the highest security level interface from which access is sought. You can set this address to **0** to specify all hosts.

- **Mask** The network mask of *local_ip*. You can use **0** to specify all hosts.

- **Foreign_ip** The IP address of the lowest security level interface to which access is sought. You can use **0** to specify all hosts.

- **Foreign_mask** The network mask of *foreign_ip*. Always specify a mask value. You can use **0** to specify all hosts.

- **Allow** Filters URLs only when the server is unavailable; lets outbound connections pass through the PIX firewall without filtering. If you omit this option and if the WebSENSE server goes offline, PIX firewall stops outbound port 80 traffic until the WebSENSE server is back online.

Once filtering has been enabled on the PIX, to successfully filter URLs, you must designate a WebSENSE server with the *url-server* command.

```
url-server (if_name) host ip_address timeout seconds
```

To further explain:

- **If_name** The network interface where the authentication server resides. Default is inside.

- **Host ip_address** The server that runs the WebSENSE URL filtering application.

- **Timeout seconds** The maximum idle time permitted before PIX switches to the next server you specify. Default is 5 seconds.

```
pixfirewall>enable
pixfirewall#configure terminal
pixfirewall(config)#filter url http 0 0 0 0
pixfirewall(config)#filter activex 80 0 0 0 0
pixfirewall(config)#filter java 80 0 0 0 0
pixfirewall(config)#url-server (inside) host 172.16.0.38 timeout 5
```

The *filter url* statement specifies that all http traffic passing through the PIX will be filtered. In addition, the *url-server* statement will specify which server is running WebSENSE to provide the actual filtering.

The *filter activex* and *filter java* statements specify that all http traffic will be filtered for ActiveX controls and Java applets.

PIX Configuration Examples

The following examples illustrate how a PIX firewall can be used in various real-world scenarios as well as the configuration needed on the PIX.

Protecting a Private Network

Due to security reasons, Company XYZ management has decided to restrict access to the Finance servers. Management has assigned the task of securing the Finance network from unauthorized access. Only individuals who are in the Finance departments network will have access to any of the Finance resources, any traffic originating from the Finance LAN will be permitted to any destination and all other departments will not be permitted to access the Finance LAN. Figure 3.6 illustrates how the LAN will be set up.

Figure 3.6 Secure Department to Department

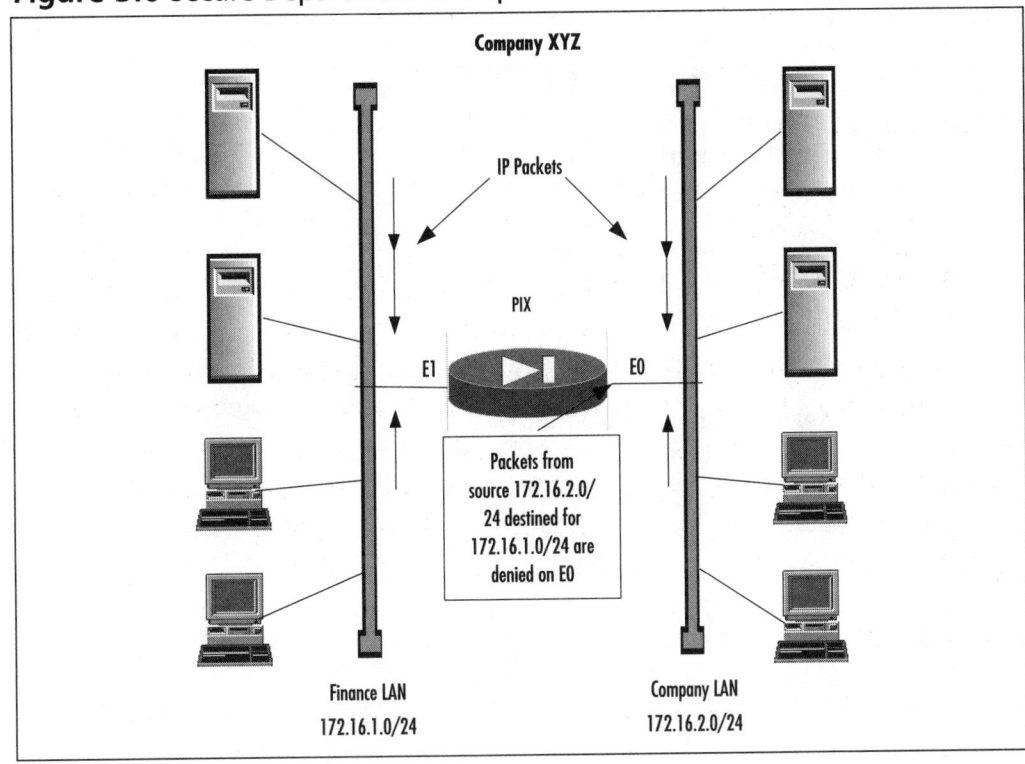

To begin, execute the following:

```
pixfirewall(config)#write terminal
nameif ethernet0 public security0
nameif ethernet1 finance security100
```

This assigns names and security values to each of the interfaces.

```
interface ethernet0 inside auto
interface ethernet1 outside auto
```

This sets each Ethernet interface to 10/100 auto negotiation.

```
ip address public 172.16.2.1 255.255.255.0
ip address finance 172.16.1.1 255.255.255.0
```

This assigns unique RFC 1918 IP addresses to each of the interfaces.

```
access-list deny tcp any 172.16.1.0 255.255.255.0
>eq any
```

```
access-list deny udp any 172.16.1.0 255.255.255.0
>eq any
```

This specifies that TCP and UDP traffic from any source will be denied if the destination is the network 172.16.1.0/24. By applying this access list inbound on the public interface (E0), traffic originating from the 172.16.2.0/24 subnet will be denied access to the Finance LAN.

This applies access-list acl_out to the public interface.

```
telnet 172.16.1.0 255.255.255.0 public
telnet 172.16.2.0 255.255.255.0 finance
```

This specifies that only clients from the 172.16.1.0/25 and 172.16.2.0/24 subnets will be able to Telnet to the PIX.

NOTE

This configuration, where two departments are separated for security reasons, can easily be achieved by using a router with Access Control Lists. The PIX is a very versatile device and can also be used to protect internal networks as shown in this example.

Protecting a Network Connected to the Internet

Company XYZ management has decided that in order to keep up with the rapidly evolving world of technology, Internet access is a necessity. Managers and administrators have decided that a T1 leased line will be sufficient for their users to access the Internet and an ISP has already been chosen. Since the LAN uses an IP address scheme employing the private 172.16.0.0 network, Network Address Translation, or Network Address Port Translation will be needed in order to translate internal IP addresses to global IP addresses. The ISP has also provided the company with eight public addresses which consist of 207.139.221.1 to 207.139.221.8. A Cisco Secure PIX 515 Firewall has been chosen to provide security for Company XYZ.

Management and administrators have established a security policy in which users will only be permitted to access HTTP, FTP, Telnet, e-mail, DNS, and News. Web site filtering will be performed by a third-party application called WebSENSE Web filtering software (www.websense.com). ActiveX controls will also be filtered due to the security problems associated with them. The ability to Telnet to the inside interface will be restricted to the administrator's workstation. Figure 3.7 shows how the network will be set up.

Figure 3.7 Two Interfaces

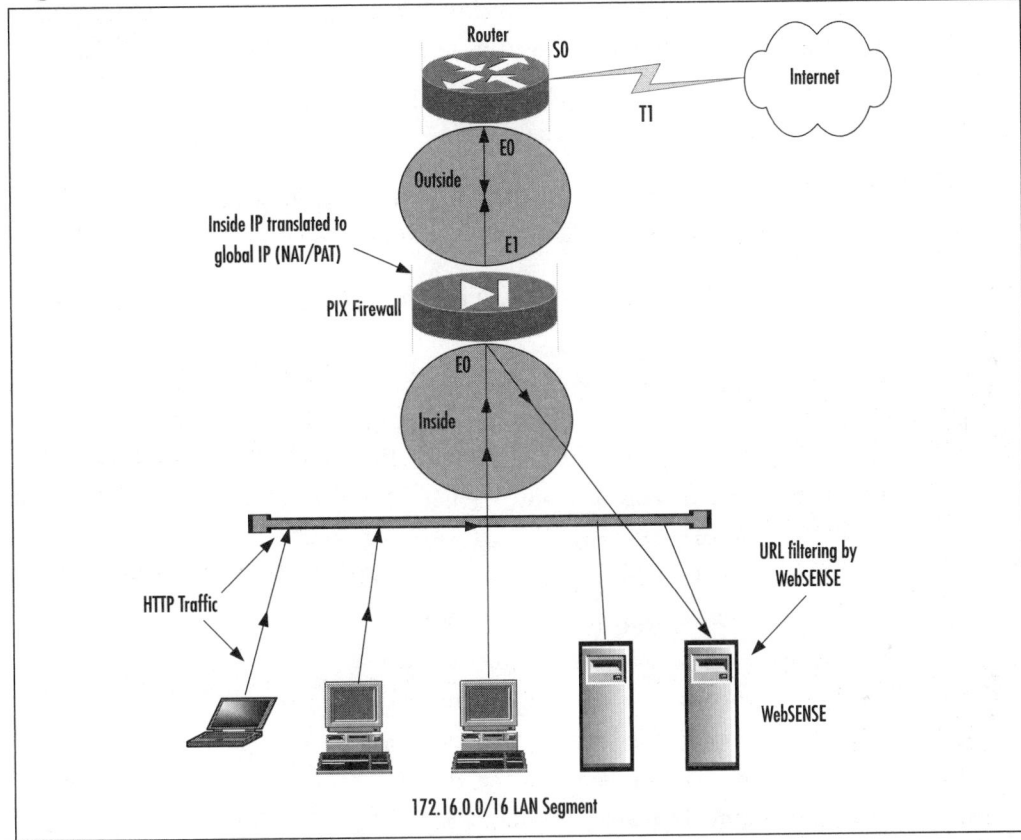

To begin, execute the following:

```
pixfirewall(config)#write terminal
interface ethernet0 inside auto
interface ethernet1 outside auto
```

This sets each Ethernet interface to 10/100 auto-negotiation ip address inside 172.16.0.1 255.255.0.0.

```
ip address outside 207.139.221.2 255.255.255.248
```

This assigns unique IP addresses to each of the interfaces.

```
route outside 0.0.0.0 0.0.0.0 207.139.221.1
```

This adds a static route for the outside interface.

```
nat (inside) 1 0.0.0.0 0.0.0.0
```

This allows any address on the inside interface to be NATed.

```
global (inside) 1 207.139.221.3
```

This sets up a global pool using the unique IP address 207.139.221.3 for NAPT.

```
filter url http 0 0 0 0
```

This filters any HTTP URL requests to any destination address.

```
filter activex 0 0 0 0
```

This filters any ActiveX controls in the HTML pages to any destination address.

```
url-server (inside) host 172.16.0.10 timeout 5
```

This specifies the server in which WebSENSE is running for URL filtering.

```
access-list acl_out permit tcp any any eq http
access-list acl_out permit tcp any any eq ftp
access-list acl_out permit tcp any any eq ftp-data
access-list acl_out permit tcp any any eq smtp
access-list acl_out permit tcp any any eq telnet
access-list acl_out permit tcp any any eq nntp
access-list acl_out permit tcp any any eq domain
access-list acl_out permit udp any any eq domain
access-list acl_out deny tcp any any
access-list acl_out deny udp any any
```

This specifies types of traffic that will be permitted through the PIX (inside, outside) with an explicit *deny all* statement to block any other traffic.

```
access-group acl_out in interface inside
```

Applies access-list acl_out to the inside interface.

```
telnet 172.16.0.50 255.255.255.255. inside
```

Only permits host 172.16.0.50 for Telnet sessions on the inside interface.

Protecting Server Access Using Authentication

The Finance department in Company XYZ is concerned about users in other departments accessing their Finance Web server. To alleviate this concern, IT has decided to limit access to the Finance server using the PIX firewall. A new server has been provided which will serve as the AAA server running Cisco Secure ACS. Figure 3.8 illustrates this scenario.

Figure 3.8 Protecting a Server Using AAA

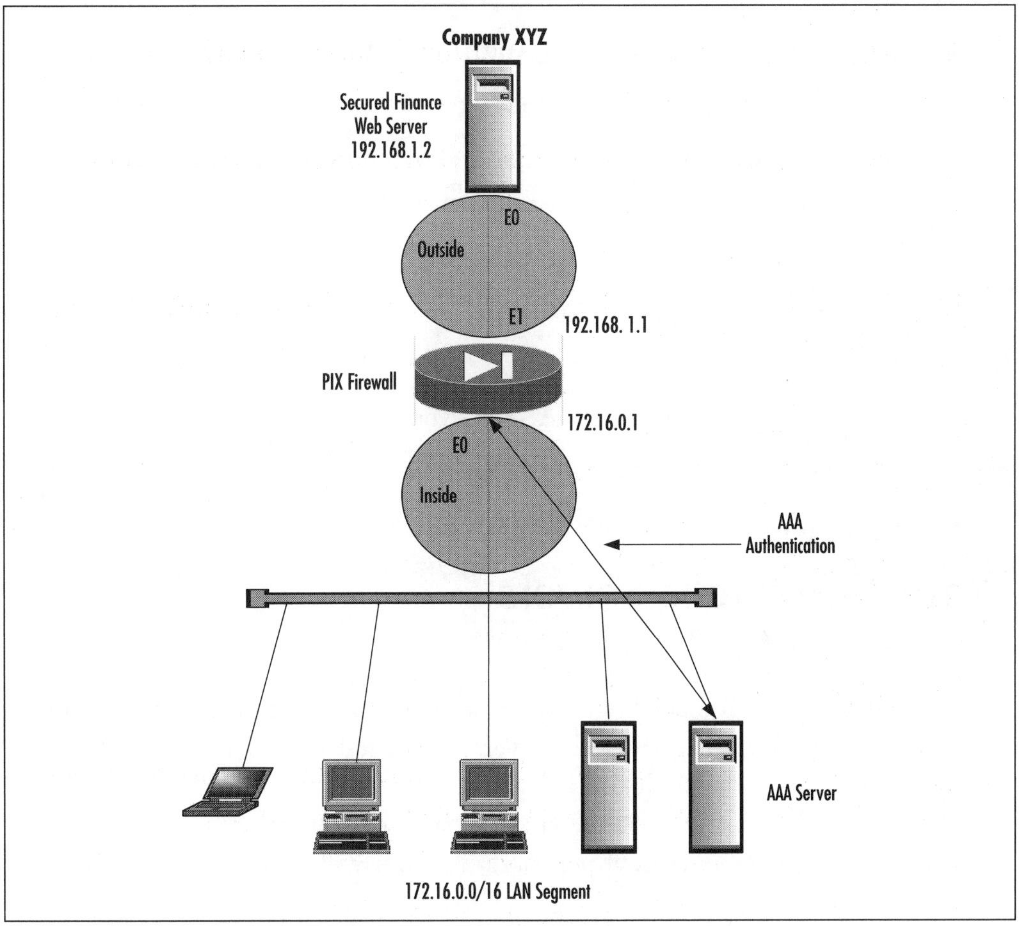

To begin, execute the following:

```
pixfirewall(config)#write terminal
interface ethernet0 inside auto
interface ethernet1 outside auto
```

This sets each Ethernet interface to 10/100 auto negotiation.

```
ip address outside 192.168.1.1 255.255.255.0
ip address inside 172.16.0.1 255.255.255.0
```

This assigns unique IP addresses to each of the interfaces.

```
nat (inside) 1 0 0
```

This allows any address on the inside interface to be NATed.

```
global (outside) 1 192.168.10-192.168.20 netmask >255.255.255.0
```

Sets up a global pool using address 192.168.10-192.168.20 for NAT.

```
global (outside) 1 192.168.10.21 netmask >255.255.255.255
```

Sets up a global pool using 192.168.10.21 for PAT. This is used when addresses from the NAT pool have been exhausted.

```
aaa-server AuthOutbound protocol tacacs+
```

Specifies TACACS+ for AAA protocol.

```
aaa-server AuthOutbound (inside) host 172.16.0.10 >cisco timeout 20
```

Specifies host 172.16.0.10 as the AAA server.

```
aaa authentication include any outbound host >192.168.1.2 0 0
```

Authorizes any traffic with a destination address of 192.168.1.2.

Protecting Public Servers Connected to the Internet

Company XYZ management has discussed the possibility of hosting their public servers internally. Currently the Web servers are hosted elsewhere by another company in which connectivity, security, and maintenance is provided by them. The security policy dictates that the risks of having public servers on the internal network are unacceptable. A new perimeter (DMZ) will need to be defined to secure the public servers.

Three Web servers, one e-mail server, and one DNS server will be placed in the DMZ.

A class C subnet has been assigned to the company by their ISP. To allow the company to utilize as many of the class C public addresses, PAT will be used instead of NAT.

Management would like to restrict the amount of traffic that traverses the PIX from their local LAN to the Internet. Administrators have decided that the only traffic permitted from the LAN will be HTTP, FTP, Telnet and DNS requests to their DNS server. Figure 3.9 illustrates how the LAN will be set up.

Figure 3.9 Three Interfaces without NAT

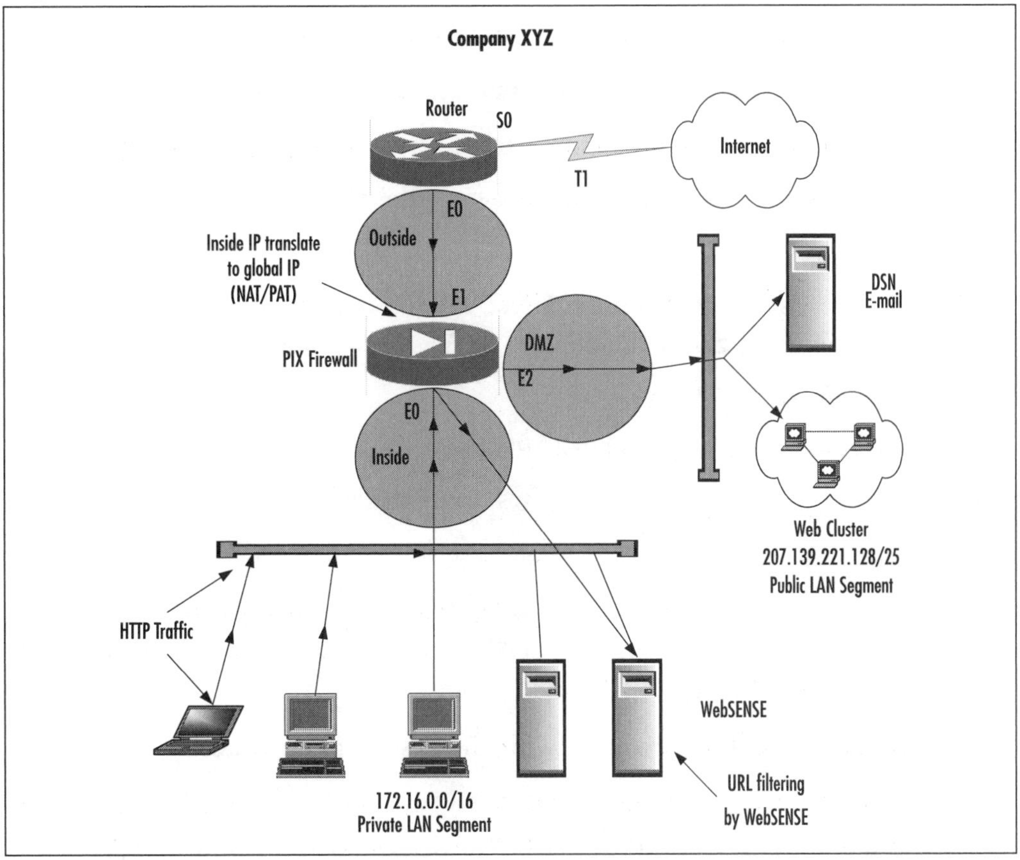

To begin, execute the following:

```
pixfirewall(config)#write terminal
nameif ethernet2 dmz security 50
```

Names and assigns security values to an ethernet2 interface.

```
interface ethernet0 inside auto
interface ethernet1 outside auto
interface ethernet2 dmz1 auto
```

Sets each Ethernet interface to 10/100 auto negotiation.

```
ip address inside 172.16.0.1 255.255.0.0
ip address outside 207.139.221.2 255.255.255.128
ip address dmz 207.139.221.129 255.255.255.128
```

Assigns unique IP addresses to each interface.

```
route (outside) 0.0.0.0 0.0.0.0 207.139.221.1
```

Sets static routes for the outside interface.

```
nat (inside) 1 0.0.0.0 0.0.0.0
```

Enables NAT for all traffic originating from the inside interface.

```
Nat (dmz) 0 0.0.0.0 0.0.0.0
```

Disables the NAT feature on the DMZ interface. Since hosts on the DMZ interface will be using global IP addresses, NAT translations are not necessary.

```
global (inside) 1 207.139.221.3
```

Sets up a global pool using global IP address 207.139.221.3 for NAPT.

```
static (dmz,outside) 207.139.221.129 207.139.221.129 >netmask 255.255.255.128
```

Creates a static translation for:

```
static (dmz,outside) 207.139.221.130 207.139.221.130 >netmask 255.255.255.128
static (dmz,outside) 207.139.221.131 207.139.221.131 >netmask 255.255.255.128
filter url http 0 0 0 0
```

Filters any HTTP URL requests with any destination address.

```
filter activex 0 0 0 0
```

Filters any ActiveX controls in HTML pages to any destination address.

```
url-server (inside) host 172.16.0.10 timeout 5
```

Specifies the server in which WebSENSE is running for URL filtering.

```
access-list acl_out permit tcp any any eq http
access-list acl_out permit tcp any any eq ftp
access-list acl_out permit tcp any any eq ftp-data
access-list acl_out permit tcp any any eq smtp
access-list acl_out permit tcp any any eq telnet
access-list acl_out permit tcp any any eq domain
```

```
access-list acl_out permit udp any any eq domain
access-list acl_out deny tcp any any
access-list acl_out deny udp any any
```

Specifies types of traffic that will be permitted through the PIX (inside, outside) with an explicit *deny all* statement to block any other traffic.

```
access-list dmz_in permit tcp any 207.139.221.128
>255.255.255.128 eq http
access-list dmz_in permit tcp any 207.139.221.128
>255.255.255.128 eq domain
access-list dmz_in permit udp any 207.139.221.128
>255.255.255.128 eq domain
access-list dmz_in permit tcp any 207.139.221.128
>255.255.255.128 eq smtp
access-list dmz_in permit tcp any 207.139.221.128
>255.255.255.128 eq pop3
```

Specifies types of traffic that will be permitted through the PIX (outside, dmz). All traffic not explicitly permitted will be denied.

```
access-group acl_out in interface inside
```

Applies *access-list acl_out* to the inside interface.

```
access-group dmz_in in interface outside
```

Applies *access-list acl_in* to the DMZ interface.

```
telnet 172.16.0.0 255.255.0.0 inside
```

Permits Telnet access on the inside interface from any host on the 172.16.0.0/16 network.

Figure 3.10 illustrates an example of a DMZ which uses private IP addresses, therefore requiring NAT.

To continue with the configuration:

```
pixfirewall(config)#write terminal
nameif ethernet2 dmz security 50
```

Names and assigns security values to an ethernet2 interface.

```
interface ethernet0 inside auto
interface ethernet1 outside auto
interface ethernet2 dmz1 auto
```

Figure 3.10 Three Interfaces with NAT

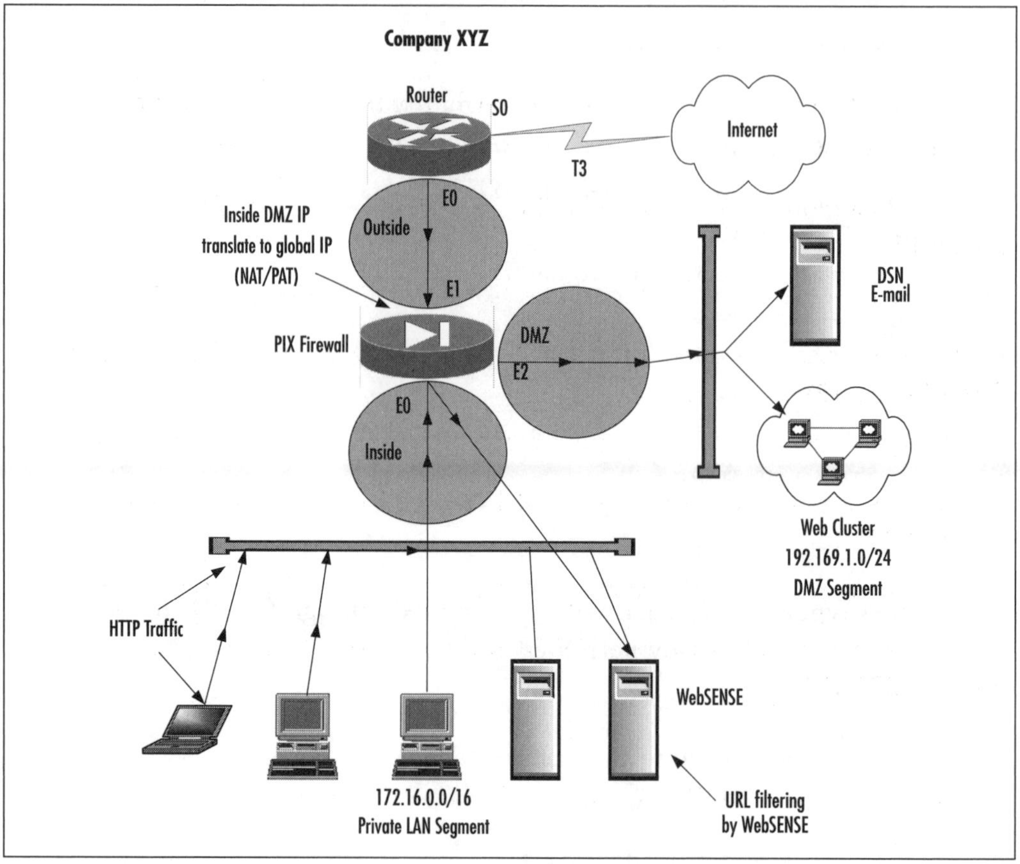

Sets each Ethernet interface to 10/100 auto negotiation.

```
ip address inside 172.16.0.1 255.255.0.0
ip address outside 207.139.221.2 255.255.255.0
ip address dmz 192.168.1.1 255.255.255.0
```

Assigns unique IP addresses to each interface.

```
route 0.0.0.0 0.0.0.0 207.139.221.1
```

Sets the static route for the outside interface.

```
nat (inside) 1 172.16.0.0 255.255.0.0
```

Enables NAT for all traffic originating from the inside interface.

```
nat (dmz) 1 0.0.0.0 0.0.0.0
```

Enables NAT for all traffic originating from the DMZ interface.

```
global (inside) 1 207.139.221.3
```

Sets up a global pool using the global IP address 207.139.221.3 for PAT.

```
global (dmz) 1 192.168.1.10-192.168.1.30
```

Sets up a global pool using IP addresses 192.168.1.10 thru 192.168.1.30 for DMZ.

```
static (dmz,outside) 207.139.221.129 192.168.1.2 >netmask 255.255.255.0
```

Creates a static translation for DMZ host 192.168.1.2 to global unique IP 207.139.221.129.

```
static (dmz,outside) 207.139.221.130 192.168.1.3 >netmask 255.255.255.0
```

Creates a static translation for DMZ host 192.168.1.3 to global unique IP 207.139.221.130.

```
static (dmz,outside) 207.139.221.131 192.168.1.4 >netmask 255.255.255.0
```

Creates a static translation for DMZ host 192.168.1.4 to global unique IP 207.139.221.131.

```
filter url http 0 0 0 0
```

Filters any HTTP URL requests with any destination address.

```
filter activex 0 0 0 0
```

Filters any ActiveX controls in HTML pages to any destination address.

```
url-server (inside) host 172.16.0.10 timeout 5
```

Specifies the server in which WebSENSE is running for URL filtering.

```
access-list acl_out permit tcp any any eq http
access-list acl_out permit tcp any any eq ftp
access-list acl_out permit tcp any any eq ftp-data
access-list acl_out permit tcp any any eq smtp
access-list acl_out permit tcp any any eq telnet
access-list acl_out permit tcp any any eq domain
access-list acl_out permit udp any any eq domain
access-list acl_out deny tcp any any
access-list acl_out deny udp any any
```

Specifies types of traffic that will be permitted through the PIX (inside, outside) with an explicit *deny all* statement to block any other traffic.

```
access-list dmz_in permit tcp any 207.139.221.129
>255.255.255.255 eq http
access-list dmz_in permit tcp any 207.139.221.130
>255.255.255.255 eq domain
access-list dmz_in permit udp any 207.139.221.130
>255.255.255.128 eq domain
access-list dmz_in permit tcp any 207.139.221.131
>255.255.255.131 eq smtp
```

Specifies types of traffic that will be permitted through the PIX (outside, dmz). All traffic not explicitly permitted will be denied.

```
access-group acl_out in interface inside
```

Applies *access-list acl_out* to the inside interface.

```
access-group dmz_in in interface outside
```

Applies *access-list acl_dmz* to the outside interface.

```
telnet 172.16.0.0 255.255.0.0 inside
```

Securing and Maintaining the PIX

Part of creating a security policy is not only protecting the network resources but also protecting the PIX itself. PIX provides several mechanisms to assist an administrator in limiting access to the PIX and reporting various items such as security violations.

System Journaling

As with most Cisco products, the system message logging feature can save messages in a buffer or redirect the messages to other devices such as a system logging server to be analyzed or archived. This feature allows administrators to reference these logs in case of security violations.

System journaling is an often overlooked security mechanism. Logging is essential to the security of the network. It can be used to detect security violations, and help determine the type of attack. If logging is done in real time, it can be used to detect an ongoing intrusion (more on this is covered in Chapter 13).

PIX also has the added feature that if for some reason or another, the syslog server is no longer available, the PIX will stop all traffic.

UNIX servers, by default, provide a syslog server. On Windows NT/2000 servers, a syslog server must be downloaded. Cisco provides a syslog server on their Web site (www.cisco.com).

By default, system log messages are sent to the console and Telnet sessions. In order to redirect logging messages to a syslog server use the *logging* command. Some of the variables used with the *logging* command are as follows:

- **On** Starts sending syslog messages to all output locations. Stop all logging with the *no logging on* command.

- **Buffered** Sends syslog messages to an internal buffer which can be viewed with the *show logging* command. To clear the buffer, use the *clear logging* command.

- **Console** Specifies that syslog messages appear on the console. You can limit which type of messages appear by using the *level* option.

- **Host** Specifies a syslog server that will receive the messages sent from the PIX. You may use multiple *logging host* commands to specify multiple syslog servers.

- **In_if_name** Interface in which the syslog server resides.

- **Ip_address** The IP address of syslog server.

- **Protocol** Protocol in which the syslog message is sent—either tcp or udp. PIX will only send TCP messages to the PIX syslog server unless otherwise specified. You cannot send both protocols to the same syslog server. Use multiple syslog servers in order to log both UDP and TCP traffic.

- **Level** Specifies the syslog message level as a number or string. See Table 3.2 for the different syslog levels.

- **Port** Port in which the PIX sends either UDP or TCP syslog messages. Default for UDP is port 514 and port 1470 for TCP.

- **Timestamp** Specifies that the syslog messages sent to the syslog server should have a time stamp value on each message.

Table 3.3 lists the different SNMP trap levels.

Table 3.3 SNMP Trap Levels

Level	Type	Description
0	Emergencies	System unusable messages
1	Alerts	Take immediate action
2	Critical	Critical condition
3	Errors	Error messages
4	Warnings	Warning message
5	Notifications	Normal but significant condition
6	Informational	Information message
7	Debugging	Debug messages, log FTP commands, and WWW URLs

An example of sending warnings to a syslog server is:

```
pixfirewall>enable
pixfirewall#configure terminal
pixfirewall(config)#logging trap 4
pixfurewall(config)#logging host inside 172.16.0.38 tcp
```

NOTE

Syslog is *not* a secure protocol. The syslog server should be secured and network access to the syslog server should be restricted.

Securing the PIX

Since the PIX is a security device, limiting access to the PIX to only those who need it is extremely important. What would happen if individuals where able to freely Telnet to the PIX from the inside network? Limiting access to the PIX can be achieved by using the *telnet* command. Telnet is an insecure protocol. Everything that is typed on a telnet session, including passwords, is sent in cleartext. Individuals using a network monitoring tool can then capture the packets and discover the password to log in and enable a password if issued. If remote management of the PIX is necessary, the network communication should be secured.

It is also a good idea to limit the idle-time of a Telnet session and log any connections to the PIX through Telnet. When possible, use a RADIUS, Kerberos or TACACS+ server to authenticate connections on the console or vty (telnet) ports.

```
telnet ip_address netmask interface_name
```

- **Ip_address** An IP address of a host or network that can access the PIX Telnet console. If an interface name is not specified, the address is assumed to be on the internal interface. PIX automatically verifies the IP address against the IP addresses specified by the *ip address* commands to ensure that the address you specify is on an internal interface.

- **Netmask** Bit mask of *ip_address*. To limit access to a single IP address, use 255.255.255.255 for the subnet mask.

- **Interface_name** The name of the interface to apply the security to.

- **Timeout** The number of minutes that a Telnet session can be idle before being disconnected by the PIX. Default is 5 minutes.

NOTE

When permitting Telnet access to an interface, be as specific as possible. If an administrative terminal uses a static IP address, only permit that IP address for Telnet access.

The following is an example of limiting Telnet access to the PIX to one host on the inside network.

```
pixfirewall>enable
pixfirewall#configure terminal
pixfirewall(config)#telnet 172.16.0.50 255.255.255.255 inside
pixfurewall(config)#telnet timeout 5
```

If features are not used on the PIX, they should then be disabled. If SNMP is not used, deactivate it. If it is used, change the default communities and limit access to the management station only.

Finally, a security measure that is often forgotten is to keep the PIX is a secure area. By locking it away in a server room or wiring closet, only authorized individuals will be able to physically reach the PIX. How would your security policy be enforced in an individual was able to walk up to the PIX and pull out the power cable?

Take the extra time to secure the PIX according to the security policy. The PIX is typically the device that enforces the majority of a company's security policy. If the PIX itself is not secured, and an unauthorized individual gains access to it, the security of the network will be compromised.

Summary

The Cisco PIX Firewall is a very versatile security device. From the PIX 501 SOHO model to the Enterprise class PIX 535 model, the PIX can fulfill the security needs of any size network.

In this chapter, we covered numerous topics including the design of a security policy and then implementing that security policy on the PIX. It is extremely important to thoroughly design a policy before implementing it. By identifying the resources to protect, the services you wish to allow (HTTP, FTP, and so on), and requiring users to be authenticated in order to access a resource ahead of time will permit an organization to implement a security policy in a quick and efficient manner. By creating a security policy on the fly, your resources can be compromised and data can be corrupted. Instead of being reactive to attacks and other security holes, creating a detailed security policy beforehand is a proactive, and superior, way of protecting your network.

Remember the key security features of the PIX, such as URL filtering, ActiveX and Java filtering, Access Control Lists, DMZs, AAA authentication and authorization, DNS Guard, IP Frag Guard, Mail Guard, Flood Defender, Flood Guard, IPSec, Stateful filtering, securing access to the PIX, and syslog. These features will aid you in creating and implementing your security policy. NAT and NAPT should not be relied on as a security measure. Using a syslog server will allow you to archive all of the traffic that passes through your firewall. By using syslog, you will always have a record of anyone attempting to attack your firewall from the inside or outside.

Solutions Fast Track

Overview of the Security Features

- ☑ PIX firewalls provide security technology ranging from stateful inspection to IPSec and L2TP/PPTP-based VPN. Also provides content filtering capability.

- ☑ Working with Cisco Intrusion Detection System can help secure the network environment.

- ☑ The PIX firewalls also contain the adaptive security algorithm. This maintains the secure perimeters between the networks controlled by the firewall.

Initial Configuration

☑ Easy setup with the use of Cisco PIX Device Manager.

☑ The same command-line interface spans all PIX firewalls.

☑ The PIX 501 is a basic Plug-and-Play for your SOHO network.

The Command-Line Interface

☑ The command-line interface (CLI) used on the PIX is very similar to that used on routers.

☑ Three modes exist in order to perform configuration and troubleshooting steps. These modes are unprivileged, privileged, and configuration mode.

Configuring NAT and PAT

☑ The information that PIX stores in the translation table includes the inside IP address and a globally unique IP address assigned by the Network Address Translation (NAT) or Network Address Port Translation (PAT).

☑ In order to allow traffic to flow from a higher level security interface to a lower level security interface (inside, outside), you must use the *nat* and *global* commands.

☑ NAT is a feature that dynamically maps IP addresses originating from the higher security level interface into IP addresses on the same subnet as the lower level security interface.

Security Policy Configuration

☑ The security policy is the most important element when designing a secure network.

☑ Remember, the PIX will deny everything that is not explicitly permitted.

☑ Planning in advance will help avoid making unnecessary changes in the way the PIX operates while in production.

☑ Once authentication and authorization have been enabled on the PIX, it will provide credential prompts on inbound and outbound connections for FTP, Telnet, and HTTP access.

☑ Perimeters must be established in order to help with designing a security policy.

☑ Java filtering is accomplished by denying applets downloaded to a client once they access a URL.

☑ In order to create a translation for an internal IP address to a public IP address, use the *static* command.

☑ Access control can be achieved through the use of Access Control Lists (ACLs).

PIX Configuration Examples

☑ **pixfirewall(config)#write terminal** shows configuration.

☑ **global (outside) 1 192.168.10.21 netmask 255.255.255.255** sets up a global pool using 192.168.10.21 for NAPT. This is used when addresses from the NAT pool have been exhausted.

☑ **access-list deny udp any 172.16.1.0 255.255.255.0 eq any** specifies that TCP and UDP traffic from any source will be denied if the destination is the network 172.16.1.0/24.

Securing and Maintaining the PIX

☑ Limit the access of the PIX to only those people who really need it. This will help the security of the network.

☑ Remember to give your PIX a unique name for the Interface Name.

☑ Be sure to put your Routers, Hubs, and PIXs in a secure location that is locked. This will stop any threats that are physical in nature, and will help secure your network.

Frequently Asked Questions

The following Frequently Asked Questions, answered by the authors of this book, are designed to both measure your understanding of the concepts presented in this chapter and to assist you with real-life implementation of these concepts. To have your questions about this chapter answered by the author, browse to **www.syngress.com/solutions** and click on the **"Ask the Author"** form.

Q: I have two inside networks. I would only like one of them to be able to access the Internet (outside network). How would I accomplish this?

A: Instead of using the NAT (inside) *1 0 0* statement which specifies all inside traffic, use the NAT (inside) 1 *xxx.xxx.xxx.xx yyy.yyy.yyy.yyy* statement where *x* is the source network you wish to translate, and *y* is the source network subnet mask.

Q: I am setting up my outbound Access Control Lists to specify which traffic I will permit users to use. How do I know which TCP or UDP port a particular application uses?

A: Usually the application vendor will have the TCP or UDP port(s) listed in the documentation, or available on their Web site. For a comprehensive list of Well Known Ports, Registered Ports, and Dynamic/Private ports, visit: www.isi.edu/in-notes/iana/assignments/port-numbers.

Q: My organization uses Microsoft Exchange server for our mail. How would I allow our Exchange server to receive external mail if the server is located on the inside network and a PIX firewall is in place?

A: Since the server is physically located on the inside network, a static translation will need to be created to assign the Exchange server a global IP address. Once the translation has been created, use ACLs to limit the type of traffic able to reach the server. In SMTP, for example, the Exchange server's internal IP address is 172.16.0.16, and the globally assigned IP address will be 207.139.221.40:

```
pixfirewall(config)#static (inside,outside) 207.139.221.40 172.16.0.16
    >netmask 255.255.255.255
pixfirewall(config)#access-list acl_mailin permit tcp any host
    207.139.221.40 eq smtp
pixfirewall(config)#access-group acl_mailin in interface outside
```

Q: If you were going to buy one new PIX for your office, but wanted to make sure you could expand or upgrade it sometime down the road. Which model would you chose?

A: PIX model 515 since the 501 and 506 are not upgradeable.

Q: While trying to connect to the PIX through the COM port, my connections keeps timing out. What are some settings to review on your terminal setup?

A: 9600 baud, 8 data bits, No parity, 1 stop bit, and Hardware flow control

Q: If I was looking to put a new server on my network but did not want to add it to the hidden network behind my PIX, where would be a good place to add it?

A: Adding it to the DMZ off of the PIX will put the new server on a different part of your network.

Q: Searching for a network interface that someone else has added to the network can be a problem. If you do not know the name of the interface you are looking for and would like to see a list of interface names on your PIX, what command would you use?

A: Type **show nameif** at the command prompt.

Q: What is the most important thing to remember when trying to sell your security plan to management?

A: Does the cost of the plan outweigh the cost of the data or network being protected?

## Chapter 4

Traffic Filtering in the Cisco Internetwork Operating System

Solutions in this chapter:

- **Access Lists**
- **Lock-and-key Access Lists**
- **Reflexive Access Lists**
- **Context-based Access Control**
- **Configuring Port to Application Mapping**

- ☑ **Summary**
- ☑ **Solutions Fast Track**
- ☑ **Frequently Asked Questions**

Introduction

As the use of technology continues to grow in business, the volume of data that companies need to exchange is increasing to match that growth. To facilitate the exchange of this data, a connection must be established between the networks of these companies. Without some form of security, each network will have complete access to the other with no way of controlling what data someone will be able to see.

One of the easiest ways to protect your network from unauthorized access is to filter the traffic at the point where it enters your network. By catching all traffic before it can be forwarded into your network, you can minimize the chance someone will be able to sidestep your security measures and find an alternate path to the data they are trying to access.

In many cases, the device used to connect two or more networks together is a router. To allow traffic filtering at the connection point to other networks, we need some method of filtering traffic on the router itself. This chapter will cover the different traffic filtering mechanisms available in a Cisco router.

In the simplest case, traffic filtering can consist of a list that permits or denies traffic based on the source or destination IP address. But very often, basic traffic filtering is not sufficient to provide adequate security in a network. Today, modern security products provide more control over the network traffic entering and exiting the network. To achieve that, the traffic must be inspected and the state of the connection must be kept. These advanced features require the router or firewall to understand the internal workings of the protocol it is trying to secure.

Access Lists

A very important step to security is the capability to control the flow of data within a network. A way to accomplish this is to utilize one of the many features of the Cisco Internetwork Operating System (IOS) known as an access list, or Access Control List (ACL). The function of an access list depends on the context in which it is used. For instance, access lists can:

- Control access to networks attached to a router or define a particular type of traffic allowed to pass to and from a network.

- Limit the contents of routing updates advertised by various routing protocols,

- Secure the router itself by limiting access to services such as SNMP and Telnet.

- Define "interesting traffic" for Dial on Demand routing. Interesting traffic defines which packets allow the dial connection to occur.

- Define queuing features by determining what packets are given priority over others.

An access list is comprised of a sequential series of filters defined globally on the router. Think of each filter as a statement you enter into the router. Each of these filters performs a comparison or match and permits or denies a packet across an interface. The decision to permit or deny is determined by the information contained inside the packets. This process is commonly referred to as *packet filtering*. The criteria that must be met for action to be taken can be based on only a source address or a source and destination address, a protocol type, a specific port or service type, or other type of information. This information is typically contained within the Layer 3 and Layer 4 headers.

Once an access list is defined, it will need to be applied on the interface where access control is required. It was previously stated that we define access lists globally on the router. The key here is to remember that after defining the access list, it must be applied on the interface or your access list will have no effect. Also remember that traffic moves both in and out of the interface of the router. So, access lists can be applied either in the inbound or in the outbound direction on a specific interface. One method commonly used to avoid confusion here is to assume you are inside the router. Simply ask yourself if you want to apply the access list statements as traffic comes in (inbound) or as traffic moves out (outbound). You can have one access list, per protocol, per interface, per direction. So, for example, it is possible to have one access list for outbound IP traffic and one access list for inbound IP traffic applied to the same interface. See Figure 4.1 for an illustration of this concept.

Figure 4.1 Inbound and Outbound Traffic on an Interface

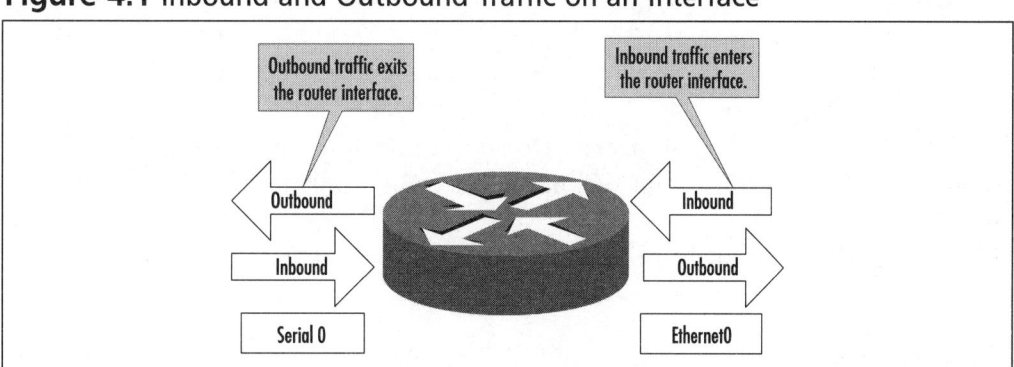

Access List Operation

When a packet enters a router, the destination address in the packet is compared to the routing table, and the exit interface for the packet is determined. When using access lists, before the packet can enter or exit the router there is a "stack" of filters applied to the interface in which the packet must pass through. The stack we are referring to here would be the commands you entered on your router with the *access-list* global configuration command. Think of each line of your access list as a filter. The following example represents a user-defined access list with three filters. A complete description on the access list syntax is given in a later section.

```
access-list 1 permit 192.168.10.15
access-list 1 permit 192.168.10.16
access-list 1 deny 192.168.10.17
```

Assuming this list is applied in the outbound direction, the packet exiting the router will be tested against each condition until a match occurs. If no match occurs on the first line, the packet moves to the second line and the matching process happens again. When a match is established, a permit or deny action, which is specified on each filter statements, will be executed. What happens if the packet ends up at the end of the stack, or last line of our access list, and a match has never occurred? There is an implicit *deny all* command at the end of every access list. So any packet that passes through an access list with no match is automatically dropped. You will not see this line on any access list you build, just think of it as a default line that exists at the end of your access list. In Figure 4.2, we can see the direction of a packet as it flows through the access list.

In some cases, you may want to enter the last line of the access list as a *permit any* statement, as shown next:

```
access-list 1 deny 192.168.10.15
access-list 1 deny 192.168.10.16
access-list 1 permit any
```

With this line in place all packets that don't match the first two lines will be permitted by the third line and will never reach the implicit *deny all*.

Figure 4.2 Flowchart of Packets Matching an Access List

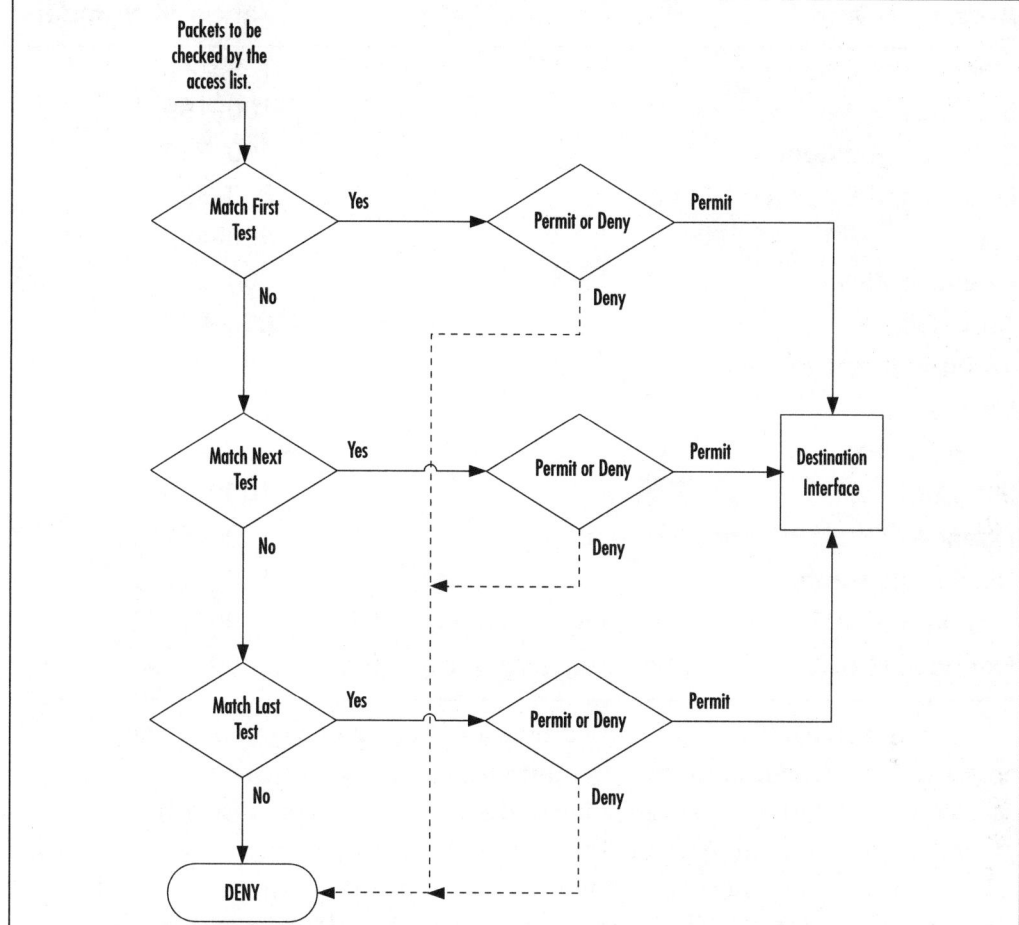

Types of Access Lists

There are several types of access lists available on Cisco routers, which can be used to filter just about any protocol that can run on the router. Access lists are usually referred to by a number, which uniquely identifies a particular list as well as specifying what type of access list it is. For example, when creating a standard IP access list, you must use any number between 1 and 99. If you use the number 100 for an access list, it will have to be an extended IP access list, which uses a different format. Table 4.1 shows the various number ranges of access lists, and what type of traffic they are meant to filter.

Table 4.1 Access List Numbers

Access List Type	Range of Numbers
Standard IP	1–99
Extended IP	100–199
Ethernet Type Code	200–299
DECnet and Extended DECnet	300–399
XNS	400–499
Extended XNS	500–599
AppleTalk	600–699
48-bit Ethernet Address	700–799
Standard IPX	800–899
Extended IPX	900–900
IPX SAP	1000–1099
Extended 48-bit Ethernet Address	1100–1199
NLSP route summary	1200–1299
Standard IP (IOS 12.1 number ranges were extended)	1300–1999
Extended IP (IOS 12.1 number ranges were extended)	2000–2699

Access lists may also be identified by name instead of a number. Named access lists are beneficial to the administrator when dealing with a large number of access lists for ease of identification and also if more than 99 standard or extended access lists are needed. Another advantage of a named access list over a numbered access list is in modifying the access list. With numbered access lists, the entire access list and all its statements are considered one entity. To delete or change a statement, you will have to delete the entire numbered access list and reenter the statements you want to keep. Named access lists allow you to delete one statement within the access list, although you are still limited to only adding new entries at the bottom of the list.

Although a Cisco router is designed to operate with multiple protocols, this chapter will only cover access lists as they relate to the IP protocol. We will discuss, in detail, the two basic types of IP access lists, standard and extended. In addition, we will cover more advanced filtering techniques that employ the use of access lists, such as lock-and-key access lists, reflexive access lists, and Context-based Access Control (CBAC).

Standard IP Access Lists

The standard IP access list is the most basic IP access list that can be created because it only looks at the source address and ignores all other information in the IP header. This allows you to easily permit or deny access to your entire network for a list of addresses and/or subnets.

As with all access lists, you must define the list in the global configuration mode of the router. In the following example any field represented by {} is mandatory for the access list. Any field represented by [] is optional. The syntax of the standard IP access list is:

```
access-list list-number {permit | deny} source-address [wildcard-mask][log]
```

Table 4.2 breaks down each section of this command and describes its function.

Table 4.2 Standard IP Access List Configuration

Command	Description
access-list list number	Defines the number of the access list. The standard access list numbers range from 1–99.
Permit	If conditions are met, traffic will be allowed.
Deny	If conditions are met, traffic will be denied.
source-address	Identifies the host or network from which the packet is being sent. The source can be specified by an IP address or by using the keyword *any*.
Wildcard-mask	By default, this field will be 0.0.0.0. This defines the number of wildcard bits assigned to the source address. The default value (0.0.0.0) specifies a single IP address. Wildcard masks will be explained further in the following section.
Log	This keyword results in the logging of packets that match the *permit* or *deny* statement.

Notice that a hyphen is required between the words *access* and *list*. Next is the list number. Since we are referencing a standard IP access list, the numbers would range from 1 to 99. The access list number actually serves a dual purpose here. Typically, you will find several access lists on one router, therefore the router must have a way to distinguish one access list from another. The number performs this purpose along with tying the lines of an access list together. The number also tells the router the type of access list it is.

The keywords *permit* or *deny* indicate the action to be performed if a match occurs. For example the keyword *permit* would allow the packet to be forwarded by the interface. The keyword *deny* will drop the packet if a match is found. If a packet is dropped, an ICMP error message of destination unreachable will be sent back to the source.

Source Address and Wildcard Mask

When using a standard IP access list, the source address must always be specified. The source address can refer to the address of a host, a group of hosts, or an entire subnet. The scope of the source address is specified by the wildcard mask.

The wildcard mask is typically one of the most misunderstood topics when dealing with access lists. When using the wildcard mask, think of the reverse manner in which a subnet mask works. The job of a subnet mask is to specify how many bits of an IP address refer to the subnet portion. Remember, a binary 1 in the subnet mask indicates the corresponding bit is part of the subnet range and a binary 0 in the subnet mask indicates the corresponding bit is part of the host portion. For example, take the following IP address and subnet mask:

```
Source address   - 10101100.00010000.10000010.01000110  =  172.16.130.77
Subnet Mask      - 11111111.11111111.11111111.00000000  =  255.255.255.0
Subnet           - 10101100.00010000.10000010.00000000  =  172.16.130.0
```

In the first three octets of the subnet mask, we have set all the bits to one (decimal 255 = 11111111 in binary). This tells us that all of the bits in the first three octets are now part of the subnet field, while the last eight bits are used for the host addresses.

Now, let's move from the subnet mask to the wildcard mask. When using a wildcard mask a zero is used for each bit that should be matched and a one is used when the bit position doesn't need to be matched. The easiest way to create a wildcard mask is to first decide what subnet mask applies to the traffic you want to filter, and then use it to create the wildcard mask. To get a wildcard mask for a subnet mask, all you need to do is change all the 1s to 0s, and the 0s to 1s. You will see this in the following example. Assume that we want to deny the IP entire subnet 172.16.130.0 with a mask of 255.255.255.0.

```
Source address   - 10101100.00010000.10000010.00000000 = 172.16.130.0
Subnet Mask      - 11111111.11111111.11111111.00000000 = 255.255.255.0
Wildcard Mask    - 00000000.00000000.00000000.11111111 = 0.0.0.255
```

So, the following access list line will deny any traffic that has a source address in the range 172.16.130.0 – 172.16.130.255, because the wildcard mask tells us that the first three octets (24 bits) must match, but the last octet (8 bits) can be anything.

```
Router(config)#access-list 5 deny 172.16.130.0 0.0.0.255
```

As a more complicated example, let's say we want to only deny the IP address range of 172.16.130.32 through 172.16.130.63. The mask associated with this range is 255.255.255.224, so we would write this in binary and derive the wild-card mask as shown next.

```
Source address  - 10101100.00010000.10000010.00100000 = 172.16.130.32
Subnet Mask     - 11111111.11111111.11111111.11100000 = 255.255.255.224
Wildcard Mask   - 00000000.00000000.00000000.00011111 = 0.0.0.31
```

So, to create an access list that allowed all traffic except those packets that come from the range 172.16.130.32 to 172.16.130.63, we would type the following:

```
Router(config)#access-list 8 deny 172.16.130.32 0.0.0.31
Router(config)#access-list 8 permit 0.0.0.0 255.255.255.255
```

Keywords *any* and *host*

In an effort to make access lists a little easier to deal with, the keywords *any* and *host* were created. For example, if you want to create a statement that allowed all traffic through, you would have to create the following command:

```
Router(config)#access-list 14 permit 0.0.0.0 255.255.255.255
```

In the previous section, we learned that a 1 bit in the wildcard mask means you don't match that bit in the source address. So, a wildcard mask of all 1s (255.255.255.255) means you do not match any of the bits in the source address, and it will permit all traffic. To save yourself from having to type all those 0s and 255s, you can use the *any* keyword, as seen in the command that follows.

```
Router(config)#access-list 14 permit any
```

Another example is when you only want to match one specific address. To do this, you would have to type in the command:

```
Router(config)#access-list 15 permit 172.16.134.23 0.0.0.0
```

Because the wildcard mask is all 0s, you are telling the router you want to match every single bit of the source address. So, you would permit

172.16.134.23, but it would deny any other address (due to the implicit *deny* statement at the end). Another way of typing this command is:

```
Router(config)#access-list 15 permit host 172.16.134.23
```

Using the *any* and *host* keywords in the *access-list* command makes them easier to read and saves you from having to type out the whole wildcard mask when you are matching on all of the bits, or on none of the bits.

Keyword Log

When including the keyword *log* in an *access-list* statement, a match of that statement will be logged. That is, any packet that matches the access list will cause a message to be sent to the console, memory, or to a syslog server.

Configuring & Implementing…

Logging Commands

You can control how your router handles log messages with the *logging* commands in global configuration mode. To see what logging features are configure on your router, use the *show logging* command as shown next:

```
Router#show logging

Syslog logging: enabled (0 messages dropped, 0 flushes, 0 overruns)

    Console logging: level debugging, 2966 messages logged

    Monitor logging: level debugging, 2695 messages logged

    Buffer logging: level informational, 54 messages logged

    Trap logging: level informational, 59 message lines logged
```

The preceding output shows us three different items: the destination of the log messages, the severity of messages logged to that destination, and the number of messages that have been logged.

As seen previously, there are four different destinations that the router can send logging messages. *Console logging* refers to the messages sent to the screen while connected to the console port. When you are connected to the router via Telnet, you cannot see console messages, but you can type **terminal monitor**, and you will be able to see any messages that are sent to *Monitor Logging*. The router also has in internal

Continued

buffer that can be used to store messages, which are collected by the *Buffer Logging* settings. When you use the *show logging* command, the buffered messages will be shown immediately after the preceding output. Finally, if you would like to keep a history of all messages generated, you can configure a syslog server and choose which messages are sent to it with the *Trap Logging* destination.

There are also eight different levels of messages, which will be listed from most severe (Emergency Level 0) to least severe (Debugging Level 7):

- **Emergency** Level 0
- **Alerts** Level 1
- **Critical** Level 2
- **Errors** Level 3
- **Warning** Level 4
- **Notification** Level 5
- **Informational** Level 6
- **Debugging** Level 7

The level set in the previous *show logging* output shows the least severe message type that will be logged. The router will also log all severity levels above what is shown. For example, Level 0 through Level 6 messages will be logged to the buffer in the preceding example. All messages generated by adding the *log* keyword to an access list are classified as Level 6, or informational messages.

This feature is available with standard access lists since IOS 11.3. Previously, this capability was only available in extended IP access lists. When using the *log* keyword, the first packet that matches the access list causes a logging message immediately. Following matching packets are gathered over a five-minute interval before they are displayed or logged. Let's look at how this would work in the following example:

```
Router(config)#access-list 17 deny 172.16.130.88 log
Router(config)#access-list 17 deny 172.16.130.89 log
Router(config)#access-list 17 deny 172.16.130.90 log
Router(config)#access-list 17 permit any
```

Suppose the interface receives 10 packets from host 172.16.130.88, 15 packets from host 172.16.130.89, and 20 packets from host 172.16.130.90 over a five-minute period. The first log would look as follows:

```
list 17 deny 172.16.130.88 1 packet
list 17 deny 172.16.130.89 1 packet
list 17 deny 172.16.130.90 1 packet
```

After five minutes, the log would display as follows:

```
list 17 deny 172.16.130.88 9 packets
list 17 deny 172.16.130.89 14 packets
list 17 deny 172.16.130.90 19 packets
```

When using the keyword *log*, we are provided with an observant capability. Here you are able to analyze not only who has tried to access your network but you are also able to tell the number of attempts. The log message will indicate the number of packets, whether the packet was permitted or denied, the source address, and the access list number. There will be a message generated for the first packet that matches the test and then at five-minute intervals you will receive a message stating the number of packets matched during the previous five minutes.

Applying an Access List

Now that we've learned how to structure the access list, we will learn how to apply it to an interface. In this section, we will assume we have a router with two interfaces: Serial0 and Ethernet0. The network we want to protect is on the Ethernet 0 interface and we want to filter traffic as it enters the router on the Serial0 interface. The only network we want to be able to pass through our router is the 192.168.10.0 255.255.255.0 network, while all other traffic is denied. In addition, the host 192.168.10.5 should also be denied access to our network, even though it is a part of the 192.168.10.0 subnet.

The first step is to create our access list. In this example, we've decided to use access list number 25. We create the list by typing:

```
Router(config)#access-list 25 deny host 192.168.10.5
Router(config)#access-list 25 permit 192.168.10.0 0.0.0.255
```

Our first statement in our access list is to deny the host 192.168.10.5. The next statement is to allow the entire Class C subnet 192.168.10.0. The implicit *deny* statement at the end of the access list will prevent any other traffic from being permitted through the list.

NOTE

Remember that access lists are processed in sequential order. If our first statement were to permit the 192.168.10.0 network, then 192.168.10.5 would be able to access our network, even though we want to deny it. This would happen because 192.168.10.5 would match the *permit* statement and would not process any farther. To remedy this situation, we must deny the specific IP first, and then allow the rest of the network.

Next, we must specify the interface where we plan to apply the access list. Since all traffic from outside our network must come to us over the Serial0 link, we want to apply this access list to that interface. To enter interface configuration mode, we would type:

```
Router(config)#interface serial 0
```

The next step is to apply the access list to the interface and define the direction of the access list. This is accomplished by using the *ip access-group* command. Table 4.3 describes the *ip access-group* command.

```
ip access-group {list number} {in|out}
```

Table 4.3 The *ip access-group* Command

Command	Description
ip	Defines the protocol used.
access-group	Applies the access list to the interface.
List number	Identifies the access list you wish to apply.
in | out	Keyword in or out defines the direction in which the access list will be applied. This indicates whether packets are examined as they leave the interface (outside), or as they enter the router (inside).

To complete our example, we would use the following command to apply the access list. This command will apply the access list we just created to filter traffic that comes towards us into the serial interface. Before it is routed to the Ethernet interface, it must pass through the access list or else it will be dropped.

```
Router(config-if)#ip access-group 25 in
```

Extended IP Access Lists

Although there are times when we only need to filter traffic based on the source address, more often than not we will need to match traffic with a higher level of detail. An option for more precise traffic-filtering control would be an extended IP access list. Here, both the source and destination address are checked. In addition, you also have the ability to specify the protocol and optional TCP or UDP port number to filter more precisely. In the following example, any field represented by {} is mandatory for the access list, while any field represented by [] is optional. The format of an extended IP access list is:

```
access-list access-list-number {permit | deny} protocol source
    source-wildcard [operator source-port] destination destination-wildcard
    [operator destination-port] [precedence precedence-number] [tos tos]
    [established] [log | log-input]
```

Bold items represent keywords that are part of the access list syntax. Table 4.4 lists the configuration for a standard IP access list.

Table 4.4 Extended IP Access List Configuration

Command	Description
Access-list list number	Defines the number of the access list. The extended access list numbers range from 100–199.
Permit	If conditions are met, traffic will be allowed.
deny	If conditions are met, traffic will be denied.
Protocol	Defines the Internet protocol for filtering. Available options here are keywords such as *TCP* or *UDP*, or the number of the protocol as seen in the IP header.
source-address	Identifies the host or network from which the packet is being sent. The source can be specified by an IP address or by using the keyword *any*.
source wildcard-mask	This defines the number of wildcard bits assigned to the source address. The source wildcard-mask can be specified by an IP address or by using the keyword *any*.

Continued

Table 4.4 Continued

Command	Description
Operator source-port	Defines the name or number of a *source* TCP or UDP port. A list of operators is shown next.
Destination-address	Identifies the host or network to which the packet is being sent. The destination can be specified by an IP address or by using the keyword *any*.
Destination wildcard-mask	This defines the number of wildcard bits assigned to the destination address. The destination wildcard-mask can be specified by an IP address or by using the keyword *any*.
Operator destination-port	Defines the name or number of a *destination* TCP or UDP port. A list of operators is shown next.
precedence precedence-number	Used for filtering by the precedence level name or number (0 thru 7).
tos tos-number	Used for filtering by the Type of Service level specified by a name or number (0 thru 15).
established	Allows established TCP sessions through the list.
log | log-input	Log the event when a packet matches the access list statement. Log-input shows the same information as the *log* keyword, except it also adds the interface name the packet was received on.

In the following access list, we get very specific about what host we want to access a particular network or host on a network. In the first three lines, we are permitting or allowing packets from individual hosts on subnet 172.16.130.0 to any host on network 10.0.0.0. In line 4, we are denying packets with the source address that belongs to subnet 172.16.130.0 to the destination of host 192.168.10.118. Line 5 tells us that we are permitting all IP packets with no concern of a source or destination address. The implicit *deny all* at the end of the list will never be matched against a packet because the previous *permit* statement will match all packets. In Figure 4.3, we would apply this access list on the serial 0 interface in the outbound direction as follows:

```
Router(config)# interface serial 0
Router(config-if)# ip access-group 141 out
```

Figure 4.3 An Example Network

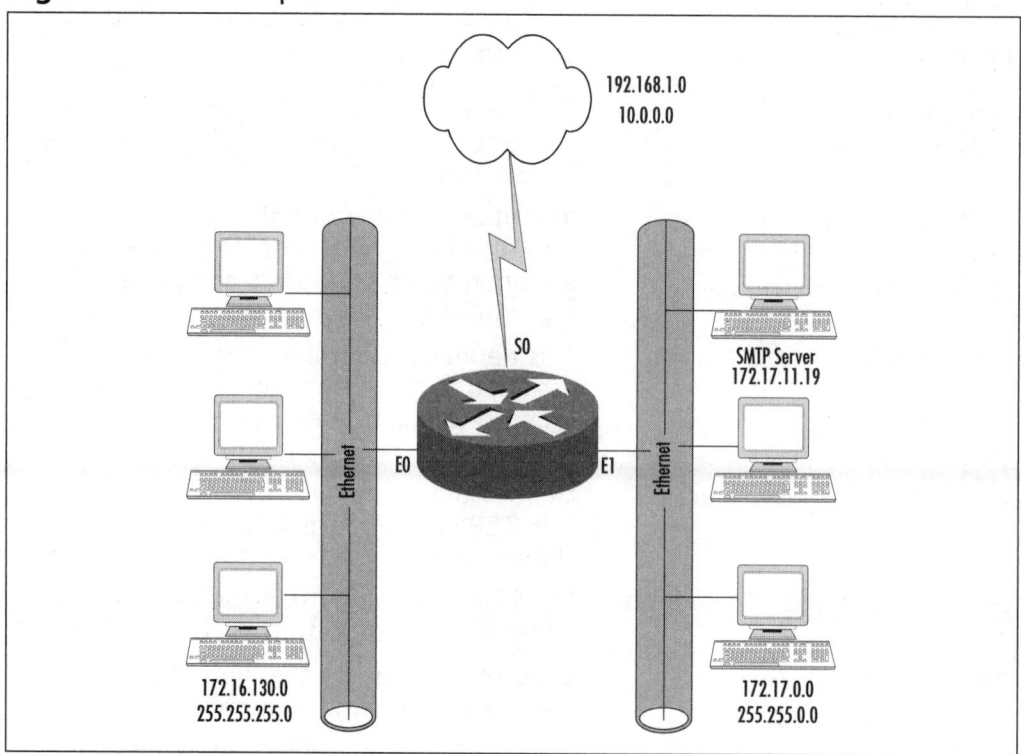

An example of an extended access list is as follows:

```
access-list 141 permit icmp host 172.16.130.88 10.0.0.0 0.255.255.255
access-list 141 permit tcp host 172.16.130.89 eq 734 10.0.0.0 0.
    255.255.255 range 10000 10010
access-list 141 permit udp host 172.16.130.90 10.0.0.0 0.255.255.255
    eq tftp
access-list 141 deny ip 172.16.130.0 0.0.0.255 host 192.168.10.118
access-list 141 permit ip any any
```

Table 4.5 describes the extended access list commands.

Table 4.5 A Description of *Access List* Commands

Command	Description
access-list 141 permit icmp host 172.16.130.88 10.0.0.0 0.255.255.255	Allows host 172.16.130.88 to send ICMP messages to any host on network 10.0.0.0.
access-list 141 permit tcp host 172.16.130.89 eq 734 10.0.0.0 0.255.255.255 range 10000 10010	Allows host 172.16.130.89 to initiate TCP sessions from port 734 to any port between 10000 and 10010 on any host on network 10.0.0.0.
access-list 141 permit udp host 172.16.130.90 10.0.0.0 0.255.255.255 eq tftp	Allows host 172.16.130.90 to send files via TFTP (UDP port 69) to any host on network 10.0.0.0.
access-list 141 deny ip 172.16.130.0 0.0.0.255 host 192.168.10.118	Denies any host on network 172.16.130.0 to host 192.168.10.118. Since we configured some *permit* statements from hosts within these previous two subnets, this entry will deny everything between these two networks that isn't explicitly permitted in the earlier listing.
access-list 141 permit ip any any	Allows all hosts from any network to any network, if it has not matched one of the preceding lists. Take a good look at the order of these commands to get a feel for the importance of the list order. Remember this is processed in a top-down manner, as shown in Figure 4.2.

Just as in our standard access list, the extended access list will require a hyphen between the words *access* and *list*. Next is the list number. Since we are referencing an extended IP access list, the numbers would range from 100 to 199.

The access list number serves the same dual purpose here as we looked at earlier with the standard access list. The router must have a way to distinguish between access lists. The number performs this purpose along with tying the lines of an access list together and designates which access list the filter is part of. The number also tells the router the type of access list.

Designing & Planning…

Placement of Access Lists

Often you have a few options about how to apply your access lists and still achieve the same affect on the traffic flowing through the router. In the case of the previous example, access list 141 was applied outbound on the serial 0 interface. Because access list 141 was designed to only filter traffic originating from the 172.16.130.0 network, and not traffic from 172.17.0.0, this list could have been applied in the inbound direction on Ethernet 0. Both approaches will have the same affect on the traffic flowing through the router.

There is a minor difference between these two approaches, though. When the ACL is applied outbound on the Serial0 interface, the traffic enters the Ethernet0 interface and is processed against the routing table. The packet is then passed to the outbound interface, where it is checked against any outbound ACLs. If the outbound interface is Serial 0, it checks packets against access list 141 and will permit or deny the traffic based on the rules defined in that list.

When the ACL is applied inbound on the Ethernet0 interface, the traffic is permitted or denied before it is processed against the routing table. On a router under heavy traffic loads, this could make a considerable difference in the delay that is introduced because the router does not have to process packets that will be dropped by the outbound interface.

Although inbound filtering has the advantage with respect to route processing, that does not necessarily make it the better way to apply access lists. Under different circumstances, you may want to prevent access to an external subnet from both Ethernet interfaces. In this case, it may be easier to apply the access lists in the outbound direction of Serial0 because packets from both Ethernet interfaces will have to pass through Serial0 to get to the external subnet. In other words, you are applying the access list to the bottleneck in traffic. Otherwise, you will

Continued

> have to keep two separate access lists, one specific for Ethernet0 and the other specific for Ethernet1. If the router is under light traffic loads, it may be easier to maintain a single access list.
>
> There is disagreement among network and security professionals about which approach is better, but neither approach should be considered better than the other in all cases. It is up to you to decide which is best for your situation.

Keywords *permit* or *deny*

A keyword *permit* or *deny* specifies to the router the action to be performed. For example, the keyword *permit* would allow the packet to exit or enter the interface, depending on whether you specify the filtering to be performed in or out. Again, this option provides the same function as in our standard access list. The last line of our extended access list example could have read as follows:

```
access-list 141 permit ip any any
```

Protocol

You have the option of filtering several different protocols using the extended access list. The protocol field in the IP header is an 8-bit number that defines what protocol is used inside the IP packet. TCP and UDP are only two of the possible protocols that can be filtered on, although they are most common. Other protocols, such as ICMP and EIGRP, have their own protocol numbers because they are not encapsulated inside TCP or UDP. If we use a question mark when defining an access list, we can see the protocol numbers that have been defined by name inside the router.

```
Router(config)#access-list 191 permit ?
  <0-255>  An IP protocol number
  ahp      Authentication Header Protocol
  eigrp    Cisco's EIGRP routing protocol
  esp      Encapsulation Security Payload
  gre      Cisco's GRE tunneling
  icmp     Internet Control Message Protocol
  igmp     Internet Gateway Message Protocol
  igrp     Cisco's IGRP routing protocol
  ip       Any Internet Protocol
```

```
ipinip    IP in IP tunneling

nos       KA9Q NOS compatible IP over IP tunneling

ospf      OSPF routing protocol

pcp       Payload Compression Protocol

pim       Protocol Independent Multicast

tcp       Transmission Control Protocol

udp       User Datagram Protocol
```

Protocols not on the preceding list may also be filtered with extended access lists, but they must be referenced by their protocol number. A full list of assigned IP protocol numbers can be found at www.iana.org/assignments/protocol-numbers.

It is important to remember that the IP keyword in the protocol field matches all protocol numbers. You must use a systematic approach here when designing your access list. For example, if your first line in the access list permits IP for a specific address, and the second line denies UDP for the same address, the second statement would have no effect. The first line would permit IP, including all the above layers. An option here may be to reverse the order of the statements. With the statements reversed, UDP would be denied from that address and all other protocols would be permitted.

Source Address and Wildcard-mask

The source address and source wildcard-mask perform the same function here as in a standard IP access list. So, in the preceding example we could have used the wildcard mask instead of the *host* and *any* keywords. The access list would then look as follows:

```
access-list 141 permit ip 172.16.130.88 0.0.0.0 10.0.0.0 0.255.255.255

access-list 141 permit ip 172.16.130.89 0.0.0.0 10.0.0.0 0.255.255.255

access-list 141 permit ip 172.16.130.90 0.0.0.0 10.0.0.0 0.255.255.255

access-list 141 permit ip 172.16.130.0 0.0.0.255 192.168.10.118 0.0.0.0

access-list 141 permit ip 0.0.0.0 255.255.255.255 0.0.0.0 255.255.255.255
```

In the first three lines, we are permitting or allowing packets from individual hosts on subnet 172.16.130.0 to any host on network 10.0.0.0. In line 4, we are permitting packets with the source address that belongs to subnet 172.16.130.0 to the destination of host 192.168.10.118. Line 5 tells us that we are permitting all packets regardless of the source or destination address. Remember that standard IP access lists have a default mask of 0.0.0.0. This does not apply to extended access lists so we must specify one.

Destination Address and Wildcard-mask

The destination address and wildcard-mask have the same effect and structure as the source address and wildcard-mask. So, here the keywords *host* and *any* are also available. You can utilize these keywords to specify any destination address as well as a specific destination without using the wildcard mask. Remember that extended access lists try a match on both source and destination. A common mistake here is trying to build an extended access list with the idea of only filtering the source address, and forgetting to specify the destination address.

Source and Destination Port Number

Many times, we don't want to deny all access to a particular server. When you put a Web server out on the Internet, you want everyone to be able to access it on port 80 (WWW), but you don't want to allow access to any other ports, because it gives hackers the opportunity to exploit other services you may not be aware of (although you should know of them in the first place). Restricting access to this level of detail is another benefit of extended ACLs. We have the option of specifying a source and destination port number in the access list. Let's look at a simple example:

```
Router(config)# interface Serial 0
Router(config-if)# ip access-group 111 in


Router(config)#access-list 111 permit tcp any host 172.17.11.19 eq 25
Router(config)#access-list 111 permit tcp any host 172.17.11.19 eq 23
```

These commands are explained in Table 4.6.

Table 4.6 Router Commands

Router Commands	Description
access-list 111 permit tcp any host 172.17.11.19 eq 25	Permits SMTP from anywhere to host 172.17.11.19.
access-list 111 permit tcp any host 172.17.11.19 eq 23	Permits Telnet from anywhere to host 172.17.11.19.
interface Serial 0	Enters interface submode.
ip access-group 111 in	Applies access list inbound on interface.

In line 1, we are permitting TCP packets from any source to the destination of host 172.22.11.19 if the destination port is 25 (SMTP). In line 2, we are permitting TCP packets from any source to the destination of host 172.22.11.19 if the destination port is 23 (Telnet). The implicit *deny* statement at the end of this access list will prevent all other traffic from making it into our network.

Let's take a look at filtering with TCP and UDP. When using TCP, for example, the access list will examine the source and destination port numbers inside the TCP segment header. So, when using an extended access list, you have the capability to filter to and from a network address and also to and from a particular port number. You have several options when deciding which operator to use, such as:

- **eq** equal to
- **neq** not equal to
- **gt** greater than
- **lt** less than
- **range** specifies an inclusive range or ports (Here, two port numbers are specified.)

Established

One of the options available for use with an extended access list is the established option. This option is only available with the TCP protocol. The idea here is to prevent someone outside your network from initiating a connection to a host on the inside, but still letting traffic through if it is a response to something that originated from inside your network. To demonstrate this, let's take a look at the following access list, which will apply later to Figure 4.4.

```
Router(config)# interface Serial 0
Router(config-if)# ip access-group 110 in


access-list 110 permit tcp any host 172.17.11.19 eq 25
access-list 110 permit tcp 12.0.0.0 0.255.255.255 172.22.114.0 0.0.0.255 eq
23
```

We created this access list so the server 172.17.11.19 can receive mail messages on the SMTP port, and to allow the 12.0.0.0 255.0.0.0 network Telnet access to the 172.22.114.0 255.255.255.0 network. What you may not realize is that while this access list will protect our network from access except on the specified servers and ports, it will also prevent anyone on our network from surfing the Web. It is important to realize that if you are permitting a very specific list of traffic, and denying everything else, responses to traffic initiated inside your network will be blocked. Let's go over the steps when the host 172.17.10.10 tries to visit a Web page at 10.15.25.35, which is somewhere on the Internet. (If you need a refresher on the TCP handshake process, you can look at Figure 4.5 later in this section.)

1. Host 172.17.10.10 initiates a TCP from a random port above 1024 (let's assume 10000) and tries to connect to port 80 (WWW) on server 10.15.25.35.

2. Host 10.15.25.35 will receive a TCP packet with the SYN flag set, destined for port 80 and sourced from 172.17.10.10:10000.

3. Host 10.15.25.35 will send a TCP packet with the SYN and ACK flag set to acknowledge the TCP session. The TCP segment will be sourced from port 80 and sent to port 10000 on 172.17.10.10.

4. The SYN/ACK TCP packet will enter the router through Serial0, which has access list 110 applied in the inbound direction

5. The packet will not match either the first or second lines in the access list, so it will match the implicit *deny all* and the packet will be dropped. This will prevent all hosts inside your network from communicating on the Internet.

In this case, we want to allow all workstations access to the Internet, but obviously, we cannot create individual lines in an access list to permit traffic back from every Web server on the entire Internet. To solve this problem, the established keyword was added to the extended access list. If the established keyword is used on a line of the access list, it will only allow a packet through if it matches the line of the list, and has either the ACK or RST bit set in the TCP header. Let's look at another access list to demonstrate this.

Figure 4.4 shows an example of our network with the access list applied inbound on interface Serial0 (S0). The first line of the access list permits TCP packets from any source to the network 172.17.0.0 with the TCP flag ACK or RST bit set. This will allow traffic back into our network if it is a response to something that was originated inside. The second line tells the router to permit TCP packets from any source if the destination is 172.17.11.19 and the destination port is 25 (SMTP). Line 3 is allowing a TCP segment with a source address from network 12.0.0.0 to port 23 (Telnet), to any address on subnet 172.22.114.0. What will happen to all other packets? Once again the implicit *deny all* will drop any other packets.

Figure 4.4 The Access List Applied to Serial 0 Inbound

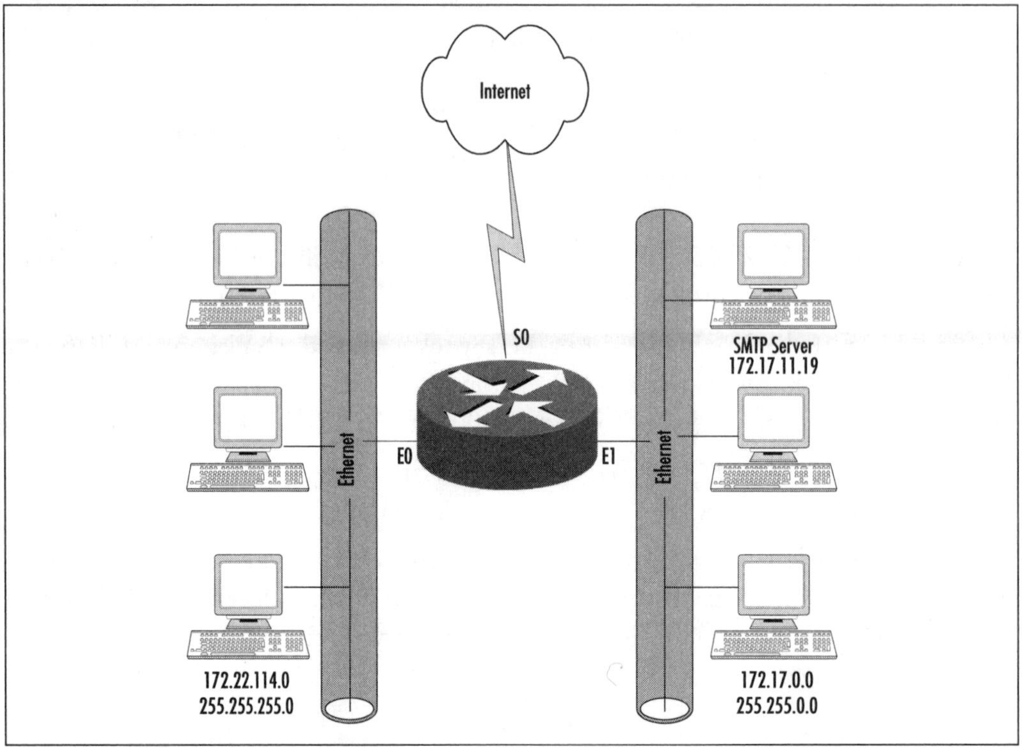

```
Router(config)# interface Serial 0
Router(config-if)# ip access-group 111 in

access-list 111 permit tcp any host 172.17.0.0 0.0.255.255 established
access-list 111 permit tcp any host 172.17.11.19 eq 25
access-list 111 permit tcp 12.0.0.0 0.255.255.255 172.22.114.0 0.0.0.255 eq
23
```

In the TCP segment there are 6 flag bits, two of which are the ACK and RST. If one of these two bits is set, then a match on the established keyword will occur. The SYN bit indicates that a connection is being established. A packet with a SYN bit without an ACK bit is the very first packet sent to establish a connection, and will be denied by a line with the established keyword due to the lack of an ACK flag. Figure 4.5 shows the TCP setup handshake.

Figure 4.5 A TCP Session Being Established

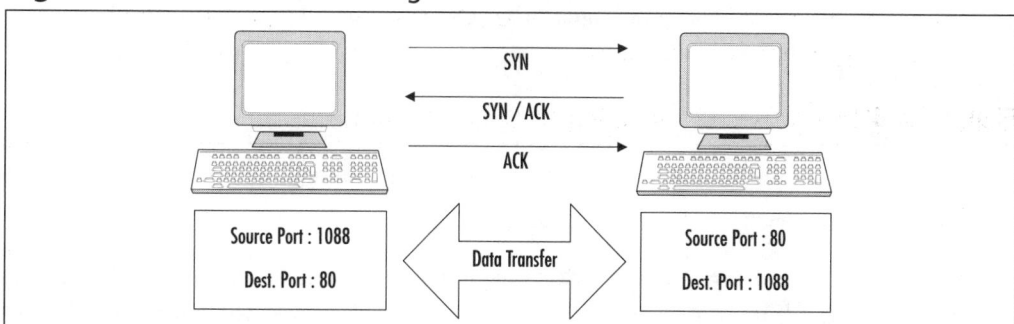

Another issue to consider here is that you, as the administrator, may not be certain what protocols the host may be using. However, we do know ports are chosen by workstations randomly between the port ranges of 1024 and 65535. Keeping that in mind, we could modify the first line of the access list as follows:

```
access-list 111 permit tcp any host 172.17.0.0 0.0.255.255 gt 1023
established
```

This would insure that no packets are accepted inbound to our network unless the destination port is higher that 1023. The hacker could spoof the ACK or RST bit in the packet but the destination port would still have to be higher that 1023. Typically, our servers running services such as DNS run below port 1024. However, it is not a good idea to let through all ports over 1023. You become vulnerable to network scans and denial of service attacks (RST).

SECURITY ALERT

The established keyword is not a secure way of protecting your network, because a hacker can easily forge a packet with the RST or ACK flag set and it will be allowed through the access list. To solve this problem, use either reflexive access lists or CBAC, which are covered later in this chapter.

Now, let's look at what happens when we decide to allow restricted TFTP access to host 172.17.11.19, unrestricted DNS access to host 172.17.11.20, and unrestricted SNMP access to the entire network. TFTP, DNS, and SNMP are UDP-based protocols. We have added to our extended access list again in the following example:

```
access-list 111 permit tcp any host 172.17.0.0 0.0.255.255 established
access-list 111 permit tcp any host 172.17.11.19 eq 25
access-list 111 permit tcp 12.0.0.0 0.255.255.255 172.22.114.0 0.0.0.255 eq
  23
access-list 111 permit udp 192.168.10.0 0.0.0.255 host 172.17.11.19 eq 69
access-list 111 permit udp any host 172.17.11.20 eq 53
access-list 111 permit udp any any eq 161
```

You will notice there is no keyword established on the lines for UDP packets. Remember that UDP is a connectionless protocol, therefore no connections will be established between hosts. A UDP packet is sent without any acknowledgement; the sending host just assumes the packet arrived at the destination. Since we have not changed the first three lines of our access list, we will begin by discussing line 4. Line 4 is allowing UDP datagrams from subnet 192.168.10.0 to port 69 (TFTP) on host 172.17.11.19. Line 5 is allowing UDP datagrams from any source to host 172.17.11.20 with a destination port of 53 (DNS). Line 6 allows all SNMP (port 161) to and from any destination. Remember, any packets not matching the list will be dropped by the implicit *deny all*. Figure 4.6 shows the addition of a DNS server in our network. Here, we would apply the access list inbound on interface serial 0. Also, be aware that the 172.22.114.0 network would still be unable to surf the Web with the current ACL applied.

Figure 4.6 Example Network with a DNS Server Added

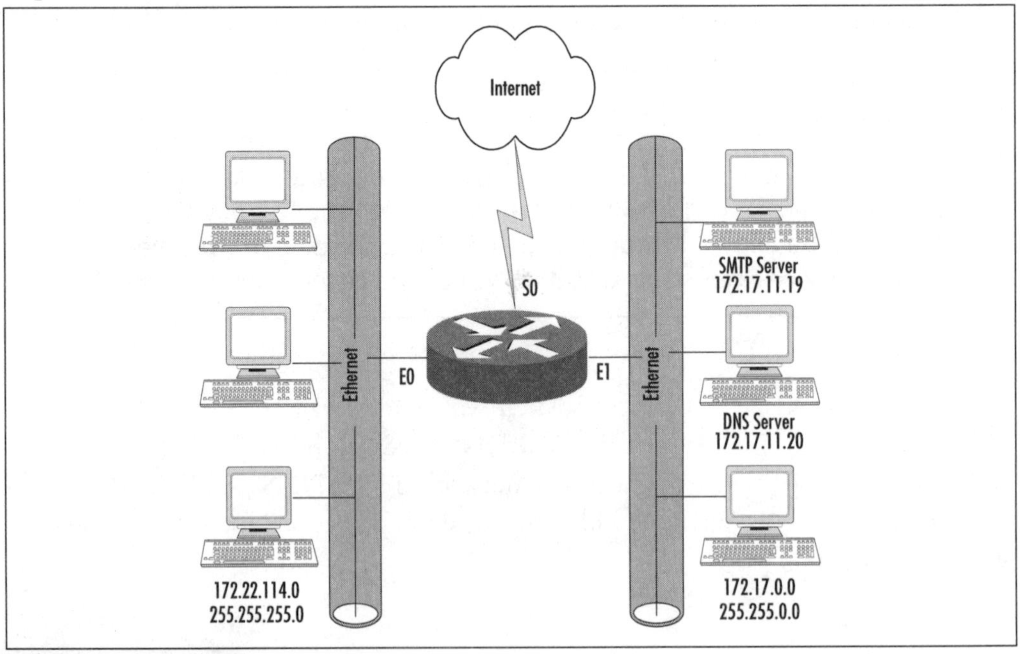

Log and Log-input

When we were discussing standard access lists we covered the *log* keyword, and what sort of information this presents us. This keyword is also available for extended access lists. Just as extended access lists allow us to filter on much more information than a standard access list, the *log* keyword gives us much more information when used with an extended access list, than a standard access list. When used with an extended ACL, we will be told the protocol, destination IP, source port and destination port, in addition to the other information returned from a standard ACL.

In some cases, for example when assigning an outbound ACL to an interface, we may not be able to tell where a packet has originated, especially in large networks. Of course, we will be given the source address, but to figure out where the packet originated, we would have to look at the routing table to see which interface the packet should have arrived on. To make this process a little easier, Cisco added the *log-input* keyword for the ACL. This will give us the interface name on which the packet arrived, in addition to all the information gathered from the *log* keyword.

The *log-input* command can also be useful in discovering if a source address has been spoofed. If your router logs are showing a packet entering on a different interface from where the route table says the network is supposed to be, you may be dealing with a packet that has a spoofed source address.

Named Access Lists

Each access list type has a range of acceptable numbers that can be used. For example, there are 99 standard (1 thru 99) and 100 extended (100 thru 199) access lists available in the Cisco IOS. This seems to be more than enough—however, maybe you need to create more that 100 extended IP access lists on your enterprise router. Named access lists provide an alternative to allow this. Also, named access lists provide a description that is typically more manageable than a large group of numbers.

Named access lists are just as the title implies, an access list that is referenced by name instead of a number. They also allow you to delete a specific entry in your access list. When using numbered access lists, this is not an option. When using a numbered access list, you must recreate the entire access list to remove an unwanted entry. When adding to an access list, both the named and numbered will place the new line at the bottom of the access list.

When creating a named access list, it must begin with a standard alphabetic character. Names are case sensitive so the access list SYDNEY and Sydney will be looked at as two unique names or two different access lists. Named access lists use the same syntax as numbered access lists, but the creation is slightly different. Notice that you must use the keyword *ip* before the main access list statement. You also enter a new configuration mode specifically for the named access lists. In this mode, you start with the *permit* or *deny* keyword, so you do not have to type **access-list** at the beginning of every line. Just type **exit** when you are finished to exit the named ACL configuration mode. Named access lists are applied with the *ip access-group* command just like numbered ACLs.

```
Router(config)#ip access-list extended filter_tx
Router(config-ext-nacl)#permit tcp any 172.17.0.0 0.0.255.255 established
Router(config-ext-nacl)#permit tcp any host 172.17.11.19 eq smtp
Router(config-ext-nacl)#permit tcp 12.0.0.0 0.255.255.255 172.22.114.0
    0.0.0.255 eq 23
Router(config-ext-nacl)#permit udp 192.168.10.0 0.0.0.255 host
    172.17.11.19 eq 69
Router(config-ext-nacl)#permit udp any host 172.17.11.20 eq 53
Router(config-ext-nacl)#permit udp any any eq 161
Router(config-ext-nacl)#exit
Router(config)#
```

Editing Access Lists

When applying access lists, there are several factors to consider. One of the most important things to remember is that access lists are evaluated from the top down. So packets will always be tested starting with the top line of the access list. Careful consideration should be taken regarding the order of your access list statements. The most frequent match should always be at the beginning of the access list.

Another thing to consider is the placement of the access list. When looking at your network, a standard access list should be placed closest to the destination of where you are trying to block the packets. Remember that a standard IP access list filters on the source IP address. If the IP address is blocked, then the entire protocol suite (IP) would typically be denied. So, if you denied an IP address close to the source, the user would basically be denied access anywhere on the network.

> **NOTE**
>
> Packets generated by the router are not affected by an outbound access list. So, to filter routing table updates or any traffic generated by the router, you should consider inbound access lists.

When using a named access list, we can delete a specific entry—however, with a numbered access list, we do not have this option. We have learned that when you need to add an entry into the access list in a specific position (such as the fifth line) the entire access list must be deleted and then re-created with new entries. This applies to both numbered and named access lists. So if this tells me I have just created a 35-line access list and need to make a change, is the only option I have to simply start over? Not really. There are several ways to avoid re-creating your entire access list. One option to explore here may be the use of the TFTP protocol. When utilizing TFTP we have the ability to copy our configuration to a server as a text file. Remember, when you copy from anywhere to the running configuration, a merge will occur. So, if your intention is to change line 14, make your changes to the configuration file while on the TFTP server, then when you copy the file to the running configuration, the merge will replace line 14 with your new changes. Once on the server, we can use a text editor to modify then reload the configuration to our router. Another option may be to have a template of an access list on your TFTP server. Having the template will help to ensure you enter the command correctly. Remember, the commands you use here will be the exact commands you would enter at the command line of the router. When copying this file to your running configuration, it will merge the new access list with your current configuration. If the syntax is incorrect, the operation will fail. The following is an example of how a session would look when loading an access list from a TFTP server. We will merge the access list with the running configuration.

```
Router# copy tftp running-config
Address or name of remote host []? 172.16.1.1
Source filename []? accesslist.txt
Destination filename [running-config]?
Accessing TFTP://172.16.1.1/accesslist.txt… OK - 1684/3072 bytes]
Loading accesslist.txt from 172.16.1.1 (via Ethernet 0): !!
    [OK - 1388/3072 bytes]
1388 bytes copied in 3 secs (462 bytes/sec)
```

If you do not have access to a TFTP server, another option for editing access lists is to just use the cut and paste feature of your terminal program. You can copy the current access list out of the *show running-config* output, and paste it into a text editor like Notepad. Once in Notepad, you can make the needed changes and paste the list back into the router.

WARNING

Be aware that if you want to paste the ACL back into the router with the same name or number, you must delete the old ACL first. If you do not, then the two access lists will combine and contain lines from both the new and old list. It is best to use a slightly different name or number for the revised ACL and then go back and change the *ip access-group* command to avoid any unexpected complications. This also avoids the small amount of time that you would be unsecured while you delete your old ACL and paste in the new one.

Problems with Access Lists

As you've seen so far, access lists are very useful in controlling what type of traffic is allowed to flow through the router. Unfortunately, in most situations, basic access lists cannot be relied upon to properly secure a network. Many times a basic access list is not flexible enough to provide a good solution for the problem. For example, using the access lists we've discussed thus far, we don't have any way of creating temporary entries in a list. Some other issues you may encounter with access lists are their limited capability to test information above the IP layer. Extended access lists have the capability to check on Layer 4, but not in the detailed sense.

Another problem to consider is that the access list will examine each packet individually and does not have the capability of detecting if a packet is part of an upper layer conversation. The keyword *established* can be used to match TCP packets that are part of an established TCP session, but you need to be cautious when using it. Remember that *established* only checks the TCP header for the presence of an RST or ACK flag, and does not perform any checks to verify that a packet is truly part of an established conversation. Although this filtering technique is suitable in many cases, it does not protect against forged TCP packets (commonly used to probe networks), nor does it offer any facility to filter UDP sessions. Reflexive access list and CBAC, introduced later in this chapter, offer better control and more facilities to do session filtering.

To help solve some of these problems, Cisco has added some advanced features to the IOS software. We will go through some of these features and discuss the problems they were designed to handle, as well as when it is best to use them.

Lock-and-key Access Lists

Lock-and-key is a traffic filtering security feature that can automatically create an opening in an access list on the router to allow incoming traffic from an authenticated source. These access lists are also referred to as dynamic access lists. When using the basic access lists discussed earlier in this chapter, the list will never change unless an administrator makes a change. With lock-and-key access lists, you can add dynamic entries that are only active after the user has been authenticated with the router. After the authentication process, the dynamic entry will disappear after the configured timeout value, or after the maximum lifetime of the temporary entry has been reached. Once the entry is terminated, the interface is configured back to its original state.

Let's say, for example, that a user in Figure 4.7 is working at a branch office and needs to log in to the corporate office. The user will attempt to log in from a PC that is connected to a router (typically via LAN). A Telnet session will be opened to the router to provide authentication. The router at the corporate site (which is configured for lock-and-key) receives the Telnet packet and opens a Telnet session. Next, the router will prompt for a password and then perform authentication by using a test that is configured by the administrator, such as a name and password. The authentication process can be done locally by the router using a local username/password configuration, or through an external AAA server such as TACACS+ or RADIUS. When the user successfully authenticates, the Telnet session closes and a temporary entry is created in the dynamic access list. This dynamic access list will typically permit traffic from the user's source IP address to some predetermined destination. This dynamic access list will be deleted when a timeout is reached, or can be cleared by the administrator. A timeout can be configured as an idle-timeout or maximum-timeout period expires.

A user may not have a static IP address in a situation where a DHCP is in use in a LAN environment or when a user is connected through a dialup to an Internet Service Provider (ISP). In both cases, users may typically get a different IP address. Lock-and-key access lists can be used to implement a higher level of security without creating large holes in your network. The format of a lock-and-key

ACL is identical to an extended access list, except for two extra fields, as seen in Table 4.7.

```
access-list access-list-number [dynamic dynamic-name[timeout minutes]]
    {deny | permit} protocol source source-wildcard destination
    destination-wildcard[precedence precedence] [tos tos] [established]
    [log | log-input]
```

Figure 4.7 Using Lock and Key

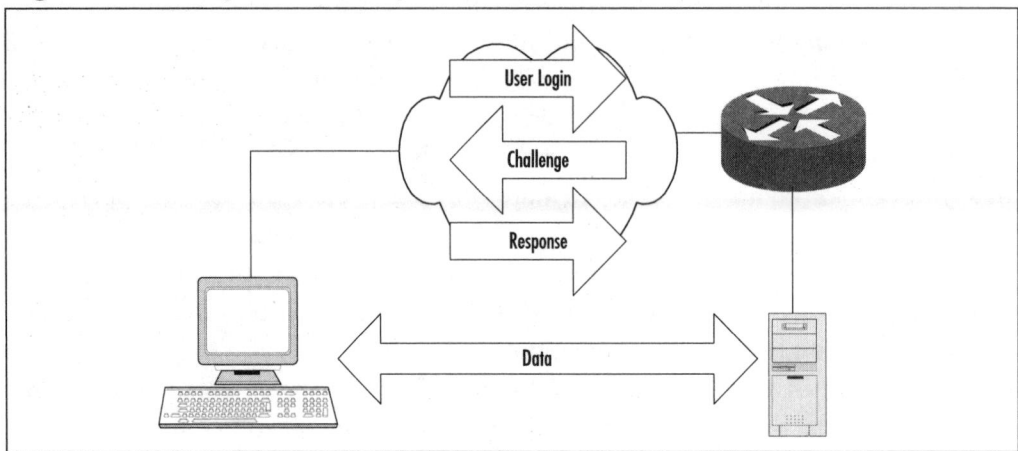

Table 4.7 Lock-and-Key Access List Configuration

Command	Description
access-list list number	Defines the number of the access list. The usable access list numbers range from 100–199.
dynamic dynamic-name	Designates this particular entry as part of a dynamic ACL. The *dynamic-name* field is a name assigned to the dynamic entries. If multiple entries need to be triggered at the same time, they all should have the same *dynamic-name*.
Timeout minutes	The *timeout* is optional and designates the absolute timeout for dynamic entries. No matter if the session is being used or not, the entry will be removed from the ACL after this timeout expires.
permit	If conditions are met, traffic will be allowed.
deny	If conditions are met, traffic will be denied.
Protocol	Defines the protocol for filtering, as discussed in the section about extended access lists.

Continued

Table 4.7 Continued

Command	Description
source-address	Identifies the host or network from which the packet is being sent. The source can be specified by an IP address or by using the keyword *any*.
source-wildcard	This defines the number of wildcard bits assigned to the source address. The source wildcard-mask can be specified by an IP address or by using the keyword *any*.
destination-address	Identifies the host or network to which the packet is being sent. The destination can be specified by an IP address or by using the keyword *any*.
destination-wildcard	This defines the number of wildcard bits assigned to the destination address. The destination wild-card-mask can be specified by an IP address or by using the keyword *any*.
precedence precedence-number	Used for filtering by the precedence level name or number.
tos	Defines filtering by service level, specified by a name or number (01-5).
established	When using TCP filtering, will occur if RST or ACK bits are set.
log | *log-input*	This keyword results in the logging of packets that match the *permit* or *deny* statement.

NOTE

Lock-and-key will only install one dynamic access list in any given access list. Although the router will allow you to specify multiple dynamic entries with different *dynamic-name* fields, these will not have any effect. You will see all the entries when viewing the list with *show ip access-list*, but if a user authenticates, it will only activate the first dynamic list. If you wish to use multiple lines when a user authenticates, make sure each entry has the same *dynamic-name* field.

Previously, when defining standard and extended access lists, we had two steps: Build the access list and apply it to an interface. Those steps are still required for lock-and-key access lists, but a few extra steps must be taken. Any entry in the ACL not marked as dynamic will filter just like a basic extended ACL. The dynamic entries will not be used until the authentication process takes place. To activate the dynamic entries, the user must Telnet into the router. With no additional configuration, the user will be at the standard user mode prompt. To open the temporary entries defined in the list, the user must type the *access-enable* command at the prompt. The format of the command is as follows:

```
access-enable [host] [timeout minutes]
```

We will look at each component of this command in Table 4.8.

Table 4.8 The Lock-and-key Access List Configuration

Command	Description
access-enable	Tells the router to activate the temporary entries in a lock-and-key ACL.
host	This keyword specifies that only the authenticating host should be allowed through the dynamic ACL, instead of activating the entire statement.
timeout minutes	This timeout value is an idle-timeout, unlike the one specified in the *access-list* command. If no traffic matches the dynamic entry in the number of minutes specified, the temporary entry will be removed from the list.

SECURITY ALERT

If your dynamic entries are configured to allow anyone to authenticate, you must make sure that the *host* keyword is used with the *access-enable* command. If not, you will open up your network to everyone. To avoid relying on the users to employ the command properly, configure the router with the *autocommand* feature. This will be discussed later in this section.

Under normal circumstances, you will be trusting the user to enter the correct command to allow himself access through the network. This can be a very dangerous thing to do because the user could accidentally open more access than you would wish.

Let's assume we have a router connected to the Internet. Our serial interface, which is connected to our ISP, has the address 10.10.100.2 assigned. The server that we are trying to protect is using the IP address 10.150.200.25. Let's also assume that we have users connecting to the Internet via dial-up accounts, and they could have IP addresses from almost any network connected to the Internet. In this case, we may decide to create a dynamic access entry such as:

```
Router(config)#access-list 120 dynamic remoteuser timeout 60 permit tcp
    any host 10.150.200.25 eq ftp
Router(config)#access-list 120 permit tcp any host 10.10.100.2 eq telnet

Router(config)#int s0
Router(config-if)#ip access-group 120 in
```

Next, we will verify the configuration.

```
Router#show ip access-list 120
Extended IP access list 120
    Dynamic remoteuser permit tcp any host 10.150.200.25 eq ftp
    permit tcp any host 10.10.100.2 eq telnet
```

In the preceding output, we see that only Telnet access to 10.10.100.2 is currently allowed. The preceding *dynamic* command will allow anyone who can authenticate with the router to FTP to the host 10.150.200.25. If the user types the command *access-enable host*, then they will allow their specific address through the access list. We can see this in the following output (assume that the user is assigned the address 192.168.100.43):

```
Router#show ip access-list 120
Extended IP access list 120
    Dynamic remote permit tcp any host 10.150.200.25 eq ftp
      permit tcp host 192.168.100.43 host 10.150.200.25 eq ftp
    permit tcp any host 10.10.100.2 eq telnet
```

Now we can see that a user has been authenticated and a specific IP is being allowed FTP access to the server. Now, let's assume that a second user wants to access the server. This user logs in correctly, but only types *access-enable* at the prompt, and does not include the *host* keyword. Let's look at the output from this command:

```
Router#show ip access-list 120
Extended IP access list 120
```

```
Dynamic remote permit tcp any host 10.150.200.25 eq ftp
   permit tcp host 192.168.100.43 host 10.150.200.25 eq ftp
   permit tcp any host 10.150.200.25 eq ftp
permit tcp any host 10.10.100.2 eq telnet
```

Now we see that our second user has just opened up the FTP server to anyone on the Internet. Obviously, this just defeated the purpose of us setting up a lock-and-key access list to begin with. To solve this problem, we will rely on the *autocommand* feature of the Cisco IOS that will allow us to make a user automatically run a command upon login.

By default, the router has five Virtual Terminal (VTY) ports available for Telnet sessions, which are numbered 0 thru 5. When a user connects to a router, the connection will reserve a VTY port for the duration of that session. So five different Telnet sessions can be established on the router simultaneously. If you specify multiple VTY ports, they must all be configured identically because the software hunts for available VTY ports on a round-robin basis. If you do not want to configure all your VTY ports for lock-and-key access, you can specify access on a per-user basis.

First, we will cover the VTY configuration to allow users lock-and-key access:

```
Router(config)#line vty 0 4
Router(config-line)#login
Router(config-line)#password OpenUp
Router(config-line)#autocommand access-enable host timeout 10
```

Using the previous configuration, as soon as someone enters the appropriate password into the Telnet session, the command *access-enable host timeout 10* will be executed and the Telnet session will be disconnected. This will ensure that the appropriate command is used every time someone authenticates with the router. Unfortunately, this also means you will be unable to use the VTY ports for administrative purposes, so this solution isn't usually very appealing. A better way to configure the router for lock-and-key is as follows:

```
Router(config)#username susan password OpenUp
Router(config)#username susan autocommand access-enable host timeout 10
Router(config)#username admin password supersecret

Router(config)#line vty 0 4
Router(config)#login local
```

The previous commands create two users: *susan* and *admin*. If someone logs into the router as Susan, then the command *access-enable host timeout 10* will be executed and the session disconnected. If, on the other hand, someone logs in with the admin user, then they will have regular access to the router for configuration purposes.

Designing & Planning…

Security Risks Using Lock-and-key ACLs

One thing to consider is an attacker using IP spoofing. IP spoofing is where a hacker changes the source IP address of the packets that are sent to an IP address believed trusted by the network. When packets arrive at your router it is nearly impossible to determine if the packets are from a real host. Lock-and-key access lists play a big role in assisting here, due to the fact that the opening is only temporary. This lowers the chance of the hacker determining the trusted source IP address. It doesn't lower the chance of determining the source IP, but it does reduce the window of opportunity to exploit the temporary opening.

One drawback to consider is when a client is behind NAT or NAPT (PAT in Cisco nomenclature). If this user is allowed to authenticate using lock-and-key to access a remote site, the dynamic access list on the router will use the external or public address of the PAT device. That address is potentially used by a number of users and they will automatically be allowed access without any authentication. This is a serious security consideration.

You must also be extremely careful when configuring the dynamic statements in the access list. If you do not specify a timeout, then the dynamic opening will stay open until the router is reset. In addition, you want to take precautions to prevent a user from accidentally making a giant hole in your router security as discussed in this section.

Reflexive Access Lists

The reflexive access list alleviates some of the limitations of the basic and extended access list. Reflexive access lists allow IP packets to be filtered based on upper-layer session information as in extended access lists—however, the reflexive access list can do session filtering by creating dynamic openings for IP traffic that are part of the allowed session. By so doing, reflexive access lists provide a way to maintain information about existing connections. You have the option to permit

IP traffic for sessions originating from within your network, but to deny IP traffic for sessions originating outside your network. This sounds the same as an extended access list. Reflexive access lists are referred to as a separate type of access list, however it is important to note that a reflexive access list is a feature added to an extended access list and can only be defined using extended named IP access lists.

One instance where a reflexive access list could be used is when an IP upper-layer session (such as TCP or UDP) is initiated from inside the network, with an outgoing packet traveling to the external network. In this case, a new, temporary entry will be created to allow the return traffic back into the network. The ingoing traffic will only be permitted if it is part of the session and all other traffic will be denied. This happens because a temporary access list will be created inside the reflexive access list when an outbound TCP packet is forwarded outside of your network. This temporary access list will permit ingoing traffic corresponding to the outbound connection.

Reflexive access lists are similar to other access lists in several ways. As with other access lists, reflexive access lists contain entries that define criteria for permitting IP packets. These entries are evaluated in a top-down process in form until a match occurs. Reflexive access lists have significant differences—for example, they contain only temporary entries. The idea here is to create a reflexive access list that is embedded within the extended access list that is protecting an interface. As stated earlier, temporary entries are created within the reflexive ACL automatically when a new IP session begins and matches a reflexive permit entry (for example, with an outbound packet); the entries are removed when the session ends. Reflexive access lists are not applied directly to an interface. They are placed within an extended named IP access list that is applied to the interface. Reflexive access lists do not have the implicit *deny all* at the end of the list. Remember, they are nested in another access list, so once the reflexive ACL has been processed, the router will continue with the rest of the extended ACL.

The idea of a reflexive access list is to basically create a mirror image of the reflected entry. For example, in Figure 4.8, host0 on network 172.22.114.0 initiates a Telnet session to host1 on network 172.17.0.0. Telnet uses the TCP protocol, therefore host0 will pick a random source port number—let's use port 1028. Also, here we will have a source IP address, destination IP address, and destination TCP port number. Since we are using Telnet, the destination port number will be 23. So far, we have the following information:

Figure 4.8 Example Network Using Reflexive ACLs

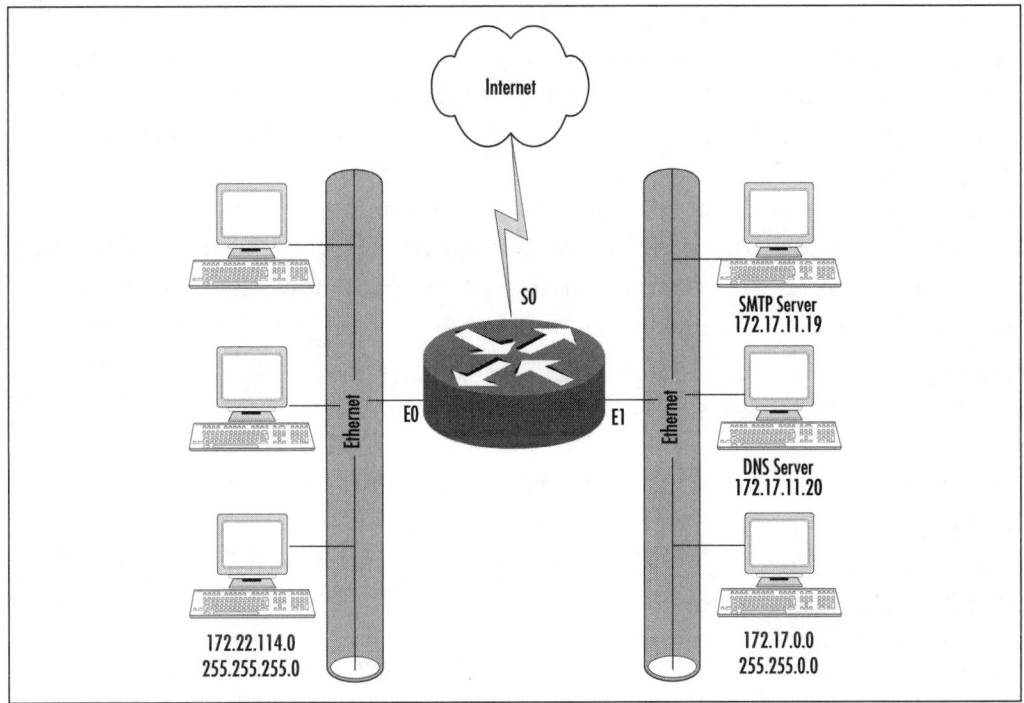

```
Source TCP port-1028
Destination TCP port-23
Source IP address-172.22.114.1
Destination IP address-172.17.0.1
```

In our configuration, we will have a *reflexive access-list* statement that will trigger a reflected access list entry. This will allow inbound return traffic and would look as follows:

```
Source TCP port-23
Destination TCP port-1028
Source IP address-172.17.0.1
Destination IP address-172.22.114.1
```

The following shows our information as a reflected access list entry:

```
permit tcp host 172.17.0.1 eq 23 host 172.22.114.1 eq 1028
```

In the preceding example of a reflected entry, the source and destination address have been swapped, along with the source and destination port numbers giving the "mirror image."

Building Reflexive Access Lists

When building a reflexive access list, we must first design an extended named access list. Remember from earlier that you must use an extended named access list when defining your reflexive access list and there is no implicit *deny all* at the end. Here, we enter a *permit* statement to allow all protocols in which you want a reflected entry created. So, what must we do to indicate a reflexive opening? You need to use the keyword *reflect* in each of your *permit* statements. This tells us that a reflexive opening will occur. The following example shows the format of a reflexive access list.

```
permit protocol source source-wildcard destination destination-wildcard
     reflect name [timeout seconds]
```

Table 4.9 describes reflexive access lists.

Table 4.9 Reflexive Access Lists

Command	Description
Permit	This entry will always use the keyword *permit*.
Protocol	Any TCP/IP protocol supported by an extended named IP access list.
Source	Identifies the host or network from which the packet is being sent. The source can be specified by an IP address or by using the keyword *any* or *host*.
Destination	Identifies the host or network to which the packet is being sent. The destination can be specified by an IP address or by using the keyword *any* or *host*.
Reflect	Allows the *permit* statement to create a temporary opening.
Name	This is the name of the reflexive access list. A name must be specified so the router can add the reflected entries into this list. This list will also be referenced within the ACL that filters traffic coming into the network.
Timeout	Timeout is optional and has a default value of 300 seconds.

The format here is very comprehensible:

- This entry will always use the keyword *permit*. The keywords *permit* and *reflect* work hand in hand. To allow the *permit* statement to create a temporary opening, you must use the *reflect* statement.

- The protocol field can depict any UDP, TCP, IP, and ICMP protocols supported by an extended named IP access list.

- The source field represents the source IP address. Keywords such as *any* and *host* are applicable here.

- The destination field represents the destination IP address. Keywords such as *any* and *host* are applicable here.

- You must include the name of the access list. Remember, a reflexive entry can only be used with an extended IP named access list.

- The timeout field is optional. If no value is specified, a default of 300 seconds will be used. The timeout is necessary when using connection-less protocols such as UDP. UDP offers nothing in the header to determine when the entry should be deleted. When using TCP, the timeout is not used. Instead, the reflexive access list is deleted after receiving a packet with the RST flag set—or when the TCP session closes (both ends have sent FIN packets), the reflexive access list is deleted within five seconds of detecting the bits.

To nest our reflexive access list within an access list, we use the *evaluate* command. By default, an access list does not evaluate. This command is used as an entry in the access list and points to the reflexive access list to be evaluated, therefore traffic entering your network will be evaluated against the reflexive access list.

NOTE

Reflexive access lists are *not* defined like extended access lists. They are created within an extended access list, although you will be able to see the reflexive ACL with the *show ip access-lists* command.

Given the information about the preceding Telnet session, we will be creating three access lists: *Outbound-List*, *Inbound-List*, and *Reflected-List*. The *Outbound-List ACL* will look at the outbound traffic and decide what should be reflected. *Inbound-List ACL* is the access list that will deny all inbound traffic to the network except for the traffic we will be evaluating. *Reflected-List ACL* is the reflexive access list.

```
Router(config)#ip access-list extended Outbound-List
Router(config-ext-nacl)#permit tcp any any reflect Reflected-List
```

```
Router(config-ext-nacl)#exit
Router(config)#ip access-list extended Inbound-List
Router(config-ext-nacl)#evaluate Reflected-List
Router(config-ext-nacl)#exit
```

Now we have created two extended access lists, and one reflexive access list. As traffic leaves our network, it will match the traffic in the *Outbound-List ACL*. The *reflect* statement will add the mirror image entry to the *Reflected-List ACL*. When return traffic is checked against the *Inbound-List ACL*, which runs the *evaluate* command on *Reflected-List ACL*, it will be allowed back to the original host. If the *evaluate* statement was not in place within *Inbound-List ACL*, then no traffic will be allowed back into the network.

Please note that while I have stated that there is not an *implicit deny* at the end of a reflexive access list, there is an *implicit deny* at the end of the *Inbound-List ACL*. If the *implicit deny* was at the end of *Reflected-List ACL*, then the router would never check any other statements that might be in *Inbound-List ACL* after the *evaluate* command.

You can use the keyword *timeout* to specify a timeout period for individual entries. If the timeout field is not used, a default value of 300 seconds is applied. Remember, this will not apply when using TCP. Also keep in mind that when using TCP, the access list will close immediately after receiving the RST bit or within five seconds after both ends have closed the TCP session. The timeout can be set on a line-by-line basis in the extended ACL configuration, or you can set a global timeout with the following command:

```
ip reflexive-list timeout seconds
```

Even though reflexive access lists give more control in our networks, they do have a major shortcoming. Reflexive access lists are only capable of handling single channel applications such as Telnet, which uses a single static port that stays the same throughout the conversation. Reflexive access lists do not offer the ability to support applications that change port numbers in a session. So how do we handle FTP? Normal mode FTP is a multichannel operation that uses one channel for control and the second channel for data transmission and is not supported by reflexive access lists because the server chooses the data port, not the client. If using the passive mode FTP, we can generally have a more favorable result. With passive mode, the server does not perform an active open to the client. Instead, the client uses the command channel to exchange port information. The client then performs an open to the server on an agreed port. So, both of the sessions we just discussed are outbound from the client, and the reflexive access list would create an additional entry. Here we would have success! FTP is not the only protocol that might be a potential problem here. Many other protocols with similar behavior, such as RPC, SQL*Net, Streamworks, and multimedia such as H.323 (Netmeeting, Proshare) will have problems.

Applying Reflexive Access Lists

The first step in applying a reflexive access list is to decide which interface the ACLs should be applied on. While referring to Figure 4.8, we need to determine which interface the ACLs, which we created previously, should be applied to. Because we want to be able to reflect sessions if they go out ethernet1 or serial0, we need to apply both ACLs to the ethernet0 interface as shown here:

```
Router(config)#interface ethernet0
Router(config-if)#ip access-group Outbound-List in
Router(config-if)#ip access-group Inbound-List out
```

Don't be confused by the names and directions in the *access-group* commands. Remember that access lists are applied with respect to the interface. So, any traffic that is heading outbound *from our network* will be considered inbound *to the ethernet0 interface*. The same logic applies to traffic flowing in the opposite direction.

In the preceding example, we must apply both ACLs to the ethernet0 interface, so we can use the reflexive operation regardless of which interface the traffic exits (serial0 or ethernet1). The previous configuration will allow any traffic that originates from the 172.22.114.0 network to the other interfaces, but only packets that are sent in response to that traffic will be allowed back onto the ethernet0 segment.

Normally, when a packet is tested against entries in an access list, the entries are tested in sequential order, and when a match occurs, no more entries are tested. When using a reflexive access list nested in an extended access list, the extended access list entries are tested sequentially up to the *evaluate* command. Then the reflexive access list entries are tested sequentially, and finally the remaining entries in the extended access list are tested sequentially. After a packet matches *any* of these entries, no more entries will be tested.

Context-based Access Control

As discussed earlier, the reflexive access list can only handle single channel applications. This could prove to be detrimental in your enterprise network. Now we will discus how CBAC overcomes some of these issues. Provided in Cisco Secure

Integrated Software, Context-based Access Control (CBAC) includes an extensive set of security features. The idea of CBAC is to inspect outgoing sessions and create temporary openings to enable the return traffic. Sound familiar? We just described a reflexive access list. The difference here is that CBAC can examine and securely handle various types of application-layer information. This is called stateful inspection, because it continually monitors the state of each connection to decide how it should be handled. For example, when the traffic you specify leaves the internal network through an interface, an opening is created that allows returning traffic based on the traffic being part of a data session that was initiated from an internal network. These openings are created when specified traffic exits your internal network through the router and allows returning traffic that would normally be blocked similar to a reflexive access list. The openings also allow additional data channels to enter your internal network back through the router if it is part of the same session as the originating traffic.

With other types of access lists, such as reflexive or extended access lists, traffic filtering is limited to filtering packets at the network layer or transport layer. CBAC examines the network layer and transport layer along with application-layer protocol information to learn about the state of the TCP or UDP session. Some protocols create multiple channels as a result of negotiations used in the control channel, and it is not possible to filter those protocols using only the information available in the IP and transport layers. By examining the information at the application layer, CBAC provides support for some of these protocols. As previously stated, CBAC inspects outgoing sessions and creates temporary openings to enable the return traffic just as a reflexive access list does. However, unlike reflexive access lists CBAC has the ability to make decisions based on the behavior of the application up to and including Layer 7. When using CBAC, the packets are examined when leaving or entering an interface on the router and the information will be placed in a packet state information table. The information may be an IP address and port numbers from Layer 4. This state table is used by CBAC to create a temporary opening in the access list for return traffic. This shows us another difference between CBAC and reflexive access lists. We had to specifically configure an access list to evaluate the reflexive ACL. With CBAC, the router will automatically determine which access lists would block the return traffic and will add the temporary entry as the very first line in the ACL. CBAC also inspects application-layer information to ensure that the traffic being allowed back through the router is applicable. Recall the issue we had with FTP earlier. Reflexive access list could only support passive mode where all communications are initiated from the client. Now we can use normal mode where multiple channels are used. CBAC would observe the outgoing session, then permit the data connection that will be established from the server to the client by creating an opening in the inbound access list. The following is a listing of the protocols where CBAC performs the equivalent function:

- Single-channel TCP
- Single-channel UDP
- CU-SeeME
- FTP
- H.323
- Java applets transported via HTTP
- Microsoft NetShow
- UNIX "r" commands
- RealAudio
- RPC
- SMTP
- SQL*Net
- StreamWorks
- TFTP
- VDOLive

Just as with everything, there are a few limitations when using CBAC.

- Any packets with the router as the source address or destination address will not be inspected. Only TCP and UDP packets are inspected. So traffic originating or in destination for the router itself cannot be controlled with CBAC.
- CBAC cannot inspect IPSec traffic. If the traffic needs to be inspected, the router must be configured as the IPSec tunnel endpoint.

UDP and ICMP traffic is stateless, so CBAC is unable to track state information for these types of sessions. UDP replies are allowed through temporary openings that timeout after a specified period of time, but ICMP traffic must be permitted or denied by extended ACL commands and will not be tracked by CBAC.

The Context-based Access Control Process

The following section describes a sample process of the events that occur when we configure CBAC on a router. We will assume that the router only has two interfaces: One that connects to the internal network we want to protect, and another connecting to the external network. Assume that *outbound* traffic is traveling from the internal to external network, and *inbound* traffic is flowing from the external to the internal network.

- The outgoing packet reaches the router and is evaluated against the outbound access list. If the access list allows the traffic, then it will be inspected by CBAC. Otherwise, it will be dropped and a CBAC inspection will never occur.

- During CBAC inspection, information is recorded, including the source and destination IP address and port numbers. The information is recorded in a state table entry created for the new connection.

- A temporary access list entry is created based on the previous state information. This access list entry is placed at the beginning of the extended access list that is configured to filter inbound traffic.

- This temporary opening is designed to permit inbound packets that are part of the same connection as the outbound packet that was inspected previously. The outbound packet now leaves the interface.

- The return packet is tested against the inbound access list and permitted because of the temporary entry created by CBAC. Here CBAC will modify the state table and inbound access list, if necessary.

- All inbound and outbound traffic in the future will be tested; therefore, the state table access list will be modified as required.

- When the connection is closed, the state table entry is deleted along with the temporary access list.

Configuring Context-based Access Control

There are several steps to follow here. We must specify which protocols you want inspected. We must also specify an interface and direction where the inspection originates. CBAC will only inspect the protocols we specify. As mentioned earlier, we must configure an outbound access list so that CBAC will know what traffic to inspect. This list can be either a standard or extended ACL, but the inbound ACL must be extended. This is because CBAC must have the facility to allow traffic back in based on Layer 4 header information. These steps are:

1. **Choose the interface**   Here the decision is to configure CBAC on an internal or external interface, such as Ethernet0 or Serial0. The internal interface is where the client sessions originate. The external interface is where the client sessions exit the router. In the network shown in Figure 4.9, we will be inspecting traffic inbound to the Ethernet interface, and the return ACL will be applied inbound to the Serial interface.

Figure 4.9 Configuring Context-based Access Control

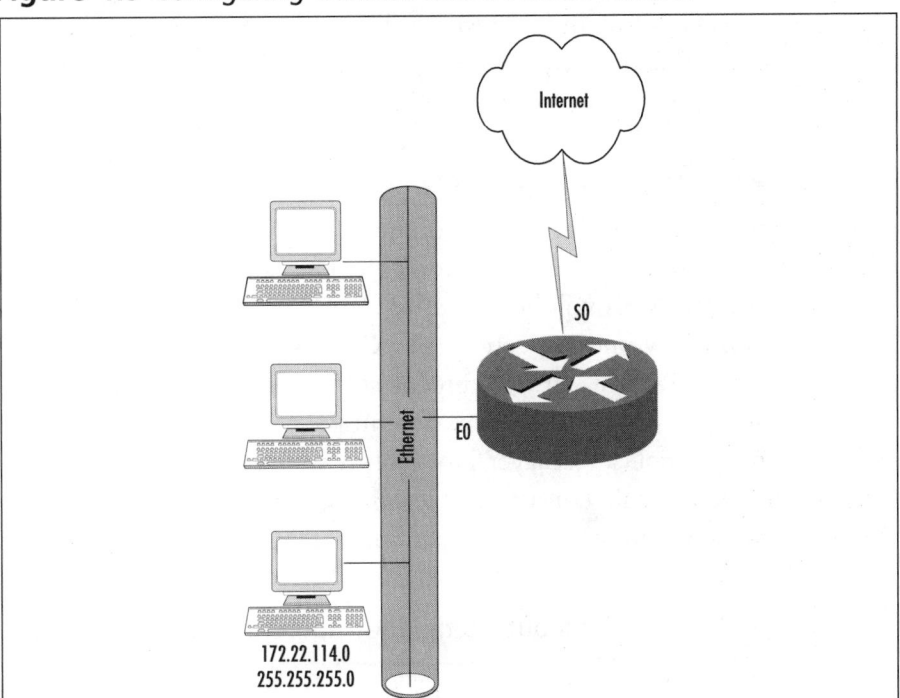

2. **Configure Access Lists**   Next, we need to create the access lists for the CBAC configuration. One access list should define all traffic that will be allowed outbound to the Internet. This could be a very specific list, or just a single *permit any* command. The second list that must be created is the inbound list, which controls which traffic should be allowed through regardless of CBAC inspection. For example, you may want to allow certain types of ICMP in, or a connection to a Web server that needs to be initiated from the Internet.

3. **Configuring Global Timeouts and Thresholds** CBAC uses time-outs and thresholds to determine the duration of an inactive session before it is deleted. This helps prevent certain denial of service (DoS) attacks by monitoring the number and frequency of half-open connections. With TCP, a half-open session is one that has not completed the three-way handshake, or if using UDP, a session which the firewall has not detected returning traffic. CBAC counts both TCP and UDP when determining the number of half-open sessions. Half-open sessions are only monitored for connections configured for inspection by CBAC. These timeouts and thresholds apply globally to all sessions. You can use the default timeout and threshold values, or you can change to values more suitable to your security requirements. You should make any changes to the timeout and threshold values before you continue configuring CBAC. Table 4.10 lists available CBAC commands used to configure timeouts and thresholds.

4. **Inspection Rules** After configuring global timeouts and thresholds, you must define an inspection rule. This specifies which application-layer protocols will be tested by CBAC at an interface. Typically, you define only one inspection rule. One exception might be if you want to enable CBAC in two directions. In this case, you should define two rules, one in each direction. The inspection rule should specify each desired application-layer protocol, as well as TCP or UDP, if desired. The inspection rule consists of a series of statements, each listing a protocol and specifying the same inspection rule name.

Table 4.10 Available Timeout Commands and Thresholds

Command	Description	Default Values
ip inspect tcp synwait-time *seconds*	Length of time of wait for TCP session to be established	30 seconds
ip inspect tcp finwait time *seconds*	Length of time TCP is managed after FIN exchange	5 seconds
ip inspect tcp idle-time *seconds*	TCP idle timeout	3600 seconds
ip inspect udp idle-time *seconds*	UDP idle timeout	30 seconds

Continued

Table 4.10 Continued

Command	Description	Default Values
ip inspect dns-timeout *seconds*	DNS lookup idle timer	5 seconds
ip inspect max-incomplete high *number*	Max number of half-open connections before CBAC begins closing connections	500 sessions
ip inspect max-incomplete low *number*	Max number of half-open connections causing CBAC to stop closing connections	400 sessions
ip inspect one-minute high *number*	Rate of half-open sessions per minute before CBAC begins closing connections	500 sessions
ip inspect one-minute low *number*	Rate of half-open sessions per minute causing CBAC to stop deleting connections	400 sessions
ip inspect tcp max-incomplete host *number* block-time *seconds*	Number of existing half-open sessions with the same destination address before CBAC begins closing sessions	50 sessions

Inspection Rules

The following is the format for defining inspection rules:

```
ip inspect name inspection-name protocol [alert {on|off} [audit-trail
    {on|off}][timeout seconds]
```

The keyword *alert* allows CBAC to send messages to a syslog server when a violation occurs in a monitored application. Each application will have an individual alert that the router will send to the server for illegal conditions. The keyword *audit trail* permits the tracking of connections used for a protected application. Here, the router logs information about each connection, including ports used, number of bytes transferred, and source and destination IP address. A key issue here is if a large amount of traffic is being monitored, the logging produced will be significant!

Applying the Inspection Rule

Now that we have defined the inspection rule, the final step is to apply it to an interface. You will apply the inspection rule the same way you apply access lists on the interface. You must also specify inbound (for traffic entering the interface) or outbound (for traffic exiting the interface). The command is as follows:

```
ip inspect inspection-name {in | out}
```

The following is an example of Java blocking. A list of permitted IP addresses must be created using a standard IP access list. The following is an example:

```
access-list list-number {permit | deny} source-address [wildcard-mask]
    [log]
```

```
ip inspect name inspection-name http [java-list access-list] [alert
    {on | off}] [audit-trail {on | off}] [timeout seconds}
```

By default, an undefined access list in the java-list definition will deny all Java applets. CBAC can only block Java applets and not ActiveX.

There are several commands that are useful in gathering information about CBAC. The *show ip inspect config* command will be discussed first. This command allows all specific portions of a configuration. The following is an example:

```
Router# show ip inspect config
Session alert is enabled
One-minute (sampling period) thresholds are [400:500] connections
max-incomplete sessions thresholds are [400:500]
max- incomplete tcp connections per host is 50.
Block-time 0 minute.
tcp synwait-time is 30 sec - tcp finwait - time is 5 sec
tcp idle - time is 3600 sec - udp idle - time is 30 sec
dns - timeout is 5 seconds
```

The *show ip inspect interfaces* command shows the interfaces where CBAC inspection is configured. Here's an example:

```
Router# sh ip inspect interfaces
Interface FastEthernet 3/0
Inbound inspection rule is Protector
tcp alert is on audit-trail is off timeout 3600
udp alert is on audit-trail is CBAC off timeout 30
```

```
fragment Maximum 50 In Use 0 alert is on audit-trail is off timeout 1
Inbound access list is 114
Outbound access list is not set
```

Refer to the "Protecting Public Servers Connected to the Internet" section for the required configuration for CBAC.

Configuring Port to Application Mapping

A limitation of CBAC is the fact that only services running on standard ports can be controlled. For example, traffic going to a Web server running on a port other than the standard HTTP port (80) cannot be inspected and protected using CBAC. Port to Application Mapping (PAM) can be used to override this limitation. PAM gives you the capability to customize TCP or UDP port numbers for network services or applications. Upon startup, PAM will build a table of ports associated with their default application, known as a PAM table or database. Kept in this table are all of the services supported by CBAC. Here is where the link with CBAC comes into play. The information built into the PAM table will give CBAC the ability to function on a non-standard port. If you are running applications on non-standard ports, PAM and CBAC have the ability to work together to identify the ports associated with their applications. Without the use of PAM, CBAC is limited to well-known ports and their applications.

PAM comes standard with the Cisco Secure Integrated Software Feature Set. Network services or applications that use non-standard ports will require you to place entries in the PAM table manually. You can also specify a range of ports used by an application by establishing a separate entry in the PAM table for each port number in the range. All manual entries are saved with the default mapping information when you save the router configuration, so upon startup, the mapping will be in the PAM table. If you use an application that requires a non-standard port, you will need to enter this manually in the PAM table (for example, if you use the Telnet application with port 8000 instead of port 23).

Configuring PAM

When configuring PAM, the following format is used:

ip port-map application_name **port** port-number

The following is a mapping for well-known port 23 (Telnet) to port 8000, and may look as follows:

```
ip port-map telnet port 8000
```

Now let's take this example a step farther and define a range of non–standard ports for use with telnet. An example may look as follows:

```
ip port-map telnet port 8001
ip port-map telnet port 8002
ip port-map telnet port 8003
ip port-map telnet port 8004
```

We also have the option of mapping an application to a port for a specific host or subnet. Mapping an application to a host would look as follows:

```
access-list 1 permit host 172.16.144.1
ip port-map telnet port 8000 list 1
```

When mapping to a specific subnet, the list may look like this:

```
access-list 1 permit 172.16.144.0 0.0.0.255
ip port-map telnet port 8000 list 1
```

Protecting a Private Network

In this section, we will apply some of the concepts we discussed in this chapter to different situations. Please keep in mind that these solutions are meant to demonstrate the application of some of the different security techniques available in a Cisco router, and may not present the most secure or appropriate solution possible. Currently, CBAC is the most secure means of protecting your network, but the licensing cost for the firewall feature set (CBAC) may cause you to decide to use some other feature when deploying security on your network. You will have to weigh your options and decide which solution works best for your network.

In this first example, we are assuming a simple connection between two companies over a point-to-point T1 connecting to the Serial0 interface on your router. As far as this exercise is concerned, we either do not have an Internet connection, or we are using a separate device to secure the Internet connection, which we need not worry about here. We are focusing on securing the connection between our company, Company A, and the remote company, Company B.

Although the risk of being hacked is considerably less from a single company as compared with an Internet connection, we still need to apply some sort of security to prevent access to unauthorized services. Figure 4.10 shows a basic layout of this connection. I purposefully did not show anything beyond the router of Company B because in most cases you will not know the topology of the other company's network. You will know the next hop router you are connecting to, but nothing beyond that point. The following is a summary of requirements that need to be properly secured:

1. All hosts belonging to Company A need to be able to access 10.150.200.5 on TCP port 1000.

2. Host 172.20.100.130 needs access to 10.150.150.56 on TCP port 1299.

3. Company B server 10.150.100.5 needs to have access to 172.20.100.155 on TCP ports 13000 thru 13010.

4. Company B server 10.150.100.6 needs to have access to 172.20.100.156 on TCP port 12050.

Figure 4.10 Connection to a Private Network

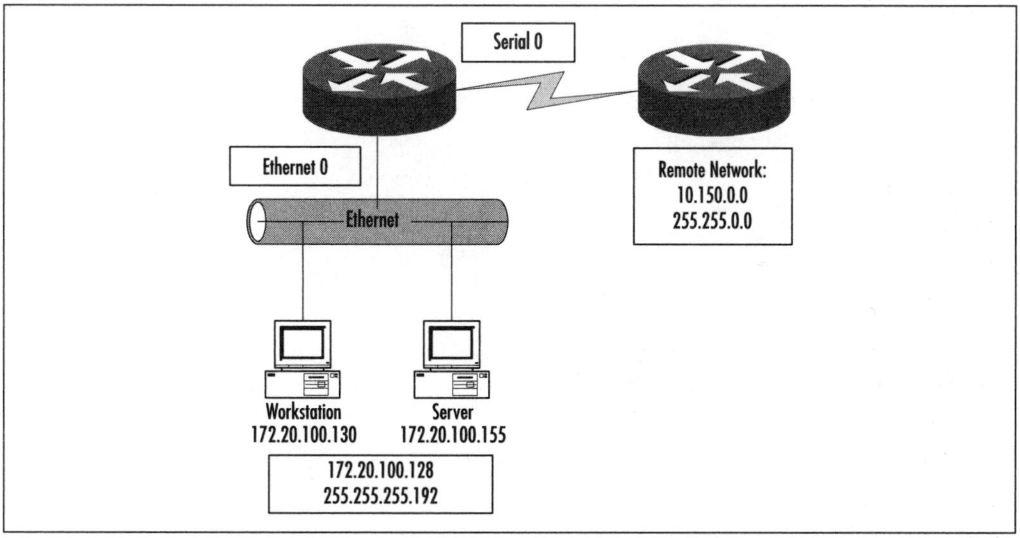

Fortunately, we have a fairly strict set of requirements defining the access between these two companies. This means that we can lock down the access lists to prevent unauthorized access to certain servers. For example, we know that only one server needs access to our 172.20.100.155 server, so we do not need to define the entire 10.150.0.0 subnet access to our servers.

We could filter traffic down to this specific list only using extended access lists, but we will use reflexive access lists to allow us to add a little extra security to the network. That way we do not have to define statements for return traffic that would be always open; we can just allow the reflexive list to handle that part. The reflexive list will prevent someone from having full access to our subnet if they source the packets from 10.150.200.5:1000. This is because if we were going to allow the return traffic through by hand, we would have to create an access list entry that permitted the one server on port 1000 to access our entire subnet on any port. The reflexive list will only allow traffic through if it is response traffic coming from, and going to, a very specific port, and the session was originated from our network.

Since we only have two interfaces on this router, we will apply the ACL that filters outgoing (from our network) traffic on Ethernet0 in the inbound direction. This will allow us to drop traffic we do not wish to pass before it reaches the route engine within the router. This will save CPU cycles. Also, we will apply the ACL that filters incoming traffic in the inbound direction on Serial0 for the same reasons as before.

The following is the configuration we will need to create to protect our network.

```
interface Ethernet0
ip address 172.20.100.129 255.255.255.192
ip access-group ToCompanyB in


interface Serial0
ip address 172.16.0.1 255.255.255.252
ip access-group FromCompanyB in

ip access-list extended ToCompanyB
   evaluate EstSessionB
   permit tcp 172.20.100.128 0.0.0.63 host 10.150.200.5 eq 1000 refelct
      EstSession
   permit tcp host 172.20.100.130 host 10.150.150.56 eq 1299 reflect
      EstSession
   deny ip any any log

ip access-list extended FromCompanyB
   evaluate EstSessionA
   permit tcp host 10.150.100.5 host 172.20.100.155 range 13000 13010
      reflect EstSessionB
```

```
   permit tcp host 10.150.100.6 host 172.20.100.156 eq 12050 reflect
      EstSessionB
deny ip any any log
```

Notice that we are reflecting in both directions. We could have easily allowed any access out of our network, but since we had a small and strict list of communications that should be allowed, we are securing both networks. We may not have a responsibility to protect Company B's network, but by doing so, we are decreasing the liability that our company is exposed to should one of our employees try to hack into a server at Company B.

Also be aware that we manually entered the *deny ip any any* statement so that we could use the *log* keyword with it. This will allow us to see any traffic that is denied by our access list and see if someone is attempting to find a way around it.

Protecting a Network Connected to the Internet

This next example will cover how to put basic protection in place when you have connected your network to the Internet. Due to the security risks associated with attaching your network to the Internet, we will use the Firewall IOS (CBAC) to secure our network. Another reason we would rather use CBAC is to cause less problems with applications that are in use on the network. For example, people may need to download files from an FTP server, or use RealAudio to stream a newscast. CBAC can handle these applications, while reflexive access lists cannot.

The following is the configuration we will use to protect our network, which is shown in Figure 4.11:

```
ip inspect name CompanyA-FW tcp
ip inpsect name CompanyA-FW udp
ip inspect name CompanyA-FW ftp
ip inspect name CompanyA-FW http
ip inspect name CompanyA-FW realaudio

interface ethernet 0
  ip address 10.150.130.0 255.255.255.0
  ip access-group Outbound in
  ip inspect CompanyA-FW in

interface serial 0
```

```
ip address 192.168.5.1 255.255.255.252
ip access-group Inbound in

ip access-list extended Outbound
  permit ip 10.150.130.0 0.0.0.255 any
  deny ip any any log

ip access-list extended Inbound
  permit icmp any 10.150.130.0 0.0.0.255 echo-reply
  permit icmp any 10.150.130.0 0.0.0.255 traceroute
  permit icmp any 10.150.130.0 0.0.0.255 time-exceeded
  permit icmp any 10.150.130.0 0.0.0.255 unreachable
  deny ip any any log
```

Figure 4.11 A Network Attached to the Internet

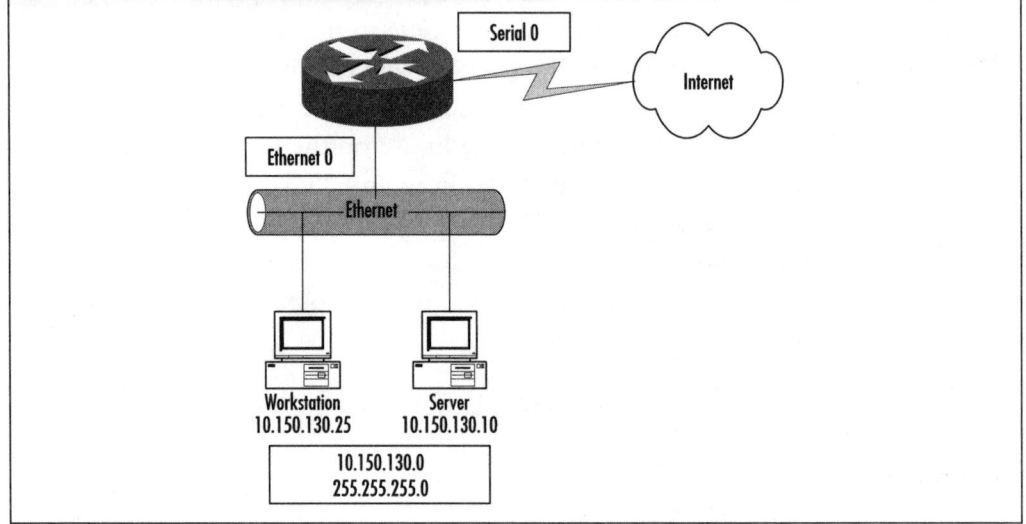

The previous configuration will allow all IP traffic outbound to the Internet. If we are worried about someone running a VPN connection from our network, we could allow protocols such as TCP, UDP, and ICMP but deny all other IP traffic. In this case, we do not care where our users go. One protective step we did take was to only allow traffic that is sourced from our subnet to be allowed through the router. We have done this to prevent someone on our network from launching an attack with spoofed source addresses. The only address spoofing that could make it through the router is if a host spoofed their address to an address used by another host on our network.

The CBAC portion of this will keep a state for all traffic that flows out to the Internet and allow the responses back in. As you can see, we specifically told CBAC to inspect FTP, HTTP, and RealAudio traffic because we think our users may be running applications that use those protocols. The other protocols CBAC can handle, such as SQLNet, are not expected to originate from our users toward the Internet. If we find that we need to use one of these protocols in the future, we can quickly and easily add another command to the inspect list.

We have also allowed specific types of ICMP traffic back through the router for troubleshooting purposes. While we don't want someone on the Internet to be able to ping our hosts, we do want to receive replies to the pings and tracer-outes that we send into the Internet. In addition to only allowing our users' replies to their pings, they can also see when a TTL has expired on their packets, indicating a routing loop, as well as unreachable messages if there are other routing or access problems somewhere on the Internet.

Protecting Server Access Using Lock-and-key

As a continuation of our last example, we need to allow two of our users access to a particular server from outside our network. This access will not be constant, so we do not want to make a permanent entry into our access lists. The best way to perform this with the tools we have available will be to use a lock-and-key access list. We are working in the same network shown in Figure 4.11, and the configuration from the previous example is applied, so we will need to modify our configuration to allow this access through.

Our two employees need to access the 10.150.130.10 server on port 110 (POP3) from their home computers. This will allow them to pull their e-mail from the server across the Internet, while prohibiting access to the mail server from everywhere else. We will be setting a very short idle timeout on the dynamic entry (one minute) because the user will only need to authenticate and then download his e-mail once during that session. If an e-mail has a large file attachment, the temporary entry will stay in place while the download occurs, but will be deleted after no traffic passes through for one minute. Since our users only need access from their home machines, we won't need to configure the dynamic ACLs to allow users to authenticate from everywhere (using the *any* keyword), and we can further reduce our risks by tightening down the dynamic lists. Their ISPs use DHCP, so they won't have the same IP every time they connect, but we do know which subnets our two users will be connecting from: 172.20.128.0 255.255.252.0, and 172.21.64.0 255.255.255.254.0.

After making the changes to our configuration, it should look like this:

```
username bill password needmyemail
username bill autocommand access-enable host timeout 1
username susan password letmein
username susan autocommand access-enable host timeout 1
username admin password supersecret


ip inspect name CompanyA-FW tcp
ip inpsect name CompanyA-FW udp
ip inspect name CompanyA-FW ftp
ip inspect name CompanyA-FW http
ip inspect name CompanyA-FW realaudio
!
interface Ethernet 0
  ip address 10.150.130.0 255.255.255.0
  ip access-group Outbound in
  ip inspect CompanyA-FW in
!
interface Serial 0
  ip address 192.168.5.1 255.255.255.252
  ip access-group Inbound in
!
ip access-list extended Outbound
   permit ip 10.150.130.0 0.0.0.255 any
   deny ip any any log
!
ip access-list extended Inbound
   permit icmp any 10.150.130.0 0.0.0.255 echo-reply
   permit icmp any 10.150.130.0 0.0.0.255 traceroute
   permit icmp any 10.150.130.0 0.0.0.255 time-exceeded
   permit icmp any 10.150.130.0 0.0.0.255 unreachable
   permit tcp 172.20.128.0 0.0.3.255 host 192.168.5.1 eq telnet
   permit tcp 172.21.64.0 0.0.1.255 host 192.168.5.1 eq telnet
   dynamic POPAccess permit tcp 172.20.128.0 0.0.3.255 host 10.150.130.1
```

```
     eq 110
  dynamic POPAccess permit tcp 172.21.64.0 0.0.1.255 host 10.150.130.1
     eq 110
  deny ip any any log
!
line vty 0 4
login local
exec-timeout 15 0
```

Protecting Public Servers Connected to the Internet

Our final example covers a situation when you not only have users that need protection while accessing the Internet, but also have servers that need to be accessed by anyone on the Internet, such as Web and mail servers. In this case, it is best to divide your network into two separate entities: an internal network and a DMZ.

The whole purpose of the DMZ is to protect the rest of your network in case one of your servers is compromised. When you have a publicly accessible server, such as your Web server or mail server, you must allow complete access on the port that is being used, such as port 80 for the Web. This increases your chances of being attacked since you cannot limit who is able to access your server. Even if a hacker is able to gain control of your box through the Web port, they still cannot access your internal network, because it is protected from the DMZ. If you had your public Web server on your internal network and someone gained control of it, that person would have complete access to all other hosts on your network. The DMZ serves as a way to isolate your public servers from your private ones.

The network shown in Figure 4.12 has the internal network on Ethernet0, the DMZ network on Ethernet1, and our Internet connection on Serial0. In a case where we have public servers, we definitely need to use the best security available to us, so we will use CBAC to protect this network. The configuration will be somewhat different from the other configurations we have covered, because we will have both inbound and outbound ACLs on both Ethernet interfaces and an inbound list on the serial interface, which gives us a total of five access lists. We are configuring the router this way because once you have more than two interfaces, the easiest approach for securing your networks is to look at each interface and decide what should be allowed through it in each direction. We will cover these lists one by one after we take a look at the configuration that follows.

Figure 4.12 A Network with a DMZ and Internet Connection

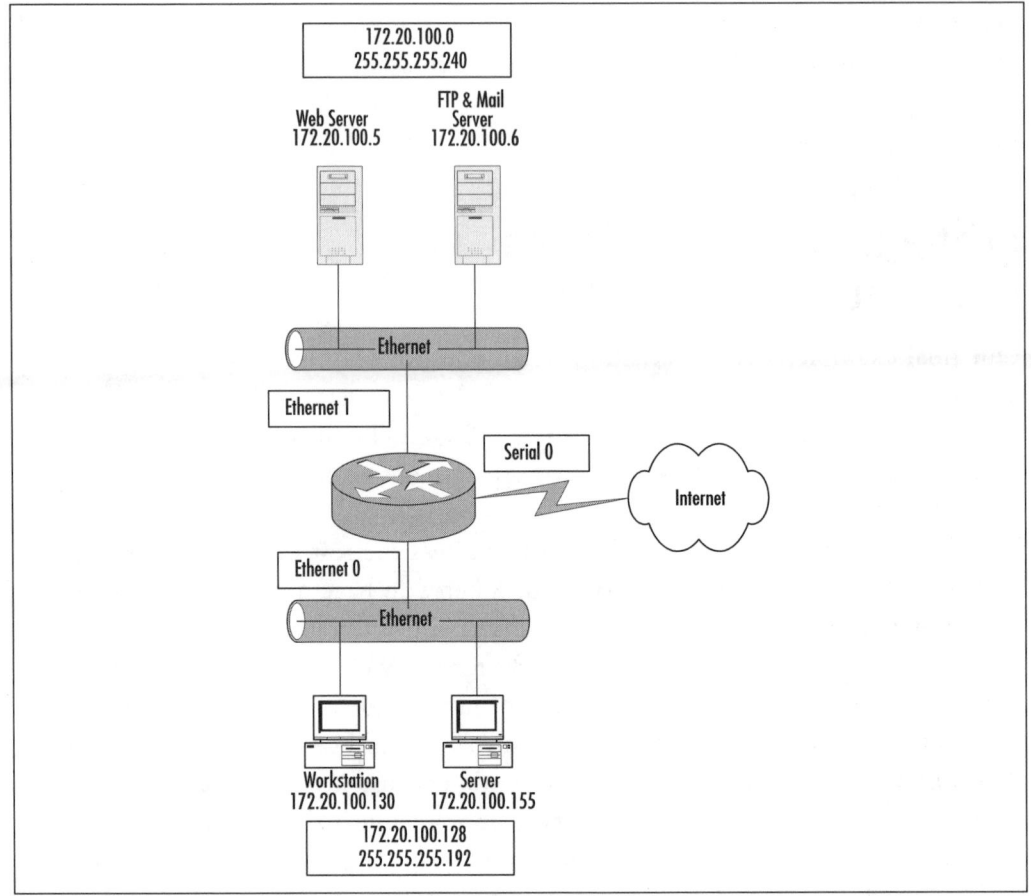

```
ip inspect name DMZ-FW tcp
ip inspect name DMZ-FW ftp
ip inspect name DMZ-FW http
ip inspect name DMZ-FW smtp
ip inspect name Internal-FW tcp
ip inpsect name Internal-FW udp
ip inspect name Internal-FW http
ip inspect name Internal-FW ftp
ip inspect name Internal-FW smtp
ip inspect name Internal-FW realaudio
```

```
interface ethernet 0
  ip address 172.20.100.129 255.255.255.192
  ip access-group Eth0-in in
  ip access-group Eth0-out out
  ip inspect Internal-FW in

interface ethernet 1
 ip address 172.20.100.1 255.255.255.240
 ip access-group Eth1-in in
 ip access-group Eth1-out out
 ip inspect DMZ-FW out

interface serial 0
  ip address 192.168.5.1 255.255.255.252
  ip access-group Serial-in in

ip access-list extended Eth0-in
   permit ip 172.20.100.128 0.0.0.63 any
   deny ip any any log-input

ip access-list extended Eth0-out
   permit icmp any 172.20.100.128 0.0.0.63 echo-reply
   permit icmp any 172.20.100.128 0.0.0.63 packet-too-big
   permit icmp any 172.20.100.128 0.0.0.63 time-exceeded
   permit icmp any 172.20.100.128 0.0.0.63 unreachable
   deny ip any any log-input

ip access-list extended Eth1-in
   permit icmp 172.20.100.0 0.0.0.15 any echo-reply
   deny ip any any log-input

ip access-list extneded Eth1-out
   permit tcp any host 172.20.100.5 eq www
   permit tcp any host 172.20.100.6 eq ftp
   permit tcp any host 172.20.100.6 eq smtp
   permit tcp 172.20.100.128 0.0.0.63 host 172.20.100.6 eq pop3
```

```
    permit icmp any 172.20.100.0 0.0.0.15 echo
    permit icmp any 172.20.100.0 0.0.0.15 echo-reply
    permit icmp any 172.20.100.0 0.0.0.15 packet-too-big
    permit icmp any 172.20.100.0 0.0.0.15 time-exceeded
    permit icmp any 172.20.100.0 0.0.0.15 unreachable
    deny ip any any log-input


ip access-list extended Serial-in
    deny ip 172.20.100.0 0.0.0.15 any log-input
    deny ip 172.20.100.128 0.0.0.63 any log-input
    permit ip any any
```

Now we will cover each section of this configuration individually. First, we have the *ip inspect* rules that are configured. We have created two rules: one for the DMZ, and another for our internal network. Both networks could be protected by a single inspect list, but we have tailored each one to fit the types of traffic expected for each network. Our DMZ farm only accepts TCP connections for HTTP, SMTP, and FTP, so those are the only protocols configured for inspection. Our internal network, on the other hand, will need inspection for UDP, and possibly other protocols such as RealAudio, so we have created a separate inspection list for the internal network.

When securing our two networks, we have used a different approach for each one. Our internal network is protected using the same logic as our previous example: Our users are permitted to go anywhere they want, but only responses to our traffic should be let back into our network, as well as a few types of ICMP to allow us to troubleshoot connectivity issues. The only difference between the two examples is the placement of the access lists. On the two-interface router in Figure 4.11, we configured one list on the Ethernet interface, and the second on the Serial interface. On our three-interface router in Figure 4.12, we have put both the inbound and outbound access lists on the Ethernet interfaces. It ends up being much simpler to secure a network with more than two interfaces with this approach because we are applying the security at the choke point. Traffic that is received on our Ethernet0 interface can either be routed to the ethernet1 interface, or the Serial0 interface. Much less administrative work is needed if we have a single list on Ethernet0 to handle the return traffic, instead of two lists: one on Ethernet1 and one on Serial0.

The DMZ network has security applied in the opposite direction. Because these servers are publicly accessible and exposed to more risk than our internal network, we want to be very strict about what traffic is allowed to originate from that network. We are allowing anyone to access the DMZ servers on a list of specific ports (HTTP, FTP, and so on) but we only want to allow response traffic back out from our DMZ. This is the opposite behavior we applied to our internal network, where only response traffic is allowed back in. If someone manages to take control of one of our DMZ servers, they will not be able to initiate any attacks, since only response traffic is allowed from them. Keep in mind that this means our DMZ servers will not have access to the Web, so if you need to download a patch, you will need to use another means of transferring the file, such as having an internal host upload it to the FTP server on the DMZ, or copy it to a floppy disk or CD and loading it directly onto the server.

To help in your understanding of how we are restricting traffic flows through our router, we will cover each access list one by one.

- **Eth0-in** This ACL checks traffic going into our Ethernet0 interface, meaning that it watches traffic sent from our internal hosts. This is a very basic list that allows all traffic from our internal network as long as it is sourced from the appropriate subnet. This will prevent spoof attacks from being launched inside our network, since the router will drop any packets not sourced from our assigned subnet. Any packets allowed through this ACL will be inspected by CBAC and the return traffic will be allowed through the Eth0-out interface.

- **Eth0-out** This ACL filters traffic coming back into our internal network. We have allowed certain types of ICMP to come back into the network, by default, because CBAC is not able to perform state checks on ICMP traffic. We do not want to remove our ability to ping other hosts outside of our network, but we also don't want to be exposed to the entire ICMP suite, so we are only allowing reply packets that can tell us about common problems found on the Internet, such as unreachable destinations and TTL expired packets, which signal a possible routing loop. All other traffic is denied because CBAC will allow response traffic back through by adding temporary entries at the top of this list.

- **Eth1-in** This is the list that decides which traffic should be allowed to originate from the DMZ hosts. As mentioned earlier, we do not want our public servers to be able to initiate connections anywhere because that will prevent our servers from being used as a launch pad if a hacker manages to gain control of it.

- **Eth1-out** This list defines what traffic is allowed to reach our DMZ. This should cover all the services we are providing with these servers. The Web site, FTP site, and mail (SMTP) server should be publicly accessible from anywhere on the Internet. The only restricted service is POP3, which only allows people to download e-mail messages if they are coming from our internal network. Again, we are restricting the types of ICMP that can enter our network, but in this case, we are also allowing echo so that people can ping the servers to test for connectivity. Anything allowed through this list is inspected by CBAC and allowed to return back through the Eth1-in access list.

- **Serial-in** This access list only has one basic function: To prevent certain types of spoofing attacks from outside our network. If any packets enter our serial interface (in the inbound direction), which are sourced from an address that is part of our internal network or DMZ, they will be dropped before they can be forwarded to either network. Hackers may try using one of our addresses as the source for their packets in an attempt to bypass our access lists. For example, if a packet was sourced from our internal network, it will be passed through the POP3 rule on our DMZ network. To prevent hackers from slipping malicious packets through our access lists rules, we must make sure that addresses on our network can only be sourced from one of our Ethernet interfaces.

SECURITY ALERT!

Keep in mind that ICMP can be a very useful and very dangerous protocol. You will have to decide if you really want ICMP access allowed within your network. ICMP is very useful for troubleshooting connectivity issues, but hackers can also use ICMP to try and gather information about your network. The more information someone is able to gather about how you are configured, the easier time they will have finding a flaw to exploit. It is also very important to be aware of the fact that a firewall is not the end-all solution for security. In this example, we must allow unrestricted access to port 80 on our Web server. At this point, the firewall will have absolutely no affect on any attacks that exploit flaws in the web server software, since the hackers have open access to your server on port 80. To help reduce this risk, we would need to install an application layer gateway that could filter malformed HTTP requests before they reach the Web server.

Summary

As we have seen, Cisco offers a variety of methods for securing your network at the router. For basic traffic filtering, we have the option to use standard and extended access lists. These can be especially useful in protecting the router itself when a firewall behind the router is protecting your network. For example, you may want to deny all traffic being sent to the router except for the BGP session coming from the next upstream hop.

Lock-and-key and reflexive access lists were designed to help solve some of the shortcomings of the basic access lists by allowing dynamic entries to be placed in the ACL. This is especially useful when you want to protect your network but still allow return traffic back through the router. Although the *established* keyword was meant for this purpose, these new additions provided a much more secure method of performing the same task.

Of course, as people continually find new ways to break through the latest security techniques, networking and security companies continually develop new ways to secure a network. CBAC was created to help bring additional security to the router platform. CBAC is designed to watch the state of all sessions passing through the router so that attackers have a harder time fooling the router into letting a packet through. Although CBAC is not impenetrable, it is one of the most secure methods of protecting a network that is currently offered by Cisco. As time passes, we can be sure that as new vulnerabilities are found, new ways to defend against them will be implemented into the devices that carry the data over our networks.

Solutions Fast Track

Access Lists

☑ Standard access lists only filter on source address, while extended access lists can filter based on much more information, such as source address, destination address, source port, destination port, and protocol number, to name a few.

☑ Access lists can either be named or numbered. Named access lists were created to make access list administration easier by allowing them to be better identified and allowing the deletion of a single line.

☑ When applying access lists, make sure to think about them with respect to the interface they will be applied on. If you are blocking inbound traffic on the serial interface, all other interfaces connected to the router will still have full access to each other. For example, if you block Telnet sessions coming inbound through your serial interface, a host on the Ethernet interface could still Telnet to the router.

Lock-and-key Access Lists

☑ Allows authenticated access through an access list via a Telnet session.

☑ The *autocommand* feature can be used to prevent users from entering the wrong commands. This can be done across all VTY ports, or on a per-user basis.

☑ Remember to use the *host* keyword with the *access-enable* command, or else the entire dynamic ACL will be opened, instead of one particular host address.

☑ Be sure your inbound access list doesn't restrict Telnet access to your router, or else you will not be able to use the lock-and-key feature.

☑ You can only create one dynamic access list per extended access list. Anything beyond the first one will be ignored. You can have multiple entries using the same *dynamic-name* in an extended ACL.

☑ Dynamic access lists must have different names from any other named access lists defined in the router.

Reflexive Access Lists

☑ Allows increased security by only allowing traffic through an ACL if it is a response to a request initiated from inside your network.

☑ Reflexive ACLs can only look at transport layer (Layer 4) information when deciding what traffic should be allowed into the network. This can cause problems with applications such as FTP, if it is not running in passive mode.

☑ There are three separate parts to a reflexive access list: the inbound ACL, outbound ACL, and the reflexive ACL. The reflexive portion of the ACL is not defined like a regular access list, but created within an extended ACL.

☑ Cannot be used with applications that change port numbers during a session or ask a server to initiate a connection back towards the client on a different port.

Context–based Access Control

☑ Provides more protection than reflexive access lists, because it keeps a detailed state table of all connections through the router, while reflexive access lists only add a mirror image of an extended ACL to the reflexive list.

☑ CBAC is able to read the application layer data for certain applications such as FTP and RealAudio. This allows for more flexibility and security in your router because you are not faced with the choice of making large openings in your access lists versus not using a particular application.

☑ Requires you to create an inspect list to specify which applications CBAC should watch for. When using CBAC as an Internet firewall, your minimum configuration should include TCP and UDP inspection to allow basic connectivity to the Internet. Other inspection statements may need to be configured to allow certain applications to function properly.

Configuring Port to Application Mapping

☑ Allows you to configure known services on nonstandard ports for use with CBAC.

☑ PAM can be configured on a per-host basis, which allows only certain hosts to access a service on the configured port. Hosts can also use different services on the same port number if PAM is configured this way.

☑ You cannot assign a service to a system-defined port. For example, you cannot configure Telnet to run on port 25, which is SMTP.

Frequently Asked Questions

The following Frequently Asked Questions, answered by the authors of this book, are designed to both measure your understanding of the concepts presented in this chapter and to assist you with real-life implementation of these concepts. To have your questions about this chapter answered by the author, browse to **www.syngress.com/solutions** and click on the **"Ask the Author"** form.

Q: I have created an access list, but it does not seem to have any affect. Why?

A: Once you've created your access list, be sure you apply it to an interface with the *ip access-group interface* command. Also make sure that you apply your access list at the appropriate interface. If you apply a list inbound on the Serial0 interface, traffic flowing from Ethernet0 to Ethernet1 will not be checked against that access list.

Q: After applying an access list on your enterprise router, there has been a drastic decrease in throughput. What could be a potential problem here?

A: First recall how an access list works. An access list utilizes "top-down" processing when testing traffic. Typically, access lists can get quite lengthy on an enterprise router. A problem here could be that the majority of your traffic is permitted or denied near the end of the access list. When creating an access list, it is important to test the majority of your traffic first.

Q: I am using reflexive access lists and traffic is being allowed back into my network that I am specifically denying with my inbound ACL. How can I fix this?

A: Make sure you have placed your *evaluate* statement correctly. If you want traffic to be denied even when one of your users has initiated the connection, be sure to place that *deny* statement before the *evaluate* statement. Once the first match is found, whether it is in the inbound ACL, or the evaluated ACL, the router will not process any farther.

Q: I forgot to set a timeout on my lock-and-key access list, and now I have entries that will not expire. It is peak usage time for this router and I do not want to reboot it, but I need to remove this entry. How can I do this without bringing down my network?

A: Cisco has added a command specifically to delete temporary entries if they don't have a timeout, or if they need to be removed before a timeout has expired. This command is used in privileged exec mode and has the syntax *clear access-template* [*access-list number | name*] [*dynamic-name*] [*source-address*] [*destination-address*].

Q: How do I know CBAC is working properly?

A: You can check to see if CBAC is making any changes by doing a *show ip access-list* command. When you view the ACL with that command, you should see a bunch of entries at the top of the list that you didn't put there. If you view the list under *show running-config*, you will see your access list as you originally wrote it.

## Chapter 5

Network Address Translation/Port Address Translation

Solutions in this chapter:

- NAT Overview
- NAT Architectures
- Guidelines for Deploying NAT and PAT
- IOS NAT Support for IP Telephony
- Configuring NAT on Cisco IOS
- Considerations on NAT and PAT

- ☑ Summary
- ☑ Solutions Fast Track
- ☑ Frequently Asked Questions

Introduction

In today's world of enterprise networks, one of the major problems facing IT professionals is the rapidly depleting supply of globally unique Internet network addresses. Measures have been taken to slow the rate at which IP addresses are being allocated—including strategies such as Classless Inter-Domain Routing (CIDR), Network Address Translation (NAT), and Port Address Translation (PAT). This chapter will discuss NAT and PAT and how they can contribute to a security policy, the implications of NAT, and considerations when implementing NAT.

Network Address Translation is designed for IP address simplification and conservation. It enables private IP networks that use non-registered RFC1918 IP addresses to connect to the Internet. NAT operates on a device, usually connecting two networks together, that allows them to communicate. Typically, one network uses RFC1918 IP addresses, which are translated into globally unique IP addresses. Other scenarios in which NAT can be utilized will be discussed later in this chapter.

NAT by itself is not a security measure and should not be implemented in such a fashion. A common misconception is that NAT will allow a company to "hide" its internal network. This can be an added security benefit, but should not be relied upon as the only security measure. Although typical private networks use addresses that are never intended to be publicly issued, a company's ISP may have knowledge of that particular network. If routing between the company and the ISP is not done properly, a route to the company may be leaked throughout the ISP, possibly exposing its network to the public.

NAT Overview

Generally, NAT is used when a company's internal addresses are not globally unique and thus cannot be routed on the Internet (for instance, using RFC1918 private addresses), or because two separate networks which need to communicate are using an overlapping IP address space.

NAT allows (in most cases) hosts in a private network (inside network) to transparently communicate with destination hosts (outside network) in a global or public network. This is achieved by modifying the *source address* portion of an IP packet as it traverses the NAT device. The NAT device will keep track of each translation (conversation) between the source host (inside network) and destination host (outside network), and vice versa. This means that NAT is a stateful technique and devices implementing NAT are stateful devices.

Throughout this chapter and in the Cisco documentation, networks will be described as being either an *inside* network or an *outside* network. An *inside* network is the set of networks subject to translation. All other networks are considered *outside* networks.

One of the variations of NAT is PAT. This solution only works if the application does not rely on an IP address in the data portion of the packet for functionality. In such cases, Application Layer Gateways included inside the NAT (discussed later) may be needed to assist a NAT device.

The following is a list of terms used when referring to NAT and their descriptions. Keep in mind that different vendors may refer to these terms in varying contexts.

Address Realm

An address realm is a network in which the network addresses (IP addresses) are uniquely assigned to hosts so traffic can be routed to them. Routing protocols used within the network are responsible for routing traffic to the destination network. Often referred to as *inside* and *outside* networks, address realms help define zones which are separated and need to communicate with each other. For example, a company's internal network could be seen as one address realm. This realm is under a single administrative authority which needs to communicate with networks outside its jurisdiction. These outside networks, which could be another company's network or even the Internet, are also considered address realms. The definition of realm will vary depending on the context in which it is used.

Designing & Planning…

RFC 1918 Private Addressing

Throughout this chapter, we have discussed private addressing and the mysterious RFC 1918. Now would be a good time to discuss exactly what private addressing is and how RFC 1918 is involved with all of it. To begin, though, we need a brief history lesson.

The Internet, as we know it today, can trace its roots back to the Department of Defense's DARPA Project in the late 1960s and early 1970s. The original Internet was envisioned to consist of only a few organizations with a limited number of hosts utilizing it. As such, efficient

Continued

address allocation was not a primary consideration. The early to mid 1990s saw exponential growth in the utilization of networking. This growth, fueled by the increased home and business use of the Web, caused IP address allocation to grow at an alarming rate, to the point where the limited address space capacity began to be a serious concern. In order to counter this, RFC 1918 was proposed.

RFC 1918 proposed that three groups of IP addresses be set aside for organizations to use on their internal networks. The private address allocation is as follows:

- One Class A network address: 10.0.0.0 with 16277216 possible host addresses

- 16 Class B network addresses: 172.16.0.0 thru 172.31.0.0, each with 65526 possible host addresses

- 256 Class C network addresses: 192.168.0.0 thru 192.168.255.0, each with 256 possible host addresses

These address spaces are available to any organization that wishes to use them. In fact, if your organization is medium to large in size, you are very likely utilizing one of these address spaces already. A couple of key points to remember when utilizing them are:

- These addresses CANNOT be advertised on the Internet or to other outside networks. Although almost every service provider has provisions and safeguards built into there networks to prevent such an occurrence, imagine the traffic that an organization would face if they received all of the traffic destined for these generic private networks

- In order to communicate to outside networks, a NAT device must be incorporated in order to translate private addresses to valid global IP addresses. This can come in the form of a router or firewall device.

- Devices outside of the internal network will not be able to see resources such as Web or e-mail servers, and will require utilization of NAT coming into the network, or utilization of a demilitarized zone (DMZ) between the internal and external networks.

Private addressing is a very useful and efficient solution for a growing network. It allows an administrator to utilize an internal network-addressing scheme exclusive to the addresses given a company by its ISP. Also, it gives organizations a great deal of flexibility in the selection of an

Continued

ISP. By utilizing private addressing space, an organization can easily change from one ISP to another with very little reconfiguration, usually only on the network edge devices. Overall, RFC 1918 private addressing offers scalability and flexibility to organizations of almost every size and, as such, is a viable solution for organizations.

NAT

The basic configuration of NAT operates on a device which connects two networks together. One of these networks (designated as "inside") is addressed with either private RFC 1918 addresses or others which need to be converted into legal addresses before packets are forwarded to their destination network (designated as "outside").

NAT is a method by which IP addresses are mapped from one Address Realm to another. This type of translation provides transparent routing from host to host. There are many variations of address translation that assist in translating different applications; however, all NAT implementations on various devices should share the following characteristics:

- Transparent address assignment

- Transparent routing through address translation (routing refers to forwarding packets and not exchanging routing information)

- ICMP error packet data translation

Transparent Address Assignment

NAT translates addresses from an "inside" network to addresses in an "outside" network, and vice versa. This provides transparent routing for the traffic traversing both networks. The translation in some cases may extend to transport level identifiers such as TCP/UDP ports. Address translation is done at the start of a session. The following describes two types of address assignment:

- **Static address assignment** Static address assignment is a one-to-one address mapping for hosts connecting an "inside" network with an "outside" network for the duration of the NAT session. Static address assignment ensures that the translation table is static and not dynamic. Using static address assignment, your internal host is visible from the outside network since it is always assigned the same global IP address. This can be useful for some applications, but care must also be taken to secure each machine.

- **Dynamic address assignment** Dynamic address assignment is the process in which addresses are translated by the NAT device dynamically based on usage requirements. Once a NAT is no longer being used, it is terminated. NAT then frees that translation so the global address can be used in another translation.

Transparent Routing

Transparent routing refers to routing traffic between separate address realms (from an "inside" network to an "outside" one), by modifying address contents in the IP header to be valid in the address realm into which the traffic is routed to. A NAT device is placed at the border between two address realms and translates addresses in IP headers so that when the packet leaves one realm and enters another, it can be routed properly. Typically, there are three phases to address translation.

- **Address Binding** Address binding is the phase in which an "inside" IP address is associated with an "outside" address, or vice versa. This assumes that dynamic NAT is being used and not static NAT. Address binding is fixed, with a pool of assigned static addresses. These addresses are dynamically assigned on a per-session basis. For example, whenever a host on the "inside" network must reach another host on the "outside" network, it will begin a session with that host. A translation will occur on the NAT device associating a global IP address on the "outside" network with the IP address of the host on the "inside" network. Once a session is created, all traffic originating from the same "inside" host will use an identical translation. The start of each new session will result in the creation of a new translation. A NAT device will support many simultaneous sessions. (Consult the vendor's documentation for specific information.)

- **Address Lookup and Translation** Once a translation is established for a session, all packets belonging to the session will be subject to address lookup and translation.

- **Address Unbinding** Address unbinding is the phase in which an "inside" host IP address is no longer associated with a global address. NAT will perform address unbinding when it believes the last session using an address binding has terminated.

An example of transparent routing is when a Company's "inside" network uses the subnet 192.168.1.0/24, and the "outside" network uses the subnet 207.139.221.0/24. Transparent routing would occur on the device that separates the two subnets. Instead of using a router to route packets based on destination address, NAT alters the source address of an IP packet originating from the "inside" network and changes it to a valid IP address in the "outside" network. The NAT device then builds a table to keep track of the translations that have occurred to maintain communications between a host on the "inside" network and a host on the "outside" network. Figure 5.1 illustrates this example.

Figure 5.1 NAT Translation

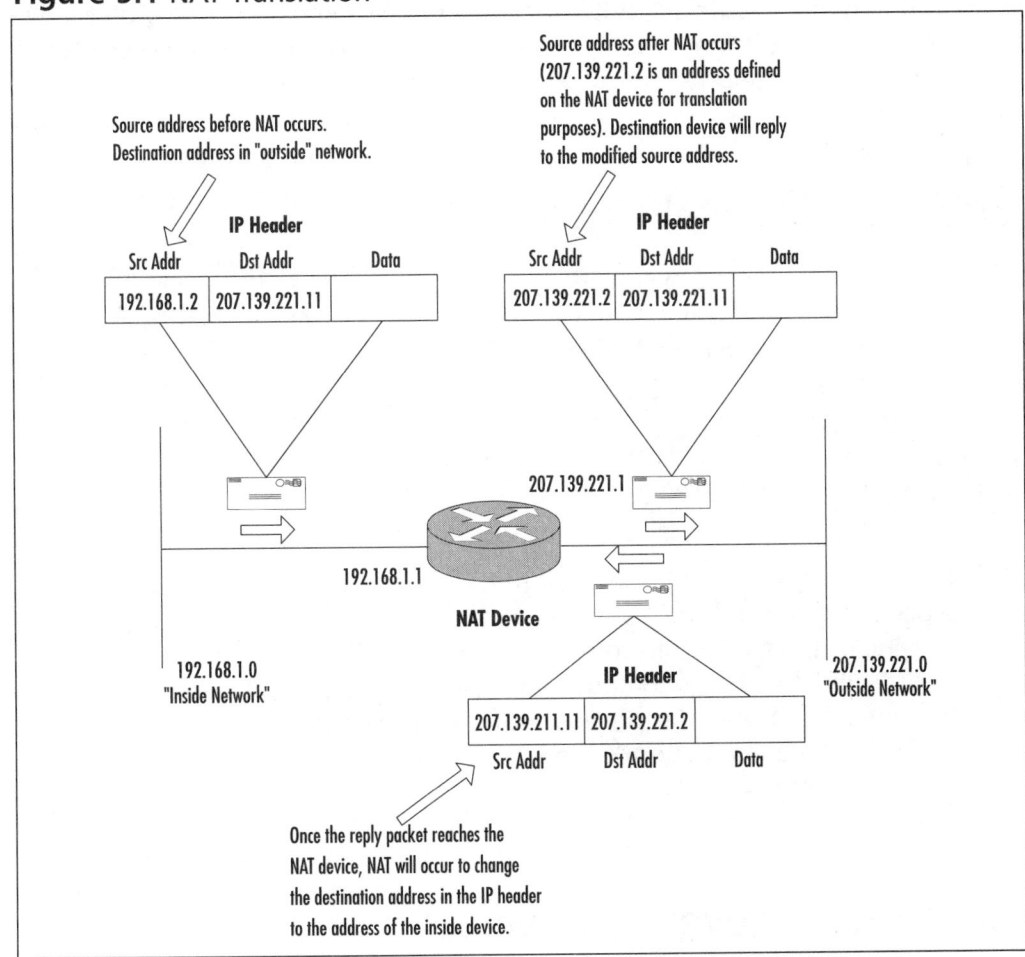

Public, Global, and External Networks

A global, public, or external network is an address realm with a unique network address assigned by the Internet Assigned Numbers Authority (IANA), or an equivalent address registry.

NOTE

Do not confuse public, global, and external networks with the term "outside" network. "Outside" is more of a generic term to describe a destination network in which NAT must occur in order to communicate with that network. "Outside" networks may refer to networks using global IP addresses, but it may also refer to the destination network in a situation where both networks use private IP addresses.

Private and Local Networks

A private or local network is an address realm independent of external network addresses. A private or local network uses IP addresses specified in RFC 1918. These addresses are private and therefore should never be used globally. Transparent routing between hosts in a private realm and external realm is made possible by a NAT device.

NOTE

Do not confuse private and local networks with the term "inside" network. As with the term "outside" network, "inside" network is more of a generic usage to describe the source network in which NAT must occur in order for two hosts to communicate. An "inside" network may refer to a network that uses the private IP addresses (RFC1918), but it may also refer to the source network used by a NAT device to communicate between global IP addresses.

Application Level Gateways

Not all applications are easily translated by NAT devices. This is especially true of those that include IP addresses and TCP/UDP ports in the data portion of the packet. Simple NAT may not always work with certain protocols. This is why most modern implementations of NAT include Application Layer Gateway functionality built in. Application Level Gateways (ALGs) are application-specific translation agents that allow an application on a host in one address realm to connect to another host running a translation agent in a different realm transparently. An ALG may interact with NAT to set up state, use NAT state information, alter application-specific data, and perform whatever else is necessary to get the application to run across different realms.

For example, recall that NAT and PAT can alter the IP header source and destination addresses, as well as the source and destination port in the TCP/UDP header. RealAudio clients on the "inside" network access TCP port 7070 to initiate a conversation with a RealAudio server located on an "outside" network and to exchange control messages during playback such as pausing or stopping the audio stream. Audio session parameters are embedded in the TCP control session as a byte stream. The actual audio traffic is carried in the opposite direction (originating from the RealAudio server, and destined for the RealAudio client on the "inside" network) on ports ranging from 6970 to 7170.

As a result, RealAudio will not work with a traditional NAT device. One workaround is for an ALG to examine the TCP traffic to determine the audio session parameters and selectively enable inbound UDP sessions for the ports agreed upon in the TCP control session. Another workaround could have the ALG simply redirecting all inbound UDP sessions directed to ports 6970 thru 7170 to the client address on the "inside" network.

ALGs are similar to proxies in that both ALGs and proxies aid application-specific communication between clients and servers. Proxies use a special protocol to communicate with proxy clients and relay client data to servers and vice versa. Unlike proxies, ALGs do not use a special protocol to communicate with application clients, and do not require changes to application clients.

NAT Architectures

There are many variations of NAT that aid to different applications. The following is a list of some of the variations of NAT.

Traditional NAT or Outbound NAT

Traditional NAT is a dynamic translation that allows hosts within the "inside" network to transparently access hosts in the "outside" network. In traditional NAT, the initial outbound session is unidirectional (one-way)—outbound from the private network. Once a session has been established with a device on the "outside" network, bidirectional communication will occur for the duration of that session.

IP addresses of hosts in the "outside" network are unique, while IP addresses of hosts in the "inside" network use RFC 1918 private IP addresses. Since the IP addresses of the "inside" network are private and cannot be used globally, they must be translated into global addresses.

A traditional NAT router in Figure 5.2 would allow Host A to initiate a session to Host Z, but not the other way around. Also, the address space from the global address pool used on the "outside" is routable, whereas the "inside" address space cannot be routed globally.

Figure 5.2 Traditional NAT

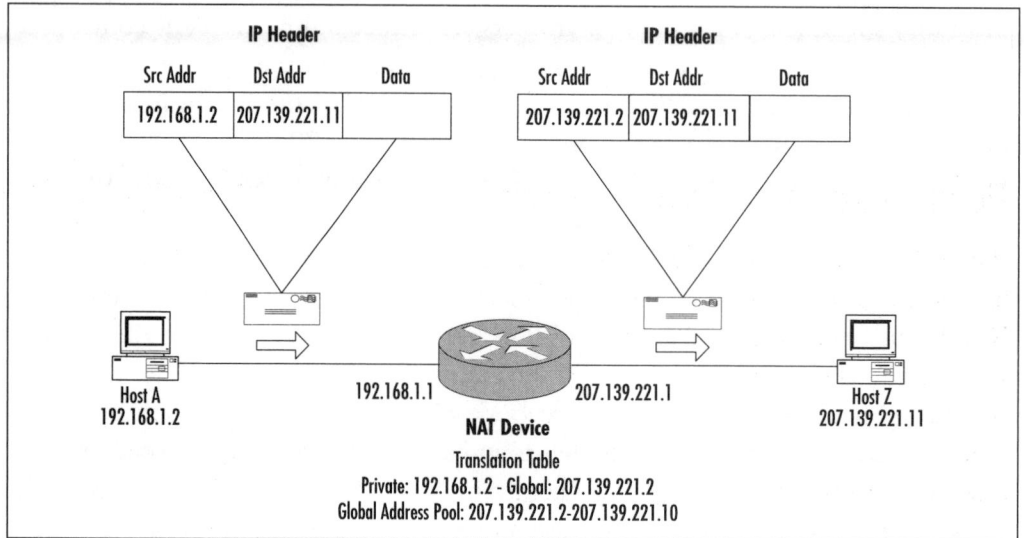

Figure 5.3 shows the reply packets sent by Host Z to Host A. Since Host A originated a session from inside, any packets originating from Host Z in response to Host A will be permitted provided that the security rules on the NAT device permit it. If Host Z attempted to initiate a session with Host A, traditional NAT will not permit this because Host A has a private IP address. This IP address is reserved for private networks and will therefore never be routed globally. From the perspective of Host Z, Host A's IP address is 207.139.221.2 (the translated address). If Host Z attempts to initiate a session with this IP address, the NAT device will not be able to associate 207.139.221.2 with an "inside" IP address with traditional NAT. In order to allow Host Z to initiate a session with Host A, Static NAT (explained later) will need to be configured.

Figure 5.3 A Traditional NAT Reply

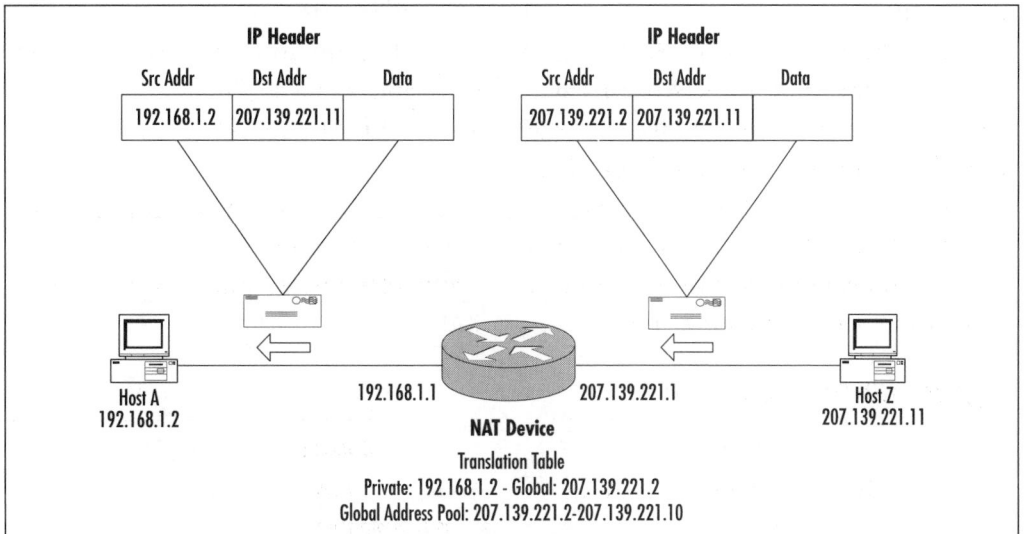

Port Address Translation

Port Address Translation (PAT) extends the concept of translation one step further by also translating transport identifiers like TCP and UDP port numbers, and ICMP query identifiers. This allows the transport identifiers of a number of private hosts to be multiplexed into the transport identifiers of a single global IP address. PAT allows numerous hosts from the "inside" network to share a single "outside" network IP address. The advantage of this type of translation is that only one global IP address is needed, whereas with NAT, each "inside" host must translate to a unique "outside" IP address.

> **NOTE**
>
> Both NAT and PAT can be combined. The advantage being that when NAT exhausts the pool of global IP addresses, PAT can then be used until one of the NAT translations times out. This method ensures that all "inside" hosts can be successfully translated into "outside" global IP addresses.

Figure 5.4 illustrates PAT. Host A on the "inside" network needs to communicate with Host Z on the "outside" network. Because these two hosts are on different networks and the "inside" network uses IP addresses from a private address space, NAT/PAT is needed to allow the two hosts to communicate. Unfortunately, the administrator only has a limited number of global IP addresses, many of which have already been assigned to various devices. Therefore, NAT cannot be used for translations. As an alternative, PAT can be used instead.

Figure 5.4 PAT

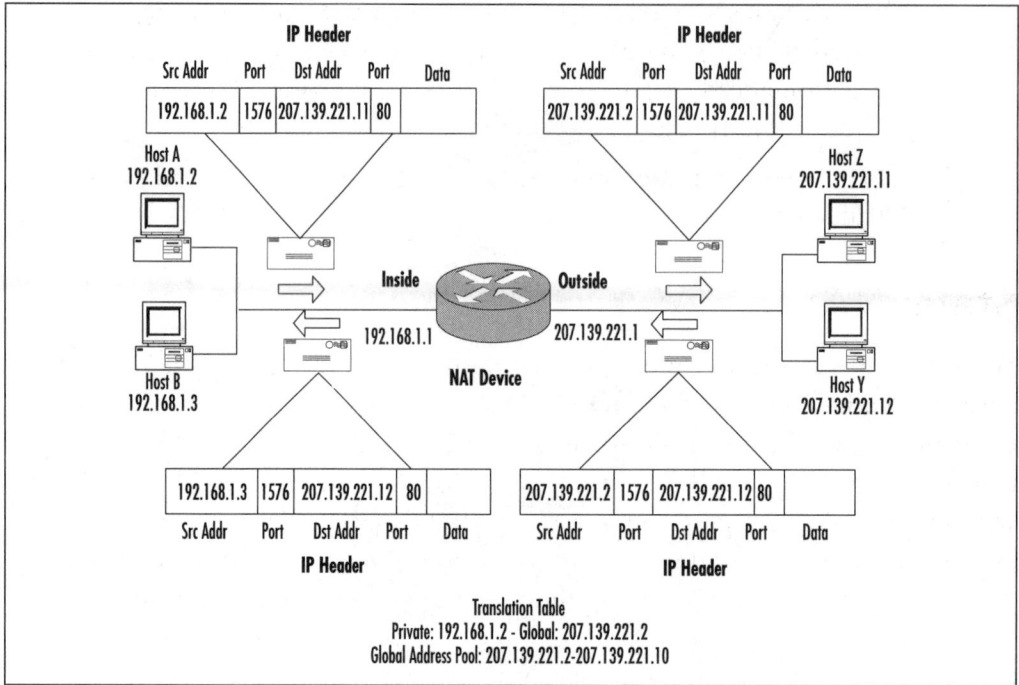

The steps taken in order to perform PAT are:

1. Host A attempts to initiate a session with Host Z. Since Host Z is not on the same network as Host A, Host A must send the packet to the router (default gateway) in order for it to be routed correctly.

2. Once the packet reaches the "inside" interface of the router in which PAT is enabled, the router examines the translation table for an existing translation. Since this is a new session, the router creates a new translation record in the table. Since only one IP address is assigned to the pool of IP addresses to translate to, a unique port number is added to the *source address*. This will allow the router to keep track of the translation for the duration of the session: PAT Global 207.139.221.2(1576) Local 192.168.1.2

The router then alters the IP header and changes the source address to the IP address of the "outside" interface of the router.

3. The packet is then transparently routed to Host Z.

4. Host Z replies to Host A by sending the packet to the "outside" interface of the router (*destination address*).

5. Once the packet reaches the "outside" interface, the router examines the IP header, checks the translation table for an existing translation. Since a translation already exists in the table, the router changes the destination address to the IP address of Host A.

6. The process is repeated until the session between Host A and Host Z is terminated.

Static NAT

With static NAT, sessions can be initiated from hosts in the "inside" or "outside" network. "Inside" addresses are bound to globally unique addresses using static translations since the connections are established in either direction. A translation that occurs from the "inside" network to the "outside" network will be translated with the statically configured address on the NAT device. When a session must be established from an "outside" network to an "inside" network, the static translation must already be manually set up on the router. By creating a static translation, you are translating an "inside" IP address to a fixed "outside" global IP address. This translation will never change and will always remain in the translation table. For example, if there is a resource on the "inside" network that must be made accessible to the "outside" network, the global IP address of the resource can be advertised worldwide through the DNS. Since this resource has been statically translated into a global IP, this IP can be advertised in a DNS record. If the resource is a mail server, an MX record may be created in the company's zone associating the MX record with the global IP that was statically assigned to the resource in the "inside" network. By doing this, even though the mail server is not physically located in the "outside" network, it can still be accessed as if it were.

Figure 5.5 illustrates a static NAT translation. A session is initiated from Host Z on the "outside" network. Since the NAT device has a static translation for Host A's IP address to a global IP address, the NAT device can forward the packet from Host Z to Host A's static NAT public IP address. Recall that with traditional or outbound NAT, a session can only be initiated from the "inside" host, which causes a dynamic translation to occur on the NAT device. Once this translation has been created, only then can the "outside" host reply back to the "inside" host. Once the session times out, the "inside" host will need to start a new session with the "outside" host causing the NAT device to create a new translation and possibly allocating a new global IP address to the "inside" host for the duration of the session (if NAT is used). With a static NAT, the translation is always active; the global IP address will never be allocated dynamically to another host on the "inside" network for translation purposes.

Figure 5.5 Static NAT

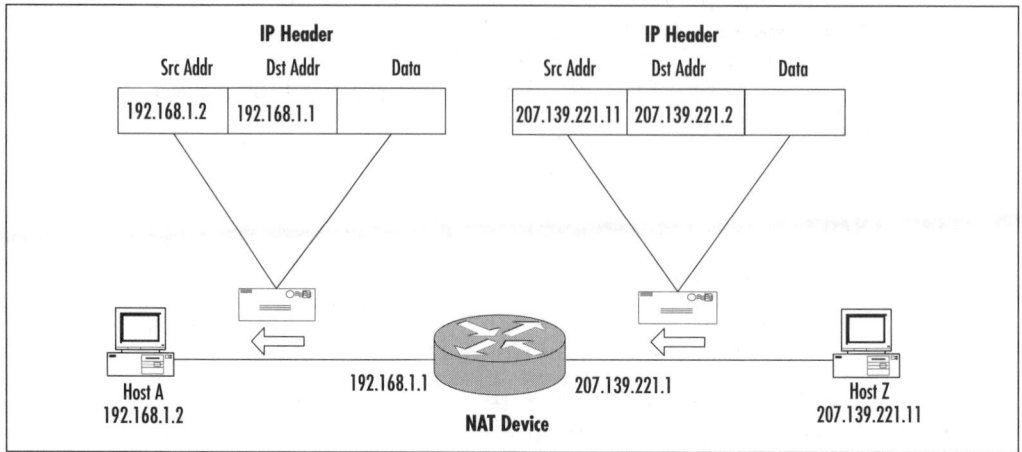

NOTE

Using this type of configuration to allow global access to resources has security-related advantages. If the NAT device is a Cisco PIX firewall or Cisco Router running FW IOS, Access Control Lists can be used to limit the type of traffic permitted to reach the resource. Compare this with having a server that is physically placed in the "outside" network allowing global access. In this case, limiting the type of traffic would be very difficult, if not impossible, creating a security risk.

Twice NAT

Twice NAT is a variation of NAT in that both the source and destination addresses are modified by the NAT device as the packet crosses address realms. Compare this to traditional NAT where only one of the addresses (either source or destination) is translated when traversing the NAT device.

Twice NAT is necessary when both "inside" and "outside" networks have overlapping address space. Although this type of problem does not occur often, a need for Twice NAT would arise when two companies merge their networks together and use overlapping address spaces, or when a company chooses an IP subnet that is already in use on the Internet. Figure 5.6 illustrates Twice NAT.

Figure 5.6 Twice NAT

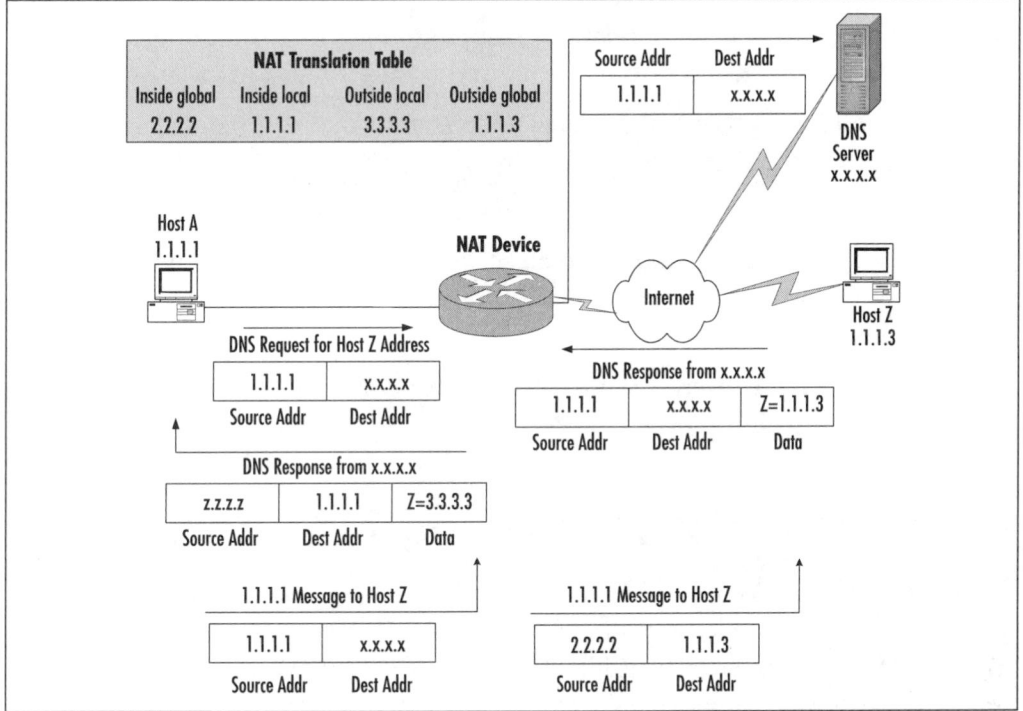

The router performs the following process when translating overlapping addresses:

1. The device Host 1.1.1.1 opens a connection to Host C by DNS name. A name-to-address lookup request is sent to DNS server x.x.x.x.

2. The router intercepts the DNS reply and translates the returned address (data portion of packet) if there is an overlap (that is, the resulting legal address resides illegally in the "inside" network). To translate the return address, the router creates a simple translation entry mapping the overlapping address 1.1.1.3 to an address from a separately configured, outside local address pool.

The router examines every DNS reply, ensuring that the IP address is not in the "inside" network. If it is, the router translates the address.

3. Host 1.1.1.1 opens a connection to 3.3.3.3.

4. The router sets up translations mapping inside local and global addresses to each other, and outside global and local addresses to each other.

5. The router replaces the source address with the inside global address and replaces the destination address with the outside global address.

6. Host C receives the packet and continues the conversation.

7. The router does a lookup, replaces the destination address with the inside local address, and replaces the source address with the outside local address.

8. Host 1.1.1.1 receives the packet and the conversation continues, using this translation process.

Guidelines for Deploying NAT and PAT

When deploying NAT and PAT in a network, there are many things to take into consideration. Various factors will contribute to which type of NAT is used, factors such as the number of available global IP addresses for translations, or whether the "inside" network uses global or RFC 1918 IP addresses. The following outlines some general guidelines for deploying NAT.

■ How many public IP addresses are available for translation from "inside" IP addresses? If there are only a limited number of global IP addresses for many "inside" hosts (for example, 8 global addresses for 250 "inside" hosts), PAT, or a combination of dynamic NAT and PAT, may be necessary.

■ Router performance needs to be considered for all types of NAT. NAT increases the time it takes for a packet to arrive at a destination address. When a packet traverses a NAT device, the IP header must be modified. This is currently done using process switching which places considerable load on the system.

- What type of addressing scheme is being used on the "inside" network? Are private RFC 1918 addresses being used? If so, then NAT will need to occur for the "inside" network(s) to be able to reach the "outside" networks.

- Not all applications will work with NAT. Be aware of what type of traffic will be translated and if the functionality of those applications will be affected by NAT. If this is the case, an ALG may need to be implemented to assist in the translation process. Application types that do not need an ALG, or where an ALG is built into Cisco's NAT implementation, are listed later in this chapter. Not all applications can be used with ALGs.

- A disadvantage of NAT is the loss of end-to-end IP connectivity. It becomes much harder to trace packets that undergo numerous IP address changes over multiple NAT hops. On the other hand, an advantage to this is that it becomes difficult if not impossible for hackers to determine a packet's source to trace or obtain the original source or destination addresses.

Designing & Planning…

What Applications Need an ALG?

ALGs (Application Level Gateways) have been mentioned several times throughout this chapter, but the question of what applications may or may not need an ALG has not been answered. The following lists summarize traffic types that may or may not be supported in Cisco IOS NAT.

Some examples of traffic types supported in the Cisco IOS NAT are as follows:

- Any TCP/UDP traffic that does not carry source and/or destination IP addresses in the data portion of an IP packet.
- HTTP
- TFTP
- Telnet
- Archie
- Finger

Continued

www.syngress.com

- NTP
- NFS
- rlogin, rsh, rcp

Although the following traffic types carry IP addresses in the data portion of an IP packet, Cisco IOS NAT will provide ALG functions for the following applications:

- ICMP
- FTP (including PORT and PASV commands)
- NetBIOS over TCP/IP
- RealAudio
- CuSeeMe
- Streamworks
- DNS name-lookup queries and reverse name-lookup queries.
- H.323/NetMeeting (IOS 12.0(1)/12.0(1)T or later)
- H.323 v2 (IOS 12.1(5) or later)
- Selsius Skinny Client Protocol (IOS 12.1(5) or later)
- VDOLive (IOS 11.3(4), 11.3(4)T or later)
- Vxtreme (IOS 11.3(4), 11.3(4)T or later)
- IP Multicast (IOS 12.0(1)T source address translation only)

The following traffic types are not currently supported by Cisco IOS NAT:

- Routing table updates
- DNS zone transfers
- BOOTP
- Talk, ntalk
- SNMP
- NetShow

Some guidelines to follow for implementing static NAT are:

- How many "inside" devices need to be statically translated? Remember that each global IP used for static translations cannot be used for dynamic translations.

- A security policy should be in place to limit the type of traffic permitted to reach that statically translated device. When an "inside" device is statically translated into a global IP address, any devices on the "outside" networks can initiate a session with the "inside" device.

IOS NAT Support for IP Telephony

Recent enhancements to the Cisco IOS support for Network Address Translation have allowed the support for several of Cisco's converged and IP telephony product solutions. Some of the technologies that these newly expanded features support include:

- H.323 v2
- Call Manager Support
- Session Initiation Protocol (SIP)

H.323 v2 Support

Previous to IOS release 12.1(5), Cisco IOS NAT support of the H.323 standard was limited solely to the support of H.323 v1 implementation for Microsoft Net meeting. However, with the release of 12.1(5) and later, NAT supports version H.323 v2. Although a detailed discussion of the H.323 protocol is outside the scope of this chapter, a brief introduction is in order. H.323 is an industrywide, open standard for real-time audio, video, and data over packet networks. H.323 is an ITU-T standard and is part of the H.32x family of protocols. Cisco's IP telephony architecture can use H.323 to communicate with IP phones and IP telephony gateways. In addition, because it is an open protocol, it can be used to communicate with dissimilar systems such as PBXs and other vendors' equipment.

This support also includes the H.225 and H.245 message types, as well as Fast Connect and Alerting messages. The support for H.323 v2 NAT does not, however, include support for Registration Admission and Status messages (RAS), which is a messaging format for gateway-to-gateway communications. The IOS version of PAT does not support H.323 in any of its versions, so NAT is the only solution for this technology. However, Version 6.2 of the PIX software will support it. No added configuration is required in order for the IOS to support H.323 NAT; only the correct IOS release is required.

CallManager Support

Cisco CallManager is the IP PBX component of the Cisco Architecture for Voice Video and Integrated Data, or AVVID as it is commonly known. Cisco CallManager communicates connection information with the endpoint IP phones through the use of a protocol known as *Skinny Station Protocol*. Skinny Station Protocol is also often used to connect the CallManager servers with gateway devices; however, its primary use remains that of communicating between IP phones and CallManager servers.

NAT support for CallManager/Skinny Station Protocol also came with the release of the 12.1(5) IOS. This support allows a router running NAT to be placed between the CallManager server(s) and the IP telephone set. When the IP phone performs a session request, the router will detect the Skinny Station Protocol request and automatically perform the port translation. This functionality is present with no configuration on IOS 12.1(5). However, if you wish to use a TCP port other than the default port, you can use the *ip nat skinny service tcp port* command. Once again, this functionality is limited to NAT; PAT cannot support this.

Session Initiation Protocol

Session Initiation Protocol or SIP is an alternative to H.323 messaging for Voice over IP (VoIP) and similar real-time transmission protocols. Like H.323, it provides support for call setup and processing in an IP environment. Session Description protocol (SDP) is a protocol that resides within SIP and is used for control and creation of multimedia sessions.

NAT support for SIP and SDP came with the release of the 12.2(8) IOS software. NAT can allow SIP/SDP messages to pass through the router and encode the messages back to the original at the packet level. In order for NAT to work with SIP and SDP, an Application Level Gateway (ALG) must be incorporated. NAT support for SIP is automatic with IOS 12.2(8), however the port used by NAT for SIP can be changed by use of the *ip nat service* command. PAT support is not available for this solution in the IOS, but it is available in the 6.2 version of the PIX firewall software.

Configuring NAT on Cisco IOS

Cisco's implementation of NAT functionality on a router is fundamentally the same as the implementation of NAT on a PIX firewall (PIX was covered in

Chapter 3). Performance-wise, the NAT session limit on a router depends on the amount of DRAM available on the router, and the load on the router. Each NAT translation consumes approximately 160 bytes of DRAM. As a result, ten thousand translations would consume about 1.6MB. This should not impose a burden on a typical router provided it is not overloaded by other processes. PAT, as described previously, is handled differently. The translations occur with one global IP address. The translation table maintains each translation by assigning a unique port number to each translation. Since TCP/UDP port numbers are encoded in 16 bits, there are theoretically 65,536 possible values, resulting in 65,536 simultaneous sessions for each protocol.

The following section will outline the commands necessary to implement, and verify, NAT operation on a Cisco router. The commands necessary to configure NAT on the Cisco PIX firewall differ from the ones used in the IOS. These commands will be covered in detail in Chapter 3.

Configuration Commands

This section will cover the commands necessary to implement NAT on a Cisco router. The configuration commands necessary to implement NAT on a Cisco Secure PIX firewall will be covered in the next chapter.

Before NAT can be implemented, the "inside" and "outside" networks must be defined. To define the "inside" and "outside" networks, use the *ip nat* command.

```
ip nat inside | outside
```

- **Inside** Indicates the interface is connected to the inside network (the network is subject to NAT translation).
- **Outside** Indicates the interface is connected to the outside network.

Mark the interface as being on the inside or outside realms with the following:

```
interface ethernet0
ip nat inside
```

Enter interface configuration mode and designate *ethernet0* as the "inside" network interface.

```
interface serial1
ip nat outside
```

Enter interface configuration mode and designate *serial0* as the "outside" network interface.

Once the "inside" and "outside" network interfaces have been defined, an access list must be created to define the traffic that will be translated. This will only define the traffic to be translated and will not control any NAT functions by itself. To create an access list, use the *access-list* command:

```
access-list access-list-number permit source [source-wildcard]
```

- **Access-list-number** Number of an access list. This is a decimal number from 1 to 99.

- **Deny** Denies access if the conditions are matched.

- **Permit** Permits access if the conditions are matched.

- **Source** Number of the network or host from which the packet is being sent. Use the keyword *any* as an abbreviation for source 0.0.0.0 and source-wildcard 255.255.255.255.

- **Source-wildcard** (optional) Wildcard bits to be applied to the source. Use the keyword *any* as an abbreviation for source 0.0.0.0 and source-wildcard 255.255.255.255.

```
access-list 10 permit ip 192.168.1.0 0.0.0.255 any
```

This specifies that traffic originating from the 192.168.1.0 subnet destined for any other network should be translated. By itself, the access list will not translate the specified traffic.

A pool of IP addresses must be defined for dynamic NAT translations. To do this, use the *ip nat* command:

```
ip nat pool name start-ip end-ip {netmask netmask | prefix-length
    prefix-length} [type rotary]
```

- **Name** Name of the pool.
- **Start-ip** Starting IP address for range of addresses in address pool.
- **End-ip** Ending IP address for range of addresses in address pool.
- **Netmask** *netmask* Specify the netmask of the network to which the pool addresses belong.
- **Prefix-length** *prefix-length* Number that indicates how many bits of the netmask are ones.

- **Type-rotary** (optional) Indicates that the range of addresses in the address pool identify real, inside hosts where TCP load distribution will occur.

Define a pool of global addresses to be allocated as needed.

```
ip nat pool net-208 207.139.221.10 207.139.221.128 netmask >255.255.255.0
```

Specifies a pool of global IP addresses with the name *net-208* will contain the range of IP addresses 207.139.221.10 thru 207.139.221.128.

To enable NAT for the inside destination address, the *ip nat inside destination* command will be used:

```
ip nat inside destination list {access-list-number | name} pool name
```

- **list** *access-list-number* Standard IP access list number. Packets with destination addresses that pass the access list are translated using global addresses from the named pool.
- **list** *name* Name of a standard IP access list.
- **pool** *name* Name of the pool from which global IP addresses are allocated during dynamic translation.

```
ip nat pool net-208 207.139.221.10 207.139.221.128 netmask >255.255.255.0
```

Define a pool of global IP addresses called *net-208* with the IP addresses 207.139.221.10 thru 207.139.221.128.

```
access-list 10 permit any 204.71.201.0 0.0.0.255
```

Specify that traffic destined for the network address 204.71.201.0 will be translated to global addresses defined in the pool *net-207*.

```
ip nat inside destinationn list 10 pool net-207
```

Enable NAT for traffic defined in access list 10 to be translated to addresses from the *net-207* pool. This will translate the destination address, not the source.

To enable NAT for the inside source address, use the *ip nat inside source* command.

```
ip nat inside source {list {access-list-number | name} pool name
    [overload] | static local-ip global-ip
```

- **List *access-list number*** Standard IP access list number. Packets with source addresses that pass the access list are dynamically translated using global addresses from the named pool.

- **List *name*** Name of the standard IP access list.

- **Pool *name*** Name of the pool from which global IP addresses are allocated dynamically.

- **Overload** (optional) Enables the router to use one global address for many local addresses (PAT).

- **Static *local-ip*** Sets up a single static translation.

- **Global-ip** Sets up a single static translation. This argument establishes the globally unique IP address which an inside host will be translated to.

Establish dynamic source translation using an access list to define the traffic to be translated based on source address.

```
ip nat pool net-207 207.139.221.10  207.139.221.128  netmask 255.255.255.0
```

Define a pool of IP addresses with the name *net-207* and a range of IP addresses from 207.139.221.10 thru 207.139.221.128.

```
access-list 10 permit ip 192.168.1.0 0.0.0.255 any
```

Specify that traffic originating from the 192.168.1.0 network will be translated.

```
ip nat inside source list 10 pool net-207
```

Enable dynamic NAT for traffic defined in access list 10 to be translated to addresses from the *net-207* pool. This will translate the source address and not the destination address. To enable static NAT translation for the "inside" host 192.168.1.10 to the global IP address 207.139.221.10 use the following command:

```
ip nat inside source static 192.168.1.10 207.139.221.10
```

To enable PAT in conjunction with, or instead of, NAT:

```
ip nat pool net-207 207.139.221.10  netmask 255.255.255.0
```

Define a single global IP address with the name *net-207* and an IP address of 207.139.221.10.

```
access-list 10 permit ip 192.168.1.0 0.0.0.255
```

Specify that traffic originating from the 192.168.1.0 network will be translated.

```
ip nat inside source list 10 pool net-207 overload
```

Enable PAT for traffic defined in access list 10 to be translated to the address defined in the *net-207* pool. This will translate the source address. To enable NAT of the outside source address, use the *ip nat outside source* command:

```
ip nat outside source {list {access-list-number | name} pool name | static
    global-ip local-ip}
```

- **List *access-list-number*** Standard IP access list number. Packets with source addresses that pass the access list are translated using the global addresses from the named pool.

- **List *name*** Name of a standard IP access list.

- **Pool *name*** Name of the pool from which global IP addresses are allocated.

- **Static *global-ip*** Sets up a single static translation. This argument establishes the globally unique IP address assigned to an outside host.

- **Local-ip** Sets up a single static translation. This argument establishes the local IP address of an outside host as it appears to the inside world.

```
ip nat translation {timeout | udp-timeout | dns-timeout | tcp-timeout |
    finrst-timeout} seconds
```

- **Timeout** Specifies that the timeout value applies to dynamic translations except for overload translations. Default is 86400 seconds (24 hours).

- **Udp-timeout** Specifies that the timeout value applies to the UDP port. Default is 300 seconds (5 minutes).

- **Dns-timeout** Specifies that the timeout value applies to connections to the Domain Naming System. Default is 60 seconds.

- **Tcp-timeout** Specifies that the timeout value applies to the TCP port. Default is 86400 seconds (24 hours).

- **Finrst-timeout** Specifies that the timeout value applies to Finish and Reset TCP packets, which terminate a connection. Default is 60 seconds.

- **Seconds** Number of seconds the specified port translation times out.

```
ip nat translation timeout 300
```

This example specifies that translations will timeout after 300 seconds (5 minutes) of inactivity.

```
ip nat translation timeout 600
```

This specifies that NAT translations will timeout after 600 seconds (10 minutes) of inactivity.

Verification Commands

The following are commands used to verify the operation of NAT on a Cisco router.

- **show ip nat statistics** Displays NAT statistics.
- **show ip nat translations [verbose]** Displays NAT translations, where *verbose* optionally displays additional information for each translation table entry, including how long ago the entry was created and used.

The following is a sample output from the *show ip nat statistics*. Table 5.1 outlines the significant fields in the sample output.

```
Router#show ip nat statistics
Total translations: 2 (0 static, 2 dynamic; 0 extended)
Outside interfaces: Serial0
Inside interfaces: Ethernet1
Hits: 135  Misses: 5
Expired translations: 2
Dynamic mappings:
- Inside Source
access-list 1 pool net-208 refcount 2
 pool net-208: netmask 255.255.255.240
        start 171.69.233.208 end 171.69.233.221
        type generic, total addresses 14, allocated 2 (14%), misses 0
```

Table 5.1 Explanation of the Significant Fields from the *show ip nat statistics* Sample Output

Field	Description
Total translations	Number of translations active in the system. This number is incremented each time a translation is created and is decremented each time a translation is cleared or times out.
Outside interfaces	List of interfaces marked as outside with the *ip nat outside* command.

Continued

Table 5.1 Continued

Field	Description
Inside interfaces	List of interfaces marked as inside with the *ip nat inside* command.
Hits	Number of times the software does a translations table lookup and finds an entry.
Misses	Number of times the software does a translation table lookup, fails to find an entry, and must try to create one.
Expired translations	Cumulative count of translations that have expired since the router was booted.

Configuring NAT between a Private Network and the Internet

Company XYZ management has decided to allow employees access to the Internet. A leased line to their ISP has been purchased and installed, and a Cisco router has been purchased to route the company's internal traffic to their ISP. The ISP has assigned a range of 128 global IP addresses (207.139.221.0/25) to the company to use as they see fit. Administrators have used a private 192.168.1.0/24 subnet for their internal hosts. Figure 5.7 illustrates the design.

Figure 5.7 NAT and the Internet

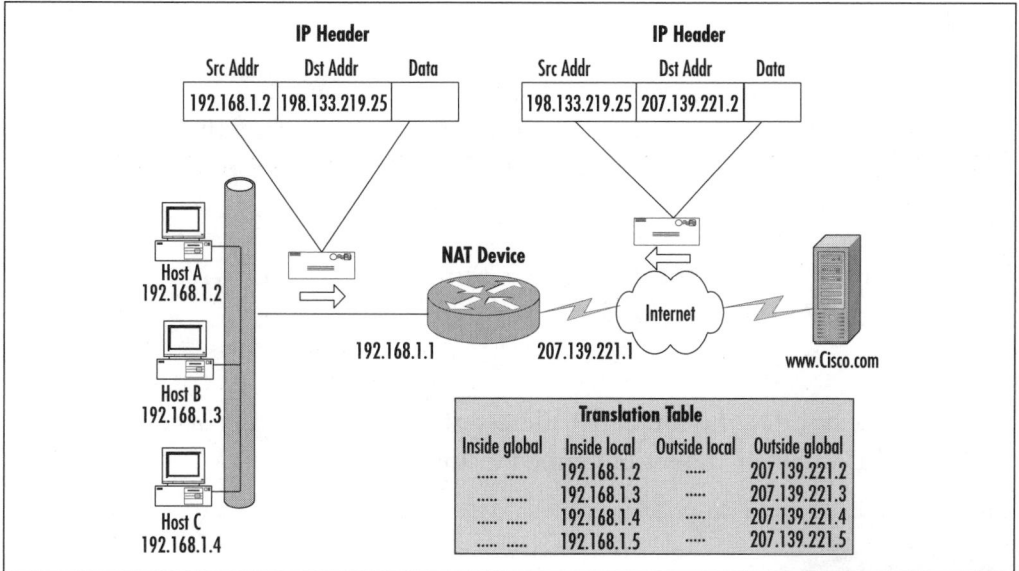

Here are the steps to follow for the configuration example, with explanations for clarification as you go through the commands:

```
configure terminal
interface ethernet0
ip address 192.168.1.1 255.255.255.0
```

This assigns an IP address to *ethernet0 interface*.

```
ip nat inside
```

This designates *ethernet0 interface* as an "inside" network.

```
no shutdown
```

This serves to remove the interface from shutdown state.

```
interface serial0
ip address 207.139.221.1 255.255.255.128
Assign IP address to serial0 interface.ip nat outside
```

This designates *serial0 interface* as an "outside" network.

```
no shutdown
```

This removes the interface from shutdown status.

```
exit
access-list 10 permit ip 192.168.1.0 0.0.0.255
```

This specifies that traffic originating from the 192.168.1.0 network will be translated.

```
ip nat pool net-207 207.139.221.2  207.139.221.126  netmask 255.255.255.128
```

This defines a pool of global IP addresses named *net-207* with an address range of 207.139.221.2 thru 207.139.221.126 to be used for NAT.

```
ip nat pool net-207-PAT  207.139.221.127  netmask 255.255.255.128
```

This defines a single global IP address named *net-207-PAT* with address 207.139.221.127 to be used for PAT.

```
ip nat inside source list 10 pool net-207
```

This specifies that the source IP address of traffic defined in access list 10 will be NAT'd with IP addresses defined in the *net-207* pool.

```
ip nat inside source list 10 pool net-207-PAT  overload
```

Lastly, this specifies that the source IP address of traffic defined in access list 10 will be PATed with IP addresses defined in *net-207-PAT* pool. PAT will occur once NAT has used all available addresses in the *net-207* pool. Once a translation has timed out due to inactivity, that global IP address will be reused for future NAT translations.

Configuring NAT in a Network with DMZ

Company XYZ has decided to host both a Web server and an e-mail server on their LAN. They would like to make these servers publicly available yet provide full security for them. It has been decided that a demilitarized zone (DMZ) will be created to keep the servers separated from the company's local LAN. The Cisco router currently used has an additional Ethernet port which will be designated as the DMZ. The DMZ subnet will use the private IP address space of 192.168.2.0/24, while the Web server and e-mail server will be statically translated into two global IP addresses currently used in the NAT global pool. Figure 5.8 illustrates the new scenario.

Figure 5.8 NAT with DMZ

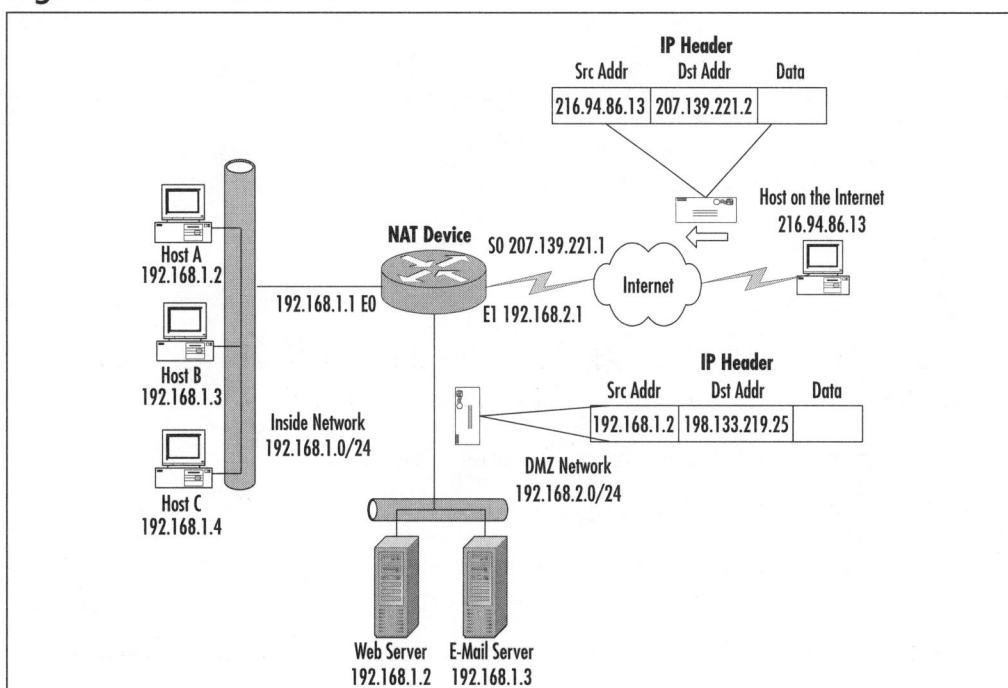

Here are the steps to follow, with explanations of the commands:

```
configure terminal
interface ethernet0
ip address 192.168.1.1 255.255.255.0
```

This assigns an IP address to *ethernet0 interface*.

```
ip nat inside
```

This designates *ethernet0 interface* as an "inside" network.

```
no shutdown
```

This removes the interface from shutdown status.

```
interface serial0
ip address 207.139.221.1 255.255.255.128
```

This assigns the IP address to *serial0 interface*.

```
ip nat outside
```

This designates *serial0 interface* as an "outside" network.

```
no shutdown
```

This removes the interface from shutdown status.

```
interface ethernet1
ip address 192.168.2.1 255.255.255.0
```

This assigns the IP address to *ethernet1 interface*.

```
ip nat inside
```

This designates *ethernet1 interface* as an "inside" network.

```
no shutdown
```

This removes the interface from shutdown status.

```
access-list 10 permit ip 192.168.1.0 0.0.0.255
```

This specifies that traffic originating from the 192.168.1.0 network will be translated.

```
ip nat pool net-207 207.139.221.4  207.139.221.126  netmask 255.255.255.128
```

This defines a pool of global IP addresses named *net-207* with an address range of 207.139.221.4 thru 207.139.221.126 to be used for NAT.

```
ip nat pool net-207-PAT  207.139.221.127  netmask 255.255.255.128
```

This defines a single global IP address named *net-207-PAT* with address 207.139.221.127 to be used for PAT.

```
ip nat inside source list 10 pool net-207
```

This specifies that the source IP address of traffic defined in access list 10 will be NATed with IP addresses defined in the *net-207* pool.

```
ip nat inside source list 10 pool net-207-PAT  overload
```

This specifies that the source IP address of traffic defined in access list 10 will be PATed with the IP address defined in the *net-207-PAT* pool. PAT will occur once NAT has used all available addresses in the *net-207* pool. Once a translation has timed out due to inactivity, that global IP address will be reused for future NAT translations.

```
ip nat inside source static 192.168.2.2 207.139.221.2 netmask 255.255.255.128
```

This creates a static translation for the "inside" IP address 192.168.2.2 to the global IP address 207.139.221.2. Any traffic destined for 207.139.221.2 will be statically translated to 192.168.2.2.

```
ip nat inside source static 192.168.2.3 207.139.221.3 netmask 255.255.255.128
```

Considerations on NAT and PAT

Even though NAT helps get around the problem of scarce globally-routable IP addresses, it does have an impact on the functionality of certain protocols, therefore complicating their deployment. This section outlines some of the problems associated with NAT.

IP Address Information in Data

Numerous applications fail when packets traverse a NAT device. These packets carry IP address or port information in the data portion of the packet. Since NAT only alters the IP header to perform the translation, the data portion is left untouched. With the aid of an ALG, a work around may be provided in some cases. But if the packet data is IPSec secured (or secured by another transport or application level mechanism), the application is going to fail.

Bundled Session Applications

Bundled session applications such as FTP, H.323, SIP, and RTSP, which use a control connection to establish data flow are also usually broken up by NAT devices. This occurs because the applications exchange address and port information within the control session to establish data sessions and session orientations. NAT cannot know the interdependency of the bundled sessions and would therefore treat each session as if they were unrelated to one another. Applications like these can fail for a variety of reasons. Two of the most common reasons for failure are:

- Addressing information in the data portion of the packet is realm-specific and is not valid once the packet crosses the originating realm.

- Control sessions create new data sessions that NAT has no information about. These will fail in many cases.

Peer-to-Peer Applications

Peer-to-peer applications are more prone to failure than client-server-based applications, and can be originated by any of the peers if those peers are located in different realms. NAT translations, however, may not be established because the hosts on the "inside" network are not visible to the host on the "outside" network. This is problematic with traditional NAT (dynamic NAT and PAT) where connections are client to server.

IP Fragmentation with PAT en Route

IP fragmentation with PAT can occur when two hosts send fragmented TCP/UDP packets to the same destination host, and they happen to use the same fragmentation identifier. When the target host receives the two unrelated packets (which carry the same fragmentation ID from the same assigned host address), the target host is unable to distinguish which of the two sessions the packets belong to (due to the translation of the local source address when compared to the global PAT address), causing both sessions to be corrupted.

Applications Requiring Retention of Address Mapping

When a session is established across realms through the use of NAT, the translation for that session will eventually timeout and then be utilized by another session traversing realms. This can be a problem for applications that require numerous sessions to the same external address. NAT cannot know this requirement ahead of time and may reassign the global address between sessions. For example, if Host A on the "inside" network has established a session with Host Z on the "outside" network, the application will function properly. Once the session stops sending traffic and the NAT timer expires, the translation will be terminated and the global IP allocated for that specific translation will be used for another translation. What happens if Host Z requires more data and tries to initiate a session with the IP address that Host A had while it was translated? At this point, the application will no longer function properly.

In order to remedy this problem, keepalive messages need to be sent between hosts to keep the translation active. This can be especially annoying and may not be possible in some situations. An alternative is to use an ALG to keep the address mapping from being discarded by NAT.

IPSec and IKE

NAT operates by modifying source addresses within the IP header while it passes through the NAT device. Due to the nature of IPSec, the AH protocol is designed to detect alterations to IP packet headers. So, when NAT alters the source address information, the destination host receiving the altered packet discards the packet since the IP headers have been altered. The IPSec AH secure packet traversing NAT will simply not reach the target application.

IPSec ESP encrypted packets may be altered by NAT devices only in a limited number of cases. In the case of TCP/UDP packets, NAT would need to update the checksum in the TCP/UDP headers whenever the IP header is changed. However, as the TCP/UDP header is encrypted by the ESP, NAT would not be able to make this checksum update because it is now encrypted. TCP/UDP packets that are encrypted and traverse a NAT device will fail because the TCP/UDP checksum validation on the receiving end will not reach the target application.

Internet Key Exchange Protocol (IKE) can potentially pass IP addresses as node identifiers during the Main, Aggressive, and Quick modes. In order for an IKE negotiation to correctly pass through NAT, these data portions should be modified. However, these payloads are often protected by encryption. For all practical purposes, end-to-end IPSec is almost impossible to accomplish with NAT translation en route.

Summary

NAT solves the problem of the limited supply of global IP addresses available. By implementing a private IP address scheme in a private network, those addresses can then be translated into global IP addresses via a NAT device. This chapter covered various generic terms used by NAT, variations of NAT, how to deploy NAT on a network, and considerations for using NAT. As I stated at the beginning of the chapter, NAT is not a security feature and should not be used for security. It simply allows private IP addresses to be translated into global IP addresses. The myth that NAT "hides" a network is exactly that, a myth. A company's ISP may have knowledge of that private network and can therefore inject a route to that network in their routing tables therefore exposing the private network.

NAT uses the concept of an address realm to separate the "inside" network (a network with private addresses) from the "outside" network (the network outside of the private, or separated, segment of the network). NAT incorporates a system known as transparent address assignment in order to assign outside or global addresses to inside hosts. There are two methods used to accomplish this: static and dynamic address assignment. This system also works with transparent routing in order to route traffic between the inside and outside address realms. There are three phases of transparent routing: *address binding, address lookup and translation,* and *address unbinding.*

Application Level Gateways (ALGs) provide NAT with the ability to translate packets for applications that include TCP/UDP ports in the data portions of the packet. A prime example of such an application is RealAudio. ALGs act as specific translation agents for this information in order to allow the application traffic to pass over NAT. There are four primary architectures for NAT:

- Traditional or outbound NAT
- Port Address Translation (PAT)
- Static NAT
- Twice NAT

The choice of which architecture to deploy depends on the type of applications being supported. When deploying NAT within your enterprise, there are a number of considerations that must be taken into account, including the following:

- Available public addresses
- Router performance capabilities

- The addressing scheme
- The type of applications that will be used

Recent updates to NAT functionality now allow much greater support for IP telephony and converged data solutions for the Cisco IOS. Currently supported protocols include:

- H.323 v2
- CallManager support with support for Skinny Station Protocol
- Session Initiation Protocol (SIP) support for an alternative Voice over IP solution to H.323

NAT is configured on the Cisco IOS through the use of the *ip nat inside | outside* command. Next comes the configuration of access list(s) to allow or disallow hosts access, which is followed by the configuration of address pools for both inside and outside addresses. NAT configuration can be verified by use of the *show ip nat statistics* command as well as the *show ip nat translation* command.

Several factors should be considered before deploying NAT within your network. These include the following:

- Problems with IP address information in data packets. Because of the inherent nature of NAT to translate only the IP address header, IP information in the packets will not be translated. This problem can be generally remedied by use of an ALG.

- Problems with bundled session applications. These arise from the fact that such applications use a control connection in order to establish and maintain data flow. The majority of such issues are resolved in the 12.1(5) and later releases of Cisco IOS.

- Problems with peer-to-peer applications. This occurs because peers that exist in different realms are not visible to peer devices on outside realms. There is little work around for this problem; it is advised that client/server applications be used instead, when possible.

- IP fragmentation with PAT en route. This rare occurrence happens when two hosts originate fragmented TCP/UDP packets to the same destination host, and they happen to use the same fragmentation identifier. This is a very rare occurrence, however, and there is no workaround.

■ Problems with applications requiring retention of address mapping. This can be a problem for applications that require numerous sessions to the same external address. NAT cannot know this requirement ahead of time and may reassign the global address between sessions. In order to remedy this problem, keepalive messages need to be sent between hosts to keep the translation active.

■ Problems with IPSec and IKE. For all practical purposes, end-to-end IPSec is almost impossible to accomplish with NAT translation en route. This is because of the nature of IPSec. The AH protocol is designed to detect alterations to IP packet header, so when NAT alters the source address information, the destination host receiving the altered packet will discard the packet since the IP headers have been altered.

Solutions Fast Track

NAT Overview

☑ NAT is incorporated by the IOS in order to allow hosts within a private addressing space to communicate to outside networks.

☑ PAT is similar to NAT, however, in that it allows multiple inside addresses to use the same outside address by utilizing several ports on the same IP address.

☑ Transparent address assignment allows inside hosts to communicate with outside addresses transparently. There are two forms of transparent address assignment: static and dynamic.

☑ Transparent routing is the process by which the inside or local address is converted to the outside or global address, and vice versa. There are three stages to transparent routing: address binding, address lookup and translation, and address unbinding.

☑ Application level gateways allow NAT to translate addresses for application that incorporate TCP/UDP information within the data portions of their headers.

NAT Architectures

☑ Traditional or outbound NAT is a dynamic translation allowing inside hosts to communicate transparently with outside hosts.

☑ Static NAT involves the static mapping of inside addresses to outside addresses. This translation will remain until it is manually changed on the router.

☑ Twice NAT involves both the source and the destination address being modified by a NAT device as packets cross address realms. This is most often incorporated when there is overlapping address space between inside and outside networks.

Guidelines for Deploying NAT and PAT

☑ The number of available global IP addresses available for NAT must be taken into consideration before incorporating NAT into your network.

☑ Router performance is a key element to consider when deploying NAT. Process switching must be incorporated in order to perform NAT translations. Ensure that the router you have selected is capable of handling the added workload.

☑ Not all application will work with NAT. In such cases, Application Level Gateways (ALGs) should be incorporated.

IOS NAT Support for IP Telephony

☑ H.323 is a protocol used for IP telephony and Voice over IP convergence. As of IOS release 12.1(5), NAT supports H.323 v2.

☑ NAT support for CallManager comes in the form of support for Skinny Station Protocol sessions between IP phones and CallManager servers. This support is also available in IOS 12.1(5).

☑ Session Initiation Protocol, a protocol that can serve as a substitute for H.323 functionality is also supported by NAT. This functionality is available with version 12.2(8) of the IOS and also requires the use of an Application Level Gateway (ALG).

Configuring NAT on Cisco IOS

☑ NAT configuration begins with the use of the *ip nat inside | outside* command at the interface level.

☑ An access list is used to determine which hosts will have access to NAT resources and the address mappings by use of address pools.

☑ Address pools are used in order to specify the available pool of inside and outside addresses. This is accomplished by use of the *ip nat pool* command.

☑ NAT operation is verified by use of the *show ip nat statistics* and *show ip nat translations* commands.

Considerations on NAT and PAT

☑ Packets that incorporate IP addressing information including TCP and UPD port numbers may encounter problems when traversing a network that incorporates NAT. In order to work around this, an ALG may be incorporated.

☑ Bundled session applications, applications that use a control connection in order to establish data flow, may encounter failures in NAT networks.

☑ Applications that require retention of address mappings will timeout when NAT is used. In order to remedy this, keepalive messages need to be used to keep the session active.

Frequently Asked Questions

The following Frequently Asked Questions, answered by the authors of this book, are designed to both measure your understanding of the concepts presented in this chapter and to assist you with real-life implementation of these concepts. To have your questions about this chapter answered by the author, browse to **www.syngress.com/solutions** and click on the **"Ask the Author"** form.

Q: Should I use NAT or PAT?

A: It is a good idea to implement both depending on how many global addresses are available and how many local hosts need to be translated. If a NAT pool is implemented, PAT can then be used once all of the NAT translations are used up. Once a translation times out, it will then be re-allocated to another local host trying to open a session with a host on the outside. Therefore, NAT is the best practice, if and when enough globally valid IP addresses are available. If not, PAT could be used to provide outside connectivity with a few globally valid IP addresses.

Q: This chapter continually used the term inside and outside addresses. How do I classify these?

A: Inside addresses are those you will need to translate in order to communicate to the outside world. This could be for a variety of reasons, but the most common is the use of private addressing space. Outside addresses are not a part of your private network's address scheme. Therefore, in order for them to communicate to the inside network, they will need to be translated to an internal address. This form of address is needed in order for internal hosts to communicate outside of their address realm.

Q: I have implemented NAT on my network. At different points in time, hosts are no longer being translated. Why is this happening?

A: Check the number of global addresses in your global pool. The number of hosts requiring translation may be out-numbering available addresses. If this is the case, remove one address from the NAT pool and assign that address to PAT.

Q: Static address assignment seems like a lot of administrative work. What possible benefit does it offer?

A: Static address assignment is useful when you want the ability to keep a resource in a private addressing space, but still require outside resources to be able to access it with the same IP address constantly. A good example of this would be a mail server sitting in your DMZ.

Q: Did support for the H.323 specification only begin with IOS release 12.1(5)?

A: Earlier versions of the IOS did support the Microsoft Net meeting version of the H.323 v1 specification. However, IOS 12.1(5) and later releases support the entire H.323 specification except for registration and status messages (RAS) services.

Q: If PAT allows me to map several inside addresses to only one global address, wouldn't it just be better to use that as a solution instead of employing traditional NAT?

A: While PAT does allow that capability, you will encounter several limitations. Specifically, PAT does not support all of the applications you may encounter, and does not, in its current release, support IP telephony applications as well. It also places more load on the system than NAT.

## Chapter 6

Cryptography

Solutions in this chapter:

- Understanding Cryptography Concepts
- Learning about Standard Cryptographic Algorithms
- Understanding Brute Force
- Knowing When Real Algorithms Are Being Used Improperly
- Understanding Amateur Cryptography Attempts

☑ Summary

☑ Solutions Fast Track

☑ Frequently Asked Questions

Introduction

Cryptography is everywhere these days, from hashed passwords to encrypted mail, to Internet Protocol Security (IPSec) virtual private networks (VPNs) and even encrypted filesystems. Security is the reason why people opt to encrypt data, and if you want your data to remain secure you'd best know a bit about how cryptography works. This chapter certainly can't teach you how to become a professional cryptographer—that takes years of study and practice—but you *will* learn how most of the cryptography you will come in contact with functions (without all the complicated math, of course).

We'll examine some of the history of cryptography and then look closely at a few of the most common algorithms, including Advanced Encryption Standard (AES), the recently announced new cryptography standard for the U.S. government. We'll learn how key exchanges and public key cryptography came into play, and how to use them. I'll show you how almost all cryptography is at least theoretically vulnerable to brute force attacks.

Naturally, once we've covered the background we'll look at how cryptography can be broken, from cracking passwords to man-in-the-middle-type attacks. We'll also look at how other attacks based on poor implementation of strong cryptography can reduce your security level to zero. Finally, we'll examine how weak attempts to hide information using outdated cryptography can easily be broken.

Understanding Cryptography Concepts

What does the word *crypto* mean? It has its origins in the Greek word *kruptos*, which means *hidden*. Thus, the objective of cryptography is to hide information so that only the intended recipient(s) can "unhide" it. In crypto terms, the hiding of information is called *encryption*, and when the information is unhidden, it is called *decryption*. A cipher is used to accomplish the encryption and decryption. Merriam-Webster's Collegiate Dictionary defines *cipher* as "a method of transforming a text in order to conceal its meaning." The information that is being hidden is called *plaintext*; once it has been encrypted, it is called *ciphertext*. The ciphertext is transported, secure from prying eyes, to the intended recipient(s), where it is decrypted back into plaintext.

History

According to Fred Cohen, the history of cryptography has been documented back to over 4000 years ago, where it was first allegedly used in Egypt. Julius Caesar even used his own cryptography called *Caesar's Cipher*. Basically, Caesar's Cipher rotated the letters of the alphabet to the right by three. For example, *S* moves to *V* and *E* moves to *H*. By today's standards the Caesar Cipher is extremely simplistic, but it served Julius just fine in his day. If you are interested in knowing more about the history of cryptography, the following site is a great place to start: www.all.net/books/ip/Chap2-1.html.

In fact, ROT13 (rotate 13), which is similar to Caesar's Cipher, is still in use today. It is not used to keep secrets from people, but more to avoid offending people when sending jokes, spoiling the answers to puzzles, and things along those lines. If such things occur when someone decodes the message, then the responsibility lies on them and not the sender. For example, Mr. G. may find the following example offensive to him if he was to decode it, but as it is shown it offends no one: V guvax Jvaqbjf fhpxf…

ROT13 is simple enough to work out with pencil and paper. Just write the alphabet in two rows; the second row offset by 13 letters:

```
ABCDEFGHIJKLMNOPQRSTUVWXYZ

NOPQRSTUVWXYZABCDEFGHIJKLM
```

Encryption Key Types

Cryptography uses two types of keys: *symmetric* and *asymmetric*. Symmetric keys have been around the longest; they utilize a single key for both the encryption and decryption of the ciphertext. This type of key is called a *secret key*, because you must keep it secret. Otherwise, anyone in possession of the key can decrypt messages that have been encrypted with it. The algorithms used in symmetric key encryption have, for the most part, been around for many years and are well known, so the only thing that is secret is the key being used. Indeed, all of the really useful algorithms in use today are completely open to the public.

A couple of problems immediately come to mind when you are using symmetric key encryption as the sole means of cryptography. First, how do you ensure that the sender and receiver each have the same key? Usually this requires the use of a courier service or some other trusted means of key transport. Second, a problem exists if the recipient does not have the same key to decrypt the ciphertext from the sender. For example, take a situation where the symmetric key for a piece of crypto hardware is changed at 0400 every morning at both ends of a circuit. What happens if one end forgets to change the key (whether it is done with a strip tape, patch blocks, or some other method) at the appropriate time and sends ciphertext using the old key to another site that has properly changed to the new key? The end receiving the transmission will not be able to decrypt the ciphertext, since it is using the wrong key. This can create major problems in a time of crisis, especially if the old key has been destroyed. This is an overly simple example, but it should provide a good idea of what can go wrong if the sender and receiver do not use the same secret key.

Tools & Traps…

Assessing Algorithmic Strength

Algorithmic security can only be proven by its resistance to attack. Since many more attacks are attempted on algorithms which are open to the public, the longer an algorithm has been open to the public, the more attempts to circumvent or break it have occurred. Weak algorithms are broken rather quickly, usually in a matter of days or months, whereas stronger algorithms may be used for decades. However, the openness of the algorithm is an important factor. It's much more difficult to break an algorithm (whether weak or strong) when its complexities are completely unknown. Thus when you use an open algorithm, you can rest assured in its strength. This is opposed to a proprietary algorithm, which, if weak, may eventually be broken even if the algorithm itself is not completely understood by the cryptographer. Obviously, one should limit the trust placed in proprietary algorithms to limit long-term liability. Such scrutiny is the reason the inner details of many of the patented algorithms in use today (such as RC6 from RSA Laboratories) are publicly available.

Asymmetric cryptography is relatively new in the history of cryptography, and it is probably more recognizable to you under the synonymous term *public key cryptography*. Asymmetric algorithms use two different keys, one for encryption and one for decryption—a *public key* and a *private key*, respectively. Whitfield Diffie and Martin Hellman first publicly released public key cryptography in

1976 as a method of exchanging keys in a secret key system. Their algorithm, called the Diffie-Hellman (DH) algorithm, is examined later in the chapter. Even though it is commonly reported that public key cryptography was first invented by the duo, some reports state that the British Secret Service actually invented it a few years prior to the release by Diffie and Hellman. It is alleged, however, that the British Secret Service never actually did anything with their algorithm after they developed it. More information on the subject can be found at the following location: www.wired.com/wired/archive/7.04/crypto_pr.html

Some time after Diffie and Hellman, Phil Zimmermann made public key encryption popular when he released Pretty Good Privacy (PGP) v1.0 for DOS in August 1991. Support for multiple platforms including UNIX and Amiga were added in 1994 with the v2.3 release. Over time, PGP has been enhanced and released by multiple entities, including ViaCrypt and PGP Inc., which is now part of Network Associates. Both commercial versions and free versions (for non-commercial use) are available. For those readers in the United States and Canada, you can retrieve the free version from http://web.mit.edu/network/pgp.html. The commercial version can be purchased from Network Associates at www.pgp.com.

Learning about Standard Cryptographic Algorithms

Just why are there so many algorithms anyway? Why doesn't the world just standardize on one algorithm? Given the large number of algorithms found in the field today, these are valid questions with no simple answers. At the most basic level, it's a classic case of tradeoffs between security, speed, and ease of implementation. Here *security* indicates the likelihood of an algorithm to stand up to current and future attacks, *speed* refers to the processing power and time required to encrypt and decrypt a message, and *ease of implementation* refers to an algorithm's predisposition (if any) to hardware or software usage. Each algorithm has different strengths and drawbacks, and none of them is ideal in every way. In this chapter, we will look at the five most common algorithms that you will encounter: Data Encryption Standard (DES), AES [Rijndael], International Data Encryption Algorithm (IDEA), Diffie-Hellman, and Rivest, Shamir, Adleman (RSA). Be aware, though, that there are dozens more active in the field.

Understanding Symmetric Algorithms

In this section, we will examine several of the most common symmetric algorithms in use: DES, its successor AES, and the European standard, IDEA. Keep in mind that the strength of symmetric algorithms lies primarily in the size of the keys used in the algorithm, as well as the number of cycles each algorithm employs. All symmetric algorithms are also theoretically vulnerable to *brute force attacks*, which are exhaustive searches of all possible keys. However, brute force attacks are often infeasible. We will discuss them in detail later in the chapter.

DES

Among the oldest and most famous encryption algorithms is the Data Encryption Standard, which was developed by IBM and was the U.S. government standard from 1976 until about 2001. DES was based significantly on the Lucifer algorithm invented by Horst Feistel, which never saw widespread use. Essentially, DES uses a single 64-bit key—56 bits of data and 8 bits of parity—and operates on data in 64-bit chunks. This key is broken into 16 separate 48-bit subkeys, one for each round, which are called *Feistel cycles*. Figure 6.1 gives a schematic of how the DES encryption algorithm operates.

Each round consists of a substitution phase, wherein the data is substituted with pieces of the key, and a permutation phase, wherein the substituted data is scrambled (reordered). Substitution operations, sometimes referred to as confusion operations, are said to occur within S-boxes. Similarly, permutation operations, sometimes called diffusion operations, are said to occur in P-boxes. Both of these operations occur in the "F Module" of the diagram. The security of DES lies mainly in the fact that since the substitution operations are non-linear, so the resulting ciphertext in no way resembles the original message. Thus, language-based analysis techniques (discussed later in this chapter) used against the ciphertext reveal nothing. The permutation operations add another layer of security by scrambling the already partially encrypted message.

Every five years from 1976 until 2001, the National Institute of Standards and Technology (NIST) reaffirmed DES as the encryption standard for the U.S. government. However, by the 1990s the aging algorithm had begun to show signs that it was nearing its end of life. New techniques that identified a shortcut method of attacking the DES cipher, such as differential cryptanalysis, were proposed as early as 1990, though it was still computationally unfeasible to do so.

Figure 6.1 Diagram of the DES Encryption Algorithm

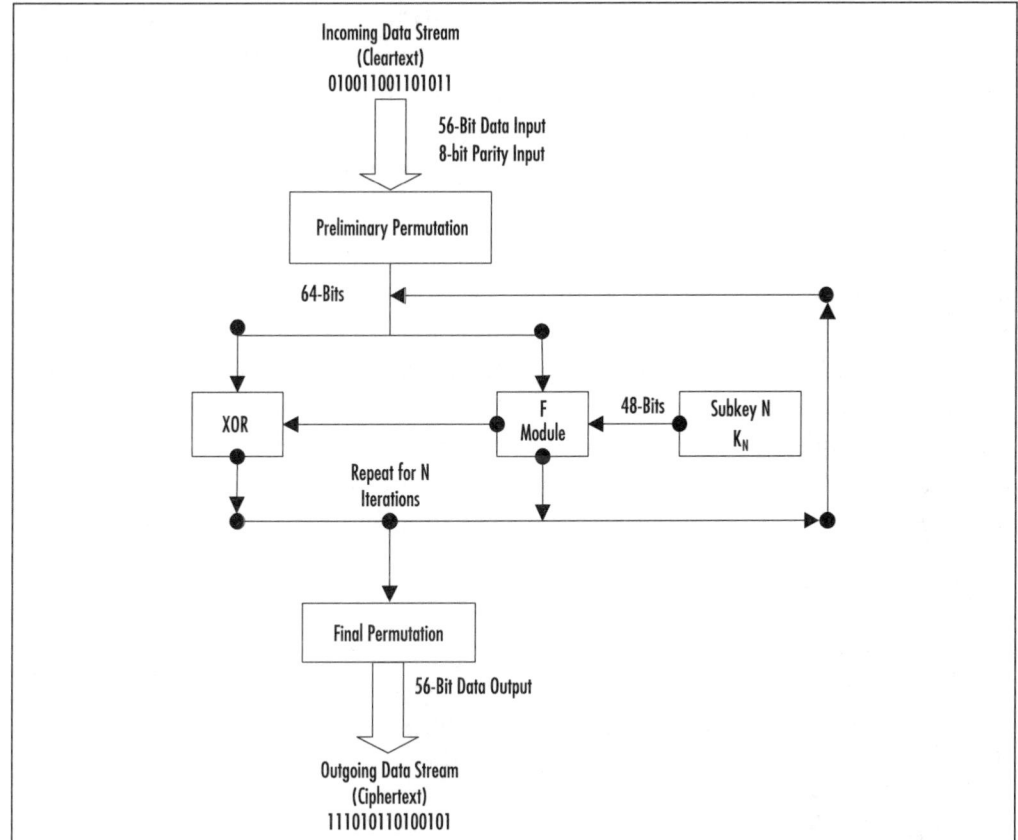

SECURITY ALERT

How can symmetric algorithms such as DES be made more secure? Theoretically, there are two ways: either the key length needs to be increased, or the number of rounds in the encryption process needs to be increased. Both of these solutions tend to increase the processing power required to encrypt and decrypt data and slow down the encryption/decryption speed because of the increased number of mathematical operations required. Examples of modified DES include 3-DES (a.k.a. Triple DES) and DESX. Triple DES uses three separate 56-bit DES keys as a single 168-bit key, though sometimes keys 1 and 3 are identical, yielding 112-bit security. DESX adds an additional 64-bits of key data. Both 3-DES and DESX are intended to strengthen DES against brute force attacks.

Significant design flaws such as the short 56-bit key length also affected the longevity of the DES cipher. Shorter keys are more vulnerable to brute force attacks. Although Whitfield Diffie and Martin Hellman were the first to criticize this short key length, even going so far as to declare in 1979 that DES would be useless within 10 years, DES was not publicly broken by a brute force attack until 1997.

The first successful brute force attack against DES took a large network of machines over 4 months to accomplish. Less than a year later, in 1998, the Electronic Frontier Foundation (EFF) cracked DES in less than three days using a computer specially designed for cracking DES. This computer, code-named "Deep Crack," cost less than $250,000 to design and build. The record for cracking DES stands at just over 22 hours and is held by Distributed.net, which employed a massively parallel network of thousands of systems (including Deep Crack). Add to this the fact that Bruce Schneier has theorized that a machine capable of breaking DES in about six minutes could be built for a mere $10 million. Clearly, NIST needed to phase out DES in favor of a new algorithm.

AES (Rijndael)

In 1997, as the fall of DES loomed ominously closer, NIST announced the search for the Advanced Encryption Standard, the successor to DES. Once the search began, most of the big-name cryptography players submitted their own AES candidates. Among the requirements of AES candidates were:

- AES would be a private key symmetric block cipher (similar to DES).

- AES needed to be stronger and faster then 3-DES.

- AES required a life expectancy of at least 20-30 years.

- AES would support key sizes of 128-bits, 192-bits, and 256-bits.

- AES would be available to all—royalty free, non-proprietary and unpatented.

Within months NIST had a total of 15 different entries, 6 of which were rejected almost immediately on grounds that they were considered incomplete. By 1999, NIST had narrowed the candidates down to five finalists including MARS, RC6, Rijndael, Serpent, and Twofish.

Selecting the winner took approximately another year, as each of the candidates needed to be tested to determine how well they performed in a variety of environments. After all, applications of AES would range anywhere from portable smart cards to standard 32-bit desktop computers to high-end optimized 64-bit computers. Since all of the finalists were highly secure, the primary deciding factors were speed and ease of implementation (which in this case meant memory footprint).

Rijndael was ultimately announced as the winner in October of 2000 because of its high performance in both hardware and software implementations and its small memory requirement. The Rijndael algorithm, developed by Belgian cryptographers Dr. Joan Daemen and Dr. Vincent Rijmen, also seems resistant to power- and timing-based attacks.

So how does AES/Rijndael work? Instead of using Feistel cycles in each round like DES, it uses iterative rounds like IDEA (discussed in the next section). Data is operated on in 128-bit chunks, which are grouped into four groups of four bytes each. The number of rounds is also dependent on the key size, such that 128-bit keys have 9 rounds, 192-bit keys have 11 rounds and 256-bit keys require 13 rounds. Each round consists of a substitution step of one S-box per data bit followed by a pseudo-permutation step in which bits are shuffled between groups. Then each group is multiplied out in a matrix fashion and the results are added to the subkey for that round.

How much faster is AES than 3-DES? It's difficult to say, because implementation speed varies widely depending on what type of processor is performing the encryption and whether or not the encryption is being performed in software or running on hardware specifically designed for encryption. However, in similar implementations, AES is always faster than its 3-DES counterpart. One test performed by Brian Gladman has shown that on a Pentium Pro 200 with optimized code written in C, AES (Rijndael) can encrypt and decrypt at an average speed of 70.2 Mbps, versus DES's speed of only 28 Mbps. You can read his other results at fp.gladman.plus.com/cryptography_technology/aes.

IDEA

The European counterpart to the DES algorithm is the IDEA algorithm, and its existence proves that Americans certainly don't have a monopoly on strong cryptography. IDEA was first proposed under the name *Proposed Encryption Standard* (PES) in 1990 by cryptographers James Massey and Xuejia Lai as part of a combined research project between Ascom and the Swiss Federal Institute of Technology. Before it saw widespread use PES was updated in 1991 to increase its strength against differential cryptanalysis attacks and was renamed Improved PES (IPES). Finally, the name was changed to International Data Encryption Algorithm (IDEA) in 1992.

Not only is IDEA newer than DES, but IDEA is also considerably faster and more secure. IDEA's enhanced speed is due to the fact the each round consists of much simpler operations than the Fiestel cycle in DES. These operations (XOR, addition, and multiplication) are much simpler to implement in software than the substitution and permutation operations of DES.

IDEA operates on 64-bit blocks with a 128-bit key, and the encryption/decryption process uses 8 rounds with 6 16-bit subkeys per round. The IDEA algorithm is patented both in the US and in Europe, but free non-commercial use is permitted.

Understanding Asymmetric Algorithms

Recall that unlike symmetric algorithms, asymmetric algorithms require more than one key, usually a *public* key and a *private* key (systems with more than two keys are possible). Instead of relying on the techniques of substitution and transposition, which symmetric key cryptography uses, asymmetric algorithms rely on the use of massively large integer mathematics problems. Many of these problems are simple to do in one direction but difficult to do in the opposite direction. For example, it's easy to multiply two numbers together, but it's more difficult to factor them back into the original numbers, especially if the integers you are using contain hundreds of digits. Thus, in general, the security of asymmetric algorithms is dependent not upon the feasibility of brute force attacks, but the feasibility of performing difficult mathematical inverse operations and advances in mathematical theory that may propose new "shortcut" techniques. In this section, we'll take a look at RSA and Diffie-Hellman, the two most popular asymmetric algorithms in use today.

Diffie-Hellman

In 1976, after voicing their disapproval of DES and the difficulty in handling secret keys, Whitfield Diffie and Martin Hellman published the Diffie-Hellman algorithm for key exchange. This was the first published use of public key cryptography, and arguably one of the cryptography field's greatest advances ever. Because of the inherent slowness of asymmetric cryptography, the Diffie-Hellman algorithm was not intended for use as a general encryption scheme—rather, its purpose was to transmit a private key for DES (or some similar symmetric algorithm) across an insecure medium. In most cases, Diffie-Hellman is not used for encrypting a complete message because it is 10 to 1000 times slower than DES, depending on implementation.

Prior to publication of the Diffie-Hellman algorithm, it was quite painful to share encrypted information with others because of the inherent key storage and transmission problems (as discussed later in this chapter). Most wire transmissions were insecure, since a message could travel between dozens of systems before reaching the intended recipient and any number of snoops along the way could uncover the key. With the Diffie-Hellman algorithm, the DES secret key (sent along with a DES-encrypted payload message) could be encrypted via Diffie-Hellman by one party and decrypted only by the intended recipient.

In practice, this is how a key exchange using Diffie-Hellman works:

- The two parties agree on two numbers; one is a large prime number, the other is an integer smaller than the prime. They can do this in the open and it doesn't affect security.

- Each of the two parties separately generates another number, which they keep secret. This number is equivalent to a *private key*. A calculation is made involving the private key and the previous two public numbers. The result is sent to the other party. This result is effectively a *public key*.

- The two parties exchange their public keys. They then privately perform a calculation involving their own private key and the other party's public key. The resulting number is the *session key*. Each party will arrive at the same number.

- The session key can be used as a secret key for another cipher, such as DES. No third party monitoring the exchange can arrive at the same session key without knowing one of the private keys.

The most difficult part of the Diffie-Hellman key exchange to understand is that there are actually two separate and independent encryption cycles happening. As far as Diffie-Hellman is concerned, only a small message is being transferred between the sender and the recipient. It just so happens that this small message is the secret key needed to unlock the larger message.

Diffie-Hellman's greatest strength is that anyone can know either or both of the sender and recipient's public keys without compromising the security of the message. Both the public and private keys are actually just very large integers. The Diffie-Hellman algorithm takes advantage of complex mathematical functions known as *discrete logarithms*, which are easy to perform forwards but extremely difficult to find inverses for. Even though the patent on Diffie-Hellman has been expired for several years now, the algorithm is still in wide use, most notably in the IPSec protocol. IPSec uses the Diffie-Hellman algorithm in conjunction with RSA authentication to exchange a session key that is used for encrypting all traffic that crosses the IPSec tunnel.

RSA

In the year following the Diffie-Hellman proposal, Ron Rivest, Adi Shamir, and Leonard Adleman proposed another public key encryption system. Their proposal is now known as the RSA algorithm, named for the last initials of the researchers. RSA shares many similarities with the Diffie-Hellman algorithm in that RSA is also based on multiplying and factoring large integers. However, RSA is significantly faster than Diffie-Hellman, leading to a split in the asymmetric cryptography field that refers to Diffie-Hellman and similar algorithms as Public Key Distribution Systems (PKDS) and RSA and similar algorithms as Public Key Encryption (PKE). PKDS systems are used as session-key exchange mechanisms, while PKE systems are generally considered fast enough to encrypt reasonably small messages. However, PKE systems like RSA are not considered fast enough to encrypt large amounts of data like entire filesystems or high-speed communications lines.

NOTE

RSA, Diffie-Hellman and other asymmetric algorithms use much larger keys than their symmetric counterparts. Common key sizes include 1024-bits and 2048-bits, and the keys need to be this large because factoring, while still a difficult operation, is much easier to perform than the exhaustive key search approach used with symmetric algorithms. The relative slowness of public key encryption systems is also due in part to these larger key sizes. Since most computers can only handle 32-bits of precision, different "tricks" are required to emulate the 1024-bit and 2048-bit integers. However, the additional processing time is somewhat justified, since for security purposes 2048-bit keys are considered to be secure "forever"—barring any exponential breakthroughs in mathematical factoring algorithms, of course.

Because of the former patent restrictions on RSA, the algorithm saw only limited deployment, primarily only from products by RSA Security, until the mid-1990s. Now you are likely to encounter many programs making extensive use of RSA, such as PGP and Secure Shell (SSH). The RSA algorithm has been in the public domain since RSA Security placed it there two weeks before the patent expired in September 2000. Thus the RSA algorithm is now freely available for use by anyone, for any purpose.

Understanding Brute Force

Just how secure are encrypted files and passwords anyway? Consider that there are two ways to break an encryption algorithm—brute force and various cryptanalysis shortcuts. Cryptanalysis shortcuts vary from algorithm to algorithm, or may even be non-existent for some algorithms, and they are always difficult to find and exploit. Conversely, brute force is always available and easy to try. Brute force techniques involve exhaustively searching the given keyspace by trying every possible key or password combination until the right one is found.

Brute Force Basics

As an example, consider the basic three-digit combination bicycle lock where each digit is turned to select a number between zero and nine. Given enough time and assuming that the combination doesn't change during the attempts, just rolling through every possible combination in sequence can easily open this lock. The total number of possible combinations (keys) is 10^3 or 1000, and let's say the frequency, or number of combinations a thief can attempt during a time period, is 30 per minute. Thus, the thief should be able to open the bike lock in a maximum of 1000/(30 per min) or about 33 minutes. Keep in mind that with each new combination attempted, the number of remaining possible combinations (keyspace) decreases and the chance of guessing the correct combination (deciphering the key) on the next attempt increases.

Brute force always works because the keyspace, no matter how large, is always finite. So the way to resist brute force attacks is to choose a keysize large enough that it becomes too time-consuming for the attacker to use brute force techniques. In the bike lock example, three digits of keyspace gives the attacker a maximum amount of time of 33 minutes required to steal the bicycle, so the thief may be tempted to try a brute force attack. Suppose a bike lock with a five-digit combination is used. Now there are 100,000 possible combinations, which would take about 55.5 hours for the thief check by brute force. Clearly, most thieves would move on and look for something easier to steal.

When applied to symmetric algorithms such as DES, brute force techniques work very similarly to the bike lock example. In fact, this happens to be exactly the way DES was broken by the EFF's "Deep Crack." Since the DES key is known to be 56 bits long, every possible combination of keys between a string of 56 zeros and a string of 56 ones is tested until the appropriate key is discovered.

As for the distributed attempts to break DES, the five-digit bike lock analogy needs to be slightly changed. Distributed brute force attempts are analogous to having multiple thieves, each with an exact replica of the bike lock. Each of these replicas has the exact same combination as the original bike lock, and the thieves work on the combination in parallel. Suppose there are 50 thieves working together to guess the combination. Each thief tries a different set of 2,000 combinations such that no two thieves are working on the same combination set (sub-keyspace). Now instead of testing 30 combinations per minute, the thieves are testing 1500 combinations per minute, and all possible combinations will be checked in about 67 minutes. Recall that it took the single thief 55 hours to steal the bike, but now 50 thieves working together can steal the bike in just over an hour. Distributed computing applications working under the same fundamentals are what allowed Distributed.net to crack DES in less than 24 hours.

Applying brute force techniques to RSA and other public key encryption systems is not quite as simple. Since the RSA algorithm is broken by factoring, if the keys being used are sufficiently small (far, far smaller than any program using RSA would allow), it is conceivable that a person could crack the RSA algorithm using pencil and paper. However, for larger keys, the time required to perform the factoring becomes excessive. Factoring does not lend itself to distributed attacks as well, either. A distributed factoring attack would require much more coordination between participants than simple exhaustive keyspace coordination. There are projects, such as the www-factoring project (www.npac.syr.edu/factoring.html), that endeavor to do just this. Currently, the www-factoring project is attempting to factor a 130-digit number. In comparison, 512-bit keys are about 155 digits in size.

Using Brute Force to Obtain Passwords

Brute force is a method commonly used to obtain passwords, especially if the encrypted password list is available. While the exact number of characters in a password is usually unknown, most passwords can be estimated to be between 4 and 16 characters. Since only about 100 different values can be used for each character of the password, there are only about 100^4 to 100^{16} likely password combinations. Though massively large, the number of possible password combinations is finite and is therefore vulnerable to brute force attack.

Before specific methods for applying brute force can be discussed, a brief explanation of password encryption is required. Most modern operating systems use some form of password hashing to mask the exact password. Because passwords are never stored on the server in cleartext form, the password authentication system becomes much more secure. Even if someone unauthorized somehow obtains the password list, he will not be able to make immediate use of it, hopefully giving system administrators time to change all of the relevant passwords before any real damage is caused.

Passwords are generally stored in what is called *hashed* format. When a password is entered on the system it passes through a *one-way hashing function*, such as Message Digest 5 (MD5), and the output is recorded. Hashing functions are one-way encryption only, and once data has been hashed, it cannot be restored. A server doesn't need to know what your password is. It needs to know that *you* know what it is. When you attempt to authenticate, the password you provided is passed through the hashing function and the output is compared to the stored hash value. If these values match, then you are authenticated. Otherwise, the login attempt fails, and is (hopefully) logged by the system.

Brute force attempts to discover passwords usually involve stealing a copy of the username and hashed password listing and then methodically encrypting possible passwords using the same hashing function. If a match is found, then the password is considered cracked. Some variations of brute force techniques involve simply passing possible passwords directly to the system via remote login attempts. However, these variations are rarely seen anymore due to account lockout features and the fact that they can be easily spotted and traced by system administrators. They also tend to be extremely slow.

Appropriate password selection minimizes—but cannot completely eliminate—a password's ability to be cracked. Simple passwords, such as any individual word in a language, make the weakest passwords because they can be cracked with an elementary *dictionary attack*. In this type of attack, long lists of words of a particular language called *dictionary files* are searched for a match to the encrypted password. More complex passwords that include letters, numbers and symbols require a different brute force technique that includes all printable characters and generally take an order of magnitude longer to run.

Some of the more common tools used to perform brute force password attacks include L0phtcrack for Windows passwords, and Crack and John the Ripper for UNIX passwords. Not only do hackers use these tools but security professionals also find them useful in auditing passwords. If it takes a security professional N days to crack a password, then that is approximately how long it will take an attacker to do the same. Each of these tools will be discussed briefly, but be aware that written permission should always be obtained from the system administrator before using these programs against a system.

L0phtcrack

L0phtCrack is a Windows NT password–auditing tool from the L0pht that came onto the scene in 1997. It provides several different mechanisms for retrieving the passwords from the hashes, but is used primarily for its brute force capabilities. The character sets chosen dictate the amount of time and processing power necessary to search the entire keyspace. Obviously, the larger the character set chosen, the longer it will take to complete the attack. However, dictionary based attacks, which use only common words against the password database are normally quite fast and often effective in catching the poorest passwords. Table 6.1 lists the time required for L0phtcrack 2.5 to crack passwords based on the character set selected.

Table 6.1 L0phtcrack 2.5 Brute Force Crack Time Using a Quad Xeon 400 MHz Processor

Test: Brute Force Crack
Machine: Quad Xeon 400 MHz

Character Set	Time
Alpha-Numeric	5.5 Hours
Alpha-Numeric-Some Symbols	45 Hours
Alpha-Numeric-All Symbols	480 Hours

Used with permission of the L0pht

L0pht Heavy Industries, the developers of L0phtcrack, have since sold the rights to the software to @stake Security. Since the sale, @stake has released a program called LC3, which is intended to be L0phtcrack's successor. LC3 includes major improvements over L0phtcrack 2.5, such as distributed cracking and a simplified sniffing attachment that allows password hashes to be sniffed over Ethernet. Additionally, LC3 includes a password–cracking wizard to help the less knowledgeable audit their system passwords. Figure 6.2 shows LC3 displaying the output of a dictionary attack against some sample user passwords.

LC3 reflects a number of usability advances since the older L0phtcrack 2.5 program, and the redesigned user interface is certainly one of them. Both

L0phtCrack and LC3 are commercial software packages. However, a 15-day trial can be obtained at www.atstake.com/research/lc3/download.html.

Figure 6.2 Output of a Simple Dictionary-Based Attack

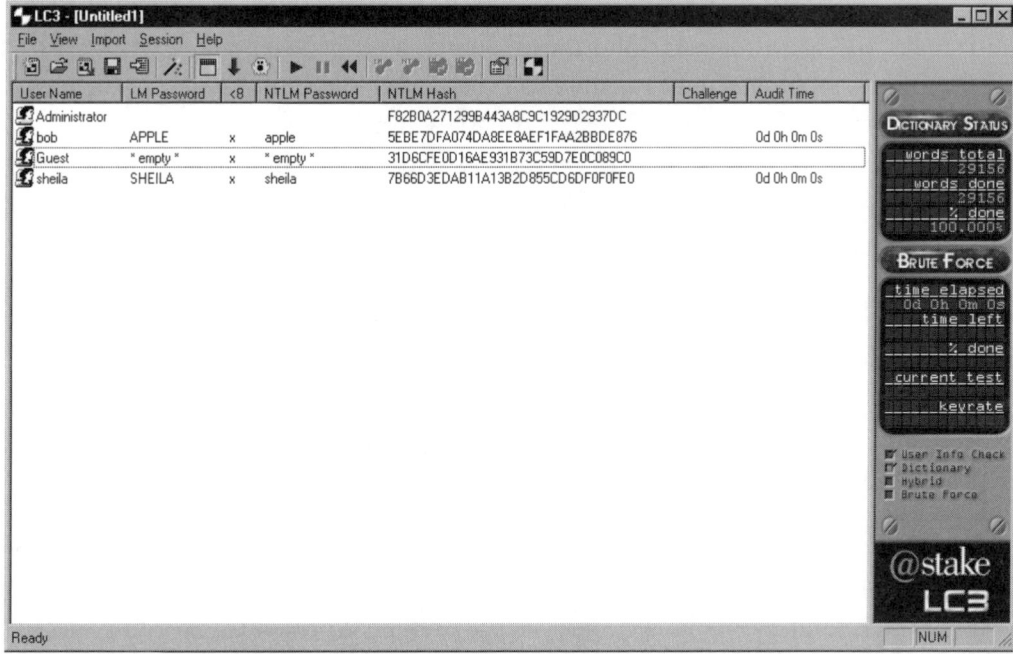

Crack

The oldest and most widely used UNIX password cracking utility is simply called *Crack*. Alec Muffett is the author of Crack, which he calls a password-guessing program for UNIX systems. It runs only on UNIX systems against UNIX passwords, and is for the most part a dictionary-based program. However, in the latest release available (v5.0a from 1996), Alec has bundled Crack7, a brute force password cracker that can be used if a dictionary-based attack fails. One of the most interesting aspects of this combination is that Crack can test for common variants that people use when they think they are picking more secure passwords. For example, instead of "password," someone may choose "pa55word." Crack has user-configurable permutation rules that will catch these variants. More information on Alec Muffett and Crack is available at www.users.dircon.co.uk/~crypto.

John the Ripper

John the Ripper is another password-cracking program, but it differs from Crack in that it is available in UNIX, DOS, and Win32 editions. Crack is great for older systems using crypt(), but John the Ripper is better for newer systems using MD5 and similar password formats. John the Ripper is used primarily for UNIX passwords, but there are add-ons available to break other types of passwords, such as Windows NT LanManager (LANMAN) hashes and Netscape Lightweight Directory Access Protocol (LDAP) server passwords. John the Ripper supports brute force attacks in *incremental mode*. Because of John the Ripper's architecture, one of its most useful features is its ability to save its status automatically during the cracking process, which allows for aborted cracking attempts to be restarted even on a different system. John the Ripper is part of the OpenWall project and is available from www.openwall.com/john.

A sample screenshot of John the Ripper is shown in Figure 6.3. In this example, a sample section of a password file in OpenBSD format is cracked using John the Ripper. Shown below the password file snippet is the actual output of John the Ripper as it runs. You can see that each cracked password is displayed on the console. Be aware that the time shown to crack all four passwords is barely over a minute only because I placed the actual passwords at the top of the "password.lst" listing, which John uses as its dictionary. Real attempts to crack passwords would take much longer. After John has cracked a password file, you can have John display the password file in unshadowed format using the **show** option.

Figure 6.3 Sample Screenshot of John the Ripper

Knowing When Real Algorithms Are Being Used Improperly

While theoretically, given enough time, almost any encryption standard can be cracked with brute force, it certainly isn't the most desirable method to use when "theoretically enough time" is longer than the age of the universe. Thus, any shortcut method that a hacker can use to break your encryption will be much more desirable to him than brute force methods.

None of the encryption algorithms discussed in this chapter have any serious flaws associated with the algorithms themselves, but sometimes the way the algorithm is implemented can create vulnerabilities. Shortcut methods for breaking encryption usually result from a vendor's faulty implementation of a strong encryption algorithm, or lousy configuration from the user. In this section, we'll discuss several incidents of improperly used encryption that are likely to be encountered in the field.

Bad Key Exchanges

Because there isn't any authentication built into the Diffie-Hellman algorithm, implementations that use Diffie-Hellman-type key exchanges without some sort of authentication are vulnerable to man-in-the-middle (MITM) attacks. The most notable example of this type of behavior is the SSH-1 protocol. Since the protocol itself does not authenticate the client or the server, it's possible for someone to cleverly eavesdrop on the communications. This deficiency was one of the main reasons that the SSH-2 protocol was completely redeveloped from SSH-1. The SSH-2 protocol authenticates both the client and the server, and warns of or prevents any possible MITM attacks, depending on configuration, so long as the client and server have communicated at least once. However, even SSH-2 is vulnerable to MITM attacks prior to the first key exchange between the client and the server.

As an example of a MITM-type attack, consider that someone called Al is performing a standard Diffie-Hellman key exchange with Charlie for the very first time, while Beth is in a position such that all traffic between Al and Charlie passes through her network segment. Assuming Beth doesn't interfere with the key exchange, she will not be able to read any of the messages passed between Al and Charlie, because she will be unable to decrypt them. However, suppose that Beth intercepts the transmissions of Al and Charlie's public keys and she responds to them using her own public key. Al will think that Beth's public key is actually

Charlie's public key and Charlie will think that Beth's public key is actually Al's public key.

When Al transmits a message to Charlie, he will encrypt it using Beth's public key. Beth will intercept the message and decrypt it using her private key. Once Beth has read the message, she encrypts it again using Charlie's public key and transmits the message on to Charlie. She may even modify the message contents if she so desires. Charlie then receives Beth's modified message, believing it to come from Al. He replies to Al and encrypts the message using Beth's public key. Beth again intercepts the message, decrypts it with her private key, and modifies it. Then she encrypts the new message with Al's public key and sends it on to Al, who receives it and believes it to be from Charlie.

Clearly, this type of communication is undesirable because a third party not only has access to confidential information, but she can also modify it at will. In this type of attack, no encryption is broken because Beth does not know either Al or Charlie's private keys, so the Diffie-Hellman algorithm isn't really at fault. Beware of the key exchange mechanism used by any public key encryption system. If the key exchange protocol does not authenticate at least one and preferably both sides of the connection, it may be vulnerable to MITM-type attacks. Authentication systems generally use some form of digital certificates (usually X.509), such as those available from Thawte or VeriSign.

Hashing Pieces Separately

Older Windows-based clients store passwords in a format known as LanManager (LANMAN) hashes, which is a horribly insecure authentication scheme. However, since this chapter is about cryptography, we will limit the discussion of LANMAN authentication to the broken cryptography used for password storage.

As with UNIX password storage systems, LANMAN passwords are never stored on a system in cleartext format—they are always stored in a hash format. The problem is that the hashed format is implemented in such a way that even though DES is used to encrypt the password, the password can still be broken with relative ease. Each LANMAN password can contain up to 14 characters, and all passwords less than 14 characters are padded to bring the total password length up to 14 characters. During encryption the password is split into a pair of seven-character passwords, and each of these seven-character passwords is encrypted with DES. The final password hash consists of the two concatenated DES-encrypted password halves.

Since DES is known to be a reasonably secure algorithm, why is this implementation flawed? Shouldn't DES be uncrackable without significant effort? Not exactly. Recall that there are roughly 100 different characters that can be used in a password. Using the maximum possible password length of 14 characters, there should be about 100^{14} or 1.0×10^{28} possible password combinations. LANMAN passwords are further simplified because there is no distinction between upper- and lowercase letters—all letters appears as uppercase. Furthermore, if the password is less than eight characters, then the second half of the password hash is always identical and never even needs to be cracked. If only letters are used (no numbers or punctuation), then there can only be 26^7 (roughly eight billion) password combinations. While this may still seem like a large number of passwords to attack via brute force, remember that these are only theoretical maximums and that since most user passwords are quite weak, dictionary-based attacks will uncover them quickly. The bottom line here is that dictionary-based attacks on a pair of seven-character passwords (or even just one) are much faster than those on single 14-character passwords.

Suppose that strong passwords that use two or more symbols and numbers are used with the LANMAN hashing routine. The problem is that most users tend to just tack on the extra characters at the end of the password. For example, if a user uses his birthplace along with a string of numbers and symbols, such as "MONTANA45%," the password is still insecure. LANMAN will break this password into the strings "MONTANA" and "45%." The former will probably be caught quickly in a dictionary-based attack, and the latter will be discovered quickly in a brute force attack because it is only three characters. For newer business-oriented Microsoft operating systems such as Windows NT and Windows 2000, LANMAN hashing can and should be disabled in the registry if possible, though this will make it impossible for Win9x clients to authenticate to those machines.

Using a Short Password to Generate a Long Key

Password quality is a subject that we have already briefly touched upon in our discussion of brute force techniques. With the advent of PKE encryption schemes such as PGP, most public and private keys are generated using passwords or passphrases, leaving the password generation steps vulnerable to brute force attacks. If a password is selected that is not of significant length, that password can be brute force attacked in an attempt to generate the same keys as the user. Thus PKE systems such as RSA have a chance to be broken by brute force, not because of any deficiency in the algorithm itself, but because of deficiencies in the key generation process. The best way to protect against these types of round-about attacks is to use strong passwords when generating any sort of encryption key. Strong passwords include the use of upper- and lowercase letters, numbers, and symbols, preferably throughout the password. Eight characters is generally considered the minimum length for a strong password, but given the severity of choosing a poor password for key generation, I recommend you use at least twelve characters for these instances.

High quality passwords are often said to have high entropy, which is a semi-finite measurement that attempts to quantify the relative quality of a password. Longer passwords typically have more entropy than shorter passwords, and the more random each character of the password is, the more entropy in the password. For example, the password "albatross" (about 30 bits of entropy) might be reasonably long in length, but has less entropy than a totally random password of the same length such as "g8%=MQ+p" (about 48 bits of entropy). Since the former might appear in a list of common names for bird species, while the latter would never appear in a published list, obviously the latter is a stronger and therefore more desirable password. The moral of the story here is that strong encryption such as 168-bit 3-DES can be broken easily if the secret key has only a few bits of entropy.

Improperly Stored Private or Secret Keys

Let's say you have only chosen to use the strong cryptography algorithms, you have verified that there are not any flaws in the vendors' implementations, and you have generated your keys with great care. How secure is your data now? It is still only as secure as your private or secret key. These keys must be safeguarded at all costs, or you may as well not even use encryption.

Since keys are simply strings of data, they are usually stored in a file somewhere in your system's hard disk. For example, private keys for SSH-1 are stored in the *identity* file located in the .ssh directory under a user's home directory. If the filesystem permissions on this file allow others to access the file, then this private key is compromised. Once others have your private or secret key, reading your encrypted communications becomes trivial. (Note that the SSH identity file is used for authentication, not encryption; but you get the idea.)

However, in some vendor implementations, your keys could be disclosed to others because the keys are not stored securely in RAM. As you are aware, any information processed by a computer, including your secret or private key, is located in the computer's RAM at some point. If the operating system's kernel does not store these keys in a protected area of its memory, they could conceivably become available to someone who dumps a copy of the system's RAM to a file for analysis. These memory dumps are called *core dumps* in UNIX, and they are commonly created during a denial of service (DoS) attack. Thus a successful hacker could generate a core dump on your system and extract your key from the memory image. In a similar attack, a DoS attack could cause excess memory usage on the part of the victim, forcing the key to be swapped to disk as part of virtual memory. Fortunately, most vendors are aware of this type of exploit by now, and it is becoming less and less common since encryption keys are now being stored in protected areas of memory.

Tools & Traps…

Netscape's Original SSL Implementation: How Not to Choose Random Numbers

As we have tried to point out in this section, sometimes it does not matter if you are using an algorithm that is known to be secure. If your algorithm is being applied incorrectly, there will be security holes. An excellent example of a security hole resulting from misapplied cryptography is Netscape's poor choice of random number seeds used in the Secure Sockets Layer (SSL) encryption of its version 1.1 browser. You no doubt note that this security flaw is several years old and thus of limited importance today. However, below the surface we'll see that this particular bug is an almost classic example of one of the ways in which vendors implement broken cryptography, and as such it continues to remain relevant to this day. We will limit this discussion to the vulnerability in the UNIX version of Netscape's SSL implementation as discovered by Ian Goldberg and David Wagner, although the PC and Macintosh versions were similarly vulnerable.

Before I can explain the exact nature of this security hole we will need to cover some background information, such as SSL technology and random numbers. SSL is a certificate-based authentication and encryption scheme developed by Netscape during the fledgling days of e-commerce. It was intended to secure communications such as credit card transactions from eavesdropping by would-be thieves. Because of U.S. export restrictions, the stronger and virtually impervious 128-bit (key) version of the technology was not in widespread use. In fact, even

Continued

domestically, most of Netscape's users were running the anemic 40-bit international version of the software.

Most key generation, including SSL key generation, requires some form of randomness as a factor of the key generation process. Arbitrarily coming up with random numbers is much harder than it sounds, especially for machines. So we usually end up using pseudo-random numbers that are devised from mostly random events, such as the time elapsed between each keystroke you type or the movement of your mouse across the screen.

For the UNIX version of its version 1.1 browser, Netscape used a conglomeration of values, such as the current time, the process ID (PID) number of the Netscape process and its parent's process ID number. Suppose the attacker had access to the same machine as the Netscape user simultaneously, which is the norm in UNIX-based multi-user architectures. It would be trivial for the attacker to generate a process listing to discover Netscape's PID and its parent's PID. If the attacker had the ability to capture TCP/IP packets coming into the machine, he could use the timestamps on these packets to make a reasonable guess as to the exact time the SSL certificate was generated. Once this information was gathered, the attacker could narrow down the keyspace to about 10^6 combinations, which is then brute force attacked with ease at near real-time speeds. Upon successfully discovering Netscape's SSL certificate seed generation values, he can generate an identical certificate for himself and either eavesdrop or hijack the existing session.

Clearly, this was a serious security flaw that Netscape would need to address in its later versions, and it did, providing patches for the 1.x series of browsers and developing a new and substantially different random number generator for its 2.x series of browsers. You can read more details about this particular security flaw in the archives of Dr. Dobbs' Journal at www.ddj.com/documents/s=965/ddj9601h.

Understanding Amateur Cryptography Attempts

If your data is not being protected by one of the more modern, computationally secure algorithms that we've already discussed in this chapter, or some similar variant, then your data is probably not secure. In this section, we're going to discover how simple methods of enciphering data can be broken using rudimentary cryptanalysis.

Classifying the Ciphertext

Even a poorly encrypted message often looks indecipherable at first glance, but you can sometimes figure out what the message is by looking beyond just the stream of printed characters. Often, the same information that you can "read between the lines" on a cleartext message still exists in an enciphered message.

For the mechanisms discussed below, all the "secrecy" is contained in the algorithm, not in a separate key. Our challenge for these is to figure out the algorithm used. So for most of them, that means that we will run a password or some text through the algorithm, which will often be available to us in the form of a program or other black box device. By controlling the inputs and examining the outputs, we hope to determine the algorithm. This will enable us to later take an arbitrary output and determine what the input was.

NOTE

The techniques described in this section are largely ineffective on modern algorithms such as DES and its successors. What few techniques do exist to gain information from modern ciphertext are quite complicated and only work under special conditions.

Frequency Analysis

The first and most powerful method you can employ to crack simple ciphertext is *frequency analysis*, which is based on the idea that certain letters are used more often than others. For example, I can barely write a single word in this sentence that doesn't include the letter *e*. How can letter frequency be of use? You can create a letter frequency table for your ciphertext, assuming the message is of sufficient length, and compare that table to one charting the English language (there are many available). That would give you some clues about which characters in the ciphertext might match up with cleartext letters.

The astute reader will discover that some letters appear with almost identical frequency. How then can you determine which letter is which? You can either evaluate how the letters appear in context, or you can consult other frequency tables that note the appearance of multiple letter combinations such as *sh*, *ph*, *ie* and *the*.

Crypto of this type is just a little more complicated than the Caesar Cipher mentioned at the beginning of the chapter. This was state-of-the-art hundreds of years ago. Now problems of this type are used in daily papers for commuter entertainment, under the titles of "Cryptogram," "CryptoQuote," or similar. Still, some people will use this method as a token effort to hide things. This type of mechanism, or ones just slightly more complex, show up in new worms and viruses all the time.

Ciphertext Relative Length Analysis

Sometimes the ciphertext can provide you with clues to the cleartext even if you don't know how the ciphertext was encrypted. For example, suppose that you have an unknown algorithm that encrypts passwords such that you have available the original password and a ciphertext version of that password. If the length or size of each is the same, then you can infer that the algorithm produces output in a 1:1 ratio to the input. You may even be able to input individual characters to obtain the ciphertext translation for each character. If nothing else, you at least know how many characters to specify for an unknown password if you attempt to break it using a brute force method.

If you know that the length of a message in ciphertext is identical to the length of a message in cleartext, you can leverage this information to pick out pieces of the ciphertext for which you can make guesses about the cleartext. For example, during WWII while the Allies were trying to break the German Enigma codes, they used a method similar to the above because they knew the phrase "Heil Hitler" probably appeared somewhere near the end of each transmission.

Similar Plaintext Analysis

A related method you might use to crack an unknown algorithm is to compare changes in the ciphertext output with changes in the cleartext input. Of course, this method requires that you have access to the algorithm to selectively encode your carefully chosen cleartext. For example, try encoding the strings "AAAAAA," "AAAAAB" and "BAAAAA" and note the difference in the ciphertext output. For monoalphabetic ciphers, you might expect to see the first few characters remain the same in both outputs for the first two, with only the last portion changing. If so, then it's almost trivial to construct a full translation table for the entire algorithm that maps cleartext input to ciphertext output and vice versa. Once the translation table is complete, you could write an inverse function that deciphers the ciphertext back to plaintext without difficulty.

What happens if the cipher is a polyalphabetic cipher, where more than one character changes in the ciphertext for single character changes in cleartext? Well, that becomes a bit trickier to decipher, depending on the number of changes to the ciphertext. You might be able to combine this analysis technique with brute force to uncover the inner workings of the algorithm, or you might not.

Monoalphabetic Ciphers

A monoalphabetic cipher is any cipher in which each character of the alphabet is replaced by another character in a one-to-one ratio. Both the Caesar Cipher and ROT13, mentioned earlier in the chapter, are classic examples of monoalphabetic ciphers. Some monoalphabetic ciphers scramble the alphabet instead of shifting the letters, so that instead of having an alphabet of *ABCDEFGHIJKLMNOPQRSTUVWXYZ*, the cipher alphabet order might be *MLNKBJVHCGXFZDSAPQOWIEURYT*. The new scrambled alphabet is used to encipher the message such that M=A, L=B…T=Z. Using this method, the cleartext message "SECRET" becomes "OBNQBW."

You will rarely find these types of ciphers in use today outside of word games because they can be easily broken by an exhaustive search of possible alphabet combinations and they are also quite vulnerable to the language analysis methods we described. Monoalphabetic ciphers are absolutely vulnerable to frequency analysis because even though the letters are substituted, the ultimate frequency appearance of each letter will roughly correspond to the known frequency characteristics of the language.

Other Ways to Hide Information

Sometimes vendors follow the old "security through obscurity" approach, and instead of using strong cryptography to prevent unauthorized disclosure of certain information, they just try to hide the information using a commonly known reversible algorithm like UUEncode or Base64, or a combination of two simple methods. In these cases, all you need to do to recover the cleartext is to pass the ciphertext back through the same engine. Vendors may also use XOR encoding against a certain key, but you won't necessarily need the key to decode the message. Let's look at some of the most common of these algorithms in use.

XOR

While many of the more complex and secure encryption algorithms use XOR as an intermediate step, you will often find data obscured by a simple XOR operation. XOR is short for *exclusive or*, which identifies a certain type of binary operation with a truth table as shown in Table 6.2. As each bit from A is combined with B, the result is "0" only if the bits in A and B are identical. Otherwise, the result is 1.

Table 6.2 XOR Truth Table

A	B	A XOR B
0	0	0
0	1	1
1	0	1
1	1	0

Let's look at a very simple XOR operation and how you can undo it. In our simple example, we will use a single character key ("a") to obscure a single character message ("b") to form a result that we'll call "ciphertext" (see Table 6.3).

Table 6.3 XOR of "a" and "b"

Item	Binary Value
a	01100001
b	01100010
ciphertext	00000011

Suppose that you don't know what the value of "a" actually is, you only know the value of "b" and the resulting "ciphertext." You want to recover the key so that you can find out the cleartext value of another encrypted message, "cipher2," which is 00011010. You could perform an XOR with "b" and the "ciphertext" to recover the key "a," as shown in Table 6.4.

Table 6.4 XOR of "ciphertext" and "b"

Item	Binary Value
ciphertext	00000011
b	01100010
a	01100001

Once the key is recovered, you can use it to decode "cipher2" into the character "z" (see Table 6.5).

Table 6.5 XOR of "cipher2" and "a"

Item	Binary Value
cipher2	00011010
a	01100001
z	01111010

Of course, this example is somewhat oversimplified. In the real world, you are most likely to encounter keys that are multiple characters instead of just a single character, and the XOR operation may occur a number of times in series to obscure the message. In this type of instance, you can use a null value to obtain the key—that is, the message will be constructed such that it contains only 0s.

Abstract 1 and 0 manipulation like this can be difficult to understand if you are not used to dealing with binary numbers and values. Therefore, I'll provide you with some sample code and output of a simple program that uses a series of 3 XOR operations on various permutations of a key to obscure a particular message. This short Perl program uses the freely available IIIkey module for the backend XOR encryption routines. You will need to download IIIkey from www3.marketrends.net/encrypt/ to use this program.

```perl
#!/usr/bin/perl
# Encodes/Decodes a form of XOR text
# Requires the IIIkey module
# Written specifically for HPYN 2nd Ed.
# by FWL 01.07.02


# Use the IIIkey module for the backend
# IIIkey is available from http://www3.marketrends.net/encrypt/
use IIIkey;

# Simple input validation
sub validate() {
        if (scalar(@ARGV) < 3) {
        print "Error: You did not specify input correctly!\n";
```

```
            print "To encode data use ./xor.pl e \"Key\" \"String to
                Encode\"\n";
            print "To decode data use ./xor.pl d \"Key\" \"String to
                Decode\"\n";
            exit;
            }
    }


validate();


$tmp=new IIIkey;
$key=$ARGV[1];
$intext=$ARGV[2];


if ($ARGV[0] eq "e") {   # encode text
            $outtext=$tmp->crypt($intext, $key);
            print "Encoded $intext to $outtext";
} elsif ($ARGV[0] eq "d") { # decode text
            $outtext=$tmp->decrypt($intext, $key);
            print "Decoded $intext to $outtext";
} else { # No encode/decode information given!
            print "To encode or decode? That is the question.";
            exit;
}
```

Here's some sample output:

```
$ ./xor.pl e "my key" "secret message"
Encoded secret message to 8505352480^0758144+510906534

$ ./xor.pl d "my key" "8505352480^0758144+510906534"
Decoded 8505352480^0758144+510906534 to secret message
```

UUEncode

UUEncode is a commonly used algorithm for converting binary data into a text-based equivalent for transport via e-mail. As you probably know, most e-mail systems cannot directly process binary attachments to e-mail messages. So when you attach a binary file (such as a JPEG image) to an e-mail message, your e-mail client takes care of converting the binary attachment to a text equivalent, probably through an encoding engine like UUEncode. The attachment is converted from binary format into a stream of printable characters, which can be processed by the mail system. Once received, the attachment is processed using the inverse of the encoding algorithm (UUDecode), resulting in conversion back to the original binary file.

Sometimes vendors may use the UUEncode engine to encode ordinary printable text in order to obscure the message. When this happens, all you need to do to is pass the encoded text through a UUDecode program to discern the message. Command-line UUEncode/UUDecode clients are available for just about every operating system ever created.

Base64

Base64 is also commonly used to encode e-mail attachments similar to UUEncode, under Multipurpose Internet Mail Extensions (MIME) extensions. However, you are also likely to come across passwords and other interesting information hidden behind a Base64 conversion. Most notably, many Web servers that implement HTTP-based basic authentication store password data in Base64 format. If your attacker can get access to the Base64 encoded username and password set, he or she can decode them in seconds, no brute force required. One of the telltale signs that a Base64 encode has occurred is the appearance of one or two equal signs (=) at the end of the string, which is often used to pad data.

Look at some sample code for converting between Base64 data and cleartext. This code snippet should run on any system that has Perl5 or better with the MIME::Base64 module from CPAN (www.cpan.org). We have also given you a couple of usage samples.

```
#!/usr/bin/perl
# Filename: base64.pl
# Encodes/Decodes Base-64 text
# Requires the MIME::Base64 module
# Written specifically for HPYN 2nd Ed.
```

```perl
# by FWL 01.07.02


# Use the MIME module for encoding/decoding Base-64 strings
use MIME::Base64;


# Simple input validation
sub validate() {
        if (scalar(@ARGV) < 2) {
        print "Error: You did not specify input correctly!\n";
        print "To encode data use ./base64.pl e \"String to Encode\"\n";
        print "To decode data use ./base64.pl d \"String to Decode\"\n";
        exit;
        }
}


validate();


$intext=$ARGV[1];


if ($ARGV[0] eq "e") {   # encode text
        $outtext=encode_base64($intext);
        print "Encoded $intext to $outtext";
} elsif ($ARGV[0] eq "d") { # decode text
        $outtext=decode_base64($intext);
        print "Decoded $intext to $outtext";
} else { # No encode/decode information given!
        print "To encode or decode? That is the question.";
        exit;
}
```

Here's some sample output:

```
$ ./base64.pl e "Secret Password"
Encoded Secret Password to U2VjcmV0IFBhc3N3b3Jk
```

```
$ ./base64.pl d "U2VjcmV0IFBhc3N3b3Jk"
Decoded U2VjcmV0IFBhc3N3b3Jk to Secret Password
```

Compression

Sometimes you may find that compression has been weakly used to conceal information from you. In days past, some game developers would compress the size of their save game files not only to reduce space, but also to limit your attempts to modify it with a save game editor. The most commonly used algorithms for this were SQSH (Squish or Squash) and LHA. The algorithms themselves were somewhat inherited from console games of the 1980s, where they were used to compress the ROM images in the cartridges. As a rule, when you encounter text that you cannot seem to decipher via standard methods, you may want to check to see if the information has been compressed using one of the plethora of compression algorithms available today.

Notes from the Underground…

Consumer-Oriented Crypto— The SDMI Hacking Challenge

Sometimes organizations decide to use cryptography that isn't necessarily amateur, but shouldn't really be considered professional grade either. For example, the Secure Digital Music Initiative (SDMI) is trying to develop a watermarking scheme for digital music that carries an extra-encoded signal that prevents the music from being played or copied in an unauthorized manner. In developing its watermarking scheme, the SDMI proposed six watermarking schemes to the hacking community and offered up a $10,000 prize to whoever could break the watermarking technology, producing a song without any watermark from a sample song with a watermark. Only samples of the watermarked songs were made available; the SDMI did not release any details about how the watermarking schemes themselves worked. A before-and-after sample of a different song was provided for each of the watermarking schemes, so that differences could be noted.

Two of the six watermarking schemes were dropped shortly after the contest began, and the remaining four were ultimately broken

Continued

within weeks by a team of academic researchers led by Princeton Professor Edward W. Felten. Felten and his associates chose not to accept the $10,000 bounty, opting instead to publicly publish the results of their research. It seems there was a small loophole in the agreement that was presented to challengers before they would be given the files. It said that they had to agree to keep all information secret in order to collect the $10,000. It didn't say anything about what would happen if the challenger wasn't interested in the money. Shortly thereafter, the seemingly upset SDMI threatened a lawsuit under the provisions of the Digital Millennium Copyright Act (DMCA) that prevented the sharing of knowledge that could be used to circumvent copyright protection schemes. Ultimately the SDMI chose not to pursue the matter, and Felten and his associates presented their findings at the 10th USENIX Security Symposium. Felten's conclusion, which is generally shared by the security community at large, was that any attempts at watermarking-type encryption would ultimately be broken. Also of interest is the fact that Felten's team identified that no special knowledge in computer science was needed to break the watermarking schemes; only a general knowledge of signal processing was required.

You might view this story as yet another example of a vendor attempting to employ what they proclaim to be "highly secure proprietary algorithms," but it is also an example of the continuing evolution of cryptography and its applications in new ways. Even if these new applications of cryptography don't lend themselves well to the use of conventional algorithms, you would be wise to remain skeptical of newly proposed unproven algorithms, especially when these algorithms are kept secret.

Summary

This chapter looked into the meaning of cryptography and some of its origins, including Caesar's Cipher. More modern branches of cryptography are *symmetric* and *asymmetric* cryptography, which are also known as *secret key* and *public key* cryptography, respectively.

The most common symmetric algorithms in use today include DES, AES, and IDEA. Since DES is showing its age, we looked at how NIST managed the development of AES as a replacement, and how Rijndael was selected from five finalists to become the AES algorithm. From the European perspective, we saw how IDEA came to be developed in the early 1990s and examined its advantages over DES.

The early development of asymmetric cryptography was begun in the mid-1970s by Diffie and Hellman, who developed the Diffie-Hellman key exchange algorithm as a means of securely exchanging information over a public network. After Diffie-Hellman, the RSA algorithm was developed, heralding a new era of public key cryptography systems such as PGP. Fundamental differences between public key and symmetric cryptography include public key cryptography's reliance on the factoring problem for extremely large integers.

Brute force is an effective method of breaking most forms of cryptography, provided you have the time to wait for keyspace exhaustion, which could take anywhere from several minutes to billions of years. Cracking passwords is the most widely used application of brute force; programs such as L0phtcrack and John the Ripper are used exclusively for this purpose.

Even secure algorithms can be implemented insecurely, or in ways not intended by the algorithm's developers. Man-in-the-middle attacks could cripple the security of a Diffie-Hellman key exchange, and even DES-encrypted LANMAN password hashes can be broken quite easily. Using easily broken passwords or passphrases as secret keys in symmetric algorithms can have unpleasant effects, and improperly stored private and secret keys can negate the security provided by encryption altogether.

Information is sometimes concealed using weak or reversible algorithms. We saw in this chapter how weak ciphers are subject to frequency analysis attacks that use language characteristics to decipher the message. Related attacks include relative length analysis and similar plaintext analysis. We saw how vendors sometimes conceal information using XOR and Base64 encoding and looked at some sample code for each of these types of reversible ciphers. We also saw how, on occasion, information is compressed as a means of obscuring it.

Solutions Fast Track

Understanding Cryptography Concepts

☑ Unencrypted text is referred to as *cleartext*, while encrypyted text is called *ciphertext*.

☑ The two main categories of cryptography are *symmetric key* and *asymmetric key* cryptography. Symmetric key cryptography uses a single secret key, while asymmetric key cryptography uses a pair of public and private keys.

☑ Public key cryptography was first devised as a means of exchanging a secret key securely by Diffie and Hellman.

Learning about Standard Cryptographic Algorithms

☑ The reason why so many cryptographic algorithms are available for your use is that each algorithm has its own relative speed, security and ease of use. You need to know enough about the most common algorithms to choose one that is appropriate to the situation to which it will be applied.

☑ Data Encryption Standard (DES) is the oldest and most widely known modern encryption method around. However, it is nearing the end of its useful life span, so you should avoid using it in new implementations or for information you want to keep highly secure.

☑ Advanced Encryption Standard (AES) was designed as a secure replacement for DES, and you can use several different keysizes with it.

☑ Be aware that asymmetric cryptography uses entirely different principles than symmetric cryptography. Where symmetric cryptography combines a single key with the message for a number of cycles, asymmetric cryptography relies on numbers that are too large to be factored.

☑ The two most widely used asymmetric algorithms are Diffie-Hellman and RSA.

Understanding Brute Force

☑ Brute force is the one single attack that will always succeed against symmetric cryptography, given enough time. You want to ensure that "enough time" becomes a number of years or decades or more.

☑ An individual machine performing a brute force attack is slow. If you can string together a number of machines in parallel, your brute force attack will be much faster.

☑ Brute force attacks are most often used for cracking passwords.

Knowing When Real Algorithms Are Being Used Improperly

☑ Understand the concept of the man-in-the-middle attack against a Diffie-Hellman key exchange.

☑ LANMAN password hashing should be disabled, if possible, because its implementation allows it to be broken quite easily.

☑ Key storage should always be of the utmost importance to you because if your secret or private key is compromised, all data protected by those keys is also compromised.

Understanding Amateur Cryptography Attempts

☑ You can crack almost any weak cryptography attempts (like XOR) with minimal effort.

☑ Frequency analysis is a powerful tool to use against reasonably lengthy messages that aren't guarded by modern cryptography algorithms.

☑ Sometimes vendors will attempt to conceal information using weak cryptography (like Base64) or compression.

Frequently Asked Questions

The following Frequently Asked Questions, answered by the authors of this book, are designed to both measure your understanding of the concepts presented in this chapter and to assist you with real-life implementation of these concepts. To have your questions about this chapter answered by the author, browse to **www.syngress.com/solutions** and click on the **"Ask the Author"** form.

Q: Are there any cryptography techniques which are 100 percent secure?

A: Yes. Only the One Time Pad (OTP) algorithm is absolutely unbreakable if implemented correctly. The OTP algorithm is actually a Vernam cipher, which was developed by AT&T way back in 1917. The Vernam cipher belongs to a family of ciphers called *stream ciphers*, since they encrypt data in continuous stream format instead of the chunk-by-chunk method of block ciphers. There are two problems with using the OTP, however: You must have a source of truly random data, and the source must be bit-for-bit as long as the message to be encoded. You also have to transmit both the message and the key (separately), the key must remain secret, and the key can *never* be reused to encode another message. If an eavesdropper intercepts two messages encoded with the same key, then it is trivial for the eavesdropper to recover the key and decrypt both messages. The reason OTP ciphers are not used more commonly is the difficulty in collecting truly random numbers for the key (as mentioned in one of the sidebars for this chapter) and the difficulty of the secure distribution of the key.

Q: How long is DES expected to remain in use?

A: Given the vast number of DES-based systems, I expect we'll continue to see DES active for another five or ten years, especially in areas where security is not a high priority. For some applications, DES is considered a "good enough" technology since the average hacker doesn't have the resources available (for now) to break the encryption scheme efficiently. I predict that DES will still find a use as a casual eavesdropping deterrent, at least until the widespread adoption of IPv6. DES is also far faster than 3-DES, and as such it is more suitable to older-style VPN gear that may not be forward-compatible with the new AES standard. In rare cases where legacy connections are required, the government is still allowing new deployment of DES-based systems.

Q: After the 9/11 attacks I'm concerned about terrorists using cryptography, and I've heard people advocate that the government should have a back door access to all forms of encryption. Why would this be a bad idea?

A: Allowing back-door access for anyone causes massive headaches for users of encryption. First and foremost, these back door keys are likely to be stored all in one place, making that storage facility the prime target for hackers. When the storage facility is compromised, and I have no doubt that it would be (the only question is how soon), everyone's data can effectively be considered compromised. We'd also need to establish a new bureaucracy that would be responsible for handing out the back door access, probably in a manner similar to the way in which wiretaps are currently doled out. We would also require some sort of watchdog group that certifies the deployment group as responsible. Additionally, all of our encryption schemes would need to be redesigned to allow backdoor access, probably in some form of "public key + trusted key" format. Implementation of these new encryption routines would take months to develop and years to deploy. New cracking schemes would almost certainly focus on breaking the algorithm through the "trusted key" access, leaving the overall security of these routines questionable at best.

Q: Why was CSS, the encryption technology used to protect DVDs from unauthorized copying, able to be broken so easily?

A: Basically, DVD copy protection was broken so easily because one entity, Xing Technologies, left their key lying around in the open, which as we saw in this chapter is a cardinal sin. The data encoded on a DVD-Video disc is encrypted using an algorithm called the Content Scrambling System (CSS) which can be unlocked using a 40-bit key. Using Xing's 40-bit key, hackers were able to brute force and guess at the keys for over 170 other licensees at a rapid pace. That way, since the genie was out of the bottle, so to speak, for so many vendors, the encryption for the entire format was basically broken. With so many keys to choose from, others in the underground had no difficulty in leveraging these keys to develop the DeCSS program, which allows data copied off of the DVD to be saved to another media in an unencrypted format. Ultimately, the CSS scheme was doomed to failure. You can't put a key inside millions of DVD players, distribute them, and not expect someone to eventually pull it out.

## Chapter 7

Cisco LocalDirector and DistributedDirector

Solutions in this chapter:

- **Improving Security Using Cisco LocalDirector**

- **LocalDirector Security Features**

- **Securing Geographically Dispersed Server Farms Using Cisco DistributedDirector**

- **DistributedDirector Security Features**

- ☑ **Summary**

- ☑ **Solutions Fast Track**

- ☑ **Frequently Asked Questions**

Introduction

When it was first deployed, Cisco Systems' LocalDirector was positioned as a replacement solution for the "round-robin" redundancy and load-balancing methods used on the Internet. The networking and computing trade sheets referred to these devices as *load balancers*. However, when applied to LocalDirector, the load balancing term is actually a misnomer. While load balancers are able to equally distribute traffic loads across multiple servers, LocalDirector is capable of additional functions like scalability, high availability, server connection management, and server security.

Even with a highly secure network, one also needs to be certain there is some level of redundancy built into the network. This will ensure that attacks intended to suck up your bandwidth meet with a minimum of success.

LocalDirector can help you with this. On the other hand, there are many other devices that can complete this job more efficiently. The LocalDirector technology is somewhat outdated, and even Cisco is beginning to suggest other devices to perform these same functions. The replacement for LocalDirector is now Cisco Content Services Switch (detailed information on CSSs can be found in Chapter 10). Therefore, if you are only starting to add redundancy and distribution features to your server network, you might be interested in looking into CSS solutions first.

DistributedDirector is also a load-balancing solution used to distribute traffic between geographically distant servers. Again, these features were improved and further developed in the CSS product line.

Improving Security Using Cisco LocalDirector

Cisco's LocalDirector allows you to load-balance Internet resource requests among multiple local servers. One would typically use this solution to front-end a Web server farm, based in the same location, and thus load-balance Web traffic to the most appropriate server.

Using this technology, LocalDirector allows you to publish a Web address, along with a single Internet Protocol (IP) address associated with that address, and yet have one of many Web servers respond to that resource request. Redundancy, introduced by this feature, allows for increased availability and stability of the server network in case of attacks (especially in regards to denial of service (DoS) attacks).

LocalDirector Technology Overview

Cisco's LocalDirector uses the Open System Interconnection (OSI) Layers 3 and 4 (Network and Transport Layers respectively) as a load-balancing technology that allows you to publish a single Uniform Resource Locator (URL) and a single IP address for an entire server farm. From a technical point of view, it acts as a transparent TCP/IP bridge within the network.

The LocalDirector determines which server is most appropriate by tracking network sessions and server load conditions in real time.

Such technology helps decrease the response time of your service while increasing service reliability. Service response time is decreased because resource requests for a URL or IP address are directed to the most appropriate server (the least busy server, for example) within the server farm. Likewise, service reliability is increased because LocalDirector monitors individual servers in the server farm and forwards resource requests only to servers that are operating correctly.

Before the inception of this technology, you would have to know the name or IP address of every individual Web server in the server farm, or you would have to make use of multiple IP addresses associated with a single DNS name (the so-called DNS round-robin load balancing). Neither of these techniques were user friendly, nor did they result in appropriate load distribution. They were also unreliable, because no attempt was made to verify the servers' availability in real time.

Cisco's LocalDirector can be compared to an Automatic Call Distributor (ACD) in the telephony world. LocalDirector is similar to an ACD in that incoming telephone calls are routed to a pool of agents and answered as soon as an agent is available. It works as a front-end for a Web server farm and redirects resource requests to the most appropriate server. Figure 7.1 depicts a typical LocalDirector implementation.

LocalDirector Product Overview

The LocalDirector product is available in three different ranges:

- **LocalDirector 416** This is both the entry-level product as well as the medium-size product. It supports up to 90 Mbps throughput and 7,000 connections per second.

- **LocalDirector 430** This is the high-end product. It supports up to 400 Mbps throughput and 30,000 connections per second.

- **LocalDirector 417** Newer platform with different mounting features. It is even more productive than 430 series and has more memory—two Fast Ethernet and one Gigabit Ethernet interfaces.

Figure 7.1 A Typical LocalDirector Implementation

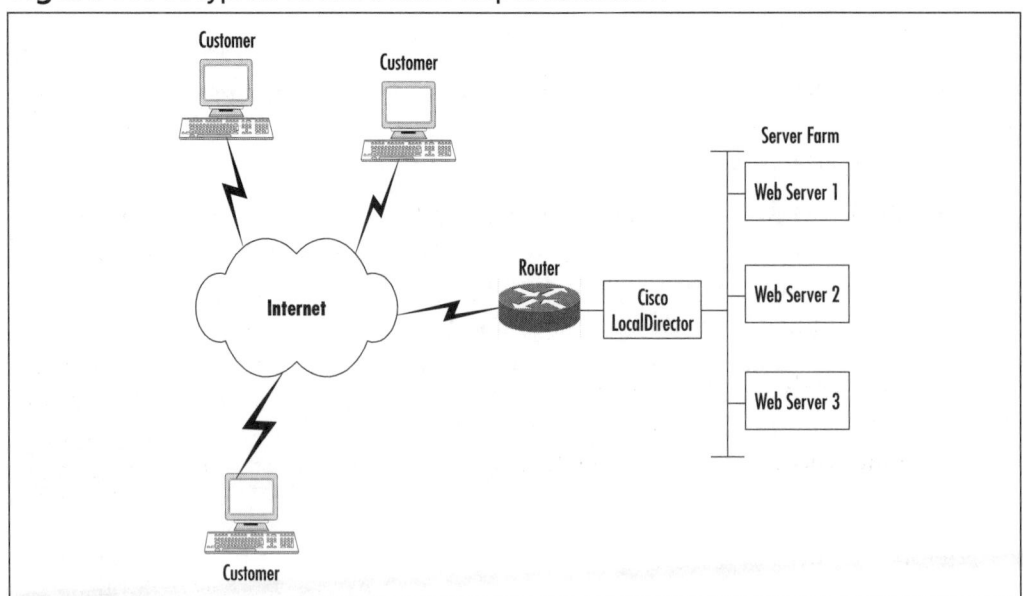

For additional performance, LocalDirector can be used with the Accelerated Server Load Balancing (ASLB) feature of the Catalyst 6000 series switches to increase throughput to 15 million packets per second (mpps).

LocalDirector Security Features

The following information about the security features of LocalDirector will allow you to better understand the security mechanisms it uses and enable you to configure or change these features. Although there are not many of them, correct usage of those present will help you protect the server farm from attacks and network hiccups.

Filtering of Access Traffic

Since LocalDirector maintains and tracks the state of communications for all clients and server hosts, it can control access to specific servers based on various conditions—for example, by source IP address or service port number. This allows you to increase security by restricting which resources the client is allowed to access.

LocalDirector protects your network by only allowing specific traffic to pass between virtual and real servers, restricting both external and internal access to servers. It does not have full Access Control List (ACL) features, but several options are provided:

- **SecureAccess** Allows you to manipulate a connection based on the source IP address of the client. Traffic from certain clients can be directed to a specific virtual server or dropped altogether.

- **SecureBind** Allows you to restrict traffic to a specific port using port-bound (as opposed to IP-bound) servers. Incoming TCP traffic to a port that is not specified as available is terminated by a reset packet (TCP RST). This feature is not available for UDP-based traffic.

- **SecureBridging** Because LocalDirector acts as a transparent TCP/IP bridge, it will pass traffic to the real server's IP addresses. Thus, clients who know the real server's IP address can access it directly if the server is configured to be bridged (the default setting). Bridging can be turned off, thereby forcing client traffic through the LocalDirector virtual address.

- **Secure IP Address** This is similar to static NAT. It allows LocalDirector to translate the IP address of a real server to a virtual IP address, thereby hiding the IP address of the real server while still allowing the physical server to connect to the outside world.

The following is an example of a configuration using SecureAccess, SecureBind, and SecureBridging features. Suppose in Figure 7.1 that LocalDirector is on the local network 192.168.2.0, which has two Web servers: 192.168.2.1 and 192.168.2.2. These hosts run public Web services on port 80 and intranet services (which have to be available only to internal clients from the 192.168.2.0 network) on port 8080. We will create one virtual server—server 192.168.2.10—and using the SecureAccess feature, redirect external clients to 192.168.2.1:80 and 192.168.2.2:80, while redirecting clients from the internal network to 192.168.2.1:8080 and 192.168.2.2:8080.

```
secure 0
secure 1
virtual 192.168.2.10:80:0:tcp is
virtual 192.168.2.10:80:1:tcp is
real 192.168.2.1:80:tcp is
real 192.168.2.2:80:tcp is
```

```
real 192.168.2.1:8080:tcp is
real 192.168.2.2:8080:tcp is
bind 192.168.2.10:80:0:tcp 192.168.2.1:80:tcp
bind 192.168.2.10:80:0:tcp 192.168.2.2:80:tcp
bind 192.168.2.10:80:1:tcp 192.168.2.1:8080:tcp
bind 192.168.2.10:80:1:tcp 192.168.2.2:8080:tcp
assign 192.168.2.10:80:1:tcp 192.168.2.0 255.255.255.0
```

The first two lines turn off transparent bridging on both interfaces (the SecureBridging feature). The next two lines are used to define two virtual servers, both running on port 80 at IP address 192.168.2.10. Four real port-bound servers are described after that (the SecureBind feature). Then (*bind* commands) four real servers are assigned to instances of the virtual server. Lastly, the *assign* command is used to redirect internal clients to a specific instance of the virtual server, the one that is redirected to intranet servers on 192.168.2.1:8080 and 192.168.2.2:8080. This is an example of the SecureAccess feature.

Using *synguard* to Protect Against SYN Flood Attacks

The SYN flood attack is a form of DoS strike that occurs when a server receives many SYN packets (which are used for connection initiation in TCP) without any follow-up. By definition, these potential connections have to be put on hold for some time before they are considered expired. This causes connection queues to fill up, preventing any other TCP connections from being established until the backlog is cleared.

On host systems (for example, on Web servers), you will need to employ techniques for minimizing the effect of a SYN attack. One of these techniques is to increase the size of the connection queue so the attacker needs more time and resources to cause problems—a condition that will apply to the host itself as well, causing it to consume more resources than normal. Another technique is to determine whether or not your host software vendor has any patches that help protect against SYN attacks. Many products, including IBM's AIX, Microsoft's NT, and Sun's Solaris now have these types of patches, although they generally do not eliminate the cause of the problem, but instead only try to ease the consequences. LocalDirector, on the other hand, has a *synguard* feature which is used to protect servers from excessive SYN packets. It counts incoming SYNs and SYN-ACK replies from the server. Once the number of unanswered SYNs reaches a certain limit, all incoming SYN packets to this virtual server are dropped.

By default, this feature is disabled, making the default value 0. The maximum number of SYNs allowed needs to be configured before the feature is enabled.

The following syntax is used to configure the *synguard* feature (from configuration mode):

```
synguard virtual_id count
```

where *virtual_id* is the virtual server IP address or name and port (if a server is port-bound), and *count* is the maximum number of unanswered SYNs allowed to this virtual server.

To disable *synguard*, either set the count back to zero, or use the *no* command:

```
no synguard virtual_id count
```

Note that the *synguard* command provides limited protection against SYN attacks to the virtual server. One of its uses is to notify a system administrator that something bad is happening—LocalDirector always sends a syslog message when it enters protection mode (that is, when the number of unanswered SYN packets exceeds the threshold). After the feature is activated, LocalDirector begins protecting the real network and servers from SYN flood attacks.

The following example illustrates the use of *synguard*:

```
LocalDirector(config)# show synguard
       Machine     Port    SynGuard      Status
   www.test.com  default          0
```

No threshold is set for server www.test.com, so we'll set it to 500 SYN packets.

```
LocalDirector(config)# synguard www.test.com 500
LocalDirector(config)# show synguard
       Machine     Port    SynGuard      Status
   www.test.com  default        500
LocalDirector(config)# show syn
       Machine     Port     Conns   Syn Count
   www.test.com  default      648        176
```

The *show syn* command displays the total number of active connections and current number of active TCP handshakes (unanswered SYN packets).

The following example shows *synguard* in active mode. Notice how the status changes to Active after the number of unanswered SYNs has increased to the threshold.

```
LocalDirector(config)# show synguard
           Machine      Port    SynGuard       Status
      www.site.com   default         500       Active
LocalDirector(config)# show syn
           Machine      Port    Conns  Syn Count
      www.site.com   default      892        500
LocalDirector(config)#
```

Using NAT to Hide Real Addresses

LocalDirector supports Network Address Translation (NAT). This allows you to use unregistered IP addresses on your inside network (usually the server farm) and prevents hackers from being able to directly target the real server's IP address.

RFC 1918 reserves three address ranges—often referred to as *private, internal,* or *unregistered* address ranges—for internal use. These address ranges are not routed on the Internet and packets need to be converted to registered IP addresses before they can be sent to the Internet. NAT performs this conversion from private IP addresses to registered IP addresses, and vice versa, allowing devices access to and from the Internet. This also conserves registered IP addresses.

Increased security is provided through NAT by hiding the internal IP address range and making it more difficult for potential hackers to access as well as learn about the internal structure of your network.

Figure 7.2 shows an example of a device performing NAT. The 10.0.0.x IP address range is not accessible via the Internet, without first going through the NAT conversion process where the registered IP address range is converted to the private IP address range.

Figure 7.2 The NAT Conversion Process

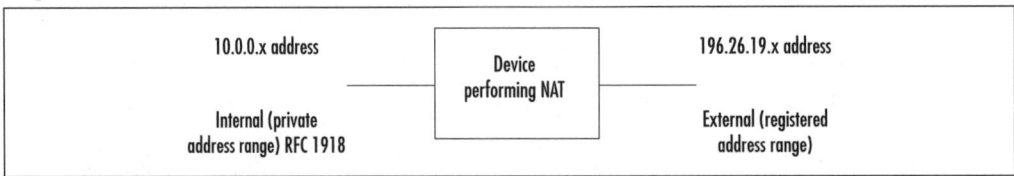

Incoming connections to virtual servers are not subject to NAT, as forwarding and load balancing is performed on the Ethernet level by manipulating MAC addresses in packets, with LocalDirector working as a bridge. There is a possibility of making it translate IP addresses instead, although it is not recommended.

Other NAT capabilities of LocalDirector can be used to statically translate IP addresses of outgoing connections from the real server to the outside world. For example, you can translate this IP to the IP of the virtual server, so the actual IP address of the real server is never revealed, even if the server connects to the hosts outside LocalDirector.

Restricting Who Is Authorized to Have Telnet Access to LocalDirector

You can specify who is authorized to have Telnet access to the LocalDirector. This can be entered either in the form of an IP address or a network address. Limiting who can Telnet into the LocalDirector is an easy and highly effective way of keeping unauthorized persons from trying to gain access to, or cause the disruption of, your systems.

The following syntax is used to configure who has Telnet access (from configuration mode):

```
telnet ip mask
```

Here, *ip* is the IP address or network of the host that is authorized to access the LocalDirector Telnet management interface, and *mask* is the subnet mask for the network specified in this command. Use 255.255.255.255 if you specified a single IP address.

To disable this feature, use the *no* command:

```
no telnet ip mask
```

You can use the following syntax to view allowed IP addresses or networks:

```
show telnet
```

Password Protection

Like most Cisco devices, LocalDirector supports two levels of password protection: *privileged* and *nonprivileged*. The *enable* password is used to enter the privileged level and allows you to view settings, as well as make configuration changes. The *telnet* password is used for the nonprivileged level that allows you to view certain settings but not change them. Passwords can consist of up to 16 alphanumeric symbols and are not case-sensitive; they are converted into lowercase and stored in an encrypted MD5 form.

The *enable* Password

The *enable* password is the privileged-level password. There is no default *enable* password. Be sure to set one before you deploy LocalDirector. The following syntax is used to create an *enable* password (from configuration mode):

```
enable password password
```

The *telnet* Password

The *telnet* password is a user-level password. The default *telnet* password is *cisco*.

The following syntax is used to change the default *telnet* password (from configuration mode):

```
password password
```

Here, *password* is a password of up to 16 alphanumeric characters.

Configuring & Implementing...

Password Protection

For maximum protection, configure Telnet access restriction to allow only a minimal amount of IP addresses to access LocalDirector. One is ideal, although this is not always possible—for example, if you have several management stations.

Always use a different password for each of the password levels. Having the same password for each security level is a frequently encountered misconfiguration and is strongly discouraged.

A common security mistake is failing to change the default *telnet* password (*cisco*) before deploying LocalDirector.

Syslog Logging

Often, knowing when your network is under attack is as important as taking steps to protect yourself against the attack. This is where logging plays an important role.

If a syslog server is configured, LocalDirector will log error and event messages to an external syslog server. For example, a syslog message will be generated if LocalDirector enters synguard protection mode.

The following syntax is used to configure the syslog feature (from configuration mode):

```
syslog {host ip |console}
```

Here the word *host* defines that syslog messages should be sent to a syslog server with IP address *ip*, while *console* specifies that syslog messages will be displayed on the local console (connected to the console port).

To disable syslog messaging, use the *no* command:

```
no syslog {host ip |console}
```

You can use the following syntax to view previously sent syslog messages:

```
show syslog
```

Securing Geographically Dispersed Server Farms Using Cisco DistributedDirector

Cisco's DistributedDirector is a product that allows you to load-balance Internet resource requests among geographically dispersed servers. Its typical application is for a corporation to make use of Web servers, or Web server farms, in multiple locations to service Web requests.

DistributedDirector achieves this by redirecting resource requests to servers located closest to the customer requesting that service. This feature was greatly developed and improved in the Cisco Content Services Switch product—a sophisticated device for Web traffic distribution (see Chapter 10 for additional details about the CSS product line).

DistributedDirector Technology Overview

Cisco's DistributedDirector uses routing table intelligence in the network infrastructure to transparently redirect a customer's service requests to the closest server, as determined by the client-to-server proximity or client-to-server latency.

By using this technology, you can decrease the service response time and increase the service reliability, as well as reduce the cost of long distance communication. The service response time is decreased, and the cost of long distance communications reduced because resource requests to a URL or IP address are redirected to the server closest to the customer requesting the service. The service reliability is increased because DistributedDirector monitors individual servers and does not direct resource requests to servers that are not operating correctly.

Designing & Planning...

Using LocalDirector and DistributedDirector Together

These two products are complimentary in the sense that they can be used together to provide both global scalability of topologically (and geographically) distant server farms and local scalability for redundant clusters. In this scenario, DistributedDirector is responsible for global traffic distribution between virtual servers, where each in its turn is represented by LocalDirector, which provides the local load balancing, ensuring traffic is directed to the highest-available physical server at each distribution site.

DistributedDirector doesn't know anything about the structure of the sites it distributes traffic to. It simply treats them as single servers. When its server availability check fails, it means no physical server behind the corresponding LocalDirector is available or that LocalDirector itself is unavailable at that site. So, provided LocalDirector is itself functioning (this can be ensured by using the failover features), the site will be considered operational by a DistributedDirector as long as it has at least one physical server working. This is a serious availability enhancement—as long as at least one physical server in one geographical location is operational, people will be able to reach your site without knowing of your problems.

Director Response Protocol (DRP) is a protocol that allows DistributedDirector to query routers (DRP server agents) for routing table topological metrics. (DRP agent functionality has been available in IOS releases since 11.3(2)T.) Various Internal Gateway Protocols can be used—RIP, OSPF, IGRP, EIGRP, Integrated, IS-IS, and so on DistributedDirector uses this information to calculate the distance from the client to the servers and redirect the customer's service requests to the closest server. DistributedDirector can function in two modes—Caching DNS mode and HTTP Session Redirect mode. In the first instance, it acts as a caching DNS server, resolving DNS requests for a Web server's name to the IP address of the closest server. In the second mode, it acts as a Web server itself, issuing HTTP redirect messages to the client (HTTP status code 302), and providing the IP address of the nearest real Web server.

Cisco's DistributedDirector can be compared to a regionalized 1–800 number in the telephony world, where incoming calls to a toll-free number are routed to agents located in the same region the call originated, saving on long-distance charges that would otherwise be incurred if the call were answered at a centralized location.

Figure 7.3 depicts a typical DistributedDirector implementation. Web requests are sent to the DistributedDirector, which redirects them to the most appropriate Web server. Often, this is the nearest server from a geographical standpoint. For example, the Web server in San Francisco might best service a Web request from Customer 1 and Customer 2 (who are in the U.S.), whereas the Web server in London might better service a Web request from Customer 3 (who is in Ireland, for example).

Figure 7.3 A Typical DistributedDirector Implementation

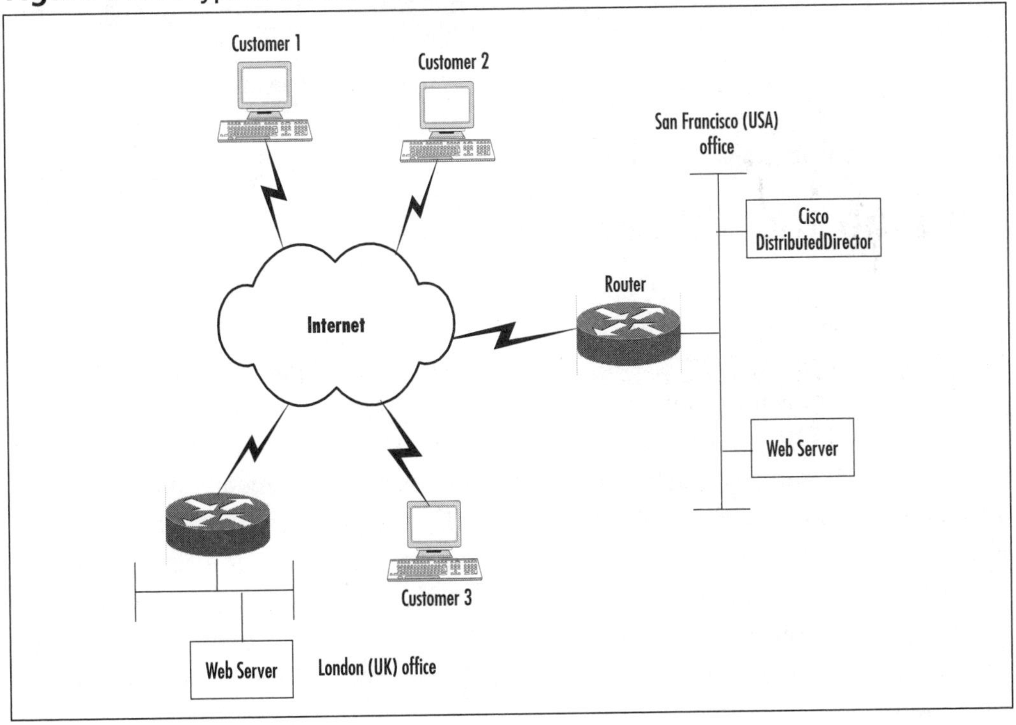

DistributedDirector Product Overview

The DistributedDirector product is available in three different ranges:

- **DistributedDirector 2501/2502** This is the entry-level product. DistributedDirector 2501 has an Ethernet interface, and DistributedDirector 2502 has a Token Ring.

- **DistributedDirector 4700M** This is the medium-level product and comes in models that have Ethernet, Fast Ethernet, Token Ring, and FDDI interfaces.

- **The Cisco 7200 Series Router** This is the high-end product, and is based on the modular Cisco 7200 router, with the DistributedDirector feature set.

DistributedDirector Security Features

The following information about the security features of DistributedDirector will allow you to better understand the security mechanisms they use, and enable you to configure or change these features. DistributedDirector does not provide many security features for the network. Its use in security architecture is based on the enhanced redundancy it provides. Therefore, this section describes securing the product itself from various attacks.

Limiting the Source of DRP Queries

Security of the whole system can be increased by limiting DRP server agents' access to devices having specific source IP addresses. This is done using standard Cisco Access Control Lists (ACLs) together with the *ip drp access-group* command.

If this feature is not implemented, intruders can exploit this vulnerability by creating forged DRP queries and disrupting the normal DRP process by providing incorrect DRP information, thus creating DoS attacks or redirecting clients to false servers. The possibility of a DoS attack against DistributedDirector itself also exists—it can be flooded with illegitimate DRP packets. Protection against this attack is provided by the same feature, because DRP queries that do not originate from authorized DRP sources are discarded even before they can be processed.

The following syntax is used to configure this feature (from global configuration mode):

```
ip drp access-group access-list-number
```

Here *access-list-number* is the standard IP access list describing agents' permissions to connect to the device.

Authentication between DistributedDirector and DRP Agents

In order to increase security and help prevent DoS attacks based on DRP, authentication of DRP queries and responses between the DistributedDirector and the Director Response Protocol (DRP) agents is supported.

By using DRP authentication, DistributedDirector stops intruders from forging DRP queries and disrupting or interfering with the service request redirection function. The authentication feature is based on Keyed-Hashing for Message Authentication Code (HMAC) – Message Digest 5 (MD5) digital signatures. The following syntax is used to configure this feature (from global configuration mode):

```
ip drp authentication key-chain key-chain-name
```

Here *key-chain-name* is the name of the key chain (a string of characters without spaces) containing one or more authentication keys.

To disable this feature, use the *no* command:

```
no ip drp authentication key-chain key-chain-name
```

SECURITY ALERT!

For additional security, use multiple keys on a key chain so you can set key lifetimes using the *accept-lifetime* and *send-lifetime* commands.

You will also need to configure a key chain itself, including actual keys and key-strings, using the *key chain*, *key*, and *key-string* commands.

The *key chain* Command

The *key chain* command is the structure that holds the authentication keys and key-strings together. The following syntax is used to configure this feature (from global configuration mode):

```
key chain name-of-chain
```

Here *name-of-chain* is the name of the key chain.
To disable this feature, use the *no* command:

```
no key chain name-of-chain
```

Use the following syntax to verify key chain information:

```
show key chain
```

The *key* Command

The *key* is a number used to identify the authentication key on a key chain. The following syntax is used to configure this feature (from the key chain configuration):

```
key number
```

Here *number* is the identification number of an authentication key on a key chain. The range of keys is 0 to 2147483647. The key numbers do not have to be consecutive.

To disable this feature, use the *no* command:

```
no key number
```

The *key-string* Command

The *key-string* command is used to identify the authentication string for the key. The following syntax is used to configure this feature (from the key configuration):

```
key-string text
```

Here, *text* is the authentication string, which can contain from 1 to 80 upper-case and lowercase alphanumeric characters (the first character cannot be a number, however). This string must be contained in the DRP packets received in order for them to be authenticated.

To disable this feature, use the *no* command:

```
no key-string text
```

There are two options *accept-lifetime* and *send-lifetime* that define when this specific string will be used for authentication.

The following is an example of DRP authentication using a *key chain, keys, key-strings,* and *accept-lifetime,* as well as *send-lifetime.* In this example, the password *xonix* will always be a valid key for accepting and receiving. The *tetris* key, on the other hand, will be accepted from 15:30 to 17:30 (7,200 seconds) on May 14, 2002 and be sent from 16:00 to 17:00 (3,600 seconds) on May 14, 2002. The overlap allows for a migration of keys or a discrepancy in the router's time. The *klingons* key-string works in the same way but with different times.

```
ip drp authentication key-chain gameboy
!
key chain gameboy
 key 1
  key-string xonix
 key 2
  key-string tetris
  accept-lifetime 15:30:00 May 14 2002 duration 7200
  send-lifetime 16:00:00 May 14 2002 duration 3600
 key 3
  key-string klingons
  accept-lifetime 16:30:00 May 14 2002 duration 7200
  send-lifetime 17:00:00 May 14 2002 duration 3600
```

Password Protection

Because DistributedDirector runs a modified copy of Cisco's Internet-working Operating System (IOS), the procedure for changing passwords on DistributedDirector is the same as for regular IOS. DistributedDirector supports three different levels of password protection: *enable secret, enable,* and *telnet.*

SECURITY ALERT!

For maximum protection, use a different password for the three different password levels that DistributedDirector supports. Although IOS allows you to make all the passwords the same, this is strongly discouraged for security reasons.

The *enable secret* Password

The *enable secret* password is the most secure, encrypted privileged-level password, and can be used even if an *enable* password is configured. The following syntax is used to create an *enable secret* password (from configuration mode):

```
enable secret password password
```

Here, *password* is the *enable secret* password.

The *enable* Password

The *enable* password is a less secure, non-encrypted privileged-level password. It's used when the *enable secret* password does not exist. The following syntax is used to create an *enable* password (from configuration mode):

```
enable password password
```

Here, *password* is the *enable* password.

The *telnet* Password

The *telnet* password is a user-level password that allows you to look at some of the configuration information, but not change any configuration. By default, Telnet is not allowed and there is no default *telnet* password. You will need to configure both the *telnet* password as well as an *enable* password for you to be able to Telnet into DistributedDirector. The following syntax is used to configure a *telnet* password (from vty configuration mode):

```
password password
```

Here, *password* is the *telnet* password.

Syslog Logging

As already noted, knowing that an attack is occurring is an important way to protect against it. Logging plays an imperative role in this.

Again, because DistributedDirector runs a modified copy of Cisco's IOS, the procedure for configuring logging to an external syslog server is the same as with regular IOS.

The following syntax is used to configure the *syslog* feature (from configuration mode):

```
logging ip
```

Here, *ip* is the IP address of the log host.

To disable syslog, use the *no* command:

```
no logging ip
```

Use the following syntax to view syslog messages in the buffer:

```
show logging
```

Summary

Load-balancing solutions provide extra redundancy and availability for network servers—both Web and generic TCP servers—by distributing traffic destined for one virtual server between several physical servers. Cisco LocalDirector and DistributedDirector can be used for this purpose. LocalDirector acts as a front-end for a local server farm, while DistributedDirector provides traffic distribution among geographically distant servers.

The LocalDirector product range consists of three appliances, from entry-level to high-level devices. The high-level product, LocalDirector 417, is able to support Gigabit Ethernet speeds. There is also a possibility of cooperation with Catalyst 6000 switches for increase of throughput (to 15 million packets per second).

LocalDirector features various security-related technologies: SecureAccess, which provides for traffic filtering by source of connection; SecureBind, which allows port-bound servers (instead of only IP-based redirection); and SecureBridging, which helps to protect real servers from direct connections from the outside world. It also has static NAT features, and the capability to protect against SYN flood attacks.

The device itself has common Cisco-style password protection and is capable of sending syslog messages to remote servers.

DistributedDirector works together with Cisco routers, which provides it with IGP metrics of corresponding networks. This allows it to select the server nearest to each specific client, thus saving on long-distance communications and decreasing delays in service. Product range consists of two appliances that run modified Cisco IOS software and one device based on a modular 7200 series router.

Security features of DistributedDirector are limited to authentication of its communications with routers (DRP agents). This authentication is based on the HMAC-MD5 hashing algorithm. It also has the Cisco common password system (non-privileged mode and enable mode) and syslog subsystem.

Solutions Fast Track

Improving Security Using Cisco LocalDirector

☑ Security-related use of LocalDirector mainly comes from its increased reliability and redundancy features.

☑ LocalDirector also serves to protect against SYN flood attacks.

☑ It can balance stateless TCP and UDP servers.

☑ The LocalDirector product range consists of three series—the 416, 430, and 417 product lines.

☑ The 417 series, in addition to two Fast Ethernet interfaces, has a one Gigabit Ethernet interface.

☑ When used together with the Catalyst 6000 Accelerated Server Load Balancing feature, LocalDirector can achieve throughput of up to 15 million packets per second.

LocalDirector Security Features

☑ LocalDirector has some restricted traffic filtering abilities.

☑ It can also perform static NAT for outgoing connections, helping hide an internal server's IP address.

☑ The LocalDirector command interface is password protected in a manner similar to other Cisco devices. It has the capability to restrict Telnet access to a device based on its IP address.

Securing Geographically Dispersed Server Farms Using Cisco DistributedDirector

☑ Cisco's DistributedDirector is a product that allows load balancing of Internet resource requests among geographically dispersed servers.

☑ DistributedDirector achieves this by redirecting resource requests to servers located closest to the customer requesting that service.

☑ DistributedDirector works in cooperation with Cisco routers, which provide information on network topology and distance.

☑ DistributedDirector can function in two modes—Caching DNS mode and HTTP Session Redirect mode.

☑ The DistributedDirector product line includes two appliances—entry-level and medium-level devices—plus a high-end product based on the 7200 series modular Cisco router.

☑ In the process of calculating network distances, DistributedDirector can use various IGP protocols, such as RIP, OSPF, IGRP, EIGRP, Integrated IS-IS, and so on.

DistributedDirector Security Features

☑ Security of the system is achieved by limiting the source/destination of DRP communications of DistributedDirector with participating routers.

☑ DRP communications can be also authenticated using MD5 keyed hashing algorithms.

☑ Command-line interface is protected in the same way as all IOS devices. This is because DistributedDirector runs a modified copy of Cisco IOS software.

Frequently Asked Questions

The following Frequently Asked Questions, answered by the authors of this book, are designed to both measure your understanding of the concepts presented in this chapter and to assist you with real-life implementation of these concepts. To have your questions about this chapter answered by the author, browse to **www.syngress.com/solutions** and click on the **"Ask the Author"** form.

Q: How are SSL connections supported by LocalDirector?

A: When load-balancing SSL connections (HTTPS servers), LocalDirector has to ensure that once a connection is established, all requests from the same client are redirected to the same server since this encrypted connection uses a unique key that is established during session setup. To achieve this, the device supports the so-called "sticky" mode for connections. A connection can be made sticky based on the client source IP address or SSL session ID (which is provided by the client's browser).

Q: What is the major problem with stickiness based on source IP address?

A: The major problem in such cases is that all connections from the same source IP address are redirected to the same physical server. This does not work well when several clients behind a firewall try to connect to the same server. If a firewall performs while hiding NAT (so all source IPs are translated to the same address), then from the point of view of a LocalDirector they come from the same client. When one of these clients finishes the connection, tearing it up in a proper way (by exchanging FIN packets with the server), LocalDirector loses its state, and packets from other clients who did not finish their session yet can be redirected to another physical server, causing disruption of the SSL connection. This is not an implementation error since all IP-based stickiness solutions suffer from the same problem.

Q: What is the major problem with SSL ID-based stickiness?

A: With SSL ID-based stickiness, LocalDirector forwards packets based on their SSL ID, which is provided by the client's browser inside a TCP packet. This works well even when there are many clients with the same IP address since persistence of the connection is not based on IP address. Unfortunately, Microsoft Internet Explorer 5 users experience problems with this mode because the browser randomly clears this field approximately once every 30 to 120 seconds, which causes LocalDirector to redirect the connection randomly to one of the physical servers. This problem appears to be fixed in IE 6.0. Netscape Navigator does not suffer from it either.

Q: Does DistributedDirector experience problems with SSL connections?

A: No, because it uses DNS or HTTP redirect to inform the client of the IP address of a real server, so all communications after redirection are performed between client and server directly, without interference from the DistributedDirector.

Q: Can DistributedDirector work without DRP agents?

A: Not always. However, the device has some balancing modes that do not require any external information. They share equally load balancing, primary/backup server balancing, and random server balancing.

## Chapter 8

Virtual Private Networks and Remote Access

Solutions in this chapter:

- **Overview of the Different VPN Technologies**
- **Layer 2 Transport Protocol**
- **IPSec**

☑ **Summary**

☑ **Solutions Fast Track**

☑ **Frequently Asked Questions**

Introduction

When you think about the world today, with hackers everywhere, you need something to reassure you that you have a little privacy. The Virtual Private Network (VPN) provides that—on a LAN, WAN, and Remote Access scale for many different types of people.

If you think about it, you can have people anywhere in the world using a VPN on a WAN, sending secure messages over a service provider's network in the middle. Also, you could have people working on the road or from home using a VPN to securely connect to the company infrastructure over an Internet Service Provider (ISP). The latest, and possibly best, way is to use a VPN over some wireless device such as a Cisco Aironet Card or other type of wireless device.

All network administrators are focused on securing their network from the outside world. With the implementation of a VPN from a PC to a Cisco piece of equipment (in other words, a Cisco VPN Concentrator) using IPSec, you are able to securely send information to and from both sides of the VPN. This makes for a very secure environment for remote access users to perform work on a WAN. VPNs can be utilized on different levels of the OSI model, depending on what they are being used for at that time.

In the following chapter, you will learn how IPSec works within a VPN to help prevent security breaches on a network. Also, you will understand the different types of VPNs used today, and discover how IPSec works from end-to-end. To describe it simply, a VPN is a network deployed on a shared infrastructure, employing the same security, management, and throughput policies applied in a private network. Figure 8.1 shows how VPN works in the real world.

Overview of the Different VPN Technologies

As discussed in the introduction, VPNs can take many different forms and be implemented in various ways. Not only can a VPN be classified by the OSI Reference model layer it is implemented on, but also by which VPN model it employs.

The Peer Model

A *peer* VPN model is one in which the path determination at the network layer is done on a hop-by-hop basis. The edge nodes (customer sites) form a network layer peering relationship with the VPN service provider network and use the best route through the network, rather than connecting to other edge nodes (customer sites) via a predetermined path though the network.

Figure 8.1 A Typical VPN

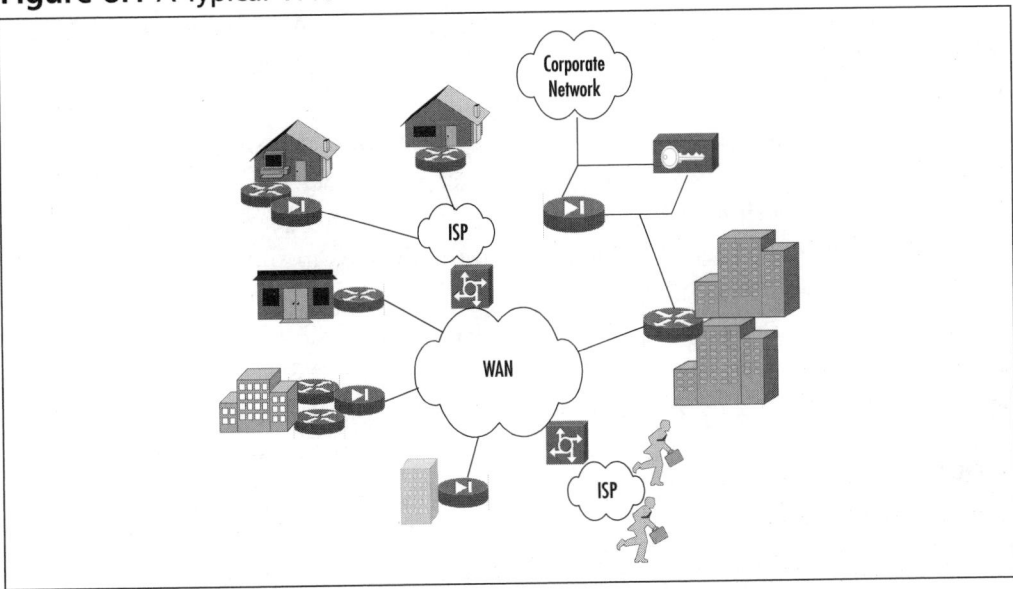

One of the major drawbacks of this model is that all network layer addressing must be unique within the VPN service provider network and the individual VPNs. A traditional routed network is an example of a *peer* model.

In Figure 8.2, a packet from Network 1, destined for Network 2, is first sent to router A. Router A determines that the best path for this packet to follow is via router B. Router B determines that the best path for this packet to follow is via router C. Router C determines that the best path for this packet to follow is via router D, which in turn delivers the packet to Network 2.

Figure 8.2 A Typical Peer Model

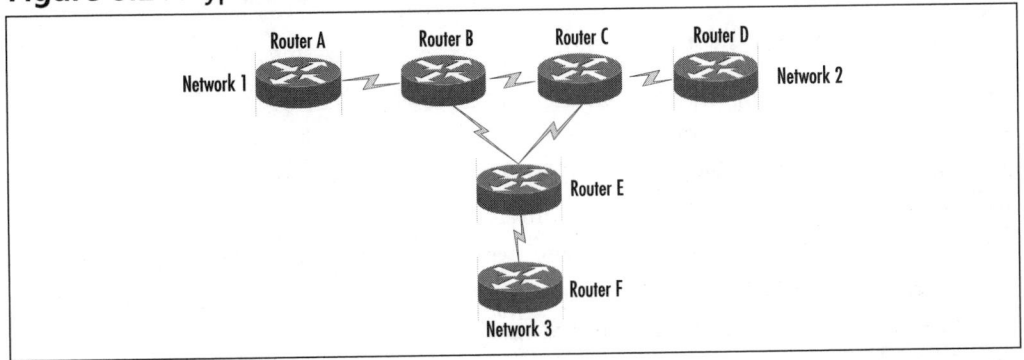

The Overlay Model

An *overlay* VPN model is one in which path determination at the network layer is done on a "cut-through" basis to another edge node (customer site). The network layer has no knowledge of the underlying infrastructure. All edge nodes (customer sites) are effectively one hop away from each other, no matter how many physical hops are between them.

An advantage of this type of VPN is that network addressing between the different VPNs and the VPN service provider networks does not have to be unique, except for within a single VPN.

It is generally accepted that the *overlay* model results in suboptimal routing in larger networks and that full mesh *overlay* topologies have scalability problems, since they create large numbers of router adjacencies. Examples include ATM, Frame Relay, and tunneling implementations. In Figure 8.3, Network 1 is one hop away from Network 2, no matter how many physical hops are between them.

Figure 8.3 A Typical Overlay Model

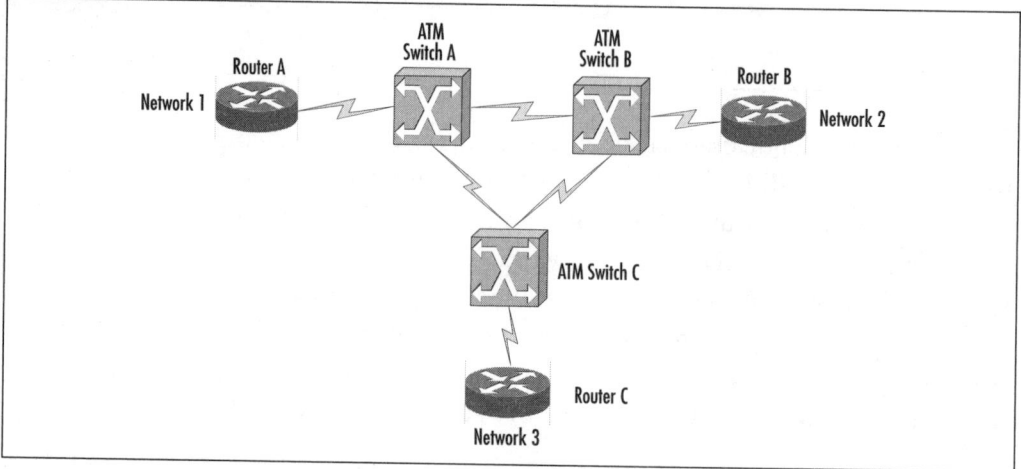

Link Layer VPNs

Link layer VPNs are implemented at the link layer (Layer 2) of the OSI Reference model. The link layer provides the networking platform, while discrete networks are built at the network layer. The different VPNs share the same infrastructure, but have no visibility of one another. The difference between this model and that of dedicated circuits is that there is no synchronized data clock shared by the sender and receiver, as well as no dedicated transmission path provided by the underlying network. Frame Relay and ATM networks are examples of link layer VPNs.

Network Layer VPNs

Network layers are VPNs implemented at the network layer (Layer 3) of the OSI Reference model. We will now look at the two types of VPNs that work within the network layer: Tunneling and Virtual Private Dial Networks (VPDN).

Tunneling VPNs

Tunneling VPNs are becoming increasingly popular and most VPN growth is expected in this area. Tunnels can be created either between a source and destination router, router-to-router, or host-to-host. Tunneling can be point-to-point or point-to-multipoint, but point-to-point tunneling is much more scaleable than point-to-multipoint. This is due to point-to-point tunneling requiring substantially less management overhead, both from an establishment as well as a maintenance point of view.

One of the major advantages of tunneling is that the VPN backbone and the VPN connected subnets do not have to have unique network addresses. This is particularly important when you consider that the majority of organizations today use private address space.

A VPN using tunneling could be constructed with or without the knowledge of the network provider, and could span multiple network providers. Obviously, performance might be a problem if the service provider is not aware of the tunneling and does not provide adequate Quality of Service (QoS).

Cisco's Generic Routing Encapsulation (GRE) is used for tunneling between source and destination router, or router-to-router. GRE tunnels provide a specific pathway across a shared WAN and encapsulate traffic with new packet headers to ensure delivery to a specific destination. A GRE tunnel is configured between the source (*ingress*) router and the destination (*egress*) router. Packets designated to be forwarded across the tunnel are encapsulated with a GRE header, transported across the tunnel to the tunnel end-point address, and stripped of their GRE header.

The IETF's Layer 2 Tunneling Protocol (L2TP) and Microsoft's Point-to-Point Tunneling Protocol (PPTP) are used for host-to-host tunneling. PPTP should not be used without additional security features, such as those provided by IPSec, as it is known to have several security vulnerabilities. Some of these vulnerabilities have been addressed by the strengthening of PPTP's authentication mechanism, MS-CHAP, in the revised MS-CHAP version 2. Even with these changes, PPTP's security mechanisms provide only weak security and are vulnerable to attack.

Host-to-host tunneling is considerably more secure than router-to-router tunneling due to the fact that with host-to-host tunneling the entire "conversation" can be encrypted. This is not the case in router-to-router tunneling, since only the tunnel can be encrypted while the host-to-router and router-to-host parts on both sides of the "conversation" remain in cleartext. Tunneling is considered an *overlay* VPN model.

Virtual Private Dial Networks

VPDNs that utilize the Internet as a carrier for remote access (RAS) traffic are becoming very popular.

Not only do they offer substantial cost savings compared to traditional RAS solutions, they also provide substantial flexibility. Any ISP point of presence (PoP) could be used to provide secure RAS access services at a fraction of traditional costs.

L2TP and PPTP are fundamental to VPDN design and provide the tunneling features through which the RAS traffic reaches the desired services. A VPDN could be considered an *overlay* VPN model.

Controlled Route Leaking

This method uses route filtering to control route propagation to only the members of a particular VPN. Multiple VPNs sharing the same network layer infrastructure are only separated from one another by the fact that routes to the other VPNs are blocked from each other. This is a rather simple and unsophisticated method of implementing a VPN, but it might be very effective for extranets or smaller network applications. Controlled route leaking is considered a *peer* VPN model.

Transport and Application Layer VPNs

These are VPNs implemented at the transport and application layer (Layers 4 and 5) of the OSI Reference model. These implementations require the application to be VPN-aware and hence need to be written with this in mind. While certainly possible, this form of VPN is not common.

With the IETF developing their Transport Layer Security (TLS) protocol, this form of VPN might become more important in the future. TLS 1.0 is at the proposed standard stage as RFC 2246.

Intranet VPNs

An intranet VPN links enterprise customer headquarters, remote offices, and branch offices to an internal network over a shared infrastructure using dedicated connections. Intranet VPNs differ from extranet VPNs in that they only allow access to the enterprise customer's employees. In Figure 8.4, we see a typical VPN dial-up scenario.

Figure 8.4 VPN Client to Router VPN via Dial-up

Extranet VPNs

An *extranet* VPN links outside customers, suppliers, partners, or communities of interest to an enterprise customer's network over a shared infrastructure using dedicated connections (see Figure 8.5). Extranet VPNs differ from intranet VPNs in that they allow access to users outside the enterprise.

Figure 8.5 Router-to-Router VPN Gateway

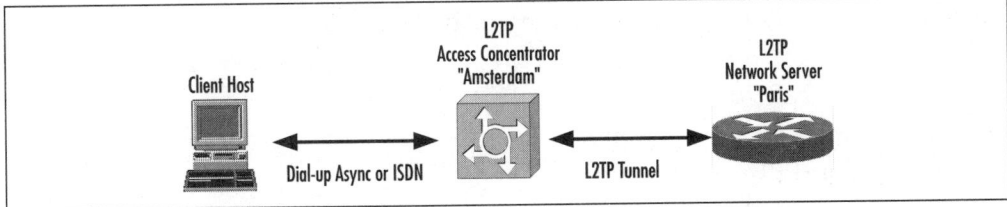

Access VPNs

An *access* VPN provides remote access to an enterprise customer's intranet or extranet over a shared infrastructure (see Figure 8.6). Access VPNs use analog, dial, ISDN, digital subscriber line, mobile IP, and various cable technologies. They securely connect mobile users, telecommuters, and branch offices.

Figure 8.6 Other Vendors to the Router VPN

Layer 2 Transport Protocol

L2TP is an Internet Engineering Task Force (IETF) standard that combines the best features of two existing tunneling protocols: Cisco's Layer 2 Forwarding Protocol (L2F) and PPTP. L2TP has replaced Cisco's own proprietary L2F protocol.

L2TP is a key building block for VPNs in the dial access space. Using L2TP tunneling, an ISP, or other access provider, can create a virtual tunnel to link customer's remote sites or remote users with corporate networks. L2TP allows organizations to provide connectivity to remote users by leveraging a service provider's existing infrastructure. This can often be achieved at a lower cost and without the delays caused by establishing your own infrastructure.

The L2TP access controller (LAC) located at the ISP's PoP exchanges messages with remote users and communicates by way of L2TP requests and responses with the customer's L2TP network server (LNS) to set up tunnels (see Figure 8.7). L2TP passes packets through the virtual tunnel between end points of a point-to-point connection. Frames from remote users are accepted by the ISP's PoP, stripped of any linked framing or transparency bytes, encapsulated in L2TP, and forwarded over the appropriate tunnel. The customer's home gateway accepts these L2TP frames, strips the L2TP encapsulation, and processes the incoming frames for the appropriate interface. L2TP is an extension of Point-to-Point Protocol (PPP) and is vendor interoperable.

Figure 8.7 L2TP Architecture

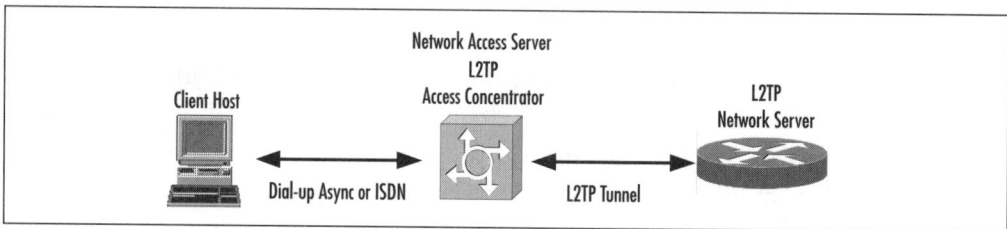

> **NOTE**
>
> L2TP is *not* a security protocol. It is, however, crucial to the operation of VPNs—in particular, to dial VPNs. Security for L2TP is provided through IPSec.

L2TP uses a *compulsory* tunneling model, which means that the tunnel is created without any action from the user, and without giving the user a choice in the matter.

In this scenario, a user dials into a Network Access Server (NAS), authenticates either against a locally configured profile or against a policy server, and after successful authentication, a L2TP tunnel is dynamically established to a predetermined endpoint, where the user's PPP session is terminated.

L2TP is supported in IOS from version 11.3(5)AA on limited platforms such as the Cisco AS5200, AS5300, AS5800, and the 7200 series. Platform support was extended to the 1600, 2500, 2600, 3600, 4000, 4500, 7500, and UAC 6400 in version 12.0(5)T.

Configuring Cisco L2TP

The following example illustrates how L2TP can be used to provide enterprise connectivity to remote users using a shared network such as a service provider. In this example, the user's domain name is very important, as this is what the LAC uses to determine which L2TP tunnel it needs to send the packet through.

It is also important to understand that the client host gets an IP address from the remote network. The connection between the LAC and the LNS can typically be a series of IP networks, such as the Internet. Figure 8.8 shows a typical L2TP scenario, displaying LAC as well as the LNS.

Figure 8.8 L2TP Configuration

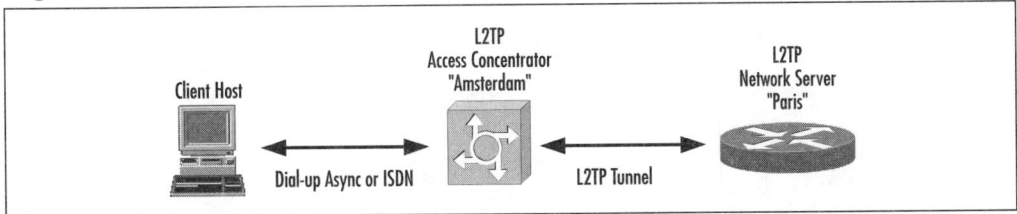

NOTE

Within this chapter, the asterisks (*) within the code listings represent a password being entered. Be sure you do not use simple passwords, as this is the most common security mistake made by network and security administrators. Either pick some good random password or mask the password, since this is a simple way to improve your security.

An LAC Configuration Example

The following is a basic LAC configuration for the scenario shown previously in Figure 8.8.

```
aaa new-model
```

Enables AAA.

```
aaa authentication ppp default local
```

Enables AAA authentication for PPP.

```
username Amsterdam password 7 *********
```

Defines the username as "Amsterdam."

```
vpdn enable
```

Enables VPDN.

```
vpdn-group 1
```

Defines VPDN group number 1.

```
request dialin l2tp ip 172.25.1.19 domain test.com
```

Allows the LAC to respond to dial in requests using L2TP from the IP address 172.25.1.19 domain test.com.

A LNS Configuration Example

The following is a basic LNS configuration for the scenario shown previously in Figure 8.8.

```
01:    aaa new-model
```

Enables AAA.

```
02:    aaa authentication ppp default local
```

Enables AAA authentication for PPP.

```
03:    username Paris password 7 *********
```

Defines the username as "Paris."

```
04:    interface Virtual-Template1
```

Creates virtual-template 1 and assigns all values for virtual access interfaces.

```
05:        ip unnumbered Ethernet0
```

Uses the IP address from interface Ethernet 0.

```
06:    no ip mroute-cache
```

Disables multicast fast switching.

```
07:    ppp authentication chap
```

Uses CHAP to authenticate PPP.

```
08:    vpdn enable
```

Enables VPDN.

```
09:    vpdn-group 1
```

Creates vpdn-group number 1.

```
10:    accept dialin l2tp virtual-template 1 remote Amsterdam
```

Accepts all dial-in l2tp tunnels from virtual-template from remote peer Amsterdam.

IPSec

IPSec, or Internet Protocol Security as it is known by its full name, was developed by the IETF to address the issue of network layer security. It is not a single protocol or specification, but rather a framework of open standards for ensuring secure private communications over public IP networks. IPSec is documented in a series of RFCs. The overall IPSec implementation is guided by RFC 2401, "Security Architecture for the Internet Protocol."

NOTE

IPSec's strength lies in the fact that it allows organizations to implement strong security, without the need to change any of their applications. Only network layer infrastructures change, such as routers, firewalls, and cases where a software client is required. As with IP, IPSec is completely transparent from the end-user perspective.

The IETF maintains an official depository for its work on IPSec. This information can be found at www.ietf.org/html.charters/ipsec-charter.html.

While IP dwarfs all other network protocols in sheer deployment numbers and has been more successful than its inventors could ever imagine, it was not designed to be secure. IP has long been vulnerable to many forms of attack, including spoofing, sniffing, session hijacking, and man-in-the-middle attacks.

Initial security standards focused on application level protocols and software, such as Secure Sockets Layer (SSL) which is used mainly for securing Web traffic, Secure Shell (SSH) which is used for securing Telnet sessions and file transfers, and Pretty Good Privacy (PGP) which is used for securing e-mail. These forms of security can be limiting, as the application itself needs to support them. However, in some cases application layer security provides additional features not supported by network layer security. Open PGP's digital signature is an example of such a feature.

Another way of implementing security is at the network layer, as the applications are secured, even if they are not themselves aware of the security mechanisms. IPSec is based on this model.

Cisco has made IPSec support available since IOS release 11.3(3)T. It also supports IPSec in its PIX firewall product range as well as its Cisco Secure VPN Client software available for the Microsoft Windows operating systems. It uses the approach that no matter what application is used, all packet level information has to travel through the network layer. By securing the network layer, the applications can automatically benefit from the security offered by that layer.

Due to its flexibility and strong security, as well as its vendor interoperability feature, IPSec has found favour with all of the major networking and operating systems vendors. Most of these vendors have replaced, or at least supplemented, their own proprietary network layer security mechanism with IPSec.

Before the development of IPSec, the acceptance and large scale deployment of VPNs was often hampered by security concerns. Existing solutions were either proprietary or used weak security algorithms.

The strength of proprietary solutions is often difficult to assess, since little information about them is made available and their deployment is usually limited to a specific vendor.

Multivendor interoperability was also a problem. This requirement was spurred on by the new economy, where mergers and acquisitions and unlikely partnerships are becoming commonplace. IPSec addresses these concerns.

IPSec Architecture

In simplified terms, IPSec provides three main functions:

- Authentication only, provided through the Authentication Header (AH) protocol

- Authentication and confidentiality (encryption), provided through the Encapsulating Security Payload (ESP) protocol

- Key exchange, provided either manually or through the Internet Key Exchange (IKE) protocol

Table 8.1 and 8.2 show the standards and features of IPSec on Cisco IOS. These tables provide a basic understanding of how IPSec works through each standard.

Table 8.1 IPSec Standards Supported by Cisco IOS and PIX Firewall

Standard	Description
IPSec	AH provides data authentication and integrity for IP packets passed between two different systems. AH does not provide data confidentiality (such as encryption) of packets. Authentication is achieved by applying a keyed one-way hash function to the packet to create a message digest.
	ESP is a security protocol used to provide confidentiality (such as encryption), data origin authentication, integrity, and optional anti-replay. It also provides confidentiality by performing encryption at the IP packet layer. It supports a variety of symmetric encryption algorithms. (The default algorithm for IPSec is DES.)
DES	DES employs a 56-bit key used for ensuring high encryption. DES is used to encrypt and decrypt packet data. It also turns cleartext into ciphertext through an encryption algorithm.
Triple DES (3DES)	3DES is an encryption protocol for use in IPSec on Cisco products. The 3DES algorithm is a variant of the 56-bit DES. 3DES operates similarly to DES but in that data is broken into 64-bit blocks. 3DES then processes each block three times (that would be one time within each 56-bit key).
Diffie-Hellman (DH)	DH is a public key cryptography protocol. It allows two parties to establish a shared secret key used by encryption algorithms over some type of insecure channel.

Continued

www.syngress.com

Table 8.1 Continued

Standard	Description
Message Digest 5 (MD5) and Secure Hash Algorithm (SHA1)	These are both hash algorithms used to authenticate packet data.
RSA Signatures: Rivest, Shamir, and Adelman Signatures (RSA)	RSA is a public-key cryptographic system used for authentication.
Internet Key Exchange (IKE)	IKE is a protocol that provides authentication of the IPSec peers, negotiation of IKE and IPSec security associations (SA). Also, it establishes keys for encryption algorithms used by IPSec.
Certificate Authorities (CA)	Provides a so-called digital identification card to each querying device.

Table 8.2 IPSec-VPN Features on Cisco IOS

Feature	Description
Data confidentiality	The IPSec sender can encrypt packets before transmitting them across a network; this improves security.
Data integrity	The IPSec receiver can authenticate packets sent by the IPSec sender; this ensures the data has not been altered during transmission.
Data origin authentication	The IPSec receiver can authenticate the source of the IPSec packets sent.
Anti-replay	The IPSec receiver can detect and reject replayed packets.

IPSec provides secure communications between two end–points, called IPSec peers. These communications are essentially sets of security associations (SAs) and define which protocols should be applied to sensitive packets, as well as the keying between the two peers. Multiple IPSec tunnels can exist between two peers, securing different data streams, with each communication having a separate set of security associations.

In Figure 8.9, IPSec is used in tunnel mode to protect the traffic between the two private networks connected via the public network.

Figure 8.9 IPSec Deployed across a Public Network

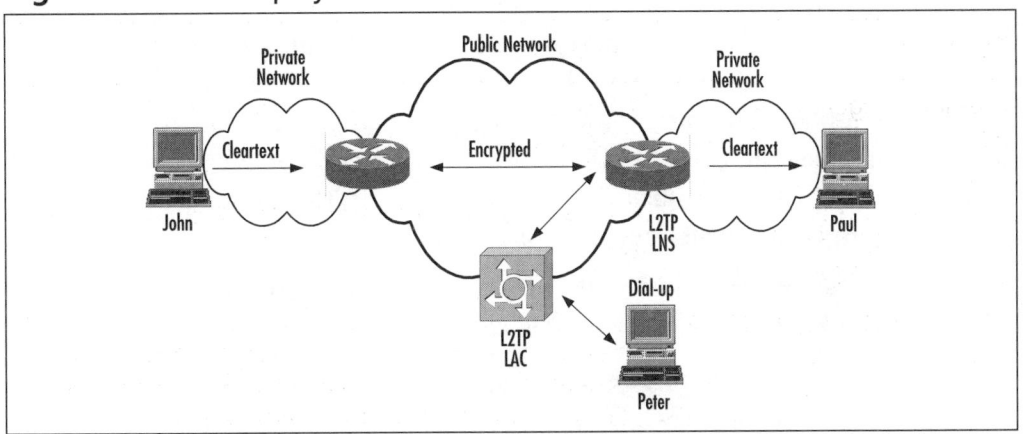

In this scenario, the end hosts (John and Paul) do not need to support IPSec. Only the routers that connect the private networks to the public network need to support IPSec. Traffic on the private network is not encrypted (cleartext) and only gets encrypted when it has to pass over the public network.

IPSec over L2TP is also shown to provide secure remote access support for Peter, via PSTN dial-up, to access the corporate network. In this case, the end host (Peter) must also support IPSec.

Security Associations

IPSec SAs define how two or more IPSec parties will use security services in the context of a particular security protocol (AH or ESP) to communicate securely on behalf of a particular flow. Amongst other information, SAs contain the shared secret keys used to protect data in a particular flow, as well as their lifetimes.

SAs are unidirectional connections and are unique per security protocol (AH or ESP). This means that if both AH and ESP services are required, two or more SAs have to be created.

SAs can be created manually, or automatically by using IKE. If created manually, the SAs are established as soon as they are created and do not expire. When created through IKE, SAs are established when needed and expire after a certain amount of time, or after a certain volume of traffic, whichever is reached first. The default Cisco IOS lifetimes are 3600 seconds (one hour) and 4,608,000 KB. An additional level of security is provided by this, as it forces a periodic security association renegotiation, thus periodically renewing the encryption key material.

An SA is identified by three parameters:

- **Security Parameter Index (SPI)** A pseudo-arbitrary 32-bit value that is assigned to an SA when it is first created. Together with an IP address and security protocol (either AH or ESP) it uniquely identifies a particular SA. Both AH and ESP always contain a reference to an SPI. When SAs are manually created (for example, IKE is not used), the SPI has to be manually specified for each SA.

- **IP Destination Address** The destination endpoint of the SA. This could be a host or network device such as a router or firewall.

- **Security Protocol Identifier** This could be either AH or ESP. SAs specify whether IPSec is used in *transport* or *tunnel* mode.

  - A *transport* mode SA is a security association between two hosts.

  - A *tunnel* mode SA is essentially an SA applied to an IP tunnel. Whenever either end of a security association is a security gateway, the SA is a tunnel mode SA. Thus tunnel mode is always used between two gateways or between a gateway and a host.

Use the *show crypto IPSec security-association-lifetime* syntax to view the lifetimes.

```
show crypto ipsec security-association-lifetime
Security association lifetime: 4608000 kilobytes/3600 seconds
```

Anti-replay Feature

Anti-replay is an important IPSec feature that uses sequence numbers together with data authentication to reject old or duplicate packets that could be used in an attack.

Replay attacks occur when an attacker intercepts an authenticated packet and later transmits it in order to disrupt service or use it with some other malicious intent in mind.

Cisco IOS always uses anti-replay protection when it provides data authentication services, except when security associations are manually established without the use of IKE.

A Security Policy Database

Security Associations are used by IPSec to enforce a security policy. A higher level Security Policy Database (SPD) specifies what security services are to be applied to IP packets and how.

An SPD discriminates between traffic that is to be IPSec-protected and traffic allowed to bypass IPSec. If the traffic is to be IPSec-protected, it also determines which specific SA the traffic should use.

Each SPD entry is defined by a set of IP and upper-layer protocol field values, called selectors. In effect, these selectors are used to filter outgoing traffic in order to map it into a particular SA.

Authentication Header

The AH is an important IPSec security protocol that provides packet authentication and anti-replay services. AH is defined in RFC 2402 and uses IP Protocol 51. AH can be deployed in either *transport* or *tunnel* mode.

Transport mode is generally used when the client host initiates the IPSec communication. It provides protection for upper-layer protocols, in addition to selected IP header fields. In transport mode, the AH is inserted after the IP header and before an upper-layer protocol (such as TCP, UDP, and ICMP), or before any other previously inserted IPSec headers.

In Figure 8.10 and Figure 8.11, the mutable fields referred to are fields like time-to-live, which cannot be included in authentication calculations because they change as the packet travels.

Figure 8.10 AH in *Transport* Mode

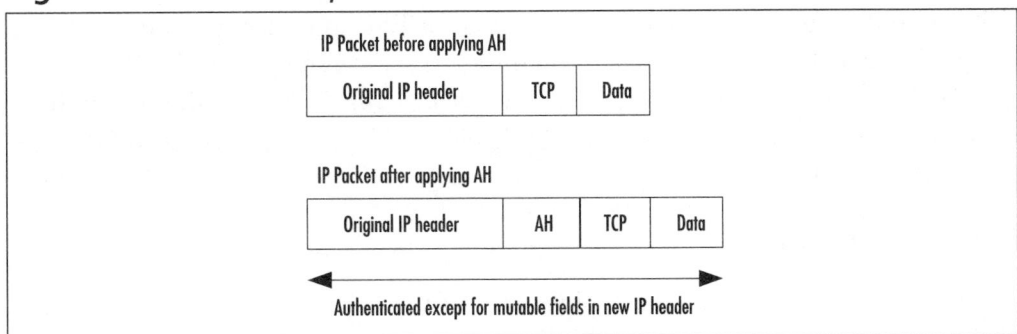

Figure 8.11 AH in *Tunnel* Mode

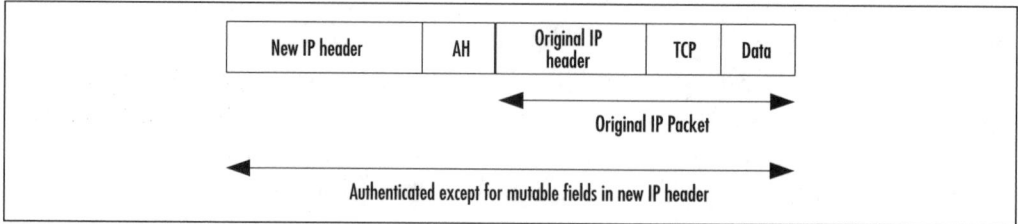

Encapsulating Security Payload

ESP is an important IPSec security protocol that provides data encryption, data authentication, and optional anti-replay services. ESP can be used on its own or with AH packet authentication. ESP encapsulates the data that is to be protected and can be deployed in either transport or tunnel mode. ESP is defined in RFC 2406 and uses IP Protocol number 50.

Transport mode provides protection for upper layer protocols, but not for the IP header. This means that the ESP is inserted after the IP header and before an upper-layer protocol or any other IPSec header. With IPv4, this means the ESP is placed after the IP header (and any options that it contains), and before the upper layer protocol. This makes ESP and AH compatible with non–IPSec-compliant routers.

Tunnel mode ESP may be employed in either hosts or security gateways. In tunnel mode, the "inner" IP header carries the ultimate source and destination addresses, while an "outer" IP header may contain distinct IP addresses (of security gateways, for example). In tunnel mode, ESP protects the entire inner IP packet, including the entire inner IP header. The position of ESP in tunnel mode relative to the outer IP header, is the same as for ESP in transport mode.

In order to use NAT, you need to configure static NAT translations. This is due to AH being incompatible with NAT because NAT changes the source IP address. This, in turn, will break the AH header and cause the packets to be rejected by the IPSec peer or peers.

Manual IPSec

In manual IPSec, the device keys, plus those of the systems it will be communicating with are manually configured. This makes manual IPSec very configuration intensive and prone to misconfiguration. This method is generally only practical for small, relatively static environments.

In manual IPSec, security associations need to be manually defined, a function that is automated when IKE is used. For larger, more complex environments, the use of IKE is strongly advised to automate key management.

Internet Key Exchange

IKE is a key management protocol used in IPSec to create an authenticated, secure communication channel between two entities and then negotiate the security associations for IPSec. This process requires that the two entities authenticate themselves to each other and exchange the required key material.

IPSec assumes that a security association is in place, but does not itself have a mechanism for creating this association. IPSec uses IKE to automatically create and maintain these security associations.

IKE is defined in RFC 2409 and is a hybrid protocol which implements Oakley and SKEME key exchanges inside the Internet Security Association Key Management Protocol (ISAKMP) framework, which, in turn, is defined by RFC 2408.

IKE offers several advantages over manually defined keys (manual keying):

- Eliminates manual configuration of keys

- Allows you to specify a lifetime for IPSec security association

- Allows encryption keys to change during IPSec sessions

- Supports the use of public key-based authentication and CAs, making IPSec scalable

- Allows dynamic authentication of peers

IKE negotiation has two phases:

1. **Phase One** The two peers negotiate and set up a bidirectional ISAKMP SA which they then use to handle phase-two negotiation. One such SA between a pairs of peers can handle negotiations for multiple IPSec SAs.

2. **Phase Two** Using the ISAKMP SA, the peers negotiate IPSec (ESP and/or AH) as required. IPSec SAs are unidirectional (a different key is used in each direction) and are always negotiated in pairs to handle two-way traffic. There may be more than one pair defined between two peers.

Both of these phases use the UDP protocol and port 500 for their negotiations. The actual IPSec SAs use the ESP or AH protocols.

In selecting a suitable key management protocol for IPSec, the IETF considered several different protocols and eventually chose IKE. Sun's Simple Key management for Internet Protocols (SKIP) seemed to be a favorite, but was eventually not chosen. In an effort to be standards-compliant, Sun is now also offering IKE support. Another protocol, Photorus, described in RFC 2522 and RFC 2523, was considered too experimental.

> **NOTE**
>
> Don't confuse IPSec SAs with IKE SAs. IKE SAs create the tunnel used by IPSec SAs. There is only one IKE SA between two devices, but there can be multiple IPSec SAs for the same IKE SA.

Authentication Methods

IPSec peers must be authenticated to each other. The peers must agree on a common authentication protocol through a negotiation process.

Multiple authentication methods are supported.

- **Preshared keys** The same key is preconfigured in each device. The peers authenticate each other by computing and sending a keyed hash of data that includes the preshared key. If the receiving side can independently recreate the same hash using its preshared key, it knows that both parties must share the same key.

- **Public key encryption** Each party generates a pseudo-random number (nonce) and encrypts it in the other party's public key. The parties authenticate each other by computing a keyed hash containing the other peer's nonce, decrypted with the local private key as well as other publicly and privately available information.

- **Digital signatures** Each device digitally signs a set of data and sends it to the other party. This method is similar to the public key cryptography one, except that it provides nonrepudiation (the ability for a third-party to prove that a communication between the two parties took place).

IKE and Certificate Authorities

Even with IKE, the keys for enabling the strong security offered by IPSec become difficult to manage in larger secure networks. Digital certificates together with trusted third-party CAs offer a mechanism to scale IPSec to the Internet.

IKE interoperates with the X.509 certificate standard. X.509 certificates, are the equivalent of digital ID cards and are the building block with which CAs like Verisign and Entrust authenticate IPSec connections.

Cisco and VeriSign, Inc. co-developed a certificate management protocol called Certificate Enrollment Protocol (CEP). CEP is an early implementation of Certificate Request Syntax (CRS), an emerging standard proposed by the IETF. CEP specifies how a device communicates with a CA, including how to retrieve the CA's public key, how to enroll a device with the CA, and how to retrieve a Certificate Revocation List (CRL). CEP uses RSA's PKCS (public key cryptography standards) 7 and 10 as key technologies. The IETF's Public Key Infrastructure Working Group is working to standardize a protocol for these functions.

Figure 8.12 shows an example of multiple routers in a mesh topology where key management is not performed via a CA. Every time a new router is added, keys need to be created between each of the participating IPSec routers.

Figure 8.12 Key Management without CA

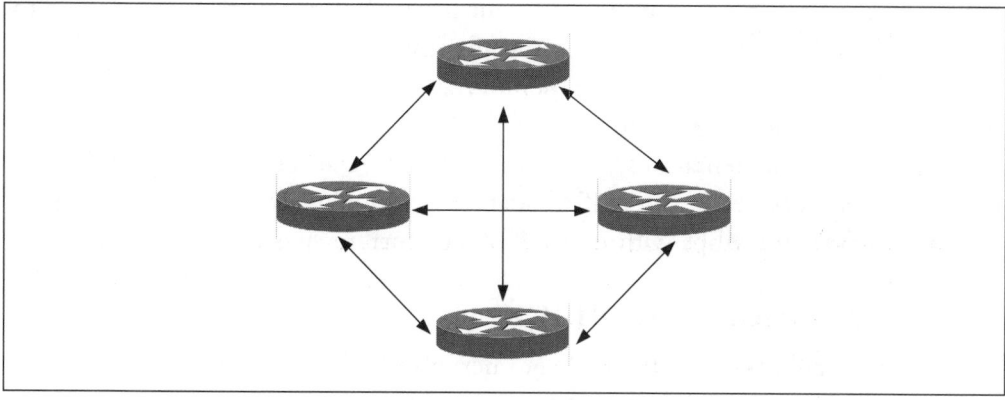

As an example, if you wanted to add an additional router to Figure 8.12, four additional two-part keys would be required to add just a single encryption router. The key's numbers grow exponentially as you add more routers and the configuration and management of these keys becomes problematic. CAs offer an ideal solution to such an environment.

Figure 8.13 shows a typical scenario where key management is performed through a CA.

Figure 8.13 Key Management with CA

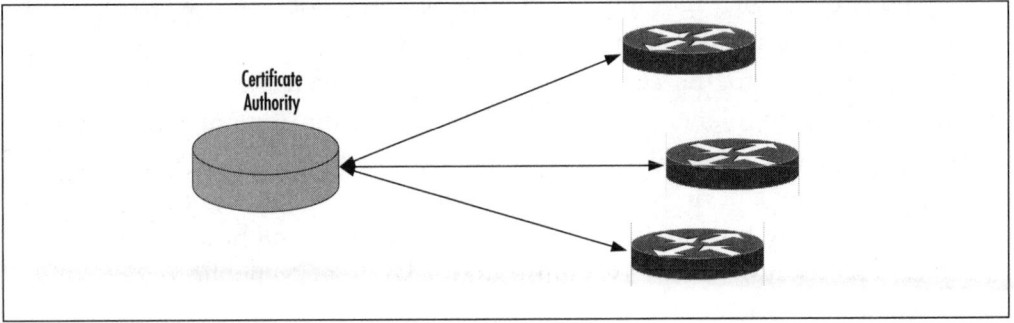

IPSec limitations

One of the few limitations of IPSec is that it only supports unicast IP datagrams. No support for multicasts or broadcasts is currently provided.

Network Performance

IPSec can have a significant impact on your network performance. The degree to which it does so is dependant on the specific implementation. Ensuring that the routers and firewalls have sufficient memory and processor capacity helps in minimizing performance degradation.

For larger implementations, hardware-based IPSec acceleration provided by the Integrated Services Adapter (ISA) adapter is strongly advised. The ISA can encrypt traffic at 90 Mbps with up to 2000 concurrent sites or users.

Network Troubleshooting

One of the drawbacks of network layer encryption is that it does complicate network troubleshooting and debugging.

Intrusion detection, such as that offered by the Cisco Secure Intrusion Detection System (IDS) is also affected by IPSec. In order to determine if suspicious activity is occurring, the Cisco Secure IDS sensor analyzes both the packet header information and packet data information. If these are encrypted by IPSec, then the sensor cannot analyze the packet and determine if the packet contains any suspicious information.

IPSec and Cisco Encryption Technology

Prior to IPSec's development and standardization, Cisco developed a proprietary network layer encryption technology called Cisco Encryption Technology (CET). CET was first introduced in IOS release 11.2 and was based on the 40- and 56-bit DES encryption algorithm.

CET has now largely been replaced by the standards-based IPSec, although Cisco still maintains support for it. While specific CET images will no longer be available in release 12.1, CET will continue to be included as part of the IPSec images (CET End-of-Life announced in Cisco Product Bulletin, No. 1118).

In many aspects, CET is very similar to IPSec. IPSec does however have some major advantages over CET, namely:

- **Multivendor interoperability** Since IPSec is standardized, it interoperates not only with other vendors' equipment, but also on a variety of platforms such as routers, firewalls, and hosts.

- **Scalability** IPSec deploys the IKE key management technique, and includes support for CAs that allow virtually unlimited scalability.

- **Data authentication** CET provides only for data confidentiality.

- **Anti-replay** CET does not support this important feature and is vulnerable to this form of attack.

- **Stronger encryption** CET only supports 40- and 56-bit DES, which is now considered unsecure.

- **Host implementations** CET only supports router-to-router implementations. It does, however, have an advantages over IPSec:

  - **Speed** It's faster than IPSec; however, this is mainly because it isn't as thorough. For instance, CET does not offer per-packet data authentication, nor packet expansion.

Like L2F and many other technologies developed by Cisco, CET is another prime example of where Cisco has developed a technology, worked with the Internet community to standardize it and then replaced it's own proprietary solution with the standardized version.

Configuring Cisco IPSec

The following examples show how IPSec can be used to encrypt and protect network traffic between two networks. The first example demonstrates IPSec manual keying, while the second shows IPSec over a GRE Tunnel.

NOTE

When using access-lists or any form of filtering, remember that IKE uses UDP port 500 and IPSec ESP and AH use protocol numbers 50 and 51. These ports and protocols must not be blocked.

In very simplified terms IPSec is configured by:

1. Creating a SA (either manually or by using IKE)
2. Defining the SPD (access-lists which specify which traffic is to be secured)
3. Applying these access lists to an interface by way of crypto map sets

IPSec Manual Keying Configuration

The following example illustrates the use of IPSec Manual Keying to encrypt TCP/IP traffic between the 10.1.1.0/24 and 10.1.3.0/24 networks.

If a host on network 10.1.1.x wants to send a packet to a host on network 10.1.3.x, the packet from host 10.1.1.x is sent in cleartext to the Capetown router. The Capetown router uses the IPSec tunnel between the Capetown and London router to encrypt the packet and sends it to the London router that decrypts the packet and sends it to the host on network 10.1.3.x in cleartext. Cisco 3640s with IOS release 11.3(8)T1 (Enterprise Plus IPSec 56 feature set) were used for this example.

NOTE

In IOS release 12.0, the crypto map statement *set security-association inbound...* has changed to *set session-key inbound...*

In this example (Figure 8.14), DES was used as the encryption cipher. This was mainly done to accommodate an international audience, where export restrictions might limit the availability of strong encryption. Please note that DES is no longer considered secure and, wherever possible, a stronger cipher such as 3DES should be used.

Figure 8.14 Network Diagram for IPSec Manual Keying

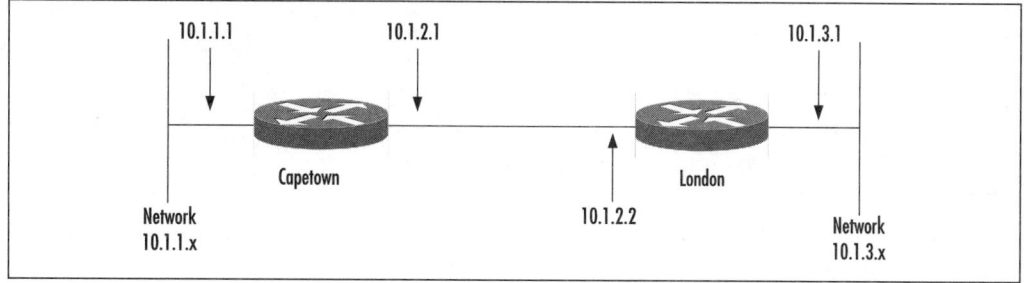

Here is the configuration of the Capetown router:

```
version 11.3
service timestamps debug uptime
service timestamps log uptime
no service password-encryption
!
hostname capetown
!
enable password a
!
ip subnet-zero
!
!
no crypto isakmp enable
!
!
crypto ipsec transform-set encrypt-des esp-des
!
 !
 crypto map test 8 ipsec-manual
 set peer 10.1.2.2
 set security-association inbound esp 1000 cipher ****************
    authenticator 01
```

```
   set security-association outbound esp 1001 cipher ****************
      authenticator 01
  set transform-set encrypt-des
  match address 100
 !
 !
 !
interface Serial0/0
  ip address 10.1.2.1 255.255.255.0
  no ip route-cache
  no ip mroute-cache
  crypto map test
 !
interface Serial0/1
  no ip address
  shutdown
 !
interface Serial0/2
  no ip address
  shutdown
 !
interface Serial0/3
  no ip address
  shutdown
 !
interface Ethernet1/0
  ip address 10.1.1.1 255.255.255.0
 !
ip classless
ip route 0.0.0.0 0.0.0.0 10.1.2.2
 !
access-list 100 permit ip 10.1.1.0 0.0.0.255 10.1.3.0 0.0.0.255
 !
 !
line con 0
line aux 0
line vty 0 4
```

```
 login
 !
end
```

The following is the configuration of the London router:

```
version 11.3
service timestamps debug uptime
service timestamps log uptime
no service password-encryption
!
hostname london
!
enable password a
!
ip subnet-zero
!
!
no crypto isakmp enable
!
!
crypto ipsec transform-set encrypt-des esp-des
!
  !
 crypto map test 8 ipsec-manual
 set peer 10.1.2.1
 set security-association inbound esp 1001 cipher ***************
     authenticator 01
 set security-association outbound esp 1000 cipher ***************
     authenticator 01
 set transform-set encrypt-des
 match address 100
!
!
!
interface Ethernet0/0
 ip address 10.1.3.1 255.255.255.0
!
```

```
interface Serial0/0
 ip address 10.1.2.2 255.255.255.0
 no ip route-cache
 no ip mroute-cache
 no fair-queue
 crypto map test
!
interface Serial0/1
 no ip address
 shutdown
!
ip classless
ip route 0.0.0.0 0.0.0.0 10.1.2.1
!
access-list 100 permit ip 10.1.3.0 0.0.0.255 10.1.1.0 0.0.0.255
!
!
line con 0
line aux 0
line vty 0 4
 login
!
end
```

To verify and debug the preceding example, use the *show crypto engine connections active* and *show crypto ipsec sa* commands.

```
capetown#show crypto engine connections active
ID   Interface   IP-Address   State   Algorithm     Encrypt   Decrypt
1    Serial0/0   10.1.2.1     set     DES_56_CBC    235       0
2    Serial0/0   10.1.2.1     set     DES_56_CBC    0         236
capetown#
```

The command *show crypto engine connections active* shows active encryption connections for all crypto engines. Of particular interest are the encrypt counters that show encryption is working.

```
capetown#show crypto ipsec sa

interface: Serial0/0
```

```
 Crypto map tag: test, local addr. 10.1.2.1


local  ident (addr/mask/prot/port): (10.1.1.0/255.255.255.0/0/0)
remote ident (addr/mask/prot/port): (10.1.3.0/255.255.255.0/0/0)
current_peer: 10.1.2.2
  PERMIT, flags={origin_is_acl,}
 #pkts encaps: 235, #pkts encrypt: 235, #pkts digest 0
 #pkts decaps: 236, #pkts decrypt: 236, #pkts verify 0
 #send errors 0, #recv errors 0


  local crypto endpt.: 10.1.2.1, remote crypto endpt.: 10.1.2.2
  path mtu 1500, media mtu 1500
  current outbound spi: 3E9


  inbound esp sas:
   spi: 0x3E8(1000)
     transform: esp-des ,
     in use settings ={Tunnel, }
     slot: 0, conn id: 2, crypto map: test
     no sa timing
     IV size: 8 bytes
     replay detection support: N



  inbound ah sas:



  outbound esp sas:
   spi: 0x3E9(1001)
     transform: esp-des ,
     in use settings ={Tunnel, }
     slot: 0, conn id: 1, crypto map: test
     no sa timing
     IV size: 8 bytes
     replay detection support: N
```

```
outbound ah sas:
```

```
capetown#
```

The *show crypto ipsec sa* command shows the settings used by current security associations. Of particular interest are local and remote crypto endpoints, the transform set used (encryption algorithm), as well as statistics of the packets encrypted and decrypted.

IPSec over GRE Tunnel Configuration

Figure 8.15 illustrates the use of IPSec over a GRE Tunnel to encrypt non-IP-based traffic. In this example, Novell's Internetwork Packet Exchange (IPX) was used, but the same example holds true for other non-IP-based protocols such as AppleTalk.

Cisco 3640s with IOS release 11.3(8)T1 (Enterprise Plus IPSec 56 feature set) were used for this example. DES was used as the encryption cipher. This was mainly done to accommodate an international audience, where export restrictions might limit the availability of strong encryption. Please note that DES is no longer considered secure and wherever possible, a stronger cipher such as 3DES or AES should be used.

Figure 8.15 Network Diagram for IPSec over a GRE Tunnel

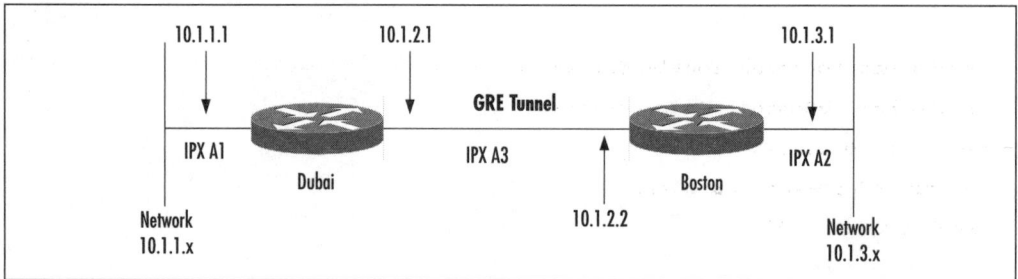

Cisco 3640s with IOS release 11.3(8)T1 (Enterprise Plus IPSec 56 feature set) were used for this example. DES was used as the encryption cipher. This was mainly done to accommodate an international audience, where export restrictions might limit the availability of strong encryption. Please note that DES is no longer considered secure and wherever possible, a stronger cipher such as 3DES or AES should be used.

The following is the configuration of the Dubai router:

```
version 11.3
service timestamps debug uptime
service timestamps log uptime
no service password-encryption
!
hostname dubai
!
!
ip subnet-zero
ipx routing 0001.425f.9391
!
!
!
crypto isakmp policy 10
 authentication pre-share
 group 2
 lifetime 3600
crypto isakmp key ****** address 10.1.5.1
!
!
crypto ipsec transform-set tunnelset esp-des esp-md5-hmac
!
  !
 crypto map toBoston local-address Loopback0
 crypto map toBoston 10 ipsec-isakmp
 set peer 10.1.5.1
 set transform-set tunnelset
 match address 101
!
!
!
interface Loopback0
 ip address 10.1.4.1 255.255.255.0
!
interface Tunnel0
 no ip address
 no ip route-cache
```

```
 no ip mroute-cache
 ipx network A3
 tunnel source Serial0/0
 tunnel destination 10.1.2.2
 crypto map toBoston
!
interface Serial0/0
 ip address 10.1.2.1 255.255.255.0
 no ip route-cache
 no ip mroute-cache
 no fair-queue
 crypto map toBoston
!
interface Serial0/1
 no ip address
 shutdown
!
interface Serial0/2
 no ip address
 shutdown
!
interface Serial0/3
 no ip address
 shutdown
!
interface Ethernet1/0
 ip address 10.1.1.1 255.255.255.0
 ipx network A1
!
ip classless
ip route 0.0.0.0 0.0.0.0 10.1.2.2
!
access-list 101 permit gre host 10.1.2.1 host 10.1.2.2
!
!
!
!
```

```
!
line con 0
line aux 0
line vty 0 4
 login
!
end
```

Here is the configuration of the Boston router:

```
version 11.3
service timestamps debug uptime
service timestamps log uptime
no service password-encryption
!
hostname boston
!
!
ip subnet-zero
ipx routing 0001.42a5.79a1
!
!
!
crypto isakmp policy 10
 authentication pre-share
 group 2
 lifetime 3600
crypto isakmp key ****** address 10.1.4.1
!
!
crypto ipsec transform-set tunnelset esp-des esp-md5-hmac
!
 !
 crypto map toDubai local-address Loopback0
 crypto map toDubai 10 ipsec-isakmp
 set peer 10.1.4.1
 set transform-set tunnelset
 match address 101
```

```
!
!
!
interface Loopback0
 ip address 10.1.5.1 255.255.255.0
!
interface Tunnel0
 no ip address
 no ip route-cache
 no ip mroute-cache
 ipx network A3
 tunnel source Serial0/0
 tunnel destination 10.1.2.1
 crypto map toDubai
!
interface Ethernet0/0
 ip address 10.1.3.1 255.255.255.0
 ipx network A2
!
interface Serial0/0
 ip address 10.1.2.2 255.255.255.0
 no ip route-cache
 no ip mroute-cache
 no fair-queue
 crypto map toDubai
!
interface Serial0/1
 no ip address
 shutdown
!
ip classless
ip route 0.0.0.0 0.0.0.0 10.1.2.1
!
access-list 101 permit gre host 10.1.2.2 host 10.1.2.1
!
!
!
```

```
!
!
line con 0
line aux 0
line vty 0 4
 login
!
end
```

To verify and debug the preceding example, use the *show crypto engine connections active, show ipx route ping ipx* …, and *show crypto ipsec sa* commands.

```
dubai#show crypto engine connections active
ID    Interface    IP-Address    State  Algorithm              Encrypt  Decrypt
17    no idb       no address    set    DES_56_CBC                0        0
22    Tunnel0      unassigned    set    HMAC_MD5+DES_56_CB 0             20
23    Tunnel0      unassigned    set    HMAC_MD5+DES_56_CB 20           0
dubai#
```

The command *show crypto engine connections active* displays all active encryption connections for all crypto engines. Of particular interest are the encrypt counters that show that the encryption is working.

```
dubai#show ipx route
Codes: C - Connected primary network,
       c - Connected secondary network
       S - Static
       F - Floating static
       L - Local (internal)
       W - IPXWAN
       R - RIP
       E - EIGRP
       N - NLSP
       X - External
       A - Aggregate
       s - seconds
       u - uses
       U - Per-user static
```

```
3 Total IPX routes. Up to 1 parallel paths and 16 hops allowed.

No default route known.

C         A1 (NOVELL-ETHER),    Et1/0
C         A3 (TUNNEL),          Tu0
R         A2 [151/01] via       A3.0001.42a5.79a1,    27s, Tu0
dubai#
```

The *show ipx route* command displays the ipx routing table and shows that network A2 is known via RIP through Tunnel 0. IPX traffic between network A1 and A2 is being encapsulated in TCP/IP and tunneled through the network.

```
dubai#ping ipx a2.0001.42a5.79a1
Type escape sequence to abort.
Sending 5, 100-byte IPX cisco Echoes to A2.0001.42a5.79a1, timeout is
    2 seconds:
!!!!!
Success rate is 100 percent (5/5), round-trip min/avg/max = 8/8/8 ms
dubai#
```

The *ping ipx …* command proves that the remote IPX device is accessible through the encrypted IPSec Tunnel interface. The output of *show crypto engine connections active* and *show crypto ipsec sa* will confirm that five packets have been encrypted—the five IPX ping packets.

```
dubai#show crypto ipsec sa

interface: Tunnel0
    Crypto map tag: toBoston, local addr. 10.1.4.1

    local  ident (addr/mask/prot/port): (10.1.2.1/255.255.255.255/47/0)
    remote ident (addr/mask/prot/port): (10.1.2.2/255.255.255.255/47/0)
    current_peer: 10.1.5.1
      PERMIT, flags={origin_is_acl,}
    #pkts encaps: 57, #pkts encrypt: 57, #pkts digest 57
    #pkts decaps: 57, #pkts decrypt: 57, #pkts verify 57
    #send errors 1, #recv errors 0
```

```
      local crypto endpt.: 10.1.4.1, remote crypto endpt.: 10.1.5.1
      path mtu 1514, media mtu 1514
      current outbound spi: 71313FA


      inbound esp sas:
       spi: 0x111214EE(286397678)
          transform: esp-des esp-md5-hmac ,
          in use settings ={Tunnel, }
          slot: 0, conn id: 22, crypto map: toBoston
          sa timing: remaining key lifetime (k/sec): (4607992/2989)
          IV size: 8 bytes
          replay detection support: Y



      inbound ah sas:



      outbound esp sas:
       spi: 0x71313FA(118690810)
          transform: esp-des esp-md5-hmac ,
          in use settings ={Tunnel, }
          slot: 0, conn id: 23, crypto map: toBoston
          sa timing: remaining key lifetime (k/sec): (4607992/2989)
          IV size: 8 bytes
          replay detection support: Y



      outbound ah sas:



interface: Serial0/0
     Crypto map tag: toBoston, local addr. 10.1.4.1


    local  ident (addr/mask/prot/port): (10.1.2.1/255.255.255.255/47/0)
    remote ident (addr/mask/prot/port): (10.1.2.2/255.255.255.255/47/0)
    current_peer: 10.1.5.1
```

```
    PERMIT, flags={origin_is_acl,}
  #pkts encaps: 57, #pkts encrypt: 57, #pkts digest 57
  #pkts decaps: 57, #pkts decrypt: 57, #pkts verify 57
  #send errors 1, #recv errors 0


   local crypto endpt.: 10.1.4.1, remote crypto endpt.: 10.1.5.1
   path mtu 1514, media mtu 1514
   current outbound spi: 71313FA


   inbound esp sas:
    spi: 0x111214EE(286397678)
       transform: esp-des esp-md5-hmac ,
       in use settings ={Tunnel, }
       slot: 0, conn id: 22, crypto map: toBoston
       sa timing: remaining key lifetime (k/sec): (4607992/2989)
       IV size: 8 bytes
       replay detection support: Y



   inbound ah sas:



   outbound esp sas:
    spi: 0x71313FA(118690810)
       transform: esp-des esp-md5-hmac ,
       in use settings ={Tunnel, }
       slot: 0, conn id: 23, crypto map: toBoston
       sa timing: remaining key lifetime (k/sec): (4607992/2989)
       IV size: 8 bytes
       replay detection support: Y



   outbound ah sas:

dubai#
```

Here, the *show crypto ipsec sa* shows the settings used by current security associations. Of particular interest are local and remote crypto endpoints, the transform set used (encryption algorithm), as well as the statistics of the packets encrypted and decrypted.

Connecting IPSec Clients to Cisco IPSec

A common design is to use IPSec between an IPSec-aware host client (such as a remote PC) and an IPSec router or firewall.

This means that the host client needs to be IPSec-aware. This can be achieved though either the host client's operating system being IPSec-aware or through a third-party IPSec software client.

Cisco Secure VPN Client

The Cisco VPN Client is a software program that runs on Windows, Linux, and Mac OS X-based PCs. The Cisco VPN Client on a remote PC communicates with a Cisco VPN device on an enterprise network, or with an ISP creates a secure connection over the Internet. Through this connection, you can access a private network as if you were an onsite user, hallmarks of a virtual private network.

Cisco Secure VPN Client is a software program that provides IPSec support to Windows 95, Windows 98, and Windows NT operating systems which do not have native IPSec support. It does this by integrating into the existing IP stack.

The latest Windows release is Cisco Secure VPN Client 3.5.1 which is a component of the Cisco Secure VPN software. Version 3.5.1 also supports Linux, Solaris, and Mac OS X.

New Feature in Release 3.5.1

There is only one new feature in Release 3.5.1:

■ **Zone Lab Support** This feature maintains policies for the firewall on remote VPN Client PCs.

New Features in Release 3.5

The following are new features in Release 3.5:

■ **Integrated Firewall** The VPN Client on the Windows platform will include a stateful firewall integrated within. This firewall will be transparent to the user.

■ **Centralized Protection Policy (CPP) on a VPN Concentrator** The Concentrator may be configured for CPP, in which an administrator may set up firewall rules on the Concentrator then send them to the VPN Clients.

- **Support for Personal Firewalls** If there were rules configured on the firewall that are on the VPN Client PC, the VPN Client polls the firewall to determine whether the firewall software is still running on the PC.

- **Smart Card** The VPN Client does support authentication using digital certificates. This is by way of electronic tokens and smart cards.

- **IPSec over TCP** IPSec over TCP encapsulates encrypted data traffic in each TCP packet. This will allow the VPN Concentrator to operate in a way in which ESP and IKE cannot.

Windows 2000

The Microsoft Windows 2000 operating system (Server, Professional, Advanced Server, and Datacenter Server versions) now has native support for IPSec, without the use of any third-party software. Full support of industry IETF standards is provided.

Microsoft makes available a tool called IP Security Monitor that administrators can use to confirm whether IPSec communications are successfully secured. The tool shows how many packets have been sent over the AH or ESP security protocols and how many security associations and keys have been generated since the computer was last started.

IP Security Monitor also indicates whether or not IPSec is enabled in a given computer. This information is located in the lower-right corner of the window. To start IP Security Monitor, click **Start | Run**, type **ipsecmon** and then click **OK**.

For remote Windows 2000 clients to use IPSec across a public IP network on a dial-up basis, the use of L2TP or Microsoft's PPTP protocol are required to establish a tunnel through the public IP network. Once the tunnel is established, IPSec can be used in transport mode to secure communications through the tunnel.

Linux FreeS/WAN

The Secure Wide Area Network project or FreeS/WAN aims to make IPSec freely available on Linux platforms. It does so by providing free source code for IPSec. The project's official Web site can be found at www.freeswan.org.

It all started with John Gilmore, the founder and main driving force behind FreeS/WAN, who wanted to make the Internet more secure and protect traffic against wiretapping.

To avoid export limitations imposed by the U.S. Government of cryptographic products, FreeS/WAN has been completely developed and maintained outside of the United States of America. As a result, the strong encryption supported by FreeS/WAN is exportable.

Those interested in large scale FreeS/WAN implementations should read a paper called "Moat: a Virtual Private Network Appliance and Services Platform" that discusses a large VPN deployment using FreeS/WAN. It was written by John S. Denker, Steven M. Bellovin, Hugh Daniel, Nancy L. Mintz, Tom Killian, and Mark A. Plotnick, and is available for download from www.research.att.com/~smb/papers/index.html.

Summary

VPN will help scale network security in a way that will be more manageable and reliable. With the use of IPSec within the VPN, you are addressing the concerns of network security from end to end. This provides a secure means for the transmission of data to and from your intended source.

Since VPNs are so widely used now by companies for WANs to Remote Access, we should soon see them in all wireless devices. Wireless is quickly becoming as secure as a remote user using a VPN to connect to a corporate LAN.

With Cisco leading the way in the use of IPSec with their line of IOS Routers, PIX firewalls, and VPN Concentrators, network security breaches should be reduced. With the multivendor interoperability possibilities that Cisco is currently working on, you will see VPNs being widely used by all network administrators.

Solutions Fast Track

Overview of the Different VPN Technologies

☑ A *peer* VPN model is one in which the path determination at the network layer is done on a hop-by-hop basis.

☑ An *overlay* VPN model is one in which path determination at the network layer is done on a "cut-through" basis to another edge node (customer site).

☑ Link layer VPNs are implemented at link layer (Layer 2) of the OSI Reference model.

Layer 2 Transport Protocol

☑ Layer 2 Transport Protocol (L2TP) is a key building block for VPNs in the dial access space.

☑ It is important to understand that the client host gets an IP address from the remote network.

☑ L2TP is an extension to Point-to-Point Protocol (PPP) and is vendor interoperable.

IPSec

☑ IPSec, or Internet Protocol Security as it's known by its full name, was developed by the IETF to address the issue of network layer security.

☑ Authentication only is provided through the Authentication Header (AH) protocol.

☑ Authentication and confidentiality (encryption) are provided through the Encapsulating Security Payload (ESP) protocol.

☑ Key exchange is provided either manually or through the Internet Key Exchange (IKE) protocol.

☑ IPSec Security Associations (SAs) define how two or more IPSec parties will use security services in the context of a particular security protocol (AH or ESP) to communicate securely on behalf of a particular flow.

Frequently Asked Questions

The following Frequently Asked Questions, answered by the authors of this book, are designed to both measure your understanding of the concepts presented in this chapter and to assist you with real-life implementation of these concepts. To have your questions about this chapter answered by the author, browse to **www.syngress.com/solutions** and click on the **"Ask the Author"** form.

Q: In which IOS release was IPSec first made available?

A: IPSec was first introduced in IOS version 11.3(3)T.

Q: Which two main protocols does IPSec consist of?

A: Authentications Header (AH) and Encapsulating Security Protocol (ESP). AH provides data authentication and integrity for IP packets passed between two different systems. ESP is a security protocol used to provide confidentiality (such as encryption), data origin authentication, integrity and optional anti-replay.

Q: I need to provide authentication between two IPSec peers. What negotiates the IPSec Security Associations between those two peers?

A: IKE is a protocol that provides authentication of the IPSec peers, negotiation of IKE and IPSec Security Associations (SA). It also establishes keys for encryption algorithms used by IPSec.

Q: If I am asked to enable IKE while on a Cisco Router or PIX firewall, which command should I use?

A: *crypto isakmp enable*

Q: In which phase does IKE negotiate IPSec SA parameters and set up matching IPSec SAs in the peer?

A: IKE Phase Two.

Q: I am designing a VPN for my company. What are the different types of VPNs and what do they do?

A: The three types of VPNs are:

- **Access VPN** Provides remote access to an enterprise customer's intranet or extranet over a shared infrastructure. Access VPNs use analog, dial, ISDN, digital subscriber line, mobile IP, and different cable technologies.

- **Intranet VPN** Links enterprise customer headquarters, remote offices, and branch offices to an internal network over a shared infrastructure using dedicated connections.

- **Extranet VPN** Links outside customers, suppliers, partners, or communities of interest to an enterprise customer's network over a shared infrastructure using dedicated connections.

## Chapter 9

Cisco Authentication, Authorization, and Accounting Mechanisms

Solutions in this chapter:

- Cisco AAA Overview

- Cisco AAA Mechanisms

- Authentication Proxy

☑ Summary

☑ Solutions Fast Track

☑ Frequently Asked Questions

Introduction

Authentication, authorization, and accounting (AAA) is an architectural framework for providing the independent but related functions of authentication, authorization, and accounting, and is critical to providing secure remote access to both network devices and resources. The AAA framework typically consists of both a client and a server. The AAA client (for example, a router or network access server (NAS)) requests authentication, authorization, and/or accounting services from a AAA server (for instance, a UNIX or Windows server with appropriate software) that maintains databases containing the relevant AAA information.

Typically, an AAA framework is effective in three ways:

1. It provides centralized authentication for the administration of a large number of routers. An example is a small- to medium-sized business that has a relatively high ratio of routers to network administrators. Centralized authentication would ease the administrative burden of the routers, but because the number of administrators is low, centralized authorization and accounting would not be beneficial.

2. It provides flexible authorization capabilities. An example is a global enterprise that has a large number of both routers and administrators. Administrative duties might be divided along operational and configuration lines such that the implementation of centralized authorization would be an effective addition to centralization authentication.

3. It provides relevant usage or billing information. An example is a service provider that charges customers based on network usage statistics. In this case, the centralized authentication and authorization would be an effective means of supporting the router and NAS administration, while centralized accounting would provide the business with network usage information for billing.

Examples of AAA happen in every day life outside of computers and Cisco devices. For instance, when you go to an ATM machine to withdraw money, you must first insert your bank card and enter your personal identification number (PIN). At this point, you are now authenticating yourself as someone who has the authority to withdraw money. If both your card and PIN are valid, you are successfully authenticated and can now continue the task of withdrawing money. If you have entered an incorrect PIN number, or your card has been damaged (or stolen) and the criteria cannot be validated, you will not be able to continue.

Once authenticated you will be permitted to perform certain actions, such as withdraw, deposit, check your balance on various accounts, and so on. Based on your identity (your bank card and your PIN), you have been preauthorized to perform certain functions, which include withdrawing your hard-earned money. Finally, once you have completed the tasks in which you are authorized to perform, you are then provided with a statement describing your transactions, as well as the remaining balance in your account. The bank will also record your transactions for accounting purposes.

This chapter provides an overview of AAA and its benefits, a description of the RADIUS, TACACS+, and Kerberos security protocols, and a discussion (with examples) of how to configure each of the AAA services on Cisco IOS devices.

Cisco AAA Overview

AAA is comprised of the three independent but related functions of authentication, authorization, and accounting, defined in the following:

- Authentication is the process of identifying and authenticating a user prior to allowing access to network devices and services. User identification and authentication is critical for the accuracy of the authorization and accounting functions.

- Authorization is the process of determining a user's privileges and access rights after they have been authenticated.

- Accounting is the process of recording user activities for accountability, billing, auditing, or reporting purposes.

In some cases, it may not be necessary to implement all AAA mechanisms. For example, if a company simply wishes to authenticate users when they access a certain resource, authentication would be the only element needed. If a company wishes to create an audit trail to reference which users logged in to the network at what times, authentication and accounting will be needed. Typically, AAA is used in remote access scenarios such as end users dialing into an Internet service provider (ISP) to access the Internet, or dialing into their company LAN to access resources. Figure 9.1 illustrates a common implementation of AAA.

In Figure 9.1, Client A is attempting to access the Web site, www.syngress.com. Client A must first connect to their local ISP to gain access to the Internet. When Client A connects to the ISP, they are then prompted for a set of logon credentials (authentication) by the NAS before they can fully access the Internet.

Figure 9.1 An AAA ISP Implementation Example

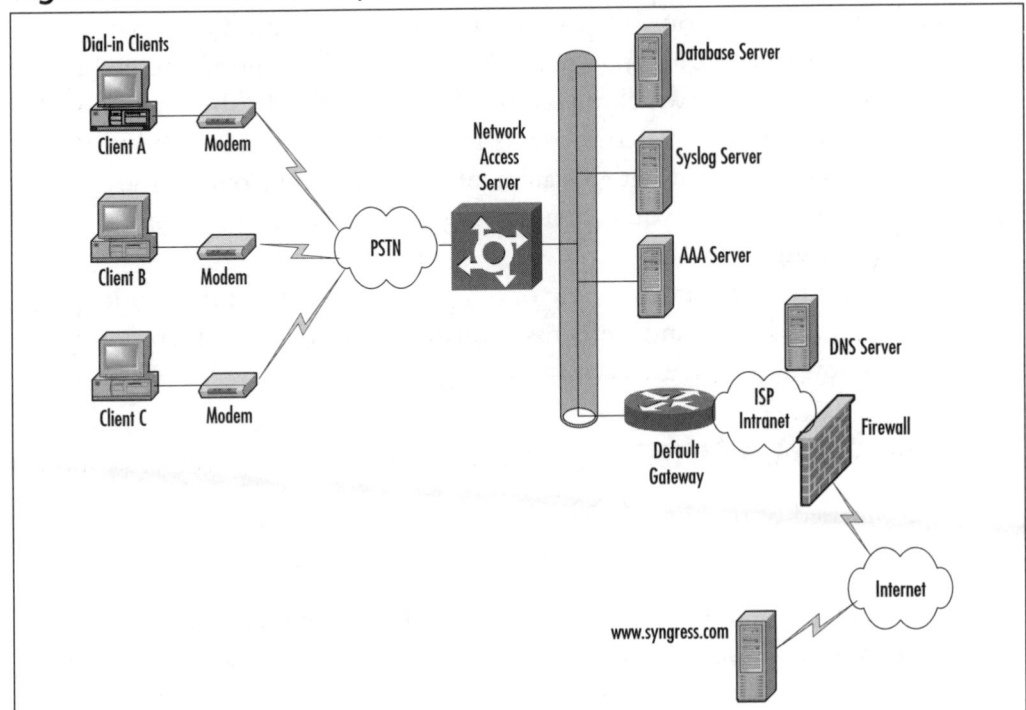

A NAS is a device that usually has interfaces connected to both the backbone and to the Telco (analog or ISDN modems) and receives calls from remote clients who wish to access the backbone via dial-up services. A security server is typically a device such as a Windows NT, UNIX, or Solaris server that is running TACACS+, RADIUS, or another service that enforces security. In Figure 9.1, the AAA server and the syslog server are examples of security servers. Once they have entered their credentials and the AAA server has validated them, if the security policy permits them to use the Internet (authorization), they can now connect to the desired Web site (www.syngress.com). As a policy, the ISP has decided to log all their customer connections on a syslog server (Accounting). This example illustrates all the elements of AAA: Authentication, Authorization, and Accounting.

AAA Authentication

Authentication is the process of identifying and authenticating a user, and typically relies on one or more of the following general methods:

- **Something the user knows** This approach is authentication by knowledge, where the identity is verified by something known only by the user. This is both the most common approach being used today and the weakest method of authentication. Examples include both the UNIX and Windows NT login process, where the user is prompted to enter a password. The integrity of this authentication process depends on the "something" being both secret and hard to guess, which is not something that is easily ensured.

- **Something the user possesses** This approach is authentication by possession, where the identity is verified by something possessed only by the user. This is becoming a more common authentication approach, and is used in most people's daily lives in the form of credit cards and ATM cards. The integrity of this authentication process depends on the "something" being unique and possessed only by the user. If it is lost or stolen, the authentication process is compromised. This form of authentication is typically stronger than something the user knows.

- **Something the user is** This approach is authentication by user characteristic, where the identity is verified by something that is unique *about* the user. This is known as the field of biometrics, and there are many products currently being developed and produced that use techniques such as fingerprint scans, retina scans, and voice analysis. ATM machines are beginning to be deployed with biometric authentication. This is the strongest approach to authentication that avoids the common problems with the other approaches (for example, the password being guessed, a card being lost or stolen); however, it is more difficult to implement.

Two-factor authentication uses a combination of two of the previous approaches to authenticate user identities. Typically, it is a combination of something the user possesses and something the user knows. A common example is the use of an ATM card (something possessed) and an associated PIN (something known) to access an account via an ATM machine.

Within the AAA framework, authentication occurs when a AAA client passes appropriate user credentials to a AAA server, and requests that the server authenticate the user. The AAA server will attempt to validate the credentials, and respond with either an accept or deny message. AAA authentication is typically used in the following scenarios:

- To control access to a network device such as a router or NAS
- To control access to network resources by remote users

Configuring & Implementing...

Remote Administration: Telnet versus Secure Shell

While the use of AAA authentication can provide centralized and robust authentication services for the management of network devices, there is still a risk related to authentication if remote administration is permitted. Many people use Telnet, which is a remote access protocol that allows you to have a "virtual terminal" (vty) over the network, to connect to the vty ports on a network device to administer and manage it remotely. The risk of using Telnet to remotely manage devices across a network is that all data is transmitted across the network in cleartext. There is no encryption protecting the passwords, so anyone with a network sniffer connected to the network in the right manner could capture them.

An alternative to Telnet is secure shell (SSH), which is a Telnet-like protocol that provides traffic encryption and authentication. Both the PIX firewall and Cisco IOS 12.1 (and later) support SSH (version 1). The IOS supports both a SSH server and an integrated SSH client. This means you can use SSH to connect to a SSH server on a network device to perform remote administration tasks, then use a SSH client on that network device to connect to the SSH server on another network device.

In order to use SSH to manage an IOS device, you need to:

- Ensure you have an image that supports it.

- Configure a host name and host domain on your device using the *hostname* and *ip domain-name* global configuration commands.

- Generate an RSA key pair for your device, which automatically enables SSH, using the *crypto key generate rsa* global configuration command.

- Configure the SSH server using the *ip ssh* global configuration command.

In addition, you need to download and install an SSH client onto the workstation you use to perform remote administration. The following sites let you download an SSH v1 client. Make sure you download a v1 client, not a v2 client:

- Windows 3.1, Windows CE, Windows 95, and Windows NT 4.0—download the free Tera Term Pro terminal emulator

Continued

> from the following site: hp.vector.co.jp/authors/VA002416/
> teraterm.html. Download the SSH extension for Tera Term Pro
> from the following site: www.zip.com.au/~roca/ttssh.html.
>
> - Linux, Solaris, OpenBSD, AIX, IRIX, HP/UX, FreeBSD, and
>   NetBSD—download the SSH v1 client from the following site:
>   www.openssh.com.
> - Macintosh (international users only)—download the Nifty
>   Telnet 1.1 SSH client from the following site:
>   www.lysator.liu.se/~jonasw/freeware/niftyssh/.

AAA Authorization

Authorization can be described as the act of permitting predefined rights or privileges to a user, group of users, system, or a process. Within the AAA framework, the client will query the AAA server to determine what actions a user is authorized to perform. The AAA server will then return a set of attribute-value (AV) pairs that defines the user's authorization. The client is then responsible for enforcing user access control based on those AV pairs. AAA authorization is typically used in the following scenarios:

- To provide authorization for actions attempted while logged into a network device.
- To provide authorization for attempts to use network services.

AAA Accounting

Accounting is a method which records (or accounts) the who, what, when, and where of an action that has taken place. Accounting enables you to track both the services that users are accessing and the amount of resources they are consuming. This data can later be used for accountability, network management, billing, auditing, and reporting purposes. Within the AAA framework, the client sends accounting records that consist of accounting AV pairs to the AAA server for centralized storage. An accounting record consists of accounting AV pairs

AAA Benefits

AAA provides a security mechanism to protect a company's resources by authenticating entities (such as individuals or system processes) prior to permitting access to those resources, determining and controlling what those entities can do once they have authenticated, and logging the actions that were performed for accountability, billing, auditing, reporting, or troubleshooting purposes.

AAA provides several benefits when implemented correctly. Picture a very large network consisting of over one hundred Cisco devices (routers, PIX firewalls) located around the world. By default, each Cisco device requires a password to access EXEC mode (if configured on the console or vty lines) as well as a password to enter privileged EXEC mode. In addition, if any of those devices function as a NAS, individual user accounts will require management as well. If good security practices are implemented, such as different passwords (changed regularly) on each device, then this quickly becomes an administrative nightmare.

Instead of configuring and managing accounts and passwords individually on each device, imagine if there was a centralized database in which user accounts were established, access rights defined, and logging information maintained. AAA is the framework that allows dynamic configuration of the type of authentication, authorization, and accounting that can be done on a per-entity (user, group, system, or system process) basis. You have the ability to define the type of authentication, authorization, and accounting you want by creating lists which define the method by which those functions will be performed, then applying those lists to specific services or interfaces. Cisco documentation refers to these lists as *method lists*. For the purpose of clarity, these lists will be referred to method lists throughout this chapter to avoid confusion.

AAA provides many benefits, such as increased flexibility and control, the ability to scale as networks grow larger, the use of standard protocols such as RADIUS, TACACS+, and Kerberos for authentication, and the ability to define backup AAA servers in case the primary one fails.

Cisco AAA Mechanisms

The previous section provided a high-level overview of AAA and identified the benefits of using it. This section describes how to implement AAA services on Cisco network devices.

As discussed previously, AAA is an architectural framework for providing the independent but related functions of authentication, authorization, and accounting. The AAA framework typically consists of both a client and a server. The AAA client (typically a router or NAS) requests authentication, authorization, and/or accounting services from an AAA server (typically a UNIX or

Windows server with appropriate software) that maintains databases containing the relevant AAA information.

You can configure most Cisco devices, including routers, access servers, firewalls, and virtual private network (VPN) gateways to act as an AAA client. You can configure network devices such as routers to request AAA services to protect the router itself from unauthorized access. You can configure network devices such as access servers and VPN gateways to request AAA services to protect the network itself from unauthorized access by users attempting to utilize the device as an access point. For most of these devices, you configure the desired AAA services through the creation of method lists that define both the AAA mechanisms to be used, and the order in which they should be used. You then apply the method lists to the desired interface or line.

NOTE

Cisco Secure Access Control Server (ACS) is an AAA server that runs on Windows and Solaris platforms, and supports protocols such as RADIUS and TACACS+. For more information about Cisco Secure ACS, please refer to Chapter 14.

To configure AAA on a Cisco network device, you need to perform the following high-level tasks:

1. Enable AAA by using the *aaa new-model* global configuration command.

2. If you are using a separate AAA server, configure the appropriate protocol parameters (for example, RADIUS, TACACS+, or Kerberos). These security protocols are discussed in the next section.

3. Define the appropriate method lists for the desired service (authentication, authorization, accounting).

4. Apply the method lists to the desired interface or line, if required.

Supported AAA Security Protocols

After you have enabled AAA on the device by using the *aaa new-model* global configuration command, you then need to configure the appropriate protocol parameters on the device. Cisco devices generally support the RADIUS, TACACS+, and Kerberos security protocols for use within an AAA mechanism. In the following paragraphs, each of these protocols is briefly described, and the relevant Cisco configuration commands for that protocol are identified and described.

As today's networks grow larger and larger, the need for remote dial-in access increases. In a company such as an ISP, managing NASs with modem pools for a large number of users can be an administrative headache. Since a pool of modems are typically how remote users will gain access to the Internet, great care and attention must be taken to secure them. In a company such as an ISP, their business revolves around granting access to the Internet for remote users. If the method in which remote users access the Internet is compromised, the ISP could lose a lot of money due to their customers being unable to use the services for which they have paid. Typically, users accounts will be stored in a single database which is then queried for authentication requests by a NAS or router.

RADIUS

The Remote Access Dial-In User Service (RADIUS) protocol was developed by Livingston Enterprises, Inc. as an access server authentication and accounting protocol. The RADIUS specification (RFC 2138 was made obsolete by RFC 2865 and updated in RFC 2868) is a proposed standard security protocol and RADIUS accounting standard (RFC 2139 was made obsolete by RFC2866 and updated in RFC2867) is informational and for accounting purposes.

From large enterprise networks such as ISPs to small networks consisting of a few users requiring remote access, RADIUS can be used as a security protocol on any size network. RADIUS uses less CPU overhead, and consumes less memory than TACACS+.

RADIUS is a client/server protocol. The RADIUS client is typically a NAS, router or switch, which requests a service such as authentication or authorization from the RADIUS server. A RADIUS server is usually a daemon running on a UNIX machine or service running on a Windows NT/2000 server machine. The daemon is the software, such as Cisco Secure ACS or another RADIUS or TACACS+ server program, that fulfills requests from RADIUS clients.

When authorization information is needed by the client, it queries the RADIUS server and passes the user credentials to the designated RADIUS server. The server then acts on the configuration information necessary for the client to deliver services to the user. A RADIUS server can also act as a proxy client to other RADIUS servers or other kinds of authentication servers. Figure 9.2 illustrates what happens when a user attempts to log in and authenticate to a NAS or router using RADIUS.

Figure 9.2 Authenticating with RADIUS

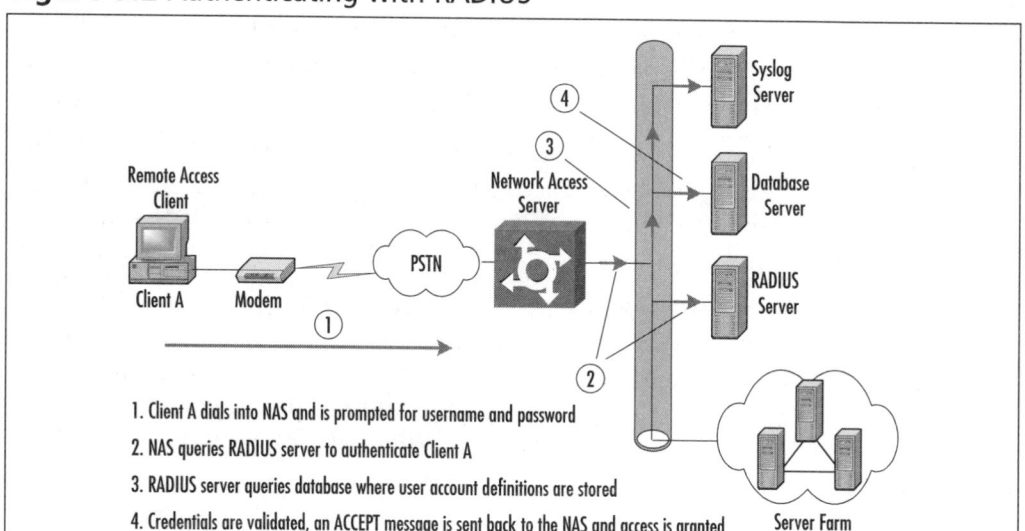

1. Client A dials into NAS and is prompted for username and password
2. NAS queries RADIUS server to authenticate Client A
3. RADIUS server queries database where user account definitions are stored
4. Credentials are validated, an ACCEPT message is sent back to the NAS and access is granted

1. The remote user dials into a NAS and is prompted for credentials such as a username and password by the NAS.

2. The username and encrypted password are sent from the RADIUS client (NAS) to the RADIUS server via the network.

3. The RADIUS server queries the database where user account definitions are stored.

4. The RADIUS server evaluates the credentials and replies with one of the following responses:

   - **REJECT** The user is not authenticated; they are prompted to re-enter the username and password, otherwise access is denied.

   - **ACCEPT** The user is authenticated.

   - **CHALLENGE** A challenge is issued by the RADIUS. The challenge may request additional information from the user.

   - **CHANGE PASSWORD** A request from the RADIUS server specifying that the user must change their current password.

Configuring RADIUS on Cisco

To use RADIUS as an AAA mechanism, you must specify the host running the RADIUS server software, and a secret text string that it shares with the RADIUS client. Table 9.1 identifies and describes the global configuration commands needed to define a RADIUS server and its parameters.

Table 9.1 RADIUS Global Configuration Commands

Command	Task
radius-server host {*hostname* | *ip-address*} [auth-port *port-number*] [acct-port *port-number*] [timeout *seconds*] [retransmit *retries*] [key *string*] [alias {*hostname* | *ip-address*}]	Specifies the IP address or host name of the remote RADIUS server, and optionally specifies additional parameters identified in the following. Use the *no* form of the command to delete a specified RADIUS server. *hostname* – enters the host name of the server to which RADIUS requests will be directed. -or- *ip-address* – enters the IP address of the server to which RADIUS requests will be directed. (optional) auth-port *port-number* – enters the UDP port for authentication requests (default is 1645). (optional) acct-port *port-number* – enters the UDP port for accounting requests (default is 1646). (optional) timeout *seconds* – designates the time interval to wait for the RADIUS server reply before retransmitting (1 to 1000). This setting overrides the global value of the *radius-server timeout* command. If no timeout value is specified, the global value is used. (optional) key *string* – the authentication and encryption key used between the router and the RADIUS daemon running on this RADIUS server. This key overrides the global setting of the *radius-server key* command. If no key string is specified, the global value is used. (optional) alias {*hostname* | *ip-address*} – allows up to eight aliases per line for any given RADIUS server.

Continued

Table 9.1 Continued

Command	Task
radius-server key {0 *string* | 7 *string* | *string*}	Sets the authentication and encryption key for all RADIUS communications between the device and the RADIUS server. To disable the key, use the *no* form of this command. 0 *string* – the 0 specifies that an unencrypted (*string*) key will follow. 7 *string* – the 7 specifies that a hidden key (*string*) will follow. *string* – the unencrypted (cleartext) shared key. The specified key must be the same on both the RADIUS client and RADIUS server.
radius-server retransmit *retries*	Specifies the number of times the router transmits each RADIUS request to the server before giving up (default is 3). To disable retransmission, use the *no* form of this command.
radius-server timeout *seconds*	Specifies the number of seconds a router waits for a reply to a RADIUS request before retransmitting the request (default is 5). To restore the default, use the *no* form of this command.
radius-server deadtime *minutes*	Specifies the number of minutes a RADIUS server, which is not responding to authentication requests, is passed over by requests for RADIUS authentication. To set deadtime to 0, use the *no* form of this command.
aaa group server radius *group-name*	By default, all RADIUS servers are considered part of one group with respect to method lists. In other words, the device will request services from all defined RADIUS servers in the order in which they are listed. This command allows you to group different RADIUS server hosts into distinct lists and distinct methods. Use the *no* form of the command to remove a group server from the configuration.

Continued

Table 9.1 Continued

Command	Task
	group-name – the character string used to name the group of servers. Employ the *server* command to specify a server that belongs in the group server.
server *ip-address* [auth-port *port-number*] [acct-port *port-number*]	After using the *aaa group server* command to define a RADIUS group server, use this command to specify the IP address of a RADIUS server that belongs in the group server. Use the *no* form of the command to remove a server from the server group. *ip-address* – enters the IP address of the RADIUS server (optional) auth-port *port-number* – the UDP port for authentication requests (default is 1645). (optional) acct-port *port-number* – the UDP port for accounting requests (default is 1646).

NOTE

If you specify the key in the *radius-server host* command, you must make sure the text string matches the encryption key defined on the RADIUS server. In addition, because leading spaces are ignored, but spaces within and at the end of the key are used, you should always configure the key as the last item in the command. If you use spaces in your key, do not enclose the key in quotation marks.

The following example enables AAA and defines multiple RADIUS servers with different IP addresses, different ports for authentication requests, and timeout or retry settings that are different from the default. If RADIUS authentication is specified in a method list, then the defined RADIUS servers will be queried in their order of definition.

```
aaa new-model
radius-server host 192.168.1.10 auth-port 4645 timeout 10 retries 5 key
```

```
     RadiusPassword1
radius-server host 192.168.2.10 auth-port 5645 timeout 10 retries 5 key
     RadiusPassword2
```

NOTE

You can use multiple *radius-server host* commands to specify multiple hosts. The software searches for hosts in the order in which you specify them. If no host-specific timeout, retransmit, or key values are specified, the global values apply to each host

TACACS+

Another available security protocol is Terminal Access Controller Access System (TACACS). TACACS provides a method to validate users attempting to gain access to a service through a router or NAS. The original Cisco TACACS was modeled after the original Defense Data Network (DDN) application. Similar to RADIUS, a centralized server running TACACS software responds to client requests in order to perform AAA requests.

TACACS+ allows an administrator to separate the authentication, authorization, and accounting AAA mechanisms, therefore providing the ability to implement each service independently. Each of the AAA mechanisms can be tied into separate databases.

Currently, the Cisco IOS software supports three versions of the TACACS security protocol. They are:

- **TACACS** The original specification of TACACS. This version has the ability to perform authentication requests only.

- **XTACACS** In addition to authentication, extended TACACS has the ability to perform the accounting element of AAA.

- **TACACS+** The latest version of TACACS is TACACS+. This version enhances the previous versions by providing all elements of AAA. Packets rely on TCP as the transport protocol, therefore making the connection reliable. TACACS+ can also encrypt the body of traffic traveling between the TACACS+ server and client. Only the TACACS+ header is left unencrypted.

TACACS and XTACACS are now deprecated and are not compatible with the AAA security features in Cisco. This section will focus on the operation and configuration of TACACS+.

TACACS+ separates each of the functions of AAA by allowing configurations of each element independently of one another.

Figure 9.3 illustrates the process that occurs when a user attempts to log in by authentication to a NAS using TACACS+.

Figure 9.3 Logging on Using TACAS+

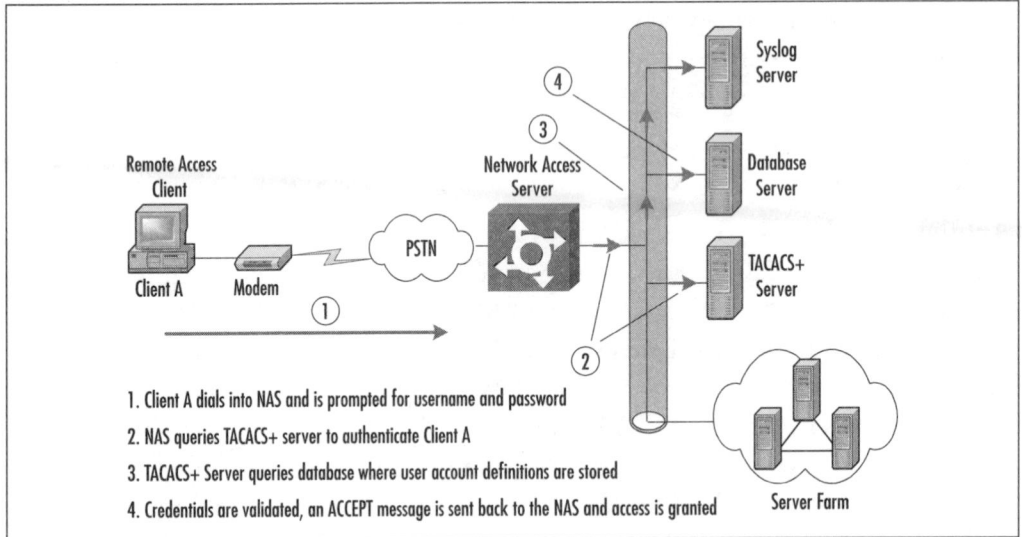

1. Client A dials into NAS and is prompted for username and password
2. NAS queries TACACS+ server to authenticate Client A
3. TACACS+ Server queries database where user account definitions are stored
4. Credentials are validated, an ACCEPT message is sent back to the NAS and access is granted

1. When the connection is established, the network access server will contact the TACACS+ server to obtain an authentication prompt, which is then displayed to the user. The user enters their username and the NAS then contacts the TACACS+ server to obtain a password prompt. The NAS displays the password prompt to the user, and the user enters their password.

2. These credentials are then sent to the TACACS+ daemon running on a server.

3. The TACACS+ server will query either a user database and compare Client A's credentials with those stored in the database server.

4. The NAS will eventually receive one of the following responses from the TACACS+ daemon:

- **ACCEPT** The user is authenticated and the service may begin.

- **REJECT** The user failed authentication. The user may be denied further access, or will be prompted to retry the login sequence depending on the TACACS+ daemon.

- **ERROR** An error occurred at some time during authentication. This can be either at the daemon or in the network connection between the daemon and the network access server. If an ERROR response is received, the network access server will typically try to use an alternative method for authenticating the user.

- **CONTINUE** The user is prompted for additional authentication information.

If the user is employing PPP to authenticate to a NAS, either PAP (Password Authentication Protocol) or CHAP (Challenge Handshake Authentication Protocol) can be used for authentication. Both PAP and CHAP automatically and transparently send authentication credentials (e.g., username and password) through the PPP link instead of prompting the user for the information. For example, when a user connects to an ISP with their modem, PPP is used to encapsulate the traffic to and from the remote user and the NAS. PPP can send authentication information in the form of PAP and CHAP to the NAS for authentication and authorization purposes. PAP sends passwords in cleartext that can easily be viewed using a packet sniffer. CHAP uses a three-way handshake process to validate each side of the point-to-point link, and also encrypts the username and password exchanged during that handshake. CHAP is a much more secure protocol than PAP and should be used whenever possible.

Configuring TACAS+ on Cisco

To configure TACACS+ as your security protocol for AAA, you must specify the host running the TACACS+ server software, and a secret text string that it shares with the TACACS+ client. Table 9.2 identifies and describes the global configuration commands needed to define a TACACS+ server and key.

Table 9.2 TACACS+ Global Configuration Commands

Command	Task
tacacs-server host *name* [single-connection] [port *integer*] [timeout *integer*] [key *string*]	Specifies the IP address or host name of the remote TACACS+ server host, as well as the assigned authentication and accounting destination port numbers. *name* – enters the host name or IP address of the server in which TACACS+ requests will be directed. (optional) single-connection – specifies that the client should maintain a single open connection when exchanging information with the TACACS+ server. (optional) port *integer* – specifies the TCP port in which the TACACS+ client will send TACACS+ requests. This value should match the configuration of the TACACS+ server (default is 49). (optional) timeout integer – specifies the time (in seconds) that the TACACS+ client will wait for the TACACS+ server to respond. This setting overrides the default timeout value set with the tacacs-server timeout command for this server only. (optional) key *string* – specifies the shared secret text string used between the TACACS+ client and server. The specified key must be the same on both devices. The key specified here will override the key specified in the tacacs-server key command.
tacacs-server key *key*	Specifies the shared secret text string used between the TACACS+ client and server.
aaa group server tacacs+ *group-name*	By default, all TACACS+ servers are considered part of one group with respect to method lists. In other words, the device will request services from all defined TACACS+ servers in the order in which they are listed. This command allows you to group different TACACS+ server hosts into distinct lists and distinct methods. Use the *no* form of the command to remove a

Continued

Table 9.2 Continued

Command	Task
	group server from the configuration. *group-name* – specifies the character string name used by the group of servers. Use the *server* command to specify a server that belongs in the group server.
server *ip-address*	After using the *aaa group server* command to define a TACACS+ group server, use this command to specify the IP address of a TACACS+ server that belongs in the group server. Use the *no* form of the command to remove a server from the server group. *ip*-address – specifies the IP address of the TACACS+ server.

NOTE

Specifying the *key* string with the *tacacs-server host* command overrides the default key set by the global configuration *tacacs-server key* command.

The following example enables AAA and defines multiple TACACS+ servers with different IP addresses, different ports for authentication requests, and timeout or retry settings different from the default. If RADIUS authentication is specified in a method list, then the defined RADIUS servers will be queried in their order of definition.

```
aaa new-model
tacacs-server host 192.168.1.11 port 1149 timeout 10 key TacacsPassword1
tacacs-server host 192.168.2.11 port 2149 timeout 10 key TacacsPassword 2
```

Kerberos

A major security concern for today's networks is the usage of network monitoring tools to capture packets traversing a network. Contained in these packets is sensitive information such as a users login ID and password. Protocols such as Telnet, FTP, POP3, and many others, send the information in cleartext. What this means, is that anyone who looks at the contents of the packet (data portion), will be able to see everything in plaintext.

Firewalls have been put in place to protect a network from intrusion that originates from the "outside," this assumption does not protect a network from attacks that originate from the "inside." An often overlooked security measure is having users on the "inside" network prove their identity to the services they are accessing.

The name "Kerberos" originates from Greek mythology, and describes the three-headed dog that guards the entrance to Hades. It was developed by MIT as a solution to the aforementioned security problems. Kerberos uses strong cryptography protocol, which means that a client must prove their identity to a server or service, and a server or service must prove its identity to the client across an insecure network (such as the Internet). After a client has used Kerberos to prove their identity, data exchanged between the client and server will be encrypted, thereby making network monitoring tools useless when capturing packets that contain sensitive data.

How does Kerberos work? Well, Kerberos works similar to how your driver's license works as identification. For example, in a situation where you need to prove your identity, your driver's license contains enough unique information on it (photo, name and address, birth date) to prove who you are without any other ID. In addition to the unique information, your driver's license is issued by a single recognized authority—in the U.S., the DMV. It must be renewed periodically (typically on your birthday), and once it has expired, it's no longer valid. In the Kerberos world, the governing agency would be the Kerberos *authentication server* (AS), and your driver's license would be called a *ticket*. The following steps outline the process in which Kerberos authenticates a client so it can use a service. Before the process actually occurs, both the user and service are required to register keys with the AS. The user's key is derived from a password they choose. The service key, on the other hand, is a randomly chosen key since no user is required to type in a password for the service.

1. First, the user sends a message to the AS requesting that the "user would like to talk to server."

2. When the AS receives this message, it makes two copies of a brand new key. This key is called the *session* key, and will be used in the exchange between user and service.

3. It then places one of the session keys in a packet (for clarity, the packet will be called *packet1*), along with the name of the service—for example,

sessionkey@email. It then encrypts this packet with the user's key (recall that the user's key is derived from the password they choose).

4.   It places the other session key in another packet (for clarity, the packet will be called *packet2*), along with the name of the user—for example, *sessionkey@rlusignan*. It then encrypts this packet with the services key.

5.   Both packet1 and packet2 are then returned to the user.

6.   The user decrypts packet1 with their key, extracting the session key and the name of the service in it—for example, *email*.

7.   The user will be unable to decrypt packet2 (since it is encrypted with the service's key). Instead, they place a note with the current time in another packet (for clarity, the packet will be called *packet3*), and encrypts this packet with the session key and then passes both packet2 and packet3 to the service.

8.   The service decrypts packet2 with its own key, extracting the session key and note with the user on it. It then decrypts packet3 with the session key to extract the note with the current time on it. This process identi-fies the user.

The timestamp on packet3 is to prevent another individual from copying pacekt2 and using it to impersonate the user at a later time. What happens if the clocks on both machines are slightly off? A little leeway is given between the two computers (five minutes is a common time interval).

In Kerberos language, packet2 is called the *ticket*, and packet3 is called the *authenticator*. The authenticator usually contains more information than what is listed in the example, some of this which comes from other fields in the packet such as the checksum.

In the previous example, there is a small problem. This process must occur every time a user attempts to use a service. The user must enter a password each time this occurs (to decrypt packet1). The most obvious way around this problem is to cache the key that was derived from the user's password. This poses another security problem, caching keys and having them around is very dangerous. An attacker can used a copy of this cached key to impersonate the user at anytime (or until the password was changed by the user).

The solution is for Kerberos to introduce a new agent, called the *ticket granting server* (TGS). The TGS is logically separated from the AS; in other words, even though both agents may be running on the same machine, they remain sep-arate entities. These two entities are commonly referred to as the *key distribution center* (KDC). The KDC's purpose is as follows; before accessing any service, the user requests a ticket to contact the AS. This ticket is called the *ticket granting ticket* (TGT). After receiving the TGT, any time the user wishes to contact a service, they request a ticket not from the AS, but from the TGS. In addition, the reply is encrypted not with the user's key, but with the session key that the AS provided for use with the TGS. Inside that packet is a new session key for use with the regular service. The rest of the process continues as explained previously.

If this extra process confuses you (how could it not?), think about it in this manner. When a visitor arrives at a company to take a tour, that visitor typically exchanges their regular ID (such as a driver's license) for a guest ID. During the tour, in order to get into the various areas of the company, the visitor will show their guest ID each time it's needed. If this guest ID was dropped or stolen, since it is only valid for a limited time (until the visitor realizes that they have lost their guest ID, and in order to get their driver's license back, they report the guest ID as being lost or stolen), a new guest ID would be issued.

Kerberos 5 is used in Windows 2000 as the default authentication protocol. This allows for the "single logon" concept that permits a user to enter their username and password only once. From that point on (assuming authorization has been granted) they will be able to access services available in foreign realms.

In the AAA model, Kerberos only fulfills the authentication mechanism. It does not provide any authorization or accounting functionality. If Kerberos is used for authentication, TACACS+ may be used in conjunction with Kerberos to provide authorization or accounting mechanisms.

Configuring Kerberos

In order to configure a Cisco router or NAS to authenticate users using the Kerberos 5 protocol, the following steps must first be taken:

1. Define a Kerberos Realm in which the router or NAS resides in.

2. Copy SRVTAB file from the KDC to the router or NAS.

3. Specify Kerberos authentication on the router or NAS.

4. Enable credential forwarding on the router or NAS.

NOTE

SRVTAB (also known as KEYTAB) is a password that a network service shares with the KDC.

Note that the previous steps assume that a Kerberos server is running and configured. Configuration of a Kerberos server is outside the scope of this chapter. For more information on configuration of a Kerberos server, refer to the relevant vendor documentation. To configure the router to authenticate to a specified Kerberos realm, perform the following tasks in Table 9.3 in global configuration mode.

Table 9.3 Configuring the Router to a Kerberos Realm

Command	Task
kerberos local-realm *kerberos-realm*	Define the default realm for the router.
kerberos server *kerberos-realm* [*hostname* | *ipaddress*] [*port-number*]	Specifies the KDC the router or NAS will use in a given realm. *hostname* – hostname of the KDC. -or- *ipaddress* – IP address of the KDC. (optional) *port-number* – specifies the port number Kerberos will use. The default port is 88.
kerberos realm [dns-domain | host] kerberos-realm	Optionally, map a host name or DNS domain to a Kerberos realm. dns-domain – name of the DNS domain. -or- host – name of the DNS host. kerberos-realm – name of the Kerberos realm to which the specified domain belongs to.

In order for users to authenticate to the router or NAS using Kerberos, the device must share a secret key with the KDC. In order to accomplish this, the device needs a copy of the SRVTAB file located on the KDC. To copy the SRVTAB file, it should be transferred over the network via the Trivial File Transfer Protocol (TFTP).

NOTE

A TFTP server must be running on a network host in order for the router to successfully download the SRVTAB. A copy of a Cisco's version of a TFTP server is available at www.cisco.com.

To copy the SRVTAB files from the KDC to the router or NAS, use the *kerberos srvtab remote* command in global configuration mode, as shown in Table 9.4.

Table 9.4 The kerberos srvtab remote Command

Command	Task
kerberos srvtab remote [*hostname* | *ip-address*] [*file name*]	Retrieve a SRVTAB file from the KDC. *hostname* – specifies the host name of the KDC that the SRVTAB files will be downloaded from. -or- *ip-address* – specifies the IP address of the KDC that the SRVTAB files will be downloaded from. *file name* – specifies the name of the SRVTAB file to download from the KDC.

WARNING

The SRVTAB is the core of Kerberos security. Using TFTP to transfer this key is an IMPORTANT security risk! Be very careful about the networks in which this file crosses when transferred from the server to the router. To minimize the security risk, use a cross-over cable that is directly connected from a PC to the router's Ethernet interface. Configure both interfaces with IP addresses in the same subnet. By doing this, it is physically impossible for anyone to capture the packets as they are transferred from the Kerberos server to the router.

Once the SRVTAB file has been copied, Kerberos must now be specified as the authentication protocol using the *aaa authentication* command. For example:

```
aaa authentication login default krb5
```

Optionally, you can configure the router or NAS to forward users' TGTs with them as they authenticate from the router to another host that uses Kerberos for authentication. For example, if a user Telnets to the router, and Kerberos is used for authentication, their credentials can be forwarded to a host they are attempting to access (from the router). This host must also be using Kerberos as its authentication protocol. To have all clients forward users' credentials as they connect to other hosts in the Kerberos realm, use the command shown in Table 9.5.

Table 9.5 Forwarding Credentials

Command	Task
kerberos credential forward	Forward user credentials upon successful Kerberos authentication.

To use Kerberos to authenticate users when they connect to a router or NAS using Telnet, use the following command shown in Table 9.6 in global configuration mode.

Table 9.6 Authenticating Users

Command	Task
aaa authentication login [default | list-name] krb5_telnet	Set login authentication to use Kerberos 5 Telnet authentication protocol when using Telnet to connect to the router. default – keyword to modify the *default* method list which will automatically be applied to all interfaces. *list-name* – name of the method list to be referenced when applying the method list to an interface. krb_telnet –keyword to specify Kerberos as the authentication protocol when users establish telnet sessions to the router or NAS. This is different than using krb5 keyword which specifies that Kerberos will be used for any login authentication, not just Telnet authentication.

Users have the ability to open Telnet sessions to other hosts from the router or NAS they are currently logged in on. Kerberos can be used to encrypt the Telnet session using 56-bit Data Encryption Standard (DES) with 64-bit Cipher Feedback (CFB). To enable this when a user opens a Telnet session to another host, use the command shown in Table 9.7.

Table 9.7 Enabling 56-bit DES with 64-bit CFB

Command	Task
connect *host* [*port*] /encrypt kerberos or telnet *host* [*port*] /encrypt kerberos	Establishes an encrypted Telnet session. *host* – specifies the host name or IP address of the host to establish a Telnet session to. (optional)*port* – specifies the port in which the Telnet session will be established. /encrypt kerberos – specifies that data transferred during the Telnet session will be encrypted.

The following configuration example shows how to enable user authentication on a router via the Kerberos database. Remember that in order to enable Kerberos on a router, the necessary steps for configuring a Kerberos server must be done before configuring the router.

```
aaa new-model
```

Enable the AAA security services.

```
kerberos local-realm syngress.com
```

Set the Kerberos local realm to *syngress.com*.

```
kerberos server syngress.com krbsrv
Translating "krbsrv"...domain server (192.168.1.10) [OK]
```

Specify the KDC for the *syngress.com* realm.

```
kerberos credentials forward
```

Enable the forwarding of credentials when initiating sessions from the router or NAS to another device using Kerberos authentication when the */encrypt kerberos* command is specified.

```
kerberos srvtab remote krbsrv srvtab
[output ommitted]
```

Specify the server in which the file *srvtab* will be downloaded from via TFTP.

```
aaa authentication login default krb5
```

Specify that the *default* method list will use Kerberos as the authentication protocol.

Choosing RADIUS, TACAS+, or Kerberos

The two most widely used security protocols are RADIUS and TACACS+. Which one should be implemented in your enterprise?

Several factors will influence your decision on which protocol to implement. Vendor interoperability and how the protocols are structured are typical factors that lead to the final decision.

Designing & Planning...

Security Protocol Considerations

Selecting a security protocol can be a daunting task for administrators. Many factors have to be taken into consideration. For example, will this security protocol facilitate only Cisco routers? Should I dedicate only one server or use two servers in case of failure? What services should I configure any of the AAA mechanisms on? Or simply: Which protocol is easier to configure then the others.

Remember the key differences between RADIUS and TACACS+. At the transport layer of the OSI model TACACS+ uses TCP while RADIUS uses UDP. TCP is a connection-oriented protocol, therefore RADIUS does not have the ability to resend lost or corrupted packets, RADIUS packets are sent on a "best effort" basis.

TACACS+ follows the AAA architecture by separating each of the AAA elements. This can be taken advantage of in an environment where Kerberos is already used as an authentication protocol. In such cases, TACACS+ can be used as an authorization or accounting protocol.

Transport Protocol Considerations

Like the title states, RADIUS uses User Datagram Protocol (UDP) as the transport layer protocol, whereas TACACS+ uses Transport Control Protocol (TCP) as its transport layer protocol. What this means is that TACACS+ traffic is more reliable than RADIUS traffic. If any disruption occurs (such as corrupted or dropped packets), TACACS+ will retransmit those unacknowledged packets, while RADIUS will not.

Packet Encryption

RADIUS only encrypts the password portion of the access–request packet from the client to the server. The rest of the packet is sent in cleartext, which can be captured and viewed by a network monitoring tool.

TACACS+ encrypts the entire body of the packet, but does not encrypt the TACACS+ header. The header contains a field that indicates whether the body of the packet is encrypted or not.

Authentication and Authorization

RADIUS combines both the AAA elements of authentication and authorization. The *access-accept* packet exchanged by the RADIUS client and server contain authorization information. This makes it difficult to separate the two elements.

TACACS+ uses the AAA architecture. This architecture separates authentication, authorization, and accounting allowing for advantages such as multiprotocol use. For example, TACACS+ could provide the authorization and accounting elements, and Kerberos may be used for the authorization element.

Protocol Support

RADIUS does not support the following protocols, but TACAS+ does:

- AppleTalk Remote Access (ARA) protocol
- NetBIOS Frame Protocol Control protocol
- Novell Asynchronous Services Interface (NASI)
- X.25 PAD connection

Designing & Planning…

AAA Server Protection and the Loopback Interface

Because AAA servers are critical components of any organization's security infrastructure, they need to be protected accordingly. Whether they are used for only one of the AAA services or all three, the information they contain and the services they provide need to be protected. The AAA authentication service and data provide the mechanisms to reliably establish the identities of users connecting to the network devices or

Continued

using network resources. The AAA authorization service and data provide the mechanism for ensuring that authenticated users are prevented from unauthorized access to resources. The AAA accounting service and data provide critical usage information, especially for an ISP that uses the information for billing purposes.

Because the AAA services need to be available and the AAA data needs to be accurate, protection of the servers is critical and can be achieved using a defense-in-depth approach. In addition, hardening the platform configurations of AAA servers, firewalls or packet-filtering routers can be used to ensure that only authorized devices (valid AAA clients) communicate with servers. Because this protection is based on the IP addresses of the AAA clients, ensuring that the source IP address of AAA clients is standard and consistent can reduce the administration of the packet-filtering protection. By assigning all IP addresses used for loopback interfaces from one address block and by using the *ip tacacs source-interface* and *ip radius source-address* commands on AAA clients to use the loopback interface of AAA communications, the maintenance of the packet-filtering protection is reduced. The packet-filtering rules can be established to only allow communication with the AAA servers from the defined loopback interface block. As new devices are added, the packet-filtering rules do not need to be modified.

While this approach may not be required for small organizations, it can be effective for larger ones with complex networks (ISPs).

Configuring AAA Authentication

Authentication on Cisco devices comes in many forms. There are many features that Cisco devices (especially PIX and routers) perform which authentication would benefit. For example, accessing a router either through the console or vty (Telnet) lines in order to perform configuration, diagnostics, or troubleshooting tasks. In an ISP environment, users dialing in to a NAS must be authenticated before access will be granted to the Internet. Depending on how the device has been configured, authentication may be provided by security protocols such as RADIUS, TACACS+, Kerberos, or a local user database on the device.

A basic form of authentication is, by default, already provided on Cisco devices. During the initial configuration of a router, you will be asked to enter an *enable* password. This password will allow access to a privileged EXEC mode where modifications and diagnostics (which were not available in EXEC mode) may be done. The default authentication on these devices only requires one set of credentials (a password) in order to continue. Worse yet, the Telnet protocol sends data in cleartext over the network. If a user Telnets into a device, the login and enable passwords will be readily available to anyone who captures the packets.

In order to configure authentication on Cisco devices, you must first define a method list of authentication methods, and then apply that list to the various interfaces. A method list defines the various types of authentication (network, login, or privileged EXEC mode authentication) to be performed, and the order in which they will occur.

Once the list has been defined, it must then be applied to a specified interface such as vty lines (Telnet), console lines, or groups of asynchronous interfaces (modems) and services such as the ability to use HTTP through a router or PIX before it will become active. There is also a default method list which may be altered. This default list is automatically applied to interfaces or services which require a login unless another method list is applied to that interface or service, overriding the default method list. For example, a method list named *admin* is created and then applied to the vty lines. This done, the default method list will no longer apply to that interface because the *admin* method list was explicitly applied.

The purpose of a method list is to identify one or more authentication methods and the order in which they will be attempted to authenticate a user. This is where the security protocols (RADIUS, TACACS+, and Kerberos) may be specified. For example, a method list can be configured to query a RADIUS server first in order to validate a username and password. If the RADIUS server is nonresponsive, the method list could specify that a TACACS+ server be queried next to validate that same username and password. If the TACACS+ server is nonresponsive, the method list could specify that the local user database on the device be queried to validate the same username and password as a last resort. This process only occurs in the event that a security server has failed and is unable to perform validation. If the RADIUS server denies the credentials of the user (an incorrect password or invalid username), the TACACS+ server and local user database would never be queried in this case.

The next few sections discuss how to enable AAA authentication for the three primary scenarios you will encounter:

- Configuring Login Authentication Using AAA

- Configuring PPP Authentication Using AAA

- Enabling Password Protection for Privileged EXEC Mode

Configuring Login Authentication Using AAA

Login authentication using AAA controls login access to the device itself. The steps you need to follow to enable login authentication using AAA are identified and described next. The commands used in these steps are identified and described in Table 9.8.

1. Enable AAA on the device by issuing the *aaa new-model* command while in global configuration mode.

   ```
   aaa new-model
   ```

2. Once AAA has been enabled, you then need to specify security protocol parameters such as the IP address of the AAA authentication server and the secret key that the device will exchange with it. To specify the parameters for a RADIUS server within global configuration mode, use the following commands:

   ```
   radius-server host 192.168.1.10
   radius-server key RadiusPassword1
   ```

3. To specify the parameters for a TACACS+ server, use these commands:

   ```
   tacacs-server host 192.168.1.11
   tacacs-server key TacacsPassword1
   ```

4. You must then define a login authentication method list that specifies one or more authentication mechanisms and the order in which they will be attempted. Use the *aaa authentication login* command to define a method list. The following command example creates a named method list called *login_auth_example*, and specifies that the default group of RADIUS servers be queried first, then the default group of TACACS+ servers, followed by the local database.

   ```
   aaa authentication login login_auth_example group radius group
   tacacs+ local
   ```

5. Finally, apply the method lists to a particular interface, line, or service if required.

   ```
   line vty 0 4
        login authentication auth_example
   ```

Table 9.8 Login Authentication Commands

Command	Task
aaa new-model	Enables AAA globally on the device.
aaa authentication login {default | *list-name*} *method1* [*method2...*]	Creates a login authentication method list. default – enters keyword to modify the *default* method list which will automatically be applied to all interfaces that do not have a method list explicitly applied to them. *list-name* – name of the method to be referenced when applying the method list to an interface. *method1* [*method2...*] – one or more keywords to specify authentication mechanisms. See Table 9.9 for a list of method keywords that can be used in this command.
line [aux | console | tty | vty] *line-number* [*end-line-number*]	Enter interface configuration mode for the interface to which you want to apply the authentication list. aux – enters configuration mode for the aux port. console – enters configuration mode for the console port. tty – enters configuration mode for tty line. vty – enters configuration mode for vty (Telnet) line. *line-number* – enters the starting line number. *end-line-number* – enters the end line number.
login authentication [default | *list-name*]	Applies the authentication list to a line or set of lines. default – specifies that the default method list should be used for authentication. *list-name* – specifies the method list to use for authentication.

WARNING

When AAA is enabled, then authentication will use the local database, by default, on all lines. To avoid being locked out of a device, make sure you add an administrator account to the local username database *prior* to enabling AAA. In addition, be certain the default method list for authentication includes a local method that guarantees access to the device.

A login authentication method list defined using the *aaa authentication login* command must specify one or more of the *method* keywords identified and described in Table 9.9.

Table 9.9 AAA Authentication Login Methods

Method Keyword	Description
enable	Uses the enable password for authentication.
krb5	Uses Kerberos 5 for authentication.
krb5-telnet	Uses Kerberos 5 Telnet authentication protocol when using Telnet to connect to the device.
line	Uses the line password for authentication.
local	Uses the local username database for authentication.
local-case	Uses case-sensitive local username authentication.
none	Uses no authentication.
group radius	Uses the list of all RADIUS servers for authentication.
group tacacs+	Uses the list of all TACACS+ servers for authentication.
group group-name	Uses a subset of RADIUS or TACACS+ servers for authentication, as defined by the *aaa group server radius* or *aaa group server tacacs+* command.

WARNING

Be careful when stating that no password is necessary for login authentication. This option defeats the purpose of a security policy entirely.

```
aaa authentication login local
```

This specifies that the local database on the device will be queried to perform authenticated requests.

```
aaa authentication login krb5
```

This specifies that a Kerberos 5 server will be queried to perform authentication requests.

```
aaa server group radius radiuslogin
server 192.168.1.1
server 192.168.1.2
server 192.168.1.3
aaa authentication login group radiuslogin none
```

This specifies that servers at IP addresses 192.168.1.1, 192.168.1.2, and 192.168.1.3 are members of the *radiuslogin* group. Login authentication will use this group of servers to perform authentication requests. If the RADIUS server at IP address 192.168.1.1 is unavailable to perform the authentication request, the next server (192.168.1.2) will be queried, if the server at IP address 192.168.1.2 is unavailable, the next server (192.168.1.3) will be queried to perform the authentication request. If all of the RADIUS servers are unavailable, then no authentication will be required.

```
aaa server group tacacs+ logintacacs
server 172.16.1.1
server 172.16.1.2
server 172.16.1.3
aaa authentication login group logintacacs local
```

This specifies that servers at IP addresses 172.16.1.1, 172.16.1.2, and 172.16.1.3 are members of the *logintacacs* group. Login authentication will use this group of servers to perform authentication requests. If the TACACS+ server at IP address 172.16.1.1 is unavailable to perform the authentication request, the next server (172.16.1.2) will be queried. If the server at IP address 172.16.1.2 is unavailable, the next server (172.16.1.3) will be queried to perform the authentication request. If all of the TACACS+ servers are unavailable, the local user database will be used to perform authentication requests.

Configuring PPP Authentication Using AAA

In an environment such as an ISP, users often access network resources through dialup via async (analog modem) or ISDN. When this occurs, a network protocol (such as PPP) takes charge of the network connection setup and authentication. PPP authentication is very similar to login authentication. When a user configures a workstation to dial up to their ISP, they must enter their login ID and password (as well as the phone number of the ISP). When the user connects to the NAS, the login ID and password is transmitted over the phone line. If they are successfully authenticated, they will then be able to access the Internet (or other services in which they are authorized to access).

The steps you need to follow to enable PPP login authentication using AAA are identified and described next. The commands used in these steps are identified and described in Table 9.10.

1. Enable AAA on the device by issuing the *aaa new-model* command while in global configuration mode.

   ```
   aaa new-model
   ```

2. Once AAA has been enabled, you then need to specify security protocol parameters such as the IP address of the AAA authentication server and the secret key that the device will exchange with it. To specify the parameters for a RADIUS server within global configuration mode, use the following commands:

   ```
   radius-server host 192.168.1.10
   radius-server key RadiusPassword1
   ```

   To specify the parameters for a TACACS+ server, use the following commands:

   ```
   tacacs-server host 192.168.1.11
   ```

3. You must then define a PPP authentication method list that specifies one or more authentication mechanisms and the order in which they will be attempted. Use the *aaa authentication ppp* command to define a method list. The following example of the command creates a named method list called *ppp_auth_example*, and specifies that the default group of RADIUS servers be queried first, followed by the default group of TACACS+ servers, and then the local database.

   ```
   aaa authentication ppp ppp_auth_example group radius group
       tacacs+ local
   ```

4. Finally, apply the method lists to a particular interface, line, or service if required.

```
interface async 4
    encapsulation ppp
    ppp authentication chap ppp_auth_example
```

Table 9.10 PPP Authentication Commands

Command	Task
aaa new-model	Enables AAA globally on the device.
aaa authentication ppp {default | *list-name*} *method1* [*method2...*]	Creates a local authentication list. default – enters a keyword to modify the *default* method list which will automatically be applied to all interfaces. *list-name* – enters the name of the method list to be referenced when applying the method list to an interface. *method1* [*method2...*] – one or more keywords to specify authentication mechanisms. See Table 9.11 for a list of method keywords that can be used in this command.
ppp authentication {chap | pap | chap pap} [if-needed] [default | *list-name*] [callin] [one-time]	Applies the authentication list to a line or set of lines selected on the previous command. chap – selects the challenge handshake authentication protocol when exchanging login credentials. pap – selects the password authentication protocol when exchanging login credentials. chap pap – selects CHAP first, if the client does not support CHAP, then use PAP when exchanging login credentials. if-needed – if specified, users will not need to authenticate if user has already provided authentication (used on async interfaces). This is useful if a user has already authenticated via normal login procedure, and keeps the user from entering their username and password twice.

Continued

Table 9.10 Continued

Command	Task
	default – keyword to modify *default* method list which will automatically be applied to all interfaces.
	list-name – name of the method to be referenced when applying the method list to an interface.
	callin – specifies that authentication will be performed on incoming calls only.
	one-time – designates use of one-time passwords such as token card passwords. Note that one-time passwords are not supported by CHAP.

A PPP authentication method list defined using the *aaa authentication ppp* command must specify one or more of the *method* keywords identified and described in Table 9.11.

Table 9.11 AAA Authentication PPP Methods

Method Keyword	Description
if-needed	Does not authenticate if the user has already been authenticated on a TTY line.
krb5	Uses Kerberos 5 for authentication.
Local	Uses the local username database for authentication.
local-case	Uses case-sensitive local username authentication.
none	Uses no authentication.
group radius	Uses the list of all RADIUS servers for authentication.
group tacacs+	Uses the list of all TACACS+ servers for authentication.
group *group-name*	Uses a subset of RADIUS or TACACS+ servers for authentication, as defined by the *aaa group server radius* or *aaa group server tacacs+* command.

NOTE

You can use the AAA Scalability feature to specify the number of background processes that will be used within the device to handle AAA authentication and authorization requests. Because previous IOS releases only had one background process to handle all requests, the parallelism of AAA servers could not be exploited fully. Because increasing the number of background processes can be expensive for the AAA client (router or NAS), you should be careful when using this feature and ensure the device is appropriately configured with respect to memory and CPU. To specify the number of processes, use the following global configuration command:

    aaa processes number

    where *number* is the number of background processes you want to handle the AAA authentication and authorization requests.

Enabling Password Protection for Privileged EXEC Mode

When a user successfully authenticates on a device via the console (if configured) or via Telnet, they are in EXEC mode. In order to enter privileged EXEC mode, the user must use the *enable* command. Typically, the *enable* password is stored locally on the device, by using the *aaa authentication enable default* command, a method list can be used to specify the authentication mechanisms that will be used for anyone attempting to enter privileged EXEC mode. Table 9.12 describes the command you should use to specify a method list that will be used with the *enable* command.

Table 9.12 The Enable Authentication Command

Command	Task
aaa authentication enable default *method1 [method2...]*	Enables user ID and password checking for users attempting to enter privileged EXEC mode. *method [method2...]* – one or more keywords to specify authentication mechanisms. See Table 9.13 for a list of method keywords that can be used in this command.

An enable default authentication method list defined using the *aaa authentication enable default* command must specify one or more of the *method* keywords identified and described in Table 9.13.

Table 9.13 AAA Authentication Enable Default Methods

Method Keyword	Description
enable	Uses the enable password for authentication.
line	Uses the line password for authentication.
none	Uses no authentication.
group radius	Uses the list of all RADIUS servers for authentication.
group tacacs+	Uses the list of all TACACS+ servers for authentication.
group *group-name*	Uses a subset of RADIUS or TACACS+ servers for authentication as defined by the *aaa group server radius* or *aaa group server tacacs+* command.

The following example creates a named method list called *admin-enable*. When users attempt to enter privileged EXEC mode, the TACACS+ group server will be queried to authenticate the user. If the TACACS+ server is unavailable, the previously configured enable password will be used for authentication.

```
aaa authentication enable admin-enable group tacacs+ enable
```

Authorization

The second mechanism in AAA is authorization. Authorization can be defined as the act of granting permission to a user, group of users, a system, or system process. For example, if a user logs in to a server, their user account will be preauthorized to use certain services such as file access or printing. On a router or NAS, authorization may include the ability to access the network when logging in via PPP, or the ability to use a certain protocol such as FTP.

A Cisco device can be used to restrict user access to the network so that users can only perform certain functions after they have successfully authenticated. Like authentication, a remote or local database can be used to define the ability of a user once they have authenticated.

An example of authorization that is enabled by default on Cisco devices is the ability to enter privileged EXEC mode. Once a user types **enable** at the EXEC prompt, they are prompted for a password (if the router or NAS is configured with an enable password). If the correct enable password is entered, the user is now authorized to use privileged EXEC mode. Instead of the enable password, a database of users may be used that previously defines whether a user may or may not access privileged EXEC mode. If a RADIUS or TACACS+ server is configured for use with authorization, then the ability to enter privileged EXEC mode will be defined on the security server, and may not rely on the configured enable password, or may rely on it in a fail-safe configuration on the Cisco device.

The following list defines the authorization types that may be used on a router or NAS:

- **EXEC** Applies to the attributes associated with a user EXEC terminal session.

- **Command** Applies to EXEC mode commands that a user issues. Command authorization attempts authorization for all EXEC mode commands, including global configuration commands associated with a specific privilege level.

- **Network** Applies to network connections. This can include a PPP, SLIP, or ARAP connection.

- **Reverse Access** Applies authorization to reverse-Telnet sessions.

The following list defines the methods in which a user may be authorized:

- **TACACS+** As with authentication, a TACACS+ server is queried to authorize a user to perform a certain action. TACACS+ authorization defines specific rights for users by associating the appropriate user with the authorized services.

- **If-Authenticated** The user is allowed to access the requested function provided the user has been authenticated successfully.

- **Local** Similar to authentication, the router or NAS consults its local database, as defined by the *username* command, to authorize specific rights for users. Only a limited set of functions can be controlled via the local database.

- **RADIUS** As with authentication, a RADIUS server is queried to authorize a user to perform a certain action. RADIUS authorization defines specific rights for users by associating the appropriate user with the authorized services.

- **Kerberos Instance Map** The router or NAS uses the instance defined by the *kerberos instance map* command for authorization.

- **None** No authorization will occur.

Configure Authorization

The steps you need to follow to configure authorization using AAA are identified and described next. The commands used in these steps are identified and described in Table 9.14.

1. Enable AAA on the device by issuing the *aaa new-model* command while in global configuration mode.

    ```
    aaa new-model
    ```

2. Because authorization relies on authentication and occurs after it, you must configure AAA authentication as described in the previous section.

3. As discussed in the preceding section, you need to specify security protocol parameters such as the IP address of the AAA authorization server and the secret key that the device will exchange with it. To specify the parameters for a RADIUS server within global configuration mode, use the following commands:

    ```
    radius-server host 192.168.1.10
    radius-server key RadiusPassword1
    ```

    To specify the parameters for a TACACS+ server, use these commands:

    ```
    tacacs-server host 192.168.1.11
    tacacs-server key TacacsPassword1
    ```

4. You must then define a AAA authorization method list that specifies one or more authorization mechanisms and the order in which they will be attempted. Use the *aaa authorization* command to define a method list. The following examples specify that for both EXEC and network attempted actions, the default method list will send authorization requests first to the default group of TACACS+ servers, and then to the local database.

    ```
    aaa authorization exec default group tacacs+ local
    aaa authorization network default group tacacs+ local
    ```

Table 9.14 identifies and describes the commands used to specify and apply an AAA authorization method list.

Table 9.14 AAA Authorization Commands

Command	Task
aaa authorization {network | exec | commands *level* | reverse-access | configuration} {default | *list-name*} *method1* [*method2*...]	Sets parameters that restrict a user's network access. network – enters keyword to specify that authorization will run for all network-related service requests. -or- exec – keyword to specify that authorization will run to determine if the user is permitted to run an EXEC shell. -or- commands *level* – keyword to specify that authorization will run for all commands at the specified privilege *level*. Valid *level* entries are 0 – 15. -or- reverse-access – keyword to specify that authorization will run for reverse access connections, such as reverse Telnet. -or- configuration – keyword to specify that the configuration will be downloaded from the AAA server. default – keyword to modify the *default* method list which will automatically be applied to all interfaces. *list-name* – name of the method list to be referenced when applying the method list to an interface. *method1* [*method2*...] – one or more keywords to specify authorization mechanisms. See Table 9.15 for a list of method keywords that can be used in this command.
aaa authorization config-commands	If aaa authorization command's *level method* command is enabled, all commands, including configuration commands, are authorized by AAA using the method specified. Because there are configuration commands that are identical to some EXEC-level commands, there can be some confusion in the authorization process. Using the no aaa authorization

Continued

Table 9.14 Continued

Command	Task
	config-commands command stops the network access server from attempting configuration command authorization.
authorization {arap | commands *level* | exec | reverse-access} [default | *list-name*]	In line configuration mode, this enables authentication, authorization, and accounting (AAA) for a specific line or group of lines. To disable authorization, use the *no* form of this command. Arap – enables authorization for lines configured for AppleTalk Remote Access (ARA) protocol. commands *level* – enables authorization on the selected lines for all commands at the specified privilege *level*. Valid entries are 0 through 15. exec – enables authorization to determine if the user is allowed to run an EXEC shell on the selected lines. reverse-access – enables authorization to determine if the user is allowed reverse access privileges. (optional) default | *list-name* – enables the default method list created with the aaa authorization command or specifies the name of a list of authorization methods to use.
ppp authorization [default | *list-name*]	In interface configuration mode, enables authentication, authorization, and accounting (AAA) authorization on the selected interface. To disable authorization, use the *no* form of this command. (optional) default | *list-name* – enters the default method list created with the aaa authorization command or specify the name of a list of authorization methods to use.

An authorization method list defined using the *aaa authorization* command must specify one or more of the *method* keywords identified and described in Table 9.15.

Table 9.15 AAA Authorization Methods

Method Keyword	Description
if-authenticated	Allows the user to access the requested function if the user is authenticated.
krb5-instance	Uses the instance defined by the *kerberos instance map* command.
local	Uses the local username database for authorization.
none	Uses no authorization.
group radius	Uses the list of all RADIUS servers for authorization.
group tacacs+	Uses the list of all TACACS+ servers for authorization.
group *group-name*	Uses a subset of RADIUS or TACACS+ servers for authorization as defined by the *aaa group server radius* or *aaa group server tacacs+* command.

NOTE

AAA authorization does not apply to the console line, even if a named method list is created and applied to it, the method list will be ignored.

TACACS+ Configuration Example

The following example defines two TACACS+ servers that provide both authentication and authorization services. The example does the following:

1. Enables AAA.
2. Defines two TACACS+ servers and defines the key they will use for communication with clients.
3. Defines the login authentication named method list called *admins*.
4. Defines the PPP authentication named method list called *remote*.

5. Defines the *default* authorization method list for users attempting to enter privileged EXEC mode. The TACACS+ group server will be queried first, then the local database.

6. Defines the *default* AAA authorization method list for users attempting to use network services. Only the TACACS+ group server will be queried.

7. Applies the *remote* named method for PPP authentication.

8. Applies the *admins* named method list to the console.

9. Applies the *admins* named method list to the vty (Telnet) lines 0 through 4.

```
aaa new-model
tacacs-server host 192.168.1.11
tacacs -server host 192.168.2.11
tacacs-server key TacacsPassword
aaa authentication login admins group tacacs+ local
aaa authentication ppp remote group tacacs+ local
aaa authorization exec default group tacacs+ local
aaa authorization network default group tacacs+
interface group-async1
 ppp authentication chap remote
group-range 1 16
line console 0
 login authentication admins
line vty 0 4
login authentication admins
```

WARNING

Be extremely careful when specifying authentication to the console. It is very easy to lock yourself out of the device. The *admins* method list specifies that a TACACS+ server will be queried for authentication. If that TACACS+ is not available, the local user database on the device will be used. If *local* was not specified and the TACACS+ server was unavailable, you would then be locked out of the device until the TACACS+ was again available.

Accounting

Finally, the last mechanism of AAA is accounting. Accounting provides the method for collecting and sending information used for billing, auditing, and reporting, such as user identities, start and stop times, commands executed, number of packets sent and received, and the number of bytes sent and received.

Accounting enables you to track the services users are accessing as well as the amount of network resources they are consuming. When accounting is activated, the router or NAS reports user activity to the TACACS+ or RADIUS security server (depending on which security method you have implemented) in the form of accounting records. Each accounting record consists of accounting attribute value (AV) pairs, meaning that an attribute will have a specific value. For example, for the pair "address=192.168.2.1", address is the attribute and 192.168.2.1 is the value. These AV pairs are stored on the accounting server, which may be analyzed for network management, client billing, and/or auditing purposes.

All accounting methods must be defined through AAA. When accounting is activated, it is globally applied to all interfaces on the router or NAS; therefore, you do not have to specify whether accounting is enabled or not on an interface-by-interface or line-by-line basis. The following lists the different types of accounting available on the Cisco IOS:

- **Network Accounting** Provides information for all network sessions (PPP, SLIP, or ARAP) such as packet and byte counts.

- **Connection Accounting** Provides information about all outbound connections originating from the router or NAS, such as Telnet.

- **EXEC Accounting** Provides information about user EXEC terminal sessions (user shells) on the NAS or router, including username, date, start and stop times, the NAS or router IP address, and (for dial-in users) the telephone number the call originated from if caller ID is enabled.

- **System Accounting** Provides information about all system-level events such as system reboots.

- **Command Accounting** Provides information about EXEC shell commands being used for a specific privilege level on a NAS or router. Each accounting record will include a list of the commands executed for that privilege level, as well as the date and time the command was executed, and the user who executed it.

Configuring Accounting

In order to enable accounting on a router or NAS, you must first issue the *aaa accounting* command.

Table 9.16 describes the command you should use to specify a method list that will be used for accounting.

Table 9.16 The Enable Accounting Command

Command	Description
aaa accounting {auth-proxy | system | network | exec | connection | commands *level*} {default | *list-name*} {start-stop | stop-only | wait-start | none} [broadcast] *group groupname*	In global configuration mode, this enables AAA accounting of requested services for billing or security purposes when using RADIUS or TACACS+. To disable AAA accounting, use the *no* form of this command. auth-proxy – enters the keyword to provide information about all authenticated-proxy user events. -or- system – designates keyword to perform accounting for all system-level events. -or- network – enters keyword to perform accounting for all network-related service requests such as PPP,. SLIP, and ARAP. -or- exec – enters keyword to perform accounting for EXEC sessions (user shells). -or- connection – enters keyword to provide information about all outbound connections from the router or NAS. -or- commands – enters keyword to perform accounting for all commands at the specified privilege *level*. Valid entries are 0 thru 15 in increasing level of privilege. default – enters keyword to specify that the listed accounting methods that follow will be used as the default list of methods for accounting services.

Continued

Table 9.16 Continued

Command	Description
	-or- *list-name* – specifies a named method list of accounting methods that can be applied to an interface or line. start-stop – specifies that accounting notices be sent at both the beginning and the end of a process. The requested user process begins regardless of whether the "start" accounting notice was received by the accounting server. -or- wait-start – specifies that accounting notices be sent at both the beginning and the end of a process. In this case the user process can continue only if the "start" accounting notice was received and acknowledged by the accounting server. If not, the user process will be terminated. -or- stop-only – specifies that accounting notices be sent only at the end of a process. -or- none – specifies that accounting services be disabled on this line or interface. (optional) broadcast – keyword that enables sending accounting records to multiple AAA servers. Simultaneously sends accounting records to the first server in each group. If the first server is unavailable, fail over occurs using the backup servers defined within that group. *group groupname* – one or more keywords to specify accounting mechanisms. See Table 9.17 for a list of method keywords that can be used in this command.
aaa accounting update [newinfo] [periodic *number*]	In global configuration mode, enables periodic interim accounting records to be sent to the accounting server. To disable interim accounting updates, use the *no* form of this command.

Continued

Table 9.16 Continued

Command	Description
	(optional) newinfo – specifies that an interim accounting record be sent to the accounting server whenever there is new accounting information to report. (optional) periodic *number* – specifies that an interim accounting record be sent to the accounting server periodically, as defined by the argument *number*, which specifies the number of minutes.
accounting {arap | commands *level* | connection | exec} [default | *list-name*]	In line configuration mode, enables AAA accounting services to a specific line or group of lines. To disable AAA accounting services, use the *no* form of this command. arap – specifies that accounting be enabled on lines configured for AppleTalk Remote Access Protocol (ARAP). -or- commands *level* – specifies that accounting be enabled on the selected lines for all commands at the specified privilege *level*. Valid privilege level entries are 0 thru 15. -or- connection – specifies both CHAP and PAP be enabled, and that PAP authentication be performed before CHAP. -or- exec – specifies that accounting be enabled for all system-level events not associated with users. (optional) default – specifies the default method list. -or- (optional) *list-name* – specifies a named accounting methods list (*list-name*).
ppp accounting [default | *list-name*]	In interface configuration mode, enables AAA accounting services on the selected interface. To disable AAA accounting

Continued

Table 9.16 Continued

Command	Description
	services, use the *no* form of this command. (optional) default – specifies the default method list. -or- (optional) *list-name* – specifies a named accounting methods list (*list-name*).

WARNING

Be careful when specifying wait-start accounting on an interface or line. If none of the accounting servers are available for receiving the accounting record, then the user process associated with that interface or line will be locked out. Because of this, make sure you don't use wait-start accounting on the console line. A reasonable general practice would be to use wait-start accounting for remote users, start-stop accounting for local users, and stop-only accounting for any command accounting; however, you should make sure these recommendations satisfy your requirements before implementing them.

An accounting method list defined using the *aaa accounting* command must specify one or more of the *method* keywords identified and described in Table 9.17.

WARNING

Because it can cause congestion when many users are logged in to the network, be careful when using the *aaa accounting update periodic* command.

Table 9.17 AAA Accounting Methods

Method Keyword	Description
group radius	Uses the list of all RADIUS servers for accounting.
group tacacs+	Uses the list of all TACACS+ servers for accounting.
group *group-name*	Uses a subset of RADIUS or TACACS+ servers for accounting as defined by the *aaa group server radius* or *aaa group server tacacs+* command.

WARNING

Be careful when enabling command accounting using the *aaa accounting command*, especially for higher privilege levels such as 15, because all keystrokes sent to the device during a privileged EXEC session will be logged in the AAA accounting database. For example, when changing sensitive configurations on the device (for instance, enable secret), the changes will be recorded in the AAA accounting database (for example, new enable secret).

Suppress Generation of Accounting Records for Null Username Sessions

There may be a situation in which authentication is set to *none*. This means that users who connect to lines (vty, tty, or con) are not required to authenticate. If accounting is activated, an accounting record will be created with NULL as their username. To avoid seeing these records, you can disable accounting of records with a username of NULL. To do this, use the command:

```
aaa accounting suppress null-username
```

This will prevent accounting records from being generated for users whose username string is NULL.

RADIUS Configuration Example

The following example uses RADIUS to implement AAA accounting, including implementing wait-start accounting for remote users, start-stop accounting for local users, and stop-only accounting for any commands. The example does the following:

1. Enables AAA.

2. Defines two RADIUS servers and the key they will use for communication with clients.

3. Defines the login authentication named method list called *admins*. The RADIUS group server will be used for authentication, then the local database.

4. Defines the *default* PPP authentication method list. The RADIUS group server will be used for authentication, then the local database.

5. Defines the EXEC authorization named method list called *adminauth* for all EXEC sessions. The RADIUS group server will be used for authorization. If the RADIUS servers are not available, then it will allow the user to perform the function if they have been successfully authenticated.

6. Defines the *default* authorization method list for network-related service requests. The RADIUS group server will be used for authorization. If the RADIUS servers are not available, then it will allow the user to perform the function as if they had been successfully authenticated.

7. Defines the *default* accounting method list for all exec sessions. Start-stop accounting records will be sent to the RADIUS group server.

8. Defines the exec accounting named method list called *remoteacc*. Wait-start accounting records will be sent to the RADIUS group server.

9. Defines the default accounting method list for all network-related service requests. Wait-start accounting records will be sent to the RADIUS group server.

10. Applies the *admins* named method list to the console.

11. Applies the login authentication named method list called *admins* to the vty (Telnet) lines 0 thru 4.

12. Applies the EXEC authorization named method list called *adminauth* to the vty (Telnet) lines 0 thru 4.

13. Applies the EXEC accounting named method list called *remoteacc* to vty (Telnet) lines 0 thru 4.

```
aaa new-model
radius-server host 192.168.1.10
radius -server host 192.168.2.10
radius-server key RadiusPassword
```

```
aaa authentication login admins group radius local
aaa authentication ppp default group radius local
aaa authorization exec adminauth group radius if-authenticated
aaa authorization network default group radius if-authenticated
aaa accounting exec default start-stop group radius
aaa accounting exec remoteacc wait-start group radius
aaa accounting network default wait-start group radius
line console 0
     login authentication admins
line vty 0 4
     login authentication admins
     authorization exec adminauth
     accounting exec remoteacc
```

Typical RAS Configuration Using AAA

In the following example, an ISP is using a Cisco AS5200 access server to enable remote analog customers to dial in to the AS5200 (NAS) and access the Internet. The ISP has decided that authentication and accounting will be enabled and the security protocol of choice will be RADIUS. Login authentication will occur on each of the asynchronous interfaces (modems), vty lines on the NAS (Telnet), and the console. The AAA configuration examples are outlined in bold. Figure 9.4 illustrates this configuration.

Figure 9.4 An AAA ISP Example

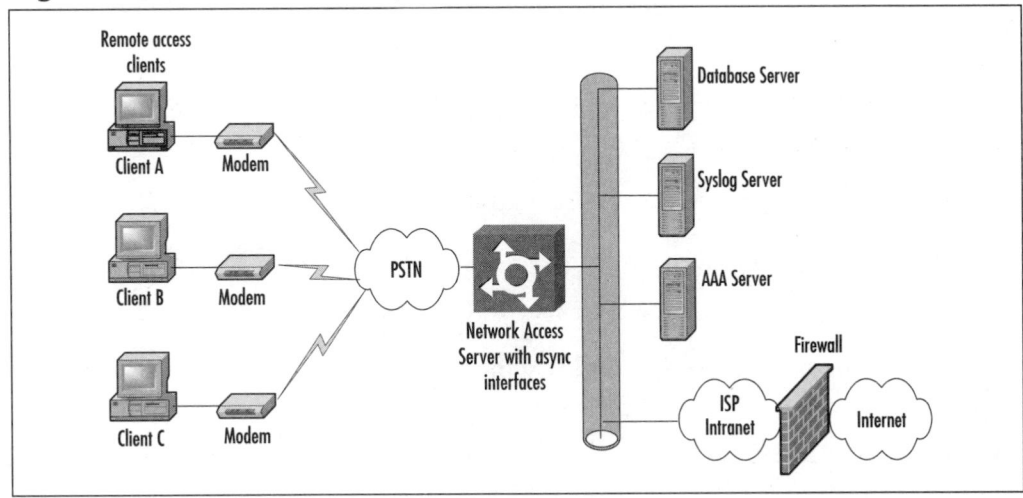

```
!
version 11.3
service timestamps debug datetime msec
service timestamps log datetime msec
service password-encryption
no service udp-small-servers
no service tcp-small-servers
!
hostname NAS
!
```

aaa new-model
Enable AAA globally
aaa server group radius loginradius
server 172.16.1.200
server 172.16.1.210

Define a group of RADIUS servers which will be used for authentication and accounting. If the server is at IP address 172.16.1.200, RADIUS will query the server at 172.16.1.210 as a backup.

```
aaa authentication login console enable
```

Enable login authentication for users accessing the AS5200 by the console port. The authentication uses the enable password:

```
aaa authentication login vty group loginradius.
```

Enable RADIUS authentication when accessing the AS5200 by Telnet.

```
aaa authentication login dialin group loginradius
```

Create a method list named **dialin** which will query a RADIUS server for authentication.

```
aaa authentication ppp default loginradius
```

Set RADIUS authentication for the *default* method list for PPP sessions.

```
aaa authentication ppp dialin if-needed loginradius
```

Create a method list named **dialin** which will query a RADIUS server for authentication unless the user has already been authenticated (if-needed).

```
aaa accounting login isp-accounting start-stop group loginradius
```

Create a method list named **isp-accounting** which will execute accounting during login attempts and the accounting servers will be defined in the *loginradius* server group.

```
enable secret secretpass
!
async-bootp dns-server 172.16.1.5 172.16.1.6
isdn switch-type primary-5ess
!
controller T1 0
 framing esf
 clock source line primary
 linecode b8zs
 pri-group timeslots 1-24
!
controller T1 1
 framing esf
 clock source line secondary
 linecode b8zs
 pri-group timeslots 1-24
!
interface Loopback0
 ip address 172.16.1.254 255.255.255.0
!
interface Ethernet0
 ip address 172.16.1.2 255.255.255.0
!
interface Serial0
 no ip address
 shutdown
!
interface Serial1
 no ip address
 shutdown
!
interface Serial0:23
 no ip address
```

```
 encapsulation ppp
 isdn incoming-voice modem
!
interface Serial1:23
 no ip address
 isdn incoming-voice modem
!
interface Group-Async1
 ip unnumbered Loopback0
 encapsulation ppp
 async mode interactive
 peer default ip address pool dialin_pool
 no cdp enable
 ppp authentication chap pap dialin
```

Set the authentication method for *Group-Async1* to be CHAP, then PAP (if the connecting party does not support CHAP) using the *dialin* method-list for authentication.

```
ppp accounting isp-accounting
```

Enable the accounting method defined in the *isp-accounting* method list on all async interfaces defined by *Group-Async1*.

```
 group-range 1 48
!
router eigrp 10
 network 172.16.1.0
 passive-interface Dialer0
 no auto-summary
!
ip local pool dialin_pool 172.16.1.10 172.16.1.250
ip default-gateway 172.16.1.1
ip classless
!
dialer-list 1 protocol ip permit
!
line con 0
 login authentication console
line 1 48
```

```
autoselect ppp
autoselect during-login
login authentication dialin
```

Set the authentication method for lines 1 to 48 to that specified in the *dialin* method list.

```
modem DialIn
line aux 0
login authentication console
```

Set the authentication method for the console to that specified in the *console* method list.

```
line vty 0 4
login authentication vty
```

Set the authentication method for Telnet to that specified in the *vty* method list.

```
transport input telnet rlogin
!
end
```

Typical Firewall Configuration Using AAA

The following sample configuration displays how authentication and authorization can be used on a Cisco Secure PIX firewall. In this example, the following services will be permitted when authentication and authorization are enabled:

- **Telnet** When the user connects to a host on the outside network via Telnet, they will see a username and password prompt before the connection to the host is established. This is the PIX perform authorization (for the use of Telnet). If the authentication succeeds, a connection will be established to the target host and another prompt will appear from the host beyond the PIX.

- **FTP** When the user initiates an FTP session to a remote host, a username prompt will appear. The user needs to enter **local_username@ remote_username** for username and **local_password@remote_ password** for password. The PIX sends the *local_username* and *local_password* to the security server, and if the authentication (and authorization) succeeds at the PIX, the *remote_username* and *remote_password* are passed to the destination FTP server beyond.

- **HTTP** A window is displayed in the browser requesting a username and password. If authentication (and authorization) succeeds, the user arrives at the destination Web site beyond the PIX. Keep in mind that browsers cache usernames and passwords.

Figure 9.5 illustrates AAA on a Cisco Secure PIX firewall. For more information on the Cisco Secure PIX firewall, see Chapter 3.

Figure 9.5 An AAA PIX Example

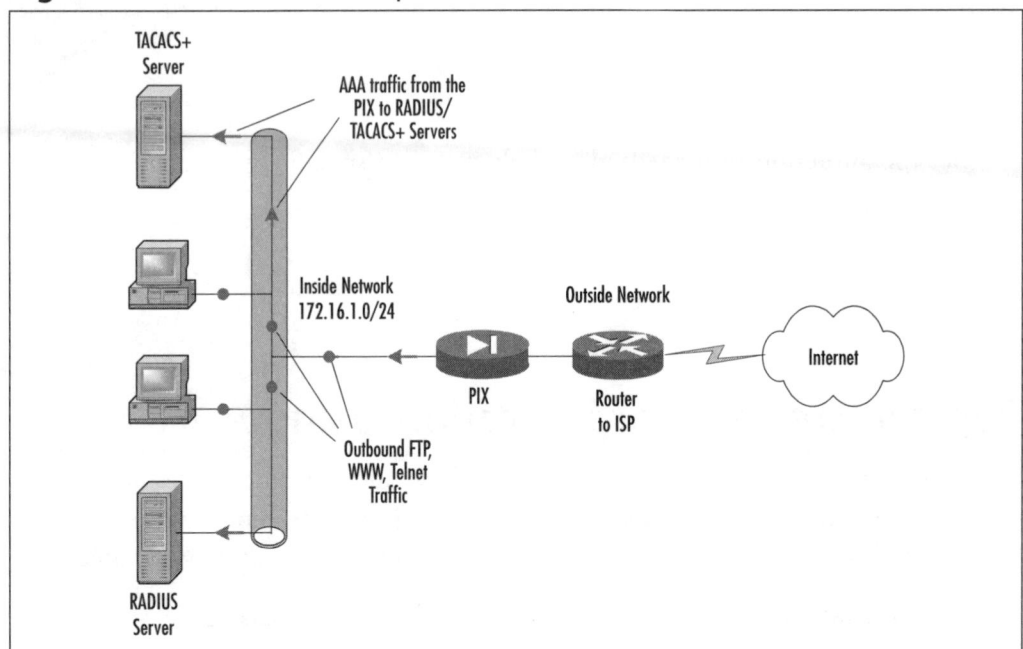

If it appears that the PIX should be timing out an HTTP connection but is not doing so, it is likely that reauthentication is taking place with the browser sending the cached username and password to the PIX, which then forwards this to the authentication server. If this problem occurs, clear the cache in the Web browser settings.

```
PIX Version 5.2
nameif ethernet0 outside security0
nameif ethernet1 inside security100
nameif ethernet2 dmz security10
```

```
enable password 8Ry2YjIyt7RRXU24 encrypted
passwd 2KFQnbNIdI.2KYOU encrypted
hostname firewall
fixup protocol ftp 21
fixup protocol http 80
fixup protocol smtp 25
fixup protocol h323 1720
fixup protocol rsh 514
fixup protocol sqlnet 1521
names
pager lines 24
no logging timestamp
no logging standby
logging console debugging
no logging monitor
no logging buffered
no logging trap
no logging history
logging facility 20
logging queue 512
interface ethernet0 auto
interface ethernet1 auto
interface ethernet2 auto
mtu outside 1500
mtu inside 1500
mtu dmz 1500
ip address outside 207.139.221.2 255.255.255.0
ip address inside 172.16.1.1 255.255.255.0
ip address dmz 127.0.0.1 255.255.255.255
no failover
failover timeout 0:00:00
failover ip address outside 0.0.0.0
failover ip address inside 0.0.0.0
failover ip address dmz 0.0.0.0
arp timeout 14400
global (outside) 1 207.139.221.10-207.139.221.50 netmask 255.255.255.0
nat (inside) 1 172.16.1.0 255.255.255.0 0 0
```

```
static (inside,outside) 207.139.221.5 172.16.0.22 netmask 255.255.255.255 >0
0
conduit permit icmp any any
conduit permit tcp any any
conduit permit udp any any
route outside 0.0.0.0 0.0.0.0 207.139.221.1
timeout xlate 3:00:00 conn 1:00:00 half-closed 0:10:00 udp 0:02:00
timeout rpc 0:10:00 h323 0:05:00
timeout uauth 0:05:00 absolute
access-list 100 permit tcp any any eq telnet
access-list 100 permit tcp any any eq ftp
access-list 100 permit tcp any any eq www
```

Create an access list that defines the traffic that will trigger authentication. This access list will be referenced by the *aaa authentication match* command.

```
aaa-server TACACS+ protocol tacacs+
aaa-server RADIUS protocol radius
aaa-server AuthInbound protocol tacacs+
```

Specify that TACACS+ will be used to authenticate inbound traffic.

```
aaa-server AuthInbound (inside) host 171.68.118.101 cisco timeout 5
```

Specify the TACACS+ server IP address to query for authentication requests.

```
aaa-server AuthOutbound protocol radius
```

Specify that RADIUS will be used to authenticate outbound traffic.

```
aaa-server AuthOutbound (inside) host 171.68.118.101 cisco timeout 5
```

Specify the RADIUS server IP address to query for authentication requests.

```
aaa authentication match 100 outside AuthInbound
```

Perform an inbound authentication on any traffic defined in access list 100.

```
aaa authentication match 100 inside AuthOutbound
```

Perform outbound authentication on any traffic defined in access list 100.

```
no snmp-server location
no snmp-server contact
snmp-server community public
no snmp-server enable traps
```

```
floodguard enable
telnet timeout 5
terminal width 80
Cryptochecksum:b26b560b20e625c9e23743082484caca
: end
[OK]
```

Authentication Proxy

Authentication proxy (auth-proxy), which is available in Cisco IOS Software Firewall version 12.0.5.T and later, allows administrators to apply security policies on a per-user basis. Typically, authorization was associated with a user's IP address, or a subnet. For example, if an administrator wanted to restrict access to the FTP protocol, they would create an access list denying (or permitting) use of a single IP address or specific range of IP addresses. This is difficult to implement, especially if a DHCP server is dynamically assigning IP addresses to workstations. Careful IP management is needed to make sure that a group of workstations is assigned an IP from the correct pool; otherwise, use of FTP may be denied because of their IP address.

Instead of implementing access control lists based on the IP address only, the authentication proxy allows the enforcement of a security policy on a per-user basis. Users can be identified by their username (instead of IP address), and based on their username, access profiles are automatically retrieved and applied from a Cisco Secure ACS server or some other RADIUS or TACACS+ authentication server. These profiles are only in use while traffic is being passed to and from the specific user. For example, if a user initiates an HTTP connection to a Web site, the profile will be in use, after a certain amount of time where no HTTP traffic unique to that profile passes through the firewall, the profile will no longer apply to that user.

How the Authentication Proxy Works

The authentication proxy works like this:

1. A user initiates an HTTP session via a Web browser through the IOS Software Firewall and triggers the authentication proxy.

2. The authentication proxy checks if the user has already been authenticated. If the user has been authenticated, the connection is completed. If

the user has not been authenticated, the authentication proxy prompts the user for a username and password.

3. After the user has entered their username and password, the authentication profile is downloaded from the AAA (RADIUS or TACACS+) server. This information is used to create dynamic access control entries (ACEs) which are added to the inbound access control list (ACL) of an input interface, and to the outbound ACL of an output interface (if an output ACL exists). For example, after successfully authenticating by entering my username and password, my profile will be downloaded to the firewall and ACLs will be dynamically altered and then applied appropriately to the inbound and outbound interfaces. If my profile permits me to use FTP, then an outbound ACL will be dynamically added to the outbound interface (typically, the *outside* interface) allowing this. If the authentication fails, then the service will be denied.

4. The inbound and/or outbound ACL is altered by replacing the source IP address in the access list downloaded from the AAA server with the IP address of the authenticated host (in this case, the workstation's IP address).

5. As soon as the user has successfully authenticated, a timer begins for each user profile. As long as traffic is being passed through the firewall, the user will not have to reauthenticate. If the authentication timer expires, the user must reauthenticate before traffic is permitted through the firewall again.

Comparison with the Lock-and-key Feature

Another feature which utilizes authentication and dynamic access control lists is the *lock-and-key access lists*, described in Chapter 4. Table 9.18 provides a quick comparison of the features of the authentication proxy and *lock-and-key*.

Table 9.18 Authentication Proxy versus Lock-and-key

Authentication Proxy	Lock-and-key
Triggers on HTTP connection requests.	Triggers on Telnet connection requests.
TACACS+ or RADIUS authentication and authorization.	TACACS+, RADIUS, or local authentication.

Continued

Table 9.18 Continued

Authentication Proxy	Lock-and-key
Access lists are retrieved from AAA server only.	Access lists are configured on the router only.
Access privileges are granted on a per-user and host IP address basis.	Access privileges are granted based on the user's host IP address.
Access lists can have multiple entries as defined by the user profiles on the AAA server.	Access lists are limited to one entry for each host IP address.
Allows DHCP-based host IP addresses, meaning that users can log in from any host location and obtain authentication and authorization.	Associates a fixed IP address with a specific user. Users must log in from the host with that IP address.

Benefits of Authentication Proxy

Every policy or networking concept has its advantages and disadvantages, the following are some of the benefits provided by the authentication proxy:

- Provides dynamic, per-user AAA authentication and authorization using either TACACS+ or RADIUS security protocols.

- Does not require static IP addresses to authenticate and authorize users. This makes it easier for administrators who use DHCP assigned IP addresses.

- Since authentication and authorization are being used, it aids in the overall security policy of a company.

- User profiles can be configured on a case-by-case basis, permitting varying levels of authorization based on the duties of the user.

- No special client software is needed. Only an HTTP browser (which is typically installed on clients anyhow) is needed, therefore making this completely transparent to the client (apart from entering their username and password).

WARNING

The authentication proxy will not operate correctly with network address translation unless context-based access control (CBAC) has been config-ured. To ensure the compatibility of authentication proxy with any con-figuration, ensure you have configured CBAC.

Restrictions of Authentication Proxy

As stated earlier, there are always some minor restrictions when implementing a protocol or policy. The restrictions of the authentication proxy are as follows:

- Only HTTP connections will trigger the authentication proxy.

- HTTP services must be running on the IOS firewall on the default (well-known) port 80.

- The authentication proxy does not yet support accounting.

- JavaScript must be enabled in the client browsers.

- The authentication proxy access lists apply to traffic passing through the IOS firewall. Traffic destined to the router is authenticated by the existing authentication methods defined in the IOS software.

- The authentication proxy does not support concurrent usage. For example, if two separate users attempt to log in from the same worksta-tion, authentication and authorization will only apply to the first user who is successfully authenticated. The second user will fail to be authen-ticated and will be unable to pass traffic through the IOS firewall until the user is authenticated.

- Load balancing through multiple AAA servers is currently not supported.

Configuring Authentication Proxy

To configure the authentication proxy, you must perform the following high-level tasks:

1. Configure AAA for the authentication proxy.
2. Configure the HTTP server on the IOS firewall.

3. Configure the Authentication Proxy itself.

The following sections describe how to perform these tasks.

This section identifies and describes the steps necessary to configure AAA for the authentication proxy on the IOS firewall:

1. Enable AAA functionality on the router.

    ```
    aaa new-model
    ```

2. Identify the AAA server (e.g., RADIUS or TACACS+) and specify its related parameters.

    ```
    tacacs-server host hostname
    tacacs-server key sting
    ```

3. Define the AAA authentication login methods.

    ```
    aaa authentication login default
    ```

4. Enable the authentication proxy for AAA methods.

    ```
    aaa authorization auth-proxy default [method1 [method2...]]
    ```

5. Create an ACL entry to allow the AAA server return traffic to the firewall.

    ```
    access-list access-list-number permit tcp host source eq tacacs
    host destination
    ```

Configuring the HTTP Server

In order to use the authentication proxy, the HTTP server must be enabled on the IOS firewall, and the authentication method should be set to use AAA. To do this, perform these commands, which are described in Table 9.19:

1. Enable the HTTP server. The authentication proxy uses the HTTP server to communicate with the client for user authentication.

    ```
    ip http server
    ```

2. Set the HTTP server authentication method to AAA.

    ```
    ip http authentication aaa
    ```

3. Specify the access list for the HTTP server. Use the access list number that was configured previously.

```
ip http access-class access-list-number
```

Table 9.19 Configuring the HTTP Server

Command	Description
ip http server	In global configuration mode, this enables the http server on the device. To disable the http server, use the *no* form of this command.
ip http authentication {aaa | enable | local | tacacs}	In global configuration mode, this specifies the authentication method for HTTP server users. To disable a configured authentication method, use the *no* form of this command. aaa – specifies that the AAA facility is used for authentication. -or- enable – specifies that the enable password method is used for authentication (default). -or- local – specifies that the local user database is used for authentication -or- tacacs – specifies that a TACACS or XTACACS server is used for authentication.
ip http access-class {*access-list-number* | *access-list-name*}	In global configuration mode, assigns an access list to the HTTP server. To remove the assigned access list, use the *no* form of this command *access-list-number* – specifies a standard IP access list number in the range 0 to 99. -or- *access-list-name* – specifies the name of a standard IP access list.

Configuring the Authentication Proxy

Finally, to configure the authentication proxy, use the following commands, described in Table 9.20, in global configuration mode:

1. Set the global authentication proxy idle timeout value in minutes.

```
ip auth-proxy auth-cache-time min
```

2. (Optional) Display the name of the firewall router in the authentication proxy login page. The banner is disabled by default.

```
ip auth-proxy auth-proxy-banner
```

3. Create authentication proxy rules.

```
ip auth-proxy name auth-proxy-name http [auth-cache-time min] [list
std-access-list
```

4. Enter interface configuration mode by specifying the interface type on which to apply the authentication proxy.

```
interface type
```

5. In interface configuration mode, apply the named authentication proxy rule at the interface.

```
ip auth-proxy auth-proxy-name
```

Table 9.20 Configuring the Authentication Proxy

Command	Description
ip auth-proxy auth-cache-time *min*	Sets the global authentication proxy idle timeout value in minutes. If the timeout expires, user authentication entries are removed, along with any associated dynamic access lists. Enter a value in the range 1 to 2,147,483,647. The default value is 60 minutes.
ip auth-proxy auth-proxy-banner	(Optional) Displays the name of the firewall router in the authentication proxy login page. The banner is disabled by default.
Ip auth-proxy name *auth-proxy-name* http [auth-cache-time *min*] [list *std-access-list*]	Creates authentication proxy rules. These rules define how you apply authentication proxy. This command associates connection initiating HTTP protocol traffic with an authentication proxy name. You can associate the named rule with an access control list, providing control over which hosts use the authentication proxy feature. If no standard access list is defined, the named authentication proxy rule intercepts HTTP

Continued

Table 9.20 Continued

Command	Description
	traffic from all hosts whose connection initiating packets are received at the configured interface. *auth-proxy-name* – name of the authentication proxy. (optional) auth-cache-time – keyword to override the global authentication proxy cache timer. This provides more control over timeout values. If no value is specified, the proxy assumes the value set with the ip auth proxy auth-cache=time command. (optional) list – designates keyword to specify the standard access list to apply to a named authentication proxy rule. HTTP connections initiated from hosts defined in the access list are intercepted by the authentication proxy. *std-access-list* – specify the standard access list for use with the list keyword.
interface *type*	Enter interface configuration mode by specifying the interface type on which to apply the proxy. For example, interface *Ethernet0*.
ip auth-proxy *auth-proxy-name*	In interface configuration mode, apply the named authentication proxy rule at the interface. This command enables the authentication proxy with that name.

Authentication Proxy Configuration Example

The following examples highlight the specific authentication proxy configuration entries. These examples do not represent a complete router configuration. Complete router configurations using the authentication proxy are included later in this document.

AAA Configuration

```
aaa new-model
aaa authentication login default tacacs+ radius
```

```
!Set up the aaa new model to use the authentication proxy.
aaa authorization auth-proxy default tacacs+ radius
!Define the AAA servers used by the router
tacacs-server host 172.31.54.143
tacacs-server key cisco
radius-server host 172.31.54.143
radius-server key cisco
```

HTTP Server Configuration

```
! Enable the HTTP server on the router:
ip http server
! Set the HTTP server authentication method to AAA:
ip http authentication aaa
!Define standard access list 61 to deny any host.
access-list 61 deny any
! Use ACL 61 to deny connections from any host to the HTTP server.
ip http access-class 61
```

Authentication Proxy Configuration

```
!set the global authentication proxy timeout value.
ip auth-proxy auth-cache-time 60
!Apply a name to the authentication proxy configuration rule.
ip auth-proxy name HQ_users http
```

Interface Configuration

```
! Apply the authentication proxy rule at an interface.
interface e0
ip address 10.1.1.210 255.255.255.0
ip auth-proxy HQ_users
```

Summary

In this chapter, we provided an overview of AAA and its benefits, described the RADIUS, TACACS+, and Kerberos security protocols, and discussed (with examples) how to configure each of the AAA services on Cisco IOS devices.

AAA is comprised of the three independent but related functions of authentication, authorization, and accounting, which are defined in the following:

- Authentication is the process of identifying and authenticating a user prior to allowing access to network devices and services. User identification and authentication is critical for the accuracy of the authorization and accounting functions.

- Authorization is the process of determining a user's privileges and access rights after they have been authenticated.

- Accounting is the process of recording user activities for accountability, billing, auditing, or reporting purposes.

The benefits of implementing AAA include scalability, increased flexibility and control, standardized protocols and methods, and redundancy. Cisco devices generally support the RADIUS, TACACS+, and Kerberos security protocols for use within an AAA mechanism. Each protocol has its advantages and disadvantages, so which protocol is right for you will depend on your situation and requirements.

On Cisco IOS devices, you enable one or more of the AAA services on a device by:

1. Enable AAA by using the *aaa new-model* global configuration command.

2. If you are using a separate AAA server, configure the appropriate protocol parameters (for example, RADIUS, TACACS+, or Kerberos).

3. Define the appropriate method lists for the desired service (authentication, authorization, accounting).

4. Apply the method lists to the desired interface or line, if required.

Solutions Fast Track

Cisco AAA Overview

☑ AAA is an architectural framework comprised of the three independent but related functions of authentication, authorization, and accounting.

☑ Authentication is the process of identifying and authenticating a user prior to allowing access to network devices and services. Authorization is the process of determining a user's privileges and access rights after they have been authenticated. Accounting is the process of recording user activities for accountability, billing, auditing, or reporting purposes.

☑ The benefits of implementing AAA can include scalability, increased flexibility and control, standardized protocols and methods, and redundancy.

Cisco AAA Mechanisms

☑ Cisco devices generally support the RADIUS, TACACS+, and Kerberos security protocols for use within an AAA mechanism. Each protocol has its advantages and disadvantages, so which protocol is right for you will depend on your situation and requirements.

☑ Within the AAA framework, authentication occurs when an AAA client passes appropriate user credentials to an AAA server, and requests that the server authenticate the user. The AAA server attempts to validate the credentials, and responds with either an accept or a deny message. AAA authentication is typically used in the following scenarios: To control access to a network device such as a router or NAS, or to control access to network resources by remote users.

☑ Within the AAA framework, authorization occurs when an AAA client queries the AAA server to determine what actions a user is authorized to perform. The AAA server returns a set of attribute-value (AV) pairs that defines the user's authorization. The client then enforces user access control based on those AV pairs. AAA authorization is typically used in the following scenarios: To provide authorization for actions attempted while logged in to a network device, or to provide authorization for attempts to use network services.

☑ Within the AAA framework, the client sends accounting records that consist of accounting AV pairs to the AAA server for centralized storage. An accounting record consists of accounting AV pairs.

☑ On Cisco IOS devices, you enable one or more of the AAA services on a device by: (1) Enabling AAA by using the *aaa new-model* global configuration command, (2) Configuring the appropriate protocol parameters (for example, RADIUS, TACACS+, or Kerberos) for your AAA servers, (3) Defining the appropriate method lists for the desired services (authentication, authorization, accounting), and (4) Applying the method lists to the desired interface or line, if required.

Authentication Proxy

☑ Authentication proxy (auth-proxy) is available in Cisco IOS Software Firewall version 12.0.5.T and later, and allows administrators to apply security policies on a per-user basis.

☑ Instead of implementing access control lists based on the IP address only, the authentication proxy allows the enforcement of a security policy on a per-user basis. It allows DHCP-based host IP addresses, meaning that the users can log in from any host location and obtain authentication and authorization.

☑ Authentication proxy is triggered only on HTTP connection requests, and can use either TACACS+ or RADIUS authentication and authorization. For authorization, it retrieves access lists from the AAA server, modifies them based on the user's IP address, and applies then dynamically to the necessary interfaces.

☑ To configure the authentication proxy, the following high-level tasks must be performed: (1) configure AAA for the authentication proxy, (2) configure the HTTP server on the IOS firewall, and (3) configure the authentication proxy itself.

Frequently Asked Questions

The following Frequently Asked Questions, answered by the authors of this book, are designed to both measure your understanding of the concepts presented in this chapter and to assist you with real-life implementation of these concepts. To have your questions about this chapter answered by the author, browse to **www.syngress.com/solutions** and click on the **"Ask the Author"** form.

Q: What is AAA?

A: Authentication, authorization, and accounting (AAA) is an architectural framework for providing the independent but related functions of authentication, authorization, and accounting, and is critical to provide secure remote access to both network devices and resources. The AAA framework typically consists of both a client and server. The AAA client (for example, a router or network access server (NAS)) requests authentication, authorization, and/or accounting services from an AAA server (for example, a UNIX or Windows server with appropriate software) that maintains databases containing the relevant AAA information.

Q: What are the functions authentication, authorization, and accounting?

A: Authentication is the process of identifying and authenticating a user prior to allowing access to network devices and services. Authorization is the process of determining a user's privileges and access rights after they have been authenticated. Accounting is the process of recording user activities for accountability, billing, auditing, or reporting purposes.

Q: What are the benefits of using AAA?

A: The benefits of implementing AAA can include scalability, increased flexibility and control, standardized protocols and methods, and redundancy.

Q: How do I configure AAA services on a Cisco device?

A: To configure AAA on a Cisco network device, you need to perform the following high-level tasks:

1. Enable AAA by using the *aaa new-model* global configuration command.

2. Configure the appropriate protocol parameters (for example, RADIUS, TACACS+, or Kerberos) for the AAA server you are using.

3. Define the appropriate method lists for the desired service (authentication, authorization, accounting).

4. Apply the method lists to the desired interface or line, if required.

Q: What are the three primary scenarios for using AAA authentication with Cisco devices?

A: For Cisco devices, AAA authentication can be used for login authentication, PPP authentication, or for enabling password protection. AAA login authentication controls login access to the device itself. PPP authentication controls access to network resources async interfaces, and enables password protection controls access to privileged EXEC mode using the *enable* command.

Q: What types of AAA authorization can be defined for Cisco devices?

A: For Cisco devices, AAA authorization can be used to control access to EXEC shells (exec), specific command privilege levels (command *level*), network related services (network), and reverse access connections (reverse-access) such as reverse Telnet. Exec and command apply to router access control and are applied to lines, while network and reverse-access primarily deal with dial-in and dial-out access control and are applied to interfaces. Also, note that AAA authentication must be configured in order to use AAA authorization.

Q: What types of AAA accounting can be defined for Cisco devices?

A: For Cisco devices, AAA accounting can be used to record network session information (network), outbound connection information (connection), EXEC shells (exec), system level events (system), and command usage (command). The collected information can be used for a variety of purposes, including accountability, resource usage tracking, and billing.

Q: Should I use RADIUS or TACACS+ as my AAA protocol?

A: Various factors come into play on this question. If encryption and a connection-oriented authorization request is important, then TACACS+ would be the best choice. Recall that TACACS+ uses TCP as its transport protocol and encrypts the entire body of the packet when sending information back and forth, while RADIUS uses UDP for its transport protocol, and only encrypts the password in the access-request packet when sending information back and forth.

Q: Where can I find a RADIUS or TACACS+ server/daemon?

A: There are several programs available for use as a RADIUS or TACACS+ server, for example:

- Cisco Secure ACS, which can be found at www.cisco.com

- Lucent RADIUS, which can be found at www.livingston.com

- RADIUS-VMS server, which can be found at www.radiusvms.com

A listing of available RADIUS and TACACS+ servers can be found at http://ing.ctit.utwente.nl/WU5/backgrounds/products/index.html.

## Chapter 10

Cisco Content Services Switch

Solutions in this chapter:

- Overview of Cisco Content Services Switch

- Cisco Content Services Switch Product Information

- Security Features of Cisco Content Services Switch

☑ Summary

☑ Solutions Fast Track

☑ Frequently Asked Questions

Introduction

The Internet has grown to the point where its value transcends IP connectivity for the support of Web pages, e-mail, and other applications. Businesses now look to the Web for high-performance, reliable transport for bandwidth-intensive applications, and multimedia content such as everything over IP (XoIP), e-commerce transactions, special events, news, and even entertainment services. Content switching is a method to remove delays that might occur in the transport of data across a network. This chapter deals with the technology that allows this to occur and with the dangers the user may face with corruption of data, and why, by using the products described in the following pages, they should be protected from such corruption.

Overview of Cisco Content Services Switch

The *Content Services Switch* (CSS) uses content switching to intelligently redirect service requests to the most appropriate server. The key difference between load balancing and content switching is that content switching makes decisions based on information from Layers 4 through 7 (including URLs, host tags, and cookies) instead of just Layer 4 information (IP addresses and port numbers) such as LocalDirector and DistributedDirector.

Some of you might know this product as the ArrowPoint Content Smart Switch (the CCS login screen still mentions ArrowPoint). Cisco Systems acquired ArrowPoint Communications in June 2000 and incorporated their products and technology into Cisco's product range.

A common implementation of this technology is for a service provider to have two types of Web services. The first service is for contracted Service Level Agreement (SLA) customers and the second for non-SLA customers. In this way, customers with SLAs can be guaranteed a faster Web response time than non-contract customers. This is typically be done using cookies. The CSS recognizes the cookie and processes that flow via the SLA policy to the most appropriate server. Given its priorities, the SLA policy might specify more Web servers than the non-SLA policy.

Cisco Content Services Switch Technology Overview

At first glance, the CSS appears to have similar features to those of LocalDirector or DistributedDirector (if you add the enhanced feature set to the CSS).

Although this observation is partly correct, Web content switching uses a completely different technology compared to load balancing, which is what both LocalDirector and DistributedDirector are based on. Load balancing uses OSI Layer 4 (transport layer) technology while content switching is based on OSI Layers 5 through 7 (session, presentation, and application layers) technology.

Content switching optimizes Web traffic by utilizing information from OSI Layers 5 through 7 to better direct the Web request to the most appropriate server. In this way, content switching can make use of URLs, host tags, and cookies to optimize content delivery.

OSI Layer 3 and 4 (network and transport) switching is simply not optimized for Web-based traffic. For a start, Web traffic is largely asymmetric, with much larger flows back out to the customer from the Web servers than inward-bound flows. It is also very different in the way sessions are constantly brought up and torn down, often with little data involved but many concurrent connections.

Figure 10.1 depicts a typical CSS implementation. The Content Services Switch redirects the Web request to the most appropriate server. The enhanced feature set is required to give the CSS the ability to load-balance geographically distributed servers.

Cisco Content Services Switch Product Information

The CSS product is available in three different ranges:

- **CSS 11050** This is the entry-level product and is suitable for small Web sites as well as points of presence (PoPs). It was designed for throughput of up to 5 Gbps and has a fixed port configuration. Use for up to eight Web servers or caches.

- **CSS 11150** This is the medium-level product and is suitable for small-to-medium-sized Web sites. It was designed for throughput of up to 5 Gbps and has a fixed port configuration. Use for up to 16 Web servers or caches.

- **CSS 11800** This is the high-end product, suitable for large, high-traffic Web sites and Web-hosting infrastructures. It was designed for throughput of up to 20 Gbps and has a modular port configuration.

Figure 10.1 Typical Content Services Switch Implementation

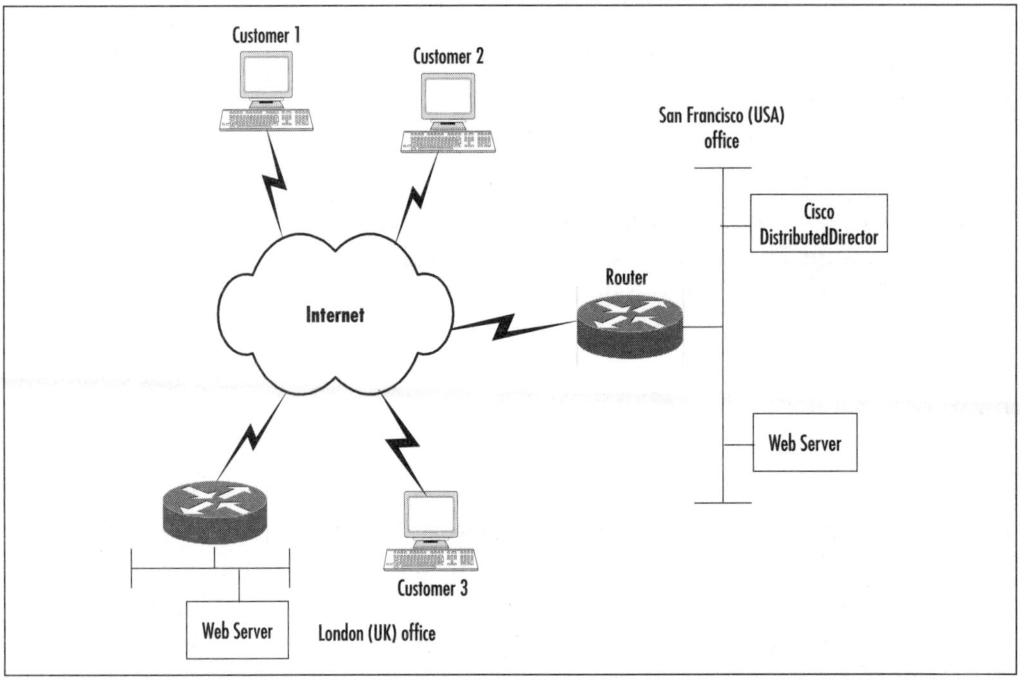

Software that runs on these switches is called Cisco Web Network Services (WebNS). A copy of the basic feature set is bundled with the switches. This software allows network managers to configure load balancing based on SLAs, and provide delivery services for various Web-related services, including streaming video and audio. It also supports "sticky" connections based on IP addresses, Secure Socket Layer IDs (SSL IDs), and cookies. "Stickiness," in short, means that once the connection is made, all other connections from this client will be redirected to the same physical server. This helps CSS ensure reliability of services for e-commerce transactions. An enhanced feature set is also available. The key difference is that the enhanced feature set also includes multisite content routing and site selection, all content replication features, and content distribution as well as delivery services. The current WebNS software version is 5.x.

Because CSS products are tailored to load-balance Web services, these devices include more sophisticated algorithms of application availability testing. Local server selection can be based on server load and application response time, as well as simpler connections and round-robin algorithms. There are global server load-balancing features based on DNS and proximity by source IP address of connection. The CSS can also load-balance any other application that uses TCP or UDP for communication, much like LocalDirector does.

Monitoring and management tools include command-line interface (CLI), Web-based graphical interface, SNMP and RMON capabilities, plus an extensive logging system. It also includes various security-related features, which will be described later, together with some recommendation on securing the device itself.

Security Features of Cisco Content Services Switch

The following information about the security features of the CSS will allow you to better understand the security mechanisms it uses and enable you to configure or change these features. Main security features of CSS include:

- **Denial of service (DoS) attack prevention** The switch checks each session flow at initial flow setup time, eliminating connection-based DoS attacks such as SYN floods. The device also drops all abnormal connections with minimal impact on performance.

- **FlowWall Security** CSS products provide firewall services, which include high-speed Access Control Lists (ACL), that control connections by IP address, TCP port, host tags, URLs, or file types.

- **Network Address Translation (NAT)** Address translation capabilities of CSS help hide the real IP addresses of devices located behind the switch. This prevents direct attacks on Web servers protected by the switch.

- **Firewall load balancing** CSS can work as a load-sharing device for complex firewall structures, preventing bottlenecks and eliminating single points of failure.

FlowWall Security

FlowWall is an integrated firewall that provides wire-speed-per-flow-based filtering of content requests, with no performance penalty. It provides firewall services such as ACLs and flow admission control. These conditions are checked as a part of the flow (session) setup process and after they are validated, packet forwarding for this flow is permitted with wire speed.

FlowWall provides intelligent flow inspection technology that screens for all common DoS attacks, such as SYN floods, ping floods, smurfs, and abnormal or malicious connection attempts.

It does this by discarding packets that have the following characteristics:

- Frame length is too short.
- Frame is fragmented.
- Source IP address = IP destination (LAND attack).
- Source address = Cisco address, or the source is a subnet broadcast.
- Source address is not a unicast address.
- Source IP address is a loop-back address.
- Destination IP address is a loop-back address.
- Destination address is not a valid unicast or multicast address.

If the flow is HTTP flow, then it is considered valid if CSS receives a valid content frame within 16 seconds of starting the flow. It this does not happen, switch will discard all frames and tear the flow down. A real physical server will be contacted only after the flow is validated, so there is no danger that its TCP state tables overflow even if the switch is under SYN flood attack or other state table overflow attack.

Other TCP flows (not HTTP) are considered valid if CSS receives a return ACK for the three-way TCP handshake during the first 16 seconds after the initial SYN packet. If any flow sends an initial SYN packet more than eight times, CSS discards this flow and does not process any SYN packets from the same source/ destination addresses or from port numbers with the same initial sequence numbers.

Using ACLs, policies can be created based on actions (deny/permit/bypass) for traffic matching some or all of the following:

- Source IP address
- Destination IP address
- TCP port
- Host tag
- URL
- File extension

SECURITY ALERT!

FlowWall does not scan for Java and ActiveX traffic, although it is possible to configure for the filtering of Java or ActiveX code by file name or extension.

ACL rules on CSS can be of three types:

- **Deny** These rules prevent any request for matching content from being forwarded to the original server or cache. These rules can be used to block access to specific content or access from specific networks.

- **Permit** These rules do the opposite. They permit traffic that matches the rule. If something is not permitted in ACL, then it is denied by default.

- **Bypass** This rule also permits traffic that matches this rule, but as an addition, all content rules for this traffic are ignored. This is more useful for cache control functions than security—for example, it can be used for specifying that matching traffic is not cached.

The commands used to manage ACLs are a bit different from Cisco IOS or PIX firewall commands. The main difference is that clauses (rules) in an ACL are numbered, so it is possible to insert a new rule between any other two rules without re-creating the whole ACL. An example of ACL configuration is provided next.

```
acl 1
clause 20 permit any 1.2.3.0 255.255.255.0 destination 1.2.3.4
clause 30 permit any 1.2.3.0 255.255.255.0 destination 1.2.3.5
clause 50 permit ICMP any destination any
clause 70 deny any any destination any
apply circuit-(VLAN1)
```

This simple access-list allows access from network 1.2.3.0 thru 1.2.3.255 to the servers 1.2.3.4 and 1.2.3.5 (virtual servers implemented by CSS). It also permits all ICMP traffic and finally denies all that is not permitted. The last line is used to apply this ACL number 1 to a specific circuit (IP interface) with the name VLAN1.

To enable ACL processing, you need to enter a global command *acl enable* in configuration mode.

Configuring & Implementing...

Access Control Lists

It is important you configure ACLs before enabling them, otherwise all traffic will be disabled because an empty access list will implicitly deny all traffic. If you do this by mistake, you can recover using console port only. Console port is not affected by ACL filtering.

The normal sequence of steps when configuring access lists would be the following:

1. Configure access lists for filtering content and apply them, either as one process or by configuring them first and applying them afterwards.

2. Configure access lists for management traffic and apply them.

3. Enable ACL.

For a more in-depth look at Access Lists, refer to Chapter 4. Note that CSS Access Lists are slightly different in configuration and functionality than IOS Access Lists

ACL configuration is described in detail in The Advanced Configuration Guide for CSS.

Example of Nimda Virus Filtering without Access Control Lists

ACL processing on CSS requires extra processor power, and because of this, sometimes it is more convenient to use content rules to provide filtering of the traffic. This filtering essentially redirects "bad" traffic to a non-existent server. It is better to redirect traffic to an existing machine, which does not run any Web server, so it will promptly respond with reset (RST) packets. If the redirection is performed to the non-existent IP address, this introduces extra time-outs while CSS waits for a server's reply and requires more resources. The following description of rules, which will filter all Nimda worm requests, assumes that a reader has some knowledge of CSS configuration commands.

As a first step, a dummy server is configured. It has IP address 10.10.0.1 and will reply with RST packets for all connection attempts.

```
service dummy
  ip address 10.10.0.1
  keepalive type none
  active
```

Now various rules are created that allow CSS to inspect incoming requests for HTTP header fields:

```
header-field-group .ida
  header-field .ida request-line contain ".ida"
header-field-group cmd.exe
  header-field cmd.exe request-line contain "cmd.exe"
header-field-group default.ida
  header-field default.ida request-line contain "default.ida"
header-field-group root.exe
  header-field root.exe request-line contain "root.exe"
header-field-group x.ida
  header-field x.ida request-line contain "x.ida"
```

Each pair of lines in this snippet defines a new group that matches specific content in the HTTP request. For example, first group matches each request that has .ida contained within it.

After that, this configuration is applied to content rules as follows:

```
owner nimdarules
  content block_.ida
    protocol tcp
    port 80
    url "/*"
    header-field-rule .ida weight 0
    add service dummy
    active
  content block_cmd.exe
    protocol tcp
    port 80
    url "/*"
    header-field-rule cmd.exe weight 0
    add service dummy
    active
```

```
content block_default.ida
   protocol tcp
   port 80
   url "/*"
   header-field-rule default.ida weight 0
   add service dummy
   active
content block_root.exe
   protocol tcp
   port 80
   url "/*"
   header-field-rule root.exe weight 0
   add service dummy
   active
content block_x.ida
   protocol tcp
   port 80
   url "/*"
   header-field-rule x.ida weight 0
   add service dummy
   active
```

Each block of content rules in this example defines a rule, which will inspect incoming traffic for connections to port 80/tcp, looking for Nimda-specific headers, and when they are found, the connection is redirected to the dummy server, which tears it down. The *show rules* command will show the number of hits for each rule, giving you a number of attack attempts. The same approach can be used in the defense against CodeRed and similar HTTP-oriented worms.

Using Network Address Translation to Hide Real Addresses

CSS supports wire-speed Network Address Translation (NAT). As described in the LocalDirector chapter, this allows you to use unregistered IP addresses on your inside network (usually the server farm) and prevents hackers from being able to directly target the real server's IP address. Cisco CSS 11000 series switches provide full two-way translation on any Ethernet port at wire speed. The device also supports source group NAT, which allows translation for server-initiated flows going back to the client (for example, as in active FTP sessions) or server-initiated flows, going to other locations.

Firewall Load Balancing

CSS can enhance security by load-balancing traffic among multiple firewalls. This not only eliminates performance bottlenecks but also guards against having a single point of failure.

This is typically done by deploying a CSS in front, and at the back, of the firewalls being load balanced. In this way, traffic for a given flow will traverse the same firewall.

Figure 10.2 depicts a typical CSS implementation to load balance multiple firewalls. This design provides not only firewall load balancing, but also redundancy, while maintaining all the usual firewall security features.

Figure 10.2 A Typical Content Services Switch Implementation to Load-Balance Multiple Firewalls

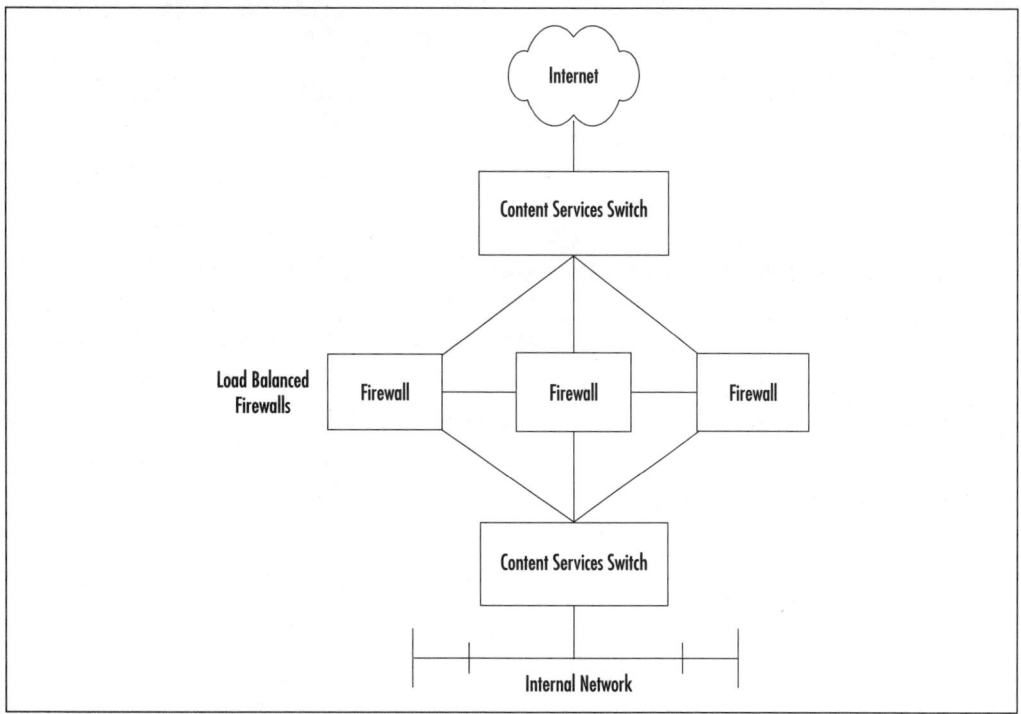

CSS firewall load balancing can be used for distribution of traffic among stateful firewalls, which have their own IP addresses. Firewall load balancing acts as a Layer 3 device. Each link between CSS and firewalls is a separate IP subnet.

CSS ensures that all flows between the same endpoints (pair of IP addresses) will pass through the same firewall in both directions. Firewall load balancing performs only routing functions. No content rules are matched during this process and it is not possible for firewalls in this scenario to perform NAT. If address translation is needed, it can be configured on CSS itself or on another device placed before CSS.

Firewall load balancing configuration essentially consists of defining firewalls' parameters and routing information by either using static routes or an OSPF routing protocol. It is rather easy and requires a minimum of commands. The redundancy of load-balancing solutions can be increased even more by using a pair of switches instead of one on each side of the firewall's array.

Designing & Planning...

Firewall Load Balancing with CSS

CSS can support up to 15 firewalls, distributing traffic between them. It is always better to use dedicated CSS switches in case of heavy traffic load, although it is technically possible to use their free ports for some content switching purposes.

Technically speaking, it is possible to use various firewall platforms at the same time—for example, you can have CSS distributing traffic between PIX and the Check Point firewall. Nevertheless, it is recommended to use the same software platform and, if possible, use firewall state synchronization of separate modules.

Example of Firewall Load Balancing with Static Routes

The following is an example of CSS configuration with two firewalls (which may be connected with a state synchronization link) using static routing.

Suppose you have two content switches—one on client (Internet) side—switch CSS1. It is connected to the Internet via an IP circuit with address 1.2.3.254/24. The circuit connected to the firewalls has IP address 192.168.1.10. Two of the firewalls' external interfaces are on the same subnet 192.168.1.0/24 and have IP addresses 192.168.1.1 and 192.168.1.2. Second switch CSS2 is on servers' side and has IP address 192.168.2.10. Internal interfaces of firewalls are 192.168.2.1 and 192.168.2.2 correspondingly. Lastly, CSS2 is connected to the server network via a circuit with IP address 10.100.1.254/24. Figure 10.3 illustrates this setup.

Figure 10.3 Firewall Load Balancing with Static Routes

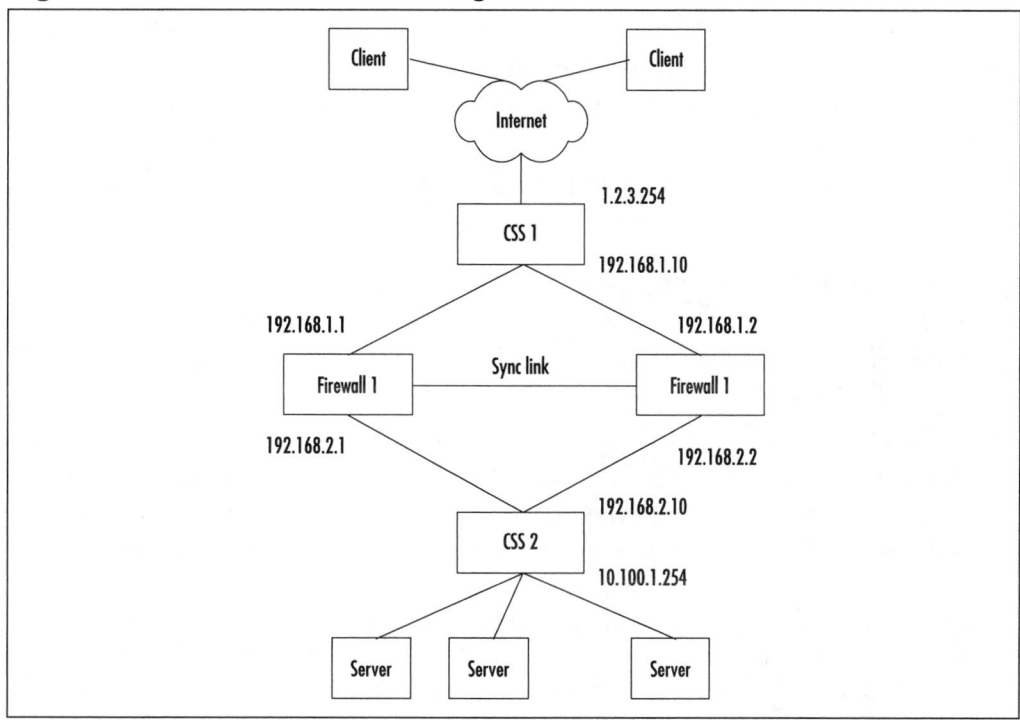

In this case, the relevant part of the configuration for CSS1 will look like the following:

```
ip firewall 1 192.168.1.1 192.168.2.1 192.168.2.10
ip firewall 2 192.168.1.2 192.168.2.2 192.168.2.10
ip route 10.100.1.0/24 firewall 1
ip route 10.100.1.0/24 firewall 2
```

The first two lines describe the configuration of two firewalls—the parameters here are the firewall index (an arbitrary number from 1 to 254), the address of the firewall interface connected to this switch, the address of the firewall interface connected to the switch on the other side, and the IP address of the second CSS. The last two lines describe static routes to the server network 10.100.1.0.24 via both firewalls. Parameters here are the network itself and the index of firewalls through which it can be reached. Second switch CSS2 will be configured in a similar way:

```
ip firewall 1 192.168.2.1 192.168.1.1 192.168.1.10
ip firewall 2 192.168.2.2 192.168.1.2 192.168.1.10
ip route 0.0.0.0/0 firewall 1
ip route 0.0.0.0/0 firewall 2
```

Here, the first two lines mean the same as in the CSS1 case with the interfaces interchanged. The last two lines describe a default route passing through both of the available firewalls.

For an example of firewall load balancing with dynamic route distribution (OSPF), see the Cisco CSS Advanced Configuration Guide.

Password Protection

Content Services Switches support two types of access levels, *User* and *SuperUser,* and up to 32 usernames, including administrator and technician.

The User Access Level

This is the user-level user. This type of access level allows you to have access to a limited set of commands that permit you to monitor and display parameters but not change them (for example, no configuration mode access is provided). The following syntax is used to create a user account (the *global configuration* command):

```
username name [des-password|encrypted-password|password] password
```

Here, *name* is the username you want to create or change (a text string with a maximum of 16 characters is supported), while des-password specifies that the provided password is encrypted with Data Encryption Standard, or DES (use this option only when you are creating a file for use as a script or a startup configuration file; the password is case sensitive and between 6 and 64 characters long). The parameter *encrypted-password* specifies that the password is encrypted (this option is also useful when creating a file for use as a script or a startup configuration file). If the *password* parameter is specified, it means the following password is unencrypted. The last mode is used when creating users online utilizing the console mode. The parameter *password* is the password itself, which must be between 6 and 16 characters long.

The SuperUser Access Level

This is the privileged-level user. This type of access level allows you to both monitor and display parameters, as well as change them. The default privileged-user username is *admin* and the default password is *system*.

The following syntax is used to create a SuperUser account (*global configuration* command):

```
username name [des-password|encrypted-password|password] password superuser
```

Here, *name* is the username you want to create or change (a text string with a maximum of 16 characters is supported). Password encryption options are the same as for other users and the word *superuser,* which is optional, specifies that the user has SuperUser rights. If this word is not present, then the user is created as a normal user.

CSS supports up to 32 different users, including SuperUser. It also has capabilities of defining more gradual access rights to parts of a device's file structure. To use this feature, you have to add to the user's definition one more parameter. For example:

```
username User1 password mypassword dir-access BBNBNBB
```

The last parameter, *dir-access XXXXXXXX,* specifies a user's access rights to the following CSS file areas:

- CSS script
- Log
- Root (contains installed CSS software)
- Archive
- Release root (contains configuration files)
- Core
- MIB directories

Each letter specifies a type of access for the corresponding directory: "N" means no access; "B" means read/write access; "W" means write; and "R" means read access. So, in the preceding example, the user has no access to the root and release root directories but does have read/write access to all other directories.

For increased security, it is also better to issue the command (in configuration mode):

```
restrict user-database
```

It will prevent users without SuperUser rights from clearing running-config and modifying or creating usernames.

The syntax to list existing usernames is:

```
username ?
```

The syntax to remove users is:

```
no username username
```

SECURITY ALERT!

A security mistake that is often made is not to change the default admin password for the Content Services Switch. CSS ships with the default SuperUsername *admin* and the password *system*. Be sure to change this before you deploy the CSS.

Disabling Telnet Access

Although it may be not be feasible for many customers with CSS deployed in more than one location, disabling Telnet access to these switches greatly increases security. Access would then be via the physical console or SSH (recommended) connection.

The syntax to disabling Telnet access is:

```
restrict telnet
```

It is also recommended to check that there is no Web management access enabled. It is disabled by default, but if it is enabled, then the following command will disable it.

```
restrict web-mgmt
```

SSH daemon allows Secure Shell connections to the CSS. It is enabled by default and has some parameters that can be changed in global configuration mode. These parameters are SSH keepalives (enabled by default), the port number for incoming connections (default is 22), and the number of bits in the server key (default is 768 bits).

Syslog Logging

Often, knowing about an attack is as important as taking steps to protect yourself against it. This is where logging plays an important role. If a syslog server is configured, the CSS will log error and event messages to an external syslog server (called *host*).

The following syntax is used to configure the syslog feature (from configuration mode):

```
logging host ip facility number
```

Here *ip* is the IP address of the log host and *number* is the syslog facility number (0 thru 7). This is discussed in greater detail in Chapter 4.

To disable syslog, use the *no* command:

```
no logging host
```

The following command will include logging of all commands entered on CSS:

```
logging commands enable
```

One of the CSS logging subsystems can log all hits for ACL rules. To enable ACL logging (it is disabled by default), you need to do the following (assume you need to enable the logging of hits for clauses 10 and 20 of access list 5, which is applied to circuit VLAN1):

```
acl 5
remove circuit-(VLAN1)
clause 10 log enable
clause 20 log enable
apply circuit-(VLAN1)
```

Unfortunately, logging settings are not saved in running-config, so you will need to reapply them after reboot. For logging commands to become active, you also need to enable the ACL logging subsystem globally. The command to be used in configuration mode is:

```
logging subsystem acl level debug-7
```

Known Security Vulnerabilities

Last year, new vulnerabilities were discovered in various Cisco products, including CSS. Detailed documentation about these and other vulnerabilities is available on

Cisco's Web site at www.cisco.com/warp/public/707/advisory.html. We will briefly list them here.

Cisco Bug ID CSCdt08730

Cisco Bug ID CSCdt08730 allows someone with a nonprivileged user level account to prompt an abnormal event that can cause the switch to reboot, which will prevent normal functioning for up to five minutes. This vulnerability can be continuously reproduced, resulting in a DoS attack.

This vulnerability has been resolved in Cisco WebNS software revision 4.01(12s) and revision 3.10(71s).

Cisco Bug ID CSCdt12748

Cisco Bug ID CSCdt12748 allows someone with a nonprivileged user level account to gain access to files on the CSS that that should not have access to. This vulnerability has been resolved in Cisco WebNS software revision 4.01(23s) and revision 4.10(13s).

Cisco Bug ID CSCdu20931

If users bookmark the URL they are redirected to after a successful authentication on the CSS 11000 series switches, they can later access the Web management interface without having to reauthenticate. This allows users to bypass access control of the Web management interface. This vulnerability has been fixed in Cisco WebNS software revisions 4.01(29s) and 4.10(17s).

Cisco Bug ID CSCdt32570

Cisco Bug ID CSCdt32570 allows someone with user-level access to escalate their privileges to superuser level by issuing a series of keystrokes, which enter the CSS in debug mode. This vulnerability has been fixed in Cisco WebNS software revisions 4.01(19s).

Cisco Bug ID CSCdt64682

A nonprivileged user (user account without administrative privileges) can open an FTP connection to a CSS 11000 series switch and use *GET* and *PUT FTP* commands, without any user-level restrictions enforced. This allows nonprivileged users to access files they normally couldn't.

Cisco Bug ID CSCdt64682 has been fixed in Cisco WebNS software revisions 4.01(23s) and 4.10(13s).

CSS devices did not escape the industrywide bugs discovered recently, nor the SSH v1.5 vulnerabilities, SNMP implementation problems, and CodeRed impact.

Multiple SSH Vulnerabilities

Like many other Cisco devices that were using SSH version 1.5 at the time, CSS contained the following SSH vulnerabilities:

- **CRC-32 integrity check vulnerability** Allows insertion of arbitrary commands in the session once it has been established. (Cisco bug ID CSCdv34668)

- **Traffic analysis** This vulnerability exposes the exact lengths of the passwords used for login authentication. (Cisco bug ID CSCdv34676)

- **Key recovery** This vulnerability may lead to the compromise of the session key. Once the session key is determined, the attacker can decrypt the stored session using any implementation of the crypto algorithm used. (Cisco bug ID CSCdv34679)

These vulnerabilities were fixed in WebNS software versions R4.01 B42s, R4.10 B22s, R5.0 B11s, and R5.01 B6s.

Malformed SNMP Message Handling Vulnerabilities

Again, many Cisco and non-Cisco products are affected by this vulnerability. It allows the attacker to conduct a denial of service by sending malformed SNMP packets to the CSS, causing it to crash and reload. (Cisco bug ID CSCdw64236)

All SNMP related vulnerabilities were fixed in WebNS releases 4.01.053s, 5.00.037s, 5.01.013s, and 5.02.005s.

CodeRed Impact

Although CSS does not contain Microsoft IIS (Internet Information Server), it was also affected by large traffic generated from hosts infected with CodeRed. When the traffic from the worm reaches a significant level, a Cisco CSS 11000 series may suffer a memory allocation error that leads to memory corruption and requires a reboot. This is documented in Cisco bug ID CSCdu76237. This vulnerability was fixed in WebNS releases R3.10 B78s, R4.01 B41s, R4.10 B21s, R5.0 B8s, and R5.01 B5.

Summary

Cisco Content Services Switch (CSS) is a device specifically designed to provide load sharing for Web-related services. It uses information from Layers 4 thru 7 of the ISO/OSI network model (from destination port numbers to browser cookies) in order to decide where to forward each request for content.

The CSS 11000 product line consists of three different models—CSS 11050 (entry-level product), CSS 11150 (medium-level), and CSS 11800 (high-end device with modular port extensions).

Security features of CSS include health checks for each new flow, Access Control Lists (ACLs), and Network Address Translation (NAT). Another application of CSS in security architecture is to provide load balancing for firewalls.

ACL features filtering of connections by their source IP address, destination IP address, TCP port, host tag, URL, or file extension. Another way of filtering can be configuring content rules so that undesired requests are forwarded to a dummy server and dropped there. Worms such as CodeRed or Nimda can be filtered out this way.

CSSs support wire-speed NAT. This allows you to use unregistered IP addresses on your inside network (usually the server farm) and prevents hackers from being able to directly target the real server's IP address.

CSS firewall load balancing can be used for distribution of traffic among stateful firewalls, which have their own IP addresses. Firewall load balancing acts as a Layer 3 device. The function of CSS is to ensure all flows between the same endpoints (pair of IP addresses) will pass through the same firewall in both directions.

Command-line interface (CLI) of CSS supports up to 32 different users and allows for configuration of access privileges, as well as distinction of privileged and nonprivileged users.

An extensive logging system can be configured to provide necessary information in the form of syslog messages, or to store data on the local hard drive.

As many other network devices, CSS has had security vulnerabilities. In particular, it was vulnerable to such industrywide problems as the incorrect handling of malformed SNMP messages and SSH 1.5 bugs.

Solutions Fast Track

Overview of Cisco Content Services Switch

☑ CSS is designed to provide effective load sharing for Web-oriented services and uses information up to the application layer of communications to find the optimal way of doing this.

☑ Information used by CSS in making decisions on forwarding requests includes browser cookies, URLs, host tags, HTTP header fields, and SSL connection IDs.

☑ The enhanced feature set of WebNS management software, which runs on CSS, allows load balancing of geographically distributed server farms.

Cisco Content Services Switch Product Information

☑ The CSS product line includes three devices for all sizes of server farms—from entry-level CSS 11050 through mid-level CSS 11150 to the high-end CSS 11800.

☑ The newest version of WebNS software is 5.x.

☑ Application availability tests (used for making decisions during the load balancing process) include server load, application response time, and global load balancing based on DNS and the proximity of the source IP address. Simpler algorithms resembling those of LocalDirector are also available.

Security Features of Cisco Content Services Switch

☑ CSS performs various checks during the initial phase of flow setup, helping to prevent denial of service attacks.

☑ FlowWall security features include traffic filtering based on various conditions.

☑ The NAT capabilities of CSS help hide real IP addresses of devices located behind the switch.

☑ CSS can work as a load-sharing device for complex firewall structures, preventing bottlenecks and eliminating single points of failure.

Frequently Asked Questions

The following Frequently Asked Questions, answered by the authors of this book, are designed to both measure your understanding of the concepts presented in this chapter and to assist you with real-life implementation of these concepts. To have your questions about this chapter answered by the author, browse to **www.syngress.com/solutions** and click on the **"Ask the Author"** form.

Q: My browser does not work with Web-based management interfaces on CSS. I cannot connect to it. What is going on?

A: First of all, it is better to disable Web-based management and use only command line configuration. If you need to use it, make sure that connections to http and https ports on CSS are allowed from your computer and hot blocked somewhere along the way. The most common problem with the Web interface is that it uses only 128-bit encryption, and browsers that do not support it (for example, Microsoft Internet Explorer earlier than version 4.0), will be refused during the SSL session establishing process. You will need to upgrade the browser.

Q: What are standard, enhanced, and optional feature sets of CSS?

A: The Enhanced feature set contains everything in the Standard feature set plus Network Address Translation (NAT) Peering, Domain Name Service (DNS), Demand-Based Content Replication (Dynamic Hot Content Overflow), Content Staging and Replication, and Network Proximity DNS. Proximity Database and SSH are optional features. In order to activate optional features such as the SSH server, you will need a special license provided with the software when you purchase this optional set.

Q: Where can I find more information on CSS?

A: On the Cisco Web site at http://cisco.com/warp/public/cc/pd/si/11000/prodlit/index.shtml. It includes configuration manuals for all product versions.

Q: Does CSS have any tools for performing automated tasks, such as log rotation?

A: CSS has a built-in scripting language, which resembles UNIX scripting languages.

Q: I forgot the administrative password for my CSS. How can I change it?

A: This procedure is easier than for Cisco routers. You need to connect to the CSS via the console cable. When the device boots, it displays a message: Press any key to access the Offline Diagnostic Monitor menu. If you press a key during the five-second period after this message is displayed, an Offline DM menu will appear. In the main menu, select option number **3** (to enter the advanced options menu), then option **2** in the submenu that appears (the selecting security options menu), then **2** again ("Set administrative user name and password"). After that, just enter the username and password of your choice at the prompt, and reboot the device (option **4** in the main menu).

## Chapter 11

Cisco Secure Scanner

Solutions in this chapter:

- Minimum System Specifications for Secure Scanner
- Searching the Network for Vulnerabilities
- Viewing the Results
- Keeping the System Up-to-Date

☑ Summary

☑ Solutions Fast Track

☑ Frequently Asked Questions

Introduction

Cisco Secure Scanner is a vulnerability scanner that maps network devices, identifies device operating systems and versions, open ports and applications listening on them, and vulnerabilities associated with those applications.

Some of the key features of Cisco Secure Scanner include the following:

- It can actively probe the open ports and attempt to confirm vulnerabilities in order to reduce false positives.

- Once you have mapped and scanned your network, the unique Grid Browser enables you to view the results of your scan from many different perspectives and at varying levels of detail. This not only provides you with the capability to identify and drill into the data that you need to implement corrective actions, but also provides you with the flexibility to generate management charts and reports that will communicate the necessary information focus management attention and resources where it is needed.

- Unlike other vulnerability scanners, since Cisco Secure Scanner is licensed without any ties or restrictions based on IP address, there is no requirement to modify your license as your network changes. Nor is its license based on platform types to be scanned; all network devices are mapped and scanned, including UNIX servers, Windows servers, firewalls, routers, switches, and printers.

Designing & Planning…

Risk Management and Vulnerability Scanning

Vulnerability scanning performed without a risk management process can provide tactical value at best. To truly leverage the value of vulnerability scanning, it should actually be a key component of a risk management process. Risk management is the process of assessing risk, implementing countermeasures to reduce the risk to an acceptable level, and maintaining that level of risk. A lifecycle process that is the core of a comprehensive information security program, risk management typically includes two primary subprocesses: *risk assessment* and *risk mitigation*.

Continued

- **Risk assessment** is the process of identifying, analyzing, and interpreting risk. Although the risk assessment process will vary among organizations, it typically includes the steps of identifying critical assets, identifying threats, and identifying vulnerabilities. These factors are analyzed to calculate a quantitative or qualitative risk level for a given system or network. Vulnerability scanning using the Cisco Secure Scanner can automatically identify the technical vulnerabilities within the vulnerability identification step of the process; management and operational vulnerabilities would still need to be identified via other mechanisms. Not only can Secure Scanner identify potential vulnerabilities and attempt to confirm their existence, but it also provides capabilities for the analyst to manipulate the data presentation into a form that is meaningful to the assessment.

- **Risk Mitigation** is the process of selecting and implementing security controls to reduce risk to a level acceptable to management. Typically, the risk level identified as an output of the risk assessment process is analyzed to determine if that level of risk is acceptable to the business. If not, then a risk mitigation plan is developed and executed to reduce the risk to an acceptable level. A key aspect of the risk mitigation plan is the prioritization of security controls and countermeasures so that resources are applied appropriately and efficiently. Because the Cisco Secure Scanner identifies vulnerability severity, attempts confirmation, and provides relevant graphic and reporting capabilities, it can provide key input for the risk mitigation plan development.

This chapter focuses on informing you about how to use Cisco Secure Scanner to scan your network for vulnerabilities, manipulate the display of the results to identify the information you need to better secure your network and communicate the desired information, and generate graphics and reports that will communicate the desired information to management.

Minimum System Specifications for Secure Scanner

Cisco Secure Scanner runs on both Windows NT and Solaris. The minimum requirements for running Secure Scanner on Windows NT are:

- Pentium II 450MHz processor

- Windows NT 4.0 Workstation/Server or Windows 2000 Professional/ Server

- Service Pack 5 or later

- 64MB RAM (96MB RAM recommended)

- Disk Space: 20MB (application), 100MB (session data), 400MB (paging file)

- TCP/IP network interface

- CD-ROM drive

- Microsoft Internet Explorer 4.0 or later (or Netscape Navigator 2.0 or later)

- Microsoft Virtual Machine 5.00.3167 (provided with Cisco Secure Scanner)

- Screen resolution of 800×600 or greater

- Local or domain administrative privileges

NOTE

Cisco Secure Scanner operates normally without Microsoft Internet Explorer; however, you must have Internet Explorer 4.0 or later installed to use Cisco Secure Scanner Help.

The minimum requirements for running Secure Scanner on Solaris are:

- Pentium 266MHz processor or Sun SPARC 5

- Solaris x86 2.5.x, 2.6, 2.7, 2.8 (for Pentium) or Solaris 2.5.x, 2.6, 2.7, 2.8 (for SPARC)

- 64MB RAM (96MB RAM recommended)

- Disk Space: 20MB (application), 100MB (session data), 400MB (paging file)

- TCP/IP network interface

- CD-ROM drive

- Netscape Navigator 2.0 or later

- Screen resolution of 800×600 or greater

- Root privileges

Searching the Network for Vulnerabilities

Once you have installed Cisco Secure Scanner, you can create and initiate a session to search your network for vulnerabilities. The session can be designated as either a passive scan or an active probe (used to confirm any vulnerabilities found). A scan is a non-intrusive session that discovers network devices, identifies open ports on those devices, and attempts to identify applications and versions listening on those ports. By collecting and analyzing banner information associated with a port, the scanner often can identify the application and its version. In order to accurately identify the application and version, the scanner also utilizes a non-intrusive and user-transparent technique called nudges. Where banner information is not provided by the server when connecting to a port, the scanner issues protocol-specific commands (nudges) to collect additional information to identify the application and version. Once the relevant information has been collected, the scanner then uses the Cisco Network Security Database (NSDB) to identify all of the potential vulnerabilities associated with that version of the application. A probe is an intrusive session that attempts to discover additional vulnerabilities and confirm potential ones through actual exploitation attempts. Sessions can also be scheduled to start on recurring or specific dates and times, or at random.

WARNING

Because it is possible to render a service or device unavailable by initiating an active and intrusive probe, you should conduct probe sessions outside peak network usage hours or omit sensitive devices from the probe to prevent loss of service. In addition, you should coordinate with the appropriate systems administrators to ensure that any lost service can be restored as quickly as possible.

In general, users should be unaware that a session is in progress; however, a performance drop may occur, especially if a probe has been selected with a heavy Active Probe Profile (see Figure 11.3 for more details).

There are three primary steps in creating a session to search your network for vulnerabilities:

1. Identifying the network addresses to scan

2. Identifying vulnerabilities to scan by specifying the TCP and UDP ports (and any active probe settings)

3. Scheduling the session

To create a session, select the **page icon** from the Cisco Secure Scanner main screen, as shown in Figure 11.1.

Figure 11.1 Cisco Secure Scanner Main Screen

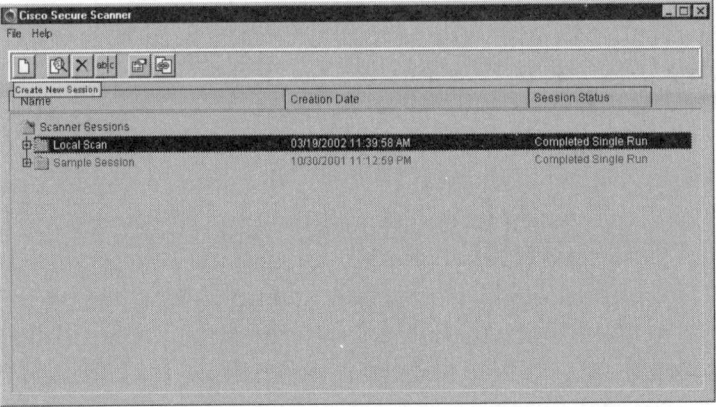

Designing & Planning...

Vulnerability Assessment versus Penetration Testing

As we stated earlier, a vulnerability scanner such as the Cisco Secure Scanner can be a useful tool in an organization's continuous risk management process. Specifically, the scanner can be used to identify and assess technical vulnerabilities as part of the risk assessment portion of the risk management process. But what exactly is vulnerability assessment, and how does it differ from penetration testing?

The differences between the phrases may not always be clear, and may convey different meanings depending on the context within which they are used. However, generally a vulnerability assessment is a systematic review of the security environment and controls of a system or network to identify the degree to which it is at risk. Its goal is to provide

Continued

more comprehensive management guidance on where and how to reduce risk. A penetration test is an attempt to circumvent the security environment and controls of a system or network to identify one or more system weaknesses. Its goal is to exploit vulnerabilities tactically and locally to demonstrate weakness. Because its intent is to circumvent the system controls, a penetration test is typically more intrusive than a vulnerability assessment, and has a higher probability of resulting in a loss of data or service.

Both vulnerability assessments and penetration tests are valuable security checks for evaluating the security of a system or network. Vulnerability assessments can be particularly important both in the pre-deployment lifecycle phases of a system to validate security controls prior to deployment and in the production lifecycle phase to ensure the security posture of the system is maintained. Penetration tests can also be valuable prior to deployment, but can also be used if a particularly reluctant system or network manager needs convincing of the need for specific security control.

Identifying Network Addresses

Once you have selected the **Create New Session** icon, the Session Configuration window appears with the Network Addresses tab selected as shown in Figure 11.2.

Figure 11.2 Session Configuration Window (Network Addresses Tab)

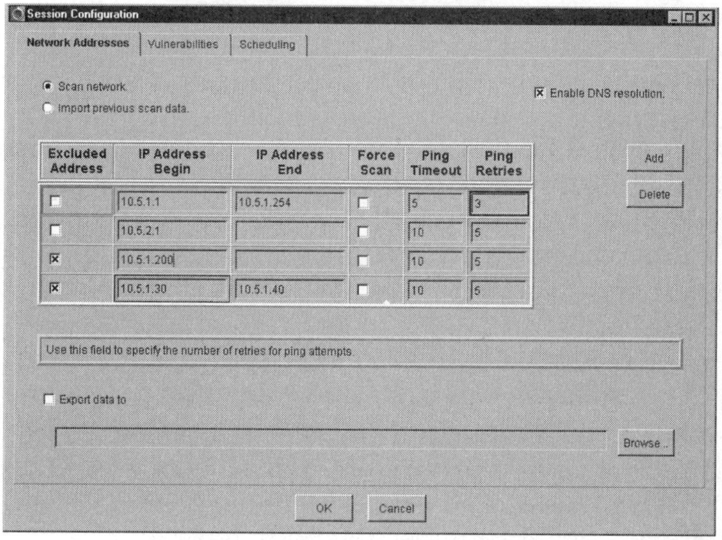

You use this screen to specify the addresses that should be included in the scan session. By default, the Scan Network check box is selected. As shown in the multiple entries in Figure 11.2, you can specify address ranges and single addresses to be included or excluded from the scan. Addresses are included unless the Excluded Address check box is selected. To add or delete a data line containing IP address entries, select either the **Add** or **Delete** buttons. If you want the scan results to include any hostnames associated with the IP addresses, select the **Enable DNS Resolution** check box.

WARNING

Cisco Secure Scanner does not respond to descending address ranges within a data line, so make sure you enter the lowest IP address in a range in the **IP Address Begin** field and the highest IP address in the **IP Address End** field.

Configuring & Implementing...

Firewalls and Cisco Secure Scanner

If some of the target addresses you are attempting to scan are located behind a firewall or packet filtering router, you may not obtain a complete scan of the addresses. If the packet filtering device blocks incoming ICMP Echo Requests, you will not discover the target hosts on the other side of the device if you use the default scan session configuration. The reason is the Secure Scanner uses ping sweeps (ICMP Echo Requests) to discover hosts on the network. If a packet filtering device blocks the ping, it will never reach the host, which will not know to respond, so Secure Scanner will not know that the host exists. If it does not know that the host exists, Secure Scanner will not attempt any port scans or probes of the host.

The good news is that you still may be able to discover hosts behind a packet-filtering device; however, your scan and probe results will be limited by the policy that is being enforced by the packet filter. In other words, you will only be able to identify ports and related vulnerabilities if the packet filter allows that particular traffic to reach the target host. In order to accomplish this, you will need to enable the **Force Scan**

Continued

option within the **Network Addresses** tab of the **Create Session** window for the appropriate addresses (see Figure 11.2). This option instructs the Secure Scanner to conduct a port scan of the IP addresses in the specified range without performing the ping sweep first. Because Secure Scanner will attempt to connect to all of the ports configured for the session for the specified addresses, the disadvantage of enabling this option is that the session will take longer to complete because the scanner will be attempting to repeatedly connect to ports on some hosts that do not exist. Therefore, make sure you limit the number of addresses for which you enable the **Force Scan** option.

The *Ping Timeout* and *Ping Retries* parameters specify the length of time (in seconds) that the scanner waits for a response from an IP address and the number of times the scanner will ping an IP address before identifying it as not alive, respectively.

NOTE

Cisco Secure Scanner may appear to hang during the ping session, particularly if the defined scan range is large compared to the number of active devices. It is functioning properly, but attempts to ping each address included in the session, and must wait for a response and retry as appropriate. You can adjust the length of time for a ping session through the *Ping Timeout* and *Ping Retries* parameters within the **Session Configuration** window.

Identifying Vulnerabilities

Once you have identified the address range(s) to be scanned, you must then specify the vulnerabilities to be scanned. Selecting the **Vulnerabilities** tab within the **Session Configuration** window displays the screen shown in Figure 11.3.

You use this screen to specify which TCP and UDP ports to scan, and the degree to which the scanner should attempt to confirm potential vulnerabilities through probes. Within the **Discovery Settings** area of the screen, you can specify the TCP or UDP ports by selecting the relevant tab, then selecting one of the predefined options in the list box on the right. You will then see the list of ports included in that option cataloged in the **Assess vulnerabilities for TCP ports** field on the left.

Figure 11.3 Session Configuration Window (Vulnerabilities Tab)

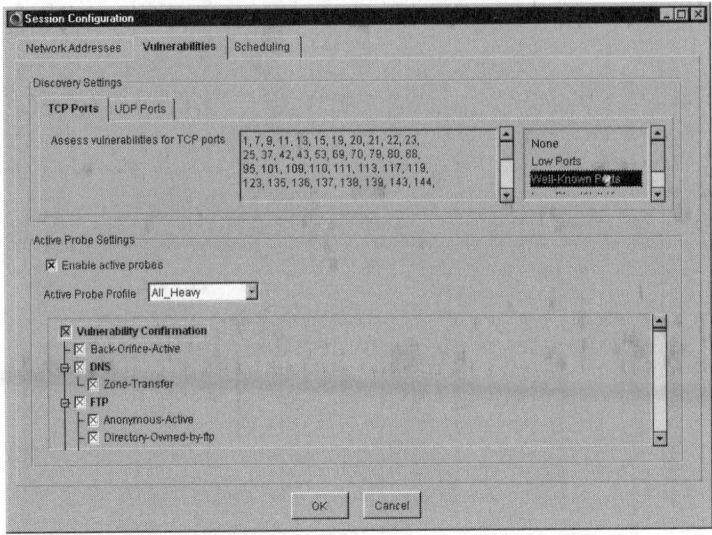

For the TCP ports, the predefined options are:

- **None** No TCP ports will be scanned
- **Low Ports** TCP ports 1 through 1024 will be scanned
- **Well-Known Ports (Default)** Specific TCP ports where common services typically listen will be scanned (for example, Telnet, FTP, SMTP, DNS, HTTP)
- **Low Plus Well-Known** TCP ports 1 through 1024 and any ports above that range where common services typically listen will be scanned
- **All Ports** TCP ports 1 through 65535 will be scanned

For UDP ports, the predefined options are:

- **None** No UDP ports will be scanned
- **Well-Known Ports (Default)** Specific UDP ports where common services typically listen will be scanned (for instance, DNS, TFTP, SNMP, NFS)

You can edit the list of predefined ports within an option by clicking within the ports list, and adding ports or ranges of ports separated by commas. In addition, you can copy lists of ports from one option to another, or from one session to another, by right-clicking the ports list and using the listed options of **Cut**, **Paste**, **Copy**, **Delete**, and **Select All**.

> **W**ARNING
>
> Change the default UDP port configuration with care. Because of the connectionless nature of UDP and the implementation of ICMP error message rate limiting by many hosts, scanning a large number of UDP ports can greatly increase the scan time.

You can also configure active and intrusive probing from the **Vulnerabilities** tab of the **Session Configuration** window to confirm potential vulnerabilities identified through the port scan. As shown in Figure 11.3, check the **Enable Active Probes** check box within the **Active Probe Settings** area of the screen. This will allow you to choose a predefined profile from the **Active Probe Profile** drop-down list. The available profiles are defined based on platform type (All, UNIX, Windows) and decreasing intrusiveness (Heavy, Severe, Lite), and are listed next:

- All Heavy
- All Lite
- All Severe
- Unix Heavy
- Unix Lite
- Unix Severe
- Windows Heavy
- Windows Lite
- Windows Severe

When you select a probe profile, the actual probes that are included in that profile are checked in the list below it. You can modify the probes included in the session by selecting or deselecting the individual probes. To obtain information about a particular probe, right-click the probe, and select **Help** from the pop-up menu. This will launch a browser window with information on the vulnerability of the NSDB. The probes are grouped into the following high-level categories:

- Back-Orifice-Active
- DNS
- FTP
- Finger
- HTTP
- MSSQL
- NFS
- NT
- NetBIOS
- RPC
- Rlogin
- Rsh
- SMTP
- SNMP
- TFTP
- Telnet
- Xwindows

NOTE

It is possible to configure user defined/custom vulnerability rules. This could be useful if you are scanning for unique devices or non-standard port numbers. Once a custom rule has been defined, you should distribute that rule throughout the enterprise to ensure consistency across the scanners. Further details on how to create user-defined rules can be found at: www.cisco.com/univercd/cc/td/doc/product/iaabu/csscan/csscan2/csscug/userrule.htm.

Scheduling the Session

Once you have identified the address range(s) and ports to be scanned, and specified the vulnerabilities to be probed, you must then schedule the session. Selecting the **Scheduling** tab within the **Session Configuration** window displays the screen shown in Figure 11.4.

Figure 11.4 Session Configuration Window (Scheduling Tab)

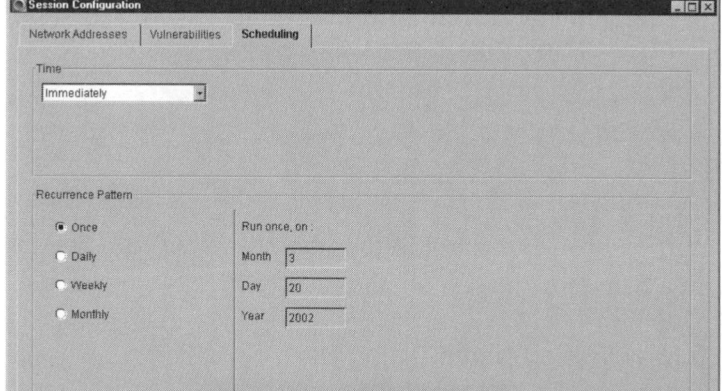

As shown in the **Recurrence** area of the screen, you can schedule a session to be run once, daily, weekly, or monthly. As you can see, the default scheduling configuration has the session being run immediately. Depending on which recurrence pattern you select, you will need to fill out the appropriate information in the area to the right of the pattern selected. For instance, for a daily recurrence pattern, you can specify that the session be run every weekday, or repeated every X number of days. Once this information has been selected, you need to select the time for the scan to run. The options include immediately, every hour of the day, or a random execution within one of four six-hour time windows:

- Midnight – 6:00 A.M.

- 6:00 A.M. – Noon

- Noon – 6:00 P.M.

- 6:00 P.M. – Midnight

Once you have configured the addresses, vulnerabilities, and scheduling, you can click the **OK** button within the **Session Configuration** window. If you have the session configured to perform active probing, you may receive a warning prompt similar to the one shown in Figure 11.5. You should choose whether or not to perform the exploit based on warning information, the criticality of the hosts being scanned, the day and time of the scan, and the degree of administrative support that you have coordinated prior to initiating the scan.

Figure 11.5 Vulnerability Confirmation Warning

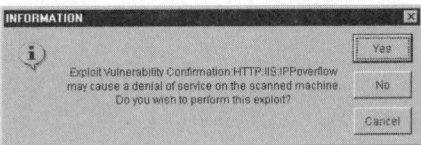

As shown in Figure 11.6, you will then be prompted to name the session. You should type in a name for the session and click **OK**.

Figure 11.6 New Session Name Dialog Box

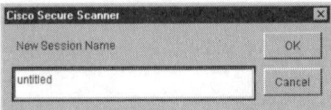

Once you have initiated the session, you will see a progress window that looks similar to the one shown in Figure 11.7.

Figure 11.7 Session Status Window

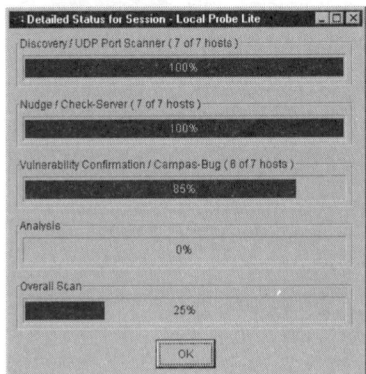

Configuring & Implementing...

Cisco Secure Scanner – General Usage Tips

Like any tool, Cisco Secure Scanner is most effective when used properly. Here are some general tips you can use for maximum benefit.

- The same person or people should perform the scan each time; this may even lead to the creation (or enhancement) of a central team in your organization responsible for security. They should be the ones to take action on the results; this will have the additional effect of creating or enforcing security standards in your organization.

- The session should be run when the network traffic levels are low, as well as during busy hours when all devices are powered up in order to give you a more comprehensive set of results.

- Run unscheduled scans to increase the likelihood of catching devices that may only be active occasionally. An example might be a traveling sales representative who only comes to the office once a week.

- As soon as new devices are added to the network, a scan should be run. Ideally, this should be integrated into both the company change management system and the company system development lifecycle.

- Report any anomalies or new vulnerabilities you have found to Cisco Systems using the NSDB reporting mechanism. As a responsible user of the system, you could help protect other companies from similar attacks. However, be sure you obey your company's policies and don't provide information which may be used against your company, or information which is illegal to provide.

Viewing the Results

Following the completion of a session, the message "Completed Single Run" appears in the Session Status column, and a Result Set subfolder is created within the session folder in the main Secure Scanner screen, as shown in Figure 11.8. The Result Set contains additional subfolders for charts, grids and reports that you create as you analyze the session results. To begin analyzing your data, right click the **Result Set** subfolder and then select **View Grid Data**.

Figure 11.8 Opening the Grid Browser

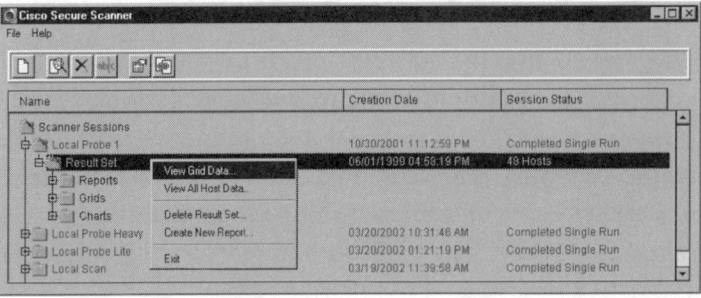

The Grid Browser, shown in Figure 11.9, is a two-dimensional hyperlinked spreadsheet that is used to view session results. You can change the information displayed on the *x* and *y* axes, drill down into selected data cells, perform "data pivoting," view different levels of detail by zooming in or out, show/hide totals or percentages for rows or columns, and create charts. Once you have created grid browser views and charts, you can save them for later use.

Figure 11.9 The Grid Browser

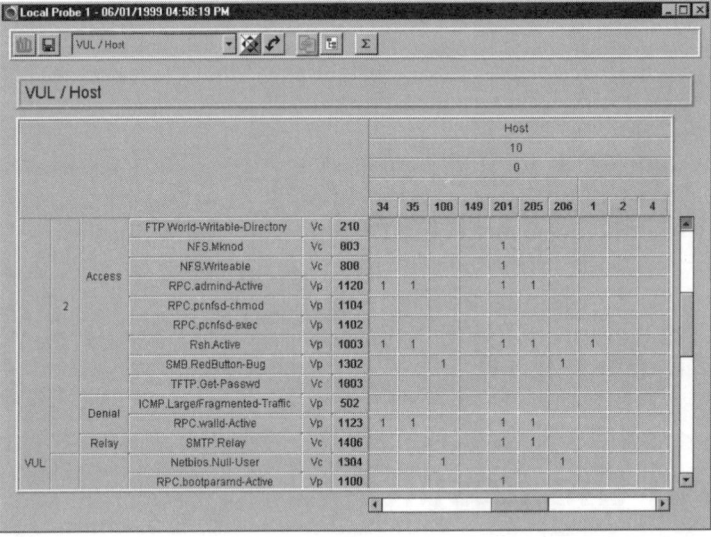

In Figure 11.9, the IP addresses of the hosts are displayed along the *x*-axis, and the vulnerabilities are displayed along the *y*-axis.

The leading six columns on the left provide the vulnerability details. Let's examine a row from left to right. Column one identifies the data displayed along the y-axis (vulnerabilities). Column two shows a value that represents the severity level of the vulnerability (the higher the number, the worse the vulnerability). Column three classifies the type of exploit. Column four identifies the name of the exploit. Column five identifies whether the vulnerability is potential (Vp) or confirmed (Vc). Column six identifies the corresponding ID in the NSDB database.

The top six rows provide the host details. The first row identifies the data that is displayed along the x-axis (host). The second row displays the first octet of the host IP address, the third row displays the second octet of the host IP address, the fourth row identifies the third octet of the host IP address, and the fifth row identifies the fourth octet of the host IP address.

Within the grid area, the numbers in the cells represent the number of intersections of a row and column value. For this particular view, the value is always 1; however, the number can vary within other views.

Changing Axis Views

As shown in Figure 11.10, you can change the information displayed along the axes by selecting the **Axis** drop-down menu and selecting a new pair.

Figure 11.10 Changing the Axis Pair

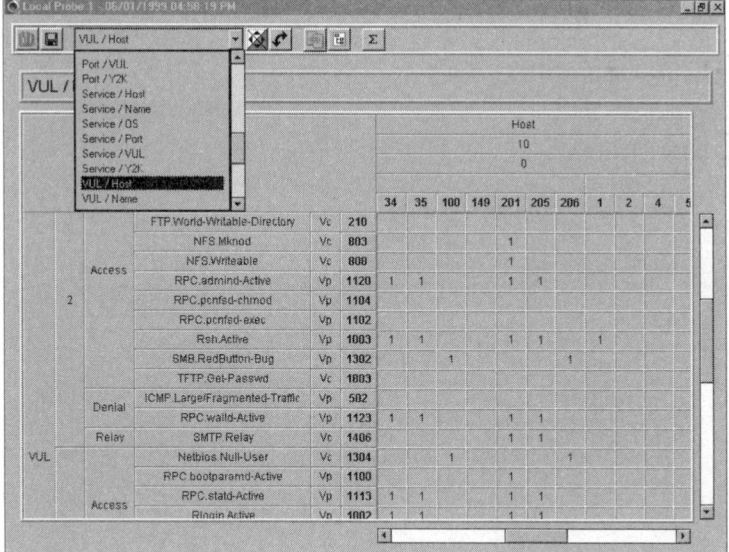

For example, changing the axis pair from Vul / Host to OS / Host results in the view shown in Figure 11.11. This view displays the operating system and version that the scanner identified for each host.

Figure 11.11 OS / Host Grid View

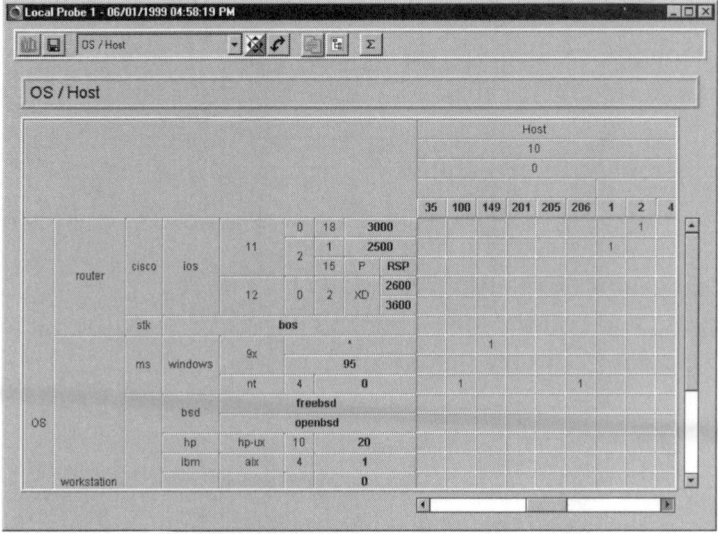

You can swap the axes display by clicking the **Swap Axis** icon on the toolbar, as shown in Figure 11.12.

Figure 11.12 Swapping the Axes

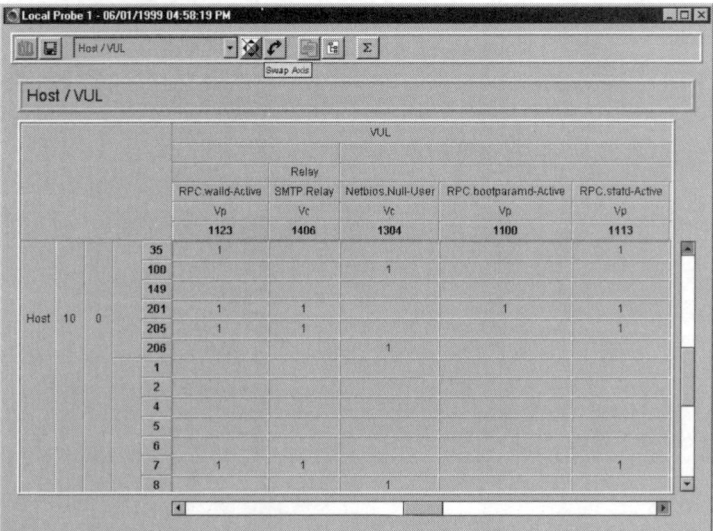

You can change an individual axis within the a view by right-clicking the axis you want to change, selecting **Change Y Axis** (or **Change X axis**), and then selecting the information you want to display, as shown in Figure 11.13.

Figure 11.13 Changing an Individual Axis

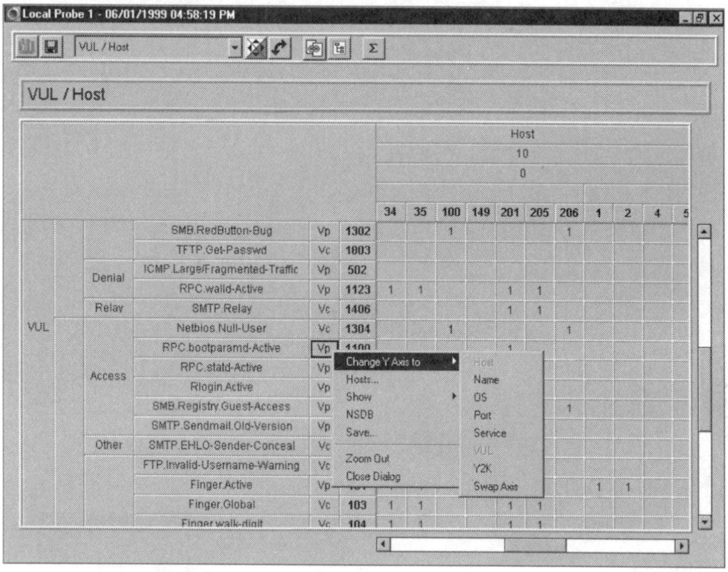

Drilling into Data

Within the Grid Browser, you can also drill down into the data to identify all of the hosts that share a particular attribute such as operating system, specific vulnerability, vulnerability type, open TCP or UDP port, or listening service. This can be valuable in identifying which hosts require a particular patch or countermeasure. To drill into data, you simply select the attribute you are interested in, right-click it, and select **Hosts**. Figure 11.14 illustrates the process of drilling into the hosts that share a particular vulnerability.

After drilling into the data, you will see a window similar to the one shown in Figure 11.15. Notice that the title within the window is the name of the attribute you selected to drill into. All of the hosts that share the particular attribute, in this case a vulnerability, as listed in the window. In addition, Figure 11.15 shows that by clicking on the **+** next to the host, you will see a listing of all the services and vulnerabilities for that host.

Figure 11.14 Drilling into Data

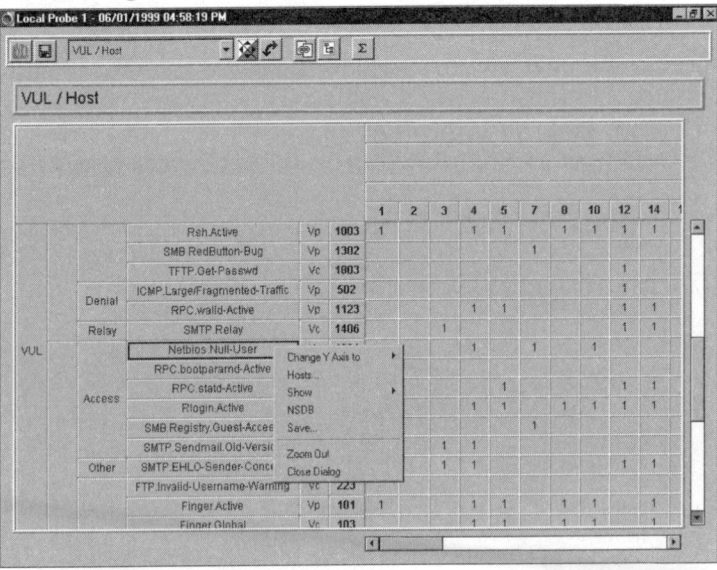

Figure 11.15 Host Detail

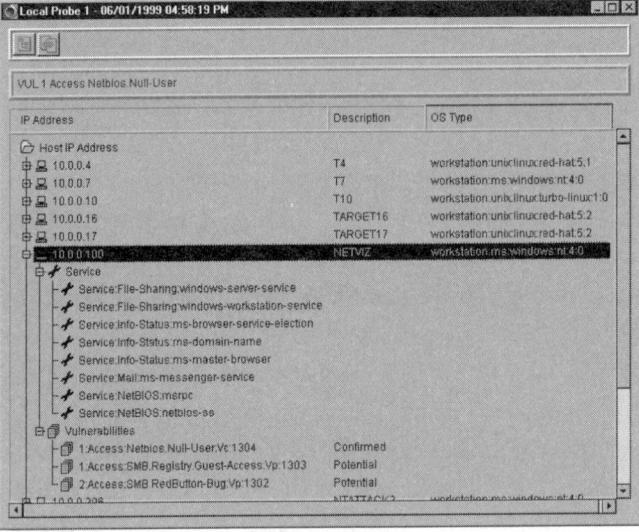

Pivoting Data

Once you have drilled into data and are viewing the services and vulnerabilities associated with a particular host, as shown in the previous figure, you can also perform a manipulation called *data pivoting*. If you see a particular service or vulnerability listed under a host entry, and want to know what other hosts share that service or vulnerability, simply right-click the entry and select **Hosts** as shown in Figure 11.16. You have now pivoted on the data to obtain another view.

Figure 11.16 Pivoting on Data

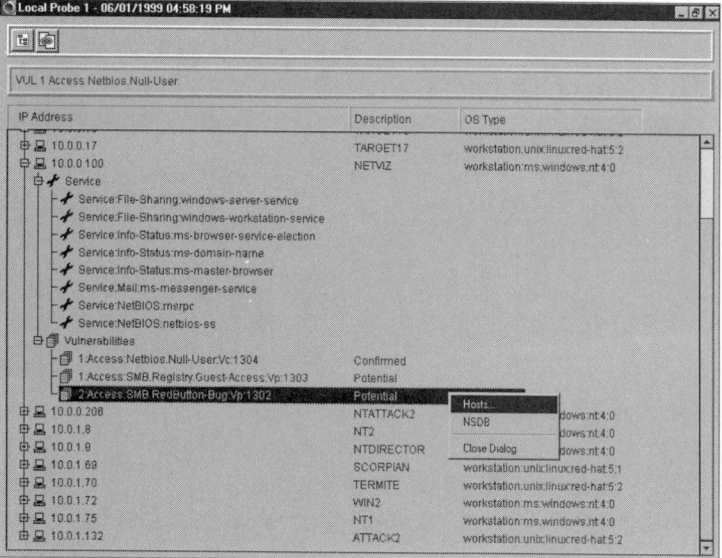

The preceding pivot results in the view illustrated in Figure 11.17. Notice that the format is the same as that shown in Figure 11.15, but the title within the window reflects the attribute selected for pivoting.

Figure 11.17 Pivoted Data View

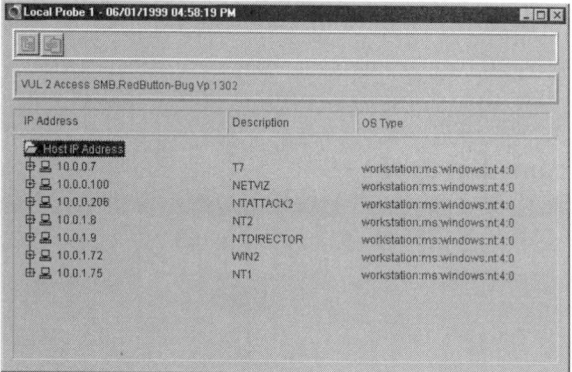

Zooming In and Out

You can also change the level of detail displayed within the Grid Browser through the zooming capability. Let's say you want to change the grid to display the number of vulnerabilities of each severity level for the hosts. As shown in Figure 11.18, simply right-click anywhere within column 2 and then select **Zoom Out**.

Figure 11.18 Zooming Out

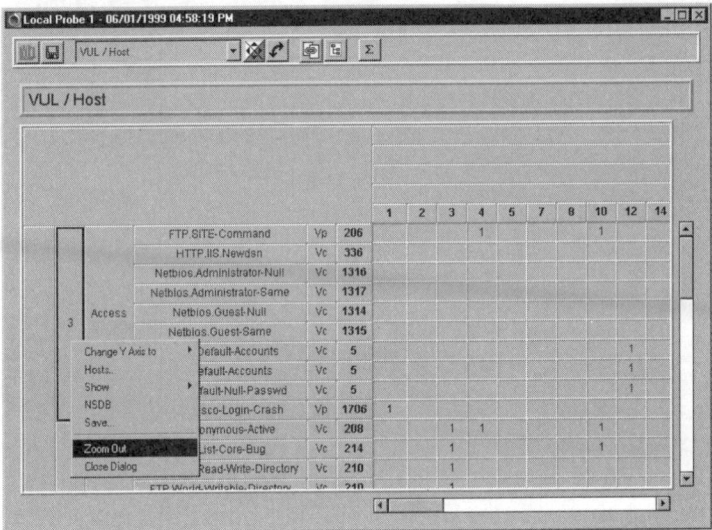

As you can see in Figure 11.19, the cell values change to the total number of vulnerabilities of each severity level for each host. You could also use the zooming capability to view more or less details about operating system types, services, and open ports on the network. You could view the number of hosts running a particular operating system, the number of hosts running a particular service, or the number of hosts with a particular port open.

Figure 11.19 Zoomed-in Data

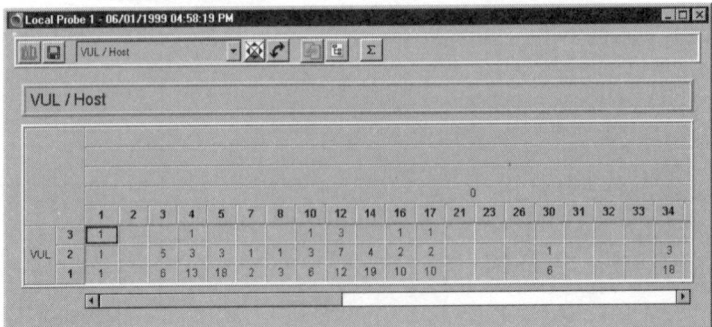

Creating Charts

From within the Grid Browser, you can create charts to represent the data graphically. This is particularly useful for communicating assessment results to management. The Chart Wizard enables you to create many different types of charts, including 2D and 3D, line, area, pie, bar, and stacked charts. You can then use the chart in the generation of a report, or export it for use in a Microsoft PowerPoint slide show. You create a chart by selecting the desired cells and clicking the **Chart** button on the tool bar, as shown in Figure 11.20.

Figure 11.20 Creating a Chart

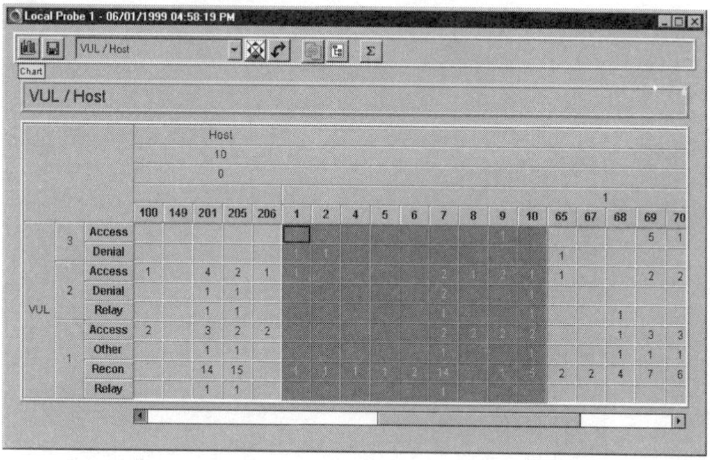

This will launch the Chart Wizard, as shown in Figure 11.21, where you can choose the type of chart you want to create. The chart types available will depend on the data you have selected. For example, a pie chart will only appear as an option if you choose a single row of data.

By selecting the first option (**3D Row**), the chart in Figure 11.22 is created.

Charts like the one shown in the previous figure are often invaluable in communicating effectively to both system managers and executive management because they can instantly communicate where mitigation or compliance efforts should be focused.

The chart is easily manipulated by right-clicking it and choosing the appropriate option, as shown in Figure 11.22. You can show/hide/manipulate the legend, change the chart type, change the background color, and tilt or pan the view. In the preceding example, the height of the bars represents the number of vulnerability types exhibited by a host. Once you save a graph, it can be incorporated into a NetSonar report or used externally as a .bmp or .gif file.

Figure 11.21 The Chart Wizard

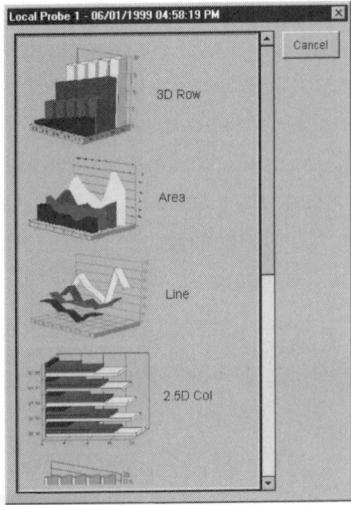

Figure 11.22 3D Row Chart

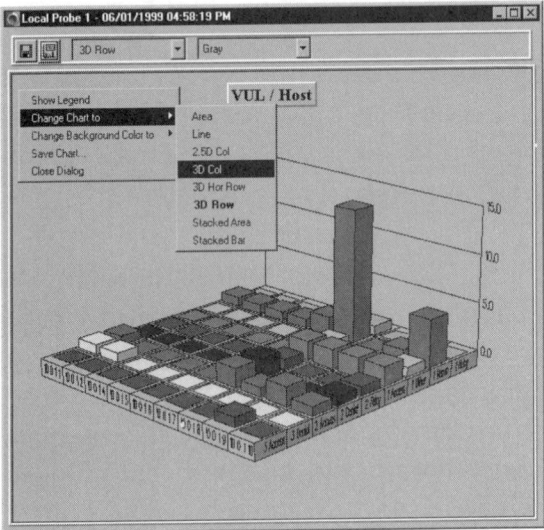

Saving Grid Views and Charts

After you have created grid views and charts, you can save them for later reference or inclusion in a report by simply right-clicking anywhere on the view or chart and clicking **Save** or **Save Chart** options, respectively. When prompted, enter a title and click **OK**. The grid view or chart will now appear in the **Grids** or **Charts** subfolder (respectively) of the **Session** folder on the main screen of the Cisco Secure Scanner.

> **NOTE**
>
> You can also save any portion of a grid view by highlighting the desired data, right-clicking it, and selecting **Save**.

Reports and Wizards

Cisco Secure Scanner includes a flexible reporting and analysis tool that can generate three types of HTML reports: executive, brief technical, and full technical. As the names suggest, each type of report is aimed at different groups of people as identified in Table 11.1.

Table 11.1 Scanner Report Types

Report Type	Target Audience	Description
Executive	Executive Management	High-level overview of security vulnerabilities
Brief Technical	Corporate Security Management	Technical summary of security vulnerabilities
Full Technical	System/Network Management	Detailed technical information about security vulnerabilities

To generate a report via the Scanner Report Wizard, simply right-click the desired **Result Set** and select **Create New Report** as shown in Figure 11.23.

Figure 11.23 Creating a Scanner Report

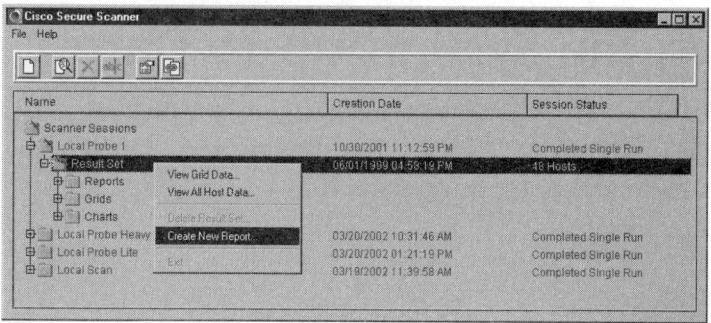

This will launch the Scanner Report Wizard shown in Figure 11.24. The wizard is easy to use to generate a report, and allows you to: Customize report types by changing the set of report components included in a report type (Executive, Brief Technical, Full Technical), change the order of report components, and include grids and charts you created and saved previously. The generated report is in HTML format, but can be manually converged into one Microsoft Word file.

Figure 11.24 The Scanner Report Wizard

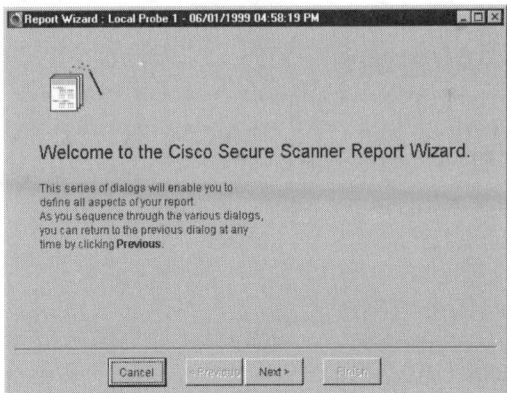

> **NOTE**
>
> You can customize both reports and report templates. The advantage of customizing report templates is that you can customize it once and apply it to all reports you subsequently generate using the scanner. You can find detailed guidance on customizing reports and templates at www.cisco.com/univercd/cc/td/doc/product/iaabu/csscan/csscan2/csscug/custrep.htm.

Keeping the System Up-to-Date

As Cisco Secure Scanner vulnerability exploits are updated and added, a new list will appear on the Cisco Web site. You should check the following location for new updates: www.cisco.com/kobayashi/sw-center/ciscosecure/scanner-updates.shtml.

When vulnerability exploits are updated or added, Cisco makes the appropriate updates in its Network Security Database (NSDB), which is an online HTML reference guide that provides information on the vulnerabilities detected by the Cisco Secure Scanner. The NSDB main screen is shown in Figure 11.25.

Figure 11.25 The NSDB Main Screen

For each vulnerability, the NSDB provides the information identified in Table 11.2.

Table 11.2 NSDB Vulnerability Information

Information	Description
Vulnerability Name	The name by which the vulnerability is known in the Scanner and the NSDB.
Alias	Other names by which the vulnerability may be known.
ID Number	A number assigned to the vulnerability in the NSDB.
Severity Level	A level of 1, 2, or 3 (refer to Table 11.3).
Vulnerability Type	The type of damage the vulnerability causes.
Exploit Type	The network service the vulnerability affects.
Affected Systems	The operating systems affected by the vulnerability.
Affected Programs	The programs affected by the vulnerability.
Description	A description of the vulnerability.

Continued

Table 11.2 Continued

Information	Description
Consequences	A discussion of the vulnerability's consequences.
Countermeasures	The recommended countermeasure for the vulnerability.
Related Links	Any other sites that offer more information on the vulnerability.
User Notes	An HTML page where you can add any information you find about that vulnerability.

The severity levels that are assigned to vulnerabilities in the NSDB are identified and described in Table 11.3.

Table 11.3 NSDB Vulnerability Severity Levels

NSDB Severity Level	Description
Level 1	Generally, most Level 1 vulnerabilities permit reconnaissance activities that allow attackers to collect information that can be used to stage an attack. Examples include network topology and configuration information, including active IP addresses, active network services, operating system type and version, and valid usernames. These vulnerabilities do not directly lead to unauthorized access, but they should be corrected to make it difficult for intruders to become knowledgeable about your network and systems.
Level 2	Generally, most Level 2 vulnerabilities permit some level of unprivileged unauthorized access or denial of service. These vulnerabilities can frequently be leveraged to allow attackers to eventually gain more privileged and complete control of your network or systems. Level 2 vulnerabilities should be corrected as soon as possible.
Level 3	Generally, most Level 3 vulnerabilities permit an attacker to execute arbitrary commands on systems. The ability to execute commands on a system implies the ability either to cause denial of service or to gain unauthorized data access. These vulnerability types frequently allow attackers to establish a base of operations within your network from which they compromise other systems. Level 3 vulnerabilities should be corrected immediately.

Figure 11.26 shows the typical information provided by the NSDB for a given vulnerability.

Figure 11.26 NSDB Vulnerability Information Display

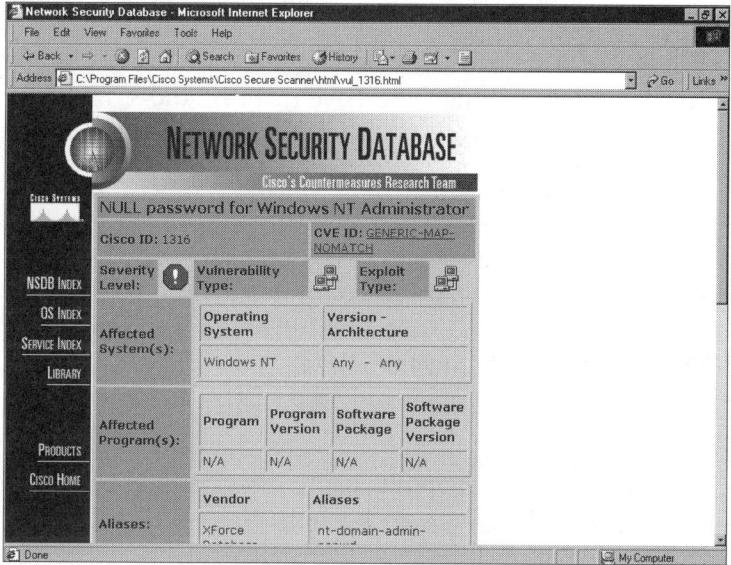

The NSDB can be accessed from within Cisco Secure Scanner in the following ways:

- From the scanner main window by selecting **File | Show NSDB**.

- From within the Grid Browser by selecting a vulnerability, service, or data cell, right-clicking it, and selecting **NSDB**.

- While data pivoting, by selecting a service or vulnerability, right-clicking it, and selecting **Vulnerabilities | NSDB**.

- From within the **Vulnerabilities** tab in the **Session Configuration** window by selecting **Enable active probes**, right-clicking any vulnerability in the **Vulnerability Confirmation** group box, and selecting **Help**.

Summary

Cisco Secure Scanner is a vulnerability scanner that maps network devices, identifies device operating systems and versions, identifies open ports and applications listening on them, and identifies vulnerabilities associated with those applications.

It can actively probe the open ports and attempt to confirm vulnerabilities in order to reduce false positives. Once you have mapped and scanned your network, the unique Grid Browser enables you to view the results of your scan from many different perspectives and at varying levels of detail. This not only provides you with the capability to identify and drill into the data that you need to implement corrective actions, but also provides you with the flexibility to generate management charts and reports that will communicate the necessary information to focus management attention and resources where it is needed. Unlike other vulnerability scanners, Cisco Secure Scanner is licensed without any ties or restrictions based on IP address; there is no requirement to modify your license as your network changes. Nor is its license based on the platform types to be scanned; all network devices are mapped and scanned, including UNIX servers, Windows servers, firewalls, routers, switches, and printers.

Solutions Fast Track

Minimum System Specifications for Secure Scanner

- ☑ Windows NT or Solaris
- ☑ 64MB RAM (96MB RAM recommended)
- ☑ Disk Space: 20MB (application), 100MB (session data), 400MB (paging file)
- ☑ TCP/IP network interface
- ☑ Microsoft Internet Explorer 4.0 or later (or Netscape Navigator 2.0 or later)

Searching the Network for Vulnerabilities

- ☑ Specify IP address ranges and details through the Network Addresses tab of the Session Configuration window.

☑ Specify the TCP/UDP ports to scan, and the vulnerabilities to attempt to confirm through the Vulnerabilities tab of the Session Configuration window.

☑ Schedule the scan session through the Scheduling tab of the Session Configuration window.

Viewing the Results

☑ The Grid Browser can manipulate the data display by changing axis views, drilling into data, pivoting on data, zooming in and out, and saving grid views.

☑ Using the Chart Wizard, you can create and save charts that graphically illustrate a particular grid view.

☑ Using the Report Wizard, you can create different report types (executive, brief technical, full technical) that are targeted at different audiences, including previously saved grid views and charts.

Keeping the System Up-to-Date

☑ Check the Cisco Web site for Cisco Secure Scanner updates that include new or updated vulnerability exploits.

☑ Use the NSDB as a resource to become knowledgeable about particular vulnerabilities.

Frequently Asked Questions

The following Frequently Asked Questions, answered by the authors of this book, are designed to both measure your understanding of the concepts presented in this chapter and to assist you with real-life implementation of these concepts. To have your questions about this chapter answered by the author, browse to **www.syngress.com/solutions** and click on the **"Ask the Author"** form.

Q: What is vulnerability scanning and how can it be leveraged?

A: Security scanning is the process of identifying security vulnerabilities associated with network devices and hosts. It can be leveraged within a company's system lifecycle process, change management process, and comprehensive risk management process. Scanning can be used in a proactive manner to identify vulnerabilities before a system is deployed, or after a significant change has occurred. In addition, it can be used as part of the vulnerability assessment phase of a continual risk management process.

Q: Do Cisco Secure Scanner users need to be experts in security in order to use it?

A: No. The graphical user interface makes it easy to initiate scan sessions, and the Grid Browser, Chart Wizard, and Report Wizard enable you to view the information needed to take corrective action. In addition, the Network Security Database provides you with comprehensive information for identified vulnerabilities so you can develop and implement effective action plans.

Q: Is Cisco Secure Scanner customizable?

A: Yes. You can define custom vulnerability rules, and customize reports and report templates.

Q: How do firewalls effect the operation of Cisco Secure Scanner?

A: If some of the target addresses you are attempting to scan are located behind a firewall or packet filtering router, you may not obtain a complete scan of the addresses. Because Secure Scanner uses ping sweeps to discover network hosts, if the packet filtering device blocks incoming pings, you will not discover the target hosts on the other side of the device if you use the default scan session configuration. The good news is that you still may be able to discover hosts behind a packet filtering device by configuring your scan session appropri-ately. However, your scan and probe results will be limited by the policy being enforced by the packet filter. In other words, you will only be able to identify ports and related vulnerabilities if the packet filter allows that partic-ular traffic to reach the target host.

Q: What impact will Scanner scans have on my traffic load?

A: In general, users should be unaware that a session is in progress; however, a performance drop may occur, especially if a probe has been selected with a heavy active probe profile. The network impact will be a function of the duration of the scan and the depth of penetration. In addition, because it is possible to render a service or device unavailable by initiating an active and intrusive probe, you should conduct probe sessions outside peak network usage hours, or you should omit sensitive devices to prevent loss of service.

## Chapter 12

Cisco Secure Policy Manager

Solutions in this chapter:

- **Overview of the Cisco Secure Policy Manager**

- **Features of the Cisco Secure Policy Manager**

- **Using the Cisco Secure Policy Manager**

☑ **Summary**

☑ **Solutions Fast Track**

☑ **Frequently Asked Questions**

Introduction

Network security has become more critical to organizations than ever before. The associated security risks have become very high, with most organizations configuring and deploying firewalls to improve network boundary security and virtual private networks (VPNs) to protect the integrity of the network and establish secure business-to-business communications.

As you will see, the Cisco Secure Policy Manager (CSPM) is an excellent tool that allows you to minimize costs and ensure a consistent security policy on your network. It also allows you to manage your network and associated services with a consolidated management system. It supports the different network requirements of your organization that are used to establish a secure connection for your intranets with multiple firewalls and VPN routers, and allows real-time monitoring of alerts from Intrusion Detection sensors.

In this chapter, we will take a look at the CSPM as a whole, the features that come with it, and then take some time to examine exactly how it should be used.

Overview of the Cisco Secure Policy Manager

The CSPM is a powerful policy-driven management system for Cisco PIX firewalls, IP Security (IPSec) routers, and Cisco Intrusion Detection System (Cisco IDS) sensors. With CSPM, you can define, distribute, enforce, and audit your entire network security policies from a central location. You can use CSPM to configure your PIX firewalls on the boundary of your enterprise network as well as configure Network Address Translation (NAT) and IPSec based VPNs. This allows for easy and simple deployment of your security policy to your PIX firewalls and your VPN, which should be the cornerstone of your security policy. CSPM is also capable of configuring IDS sensors and monitoring the security alerts produced by them, so you are able to see the status of your security measures at any given time.

CSPM's distributed architecture, combined with its secure remote management features, allows you to deploy the security policy in various environments by using more than one policy enforcement point. If you are administrating a large enterprise network, you can install the policy administrator, the graphical user interface (GUI) used for policy administration, in different locations across your network for distributed management of your network security policy.

The CSPM software is an immense product and could be the subject of an entire book, so this will only be a brief summary of the benefits, features, and sample configurations included in this application.

The Benefits of Using Cisco Secure Policy Manager

Using CSPM on your network gives you a great number of products to use for creating, deploying, and changing your enterprise network security policy. Some benefits of using CSPM and all the related products include:

- Scalability enables you to meet large-scale security policy requirements and network growth. It provides the capability to manage up to several hundred PIX firewall and VPN routers on your network plus corresponding number of IDS sensors.

- The built-in auditing and reporting provides up-to-date information on network and system events. It allows you to configure notifications according to your needs—from real-time alerting of urgent events to generation of scheduled reports on other events of interest.

- It allows you to define networkwide security policies based on your organization's business objectives. You can accurately define your security policies for different devices on your network and can reduce the time needed to deploy the security configurations.

- It also allows you to define networkwide monitoring for possible security policy violations by integrating IDS management features.

- You can either use a centralized standalone policy management environment, or a distributed architecture policy management environment to support your needs on the Internet, intranet, and extranet environments.

- Now you can configure and test your security policies without connecting to your live network. You can do your configurations offline and verify that your security policies are working correctly, as attended, and then deploy the policy to your live network.

- A Windows NT-based system provides you with an easy-to-use GUI to manage your security policy.

The version discussed in this chapter is CSPM 2.3.2.

Since version 2.3, the functionality of CSPM has been split into two branches. The bulk of firewall and VPN management features are implemented in the "f" series of the product. For example, 2.3f is a CSPM version with enhanced firewall/VPN management. Installation images of this series also contain basic IDS management (setup and monitoring), although another version ("i" series) contains the full range of IDS capabilities plus basic firewall/VPN features. Most of the time, this chapter will discuss the "f" series since intrusion detection is dealt with in Chapter 13. In any case, both series share the same interface and internals.

The newest version of the "f" series is 3.0f, which is offered exclusively as a part of the VPN Management Solution (VMS) for Cisco Works 2000. This version (which is very recent and still a bit "raw") continues the integration of CSPM with Cisco Works, which was started in 2.3. The most interesting feature of 3.0 that is not offered in 2.3 is a policy import from already configured devices, which allows (to some extent) automatic creation of network topology and the importing of existing device configurations into the CSPM database.

Installation Requirements for the Cisco Secure Policy Manager

Before installing CSPM on your target server, you should ensure that all the devices on the network you intend to manage are configured properly and are active on your network. You should have IP communication between the device and the target CSPM server on your network for Telnet sessions. CSPM can only be installed on Windows NT computers. Only Intel architecture is supported, a version for DEC Alpha is not available.

Next, you should insure that your target CSPM server meets the following hardware requirements:

- Pentium-compatible processor, 600MHz or better
- 256MB RAM
- System must be partitioned using NTFS, not FAT
- 8GB free hard drive space available
- One or more properly configured network adapters
- Video Display—1024×768, with 64K color support
- CD-ROM and 3.5-inch diskette drive

If you are installing the stand-alone or client-server system option on your target CSPM server, these minimum requirements would be sufficient, but would not be optimal for a distributed system. The Policy Server component is a multi-threaded application that can benefit from multiple processors and available memory.

You can install the GUI client for CSPM on a computer that runs Windows NT 4.0, Windows 95, Windows 98, or Windows 2000. This allows you to manage the network security policy from any host on your network.

The following minimum software requirements should be met before attempting the CSPM installation:

- Windows NT 4.0 with Service Pack 6a or Windows 2000 with Service Pack 1 (the latter for GUI only)

- Microsoft Internet Explorer 5.5

- TCP/IP protocol stack installed and working properly

- Static IP address with DHCP disabled

- TAPI for pager notifications

- MAPI for e-mail notifications

Configuring & Implementing...

Upgrading CSPM

If you are currently running an earlier version of CSPM (version 2.0, for example) and would like to upgrade to CSPM version 2.3f, you need to run the installation for all intermediate versions first (2.1 and 2.2). This will ensure that all data are converted properly. After this upgrade is completed successfully, you can run the installation for CSPM version 2.3f and upgrade the older version.

Upgrading to the 3.0f version is performed in the same way. Upgrade to 2.3f first and then to 3.0f. It is not possible to upgrade from 2.3i (IDS series) to 3.0f.

Before installing CSPM on your target server, you should check the Cisco Web site for the latest compatible software list with information on various softwares that have been tested for coexistence with CSPM on the same host. CSPM already supports the coexistence of Cisco Secure VPN Client 1.1, CiscoWorks 2000 with Resource Management Essentials version 3.0, and the QoS Policy Manager version 1.1 on the same computer. On the other hand, the "f" and "i" series cannot coexist on the same machine, so if you plan to use the extra IDS management features of "i" series, you will need to install it on a separate host. It is also recommended you turn off anti-virus programs while installing CSPM as they may interfere with the installation process. You can safely turn them on after CSPM has been installed.

Features of the Cisco Secure Policy Manager

The main features included in the CSPM product will be discussed in this section. Some of the features included in the CSPM product have the same function as the PIX Firewall Manager and the Access Control List (ACL) Manager. CSPM was meant to replace and improve the features provided by these products. The difference with CSPM is that you have a more centralized management approach that includes more functionality for managing your enterprise network security policy.

The main CSPM features include the following:

- **Cisco firewall management** Allows definition and management of perimeter security policies for Cisco PIX Firewalls and Cisco IOS routers running the Cisco Secure Integrated Software feature set.

- **Cisco VPN gateway management** Configuration of site-to-site IPSec VPNs based on Cisco Secure PIX Firewalls and the Cisco suite of VPN routers running Cisco IOS IPSec software.

- **Intrusion detection sensors management** Configuration and monitoring of Cisco intrusion detection sensors and Cisco Catalyst 6000 line cards.

- **Security policy management** Allows usage of enterprisewide policies for managing hundreds of Cisco security devices without dependency on the command-line interface (CLI).

- **Notification and reporting system** Provides tools to monitor, alert, and report Cisco device and policy-related activity.

Let's take a look at each of these in detail.

Cisco Firewall Management

This feature allows you to easily define the boundary security policy on PIX firewall and Cisco IOS routers running the firewall feature set. This allows for centralized configuration management of Cisco PIX firewalls and Cisco routers using the firewall feature set on your enterprise network. It will simplify your networkwide firewall and NAT management and reduce the need for management skills to manage the security policy, as well as reduce costs.

NOTE

A Cisco router running the firewall feature set is called a *Cisco Router/Firewall*, while a Cisco router running the IPSec VPN feature set is called a *Cisco VPN Gateway*. These feature sets are part of the *Cisco Secure Integrated Software* and *Cisco Secure Integrated VPN Software* solutions for Cisco routers.

Using this component within CSPM you can specify the outside and inside interface addresses of the specific PIX firewall. When you configure either one of the interface settings, you need to define the network the interface is connected to and specify the IP address assigned to the interface on the specific network. New versions of CSPM support multiple interfaces and failover configurations. Figure 12.1 shows what the PIX Firewall Properties panel looks like.

Figure 12.1 PIX Firewall Properties Panel

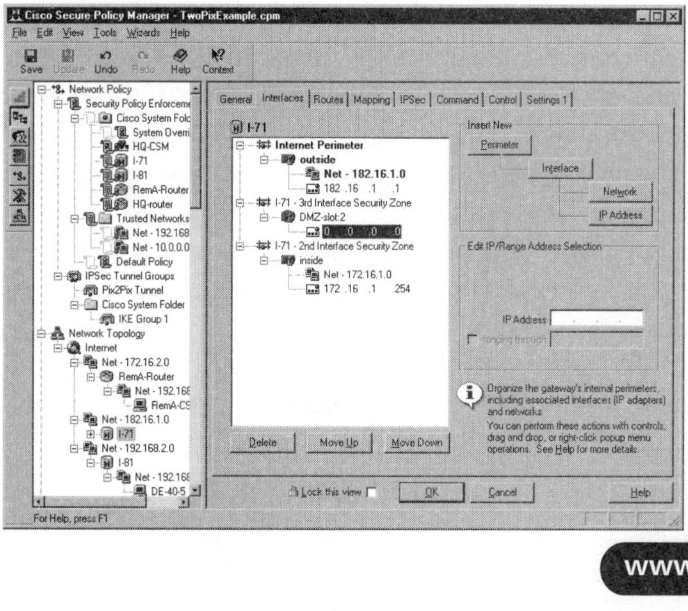

You can use the Mapping tab of the PIX Firewall Properties panel to define any NAT handled by the PIX firewall. Network routes can also be configured on the Routes tab. On the other hand, you would not use the Firewall management component to configure any of the security rules that apply to the PIX firewall on your network. For this, you should use the security policies abstractors to define any traffic filter rules that are part of your firewall security policy.

VPN and IPSec Security Management

The IPSec suite is used to seamlessly integrate security features, such as authentication, integrity, and confidentiality into IP packets. You can configure an encrypted and authenticated communication path between two clients, routers, or firewalls.

IPSec can function in two modes: tunnel and transport mode. Transport mode is used to provide end-to-end security between two nodes. Transport mode will protect all traffic between the source and destination with IPSec. In tunnel mode IPSec, the end nodes do not necessarily use or support IPSec. Instead, an IPSec-enabled security gateway or firewall functions as an IPSec peer for the communication between the end nodes. For example, a roaming user on the Internet connects to the enterprise e-mail server using an IPSec tunnel to the enterprise firewall. The traffic between the roaming user and the e-mail server is protected with IPSec up to the firewall. From there, the traffic is forwarded to the e-mail server unprotected.

IPSec uses two security protocols to provide data protection. The first one is Authentication Header (AH) protocol, which provides data integrity, data source authentication, and protection against replay attacks. When this protocol is used, the original IP packet is encapsulated into a packet that contains an extra header (AH), which contains an authentication value calculated from the contents of the packet. This value is checked when the packet arrives at its destination, ensuring the its contents were not modified on the way. The AH protocol does not provide data confidentiality, because information is not encrypted.

The second is the Encapsulation Security Payload (ESP) protocol, which provides data confidentiality, data integrity, data source authentication, and protection against replay attacks. The data confidentiality is accomplished by encrypting the original IP packet and encapsulating it into a new IP packet with the ESP header attached. The ESP header contains connection-specific encryption information in the form of reference to the Security Association (SA). This information is used on the other end of the connection to decrypt the packet after its arrival and check that the original data was not modified in any way.

The SA contains information on security protocols and encryption algorithms used to protect data for a specific connection, along with what data should be protected and which endpoints are used.

CSPM supports the configuration for IPSec SAs through the use of tunnel templates, tunnel groups, and policies. You can use the tunnel template to define the algorithms and protocols that will be used for encryption of data across the tunnel for confidentiality or authentication purposes. The tunnel group is based on one associated tunnel template and defines the tunnel peers or endpoints. This ensures that peers which are part of one tunnel group will reference the same protocols and algorithms. This will reduce risks of introducing errors when manually configuring each peer or endpoint for the tunnels. You can use the security policies to determine between services that should be routed through the tunnels, and services that should be routed using other methods.

For more information on IPSec, see Chapter 8.

CSPM allows you to create three basic types of tunnels:

- **Managed Device-to-Managed Device** Managed Device-to-Managed Device tunnels are used to securely transmit data between two managed devices (PIX firewalls or IPSec routers) across a public network, creating a VPN between two locations.

- **Policy Distribution Point-to-Managed Device** A policy distribution point is the component of CSPM that issues commands to managed devices (such as routers or Cisco Secure IDS sensors). Policy Distribution Point-to-Managed Device tunnels are used to securely transmit Managed Device configuration information to the Managed Devices over a public network. They can be used, for example, to configure and monitor remote devices over the Internet.

- **Remote User Tunnels** Remote user tunnels allow remote users secure access to internal network resources over a public network.

CSPM supports both manual and IKE tunnels. There are many preconfigured templates that can be used for creating your own tunnels. You can use them as they are or change any parameters so they suit your network setup. Figure 12.2 demonstrates one of these templates.

Figure 12.2 The IPSec Tunnel Template

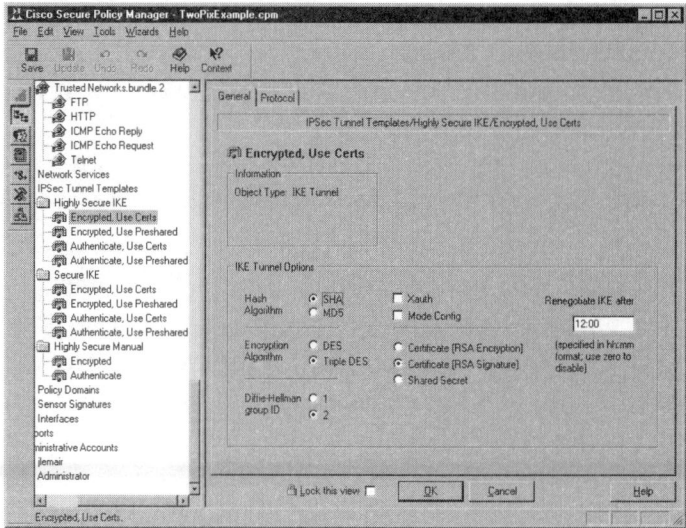

As you can see, CSPM supports all standard Cisco IPSec configuration parameters. After the template is configured, it is applied to a tunnel group to provide peers with protocol information.

Security Policy Management

CSPM is a centralized, policy-based management solution for Cisco security devices on your network. You can use CSPM to deploy a company network security policy throughout your network. The main goal of CSPM is to make the management of these policies easier. The process of policy management consists of its definition, enforcement, and auditing.

Security Policy Definition

Using CSPM, you can create high-level security policies based on the company security objectives. You can create security policy abstracts that define access and the associated level of security to specific network devices. Policy abstracts are created independently from managed devices and later assigned to them. By adjusting the parameters for the type of network service, or application, and the source and destination address of the abstracts, you can control network traffic across your enterprise network.

To simplify the creation of the policies on your network, policy abstracts can be created for a collection of services to reduce the number of policies created. When you first install the CSPM software on your server, there will be predefined abstract bundles ready for you to use in your security policies. CSPM also provides you grouping constructs for supported devices and hosts that allow you to reference multiple networks or hosts in a single policy. Figure 12.3 shows the appearance of Policy Builder—the tool used for policy creation.

Figure 12.3 Policy Builder

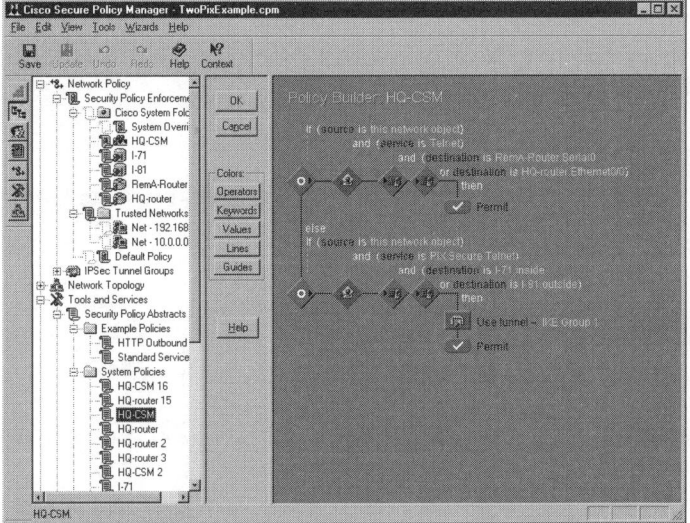

You can also use CSPM to easily define NAT policies on your PIX firewall or router on the boundary of your network. CSPM considers NAT configuration a part of device properties, not a "security policy" in the proper sense of the word. Security policies configured using Policy Builder are concerned with:

- Permitting or denying traffic for a specific user or device under certain conditions

- Use of IPSec tunnels

- Authentication, Authorization, and Accounting (AAA)

- Blocking Java in HTTP sessions

Other aspects of network traffic flow (routing, traffic shaping, general settings) are configured as the properties of corresponding devices.

Security Policy Enforcement

After you have defined the security policy, you need to apply the policy to the specific Cisco security device on your network. After the network topology is configured, you can use a simple drag-and-drop method to apply the security policies to the target network segments where they should be deployed (see Figure 12.4). The CSPM translates the policy into the device commands to apply it to the necessary PIX firewalls and VPN routers on the specified network section. You don't need to use the time-consuming CLI to configure each router for the new security policy deployed. On the other hand, if you are interested in reviewing generated commands, CSPM provides many tools for this. You can view entire sets of commands or only changes introduced by recent reconfigurations. There is also a version management utility available.

Figure 12.4 Policy Assignment

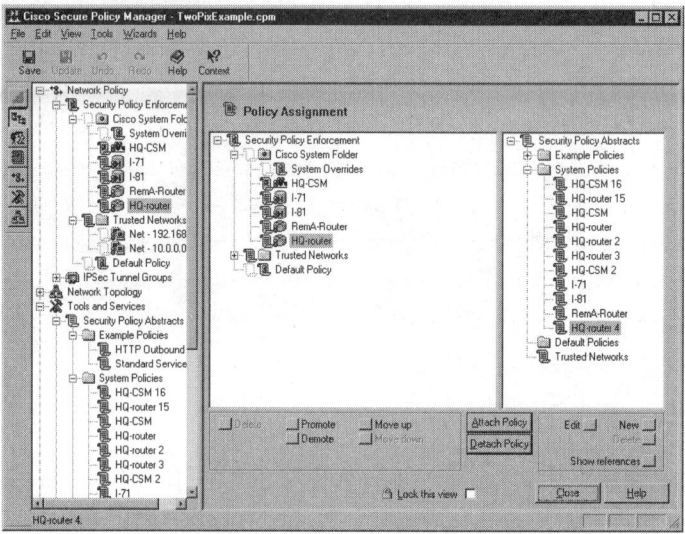

Depending on your preferences and needs, you can deploy the policy to the network automatically or manually. Manual deployment means you will need to approve each command set before it is sent to a device. Automatic approval means that commands are distributed to all devices when needed. The communication between the CSPM host and the managed devices is secure and safe to use across the network. It provides a flexible, robust mechanism to distribute configurations and enforce policies.

It allows you to have a consistent and proper policy enforcement on your network that you can easily verify and modify as required. The separate "Security Policy Enforcement" folder contains all policy enforcing devices, their hierarchy and assigned policy abstracts. You can, at any time, use the consistency check feature to ensure your network policy integrity and enforce status, or you can configure a notification if an error occurs with the policy enforcement.

Security Policy Auditing

The final part of the policy management process is the policy auditing. CSPM provides for an auditing system that enables you to log, monitor, alert, and report on the security policy events on your network where you enforced a policy. This is critical for checking the status of the policies on your network. There are two types of messages generated by Cisco security devices—firewalls and routers produce SYSLOG messages, and Cisco IDS sensors produce IDS alerts which are communicated to CSPM using Cisco proprietary protocol.

You can define filters and actions for the events related to SYSLOG messages generated on your network for the policies enforced. Any messages regarding possible network attacks and security breaches on your network can be configured for a real-time automated delivery to you using e-mail or a visual display. You can categorize the alerts based on specific events and messages for your policies to trigger only important notifications when needed. All the SYSLOG messages can be redirected to other servers on your network that could be used by third-party applications for reporting and analysis.

Cisco IDS messages are stored separately and can be viewed with the help of Event Viewer in CSPM (see Figure 12.5). This view can be manipulated by clicking plus signs (+) to open further details of the event. The special "i" series of CSPM has many extra IDS-related reports preconfigured.

Figure 12.5 Cisco IDS Sensor Events View

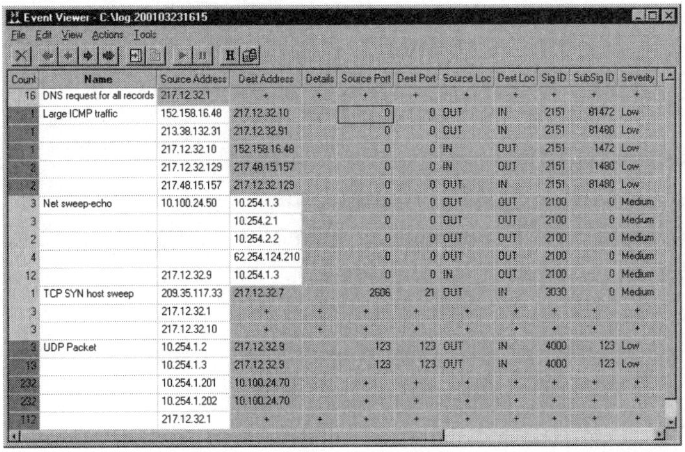

The other useful auditing and reporting CSPM tool is the Web-based reporting system that enables you to easily diagnose system security and integrity of your policies by using any host with an Internet browser. This tool allows setting access passwords and access privileges, so the reports will be open only for authorized administrators.

Network Security Deployment Options

CSPM can be used for a wide range of networks ranging from small- or medium-sized businesses that need a secure intranet connection to the Internet for networks distributed across multiple geographical locations using PIX firewalls and VPN routers for intercommunication.

When using CSPM on a large-scale enterprise network, you can deploy secure intranet connections between multiple remote sites. Using CSPM as a centralized solution for your network security management will benefit from the flexible and distributed architecture. On a large enterprise network, you could deploy CSPM in a distributed mode in which the GUI, or policy administrator, is installed on hosts in different locations on the network. The policy server includes the fundamental database, the policy translation, and the configuration distribution for CSPM. Policy server can also be installed on multiple servers in different locations on the network.

If you administer a small- to medium-sized network, you would use the perimeter, or boundary, security deployment policy available from CSPM. This gives you a simple security model and requires minimum configuration and ongoing maintenance for your security policy. Small companies usually enforce this deployment option to protect them from the Internet.

Cisco Secure Policy Manager Device and Software Support

When you use CSPM to manage your security policies in your enterprise network, you need to ensure that the managed devices comply with the list of devices and software or IOS version supported by CSPM before attempting to enforce any policies.

For all the Cisco PIX firewalls, Cisco IOS routers, and VPN routers on your network, you need to verify that they support the platform or model, as well as the software or IOS version shown in Table 12.1.

Table 12.1 Devices and Related Software Supported by CSPM 2.3.2

Device Platform	Supported Software Version
Cisco PIX Firewall	4.2(4), (5) 4.4(x) 5.1(x) 5.2.1 5.3(x) 6.0
Cisco Router/Firewall and Cisco's VPN router	IOS 12.0(5)T, XE IOS 12.0(7)T IOS 12.1(1)T, E1, XC IOS 12.1(2), T, (2) T, E, XH, (3) T, X1 IOS 12.1(4), E, T 12.1(5), 12.1(5)T

To ensure the appropriate device types are managed, CSPM includes a software version-checking mechanism that will display a warning message indicating a difference in software versions. There are also tools that allow you to manage new versions of these devices. This is called *version mapping*. Using the Version Management utility allows mapping of unsupported versions to those already known to CSPM. For example, you could create a rule that will manage Cisco PIX 6.1 using commands from the 6.0 version set.

When it comes to access control lists that need to be deployed to the specific device on the network, you would use the Policy Abstract tool to define, store, and manage your security policy abstracts that will be changed to access control lists before you enforce the policy to devices. The policy abstracts you create with this tool will support the following configuration settings:

- **Source** IP address range, specific host name, network object, policy domain, or interface defined in the network topology.

- **Destination** IP address range, specific host name, network object, policy domain or interface defined in the network topology.

- **Service type** Single or defined bundle of service types.

- **Tunnel** Uses specific IPSec tunnel groups.

- **Java** Blocks Java.

As you can see from the earlier list of allowed configuration settings to use in Policy Builder, these abstracts are mapped to standard IP ACLs and extended IP ACLs only. All other access lists have to be configured using the CLI. For example, CSPM does not support Content-Based Access-Control (CBAC) access lists. After a policy is created, you can browse the generated device commands and review to which parts of the security policy specific command sets are mapped. This is called *command to policy mapping*.

Using the Cisco Secure Policy Manager

To successfully install the CSPM on your network servers, you first need to identify the type of deployment option you will use, as discussed earlier. This will affect the number of servers you need to run the CSPM installation on, the physical location of the servers on your network, and which option you would choose during the installation based on the servers' responsibility on your enterprise network.

You have to verify that your network devices meet the necessary requirements before you can enforce any of the policies to the selected network section and related devices. In addition, you should check the minimum hardware requirements needed for your target hosts that you install the CSPM software on.

The next topics discuss the steps necessary to get CSPM installed, as well as some basic examples for configuring CSPM, and how to get CSPM up and running. Given the large amount of configuration and optional tools available in CSPM, it will be impossible to fit them all into this small section of the book. Consequently, only a few of the configurations and examples will be discussed that relate to the CSPM product. You can find additional information on the Cisco Web site at www.cisco.com. You can find almost everything you need here—from release notes for all currently supported versions of CSPM to detailed deployment guides.

Configuration

When you insert the CSPM software installation CD-ROM into the CD drive of your computer, it should autostart the Installation Wizard for CSPM. Select the **Install Product** option and then click **Next**. This will start the installation and you can follow the onscreen instructions to complete the installation. If there is no Install Product option there, this means some of the prerequisites are not fulfilled—for example, the required service pack is not installed. You will need to install it and restart installation. It is also possible to install a demo interface without installing the full product.

After installation starts, it will ask you for the location of the licence file. You can use the one supplied with the CD-ROM, which will grant you limited use of the software, and you can use the password **cisco** to continue. If you do have a licence file you purchased from Cisco, you can specify the location and enter the appropriate password.

The next option selection screen will be determined by your deployment option type on your network. You can select **Standalone CSPM** or **Client-Server CSPM,** which has two subselections to pick from, namely "Policy Server" or "Policy Client." You can also choose **Distributed CSPM** with a subselection of one of the following:

- Policy Server
- Policy Proxy-monitor
- Policy Proxy
- Policy Monitor
- Policy Admin

Designing & Planning…

Selecting between Various Deployment Types

There are many issues that affect the choice between standalone, client-server, and distributed configuration of CSPM. Some of them are:

- **Encryption of data traffic between managed devices and CSPM** This traffic will be encrypted only if the device supports IPSec and you defined IPSec tunnels for communication between the device and CSPM host. For example, if you place any part of CSPM (in a distributed configuration) on an unprotected network between the outermost managed device and your Internet provider, control traffic to that part will not be encrypted.

- **Syslog traffic** Almost all messages about the status of security policy are sent from managed devices using syslog UDP packets (the only exclusion is IDS sensors, which use their own protocol). In case of heavy attack, this UDP traffic can

Continued

flood the network if it's busy enough, therefore it's not recommended a standalone system or Policy Monitor component be placed on a busy network.

■ **IDS sensors management** CSPM does not support IDS sensors in a distributed configuration. If you plan to use Cisco
Secure IDS sensors on the network, you will need either a
standalone or client-server configuration. Note that only dedicated sensors are supported (as standalone devices or
Catalyst 6000 blades). There is no support for IOS IDS features yet.

A brief description for your selection can be found in the Installation Option
box. In this window, you also specify the installation path for CSPM. The next
screen allows you to enter the password for the username that will be used to
install and start the relevant services on your server.

Next, you can specify the IP address on your target installation server that
will be used to access and configure your CSPM. This IP address is associated
with a port number, or so called service port, used for the connection to the primary policy database. You can export the primary policy database key to a file in
a selected path, if required. If you export the primary database key, make sure to
keep it safe and secure, otherwise you might compromise the security of your
network. This will start the installation of the files needed to run CSPM and
configure your preferred settings.

Now that you're ready to start your CSPM, you need to get the access information for the routers and PIX firewalls you would like to manage. You will need
the usernames and password to add the relevant devices to your CSPM application.

CSPM Configuration Example

The examples in this section will give you a general view of the related configuration screens available in CSPM. You can see some of the settings for the topics
discussed previously. All the configurations can be used without connecting to
your network devices and you only need to deploy your new security policy if
you are satisfied with the new configuration.

Initial configuration of CSPM consists of three steps:

1. Network topology definition

2. Network policy definition and deployment

3. Generation and distribution of device commands

The first step is defining the network topology in the "Network Topology" tree in CSPM. You do not have to map your entire network to it, only devices used in security policy definition are needed here. The second step is concerned with defining security policy in terms of services permitted for different users, as well as the parameters of these services. In the last step, CSPM generates actual commands for Cisco security devices on your network based on the topology and security policies you have defined and then distributes these commands.

Network Policy Definition

Consider the following network (Figure 12.6). It is a standard example from a default installation of CSPM. It features three different remote networks connected to the Internet using Cisco routers and PIX firewalls.

Figure 12.6 Two PIX Examples

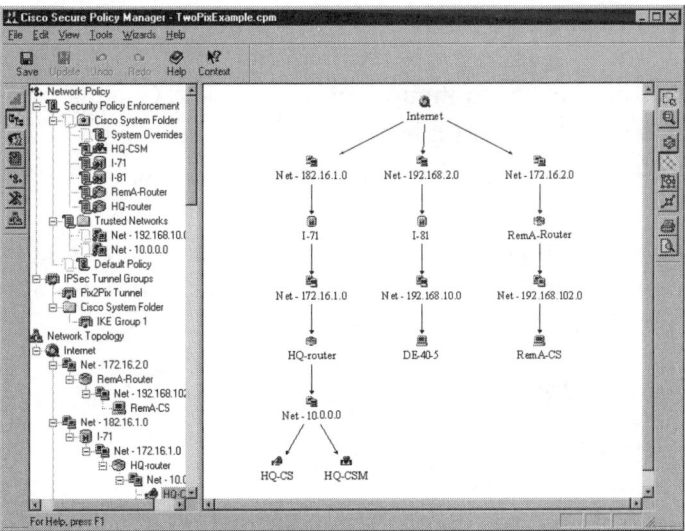

Here you will need to define hosts (servers on a network), networks, routers, and PIX firewalls in a "Network Topology" subtree. It can be done manually or by using specific wizards. For example, router configuration (probably the most complicated one judging by the amount of options available) is displayed in Figure 12.7

You can add a device by simply right-clicking the network it belongs to and clicking **New**. If you prefer to use a wizard, it is even simpler; you can select where the device has to be connected during the configuration process.

Figure 12.7 The Router Properties Panel

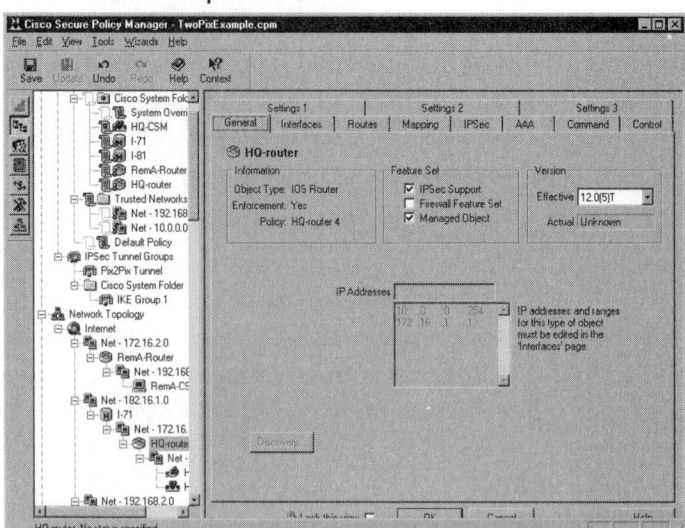

Cisco routers have many configuration options. The General tab defines general settings, such as IOS version number and feature set used. The Interfaces tab defines network perimeters, interfaces, and their IP addresses. Other panels are used to set up static routes, NAT pools, IPSec properties, authentication features, and so on. The PIX firewall configuration has fewer details (as seen in Figure 12.1). Do not forget to define your CSMP server on the network since it is a special device type (host HQ-CSM in Figure 12.6).

Network Security Policy Definition

Now that we have defined all our network assets, we need to create a security policy for the network. In order to perform this task, you will first need to place the objects, which are used to enforce the policy, in the "Security Policy Enforcement" branch of the "Network Policy" tree. The next step is to build some security policy abstracts and then assign these abstracts to the enforcement devices. If your security policy uses more complicated services than those already defined in CSPM, you will need to define them before creating policy abstracts.

Placing objects into the Security Policy Enforcement branch can be done by simply dragging-and-dropping. Policy abstracts are created using Policy Builder as in Figure 12.3. This is a context-sensitive visual tool—if you click an operator, you will be presented with a choice of possible actions, such as creating another if-then–else branch and security action selection (permit/deny/use IPSec tunnel and so on). For example, if you add another if-then branch, you are allowed to select source/destination hosts or services. Figure 12.8 shows the selection of a source of the connection.

Figure 12.8 Selecting Source Conditions for an if-then Operator

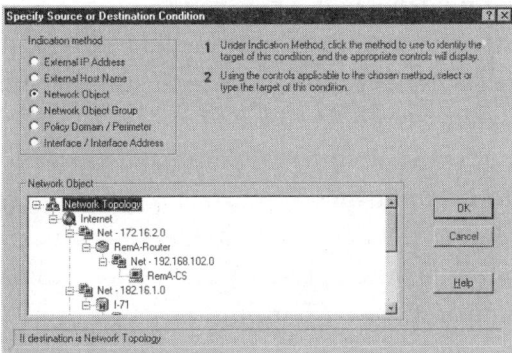

After policy abstracts are created, they need to be assigned using the policy assignment tool (as in Figure 12.4). The assignment process is very simple—just drag-and-drop policy abstracts onto corresponding enforcement points. Now everything is ready for implementation and distribution of the actual commands that will be generated by the CSPM based on your definitions. There is also a way to check some actual connections against the defined policies through use of the Policy Query tool (Figure 12.9). Using this, you can specify the source, destination, and network service of a connection and query the Policy Database on which rules actually affect this connection and what the result will be.

Figure 12.9 Policy Query

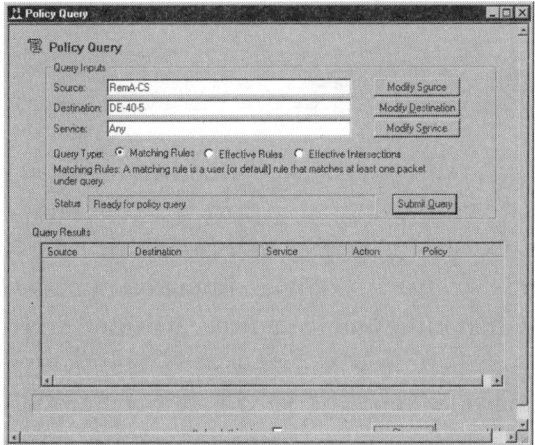

Generation and Distribution of Device Commands

The final task in the initial configuration of CSPM is generation, verification, and publishing (distribution to the actual devices) of device commands.

Device commands are generated when you select **Save and Update** from the **File** menu. The resulting command sets include all security-related commands—access lists, IPSec tunnels, and so on, plus routing and network mapping (NAT) commands, which are produced based on defined device properties. Each managed device (router or firewall) has a Command tab which allows the browsing of the resulting commands. You can also specify here any extra commands you need to send to the device (Prologue/Epilogue sections). Figure 12.10 shows the editor window for the *Epilogue* section. No commands have been generated yet, so the Command Viewer button is inactive.

Figure 12.10 Command Viewer

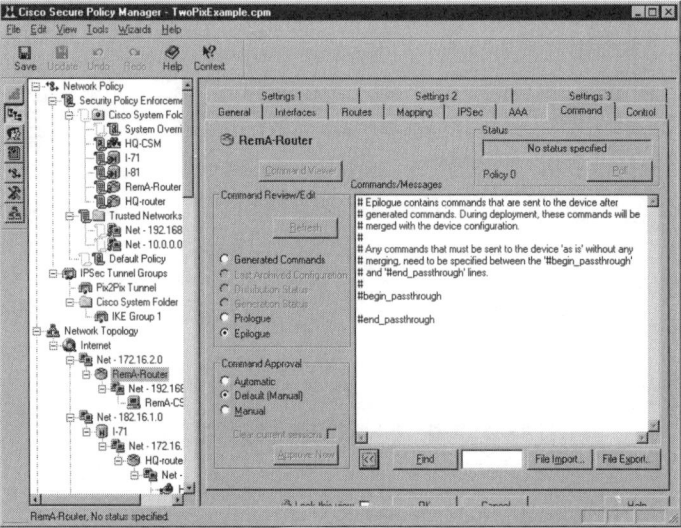

After you have reviewed the generated commands, you can distribute them to the device. This is done by clicking the **Approve Now** button. If you think you are familiar with what CSPM generates, you can change the command approval method to **Automatic** so that all commands will be published to the corresponding devices right after they are generated, meaning you aren't required to review them.

Now you are familiar with basic CSPM configuration steps from installation to the deployment of enterprisewide security policy. Of course, this was a rather sketchy description. If you plan to deploy CSPM in the real world, do not forget to consult the Cisco documentation on their Web site.

Summary

Cisco Secure Policy Manager is a scalable policy-based security management system for Cisco PIX firewalls, IPSec routers, and intrusion detection sensors. It allows network administrators to deploy their security policy from one location, or to use distributed deployment from multiple locations on the network. In addition, you can configure all the VPN tunnels using IPSec and NAT on the boundary of your network to change your private IP address range so you can communicate with outside networks.

CSPM is being distributed in two product lines: the "f" series, with enhanced support for firewalls/VPNs; and the "i" series with extended IDS reporting tools. These products cannot coexist on one host. The current version of both products is 2.3.2, with a new 3.0f version just starting to be distributed as part of CiscoWorks VMS 2.0 (VPN Management Solution) 2.0. It is also promised by Cisco that 3.0i will be released this year.

Implementation of security policies with CSPM consists of three main steps:

- Defining network topology
- Creating security policies
- Publishing generated command sets to the managed devices

All these tasks are performed inside the GUI interface. It is possible to use the various wizards or to fine-tune everything by changing the default values manually. The GUI also features many tools for checking the results of your work, such as the network graph or Policy Query tool.

CSPM can even be used for managing new, originally unsupported versions of IOS/PIX software by mapping them into supported ones with the *Version Management* utility.

Solutions Fast Track

Overview of the Cisco Secure Policy Manager

☑ CSPM is an integrated solution for management of Cisco security devices. It has distributed architecture and is policy-based. There are two product lines: The "i" series with enhanced IDS support and the "f" series with full VPN/firewall configuration capabilities.

www.syngress.com

☑ CSPM has built-in auditing and reporting tools, which provide up-to-date information on network and system events. It also supports Cisco Secure IDS sensors, which produce signature-based events, allowing you to track down network intrusions.

☑ CSPM is a Windows NT-based application. One requirement of the installation is Service Pack 6a. CSPM can coexist on the same host with Cisco Secure VPN Client 1.1, CiscoWorks 2000 with Resource Management Essentials version 3.0, and the QoS Policy Manager version 1.1. On the other hand, two different product lines, namely the "i" series and the "f" series, cannot be installed on the same computer.

Features of the Cisco Secure Policy Manager

☑ CSPM is designed to replace the PIX firewall manager and ACL manager, so it includes their functionality and enhances it with centralized management.

☑ Firewall management features of CSPM allow definition and management of perimeter security policies for Cisco PIX firewalls and Cisco IOS routers running the Cisco Secure Integrated Software feature set.

☑ Cisco IPSec VPN gateway management allows onfiguration of site-to-site IPSec VPNs based on Cisco Secure PIX firewalls and the Cisco suite of VPN routers running Cisco IOS IPSec software.

☑ Intrusion detection sensors management supports configuration and monitoring of Cisco intrusion detection sensors and Cisco Catalyst 6000 line cards. The Cisco IDS feature set of PIX firewalls and IOS routers is not supported.

☑ Another feature is security policy management. It allows usage of enterprisewide policies for managing hundreds of Cisco security devices without dependency on the command-line interface.

☑ The notification and reporting system provides tools to monitor, alert, and report Cisco device- and policy-related activity.

Using the Cisco Secure Policy Manager

- ☑ CSPM can be installed in standalone, client-server, or distributed mode (the latter is possible only for the "f" series). Selection between these modes depends on the size and structure of your network.

- ☑ Initial CSPM configuration process consists of three tasks—defining network topology, creating security policies, and distributing generated commands to managed devices.

- ☑ Network topology definition can be performed manually or by using wizards. There is no need to map the whole network to the CSPM database—only devices used in formulation and enforcement of security policies are important.

- ☑ Security policy determines user access to various services and is defined using the graphical Policy Builder. After that, it is mapped to corresponding enforcement points.

- ☑ The last step is command generation and distribution. There are various possibilities here—each command set may be modified (manually or automatically by adding specified prologues/epilogues) and applied to the corresponding device (again, by manually approving it or having the task performed automatically).

- ☑ Command differences between existing device configurations and new configurations can be viewed and checked. CSPM also supports commands to policy mapping, which allows the browsing of specific commands related to parts of security policy.

Frequently Asked Questions

The following Frequently Asked Questions, answered by the authors of this book, are designed to both measure your understanding of the concepts presented in this chapter and to assist you with real-life implementation of these concepts. To have your questions about this chapter answered by the author, browse to **www.syngress.com/solutions** and click on the **"Ask the Author"** form.

Q: Which IDS platforms are supported in CSPM?

A: Only Cisco Secure IDS sensors (former NetRanger sensors) are supported, either in standalone configuration or as Catalyst 6000 blades. Embedded IDS features of Cisco PIX firewalls and Cisco IOS routers are not supported.

Q: What network topologies are best managed by CSPM?

A: CSPM supports Cisco firewall and VPN router deployments within Internet, intranet, and extranet topologies. For VPN environments, the product supports site-to-site (router-to-router) network topologies only. RAS (client-to-router) VPN networks are not supported. The network topology discovery feature in the 3.0f version supports only "flat" networks—that is, networks without multiple layers of firewalls.

Q: Does CSPM offer user-based security policy management?

A: No, CSPM does not currently provide comprehensive management of user policies (especially user-based authentication and authorization). On the other hand, it is possible to configure AAA (authentication, authorization, and accounting) for pass-through and administrative traffic.

Q: Are there different administrator levels within CSPM?

A: Yes, the product provides three levels of administration:

- **Full access** Provides read and write access to all policy administration functions within CSPM and allows creation of other administrator accounts. Only one network security administrator can have full access rights to the system at any moment in time.

- **Read only** Provides read-only access to all policy administration functions within CSPM. This would be appropriate for help-desk personnel or network security administrators with audit/documentation responsibilities.

- **Report viewing** Provides read-only access to Web-based reports created with CSPM. This is appropriate for help-desk personnel or managers.

Q: What kind of database does CSPM use?

A: CSPM uses a proprietary object-oriented database that has been optimized for use in the policy-based management system. There are possibilities for the importing and exporting of events or topology structures into other systems, although the database itself cannot be moved to any common DBMS platform.

Q: Where can I find more information about CSPM features and requirements?

A: There is plenty of information available on the Cisco Web site at www.cisco.com/go/policymanager/.

Q: Can CSPM be integrated with third-party network management applications?

A: No, CSPM has no support for integration with any third-party applications for network management.

## Chapter 13

Intrusion Detection

Solutions in this chapter:

- **What Is Intrusion Detection?**
- **IDS Tuning**
- **Network Attacks and Intrusions**
- **The Cisco Secure Network Intrusion Detection System**

☑ **Summary**

☑ **Solutions Fast Track**

☑ **Frequently Asked Questions**

Introduction

A properly configured firewall appliance is considered a first line of network defense, and controls the flow of information to your servers. Unfortunately, if the server receives information from the network, it runs a risk of compromise from the unlikely event that the firewall fails. A more likely type of failure is that the firewall does its job passing traffic but that the server itself is vulnerable to an unusual request.

Other elements of that first line of defense would include Access Control Lists (ACLs) on perimeter routers, perhaps Web caching, or load-balancing appliances. It would include operating system (OS) hardening and application configuration controls on the server, as well as ensuring that the vendor software is current according to vendor recommendations. All these things contribute to the security of the service. But because we can never be completely sure that best practices have been followed, a second line of defense is a good plan. This is known as "defense in depth." We put everything we can into the front lines, but in case that fails, we have a backup plan. A detective control is an excellent element of that second line of defense.

An intrusion detection system gives the network or security manager a tool to detect and react rapidly to an attack on the network. This chapter will investigate the various types of attacks and intrusions as well as describe the tools available from Cisco to implement an intrusion detection system.

What Is Intrusion Detection?

An intrusion detection system (IDS) is a software program, or a suite of hardware and software, that automates the investigation of unusual or potentially inappropriate activity in or around computers. It is an example of a technical security control, where the direct application of technology (as opposed to procedure or management guidance) attempts to solve security problems.

Technical controls can be classified as preventative or detective. Preventive controls attempt to avoid the occurrence of unwanted events, whereas detective controls attempt to identify unwanted events after they have occurred. An IDS is typically used as a detective control, alerting to misuse, and providing information about the frequency of the event. These detective controls typically combine signature-based approaches (similar to antivirus scanners) as well as unusual traffic analysis. This allows for more broadly based detection, but suffers from problems of false alerts.

An IDS can also be used in a preventative fashion: modern IDS can take action to interrupt a system call on a host, or interrupt network activity. In this case, the IDS must be adjusted so that this kind of activity only occurs when very clear identification of malicious activity is present.

Types of IDSs

IDSs fall into two types: network-based IDSs (NIDSs), where traffic is analyzed as it passes by a sensor on a wire; and host-based IDSs (HIDSs), where traffic is analyzed as it is accepted by the OS. The former is more readily deployed since it can be done with appliance devices rather than requiring modification of an existing server, and can provide a broader area of coverage. The latter is more precise, since it is able to understand what is occurring at the host itself: thus if an unknown form of attack attempted to cause a system to fail in a known fashion, the network-based sensor would probably miss the attack, but the host-based sensor would see the fault. This allows host-based IDS to function effectively as a preventative control, and is generally considered an appropriate use of the technology.

The Cisco Secure Network IDS product has the capability to do *shunning*. With shunning, the intrusion detection system alerts actually cause configuration changes in firewalls and routers, and block traffic from those networks.

IDS Architecture

IDSs are generally composed of a management station and one or more sensors. Because the control must see traffic to analyze it, it is generally distributed throughout a network at key locations. The management station integrates information from the distributed sensors (host and network) to provide a comprehensive and comprehensible view of the network. An operator usually interacts with the management station via a Web front-end or dedicated graphical user interface (GUI), and does not directly interact with the sensors. With the Cisco IDS, the management station can be either the IDS Director or a Cisco Secure Policy Manager (CSPM). The CSPM is documented in Chapter 12. In the fall of 2002, Cisco will be announcing a new management device to replace both the CSPM and Director consoles.

Ideally, the management station should integrate with any other operations management platforms in use. In an all-Cisco network, integration with the CSPM is helpful. In larger or nonhomogeneous networks, third-party products, such as HP OpenView, are often used to provide that integration.

Designing & Planning…

Controlling the Communication between Sensor and Manager

Often people deploy the sensor and manager focusing on bandwidth issues, and don't think about the security issues. Remember, security usually revolves around CIA: confidentiality, integrity, and availability. These issues come up in spades for the sensor/manager communication:

- **Confidentiality** The output from the sensors will contain highly sensitive information, including passwords, URLs visited, and the like.

- **Integrity** If a bad guy can forge data from the sensor, he can implicate other innocent users.

- **Availability** If a bad guy can prevent the data from getting from the sensor to the manager, he can work his evil undetected.

While other IDSs may communicate using unencrypted protocols such as syslog, Cisco has thoughtfully provided for confidentiality and integrity in its Post Office protocol, used to communicate between sensor and manager. However, don't forget to protect the communication channel, and don't forget that the sensors and the managers are prime targets for the attackers!

Why Should You Have an IDS?

The security events detected by an IDS are typically of three types:

- Malicious events, such as those present at an intrusion

- Misconfigured events, such as incorrect configuration data causing system malfunction

- Ineffective events, such as ineffective network traffic

These security events are also usually classified by severity (that is, the ability of the event to harm the enterprise) and frequency (the likelihood of the occurrence). As an example of two types of malicious events, those that are severe or frequent (for example, the recent Nimda worm) are more important to identify and act upon than those that are minor or rare (for instance, a curious employee performing a port scan on his buddy's machine). Perhaps even more important is distinguishing between that curious employee port scan on an unimportant machine and a port scan on a core business asset that may signal a prelude to a determined attack.

The business drivers for each of the three types are slightly different. The driver for the first is to reduce the risk associated with a systems compromise. They may be a required part of due diligence for protection of corporate assets. The driver for the second is to identify errors in configuration so that they can be corrected. This reduces the overall cost of maintenance. The driver for the third is to optimize the use of corporate assets.

Benefits of an IDS in a Network

As stated, the tuning process can take different approaches depending upon the desired result. Usually, the desired result should follow the business driver. These are examined in turn.

Reduce the Risk of a Systems Compromise

This is the most direct driver associated with an intrusion detection system. Risk can be reduced indirectly through detection and response or through direct corrective action. As a part of the response, a forensic element can be applied. If the enterprise has the ability to document the root causes of an attack, this can reduce the frequency of occurrence, particularly among the local user community (they are put on notice that malicious activity can have severe consequences). Forensic analysis may also be of some use in recovering damages, if the activity is careful enough to survive the necessary legal proceedings.

Indirect Action

Indirect action through an incident response procedure is flexible, and can tolerate potential errors in alerting. The trade off is increased work for reduced risk. The key is to have a prepared incidence response protocol for handling events.

Direct Action

Direct corrective action can be both automated and inherent to the alert, or provide notice to a security officer so that an incident response procedure can be initiated. Examples of direct action are blocking an offending system call (for a host-based system) or reconfiguring a firewall (for a network-based system). These kinds of activity require a high degree of confidence in the alert.

Identifying Errors of Configuration

Identifying errors of configuration is an immediate benefit of an IDS. A complex environment, such as a server or a network, is usually misconfigured in several small ways. Luckily, our systems are redundant enough that the error conditions are handled by secondary systems. However, there is a risk that the secondary system may fail, causing a systemic failure; in addition, there may be improvements to service possible if the original device is correctly configured.

An IDS can usually identify this sort of invalid traffic. For example, a device may be misconfigured to have an invalid password for file access. The IDS will track this as an attempt to "break into" the file server by noting an excessive number of password failures. The detective control will allow the owner of the system to correct the password, and allow improved functionality.

Optimize Network Traffic

A third benefit of an IDS is to optimize network flows, or at least to provide insight into how networks are being used. A common component of an IDS is a statistical anomaly detection engine. Cisco calls this *profile-based detection* and notes it "involves building statistical profiles of user activity and then reacting to any activity that falls outside these established profiles." The immediate reason is to identify an intrusion through unusual behavior. However, this also permits the operator to get a feel for the behavior of the network under normal operating conditions, and that insight can provide assistance on larger network maintenance and design issues.

Documenting Existing Threat Levels
for Planning or Resource Allocation

When you are drawing up a budget for network security, it often helps to substantiate claims that the network is likely to be attacked or is even currently under attack. Understanding the frequency and characteristics of attacks allows you to understand what security measures are appropriate to protect the network against those attacks.

IDSs verify, itemize, and characterize threats from both outside and inside the enterprise network, assisting security management in making sound decisions regarding the allocation of computer security resources. Using IDSs in this manner is important, as many people mistakenly deny that anyone (outsider or insider) would be interested in breaking into their networks. Furthermore, the information that IDSs give you regarding the source and nature of attacks allows you to make decisions regarding security strategy driven by demonstrated need, not guesswork or folklore.

Changing User Behavior

A fundamental goal of computer security management is to affect the behavior of individual users in a way that protects information systems from security problems. Intrusion detection systems help organizations accomplish this goal by increasing the perceived risk of discovery and punishment of attackers. This serves as a significant deterrent to those who would violate security policy.

Deploying an IDS in a Network

The placement of a NIDS requires careful planning. Cisco's Secure IDS product (NetRanger) is made up of a probe and a central management station called a Director (old style) or the CSPM (new style). Each probe has two interfaces: a *command interface*, on which configuration information is accepted and logging information is sent, and a *sensor interface*. The sensor interface has an unnumbered interface; some feel that this allows placement of the command interface on a different network than the command interface. If that is your policy, it is helpful to place the command interface on a management network. If you are concerned about the potential for a compromise through the sensor interface, then it is best to place the command interface on the same network as the sensor interface. Let's look at the best place to put the Sensor interface.

Sensor Placement

Most companies have a firewall that separates the internal network from the outside world. They typically have one or more service networks, and the internal network may also be subdivided.

Should we place the probe outside or inside? If the probe is outside, then it can monitor external traffic. This is useful against attacks from the outside but does not allow for detection of internal attacks. Of course, understanding attacks against the outside net may not be particularly valuable, since generally they would be stopped by the firewall. Also, the probe itself may become the target of an attack so it must be protected.

If you place the probe inside, it will detect internally-initiated attacks and can highlight firewall rules that are not working properly or are incorrectly configured.

Generally, the reason to put a probe outside the firewall would be to "take the temperature" of the Internet. This can be valuable to demonstrate the value of the firewall. More importantly, you should deploy sensors so they can view traffic worth sensing.

One effective strategy is to deploy probes to capture the interface of the firewall that faces the service net (or nets) so you can capture traffic from networks headed toward the service net. Other appropriate monitoring points would be near server clusters, or near router transit networks/interfaces. When you review your security policy, you may decide you need to install more probes at different points in the network according to security risks and requirements.

Here are some example locations:

- The Accounts department's Local Area Network (LAN)
- Company strategic networks (for example, the Development LAN)
- Technical department's LAN
- LANs where staff turnover is rapid or hot-desk/temp locations exist
- the Server LAN

Difficulties in Deploying an IDS

There are several difficulties associated with successful IDS deployments. One fundamental problem is that the underlying science behind intrusion detection systems is relatively new. While everyone agrees that some things can be achieved, the January 1998 paper *Insertion, Evasion, and Denial of Service: Eluding Network Intrusion Detection* by Thomas H. Ptacek and Timothy N. Newsham seemed to throw the field for a loop. They described techniques by which a properly designed IDS can be deceived, with a follow-up discussion that seemed to indicate the loftiest goal of an IDS is not achievable without a complete recreation of all network hosts. In the paper they note:

> The number of attacks against network intrusion detection systems, and the relative simplicity of the problems that were actually demonstrated to be exploitable on the commercial systems we tested, indicates to us that network intrusion detection is not a mature technology. More research and testing needs to occur before network intrusion detection can be looked to as a reliable component in a security system.

However, it should not be taken that this is seen as an unusable technology. An IDS is one of the most common security purchases today. Current (2002) Computer Security Institute (CSI)/FBI statistics show that approximately 60 percent of Fortune 500 companies deploy an IDS; in just a few years, an IDS suite will likely be as ubiquitous as firewalls. What this does point out is that this is a technology in a state of rapid change. It is also worth noting that Cisco engineering took the flaws identified to heart; today, their analysis engine is vulnerable to none of these flaws.

A second difficulty is that of expectation. Management may feel that simply purchasing an IDS will make them safe. It doesn't. It can be of assistance in identifying, imperfectly, attacks on a host or network, and can also be of use in tracking human events. But IDS tools should probably be combined with additional tools to provide a more robust detection environment.

A third difficulty is associated with the deployment phase. The network deployment is relatively straightforward but non-trivial, and coordination between multiple groups is often required. In a larger enterprise, the people who "own" the network are different from the people who "own" security, and clear communication may not always be possible. A host deployment involves interaction with a complex environment, and may involve further unknown interactions.

A fourth difficulty concerns incidence response. An incidence response procedure is a nontrivial task for most enterprises. A significant development effort is usually required. For most enterprises, such programs have not been required before. In many environments, the program is developed after the first incident, as part of a "lessons learned" analysis.

A fifth difficulty revolves around IDS tuning, described next. An IDS, out of the box, is generally not very useful. It must be adjusted to be in harmony with the local environment and the resources available to explore events. It's this level of effort associated with IDS tuning that management often underestimates.

It should be recognized that most IDS programs are at their most effective several months or even years after their initial deployment.

IDS Tuning

A detective control makes an assertion that a particular event has occurred (by flagging one or more network packets or system calls). An important aspect is to tune the tool so that the accuracy of the assertion provides maximum relevancy to the enterprise. In other words, the IDS makes a call that either something is wrong or that everything is fine. You want it to be right more often than not.

To quantify this, the language of hypothesis testing applies. Note that in the following, native errors to the tool (such as dropped packets for the NIDS or incorrect configuration of the HIDS) are not considered. An IDS makes a decision on whether a security event is taking place. Let's suppose the chance that a particular packet is an attack is "p." In most enterprises, "p" would be fairly small. This is the chance that, if you were just poking about using a sniffer, you would be able to view a malicious packet.

In hypothesis testing, a matrix is developed, as shown in Table 13.1.

Table 13.1 IDS Decision versus Truth

Truth	IDS Decision: Alert Is Generated	IDS Decision: Alert Is Not Generated
No security event is in progress (prob. 1-p)	Type I error (alpha)	Correct result
A security event is in progress (prob. p)	Correct result	Type II error (beta)

The error probability alpha represents the amount of "work" assumed by the enterprise. It is the number of stray alarms that might need to be checked out—the probability that an alert is generated even though no security event is in progress. It is often normalized by multiplying by the number of alerted events, producing the frequency of *false positives*. Thus, we say "nine out of ten of the alerts were false positives." In conventional hypothesis testing, much effort is spent to minimize alpha. The error probability beta represents the amount of "risk" assumed by the enterprise. It is also often normalized by dividing by p, the probability that a security event is occurring. This number is typically difficult to estimate, but is based upon the threat model.

With a "full bore" signature load, the error probability "alpha" is very high. By way of example, let's look at some numbers. At a recent deployment, the probes saw about 38 billion packets a day. The probes reported nearly a million events after three days. Sifting through the alerts, the security engineers found some ICMP traffic that corresponded to unauthorized test equipment; this corresponded to about ten thousand packets. They also found one server that had apparently been compromised; this probably corresponded to about a thousand packets. Therefore:

p = 11 thousand packets / 38 billion packets = 0.00000029

Without an IDS (say by using a sniffer) this would clearly be a "needle in a haystack" problem – you would have to go through about 30 million packets before finding one corresponding to a bad guy. The fact that the analysts were able to find a compromised server is a great testimonial to the power of the tool.

On the other hand, note that computing the normalized alpha, we get:

$$\text{False positive ratio} = \frac{(1 \text{ million alerts}) - (11 \text{ thousand real alerts})}{1 \text{ million alerts}} = 0.989$$

so that 99 out of 100 alerts are false positives. To be fair, with a million alerts, it is possible there were more "real" security events that were just missed. This analysis also assumes that there are no false negatives, that there were alerts on all security events, so the accuracy numbers may be lower than expected. The sheer number of packets is part of the problem with an untuned IDS deployment. It is a *lot* of work to try to classify these events. It's nice that the analyst found the compromised server, but having to explore a hundred alerts to find the smoking gun is probably not tenable over the long run.

Tuning

After the IDS is installed, a tuning phase is performed. This is to modify the performance of the tool to optimize alpha and beta. Note that it is very easy to optimize each separately: you can drop alpha to zero by never generating an alert; in this case, beta is now 100 percent. You can optimize beta by flagging every packet; unfortunately, now alpha is at nearly 100 percent error. Experience has shown that in this case, while the formal value of beta is excellent, in practice no system can respond to the high number of alarms. Managers simply turn off the system, and while the security event is detected, no action is taken, which in some respects is an even more undesirable result. This is similar to what was seen in the preceding deployment: A million alerts is too daunting.

The trick is to train the tool to provide a reasonable degree of accuracy, so the error rates of alpha and beta are both close to zero—the enterprise trades the work of investigating false positives for the risk of missing an event.

Turn It Up

There are two traditional approaches. One approach is to work through the alert information, selectively enabling only those alerts that are known to be desirable. This approach typically minimizes alpha, and is most suited to strongly controlled environments or those for which the detective control has severe consequence, such as alarms that reconfigure devices or directly notify third parties.

Tone It Down

The more common approach is to apply all possible sensitivity and slowly "tone it down," eliminating those alerts that have too high an alpha in the given environment. The best approach is to identify an acceptable false positive rate for a particular type of alert, and then enable the signature only if the observed rate is less than the desired rate. For example, if an alert indicated traffic showing a systems compromise, the acceptable false positive rate may be nine out of ten, while if the alert merely indicates traffic of a suspicious nature, the acceptable false positive rate may be one in three. The system is then allowed to run for a period, observing the environment. At the end of that time, the alerts are assessed. If more than nine out of ten of the more serious alerts prove false, the alert is disabled; if more than one out of three of the lesser severity alerts prove false, that signature is disabled.

In addition, the alerts can often be refined; the alerting procedure can selectively disable based upon known behaviors. For example, one signature may identify large numbers of User Datagram Protocol (UDP) packets in a short period as a UDP flood, often associated with malicious activity. However, large numbers of UDP packets destined to, or from, a name server is normal; thus the alert signature is revised to specify "large numbers of UDP packets in a short period EXCEPT to this host."

Network Attacks and Intrusions

An IDS provides information about network attacks and intrusions. We need to classify what these alarms are saying, which means the first step is for us to identify what an attack or intrusion is. Any action that violates the security policy of your organization should be considered a potential harm, but broadly speaking, attacks and intrusions can be summarized as an exploitation of:

- Poor network perimeter/device security
- Poor physical security
- Application and operating software weaknesses
- Human failure
- Weaknesses in the IP suite of protocols

Before we look at these threats in more detail let me suggest that you assume a devious mind, something which helps when it comes to learning about intrusion detection.

Poor Network Perimeter/Device Security

This can be described as the ease of access to devices across the network. Without access control using a firewall or a packet filtering router, the network is vulnerable.

Packet Decoders

It is very common to place packet decoders, such as Network General's Sniffer or open source products like Ethereal, onto your network to try to debug applications or diagnose network problems. The invisible becomes visible, and things on the wire are visible in text. This means that applications that send password information in the clear—Telnet, FTP, POP3 (how many users read mail), Web applications—are obvious examples.

For instance, here is a quick trace of an FTP session: This first portion is what is visible only on my private workstation.

```
C:\>ftp fred.callisma.com
Connected to fred.callisma.com.
220 ProFTPD 1.2.2 Server (ProFTPD Default Installation)
    [fred.callisma.com]
User (fred.callisma.com:(none)): luser
331 Password required for luser.
Password:
230 User luser logged in.
```

Here is what flows over the wire, visible to someone with a packet decoder—this is the "Follow TCP stream" tool from Ethereal.

```
220 ProFTPD 1.2.2 Server (ProFTPD Default Installation)
    [fred.callisma.com]
USER luser
331 Password required for luser.
PASS SeCrEt!
230 User luser logged in.
QUIT
221 Goodbye.
```

Wireless LANs suffer from the same sort of problem. It's even more sneaky, since this data can be captured without being physically present and with a much more difficult chance of being detected.

This method of intrusion is called *eavesdropping* or *packet snooping* and the type of network technology implemented directly influences its susceptibility. For instance, shared networks are easier to eavesdrop on than switched networks. Of course, confidential material should not flow across uncontrolled networks in the clear.

Scanner Programs

Certain types of software, such as Nmap, Nessus, and John the Ripper, are able to scan entire networks, produce detailed reports on what ports are in use, perform password cracking and view account details on servers. Although these are very useful tools if used for the purpose of legitimate network auditing, in the wrong hands they can be devastating. Scanning software commonly uses one or more of the following methods:

- Ping sweep
- SNMP sweep
- TCP/UDP port scans
- Scanning logon accounts

Approaching the millennium, I performed a global scan for a company using an SNMP sweep program. The objective was to ensure that all network devices were running at a compliant release of software. This was surprisingly easy and I even ended up accidentally scanning some devices outside the perimeter of our network that were inside the carrier's network. Incidentally, one device in their network was not Y2K-compliant and was upgraded on our request!

Network Topology

Shared networks are easier to eavesdrop on, as all traffic is visible from everywhere on that shared media. Switched networks, on the other hand, are more secure as, by default, there is no single viewpoint for traffic: An intruder would have to take action such as CAM table flooding, ARP cache poisoning, or route table corruption to see the packets.

Luckily, this topology does not forbid the use of IDS appliances. On Cisco Catalyst switches there is a feature where you can mirror traffic from VLANs or switch ports to a single designated switch port called the span port. Once you plug your IDS into the span port, you can easily view traffic in different VLANs by making configuration changes, allowing analysis of LAN traffic.

Configuring & Implementing...

Deploying a Cisco IDS 4230 in a LAN

The Cisco IDS 4230 is a standalone appliance used to monitor high-speed networks. In a modern switched environment, the interesting task is to see enough traffic. If you just drop the sensor interface into an unused port, you will see no traffic!

There are several approaches. One technique is to use dedicated hardware, such as a Shomiti Tap, which acts like a "mini hub" so you can monitor critical interfaces, such as areas just before a router, switch uplink, or key server.

Another technique is to use the Switched Port Analyzer (SPAN) port feature. The technique is to configure the switch with a span port combining the networks you want to monitor. The 4230 sensor interface is then plugged into the SPAN port. The problem with this is that if someone reconfigures the switch, your probe ceases to function! In that environment, it is important to verify strong change control over the LAN switch configurations, and to monitor for unexpected loss of traffic at the probe.

Unattended Modems

Installing a modem on a PC for remote access allows a quick and easy way to access the network from home. Unfortunately, this also means that the modem and PC may be prone to attack when you are not there. Detecting modems attached to PCs can be done using host auditing systems, or via network auditing systems that have direct access to the host (for instance, by inspecting the registry hive, or reviewing route tables) but this is a complex task. A better approach is to use POTS auditing software: A "war dialer" that periodically reviews all owned phone numbers to look for carriers. The problem with this approach is that the user could configure "ring back" approaches, so that the modem doesn't pick up on the first few rings. This way the war dialer would fail.

In such cases, technical controls are not the best solution: Instead use cooperation with the user community. If access is essential, you should explain the benefits of employing the (secure) corporate remote access solution instead.

Poor Physical Security

Simple measures can be taken in the physical world to ensure better security for your systems. Locking your doors is obviously a good commonsense start, but there are often a number of straightforward procedures and safeguards that companies could perform and implement that, for one reason or another, they do not.

I recently read an article in the Cisco's Packet magazine that described a theft in the Redwood City, California office of VISA of a file server that contained over 300,000 credit card numbers. The thief just unplugged the server and walked out with it. A simple tagging system would have done the trick, as alarms would have sounded when the machine was removed; even a paper authorization system would have worked. After all, it's pretty simple to bypass security on routers and switches if you can get to the console port, or in the case of servers you can remove the hard disks and reinstall them elsewhere.

Microsoft, in its Ten Immutable Laws, captures this as law number three: "If a bad guy has unrestricted physical access to your computer, it's not your computer anymore."

Application and Operating Software Weaknesses

In this context, software is a term that describes the operating system as well as the packages that run under its control. Most commercial software is, or has been, deficient at some point in its life due to poor programming compounded by commercial pressures to release software early, before it is debugged completely.

Software Bugs

Software bugs can be characterized into one of several types. The BugTraq classification scheme recognizes nine types: *boundary condition errors* (which includes buffer overflows), *access validation errors* (errors in trust), *input validation errors* (poor defensive programming), *failure to handle exceptional conditions* (more poor programming), *race conditions, serialization errors, atomicity errors* (belief that things will happen "all at once" when they might happen in stages), *environment errors*, and *configuration errors*.

Getting Passwords—Easy Ways of Cracking Programs

Most people, at some point or other, have created a simple password based on objects that are easy to remember, such as a name or favorite color. In 10 of the 15 companies I've worked for, good password management practices were rarely enforced.

It's quite simple to get someone else's password; many times, all you have to do is ask. Some other ways passwords might be obtained are:

- "Shoulder surfing," observation over the shoulder.

- Gaining access to password files.

- Using a sniffer or Trojan software to look for cleartext passwords.

- Replaying logon traffic recorded on a sniffer that contains the encrypted password.

- Dictionary-based attacks, where a software program runs through every word in a dictionary database.

- Brute force attacks, where the attacker runs a program that tries variations of letters, numbers, and common words in the hope of getting the right combination. Typical programs can try around 100,000 combinations per minute.

Human Failure

Henry Ford once said, "If there is any one secret of success, it lies in the ability to get the other person's point of view and see things from that person's angle as well as from your own."

Everyone is an individual; we all have our own thoughts, feelings, and moods. Of course, the human failure factor spans far and wide across the security spectrum and is usually a common contributing cause for security breaches. These can be caused as a result of malicious motives or innocent mistakes.

Poorly Configured Systems

The very first time I configured a Cisco router on a network I used the default password *cisco*. If anyone had decided to choose that router to attack they could have logged on, looked at the routing tables, reloaded the router (causing user disruption), or changed the password.

Many new systems when taken out of the box use default accounts or passwords that are easy to obtain. Most allow you to decide whether or not to use security features without any objections. In brief, systems are poorly configured because of:

- A lack of thought during configuration
- Insufficient time to configure the product properly
- Poor knowledge of the product

Information Leaks

Rather than a sinister individual "leaking" information to the outside, this is usually a little more straightforward. You may have seen security personal identification numbers (PINs), passwords in diaries or written on post-it notes. The list is long and an absolute feast for a nocturnal attacker wandering around the office late at night. Not shredding sensitive documents and drawings can also be a risky practice. If someone gets hold of the network diagram, they can start targeting devices and choosing points for maximum impact.

One time I was sitting in an open office one day when the LAN administrator was asked by a colleague from across the room what the supervisor account password was—he shouted it back to him. Need I say more?

Malicious Users

For various reasons, people will carry out malicious attacks or intrusions on your network—for example, downloading all customer account information onto a laptop, which can then be removed from the building. Such things are, obviously, bad for business.

Weaknesses in the IP Suite of Protocols

When most of the TCP/IP family of protocols were originally developed, the world was a nicer place; perhaps, back then, there was no need for the security we have today. Nowadays, however, it is possible for you to stroll into a bookshop and pick up a volume on how to crack a network. The success of the Internet unfortunately ensures that this type of information is readily available.

The TCP/IP stack is code written by programmers/developers, and as such, it is probable that some implementations will contain errors. If the implementation of TCP/IP is poor, then the system can be compromised in spite of the upper-layer applications being used.

Taking advantage of these weaknesses requires an in-depth knowledge of TCP/IP protocols. Flaws exploited by attackers are being countered by software developers and then recountered by attackers again.

One example of improvement is IPSec, which is an addition to the IP protocol suite. IPSec provides privacy and authentication methods creating traffic security on a network.

> **NOTE**
>
> Although we have discussed TCP/IP weaknesses in this section, application programs can also be poorly written or badly designed in the way that they interface with the lower-layer protocols. Bad application software can provide the attacker with a foothold to penetrate a system.
>
> Conversely, a server running well-written applications with solid code but using a bad TCP/IP implementation can still be compromised since the application relies on the TCP/IP stack for network services.

Any member of the TCP/IP suite can be the target of an attack. Some have flaws that are easier to exploit by the cracker than others.

Layer 7 Attacks

The next sections highlight some examples of the more common attacks to date; for the purpose of our discussion, I've assumed that an Attacker (station C) can see traffic returning from its victims (stations A and B). In practice, this may not be the case, but the attack can still succeed nevertheless—it just takes a little more skill on their part. For each type of attack, I've tried to list the URL of the related CERT document for you to read.

SMTP Attacks

Simple Mail Transport Protocol (SMTP) has been used to send mail using a wide variety of mail programs, and for many years has been the e-mail standard of the Internet. A common method of attack is the buffer overrun where the attacker enters a larger number of characters in an e-mail field than expected by the e-mail server. The extra characters contain executable code that is run by the e-mail server following an error in the application. The code then facilitates further cracking. Installing the latest security patches for the e-mail system may avoid this kind of attack.

It is good practice to use digital signatures and cryptography techniques in cases where sensitive information is to be sent across shared networks. These methods can offer you excellent protection when it comes to the confidentiality and integrity of information. Digital signatures, for their part, will ensure that each message is signed and verified, while encryption techniques will make certain the mail content is viewable only by the intended receiving e-mail address. Details of these types of attack can be found at: www.cert.org/tech_tips/email_spoofing.html and www.cert.org/advisories/CA-97.05.sendmail.html

SMTP Spam

Spam is defined as unsolicited commercial e-mail (UCE). Internet service providers can restrict spamming by the implementation of rules that govern the number of destination addresses allowed for a single message. For further information, see www.cert.org/tech_tips/e-mail_bombing_spamming.html.

FTP

Anonymous connections to servers running the FTP process allow the attacking station C to download a virus, overwrite a file, or abuse trusts that the FTP server has in the same domain.

FTP attacks are best avoided by preventing anonymous logins, stopping unused services on the server, as well as creating router access lists and firewall rules. If you require the use of anonymous logons, the best course of action is to update the FTP software to the latest revision and keep an eye on related advisories. It's probably a good idea to adopt a general policy of regular checks of advisories for all software you are responsible for protecting. For further information, visit www.cert.org/advisories/CA-93.10.anonymous.FTP.activity.html.

SNMP

The Simple Network Management Protocol (SNMP) has recently been in the news for having vulnerability in ASN encoding that allowed for its compromise on essentially every implementation, including Cisco's. The basic problem is that SNMP is an unauthenticated (and because it is based upon UDP) easily spoofed service. Using *SNMP get* queries, it is possible to gain detailed information about a device. Armed with this information, the cracker can facilitate further types of attack. By using *SNMP set* queries, it is also possible to change the values of Managed Information Base (MIB) instances. In particular, one SNMP set will cause a router configuration to be written to a server, while another SNMP set will download a new configuration from a server. SNMP, and *SNMP set* in particular, are dangerous protocols, meaning access to SNMP should be carefully controlled.

Layer 3 and Layer 4 Attacks

These occur at the Network and Transport layers of the OSI model. Here are some examples of the more common attacks to date.

TCP SYN Flooding

This is best described in stages:

1. Station C sends lots of SYN packets to station B in rapid succession from nonexistent host addresses.

2. B sends back SYN/ACKs and maintains the half-opened connections in a queue as it waits for ACKs from the nonexistent hosts at the source addresses.

3. B runs out of resources waiting for ACKs back from nonexistent hosts.

4. At this point, B drops legitimate connections and is likely to hang/crash.

There is no widely accepted solution for this problem. On Cisco routers, it is possible to configure TCP Intercept that protects against SYN Floods.

TCP Intercept Configurations

This section covers the TCP Intercept feature available on Cisco routers that have Cisco Secure IS (Firewall Feature Set) installed. Here's how you configure it:

1. Make certain you have the necessary IOS Firewall Feature Set installed.

2. Create an extended access list where the source is "any" and designate internal networks to protect against SYN flooding attack.

3. In global configuration mode, enter the command:

   ```
   ip tcp intercept list <access-list number>
   ```

4. Choose what mode you want to operate in. If you don't specify it, it will be in intercept mode. In watch mode, the router "watches" TCP connection requests, if they do not become established within 30 seconds, the router sends a TCP RST to the receiving station, thus allowing it to free its resources. When operating in intercept mode, the router acts as a

"middle man" in the TCP handshake. It will keep the original SYN request, and respond back to the originator with a SYN/ACK pending the final ACK. Once this happens, the router sends the original SYN and performs a three-way handshake with the destination, it then drops out of the way allowing direct communications between source and destination. To choose the mode, enter the command:

```
ip tcp intercept mode [intercept|watch ]
```

TCP intercept will monitor for the number of incomplete connections. When this figure goes over 1100, or if a "surge" of over 1100 connections is received within 60 seconds, the router deletes the oldest connection request (like a conveyor belt) and reduces TCP retransmission time by 50 percent. This "aggressive" behavior can be adjusted to fit security policy. For further information on TCP SYN flooding, visit www.cert.org/advisories/CA-96.21.tcp_syn_flooding.html.

Smurf Spoofing Attack

This is based on IP spoofing where multiple broadcast pings are sent out by station C with victim A's IP address as the source. A could be overwhelmed with ICMP response packets. Recommended solutions are:

- To disable IP-directed broadcasts at the router by entering the global command *no ip directed-broadcast* in the router configuration.

- If possible, to configure the operating system not to respond to broadcast pings. For more information, go to: www.cert.org/advisories/CA-98.01.smurf.html.

- Use the global command *ip verify unicast reverse-path* on the router. This will match the routing entries in the Cisco Express Forwarding (CEF) table against the source IP addresses of incoming packets. If there is no route back out of the interface, then the router drops the packet. This will only work if CEF is enabled on the router.

- Use Committed Access Rate (CAR) on the Cisco routers to limit the inbound levels of ICMP traffic. Note that CAR configurations can also reduce the amount of SYN traffic to help against SYN flooding and DDoS Attacks (discussed later in this section).

TCP/IP Sequence Number Spoofing/Session Hijacking

Let's imagine C wants to spoof B into thinking it is A.

1. Station C initiates a denial of service (DoS) attack on A and then impersonates A by spoofing its IP address. The purpose of this is to prevent the real A from interfering with the attack.

2. C initiates a connection to B and tries to guess the sequence number from frames it has sniffed.

3. If B is fooled into believing C is actually A, then data will flow freely between the two.

Older TCP/IP implementations increment SEQ numbers in a predictable manner that makes the exchange easier to intercept and spoof.

> **NOTE**
>
> Modern TCP/IP implementations are able to take advantage of a SYN "cookie." The idea is to eliminate the TCP_RCVD state, thus avoiding the problems of resource starvation in that state. The technique is to delay creation of the TCB until the third packet of the handshake (the final ACK) is received. This is done by responding to the initial SYN with a secure one-way hash as the sequence number, allowing for detection of bogus ACKs.

Hijack attacks from outside the network can be prevented by applying an access list to the WAN interfaces of the company router. This would prevent traffic with internal source addresses from being accepted from the outside. This type of filtering is known as input filtering and does not protect against attempts to hijack connections between hosts inside the network.

Another access list to prevent unknown source addresses from leaving the internal network should also be applied. This is to prevent attacks to outside networks from within the company. For more information on spoofing and session hijacking, visit www.cert.org/advisories/CA-95.01.IP.spoofing.attacks.and .hijacked.terminal.connections.html.

Denial of Service Type Attacks

In DoS attacks, a victim is unable to provide services due to all its resources being consumed. This is caused by a weakness in the implementation of an application, prompting its failure, or when a victim is overwhelmed by attack traffic.

Ping of Death

The ping of death attack takes advantage of the inability of poor IP implementations to cope with abnormally large IP packets. In this example, ICMP packets transmitted by the attacking station exceed 65535 bytes (the maximum IP packet size). The packet is then fragmented and the receiving station fails the reassembly process, and thereby crashes or hangs.

Several vendors have released software patches to overcome this problem. For more information, see www.cert.org/advisories/CA-1996-26.html.

Teardrop Attack

A teardrop attack targets a specific weakness in some TCP/IP implementations where the reassembly fails to work correctly because incorrect offset values are injected into IP traffic. The attack is based on the same principle as the Ping of Death attack.

The Land Attack

The land attack spoofs IP types. Here's how it works:

1. C sends a SYN packet to B using B's IP address, along with identical source and destination port numbers.

2. B is never able to complete this connection and may go into an infinite loop.

3. If B is susceptible to this type of attack, it will hang or crash.

The recommended solution is to install vendor patches. For Land attacks, it is also advisable to install input filters to combat IP spoofing. For more information, visit www.cert.org/advisories/CA-97.28.Teardrop_Land.html.

Distributed Denial of Service Attacks

Recently, distributed denial of service (DDoS) attacks have become more common. Typical tools used by attackers are Trinoo, TFN, TFN2K and Stacheldraht ("barbed wire" in German). How does a DDoS attack work? The attacker gains access to a Client PC. From there, the cracker can use tools to send commands to the nodes. These nodes then flood or send malformed packets to the victim.

Coordinated traceroutes from several sources are used to probe the same target to construct a table of routes for the network. This information is then used as the basis for further attacks.

So what makes it so nasty? In practice, there may be thousands of nodes, meaning billions of packets can be directed at the victim, taking up all available bandwidth and perhaps causing DoS.

At present, there is no solution to the problem, nor is it easy to trace the attack origin.

A list of general suggestions is as follows:

- Prevent initial compromise of the client through good security practice.

- Keep software up to date with patches and upgrades.

- Keep all antivirus software up to date.

- Run desktop firewall software where available.

- Install and activate the Cisco IDS.

Cisco also suggests the following recommendations:

- Use the *ip verify unicast reverse-path* global command (discussed earlier).

- Use ACLs to block inbound private address range traffic.

- Use input filtering (discussed earlier).

- Use CAR to limit inbound ICMP and SYN packets.

For more information, visit www.cert.org/advisories/CA-99-17-denial-of-service-tools.html and www.cert.org/reports/dsit_workshop.pdf. For more details on Cisco's recommendations, check out www.cisco.com/warp/public/707/newsflash.html#prevention.

The Cisco Secure Network Intrusion Detection System

NetRanger was originally developed by Wheelgroup, Inc. but is now owned by Cisco Systems. We will tackle this product by dividing it into five sections—overview, managing probe setup, configuration, management, and the dedicated IOS product.

What Is the Cisco Secure Network Intrusion Detection System?

This is a solution that can be added to your network to perform dynamic intrusion detection. Cisco Secure IDS will monitor for, and respond to, intrusions in real time. A simple IDS solution is made up of a distributed model with three main components: the probe, the Director, and the CSPM.

The Probe

The probe is a specialized device that uses a rule-based inference engine to process large volumes of traffic in order to identify security issues in real time. The probe is either a ready-made appliance purchased from Cisco, or it can be software-based and installed on a Windows x86 (the Catalyst 6000 IDS module) or SPARC Solaris station (the IDS 4230 and IDS 4210). The software to create your own probe can be found on the IDS CD, and can either capture traffic itself or monitor syslog traffic from a Cisco router. Once an attack or security event is detected, the probe can respond by generating alarms, logging the event, resetting TCP connections or *shunning* the attack (by reconfiguration of managed router ACLs). Probe events are forwarded to a central facility via a control/command interface.

Probes have two interfaces, one for monitoring and one for control. The monitoring interface of the probe does not have an IP address and will not respond to Layer 3 detection attempts. There are several types of monitor interfaces available from Cisco, each selected for a particular network scenario. An example is the IDS 4230 Sensor, which is capable of supporting LAN speeds of up to 100 Mbps LAN or T3 WAN speeds. Another is the Catalyst 6000 IDS module that is designed for switched networks.

The Director

The Director is a GUI software solution used to "direct" or manage Cisco IDS from a HP OpenView platform. It is installed on a HP UX or Solaris workstation. Directors are used to complete initial probe configuration, process and present information sent from sensors (in HP OpenView) and specify sensor behavior. The Director contains drivers for the Oracle RDBMS and the Remedy Trouble Ticket system. It is possible to modify these drivers to interface with Sybase or Informix systems, if required. When the Director receives information from the probes it will initially log to a flat file and then push the data to a relational database. Once stored in the database, RDBMS tools such as SQL can be used to interrogate the data. Database details such as location of files and account information have to be configured using the nrConfigure utility (discussed later in this chapter). Systems such as Oracle contain tools to generate reports containing graphical as well as numerical representation of data. To get you started, each Director ships with a sample set of SQL queries that can be easily modified and run from within your RDBMS system. It is possible to define custom actions based on events, too (this is covered in more detail later in this section). The Director also provides you with access to the NSDB for reference material on exploits.

The Cisco Secure Policy Manager

The Cisco Secure Policy Manager is a Windows-based GUI software solution that can also manage Cisco IDS. It is installed on a modern Windows NT platform. The software is very memory sensitive—specifications call for 0.5GB, but more is better. Because of the native Windows environment, it is easy for an analyst to explore the alerts generated by the platform.

Because the CSPM is documented in Chapter 12, this chapter will go over configuration and management using the Director platform.

NOTE

Cisco recommends that no more than 25 probes be configured to send information to a single Director. Cisco suggests between three and six Probes be configured per CSPM. If more probes are required for your network, you should install multiple CSPM/Directors and build a hierarchical structure of probes and Directors.

The Post Office

The Post Office is a messaging facility between management stations and sensors that uses a proprietary UDP transport protocol for communication. Rather than being unacknowledged, the protocol guarantees transmissions, maintains connection status and provides acknowledgement for packets received with lower overhead than TCP/IP. It uses an enhanced addressing structure that is ideal for building hierarchical fault-tolerant structures. Up to 255 alternate routes between each probe and its Director can be supported. The structures are comprised of multiple Directors and probes; in this way, you can support a theoretically unlimited number of probes. Probes can forward updates onto one or more Directors which can then propagate the message to other Directors in the hierarchy.

> **NOTE**
>
> If you need to perform any traffic filtering on routers between Directors and probes (control interfaces), you must allow traffic using UDP port 45000 to pass between the two.

Figure 13.1 shows these basic components in context.

Figure 13.1 IDS Protocols and Associated Components

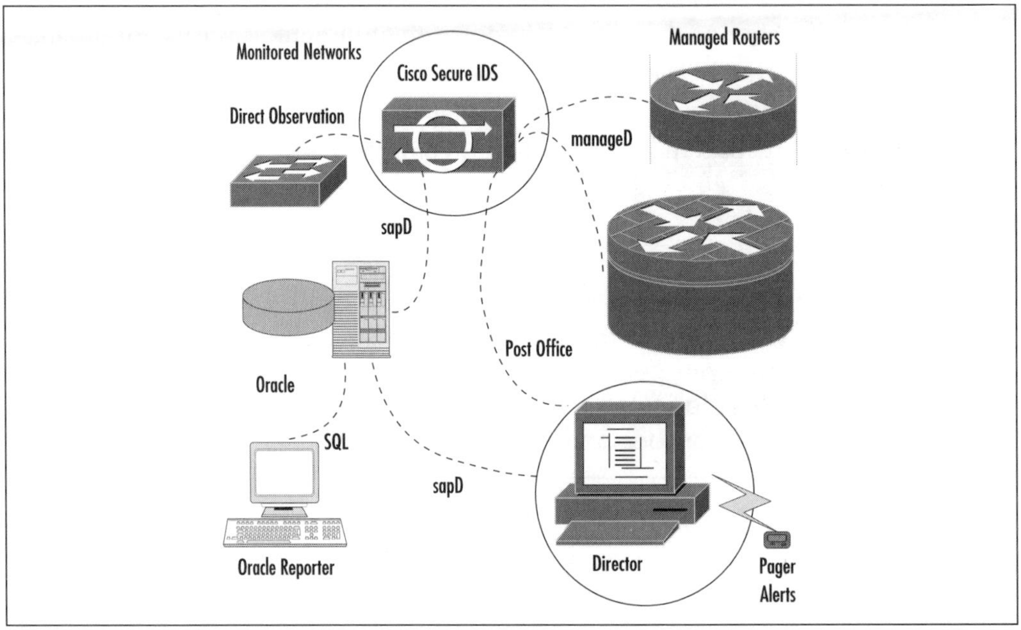

You can see the IDS components with the main daemons that are responsible for running the system. Each daemon performs a specific function, which is explained in more detail next:

- **sensord/packetd** Sensord is used to relay intrusion detection information sent from other devices capable of detecting attacks and sending data; packetd is used when the sensor itself does the intrusion detection.

- **loggerd** Used to write to log files and record events such as alarms and command instructions.

- **sapd** Provides file and data management functions, including the transfer of data to database systems such as Oracle.

- **postofficed** Manages and provides all communications between the Director and probes.

- **eventd** Performs notification management on events to pager and e-mail systems.

- **managed** Controls configuration of managed Cisco routers.

Here are some other daemons not displayed on the diagram:

- **smid** A Director daemon that converts raw information into data that ndirmap uses.

- **nrdirmap** Displays icons for NetRanger components and events such as alarms and status conditions for other daemons.

- **configd** Interprets and manages commands entered through ndirmap to interface with the other daemons.

Now we understand the components, let's discuss some of the more general features. Cisco Secure IDS is a network-based IDS system that captures packets and then performs signature analysis using an inferencing engine. The analysis involves examination of each packet's payload for content-based attacks and the examination of the header for patterns of misuse. Cisco Secure IDS classifies the types of attacks into two types: atomic (single, directed at one victim) and composite (multiple, over a period of time and involving many victims).

The Director uses an internal (upgradeable) security database (NSDB) for signature analysis, which provides information about exploits and matching countermeasures. There are two types of signatures, embedded and string matching. As the name suggests, embedded signatures are contained within the probe's system files; they cannot be modified and protect against misuse by matches against the packet header fields. String matching signatures, on the other hand, are user configurable and work by examining the payload of the packet. A description of how to do this is included later in this section.

Before You Install

It is imperative you spend time thinking out your Cisco Secure IDS design. Without this, it may end up being ineffective. You should consider all connections from your network to the outside, as well as the volumes and types of traffic in use. Also, if your network is large, perhaps multinational in nature, then you may want to consider internal boundaries. You should decide how many probes are required to monitor the network effectively.

Probes have two interfaces, one for data collection and the other, the control interface, which is used for remote communication (always Ethernet-based). The placement of the probe is important in order to protect the control port and to "sense" correctly.

Director placement is also important. It is a focal point and compromise could have serious consequences. The Director must be easily accessible for security staff yet be physically secure (in other words, protected on the network—perhaps through a firewall), and still be able to communicate with its probes.

Director and Probe Setup

Here are the minimum requirements for Director installation; the amount of RAM required varies depending on the configuration.

HP UX 10.20 (with HP OpenView 4.1) requires 125MB disk space for software directories, whereas Sun Solaris 2.5.1 or 2.6 requires 172MB. Both platforms require 1GB disk space for logging, 96MB RAM, a CD drive, a TCP/IP-enabled network card, and a current HTML browser.

Next, we will investigate how to install and configure the Director and probe. Let's start with the Director installation procedure for Unix.

Director Installation

Once you have decided on where you want to place the Director, and you have a workstation that meets the minimum system requirements, we can power up and begin the installation.

1. Log in as **root** on the chosen Director station.
2. Check that the date and time are correct.
3. Ensure /usr/sbin is in the PATH.
4. Enter **/etc/set_parms initial** and restart the machine.
5. Configure the IP address, subnet mask, default gateway, and hostname.
6. Install HP OpenView.
7. Add these lines to the root profile (watch the space between . and /)

```
.  /opt/OV/bin/ov.envvars.sh
PATH=$PATH:$OV_BIN
```

8. Modify semaphores to read:

    ```
    semmns - 256, semmni - 128, semmnu - 90, semume - 20
    ```

9. Now, restart the machine.

10. Insert the Cisco Secure IDS CD into the drive and exit OpenView.

11. From the CD type **./install**. Follow the onscreen instructions and lastly restart the machine again.

Director Configuration

So, now that we have completed the basic installation of NetRanger, we must perform the following steps to configure it:

1. Log in as **netrangr.**

2. Stop all services by typing **nrstop** at the prompt.

3. Start configuration by typing **sysconfig–director**.

4. Enter all Director information, Host ID & Name, Organization ID & Name, and the IP address.

5. Exit sysconfig-director and then type **nrstart** at the prompt to restart services.

Probe Installation

Once the Director base configuration is complete, you should already know where you want to place your probe. Probe installation and configuration is done using a program called sysconfig-sensor. Here's how it works:

1. Connect all cables, and attach the probe to the network where required.

2. Sign on as **root** and enter **sysconfig-sensor** at the prompt.

3. A menu will appear where you can enter values for the IP address, subnet mask, default gateway and hostname. Figure 13.2 shows how it should look.

Figure 13.2 The Sysconfig-sensor Menu

```
#sysconfig-sensor

NetRanger Sensor Initial Configuration Utility

Choose a value to configure one of the following parameters:

1 - IP Address

2 - IP Netmask

3 - IP Hostname

4 - Default Route

5 - Network Access Control

6 - Netranger Communications Infrastructure

7 - System Date, Time and Timezone

8 - Passwords

x - Exit


Selection:
```

4. Connect a terminal server to the COM1 port for out of band access.

5. Using option 5, define IP addresses that are allowed to Telnet or perform file transfers to the probe.

6. Using option 6, set the Probe Host and Organization details. The corresponding Director details must also be entered.

7. Exit sysconfig-sensor and restart the Sensor device.

8. Using Unix system administration tools, modify the *netrangr* password. By default, the password is *attack*.

Completing the Probe Installation

We have almost finished. All that remains is to relate the Director and probe configurations together. Here are the steps required:

1. On the Director station, select **Security, Configure**.

2. Select **File | Add Host**, choose **Next**.

3. Enter the probe details in the next screen, select **Next**.

4. Choose **Add New Sensor Reporting To This Director**.

5. Next, enter Shunning preferences—the amount of time to wait before shun and how long to log for.

6. Enter the probe interface performing the data collection (for example, **/dev/spwr0** for Ethernet).

7. Select **Add** and then choose the IP subnets the probe is protecting.

8. The next screen is optional. Here you can enter details of a Cisco router managed by the probe.

9. Select **Next** and then **Finish.**

General Operation

The Director runs under HP OpenView. The top-level icon is **NetRanger**, which once double-clicked, shows submaps containing NetRanger nodes. As more Directors and probes are configured, these will also become visible. Each submap can represent different security regions across the company. Once you select the Director or probe icon, the application daemons running on that machine are displayed. These can be selected in turn to show alarm icons generated by each. Each type of icon describes a different classification of attack based on the signatures found in the NSDB.

From HP OpenView, selecting the **Security** option displays further NetRanger options. Some of the more significant are:

- **Show** (select icon first) Provides information on devices, configuration, alarms, the NSDB, and others.

- **Configure** (select sensor first) Starts *nrConfigure*, which is used to configure probes and Directors.

- **Network Device** (select device first) Starts the *network device configuration* utility.

- **Shun** (select alarm first) Allows you to shun devices and networks.

- **Advanced** (select probe first) Allows various options; one of the most useful is the *Statistics, Show* option.

nrConfigure

When started, nrConfigure shows information regarding the device selected. You can configure communications, notification information, setup device management, log policy violations, configure shunning, and perform intrusion detection. Here are some examples of how to use nrConfigure:

Configuring Logging from a Router to a Sensor

On the router in privileged exec mode, enter global configuration mode and type these lines:

```
logging <ip address of Sensor control interface>
logging trap info
```

Modify your access list entries to include the *log* extension where required. This completes half of the configuration; the next step is to configure the probe. To do this:

1. In HP OpenView, highlight the probe.

2. From nrConfigure, select **Configure**, then select **Intrusion Detection**, **Data Sources**, and **Add**.

3. Enter the IP address of the sending router, then select **Profile**, **check the Manual box**, and **Modify Sensor**.

4. Pull down and select **Security Violations**.

5. Choose the ACL, choose the level of severity, and then select **Apply**.

Syslog traffic between the router and the probe is sent in the clear; if any networks the traffic traverses is untrusted, then this constitutes a security risk and should be avoided at all costs.

Configuring Intrusion Detection on Sensors

This can be done by using manual- or profile-based methods. The manual method allows you to configure individual signatures with complete control over configuration, whereas the profile-based one only allows selection of predefined groups of signatures. You would probably use profiles if you were integrating new signatures following a software upgrade.

Highlight the probe you wish to configure, then select one of the following methods for configuration:

1. **Profile-based** Select **Configure, Intrusion Detection, Profile**, then choose the **Profile-based** radio button, **Response**. You can then set the type of **Response**, disable Signatures, if required, or choose the **View Sensor button** to view settings. Once complete, select **OK** in the **Signatures box** and then **OK**.

2. **Manual-based** Select **Configure, Intrusion Detection, Profile** then choose the **Manual radio button**. Now choose **Modify Probe**. From the General Signatures box, configure corresponding actions. Select **OK** and choose **OK** again to exit.

By selecting **Configure | Intrusion Detection | Protected Networks tab** you can set up networks upon which you wish to perform IP packet logging using the probe.

Customizing the NSDB

This is useful for protection against vulnerabilities that are not defined in the NSDB. You can create an NSDB record that the inference engine will use as part of its analysis. Custom signatures can also be used to track host and port usage for general information. For example, you might want to look for a particular string inside the content of the packet.

Here are the steps involved in adding your own signature to the NSDB to look for the string "do not ftp" in an FTP session and then perform a session reset.

1. On the Director station, select the probe then choose **Security | Configure**.

2. Select **Intrusion Detection | Profile**.

3. Select **Manual Configuration | Modify Sensor**.

4. Choose **Matched Strings** from the **Expand** scroll box**.**

5. Select **Add,** then enter **do not ftp** in the **String** column.

6. Enter a unique ID for the signature.

7. Enter port **20** for FTP data.

8. To specify the direction, select **To & From**.

9. Enter the **Occurrences** as **1** to specify a condition to initiate an action.

10. Specify the **Action** as **Reset** and enter **5** in the destination.

11. Select **OK**, then **OK**, and finally, choose **Apply**.

The new rule will reset any FTP connections where the data contains one occurrence of the words "do not ftp" and will send out level 5 alarms to all configured logging destinations.

Upgrading the NSDB

To upgrade the NSDB, you must have a valid CCO logon. Download instructions for the NSDB file can be found at www.cisco.com by searching for "Cisco Secure IDS Update" then following instructions in the update readme file.

The Data Management Package

The Data Management Package (DMP) is contained within Cisco Secure IDS and performs two functions: 1) The collection of data in flat file logs; and 2) The manipulation of data into a relational database file format to facilitate Oracle SQL analysis (on the normalized data).

You can configure these options through *nrConfigure* and the *Data Management* options on the Director. It is possible to create triggers for execution on condition, determining log file size, and other settings. The DMP contains a basic set of SQL reports that provide detail on attack signatures with dates and times. What other components do we need to make this work? Oracle server will have to be installed either remotely or locally. It must reference the NetRanger data. Using nrConfigure, tokens must be created to allow the Oracle server access. Further details of this can be found at www.cisco.com/univercd/cc/td/doc/product/iaabu/netrangr/nr220/nr220ug/rdbms.htm#27755. Once viewable from Oracle, you can either use native scripts or third-party tools to manage the data, create graphs, and draw correlations to highlight specific areas.

An E-mail Notification Example

First of all, you must configure event notification. To do so:

1. In HP OpenView, select **Configure | Security** then **Event Processing**.

2. Select the **Application tab**.

3. Add a severity level to execute a script, and then reference the script. Enter the path to **/bin/eventd/event** in the script name field.

4. Select the **Timing option** and set the thresholds of events which will trigger the script and the interleave between sampling the event data.

5. Select **OK**, then ensure that **Daemons, nr.eventd** has a status of **Yes**. Select **OK**.

6. Configure the probe to send notifications to eventd. Select **Destinations** from **nrConfigure** then **Add**.

7. Enter the probe ID. Choose the application of eventd and a security level required to send the notification. Lastly, select the type of event to act upon.

8. Select **Event Processing | E-mail**.

9. Enter the Organization ID, the Type of event, and the Severity Level to trigger the mail.

10. Enter the e-mail addresses of the person(s) you wish to notify, then select **OK**.

The next time the event occurs, an e-mail notification will be sent.

NOTE

Whenever a change is made to the system using nrConfigure, it is advisable to use nrstop and nrstart to restart the services.

Cisco IOS Intrusion Detection Systems

This is one feature that puts the Cisco solution "streets ahead" of the competition because intrusion detection is integrated into the router IOS. Any traffic that passes through the router can be scrutinized for intrusions. The router acts as a probe checking for intrusions in a similar fashion to a Cisco Secure IDS Sensor device.

IOS IDS is useful to install at network perimeters, such as intranet/extranet borders or branch office routers. You may decide to deploy this method of intrusion detection where a Cisco Secure IDS Sensor is not financially viable or where a reduced set of signatures to be checked will suffice. Despite not having the same level of granularity during signature identification, and checking against a much smaller signature base than Cisco Secure IDS, it is still capable of detecting severe breaches of security, reconnaissance scans, and common network attacks. The signatures it uses constitute a broad cross section selected from the NSDB. IOS IDS will protect against 59 different types of network intrusions. It is possible to disable checking for individual signatures through modification of the router config in order to avoid false positives. The signatures can be categorized into two main types: *Info* and *Attack*. Info refers to reconnaissance scans for information gathering, and Attack refers to DoS or other intrusions. Each type can also be further divided into atomic (directed at an individual station) or compound (directed at a group of stations perhaps over an extended period of time).

IOS IDS is fully compatible with Cisco Secure IDS and can appear as an icon on the Director GUI. The router can send alarms back to a syslog server, a Cisco Secure IDS sensor, or take action by dropping unwanted packets or terminating TCP/IP sessions. Dropping packets happens transparently without the router interacting with end stations, but session termination does involve the router sending a TCP RST to source and destination devices; it is usually best to use both these actions together when configuring the router.

One important consideration is that of the impact of IOS IDS on the router. This will vary depending upon the specification of the router, the number of signatures configured, and how busy the router is. The most significant impact on the router is caused by audit rules that refer to Access Control Lists. It is probably a good idea to keep an eye on the router memory by using the *sh proc mem* command from the privileged exec prompt after configuration.

Unlike Cisco Secure IDS, IOS IDS (as the name suggests), contains the signatures within the image. For future updates to the IOS IDS signature base, the image on the router flash has to be upgraded. It is not possible to modify or add new signatures to the existing set, which is a useful feature available on Cisco Secure IDS (discussed in the previous section).

We can divide our discussion of IOS IDS into two main sections: Configuring Cisco IOS IDS features and associated commands.

Configuring Cisco IOS IDS Features

Configuration begins by initializing the IOS IDS software and then creating audit rules to specify signatures and associated actions. Rules can be applied inbound or outbound on the router interfaces. The audit rule command *ip audit* has the following extensions available:

- **smtp spam** Sets e-mail spamming restrictions.
- **po** Employed for all Post Office configurations when using a Cisco Secure IDS Director.
- **notify** Sends event information to syslog servers or a Cisco Secure IDS Director.
- **info** Specifies the action on a reconnaissance scan.

- **attack** Specifies the action to take when an attack is detected.

- **name** Specifies the name of the rule; also used to apply the rule to an interface.

- **signature** Disables individual signatures and sources of false alarms.

- **po protected** Selects which interfaces are to be protected by the router.

To investigate these commands further, we can look at an example based upon the scenario shown in Figure 13.3.

Figure13.3 The Secure IS (IOS IDS) Configuration Scenario

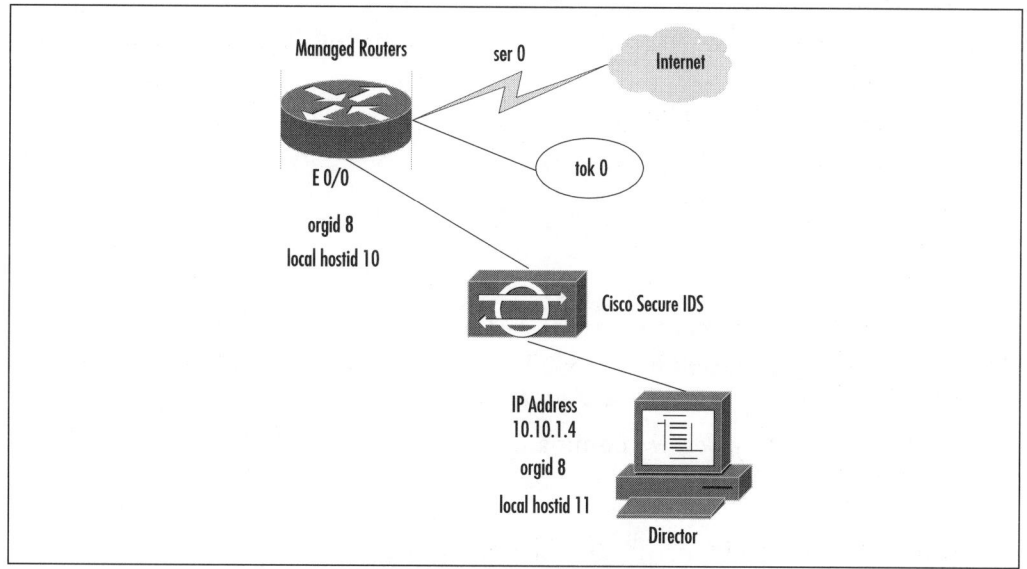

Here is the configuration for Figure 13.3:

```
ip audit smtp spam 50
ip audit po max-events 20
ip audit notify nr-director
ip audit po local hostid 10 orgid 8
ip audit po remote hostid 11 orgid 8 rmtaddress 10.10.1.4 localaddress
10.10.1.3 port-number 32000 application director
ip audit info action alarm
ip audit attack action alarm drop reset
ip audit name TEST info list 3 action alarm
```

```
ip audit name TEST attack list 3 action alarm reset drop
interface e 0/0
        ip address 10.10.1.3 255.255.0.0
        ip audit TEST in
interface tokenring 0
        ip address 11.1.3.1 255.255.255.0
        access-list 3 deny 11.1.3.1 0.0.0.255
ip audit po protected 10.10.0.0 to 10.10.255.254
```

Our objective is to protect the Ethernet network from attackers from the untrusted Internet. The example assumes that a NetRanger Director is present and that there is a trusted token ring network also attached to the router. The configuration displayed shows a subsection of commands from the router configuration.

Let's describe the commands in turn:

```
ip audit smtp spam 50
```

This sets a threshold of 50 recipients in an e-mail to denote a spam e-mail.

```
ip audit po max-events 20
```

This defines that 20 entries can be queued up for sending to the Director; above this value, events will be dropped. You need to be careful when using this command as each queue entry uses 32KB of RAM; you can monitor levels of RAM using the *show proc mem* command.

```
ip audit notify nr-director
```

This configures the Cisco Secure IDS Director as the destination for the alarms.

```
ip audit po local hostid 10 orgid 8
```

This defines the local router's Post Office details. hostid is unique, and orgid is the same as the Cisco Secure IDS Director group.

```
ip audit po remote hostid 11 orgid 8 rmtaddress 10.10.1.4 localaddress
    10.10.1.3 port-number 32000 application director
```

This is the same as the previous command but defines the Cisco Secure IDS Director hostid as 11, the Director orgid as 8, the IP address for the Director, the router's IP address, the UDP port the Director is listening on as 32000, and the type of application being used as Director (*logger* would be used in this field if logging to a syslog server).

Note that the router has to be reloaded after all Post Office config changes.

```
ip audit info action alarm
```

The default response to take on an information signature is to send an alarm.

```
ip audit attack action alarm drop reset
```

The default response to take on an attack signature is to send an alarm, drop the packet, and reset the audited session.

```
ip audit name TEST info list 3 action alarm
```

This defines an audit rule called TEST where traffic permitted by access list 3 will be processed and an alarm will be raised on an information signature match.

```
ip audit name TEST attack list 3 action alarm reset drop
```

This defines an audit rule called TEST where traffic permitted by access list 3 will be processed and an alarm will be raised, the connection reset, and the packet dropped on an attack signature match.

```
interface e 0/0
ip address 10.10.1.3 255.255.0.0
ip audit TEST in
```

This applies the audit rule to inbound traffic on the Ethernet interface.

```
interface tokenring 0
ip address 11.1.3.1 255.255.255.0
access-list 3 deny 11.1.3.1 0.0.0.255
```

This prevents Token Ring traffic from being audited since the token ring can be considered a trusted network.

```
ip audit po protected 10.10.0.0 to 10.10.255.254
```

This specifies the IP address range of the Ethernet network to be protected. Note that you can omit addresses from being protected by defining multiple ranges.

By using another command, *no ip audit signature <signature-id>* or *ip audit signature <signature-id> <disable / list ACL number>*, it is possible to omit the auditing of a particular signature globally, or for a range of addresses.

Associated Commands

These are IOS IDS commands you can enter at the Privileged EXEC prompt:

`clear ip audit configuration`

This disables IOS IDS and removes all IDS entries from the configuration.

`show ip audit interface`

Shows IOS IDS configuration from an interface perspective.

`show ip audit configuration`

Used to display the active IOS IDS configuration on the router.

`show ip audit debug`

Shows the current IDS debug flag entries.

`show ip audit statistics`

This will show you signature audited counts and TCP session statistics. You would use the *clear ip audit statistics* command to reset these figures.

Summary

An intrusion detection system (IDS) is a suite of devices, hardware and software, that automates the investigation of odd activity in or around computers. It is generally used as a detective device, highlighting unwanted events after they have occurred. The Cisco IDS can also act as a preventative device, taking steps to prevent unwanted action.

IDSs fall into two types: network-based IDSs (NIDSs), where traffic is analyzed as it passes by a sensor on a wire; and host-based IDSs (HIDSs), where traffic is analyzed as it is accepted by the operating system. Network appliances or infrastructure plug-ins are readily deployed arbitrarily into the network, while host-based solutions must be customized to the operating system of the existing server. On the other hand, host systems have better insight into how the host actually handles the event, and so the alarms are of much higher fidelity than the equivalent network solution.

The IDS architecture consists of one or more probes combined with one or more management stations. The probes have two interfaces: a sensor interface that samples traffic, and a command interface for configuration information. The sensors are generally distributed throughout the network at key locations. Sensors report back to the management station, and users will poll the management station to interpret alerts.

There are several business drivers leading to IDS deployment. The most natural one is to reduce the risk of a systems compromise. Having the detective control will reduce the frequency of events (because the vulnerabilities can be identified and addressed) and the impact of events (because root cause can be known, thus leading more rapidly to remediation). They are also good at identifying misconfigured events, such as incorrect configuration data causing system malfunction, or ineffective events, such as ineffective network traffic. Thus, in addition to traditional intrusion features, it can also help with network administration and management. Other business drivers are document existing threat levels, for planning or resource allocation purposes, and to change user behavior.

An important planning function is to determine exact placement of probes. Placing the probe outside the firewall allows you to "take the temperature" of the Internet, while placing the probe just inside the firewall allows testing of the firewall rulebase, and the possibility to identify intrusions if they pass the firewall. Other likely locations are on a service network, near server clusters, or near router transit networks/interfaces.

There are many difficulties associated with IDS deployments. One is that the underlying science behind intrusion detection systems is relatively new. Another is that management has unrealistic expectations of the capabilities of an IDS. A third is the deployment phase, since this is a security device that needs to cross organizational boundaries. A fourth is that the incidence response procedure associated with an IDS is nontrivial, and takes time to develop. A fifth is the complexity of IDS tuning, to make it a more effective product.

IDS tuning is the process of training a sensor to understand the enterprise network, so it provides a reasonable number of alerts of high fidelity. An IDS is a decision tool, and suffers from two types of errors: the Type I error, the "false positive," where it dispatches an alarm even though no event has occurred; and the Type II error, the "false negative," where it fails to send out an alarm even though an event has occurred. With a default signature load, the ratio of Type I errors to true alerts is so high that it is difficult to use on an enterprise network. In a sample data, 98.9 percent of the alerts were false positives.

There are two typical strategies for tuning. One is to "turn it up," where you review the signature database, and enable only those signatures that are of high fidelity and of interest to the site. Another (the more common of the two) is to "tone it down," where all possible sensitivity is first set, and then false positive alerts are slowly weeded out.

An IDS provides alerting for a network attack, so it's important to look at what kind of attacks occur. One type is loss of confidentiality due to packet capture on the wire. Another is reconnaissance from scanning programs. The network topology itself can help or harm you in deployments. Out-of-band communication due to unattended modems is also a risk.

Physical security of your network is always a concern. Poor physical security trumps strong technical controls.

Applications and operating systems themselves often have weaknesses, and software bugs are common in today's market. Nine types of software bugs are: boundary condition errors, access validation errors, input validation errors, failure to handle exceptional conditions, race conditions, serialization errors, atomicity errors, environment errors, and configuration errors.

Compromise of the authentication services can occur through discovery of a password. There are many ways to capture a password, from "shoulder surfing" to a brute force attack in which all possible passwords are tried in turn. Malicious code can be a source of attacks as well, and may include Trojan horses, viruses, or worms.

Errors and omissions are a major source of vulnerabilities in systems. Poorly configured systems are common as well. In addition, information leakage often occurs, simply because people don't think about what the leakage implies. Of course, malicious users are also a concern.

The IP protocols themselves can be targets of attacks. Services can be attacked, such as problems with mail bombing or spamming, together with mail impersonations. FTP is a common source of problems, particularly if anonymous ftp is permitted. SNMP has recently made news for being a source of many vulnerabilities, and unfortunately is widespread. The usual guidance of limiting access to services if they are not needed applies here.

Below the application itself, some infrastructure protocols can be vulnerable. DNS can be subject to host compromise, transparent fraudulent caching, and cache poisoning. DoS floods are also common; TCP SYN floods, an attack that sends a large number of SYN packets that never complete the handshake, in order to exhaust the TCB queue is similarly popular. A Cisco router or firewall can provide protection against this sort of flood through the use of TCP Intercept. Another common strike is the smurf attack, which depends upon forged source addresses aimed at broadcast addresses to harm hosts. TCP can also be subject to session hijacking, and various sorts of low-level packet attacks such as the Ping of Death, Teardrop, and Land attacks.

Distributed denial of service attacks are common, too, where the attacker compromises multiple computers, and installs programs like Trinoo, Tribal Flood Network, or Stacheldraht to provide an attacking agent.

As far as the equipment itself goes, the Cisco Secure IDS is either the Catalyst 6000 IDS module or a standalone Unix-based appliance. The Catalyst module is designed to be integrated natively into a switched environment, while the IDS 4230 is designed to monitor fast Ethernet links. The Director is a GUI-based plug-in for HP OpenView. The Director integrates with an Oracle relational database, and permits query of the stored information. The sensors can also report back to a Cisco Secure Policy Manager console, which provides a native Windows NT application for easy use.

In terms of the underlying communication architecture, the sensors and management console use a proprietary communication channel on UDP port 45000. This provides for native encryption, and includes reliable, acknowledged transport of the sensor data.

The IDS has several daemons responsible for successful operations. The nine daemons are sensord/packetd, loggerd, sapd, postofficed, eventd, managed, smid, nrdirmap, and configd. Signature information is stored on the sensor hard drive, and consists of a contained signature base together with a customizable string search approach.

The Director installation is an extension of HP OpenView. After that is complete, running the install script from the Cisco Secure IDS CD, and following the prompts completes the installation. The director parameter configuration is achieved with the *sysconfig-director* script; you need to specify HostID, Name, Organizational ID, Name, and IP address. Building the sensors is similar: launch an install script from the CD, and execute *sysconfig-sensor*, then follow the prompts to set up the initial communication information. Finally, the sensor is introduced to the director by selecting Add Host from the file menu, and following the prompts.

Further configuration of the sensors from inside of HP OpenView is similar to any HP OpenView plug-in. Selecting the NetRanger icon from the top-level map provides submaps containing IDS nodes. Submaps represent security zones, and various options are available from the Security menu. You can configure logging from routers to a sensor (the data is uploaded to the manager via Post Office from the sensor), and configure the IDS directly on the sensor. You can also update the network string search signatures directly from HPOV.

Other important configurations for global management are establishing the data management package (reflects flat file management and integration into Oracle) and e-mail alerting.

Cisco also has an IDS as part of the IOS firewall feature set. This is useful in integrating IDS into the infrastructure, where the expense of a dedicated probe is not justified. Its feature set is a limited subset of the probe signature-matching engine. The data will report back via a Cisco Secure IDS sensor to the management platform. Again, it is capable of alerting, and offers protective capabilities through TCP resets.

It's important to keep an eye on the performance of the router. The *sh proc mem* command is helpful in monitoring memory use. Additional commands are available under the *ip audit* menu tree; they include *smtp spam*, *po*, *notify*, *info*, *attack*, *name*, *signature*, and *po protected*. Typical Cisco IOS help systems apply. In addition, privileged commands include *clear ip audit conf*, *show ip audit int*, *show ip audit conf*, *show ip audit debug*, and *show ip audit stat*.

Solutions Fast Track

What Is Intrusion Detection?

☑ An IDS is a software or a suite of devices that helps investigate unusual traffic on the network. It is primarily used in a detective capability, but can also be used in a protective capability (through interrupting system calls for the host-based product, or through shunning for the network product).

☑ Usually the architecture is a typical client/server model, where the probes send data up to management consoles. Users interact with the management console to address data.

☑ The primary purposes for an IDS deployment are to reduce risk, identify error, optimize network use, provide insight into threat levels, and change user behavior. Thus, an IDS provides more than just detection of intrusion.

☑ Determining where to place the probes is not straightforward. You can place them outside the firewall if you want to gather data on attacks from the Internet, but typical locations are near critical servers, or covering interfaces between security zones.

☑ There are many difficulties associated with IDS deployment. Five important issues to overcome are: the newness of the technology, management expectation, coordination with other internal organizations, incident response procedures, and tuning IDS.

IDS Tuning

☑ What an IDS does is make a decision whether or not to alarm on a packet. The tuning process is designed to make the decision as accurate as possible.

☑ Any decision process suffers from two types of errors: the Type I error, known as the "false positive," is an alert that does not correspond to a security event. These lead to additional work as the security analyst needs to review these messages. The second is the Type II error, or the "false negative," which is a security event that isn't alarmed. This type of error leads to risk assumed by the enterprise.

☑ Untuned, an IDS deployment has a high ratio of false positives to true alerts. Based upon sample data, 99 out of 100 alerts were invalid. However, even with the high level of work, it is possible to explore the alerts to find the actual attacks.

☑ The tuning process usually follows one of two paths: "turn it up," where alerts are selectively enabled, or "tone it down," where alerts are disabled. One good approach in the "tone it down" phase is to let the appliance run, and for each alert type, disable it if the ratio of false positives exceeds the importance of the signature.

Network Attacks and Intrusions

☑ Understanding network attack and intrusion types is essential to interpreting IDS data.

☑ Five categories that correspond to network attacks are: breakdowns in perimeter/device security, harm to physical security, attacks on application/OS integrity, effects of human error and omission, and taking advantage of weaknesses in the underlying IP suite.

The Cisco Secure Network Intrusion Detection System

☑ The probe types are the Windows x86-based Catalyst 6000 IDS module, or the SPARC Solaris-based IDS 4230 and IDS 4210. Management types include the Director, a Unix-based HPOV plug-in, and the CSPM, a Windows NT-based standalone application.

☑ The Post Office is a proprietary UDP-based communication protocol between the Sensor and the management platform. It provides an encrypted channel, with reliable communications handled by the application.

☑ Nine Unix daemons handle communication between sensor and database and up to HPOV.

☑ The installation process is fairly straightforward, and is primarily prompt driven after running an install script from provided installation media. Key parameters are the IP address/routing information, host ID and Name, and Organization ID and name. Finally, the information on any new probe needs to be introduced to the management database.

☑ Probes have an atomic database, updated about every month by Cisco, and a locally customizable database. The customizable portion of the detection engine is configured from the management station and pushed out to the sensor.

☑ In addition to the conventional probes, a subset of the IDS features are available on the routers themselves. IOS IDS is useful to install at network perimeters such as branch routers. This is fully compatible with the management platform for the probes, and allows for a widespread IDS deployment.

Frequently Asked Questions

The following Frequently Asked Questions, answered by the authors of this book, are designed to both measure your understanding of the concepts presented in this chapter and to assist you with real-life implementation of these concepts. To have your questions about this chapter answered by the author, browse to **www.syngress.com/solutions** and click on the **"Ask the Author"** form.

Q: I already have a firewall. Why do I need an IDS?

A: Firewalls are gatekeepers. They allow traffic in and out of a network, and are the first line of defense. They aren't a complete solution, however. For one thing, they don't address traffic they can't see—if an internal user is playing around with a core asset and both are "internal," the firewall won't see it. For another, an IDS provides a "defense in depth." They have a different focus, and so if an attack technology penetrates the first layer of defense, there is a chance they will be picked up by the IDS. And of course, there are other advantages mentioned earlier: an IDS provides visibility into your network that can help with maintenance of applications and the network itself. An IDS is a flexible tool!

Q: I'm seeing lots of network scans on my IDS. Should I worry?

A: It depends. If your sensor covers Internet-based hosts, then port scans are a routine fact of life. Some security administrators make an effort to report the intrusion back to the owning ISP, but many do not.

On the other hand, if the scanning is going on internally, then its probably inappropriate traffic. It may be unintentional: many users install software (such as printer drivers or Visio 2000) which will attempt network scans. While harmless, eliminating this unnecessary traffic is desirable. If intentional, it could indicate someone unwilling to comply with your security policy, and a headache in development. Addressing the headache early on is the best way to keep the problem small. On the other hand, it could also indicate a compromised machine, and that is definitely worth addressing.

Q: I'm seeing an alert indicating something on my network. What should I do?

A: The first thing is to review your event management protocol; it's best to have these things thought out and documented. But essentially, if an alert comes in, you need to review the nature of the alert. For example, if the alert relates to an IIS server, and the target is a Unix host running apache, you can ignore the alert as a false positive, and perhaps tune the signature. If the event management protocol allows it, the next step might be to contact the owner of the information asset, inform them of what you are seeing, and ask them to verify the vulnerability of the device to the indicated alarm.

Q: I'm seeing an alert indicating something on my network. What does it mean?

A: Many signatures provide a context buffer; this can help you understand what it means. However, your first stop is probably the included signature database information. That provides information about the nature of the alert, and the fidelity of the signature. If you need more information, you might try the SecurityFocus database, or the ISS database. Web searches usually provide a wealth of information on the alert.

Q: How can I stay current on the various attacks?

A: CERT, the Computer Emergency Response Team at the Software Engineering Institute (SEI) of the Carnegie Mellon University (CMU), is a good source of validated information. They are online at www.cert.org. AUSCERT is the Australian CERT, available at www.auscert.org.au. Another reputable source of information on attacks is the Department of Energy's CIAC, at www.ciac.org.

While not related directly to attack information, SANS, the System Administration and Network Security Institute <http://www.sans.org>, is a good resource as well. They have a wide variety of security information, and have their own FAQ site at www.sans.org/newlook/resources/IDFAQ/ ID_FAQ.htm.

Q: Should I build a full infrastructure, or should I outsource?

A: A difficult question, as the jury is still out. On the one hand, few care as much about security on your network or have as much information about what is normal on your network as you do—and effective use of a network requires intimate knowledge of the network. On the other hand, because an IDS remains a complex and sharp tool, with skill sets that are not common, it is difficult to staff adequately. The "Managed Security Services" and "Managed Security Monitoring" companies offer services with a wide area of coverage. You need to look at your own staffing ability, your own costs and budgets, and make a decision regarding your business drivers.

## Chapter 14

Network Security Management

Solutions in this chapter:

- PIX Device Manager
- CiscoWorks2000 Access Control List Manager
- Cisco Secure Policy Manager
- Cisco Secure Access Control Server

- ☑ Summary
- ☑ Solutions Fast Track
- ☑ Frequently Asked Questions

Introduction

The frequency and complexity of network security-related incidences has increased dramatically in recent years. Additionally, network infrastructure and services have grown larger and more intricate to meet continually evolving user demands for bandwidth and functionality. As a result, managing security in enterprise environments has become a challenge for administrators in companies large and small.

To overcome security management issues, Cisco has developed several security management applications including those listed next:

- PIX Device Manager (PDM)

- CiscoWorks2000 Access Control Lists Manager (ACLM)

- Cisco Secure Policy Manager (CSPM)

- Cisco Secure Access Control Server (ACS)

These applications are designed to ease the burden of security management through intuitive graphical interfaces, configuration automation, report generation, and enhanced monitoring capabilities among others. Each application is suited for a different purpose, yet the combination of these tools can represent a holistic management solution in many environments.

In addition to the applications in the preceding list, administrators can also use other tools to support and configure Cisco security devices such as the convenient command-line interface (CLI) via methods including Telnet, Secure Shell (SSH), and the out-of-band console port. Additionally, Cisco security devices can also be remotely monitored using Simple Network Management Protocol (SNMP) and syslog.

This section includes a discussion regarding the applications listed earlier. For additional information regarding more basic, CLI-based management techniques, refer to Cisco documentation.

PIX Device Manager

Companies and organizations with one or two PIX firewall devices require a tool to effectively and efficiently manage the configuration and functionality of their firewalls. PDM is an application ideally suited for such small enterprises as it enables full control over individual PIX firewalls from virtually any authorized client management platform inside an organization.

Whether it is a simple access rule change or a more advanced Network Address Translation (NAT) configuration, PDM eases administrative burdens by providing an intuitive, Web-based graphical interface to each PIX device.

With security incidents on the rise, administrators also require insight into the events and traffic patterns detected on their firewall devices. PDM provides excellent reporting and proactive IDS configuration capabilities to firewall administrators all through the Web-based interface.

PIX Device Manager Overview

The PDM is a Java-based graphical user interface used to manage the Cisco PIX firewall. It is imbedded in the PIX firewall software in all versions 6.0 and later. The PDM replaces the PIX Firewall Manager (PFM) software as of PIX Firewall software version 5.3. PDM allows firewall administrators to work from a variety of authorized workstations configured with a JDK 1.1.4-compliant browser and includes nearly all PIX command-line interface (CLI) functionalities. For example, using PDM, administrators can add, modify, and delete firewall rule sets or configure Authentication, Authorization, and Accounting (AAA). Furthermore, firewall administrators can issue command line configurations directly from the Web interface for swifter management. A more comprehensive list of capabilities is included in the sections that follow.

Using PDM for firewall management, administrators do not compromise security thanks to Secure Sockets Layer (SSL) encryption capabilities and authentication mechanisms on the PIX firewall.

PIX Device Manager Benefits

Administrators using PDM can enjoy a host of benefits over more traditional management techniques. Foremost is the ability to make configurations to PIX devices from various authorized client locations using the Web-based GUI. Doing so avoids potential configuration problems due to syntax errors and enables the administrator to swiftly alter configurations without constantly returning to a centralized management station.

Since Cisco developed PDM in Java and because the Java applets actually reside on the PIX platform, management from multiple platforms without time-consuming software installations is possible. Administrators simply need to launch a JDK 1.1.4 capable browser and connect to the PIX firewall from an authorized location.

PDM also includes helpful wizards such as the Initial Setup Wizard. The Initial Setup Wizard allows for rapid and simplified deployment of PIX firewall devices by prompting the administrator for typical information required in all firewall configurations.

With the PDM interface, administrators can also visually monitor and baseline connections, PIX system internal metrics, traffic load, IDS, and other useful information. Because PDM clients use SSL (HTTPS) to connect to the PIX, these connections are reasonably secure. However, it is recommended to further control access to PIX for administrative tasks through an Access Control List (ACL).

Finally, while PDM is designed to manage and monitor individual PIX firewalls, multiple browser windows may be opened on the management client desktop enabling the concurrent and easy management of multiple firewalls across the enterprise.

Supported PIX Firewall Versions

The PIX Device Manager application is new as of PIX Firewall software version 6.0 and replaces the PIX Firewall Management software as of PIX Firewall software version 5.3. To facilitate multiple management platforms, Cisco created the software using Java and imbedded applets directly in the OS image. All versions of the PIX Firewall software version 6.0 or later support PDM.

PIX Device Requirements

PDM is supported on all PIX 501, 506, 515, 520, 525, and 535 platforms running PIX Firewall software version 6.0 or later. Additionally, the PIX platform must meet the following requirements to run PDM:

- 8MB Flash memory
- A Data Encryption Standard (DES) or 3DES activation key

The DES or 3DES activation key supports the SSL-based communication between the remote Java management client and the Cisco PIX device. PIX devices shipped with firewall software version 6.0 and later already include DES capabilities. 3DES, which enables stronger encryption capabilities, is available from Cisco as an additional license.

Those PIX devices shipped with Firewall software versions prior to version 6.0 must be upgraded to version 6.0 or later and configured with a DES activation key before PDM will function. DES activation keys are available for free from Cisco on their Web site at www.cisco.com/kobayashi/sw-center/internet/pix-56bit-license-request.shtml.

NOTE

Check the PIX firewall software version and DES capabilities using the *show version* console command on the selected PIX firewall.

Requirements for a Host Running the PIX Device Management Client

Because Cisco created PDM using Java technology, several client workstations are capable of running the PDM client software. However, PDM will not function on MacOS, Windows 3.1, or Windows 95 operating systems. PDM can be run from Solaris, Linux, MacOS X, and Windows 98+. The corresponding PIX Firewall IOS versions are shown in Table 14.1.

Table 14.1 PIX Device Manager Client OS Requirements

Client Operating Systems	PIX Firewall IOS Version
Solaris	Solaris 2.6 and later
Linux	Red Hat 7.0 and later
Windows	Windows 98, Windows NT 4.0 (SP4), Windows2000 (SP1), and Windows ME

When running PDM on a Solaris operating system, the following requirements apply:

- **Processor** SPARC Processor
- **Memory** 128MB RAM
- **Display** 800×600 pixel display with at least 256 colors
- **Display** CDE or OpenWindows window manager
- **Browser** Netscape Communicator 4.51 or later (4.76 recommended)

When running PDM on a Linux operating system, the following requirements apply:

- **Memory** 64MB RAM
- **Display** An 800×600 pixel display with at least 256 colors

- **Display** GNOME or KDE 2.0 desktop environment
- **Browser** Netscape Communicator 4.75 or later version

When running PDM on a Windows operating system, the following requirements apply:

- **Processor** Pentium-compatible running at 350MHz or later
- **Memory** 128MB RAM
- **Display** 800×600 pixel display with at least 256 colors
- **Browser** Either Internet Explorer 5.0 (SP1) or later (5.5 recom-
  mended), or Netscape Communicator 4.51 or later (4.76 recommended)

Regardless of the client operating system, a Web browser is required to connect to PDM on the PIX firewall. To successfully launch PDM, the Web browser
must have JavaScript and Java enabled and must support JDK 1.1.4 or later.
Finally, the browser must support SSL connectivity. All browsers listed previously
include this functionality.

Using PIX Device Manager

This section of the chapter provides insight into the logical steps and procedures
required to get PDM working and includes examples that administrators can use
to compare to their own environment. Perform the following configuration steps
to make PFM functional. Then connect to the PIX firewall via PDM and begin
changing rules for inbound and outbound connections to and from the network.
This section also includes information regarding other configuration features discussed in the previous pages.

Configuring the PIX Device Manager

Before attempting to use PDM or configure a PIX device using PDM, verify that
the PIX firewall version of the device is 6.0 or later. If the PIX firewall device
was shipped from Cisco with 6.0 or later installed, PDM is probably already
installed as part of the PIX OS. If the PIX firewall version is not 6.0 or later, the
firewall version must be upgraded and DES must be activated before PDM will
function.

To verify the PIX firewall version, log in to the command-line interface via
Telnet or a console connection and type **show version**. The first two lines of
response should display the current PIX firewall version and indicate whether

PDM is installed. Figure 14.1 shows a PIX firewall with Firewall version 6.1(1) and PDM version 1.0(2) installed.

Figure 14.1 PIX Firewall with Firewall version 6.1(1) and PDM version 1.0(2) Installed

```
Pix> show version
Cisco PIX Firewall Version 6.1(1)
Cisco PIX Device Manager Version 1.0(2)
```

If the PIX firewall version is 6.0 or later and PDM is installed, proceed to the Configuration Example Section included on the following pages. If not, perform the following steps to upgrade the PIX firewall and install the DES activation key.

Installing the PIX Device Manager

As with all upgrade and installation procedures, begin by backing up all configuration data on the existing PIX firewall devices to upgrade. If the PIX firewall is a production device, schedule the upgrade procedure during off hours and notify the users in the company of the potential service outage. Doing so helps ensure a smooth upgrade process and prevents unwarranted complaints from the user community.

> **NOTE**
>
> Administrators with a valid CCO login can find Cisco PIX firewall software and PDM images on the Cisco Web site at www.cisco.com/kobayashi/sw-center/ciscosecure/pix.shtml.

Verify the PIX firewall meets all requirements listed previously in this chapter before starting with the upgrade and installation. Finally, be sure to obtain the correct version of the PIX firewall software and have a version of the PIX firewall software currently running on the PIX device in the event the new version upgrade fails. This procedure is generally trouble free, but best practice always dictates the preparation for version rollback.

The basic steps for PDM installation are:

- Obtain a DES activation key.
- Configure the PIX firewall for basic network connectivity.

- Install a TFTP server and make it available to the PIX firewall.

- Upgrade to a version of PIX firewall software 6.0 or later and configure the DES activation key on the PIX device.

- Install PDM on the PIX device.

These installation tasks are described in further detail next, and on the following pages.

Obtaining a DES Activation Key

The first step in configuring PDM on a PIX firewall is obtaining a new activation key to enable DES. This activation key is free from Cisco and required for PDM functionality. Because it may take some time for Cisco to issue the new key, it is best to start the request process early. Perform the following steps to request a DES activation key.

1. Establish a CLI connection to the PIX device via Telnet or the console.

2. From the command prompt, type **show version**. Note the current PIX serial number in the display. This will be required to request a new serial number and activation key.

3. From a Web browser, go to www.cisco.com/cgi-bin/Software/ FormManager/formgenerator.pl?pid=221&fid=324 and fill out the key request form. The key will be sent to you via e-mail.

Configuring the PIX Firewall for Basic Network Connectivity

To upgrade a PIX firewall and install PDM, the PIX firewall must first be capable of basic network connectivity. If the PIX firewall device is already on the network and capable of connecting to other devices, proceed to the next section and install a Trivial File Transfer Protocol (TFTP) server.

1. Establish a connection to the console port of the PIX device and log in to the CLI.

2. Enter enable mode by typing **enable** at the console prompt.

3. Type **configure terminal** to enter configuration mode on the PIX firewall.

4. Enter the setup dialog by typing **setup** after entering configure mode.

5. Follow the setup dialog prompts and enter information for the following variables:

- Enable password

- Clock variables

- IP address information

- Hostname

- Domain name

6. Save the information when prompted to write the configuration to memory.

Installing a TFTP Server and Making It Available to the PIX Firewall

After the PIX firewall is successfully placed on the network, a TFTP server must be configured to accommodate the new PIX firewall software and PDM software upload. Like other Cisco devices, using TFTP for software upload is the recommended method for performing software upgrades. If a TFTP server already exists, proceed to the next section and upgrade the PIX firewall software.

TFTP servers are usually included in all Unix and Linux distributions and can easily be configured. For information regarding TFTP configuration on a Unix or Linux platform, refer to the specific operating system documentation.

Cisco conveniently offers a TFTP server for Windows 95, Windows 98, Windows NT 4.0, and Windows2000 operating systems. The example that follows assumes the use of this software. Perform the following steps to install the Cisco TFTP server.

1. Allocate a machine to be used as the TFTP server. The Cisco software runs on the Windows 95, Windows 98, Windows NT 4.0, and Windows2000 operating systems.

2. Download the Cisco TFTP software. Administrators with a valid CCO account can find the software at www.cisco.com/cgi-bin/tablebuild.pl/tftp.

3. Run the self-extracting executable and follow the instructions included on the TFTP server download page to install the software.

Upgrading to PIX Firewall Software 6.0 and Configuring the DES Activation Key on the PIX Device

Because PDM only functions on PIX firewall software 6.0 and later, PIX devices with versions released before 6.0 must be upgraded. Furthermore, the use of PDM requires the activation of DES. To enable DES, the new key requested in previous steps must be activated during a new PIX image load using the monitor mode method on the PIX firewall. The key on the PIX firewall cannot be changed via typical copy tftp Flash upgrade procedures.

The upgrade of any operating system is a potentially difficult operation and should be thoroughly planned. Always back up configuration files and software versions before proceeding with the upgrade. Likewise, always verify that the PIX firewall meets the requirements specified for the PIX firewall software. There are several versions of PIX firewall software version 6.0 and later available on the Cisco Web site. Be sure to select the appropriate version for the installation.

To upgrade the PIX firewall software, follow these steps:

1. From the TFTP server, log in to Cisco Connection Online and download the appropriate version of the PIX firewall software. It can be found at www.cisco.com/cgi-bin/tablebuild.pl/pix.

2. Save the software in a location that can be accessed via TFTP. Note the name of the software image for later reference.

3. Log in to the PIX firewall CLI via a console connection.

4. Reboot the PIX device. As the PIX device is booting, issue a **BREAK** or **ESC** command when prompted to interrupt the Flash boot process. If using Windows HyperTerminal, the BREAK command is issued by pressing **Ctrl+Break**. The *monitor>* prompt should appear once in monitor mode.

NOTE

In monitor mode, use the ? key to see a list of available options.

5. From the monitor prompt, type **interface 1**. This command instructs the PIX firewall to use the inside interface to connect to the TFTP server.

6. Type **address** *pix_interface_ip_address* where *pix_interface_ip_address* is the IP address of the PIX internal interface.

7. Type **server** *tftp_server_ip_address* where *tftp_server_ip_address* is the IP address of the TFTP server with the new PIX firewall software image.

8. Type **file** *filename* where *filename* is the name of the new PIX firewall software image on the TFTP server.

9. If the TFTP server is on a remote network, the gateway command must be issued to configure the PIX firewall with a default gateway. Type **gateway** *ip_address_of_default_gateway* where *ip_address_of_default_gateway* is the ip address of the default router.

10. Type **tftp** to initiate the TFTP download of the new PIX firewall software from the TFTP server.

11. When prompted, type **yes** to install the new PIX Firewall software.

12. When prompted, type **yes** to enter a new activation key. Enter the new activation key acquired from Cisco in previous steps.

Here is an example of a successful PIX firewall software upgrade:

```
monitor> interface 1

0: ethernet0: address is 0050.54ff.59cc, irq 10

1: ethernet1: address is 0050.54ff.59cd, irq 7


Using 1: i82557 @ PCI(bus:0 dev:13 irq:11), MAC: 0050.54ff.59cd

monitor> address 172.20.1.1

address 172.20.1.1

monitor> server 172.20.1.20

server 172.20.1.20

monitor> file pix613.bin

file pix613.bin

monitor> tftp

tftp pix613.bin@172.20.1.20.........................................

......

Received 2562368 bytes


Cisco Secure PIX Firewall admin loader (3.0) #0: Tue Dec  517:35:46
    EST2000

System Flash=E28F128J3 @ 0xfff00000
```

```
BIOS Flash=am29f400c @ 0xd8000
Flash version 6.1.3, Install version 6.1.3
Do you wish to copy the install image into flash? [n] y

Installing to flash

Serial Number: 480501351 (0x1ca20729)
Activation Key: 12345678 12345678 12345678 12345678

Do you want to enter a new activation key? [n] y
Enter new activation key: 87654321 87654321 87654321 87654321
Updating flash...Done.
Serial Number: 480501351 (0x1ca20729)

Flash Activation Key: 87654321 87654321 87654321 87654321

Writing 2562368 bytes image into flash...
```

Installing PDM on the PIX Device

The final step to enable PDM on the PIX firewall is to install PDM into Flash. As with the PIX firewall software upgrade, the installation of PDM is a potentially difficult operation. Always back up configuration files and software versions before proceeding with the installation. Always verify that the PIX firewall meets the requirements specified for PDM. To install PDM, follow these steps:

1. From the TFTP server, log in to CCO and download the PDM image. PDM can be found at www.cisco.com/cgi-bin/tablebuild.pl/pix.

2. Save the software in a location that can be accessed via TFTP. Note the name of the software image for later reference.

3. Log in to the PIX CLI via Telnet or the console.

4. Enter enable mode by typing **enable** at the command prompt.

5. Type **copy tftp flash:pdm**.

6. When prompted for the remote address of host, type the **ip address of the TFTP server**.

7. When prompted for the source filename, type the name of the PDM software on the TFTP server.

8. When prompted, type **yes** to proceed with the PDM installation.

9. After the installation is complete, type **show version** to verify that PDM is installed and that DES is enabled. Output similar to the following should appear:

```
pix# sh ver

Cisco PIX Firewall Version 6.1(3)
Cisco PIX Device Manager Version 1.0(2)

Compiled on Tue 11-Sep-01 07:45 by morlee

pix up 326 days 19 hours

Hardware:    PIX-515, 32 MB RAM, CPU Pentium 200 MHz
Flash i28F640J5 @ 0x300, 16MB
BIOS Flash AT29C257 @ 0xfffd8000, 32KB

0: ethernet0: address is 0050.54ff.59cc, irq 10
1: ethernet1: address is 0050.54ff.59cd, irq 7

Licensed Features:
Failover:          Disabled
VPN-DES:           Enabled
VPN-3DES:          Disabled
Maximum Interfaces:       3
Cut-through Proxy:        Enabled
Guards:            Enabled
Websense:          Enabled
Inside Hosts:      Unlimited
Throughput:        Unlimited
ISAKMP peers:      Unlimited

Serial Number: 480501351 (0x1ca20729)
Activation Key: 12345678 12345678 12345678 12345678
```

10. Type **configure terminal** to enter terminal configuration mode.

11. Enable the PDM http server on the PIX firewall by typing **http server enable**.

12. Configure internal PDM management clients by typing **http *ip_address_of_client netmask* inside** where *ip_address_of_client* is a specific client ip address or network ip address and *netmask* is the appropriate netmask of the client or network.

13. Save the new configuration by typing **write memory** and exit the CLI.

Configuration Examples

Configuring a PIX firewall, whether through PDM or the PIX CLI, should be the technical application of a well-developed and understood security policy. Moreover, the rules implemented on the PIX firewall often represent the enforcement of the security policy. Before configuring any security device, the firewall administrator should be aware of the specific security policy of the organization. A cohesive and comprehensive technical security solution is more likely with such an approach.

Designing & Planning…

Security Policy Development

A good security practice within any organization begins with a sound and well-developed security framework. It is from this framework that policies, standards, guidelines, and standard operating procedures flow. Organizations should clearly define this framework before embarking upon device configurations to ensure a uniform and predictable security stance.

After successfully installing PDM, connect to the PIX firewall via PDM and begin configuring a specific security policy appropriate for the company. This section includes configuration steps and examples typical of PIX firewall installations such as the following:

- Connecting to the PIX with PDM

- Configuring basic firewall properties

- Implementing Network Address Translation (NAT)
- Allowing inbound traffic from external sources

These examples represent a small portion of PDM's capabilities and are intended as a representative tour through some of the functionality PDM offers. For complete information regarding PDM functionality and methodical configuration details, refer to the Cisco PIX firewall and PDM software technical documentation.

The examples included next and on the following pages are based on the network architecture as shown in Figure 14.2.

Figure 14.2 Example Network Architecture

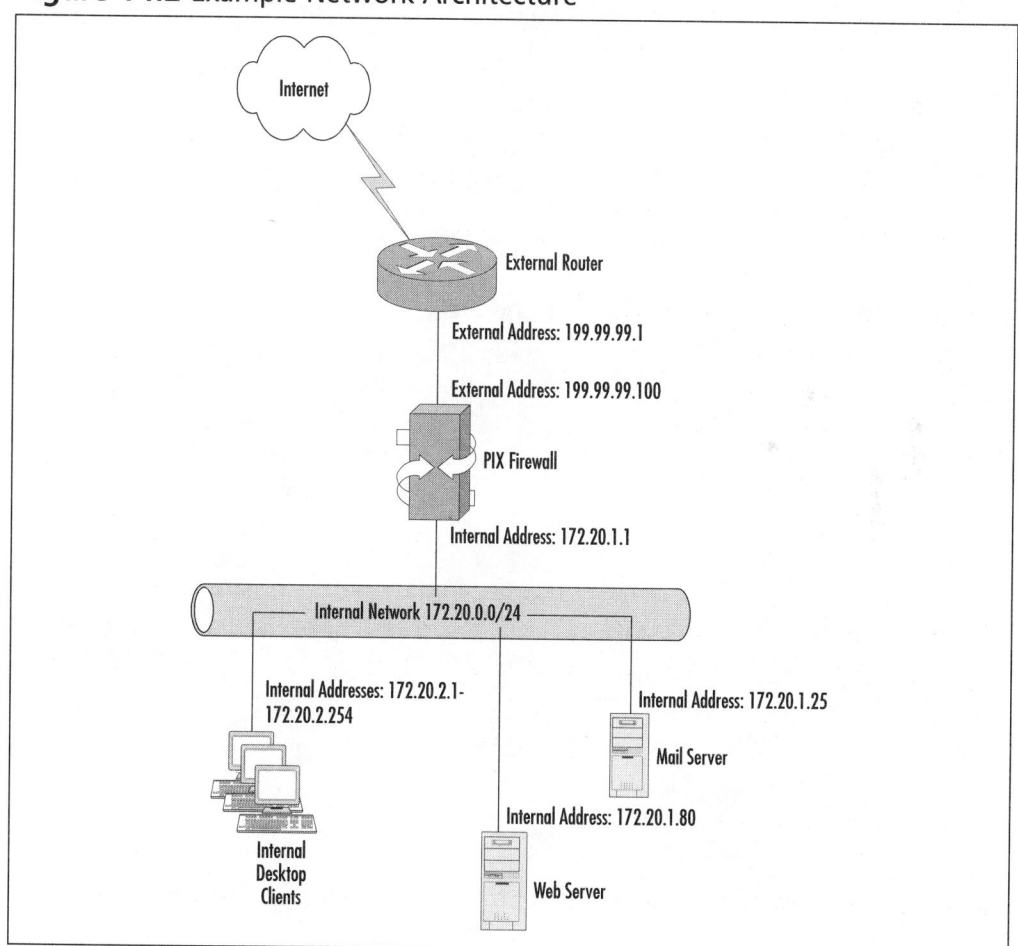

Connecting to the PIX with PDM

PDM management clients are only permitted from authorized ip addresses as specified previously using the http command. Before attempting to connect to the PIX via PDM, verify that the management workstation meets all functional requirements previously detailed. In addition, verify the PDM management client is included in the http configuration statement on the PIX firewall.

Complete the following steps to connect to the PIX firewall with PDM.

1. Launch a JDK 1.1.4 capable browser on an authorized PDM management workstation and connect to the PIX firewall internal ip address using SSL. Using the example network architecture shown previously, the URL should be entered as follows: **https://172.20.1.1**. Be sure to use https:// and not http:// in the URL string.

2. Choose to accept the SSL security certificate when prompted.

3. When prompted for authentication credentials, do not enter a username. Enter the enable password in the password field and click **OK**.

4. PDM will launch in a separate window similar to Figure 14.3.

Figure 14.3 PDM Launch Window

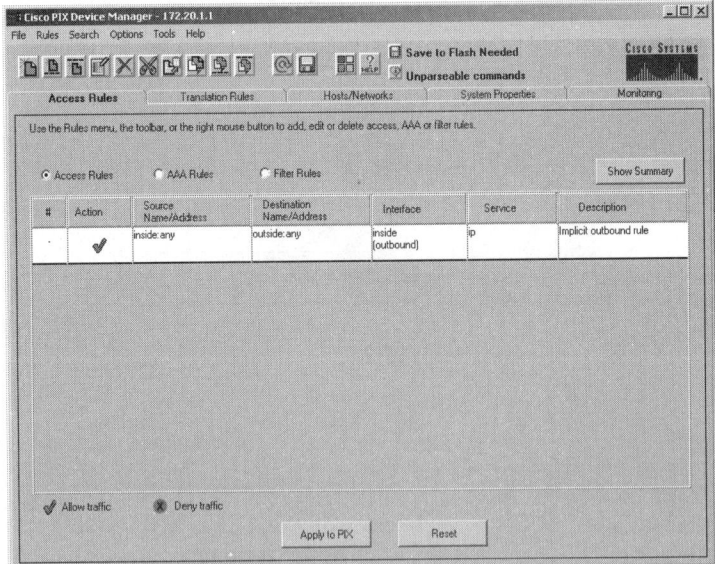

NOTE

A complete PDM troubleshooting guide is located on the Cisco Web site at www.cisco.com/univercd/cc/td/doc/product/iaabu/pix/pix_61/pdm_ig/pdm_tsht.htm.

From the main PDM screen, notice that there are pull-down menus, toolbar buttons, and five tabbed screens to use for configuration. Click the tabs and pull-down menus to become familiar with the interface. The five tabbed screens are as follows:

- **Access Rules** The Access Rules screen is used to permit and deny specific network traffic traversing the PIX firewall. From this screen, AAA authentication and URL filters are configured as well.

- **Translation Rules** Administrators configure NAT properties from the Translation Rules screen.

- **Hosts/Networks** Entities such as networks and hosts are delineated from the Hosts/Networks screen.

- **System Properties** The basic maintenance of the PIX firewall system is performed from the System Properties screen. Properties such as DHCP client behavior, IDS configuration, interface attributes, and others are configured from this screen.

- **Monitoring** The monitoring screen is used to configure monitoring for the PIX firewall.

These screens, in addition to the pull-down menus and toolbar buttons, will be used in the following configuration examples.

Configuring Basic Firewall Properties

After connecting to the PIX firewall using PDM, click the **System Properties tab** to modify some basic firewall properties. The System Properties screen is shown in Figure 14.4.

This example includes changing the PIX firewall interface ip configuration, adding a default route, and changing the administrative password.

To alter PIX interface ip configuration information, click the **Interface Category** listed in the left portion of the System Properties screen as seen in

Figure 14.4. Highlight the specific interface to modify and click the **Edit** button. The Edit Interface screen is shown in Figure 14.5.

Figure 14.4 The System Properties Tab

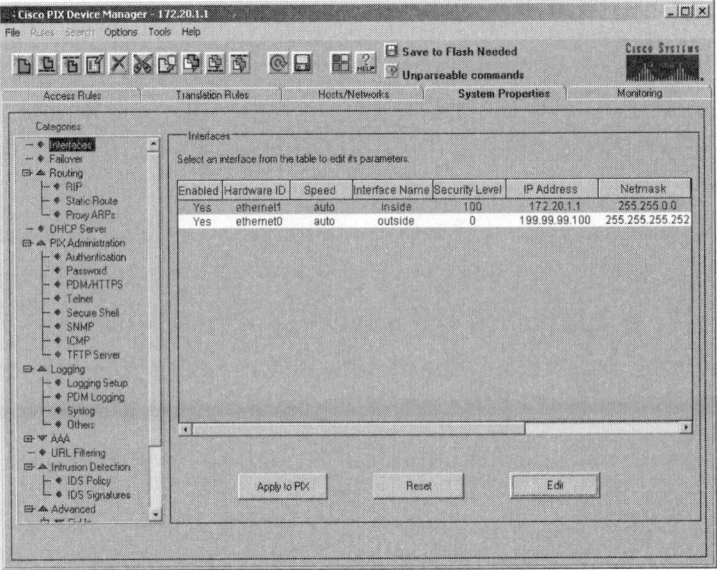

Figure 14.5 The Edit Interface Screen

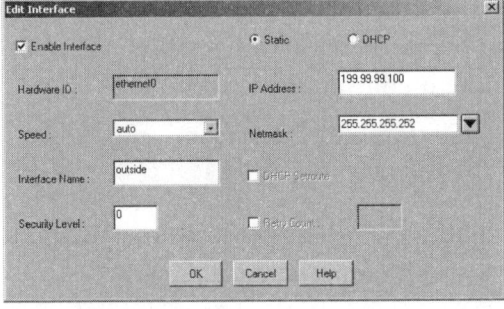

Modify the attributes that require change and click **OK**. From the System Properties screen, click the **Apply To PIX button** to save changes to Flash memory on the PIX device.

To add a default route, click the **Routing Category** listed in the left portion of the System Properties screen. From the expanded category list, click **Static Routes** as shown in Figure 14.6.

Figure 14.6 Adding a Default Route

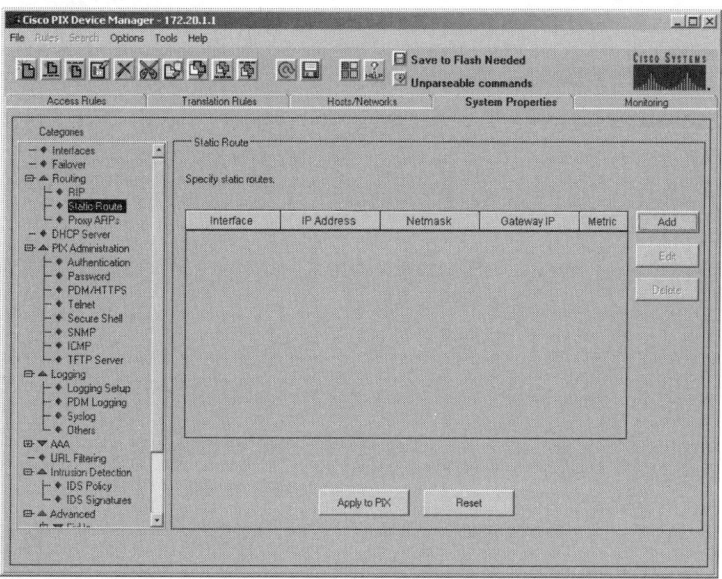

Click **Add** to add a new default route. The Add Static Route window appears, similar to the window shown in Figure 14.7. Add the required default route information as shown next and click **OK**.

Figure 14.7 The Add Static Route Window

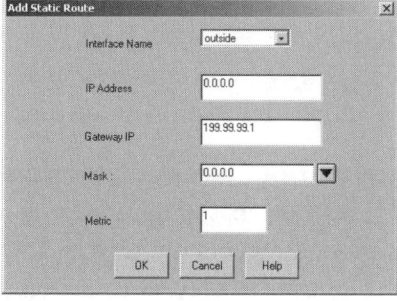

From the System Properties screen, click the **Apply To PIX button** to save changes to Flash memory on the PIX device.

To change administrative authentication variables on the PIX firewall, click the **PIX Administration** category listed in the left portion of the System Properties screen. From the expanded category list, click **authentication** as shown in Figure 14.8.

Figure 14.8 Changing the Administrative Authentication Variables

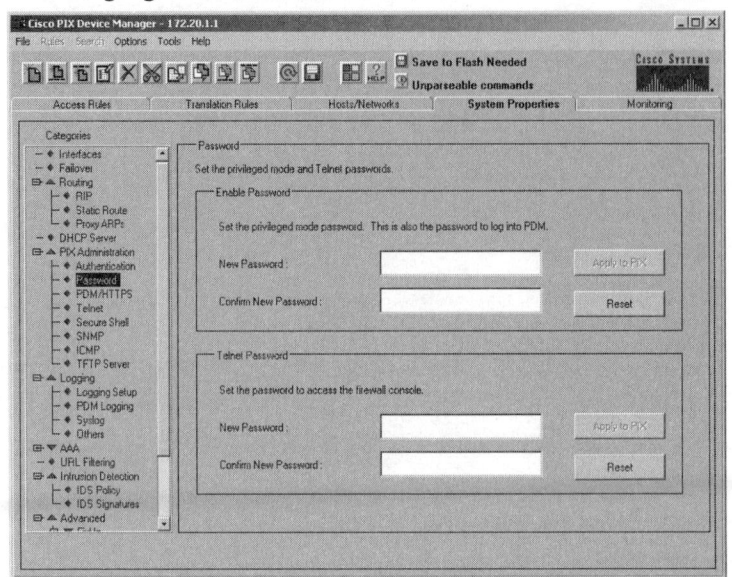

Type the new enable or Telnet (vty) password in the space provided. To confirm the password, retype the password in the space provided and click **Apply To PIX**. A dialog box will appear confirming the new password.

Implementing Network Address Translation

Network Address Translation (NAT) is widely used in networked environments to add additional layers of security and to conserve ip address space. With the PIX firewall, three types of address translation are available.

- **Static address translation** Static address translation is used to map external ip addresses to internal ip addresses on a one-to-one basis. Static mappings such as these are generally required when allowing externally originated traffic through the firewall to internal servers.

- **Dynamic address translation (PAT)** Dynamic address translation allows many internal ip addresses to be hidden behind one external IP address. Because the firewall uses ports to maintain discrete connectivity for each translated ip address, this configuration is commonly referred to as PAT. This configuration is useful for conserving external ip addresses, but cannot be used to direct externally originated traffic through the firewall to internal servers.

■ **Static PAT** Static PAT is similar to dynamic address translation as described earlier. Static PAT can be used, however, to allow externally originated traffic through the firewall to internal servers. Using ports to differentiate where specific services should be sent internally, static PAT is useful in environments where only one external ip address is available for the PIX firewall. PDM does not support the configuration of static PAT.

WARNING
_____

If static PAT is configured on the PIX device via the CLI, administrators will be unable to manage the firewall via PDM. PDM will only be able to perform monitoring on the firewall in this situation.

This configuration example includes both static address translation and dynamic address translation.

To configure NAT on the PIX firewall, click the **Translation Rules tab** as shown in Figure 14.9.

Figure 14.9 The Translation Rules Tab

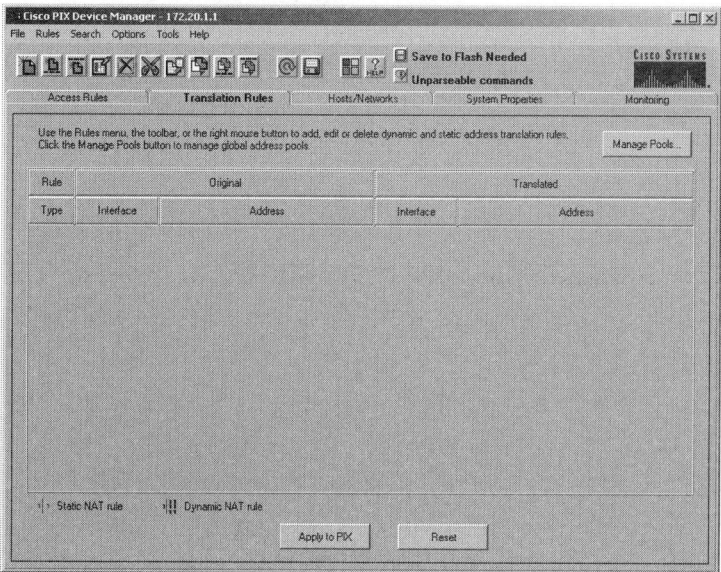

A pool must first be created on which the NAT will be based. Click the **Manage Pools...** button to add a new address pool. The Add Global Pool Item screen appears. Populate the fields with the values shown in Figure 14.10 and click **OK**.

Figure 14.10 The Add Global Pool Item Window

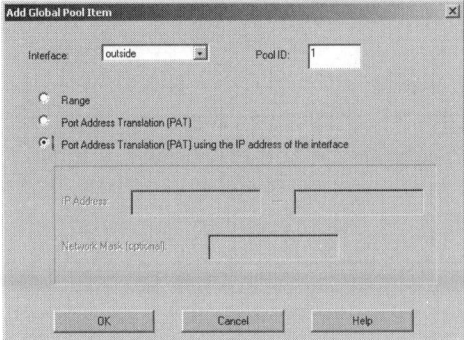

This design allows the external ip address of the firewall to be used in a dynamic NAT configuration. Next, from the Rules drop-down menu, select **Add** to create a new dynamic address translation on the firewall. Populate the Add Address Translation Rule fields with the values shown in Figure 14.11.

Figure 14.11 The Edit Address Translation Rules Window

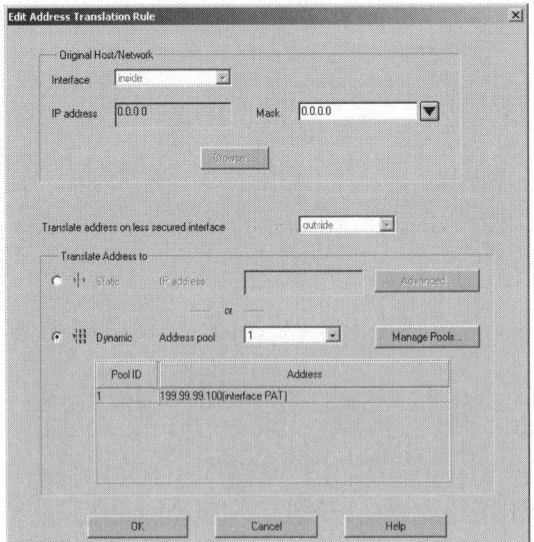

When finished, click the **OK** button. From the Translation Rules screen, click **Apply To PIX** to update Flash memory on the firewall and make the changes effective.

Now add a static NAT configuration in preparation for the next exercise of allowing inbound traffic from external sources. To do so, click the **Add From The Rules** drop-down menu again. This time, populate the Add Address Translation Rule fields with the values shown in Figure 14.12.

Figure 14.12 Adding Static NAT Configuration

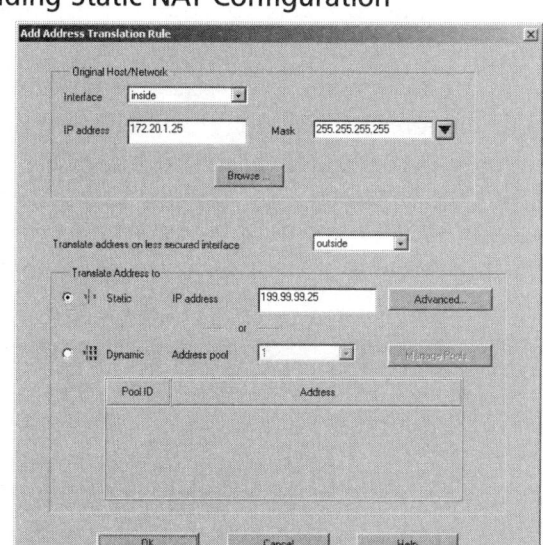

This configuration creates a static address translation mapping between the external ip address 199.99.99.25 and the internal ip address 172.20.1.25. Click **OK** to add the rule. PDM may request to add a host entity to support the rule. If so, click **OK**, then click **Add To PIX** to update the PIX firewall Flash memory. Next, add an access rule to allow traffic for this new NAT rule through the firewall.

Allowing Inbound Traffic from External Sources

Once NAT has been successfully configured, as shown in the previous exercise, internal clients should be able to access external resources. Even though a specific rule has not been manually added to allow such outbound access, it is implied through Cisco's interpretation of interface security levels.

Using Cisco parlance, traffic is always permitted from firewall interfaces with a higher security level to firewall interfaces with a lower security level. For instance, in the example network architecture previously described, the external interface of the firewall at address 199.99.99.100 has a security level of 0 and the internal interface of the firewall at address 172.20.1.1 has a security level of 100. This allows internal traffic to traverse the firewall outbound without expressly permitting it.

However, this implied rule is reversed for traffic originating on a firewall interface with a lower security level that is traversing to a higher security level. Such traffic coming from outside networks to inside networks is implicitly denied. Therefore, an access rule must be manually added to permit such traffic. The next exercise includes the configuration of such a rule and will be based on the NAT rule added previously to the mail server in the example network architecture.

To permit access to the internal mail server, click the **Access Rules tab**. Next, from the Rules drop-down menu, select **Add** to create a new access list on the firewall. The Add Rule window appears (Figure 14.13).

Figure 14.13 Permitting Access to the Internal Mail Server through the Add Rule Window

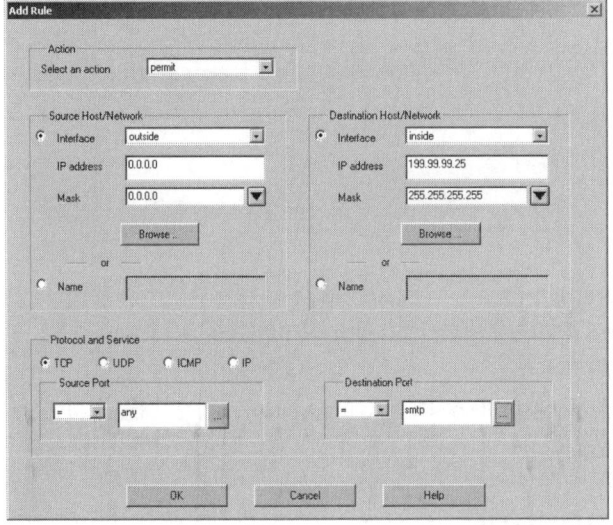

This configuration permits SMTP traffic to the external ip address 199.99.99.25. Click **OK** to add the rule. Then click **Add To PIX** to update the PIX firewall Flash memory.

The configuration of security on PIX firewall is one of many methods to protect critical network and systems resources from attack. While, PDM is oriented specifically toward the management of individual PIX firewall devices, other security devices and management applications exist in the Cisco security arsenal. The next section includes information regarding another tool, CiscoWorks2000 ACLM, and its benefits to the enterprise security suite.

CiscoWorks2000 Access Control List Manager

Another line of defense against potential intruders and malicious hackers is the configuration of Access Control Lists (ACLs) on routers, switches, and other Cisco devices. The PIX firewall is adept at providing boundary defense and other critical security functionality such as VPN termination. Moreover, the PIX firewall actually relies on ACL constructs to delineate permissible traffic from denied traffic. However, companies often require additional security throughout the network to limit access to critical resources behind boundary defenses or to simply segment certain internal network traffic. This additional security can be provided through ACLs on Cisco devices across the network.

The maintenance of ACLs on multiple devices can quickly become difficult due to complexity and quantity in a large network. To mitigate this management issue, Cisco developed a component within CiscoWorks2000 called Access Control List Manager. This section details the capabilities and functionality of the ACLM and includes examples on deployment and management within a typical network infrastructure.

ACL Manager Overview

ACLM is a component within the network management software system known as CiscoWorks2000. CiscoWorks2000 is a highly extensible application suite ideally suited for managing Cisco enterprise networks and devices. For convenience and appropriate application, CiscoWorks2000 has numerous sub-components that integrate under the CiscoWorks2000 software framework. Theses components provide management solutions for local area networks (LAN) and wide area networks (WAN) of the enterprise.

ACLM is included in the CiscoWorks2000 Routed WAN Management Solution set. In addition to ACLM, this set of applications includes the following components:

- Cisco nGenius Real-Time Monitor
- CiscoView

- Resource Manager Essentials
- Internetwork Performance Monitor

With these tools, administrators greatly increase configuration, administration, monitoring, and troubleshooting capabilities in large-scale network deployments. Furthermore, long-term performance insight and network traffic optimization are possible with the CiscoWorks2000 Routed WAN Management Solution. For additional information regarding the CiscoWorks2000 suite of productions and functionality, refer to the Cisco Web site.

As the name implies, ACLM is used to develop and maintain ACLs on Cisco devices. ACLM runs as an integrated component of Resource Manager Essentials and can manage most Cisco IOS routers, access servers, and hubs with an IOS of 10.3 through 12.1. ACLM can also manage Catalyst switches running Catalyst IOS version 5.3 through 5.5.

The Web-based Windows Explorer-like graphical interface provides powerful control of IP and IPX access lists and device access control from virtually anywhere on the network. VLAN and SNMP access control list management is also possible via ACLM. The interface eliminates the complexity and syntactical accuracy required to implement lengthy ACLs via the CLI. Furthermore, ACLM saves time and resources through batch configuration of new filters and the consistent and accurate management of existing access lists in a large-scale network.

ACLM includes several modules used to perform specific actions within the manager functionality suite. These modules are as follows:

- **Template Manager** The Template Manager module is used to construct and maintain ACL templates for the predictable and error-free security management of numerous Cisco devices. Using template manager, administrators can create appropriate templates for many devices instead of reinventing the wheel for each new network component.

- **Class Manager** This module enables the creation of service and network groups or classes. With this module, administrators can save time by designating typical groupings of rules to be quickly implemented via ACLM.

- **Template Use Wizard** Administrators use the Template Use Wizard to apply previously created packet and VLAN filtering ACLs, and line and SNMP ACLs across the network. In conjunction with Template Manager, the wizard module allows administrators to be more efficient when deploying or modifying numerous ACL configurations to devices on the network.

- **Optimizer** For additional ACL efficiency of a Cisco device, the Optimizer module can be used to inspect ACL statement ordering and syntax. Optimizer removes redundant statements and consolidates entries. Moreover, the optimizer module can automatically reorder ACL statements against hit rate utilization statistics to provide the utmost in efficiency.

- **DiffViewer** DiffViewer assists the administrator in discerning changes to ACLs of different versions. Using this module, alteration is easily identifiable making version control and version rollback simple.

- **ACL Downloader** This modules enables the scheduled or manual download of ACLs from Cisco devices in the network.

ACL Manager Device and Software Support

ACLM version 1.3 supports most Cisco IOS routers, access servers, and hubs with an IOS of 10.3 through 12.1. ACLM can also manage Catalyst switches running Catalyst OS version 5.3 through 5.5. Using ACLM, administrators can view all ACLs, regardless of type. ACLM includes full support for the following access lists:

- IP, IP_EXTENDED
- IPX, IPX_EXTENDED
- IPX_SAP, IPX_SUMMARY
- RATE_LIMIT_MAC
- RATE_LIMIT_PRECEDENCE
- VACL_Catalyst 6000

Installation Requirements for ACL Manager

Before installing ACLM, verify that the intended server meets all software and hardware requirements listed in the following. CiscoWorks2000 and Cisco Resource Manager Essentials (RME) are both prerequisites for the installation of ACLM. The software runs on either Windows NT 4.0 and Windows2000, or Solaris 2.6 and 2.7 operating systems.

When running ACLM server on a Solaris operating system, the following requirements apply:

- **System** Sun UltraSPARC 60
- **Processor** 400MHz or faster
- **Memory** 512MB RAM with 1GB swap space
- **Disk** 9GB

When running ACLM server on a Windows operating system, the following requirements apply:

- **System** Pentium-compatible
- **Processor** 500Mhz or faster
- **Memory** 512MB RAM with 1GB swap space
- **Disk** 9GB

Because the ACLM user interface is run from a browser on an authorized client machine, certain software and hardware requirements are needed on the client as well. ACLM will function on several different client platforms and operating systems as follows:

- **IBM PC-Compatible** Windows 95, Windows 98, Windows NT 4.0, and Windows2000
- **Sun Microsystems** Solaris versions 2.5.1, 2.6, or 2.7
- **IBM RS/6000** Any version of AIX supporting the required browsers listed next
- **HP-UX Workstation** Any version of HP-UX supporting the required browsers listed next

All client systems connecting to ACLM must also have either an Internet Explorer 5.0 or 5.1 browser or the Netscape Communicator 4.6 or 4.7 Internet Web browser.

ACL Manager Features

The features added when ACLM is installed concern the management of ACLs on Cisco devices in the enterprise network. ACLM is accessed through CiscoWorks2000 from any client host with an Internet browser, hardware, and that is OS-compatible with the client requirements specified earlier. All ACLM tools are found under the RME section on the left panel of CiscoWorks2000. In the following, some of the ACLM features used to manage Cisco devices are described.

Using a Structured Access Control List Security Policy

In an infrastructure consisting of multiple routers and switches, it is important to consistently manage and configure ACLs to control traffic across the network. ACLM can help ensure the uniform application of the security policy across the enterprise through Template Manager and Class Manager. These modules facilitate the creation of standardized ACL templates and classes consistent with policy on the entire network.

Decreasing Deployment Time for Access Control Lists

After creating appropriate ACL templates using Template Manager, all security policy changes and new device installations are expedited by quickly pushing the prefabricated ACL configuration to the Cisco infrastructure. In this manner, the deployment and maintenance network infrastructure is optimized for operation. When managing network security policy with ACL templates, only the initially created template must be altered to reflect policy changes. Thereafter, ACLM identifies the devices affected by the policy change and automatically generates the appropriate configurations to be deployed to the specific Cisco devices.

Using the ACL Use Wizard also decreases the deployment time for new ACLs required to enforce evolving security policy on a network. Through a methodical process, device access control or ACL filtering can be configured for devices by applying already defined templates to the device. This eases maintenance complexity and allows for quick deployment of network configuration changes across multiple devices.

Ensure Consistency of Access Control Lists

When defining ACLs on network devices, it is essential to ensure consistency of configuration throughout the enterprise. This reduces the likelihood of unauthorized network traffic by preventing unanticipated backdoor access and poorly configured ACLs. Using Template Manager with Class Manager to define network classes and services allows for the fast and consistent implementation of security policy.

ACLM always indicates the devices affected by template changes when using Template Manager, allowing administrators to confirm the new ACL configuration and fix errors before making changes to the production environment.

Furthermore, all changes to ACLs and network security policy can be reviewed with DiffViewer. DiffViewer shows a list of all affected devices and displays the current and new ACL configuration side by side. This permits the review and confirmation of ACL configuration changes before deployment to reduce the possibility of errors in the enforced security policy.

Keep Track of Changes Made on the Network

Because ACLM is installed with CiscoWorks2000 and Resource Manager Essentials (RME), it uses the RME Change Audit service. The Change Audit service is a central point from which network configuration changes can be reviewed. It displays information concerning when and what type of change was made and whether the change was made from Telnet connections, from the console port, or from a CiscoWorks2000 application like ACL Manager.

> **NOTE**
>
> The RME Change Audit service can filter reports using simple or complex criteria to locate specific changes in the network. Variables such as changes in time can be used to pinpoint critical infrastructure alterations.

Troubleshooting and Error Recovery

When experiencing issues on a network, it is best to first confirm that the physical network, routing, and protocols are functioning properly. After verifying such infrastructure is functional, troubleshooting ACLs on the network may be required. Using the methods previously described, investigating the nature of recent ACL changes can provide insight into whether security-related changes have negatively affected network functionality.

If issues are detected with specific ACLs, Template Manager can be used to alter the ACL template and generate appropriate configurations required to deploy new policies to network devices. In this manner, Template Manager greatly reduces the time to recovery due to unintended and erroneous ACL configurations in the enterprise.

Another error prevention feature in ACLM is the ACL Downloader, which allows administrators to select various failsafe options when deploying new ACLs to the network. One such feature forces ACL updates to abort if errors are detected in the configuration. With the "abort on error" feature enabled, ACLM will automatically revert to the original router configuration, known in Cisco ACLM parlance as *rollback*. This option prevents potentially damaging and erroneous ACL configurations from being enabled on a critical production infrastructure.

The Basic Operation of ACL Manager

With many of the useful network management features of ACLM defined, this section focuses on some of the basic operations of ACLM components. The following operational capabilities will be covered in the following sections:

- Using Templates and Defining Classes
- Using DiffViewer
- Using the Optimizer and Hits Optimizer

There are many other basic operational capabilities within the ACLM. For additional information, refer to the Cisco ACLM documentation.

Using Templates and Defining Classes

As previously discussed, templates can help ensue consistency across the network and reduce the time in deploying ACLs. Before using Template Manager however, it is important to first configure networks, network classes, services, and service classes. To do so, administrators use the Class Manager to view, add, and change classes.

The services in the Class Manager include standard services and port numbers for well-known applications like FTP, HTTP, and Telnet. New, custom services can be added to the list of services as well. To add new services, simply select the type of IP service, UDP or TCP, enter a name to identify the new service, and enter the associated port number.

Class Manager also provides the configuration of service classes, which are customized, user-defined groups of services. To add a custom service class, first specify a name to identify the service class and select the associated IP protocol type, UDP or TCP. Finally, specify the following to be part of the services class definition:

- One or more service port numbers

- A range of ports specified with a low and high port value

- One or more previously defined service classes

Additionally, the Class Manager facilitates the creation and modification of networks and network classes. Networks are created with logical names and include the IP address and corresponding subnet mask of the network. Network entities should define the smallest logical network segment on the enterprise. This allows for increased specificity when defining ACL. If necessary, network classes can be used to define larger, generalized groups of networks.

Network classes created with the Class Manager allow for the association of one or all of the following:

- One or more specific host IP addresses

- One or more ranges of IP addresses specified using a start and end IP address

- One or more networks created in the network folder

- One or more previously created network classes created in this folder

These specific service and network entities can be removed and added to new service and network classes as necessary. By defining these entities and grouping first, administrators can easily and quickly create ACL template configurations and define a standardized security policy for replication across the network.

Using DiffViewer

ACLs created and altered on the network via ACLM do not take effect immediately. Rather, changes are applied to specific routers and devices manually or at a scheduled, off-hours time with the ACL Downloader. When finished with ACL changes on the network, administrators can use the DiffViewer, as previously described, to verify all current configurations, as well as the changes made to ACLs.

The left panel of DiffViewer contains a list of all *Modified Objects*, including all network devices to which changes have been made or that are affected by other changes. This panel has subfolders under the specific devices that include detailed information concerning the altered ACLs and the affected interfaces. Using this interface, administrators can select a more specific view of changes based on an ACL or interface.

Within DiffViewer, the middle and right portion of the screen includes the original configuration and the modified configuration of the specific device selected on the right panel, respectively. Colors are used to simplify identification of changes as follows:

- Red indicates changes to access control entries (ACEs)
- Green indicates recently added ACEs in the ACL
- Blue identifies ACEs removed from the ACL

The Config and Delta buttons supply more information regarding changes to ACLs on the devices. The Config... button displays the entire new configuration for the selected device, including all changes. The Delta... button, on the other hand, shows the IOS commands to be performed on the selected device to make the necessary changes for the new security policy.

Using the Optimizer and the Hits Optimizer

The Optimizer and Hits Optimizer in ACLM help reduce processor cycles and increase packet-forwarding throughput through intelligent ACL regrouping and reordering. ACLs negatively impact the forwarding performance of a network device. When a packet is received or forwarded out an interface, it must first be compared to all ACEs in the ACL until a match is found. Once a match for the specific traffic is located in the ACL, traffic is denied or permitted according to ACE.

To prevent latency due to lengthy ACLs on network devices, the ACL Optimizer minimizes the number of ACEs used in ACLs. This is achieved by merging and removing redundant ACEs. In this manner, the Optimizer frees up processing resources and improves network performance. Table 14.2 exemplifies the positive effects of the Optimizer on some ACEs in an ACL.

Table 14.2 Beneficial Effects of the Optimizer

Original ACEs	Optimized ACEs
permit ip any host 192.168.50.8 permit ip any host 192.168.50.9 permit ip any host 192.168.50.10 permit ip any host 192.168.50.11 permit ip any host 192.168.50.12 permit ip any host 192.168.50.13 permit ip any host 192.168.50.14 permit ip any host 192.168.50.15	permit ip any 192.168.50.8 0.0.0.7

As can be seen, the Optimizer uses a process similar to that employed for route summarization on the network to improve network routing performance.

Hits Optimizer is used to improve throughput performance related to ACLs on a device. Hits Optimizer rearranges ACLs by placing the most frequently matched ACEs at the top of the ACL and moving less frequently matched ACEs to the bottom. This is achieved based on the number of matches tracked by the device IOS.

WARNING

Hits Optimizer may not always change the order of ACLs based on the number of matches for the ACEs. Hits Optimizer never alters the intent of the ACL and always preserves the security of the device since the careless reordering of access list entries can completely disable the security of an ACL.

Using ACL Manager

Before using the ACLM to manage network devices, the ACLM software must be successfully installed and the network devices configured for proper management. This section includes the procedures necessary for installation and preparation of the enterprise before ACL management can take place.

Configuring the ACL Manager

Several pieces of information must be gathered when preparing the network for ACLM. Additionally, all Cisco devices to be managed must be configured to integrate with ACLM.

Domain Name Service (DNS) entries must be configured for all devices on the network including forward and reverse resolution mapping. This information is used when adding devices to the RME inventory within CiscoWorks2000. The DNS entry should be a fully qualified domain name. When adding devices to the RME, the following information for each device on the network is required:

- Read Community String for SNMP
- Read/Write Community String for SNMP

- TACACS Username and Password, if used

- Local Device Username and Password

- Telnet Username and Password

- Enable TACACS Username and Password, if used

- Enable Password

- Enable Secret Password

Managed devices must be configured with accurate public and private SNMP community strings. All devices to be managed should be added using the Add Device tool under the Inventory folder in the RME section of CiscoWorks2000. This should be accomplished before making changes to the ACLs of the device.

NOTE

To configure the SNMP service on an ACLM managed router, use one of the following two commands in global configuration mode:

```
Rt1(config)#snmp-server community community_string ro
```

This command configures SNMP read-only access for the specified community string.

```
Rt1(config)#snmp-server community community_string rw
```

This command configures read-write access for the specific community string.

Installing the ACL Manager and Associated Software

Before beginning the ACLM installation process, ensure that the server hardware and OS meets all requirements. Also, verify that the following installation CD-ROMs or files are available:

- CiscoWorks2000 CD One

- Resource Manager Essentials

- Access Control List Manager

The software in the preceding list must be installed in sequence for the successful operation of ACL Manager on the server. Begin by installing CiscoWorks2000. If installing the software on a Windows platform, verify the server is not a primary or backup domain controller for the Windows NT domain. Furthermore, a Windows-based installation can only be performed on an NTFS file system.

After successfully installing CiscoWorks2000, install Resource Manager Essentials on the same server. Follow the onscreen wizard dialogs through the installation process, which takes approximately 30 minutes to complete.

Once RME is installed, finish by integrating ACLM on the server platform. As with the previous software installations, follow the onscreen wizards to successfully complete ACLM. This process installs the ACLM add-on to RME within CiscoWorks2000.

For detailed information regarding the installation of these software packages, refer to the appropriate Cisco documentation included with the software media.

Configuration Example: Creating ACLs with ACLM

The next example includes procedures for creating ACLs on a router. To do so, the following specific exercises are included:

- Adding a new router to the CiscoWorks2000 configuration

- Opening a new scenario to edit ACLs on the new router

- Adding an ACL and a specific ACE to the router

Additional recommended self-study exercises could include the creation of templates in the ACLM Template Editor for future security policy enforcement of the newly created ACLs.

NOTE

When using CiscoWorks2000, ensure that Java, JavaScript, and Accept all cookies are enabled in the Internet browser settings on the management client workstation. If these settings are not correct, the CiscoWorks2000 client will not function properly.

To use the CiscoWorks2000 Web-based GUI, open an HTTP connection to the specific host name or IP address of the CiscoWorks2000 server. In the URL string, include the specific TCP port number of the CiscoWorks2000 server specified during installation. The default CiscoWorks2000 port number is 1741. Use the following format in the browser: http://server_ip_address:server_port.

The initial login screen, as shown in Figure 14.14, requires a username and password to log in to the CiscoWorks2000 GUI. The default username is *admin* and the default password is *admin*.

Figure 14.14 The CiscoWorks2000 Initial Login Screen

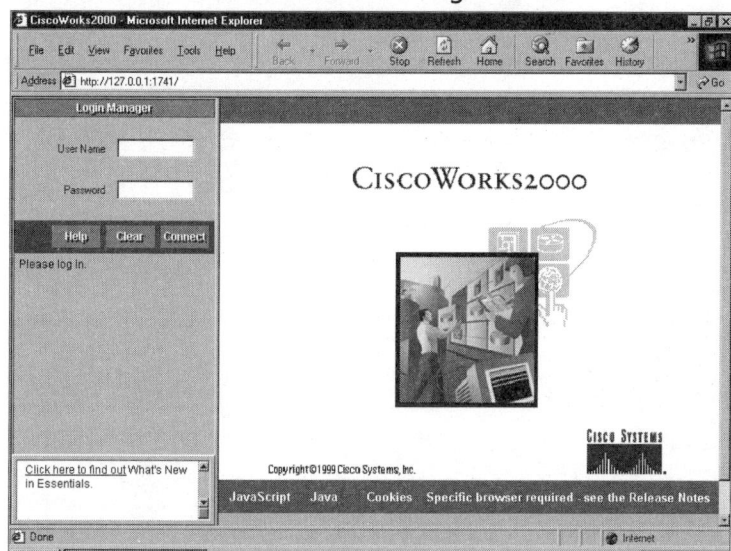

After successfully logging in to CiscoWorks2000, continue by clicking the **Resource Manager Essentials tab** on the left side of the screen. Next, click the **Administration** tree selection, followed by the Inventory subselection. Finally, click the **Add Devices** tool to add and manage the new device on the network. Figure 14.15 shows the screen used to add a device to the configuration. Enter the required information, including passwords and SNMP community strings, in the forms provided.

A scenario must be created in association with the new ACL to be configured. Figure 14.16 shows the screen on which a scenario is configured. Enter a specific name for the new scenario and select the relevant information below. Click **Next** to select the devices to be used in the scenario.

The next screen appears where the devices can be selected based on a custom view filter. Click **Add** to add the related device for the new scenario. Clicking **Next** opens a new Java applet window called "ACL Manager," which is used to configure the ACL. Apply it to the selected device. Figure 14.17 shows the ACL Manager applet window and subselections.

Figure 14.15 Adding a Device to the CiscoWorks2000 Configuration

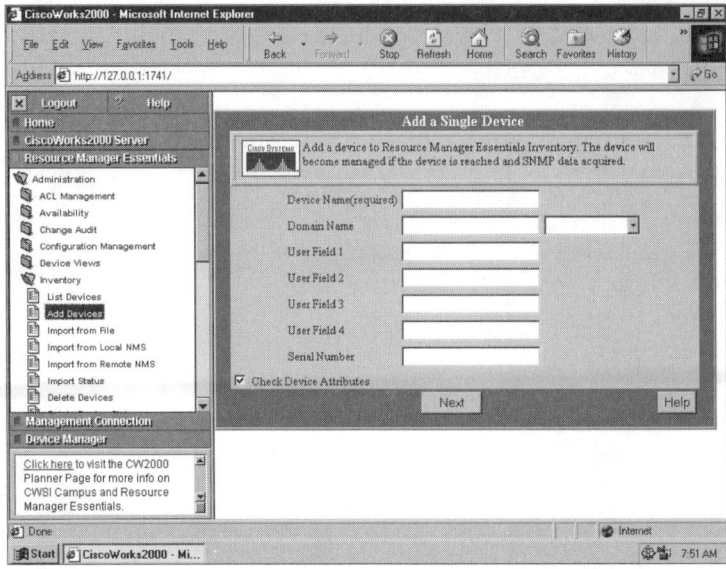

Figure 14.16 Creating a Scenario to Edit the ACL

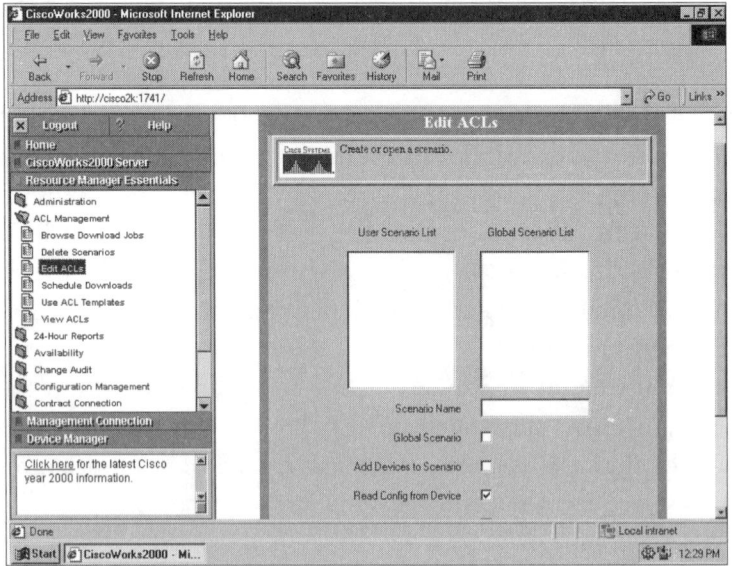

Figure 14.17 The ACL Manager Window

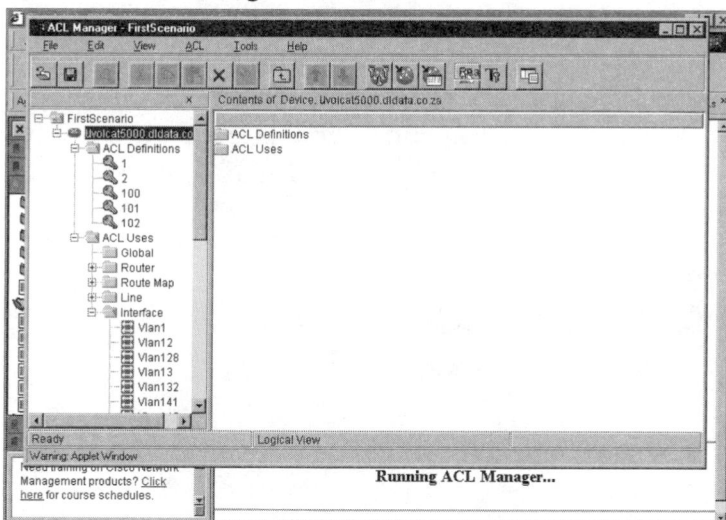

Next, add a specific ACL for the new ACE by right-clicking the **ACL Definitions folder** and selecting **New ACL**. Figure 14.18 shows the ACL Editor screen used to add an ACL to the selected router.

Figure 14.18 Adding an ACL to the Router

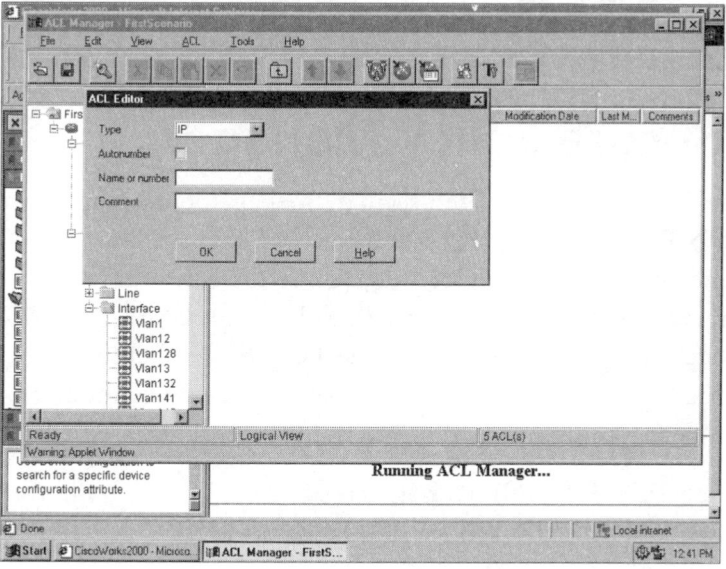

After clicking **OK**, notice the new ACL in the ACL Definition section. Right-click the new ACL to obtain a list of options related to it.

Finally, add the relevant ACEs for the specific security policy to the ACL. Figure 14.19 shows the first ACE for the new standard ACL that denies all traffic from 192.168.200.0. Click the **Expand...** button to see the list of IOS commands used to configure the selected router. To add another ACE to the ACL, click the **New** button.

Figure 14.19 Adding an ACE to the New ACL

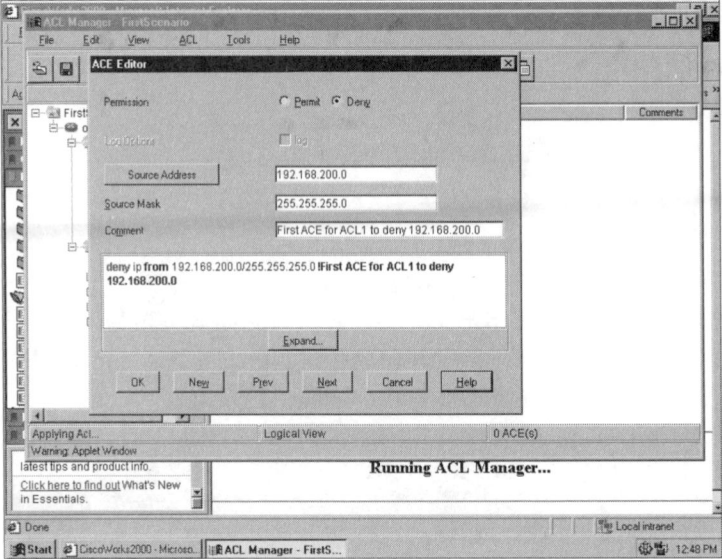

Cisco Secure Policy Manager

Another powerful tool in the Cisco security management arsenal is the CSPM. CSPM is an NT-based management tool for networks sized up to 500 devices. The application provides a complete management solution for Cisco VPN routers, IDS, and Cisco Secure PIX firewalls. Through CSPM, security administrators can effectively and securely manage the definition, enforcement and auditing of security policy from one intuitive administrative interface.

The significant features of CSPM are as follows:

- **Cisco PIX Firewall Management** With CPSM, administrators can define and maintain PIX- and IOS-based security policies via the Cisco Secure Integrated Software feature set.

- **Cisco VPN Gateway Management** VPN Gateway Management enables IPSec VPN management on PIX firewalls and Cisco VPN devices running the IOS IPSec software.

- **Config Import** Firewall administrators can import topology and security polices from PIX and IOS security network devices.

- **Security Policy Management** Up to 500 Cisco security devices can be easily managed without extensive device knowledge and dependency on the command-line interface (CLI).

- **Notification and Reporting System** CSPM includes auditing tools to monitor, alert, and report Cisco security device and policy activity.

Due to the extensive capabilities and functionality in the CSPM application, an entire chapter in this book has been devoted to the software. For additional and detailed information regarding CSPM, refer to Chapter 12.

Cisco Secure Access Control Server

In large network infrastructures, it is essential to control access to, and use of, the many diverse devices providing critical services. Without a scalable and capable management application platform to configure and monitor device access, the work of a security manager can quickly become overburdened with time-consuming and tedious administration. It is also often necessary to track specific events occurring on network devices for correlation of security breaches, configuration changes, and other access nuances.

To assist network and security administrators in these endeavors, Cisco has developed the Secure Access Control Server (Secure ACS). This application enables full control over all Cisco-based authentication, authorization, and accounting (AAA) configurations and management.

Overview of the Cisco Secure Access Control Server

Secure ACS enables centralized management of access control and accounting for dial-up access servers, VPNs and firewalls, Voice over IP (VoIP) solutions, broadband access, content networks and Cisco wireless solutions. Administrators can quickly manage user and group accounts on the entire network through security level changes and network policy alterations. Secure ACS is also designed for interoperability; administrators can leverage existing user database infrastructures such as

Lightweight Directory Access Protocol (LDAP) servers or Windows-based domain authentication mechanisms in combination with RADIUS and TACACS+ functionality to manage users. Additionally, with Secure ACS, AAA in the enterprise can be used to manage user access from disparate client mediums such as wireless networks with the Extensible Authentication Protocol (EAP) module.

Secure ACS is available on both Windows and Solaris platforms. At the time of this publication however, only the Windows release is at version 3.0, while the Solaris release remains at 2.3. All functionality described next, therefore, relates to the latest Windows release, 3.0.

Also new to Secure ACS 3.0 is a powerful new device command policy engine for TACACS+ administration control. The device command sets (DCSs) feature new, fine-grained control of administrative management, and provide for reusable policy "roles," significantly enhancing the ability to scale administrative privileges across large sets of user groups and network device groupings.

Benefits of the Cisco Secure Access Control Server

Secure ACS enables the centralized management of AAA for Cisco devices within the enterprise. The easy-to-use Web-based interface simplifies AAA configuration and permits distributed administration of Cisco device security. The capabilities of Secure ACS and AAA are described next in the following sections.

Authentication

As users require access to network resources, authentication must be used to verify the identity of the user and correlate the necessary user information. Authentication mechanisms range from simple, cleartext methods to more secure techniques such as encrypted passwords or One-Time-Password (OTP) token systems.

With Secure ACS, several methods are available for authentication between the ACS server and network components. Most simple are cleartext password mechanisms. To increase security, administrators can use encrypted methodologies such as the TACACS+ and RADIUS protocols. It should be noted, however, that this authentication connectivity is between the ACS server and the network device only. For completely secure authentication techniques, strong security measures such as OTP token systems should be implemented for user authentication to the network access device.

Finally, Secure ACS integrates with several user databases. In addition to the native Cisco Secure user database, support for the following external user databases is included:

- Windows NT/2000 User Database
- Generic LDAP
- Novell NetWare Directory Services (NDS)
- Open Database Connectivity (ODBC)-compliant relational databases
- CRYPTOCard Token Server
- SafeWord Token Server
- AXENT Token Server
- RSA SecureID Token Server
- ActivCard Token Server
- Vasco Token Server

Authorization

Authorization determines the permissible actions of a specific, authenticated user. As users access services on a network device or access server, the Secure ACS sends the users' profiles to the device to determine allowed levels of service. This enables different users and groups to possess different levels of services, access times, or security to specific devices.

Administrators can restrict users based on time of day or any one (or a combination) of the following:

- PPP
- ARA
- SLIP
- Device-based EXEC service

After the service is configured on the network, Layer 2 and 3 protocols can be restricted per user via access lists. In this manner, users or groups of users can be restricted from accessing networked devices such as FTP and HTTP servers. Additionally, authorization for Virtual Private Dial-up Networks (VPDNs) can be configured via Secure ACS to allow users and groups temporal access to secure tunnels to and from various locations. Finally, Secure ACS provides dynamic quotas for time-of-day, network usage, number of logged sessions, and day-of-week access restrictions.

> **WARNING**
>
> An important rule to remember when configuring authentication and authorization for users on the network: those with more authorization should always require stronger authentication to access network resources.

Accounting

The final piece of AAA is accounting. With accounting enabled on network devices, Secure ACS can track user actions. Secure ACS writes accounting records to Comma Delimited (CSV) log files or to ODBC-compliant data sources for integration into third-party applications to generate items such as billing reports or security audits. For more information on AAA, see Chapter 9.

In addition to the typical AAA features listed earlier, Secure ACS also includes functionality such as IEEE 802.1x support. This permits access control for switched LANs at port-level granularity. Doing so relies on the new IETF RFC Extensible Authentication Protocol (EAP) standard. EAP is an emerging PPP authentication methodology using MD5 hashing for security and is included in Secure ACS.

Finally, ACS includes new TACACS+ management functionality known as Device Command Sets (DCS). This new administrative tool provides a central CiscoSecure ACS GUI mechanism to control the authorization of each command on each device via per-user, per-group, or per-network device group mapping.

Installation Requirements for the Cisco Access Control Server

Before installing the Secure ACS software, verify the server meets the following hardware and software requirements as shown next. Although this section focuses on the recently released Windows 3.0 functionality, specifications for the Solaris-based 2.3 version are included as well.

When running Secure ACS on a Windows operating system, the following requirements apply:

- **OS** Windows NT 4.0 SP6a or Windows 2000 SP1 or SP2
- **System** Pentium-compatible

- **Processor** 550MHz or faster
- **Memory** 256MB RAM
- **Disk** 250MB; more if the database is on the same machine
- **Browser** Microsoft Internet Explorer Versions 5.0 and 5.5 or Netscape Communicator Version 4.76

When running Secure ACS on a Solaris operating system, the following requirements apply:

- **OS** Solaris 2.5, 2.6, 7, 8
- **System** Sun SPARC 20
- **Memory** 128MB RAM with 256MB swap space
- **Disk** 500MB
- **Database** Oracle 7.33 or Sybase 11.1
- **Browser** Netscape Communicator Version 4.76

Features of Cisco Secure ACS

Secure ACS is a powerful access control server with many high-performance and scalability features such as the following:

- **Intuitive User Interface** The Web-based user interface simplifies and distributes the configuration for user profiles, group profiles, and ACS configuration.
- **Scalability** Secure ACS is built to support large networked environments with support for redundant servers, remote databases, and user database backup services.
- **Extensibility** LDAP authentication forwarding supports the authentication of user profiles stored in directories from leading directory vendors such as Netscape, Novell, and Microsoft.
- **Management** Windows 2000 Active Directory and Windows NT database support consolidates Windows username/password management and uses the Windows Performance Monitor for real-time statistics viewing.
- **Administration** Different access levels for each Secure ACS administrator and the ability to group network devices enables easier control

and maximum flexibility. This facilitates enforcement and changes of security policy administration over all devices in a network.

- **Product Flexibility** Because Cisco IOS Software has embedded support for AAA, Secure ACS can be used across virtually any network access device that Cisco sells. (The Cisco IOS version must support RADIUS or TACACS+.)

- **Protocol Flexibility** Secure ACS includes simultaneous TACACS+ and RADIUS support for a flexible solution with VPN or dial support at the origin and termination of Internet Protocol Security (IPSec) and Point-to-Point Tunneling Protocol (PPTP) tunnels.

- **Integration** Tight coupling with Cisco IOS routers and VPN solutions provides features such as Multichassis Multilink Point-to-Point Protocol and Cisco IOS command authorization.

- **Third-party Support** Secure ACS offers token server support for RSA SecurID, Passgo, Secure Computing, ActiveCard, Vasco, and CryptoCard.

- **Control** Secure ACS provides dynamic quotas for time-of-day, network usage, number of logged sessions, and day-of-week access restrictions.

For more information on features available, refer to Secure ACS information on the Cisco Web site.

Placing Cisco Secure ACS in the Network

Secure ACS can control access to many devices and services on a network. Figure 14.20 depicts a typical placement of a Secure ACS server in the network.

As can be seen, Secure ACS can be used with dial-up access servers, VPNs and firewalls, voice-IP solutions, content networks and Cisco wireless solutions. Windows NT domain servers or external databases/directories, such as LDAP, can be used to manage the username database for access to network devices and dial-up user access. Centralizing control of network access simplifies access management and helps establish a constant security policy.

Between the access devices and Secure ACS, TACACS+ or RADIUS can provide authentication and authorization for network users. The ACS server checks external user databases or local accounts on the ACS server. Dial-up users from remote locations can use PPP or other methodologies to authenticate with the NAS, and the NAS can use TACACS+ or RADIUS to interact with ACS server.

Figure 14.20 A Secure ACS Server in the Network Architecture

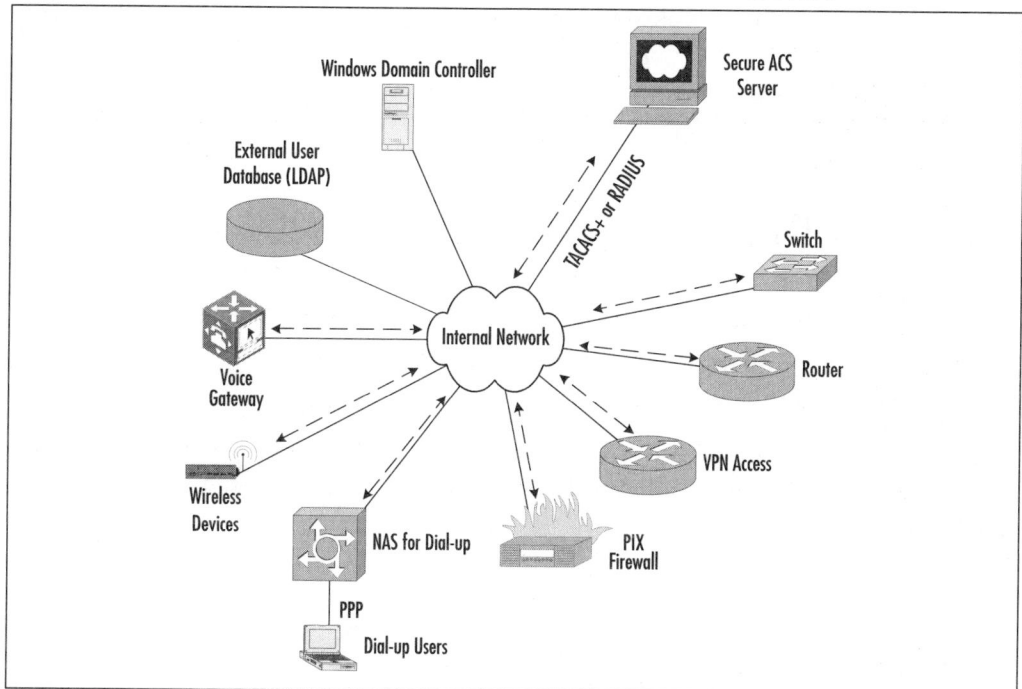

Cisco Secure ACS Device and Software Support

As previously mentioned, Secure ACS supports management of access control and accounting for dial-up access servers, VPNs and firewalls, voice-IP solutions, broadband access, content networks and Cisco wireless solutions. More specifically, Secure ACS supports all devices compliant with TACACS+ or RADIUS protocol, including non-Cisco devices. For full TACACS+ and RADIUS support on Cisco IOS devices however, verify that all AAA clients are running Cisco IOS Release 11.2 or later.

When using TACACS+ and RADIUS with third-party devices via the ACS server, verify the devices conform to the following specifications:

- Cisco Systems draft 1.77: TACACS+
- IETF RADIUS RFCs: 2138, 2139, 2865, 2866, 2867, 2868

To support both the older and newer RADIUS RFCs, Secure ACS accepts authentication requests on port 1645 and port 1812. For accounting, Secure ACS accepts accounting packets on port 1646 and 1813.

In addition to supporting standard IETF RADIUS attributes, Secure ACS includes support for RADIUS vendor-specific attributes (VSAs). The following predefined RADIUS VSAs exist in Secure ACS:

- Cisco IOS/PIX
- Cisco VPN 3000
- Cisco VPN 5000
- Ascend
- Juniper
- Microsoft
- Nortel

Finally, Secure ACS supports up to ten user-defined RADIUS VSAs to be used with AAA.

Secure ACS supports several external databases for authentication in addition to the ACS internal password database as follows:

- Windows NT/2000 User Database
- Generic LDAP
- Novell NetWare Directory Services (NDS)
- Open Database Connectivity (ODBC)-compliant relational databases
- Token Card servers as follows:
    - CRYPTOCard Token Server
    - SafeWord Token Server
    - AXENT Token Server
    - RSA SecureID Token Server
    - ActivCard Token Server
    - Vasco Token Server

When dial-up users request access to a NAS server on the network, the NAS directs the dial-in user access request to the Secure ACS for authentication and authorization of privileges using TACACS+ or RADIUS. If the Secure ACS user database is not locally configured, ACS sends the authentication request to the relevant username database for authentication. The success or failure response from the Secure ACS server is relayed back to the NAS, which permits or denies user access to a network. After the user is authenticated on the network, Secure ACS sends a set of authorization attributes to the NAS and any configured accounting functions take place.

Using Cisco Secure ACS

Before using Secure ACS to manage AAA on network devices, the Secure ACS software must be successfully installed and the network devices configured for proper management. This section includes the procedures necessary for a Windows-based installation, and preparation of the enterprise before AAA management can take place. Prior to installing the software, always verify that the ACS server software and hardware meet all requirements previously specified.

Installing Cisco Secure ACS

Before initiating the installation, some information must first be gathered. Secure ACS will request the following information during the installation process:

- The AAA protocol and vendor-specific attribute to implement
- The name of the first AAA client
- The IP address of the first AAA client
- The Windows 2000/NT server IP address
- The TACACS+ or RADIUS key (shared secret)

Once you have gathered this information, begin the installation and select a location to install the server software. Next, Secure ACS requests the database format for the authentication process. Select the local Secure ACS database or the Windows NT User Database. The use of other, external authentication databases can be configured after the installation of Secure ACS.

WARNING

If upgrading an existing ACS installation, be sure to back up all Secure ACS system files, databases, and the Windows Registry.

Proceed with the installation through the following steps:

1. **Configure the first AAA client** Determine how to authenticate users on a specific Network Access Server on the network.

2. **Configure advanced options** Select advanced options to be enabled on the server. These options can be configured later via the Advanced Options page in the Interface Configuration section.

3. **Configure Active Service Monitoring** Determine whether active service monitoring should be enabled and how monitoring should be configured. Monitoring features can be configured later via the Active Server Management page in the System Configuration section.

4. **Configure Network Access Servers** Configure AAA in detail on network access servers, if desired.

5. **Start the ACS service and launch the Secure ACS software** Begin configuring Secure ACS via the administrative browser, if desired.

After the installation process successfully completes, access the Cisco SecureACS HTML interface using the ACS Admin desktop icon on the Windows server or open the following URL in a supported Web browser on the Windows server: http://127.0.0.1:2002.

Configuration

After installing Secure ACS, several additional administrative and configuration details must be completed. The following sequence of configuration activities is typical of most post-ACS installation processes.

- **Configure Administrators** Configure at least one administrator after installation; otherwise, remote administrative access will not be possible.

- **Configure System** Configure functions within the System Configuration section such as setting the format for the display of dates, password validation, and configuring settings for database replication and RDBMS synchronization. Set up the logs and reports to be generated by Secure ACS as well.

- **Configure Network** Establish the identity, location, and grouping of AAA clients and servers, and determine the authentication protocols each is to employ.

- **Configure External User Database** If using an external database to establish and maintain user authentication accounts, configure the database. Specify requirements for Secure ACS database replication, backup, and synchronization.

- **Configure Shared Profile Components** Before configuring user groups, configure Shared Profile Components.

- **Configure Groups** Decide how to implement unknown user processing and database group mapping. Then, configure user groups with a complete plan of how Secure ACS is to implement authorization and authentication.

- **Configure Users** Establish user accounts.

- **Configure Reports** Specify the nature and scope of logging that Secure ACS performs using the Reports and Activities section of the Secure ACS HTML interface.

Configuration Example: Adding and Configuring a AAA Client

After performing the recommended configuration tasks in the preceding list, continue to add AAA clients as necessary. This example provides information regarding the addition of new AAA clients. Begin from the Network Configuration screen shown in Figure 14.21 in order to add a device within the enterprise that requires the ACS server for AAA.

Figure 14.21 Configuring Network Devices Using Secure ACS

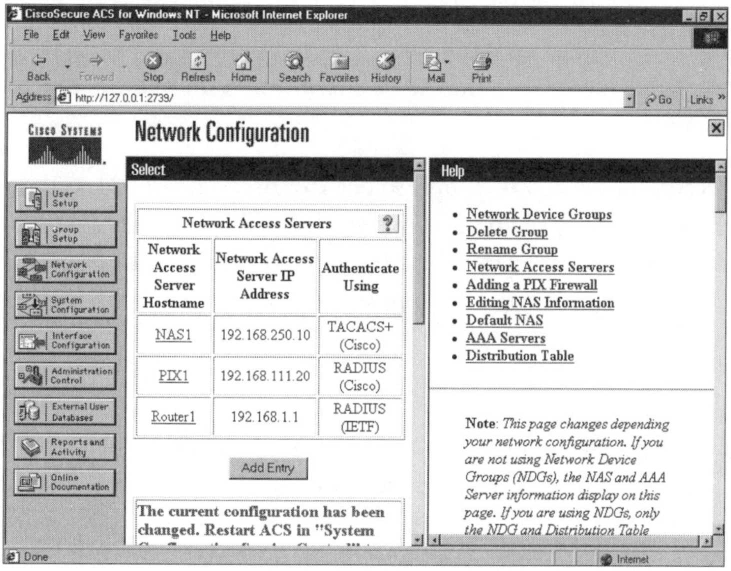

Click **Add Entry** below the AAA Clients table. The Add AAA Client page appears as shown in Figure 14.22.

Figure 14.22 Device Configuration Changes in Secure ACS

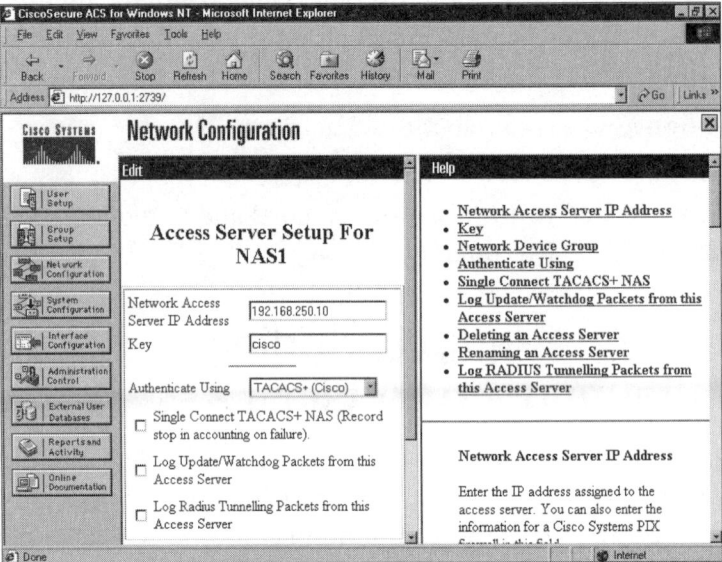

In this page, assign the following to the new AAA client:

- Hostname

- Client IP address

- The shared secret that the AAA client and Secure ACS use to encrypt data

If using Network Device Groups, select the name of the Network Device Group to which the AAA client belongs from the Network Device Group list, or select **Not Assigned**. Determine the network security protocol used by the AAA client by configuring one of the following options:

- TACACS+ (Cisco IOS)

- RADIUS (Cisco Aironet)

- RADIUS (Cisco BBMS)

- RADIUS (IETF)

- RADIUS (Cisco IOS/PIX)

- RADIUS (Cisco VPN 3000)

- RADIUS (Cisco VPN 5000)

- RADIUS (Ascend)

- RADIUS (Juniper)

- RADIUS (Nortel)

To enable a static connection for all requests from the AAA client, select the **Single Connect TACACS+ AAA Client** check box. Enable Watchdog packets by selecting the **Log Update/Watchdog Packets from this AAA Client** check box. Watchdog packets are interim packets sent periodically during a session and serve to enable an approximation of session length if the AAA client fails.

To allow RADIUS tunneling accounting packets to be logged in the RADIUS Accounting reports of Reports and Activity, select the **Log RADIUS tunneling Packets from the AAA Client** check box.

Save the changes and apply them immediately by clicking **Submit | Restart**.

NOTE

To save changes and continue working, click the **Submit** button. When finished making all changes, click **System Configuration | Service Control**. Click **Restart** to implement all changes.

Summary

Robust security management techniques are required to keep pace with the increasing complexity and frequency of security incidents. In large networks with numerous services and network ingress and egress points, the use of application tools can help administrators remain efficient and vigilant against attack while ensuring standardized security policies.

The security applications developed by Cisco (listed next) serve to enhance security management through intuitive graphical interfaces, configuration automation, report generation, and enhanced monitoring capabilities among others.

- PIX Device Manager (PDM)

- CiscoWorks2000 Access Control Lists Manager (ACLM)

- Cisco Secure Policy Manager (CSPM)

- Cisco Secure Access Control Server (ACS)

Each application is suited for different purposes, yet the combination of these applications can represent a holistic application solution in many environments. While no system or network is impervious to malicious attack, with sound management and security policy techniques, the Cisco-based solutions discussed in this chapter arm security administrators and managers with essential tools for the ongoing struggle for infrastructure security.

The Cisco-based security management solutions described in this chapter represent some of the best industry responses to the ever-evolving needs of today's security administrators and managers. Using these tools, many of the complex and tedious tasks required to manage security devices and infrastructure are simplified and automated by various application solutions.

Solutions Fast Track

PIX Device Manager

☑ PDM is designed to securely manage small numbers of PIX Firewalls.

☑ PDM has a Java-based GUI for simplified remote management.

☑ PDM has a powerful interface enabling nearly all CLI capabilities from a Web browser.

☑ PDM includes graphical reporting and monitoring capabilities.

CiscoWorks2000 Access Control Lists Manager

☑ ACLM is part of the CiscoWorks2000 Routed WAN Management Solution.

☑ ACLM enables robust control of IP and IPX access lists.

☑ ACLM automates new ACL rollout and ongoing ACL changes to multiple devices.

☑ ACLM includes version comparison tools for quick troubleshooting and change management.

Cisco Secure Policy Manager

☑ CSPM provides a complete management solution for Cisco VPN routers, IDS, and Cisco Secure PIX firewalls.

☑ CSPM is a NT-based management tool for networks sized up to 500 devices.

☑ CSPM enables the definition, enforcement, and auditing of security policy from one intuitive administrative interface.

Cisco Secure Access Control Server

☑ Secure ACS enables centralized management of access control and accounting for dial-up access servers, VPNs and firewalls, voice-IP solutions, broadband access, content networks and Cisco wireless solutions.

☑ Secure ACS provides full control over authentication, authorization, and accounting (AAA) configurations and management.

☑ Secure ACS is designed for interoperability; administrators can leverage existing user database infrastructures such as Lightweight Directory Access Protocol (LDAP) servers or Windows-based domain authentication mechanisms in combination with RADIUS and TACACS+ functionality to manage users.

Frequently Asked Questions

The following Frequently Asked Questions, answered by the authors of this book, are designed to both measure your understanding of the concepts presented in this chapter and to assist you with real-life implementation of these concepts. To have your questions about this chapter answered by the author, browse to **www.syngress.com/solutions** and click on the **"Ask the Author"** form.

Q: Is Cisco PDM compatible with other forms of management such as Cisco Secure Policy Manager (CSPM), CLI, and so forth?

A: Yes. Cisco PDM is a graphical interface to the PIX firewall, yet the resulting commands it reads and writes are CLI. PDM can read configurations that have been created via CLI or CSPM. Likewise, CLI users can view and alter configurations generated by PDM. There are some exceptions to this rule such as static PAT configurations, which cannot be interpreted by the PDM interface.

Q: Is there a limitation on the size of the configuration that Cisco PDM can handle?

A: Cisco recommends that Cisco PDM configuration files be 100KB (approximately 1500 lines) or less in size.

Q: Can Secure ACS be implemented on a platform other than Windows?

A: Yes, a Solaris version of Secure ACS exists, but is not capable of the same functionality as the Windows release at this time.

Q: Can more than one user use ACL Manager at any one time?

A: Yes, ACL Manager is designed to be a multi-user application. However, if several users are running ACL Manager and are all trying to modify ACLs on the same device, the user that downloads changes to the device first will invalidate the work of all the other users. Cisco recommends that several users use ACL Manager when the groups of devices on which they are administering ACLs do not overlap, or the user is using ACL Manager in a "read-only" manner.

Q: Will ACL Manager help reduce the time it takes to make the same changes on several devices?

A: Yes, the administrator can use the ACL Use Wizard to apply a predefined filtering policy or template to a group of devices and appropriate interfaces at one time.

Chapter 15

Looking Ahead: Cisco Wireless Security

Solutions in this chapter:

- **Understanding Security Fundamentals and Principles of Protection**

- **MAC Filtering**

- **Reviewing the Role of Policy**

- **Implementing WEP**

- **Addressing Common Risks and Threats**

- **Sniffing, Interception, and Eavesdropping**

- **Spoofing and Unauthorized Access**

- **Network Hijacking and Modification**

- **Denial of Service and Flooding Attacks**

☑ **Summary**

☑ **Solutions Fast Track**

☑ **Frequently Asked Questions**

Introduction

There is not much indication of anything slowing down the creation and deployment of new technology to the world any time in the near future. With the constant pressure to deploy the latest generation of technology today, little time is allowed for a full and proper security review of the technology and components that make it up.

This rush to deploy, along with the insufficient security review, not only allows age-old security vulnerabilities to be reintroduced to products, but creates new and unknown security challenges as well. Wireless networking is not exempt from this, and like many other technologies, security flaws have been identified and new methods of exploiting these flaws are published regularly.

Utilizing security fundamentals developed over the last few decades, you can review and protect your wireless networks from known and unknown threats. In this chapter, we recall security fundamentals and principles that are the foundation of any good security strategy, addressing a range of issues from authentication and authorization, to controls and audit.

No primer on security would be complete without an examination of the common security standards, which are addressed in this chapter alongside the emerging privacy standards and their implications for the wireless exchange of information.

We also look at how you can maximize the features of existing security standards like Wired Equivalent Protocol (WEP). We also examine the effectiveness of Media Access Control (MAC) and protocol filtering as a way of minimizing opportunity. Lastly, we look at the security advantages of using virtual private networks (VPNs) on a wireless network, as well as discuss the importance of convincing users of the role they can play as key users of the network.

You'll also learn about the existing and anticipated threats to wireless networks, and the principles of protection that are fundamental to a wireless security strategy. And although many of the attacks are similar in nature to attacks on wired networks, you need to understand the particular tools and techniques that attackers use to take advantage of the unique way wireless networks are designed, deployed, and maintained. We explore the attacks that have exposed the vulnerabilities of wireless networks, and in particular the weaknesses inherent in the security standards. Through a detailed examination of these standards, we identify how these weaknesses have lead to the development of new tools and tricks that hackers use to exploit your wireless networks. We look at the emergence and threat of "war driving" technique and how it is usually the first step in an attack on wireless networks.

Understanding Security Fundamentals and Principles of Protection

Security protection starts with the preservation of the *confidentiality*, *integrity*, and *availability* (CIA) of data and computing resources. These three tenets of information security, often referred to as "The Big Three," are sometimes represented by the CIA triad, shown in Figure 15.1.

Figure 15.1 The CIA Triad

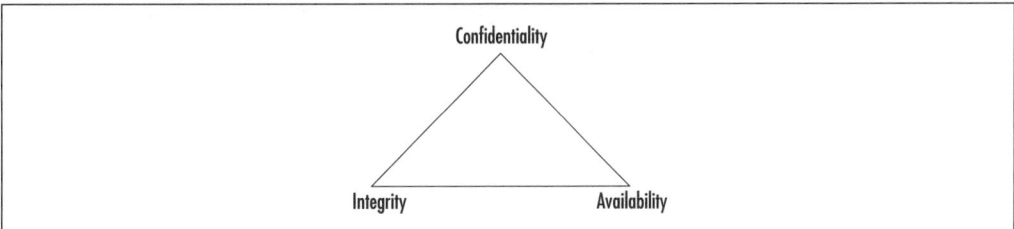

As we describe each of these tenets, you will see that in order to provide for a reliable and secure wireless environment, you will need to ensure that each tenet is properly protected. To ensure the preservation of The Big Three and protect the privacy of those whose data is stored and flows through these data and computing resources, The Big Three security tenets are implemented through tried-and-true security practices. These other practices enforce The Big Three by ensuring proper authentication for authorized access while allowing for nonrepudiation in identification and resource usage methods, and by permitting complete accountability for all activity through audit trails and logs. Some security practitioners refer to Authentication, Authorization, and Audit (accountability) as "AAA." Each of these practices provides the security implementer with tools which they can use to properly identify and mitigate any possible risks to The Big Three.

Ensuring Confidentiality

Confidentiality attempts to prevent the intentional or unintentional unauthorized disclosure of communications between a sender and recipient. In the physical world, ensuring confidentiality can be accomplished by simply securing the physical area. However, as evidenced by bank robberies and military invasions, threats exist to the security of the physical realm that can compromise security and confidentiality.

The moment electronic means of communication were introduced, many new possible avenues of disclosing the information within these communications were created. The confidentiality of early analog communication systems, such as the telegraph and telephone, were easily compromised by simply having someone connect to the wires used by a sender and receiver.

When digital communications became available, like with many technologies, it was only a matter of time until knowledgeable people were able to build devices and methods that could interpret the digital signals and convert them to whatever form needed to disclose what was communicated. And as technology grew and became less expensive, the equipment needed to monitor and disclose digital communications became available to anyone wishing to put the effort into monitoring communication.

With the advent of wireless communications, the need for physically connecting to a communication channel to listen in or capture confidential communications was removed. Although you can achieve some security by using extremely tight beam directional antennas, someone still just has to sit somewhere in between the antennas to be able to monitor and possibly connect to the communications channel without having to actually tie into any physical device.

Having knowledge that communications channels are possibly compromised allows us to properly implement our policies and procedures to mitigate the wireless risk. The solution used to ensure The Big Three and other security tenets is *encryption*.

The current implementation of encryption in today's wireless networks use the RC4 stream cipher to encrypt the transmitted network packets, and the WEP to protect authentication into wireless networks by network devices connecting to them (that is, the network adapter authentication, not the user utilizing the network resources). Both of which, due mainly to improper implementations, have introduced sufficient problems that have made it possible to determine keys used and then either falsely authenticate to the network or decrypt the traffic traveling across through the wireless network. For more information on encryption and cryptography please refer to Chapter 6.

With these apparent problems, those in charge of wireless network security should utilize other proven and properly implemented encryption solutions, such as Secure Shell (SSH), Secure Sockets Layer (SSL), or IPSec.

Ensuring Integrity

Integrity ensures the accuracy and completeness of information throughout its process methods. The first communication methods available to computers did not have much in place to ensure the integrity of the data transferred from one to another. As such, occasionally something as simple as static on a telephone line could cause the transfer of data to be corrupted.

To solve this problem, the idea of a checksum was introduced. A *checksum* is nothing more than taking the message you are sending and running it through a function that returns a simple value which is then appended to the message being sent. When the receiver gets the complete message, they would then run the message through the same function and compare the value they generate with the value that was included at the end of the message.

The functions that are generally used to generate basic checksums are usually based upon simple addition or modulus functions. These functions can sometimes have their own issues, such as the function not being detailed enough to allow for distinctly separate data that could possibly have identical checksums. It is even possible to have two errors within the data itself cause the checksum to provide a valid check because the two errors effectively cancel each other out. These problems are usually addressed through a more complex algorithm used to create the digital checksum.

Cyclic redundancy checks (CRCs) were developed as one of the more advanced methods of ensuring data integrity. CRC algorithms basically treat a message as an enormous binary number, whereupon another large fixed binary number then divides this binary number. The remainder from this division is the checksum. Using the remainder of a long division as the checksum, as opposed to the original data summation, adds a significant chaos to the checksum created, increasing the likelihood that the checksum will not be repeatable with any other separate data stream.

These more advanced checksum methods, however, have their own set of problems. As Ross Williams wrote in his 1993 paper, A Painless Guide to CRC Error Detection Algorithms (www.ross.net/crc/crcpaper.html), the goal of error detection is to protect against corruption introduced by noise in a data transfer. This is good if we are concerned only with protecting against possible transmission errors. However, the algorithm provides no means of ensuring the integrity of an intentionally corrupted data stream. If someone has knowledge of a particular data stream, altering the contents of the data and completing the transaction with a valid checksum is possible. The receiver would not have knowledge of the changes in the data because their checksum would match and it would appear as if the data was transferred with no errors.

This form of intentional integrity violation is called a "Data Injection." In such cases, the best way to protect data is to (once again) use a more advanced form of integrity protection utilizing cryptography. Today, this higher level of protection is generally provided through a stronger cryptographic algorithm such as the MD5 or RC4 ciphers.

Wireless networks today use the RC4 stream cipher to protect the data transmitted as well as provide for data integrity. It has been proven that the 802.11 implementation of the RC4 cipher with its key scheduling algorithm introduces enough information to provide a hacker with enough to be able to predict your network's secret encryption key. Once the hacker has your key, they are not only able to gain access to your wireless network, but also view it as if there was no encryption at all.

Ensuring Availability

Availability, as defined in an information security context, ensures that access data or computing resources needed by appropriate personnel is both reliable and available in a timely manner. The origins of the Internet itself come from the need to ensure the availability of network resources. In 1957, the United States Department of Defense (DoD) created the Advanced Research Projects Agency (ARPA) following the Soviet launch of Sputnik. Fearing loss of command and control over U.S. nuclear missiles and bombers due to communication channel disruption caused by nuclear or conventional attacks, the U.S. Air Force commissioned a study on how to create a network that could function with the loss of access or routing points. Out of this, packet switched networking was created, and the first four nodes of ARPANET were deployed in 1968 running at the then incredibly high speed of 50 Kbps.

The initial design of packet switched networks did not take into consideration the possibility of an actual attack on the network from one of its own nodes. As the ARPANET grew into what we now know as the Internet, many modifications have been made to the protocols and applications that make up the network, ensuring the availability of all resources provided.

Wireless networks are experiencing many similar design issues, and due to the proliferation of new wireless high-tech devices, many are finding themselves in conflict with other wireless resources. Like their wired equivalents, there was little expectation that conflicts would occur within the wireless spectrum available for use. Because of this, very few wireless equipment providers planned their implementations with features to ensure the availability of the wireless resource in case a conflict occurred.

Ensuring Privacy

Privacy is the assurance that the information a customer provides to some party will remain private and protected. This information generally contains customer personal nonpublic information that is protected by both regulation and civil liability law. Your wireless policy and procedures should contain definitions on how to ensure the privacy of customer information that might be accessed or transmitted by your wireless networks. The principles and methods here provide ways of ensuring the protection of the data that travels across your networks and computers.

Ensuring Authentication

Authentication provides for a sender and receiver of information to validate each other as the appropriate entity they are wishing to work with. If entities wishing to communicate cannot properly authenticate each other, then there can be no trust of the activities or information provided by either party. It is only through a trusted and secure method of authentication that we are able to provide for a trusted and secure communication or activity.

The simplest form of authentication is the transmission of a shared password between the entities wishing to authenticate with each other. This could be as simple as a secret handshake or a key. As with all simple forms of protection, once knowledge of the secret key or handshake was disclosed to nontrusted parties, there could be no trust in who was using the secrets anymore.

Many methods can be used to acquire a simple secret key, from something as simple as tricking someone into disclosing it, to high-tech monitoring of communications between parties to intercept the key as it is passed from one party to the other. However the code is acquired, once it is in a nontrusted party's hands, they are able to utilize it to falsely authenticate and identify themselves as a valid party, forging false communications, or utilizing the user's access to gain permissions to the available resources.

The original digital authentication systems simply shared a secret key across the network with the entity they wished to authenticate with. Applications such as Telnet, File Transfer Protocol (FTP), and POP-mail are examples of programs that simply transmit the password, in cleartext, to the party they are authenticating with. The problem with this method of authentication is that anyone who is able to monitor the network could possibly capture the secret key and then use it to authenticate themselves as you in order to access these same services. They could then access your information directly, or corrupt any information you send to other parties. They may even be able to attempt to gain higher privileged access with your stolen authentication information.

Configuring & Implementing…

Cleartext Authentication

Cleartext (non-encrypted) authentication is still widely used by many people today who receive their e-mail through the Post Office Protocol (POP), which by default sends the password unprotected in cleartext from the mail client to the server. You can protect your e-mail account password in several ways, including connection encryption as well as not transmitting the password in cleartext through the network by hashing with MD5 or some similar algorithm.

Encrypting the connection between the mail client and server is the only way of truly protecting your mail authentication password. This will prevent anyone from capturing your password or any of the mail you might transfer to your client. SSL is generally the method used to encrypt the connection stream from the mail client to the server and is supported by most mail clients today.

If you just protect the password through MD5 or a similar cryptocipher, anyone who happens to intercept your "protected" password could identify it through a brute force attack. A brute force attack is where someone generates every possible combination of characters running each version through the same algorithm used to encrypt the original password until a match is made and your password is found.

Authentication POP (APOP) is a method used to provide password-only encryption for mail authentication. It employs a challenge/response method defined in RFC1725 that uses a shared timestamp provided by the server being authenticated to. The timestamp is hashed with the username and the shared secret key through the MD5 algorithm.

There are still a few problems with this, the first of which is that all values are known in advance except the shared secret key. Because of this, there is nothing to provide protection against a brute-force attack

Continued

on the shared key. Another problem is that this security method attempts to protect your password. Nothing is done to prevent anyone who might be listening to your network from then viewing your e-mail as it is downloaded to your mail client.

You can find an example of a brute-force password dictionary generator that can produce a brute-force dictionary from specific character sets at www.dmzs.com/tools/files.

To solve the problem of authentication through sharing common secret keys across an untrusted network, the concept of Zero Knowledge Passwords was created. The idea of Zero Knowledge Passwords is that the parties who wish to authenticate each other want to prove to one another that they know the shared secret, and yet not share the secret with each other in case the other party truly doesn't have knowledge of the password, while at the same time preventing anyone who may intercept the communications between the parties from gaining knowledge as to the secret that is being used.

Public-key cryptography has been shown to be the strongest method of doing Zero Knowledge Passwords. It was originally developed by Whitfield Diffie and Martin Hellman and presented to the world at the 1976 National Computer Conference. Their concept was published a few months later in their paper, New Directions in Cryptography. Another crypto-researcher named Ralph Merkle, working independently from Diffie and Hellman, also invented a similar method for providing public-key cryptography, but his research was not published until 1978.

Public-key cryptography introduced the concept of having keys work in pairs, an encryption key and a decryption key, and having them created in such a way that generating one key from the other is infeasible. The encryption key is then made public to anyone wishing to encrypt a message to the holder of the secret decryption key. Because identifying or creating the decryption key from the encryption key is infeasible, anyone who happens to have the encrypted message and the encryption key will be unable to decrypt the message or determine the decryption key needed to decrypt the message.

Public-key encryption generally stores the keys or uses a certificate hierarchy. The certificates are rarely changed and often used just for encrypting data, not authentication. Zero Knowledge Password protocols, on the other hand, tend to use Ephemeral keys. *Ephemeral keys* are temporary keys that are randomly created for a single authentication, and then discarded once the authentication is completed.

Note that the public-key encryption is still susceptible to a chosen–ciphertext attack. This attack is where someone already knows what the decrypted message is and has knowledge of the key used to generate the encrypted message. Knowing the decrypted form of the message lets the attacker possibly deduce what the secret decryption key could be. This attack is unlikely to occur with authentication systems because the attacker will not have knowledge of the decrypted message: your password. If they had that, they would already have the ability to authenticate as you and not need to determine your secret decryption key.

Currently 802.11 network authentication is centered on the authentication of the wireless device, not on authenticating the user or station utilizing the wireless network. Public-key encryption is not used in the wireless encryption process. Although a few wireless vendors have dynamic keys that are changed with every connection, most wireless 802.11 vendors utilize shared-key authentication with static keys.

Shared key authentication is utilized by WEP functions with the following steps:

1. When a station requests service, it sends an authentication frame to the access point (AP) it wishes to communicate with.

2. The receiving AP replies to the authentication frame with its own, which contains 128 octets of challenge text.

3. The station requesting access encrypts the challenge text with the shared encryption key and returns to the AP.

4. The access decrypts the encrypted challenge using the shared key and compares it with the original challenge text. If they match, an authentication acknowledgement is sent to the station requesting access, otherwise a negative authentication notice is sent.

As you can see, this authentication method does not authenticate the user or any resource the user might need to access. It is only a verification that the wireless device has knowledge of the shared secret key that the wireless AP has. Once a user has passed the AP authentication challenge, that user will then have full access to whatever devices and networks the AP is connected to. You should still use secure authentication methods to access any of these devices and prevent unauthorized access and use by people who might be able to attach to your wireless network.

To solve this lack of external authentication, the IEEE 802.11 committee is working on 802.1x, a standard that will provide a framework for 802-based networks authenticating from centralized servers. Back in November 2000, Cisco introduced Light Extensible Authentication Protocol (LEAP) authentication to their wireless products, which adds several enhancements to the 802.11 authentication system, including the following:

- Mutual authentication utilizing Remote Access Dial-In User Service (RADIUS).

- Securing the secret key with one-way hashes that make password reply attacks impossible.

- Policies to force the user to re-authenticate more often, getting a new session key with each new session. This will help to prevent attacks where traffic is injected into the data stream.

- Changes to the initialization vector used in WEP encryption that make the current exploits of WEP ineffective.

Not all vendors support these solutions, so your best bet is to protect your network and servers with your own strong authentication and authorization rules.

Extensible Authentication Protocol (EAP)

The Extensible Authentication Protocol (EAP) was designed to provide authentication methods within the Point-to-Point-Protocol (PPP). EAP allows for the integration of third-party authentication packages that use PPP. EAP can be configured so that it can support a number of methods for authentication schemes, such as token cards, public key, certificates, PINs, and on and on.

When you install PPP/EAP, EAP will not select a specific authentication method at the Link Control Protocol (LCP) Phase, but will wait until the Authentication Phase to begin. What this does is allow the authenticator the ability to request more information, and with this information it will decide on the method of authentication to use. This delay will also allow for the implementation of a server on the backend that can control the various authentication methods while the PPP authenticator passes through the authentication exchange.

In this way, network devices like Access Points (APs) or switches do not need to understand each request type, because they will simply act as a conduit, or passthrough agent, for a server on a host. The network device will only need to see if the packet has the success or failure code in order to terminate the authentication phase.

EAP is able to define one or more requests for peer-to-peer authentication. This can happen because the request packet includes a type field, such as Generic Token, one-time password (OTP), or an MD5 challenge. The MD5 challenge is very similar to the Challenge Handshake Authentication Protocol (CHAP).

EAP is able to provide you with a flexible, link-layer security framework (see Figure 15.2), by having the following features:

- EAP mechanisms are IETF standards–based and allow for the growth of new authentication types when your security needs change:
  - Transport Layer Security (TLS)
  - Internet Key Exchange (IKE)
  - GSS_API (Kerberos)
  - Other authentication schemes (LEAP)
- There is no dependency on IP, because this is an encapsulation protocol.
- There is no windowing as this is a simple ACK/NAK protocol.
- No support for fragmentation.
- Can run over any link layer (PPP, 802.3, 802.5, 802.11, and so on).
- Does not consider a physically secure link as an authentication method to provide security.
- Assumes that there is no reordering of packets.
- Retransmission of packets is the responsibility of authenticator.

Figure 15.2 The EAP Architecture

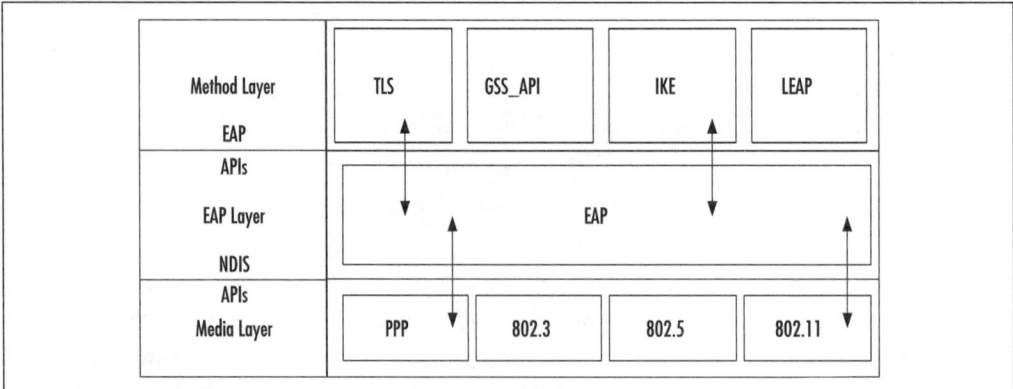

802.1x and EAP

One type of wireless security is focused on providing centralized authentication and dynamic key distribution area. By using the IEEE 802.1x standard, the EAP, and LEAP as an end-to-end solution, you can provide enhanced functionality to your wireless network. Two main elements are involved in using this standard:

- EAP/LEAP allows all wireless client adapters the capability to communicate with different authentication servers such as RADIUS and Terminal Access Controller Access Control System (TACACS+) servers that are located on the network.

- You implement the IEEE 802.1x standard for network access control that is port based for MAC filtering.

When these features are deployed together, wireless clients that are associated with APs will not be able to gain access to the network unless the user performs a network logon. The user will need to enter a username and password for network logon, after which the client and a RADIUS server will perform authentication, hopefully leading to the client being authenticated by the supplied username and password and access to the network and resources.

How this occurs is that the RADIUS server and client device will then receive a client-specific WEP key that is used by the client for that specific logon session. As an added level of security, the user's password and session key will never be transmitted in the open, over the wireless connection.

Here is how Authentication works and the WEP key is passed:

1. The wireless client will associate with an AP located on the wireless network.

2. The AP will then prevent all other attempts made by that client to gain access to network until the client logs on to the network.

3. The client will supply a username and password for network logon.

4. Using 802.1x standard and EAP/LEAP, the wireless client and a RADIUS server perform authentication through the AP. The client will then use a one-way hash of the user-supplied password as a response to the challenge, and this will be sent to the RADIUS server. The RADIUS server will then reference its user table and compare that to the response from the client. If there is a match, the RADIUS server

authenticates the client, and the process will be repeated, but in reverse. This will enable the client to authenticate the RADIUS server.

(If you are using LEAP, the RADIUS server will send an authentication challenge to the client.)

After authentication completes successfully, the following steps take place:

1. The RADIUS server and the client determine a WEP key that is unique for the client and that session.

2. The RADIUS server transmits this WEP key (also known as a session key), across the wired LAN to the AP.

3. The AP will encrypt the broadcast key and the session key so that it can then send the new encrypted key to the client. The client will then use the session key to decrypt it.

4. The client and AP then activates the WEP. The APs and clients will then use the session and broadcast WEP keys for all communications that occur during the session.

5. For enhanced security, the session key and broadcast key are regularly changed at regular periods that are configured in the RADIUS server.

A more simplified version is included in Figure 15.3.

Figure 15.3 Cisco Security Solution Using Session-Based Encryption Keys

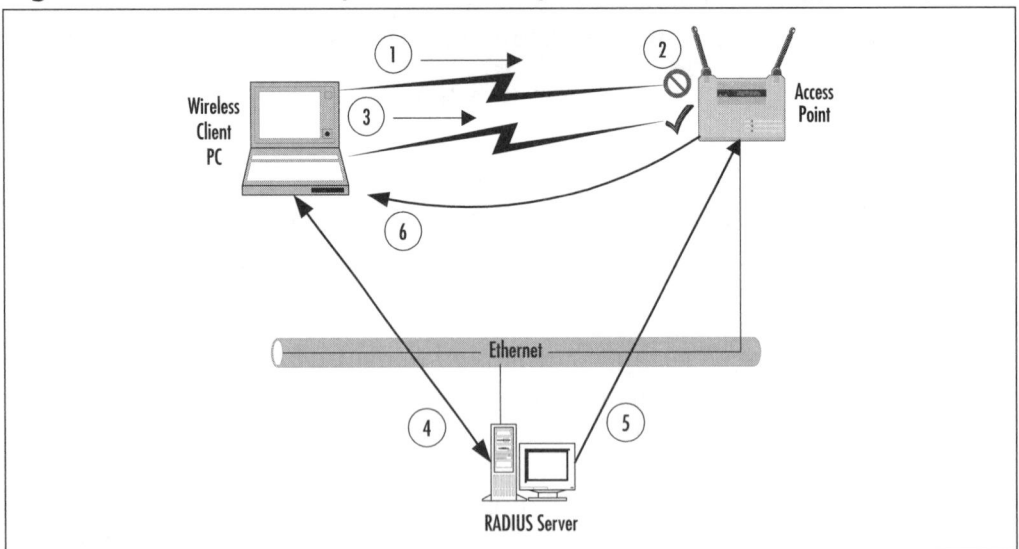

An Introduction to the 802.1x Standard

In order to better understand 802.1x, you must also understand the enhancements of current IEEE 802.11b security products and features. The current IEEE 802.11b standard is severely limited because it is available only for the current open and shared key authentication scheme, which is non-extensible.

Some of these requirements for the future security include the following:

- The creation of new 802.11 authentication methods.

- These authentication methods must be independent of the underlying 802.11 hardware.

- Authentication methods should be dynamic because hard coding it makes it difficult to fix security holes when they are found.

- It must have the ability to support Public Key Infrastructure (PKI) and certificate schemes.

Project Authorization Request (PAR) for 802.1x

Currently, no standard mechanism allows access to and from a network segment based only on the authenticated state of a port user. The problem is that network connectivity allows for the anonymous access to company data and the Internet. When 802-based networks are deployed in more accessible areas, you will need a method to authenticate and authorize basic network access. These types of projects provide for common interoperable solutions that use standards-based authentication and authorization infrastructures like those that are commonly supporting schemes such as dial-up access already.

The Objectives of the 802.1x Standard

The IEEE 802.1x Working Group was created for the purpose of providing a security framework for port-based access control that resides in the upper layers. The most common method for port-based access control is to enable new authentication and key management methods without changing current network devices.

The benefits that are the end result of this group are as follows:

- There is a significant decrease in hardware cost and complexity.

- There are more options, which allows you to pick and choose your security solution.

- You can install the latest and greatest security technology, and it should still work with your existing infrastructure.

- You are able to respond to security issues as quickly as they arise.

802.1x in a Nutshell

When a client device connects to a port on an 802.1x switch and AP, the switch port can determine the authenticity of the devices. Due to this and, according to the protocol specified by 802.1x, the services offered by the switch can be made available on that port. Only EAPOL (see the following list) frames can be sent and received on that port until the authentication is complete. When the device is properly authentication, the port switches traffic as though it were a regular port.

Here is some terminology for the 802.1x standard that you should familiarize yourself with:

- **Port** A port is a single point of connection to the network.

- **Port Access Entity (PAE)** The PAE controls the algorithms and protocols that are associated with the authentication mechanisms for a port.

- **Authenticator PAE** The authenticator PAE enforces authentication before it will allow access resources located off of that port.

- **Supplicant PAE** The supplicant PAE tries to accesses the services that are allowed by the authenticator.

- **Authentication Server** The Authentication Server is used to verify the supplicant PAE. It decides whether the supplicant is authorized to access the authenticator or not.

- **Extensible Authentication Protocol Over LAN (EAPOL)** The 802.1x defines a standard for encapsulating EAP messages so that they can be handled directly by a LAN MAC service. 802.1x tries to make authentication more encompassing, rather than enforcing specific mechanisms on the devices. Because of this, 802.1x uses Extensible Authentication Protocol to receive authentication information.

- **Extensible Authentication Protocol Over Wireless (EAPOW)** When EAPOL messages are encapsulated over 802.11 wireless frames, they are known as EAPOW.

Making it Come Together—User Identification and Strong Authentication

With the addition of the 802.1x standard, clients are identified by usernames, not the MAC address of the devices. This was designed to not only enhance security, but to streamline the process for authentication, authorization, and accountability for your network. 802.1x was designed so that it could support extended forms of authentication, using password methods (such as one-time passwords, or GSS_API mechanisms like Kerberos) and nonpassword methods (such as biometrics, IKE, and smart cards).

Key Derivation Can Be Dynamic

You can also use per-user session keys, because the 802.1x standard allows for the creation of them. Because you don't need to keep WEP keys at the client device or AP, you can dispense per-user, and/or per session–based WEP keys. These WEP keys will be dynamically created at the client for every session, thus making it more secure. The Global key, like a broadcast WEP key, can be encrypted using a unicast session key and then sent from the AP to the client in a much more secure manner.

Mutual Authentication

When using 802.1x and EAP, you should use some form of mutual authentication. This will make the client and the authentication servers mutually authenticating end-points and will assist in the mitigation of attacks from man in the middle types of devices. To enable mutual authentication, you could use any of the following EAP methods:

- **TLS** This requires that the server supply a certificate and establish that it has possession of the private key.

- **IKE** This requires that the server show possession of preshared key or private key (this can be considered certificate authentication).

- **GSS_API (Kerberos)** This requires that the server can demonstrate knowledge of the session key.

NOTE

Cisco Systems has also created a lightweight mutual authentication scheme, called LEAP (discussed later), so that your network is able to support operating systems that do not normally support EAP. LEAP also offers the capability to have alternate certificate schemes such as EAP-TLS.

Per-Packet Authentication

EAP can support per-packet authentication and integrity protection, but this authentication and integrity protection is not extended to all types of EAP messages. For example, NAK (negative acknowledgment) and notification messages are not able to use per-packet authentication and integrity. Per-packet authentication and integrity protection works for the following (packet is encrypted unless otherwise noted):

- TLS and IKE derive session key
- TLS ciphersuite negotiations (not encrypted)
- IKE ciphersuite negotiations
- Kerberos tickets
- Success and failure messages that use derived session key (through WEP)

Designing & Planning...

Preventing Dictionary Attacks Using EAP

EAP was designed to support extended authentication. When you implement EAP, you can avoid dictionary attacks by using nonpassword-based schemes such as biometrics, certificates, OTP, smart cards, and token cards.

You should be sure that if you are using password-based schemes that they use some form of mutual authentication so that they are more protected against dictionary attacks.

Possible Implementation of EAP on the WLAN

There are two main authentication methods for EAP on your wireless LAN: One is EAP-MD5, and the other is to use PKI with EAP-TLS. EAP-MD5 has a couple of issues because it does not support the capability for mutual authentication between the access server and the wireless client. The PKI schemes also has drawbacks, because it is very computation-intensive on the client systems, you need a high degree of planning and design to make sure that your network is capable of supporting PKI, and it is not cheap.

Cisco Light Extensible Authentication Protocol

LEAP is an enhancement to the EAP protocol, and as you remember, the EAP protocol was created in an effort to provide a scalable method for a PPP-based server to authenticate its clients and, hopefully allow for mutual authentication. An extensible packet exchange should allow for the passing of authentication information between the client devices and the PPP servers. The thing is that PPP servers usually rely on a centralized authentication server system that can validate the clients for them. This is where a RADIUS or a TACACS+ server usually comes into play.

This reason that the servers can work is that the servers have a protocol that will enable them to pass EAP packets between the authentication server and the PPP server. Essentially this makes the PPP server a passthrough or a relay agent, so that the authentication process happens between the client and the RADIUS server. The RADIUS server will then tell the PPP server the results of the authentication process (pass/fail) that will allow the client to access the network and its resources.

To make sure that all types of network access servers could be implemented to validate clients to network resources, the EAP protocol was created. Because we are talking about wireless connections though, the link between the AP and the client is not PPP but WLAN.

When the 802.11 specifications were standardized, it allowed for the encryption of data traffic between APs and clients through the use of a WEP encryption key. When it was first implemented, the AP would have a single key, and this key had to be configured on each client. All traffic would be encrypted using this single key. Well, this type of security has a lot of issues. In current implementations that use EAP authentication, the client and RADIUS server have a shared secret; generally this is some permutation of a username and password combination. The server will then pass certain information to the AP so that the client and AP can derive encryption keys that are unique for this client-AP pair. This is called Cisco LEAP authentication.

The previous section discussed the implementation methods of EAP (EAP-MD5, and PKI with EAP-TLS), and some of the issues that you can expect to see when you plan to implement them. LEAP may be a better option because it can offer mutual authentication, it needs only minimal support from the client's CPU, it can support embedded systems, and it can support clients whose operating system does not have the support for native EAP or allow for the use of the PKI authentication.

LEAP authentication works through three phases: the *start phase*, the *authenticate phase*, and the *finish phase*. The following sections show the process that the client and AP go through so that the client can also talk to the RADIUS server.

Start Phase for LEAP Authentication

In the start phase, information (in packet form) is transferred between the client and APs:

1. The EAPOW-Start (this is also called EAPOL-Start in 802.1x for wired networks) starts the authentication process. This packed is sent from the client to the AP.

2. The EAP-Request/Identity is sent from the AP to the client with a request for the clients Identity.

3. The EAP-Response/Identity is sent from the client to the AP with the required information.

Authentication Phase for LEAP Authentication

This sequence will change based on the mutual authentication method you choose for the client and the authentication server. If you were to use TLS for the transfer of certificates in a PKI deployment, EAP-TLS messages will be used, but because we are talking about LEAP, it would go more like this:

1. The client sends an EAP-Response/Identity message to the RADIUS server through the AP as a RADIUS-Access-Request with EAP extensions.

2. The RADIUS server then returns access-request with a RADIUS-challenge, to which the client must respond.

Cisco LEAP authentication is a mutual authentication method, and the AP is only a passthrough. The AP in the authenticate phase forwards the contents of the packets from EAP to RADIUS and from Radius to EAP.

The (Big) Finish Phase of LEAP Authentication

The steps for the finish phase are as follows:

1. If the client is considered invalid, the RADIUS server will send a RADIUS deny packet with an EAP fail packet embedded within it. If the client is considered to be valid, the server will send a RADIUS request packet with an EAP success attribute.

2. The RADIUS-Access-Accept packet contains the MS-MPPE-Send-Key attribute to the AP, where it obtains the session key that will be used by client.

The RADIUS server and client both create a session key from the user's password, when using LEAP. The encryption for the IEEE 802.11 standard can be based on a 40/64-bit or 104/128-bit key. Note that the key derivation process will create a key that is longer than is required. This is so that when the AP receives the key from the RADIUS server (using MS-MPPE-Send-Key attribute), it will send an EAPOL-KEY message to the client. This key will tell the client the key length and what key index that it should use.

The key value isn't sent because the client has already created it on its own WEP key. The data packet is then encrypted using the full-length key. The AP will also send an EAPOL-KEY message that gives information about the length, key index, and value of the multicast key. This message is encrypted using the full-length session unicast key from the AP.

Configuration and Deployment of LEAP

In this section, we talk about the installation and requirements for a LEAP solution that consists of a client, an AP and a RADIUS server for key distribution in your network.

Client Support for LEAP

You can configure your client to use LEAP mode in one of two modes:

- **Network Logon Mode** In Network logon mode, an integrated network logon provides for a single-sign on for both the wireless network as well as Microsoft Networking. This will provide users with a transparent security experience. This is probably the most common method of authenticating into the wireless network (or the wired network).

- **Device Mode** In device mode, the wireless LAN stores the username/password identification, so that you can get non-interactive authentication into the wireless LAN. You will often see this on wireless appliances where the devices that can authenticate themselves through these preconfigured credentials are enough security.

Access Point Support for LEAP

Access points can provide 802.1x for 802.11 Authenticator support. In order to make this work, you need to take the following two steps in setting up 802.1x authenticator support:

- You need to configure the AP to use 40/64- or 104/128-bit WEP mode.
- You must give the LEAP RADIUS server address and configure the shared secret key that the AP and RADIUS server use, so that they can communicate securely.

Configuring your RADIUS server for LEAP

To configure the RADIUS server for authentication and key distribution users, you will need to do the following:

- You need to create the user databases.
- You need to configure the APs as Network Access Servers (NASs). This will enable users that are configured with Cisco-Aironet RADIUS extensions on the NAS to use RADIUS. RADIUS requests from the AP with EAP extensions are passed as described earlier.

Ensuring Authorization

Authorization is the rights and permissions granted to a user or application that enables access to a network or computing resource. Once a user has been properly identified and authenticated, authorization levels determine the extent of system rights that the user has access to.

Many of the early operating systems and applications deployed had very small authorization groups. Generally, only user groups and operator groups were available for defining a user's access level. Once more formal methods for approaching various authorization levels were defined, applications and servers started offering more discrete authorization levels. You can observe this by simply looking at any standard back-office application deployed today.

Many of them provide varying levels of access for users and administrators. For example, they could have several levels of user accounts allowing some users access to just view the information, while giving others the ability to update or query that information and have administrative accounts based on the authorization levels needed (such as being able to look up only specific types of customers, or run particular reports while other accounts have the ability to edit and create new accounts).

As shown in the previous authentication example, Cisco and others have implemented RADIUS authentication for their wireless devices. Now, utilizing stronger authentication methods, you can implement your authorization policies into your wireless deployments.

However, many wireless devices do not currently support external authorization validation. Plus, most deployments just ensure authorized access to the device. They do not control access to or from specific network segments. To fully restrict authorized users to the network devices they are authorized to utilize, you will still need to deploy an adaptive firewall between the AP and your network.

This is what was done earlier this year by two researchers at NASA (for more information, see www.nas.nasa.gov/Groups/Networks/Projects/Wireless; please be aware that this URL is case sensitive). To protect their infrastructure, but still provide access through wireless, they deployed a firewall segmenting their wireless and department network. They most likely hardened their wireless interfaces to the extent of the equipments' possibilities by utilizing the strongest encryption available to them, disabling SID broadcast, and allowing only authorized MAC addresses on the wireless network.

They then utilized the Dynamic Host Configuration Protocol (DHCP) on the firewall, and disabled it on their AP. This allowed them to expressly define which MAC addresses could receive an IP address, and what the lease lifetime of the IP address would be.

The researchers then went on to turn off all routing and forwarding between the wireless interface and the internal network. If anyone happened to be able to connect to the wireless network, they would still have no access to the rest of the computing resources of the department. Anyone wishing to gain further access would have to go to an SSL protected Web site on the firewall server and authenticate as a valid user. The Web server would authenticate the user against a local

RADIUS server, but they could have easily used any other form of user authentication (NT, SecurID, and so on).

Once the user was properly authenticated, the firewall would change the firewall rules for the IP address that user was supposed to be assigned to, allowing full access to only the network resources they are authorized to access.

Finally, once the lease expired or was released for any reason from the DHCP assigned IP address, the firewall rules would be removed and that user and their IP would have to re-authenticate through the Web interface to allow access to the network resources again.

MAC Filtering

In order to fully discuss the advantages and disadvantages of MAC filtering, let's have a short review on what a MAC address is. The term *MAC* stands for Media Access Control, and forms the lower layer in the Data-Link layer of the OSI model. The purpose of the MAC sublayer is to present a uniform interface between the physical networking media (copper/fiber/radio frequency) and the Logical Link Control portion of the Data-Link layer. These two layers are found onboard a NIC, whether integrated into a device or used as an add-on (PCI card or PCMCIA card).

What Is a MAC Address?

In order to facilitate delivery of network traffic, the MAC layer is assigned a unique address, which is programmed into the NIC at the time of manufacture. The operating system will associate an IP address with this MAC address, which allows the device to participate in an IP network. Because no other NIC in the world should have the same MAC address, it is easy to see why it could be a secure way to equate a specific user with the MAC address on his or her machine.

Now, let's look at an actual MAC address. For example, my laptop has a MAC address of 00-00-86-4C-75-48. The first three octets are called the organizationally unique identifier (OUI). The Institute of Electrical and Electronic Engineers controls these OUIs and assigns them to companies as needed. If you look up the 00-00-86 OUI on the IEEE's Web site (http://standards.ieee.org/regauth/oui/index.shtml), it will state that the manufacturer of this NIC is the 3Com Corporation.

Corporations can own several OUIs, and often acquire additional OUIs when they purchase other companies. For example, when Cisco purchased Aironet

Wireless Communications in 1999, they added the 00-40-96 OUI to the many others they have.

Some other OUIs you could see on your WLAN might be the following:

- **00-02-2D** Agere Communications (previously known as ORiNOCO)

- **00-10-E7** Breezecom

- **00-E0-03** Nokia Wireless

- **00-04-5A** Linksys

The remaining three octets in a MAC address are usually burned into the NIC during manufacture, thus assuring that duplicate addresses will not exist on a network. We say "usually" because this rule has a few exceptions. For example, in some redundancy situations, one NIC on a machine is able to assume the MAC address of the other NIC if the primary NIC fails. Some early 802.11 PCMCIA cards also had the capability to change their MAC address. Although not necessarily easy to do, changing the MAC address gives a user the ability to spoof the MAC address of another PCMCIA card. This could be used to circumvent MAC filtering or be employed in a denial of service (DoS) attack against a specific user.

Where in the Authentication/Association Process Does MAC Filtering Occur?

When a wireless device wants to connect to a WLAN, it goes though a two-part process called authentication and authorization. After both have been completed, the device is allowed access to the WLAN.

As mentioned earlier, when a wireless device is attempting to connect to a WLAN, it sends an authentication request to the AP (see Figure 15.4). This request will contain the SSID of the target network, or a null value if connecting to an open system. The AP will grant or deny authentication based on this string. Following a successful authentication, the requesting device will attempt to associate with the AP. It is at this point in time that MAC filtering plays its role. Depending on the AP vendor and administrative setup of the AP, MAC filtering either allows only the specified MAC addresses—blocking the rest, or it allows all MAC addresses—blocking specifically noted MACs. If the MAC address is allowed, the requesting device is allowed to associate with the AP.

Figure 15.4 MAC Filtering

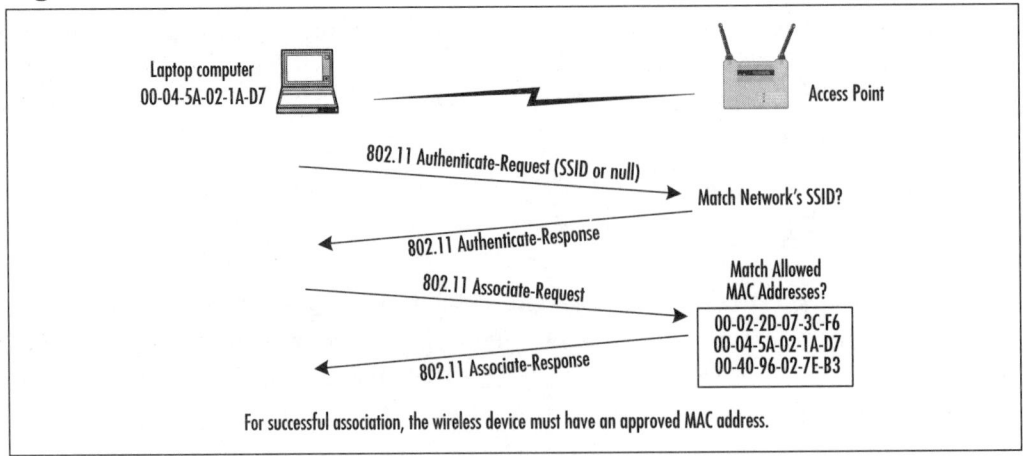

For successful association, the wireless device must have an approved MAC address.

Determining MAC Filtering Is Enabled

The easiest way to determine if a device has failed the association process due to MAC filtering is through the use of a protocol analyzer, like Sniffer Pro or AiroPeek. The difficulty here is that other factors besides MAC filtering could prevent association from occurring. RADIUS or 802.1x authentication, or an incorrect WEP key could also prevent this. These of course are costly mechanisms commonly seen in large corporate environments. Due to the costs involved with setting up the higher forms of non–AP-based authentication, most small businesses or home installations will use MAC filtering to limit access (if they use anything at all).

MAC Spoofing

If you discover that your MAC address is not allowed to associate with the AP, don't give up. There are other ways into the network besides the front door.

First off, just because you can't associate with the AP doesn't mean you can't sit there and passively watch the traffic. With 802.11b protocol analysis software, your laptop can see all the other stations' communication with any AP within range. Because the MAC addresses of the other stations are transmitted in clear text, it should be easy to start compiling a list of the MAC addresses allowed on the network.

Some early runs of 802.11 PCMCIA cards had the capability to modify their MAC addresses. Depending on the card and the level of firmware, the method to change your MAC address may vary. There are sites on the Internet that can give you more specific information on altering these parameters.

Once you have modified the MAC address, you should be able to associate it with the AP. Keep in mind however, that if the device bearing the MAC address you have stolen is still operating on the network, you will not be able to use your device. To allow the operation of two duplicate MAC addresses will break ARP tables and will attract a level of attention to your activities that is undesirable. The advanced hacker we are discussing would realize this. In attempts to subvert the security mechanisms, traffic would be monitored to sufficiently pattern the intended victim whose MAC address and identification are to be forged in order to avoid detection.

Ensuring Non-Repudiation

Repudiation is defined by West's Encyclopedia of American Law as "the rejection or refusal of a duty, relation, right or privilege." A repudiation of a transaction or contract means that one of the parties refuses to honor their obligation to the other as specified by the contract. Non-repudiation could then be defined as the ability to deny, with irrefutable evidence, a false rejection or refusal of an obligation.

In their paper "Non-Repudiation in the Digital Environment," Adrian McCullagh and William Caelli put forth an excellent review of the traditional model of non-repudiation and the current trends for crypto-technical non-repudiation. The paper was published online by First Monday—you can find it at www.firstmonday.dk/issues/issue5_8/mccullagh/index.html.

The basis for a repudiation of a traditional contract is sometimes associated with the belief that the signature binding a contract is a forgery, or that the signature is not a forgery but was obtained via unconscionable conduct by a party to the transaction, by fraud instigated by a third party, or undue influence exerted by a third party. In typical cases of fraud or repudiated contracts, the general rule of evidence is that if a person denies a particular signature, the burden of proving that the signature is valid falls upon the receiving party.

Common law trust mechanisms establish that in order to overcome false claims of non-repudiation, a trusted third party needs to act as a witness to the signature being affixed. Having a witness to the signature of a document, who is independent of the transactions taking place, reduces the likelihood that a signor is able to successfully allege that the signature is a forgery. However, there is always the possibility that the signatory will be able to deny the signature on the basis of the situations listed in the preceding paragraph.

A perfect example of a non-repudiation of submissions can be viewed by examining the process around sending and receiving registered mail. When you send a registered letter, you are given a receipt containing an identification number for the piece of mail sent. If the recipient claims that the mail was not sent, the receipt is proof that provides the non-repudiation of the submission. If a receipt is available with the recipient's signature, this provides the proof for the non-repudiation of the delivery service. The postal service provides the non-repudiation of transport service by acting as a Trusted Third Party (TTP).

Non-repudiation, in technical terms, has come to mean the following:

- In authentication, a service that provides proof of the integrity and origin of data both in an unforgeable relationship, which can be verified by any third party at any time; or

- In authentication, an authentication that with high assurance can be asserted to be genuine, and that cannot subsequently be refuted.

The Australian Federal Government's Electronic Commerce Expert group further adopted this technical meaning in their 1998 report to the Australian Federal Attorney General as:

> Non-repudiation is a property achieved through cryptographic methods which prevents an individual or entity from denying having performed a particular action related to data (such as mechanisms for non-rejection or authority (origin); for proof of obligation, intent, or commitment; or for proof of ownership.

In the digital realm, a movement is in place to shift the responsibility of proving that a digital signature is invalid to the owner of the signature, not the receiver of the signature, as is typically used in traditional common law methods.

In only a few examples does the burden of proof fall upon the alleged signer. One such example is usually found in taxation cases where the taxpayer has made specific claims and as such is in a better position to disprove the revenue collecting body's case. Another example would be in an instance of negligence. In a negligence action, if a plaintiff is able to prove that a defendant failed to meet their commitment, the burden of proof is in effect shifted to the defendant to establish that they have met their obligations.

The problem found in the new digital repudiation definitions that have been created is that they take into consideration only the validity of the signature itself. They do not allow for the possibility that the signor was tricked or forced into signing, or that their private key may be compromised, allowing the forgery of digital signatures.

With all the recent cases of Internet worms and viruses, it is not hard to imagine that one might be specifically built to steal private keys. A virus could be something as simple as a Visual Basic macro attached to a Word document, or an e-mail message that would search the targets hard drive looking for commonly named and located private key rings that could then be e-mailed or uploaded to some rogue location.

With this and other possible attacks to the private keys, it becomes difficult, under the common law position, for someone attempting to prove the identity of an alleged signatory. This common law position was established and founded in a paper-based environment where witnessing became the trusted mechanism utilized to prevent the non-repudiation of a signature. For a digital signature to be proven valid, however, it will need to be established through a fully trusted mechanism.

Thus, for a digitally signed contract to be trusted and not susceptible to repudiation, the entire document handling and signature process must take place within a secured and trusted computing environment. As we will see in some of the documentation to follow, the security policies and definitions created over the years have established a set of requirements necessary to create a secure and trusted computer system.

If we follow the definitions established in the Information Technology Security Evaluation Certification (ITSEC) to create a trusted computing environment of at least E3 to enforce functions and design of the signing process and thus prevent unauthorized access to the private key, the common law position for digitally signed documents can be maintained. E3 also ensures that the signing function is the only function able to be performed by the signing mechanism by having the source code evaluated to ensure that this is the only process available through the code. If these security features are implemented, it can be adequately assessed that under this mechanism the private key has not been stolen and as such that any digital signature created under this model has the trust established to ensure the TTP witness and validation of any signature created, preventing any possible repudiation from the signor.

One such example of a secure infrastructure designed and deployed to attempt to provide a digitally secure TTP are the PKI systems available for users of unsecure public networks such as the Internet. PKI consists of a secure computing system that acts as a certificate authority (CA) to issue and verify digital certificates. Digital certificates contain the public key and other identification information needed to verify the validity of the certificate. As long as the trust in the CA is maintained (and with it, the trust in the security of the private key), the digital certificates issued by the CA and the documents signed by them remain trusted. As long as the trust is ensured, then the CA acts as a TTP and provides for the non-repudiation of signatures created by entities with digital certificates issued through the CA.

Accounting and Audit Trails

Auditing provides methods for tracking and logging activities on networks and systems, and it links these activities to specific user accounts or sources of activity. In case of simple mistakes or software failures, audit trails can be extremely useful in restoring data integrity. They are also a requirement for trusted systems to ensure that the activity of authorized individuals on the trusted system can be traced to their specific actions, and that those actions comply with defined policy. They also allow for a method of collecting evidence to support any investigation into improper or illegal activities.

Most modern database applications support some level of transaction log detailing the activities that occurred within the database. This log could then be used to either rebuild the database if it had any errors or create a duplicate database at another location. To provide this detailed level of transactional logging, database logging tends to consume a great deal of drive space for its enormous log file. This intense logging is not needed for most applications, so you will generally have only basic informative messages utilized in system resource logging.

The logging features provided on most networks and systems involve the logging of known or partially known resource event activities. Although these logs are sometimes used for analyzing system problems, they are also useful for those whose duty it is to process the log files and check for both valid and invalid system activities.

To assist in catching mistakes and reducing the likelihood of fraudulent activities, the activities of a process should be split among several people. This segmentation of duties allows the next person in line to possibly correct problems simply because they are being viewed with fresh eyes.

From a security point of view, segmentation of duties requires the collusion of at least two people to perform any unauthorized activities. The following guidelines assist in assuring that the duties are split so as to offer no way other than collusion to perform invalid activities:

- **No access to sensitive combinations of capabilities** A classic example of this is control of inventory data and physical inventory. By separating the physical inventory control from the inventory data control, you remove the unnecessary temptation for an employee to steal from inventory and then alter the data so that the theft is left hidden.

- **Prohibit conversion and concealment** Another violation that can be prevented by segregation is ensuring that supervision is provided for people who have access to assets. An example of an activity that could be prevented if properly segmented follows a lone operator of a night shift. This operator, without supervision, could copy (or "convert") customer lists and then sell them off to interested parties. Instances have been reported of operators actually using the employer's computer to run a service bureau at night.

- **The same person cannot both originate and approve transactions** When someone is able to enter and authorize their own expenses, it introduces the possibility that they might fraudulently enter invalid expenses for their own gain.

These principles, whether manual or electronic, form the basis for why audit logs are retained. They also identify why people other than those performing the activities reported in the log should be the ones who analyze the data in the log file.

In keeping with the idea of segmentation, as you deploy your audit trails, be sure to have your logs sent to a secure, trusted, location that is separate and non-accessible from the devices you are monitoring. This will help ensure that if any inappropriate activity occurs, the person can't falsify the log to state that the actions did not take place.

Most wireless APs do not offer any method of logging activity, but if your equipment provides the feature, you should enable it and then monitor it for inappropriate activity using tools such as logcheck. Wireless AP logging should, if it's available, log any new wireless device with its MAC address upon valid WEP authentication. It should also log any attempts to access or modify the AP itself.

Using Encryption

Encryption has always played a key role in information security, and has been the center of controversy in the design of the WEP wireless standard. But despite the drawbacks, encryption will continue to play a major role in wireless security, especially with the adoption of new and better encryption algorithms and key management systems.

As we have seen in reviewing the basic concepts of security, many of the principles used to ensure the confidentiality, integrity, and availability of servers and services are through the use of some form of trusted and tested encryption. We also have seen that even with encryption, if we get tied up too much in the acceptance of the hard mathematics as evidence of validity, it is possible to be tricked into accepting invalid authorization or authentication attempts by someone who has been able to corrupt the encryption system itself by either acquiring the private key through cryptanalysis or stealing the private key from the end user directly.

Cryptography offers the obvious advantage that the material it protects cannot be used without the keys needed to unlock it. As long as those keys are protected, the material remains protected. There are a few potential disadvantages to encryption as well. For instance, if the key is lost, the data becomes unavailable, and if the key is stolen, the data becomes accessible to the thief.

The process of encryption also introduces possible performance degradation. When a message is to be sent encrypted, time must be spent to first encrypt the information, then store and transmit the encrypted data, and then later decode it. In theory, this can slow a system by as much as a factor of three.

Until recently, distribution and use of strong encryption was limited and controlled by most governments. The United States government had encryption listed as munitions, right next to cruise missiles! As such, it was very difficult to legally acquire and use strong encryption through the entire Internet. With the new changes in trade laws, however, it is now possible to use stronger encryption for internal use as well as with communications with customers and other third-parties.

Encrypting Voice Data

Voice communications have traditionally been a very simple medium to intercept and monitor. When digital cell and wireless phones arrived, there was a momentary window in which monitoring voice communications across these digital connections was difficult. Today, the only equipment needed to monitor cell phones or digital wireless telephones can be acquired at a local RadioShack for generally less than $100.

Most voice communication systems are not designed to ensure the privacy of the conversations on them, so a new industry was created to facilitate those needs. Originally designed for government and military usage, telephone encryption devices give people the option of encrypting their daily calls. A few of these devices are starting to make their way into the commercial market. Although a few are being slowed down by organizations such as the National Security Agency (NSA) and the Federal Bureau of Investigation (FBI), who argue that it will prevent their "legal" monitoring of criminal activities, consumer market needs should eventually push these devices into the mainstream.

The Internet, being a communications network, offers people the ability to communicate with anyone, anywhere. Because of this, it didn't take long for the appearance of applications enabling voice communications across the Internet. Many of the early versions, like all budding technologies, did not offer any protection methods for their users. As a result, people utilizing Internet voice communications programs could have their communications monitored by someone with access to the data stream between parties. Fortunately, encryption is making its way into some of these programs, and if you're careful, you should be able to find one that uses modern tested and secure encryption algorithms such as Twofish, a popular and publicly-available encryption algorithm created by Bruce Schneier.

Encrypting Data Systems

Data networks have traditionally been susceptible to threats from a trusted insider. However, as soon as someone connects their network to another entity, it introduces possible security compromises from outside sources. Remember, all forms of data communications, from simple modem lines to frame-relay and fiber-optic connections, can be monitored.

Reviewing the Role of Policy

Good policy is your first line of defense. A properly designed policy examines every threat (or tries to) and ensures that confidentiality, integrity, and availability are maintained (or at least cites the known and accepted risks). As we shall see, policy definition begins with a clear identification and labeling of resources being utilized that will build into specific standards that define acceptable use in what's considered an authorized and secure manner. Once a basic standard is defined, you start building specific guidelines and procedures for individual applications and services.

Many wireless manufacturers have responded to security threats hampering their initial product versions by releasing upgrades to their software and drivers. Your security policy should always require that all technology, either existing or newly deployed, have the latest security patches and upgrades installed in a timely manner. However, because the development and release of patches takes time, policy and its proper implementation tend to be the first layer of defense when confronting known and unknown threats.

A well-written policy should be more than just a list of recommended procedures. It should be an essential and fundamental element of your organization's security practices. A good policy can provide protection from liability due to an employee's actions, or can form a basis for the control of trade secrets. A policy or standard should also continue to grow and expand as new threats and technologies become available. They should be constructed with the input of an entire organization and audited both internally and externally to ensure that the assets they are protecting have the controls in place as specified in the standards, policies, and guidelines.

Designing & Planning...

The Management Commitment

Management must be aware of their needed commitment to the security of corporate assets, which includes protection of information. Measures must be taken to protect it from unauthorized modification, destruction, or disclosure (whether accidental or intentional), and ensure its authenticity, integrity, availability and confidentiality.

Fundamental to the success of any security program is senior management's commitment to the information security process and their understanding of how important security controls and protections are to the enterprise's continuity.

The senior management statement usually contains the following elements:

- An acknowledgment of the importance of computing resources to the business model

- A statement of support for information security throughout the enterprise

- A commitment to authorize and manage the definition of the lower level standards, procedures, and guidelines

Part of any policy definition includes what is required to ensure that the policy is adhered to. The prime object of policy controls is to reduce the effect of security threats and vulnerabilities to the resources being protected. The policy definition process generally entails the identification of what impact a threat would have on an organization, and what the likelihood of that threat occurring would be. Risk Analysis (RA) is the process of analyzing a threat and producing a representative value of that threat.

Figure 15.5 displays a matrix created using a small x–y graph representing the threat and the corresponding likelihood of that threat. The goal of RA is to reduce the level of impact and the likelihood that it will occur. A properly implemented control should move the plotted point from the upper right to the lower left of the graph.

Figure 15.5 Threat versus Likelihood Matrix

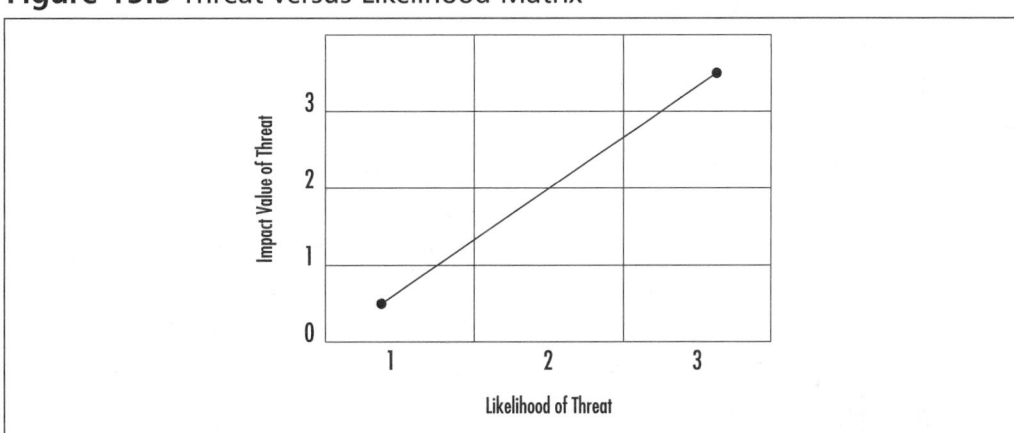

An improperly designed and implemented control will show little to no movement in the plotted point before and after the control's implementation.

Identifying Resources

To assess and protect resources, they must first be identified, classified, and labeled so that in the process of performing your risk analysis you are able to document all possible risks to each identified item and provide possible solutions to mitigate those risks.

Security classification provides the following benefits:

■ Demonstrates an organization's commitment to security procedures

- Helps identify which information is the most sensitive or vital to an organization

- Supports the tenets of confidentiality, integrity, and availability as it pertains to data

- Helps identify which protections apply to which information

- May be required for regulatory, compliance, or legal reasons

In the public sector, the common categories utilized in the classification of resources are the following:

- **Public** These are no-risk items that can be disclosed to anyone, as long as they do not violate any individual's right to privacy, and knowledge of this information does not expose an organization to financial loss or embarrassment, or jeopardize security assets. Examples of public information include marketing brochures, published annual reports, business cards, and press releases.

- **Internal Use** These are low-risk items that due to their technical or business sensitivity are limited to an organization's employees and those contractors covered by a nondisclosure agreement. Should there be unauthorized disclosure, compromise, or destruction of the documents, there would only be minimal impact on the organization, its customers, or employees. Examples of Internal Use information include employee handbooks, telephone directories, organizational charts, and policies.

- **Confidential** These are moderate-risk items whose unauthorized disclosure, compromise, or destruction would directly or indirectly impact an organization, its customers, or employees, possibly causing financial damage to an organization's reputation, a loss of business, and potential legal action. They are intended solely for use within an organization and are limited to those individuals who have a "need-to-know" security clearance. Examples of confidential items include system requirements or configurations, proprietary software, personnel records, customer records, business plans, budget information, and security plans and standards.

- **Restricted** These are high-risk critical items whose unauthorized disclosure, compromise, or destruction would result in severe damage to a company, providing significant advantages to a competitor, or causing penalties to the organization, its customers, or employees. It is intended solely for restricted use within the organization and is limited to those with an explicit, predetermined, and stringent "business-need-to-know." Examples of restricted data include strategic plans, encryption keys, authentication information (passwords, PINs, and so on), and IP addresses for security-related servers.

All information, whether in paper, spoken, or electronic form should be classified, labeled, and distributed in accordance to your information classification and handling procedures. This will assist in the determination of what items have the largest threat, and as such, should determine how you set about providing controls for those threats.

Your wireless network contains a few internal items that should be identified and classified, however the overall classification of any network device comes down the level of information that flows through its channels. While using e-mail systems or accessing external sites through your wireless network, you will likely find that your entire network contains restricted information. However, if you are able to encrypt the password, the classification of your network data will then be rated based upon the non-authentication information traveling across your wireless network.

Understanding Classification Criteria

To assist in your risk analysis, you can use a few additional criteria to determine the classification of information resources:

- **Value** Value is the most commonly used criteria for classifying data in the private sector. If something is valuable to an individual or organization, that will prompt the data to be properly identified and classified.

- **Age** Information is occasionally reclassified to a lower level as time passes. In many government organizations, some classified documents are automatically declassified after a predetermined time period has passed.

- **Useful Life** If information has become obsolete due to new information or resources, it is usually reclassified.

- **Personal Association** If information is associated with specific individuals or is covered under privacy law, it may need to be reclassified at some point.

Implementing Policy

Information classification procedures offer several steps in establishing a classification system, which provides the first step in the creation of your security standards and policies. The following are the primary procedural steps used in establishing a classification system:

1. Identify the administrator or custodian.

2. Specify the criteria of how the information will be classified and labeled.

3. Classify the data by its owner, who is subject to review by a supervisor.

4. Specify and document any exceptions to the classification policy.

5. Specify the controls that will be applied to each classification level.

6. Specify the termination procedures for declassifying the information or for transferring custody of the information to another entity.

7. Create an enterprise awareness program about the classification controls.

Once your information and resources are properly identified and classified, you will be able to define the controls necessary to ensure the privacy and security of information regarding your employees and customers. Many industries are required, either by regulation or civil law, to ensure that proper policy is in place to protect the security and privacy of nonpublic personal information. This relationship of policy, guidelines, and legal standards is shown in Figure 15.6.

Figure 15.6 The Hierarchy of Rules

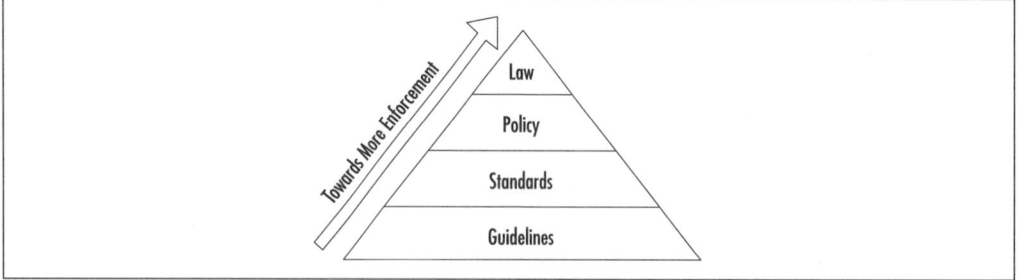

Guidelines refer to the methodologies of securing systems. Guidelines are more flexible than standards or policies and take the varying nature of information systems into consideration as they are developed and deployed, usually offering specific processes for the secure use of information resources. Many organizations have general security guidelines regarding a variety of platforms available within them: NT, SCO-UNIX, Debian Linux, Red Hat Linux, Oracle, and so on.

Standards specify the use of specific technologies in a uniform way. Although they are often not as flexible as guidelines, they do offer wider views to the technology specified. Usually, standards are in place for general computer use, encryption use, information classification, and others.

Policies are generally statements created for strategic or legal reasons, from which the standards and guidelines are defined. Some policies are based on legal requirements placed on industries such as health insurance, or they can be based upon common law requirements for organizations retaining personal nonpublic information of their customers.

Policies, standards, and guidelines must be explicit and focused, and they must effectively communicate the following subjects:

- Responsibility and authority
- Access control
- The extent to which formal verification is required
- Discretionary/mandatory control (generally relevant only in government or formal policy situations)
- Marking/labeling
- Control of media
- Import and export of data
- Security and classification levels
- Treatment of system output

The intent of policy is to delineate what an organization expects in the information security realm. Reasonable policy should also reflect any relevant laws and regulations that impact the use of information within an organization.

The System Administration, Networking, and Security Institute (SANS) offers excellent resources for implementing security standards, policies, and guidelines. You can find more information on policy implementation at the SANS Web site at www.sans.org/newlook/resources/policies/policies.htm. There you'll find example policies regarding encryption use, acceptable use, analog/ISDN lines, anti-virus software, application service providers, audits, and many others.

In this section's sidebar, "Sample Wireless Communication Policy," you will find the example wireless policy that defines the standards used for wireless communications.

Designing & Planning...

Sample Wireless Communication Policy

1.0 Purpose

This policy prohibits access to <Company Name> networks via unsecured wireless communication mechanisms. Only wireless systems that meet the criteria of this policy or have been granted an exclusive waiver by InfoSec are approved for connectivity to <Company Name>'s networks.

2.0 Scope

This policy covers all wireless data communication devices (for example, personal computers, cellular phones, PDAs, and so on) connected to any of <Company Name>'s internal networks. This includes any form of wireless communication device capable of transmitting packet data. Wireless devices and/or networks without any connectivity to <Company Name>'s networks do not fall under the purview of this policy.

3.0 Policy

To comply with this policy, wireless implementations must: maintain point-to-point hardware encryption of at least 56 bits; maintain a hardware address that can be registered and tracked (for instance, a MAC address); support strong user authentication which checks against an external database such as TACACS+, RADIUS, or something similar.

Exception: a limited-duration waiver to this policy for Aironet products has been approved if specific implementation instructions are followed for corporate and home installations.

4.0 Enforcement

Any employee found to have violated this policy may be subject to disciplinary action, up to and including termination of employment.

5.0 Definitions

Terms	Definitions
User Authentication	A method by which the user of a wireless system can be verified as a legitimate user independent of the computer or operating system being used.

6.0 Revision History

Addressing the Issues with Policy

Wireless users have unique needs that policy must address. The administrator must take diligent care in creating effective policy to protect the users, their data, and corporate assets. But just what is an effective policy for wireless users? Let's look at some common sense examples of good wireless policy.

First, wireless LANs are an "edge" technology. As such, policy should reflect a standard consistent with end users attempting to gain access to network resources from "the edge." In the case of wired LANs, typically you would set some standard physical access restrictions. This type of restriction would protect the LAN from certain types of attacks. You might also create group policy on the PC for authentication and access restrictions to corporate domains, and so long as there is no inside threat, the LAN is secured. (This scenario is unlikely in that disgruntled employees are representative of a solid portion of network hacking/misuse.) If you can't physically access the media, you cannot break in. If you do not furnish a valid username and password despite physical access, in most cases you cannot break in. Certainly some other methods of attack exist so long as you have physical access, but for all intents and purposes in this discussion, the typical, aspiring hacker is locked out. This assists in implementing the more stringent rule set as required by edge and remote access.

In a wireless environment, the rules change. How do you stop access to RF? RF travels through, around, and is reflected off objects, walls, and other physical barriers. RF doesn't have the feature-rich security support that the typical wired network has. Even though you can use the features of the wired Ethernet/IP security model after you are connected to the LAN, what about the signal from the AP to the client and vice-versa? Because of this access methodology, wireless poses some interesting policy challenges.

You can overcome one of these challenges—ease of capture of RF traffic—by preventing the broadcast of the Secure Set Identifier (SSID) to the world from the AP. Much like the Network Basic Input/Output System (NETBIOS) in the Windows world that broadcasts shares, the AP typically broadcasts the SSID to allow clients to associate. This is an advertisement for access to what you would like to be a restricted WLAN. Therefore, a good policy in the WLAN space is to prevent the AP from broadcasting this information. Instead, set up the AP to respond only to clients that already have the required details surrounding the Basic Service Set (BSS). This means that when the client attempts to associate, the AP challenges the client for the SSID and WEP encryption key information before allowing access. Of course, there are still ways to capture the traffic, but with this minor policy rule, the level of difficulty has been exponentially increased from the default implementation.

This security policy works well in the WLAN space until a technically savvy, but security ignorant, user installs a rogue AP because they wish to have their own personal AP connected to the WLAN. This poses a strong threat to the overall network security posture and must be prohibited.

What's in a name? It's imperative that you set in place a standard naming convention and WEP policy to prevent the standard defaults from being utilized. You wouldn't want your password published to the world in a set of instructions on how to access your PC, but that is exactly the case when speaking of WLAN defaults. They are published, documented, and presented as the default settings of the wireless space built from that specific hardware, and this is a *good* thing. Without this information, you would not be able to implement the hardware. However, to prevent unauthorized access, it's critical that you do not leave the default settings in place. A further consideration would be not using easily guessed names such as the company name. This should be part of your security policy for new hardware/software integration and goes toward assisting in the mitigation of capturing RF traffic.

With respect to roaming needs, these policies should not change from room to room or AP to AP. A consistent rule set (more stringent than normally internally trusted users) should be put in place across all APs where users are likely to roam while connected wirelessly. When choosing your AP, you can also add to ease of use for your wireless users by getting hardware that supports true roaming as opposed to having to lose connectivity momentarily while re-associating with another AP. The temporary loss of connectivity could lead to account lock out and the need to re-authenticate in upper layers.

Finally, strong authentication and encryption methods makes attacking the access mechanisms even more difficult, which is why the organization must include the appropriate use of authentication and encryption in its policy. Use of RADIUS or VPN solutions for authentication and tunneling sits nicely in the gap for the added protection. These authentication tools even serve as a standalone security feature for open networks where disabling the SSID is not an option.

All in all, policy should reflect these general guidelines if you intend to secure the WLAN access to corporate assets. We explore each in detail throughout this chapter to give you the information you need to secure your WLAN. Don't make the mistake of using just one of these options. Instead, look at your security policy as a tightly bound rope consisting of multiple threads. Each thread is another layer of security. In this case, your security policy will remain strong despite the failure of one or two threads. At no time do you want one solution to be the only boundary between maintaining your valuables and losing them.

Implementing WEP

Despite its critics, WEP still offers a reasonable level of security, providing that all its features are used properly. This means greater care in key management, avoiding default options, and making sure adequate encryption is enabled at every opportunity.

Proposed improvements in the standard should overcome many of the limitations of the original security options, and should make WEP more appealing as a security solution. Additionally, as WLAN technology gains popularity, and users clamor for functionality, both the standards committees as well as the hardware vendors will offer improvements. This means that you should make sure to keep abreast of vendor-related software fixes and changes that improve the overall security posture of your WLAN.

Most APs advertise that they support WEP in at least 40-bit encryption, but often the 128-bit option is also supported. For corporate networks, 128-bit encryption–capable devices should be considered as a minimum. With data security enabled in a closed network, the settings on the client for the SSID and the encryption keys have to match the AP when attempting to associate with the network, or it will fail. In the next few paragraphs, we discuss WEP as it relates to the functionality of the standard, including a standard definition of WEP, the privacy created, and the authentication.

Defining WEP

802.11, as a standard, covers the communication between WLAN components. RF poses challenges to privacy in that it travels through and around physical objects. As part of the goals of the communication, a mechanism needed to be implemented to protect the privacy of the individual transmissions that in some way mirrored the privacy found on the wired LAN. Wireless Equivalency Privacy is the mechanism created in the standard as a solution that addresses this goal. Because WEP utilizes a cryptographic security countermeasure for the fulfillment of its stated goal of privacy, it has the added benefit of becoming an authentication mechanism. This benefit is realized through a shared key authentication that allows the encryption and decryption of the wireless transmissions. Many keys can be defined on an AP or a client, and they can be rotated to add complexity for a higher security standard for your WLAN policy. This is a must!

WEP was never intended to be the absolute authority in security. Instead, the driving force was privacy. In cases that require high degrees of security, you should utilize other mechanisms, such as authentication, access control, password protection, and virtual private networks.

Creating Privacy with WEP

Let's look at how WEP creates a degree of privacy on the WLAN. WEP comes in several implementations: no encryption, and 40-bit and 128-bit encryption. Obviously, no encryption means no privacy. Transmissions are sent in the clear, and they can be viewed by any wireless sniffing application that has access to the RF propagated in the WLAN. In the case of the 40- and 128-bit varieties (just as with password length), the greater the number of characters (bits), the stronger the encryption. The initial configuration of the AP will include the setup of the shared key. This shared key can be in the form of either alphanumeric, or hexadecimal strings, and is matched on the client.

WEP uses the RC4 encryption algorithm, a stream cipher developed by noted cryptographer Ron Rivest (the "R" in RSA). Both the sender and receiver use the stream cipher to create identical pseudorandom strings from a known shared key. The process entails the sender to logically XOR the plaintext transmission with the stream cipher to produce the ciphertext. The receiver takes the shared key and identical stream and reverses the process to gain the plaintext transmission.

A 24-bit initialization vector (IV) is used to create the identical cipher streams. The IV is produced by the sender, and is included in the transmission of each frame. A new IV is used for each frame to prevent the reuse of the key weakening the encryption. This means that for each string generated, a different value for the RC4 key will be used. Although a secure policy, consideration of the components of WEP bear out one of the flaws in WEP. Because the 24-bit space is so small with respect to the potential set of IVs, in a short period of time, all keys are eventually reused. Unfortunately, this weakness is the same for both the 40- and 128-bit encryption levels.

To protect against some rudimentary attacks that insert known text into the stream to attempt to reveal the key stream, WEP incorporates a checksum in each frame. Any frame not found to be valid through the checksum is discarded. All in all this sounds secure, but WEP has well-documented flaws, which we cover in later sections. Let's review the process in a little more detail to gain a better understanding of the behind-the-scenes activities that are largely the first line of defense in WLAN security.

The WEP Authentication Process

Shared key authentication is a four-step process that begins when the AP receives the validated request for association. After the AP receives the request, a series of management frames are transmitted between the stations to produce the authentication. This includes the use of the cryptographic mechanisms employed by WEP as a validation.

Strictly with respect to WEP, in the authorization phase, the four steps break down in the following manner:

1. The requestor (the client) sends a request for association.

2. The authenticator (the AP) receives the request, and responds by producing a random challenge text and transmitting it back to the requestor.

3. The requestor receives the transmission, ciphers the challenge with the shared key stream, and returns it.

4. The authenticator decrypts the challenge text and compares the values against the original. If they match, the requestor is authenticated. On the other hand, if the requestor doesn't have the shared key, the cipher stream cannot be reproduced, therefore the plaintext cannot be discovered, and theoretically, the transmission is secured.

WEP Benefits and Advantages

WEP provides some security and privacy in transmissions to prevent curious or casual browsers from viewing the contents of the transmissions held between the AP and the clients. In order to gain access, the degree of sophistication of the intruder has to improve, and specific intent to gain access is required. Let's view some of the other benefits of implementing WEP:

- All messages are encrypted using a checksum to provide some degree of tamper resistance.

- Privacy is maintained via the encryption. If you do not have the key, you can't decrypt the message.

- WEP is extremely easy to implement. Set the encryption key on the AP, repeat the process on each client, and voilà! You're done!

- WEP provides a very basic level of security for WLAN applications.

- WEP keys are user definable and unlimited. You do not have to use pre-defined keys, and you can and should change them often.

WEP Disadvantages

As with any standard or protocol, WEP has some inherent disadvantages. The focus of security is to allow a balance of access and control while juggling the advantages and disadvantages of each implemented countermeasure for security gaps. The following are some of the disadvantages of WEP:

- The RC4 encryption algorithm is a known stream cipher. This means it takes a finite key and attempts to make an infinite pseudorandom key stream in order to generate the encryption.

- Once you alter the key—which you should do often—you have to tell everyone so they can adjust their settings. The more people you tell, the more public the information becomes.

- Used on its own, WEP does not provide adequate WLAN security.

- WEP has to be implemented on every client as well as every AP to be effective.

The Security Implications of Using WEP

From a security perspective, you have mitigated the curious hacker who lacks the means or desire to really hack your network. If you have enabled WEP as instructed in the previous pages, someone has to be actively attempting to break into your network in order to be successful. If that is the case, using the strongest form of WEP available is important. Because WEP relies on a known stream cipher, it is vulnerable to certain attacks. By no means is it the final authority and should not be the only security countermeasure in place to protect your network—and ultimately your job!

Implementing WEP on the Cisco Aironet AP 340

As you can see in the following, the Cisco AP340 supports 128-bit encryption. It is configured with either a HTTP connection pictured here, or a serial connection. The serial interface is cryptic and in no way intuitive. If you plan on administering many Cisco wireless devices, use the Web interface. In Figure 15.7, you see the Web interface for an AP340. By using the drop-down menu, you can select **Full Encryption** and then **128 bit** for the key size. Finally, select the **WEP Key** radio button for the transmission key and type the string.

Figure 15.7 WEP Configuration on the Aironet

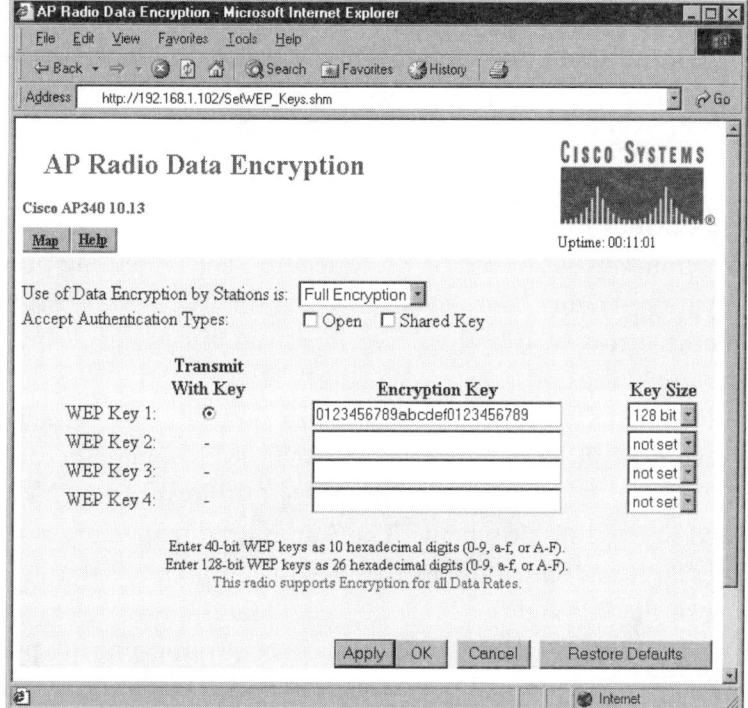

Exploiting WEP

There have been a number of well-publicized exploitations and defeats of the security mechanisms at the heart of WEP, from weaknesses in the encryption algorithm to weaknesses in key management. Although steps have been taken to overcome these weaknesses, attackers are not suffering from a lack of networks to exploit.

The first warnings regarding WEP's vulnerability to compromise came in the fall of 2000 when Jesse Walker published a document called "Unsafe at any Size: An Analysis of the WEP Encryption." In this document, Walker underscored the main weakness of WEP—the fact that it reinitializes the encrypted data stream every time an Ethernet collision occurs. Even though the 802.11 protocol attempts to avoid them with CDMA/CA, collisions are a reality that will occur. If someone is listening in on the wireless conversation, they capture the initialation vector (IV) information transmitted with each frame and in a matter of hours have all the data needed to recover the WEP key.

Although many experts have made similar discoveries regarding this and other ways to recover WEP keys, these were usually academic and only showed that the potential for vulnerability existed. This all changed with the introduction of AirSnort and WEPCrack. Both of these programs saw an initial release in the summer of 2001, and moved the recovery of WEP keys from being a theoretical to something anyone could do—if they had a wireless card based on the Prism2 chipset.

Security of 64-Bit versus 128-Bit Keys

It might seem obvious to a nontechnical person that something protected with a 128-bit encryption scheme would be more secure than something protected with a 64-bit encryption scheme. This, however, is not the case with WEP. Because the same vulnerability exists with both encryption levels, they can be equally broken within similar time limits.

With 64-bit WEP, the network administrator specifies a 40-bit key—typically ten hexadecimal digits (0–9, a–f, or A–F). A 24-bit IV is appended to this 40-bit key, and the RC4 key scheme is built from these 64-bits of data. This same process is followed in the 128-bit scheme. The Administrator specifies a 104-bit key—this time 26 hexadecimal digits (0-9, a-f, or A-F). The 24-bit IV is added to the beginning of the key, and the RC4 key schedule is built.

As you can see, because the vulnerability comes from capturing predictably weak IVs, the size of the original key would not make a significant difference in the security of the encryption. This is due to the relatively small number of total IVs possible under the current WEP specification. Currently, there are a total of 2^{24} possible IV keys. You can see that if the WEP key was not changed within a strictly-defined period of time, all possible IV combinations could be heard off of a 802.11b connection, captured, and made available for cracking within a short period of time. This is a flaw in the design of WEP, and bears no correlation to whether the wireless client is using 64-bit WEP or 128-bit WEP.

Acquiring a WEP Key

As mentioned previously, programs exist that allow an authenticated and/or unassociated device within the listening area of the AP to capture and recover the WEP key. Depending on the speed of the machine listening to the wireless conversations, the number of wireless hosts transmitting on the WLAN, and the number of IV retransmissions due to 802.11 frame collisions, the WEP key could be cracked as quickly as a couple of hours. Obviously, if an attacker attempts to listen to a WEP-protected network when there was very little network traffic, it would take much longer to be able to get the data necessary to crack WEP.

Armed with a valid WEP key, an intruder can now successfully negotiate association with an AP, and gain entry onto the target network. Unless other mechanisms like MAC filtering are in place, this intruder is now able to roam across the network and potentially break into servers or other machines on the network. If MAC filtering is occurring, another procedure must be attempted to get around this. This was covered earlier in the "MAC Filtering" section.

WARNING

Because WEP key retrieval is now possible by casual attackers, keeping the same static WEP key in a production role for an extended period of time does not make sense. If your WEP key is static, it could be published into the underground by a hacker and still be used in a production WLAN six months to a year later.

One of the easiest ways to mitigate the risk of WEP key compromise is to regularly change the WEP key your APs and clients use. Although this may be an easy task for small WLANs, the task becomes extremely daunting when you have dozens of APs and hundreds of clients to manually rekey.

Both Cisco and Funk Software have released Access Control servers that implement rapid WEP rekeying on both APs as well as the end-user client. Utilizing this form of software, even if a WEP key was to be discovered, you could rest assured that within a specified period of time, that particular key would no longer be valid.

Addressing Common Risks and Threats

The advent of wireless networks has not created new legions of attackers. Many attackers will utilize the same attacks for the same objectives they used in wired networks. If you do not protect your wireless infrastructure with proven tools and techniques, and do not have established standards and policies that identify proper deployment and security methodology, you will find that the integrity of your wireless networks may be threatened.

Finding a Target

Utilizing new tools created for wireless networks and thousands of existing identification and attack techniques and utilities, attackers of wireless networks have many avenues to your network. The first step to attacking a wireless network involves finding a network to attack. The first popular software to identify wireless networks was NetStumbler (www.netstumbler.org). NetStumbler is a Windows application that listens for information, such as the SSID, being broadcast from APs that have not disabled the broadcast feature. When it finds a network, it notifies the person running the scan and adds it to the list of found networks.

As people began to drive around their towns and cities looking for wireless networks, NetStumbler added features such as pulling coordinates from Global Positioning System (GPS) satellites and plotting that information on mapping software. This method of finding networks is very reminiscent of a way hackers would find computers when they had only modems to communicate. They would run programs designed to search through all possible phone numbers and call each one looking for a modem to answer the call. This type of scan was typically referred to as *war dialing*; driving around looking for wireless networks has come to be known as *war driving*.

NetStumbler.org created place that people can upload the output of their war drives for inclusion in a database that can graph the location of wireless networks that have been found (www.netstumbler.org/nation.php). See Figure 15.8 for output of discovered and uploaded wireless networks as of January 2002.

Similar tools soon became available for Linux and other UNIX-based operating systems, which contained many additional utilities hackers use to attack hosts and networks once access is found. A quick search on www.freshmeat.net or www.packetstormsecurity.com for "802.11" will reveal several network identification tools as well as tools to configure and monitor wireless network connections.

Finding Weaknesses in a Target

If a network is found without encryption enabled, which reports are showing to be more than half of the networks found so far, the attacker has complete access to any resource the wireless network is connected to. They can scan and attack any machines local to the network, or launch attacks on remote hosts without any fear of reprisal, as the world thinks the attack is coming from the owner of the wireless network.

If the network is found with WEP enabled, the attacker will need to identify several items to reduce the time it will take to get onto the wireless network.

First, utilizing the output of NetStumbler or one of the other network discovery tools, the attacker will identify the SSID, network, MAC address, and any other packets that might be transmitted in cleartext. Generally, NetStumbler results include vendor information, which an attacker can use to determine which default keys to attempt on the wireless network.

Figure 15.8 Networks Discovered with NetStumbler (as of January 2002)

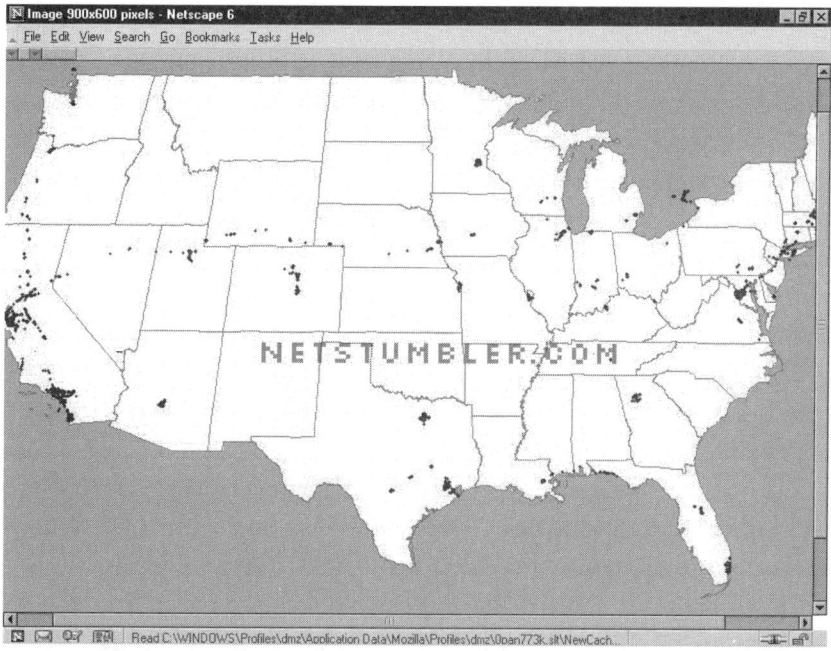

If the vendor information has been changed or is unavailable, the attacker can still use the SSID and network name and address to identify the vendor or owner of the equipment (many people use the same network name as the password, or use the company initials or street address as their password). If the SSID and network name and address has been changed from the default setting, a final network-based attempt could be to use the MAC address to identify the manufacturer.

If none of these options work, there is still the possibility of a physical review. Many public areas are participating in the wireless revolution. An observant attacker will be able to use physical and wireless identification techniques—such as finding antennas, APs, and other wireless devices that are easily identified by the manufacturer's casing and logo.

Exploiting Those Weaknesses

A well-configured wireless AP will not stop a determined attacker. Even if the network name and SSID are changed and the secret key is manually reconfigured on all workstations on a somewhat regular basis, the attacker will still take other avenues to compromise the network.

If easy access is available near to the wireless network, such as a parking lot or garage next to the building being attacked, the only thing an attacker needs is patience and AirSnort or WEPCrack. When these applications have captured enough "weak" packets (IV collisions, for example) they are able to determine the secret key currently in use on the network. Quick tests have shown that an average home network can be cracked in an overnight session. This means that to ensure your network protection, you would need to change your WEP key at least two times per day, or keep your eyes open for any vehicles that look suspicious (with an antenna sticking out the window, for instance) parked outside your home or business for hours or days at a time.

If none of these network tools help in determining which default configurations to try, the next step is to scan the traffic for any cleartext information that might be available. Some manufacturers, such as Lucent, have been known to broadcast the SSID in cleartext even when WEP and closed network options are enabled. Using tools such as Ethereal (www.ethereal.com) and TCPDump (www.tcpdump.org) allow the attacker to sniff traffic and analyze it for any cleartext hints they may find.

As a last option, the attacker will go directly after your equipment or install their own. The number of laptops or accessories stolen from travelers is rising each year. At one time these thefts were perpetrated by criminals simply looking to sell the equipment, but as criminals become more savvy, they are also after the information contained within the machines. Once you have access to the equipment, you are able to determine what valid MAC addresses can access the network, what the network SSID is, and what secret keys are to be used.

An attacker does not need to become a burglar in order to acquire this information. A skilled attacker will utilize new and specially designed malware and network tricks to determine the information needed to access your wireless network. A well-scripted Visual Basic script that could arrive in e-mail (targeted spam) or through an infected Web site can extract the information from the user's machine and upload it to the attacker.

With the size of computers so small today (note the products at www.mynix.com/espace/index.html and www.citydesk.pt/produto_ezgo.htm), it wouldn't take much for the attacker to simply create a small AP of their own that could be attached to your building or office and look just like another telephone box. Such a device, if placed properly, will attract much less attention than someone camping in a car or van in your parking lot.

Sniffing, Interception, and Eavesdropping

Originally conceived as a legitimate network and traffic analysis tool, sniffing remains one of the most effective techniques in attacking a wireless network, whether it's to map the network as part of a target reconnaissance, to grab passwords, or to capture unencrypted data.

Defining Sniffing

Sniffing is the electronic form of eavesdropping on the communications that computers have across networks. In the original networks deployed, the equipment tying machines together allowed every machine on the network to see the traffic of others. These repeaters and hubs, while very successful for getting machines connected, allowed an attacker easy access to all traffic on the network by only needing to connect to one point to see the entire network's traffic.

Wireless networks function very similar to the original repeaters and hubs. Every communication across the wireless network is viewable to anyone who happens to be listening to the network. In fact, the person listening does not even need to be associated with the network to sniff!

Sample Sniffing Tools

The hacker has many tools available to attack and monitor your wireless network. A few of these tools are Ethereal and AiroPeek (www.wildpackets.com/products/ airopeek) in Windows, and tcpdump or ngrep (http://ngrep.sourceforg.net) within a UNIX or Linux environment. These tools work well for sniffing both wired and wireless networks.

All of these software packages function by putting your network card in what is called *promiscuous mode*. When in this mode, every packet that goes past the interface is captured and displayed within the application window. If the attacker is able to acquire your WEP password, they can then utilize features within AiroPeek and Ethereal to decrypt either live or post-capture data.

Sniffing Case Scenario

By running NetStumbler, the hacker will be able to find possible targets. As shown in Figure 15.9, we have found several networks that we could attack.

Figure 15.9 Discovering Wireless LANS with NetStumbler

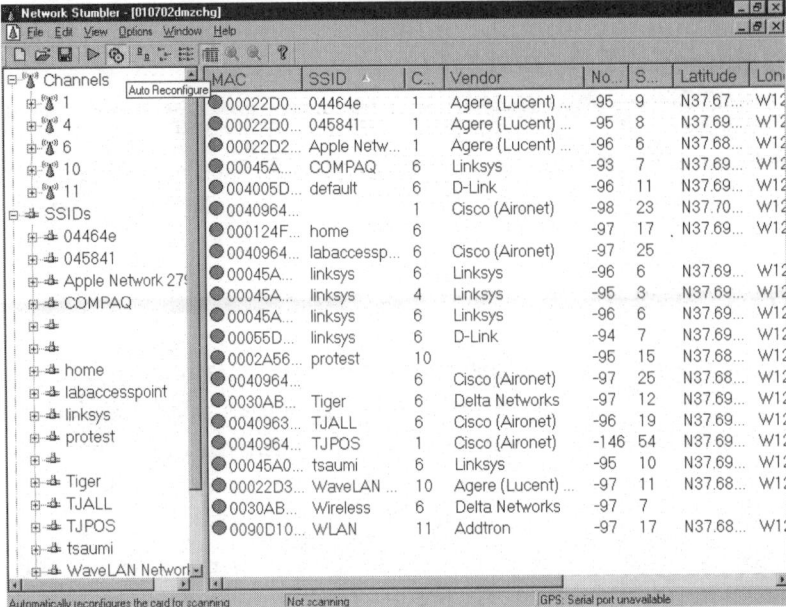

Once the hacker has found possible networks to attack, one of the first tasks is to identify who the target is. Many organizations are "nice" enough to include their name or address in the network name. For those that do not display that information, we can gather a lot from their traffic that allows us to determine who they could be.

Utilizing any of the mentioned network sniffing tools, the unencrypted network is easily monitored. Figure 15.10 shows our network sniff of the traffic on the wireless network. From this, we are able to determine who their Domain Name System (DNS) server is, and what default search domain and default Web home page they are accessing. With this information, we can easily identify who the target is and determine if they are worth attacking.

If the network is encrypted, the first place to start is locating the physical location of the target. NetStumbler has the capability to display the signal strength of the networks you have discovered (see Figure 15.11). Utilizing this information, the attacker needs to just drive around and look for where the signal strength increases and decreases to determine the home of the wireless network.

Figure 15.10 Sniffing with Ethereal

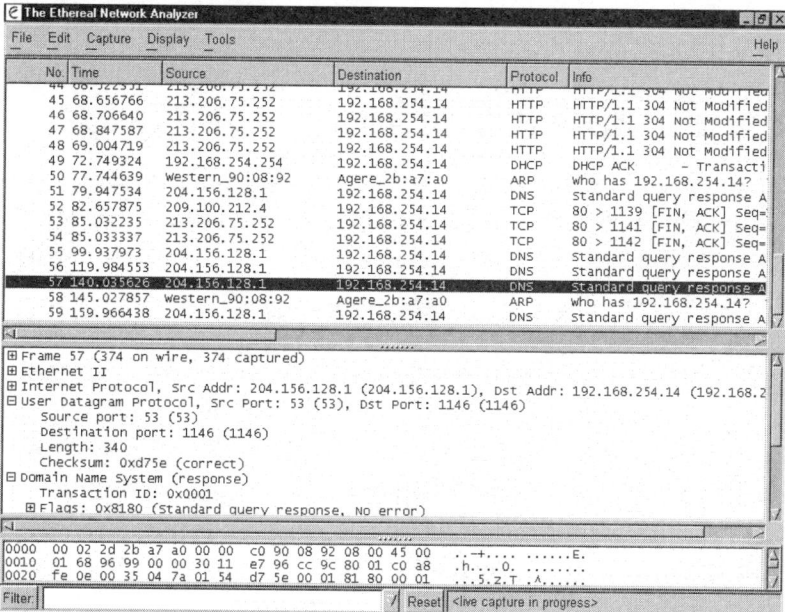

Figure 15.11 Using Signal Strength to Find Wireless Networks

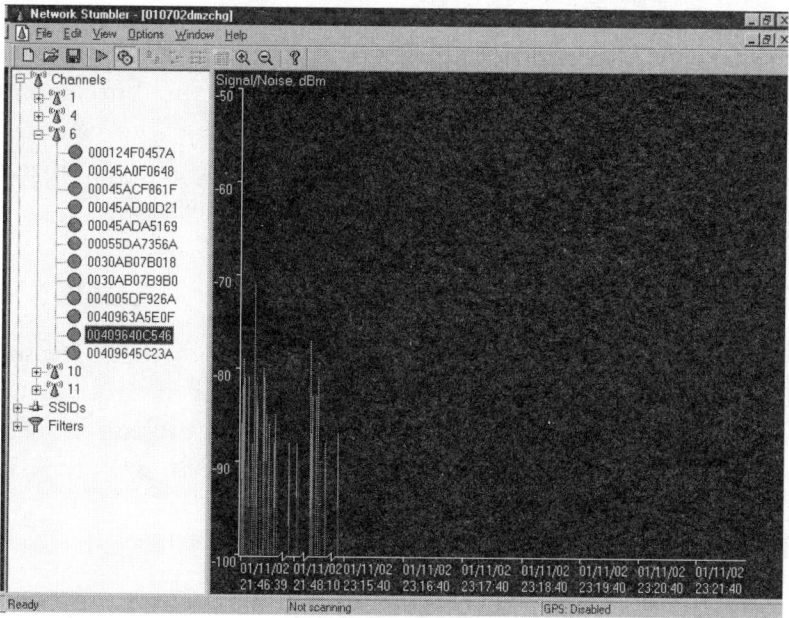

To enhance the ability to triangulate the position of the wireless network, the attacker can utilize directional antennas to focus the wireless interface in a

specific direction. An excellent source for wireless information, including information on the design of directional antennas is the Bay Area Wireless Users Group (www.bawug.org).

Protecting Against Sniffing and Eavesdropping

One protection available to wired networks was the upgrade from repeaters and hubs to a switched environment. These switches would send only the traffic intended over each individual port, making it difficult (although not impossible) to sniff the entire network's traffic. This is not an option for wireless due to the nature of wireless itself.

The only way to protect your wireless users from attackers who might be sniffing is to utilize encrypted sessions wherever possible: Use SSL for e-mail connections, SSH instead of Telnet, and Secure Copy (SCP) instead of FTP.

To protect your network from being discovered with NetStumbler, be sure to turn off any network identification broadcasts, and if possible, close down your network to any unauthorized users. This will prevent tools such as NetStumbler from finding your network to begin with. However, the knowledgeable attacker will know that just because you are not broadcasting your information does not mean that your network can't be found.

All the attacker needs to do is utilize one of the network sniffers to monitor for network activity. Although not as efficient as NetStumbler, it is still a functional way to discover and monitor networks. Even encrypted networks will show traffic to the sniffer, even if you are not broadcasting who you are. Once they have identified your traffic, the attacker will then be able to utilize the same identification techniques to begin an attack on your network.

Spoofing and Unauthorized Access

The combination of weaknesses in WEP, and the nature of wireless transmission, has highlighted the art of *spoofing* as a real threat to wireless network security. Some well publicized weaknesses in user authentication using WEP have made authentication spoofing just one of an equally well tested number of exploits by attackers.

Defining Spoofing

One definition of spoofing is where an attacker is able to trick your network equipment into thinking that the connection they are coming from is one of the valid and allowed machines from its network. Attackers can accomplish this several ways, the easiest of which is to simply redefine the MAC address of your wireless or network card to be a valid MAC address. This can be accomplished in Windows through a simple Registry edit. Several wireless providers also have an option to define the MAC address for each wireless connection from within the client manager application that is provided with the interface.

There are several reasons that an attacker would spoof your network. If you have closed out your network to only valid interfaces through MAC or IP address filtering, if an attacker is able to determine a valid MAC or IP address, he could then reprogram his interface with that information, allowing him to connect to your network impersonating a valid machine.

IEEE 802.11 networks introduce a new form of spoofing: authentication spoofing. As described in their paper "Intercepting Mobile Communications: The Insecurities of 802.11," the authors identified a way to utilize weaknesses within WEP and the authentication process to spoof authentication into a closed network. The process of authentication, as defined by IEEE 802.11, is a very simple process. In a shared-key configuration, the AP sends out a 128-byte random string in a cleartext message to the workstation wishing to authenticate. The workstation then encrypts the message with the shared key and returns the encrypted message to the AP. If the message matches what the AP is expecting, the workstation is authenticated onto the network and access is allowed.

As described in the paper, if an attacker has knowledge of both the original plaintext and ciphertext messages, it is possible to create a forged encrypted message. By sniffing the wireless network, an attacker is able to accumulate many authentication requests, each of which includes the original plaintext message and the returned ciphertext-encrypted reply. From this, the attacker can easily identify the keystream used to encrypt the response message. She could then use it to forge an authentication message that the AP will accept as a proper authentication.

Sample Spoofing Tools

The wireless hacker does not need many complex tools to succeed in spoofing a MAC address. In many cases, these changes are either features of the wireless manufacturers or easily changed through a Windows Registry modification. Once a valid MAC is identified, the attacker need only reconfigure his device to trick the AP into thinking they are a valid user.

The ability to forge authentication onto a wireless network is a complex process. There are no known "off the shelf" packages available that will provide these services. An attacker will need to either create their own tool or take the time to decrypt the secret key by using AirSnort or WEPCrack.

If the attacker is using Windows 2000, and his network card supports reconfiguring the MAC address, there is another way to reconfigure this information. If your card supports this feature, you can change it from the Control Panel by clicking the **System** icon. Once the System Properties dialog box appears, select the **Hardware** tab and choose **Device Manager**. Within the Device Manager, under the **Network Adaptors**, you should find your interface. If you open the properties to this interface, you should have an **Advanced** tab. Many network adaptors allow you to reconfigure the MAC address of the card from this area.

Now that the hacker is utilizing a valid MAC address, he is able to access any resource available from your wireless network. If you have WEP enabled, the hacker will have to either identify your secret key, or as you will see shortly, capture the key through malware or stealing the user's notebook.

Protecting Against Spoofing and Unauthorized Attacks

Little can be done to prevent these attacks. The best protection involves several additional pieces to the wireless network. Using an external authentication source, such as RADIUS or SecurID, will prevent an unauthorized user from accessing the wireless network and resources it connects with.

If the attacker has reconfigured her machine to use a valid MAC address, little can be done, except the additional external authentication. The only additional protection that you can provide is if you utilize secure connections for all host services accessed by the network. If you use SSH and SSL, you can require valid client certificates to access those resources. Even if a hacker were able to access the network, this would keep her from accessing your critical systems.

However, note that even with this, and without utilizing either a dynamic firewall or RADIUS WEP authentication, an attacker could be able to get onto your network. Even if you protect your critical systems, the attacker will still have access to all workstations on the network, as well as all networks that are connected to the wireless network. She could then compromise those resources and acquire the valid information needed to access your systems.

Network Hijacking and Modification

Numerous techniques are available for an attacker to "hijack" a wireless network or session. And unlike some attacks, network and security administrators may be unable to tell the difference between the hijacker and a legitimate passenger.

Defining Hijacking

Many tools are available to the network hijacker. These tools are based upon basic implementation issues within almost every network device available today. As TCP/IP packets go through switches, routers, and APs, each device looks at the destination IP address and compares it with the IP addresses it knows to be local. If the address is not in the table, the device hands the packet off to its default gateway.

This table is used to coordinate the IP address with what MAC addresses are local to the device. In many situations, this list is a dynamic list that is built up from traffic that is passing through the device and through Address Resolution Protocol (ARP) notifications from new devices joining the network. There is no authentication or verification that the request received by the device is valid. So a malicious user is able to send messages to routing devices and APs stating that their MAC address is associated with a known IP address. From then on, all traffic that goes through that router destined for the hijacked IP address will be handed off to the hacker's machine.

If the attacker spoofs as the default gateway or a specific host on the network, all machines trying to get to the network or the spoofed machine will connect to the attacker's machine instead of where they had intended. If the attacker is clever, he will only use this to identify passwords and other necessary information and route the rest of the traffic to the intended recipient. This way the end user has no idea that this "man-in-the-middle" has intercepted her communications and compromised her passwords and information.

Another clever attack that is possible is through the use of rogue APs. If the attacker is able to put together an AP with enough strength, the end users may not be able to tell which AP is the real one to use. In fact, most will not even know that another is available. Using this, the attacker is able to receive authentication requests and information from the end workstation regarding the secret key and where they are attempting to connect.

These rogue APs can also be used to attempt to break into more tightly configured wireless APs. Utilizing tools such as AirSnort and WEPCrack requires a large amount of data to be able to decrypt the secret key. A hacker sitting in a car in front of your house or office is easily identified, and will generally not have enough time to finish acquiring enough information to break the key. However, if they install a tiny, easily hidden machine, this machine could sit there long enough to break the key and possibly act as an external AP into the wireless network it has hacked.

Sample Hijacking Tools

Attackers who wish to spoof more than their MAC addresses have several tools available. Most of the tools available are for use under a UNIX environment and can be found through a simple search for "ARP Spoof" at http://packetstormsecurity.com. With these tools, the hacker can easily trick all machines on your wireless network into thinking that the hacker's machine is another machine. Through simple sniffing on the network, an attacker can determine which machines are in high use by the workstations on the network. If they then spoof themselves as one of these machines, they could possibly intercept much of the legitimate traffic on the network.

AirSnort and WEPCrack are freely available. And while it would take additional resources to build a rogue AP, these tools will run from any Linux machine.

Hijacking Case Scenario

Now that we have identified the network to be attacked, and spoofed our MAC address to become a valid member of the network, we can gain further information that is not available through simple sniffing. If the network being attacked is using SSH to access their hosts, just stealing a password might be easier than attempting to break into the host using any exploit that might be available.

By just ARP spoofing their connection with the AP to be that of the host they are wishing to steal the passwords from, all wireless users who are attempting to SSH into the host will then connect to the rogue machine. When they attempt to sign on with their password, the attacker is then able to, first, receive their password, and second, pass on the connection to the real end destination. If the attacker does not do the second step, it will increase the likelihood that their attack will be noticed because users will begin to complain that they are unable to connect to the host.

Protection against Network Hijacking and Modification

You can use several different tools to protect your network from IP spoofing with invalid ARP requests. These tools, such as ArpWatch, will notify an administrator when ARP requests are seen, allowing the administrator to take appropriate action to determine if indeed someone is attempting to hack into the network.

Another option is to statically define the MAC/IP address definitions. This will prevent the attacker from being able to redefine this information. However, due to the management overhead in statically defining all network adaptors' MAC address on every router and AP, this solution is rarely implemented. In fact, many APs do not offer any options to define the ARP table, and it would depend upon the switch or firewall you are using to separate your wireless network from your wired network.

There is no way to identify or prevent any attackers from using passive attacks, such as from AirSnort or WEPCrack, to determine the secret key used in an encrypted wireless network. The best protection available is to change the secret key on a regular basis and add additional authentication mechanisms such as RADIUS or dynamic firewalls to restrict access to your wired network once a user has connected to the wireless network. However, if you have not properly secured every wireless workstation, an attacker need only go after one of the other wireless clients to be able to access the resources available to it.

Denial of Service and Flooding Attacks

The nature of wireless transmission, and especially the use of spread spectrum technology, makes a wireless network especially vulnerable to *denial of service* (DoS) attacks. The equipment needed to launch such an attack is freely available and very affordable. In fact, many homes and offices contain equipment necessary to deny service to their wireless network.

Defining DoS and Flooding

A denial of service occurs when an attacker has engaged most of the resources a host or network has available, rendering it unavailable to legitimate users. One of the original DoS attacks is known as a *ping flood*. A ping flood utilizes misconfigured equipment along with bad "features" within TCP/IP to cause a large number of hosts or devices to send an ICMP echo (ping) to a specified target. When the attack occurs it tends to use much of the resources of both the network connection and the host being attacked. This will then make it very difficult for any end users to access the host for normal business purposes.

In a wireless network, several items can cause a similar disruption of service. Probably the easiest is through a confliction within the wireless spectrum by different devices attempting to use the same frequency. Many new wireless telephones use the same frequency as 802.11 networks. Through either intentional or unintentional uses of this, a simple telephone call could prevent all wireless users from accessing the network.

Another possible attack would be through a massive amount of invalid (or valid) authentication requests. If the AP is tied up with thousands of spoofed authentication attempts, any users attempting to authenticate themselves would have major difficulties in acquiring a valid session.

As you saw earlier, the attacker has many tools available to hijack network connections. If a hacker is able to spoof the machines of a wireless network into thinking that the attackers machine is their default gateway, not only will the attacker be able to intercept all traffic destined to the wired network, but they would also be able to prevent any of the wireless network machines from accessing the wired network. To do this the hacker need only spoof the AP and not forward connections on to the end destination, preventing all wireless users from doing valid wireless activities.

Sample DoS Tools

Not much is needed to create a wireless DoS. In fact, many users create these situations with the equipment found within their homes or offices. In a small apartment building, you could find several APs as well as many wireless telephones. These users could easily create many DoS attacks on their own networks as well as on those of their neighbors.

A hacker wishing to DoS a network with a flood of authentication strings will also need to be a well skilled programmer. Not many tools are available to create this type of attack, but as we have seen in the attempts to crack WEP, much of the programming required does not take much effort or time. In fact, a skilled hacker should be able to create such a tool within a few hours. When done, this simple application, when used with standard wireless equipment, could possibly render your wireless network unusable for the duration of the attack.

Creating a hijacked AP DoS will require additional tools that can be found on many security sites. See the earlier section "Sample Hijacking Tools" for a possible starting point to acquiring some of the ARP spoofing tools needed. These tools are not very complex and are available for almost every computing platform available.

DoS and Flooding Case Scenario

Many apartments and older office buildings do not come prewired for the high-tech networks that many people are using today. To add to the problem, if many individuals are setting up their own wireless networks, without coordinating the installs, many problems can occur that will be difficult to detect.

Only so many frequencies are available to 802.11 networks. In fact, once the frequency is chosen, it does not change until someone manually reconfigures it.

With these problems, it is not hard to imagine the following situation from occurring.

A person goes out and purchases a wireless AP and several network cards for his home network. When he gets home to his apartment and configures his network he is extremely happy with how well wireless actually works. Then all of a sudden none of the machines on the wireless network are able to communicate. After waiting on hold for 45 minutes to get though to tech support for the device, the network magically starts working again so he hangs up.

Later that week the same problem occurs, only this time he decides to wait on hold. While waiting he goes onto his porch and begins discussing his frustration with his neighbor. During the conversation his neighbor's kids come out and say that their wireless network is not working.

So they begin to do a few tests (still waiting on hold, of course). First the man's neighbor turns off his AP (which is generally off unless the kids are online, to "protect" their network). Once this is done the wireless network starts working again. Then they turn on the neighbor's AP again and the network stops working again.

At this point, tech support finally answers and he describes what has happened. The tech-support representative has seen this situation several times and informs the user that he will need to change the frequency used in the device to another channel. He explains that what has happened is that the neighbor's network is utilizing the same channel, causing the two networks to conflict. Once he changes the frequency, everything starts working properly.

Protecting Against DoS and Flooding Attacks

There is little that you can do to protect against DoS attacks. In a wireless environment the attacker does not need to even be in the same building or neighborhood. With a good enough antenna, the attacker is able to send these attacks from a great distance away. There is no indication that there is any reason for the disruption.

This is one of the valid times to use NetStumbler in a nonhacking context. By using NetStumbler, you can identify any other networks that might be conflicting with your network configuration. However, NetStumbler will not identify other DoS attacks or other equipment that is causing conflicts (such as wireless telephones).

Summary

Only through a solid understanding of security fundamentals, principles, and procedures will you be able to fully identify today's security risks. From this understanding, which is built upon "The Big Three" tenets of security (confidentiality, integrity, and availability, or CIA) come the basis for all other security practices. The essential practices usually associated with security build upon the concepts of "The Big Three," which provide tools for actually implementing security into systems. The ability to properly authenticate a user or process, before allowing that user or process access to specific resources, protect the CIA directly. If you are able to clearly identify the authenticated user through electronic non-repudiation techniques usually found in encryption tools such as public-key encryption, you can ensure that the entities attempting to gain access are who they say they are. Finally, if you log the activities performed, a third party can monitor the logs and ensure that all activity happening on a system complies with the policy and standards defined, and that all inappropriate activity is identified, allowing for possible prosecution or investigation into the invalid activity.

Following these practices, through the use of tested and proven identification and evaluation standards, you can fully understand the security risks associated with any object. Once you know the risks, you can provide solutions to diminish these risks as much as possible.

The standard solution is to create a formal security policy along with detailed guidelines and procedures. These guidelines describe the actual implementation steps necessary for any platform to comply with the established security procedure.

By using these standard methods to protect your wireless network, you should be able to develop a clear and concise wireless security plan that incorporates the needs of your organization's highest levels. This plan will allow for the deployment of a wireless network that's as secure as possible and will provide clear exception listings for areas where the risks to your infrastructure cannot be fully controlled.

Through a careful examination of the design of WEP, we identified significant weaknesses in the algorithm. These weaknesses, along with implementation flaws, have lead to the creation of many new tools that can be used to attack wireless networks. These tools allow for the attacker to identify a wireless network through *war driving* and then crack the secret key by passively listening to the encrypted transmissions. Once they have access to the secret key, only those that have deployed additional security measures will have some additional protection for the rest of their infrastructure.

Even if you have a incident response plan and procedure defined in your security standards, if an attack is not known to be happening, there is little you can do to mitigate or rectify the intrusion. The entire discovery and WEP-cracking process is passive and undetectable. Only at the point of attacking other wireless hosts or spoofing their attacking machine as a valid host does the attack becomes noticeable. However, many installations do not implement system logging, nor do they have standards and practices requiring monitoring of those logs for inappropriate activity.

None of these actions will provide protection against one of the oldest attacks known—theft. There is little you can do to protect your resources if critical information, such as network passwords and access definitions, can be acquired by only gaining access to notebooks or backups. High-tech criminals are creating custom malware that can access this information through spam or disguised Web sites.

Although wireless networks are making computing easier and more accessible, understanding the design and implementation weaknesses in 802.11 will help you in preventing attacks. And at times when attacks are unavoidable, by knowing how and where the attackers will come, you may be able to identify when they are attempting to gain access and respond as defined in your standards and incident response practices.

Solutions Fast Track

Understanding Security Fundamentals and Principles of Protection

- ☑ "The Big Three" tenets of security are: *confidentiality*, *integrity*, and *availability*.

- ☑ Requirements needed to implement the principles of protection include proper authentication of authorized users through a system that provides for a clear identification of the users via tested non-repudiation techniques.

- ☑ Internal or external auditors can use logging or system accounting to ensure that the system is functioning and being utilized in accordance to defined standards and policies.

☑ Logging can also be the first place to look for evidence should an attack does occur. Ensure that logging is going to a trusted third-party site that cannot be accessed by personnel and resources being logged.

☑ These tools are essential to protecting the privacy of customer, partner, or trade secret information.

☑ Encryption has provided many tools for the implementation of these security fundamentals.

☑ Encryption is not the definitive solution to security problems. For example, a known secret key could be stolen, or one of the parties utilizing encryption could be tricked or forced into performing the activity, which would be seen as a valid cryptographic operation because the system has no knowledge of any collusion involved in the generation of the request.

MAC Filtering

☑ Media Access Control (MAC) filtering is effective against casual attackers.

☑ MAC filtering can be circumvented by changing the MAC address on the client device.

☑ It is difficult to determine if the lack of association is due to MAC filtering or other reasons like an incorrect Wired Equivalent Protocol (WEP) key.

Reviewing the Role of Policy

☑ Once basic fundamentals and principles are understood, through the creation of policies and standards an organization or entity is able to clearly define how to design, implement, and monitor their infrastructure securely.

☑ Policies must have direct support and sign-in by the executive management of any organization.

☑ A properly mitigated risk should reduce the impact of the threat as well as the likelihood that that threat will occur.

☑ A clear and well-defined classification and labeling system is key to the identification of resources being protected.

☑ Information classification techniques also provide a method by which the items being classified can then have the proper policy or standards placed around them depending on the level or importance, as well as the risk associated with each identified item.

☑ Some organizations are required by their own regulations to have clear and well defined standards and policies.

Implementing WEP

☑ To protect against some rudimentary attacks that insert known text into the stream to attempt to reveal the key stream, WEP incorporates a check sum in each frame. Any frame not found to be valid through the check sum is discarded.

☑ Used on its own, WEP does not provide adequate wireless local area network (WLAN) security.

☑ WEP has to be implemented on every client as well as every Access Point (AP) to be effective.

☑ WEP keys are user definable and unlimited. You do not have to use predefined keys, and you can and should change them often.

☑ Implement the strongest version of WEP available and keep abreast of the latest upgrades to the standards.

Addressing Common Risks and Threats

☑ By examining the common threats to both wired and wireless networks, you can see how a solid understanding in the basics of security principles allows you to fully assess the risks associated with using wireless and other technologies.

☑ Threats can come from simple design issues, where multiple devices utilize the same setup, or intentional denial of service attacks which can result in the corruption or loss of data.

☑ Not all threats are caused by malicious users. They can also be caused by a conflict of similar resources, such as with 802.11b networks and cordless telephones.

☑ With wireless networks going beyond the border of your office or home, chances are greater that your actions might be monitored by a third party.

☑ Unless your organization has clear and well-defined policies and guidelines, you might find yourself in legal or business situations where your data is either compromised, lost, or disrupted. Without a clear plan of action that identifies what is important in certain scenarios, you will not be able to address situations as they occur.

Sniffing, Interception, and Eavesdropping

☑ Electronic eavesdropping, or *sniffing*, is passive and undetectable to intrusion detection devices.

☑ Tools to sniff networks are available for Windows (such as Ethereal and AiroPeek) and UNIX (such as tcpdump and ngrep).

☑ Sniffing traffic allows attackers to identify additional resources that can be compromised.

☑ Even encrypted networks have been shown to disclose vital information in cleartext, such as the network name, that can be received by attackers sniffing the WLAN.

☑ Any authentication information that is broadcast can often be simply replayed to services requiring authentication (NT Domain, WEP authentication, and so on) to access resources.

☑ The use of virtual private networks, Secure Sockets Layer (SSL), and Secure Shell (SSH) helps protect against wireless interception.

Spoofing and Unauthorized Access

☑ Due to the design of Transmission Control Protocol/Internet Protocol (TCP/IP), there is little that you can do to prevent MAC/IP address spoofing.

☑ Only through static definition of MAC address tables can you prevent this type of attack. However, due to significant overhead in management, this is rarely implemented.

☑ Wireless network authentication can be easily spoofed by simply replaying another node's authentication back to the AP when attempting to connect to the network.

☑ Many wireless equipment providers allow for end-users to redefine the MAC address within their cards through the configuration utilities that come with the equipment.

☑ External two-factor authentication such as Remote Access Dial-In User Service (RADIUS) or SecurID should be implemented to additionally restrict access requiring strong authentication to access the wireless resources.

Network Hijacking and Modification

☑ Due to the design of TCP/IP, some spoof attacks allow for attackers to hijack or take over network connections established for other resources on the wireless network.

☑ If an attacker hijacks the AP, all traffic from the wireless network gets routed through the attacker, so they are then able to identify passwords and other information other users are attempting to use on valid network hosts.

☑ Many users are easily susceptible to these man-in-the-middle attacks, often entering their authentication information even after receiving many notifications that SSL or other keys are not what they should be.

☑ Rogue APs can assist the attacker by allowing remote access from wired or wireless networks.

☑ These attacks are often overlooked as just faults in the user's machine, allowing attackers to continue hijacking connections with little fear of being noticed.

Denial of Service and Flooding Attacks

☑ Many wireless networks within a small space can easily cause network disruptions and even denial of service (DoS) for valid network users.

☑ If an attacker hijacks the AP and does not pass traffic on to the proper destination, all users of the network will be unable to use the network.

☑ Flooding the wireless network with transmissions can also prevent other devices from utilizing the resources, making the wireless network inaccessible to valid network users.

☑ Wireless attackers can utilize strong and directional antennas to attack the wireless network from a great distance.

☑ An attacker who has access to the wired network can flood the wireless AP with more traffic than it can handle, preventing wireless users from accessing the wired network.

☑ Many new wireless products utilize the same wireless frequencies as 802.11 networks. A simple cordless telephone could create a DoS situation for the network more easily than any of these other techniques.

Frequently Asked Questions

The following Frequently Asked Questions, answered by the authors of this book, are designed to both measure your understanding of the concepts presented in this chapter and to assist you with real-life implementation of these concepts. To have your questions about this chapter answered by the author, browse to **www.syngress.com/solutions** and click on the **"Ask the Author"** form.

Q: Do I really need to understand the fundamentals of security in order to protect my network?

A: While you are able to utilize the configuration options available to you from your equipment provider, without a solid background in how security is accomplished you will never be able to protect your assets from the unknown threats that will come against your network through either misconfiguration, backdoors provided by the vendor, or new exploits that have not been patched by your vendor.

Q: Am I required by law to have a security policy?

A: If your organization is a video store, deals with children's records, or is associated with the health care or financial industries (and you are located in the United States), you are most likely required by federal regulation to have a defined security policy, and in some cases you are required to have complete third-party audits of your configuration and policies. If you are not required by legislation, you might still find yourself liable under civil law to provide proper protection for customer or partner information contained within your system.

Q: Is 128-bit WEP more secure than 64-bit WEP?

A: Not really. This is because the WEP vulnerability has more to do with the 24-bit initialization vector than the actual size of the WEP key.

Q: If I am a home user, can I assume that if I use MAC filtering and WEP, that my network is secure?

A: You can make the assumption that your home network is more secure than if it did not utilize these safeguards. However, as shown in this chapter, these methods can be circumvented to allow for intrusion.

Q: Where can I find more information on WEP vulnerabilities?

A: Besides being one of the sources who brought WEP vulnerabilities to light, www.isaac.cs.berkeley.edu has links to other Web sites that cover WEP insecurities.

Q: Can my customers really sue me or my company for being hacked and having their information leaked or misused?

A: In any situation, if you have an established trust with a customer to maintain their information securely and someone breaks into the building or into their corporate servers, a a customer can possibly pursue litigation against you if you did not have any policies or procedures in place to address the risk associated with this and other threats to the customer's information.

Q: If someone can be forced into performing an activity, why should I bother setting up complex security applications?

A: Without those applications in place, you would find that it does not take direct force to attack you or your information. There has always been the possibility that threats could force individuals in key positions to reveal damaging information and secrets, but there is a greater chance that someone will trick a user into disclosing their password or some other security key. Proper training and education are the best defenses in these situations.

Q: I added a firewall to my design. Why should I also need both a policy and external auditing?

A: Again, a firewall may protect you initially, but what do you do as technology changes, or your staff is replaced? Policies and standards ensure that current and future implementations are built in accordance to the definitions laid out by the organization. Adding logging, as well as internal and third-party auditing of the implemented resources helps ensure that the implementations are built in accordance to policy, and that all activity occurring within the environment is in compliance with your standards, guidelines, and policies.

Q: If I have enabled WEP, am I now protected?

A: No. Certain tools can break all WEP keys by simply monitoring the network traffic for generally less than 24 hours.

Q: Is there any solution available besides RADIUS to perform external user and key management?

A: No, plans are available from manufacturers to identify other ways of performing the user/key management, but to date nothing is available.

Index

SYNGRESS SOLUTIONS...